Joint Committee on Taxation's

# General Explanation of Tax Legislation Enacted in the 111th Congress

*Blue Book*

ISBN 978-0-8080-2671-6



4025 W. Peterson Ave.
Chicago, IL 60646-6085
800 248 3248
CCHGroup.com



Printed in the United States of America

# About This Publication

This CCH publication reproduces the text of the Joint Committee on Taxation, "General Explanation of Tax Legislation Enacted in the 111th Congress" (JCS-2-11), including the errata issued on March 23, 2011 (JCX-20-11), as prepared by the staff of the Joint Committee on Taxation in consultation with the staffs of the House Ways and Means Committee and the Senate Finance Committee.

The General Explanation (commonly referred to as the "Blue Book") provides a detailed explanation of the tax-related provisions contained in over 40 pieces of legislation enacted in the 111th Congress during 2009 and 2010, including:

1. The Children's Health Insurance Program Reauthorization Act of 2009 (P.L. 111-3);
2. The American Recovery and Reinvestment Act of 2009 (P.L. 111-5);
3. The Worker, Homeownership, and Business Assistance Act of 2009 (P.L. 111-92);
4. Haiti tax relief (P.L. 111-126);
5. The Hiring Incentives to Restore Employment Act (P.L. 111-147);
6. The Patient Protection and Affordable Care Act (P.L. 111-148);
7. The Health Care and Education Reconciliation Act of 2010 (P.L. 111-152);
8. The Homebuyer Assistance and Improvement Act of 2010 (P.L. 111-198);
9. The Dodd-Frank Wall Street Reform and Consumer Protection Act (P.L. 111-203);
10. The Small Business Jobs Act of 2010 (P.L. 111-240);
11. The Tax Relief, Unemployment Insurance Reauthorization, and Job Creation Act of 2010 (P.L. 111-312); and
12. The Regulated Investment Company Modernization Act of 2010 (P.L. 111-325).

The Blue Book provides the legislative history for each Act, a provision-by-provision description of the prior law and new law, the reasons for the law change if the provision was reported out of committee before enactment, and the effective date of each law change. Descriptions prepared by the Joint Committee on Taxation were included in the absence of other committee reports or when the Joint Committee issued a contemporaneous technical explanation of the bill. An Appendix shows the estimated budget effects of the tax legislation enacted in the 111th Congress for fiscal years 2009–2020.

The Blue Book explains, in one document, the tax legislation enacted by a particular Congress. The Blue Book can resolve differences between a congressional committee's explanation of a bill provision and the provision as Congress finally enacts it. While a Blue Book explanation is not a legally binding interpretation of the new legislation, it may serve as a useful guide in understanding the intent and meaning of a law. Along with the committee and conference reports, a Blue Book interpretation is considered substantial authority for the tax treatment of an item for purposes of avoiding the Code Sec. 6662 accuracy-related penalty on substantial understatements of income tax (Reg. § 1.6662-4(d)(3)(iii)).

**March 2011**

[JOINT COMMITTEE PRINT]

# GENERAL EXPLANATION OF TAX LEGISLATION ENACTED IN THE 111TH CONGRESS

PREPARED BY THE STAFF

OF THE

JOINT COMMITTEE ON TAXATION

MARCH 2011

JCS–2–11

**ERRATA**
**"GENERAL EXPLANATION OF TAX LEGISLATION ENACTED IN THE 111TH CONGRESS"**

1. On page 555, add the following footnote 1582A to the word "amount" in the next to last sentence in example 3:

The provision adds new section 2010(c)(4), which generally defines "deceased spousal unused exclusion amount" of a surviving spouse as the lesser of (a) the basic exclusion amount, or (b) the excess of (i) the basic exclusion amount of the last deceased spouse of such surviving spouse, over (ii) the amount with respect to which the tentative tax is determined under section 2001(b)(1) on the estate of such deceased spouse. A technical correction may be necessary to replace the reference to the basic exclusion amount of the last deceased spouse of the surviving spouse with a reference to the applicable exclusion amount of such last deceased spouse, so that the statute reflects intent. Applicable exclusion amount is defined in section 2010(c)(2), as amended by the provision.

2. Beginning on page 706, replace the entire **Appendix: The Estimated Budget Effects of Tax Legislation Enacted in the 111th Congress** with the attached revenue table. The Appendix printed in JCS-2-11 contains errors as a result of the printing process, including unreadable characters and an omission of an outlay from footnote 38 that necessitated moving footnote 38 (to become footnote 25 in the corrected revenue table) and renumbering footnotes 25 through 37. Due to formatting differences, the pagination of the corrected revenue table differs from the pagination of the revenue table printed in JCS-2-11.

# SUMMARY CONTENTS

# CONTENTS

Page

Page

## INTRODUCTION

This document,[1] prepared by the staff of the Joint Committee on Taxation in consultation with the staffs of the House Committee on Ways and Means and the Senate Committee on Finance, provides an explanation of tax legislation enacted in the 111th Congress. The explanation follows the chronological order of the tax legislation as signed into law.

For each provision, the document includes a description of present law, explanation of the provision, and effective date. Present law describes the law in effect immediately prior to enactment. It does not reflect changes to the law made by the provision or subsequent to the enactment of the provision. For many provisions, the reasons for change are also included. In some instances, provisions included in legislation enacted in the 111th Congress were not reported out of committee before enactment. For example, in some cases, the provisions enacted were included in bills that went directly to the House and Senate floors. As a result, the legislative history of such provisions does not include the reasons for change normally included in a committee report. In the case of such provisions, no reasons for change are included with the explanation of the provision in this document.

In some cases, there is no legislative history for enacted provisions. For such provisions, this document includes a description of present law, explanation of the provision, and effective date, as prepared by the staff of the Joint Committee on Taxation. In some cases, contemporaneous technical explanations of certain bills were prepared and published by the staff of the Joint Committee. In those cases, this document follows the technical explanations. Section references are to the Internal Revenue Code of 1986, as amended, unless otherwise indicated.

Part One of this document is an explanation of the provisions of the Children's Health Insurance Program Reauthorization Act of 2009 (Pub. L. No. 111–3) relating to requirements for group health plans and revenue offsets.

Part Two is an explanation of the provisions of the American Recovery and Reinvestment Act of 2009 (Pub. L. No. 111–5) relating to tax relief for individuals and families, tax incentives for business, fiscal relief for state and local governments, energy incentives, and health insurance assistance.

Part Three is an explanation of the provisions relating to the extension of the Airport and Airway Trust Fund excise taxes and expenditure authority (Pub. L. Nos. 111–12, 111–69, 111–116, 111–153, 111–161, 111–197, 111–216, 111–249, and 111–329).

[1] This document may be cited as follows: Joint Committee on Taxation, General Explanation of Tax Legislation Enacted in the 111th Congress (JCS–2–11), March 2011.

Part Four is an explanation of the provisions relating to the extension of the Highway Trust Fund expenditure authority and restoration of the fund (Pub. L. Nos. 111–46, 111–68, 111–118, 111–144, 111–147, and 111–322).

Part Five is an explanation of the provisions of the Worker, Homeownership, and Business Assistance Act of 2009 (Pub. L. No. 111–92) relating to the first-time homebuyer credit, carryback of operating losses, exclusion of payments from the Homeowners Assistance Program, and revenue offsets.

Part Six is an explanation of the provision relating to the acceleration of the income tax benefits for charitable cash contributions for the relief of victims of the earthquake in Haiti (Pub. L. No. 111–126).

Part Seven is an explanation of the provisions of the Hiring Incentives to Restore Employment Act (Pub. L. No. 111–147) relating to incentives for hiring and retaining unemployed workers, increased expensing for certain business assets, qualified tax credit bonds, and foreign account tax compliance and other revenue offsets.

Part Eight is an explanation of the provisions of the Patient Protection and Affordable Care Act (Pub. L. No. 111–148), the Health Care and Education Reconciliation Act of 2010 (Pub. L. No. 111–152), an Act to clarify the health care provided by the Secretary of Veterans Affairs that constitutes minimum essential coverage (Pub. L. No. 111–173), and the Medicare and Medicaid Extenders Act of 2010 (Pub. L. No. 111–309) relating to incentives for quality, affordable health care and revenue offsets.

Part Nine is an explanation of the provisions of the Preservation of Access to Care for Medicare Beneficiaries and Pension Relief Act of 2010 (Pub. L. No. 111–192) relating to disclosure of return information to enhance Medicare program integrity and temporary changes to funding requirements for single and multiemployer pension plans.

Part Ten is an explanation of the provisions of the Homebuyer Assistance and Improvement Act of 2010 (Pub. L. No. 111–198) relating to the homebuyer credit and revenue offsets.

Part Eleven is an explanation of the provision of the Dodd-Frank Wall Street Reform and Consumer Protection Act (Pub. L. No. 111–203) excluding certain swaps and similar agreements from the definition of a section 1256 contract.

Part Twelve is an explanation of the provisions of the ____ Act of ____ (Pub. L. No. 111–226) relating to modifications to the foreign tax credit, the treatment of certain redemptions by foreign subsidiaries, and other revenue offsets.

Part Thirteen is an explanation of the provisions of the Firearms Excise Tax Improvement Act of 2010 (Pub. L. No. 111–237) relating to the time for payment of manufacturers' excise tax on recreational equipment and allowing assessment of criminal restitution as tax.

Part Fourteen is an explanation of the provisions of the Small Business Jobs Act of 2010 (Pub. L. No. 111–240) relating to providing access to capital, encouraging investment, promoting entrepreneurship, promoting small business fairness, promoting retirement preparation, and revenue offsets.

Part Fifteen is an explanation of the provisions of the Claims Resolution Act of 2010 (Pub. L. No. 111–291) relating to the settlement of litigation against the Federal government alleging mismanagement of individual Indian trust accounts and trust assets and the collection of past-due, legally enforceable State debts.

Part Sixteen is an explanation of the provisions of the Tax Relief, Unemployment Insurance Reauthorization, and Job Creation Act of 2010 (Pub. L. No. 111–312) relating to the temporary extension of 2001, 2003, and 2009 tax relief, individual AMT relief, estate tax relief, investment incentives, unemployment insurance and related matters, a temporary employee payroll tax cut, and the temporary extension of certain expiring provisions.

Part Seventeen is an explanation of the provision of the Regulated Investment Company Modernization Act of 2010 (Pub. L. No. 111–325) relating to the modification of certain rules applicable to regulated investment companies.

Part Eighteen is an explanation of the provisions of Omnibus Trade Act of 2010 (Pub. L. No. 111–344) relating to extension of health coverage tax credit.

Part Nineteen is an explanation of the provision of the James Zadroga 9/11 Health and Compensation Act of 2010 (Pub. L. No. 111–347) relating to the imposition of an excise tax on certain foreign procurement.

Part Twenty is an explanation of the provision authorizing the Tax Court to appoint employees (Pub. L. No. 111–366).

Part Twenty-One is an explanation of the provisions relating to the extension of custom user fees, the modification of corporate estimated tax payments and extension of assistance for COBRA continuation coverage (Pub. L. Nos. 111–3, 111–42, 111–92, 111–118, 111–124, 111–144, 111–147, 111–152, 111–157, 111–171, 111–210, 111–227, 111–237, 111–240, and 111–344).

The Appendix provides the estimated budget effects of tax legislation enacted in the 111th Congress.

The first footnote in each Part gives the legislative history of each of the Acts of the 111th Congress discussed.

# PART ONE: REVENUE PROVISIONS OF THE CHILDREN'S HEALTH INSURANCE PROGRAM REAUTHORIZATION ACT OF 2009 (PUBLIC LAW 111–3)[2]

## I. REQUIREMENTS FOR GROUP HEALTH PLANS

### A. Special Enrollment Period Under Group Health Plans (sec. 311 of the Act and sec. 9801 of the Code[3])

#### *Present Law*

A group health plan is required to permit an employee who is eligible, but not enrolled, for coverage under the terms of the plan to enroll for coverage under the plan if certain conditions are satisfied.[4] Included among the conditions are (1) the employee was covered under a group health plan or had health insurance coverage at the time coverage was previously offered to the employee, and (2) such other coverage terminated as a result of loss of eligibility for such coverage. This special enrollment right must also be extended to a dependent of an employee if the dependent is eligible, but not enrolled, for coverage under the terms of the group health plan and the dependent satisfies the conditions for special enrollment. The special enrollment rights apply without regard to the dates on which the employee (or dependent) would otherwise be able to enroll under the plan. If a plan receives a request for special enrollment, coverage under the plan must generally begin no later than the first day of the first calendar month beginning after the date that notice of the request is received by the plan.

An excise tax is imposed if a group health plan fails to comply with the special enrollment rights requirement.[5] The rate of the tax on any failure is $100 for each day in the noncompliance period with respect to each individual to whom the failure relates. In the case of a single employer plan, the tax is imposed on the employer that maintains the plan.

Special enrollment rights that are parallel to the Code's rules are set forth in the Employee Retirement Income Security Act of 1974 ("ERISA") and the Public Health Service Act ("PHSA").

[2] H.R. 2. The bill passed the House on January 14, 2009. The Senate passed the bill with an amendment on January 29, 2009. The House agreed to the Senate amendment on February 4, 2009. The President signed the bill on February 4, 2009. For a technical explanation of the bill prepared by the staff of the Joint Committee on Taxation, see *Technical Explanation of the Code Provisions of H.R. 2, the "Children's Health Insurance Program Reauthorization Act of 2009" as Passed by the House of Representatives on January 14, 2009* (JCX 3–09), January 14, 2009).

[3] Except where otherwise stated, all section references are to the Internal Revenue Code of 1986, as amended (the "Code").

[4] Sec. 9801(f).

[5] Sec. 4980D.

### *Explanation of Provision*

Under the provision, a group health plan is required to permit an employee who is eligible, but not enrolled, for coverage under the plan to enroll for coverage if either (1) the employee is covered under a Medicaid plan or a State child health plan under titles XIX and XXI of the Social Security Act, respectively (a "Medicaid plan" or a "State child health plan"), and coverage is terminated as a result of loss of eligibility for the Medicaid plan or State child health plan and the employee requests coverage under the group health plan within 60 days of coverage loss; or (2) the employee becomes eligible for assistance with respect to coverage under the group health plan under a Medicaid plan or State child health plan, and the employee requests coverage not later than 60 days after the employee is determined to be eligible for such assistance. The special enrollment rights of the provision also apply to a dependent of an employee if the dependent is eligible, but not enrolled, for coverage under the terms of the group health plan and the dependent satisfies the conditions for special enrollment. The provision requires an employer to provide employees with written notice of the availability of premium assistance programs under Medicaid or State child health plans. In addition, the administrator of a group health plan must provide information upon request of a State regarding the benefits available under the plan with respect to a participant or beneficiary who is covered under a Medicaid or State child health plan. The provision makes parallel amendments to ERISA and PHSA.

### *Effective Date*

The provision is effective on April 1, 2009.

## II. OTHER REVENUE PROVISIONS

### A. Increase Excise Tax Rates on Tobacco Products and Cigarette Papers and Tubes (sec. 701 of the Act and sec. 5701 of the Code)

### *Present Law*

#### *Rates of excise tax on tobacco products and cigarette papers and tubes*

Tobacco products and cigarette papers and tubes manufactured in the United States or imported into the United States are subject to Federal excise tax at the following rates:[6]

- Cigars weighing not more than three pounds per thousand ("small cigars") are taxed at the rate of $1.828 per thousand;
- Cigars weighing more than three pounds per thousand ("large cigars") are taxed at the rate equal to 20.719 percent of the manufacturer's or importer's sales price but not more than $48.75 per thousand;
- Cigarettes weighing not more than three pounds per thousand ("small cigarettes") are taxed at the rate of $19.50 per thousand ($0.39 per pack);

[6] Sec. 5701.

• Cigarettes weighing more than three pounds per thousand ("large cigarettes") are taxed at the rate of $40.95 per thousand, except that, if they measure more than six and one-half inches in length, they are taxed at the rate applicable to small cigarettes, counting each two and three-quarter inches (or fraction thereof) of the length of each as one cigarette;

• Cigarette papers are taxed at the rate of $0.0122 for each 50 papers or fractional part thereof, except that, if they measure more than six and one-half inches in length, they are taxable by counting each two and three-quarter inches (or fraction thereof) of the length of each as one cigarette paper;

• Cigarette tubes are taxed at the rate of $0.0244 for each 50 tubes or fractional part thereof, except that, if they measure more than six and one-half inches in length, they are taxable by counting each two and three-quarter inches (or fraction thereof) of the length of each as one cigarette tube;

• Snuff is taxed at the rate of $0.585 per pound, and proportionately at that rate on all fractional parts of a pound;

• Chewing tobacco is taxed at the rate of $0.195 per pound, and proportionately at that rate on all fractional parts of a pound;

• Pipe tobacco is taxed at the rate of $1.0969 per pound, and proportionately at that rate on all fractional parts of a pound; and

• Roll-your-own tobacco is taxed at the rate of $1.0969 per pound, and proportionately at that rate on all fractional parts of a pound.

In general, excise taxes on tobacco products and cigarette papers and tubes manufactured in the United States are determined at the time of removal.

### *Floor stocks tax and foreign trade zones*

Special tax and duty rules apply with respect to foreign trade zones. In general, merchandise may be brought into a foreign trade zone without being subject to the general customs laws of the United States. Such merchandise may be stored in a foreign trade zone or may be subjected to manufacturing or other processes there. The United States Customs and Border Protection agency of the Department of Homeland Security ("Customs") may determine internal revenue taxes and liquidate duties imposed on foreign merchandise in such foreign trade zones. Articles on which such taxes and applicable duties have already been paid, or which have been admitted into the United States free of tax, that have been taken into a foreign trade zone from inside the United States, may be held under the supervision of a customs officer. Such articles may later be released back into the United States free of further taxes and duties.[7]

[7] 19 U.S.C. sec. 81c(a).

### *Explanation of Provision*

#### *Rate increases*

Under the provision, the rates of excise tax on tobacco products and cigarette papers and tubes are increased, generally in a proportionate manner. The special rules relating to the application of the tax rates to large cigarettes and cigarette papers and tubes longer than six and one-half inches apply under the provision in the same manner as under present law. The rates under the provision are as follows:

- Small cigars are taxed at the rate of $50.33 per thousand;
- Large cigars are taxed at the rate equal to 52.75 percent of the manufacturer's or importer's sales price but not more than $0.4026 per cigar;
- Small cigarettes are taxed at the rate of $50.33 per thousand;
- Large cigarettes are taxed at the rate of $105.69 per thousand;
- Cigarette papers are taxed at the rate of $0.0315 for each 50 papers or fractional part thereof;
- Cigarette tubes are taxed at the rate of $0.0630 for each 50 tubes or fractional part thereof;
- Snuff is taxed at the rate of $1.51 per pound, and proportionately at that rate on all fractional parts of a pound;
- Chewing tobacco is taxed at the rate of $0.5033 per pound, and proportionately at that rate on all fractional parts of a pound;
- Pipe tobacco is taxed at the rate of $2.8311 per pound, and proportionately at that rate on all fractional parts of a pound; and
- Roll-your-own tobacco is taxed at the rate of $24.78 per pound, and proportionately at that rate on all fractional parts of a pound. The rate for roll-your-own tobacco is intended to approximate the rate for small cigarettes.

#### *Floor stocks tax and foreign trade zone treatment*

The provision imposes a tax on floor stocks. Taxable articles (i.e., those articles listed above), except for large cigars, manufactured in the United States or imported into the United States which are removed before April 1, 2009, and held on that date for sale by any person are subject to a floor stocks tax. The floor stocks tax is equal to the excess of the applicable tax under the new rates over the applicable tax at the prior rates. The person holding the article on any tax increase date to which the floor stocks tax applies is liable for the tax. Each such person is allowed a $500 credit against the floor stocks tax.

Notwithstanding any other provision of law, the floor stocks tax applies to an article located in a foreign trade zone on any tax increase date, provided that internal revenue taxes have been determined, or customs duties have been liquidated, with respect to such article before such date, or such article is held on a tax-and-duty-paid basis on such date under the supervision of a customs officer.

For purposes of determining the floor stocks tax, component members of a "controlled group" (as modified) are treated as one taxpayer.[8] "Controlled group" for these purposes means a parent-subsidiary, brother-sister, or combined corporate group with more than 50-percent ownership with respect to either combined voting power or total value. Under regulations, similar principles may apply to a group of persons under common control where one or more persons are not a corporation.

The floor stocks tax shall be paid on or before August 1, 2009, in the manner prescribed by Treasury regulations. In general, all of the rules, including penalties, applicable with respect to taxes on tobacco products and cigarette papers and tubes apply to the floor stocks tax. The Secretary of the Treasury or his delegate ("Secretary") may treat any person who bore the ultimate burden of the floor stocks tax as the person entitled to a credit or refund of such tax.

### *Effective Date*

The provision applies to articles removed after March 31, 2009.

## B. Modify Definition of Roll-Your-Own Tobacco (sec. 702(d) of the Act and sec. 5702 of the Code)

### *Present Law*

Federal excise taxes are imposed upon tobacco products and cigarette papers and tubes.[9] Tobacco products are cigars, cigarettes, snuff, chewing tobacco, pipe tobacco, and roll-your-own tobacco. A "cigar" is any roll of tobacco wrapped in leaf tobacco or in any substance containing tobacco, other than any roll of tobacco which is a cigarette. A "cigarette" is (i) any roll of tobacco wrapped in paper or in any substance not containing tobacco; and (ii) any roll of tobacco wrapped in any substance containing tobacco which, because of its appearance, the type of tobacco used in the filler, or its packaging and labeling, is likely to be offered to, or purchased by, consumers as a cigarette. "Roll-your-own tobacco" is any tobacco, which because of its appearance, type, packaging, or labeling, is suitable for use and likely to be offered to, or purchased by, consumers as tobacco for making cigarettes. "Cigarette paper" is paper, or any other material except tobacco, prepared for use as a cigarette wrapper. A "cigarette tube" is cigarette paper made into a hollow cylinder for use in making cigarettes.[10]

Wrappers containing tobacco are not within the definition of cigarette papers or tubes because they contain tobacco. They are also not generally within the definition of roll-your-own tobacco because they are usually used to make cigars, not cigarettes. For the same reason, loose tobacco suitable for making roll-your-own cigars is not considered to be roll-your-own tobacco.

### *Explanation of Provision*

Under the provision, the definition of roll-your-own tobacco is expanded to also include any tobacco, which because of its appearance, type, packaging, or labeling, is suitable for use and likely to

[8] Controlled group is defined in section 1563.
[9] Sec. 5701.
[10] Sec. 5702.

be offered to, or purchased by, consumers as tobacco for making cigars, or for use as wrappers for making cigars.

### *Effective Date*

The provision applies to articles removed after March 31, 2009.

## C. Permit, Inventory, Reporting, Recordkeeping Requirements for Manufacturers and Importers of Processed Tobacco (sec. 702 of the Act and secs. 5702, 5712, 5713, 5721, 5722, 5723, and 5741 of the Code)

### *Present Law*

Tobacco products and cigarette papers and tubes are subject to Federal excise tax.[11] Tobacco products are cigars, cigarettes, smokeless tobacco, pipe tobacco, and roll-your-own tobacco.[12] Manufacturers and importers of tobacco products and export warehouse proprietors must obtain a permit from the Secretary of the Treasury or his delegate ("Secretary").[13] Manufacturers and importers of tobacco products or cigarette papers or tubes, and export warehouse proprietors, must also periodically make an inventory and certain reports and keep certain records, all as prescribed by the Secretary.[14]

### *Explanation of Provision*

The provision creates a new category of manufacturers and importers who are subject to regulation but not to Federal excise tax. Under the provision, manufacturers and importers of "processed tobacco" are subject to the present-law permit, inventory, reporting, packaging, and recordkeeping requirements. Processed tobacco is any tobacco other than tobacco products.[15] A manufacturer of processed tobacco is any person who processes any tobacco other than tobacco products, and an importer includes an importer of processed tobacco. However, the processing of tobacco does not include the farming or growing of tobacco or the handling of whole tobacco leaf solely for sale, shipment, or delivery to a manufacturer of tobacco products or processed tobacco. For example, under the provision an importer of "cut rag" tobacco or a leaf processor that manufactures such tobacco is subject to the general permit, inventory, reporting, and recordkeeping requirements of the Code but is not subject to Federal excise tax (unless it also imports or manufactures tobacco products or cigarette papers or tubes).

Under the provision, any person who is engaged in business as a manufacturer or importer of processed tobacco on April 1, 2009 and who submits a permit application within 90 days of the effective date of this provision may continue to engage in such business pending action on their permit application. Such persons will be subject to the requirements of this provision to the same extent as

---

[11] Sec. 5701.
[12] Sec. 5702.
[13] Sec. 5713.
[14] Sec. 5721 (inventories); sec. 5722 (reports); sec. 5723 (packaging); sec. 5741 (records).
[15] Sec. 5702(c) defines tobacco products as cigars, cigarettes, smokeless tobacco, pipe tobacco, and roll-your-own tobacco.

if the person was a permit holder while final action on the permit application is pending.

### *Effective Date*

The provision is effective on April 1, 2009.

## D. Broaden Authority to Deny, Suspend, and Revoke Tobacco Permits (sec. 702(b) of the Act and secs. 5712 and 5713 of the Code)

### *Present Law*

Manufacturers and importers of tobacco products and proprietors of export warehouses must obtain a permit to engage in such businesses.[16] A permit is obtained by application to the Secretary. The Secretary may deny the application if: (1) the business premises are inadequate to protect the revenue; (2) the activity to be carried out at the business premises does not meet such minimum capacity or activity requirements as prescribed by the Secretary; (3) the applicant is, by reason of his business experience, financial standing, or trade connections, not likely to maintain operations in compliance with the applicable provisions of the Code; or (4) such applicant has failed to disclose any material information required or made any material false statement in the application.[17] In the case of a corporation, an applicant includes any officer, director, or principal stockholder and, in the case of a partnership, a partner.

A permit is conditioned upon compliance with the rules of the Code and related regulations pertaining to taxes and regulation of tobacco products and cigarette papers and tubes. The Secretary may suspend or revoke a permit after a notice and hearing if the holder: (1) has not in good faith complied with those rules or with any other provision of the Code involving intent to defraud; (2) has violated the conditions of the permit; (3) has failed to disclose any material information required or made any material false statement in the permit application; or (4) has failed to maintain the business premises in such a manner as to protect the revenue.[18]

### *Explanation of Provision*

The provision broadens the present-law authority of the Secretary to deny, suspend, or revoke tobacco permits. Under the provision, the Secretary may deny an application for a permit if the applicant has been convicted of a felony violation of a Federal or State criminal law relating to tobacco products or cigarette papers or tubes, or if, by reason of previous or current legal proceedings involving a violation of Federal criminal felony laws relating to tobacco products or cigarette papers or tubes, such applicant is not likely to maintain operations in compliance with the applicable provisions of the Code.

Similarly, a permit may be suspended or revoked if the holder is convicted of a felony violation of a Federal or State criminal law relating to tobacco products or cigarette papers or tubes, or if, by

---

[16] Sec. 5713.
[17] Sec. 5712.
[18] Sec. 5713.

reason of previous or current legal proceedings involving a violation of Federal criminal felony laws relating to tobacco products or cigarette papers or tubes, such applicant is not likely to maintain operations in compliance with the applicable provisions of the Code.

### *Effective Date*

The provision is effective on the date of enactment (February 4, 2009).

## E. Clarify Statute of Limitations Pertaining to Excise Taxes Imposed on Imported Alcohol, Tobacco Products and Cigarette Papers and Tubes (sec. 702(c) of the Act and sec. 514 of the Tariff Act of 1930)

### *Present Law*

Under the Code, amounts of tax must generally be assessed within three years after a tax return is filed, and no proceeding in court without assessment for the collection of such tax may begin after such period has expired.[19] If no return is filed (but is required), the tax may be assessed, or a proceeding in court for the collection of such tax may be initiated without assessment, at any time.[20]

Customs collects duties and excise taxes on imports. Importers of taxable articles relating to tobacco and alcohol must file a tax return with Customs.[21] In general, the limitations period for fixing and assessing duties and taxes with respect to an import is one year from the date of entry or removal.[22] Under the applicable customs law, with some limited exceptions, any duty or tax imposed on an import is final and conclusive upon all persons, including the United States, unless a protest is filed within 180 days or a court action is timely commenced.[23]

### *Explanation of Provision*

The provision clarifies the tax and customs law in the area of alcohol and tobacco products by providing that, notwithstanding customs law, the general statute of limitations for assessment under the Code (sec. 6501) applies with respect to taxes imposed under chapters 51 (relating to distilled spirits, wines, and beer) and 52 (relating to tobacco products and cigarette papers and tubes) of the Code.

No inference is intended regarding the applicability of the statute of limitations under the Code to pending cases or to excise taxes imposed other than under chapters 51 and 52 of the Code.

### *Effective Date*

The provision is effective for articles imported into the United States after the date of enactment (February 4, 2009).

---

[19] Sec. 6501(a).

[20] Sec. 6501(c)(3).

[21] 24 C.F.R. sec. 41.81(b) (tobacco products and cigarette papers and tubes); sec. 5061(a) (distilled spirits, wines, and beer).

[22] 19 U.S.C. sec. 1504(a). The Secretary may extend this period under certain circumstances and with notice to the importer.

[23] 19 U.S.C. sec. 1514(a), (c)(3).

## F. Impose Immediate Tax on Unlawfully Manufactured Tobacco Products and Cigarette Papers and Tubes (sec. 702(e) of the Act and sec. 5703 of the Code)

### *Present Law*

Manufacturers and importers of tobacco products and proprietors of export warehouses must obtain a permit to engage in such businesses.[24] A permit is obtained by application to the Secretary.[25] A manufacturer of tobacco products or cigarette papers or tubes, or an export warehouse proprietor, must file a bond and obtain approval of such bond from the Secretary.[26] In general, excise taxes on tobacco products and cigarette papers and tubes manufactured in the United States are determined at the time of removal. In the case of taxes on tobacco products and cigarette papers and tubes removed during any semimonthly period under bond for deferred payment of tax, payment is due no later than the 14th day after the last day of such semimonthly period.[27]

Distilled spirits, wines, and beer produced at any place other than a place required by the Code are subject to tax immediately on production.[28] There is no such rule imposing immediate tax on tobacco products and cigarette papers and tubes that are produced by an out-of-compliance manufacturer.

### *Explanation of Provision*

Under the provision, in the case of any tobacco products or cigarette papers or tubes produced in the United States at any place other than the premises of a manufacturer that has obtained a permit (if required) and approval of a bond, the excise tax is due and payable immediately upon manufacture, unless they are produced solely for the person's own personal consumption or use.

### *Effective Date*

The provision is effective on the date of enactment (February 4, 2009).

## G. Use of Tax Information in Tobacco Assessments (sec. 702(f) of the Act and sec. 6103 of the Code)

### *Present Law*

Section 6103 provides that returns and return information are confidential and may not be disclosed by the IRS, other Federal employees, State employees, and certain others having access to the information except as provided in the Code.[29] A "return" is any tax or information return, declaration of estimated tax, or claim for refund required by, or permitted under, the Code, that is filed with

---

[24] Sec. 5713. A "manufacturer of tobacco products" does not include (1) a person who produces tobacco products solely for the person's own personal consumption or use, and (2) a proprietor of a customs bonded manufacturing warehouse with respect to the operation of such warehouse. Sec. 5702(d).

[25] Sec. 5712.

[26] Sec. 5711.

[27] Sec. 5703.

[28] Sec. 5006(c)(2) (distilled spirits); sec. 5041(f) (wines); sec. 5054(a)(3) (beer).

[29] Sec. 6103(a).

the Secretary by, on behalf of, or with respect to any person.[30] "Return" also includes any amendment or supplement thereto, including supporting schedules, attachments, or lists which are supplemental to, or part of, the return so filed.

The definition of "return information" is very broad and includes any information gathered by the IRS with respect to a person's liability or possible liability under the Code.[31]

However, data in a form that cannot be associated with, or otherwise identify, directly or indirectly a particular taxpayer is not "return information" for section 6103 purposes.

Section 6103 contains a number of exceptions to the general rule of confidentiality, which permit disclosure in specifically identified circumstances when certain conditions are satisfied.[32]

For example, under section 6103(o) of the Code, returns and return information with respect to the taxes imposed on alcohol, tobacco and firearms are open to inspection by or disclosure to officers and employees of a Federal agency whose official duties require such inspection or disclosure.

The Fair and Equitable Tobacco Reform Act of 2004[33] repealed the Federal tobacco support program and created a Tobacco Trust Fund. Funds from the Tobacco Trust Fund are used to provide transitional payments to tobacco quota holders and eligible tobacco producers. The Tobacco Trust Fund is funded by quarterly assessments paid by manufacturers and importers of tobacco products. The Farm Service Agency receives tax information from the Department of the Treasury's Alcohol and Tobacco Tax and Trade Bureau as part of its administration of the Tobacco Trust Fund assessments.

A September 2008 Department of Agriculture inspector general report indicated that a number of companies were delinquent in paying their assessments and have been referred to the Depart-

---

[30] Sec. 6103(b)(1).

[31] Sec. 6103(b)(2). Return information is:

- a taxpayer's identity, the nature, source, or amount of his income, payments, receipts, deductions, exemptions, credits, assets, liabilities, net worth, tax liability, tax withheld, deficiencies, overassessments, or tax payments, whether the taxpayer's return was, is being, or will be examined or subject to other investigation or processing, or any other data, received by, recorded by, prepared by, furnished to, or collected by the Secretary with respect to a return or with respect to the determination of the existence, or possible existence, of liability (or the amount thereof) of any person under this title for any tax, penalty, interest, fine, forfeiture, or other imposition, or offense,
- any part of any written determination or any background file document relating to such written determination (as such terms are defined in section 6110(b)) which is not open to public inspection under section 6110,
- any advance pricing agreement entered into by a taxpayer and the Secretary and any background information related to such agreement or any application for an advance pricing agreement, and
- any closing agreement under section 7121, and any similar agreement, and any background information related to such an agreement or request for such an agreement.

[32] Sec. 6103(c)–(o). Such exceptions include disclosures by consent of the taxpayer, disclosures to State tax officials, disclosures to the taxpayer and persons having a material interest, disclosures to Committees of Congress, disclosures to the President, disclosures to Federal employees for tax administration purposes, disclosures to Federal employees for nontax criminal law enforcement purposes and to the Government Accountability Office, disclosures for statistical purposes, disclosures for miscellaneous tax administration purposes, disclosures for purposes other than tax administration, disclosures of taxpayer identity information, disclosures to tax administration contractors and disclosures with respect to wagering excise taxes.

[33] Title VI of the American Jobs Creation Act of 2004, Pub. L. No. 108–357.

ment of Justice for debt collection.[34] Section 6103(o) does not provide for the use of the tax information received in civil actions against the delinquent companies. The Department of Justice could proceed with the lawsuits based on information provided by other entities, other than the tax data.

### *Explanation of Provision*

The provision provides that returns and return information provided to a Federal agency under section 6103(o) may be used in an action or proceeding, or in the preparation for an action or proceeding, brought under section 625 the Fair and Equitable Tobacco Reform Act of 2004 for any unpaid assessments or penalties arising under such Act.

### *Effective Date*

The provision is effective on and after the date of enactment (February 4, 2009).

## H. Study Concerning Magnitude of Tobacco Smuggling in the United States (sec. 703 of the Act)

### *Present Law*

Present law does not require the Secretary to submit a tobacco smuggling study to Congress.

### *Explanation of Provision*

The provision requires the Secretary to submit to Congress a study concerning the magnitude of tobacco smuggling in the United States and to recommend the most effective steps to reduce it. The study would include a review of the loss of Federal tax revenue due to illicit tobacco trade in the United States, and the role of imported tobacco products in such illicit trade.

### *Effective Date*

The study will be completed no later than one year after the date of enactment (February 4, 2009).

## I. Modifications to Corporate Estimated Tax Payments (sec. 704 of the Act and sec. 6655 of the Code)

### *Present Law*

In general, corporations are required to make quarterly estimated tax payments of their income tax liability. For a corporation whose taxable year is a calendar year, these estimated payments must be made by April 15, June 15, September 15, and December 15. For tax years beginning on any date other than January 1, the payments are due in months of the fiscal year that correspond to the calendar year payment months.

---

[34] U.S. Department of Agriculture, Office of Inspector General, Southeast Region, Report No. 03601–15–At, *Audit Report: Tobacco Transition Payment Program Tobacco Assessments Against Tobacco Manufacturers and Importers* (September 2008).

Under the Tax Increase Prevention Act of 2005 ("TIPRA"),[35] as amended, in the case of a corporation with assets of at least $1 billion, the payments due in July, August, and September, 2013, shall be increased to 120.00 percent of the payment otherwise due and the next required payment shall be reduced accordingly.

### *Explanation of Provision*[36]

The provision increases the otherwise applicable percentage for 2013 by 0.50 percentage points.

### *Effective Date*

The provision is effective on the date of enactment (February 4, 2009).

[35] Pub. L. No. 109–222.

[36] All the public laws enacted in the 111th Congress affecting this provision are described in Part Twenty-One of this document.

## PART TWO: REVENUE PROVISIONS OF THE AMERICAN RECOVERY AND REINVESTMENT ACT OF 2009 (PUBLIC LAW 111–5)[37]

## TITLE I—TAX PROVISIONS

### A. Tax Relief for Individuals and Families

### 1. Making work pay credit (sec. 1001 of the Act and new sec. 36A of the Code)

#### *Present Law*

#### *Earned income tax credit*

Low- and moderate-income workers may be eligible for the refundable earned income tax credit ("EITC"). Eligibility for the EITC is based on earned income, adjusted gross income, investment income, filing status, and immigration and work status in the United States. The amount of the EITC is based on the presence and number of qualifying children in the worker's family, as well as on adjusted gross income and earned income.

The EITC generally equals a specified percentage of earned income[38] up to a maximum dollar amount. The maximum amount applies over a certain income range and then diminishes to zero over a specified phaseout range. For taxpayers with earned income (or adjusted gross income ("AGI"), if greater) in excess of the beginning of the phaseout range, the maximum EITC amount is reduced by the phaseout rate multiplied by the amount of earned income (or AGI, if greater) in excess of the beginning of the phaseout range. For taxpayers with earned income (or AGI, if greater) in excess of the end of the phaseout range, no credit is allowed.

The EITC is a refundable credit, meaning that if the amount of the credit exceeds the taxpayer's Federal income tax liability, the excess is payable to the taxpayer as a direct transfer payment. Under an advance payment system, eligible taxpayers may elect to receive the credit in their paychecks, rather than waiting to claim a refund on their tax returns filed by April 15 of the following year.

---

[37] H.R. 1. The House Committee on Ways and Means reported H.R. 598 on January 27, 2009 (H.R. Rep. No. 111–8). The text of H.R. 598 was added to H.R. 1 at Division B, Title I. H.R. 1 passed the House on January 28, 2009. The Senate Committee on Finance reported S. 350 without a written report on January 29, 2009. The Senate passed H.R. 1 with an amendment incorporating the text of S. 350, as amended, at Division B, Title I on February 10, 2009. The conference report was filed on February 12, 2009 (H.R. Rep. No. 111–16) and was passed by the House on February 13, 2009, and the Senate on February 13, 2009. The President signed the bill on February 17, 2009.

[38] Earned income is defined as (1) wages, salaries, tips, and other employee compensation, but only if such amounts are includible in gross income, plus (2) the amount of the individual's net self-employment earnings.

### *Child credit*

An individual may claim a tax credit for each qualifying child under the age of 17. The amount of the credit per child is $1,000 through 2010 and $500 thereafter. A child who is not a citizen, national, or resident of the United States cannot be a qualifying child.

The credit is phased out for individuals with income over certain threshold amounts. Specifically, the otherwise allowable child tax credit is reduced by $50 for each $1,000 (or fraction thereof) of modified adjusted gross income over $75,000 for single individuals or heads of households, $110,000 for married individuals filing joint returns, and $55,000 for married individuals filing separate returns. For purposes of this limitation, modified adjusted gross income includes certain otherwise excludable income earned by U.S. citizens or residents living abroad or in certain U.S. territories.

The credit is allowable against the regular tax and the alternative minimum tax. To the extent the child credit exceeds the taxpayer's tax liability, the taxpayer is eligible for a refundable credit (the additional child tax credit) equal to 15 percent of earned income in excess of a threshold dollar amount (the "earned income formula"). The threshold dollar amount is $12,550 (for 2009), and is indexed for inflation.

Families with three or more children may determine the additional child tax credit using the "alternative formula," if this results in a larger credit than determined under the earned income formula. Under the alternative formula, the additional child tax credit equals the amount by which the taxpayer's social security taxes exceed the taxpayer's earned income tax credit.

Earned income is defined as the sum of wages, salaries, tips, and other taxable employee compensation plus net self-employment earnings. Unlike the EITC, which also includes the preceding items in its definition of earned income, the additional child tax credit is based only on earned income to the extent it is included in computing taxable income. For example, some ministers' parsonage allowances are considered self-employment income, and thus are considered earned income for purposes of computing the EITC, but the allowances are excluded from gross income for individual income tax purposes, and thus are not considered earned income for purposes of the additional child tax credit.

## *Reasons for Change*

The Congress believes that tax relief for working families is necessary to help the economy recover. By increasing after-tax disposable income, this credit will permit taxpayers to purchase additional goods and services, make additional investments, or pay down debt more efficiently.

## *Explanation of Provision*

### *In general*

The provision provides eligible individuals a refundable income tax credit for two years (taxable years beginning in 2009 and 2010).

The credit is the lesser of (1) 6.2 percent of an individual's earned income or (2) $400 ($800 in the case of a joint return). For these purposes, the earned income definition is the same as for the earned income tax credit with two modifications. First, earned income for these purposes does not include net earnings from self-employment which are not taken into account in computing taxable income. Second, earned income for these purposes includes combat pay excluded from gross income under section 112.

The credit is phased out at a rate of two percent of the eligible individual's modified adjusted gross income above $75,000 ($150,000 in the case of a joint return). For these purposes an eligible individual's modified adjusted gross income is the eligible individual's adjusted gross income increased by any amount excluded from gross income under sections 911, 931, or 933. An eligible individual means any individual other than: (1) a nonresident alien; (2) an individual with respect to whom another individual may claim a dependency deduction for a taxable year beginning in a calendar year in which the eligible individual's taxable year begins; and (3) an estate or trust. Each eligible individual must satisfy identical taxpayer identification number requirements to those applicable to the earned income tax credit.

Also, the Act provides that the otherwise allowable making work pay credit allowed under the provision is reduced by the amount of any payment received by the taxpayer pursuant to the provisions of the bill providing economic recovery payments under the Veterans Administration, Railroad Retirement Board, and the Social Security Administration and a temporary refundable tax credit for certain government retirees.[39] The Act treats the failure to reduce the making work pay credit by the amount of such payments or credit, and the omission of the correct TIN, as clerical errors. This allows the IRS to assess any tax resulting from such failure or omission without the requirement to send the taxpayer a notice of deficiency allowing the taxpayer the right to file a petition with the Tax Court.

***Treatment of the U.S. possessions***

*Mirror code possessions*[40]

The U.S. Treasury will make payments to each mirror code possession in an amount equal to the aggregate amount of the credits allowable by reason of the provision to that possession's residents against its income tax. This amount will be determined by the Treasury Secretary based on information provided by the government of the respective possession. For purposes of these payments, a possession is a mirror code possession if the income tax liability of residents of the possession under that possession's income tax system is determined by reference to the U.S. income tax laws as if the possession were the United States.

[39] The credit for certain government employees is available for 2009. The credit is $250 ($500 for a joint return where both spouses are eligible individuals). An eligible individual for these purposes is an individual: (1) who receives an amount as a pension or annuity for service performed in the employ of the United States or any State or any instrumentality thereof, which is not considered employment for purposes of Social Security taxes; and (2) who does not receive an economic recovery payment under the Veterans Administration, Railroad Retirement Board, or the Social Security Administration.

[40] Possessions with mirror code tax systems are the United States Virgin Islands, Guam, and the Commonwealth of the Northern Mariana Islands.

*Non-mirror code possessions*[41]

To each possession that does not have a mirror code tax system, the U.S. Treasury will make two payments (for 2009 and 2010, respectively) in an amount estimated by the Secretary as being equal to the aggregate credits that would have been allowed to residents of that possession if a mirror code tax system had been in effect in that possession. Accordingly, the amount of each payment to a non-mirror Code possession will be an estimate of the aggregate amount of the credits that would be allowed to the possession's residents if the credit provided by the provision to U.S. residents were provided by the possession to its residents. This payment will not be made to any U.S. possession unless that possession has a plan that has been approved by the Secretary under which the possession will promptly distribute the payment to its residents.

*General rules*

No credit against U.S. income tax is permitted under the provision for any person to whom a credit is allowed against possession income taxes as a result of the provision (for example, under that possession's mirror income tax). Similarly, no credit against U.S. income tax is permitted for any person who is eligible for a payment under a non-mirror code possession's plan for distributing to its residents the payment described above from the U.S. Treasury.

For purposes of the payments to the possessions, the Commonwealth of Puerto Rico and the Commonwealth of the Northern Mariana Islands are considered possessions of the United States.

For purposes of the rule permitting the Treasury Secretary to disburse appropriated amounts for refunds due from certain credit provisions of the Internal Revenue Code of 1986, the payments required to be made to possessions under the provision are treated in the same manner as a refund due from the credit allowed under the provision.

***Federal programs or Federally-assisted programs***

Any credit or refund allowed or made to an individual under this provision (including to any resident of a U.S. possession) is not taken into account as income and shall not be taken into account as resources for the month of receipt and the following two months for purposes of determining eligibility of such individual or any other individual for benefits or assistance, or the amount or extent of benefits or assistance, under any Federal program or under any State or local program financed in whole or in part with Federal funds.

***Income tax withholding***

The Act also provides for a more accelerated delivery of the credit in 2009 through revised income tax withholding schedules produced by the Department of the Treasury. Under the Act, these revised income tax withholding schedules would be designed to reduce taxpayers' income tax withheld for the remainder of 2009 in such a manner that the full annual benefit of the provision is reflected in income tax withheld during the remainder of 2009.

---

[41] Possessions that do not have mirror code tax systems are Puerto Rico and American Samoa.

### *Effective Date*

The provision applies to taxable years beginning after December 31, 2008.

## 2. Increase in the earned income tax credit (sec. 1002 of the Act and sec. 32 of the Code)

### *Present Law*

#### *Overview*

Low- and moderate-income workers may be eligible for the refundable earned income tax credit ("EITC"). Eligibility for the EITC is based on earned income, adjusted gross income, investment income, filing status, and immigration and work status in the United States. The amount of the EITC is based on the presence and number of qualifying children in the worker's family, as well as on adjusted gross income and earned income.

The EITC generally equals a specified percentage of earned income[42] up to a maximum dollar amount. The maximum amount applies over a certain income range and then diminishes to zero over a specified phaseout range. For taxpayers with earned income (or adjusted gross income ("AGI"), if greater) in excess of the beginning of the phaseout range, the maximum EITC amount is reduced by the phaseout rate multiplied by the amount of earned income (or AGI, if greater) in excess of the beginning of the phaseout range. For taxpayers with earned income (or AGI, if greater) in excess of the end of the phaseout range, no credit is allowed.

An individual is not eligible for the EITC if the aggregate amount of disqualified income of the taxpayer for the taxable year exceeds $3,100 (for 2009). This threshold is indexed for inflation. Disqualified income is the sum of: (1) interest (taxable and tax exempt); (2) dividends; (3) net rent and royalty income (if greater than zero); (4) capital gains net income; and (5) net passive income (if greater than zero) that is not self-employment income.

The EITC is a refundable credit, meaning that if the amount of the credit exceeds the taxpayer's Federal income tax liability, the excess is payable to the taxpayer as a direct transfer payment. Under an advance payment system, eligible taxpayers may elect to receive the credit in their paychecks, rather than waiting to claim a refund on their tax returns filed by April 15 of the following year.

#### *Filing status*

An unmarried individual may claim the EITC if he or she files as a single filer or as a head of household. Married individuals generally may not claim the EITC unless they file jointly. An exception to the joint return filing requirement applies to certain spouses who are separated. Under this exception, a married taxpayer who is separated from his or her spouse for the last six months of the taxable year shall not be considered as married (and, accordingly, may file a return as head of household and claim the EITC), provided that the taxpayer maintains a household that constitutes the

[42] Earned income is defined as (1) wages, salaries, tips, and other employee compensation, but only if such amounts are includible in gross income, plus (2) the amount of the individual's net self-employment earnings.

principal place of abode for a dependent child (including a child, stepchild, adopted child, or a foster child) for over half the taxable year,[43] and pays over half the cost of maintaining the household in which he or she resides with the child during the year.

***Presence of qualifying children and amount of the earned income credit***

Three separate credit schedules apply: one schedule for taxpayers with no qualifying children, one schedule for taxpayers with one qualifying child, and one schedule for taxpayers with more than one qualifying child.[44]

Taxpayers with no qualifying children may claim a credit if they are over age 24 and below age 65. The credit is 7.65 percent of earnings up to $5,970, resulting in a maximum credit of $457 for 2009. The maximum is available for those with incomes between $5,970 and $7,470 ($10,590 if married filing jointly). The credit begins to phase down at a rate of 7.65 percent of earnings above $7,470 ($10,590 if married filing jointly) resulting in a $0 credit at $13,440 of earnings ($16,560 if married filing jointly).

Taxpayers with one qualifying child may claim a credit in 2009 of 34 percent of their earnings up to $8,950, resulting in a maximum credit of $3,043. The maximum credit is available for those with earnings between $8,950 and $16,420 ($19,540 if married filing jointly). The credit begins to phase down at a rate of 15.98 percent of earnings above $16,420 ($19,540 if married filing jointly). The credit phases down to $0 at $35,463 of earnings ($38,583 if married filing jointly).

Taxpayers with more than one qualifying child may claim a credit in 2009 of 40 percent of earnings up to $12,570, resulting in a maximum credit of $5,028. The maximum credit is available for those with earnings between $12,570 and $16,420 ($19,540 if married filing jointly). The credit begins to phase down at a rate of 21.06 percent of earnings above $16,420 ($19,540 if married filing jointly). The credit phases down to $0 at $40,295 of earnings ($43,415 if married filing jointly).

If more than one taxpayer lives with a qualifying child, only one of these taxpayers may claim the child for purposes of the EITC. If multiple eligible taxpayers actually claim the same qualifying child, then a tiebreaker rule determines which taxpayer is entitled to the EITC with respect to the qualifying child. Any eligible taxpayer with at least one qualifying child who does not claim the EITC with respect to qualifying children due to failure to meet certain identification requirements with respect to such children (i.e., providing the name, age and taxpayer identification number of each of such children) may not claim the EITC for taxpayers without qualifying children.

### *Reasons for Change*

The Congress recognizes the importance of the EITC as a means of providing tax relief to low- and middle-income families with children. The Congress also recognizes that larger families need addi-

---

[43] A foster child must reside with the taxpayer for the entire taxable year.
[44] All income thresholds are indexed for inflation annually.

tional tax relief. The Congress therefore believes that the EITC should be expanded to provide additional tax relief to families with three or more qualifying children.

### *Explanation of Provision* [45]

#### *Three or more qualifying children*

The provision increases the EITC credit percentage for families with three or more qualifying children to 45 percent for 2009 and 2010. For example, in 2009 taxpayers with three or more qualifying children may claim a credit of 45 percent of earnings up to $12,570, resulting in a maximum credit of $5,656.50.

#### *Provide additional marriage penalty relief through higher threshold phase-out amounts for married couples filing joint returns*

The provision increases the threshold phase-out amounts for married couples filing joint returns to $5,000 [46] above the threshold phase-out amounts for singles, surviving spouses, and heads of households) for 2009 and 2010. For example, in 2009 the maximum credit of $3,043 for one qualifying child is available for those with earnings between $8,950 and $16,420 ($21,420 if married filing jointly). The credit begins to phase down at a rate of 15.98 percent of earnings above $16,420 ($21,420 if married filing jointly). The credit phases down to $0 at $35,463 of earnings ($40,463 if married filing jointly).

### *Effective Date*

The provision is effective for taxable years beginning after December 31, 2008.

## 3. Increase of refundable portion of the child credit (sec. 1003 of the Act and sec. 24 of the Code)

### *Present Law*

An individual may claim a tax credit for each qualifying child under the age of 17. The amount of the credit per child is $1,000 through 2010, and $500 thereafter. A child who is not a citizen, national, or resident of the United States cannot be a qualifying child.

The credit is phased out for individuals with income over certain threshold amounts. Specifically, the otherwise allowable child tax credit is reduced by $50 for each $1,000 (or fraction thereof) of modified adjusted gross income over $75,000 for single individuals or heads of households, $110,000 for married individuals filing joint returns, and $55,000 for married individuals filing separate returns. For purposes of this limitation, modified adjusted gross income includes certain otherwise excludable income earned by U.S. citizens or residents living abroad or in certain U.S. territories.

The credit is allowable against the regular tax and the alternative minimum tax. To the extent the child credit exceeds the tax-

[45] The provision was subsequently amended by section 103 of the Tax Relief, Unemployment Insurance Reauthorization, and Job Creation Act of 2010, Pub. L. No. 111–312, described in Part Sixteen of this document.

[46] The $5,000 amount is indexed for inflation in the case of taxable years beginning in 2010.

payer's tax liability, the taxpayer is eligible for a refundable credit (the additional child tax credit) equal to 15 percent of earned income in excess of a threshold dollar amount (the "earned income" formula). The threshold dollar amount is $12,550 (for 2009), and is indexed for inflation.

Families with three or more children may determine the additional child tax credit using the alternative formula, if doing so results in a larger credit than determined under the earned income formula. Under the alternative formula, the additional child tax credit equals the amount by which the taxpayer's social security taxes exceed the taxpayer's earned income tax credit ("EITC").

Earned income is defined as the sum of wages, salaries, tips, and other taxable employee compensation plus net self-employment earnings. Unlike the EITC, which also includes the preceding items in its definition of earned income, the additional child tax credit is based only on earned income to the extent it is included in computing taxable income. For example, some ministers' parsonage allowances are considered self-employment income and thus are considered earned income for purposes of computing the EITC, but the allowances are excluded from gross income for individual income tax purposes and thus are not considered earned income for purposes of the additional child tax credit.

Any credit or refund allowed or made to an individual under this provision (including to any resident of a U.S. possession) is not taken into account as income and shall not be taken into account as resources for the month of receipt and the following two months for purposes of determining eligibility of such individual or any other individual for benefits or assistance, or the amount or extent of benefits or assistance, under any Federal program or under any State or local program financed in whole or in part with Federal funds.

### *Reasons for Change*

The Congress believes that it is necessary to extend the benefit of the child credit to families that currently do not benefit by virtue of the earned income threshold in the formula for determining the refundable child credit.

### *Explanation of Provision*[47]

The provision modifies the earned income formula for the determination of the refundable child credit to apply to 15 percent of earned income in excess of $3,000 for taxable years beginning in 2009 and 2010.

### *Effective Date*

The provision is effective for taxable years beginning after December 31, 2008.

[47] The provision was subsequently amended by section 103 of the Tax Relief, Unemployment Insurance Reauthorization, and Job Creation Act of 2010, Pub. L. No. 111–312, described in Part Sixteen of this document.

### 4. American Opportunity Tax Credit (sec. 1004 of the Act and sec. 25A of the Code)

#### *Present Law*

Individual taxpayers are allowed to claim a nonrefundable credit, the Hope credit, against Federal income taxes of up to $1,800 (for 2009) per eligible student per year for qualified tuition and related expenses paid for the first two years of the student's post-secondary education in a degree or certificate program.[48] The Hope credit rate is 100 percent on the first $1,200 of qualified tuition and related expenses, and 50 percent on the next $1,200 of qualified tuition and related expenses; these dollar amounts are indexed for inflation, with the amount rounded down to the next lowest multiple of $100. Thus, for example, a taxpayer who incurs $1,200 of qualified tuition and related expenses for an eligible student is eligible (subject to the adjusted gross income phaseout described below) for a $1,200 Hope credit. If a taxpayer incurs $2,400 of qualified tuition and related expenses for an eligible student, then he or she is eligible for a $1,800 Hope credit.

The Hope credit that a taxpayer may otherwise claim is phased out ratably for taxpayers with modified adjusted gross income between $50,000 and $60,000 ($100,000 and $120,000 for married taxpayers filing a joint return) for 2009. The adjusted gross income phaseout ranges are indexed for inflation, with the amount rounded down to the next lowest multiple of $1,000.

The qualified tuition and related expenses must be incurred on behalf of the taxpayer, the taxpayer's spouse, or a dependent of the taxpayer. The Hope credit is available with respect to an individual student for two taxable years, provided that the student has not completed the first two years of post-secondary education before the beginning of the second taxable year.

The Hope credit is available in the taxable year the expenses are paid, subject to the requirement that the education is furnished to the student during that year or during an academic period beginning during the first three months of the next taxable year. Qualified tuition and related expenses paid with the proceeds of a loan generally are eligible for the Hope credit. The repayment of a loan itself is not a qualified tuition or related expense.

A taxpayer may claim the Hope credit with respect to an eligible student who is not the taxpayer or the taxpayer's spouse (e.g., in cases in which the student is the taxpayer's child) only if the taxpayer claims the student as a dependent for the taxable year for which the credit is claimed. If a student is claimed as a dependent, the student is not entitled to claim a Hope credit for that taxable year on the student's own tax return. If a parent (or other taxpayer) claims a student as a dependent, any qualified tuition and related expenses paid by the student are treated as paid by the parent (or other taxpayer) for purposes of determining the amount of qualified tuition and related expenses paid by such parent (or other taxpayer) under the provision. In addition, for each taxable

[48] Sec. 25A. The Hope credit generally may not be claimed against a taxpayer's alternative minimum tax liability. However, the credit may be claimed against a taxpayer's alternative minimum tax liability for taxable years beginning prior to January 1, 2009.

year, a taxpayer may elect either the Hope credit, the Lifetime Learning credit, or an above-the-line deduction for qualified tuition and related expenses with respect to an eligible student.

The Hope credit is available for "qualified tuition and related expenses," which include tuition and fees (excluding nonacademic fees) required to be paid to an eligible educational institution as a condition of enrollment or attendance of an eligible student at the institution. Charges and fees associated with meals, lodging, insurance, transportation, and similar personal, living, or family expenses are not eligible for the credit. The expenses of education involving sports, games, or hobbies are not qualified tuition and related expenses unless this education is part of the student's degree program.

Qualified tuition and related expenses generally include only out-of-pocket expenses. Qualified tuition and related expenses do not include expenses covered by employer-provided educational assistance and scholarships that are not required to be included in the gross income of either the student or the taxpayer claiming the credit. Thus, total qualified tuition and related expenses are reduced by any scholarship or fellowship grants excludable from gross income under section 117 and any other tax-free educational benefits received by the student (or the taxpayer claiming the credit) during the taxable year. The Hope credit is not allowed with respect to any education expense for which a deduction is claimed under section 162 or any other section of the Code.

An eligible student for purposes of the Hope credit is an individual who is enrolled in a degree, certificate, or other program (including a program of study abroad approved for credit by the institution at which such student is enrolled) leading to a recognized educational credential at an eligible educational institution. The student must pursue a course of study on at least a half-time basis. A student is considered to pursue a course of study on at least a half-time basis if the student carries at least one half the normal full-time work load for the course of study the student is pursuing for at least one academic period that begins during the taxable year. To be eligible for the Hope credit, a student must not have been convicted of a Federal or State felony consisting of the possession or distribution of a controlled substance.

Eligible educational institutions generally are accredited post-secondary educational institutions offering credit toward a bachelor's degree, an associate's degree, or another recognized post-secondary credential. Certain proprietary institutions and post-secondary vocational institutions also are eligible educational institutions. To qualify as an eligible educational institution, an institution must be eligible to participate in Department of Education student aid programs.

Effective for taxable years beginning after December 31, 2010, the changes to the Hope credit made by the Economic Growth and Tax Relief Reconciliation Act of 2001 ("EGTRRA") no longer apply. The principal EGTRRA change scheduled to expire is the change that permitted a taxpayer to claim a Hope credit in the same year that he or she claimed an exclusion from a Coverdell education savings account. Thus, after 2010, a taxpayer cannot claim a Hope credit in the same year he or she claims an exclusion from a Coverdell education savings account.

### *Reasons for Change*

The Congress observes that the cost of a college education continues to rise, and thus believes that a modification of the Hope credit is appropriate to mitigate the impact of rising tuition costs on students and their families. The Congress further believes that making a portion of the credit refundable will deliver an incentive to attend college to those who do not currently benefit from the present-law credit.

### *Explanation of Provision*[49]

The provision modifies the Hope credit for taxable years beginning in 2009 or 2010. The modified credit is referred to as the American Opportunity Tax credit. The allowable modified credit is up to $2,500 per eligible student per year for qualified tuition and related expenses paid for each of the first four years of the student's post-secondary education in a degree or certificate program. The modified credit rate is 100 percent on the first $2,000 of qualified tuition and related expenses, and 25 percent on the next $2,000 of qualified tuition and related expenses. For purposes of the modified credit, the definition of qualified tuition and related expenses is expanded to include course materials.[50]

Under the provision, the modified credit is available with respect to an individual student for four years, provided that the student has not completed the first four years of post-secondary education before the beginning of the fourth taxable year. Thus, the modified credit, in addition to other modifications, extends the application of the Hope credit to two more years of post-secondary education.

The modified credit that a taxpayer may otherwise claim is phased out ratably for taxpayers with modified adjusted gross income between $80,000 and $90,000 ($160,000 and $180,000 for married taxpayers filing a joint return). The modified credit may be claimed against a taxpayer's alternative minimum tax liability.

Forty percent of a taxpayer's otherwise allowable modified credit is refundable. However, no portion of the modified credit is refundable if the taxpayer claiming the credit is a child to whom section 1(g) applies for such taxable year (generally, any child under age 18 or any child under age 24 who is a student providing less than one-half of his or her own support, who has at least one living parent and does not file a joint return).

In addition, the provision requires the Secretary of the Treasury to conduct two studies and submit a report to Congress on the results of those studies within one year after the date of enactment. The first study shall examine how to coordinate the Hope and Lifetime Learning credits with the Pell grant program. The second study shall examine requiring students to perform community serv-

---

[49] The provision was subsequently amended by section 103 of the Tax Relief, Unemployment Insurance Reauthorization, and Job Creation Act of 2010, Pub. L. No. 111–312, described in Part Sixteen.

[50] A technical correction may be necessary so that the statute reflects this intent. See section 2(a) of H.R. 4169, the "Tax Technical Corrections Act of 2009," introduced December 2, 2009.

ice as a condition of taking their tuition and related expenses into account for purposes of the Hope and Lifetime Learning credits.

Under the Act, bona fide residents of the U.S. possessions (American Samoa, the Commonwealth of the Northern Mariana Islands, the Commonwealth of Puerto Rico, Guam, and the U.S. Virgin Islands) are not permitted to claim the refundable portion of the American opportunity credit in the United States. Rather, a bona fide resident of a mirror code possession (the Commonwealth of the Northern Mariana Islands, Guam, and the U.S. Virgin Islands) may claim the refundable portion of the credit in the possession in which the individual is a resident. Similarly, a bona fide resident of a non-mirror code possession (the Commonwealth of Puerto Rico and American Samoa) may claim the refundable portion of the credit in the possession in which the individual is a resident, but only if that possession establishes a plan for permitting the claim under its internal law.

The Act provides that the U.S. Treasury will make payments to the possessions in respect of credits allowable to their residents under their internal laws. Specifically, the U.S. Treasury will make payments to each mirror code possession in an amount equal to the aggregate amount of the refundable portion of the credits allowable by reason of the provision to that possession's residents against its income tax. This amount will be determined by the Treasury Secretary based on information provided by the government of the respective possession. To each possession that does not have a mirror code tax system, the U.S. Treasury will make two payments (for 2009 and 2010, respectively) in an amount estimated by the Secretary as being equal to the aggregate amount of the refundable portion of the credits that would have been allowed to residents of that possession if a mirror code tax system had been in effect in that possession. Accordingly, the amount of each payment to a non-mirror code possession will be an estimate of the aggregate amount of the refundable portion of the credits that would be allowed to the possession's residents if the credit provided by the provision to U.S. residents were provided by the possession to its residents. This payment will not be made to any U.S. possession unless that possession has a plan that has been approved by the Secretary under which the possession will promptly distribute the payment to its residents.

### *Effective Date*

The provision is effective with respect to taxable years beginning after December 31, 2008.

## 5. Temporarily allow computer technology and equipment as a qualified higher education expense for qualified tuition programs (sec. 1005 of the Act and sec. 529 of the Code)

### *Present Law*

Section 529 provides specified income tax and transfer tax rules for the treatment of accounts and contracts established under qualified tuition programs.[51] A qualified tuition program is a program established and maintained by a State or agency or instrumentality thereof, or by one or more eligible educational institutions, which satisfies certain requirements and under which a person may purchase tuition credits or certificates on behalf of a designated beneficiary that entitle the beneficiary to the waiver or payment of qualified higher education expenses of the beneficiary (a "prepaid tuition program"). In the case of a program established and maintained by a State or agency or instrumentality thereof, a qualified tuition program also includes a program under which a person may make contributions to an account that is established for the purpose of satisfying the qualified higher education expenses of the designated beneficiary of the account, provided it satisfies certain specified requirements (a "savings account program"). Under both types of qualified tuition programs, a contributor establishes an account for the benefit of a particular designated beneficiary to provide for that beneficiary's higher education expenses.

For this purpose, qualified higher education expenses means tuition, fees, books, supplies, and equipment required for the enrollment or attendance of a designated beneficiary at an eligible educational institution, and expenses for special needs services in the case of a special needs beneficiary that are incurred in connection with such enrollment or attendance. Qualified higher education expenses generally also include room and board for students who are enrolled at least half-time.

Contributions to a qualified tuition program must be made in cash. Section 529 does not impose a specific dollar limit on the amount of contributions, account balances, or prepaid tuition benefits relating to a qualified tuition account; however, the program is required to have adequate safeguards to prevent contributions in excess of amounts necessary to provide for the beneficiary's qualified higher education expenses. Contributions generally are treated as a completed gift eligible for the gift tax annual exclusion. Contributions are not tax deductible for Federal income tax purposes, although they may be deductible for State income tax purposes. Amounts in the account accumulate on a tax-free basis (i.e., income on accounts in the plan is not subject to current income tax).

Distributions from a qualified tuition program are excludable from the distributee's gross income to the extent that the total distribution does not exceed the qualified higher education expenses incurred for the beneficiary. If a distribution from a qualified tuition program exceeds the qualified higher education expenses incurred for the beneficiary, the portion of the excess that is treated as earnings generally is subject to income tax and an additional 10-percent tax. Amounts in a qualified tuition program may be rolled over to another qualified tuition program for the same beneficiary or for a member of the family of that beneficiary without income tax consequences.

In general, prepaid tuition contracts and tuition savings accounts established under a qualified tuition program involve prepayments or contributions made by one or more individuals for the benefit of

[51] For purposes of this description, the term "account" is used interchangeably to refer to a prepaid tuition benefit contract or a tuition savings account established pursuant to a qualified tuition program.

a designated beneficiary, with decisions with respect to the contract or account to be made by an individual who is not the designated beneficiary. Qualified tuition accounts or contracts generally require the designation of a person (generally referred to as an "account owner") whom the program administrator (oftentimes a third party administrator retained by the State or by the educational institution that established the program) may look to for decisions, recordkeeping, and reporting with respect to the account established for a designated beneficiary. Generally, the person or persons who make the contributions to the account need not be the same person who is regarded as the account owner for purposes of administering the account. Under many qualified tuition programs, the account owner generally has control over the account or contract, including the ability to change designated beneficiaries and to withdraw funds at any time and for any purpose. Thus, in practice, qualified tuition accounts or contracts generally involve a contributor, a designated beneficiary, an account owner (who oftentimes is not the contributor or the designated beneficiary), and an administrator of the account or contract.[52]

### *Explanation of Provision*[53]

The provision expands the definition of qualified higher education expenses for expenses paid or incurred in 2009 and 2010 to include expenses for certain computer technology and equipment to be used by the designated beneficiary and the beneficiary's family while the beneficiary is enrolled at an eligible educational institution.

### *Effective Date*

The provision is effective for expenses paid or incurred after December 31, 2008.

## 6. Modifications to homebuyer credit (sec. 1006 of the Act and sec. 36 of the Code)

### *Present Law*

A taxpayer who is a first-time homebuyer is allowed a refundable tax credit equal to the lesser of $7,500 ($3,750 for a married individual filing separately) or 10 percent of the purchase price of a principal residence. The credit is allowed for the tax year in which the taxpayer purchases the home unless the taxpayer makes an election as described below. The credit is allowed for qualifying home purchases on or after April 9, 2008 and before July 1, 2009 (without regard to whether there was a binding contract to purchase prior to April 9, 2008).

The credit phases out for individual taxpayers with modified adjusted gross income between $75,000 and $95,000 ($150,000 and $170,000 for joint filers) for the year of purchase.

---

[52] Section 529 refers to contributors and designated beneficiaries, but does not define or otherwise refer to the term account owner, which is a commonly used term among qualified tuition programs.

[53] The provision was subsequently amended by section 742 of the Tax Relief, Unemployment Insurance Reauthorization, and Job Creation Act of 2010, Pub. L. No. 111–312, described in Part Sixteen of this document.

A taxpayer is considered a first-time homebuyer if such individual had no ownership interest in a principal residence in the United States during the three-year period prior to the purchase of the home to which the credit applies.

No credit is allowed if the D.C. homebuyer credit is allowable for the taxable year the residence is purchased or a prior taxable year. A taxpayer is not permitted to claim the credit if the taxpayer's financing is from tax-exempt mortgage revenue bonds, if the taxpayer is a nonresident alien, or if the taxpayer disposes of the residence (or it ceases to be a principal residence) before the close of a taxable year for which a credit otherwise would be allowable.

The credit is recaptured ratably over fifteen years with no interest charge beginning in the second taxable year after the taxable year in which the home is purchased. For example, if the taxpayer purchases a home in 2008, the credit is allowed on the 2008 tax return, and repayments commence with the 2010 tax return. If the taxpayer sells the home (or the home ceases to be used as the principal residence of the taxpayer or the taxpayer's spouse) prior to complete repayment of the credit, any remaining credit repayment amount is due on the tax return for the year in which the home is sold (or ceases to be used as the principal residence). However, the credit repayment amount may not exceed the amount of gain from the sale of the residence to an unrelated person. For this purpose, gain is determined by reducing the basis of the residence by the amount of the credit to the extent not previously recaptured. No amount is recaptured after the death of a taxpayer. In the case of an involuntary conversion of the home, recapture is not accelerated if a new principal residence is acquired within a two year period. In the case of a transfer of the residence to a spouse or to a former spouse incident to divorce, the transferee spouse (and not the transferor spouse) will be responsible for any future recapture.

An election is provided to treat a home purchased in the eligible period in 2009 as if purchased on December 31, 2008 for purposes of claiming the credit on the 2008 tax return and for establishing the beginning of the recapture period. Taxpayers may amend their returns for this purpose.

### *Reasons for Change*

The Congress believes that additional support for the housing sector is warranted. To encourage purchases of homes, the Committee wishes to increase the benefit of the existing temporary provision to assist first-time homebuyers by waiving the recapture of the credit. This change transforms the credit from the equivalent of an interest-free loan (under present law) into direct financial support for qualifying home purchases. To prevent artificial sales for the purpose of garnering the refundable credit, the waiver of the credit recapture is available only if taxpayers retain the home and use it as a principal residence for at least 36 months.

### *Explanation of Provision*[54]

The Act extends the existing homebuyer credit for qualifying home purchases before December 1, 2009. In addition, it increases the maximum credit amount to $8,000 ($4,000 for a married individual filing separately) and waives the recapture of the credit for qualifying home purchases after December 31, 2008 and before December 1, 2009. This waiver of recapture applies without regard to whether the taxpayer elects to treat the purchase in 2009 as occurring on December 31, 2008. If the taxpayer disposes of the home or the home otherwise ceases to be the principal residence of the taxpayer within 36 months from the date of purchase, the present law rules for recapture of the credit will apply.

The Act modifies the coordination with the first-time homebuyer credit for residents of the District of Columbia under section 1400C. No credit under section 1400C shall be allowed to any taxpayer with respect to the purchase of a residence during 2009 if a credit under section 36 is allowable to such taxpayer (or the taxpayer's spouse) with respect to such purchase. Taxpayers thus qualify for the more generous national first-time homebuyer credit rather than the D.C. homebuyer credit for qualifying purchases in 2009. No credit under section 36 is allowed for a taxpayer who claimed the D.C. homebuyer credit in any prior taxable year.

The Act removes the prohibition on claiming the credit if the residence is financed by the proceeds of a mortgage revenue bond, a qualified mortgage issue the interest on which is exempt from tax under section 103.

### *Effective Date*

The provision applies to residences purchased after December 31, 2008.

## 7. Election to substitute grants to states for low-income housing projects in lieu of low-income housing credit allocation for 2009 (secs. 1404 and 1602 of the Act and sec. 42 of the Code)

### *Present Law*

#### *In general*

The low-income housing credit may be claimed over a 10-year period by owners of certain residential rental property for the cost of rental housing occupied by tenants having incomes below specified levels.[55] The amount of the credit for any taxable year in the credit period is the applicable percentage of the qualified basis of each qualified low-income building. The qualified basis of any qualified low-income building for any taxable year equals the applicable fraction of the eligible basis of the building.

---

[54] This provision was subsequently amended by sections 11 and 12 of the Worker, Homeownership, and Business Assistance Act of 2009, Pub. L. No. 111–92, described in Part Five, and by section 2 of the Homebuyer Assistance and Improvement Act of 2010, Pub. L. No. 111–98, described in Part Ten of this document.

[55] Sec. 42.

### *Volume limits*

A low-income housing credit is allowable only if the owner of a qualified building receives a housing credit allocation from the State or local housing credit agency. Generally, the aggregate credit authority provided annually to each State for calendar year 2009 is $2.30 per resident, with a minimum annual cap of $2,665,000 for certain small population States.[56] These amounts are indexed for inflation. Projects that also receive financing with proceeds of tax-exempt bonds issued subject to the private activity bond volume limit do not require an allocation of the low-income housing credit.

### *Basic rule for Federal grants*

The basis of a qualified building must be reduced by the amount of any Federal grant with respect to such building.

## *Reasons for Change*

The current economic downturn has reduced the attractiveness of low-income housing tax credits to potential investors, in part because some potential investors have reduced or no taxable income to offset with these tax credits. The Congress believes that this provision gives State allocating agencies added flexibility and will encourage the building of more low-income housing in the short term, until investors can again use these tax credits.

## *Explanation of Provision*

### *Low-income housing grant election amount*

The Secretary of the Treasury shall make a grant to the State housing credit agency of each State in an amount equal to the low-income housing grant election amount.

The low-income housing grant election amount for a State is an amount elected by the State subject to certain limits. The maximum low-income housing grant election amount for a State may not exceed 85 percent of the product of ten and the sum of the State's: (1) unused housing credit ceiling for 2008; (2) any returns to the State during 2009 of credit allocations previously made by the State; (3) 40 percent of the State's 2009 credit allocation; and (4) 40 percent of the State's share of the national pool allocated in 2009, if any.

Grants under this provision are not taxable income to recipients.

### *Subawards to low-income housing credit buildings*

A State receiving a grant under this provision is to use these monies to make subawards to finance the construction, or acquisition and rehabilitation of qualified low-income buildings as defined under the low-income housing credit. A subaward may be made to finance a qualified low-income building regardless of whether the building has an allocation of low-income housing credit. However, in the case of qualified low-income buildings without allocations of the low-income housing credit, the State housing credit agency must make a determination that the subaward with respect to such building will increase the total funds available to the State to build

[56] Rev. Proc. 2008–66.

and rehabilitate affordable housing. In conjunction with this determination the State housing credit agency must establish a process in which applicants for the subawards must demonstrate good faith efforts to obtain investment commitments before the agency makes such subawards.

Any building receiving grant money from a subaward is required to satisfy the low-income housing credit rules. The State housing credit agency shall perform asset management functions to ensure compliance with the low-income housing credit rules and the long-term viability of buildings financed with these subawards.[57] Failure to satisfy the low-income housing credit rules will result in recapture, enforced by means of liens or other methods that the Secretary of the Treasury (or delegate) deems appropriate. Any such recapture will be payable to the Secretary of the Treasury for deposit in the general fund of the Treasury.

Any grant funds not used to make subawards before January 1, 2011, and any grant monies from subawards returned on or after January 1, 2011, must be returned to the Secretary of the Treasury.

***Basic rule for Federal grants***

The grants received under this provision do not reduce the tax basis of a qualified low-income building.

***Reduction in low-income housing credit volume limit for 2009***

The otherwise applicable low-income housing credit volume limit for any State for 2009 is reduced by the amount taken into account in determining the low-income housing grant election amount.

***Appropriations***

The provision appropriates to the Secretary of the Treasury such sums as may be necessary to carry out this provision.

### *Effective Date*

The provision is effective on the date of enactment (February 17, 2009).

## 8. Exclusion from gross income for unemployment compensation benefits (sec. 1007 of the Act and sec. 85 of the Code)

### *Present Law*

An individual must include in gross income any unemployment compensation benefits received under the laws of the United States or any State.

---

[57] The State housing credit agency may collect reasonable fees from subaward recipients to cover the expenses of the agency's asset management duties. Alternatively, the State housing credit agency may retain a third party to perform these asset management duties.

### *Explanation of Provision*

The Act provides that up to $2,400 of unemployment compensation benefits received in taxable years beginning in 2009 are excluded from gross income by the recipient.

### *Effective Date*

The provision is effective for taxable years beginning after December 31, 2008.

## 9. Deduction for State sales tax and excise tax on the purchase of qualified motor vehicles (sec. 1008 of the Act and secs. 63 and 164 of the Code)

### *Present Law*

In general, a deduction from gross income is allowed for certain taxes for the taxable year within which the taxes are paid or accrued. These include State, local, and foreign real property taxes; State and local personal property taxes; State, local, and foreign income, war profits, and excess profit taxes; generation skipping transfer taxes; environmental taxes imposed by section 59A; and taxes paid or accrued within the taxable year in carrying on a trade or business or an activity described in section 212 (relating to the expenses for production of income). At the election of the taxpayer for the taxable year, a taxpayer may deduct State and local sales taxes in lieu of State and local income taxes. No deduction is allowed for any general sales tax imposed with respect to an item at a rate other than the general rate of tax, except in the case of a lower rate of tax applicable to items of food, clothing, medical supplies, and motor vehicles. In the case of motor vehicles, if the rate of tax exceeds the general rate, such excess shall be disregarded, and the general rate shall be treated as the rate of tax.

### *Explanation of Provision*

The Act provides a deduction for qualified motor vehicle taxes. It expands the definition of taxes allowed as a deduction to include qualified motor vehicle taxes paid or accrued within the taxable year. A taxpayer who itemizes and makes an election to deduct State and local sales taxes, including for qualified motor vehicles, in lieu of State and local income taxes for the taxable year shall not be allowed an additional deduction for qualified motor vehicle taxes. A taxpayer who does not itemize deductions is allowed an increased standard deduction for qualified motor vehicle taxes.

Qualified motor vehicle taxes include any State or local sales or excise tax imposed on the purchase of a qualified motor vehicle. A qualified motor vehicle means a passenger automobile, light truck, or motorcycle which has a gross vehicle weight rating of not more than 8,500 pounds, or a motor home acquired for use by the taxpayer after the date of enactment and before January 1, 2010, the original use of which commences with the taxpayer.

The deduction is limited to the tax on up to $49,500 of the purchase price of a qualified motor vehicle. The deduction is phased out for taxpayers with modified adjusted gross income between

$125,000 and $135,000 ($250,000 and $260,000 in the case of a joint return).

### *Effective Date*

The provision is effective for purchases on or after the date of enactment (February 17, 2009) and before January 1, 2010.

## 10. Extend alternative minimum tax relief for individuals (secs. 1011 and 1012 of the Act and secs. 26 and 55 of the Code)

### *Present Law*

Present law imposes an alternative minimum tax ("AMT") on individuals. The AMT is the amount by which the tentative minimum tax exceeds the regular income tax. An individual's tentative minimum tax is the sum of (1) 26 percent of so much of the taxable excess as does not exceed $175,000 ($87,500 in the case of a married individual filing a separate return) and (2) 28 percent of the remaining taxable excess. The taxable excess is so much of the alternative minimum taxable income ("AMTI") as exceeds the exemption amount. The maximum tax rates on net capital gain and dividends used in computing the regular tax are used in computing the tentative minimum tax. AMTI is the individual's taxable income adjusted to take account of specified preferences and adjustments.

The exemption amounts are: (1) $69,950 for taxable years beginning in 2008 and $45,000 in taxable years beginning after 2008 in the case of married individuals filing a joint return and surviving spouses; (2) $46,200 for taxable years beginning in 2008 and $33,750 in taxable years beginning after 2008 in the case of other unmarried individuals; (3) $34,975 for taxable years beginning in 2008 and $22,500 in taxable years beginning after 2008 in the case of married individuals filing separate returns; and (4) $22,500 in the case of an estate or trust. The exemption amount is phased out by an amount equal to 25 percent of the amount by which the individual's AMTI exceeds (1) $150,000 in the case of married individuals filing a joint return and surviving spouses, (2) $112,500 in the case of other unmarried individuals, and (3) $75,000 in the case of married individuals filing separate returns or an estate or a trust. These amounts are not indexed for inflation.

Present law provides for certain nonrefundable personal tax credits (i.e., the dependent care credit, the credit for the elderly and disabled, the adoption credit, the child credit, the credit for interest on certain home mortgages, the Hope Scholarship and Lifetime Learning credits, the credit for savers, the credit for certain nonbusiness energy property, the credit for residential energy efficient property, the credit for plug-in electric drive motor vehicles, and the D.C. first-time homebuyer credit).

For taxable years beginning before 2009, the nonrefundable personal credits are allowed to the extent of the full amount of the individual's regular tax and alternative minimum tax.

For taxable years beginning after 2008, the nonrefundable personal credits (other than the adoption credit, the child credit, the credit for savers, the credit for residential energy efficient property, and the credit for plug-in electric drive motor vehicles) are allowed only to the extent that the individual's regular income tax liability exceeds the individual's tentative minimum tax, determined without regard to the minimum tax foreign tax credit. The adoption credit, the child credit, the credit for savers, the credit for residential energy efficient property, and the credit for plug-in electric drive motor vehicles are allowed to the full extent of the individual's regular tax and alternative minimum tax.[58]

### *Explanation of Provision*[59]

The Act provides that the individual AMT exemption amount for taxable years beginning in 2009 is $70,950, in the case of married individuals filing a joint return and surviving spouses; (2) $46,700 in the case of other unmarried individuals; and (3) $35,475 in the case of married individuals filing separate returns.

For taxable years beginning in 2009, the provision allows an individual to offset the entire regular tax liability and alternative minimum tax liability by the nonrefundable personal credits.

### *Effective Date*

The provision is effective for taxable years beginning in 2009.

## B. Tax Incentives for Business

### 1. Special allowance for certain property acquired during 2009 and extension of election to accelerate AMT and research credits in lieu of bonus depreciation (sec. 1201 of the Act and sec. 168(k) of the Code)

### *Present Law*

An additional first-year depreciation deduction is allowed equal to 50 percent of the adjusted basis of qualified property placed in service during 2008 (and 2009 for certain longer-lived and transportation property).[60] The additional first-year depreciation deduction is allowed for both regular tax and alternative minimum tax purposes for the taxable year in which the property is placed in service.[61] The basis of the property and the depreciation allowances in the year of purchase and later years are appropriately adjusted to reflect the additional first-year depreciation deduction. In addition, there are no adjustments to the allowable amount of depreciation for purposes of computing a taxpayer's alternative minimum taxable income with respect to property to which the provision applies. The amount of the additional first-year depreciation deduction is not affected by a short taxable year. The taxpayer may elect out of additional first-year depreciation for any class of property for any taxable year.

---

[58] The rule applicable to the adoption credit and child credit is subject to the EGTRRA sunset.

[59] The provision was subsequently amended by sections 201 and 202 of the Tax Relief, Unemployment Insurance Reauthorization, and Job Creation Act of 2010, Pub. L. No. 111–312, described in Part Sixteen of this document.

[60] Sec. 168(k). The additional first-year depreciation deduction is subject to the general rules regarding whether an item is deductible under section 162 or instead is subject to capitalization under section 263 or section 263A.

[61] However, the additional first-year depreciation deduction is not allowed for purposes of computing earnings and profits.

The interaction of the additional first-year depreciation allowance with the otherwise applicable depreciation allowance may be illustrated as follows. Assume that in 2008, a taxpayer purchases new depreciable property and places it in service.[62] The property's cost is $1,000, and it is five-year property subject to the half-year convention. The amount of additional first-year depreciation allowed is $500. The remaining $500 of the cost of the property is deductible under the rules applicable to 5-year property. Thus, 20 percent, or $100, is also allowed as a depreciation deduction in 2008. The total depreciation deduction with respect to the property for 2008 is $600. The remaining $400 cost of the property is recovered under otherwise applicable rules for computing depreciation.

In order for property to qualify for the additional first-year depreciation deduction it must meet all of the following requirements. First, the property must be (1) property to which MACRS applies with an applicable recovery period of 20 years or less, (2) water utility property (as defined in section 168(e)(5)), (3) computer software other than computer software covered by section 197, or (4) qualified leasehold improvement property (as defined in section 168(k)(3)).[63] Second, the original use[64] of the property must commence with the taxpayer after December 31, 2007.[65] Third, the taxpayer must acquire the property within the applicable time period. Finally, the property must be placed in service after December 31, 2007, and before January 1, 2009. An extension of the placed in service date of one year (i.e., to January 1, 2010) is provided for certain property with a recovery period of ten years or longer and certain transportation property.[66] Transportation property is defined as tangible personal property used in the trade or business of transporting persons or property.

The applicable time period for acquired property is (1) after December 31, 2007, and before January 1, 2009, but only if no binding written contract for the acquisition is in effect before January 1, 2008, or (2) pursuant to a binding written contract which was entered into after December 31, 2007, and before January 1, 2009.[67] With respect to property that is manufactured, constructed, or produced by the taxpayer for use by the taxpayer, the taxpayer must

---

[62] Assume that the cost of the property is not eligible for expensing under section 179.

[63] A special rule precludes the additional first-year depreciation deduction for any property that is required to be depreciated under the alternative depreciation system of MACRS.

[64] The term "original use" means the first use to which the property is put, whether or not such use corresponds to the use of such property by the taxpayer.

If in the normal course of its business a taxpayer sells fractional interests in property to unrelated third parties, then the original use of such property begins with the first user of each fractional interest (i.e., each fractional owner is considered the original user of its proportionate share of the property).

[65] A special rule applies in the case of certain leased property. In the case of any property that is originally placed in service by a person and that is sold to the taxpayer and leased back to such person by the taxpayer within three months after the date that the property was placed in service, the property would be treated as originally placed in service by the taxpayer not earlier than the date that the property is used under the leaseback.

If property is originally placed in service by a lessor, such property is sold within three months after the date that the property was placed in service, and the user of such property does not change, then the property is treated as originally placed in service by the taxpayer not earlier than the date of such sale.

[66] In order for property to qualify for the extended placed in service date, the property is required to have an estimated production period exceeding one year and a cost exceeding $1 million.

[67] Property does not fail to qualify for the additional first-year depreciation merely because a binding written contract to acquire a component of the property is in effect prior to January 1, 2008.

begin the manufacture, construction, or production of the property after December 31, 2007, and before January 1, 2009. Property that is manufactured, constructed, or produced for the taxpayer by another person under a contract that is entered into prior to the manufacture, construction, or production of the property is considered to be manufactured, constructed, or produced by the taxpayer. For property eligible for the extended placed in service date, a special rule limits the amount of costs eligible for the additional first-year depreciation. With respect to such property, only the portion of the basis that is properly attributable to the costs incurred before January 1, 2009, ("progress expenditures") is eligible for the additional first-year depreciation.[68]

Property does not qualify for the additional first-year depreciation deduction when the user of such property (or a related party) would not have been eligible for the additional first-year depreciation deduction if the user (or a related party) were treated as the owner. For example, if a taxpayer sells to a related party property that was under construction prior to January 1, 2008, the property does not qualify for the additional first-year depreciation deduction. Similarly, if a taxpayer sells to a related party property that was subject to a binding written contract prior to January 1, 2008, the property does not qualify for the additional first-year depreciation deduction. As a further example, if a taxpayer (the lessee) sells property in a sale-leaseback arrangement, and the property otherwise would not have qualified for the additional first-year depreciation deduction if it were owned by the taxpayer-lessee, then the lessor is not entitled to the additional first-year depreciation deduction.

The limitation on the amount of depreciation deductions allowed with respect to certain passenger automobiles (sec. 280F) is increased in the first year by $8,000 for automobiles that qualify (and do not elect out of the increased first year deduction). The $8,000 increase is not indexed for inflation.

Corporations otherwise eligible for additional first year depreciation under section 168(k) may elect to claim additional research or minimum tax credits in lieu of claiming depreciation under section 168(k) for "eligible qualified property" placed in service after March 31, 2008 and before December 31, 2008.[69] A corporation making the election forgoes the depreciation deductions allowable under section 168(k) and instead increases the limitation under section 38(c) on the use of research credits or section 53(c) on the use of minimum tax credits.[70] The increases in the allowable credits are treated as refundable for purposes of this provision. The depreciation for qualified property is calculated for both regular tax and AMT purposes using the straight-line method in place of the method that would otherwise be used absent the election under this provision.

---

[68] For purposes of determining the amount of eligible progress expenditures, it is intended that rules similar to sec. 46(d)(3) as in effect prior to the Tax Reform Act of 1986 shall apply.

[69] Sec. 168(k)(4). In the case of an electing corporation that is a partner in a partnership, the corporate partner's distributive share of partnership items is determined as if section 168(k) does not apply to any eligible qualified property and the straight line method is used to calculate depreciation of such property.

[70] Special rules apply to an applicable partnership.

The research credit or minimum tax credit limitation is increased by the bonus depreciation amount, which is equal to 20 percent of bonus depreciation[71] for certain eligible qualified property that could be claimed absent an election under this provision. Generally, eligible qualified property included in the calculation is bonus depreciation property that meets the following requirements: (1) the original use of the property must commence with the taxpayer after March 31, 2008; (2) the taxpayer must purchase the property either (a) after March 31, 2008, and before January 1, 2009, but only if no binding written contract for the acquisition is in effect before April 1, 2008,[72] or (b) pursuant to a binding written contract which was entered into after March 31, 2008, and before January 1, 2009;[73] and (3) the property must be placed in service after March 31, 2008, and before January 1, 2009 (January 1, 2010 for certain longer-lived and transportation property).

The bonus depreciation amount is limited to the lesser of: (1) $30 million, or (2) six percent of the sum of research credit carryforwards from taxable years beginning before January 1, 2006 and minimum tax credits allocable to the adjusted minimum tax imposed for taxable years beginning before January 1, 2006. All corporations treated as a single employer under section 52(a) are treated as one taxpayer for purposes of the limitation, as well as for electing the application of this provision.

### *Reasons for Change*

Congress believes that allowing additional first-year depreciation will accelerate purchases of equipment and other assets, and promote capital investment, modernization, and growth.

### *Explanation of Provision*[74]

The provision extends the additional first-year depreciation deduction for one year, generally through 2009 (through 2010 for certain longer-lived and transportation property).

The provision generally permits corporations to increase the research credit or minimum tax credit limitation by the bonus depreciation amount with respect to certain property placed in service in 2009 (2010 in the case of certain longer-lived and transportation property).[75] The provision applies with respect to extension prop-

[71] For this purpose, bonus depreciation is the difference between (i) the aggregate amount of depreciation for all eligible qualified property determined if section 168(k)(1) applied using the most accelerated depreciation method (determined without regard to this provision), and shortest life allowable for each property, and (ii) the amount of depreciation that would be determined if section 168(k)(1) did not apply using the same method and life for each property.

[72] In the case of passenger aircraft, the written binding contract limitation does not apply.

[73] Special rules apply to property manufactured, constructed, or produced by the taxpayer for use by the taxpayer.

[74] The additional first year depreciation deduction was subsequently extended for one year generally through 2010 (through 2011 for certain longer-lived and transportation property) by section 2022 of the Small Business Jobs Act of 2010, Pub. L. No. 111–240, described in Part Fourteen. The provision was temporarily expanded and extended generally through 2012 (through 2013 for certain longer-lived and transportation property) by section 401 of the Tax Relief, Unemployment Insurance Reauthorization, and Job Creation Act of 2010, Pub. L. No. 111–312, described in Part Sixteen of this document.

[75] The provision allowing a taxpayer to claim certain credits in lieu of bonus depreciation was subsequently modified and extended generally through 2012 by section 401 of the Tax Relief, Unemployment Insurance Reauthorization, and Job Creation Act of 2010, Pub. L. No. 111–312, described in Part Sixteen of this document.

erty, which is defined as property that is eligible qualified property solely because it meets the requirements under the extension of the special allowance for certain property acquired during 2009.

Under the provision, a taxpayer that has made an election to increase the research credit or minimum tax credit limitation for eligible qualified property for its first taxable year ending after March 31, 2008, may choose not to make this election for extension property. Further, the provision allows a taxpayer that has not made an election for eligible qualified property for its first taxable year ending after March 31, 2008, to make the election for extension property for its first taxable year ending after December 31, 2008, and for each subsequent year. In the case of a taxpayer electing to increase the research or minimum tax credit for both eligible qualified property and extension property, a separate bonus depreciation amount, maximum amount, and maximum increase amount is computed and applied to each group of property.[76]

### *Effective Date*

The extension of the additional first-year depreciation deduction is generally effective for property placed in service after December 31, 2008.

The extension of the election to accelerate AMT and research credits in lieu of bonus depreciation is effective for taxable years ending after December 31, 2008.

## 2. Temporary increase in limitations on expensing of certain depreciable business assets (sec. 1202 of the Act and sec. 179 of the Code)

### *Present Law*

In lieu of depreciation, a taxpayer with a sufficiently small amount of annual investment may elect to deduct (or "expense") such costs under section 179. Present law provides that the maximum amount a taxpayer may expense for taxable years beginning in 2008 is $250,000 of the cost of qualifying property placed in service for the taxable year.[77] For taxable years beginning in 2009 and 2010, the limitation is $125,000. In general, qualifying property is defined as depreciable tangible personal property that is purchased for use in the active conduct of a trade or business. Off-the-shelf computer software placed in service in taxable years beginning before 2011 is treated as qualifying property. For taxable years beginning in 2008, the $250,000 amount is reduced (but not below zero) by the amount by which the cost of qualifying property placed in service during the taxable year exceeds $800,000. For taxable years beginning in 2009 and 2010, the $125,000 amount is reduced (but not below zero) by the amount by which the cost of qualifying property placed in service during the taxable year ex-

---

[76] In computing the maximum amount, the maximum increase amount for extension property is reduced by bonus depreciation amounts for preceding taxable years only with respect to extension property.

[77] Additional section 179 incentives are provided with respect to qualified property meeting applicable requirements that is used by a business in an empowerment zone (sec. 1397A) or a renewal community (sec. 1400J), qualified section 179 Gulf Opportunity Zone property (sec. 1400N(e)), qualified Recovery Assistance property placed in service in the Kansas disaster area, Pub. L. No. 110–234, sec. 15345 (2008), and qualified disaster assistance property (sec. 179(e)).

ceeds $500,000. The $125,000 and $500,000 amounts are indexed for inflation in taxable years beginning in 2009 and 2010.

The amount eligible to be expensed for a taxable year may not exceed the taxable income for a taxable year that is derived from the active conduct of a trade or business (determined without regard to this provision). Any amount that is not allowed as a deduction because of the taxable income limitation may be carried forward to succeeding taxable years (subject to similar limitations). No general business credit under section 38 is allowed with respect to any amount for which a deduction is allowed under section 179. An expensing election is made under rules prescribed by the Secretary.[78]

For taxable years beginning in 2011 and thereafter (or before 2003), the following rules apply. A taxpayer with a sufficiently small amount of annual investment may elect to deduct up to $25,000 of the cost of qualifying property placed in service for the taxable year. The $25,000 amount is reduced (but not below zero) by the amount by which the cost of qualifying property placed in service during the taxable year exceeds $200,000. The $25,000 and $200,000 amounts are not indexed for inflation. In general, qualifying property is defined as depreciable tangible personal property that is purchased for use in the active conduct of a trade or business (not including off-the-shelf computer software). An expensing election may be revoked only with consent of the Commissioner.[79]

### *Reasons for Change*

Congress believes that section 179 expensing provides two important benefits. First, it lowers the cost of capital for property used in a trade or business. With a lower cost of capital, Congress believes businesses will invest in more equipment and employ more workers. Second, expensing eliminates depreciation recordkeeping requirements with respect to expensed property. Congress believes that the higher limitation amounts available during 2008 will continue to provide important benefits if extended, and the bill therefore extends the higher limitation amounts for an additional year. Furthermore, Congress believes that the higher dollar limits on expensing further lower the cost of capital, and make this benefit available for a greater number of taxpayers.

### *Explanation of Provision*[80]

The provision extends the $250,000 and $800,000 amounts to taxable years beginning in 2009.[81]

---

[78] Sec. 179(c)(1). Under Treas. Reg. sec. 1.179–5, applicable to property placed in service in taxable years beginning after 2002 and before 2008, a taxpayer is permitted to make or revoke an election under section 179 without the consent of the Commissioner on an amended Federal tax return for that taxable year. This amended return must be filed within the time prescribed by law for filing an amended return for the taxable year. T.D. 9209, July 12, 2005.

[79] Sec. 179(c)(2).

[80] The provision was subsequently amended by section 402 of the Tax Relief, Unemployment Insurance Reauthorization, and Job Creation Act of 2010, Pub. L. No. 111–312, described in Part Sixteen of this document.

[81] The provision was extended to taxable years beginning after 2009 and before 2011 by section 201 of the Hiring Incentives to Restore Employment Act of 2010, Pub. L. No. 111–147, described in Part Seven. Additionally, the provision was temporarily expanded and extended for taxable years beginning in 2010 and 2011 by section 2021 of the Small Business Jobs Act of

Continued

### *Effective Date*

The provision is effective for taxable years beginning after December 31, 2008.

## 3. Five-year carryback of operating losses (sec. 1211 of the Act and sec. 172 of the Code)

### *Present Law*

Under present law, a net operating loss ("NOL") generally means the amount by which a taxpayer's business deductions exceed its gross income. In general, an NOL may be carried back two years and carried over 20 years to offset taxable income in such years.[82] NOLs offset taxable income in the order of the taxable years to which the NOL may be carried.[83]

The alternative minimum tax rules provide that a taxpayer's NOL deduction cannot reduce the taxpayer's alternative minimum taxable income ("AMTI") by more than 90 percent of the AMTI.

Different rules apply with respect to NOLs arising in certain circumstances. A three-year carryback applies with respect to NOLs (1) arising from casualty or theft losses of individuals, or (2) attributable to Presidentially declared disasters for taxpayers engaged in a farming business or a small business. A five-year carryback applies to NOLs (1) arising from a farming loss (regardless of whether the loss was incurred in a Presidentially declared disaster area), (2) certain amounts related to Hurricane Katrina, Gulf Opportunity Zone, and Midwestern Disaster Area, or (3) qualified disaster losses.[84] Special rules also apply to real estate investment trusts (no carryback), specified liability losses (10-year carryback), and excess interest losses (no carryback to any year preceding a corporate equity reduction transaction). Additionally, a special rule applies to certain electric utility companies.

In the case of a life insurance company, present law allows a deduction for the operations loss carryovers and carrybacks to the taxable year, in lieu of the deduction for net operation losses allowed to other corporations.[85] A life insurance company is permitted to treat a loss from operations (as defined under section 810(c)) for any taxable year as an operations loss carryback to each of the three taxable years preceding the loss year and an operations loss carryover to each of the 15 taxable years following the loss year.[86] Special rules apply to new life insurance companies.

### *Reasons for Change*

The NOL carryback and carryover rules are designed to allow taxpayers to smooth out swings in business income (and Federal income taxes thereon) that result from business cycle fluctuations. The recent economic conditions have resulted in many taxpayers

2010, Pub. L. No. 111–240, described in Part Fourteen, and modified and extended for taxable years beginning in 2012 by section 402 of the Tax Relief, Unemployment Insurance Reauthorization, and Job Creation Act of 2010, Pub. L. No. 111–312, described in Part Sixteen of this document.

[82] Sec. 172(b)(1)(A).

[83] Sec. 172(b)(2).

[84] Sec. 172(b)(1)(J).

[85] Secs. 810, 805(a)(5).

[86] Sec. 810(b)(1).

incurring significant financial losses. Congress is concerned about the severity of the current economic downturn. A temporary extension of the NOL carryback period provides taxpayers in all sectors of the economy that experience such losses with the ability to obtain refunds of income taxes paid in prior years. These refunds can be used to fund capital investment or other expenses.

### *Explanation of Provision*

The Act provides an eligible small business with an election[87] to increase the present-law carryback period for an applicable 2008 NOL from two years to any whole number of years elected by the taxpayer that is more than two and less than six.[88] An eligible small business is a taxpayer meeting a $15,000,000 gross receipts test.[89] An applicable NOL is the taxpayer's NOL for any taxable year ending in 2008, or if elected by the taxpayer, the NOL for any taxable year beginning in 2008. However, any election under this provision may be made only with respect to one taxable year.

### *Effective Date*

The provision is effective for NOLs arising in taxable years ending after December 31, 2007.

For an NOL for a taxable year ending before the enactment of the provision (i.e., before February 17, 2009), the provision includes the following transition rules: (1) any election to waive the carryback period under either section 172(b)(3) with respect to such loss may be revoked before the applicable date; (2) any election to increase the carryback period under this provision is treated as timely made if made before the applicable date; and (3) any application for a tentative carryback adjustment under section 6411(a) with respect to such loss is treated as timely filed if filed before the applicable date. For purposes of the transition rules, the applicable date is the date which is 60 days after the date of the enactment of the provision (i.e., 60 days after February 17, 2009).

## 4. Estimated tax payments (sec. 1212 of the Act and sec. 6654 of the Code)

### *Present Law*

Under present law, the income tax system is designed to ensure that taxpayers pay taxes throughout the year based on their income and deductions. To the extent that tax is not collected through withholding, taxpayers are required to make quarterly estimated payments of tax, the amount of which is determined by reference to the required annual payment. The required annual payment is the lesser of 90 percent of the tax shown on the return or 100 percent of the tax shown on the return for the prior taxable year (110 percent if the adjusted gross income for the preceding year exceeded $150,000). An underpayment results if the required

[87] For all elections under this provision, the common parent of a group of corporations filing a consolidated return makes the election, which is binding on all such corporations.

[88] The provision was modified and extended by section 13 of the Worker, Homeownership, and Business Assistance Act of 2009, Pub. L. No. 111–92, described in Part Five of this document.

[89] For this purpose, the gross receipt test of section 448(c) is applied by substituting $15,000,000 for $5,000,000 each place it appears.

payment exceeds the amount (if any) of the installment paid on or before the due date of the installment. The period of the underpayment runs from the due date of the installment to the earlier of (1) the 15th day of the fourth month following the close of the taxable year or (2) the date on which each portion of the underpayment is made. If a taxpayer fails to pay the required estimated tax payments under the rules, a penalty is imposed in an amount determined by applying the underpayment interest rate to the amount of the underpayment for the period of the underpayment. The penalty for failure to pay estimated tax is the equivalent of interest, which is based on the time value of money.

Taxpayers are not liable for a penalty for the failure to pay estimated tax in certain circumstances. The statute provides exceptions for U.S. persons who did not have a tax liability the preceding year, if the tax shown on the return for the taxable year (or, if no return is filed, the tax), reduced by withholding, is less than $1,000, or the taxpayer is a recently retired or disabled person who satisfies the reasonable cause exception.

### *Explanation of Provision*

The Act provides that the required annual estimated tax payments of a qualified individual for taxable years beginning in 2009 is not greater than 90 percent of the tax liability shown on the tax return for the preceding taxable year. A qualified individual means any individual if the adjusted gross income shown on the tax return for the preceding taxable year is less than $500,000 ($250,000 if married filing separately) and the individual certifies that at least 50 percent of the gross income shown on the return for the preceding taxable year was income from a small trade or business. For purposes of this provision, a small trade or business means any trade or business that employed no more than 500 persons, on average, during the calendar year ending in or with the preceding taxable year.

### *Effective Date*

The provision is effective on the date of enactment (February 17, 2009).

## 5. Modification of work opportunity tax credit (sec. 1221 of the Act and sec. 51 of the Code)

### *Present Law*

#### *In general*

The work opportunity tax credit is available on an elective basis for employers hiring individuals from one or more of nine targeted groups. The amount of the credit available to an employer is determined by the amount of qualified wages paid by the employer. Generally, qualified wages consist of wages attributable to service rendered by a member of a targeted group during the one-year period beginning with the day the individual begins work for the employer (two years in the case of an individual in the long-term family assistance recipient category).

***Targeted groups eligible for the credit***

Generally, an employer is eligible for the credit only for qualified wages paid to members of a targeted group.

*(1) Families receiving TANF*

An eligible recipient is an individual certified by a designated local employment agency (e.g., a State employment agency) as being a member of a family eligible to receive benefits under the Temporary Assistance for Needy Families Program ("TANF") for a period of at least nine months part of which is during the 18-month period ending on the hiring date. For these purposes, members of the family are defined to include only those individuals taken into account for purposes of determining eligibility for the TANF.

*(2) Qualified veteran*

There are two subcategories of qualified veterans related to eligibility for food stamps and compensation for a service-connected disability.

*Food stamps*

A qualified veteran is a veteran who is certified by the designated local agency as a member of a family receiving assistance under a food stamp program under the Food Stamp Act of 1977 for a period of at least three months part of which is during the 12-month period ending on the hiring date. For these purposes, members of a family are defined to include only those individuals taken into account for purposes of determining eligibility for a food stamp program under the Food Stamp Act of 1977.

*Entitled to compensation for a service-connected disability*

A qualified veteran also includes an individual who is certified as entitled to compensation for a service-connected disability and: (1) having a hiring date which is not more than one year after having been discharged or released from active duty in the Armed Forces of the United States; or (2) having been unemployed for six months or more (whether or not consecutive) during the one-year period ending on the date of hiring.

*Definitions*

For these purposes, being entitled to compensation for a service-connected disability is defined with reference to section 101 of Title 38, U.S. Code, which means having a disability rating of 10 percent or higher for service connected injuries.

For these purposes, a veteran is an individual who has served on active duty (other than for training) in the Armed Forces for more than 180 days or who has been discharged or released from active duty in the Armed Forces for a service-connected disability. However, any individual who has served for a period of more than 90 days during which the individual was on active duty (other than for training) is not a qualified veteran if any of this active duty occurred during the 60-day period ending on the date the individual was hired by the employer. This latter rule is intended to prevent employers who hire current members of the armed services (or those departed from service within the last 60 days) from receiving the credit.

*(3) Qualified ex-felon*

A qualified ex-felon is an individual certified as: (1) having been convicted of a felony under any State or Federal law; and (2) having a hiring date within one year of release from prison or the date of conviction.

*(4) Designated community residents*

A designated community resident is an individual certified as being at least age 18 but not yet age 40 on the hiring date and as having a principal place of abode within an empowerment zone, enterprise community, renewal community or a rural renewal community. For these purposes, a rural renewal county is a county outside a metropolitan statistical area (as defined by the Office of Management and Budget) which had a net population loss during the five-year periods 1990–1994 and 1995–1999. Qualified wages do not include wages paid or incurred for services performed after the individual moves outside an empowerment zone, enterprise community, renewal community or a rural renewal community.

*(5) Vocational rehabilitation referral*

A vocational rehabilitation referral is an individual who is certified by a designated local agency as an individual who has a physical or mental disability that constitutes a substantial handicap to employment and who has been referred to the employer while receiving, or after completing: (a) vocational rehabilitation services under an individualized, written plan for employment under a State plan approved under the Rehabilitation Act of 1973; (b) under a rehabilitation plan for veterans carried out under Chapter 31 of Title 38, U.S. Code; or (c) an individual work plan developed and implemented by an employment network pursuant to subsection (g) of section 1148 of the Social Security Act. Certification will be provided by the designated local employment agency upon assurances from the vocational rehabilitation agency that the employee has met the above conditions.

*(6) Qualified summer youth employee*

A qualified summer youth employee is an individual: (1) who performs services during any 90-day period between May 1 and September 15; (2) who is certified by the designated local agency as being 16 or 17 years of age on the hiring date; (3) who has not been an employee of that employer before; and (4) who is certified by the designated local agency as having a principal place of abode within an empowerment zone, enterprise community, or renewal community. As with designated community residents, no credit is available on wages paid or incurred for service performed after the qualified summer youth moves outside of an empowerment zone, enterprise community, or renewal community. If, after the end of the 90-day period, the employer continues to employ a youth who was certified during the 90-day period as a member of another targeted group, the limit on qualified first-year wages will take into account wages paid to the youth while a qualified summer youth employee.

*(7) Qualified food stamp recipient*

A qualified food stamp recipient is an individual at least age 18 but not yet age 40 certified by a designated local employment agency as being a member of a family receiving assistance under a food stamp program under the Food Stamp Act of 1977 for a period of at least six months ending on the hiring date. In the case of families that cease to be eligible for food stamps under section 6(o) of the Food Stamp Act of 1977, the six-month requirement is replaced with a requirement that the family has been receiving food stamps for at least three of the five months ending on the date of hire. For these purposes, members of the family are defined to include only those individuals taken into account for purposes of determining eligibility for a food stamp program under the Food Stamp Act of 1977.

*(8) Qualified SSI recipient*

A qualified SSI recipient is an individual designated by a local agency as receiving supplemental security income ("SSI") benefits under Title XVI of the Social Security Act for any month ending within the 60-day period ending on the hiring date.

*(9) Long-term family assistance recipients*

A qualified long-term family assistance recipient is an individual certified by a designated local agency as being: (1) a member of a family that has received family assistance for at least 18 consecutive months ending on the hiring date; (2) a member of a family that has received such family assistance for a total of at least 18 months (whether or not consecutive) after August 5, 1997 (the date of enactment of the welfare-to-work tax credit)[90] if the individual is hired within two years after the date that the 18-month total is reached; or (3) a member of a family who is no longer eligible for family assistance because of either Federal or State time limits, if the individual is hired within two years after the Federal or State time limits made the family ineligible for family assistance.

***Qualified wages***

Generally, qualified wages are defined as cash wages paid by the employer to a member of a targeted group. The employer's deduction for wages is reduced by the amount of the credit.

For purposes of the credit, generally, wages are defined by reference to the FUTA definition of wages contained in sec. 3306(b) (without regard to the dollar limitation therein contained). Special rules apply in the case of certain agricultural labor and certain railroad labor.

***Calculation of the credit***

The credit available to an employer for qualified wages paid to members of all targeted groups except for long-term family assist-

[90] The welfare-to-work tax credit was consolidated into the work opportunity tax credit in the Tax Relief and Health Care Act of 2006, Pub. L. No. 109–432, for qualified individuals who begin to work for an employer after December 31, 2006.

ance recipients equals 40 percent (25 percent for employment of 400 hours or less) of qualified first-year wages. Generally, qualified first-year wages are qualified wages (not in excess of $6,000) attributable to service rendered by a member of a targeted group during the one-year period beginning with the day the individual began work for the employer. Therefore, the maximum credit per employee is $2,400 (40 percent of the first $6,000 of qualified first-year wages). With respect to qualified summer youth employees, the maximum credit is $1,200 (40 percent of the first $3,000 of qualified first-year wages). Except for long-term family assistance recipients, no credit is allowed for second-year wages.

In the case of long-term family assistance recipients, the credit equals 40 percent (25 percent for employment of 400 hours or less) of $10,000 for qualified first-year wages and 50 percent of the first $10,000 of qualified second-year wages. Generally, qualified second-year wages are qualified wages (not in excess of $10,000) attributable to service rendered by a member of the long-term family assistance category during the one-year period beginning on the day after the one-year period beginning with the day the individual began work for the employer. Therefore, the maximum credit per employee is $9,000 (40 percent of the first $10,000 of qualified first-year wages plus 50 percent of the first $10,000 of qualified second-year wages).

In the case of a qualified veteran who is entitled to compensation for a service-connected disability, the credit equals 40 percent of $12,000 of qualified first-year wages. This expanded definition of qualified first-year wages does not apply to the veterans qualified with reference to a food stamp program, as defined under present law.

### *Certification rules*

An individual is not treated as a member of a targeted group unless: (1) on or before the day on which an individual begins work for an employer, the employer has received a certification from a designated local agency that such individual is a member of a targeted group; or (2) on or before the day an individual is offered employment with the employer, a pre-screening notice is completed by the employer with respect to such individual, and not later than the 28th day after the individual begins work for the employer, the employer submits such notice, signed by the employer and the individual under penalties of perjury, to the designated local agency as part of a written request for certification. For these purposes, a pre-screening notice is a document (in such form as the Secretary may prescribe) which contains information provided by the individual on the basis of which the employer believes that the individual is a member of a targeted group.

### *Minimum employment period*

No credit is allowed for qualified wages paid to employees who work less than 120 hours in the first year of employment.

### *Other rules*

The work opportunity tax credit is not allowed for wages paid to a relative or dependent of the taxpayer. No credit is allowed for wages paid to an individual who is a more than fifty-percent owner of the entity. Similarly, wages paid to replacement workers during a strike or lockout are not eligible for the work opportunity tax credit. Wages paid to any employee during any period for which the employer received on-the-job training program payments with respect to that employee are not eligible for the work opportunity tax credit. The work opportunity tax credit generally is not allowed for wages paid to individuals who had previously been employed by the employer. In addition, many other technical rules apply.

#### *Expiration*

The work opportunity tax credit is not available for individuals who begin work for an employer after August 31, 2011.

### *Reasons for Change*

The Congress believes that the work opportunity tax credit can be used to improve employment opportunities for broader categories of qualified veterans and young people whose employment opportunities may have been significantly eroded by the present economic downturn.

### *Explanation of Provision*[91]

The provision creates a new targeted group for the work opportunity tax credit. That new category is unemployed veterans and disconnected youth who begin work for the employer in 2009 or 2010.

An unemployed veteran is defined as an individual certified by the designated local agency as someone who: (1) has served on active duty (other than for training) in the Armed Forces for more than 180 days or who has been discharged or released from active duty in the Armed Forces for a service-connected disability; (2) has been discharged or released from active duty in the Armed Forces during the five-year period ending on the hiring date; and (3) has received unemployment compensation under State or Federal law for not less than four weeks during the one-year period ending on the hiring date.

A disconnected youth is defined as an individual certified by the designated local agency as someone: (1) at least age 16 but not yet age 25 on the hiring date; (2) not regularly attending any secondary, technical, or post-secondary school during the six-month period preceding the hiring date; (3) not regularly employed during the six-month period preceding the hiring date; and (4) not readily employable by reason of lacking a sufficient number of skills.

For purposes of the disconnected youths, it is intended that a low-level of formal education may satisfy the requirement that an individual is not readily employable by reason of lacking a sufficient number of skills. Further, it is intended that the Internal Revenue Service, when providing general guidance regarding the various new criteria, shall take into account the administrability of the program by the State agencies.

---

[91] For further discussion of the Work Opportunity Tax Credit see section 757 of the Tax Relief, Unemployment Insurance Reauthorization, and Job Creation Act of 2010, Pub. L. No. 111–312, described in Part Sixteen of this document.

### *Effective Date*

The provisions are effective for individuals who begin work for an employer after December 31, 2008.

## 6. Clarification of regulations related to limitations on certain built-in losses following an ownership change (sec. 1261 of the Act and sec. 382 of the Code)

### *Present Law*

Section 382 limits the extent to which a "loss corporation" that experiences an "ownership change" may offset taxable income in any post-change taxable year by pre-change net operating losses, certain built-in losses, and deductions attributable to the pre-change period.[92] In general, the amount of income in any post-change year that may be offset by such net operating losses, built-in losses and deductions is limited to an amount (referred to as the "section 382 limitation") determined by multiplying the value of the loss corporation immediately before the ownership change by the long-term tax-exempt interest rate.[93]

A "loss corporation" is defined as a corporation entitled to use a net operating loss carryover or having a net operating loss carryover for the taxable year in which the ownership change occurs. Except to the extent provided in regulations, such term includes any corporation with a "net unrealized built-in loss" (or NUBIL),[94] defined as the amount by which the fair market value of the assets of the corporation immediately before an ownership change is less than the aggregate adjusted basis of such assets at such time. However, if the amount of the NUBIL does not exceed the lesser of (i) 15 percent of the fair market value of the corporation's assets or (ii) $10,000,000, then the amount of the NUBIL is treated as zero.[95]

An ownership change is defined generally as an increase by more than 50-percentage points in the percentage of stock of a loss corporation that is owned by any one or more five-percent (or greater) shareholders (as defined) within a three-year period.[96] Treasury regulations provide generally that this measurement is to be made as of any "testing date," which is any date on which the ownership of one or more persons who were or who become five-percent shareholders increases.[97]

---

[92] Sec. 383 imposes similar limitations, under regulations, on the use of carryforwards of general business credits, alternative minimum tax credits, foreign tax credits, and net capital loss carryforwards. Sec. 383 generally refers to section 382 for the meanings of its terms, but requires appropriate adjustments to take account of its application to credits and net capital losses.

[93] If the loss corporation had a "net unrealized built-in gain" (or NUBIG) at the time of the ownership change, then the section 382 limitation for any taxable year may be increased by the amount of the "recognized built-in gains" (discussed further below) for that year. A NUBIG is defined as the amount by which the fair market value of the assets of the corporation immediately before an ownership change exceeds the aggregate adjusted basis of such assets at such time. However, if the amount of the NUBIG does not exceed the lesser of (i) 15 percent of the fair market value of the corporation's assets or (ii) $10,000,000, then the amount of the NUBIG is treated as zero. Sec. 382(h)(1).

[94] Sec. 382(k)(1).

[95] Sec. 382(h)(3).

[96] Determinations of the percentage of stock of any corporation held by any person are made on the basis of value. Sec. 382(k)(6)(C).

[97] See Treas. Reg. sec. 1.382–2(a)(4) (providing that "a loss corporation is required to determine whether an ownership change has occurred immediately after any owner shift, or issuance

Section 382(h) governs the treatment of certain built-in losses and built-in gains recognized with respect to assets held by the loss corporation at the time of the ownership change. In the case of a loss corporation that has a NUBIL (measured immediately before an ownership change), section 382(h)(1) provides that any "recognized built-in loss" (or RBIL) for any taxable year during a "recognition period" (consisting of the five years beginning on the ownership change date) is subject to the section 382 limitation in the same manner as if it were a pre-change net operating loss.[98] An RBIL is defined for this purpose as any loss recognized during the recognition period on the disposition of any asset held by the loss corporation immediately before the ownership change date, to the extent that such loss is attributable to an excess of the adjusted basis of the asset on the change date over its fair market value on that date.[99] An RBIL also includes any amount allowable as depreciation, amortization or depletion during the recognition period, to the extent that such amount is attributable to the excess of the adjusted basis of the asset over its fair market value on the ownership change date.[100] In addition, any amount that is allowable as a deduction during the recognition period (determined without regard to any carryover) but which is attributable to periods before

or transfer (including an issuance or transfer described in Treas. Reg. sec. 1.382–4(d)(8)(i) or (ii)) of an option with respect to stock of the loss corporation that is treated as exercised under Treas. Reg. sec. 1.382–4(d)(2)" and defining a "testing date" as "each date on which a loss corporation is required to make a determination of whether an ownership change has occurred") and Temp. Treas. Reg. sec. 1.382–2T(e)(1) (defining an "owner shift" as "any change in the ownership of the stock of a loss corporation that affects the percentage of such stock owned by any 5-percent shareholder"). Treasury regulations under section 382 provide that, in computing stock ownership on specified testing dates, certain unexercised options must be treated as exercised if certain ownership, control, or income tests are met. These tests are met only if "a principal purpose of the issuance, transfer, or structuring of the option (alone or in combination with other arrangements) is to avoid or ameliorate the impact of an ownership change of the loss corporation." Treas. Reg. sec. 1.382–4(d). Compare prior temporary regulations, Temp. Treas. Reg. sec. 1.382–2T(h)(4) ("Solely for the purpose of determining whether there is an ownership change on any testing date, stock of the loss corporation that is subject to an option shall be treated as acquired on any such date, pursuant to an exercise of the option by its owner on that date, if such deemed exercise would result in an ownership change."). Notice 2008–76, I.R.B. 2008–39 (September 29, 2008), released September 7, 2008, provides that the Treasury Department intends to issue regulations modifying the term "testing date" under section 382 to exclude any date on or after which the United States acquires stock or options to acquire stock in certain corporations with respect to which there is a "Housing Act Acquisition" pursuant to the Housing and Economic Recovery Act of 2008, Pub. L. No. 110–289. The Notice states that the regulations will apply on and after September 7, 2008, unless and until there is additional guidance. Notice 2008–84, I.R.B. 2008–41 (October 14, 2008), provides that the Treasury Department intends to issue regulations modifying the term "testing date" under section 382 to exclude any date as of the close of which the United States owns, directly or indirectly, a more than 50-percent interest in a loss corporation, which regulations will apply unless and until there is additional guidance. Notice 2008–100, 2008–14 I.R.B. 1081 (released October 15, 2008) provides that the Treasury Department intends to issue regulations providing, among other things, that certain instruments acquired by the Treasury Department under the Capital Purchase Program (CPP) pursuant to the Emergency Economic Stabilization Act of 2008, Pub. L. No. 100–343, ("EESA") shall not be treated as stock for certain purposes. The Notice also provides that certain capital contributions made by Treasury pursuant to the CPP shall not be considered to have been made as part of a plan the principal purpose of which was to avoid or increase any section 382 limitation (for purposes of section 382(l)(1)). The Notice states that taxpayers may rely on the rules described unless and until there is further guidance; and that any contrary guidance will not apply to instruments (i) held by Treasury that were acquired pursuant to the CCP prior to publication of that guidance, or (ii) issued to Treasury pursuant to the CCP under written binding contracts entered into prior to the publication of that guidance. Notice 2009–14, 2009–7 I.R.B. 516 (January 30, 2009) amplifies and supersedes Notice 2008–100, and provides additional guidance regarding the application of section 382 and other provisions of law to corporations whose instruments are acquired by the Treasury Department under certain programs pursuant to EESA.

[98] Sec. 382(h)(2). The total amount of the loss corporation's RBILs that are subject to the section 382 limitation cannot exceed the amount of the corporation's NUBIL.

[99] Sec. 382(h)(2)(B).

[100] *Ibid.*

the ownership change date is treated as an RBIL for the taxable year in which it is allowable as a deduction.[101]

As indicated above, section 382(h)(1) provides in the case of a loss corporation that has a NUBIG that the section 382 limitation may be increased for any taxable year during the recognition period by the amount of recognized built-in gains (or RBIGs) for such taxable year.[102] An RBIG is defined for this purpose as any gain recognized during the recognition period on the disposition of any asset held by the loss corporation immediately before the ownership change date, to the extent that such gain is attributable to an excess of the fair market value of the asset on the change date over its adjusted basis on that date.[103] In addition, any item of income that is properly taken into account during the recognition period but which is attributable to periods before the ownership change date is treated as an RBIG for the taxable year in which it is properly taken into account.[104]

Notice 2003–65[105] provides two alternative safe harbor approaches for the identification of built-in items for purposes of section 382(h): the "1374 approach" and the "338 approach."

Under the 1374 approach,[106] NUBIG or NUBIL is the net amount of gain or loss that would be recognized in a hypothetical sale of the assets of the loss corporation immediately before the ownership change.[107] The amount of gain or loss recognized during the recognition period on the sale or exchange of an asset held at the time of the ownership change is RBIG or RBIL, respectively, to the extent it is attributable to a difference between the adjusted basis and the fair market value of the asset on the change date, as described above. However, the 1374 approach generally relies on the accrual method of accounting to identify items of income or deduction as RBIG or RBIL, respectively. Generally, items of income or deduction properly included in income or allowed as a deduction during the recognition period are considered attributable to period before the change date (and thus are treated as RBIG or RBIL, respectively), if a taxpayer using an accrual method of accounting would have included the item in income or been allowed a deduction for the item before the change date. However, the 1374 approach includes a number of exceptions to this general rule, including a special rule dealing with bad debt deductions under section 166. Under this special rule, any deduction item properly taken into account during the first 12 months of the recognition period as a bad debt deduction under section 166 is treated as RBIL if the item arises from a debt owed to the loss corporation at the begin-

[101] Sec. 382(h)(6)(B).

[102] The total amount of such increases cannot exceed the amount of the corporation's NUBIG.

[103] Sec. 382(h)(2)(A).

[104] Sec. 382(h)(6)(A).

[105] 2003–2 C.B. 747.

[106] The 1374 approach generally incorporates rules similar to those of section 1374(d) and the Treasury regulations thereunder in calculating NUBIG and NUBIL and identifying RBIG and RBIL.

[107] More specifically, NUBIG or NUBIL is calculated by determining the amount that would be realized if immediately before the ownership change the loss corporation had sold all of its assets, including goodwill, at fair market value to a third party that assumed all of its liabilities, decreased by the sum of any deductible liabilities of the loss corporation that would be included in the amount realized on the hypothetical sale and the loss corporation's aggregate adjusted basis in all of its assets, increased or decreased by the corporation's section 481 adjustments that would be taken into account on a hypothetical sale, and increased by any RBIL that would not be allowed as a deduction under section 382, 383 or 384 on the hypothetical sale.

ning of the recognition period (and deductions for such items properly taken into account after the first 12 months of the recognition period are not RBILs).[108]

The 338 approach identifies items of RBIG and RBIL generally by comparing the loss corporation's actual items of income, gain, deduction and loss with those that would have resulted if a section 338 election had been made with respect to a hypothetical purchase of all of the outstanding stock of the loss corporation on the change date. Under the 338 approach, NUBIG or NUBIL is calculated in the same manner as it is under the 1374 approach.[109] The 338 approach identifies RBIG or RBIL by comparing the loss corporation's actual items of income, gain, deduction and loss with the items of income, gain, deduction and loss that would result if a section 338 election had been made for the hypothetical purchase. The loss corporation is treated for this purpose as using those accounting methods that the loss corporation actually uses. The 338 approach does not include any special rule with regard to bad debt deductions under section 166.

Section 166 generally allows a deduction in respect of any debt that becomes worthless, in whole or in part, during the taxable year.[110] The determination of whether a debt is worthless, in whole or in part, is a question of fact. However, in the case of a bank or other corporation that is subject to supervision by Federal authorities, or by State authorities maintaining substantially equivalent standards, the Treasury regulations under section 166 provide a presumption of worthlessness to the extent that a debt is charged off during the taxable year pursuant to a specific order of such an authority or in accordance with established policies of such an authority (and in the latter case, the authority confirms in writing upon the first subsequent audit of the bank or other corporation that the charge-off would have been required if the audit had been made at the time of the charge-off). The presumption does not apply if the taxpayer does not claim the amount so charged off as a deduction for the taxable year in which the charge-off takes place. In that case, the charge-off is treated as having been involuntary; however, in order to claim the section 166 deduction in a later taxable year, the taxpayer must produce sufficient evidence to show that the debt became partially worthless in the later year or became recoverable only in part subsequent to the taxable year of the charge-off, as the case may be, and to the extent that the deduction claimed in the later year for a partially worthless debt was not involuntarily charged off in prior taxable years, it was charged off in the later taxable year.[111]

The Treasury regulations also permit a bank (generally as defined for purposes of section 581, with certain modifications) that is subject to supervision by Federal authorities, or State authorities

---

[108] Notice 2003–65, section III.B.2.b.

[109] Accordingly, unlike the case in which a section 338 election is actually made, contingent consideration (including a contingent liability) is taken into account in the initial calculation of NUBIG or NUBIL, and no further adjustments are made to reflect subsequent changes in deemed consideration.

[110] Section 166 does not apply, however, to a debt which is evidenced by a security, defined for this purpose (by cross-reference to section 165(g)(2)(C)) as a bond, debenture, note or certificate or other evidence of indebtedness issued by a corporation or by a government or political subdivision thereof, with interest coupons or in registered form. Sec. 166(e).

[111] See Treas. Reg. sec. 1.166–2(d)(1) and (2).

maintaining substantially equivalent standards, to make a "conformity election" under which debts charged off for regulatory purposes during a taxable year are conclusively presumed to be worthless for tax purposes to the same extent, provided that the charge-off results from a specific order of the regulatory authority or corresponds to the institution's classification of the debt as a "loss asset" pursuant to loan loss classification standards that are consistent with those of certain specified bank regulatory authorities. The conformity election is treated as the adoption of a method of accounting.[112]

Notice 2008–83,[113] released on October 1, 2008, provides that "[f]or purposes of section 382(h), any deduction properly allowed after an ownership change (as defined in section 382(g)) to a bank with respect to losses on loans or bad debts (including any deduction for a reasonable addition to a reserve for bad debts) shall not be treated as a built-in loss or a deduction that is attributable to periods before the change date."[114] The Notice further states that the Internal Revenue Service and the Treasury Department are studying the proper treatment under section 382(h) of certain items of deduction or loss allowed after an ownership change to a corporation that is a bank (as defined in section 581) both immediately before and after the change date, and that any such corporation may rely on the treatment set forth in Notice 2008–83 unless and until there is additional guidance.

### *Reasons for Change*

The Congress believes that: (1) the delegation of authority to the Secretary of the Treasury, or his delegate, under section 382(m)[115] does not authorize the Secretary to provide exemptions or special rules that are restricted to particular industries or classes of taxpayers, (2) Notice 2008–83 is inconsistent with the congressional intent in enacting section 382(m), and (3) the legal authority to prescribe Notice 2008–83 is doubtful, but that (4) as taxpayers should generally be able to rely on guidance issued by the Secretary of the Treasury, legislation is necessary to clarify the force and effect of Notice 2008–83 and restore the proper application under the Internal Revenue Code of the limitation on built-in losses following an ownership change of a bank.

### *Explanation of Provision*

The provision states that Congress finds as follows: (1) The delegation of authority to the Secretary of the Treasury, or his delegate, under section 382(m) does not authorize the Secretary to provide exemptions or special rules that are restricted to particular industries or classes of taxpayers; (2) Notice 2008–83 is inconsistent with the congressional intent in enacting such section 382(m); (3) the legal authority to prescribe Notice 2008–83 is doubtful; (4) however, as taxpayers should generally be able to rely on guidance

[112] See Treas. Reg. sec. 1.166–2(d)(3); cf. Priv. Ltr. Rul. 9248048 (July 7, 1992); Tech. Adv. Mem. 9122001 (Feb. 8, 1991).

[113] 2008–42 I.R.B. 2008–42 (Oct. 20, 2008).

[114] Notice 2008–83, section 2.

[115] Section 382(m) authorizes the Secretary to prescribe such regulations as may be necessary or appropriate to carry out the purposes of sections 382 and 383.

issued by the Secretary of the Treasury, legislation is necessary to clarify the force and effect of Notice 2008–83 and restore the proper application under the Internal Revenue Code of the limitation on built-in losses following an ownership change of a bank.

Under the provision, Notice 2008–83 shall be deemed to have the force and effect of law with respect to any ownership change (as defined in section 382(g)) occurring on or before January 16, 2009, and with respect to any ownership change (as so defined) which occurs after January 16, 2009, if such change (1) is pursuant to a written binding contract entered into on or before such date or (2) is pursuant to a written agreement entered into on or before such date and such agreement was described on or before such date in a public announcement or in a filing with the Securities and Exchange Commission required by reason of such ownership change, but shall otherwise have no force or effect with respect to any ownership change after such date.

### *Effective Date*

The provision is effective on the date of enactment (February 17, 2009).

## 7. Treatment of certain ownership changes for purposes of limitations on net operating loss carryforwards and certain built-in losses (sec. 1262 of the Act and sec. 382 of the Code)

### *Present Law*

Section 382 limits the extent to which a "loss corporation" that experiences an "ownership change" may offset taxable income in any post-change taxable year by pre-change net operating losses, certain built-in losses, and deductions attributable to the pre-change period.[116] In general, the amount of income in any post-change year that may be offset by such net operating losses, built-in losses and deductions is limited to an amount (referred to as the "section 382 limitation") determined by multiplying the value of the loss corporation immediately before the ownership change by the long-term tax-exempt interest rate.[117]

A "loss corporation" is defined as a corporation entitled to use a net operating loss carryover or having a net operating loss carryover for the taxable year in which the ownership change occurs. Except to the extent provided in regulations, such term includes any corporation with a "net unrealized built-in loss" (or NUBIL),[118]

[116] Section 383 imposes similar limitations, under regulations, on the use of carryforwards of general business credits, alternative minimum tax credits, foreign tax credits, and net capital loss carryforwards. Section 383 generally refers to section 382 for the meanings of its terms, but requires appropriate adjustments to take account of its application to credits and net capital losses.

[117] If the loss corporation had a "net unrealized built in gain" (or NUBIG) at the time of the ownership change, then the section 382 limitation for any taxable year may be increased by the amount of the "recognized built-in gains" (discussed further below) for that year. A NUBIG is defined as the amount by which the fair market value of the assets of the corporation immediately before an ownership change exceeds the aggregate adjusted basis of such assets at such time. However, if the amount of the NUBIG does not exceed the lesser of (i) 15 percent of the fair market value of the corporation's assets or (ii) $10,000,000, then the amount of the NUBIG is treated as zero. Sec. 382(h)(1).

[118] Sec. 382(k)(1).

defined as the amount by which the fair market value of the assets of the corporation immediately before an ownership change is less than the aggregate adjusted basis of such assets at such time. However, if the amount of the NUBIL does not exceed the lesser of (i) 15 percent of the fair market value of the corporation's assets or (ii) $10,000,000, then the amount of the NUBIL is treated as zero.[119]

An ownership change is defined generally as an increase by more than 50-percentage points in the percentage of stock of a loss corporation that is owned by any one or more five-percent (or greater) shareholders (as defined) within a three year period.[120] Treasury regulations provide generally that this measurement is to be made as of any "testing date," which is any date on which the ownership of one or more persons who were or who become five-percent shareholders increases.[121]

### *Explanation of Provision*

The Act amends section 382 of the Code to provide an exception from the application of the section 382 limitation. Under the provision, the section 382 limitation that would otherwise arise as a re-

---

[119] Sec. 382(h)(3).

[120] Determinations of the percentage of stock of any corporation held by any person are made on the basis of value. Sec. 382(k)(6)(C).

[121] See Treas. Reg. sec. 1.382–2(a)(4) (providing that "a loss corporation is required to determine whether an ownership change has occurred immediately after any owner shift, or issuance or transfer (including an issuance or transfer described in Treas. Reg. sec. 1.382–4(d)(8)(i) or (ii)) of an option with respect to stock of the loss corporation that is treated as exercised under Treas. Reg. sec. 1.382–4(d)(2)" and defining a "testing date" as "each date on which a loss corporation is required to make a determination of whether an ownership change has occurred") and Temp. Treas. Reg. sec. 1.382–2T(e)(1) (defining an "owner shift" as "any change in the ownership of the stock of a loss corporation that affects the percentage of such stock owned by any 5-percent shareholder"). Treasury regulations under section 382 provide that, in computing stock ownership on specified testing dates, certain unexercised options must be treated as exercised if certain ownership, control, or income tests are met. These tests are met only if "a principal purpose of the issuance, transfer, or structuring of the option (alone or in combination with other arrangements) is to avoid or ameliorate the impact of an ownership change of the loss corporation." Treas. Reg. sec. 1.382–4(d). Compare prior temporary regulations, Temp. Treas. Reg. sec. 1.382–2T(h)(4) ("Solely for the purpose of determining whether there is an ownership change on any testing date, stock of the loss corporation that is subject to an option shall be treated as acquired on any such date, pursuant to an exercise of the option by its owner on that date, if such deemed exercise would result in an ownership change."). Notice 2008–76, I.R.B. 2008–39 (September 29, 2008), released September 7, 2008, provides that the Treasury Department intends to issue regulations modifying the term "testing date" under section 382 to exclude any date on or after which the United States acquires stock or options to acquire stock in certain corporations with respect to which there is a "Housing Act Acquisition" pursuant to the Housing and Economic Recovery Act of 2008, Pub. L. No. 110–289. The Notice states that the regulations will apply on and after September 7, 2008, unless and until there is additional guidance. Notice 2008–84, I.R.B. 2008–41 (October 14, 2008), provides that the Treasury Department intends to issue regulations modifying the term "testing date" under section 382 to exclude any date as of the close of which the United States owns, directly or indirectly, a more than 50 percent interest in a loss corporation, which regulations will apply unless and until there is additional guidance. Notice 2008–100, 2008–14 I.R.B. 1081 (released October 15, 2008) provides that the Treasury Department intends to issue regulations providing, among other things, that certain instruments acquired by the Treasury Department under the Capital Purchase Program (CPP) pursuant to the Emergency Economic Stabilization Act of 2008, Pub. L. No. 100–343, ("EESA") shall not be treated as stock for certain purposes. The Notice also provides that certain capital contributions made by Treasury pursuant to the CPP shall not be considered to have been made as part of a plan the principal purpose of which was to avoid or increase any section 382 limitation (for purposes of section 382(l)(1)). The Notice states that taxpayers may rely on the rules described unless and until there is further guidance; and that any contrary guidance will not apply to instruments (i) held by Treasury that were acquired pursuant to the CCP prior to publication of that guidance, or (ii) issued to Treasury pursuant to the CCP under written binding contracts entered into prior to the publication of that guidance. Notice 2009–14, 2009–7 I.R.B. 516 (January 30, 2009) amplifies and supersedes Notice 2008–100, and provides additional guidance regarding the application of section 382 and other provisions of law to corporations whose instruments are acquired by the Treasury Department under certain programs pursuant to EESA.

sult of an ownership change shall not apply in the case of an ownership change that occurs pursuant to a restructuring plan of a taxpayer which is required under a loan agreement or commitment for a line of credit entered into with the Department of the Treasury under the Emergency Economic Stabilization Act of 2008, and is intended to result in a rationalization of the costs, capitalization, and capacity with respect to the manufacturing workforce of, and suppliers to, the taxpayer and its subsidiaries.[122]

However, an ownership change that would otherwise be excepted from the section 382 limitation under the provision will instead remain subject to the section 382 limitation if, immediately after such ownership change, any person (other than a voluntary employees' beneficiary association within the meaning of section 501(c)(9)) owns stock of the new loss corporation possessing 50 percent or more of the total combined voting power of all classes of stock entitled to vote or of the total value of the stock of such corporation. For purposes of this rule, persons who bear a relationship to one another described in section 267(b) or 707(b)(1), or who are members of a group of persons acting in concert, are treated as a single person.

The exception from the application of the section 382 limitation under the provision does not change the fact that an ownership change has occurred for other purposes of section 382.[123]

### *Effective Date*

The provision applies to ownership changes after the date of enactment (February 17, 2009).

## 8. Deferral of certain income from the discharge of indebtedness (sec. 1231 of the Act and sec. 108 of the Code)

### *Present Law*

In general, gross income includes income that is realized by a debtor from the discharge of indebtedness, subject to certain exceptions for debtors in title 11 bankruptcy cases, insolvent debtors, certain student loans, certain farm indebtedness, certain real property business indebtedness, and certain qualified principal residence indebtedness.[124] In cases involving discharges of indebtedness that are excluded from gross income under the exceptions to the general rule, taxpayers generally are required to reduce certain tax attributes, including net operating losses, general business credits, minimum tax credits, capital loss carryovers, and basis in property, by the amount of the discharge of indebtedness.[125]

The amount of discharge of indebtedness excluded from income by an insolvent debtor not in a title 11 bankruptcy case cannot exceed the amount by which the debtor is insolvent. In the case of a discharge in bankruptcy or where the debtor is insolvent, any reduction in basis may not exceed the excess of the aggregate bases

[122] This exception shall not apply in the case of any subsequent ownership change unless such subsequent ownership change also meets the requirements of the exception.

[123] For example, an ownership change has occurred for purposes of determining the testing period under section 382(i)(2).

[124] See sections 61(a)(12) and 108. But see section 102 (a debt cancellation which constitutes a gift or bequest is not treated as income to the donee debtor).

[125] Sec. 108(b).

of properties held by the taxpayer immediately after the discharge over the aggregate of the liabilities of the taxpayer immediately after the discharge.[126]

For all taxpayers, the amount of discharge of indebtedness generally is equal to the excess of the adjusted issue price of the indebtedness being satisfied over the amount paid (or deemed paid) to satisfy such indebtedness.[127] This rule generally applies to (1) the acquisition by the debtor of its debt instrument in exchange for cash, (2) the issuance of a debt instrument by the debtor in satisfaction of its indebtedness, including a modification of indebtedness that is treated as an exchange (a debt-for-debt exchange), (3) the transfer by a debtor corporation of stock, or a debtor partnership of a capital or profits interest in such partnership, in satisfaction of its indebtedness (an equity-for-debt exchange), and (4) the acquisition by a debtor corporation of its indebtedness from a shareholder as a contribution to capital.

*Debt-for-debt exchanges*

If a debtor issues a debt instrument in satisfaction of its indebtedness, the debtor is treated as having satisfied the indebtedness with an amount of money equal to the issue price of the newly issued debt instrument.[128] The issue price of such newly issued debt instrument generally is determined under sections 1273 and 1274.[129] Similarly, a "significant modification" of a debt instrument, within the meaning of Treas. Reg. sec. 1.1001–3, results in an exchange of the original debt instrument for a modified instrument. In such cases, where the issue price of the modified debt instrument is less than the adjusted issue price of the original debt instrument, the debtor will have income from the cancellation of indebtedness.

If any new debt instrument is issued (including as a result of a significant modification to a debt instrument), such debt instrument will have original issue discount equal to the excess (if any) of such debt instrument's stated redemption price at maturity over its issue price.[130] In general, an issuer of a debt instrument with original issue discount may deduct for any taxable year, with respect to such debt instrument, an amount of original issue discount equal to the aggregate daily portions of the original issue discount for days during such taxable year.[131]

*Equity-for-debt exchanges*

If a corporation transfers stock, or a partnership transfers a capital or profits interest in such partnership, to a creditor in satisfaction of its indebtedness, then such corporation or partnership is treated as having satisfied its indebtedness with an amount of money equal to the fair market value of the stock or interest.[132]

[126] Sec. 1017.
[127] Treas. Reg. sec. 1.61–12(c)(2)(ii). Treas. Reg. sec. 1.1275–1(b) defines "adjusted issue price."
[128] Sec. 108(e)(10)(A).
[129] Sec. 108(e)(10)(B).
[130] Sec. 1273.
[131] Sec. 163(e).
[132] Sec. 108(e)(8).

*Related party acquisitions*

Indebtedness directly or indirectly acquired by a person who bears a relationship to the debtor described in section 267(b) or section 707(b) is treated as if it were acquired by the debtor.[133] Thus, where a debtor's indebtedness is acquired for less than its adjusted issue price by a person related to the debtor (within the meaning of section 267(b) or 707(b)), the debtor recognizes income from the cancellation of indebtedness. Regulations under section 108 provide that the indebtedness acquired by the related party is treated as new indebtedness issued by the debtor to the related holder on the acquisition date (the deemed issuance).[134] The new indebtedness is deemed issued with an issue price equal to the amount used under regulations to compute the amount of cancellation of indebtedness income realized by the debtor (i.e., either the holder's adjusted basis or the fair market value of the indebtedness, as the case may be).[135] The indebtedness deemed issued pursuant to the regulations has original issue discount to the extent its stated redemption price at maturity exceeds its issue price.

In the case of a deemed issuance under Treas. Reg. sec. 1.108–2(g), the related holder does not recognize any gain or loss, and the related holder's adjusted basis in the indebtedness remains the same as it was immediately before the deemed issuance.[136] The deemed issuance is treated as a purchase of the indebtedness by the related holder for purposes of section 1272(a)(7) (pertaining to reduction of original issue discount where a subsequent holder pays acquisition premium) and section 1276 (pertaining to acquisitions of debt at a market discount).[137]

*Contribution of a debt instrument to capital of a corporation*

Where a debtor corporation acquires its indebtedness from a shareholder as a contribution to capital, section 118[138] does not apply, but the corporation is treated as satisfying such indebtedness with an amount of money equal to the shareholder's adjusted basis in the indebtedness.

## *Explanation of Provision*

The provision permits a taxpayer to elect to defer cancellation of indebtedness income arising from a "reacquisition" of "an applicable debt instrument" after December 31, 2008, and before January 1, 2011. Income deferred pursuant to the election must be included in the gross income of the taxpayer ratably in the five taxable years beginning with (1) for repurchases in 2009, the fifth taxable year following the taxable year in which the repurchase occurs or (2) for repurchases in 2010, the fourth taxable year following the taxable year in which the repurchase occurs.

An "applicable debt instrument" is any debt instrument issued by (1) a C corporation or (2) any other person in connection with

[133] Sec. 108(e)(4).
[134] Treas. Reg. sec. 1.108–2(g).
[135] *Ibid.*
[136] Treas. Reg. sec. 1.108–2(g)(2).
[137] *Ibid.*
[138] Section 118 provides, in general, that in the case of a corporation, gross income does not include any contribution to the capital of the taxpayer.

the conduct of a trade or business by such person. For purposes of the provision, a "debt instrument" is broadly defined to include any bond, debenture, note, certificate or any other instrument or contractual arrangement constituting indebtedness (within the meaning of section 1275(a)(1)).

A "reacquisition" is any "acquisition" of an applicable debt instrument by (1) the debtor that issued (or is otherwise the obligor under) such debt instrument or (2) any person related to the debtor within the meaning of section 108(e)(4). For purposes of the provision, an "acquisition" includes, without limitation, (1) an acquisition of a debt instrument for cash, (2) the exchange of a debt instrument for another debt instrument (including an exchange resulting from a modification of a debt instrument), (3) the exchange of corporate stock or a partnership interest for a debt instrument, (4) the contribution of a debt instrument to the capital of the issuer, and (5) the complete forgiveness of a debt instrument by a holder of such instrument.

*Special rules for debt-for-debt exchanges*

If a taxpayer makes the election provided by the provision for a debt-for-debt exchange in which the newly issued debt instrument issued (or deemed issued, including by operation of the rules in Treas. Reg. sec. 1.108–2(g)) in satisfaction of an outstanding debt instrument of the debtor has original issue discount, then any otherwise allowable deduction for original issue discount with respect to such newly issued debt instrument that (1) accrues before the first year of the five-taxable-year period in which the related, deferred discharge of indebtedness income is included in the gross income of the taxpayer and (2) does not exceed such related, deferred discharge of indebtedness income, is deferred and allowed as a deduction ratably over the same five-taxable-year period in which the deferred discharge of indebtedness income is included in gross income.

This rule can apply also in certain cases when a debtor reacquires its debt for cash. If the taxpayer issues a debt instrument and the proceeds of such issuance are used directly or indirectly to reacquire a debt instrument of the taxpayer, the provision treats the newly issued debt instrument as if it were issued in satisfaction of the retired debt instrument. If the newly issued debt instrument has original issue discount, the rule described above applies. Thus, all or a portion of the interest deductions with respect to original issue discount on the newly issued debt instrument are deferred into the five-taxable-year period in which the discharge of indebtedness income is recognized. Where only a portion of the proceeds of a new issuance are used by a taxpayer to satisfy outstanding debt, then the deferral rule applies to the portion of the original issue discount on the newly issued debt instrument that is equal to the portion of the proceeds of such newly issued instrument used to retire outstanding debt of the taxpayer.

*Acceleration of deferred items*

Cancellation of indebtedness income and any related deduction for original issue discount that is deferred by an electing taxpayer (and has not previously been taken into account) generally is accelerated and taken into income in the taxable year in which the taxpayer: (1) dies, (2) liquidates or sells substantially all of its assets (including in a title 11 or similar case), (3) ceases to do business, or (4) or is in similar circumstances. In a case under title 11 or a similar case, any deferred items are taken into income as of the day before the petition is filed. Deferred items are accelerated in a case under Title 11 where the taxpayer liquidates, sells substantially all of its assets, or ceases to do business, but not where a taxpayer reorganizes and emerges from the Title 11 case. In the case of a pass-thru entity, this acceleration rule also applies to the sale, exchange, or redemption of an interest in the entity by a holder of such interest.

*Special rule for partnerships*

In the case of a partnership, any income deferred under the provision is allocated to the partners in the partnership immediately before the discharge of indebtedness in the manner such amounts would have been included in the distributive shares of such partners under section 704 if such income were recognized at the time of the discharge. Any decrease in a partner's share of liabilities as a result of such discharge is not taken into account for purposes of section 752 at the time of the discharge to the extent the deemed distribution under section 752 would cause the partner to recognize gain under section 731. Thus, the deemed distribution under section 752 is deferred with respect to a partner to the extent it exceeds such partner's basis. Amounts so deferred are taken into account at the same time, and to the extent remaining in the same amount, as income deferred under the provision is recognized by the partner.

*Coordination with section 108(a) and procedures for election*

Where a taxpayer makes the election provided by the provision, the exclusions provided by section 108(a)(1)(A), (B), (C), and (D) shall not apply to the income from the discharge of indebtedness for the year in which the taxpayer makes the election or any subsequent year. Thus, for example, an insolvent taxpayer may elect under the provision to defer income from the discharge of indebtedness rather than excluding such income and reducing tax attributes by a corresponding amount. The election is to be made on an instrument by instrument basis; once made, the election is irrevocable. A taxpayer makes an election with respect to a debt instrument by including with its return for the taxable year in which the reacquisition of the debt instrument occurs a statement that (1) clearly identifies the debt instrument and (2) includes the amount of deferred income to which the provision applies and such other information as may be prescribed by the Secretary. The Secretary is authorized to require reporting of the election (and other information with respect to the reacquisition) for years subsequent to the year of the reacquisition.

*Regulatory authority*

The provision authorizes the Secretary of the Treasury to prescribe such regulations as may be necessary or appropriate for purposes of applying the provision, including rules extending the acceleration provisions to other circumstances where appropriate, rules requiring reporting of the election and such other information as the Secretary may require on returns of tax for subsequent taxable years, rules for the application of the provision to partnerships, S corporations, and other pass-thru entities, including for the allocation of deferred deductions.

### *Effective Date*

The provision is effective for discharges in taxable years ending after December 31, 2008.

## 9. Modifications of rules for original issue discount on certain high yield obligations (sec. 1232 of the Act and sec. 163 of the Code)

### *Present Law*

In general, the issuer of a debt instrument with original issue discount may deduct the portion of such original issue discount equal to the aggregate daily portions of the original issue discount for days during the taxable year.[139] However, in the case of an applicable high-yield discount obligation (an "AHYDO") issued by a corporate issuer: (1) no deduction is allowed for the "disqualified portion" of the original issue discount on such obligation, and (2) the remainder of the original issue discount on any such obligation is not allowable as a deduction until paid by the issuer.[140]

An AHYDO is any debt instrument if (1) the maturity date on such instrument is more than five years from the date of issue; (2) the yield to maturity on such instrument exceeds the sum of (a) the applicable Federal rate in effect under section 1274(d) for the calendar month in which the obligation is issued and (b) five percentage points, and (3) such instrument has "significant original issue discount."[141] An instrument is treated as having "significant original issue discount" if the aggregate amount of interest that would be includible in the gross income of the holder with respect to such instrument for periods before the close of any accrual period (as defined in section 1272(a)(5)) ending after the date five years after the date of issue, exceeds the sum of (1) the aggregate amount of interest to be paid under the instrument before the close of such accrual period, and (2) the product of the issue price of such instrument (as defined in sections 1273(b) and 1274(a)) and its yield to maturity.[142]

The disqualified portion of the original issue discount on an AHYDO is the lesser of (1) the amount of original issue discount with respect to such obligation or (2) the portion of the "total return" on such obligation which bears the same ratio to such total return as the "disqualified yield" (i.e., the excess of the yield to maturity on the obligation over the applicable Federal rate plus six percentage points) on such obligation bears to the yield to maturity

[139] Sec. 163(e)(1). For purposes of section 163(e)(1), the daily portion of the original issue discount for any day is determined under section 1272(a) (without regard to paragraph (7) thereof and without regard to section 1273(a)(3)).

[140] Sec. 163(e)(5).

[141] Sec. 163(i)(1).

[142] Sec. 163(i)(2).

on such obligation.[143] The term "total return" means the amount which would have been the original issue discount of the obligation if interest described in section 1273(a)(2) were included in the stated redemption to maturity.[144] A corporate holder treats the disqualified portion of original issue discount as a stock distribution for purposes of the dividend received deduction.[145]

### *Explanation of Provision*

The Act adds a provision that suspends the rules in section 163(e)(5) for certain obligations issued in a debt-for-debt exchange, including an exchange resulting from a significant modification of a debt instrument, after August 31, 2008, and before January 1, 2010.

In general, the suspension does not apply to any newly issued debt instrument (including any debt instrument issued as a result of a significant modification of a debt instrument) that is issued for an AHYDO. However, any newly issued debt instrument (including any debt instrument issued as a result of a significant modification of a debt instrument) for which the AHYDO rules are suspended under the provision is not treated as an AHYDO for purposes of a subsequent application of the suspension rule. Thus, for example, if a new debt instrument that would be an AHYDO under present law is issued in exchange for a debt instrument that is not an AHYDO, and the provision suspends application of section 163(e)(5), another new debt instrument, issued during the suspension period in exchange for the instrument with respect to which the rule in section 163(e)(5) was suspended, would be eligible for the relief provided by the provision despite the fact that it is issued for an instrument that is an AHYDO under present law.

In addition, the suspension does not apply to any newly issued debt instrument (including any debt instrument issued as a result of a significant modification of a debt instrument) that is (1) described in section 871(h)(4) (without regard to subparagraph (D) thereof) (i.e., certain contingent debt) or (2) issued to a person related to the issuer (within the meaning of section 108(e)(4)).

The provision provides authority to the Secretary to apply the suspension rule to periods after December 31, 2009, where the Secretary determines that such application is appropriate in light of distressed conditions in the debt capital markets. In addition, the provision grants authority to the Secretary to use a rate that is higher than the applicable Federal rate for purposes of applying section 163(e)(5) for obligations issued after December 31, 2009, in taxable years ending after such date if the Secretary determines that such higher rate is appropriate in light of distressed conditions in the debt capital markets.

### *Effective Date*

The temporary suspension of section 163(e)(5) applies to obligations issued after August 31, 2008, in taxable years ending after such date. The additional authority granted to the Secretary to use

---

[143] Sec. 163(e)(5)(C).
[144] Sec. 163(e)(5)(C)(ii).
[145] Sec. 163(e)(5)(B).

a rate higher than the applicable Federal rate for purposes of applying section 163(e)(5) applies to obligations issued after December 31, 2009, in taxable years ending after such date.

## 10. Special rules applicable to qualified small business stock for 2009 and 2010 (sec. 1241 of the Act and sec. 1202 of the Code)

### *Present Law*

Under present law, individuals may exclude 50 percent (60 percent for certain empowerment zone businesses) of the gain from the sale of certain small business stock acquired at original issue and held for at least five years.[146] The portion of the gain includible in taxable income is taxed at a maximum rate of 28 percent under the regular tax.[147] A percentage of the excluded gain is an alternative minimum tax preference;[148] the portion of the gain includible in alternative minimum taxable income is taxed at a maximum rate of 28 percent under the alternative minimum tax.

Thus, under present law, gain from the sale of qualified small business stock is taxed at effective rates of 14 percent under the regular tax[149] and (i) 14.98 percent under the alternative minimum tax for dispositions before January 1, 2011; (ii) 19.88 percent under the alternative minimum tax for dispositions after December 31, 2010, in the case of stock acquired before January 1, 2001; and (iii) 17.92 percent under the alternative minimum tax for dispositions after December 31, 2010, in the case of stock acquired after December 31, 2000.[150]

The amount of gain eligible for the exclusion by an individual with respect to any corporation is the greater of (1) ten times the taxpayer's basis in the stock or (2) $10 million. In order to qualify as a small business, when the stock is issued, the gross assets of the corporation may not exceed $50 million. The corporation also must meet certain active trade or business requirements.

### *Explanation of Provision*[151]

Under the Act, the percentage exclusion for qualified small business stock sold by an individual is increased from 50 percent (60 percent for certain empowerment zone businesses) to 75 percent.

---

[146] Sec. 1202.

[147] Sec. 1(h).

[148] Sec. 57(a)(7). In the case of qualified small business stock, the percentage of gain excluded from gross income which is an alternative minimum tax preference is (i) seven percent in the case of stock disposed of in a taxable year beginning before 2011; (ii) 42 percent in the case of stock acquired before January 1, 2001, and disposed of in a taxable year beginning after 2010; and (iii) 28 percent in the case of stock acquired after December 31, 2000, and disposed of in a taxable year beginning after 2010.

[149] The 50 percent of gain included in taxable income is taxed at a maximum rate of 28 percent.

[150] The amount of gain included in alternative minimum tax is taxed at a maximum rate of 28 percent. The amount so included is the sum of (i) 50 percent (the percentage included in taxable income) of the total gain and (ii) the applicable preference percentage of the one-half gain that is excluded from taxable income.

[151] The provision was subsequently modified to provide a 100-percent exclusion for stock issued after September 27, 2010, and before January 1, 2011 by section 2011 of the Small Business Jobs Act of 2010, Pub. L. No. 111–240, described in Part Fourteen. The provision was subsequently extended to stock issued during 2011 by section 760 of Tax Relief, Unemployment Insurance Reauthorization, and Job Creation Act of 2010, Pub. L. No. 111–312, described in Part Sixteen of this document.

As a result of the increased exclusion, gain from the sale of qualified small business stock to which the provision applies is taxed at effective rates of seven percent under the regular tax[152] and 12.88 percent under the alternative minimum tax.[153]

### *Effective Date*

The provision is effective for stock issued after the date of enactment (February 17, 2009) and before January 1, 2011.

## 11. Temporary reduction in recognition period for S corporation built-in gains tax (sec. 1251 of the Act and sec. 1374 of the Code)

### *Present Law*

A "small business corporation" (as defined in section 1361(b)) may elect to be treated as an S corporation. Unlike C corporations, S corporations generally pay no corporate-level tax. Instead, items of income and loss of an S corporation pass through to its shareholders. Each shareholder takes into account separately its share of these items on its individual income tax return.[154]

A corporate level tax, at the highest marginal rate applicable to corporations (currently 35 percent) is imposed on an S corporation's gain that arose prior to the conversion of the C corporation to an S corporation and is recognized by the S corporation during the recognition period, i.e., the first 10 taxable years that the S election is in effect.[155]

Gains recognized in the recognition period are not built-in gains to the extent they are shown to have arisen while the S election was in effect or are offset by recognized built-in losses. The built-in gains tax also applies to gains with respect to net recognized built-in gain attributable to property received by an S corporation from a C corporation in a carryover basis transaction.[156] The amount of the built-in gains tax is treated as a loss taken into account by the shareholders in computing their individual income tax.[157]

### *Explanation of Provision*[158]

The Act provides that, for any taxable year beginning in 2009 and 2010, no tax is imposed on an S corporation under section 1374 if the seventh year in the corporation's recognition period preceded such taxable year. Thus, with respect to gain that arose prior to the conversion of a C corporation to an S corporation, no tax will

[152] The 25 percent of gain included in taxable income is taxed at a maximum rate of 28 percent.

[153] The 46 percent of gain included in alternative minimum tax is taxed at a maximum rate of 28 percent. Forty-six percent is the sum of 25 percent (the percentage of total gain included in taxable income) plus 21 percent (the percentage of total gain which is an alternative minimum tax preference).

[154] Sec. 1366.

[155] Sec. 1374.

[156] Sec. 1374(d)(8). With respect to such assets, the recognition period runs from the day on which such assets were acquired (in lieu of the beginning of the first taxable year for which the corporation was an S corporation). Sec. 1374(d)(8)(B).

[157] Sec. 1366(f)(2).

[158] The provision was subsequently modified and extended by section 2011 of the Small Business Jobs Act of 2010, Pub. L. No. 111–240, described in Part Fourteen of this document.

be imposed under section 1374 after the seventh taxable year the S corporation election is in effect. In the case of built-in gain attributable to an asset received by an S corporation from a C corporation in a carryover basis transaction, no tax will be imposed under section 1374 if such gain is recognized after the date that is seven years following the date on which such asset was acquired.[159]

### *Effective Date*

The provision applies to taxable years beginning after December 31, 2008.

## C. Fiscal Relief for State and Local Governments

### 1. De minimis safe harbor exception for tax-exempt interest expense of financial institutions and modification of small issuer exception to tax-exempt interest expense allocation rules for financial institutions (secs. 1501 and 1502 of the Act and sec. 265 of the Code)

### *Present Law*

Present law disallows a deduction for interest on indebtedness incurred or continued to purchase or carry obligations the interest on which is exempt from tax.[160] In general, an interest deduction is disallowed only if the taxpayer has a purpose of using borrowed funds to purchase or carry tax-exempt obligations; a determination of the taxpayer's purpose in borrowing funds is made based on all of the facts and circumstances.[161]

*Two-percent rule for individuals and certain nonfinancial corporations*

In the absence of direct evidence linking an individual taxpayer's indebtedness with the purchase or carrying of tax-exempt obligations, the Internal Revenue Service takes the position that it ordinarily will not infer that a taxpayer's purpose in borrowing money was to purchase or carry tax-exempt obligations if the taxpayer's investment in tax-exempt obligations is "insubstantial."[162] An individual's holdings of tax-exempt obligations are presumed to be insubstantial if during the taxable year the average adjusted basis of the individual's tax-exempt obligations is two percent or less of the average adjusted basis of the individual's portfolio investments and assets held by the individual in the active conduct of a trade or business.

Similarly, in the case of a corporation that is not a financial institution or a dealer in tax-exempt obligations, where there is no direct evidence of a purpose to purchase or carry tax-exempt obligations, the corporation's holdings of tax-exempt obligations are presumed to be insubstantial if the average adjusted basis of the corporation's tax-exempt obligations is two percent or less of the aver-

[159] Shareholders will continue to take into account all items of gain and loss under section 1366.
[160] Sec. 265(a).
[161] See Rev. Proc. 72-18, 1972-1 C.B. 740.
[162] *Ibid.*

age adjusted basis of all assets held by the corporation in the active conduct of its trade or business.

*Financial institutions*

In the case of a financial institution, the Code generally disallows that portion of the taxpayer's interest expense that is allocable to tax-exempt interest.[163] The amount of interest that is disallowed is an amount which bears the same ratio to such interest expense as the taxpayer's average adjusted bases of tax-exempt obligations acquired after August 7, 1986, bears to the average adjusted bases for all assets of the taxpayer.

*Exception for certain obligations of qualified small issuers*

The general rule in section 265(b), denying financial institutions' interest expense deductions allocable to tax-exempt obligations, does not apply to "qualified tax-exempt obligations."[164] Instead, as discussed in the next section, only 20 percent of the interest expense allocable to "qualified tax-exempt obligations" is disallowed.[165] A "qualified tax-exempt obligation" is a tax-exempt obligation that (1) is issued after August 7, 1986, by a qualified small issuer, (2) is not a private activity bond, and (3) is designated by the issuer as qualifying for the exception from the general rule of section 265(b).

A "qualified small issuer" is an issuer that reasonably anticipates that the amount of tax-exempt obligations that it will issue during the calendar year will be $10 million or less.[166] The Code specifies the circumstances under which an issuer and all subordinate entities are aggregated.[167] For purposes of the $10 million limitation, an issuer and all entities that issue obligations on behalf of such issuer are treated as one issuer. All obligations issued by a subordinate entity are treated as being issued by the entity to which it is subordinate. An entity formed (or availed of) to avoid the $10 million limitation and all entities benefiting from the device are treated as one issuer.

Composite issues (i.e., combined issues of bonds for different entities) qualify for the "qualified tax-exempt obligation" exception only if the requirements of the exception are met with respect to (1) the composite issue as a whole (determined by treating the composite issue as a single issue) and (2) each separate lot of obligations that is part of the issue (determined by treating each separate lot of obligations as a separate issue).[168] Thus a composite issue may qualify for the exception only if the composite issue itself does not exceed $10 million, and if each issuer benefitting from the composite issue reasonably anticipates that it will not issue more than $10 million of tax-exempt obligations during the calendar year, including through the composite arrangement.

---

[163] Sec. 265(b)(1). A "financial institution" is any person that (1) accepts deposits from the public in the ordinary course of such person's trade or business and is subject to Federal or State supervision as a financial institution or (2) is a corporation described by section 585(a)(2). Sec. 265(b)(5).

[164] Sec. 265(b)(3).

[165] Secs. 265(b)(3)(A), 291(a)(3) and 291(e)(1).

[166] Sec. 265(b)(3)(C).

[167] Sec. 265(b)(3)(E).

[168] Sec. 265(b)(3)(F).

*Treatment of financial institution preference items*

Section 291(a)(3) reduces by 20 percent the amount allowable as a deduction with respect to any financial institution preference item. Financial institution preference items include interest on debt to carry tax-exempt obligations acquired after December 31, 1982, and before August 8, 1986.[169] Section 265(b)(3) treats qualified tax-exempt obligations as if they were acquired on August 7, 1986. As a result, the amount allowable as a deduction by a financial institution with respect to interest incurred to carry a qualified tax-exempt obligation is reduced by 20 percent.

### *Reasons for Change*

The Congress believes that the creation of a de minimis safe harbor to permit financial institutions to hold a limited amount of tax-exempt obligations issued in 2009 and 2010 without full reduction of their attributable interest expense deductions will stimulate demand for tax-exempt obligations issued by State and local governments in 2009 and 2010. This additional demand should increase the volume of tax-exempt bond issuances by State and local governments in 2009 and 2010 while reducing the interest costs with respect to such issuances. In addition, the Congress believes that it is appropriate to increase temporarily the volume limitation for qualified small issuers, from $10 million to $30 million, and make other modifications to allow additional issuers to qualify under the provision.

### *Explanation of Provision*

*Two-percent safe harbor for financial institutions*

The provision provides that tax-exempt obligations issued during 2009 or 2010 and held by a financial institution, in an amount not to exceed two percent of the adjusted basis of the financial institution's assets, are not taken into account for the purpose of determining the portion of the financial institution's interest expense subject to the pro rata interest disallowance rule of section 265(b). For purposes of this rule, a refunding bond (whether a current or advance refunding) is treated as issued on the date of the issuance of the refunded bond (or in the case of a series of refundings, the original bond).

The provision also amends section 291(e) to provide that tax-exempt obligations issued during 2009 and 2010, and not taken into account for purposes of the calculation of a financial institution's interest expense subject to the pro rata interest disallowance rule, are treated as having been acquired on August 7, 1986. As a result, such obligations are financial institution preference items, and the amount allowable as a deduction by a financial institution with respect to interest incurred to carry such obligations is reduced by 20 percent.

[169] Sec. 291(e)(1).

*Modifications to qualified small issuer exception*

With respect to tax-exempt obligations issued during 2009 and 2010, the provision increases from $10 million to $30 million the annual limit for qualified small issuers.

In addition, in the case of a "qualified financing issue" issued in 2009 or 2010, the provision applies the $30 million annual volume limitation at the borrower level (rather than at the level of the pooled financing issuer). Thus, for the purpose of applying the requirements of the section 265(b)(3) qualified small issuer exception, the portion of the proceeds of a qualified financing issue that are loaned to a "qualified borrower" that participates in the issue are treated as a separate issue with respect to which the qualified borrower is deemed to be the issuer.

A "qualified financing issue" is any composite, pooled or other conduit financing issue the proceeds of which are used directly or indirectly to make or finance loans to one or more ultimate borrowers all of whom are qualified borrowers. A "qualified borrower" means (1) a State or political subdivision of a State or (2) an organization described in section 501(c)(3) and exempt from tax under section 501(a). Thus, for example, a $100 million pooled financing issue that was issued in 2009 could qualify for the section 265(b)(3) exception if the proceeds of such issue were used to make four equal loans of $25 million to four qualified borrowers. However, if (1) more than $30 million were loaned to any qualified borrower, (2) any borrower were not a qualified borrower, or (3) any borrower would, if it were the issuer of a separate issue in an amount equal to the amount loaned to such borrower, fail to meet any of the other requirements of section 265(b)(3), the entire $100 million pooled financing issue would fail to qualify for the exception.

For purposes of determining whether an issuer meets the requirements of the small issuer exception, qualified 501(c)(3) bonds issued in 2009 or 2010 are treated as if they were issued by the 501(c)(3) organization for whose benefit they were issued (and not by the actual issuer of such bonds). In addition, in the case of an organization described in section 501(c)(3) and exempt from taxation under section 501(a), requirements for "qualified financing issues" shall be applied as if the section 501(c)(3) organization were the issuer. Thus, in any event, an organization described in section 501(c)(3) and exempt from taxation under section 501(a) shall be limited to the $30 million per issuer cap for qualified tax exempt obligations described in section 265(b)(3).

### *Effective Date*

The provisions are effective for obligations issued after December 31, 2008.

## 2. Temporary modification of alternative minimum tax limitations on tax-exempt bonds (sec. 1503 of the Act and secs. 56 and 57 of the Code)

### *Present Law*

Present law imposes an alternative minimum tax ("AMT") on individuals and corporations. AMT is the amount by which the tentative minimum tax exceeds the regular income tax. The tentative minimum tax is computed based upon a taxpayer's alternative minimum taxable income ("AMTI"). AMTI is the taxpayer's taxable income modified to take into account certain preferences and adjustments. One of the preference items is tax-exempt interest on certain tax-exempt bonds issued for private activities (sec. 57(a)(5)). Also, in the case of a corporation, an adjustment based on current earnings is determined, in part, by taking into account 75 percent of items, including tax-exempt interest, that are excluded from taxable income but included in the corporation's earnings and profits (sec. 56(g)(4)(B)).

### *Reasons for Change*

The Congress believes that the AMT treatment of interest on tax-exempt bonds restricts the number of persons willing to hold tax-exempt bonds, resulting in higher financing costs. This problem has become more acute as a result of the current economic downturn. Accordingly, in light of current economic circumstances, the Act eliminates the AMT adjustments for interest on tax-exempt bonds issued in 2009 and 2010.

### *Explanation of Provision*

The Act provides that tax-exempt interest on private activity bonds issued in 2009 and 2010 is not an item of tax preference for purposes of the alternative minimum tax and interest on tax exempt bonds issued in 2009 and 2010 is not included in the corporate adjustment based on current earnings. For these purposes, a refunding bond is treated as issued on the date of the issuance of the refunded bond (or in the case of a series of refundings, the original bond).

The Act also provides that tax-exempt interest on private activity bonds issued in 2009 and 2010 to currently refund a private activity bond issued after December 31, 2003, and before January 1, 2009, is not an item of tax preference for purposes of the alternative minimum tax. Also tax-exempt interest on bonds issued in 2009 and 2010 to currently refund a bond issued after December 31, 2003, and before January 1, 2009, is not included in the corporate adjustment based on current earnings.

### *Effective Date*

The provision applies to interest on bonds issued after December 31, 2008.

## 3. Temporary expansion of availability of industrial development bonds to facilities creating intangible property and other modifications (sec. 1301 of the Act and sec. 144(a) of the Code)

### *Present Law*

Qualified small issue bonds (commonly referred to as "industrial development bonds" or "small issue IDBs") are tax-exempt bonds issued by State and local governments to finance private business manufacturing facilities (including certain directly related and ancillary facilities) or the acquisition of land and equipment by certain farmers. In both instances, these bonds are subject to limits on the amount of financing that may be provided, both for a single borrowing and in the aggregate. In general, no more than $1 million of small-issue bond financing may be outstanding at any time for property of a business (including related parties) located in the same municipality or county. Generally, this $1 million limit may be increased to $10 million if, in addition to outstanding bonds, all other capital expenditures of the business (including related parties) in the same municipality or county are counted toward the limit over a six-year period that begins three years before the issue date of the bonds and ends three years after such date. Outstanding aggregate borrowing is limited to $40 million per borrower (including related parties) regardless of where the property is located.

The Code permits up to $10 million of capital expenditures to be disregarded, in effect increasing from $10 million to $20 million the maximum allowable amount of total capital expenditures by an eligible business in the same municipality or county. However, no more than $10 million of bond financing may be outstanding at any time for property of an eligible business (including related parties) located in the same municipality or county. Other limits (e.g., the $40 million per borrower limit) also continue to apply.

A manufacturing facility is any facility which is used in the manufacturing or production of tangible personal property (including the processing resulting in a change in the condition of such property). Manufacturing facilities include facilities that are directly related and ancillary to a manufacturing facility (as described in the previous sentence) if (1) such facilities are located on the same site as the manufacturing facility and (2) not more than 25 percent of the net proceeds of the issue are used to provide such facilities.[170]

## *Explanation of Provision*

### *In general*

For bonds issued after the date of enactment and before January 1, 2011, the provision expands the definition of manufacturing facilities to mean any facility that is used in the manufacturing, creation, or production of tangible property or intangible property (within the meaning of section 197(d)(1)(C)(iii)). For this purpose, intangible property means any patent, copyright, formula, process, design, knowhow, format, or other similar item. It is intended to include among other items, the creation of computer software, and intellectual property associated bio-tech and pharmaceuticals.

In lieu of the directly related and ancillary test of present law, the provision provides a special rule for bonds issued after the date

[170] The 25 percent restriction was enacted by the Technical and Miscellaneous Revenue Act of 1988, Pub. L. No. 100–647, because of concern over the scope of the definition of manufacturing facility. See H.R. Rpt. No. 100–795 (1988). The amendment was intended to clarify that while the manufacturing facility definition does not preclude the financing of ancillary activities, the 25 percent restriction was intended to limit the use of bond proceeds to finance facilities other than for "core manufacturing." The conference agreement followed the House bill, which the conference report described as follows: "The House bill clarifies that up to 25 percent of the proceeds of a qualified small issue may be used to finance ancillary activities which are carried out at the manufacturing site. All such ancillary activities must be subordinate and integral to the manufacturing process."

of enactment and before January 1, 2011. For these bonds, the provision provides that facilities that are functionally related and subordinate to the manufacturing facility are treated as a manufacturing facility and the 25 percent of net proceeds restriction does not apply to such facilities.[171] Functionally related and subordinate facilities must be located on the same site as the manufacturing facility.

### *Effective Date*

The provision is effective for bonds issued after the date of enactment and before January 1, 2011.

## 4. Qualified school construction bonds (sec. 1521 of the Act and new sec. 54F of the Code)

### *Present Law*

#### *Tax-exempt bonds*

Interest on State and local governmental bonds generally is excluded from gross income for Federal income tax purposes if the proceeds of the bonds are used to finance direct activities of these governmental units or if the bonds are repaid with revenues of the governmental units. These can include tax-exempt bonds which finance public schools.[172] An issuer must file with the Internal Revenue Service certain information about the bonds issued in order for that bond issue to be tax-exempt.[173] Generally, this information return is required to be filed no later than the 15th day of the second month after the close of the calendar quarter in which the bonds were issued.

The tax exemption for State and local bonds does not apply to any arbitrage bond.[174] An arbitrage bond is defined as any bond that is part of an issue if any proceeds of the issue are reasonably expected to be used (or intentionally are used) to acquire higher yielding investments or to replace funds that are used to acquire higher yielding investments.[175] In general, arbitrage profits may be earned only during specified periods (e.g., defined "temporary periods") before funds are needed for the purpose of the borrowing or on specified types of investments (e.g., "reasonably required reserve or replacement funds"). Subject to limited exceptions, investment profits that are earned during these periods or on such investments must be rebated to the Federal government.

#### *Qualified zone academy bonds*

As an alternative to traditional tax-exempt bonds, States and local governments were given the authority to issue "qualified zone academy bonds."[176] A total of $400 million of qualified zone acad-

---

[171] The provision is based in part on a similar rule applicable to exempt facility bonds. Treas. Reg. sec. 1.103–8(a)(3) provides: "(3) Functionally related and subordinate. An exempt facility includes any land, building, or other property functionally related and subordinate to such facility. Property is not functionally related and subordinate to a facility if it is not of a character and size commensurate with the character and size of such facility."

[172] Sec. 103.

[173] Sec. 149(e).

[174] Sec. 103(a) and (b)(2).

[175] Sec. 148.

[176] Sec. 1397E.

emy bonds is authorized to be issued annually in calendar years 1998 through 2009. The $400 million aggregate bond cap is allocated each year to the States according to their respective populations of individuals below the poverty line. Each State, in turn, allocates the credit authority to qualified zone academies within such State.

A taxpayer holding a qualified zone academy bond on the credit allowance date is entitled to a credit. The credit is includible in gross income (as if it were a taxable interest payment on the bond), and may be claimed against regular income tax and alternative minimum tax liability.

The Treasury Department sets the credit rate at a rate estimated to allow issuance of qualified zone academy bonds without discount and without interest cost to the issuer.[177] The Secretary determines credit rates for tax credit bonds based on general assumptions about credit quality of the class of potential eligible issuers and such other factors as the Secretary deems appropriate. The Secretary may determine credit rates based on general credit market yield indexes and credit ratings. The maximum term of the bond is determined by the Treasury Department, so that the present value of the obligation to repay the principal on the bond is 50 percent of the face value of the bond.

"Qualified zone academy bonds" are defined as any bond issued by a State or local government, provided that (1) at least 95 percent of the proceeds are used for the purpose of renovating, providing equipment to, developing course materials for use at, or training teachers and other school personnel in a "qualified zone academy" and (2) private entities have promised to contribute to the qualified zone academy certain equipment, technical assistance or training, employee services, or other property or services with a value equal to at least 10 percent of the bond proceeds.

A school is a "qualified zone academy" if (1) the school is a public school that provides education and training below the college level, (2) the school operates a special academic program in cooperation with businesses to enhance the academic curriculum and increase graduation and employment rates, and (3) either (a) the school is located in an empowerment zone or enterprise community designated under the Code, or (b) it is reasonably expected that at least 35 percent of the students at the school will be eligible for free or reduced-cost lunches under the school lunch program established under the National School Lunch Act.

The arbitrage requirements which generally apply to interest-bearing tax-exempt bonds also generally apply to qualified zone academy bonds. In addition, an issuer of qualified zone academy bonds must reasonably expect to and actually spend 100 percent of the proceeds of such bonds on qualified zone academy property within the three-year period that begins on the date of issuance. To the extent less than 100 percent of the proceeds are used to finance qualified zone academy property during the three-year spending period, bonds will continue to qualify as qualified zone academy bonds if unspent proceeds are used within 90 days from

[177] Given the differences in credit quality and other characteristics of individual issuers, the Secretary cannot set credit rates in a manner that will allow each issuer to issue tax credit bonds at par.

the end of such three years period to redeem any nonqualified bonds. The three-year spending period may be extended by the Secretary if the issuer establishes that the failure to meet the spending requirement is due to reasonable cause and the related purposes for issuing the bonds will continue to proceed with due diligence.

Two special arbitrage rules apply to qualified zone academy bonds. First, available project proceeds invested during the three-year period beginning on the date of issue are not subject to the arbitrage restrictions (i.e., yield restriction and rebate requirements). Available project proceeds are proceeds from the sale of an issue of qualified zone academy bonds, less issuance costs (not to exceed two percent) and any investment earnings on such proceeds. Thus, available project proceeds invested during the three-year spending period may be invested at unrestricted yields, but the earnings on such investments must be spent on qualified zone academy property. Second, amounts invested in a reserve fund are not subject to the arbitrage restrictions to the extent: (1) such fund is funded at a rate not more rapid than equal annual installments; (2) such fund is funded in a manner reasonably expected to result in an amount not greater than an amount necessary to repay the issue; and (3) the yield on such fund is not greater than the average annual interest rate of tax-exempt obligations having a term of 10 years or more that are issued during the month the qualified zone academy bonds are issued.

Issuers of qualified zone academy bonds are required to report issuance to the Internal Revenue Service in a manner similar to the information returns required for tax-exempt bonds.

### *Reasons for Change*

The Congress believes that this new category of tax credit bonds will provide an efficient mechanism to encourage the construction, rehabilitation, or repair of public school facilities and the acquisition of land on which such bond-financed facilities are to be constructed.

### *Explanation of Provision* [178]

#### *In general*

The provision creates a new category of tax-credit bonds: qualified school construction bonds. Qualified school construction bonds must meet three requirements: (1) 100 percent of the available project proceeds of the bond issue is used for the construction, rehabilitation, or repair of a public school facility or for the acquisition of land on which such a bond-financed facility is to be constructed; (2) the bond is issued by a State or local government within which such school is located; and (3) the issuer designates such bonds as a qualified school construction bond.

[178] Section 301 of the Hiring Incentives to Restore Employment Act, Pub. L. No. 111–147, added a provision to section 6431, allowing the issuer of the bonds to elect to receive a direct payment from the Treasury in lieu of providing a tax credit to the holders of the bonds. For further discussion, see Part Seven of this document.

### *National limitation*

There is a national limitation on qualified school construction bonds of $11 billion for calendar years 2009 and 2010, respectively.

### *Allocation to the States*

The national limitation is tentatively allocated among the States in proportion to respective amounts each such State is eligible to receive under section 1124 of the Elementary and Secondary Education Act of 1965 for the most recent fiscal year ending before such calendar year. The amount each State is allocated under the above formula is then reduced by the amount received by any local large educational agency within the State.

For allocation purposes, a State includes the District of Columbia and any possession of the United States. The provision provides a special allocation for possessions of the United States other than Puerto Rico under the national limitation for States. Under this special rule an allocation to a possession other than Puerto Rico is made on the basis of the respective populations of individuals below the poverty line (as defined by the Office of Management and Budget) rather than respective populations of children aged five through seventeen. This special allocation reduces the State allocation share of the national limitation otherwise available for allocation among the States. Under another special rule, the Secretary of the Interior may allocate $200 million of school construction bonds for 2009 and 2010, respectively, to Indian schools. This special allocation for Indian schools is to be used for purposes of the construction, rehabilitation, and repair of schools funded by the Bureau of Indian Affairs. For purposes of such allocations Indian tribal governments are qualified issuers. The special allocation for Indian schools does not reduce the State allocation share of the national limitation otherwise available for allocation among the States.

If an amount allocated under this allocation to the States is unused for a calendar year it may be carried forward by the State to the next calendar year.

### *Allocation to large school districts*

Forty percent of the national limitation is allocated among large local educational agencies in proportion to the respective amounts each agency received under section 1124 of the Elementary and Secondary Education Act of 1965 for the most recent fiscal year ending before such calendar year. Any unused allocation of any agency within a State may be allocated by the agency to such State. With respect to a calendar year, the term large local educational agency means any local educational agency if such agency is: (1) among the 100 local educational agencies with the largest numbers of children aged 5 through 17 from families living below the poverty level, or (2) one of not more than 25 local educational agencies (other than in (1), immediately above) that the Secretary of Education determines are in particular need of assistance, based on a low level of resources for school construction, a high level of enrollment growth, or other such factors as the Secretary of Education deems appropriate. If any amount allocated to large local educational agency is unused for a calendar year the agency may reallocate such amount to the State in which the agency is located.

***Application of qualified tax credit bond rules***

The provision makes qualified school construction bonds a type of qualified tax credit bond for purposes of section 54A. In addition, qualified school construction bonds may be issued by Indian tribal governments only to the extent such bonds are issued for purposes that satisfy the present law requirements for tax-exempt bonds issued by Indian tribal governments (i.e., essential governmental functions and certain manufacturing purposes).

The provision requires 100 percent of the available project proceeds of qualified school construction bonds to be used within the three-year period that begins on the date of issuance. Available project proceeds are proceeds from the sale of the issue less issuance costs (not to exceed two percent) and any investment earnings on such sale proceeds. To the extent less than 100 percent of the available project proceeds are used to finance qualified purposes during the three-year spending period, bonds will continue to qualify as qualified school construction bonds if unspent proceeds are used within 90 days from the end of such three-year period to redeem bonds. The three-year spending period may be extended by the Secretary upon the issuer's request demonstrating that the failure to satisfy the three-year requirement is due to reasonable cause and the projects will continue to proceed with due diligence.

Qualified school construction bonds generally are subject to the arbitrage requirements of section 148. However, available project proceeds invested during the three-year spending period are not subject to the arbitrage restrictions (i.e., yield restriction and rebate requirements). In addition, amounts invested in a reserve fund are not subject to the arbitrage restrictions to the extent: (1) such fund is funded at a rate not more rapid than equal annual installments; (2) such fund is funded in a manner reasonably expected to result in an amount not greater than an amount necessary to repay the issue; and (3) the yield on such fund is not greater than the average annual interest rate of tax-exempt obligations having a term of 10 years or more that are issued during the month the qualified school construction bonds are issued.

The maturity of qualified school construction bonds is the term that the Secretary estimates will result in the present value of the obligation to repay the principal on such bonds being equal to 50 percent of the face amount of such bonds, using as a discount rate the average annual interest rate of tax-exempt obligations having a term of 10 years or more that are issued during the month the qualified school construction bonds are issued.

As with present-law tax credit bonds, the taxpayer holding qualified school construction bonds on a credit allowance date is entitled to a tax credit. The credit rate on the bonds is set by the Secretary at a rate that is 100 percent of the rate that would permit issuance of such bonds without discount and interest cost to the issuer. The amount of the tax credit is determined by multiplying the bond's credit rate by the face amount on the holder's bond. The credit accrues quarterly, is includible in gross income (as if it were an interest payment on the bond), and can be claimed against regular income tax liability and alternative minimum tax liability. Unused credits may be carried forward to succeeding taxable years. In addition, credits may be separated from the ownership of the underlying bond in a manner similar to the manner in which interest coupons can be stripped from interest-bearing bonds.

Issuers of qualified school construction bonds are required to certify that the financial disclosure requirements and applicable State and local law requirements governing conflicts of interest are satisfied with respect to such issue, as well as any other additional conflict of interest rules prescribed by the Secretary with respect to any Federal, State, or local government official directly involved with the issuance of qualified school construction bonds.

### *Effective Date*

The provision is effective for obligations issued after the date of enactment (February 17, 2009).

## 5. Extend and expand qualified zone academy bonds (sec. 1522 of the Act and sec. 54E of the Code)

### *Present Law*

#### *Tax-exempt bonds*

Interest on State and local governmental bonds generally is excluded from gross income for Federal income tax purposes if the proceeds of the bonds are used to finance direct activities of these governmental units or if the bonds are repaid with revenues of the governmental units. These can include tax-exempt bonds which finance public schools.[179] An issuer must file with the Internal Revenue Service certain information about the bonds issued in order for that bond issue to be tax-exempt.[180] Generally, this information return is required to be filed no later the 15th day of the second month after the close of the calendar quarter in which the bonds were issued.

The tax exemption for State and local bonds does not apply to any arbitrage bond.[181] An arbitrage bond is defined as any bond that is part of an issue if any proceeds of the issue are reasonably expected to be used (or intentionally are used) to acquire higher yielding investments or to replace funds that are used to acquire higher yielding investments.[182] In general, arbitrage profits may be earned only during specified periods (e.g., defined "temporary periods") before funds are needed for the purpose of the borrowing or on specified types of investments (e.g., "reasonably required reserve or replacement funds"). Subject to limited exceptions, investment profits that are earned during these periods or on such investments must be rebated to the Federal Government.

#### *Qualified zone academy bonds*

As an alternative to traditional tax-exempt bonds, States and local governments were given the authority to issue "qualified zone

[179] Sec. 103.
[180] Sec. 149(e).
[181] Sec. 103(a) and (b)(2).
[182] Sec. 148.

academy bonds."[183] A total of $400 million of qualified zone academy bonds is authorized to be issued annually in calendar years 1998 through 2009. The $400 million aggregate bond cap is allocated each year to the States according to their respective populations of individuals below the poverty line. Each State, in turn, allocates the credit authority to qualified zone academies within such State.

A taxpayer holding a qualified zone academy bond on the credit allowance date is entitled to a credit. The credit is includible in gross income (as if it were a taxable interest payment on the bond), and may be claimed against regular income tax and alternative minimum tax liability.

The Treasury Department sets the credit rate at a rate estimated to allow issuance of qualified zone academy bonds without discount and without interest cost to the issuer.[184] The Secretary determines credit rates for tax credit bonds based on general assumptions about credit quality of the class of potential eligible issuers and such other factors as the Secretary deems appropriate. The Secretary may determine credit rates based on general credit market yield indexes and credit ratings. The maximum term of the bond is determined by the Treasury Department, so that the present value of the obligation to repay the principal on the bond is 50 percent of the face value of the bond.

"Qualified zone academy bonds" are defined as any bond issued by a State or local government, provided that (1) at least 95 percent of the proceeds are used for the purpose of renovating, providing equipment to, developing course materials for use at, or training teachers and other school personnel in a "qualified zone academy" and (2) private entities have promised to contribute to the qualified zone academy certain equipment, technical assistance or training, employee services, or other property or services with a value equal to at least 10 percent of the bond proceeds.

A school is a "qualified zone academy" if (1) the school is a public school that provides education and training below the college level, (2) the school operates a special academic program in cooperation with businesses to enhance the academic curriculum and increase graduation and employment rates, and (3) either (a) the school is located in an empowerment zone or enterprise community designated under the Code, or (b) it is reasonably expected that at least 35 percent of the students at the school will be eligible for free or reduced-cost lunches under the school lunch program established under the National School Lunch Act.

The arbitrage requirements which generally apply to interest-bearing tax-exempt bonds also generally apply to qualified zone academy bonds. In addition, an issuer of qualified zone academy bonds must reasonably expect to and actually spend 100 percent or more of the proceeds of such bonds on qualified zone academy property within the three-year period that begins on the date of issuance. To the extent less than 100 percent of the proceeds are used to finance qualified zone academy property during the three-

[183] See secs. 54E and 1397E.

[184] Given the differences in credit quality and other characteristics of individual issuers, the Secretary cannot set credit rates in a manner that will allow each issuer to issue tax credit bonds at par.

year spending period, bonds will continue to qualify as qualified zone academy bonds if unspent proceeds are used within 90 days from the end of such three-year period to redeem any nonqualified bonds. The three-year spending period may be extended by the Secretary if the issuer establishes that the failure to meet the spending requirement is due to reasonable cause and the related purposes for issuing the bonds will continue to proceed with due diligence.

Two special arbitrage rules apply to qualified zone academy bonds. First, available project proceeds invested during the three-year period beginning on the date of issue are not subject to the arbitrage restrictions (i.e., yield restriction and rebate requirements). Available project proceeds are proceeds from the sale of an issue of qualified zone academy bonds, less issuance costs (not to exceed two percent) and any investment earnings on such proceeds. Thus, available project proceeds invested during the three-year spending period may be invested at unrestricted yields, but the earnings on such investments must be spent on qualified zone academy property. Second, amounts invested in a reserve fund are not subject to the arbitrage restrictions to the extent: (1) such fund is funded at a rate not more rapid than equal annual installments; (2) such fund is funded in a manner reasonably expected to result in an amount not greater than an amount necessary to repay the issue; and (3) the yield on such fund is not greater than the average annual interest rate of tax-exempt obligations having a term of 10 years or more that are issued during the month the qualified zone academy bonds are issued.

Issuers of qualified zone academy bonds are required to report issuance to the Internal Revenue Service in a manner similar to the information returns required for tax-exempt bonds.

### *Reasons for Change*

The Congress wishes to expand and extend the qualified zone academy bond program. The Congress believes that this category of tax credit bonds will continue to provide an efficient mechanism for renovating, providing equipment to, developing course materials for use at, or training teachers and other school personnel in a "qualified zone academy."

### *Explanation of Provision* [185]

#### *In general*

The provision extends and expands the present-law qualified zone academy bond program. The provision authorizes issuance of up to $1.4 billion of qualified zone academy bonds annually for 2009 and 2010, respectively.

[185] Section 301 of the Hiring Incentives to Restore Employment Act, Pub. L. No. 111–147, added a provision to section 6431, allowing the issuer of the bonds to elect to receive a direct payment from the Treasury in lieu of providing a tax credit to the holders of the bonds. For further discussion, see Part Seven of this document. Also qualified zone academy bonds were further amended in section 758 of the Tax Relief, Unemployment Insurance Reauthorization, and Job Creation Act of 2010, Pub. L. No. 111–312, described in Part Sixteen of this document.

### *Effective Date*

The provision applies to obligations issued after December 31, 2008.

## 6. Build America bonds (sec. 1531 of the Act and new secs. 54AA and 6431 of the Code)

### *Present Law*

#### *In general*

Under present law, gross income does not include interest on State or local bonds. State and local bonds are classified generally as either governmental bonds or private activity bonds. Governmental bonds are bonds the proceeds of which are primarily used to finance governmental functions or which are repaid with governmental funds. Private activity bonds are bonds in which the State or local government serves as a conduit providing financing to nongovernmental persons (e.g., private businesses or individuals). The exclusion from income for State and local bonds does not apply to private activity bonds, unless the bonds are issued for certain permitted purposes ("qualified private activity bonds") and other Code requirements are met.

#### *Private activity bonds*

The Code defines a private activity bond as any bond that satisfies (1) the private business use test and the private security or payment test ("the private business test"); or (2) "the private loan financing test." [186]

*Private business test*

Under the private business test, a bond is a private activity bond if it is part of an issue in which:

1. More than 10 percent of the proceeds of the issue (including use of the bond-financed property) are to be used in the trade or business of any person other than a governmental unit ("private business use"); and
2. More than 10 percent of the payment of principal or interest on the issue is, directly or indirectly, secured by (a) property used or to be used for a private business use or (b) to be derived from payments in respect of property, or borrowed money, used or to be used for a private business use ("private payment test"). [187]

A bond is not a private activity bond unless both parts of the private business test (i.e., the private business use test and the private payment test) are met. Thus, a facility that is 100 percent privately used does not cause the bonds financing such facility to be private activity bonds if the bonds are not secured by or paid with private payments. For example, land improvements that benefit a privately-owned factory may be financed with governmental bonds

[186] Sec. 141.

[187] The 10 percent private business test is reduced to five percent in the case of private business uses (and payments with respect to such uses) that are unrelated to any governmental use being financed by the issue.

if the debt service on such bonds is not paid by the factory owner or other private parties.

*Private loan financing test*

A bond issue satisfies the private loan financing test if proceeds exceeding the lesser of $5 million or five percent of such proceeds are used directly or indirectly to finance loans to one or more nongovernmental persons. Private loans include both business and other (e.g., personal) uses and payments by private persons; however, in the case of business uses and payments, all private loans also constitute private business uses and payments subject to the private business test.

*Arbitrage restrictions*

The exclusion from income for interest on State and local bonds does not apply to any arbitrage bond.[188] An arbitrage bond is defined as any bond that is part of an issue if any proceeds of the issue are reasonably expected to be used (or intentionally are used) to acquire higher yielding investments or to replace funds that are used to acquire higher yielding investments.[189] In general, arbitrage profits may be earned only during specified periods (e.g., defined "temporary periods") before funds are needed for the purpose of the borrowing or on specified types of investments (e.g., "reasonably required reserve or replacement funds"). Subject to limited exceptions, investment profits that are earned during these periods or on such investments must be rebated to the Federal Government.

***Qualified tax credit bonds***

In lieu of interest, holders of qualified tax credit bonds receive a tax credit that accrues quarterly. The following bonds are qualified tax credit bonds: qualified forestry conservation bonds, new clean renewable energy bonds, qualified energy conservation bonds, and qualified zone academy bonds.[190]

Section 54A of the Code sets forth general rules applicable to qualified tax credit bonds. These rules include requirements regarding credit allowance dates, the expenditure of available project proceeds, reporting, arbitrage, maturity limitations, and financial conflicts of interest, among other special rules.

A taxpayer who holds a qualified tax credit bond on one or more credit allowance dates of the bond during the taxable year shall be allowed a credit against the taxpayer's income tax for the taxable year. In general, the credit amount for any credit allowance date is 25 percent of the annual credit determined with respect to the bond. The annual credit is determined by multiplying the applicable credit rate by the outstanding face amount of the bond. The applicable credit rate for the bond is the rate that the Secretary estimates will permit the issuance of the qualified tax credit bond with a specified maturity or redemption date without discount and with-

[188] Sec. 103(a) and (b)(2).
[189] Sec. 148.
[190] See sections 54B, 54C, 54D, and 54E.

out interest cost to the qualified issuer.[191] The Secretary determines credit rates for tax credit bonds based on general assumptions about credit quality of the class of potential eligible issuers and such other factors as the Secretary deems appropriate. The Secretary may determine credit rates based on general credit market yield indexes and credit ratings.

The credit is included in gross income and, under regulations prescribed by the Secretary, may be stripped (a separation (including at issuance) of the ownership of a qualified tax credit bond and the entitlement to the credit with respect to such bond).

Section 54A of the Code requires that 100 percent of the available project proceeds of qualified tax credit bonds must be used within the three-year period that begins on the date of issuance. Available project proceeds are proceeds from the sale of the bond issue less issuance costs (not to exceed two percent) and any investment earnings on such sale proceeds. To the extent less than 100 percent of the available project proceeds are used to finance qualified projects during the three-year spending period, bonds will continue to qualify as qualified tax credit bonds if unspent proceeds are used within 90 days from the end of such three-year period to redeem bonds. The three-year spending period may be extended by the Secretary upon the issuer's request demonstrating that the failure to satisfy the three-year requirement is due to reasonable cause and the projects will continue to proceed with due diligence.

Qualified tax credit bonds generally are subject to the arbitrage requirements of section 148. However, available project proceeds invested during the three-year spending period are not subject to the arbitrage restrictions (i.e., yield restriction and rebate requirements). In addition, amounts invested in a reserve fund are not subject to the arbitrage restrictions to the extent: (1) such fund is funded at a rate not more rapid than equal annual installments; (2) such fund is funded in a manner reasonably expected to result in an amount not greater than an amount necessary to repay the issue; and (3) the yield on such fund is not greater than the average annual interest rate of tax-exempt obligations having a term of 10 years or more that are issued during the month the qualified tax credit bonds are issued.

The maturity of qualified tax credit bonds is the term that the Secretary estimates will result in the present value of the obligation to repay the principal on such bonds being equal to 50 percent of the face amount of such bonds, using as a discount rate the average annual interest rate of tax-exempt obligations having a term of 10 years or more that are issued during the month the qualified tax credit bonds are issued.

### *Reasons for Change*

The Congress notes that borrowing by State and local governments is critically important to financing the nation's infrastructure. The Congress has observed that over the past several years, yield spreads between tax-exempt debt issued by State and local

[191] Given the differences in credit quality and other characteristics of individual issuers, the Secretary cannot set credit rates in a manner that will allow each issuer to issue tax credit bonds at par.

governments and approximately comparable taxable debt issued by corporations has narrowed, so that tax-exempt yields are now generally less than 25 percent below taxable yields.[192] The Congress further observes that not all of the benefit of the tax-exemption of interest on State and local bonds redounds to the issuing government because the exclusion of qualifying interest income is more valuable to bondholders in the highest tax brackets than to those bondholders in the lower tax brackets. The Congress, therefore, believes that the provision offers a more revenue efficient financing tool and lower net interest costs to State and local issuers.

In addition, the Congress recognizes that many States are suffering from declines in revenues and tight budgets while the need for infrastructure is great. Therefore the Congress believes it is appropriate to offer to issuers, on a temporary basis, the ability to receive a refundable credit for bonds used to fund capital expenditures in lieu of providing a tax credit to bondholders.

## *Explanation of Provision*

### *In general*

The provision permits an issuer to elect to have an otherwise tax-exempt bond treated as a "Build America Bond." A "Build America Bond" is any obligation (other than a private activity bond) if the interest on such obligation would be (but for this provision) excludable from gross income under section 103 and the issuer makes an irrevocable election to have the provision apply. In determining if an obligation would be tax-exempt under section 103, the credit (or the payment discussed below for qualified bonds) is not treated as a Federal guarantee. Further, the yield on a taxable governmental bond is determined without regard to the credit. A taxable governmental bond does not include any bond if the issue price has more than a de minimis amount of premium over the stated principal amount of the bond.

The holder of a taxable governmental bond will accrue a tax credit in the amount of 35 percent of the interest paid on the interest payment dates of the bond during the calendar year.[193] The interest payment date is any date on which the holder of record of the taxable governmental bond is entitled to a payment of interest under such bond. The sum of the accrued credits is allowed against regular and alternative minimum tax. Unused credit may be carried forward to succeeding taxable years. The credit, as well as the interest paid by the issuer, is included in gross income and the credit may be stripped under rules similar to those provided in section 54A regarding qualified tax credit bonds. Rules similar to those that apply for S corporations, partnerships and regulated investment companies with respect to qualified tax credit bonds also apply to the credit.

Unlike the tax credit for bonds issued under section 54A, the credit rate would not be calculated by the Secretary, but rather would be set by law at 35 percent. The actual credit that a tax-

---

[192] Joint Committee on Taxation, *Present Law and Issues Related to Infrastructure Finance* (JCX 83–08), October 24, 2008. pp. 23–28.

[193] Original issue discount (OID) is not treated as a payment of interest for purposes of determining the credit under the provision. OID is the excess of an obligation's stated redemption price at maturity over the obligation's issue price (section 1273(a)).

payer may claim is determined by multiplying the interest payment that the taxpayer receives from the issuer (i.e., the bond coupon payment) by 35 percent. Because the credit that the taxpayer claims is also included in income, the Congress anticipates that State and local issuers will issue bonds paying interest at rates approximately equal to 74.1 percent of comparable taxable bonds. The Congress anticipates that if an issuer issues a taxable governmental bond with coupons at 74.1 percent of a comparable taxable bond's coupon that the issuer's bond should sell at par. For example, if a taxable bond of comparable risk pays a $1,000 coupon and sells at par, then if a State or local issuer issues an equal-sized bond with coupon of $741.00, such a bond should also sell at par. The taxpayer who acquires the latter bond will receive an interest payment of $741 and may claim a credit of $259 (35 percent of $741). The credit and the interest payment are both included in the taxpayer's income. Thus, the taxpayer's taxable income from this instrument would be $1,000. This is the same taxable income that the taxpayer would recognize from holding the comparable taxable bond. Consequently the issuer's bond should sell at the same price as would the taxable bond.

***Special rule for qualified bonds issued during 2009 and 2010***

A "qualified bond" is any taxable governmental bond issued as part of an issue if 100 percent of the available project proceeds of such issue are to be used for capital expenditures.[194] The Act also allows a reasonably required reserve fund to be funded from bond proceeds.[195] The bond must be issued after the date of enactment of the provision and before January 1, 2011. The issuer must make an irrevocable election to have the special rule for qualified bonds apply.

Under the special rule for qualified bonds, in lieu of the tax credit to the holder, the issuer is allowed a credit equal to 35 percent of each interest payment made under such bond.[196] If in 2009 or 2010, the issuer elects to receive the credit, in the example above, for the State or local issuer's bond to sell at par, the issuer would have to issue the bond with a $1,000 interest coupon. The taxpayer who holds such a bond would include $1,000 on interest in his or her income. From the taxpayer's perspective the bond is the same as the taxable bond in the example above and the taxpayer would be willing to pay par for the bond. However, under the provision the State or local issuer would receive a payment of $350 for each $1,000 coupon paid to bondholders. (The net interest cost to the issuer would be $650.)

---

[194] Under Treas. Reg. sec. 150–1(b), capital expenditure means any cost of a type that is properly chargeable to capital account (or would be so chargeable with a proper election or with the application of the definition of placed in service under Treas. Reg. sec. 1.150–2(c)) under general Federal income tax principles. For purposes of applying the "general Federal income tax principles" standard, an issuer should generally be treated as if it were a corporation subject to taxation under subchapter C of chapter 1 of the Code. An example of a capital expenditure would include expenditures made for the purchase of fiber-optic cable to provide municipal broadband service.

[195] Under section 148(d)(2), a bond is an arbitrage bond if the amount of the proceeds from the sale of such issue that is part or any reserve or replacement fund exceeds 10 percent of the proceeds. As such the interest on such bond would not be tax-exempt under section 103 and thus would not be a qualified bond for purposes of the provision.

[196] Original issue discount (OID) is not treated as a payment of interest for purposes of calculating the refundable credit under the provision.

The payment by the Secretary is to be made contemporaneously with the interest payment made by the issuer, and may be made either in advance or as reimbursement. In lieu of payment to the issuer, the payment may be made to a person making interest payments on behalf of the issuer. For purposes of the arbitrage rules, the yield on a qualified bond is reduced by the amount of the credit/payment.

***Transitional coordination with State law***

As noted above, interest on a taxable governmental bond and the related credit are includible in gross income to the holder for Federal tax purposes. The provision provides that until a State provides otherwise, the interest on any taxable governmental bond and the amount of any credit determined with respect to such bond shall be treated as being exempt from Federal income tax for purposes of State income tax laws.

### *Effective Date*

The provision is effective for obligations issued after the date of enactment (February 17, 2009).

## 7. Recovery zone bonds (sec. 1401 of the Act and new secs. 1400U–1, 1400U–2, and 1400U–3 of the Code)

### *Present Law*

***In general***

Under present law, gross income does not include interest on State or local bonds. State and local bonds are classified generally as either governmental bonds or private activity bonds. Governmental bonds are bonds the proceeds of which are primarily used to finance governmental functions or which are repaid with governmental funds. Private activity bonds are bonds in which the State or local government serves as a conduit providing financing to nongovernmental persons (e.g., private businesses or individuals). The exclusion from income for State and local bonds does not apply to private activity bonds unless the bonds are issued for certain permitted purposes ("qualified private activity bonds") and other Code requirements are met.

***Private activity bonds***

The Code defines a private activity bond as any bond that satisfies (1) the private business use test and the private security or payment test ("the private business test"); or (2) "the private loan financing test."[197]

*Private business test*

Under the private business test, a bond is a private activity bond if it is part of an issue in which:

1. More than 10 percent of the proceeds of the issue (including use of the bond-financed property) are to be used in the

[197] Sec. 141.

trade or business of any person other than a governmental unit ("private business use"); and

2. More than 10 percent of the payment of principal or interest on the issue is, directly or indirectly, secured by (a) property used or to be used for a private business use or (b) to be derived from payments in respect of property, or borrowed money, used or to be used for a private business use ("private payment test").[198]

A bond is not a private activity bond unless both parts of the private business test (i.e., the private business use test and the private payment test) are met. Thus, a facility that is 100 percent privately used does not cause the bonds financing such facility to be private activity bonds if the bonds are not secured by or paid with private payments. For example, land improvements that benefit a privately-owned factory may be financed with governmental bonds if the debt service on such bonds is not paid by the factory owner or other private parties and such bonds are not secured by the property.

*Private loan financing test*

A bond issue satisfies the private loan financing test if proceeds exceeding the lesser of $5 million or five percent of such proceeds are used directly or indirectly to finance loans to one or more nongovernmental persons. Private loans include both business and other (e.g., personal) uses and payments to private persons; however, in the case of business uses and payments, all private loans also constitute private business uses and payments subject to the private business test.

*Arbitrage restrictions*

The exclusion from income for interest on State and local bonds does not apply to any arbitrage bond.[199] An arbitrage bond is defined as any bond that is part of an issue if any proceeds of the issue are reasonably expected to be used (or intentionally are used) to acquire higher yielding investments or to replace funds that are used to acquire higher yielding investments.[200] In general, arbitrage profits may be earned only during specified periods (e.g., defined "temporary periods") before funds are needed for the purpose of the borrowing or on specified types of investments (e.g., "reasonably required reserve or replacement funds"). Subject to limited exceptions, investment profits that are earned during these periods or on such investments must be rebated to the Federal Government.

### *Qualified private activity bonds*

Qualified private activity bonds permit States or local governments to act as conduits providing tax-exempt financing for certain private activities. The definition of qualified private activity bonds includes an exempt facility bond, or qualified mortgage, veterans'

[198] The 10 percent private business test is reduced to five percent in the case of private business uses (and payments with respect to such uses) that are unrelated to any governmental use being financed by the issue.
[199] Sec. 103(a) and (b)(2).
[200] Sec. 148.

mortgage, small issue, redevelopment, 501(c)(3), or student loan bond (sec. 141(e)).

The definition of an exempt facility bond includes bonds issued to finance certain transportation facilities (airports, ports, mass commuting, and high-speed intercity rail facilities); qualified residential rental projects; privately owned and/or operated utility facilities (sewage, water, solid waste disposal, and local district heating and cooling facilities, certain private electric and gas facilities, and hydroelectric dam enhancements); public/private educational facilities; qualified green building and sustainable design projects; and qualified highway or surface freight transfer facilities (sec. 142(a)).

In most cases, the aggregate volume of qualified private activity bonds is restricted by annual aggregate volume limits imposed on bonds issued by issuers within each State ("State volume cap"). For calendar year 2007, the State volume cap, which is indexed for inflation, equals $85 per resident of the State, or $256.24 million, if greater. Exceptions to the State volume cap are provided for bonds for certain governmentally owned facilities (e.g., airports, ports, high-speed intercity rail, and solid waste disposal) and bonds which are subject to separate local, State, or national volume limits (e.g., public/private educational facility bonds, enterprise zone facility bonds, qualified green building bonds, and qualified highway or surface freight transfer facility bonds).

Qualified private activity bonds generally are subject to restrictions on the use of proceeds for the acquisition of land and existing property. In addition, qualified private activity bonds generally are subject to restrictions on the use of proceeds to finance certain specified facilities (e.g., airplanes, skyboxes, other luxury boxes, health club facilities, gambling facilities, and liquor stores), and use of proceeds to pay costs of issuance (e.g., bond counsel and underwriter fees). Small issue and redevelopment bonds also are subject to additional restrictions on the use of proceeds for certain facilities (e.g., golf courses and massage parlors).

Moreover, the term of qualified private activity bonds generally may not exceed 120 percent of the economic life of the property being financed and certain public approval requirements (similar to requirements that typically apply under State law to issuance of governmental debt) apply under Federal law to issuance of private activity bonds.

### *Qualified tax credit bonds*

In lieu of interest, holders of qualified tax credit bonds receive a tax credit that accrues quarterly. The following bonds are qualified tax credit bonds: qualified forestry conservation bonds, new clean renewable energy bonds, qualified energy conservation bonds, and qualified zone academy bonds.[201]

Section 54A of the Code sets forth general rules applicable to qualified tax credit bonds. These rules include requirements regarding the expenditure of available project proceeds, reporting, arbitrage, maturity limitations, and financial conflicts of interest, among other special rules.

---

[201] See sections 54B, 54C, 54D, and 54E.

A taxpayer who holds a qualified tax credit bond on one or more credit allowance dates of the bond during the taxable year shall be allowed a credit against the taxpayer's income tax for the taxable year. In general, the credit amount for any credit allowance date is 25 percent of the annual credit determined with respect to the bond. The annual credit is determined by multiplying the applicable credit rate by the outstanding face amount of the bond. The applicable credit rate for the bond is the rate that the Secretary estimates will permit the issuance of the qualified tax credit bond with a specified maturity or redemption date without discount and without interest cost to the qualified issuer.[202] The Secretary determines credit rates for tax credit bonds based on general assumptions about credit quality of the class of potential eligible issuers and such other factors as the Secretary deems appropriate. The Secretary may determine credit rates based on general credit market yield indexes and credit ratings. The credit is included in gross income and, under regulations prescribed by the Secretary, may be stripped.

Section 54A of the Code requires that 100 percent of the available project proceeds of qualified tax credit bonds must be used within the three-year period that begins on the date of issuance. Available project proceeds are proceeds from the sale of the bond issue less issuance costs (not to exceed two percent) and any investment earnings on such sale proceeds. To the extent less than 100 percent of the available project proceeds are used to finance qualified projects during the three-year spending period, bonds will continue to qualify as qualified tax credit bonds if unspent proceeds are used within 90 days from the end of such three-year period to redeem bonds. The three-year spending period may be extended by the Secretary upon the issuer's request demonstrating that the failure to satisfy the three-year requirement is due to reasonable cause and the projects will continue to proceed with due diligence.

Qualified tax credit bonds generally are subject to the arbitrage requirements of section 148. However, available project proceeds invested during the three-year spending period are not subject to the arbitrage restrictions (i.e., yield restriction and rebate requirements). In addition, amounts invested in a reserve fund are not subject to the arbitrage restrictions to the extent: (1) such fund is funded at a rate not more rapid than equal annual installments; (2) such fund is funded in a manner reasonably expected to result in an amount not greater than an amount necessary to repay the issue; and (3) the yield on such fund is not greater than the average annual interest rate of tax-exempt obligations having a term of 10 years or more that are issued during the month the qualified tax credit bonds are issued.

The maturity of qualified tax credit bonds is the term that the Secretary estimates will result in the present value of the obligation to repay the principal on such bonds being equal to 50 percent of the face amount of such bonds, using as a discount rate the average annual interest rate of tax-exempt obligations having a term

[202] Given the differences in credit quality and other characteristics of individual issuers, the Secretary cannot set credit rates in a manner that will allow each issuer to issue tax credit bonds at par.

of 10 years or more that are issued during the month the qualified tax credit bonds are issued.

### *Reasons for Change*

Many communities have seen a significant decline in the number of individuals employed and are struggling with high concentrations of poverty and foreclosed homes. The Congress believes that additional incentives are needed to assist those communities most affected by the current economic crisis. The Congress also believes that State and local governments often are in the best position to assess economic development needs. Thus, the Congress believes it is appropriate to provide State and local governments with access to subsidized financing in order to promote economic development in communities affected by job losses and to provide needed infrastructure.

### *Explanation of Provision*

#### *In general*

The provision permits an issuer to designate one or more areas as recovery zones. The area must: (1) have significant poverty, unemployment, general distress, or home foreclosures; (2) be an area for which a designation as an empowerment zone or renewal community is in effect or; (3) be an area designated by the issuer as economically distressed by reason of the closure or realignment of a military installation pursuant to the Defense Base Closure and Realignment Act of 1990. Issuers may issue recovery zone economic development bonds and recovery zone facility bonds with respect to these zones.

There is a national recovery zone economic development bond limitation of $10 billion. In addition, there is a separate national recovery zone facility bond limitation of $15 billion. Under the Act the national recovery zone economic development bond limitation and national recovery zone facility bond limitation are allocated among the States in the proportion that each State's employment decline bears to the national decline in employment (the aggregate 2008 State employment declines for all States).[203] The Secretary is to adjust each State's allocation for a calendar year such that no State receives less than 0.9 percent of the national recovery zone economic development bond limitation and no less than 0.9 percent of the national recovery zone facility bond limitation. The Act also permits a county or large municipality to waive all or part of its allocation of the State bond limitations to allow further allocation within that State. In calculating the local employment decline with respect to a county, the portion of such decline attributable to a large municipality is disregarded for purposes of determining the county's portion of the State employment decline and is attributable to the large municipality only.

For purposes of the provision "2008 State employment decline" means, with respect to any State, the excess (if any) of (i) the num-

[203] The Bureau of Labor Statistics prepares data on regional and State employment and unemployment. See, e.g., Bureau of Labor Statistics, USDL 09–0093, *Regional and State Employment and Unemployment: December 2008* (January 27, 2009), <http://www.bls.gov/news.release/laus.nr0.htm>.

ber of individuals employed in such State as determined for December 2007, over (ii) the number of individuals employed in such State as determined for December 2008. The term "large municipality" means a municipality with a population of more than 100,000.

### *Recovery Zone Economic Development Bonds*

New section 54AA(h) of the Act creates a special rule for qualified bonds (a type of taxable governmental bond) issued before January 1, 2011, that entitles the issuer of such bonds to receive an advance tax credit equal to 45 percent of the interest payable on an interest payment date. For taxable governmental bonds that are designated recovery zone economic development bonds, the applicable percentage is 55 percent.

A recovery zone economic development bond is a taxable governmental bond issued as part of an issue if 100 percent of the available project proceeds of such issue are to be used for one or more qualified economic development purposes and the issuer designates such bond for purposes of this section. However, the Act allows for a reasonably required reserve fund to be funded from the proceeds of a recovery zone economic development bond. A qualified economic development purpose means expenditures for purposes of promoting development or other economic activity in a recovery zone, including (1) capital expenditures paid or incurred with respect to property located in such zone, (2) expenditures for public infrastructure and construction of public facilities located in a recovery zone.

The aggregate face amount of bonds which may be designated by any issuer cannot exceed the amount of the recovery zone economic development bond limitation allocated to such issuer.

### *Recovery Zone Facility Bonds*

The provision creates a new category of exempt facility bonds, "recovery zone facility bonds." A recovery zone facility bond means any bond issued as part of an issue if: (1) 95 percent or more of the net proceeds of such issue are to be used for recovery zone property and (2) such bond is issued before January 1, 2011, and (3) the issuer designates such bond as a recovery zone facility bond. The aggregate face amount of bonds which may be designated by any issuer cannot exceed the amount of the recovery zone facility bond limitation allocated to such issuer.

Under the provision, the term "recovery zone property" means any property subject to depreciation to which section 168 applies (or would apply but for section 179) if (1) such property was acquired, constructed, reconstructed, or renovated by the taxpayer after the date on which the designation of the recovery zone took effect; (2) the original use of such property in the recovery zone commences with the taxpayer; and (3) substantially all of the use of such property is in the recovery zone and is in the active conduct of a qualified business by the taxpayer in such zone. The term "qualified business" means any trade or business except that the rental to others of real property located in a recovery zone shall be treated as a qualified business only if the property is not residential rental property (as defined in section 168(e)(2)) and does not include any trade or business consisting of the operation of any facility described in section 144(c)(6)(B) (i.e., any private or commercial golf course, country club, massage parlor, hot tub facility, suntan facility, racetrack or other facility used for gambling, or any store the principal purpose of which is the sale of alcoholic beverages for consumption off premises).

Subject to the following exceptions and modifications, issuance of recovery zone facility bonds is subject to the general rules applicable to issuance of qualified private activity bonds:

1. Issuance of the bonds is not subject to the aggregate annual State private activity bond volume limits (sec. 146);
2. The restriction on acquisition of existing property does not apply (sec. 147(d));

### *Effective Date*

The provision is effective for obligations issued after the date of enactment (February 17, 2009).

## 8. Tribal economic development bonds (sec. 1402 of the Act and new sec. 7871(f) of the Code)

### *Present Law*

Under present law, gross income does not include interest on State or local bonds.[204] State and local bonds are classified generally as either governmental bonds or private activity bonds. Governmental bonds are bonds the proceeds of which are primarily used to finance governmental facilities or the debt is repaid with governmental funds. Private activity bonds are bonds in which the State or local government serves as a conduit providing financing to nongovernmental persons. For these purposes, the term "nongovernmental person" includes the Federal government and all other individuals and entities other than States or local governments.[205] Interest on private activity bonds is taxable, unless the bonds are issued for certain purposes permitted by the Code and other requirements are met.[206]

Although not States or subdivisions of States, Indian tribal governments are provided with a tax status similar to State and local governments for specified purposes under the Code.[207] Among the purposes for which a tribal government is treated as a State is the issuance of tax-exempt bonds. Under section 7871(c), tribal governments are authorized to issue tax-exempt bonds only if substantially all of the proceeds are used for essential governmental functions.[208] The term essential governmental function does not include any function that is not customarily performed by State and local governments with general taxing powers. Section 7871(c) further prohibits Indian tribal governments from issuing tax-exempt private activity bonds (as defined in section 141(a) of the Code) with the exception of certain bonds for manufacturing facilities.

---

[204] Sec. 103.
[205] Sec. 141(b)(6); Treas. Reg. sec. 1.141–1(b).
[206] Secs. 103(b)(1) and 141.
[207] Sec. 7871.
[208] Sec. 7871(c).

### *Reasons for Change*

State and local governments use tax-exempt financing for both public purposes and qualified private activities. Indian tribes, however, are restricted to issuing tax-exempt bonds for essential governmental functions. In general, Indian tribes cannot issue tax-exempt private activity bonds, except for certain manufacturing facilities. The Congress believes that in the current economic crisis, tribes should be afforded flexibility in using tax-exempt financing for economic development. Therefore, the provision permits Indian tribes to issue tax-exempt bonds for purposes not currently permitted by present law, if the bonds would have been tax-exempt if issued by a State.

### *Explanation of Provision*

#### *Tribal Economic Development Bonds*

The provision allows Indian tribal governments to issue "tribal economic development bonds." There is a national bond limitation of $2 billion, to be allocated as the Secretary determines appropriate, in consultation with the Secretary of the Interior. Tribal economic development bonds issued by an Indian tribal government are treated as if such bond were issued by a State except that section 146 (relating to State volume limitations) does not apply.

The Act defines a tribal economic development bond as any bond issued by an Indian tribal government (1) the interest on which would be tax-exempt if issued by a State or local government, and (2) that is designated by the Indian tribal government as a tribal economic development bond. The aggregate face amount of bonds that may be designated by any Indian tribal government cannot exceed the amount of national tribal economic development bond limitation allocated to such government.

Tribal economic development bonds cannot be used to finance any portion of a building in which class II or class III gaming (as defined in section 4 of the Indian Gaming Regulatory Act) is conducted, or housed, or any other property used in the conduct of such gaming. Nor can tribal economic development bonds be used to finance any facility located outside of the Indian reservation.

The Act also clarifies that for purposes of section 141 of the Code, use of bond proceeds by an Indian tribe, or instrumentality thereof, is treated as use by a State.

#### *Treasury study*

The provision requires that the Treasury Department study the effects of tribal economic development bonds. One year after the date of enactment, a report is to be submitted to Congress providing the results of such study along with any recommendations, including whether the restrictions of section 7871(c) should be eliminated or otherwise modified.

### *Effective Date*

The provision applies to obligations issued after the date of enactment (February 17, 2009).

## 9. Pass-through of credits on tax credit bonds held by regulated investment companies (sec. 1541 of the Act and new sec. 853A of the Code)

### *Present Law*

In lieu of interest, holders of qualified tax credit bonds receive a tax credit that accrues quarterly. The credit is treated as interest that is includible in gross income. The following bonds are qualified tax credit bonds: qualified forestry conservation bonds, new clean renewable energy bonds, qualified energy conservation bonds, and qualified zone academy bonds.[209] The Code provides that in the case of a qualified tax credit bond held by a regulated investment company, the credit is allowed to shareholders of such company (and any gross income included with respect to such credit shall be treated as distributed to such shareholders) under procedures prescribed by the Secretary.[210] The Secretary has not prescribed procedures for the pass through of the credit to regulated investment company shareholders.

### *Explanation of Provision*

The Act provides procedures for passing though credits on "tax credit bonds" to the shareholders of an electing regulated investment company. In general, an electing regulated investment company is not allowed any credits with respect to any tax credit bonds it holds during any year for which an election is in effect. The company is treated as having an amount of interest included in its gross income (and earnings and profits) in an amount equal that which would have been included if no election were in effect, and having made distributions of money equal to the amount of the credits. Each shareholder of the electing regulated investment company is (1) required to include in gross income an amount equal to the shareholder's proportional share of the interest attributable to its credits and (2) allowed such proportional share as a credit against such shareholder's Federal income tax.[211]

In order to pass through tax credits to a shareholder, a regulated investment company is required to mail a written notice to such shareholder not later than 60 days after the close of the regulated investment company's taxable year, designating the shareholder's proportionate share of passed-through credits and the shareholder's gross income in respect of such credits.[212] The provision gives the Secretary authority to prescribe the time and manner in which a regulated investment company makes the election to pass through credits on tax credit bonds. In addition, the provision requires the Secretary to prescribe such guidance as may be necessary to carry out the provision, including prescribing methods for determining a shareholder's proportionate share of tax credits.

A tax credit bond means a qualified tax credit bond as defined in section 54A(d), a Build America Bond (as defined in section

[209] See sections 54B, 54C, 54D, and 54E.

[210] See section 54A(h), which also covers real estate investment trusts.

[211] A technical correction may be necessary so that the statute reflects this intent.

[212] The provision was subsequently amended by section 301(d) of the Regulated Investment Company Modernization Act of 2010, Pub. L. 111–325, described in Part Seventeen of this document.

54AA(d)), and any other bond for which a credit is allowable under subpart H of part IV of subchapter A of the Code.

### *Effective Date*

The provision is applicable to taxable years ending after the date of enactment (February 17, 2009).

## 10. Delay in implementation of withholding tax on government contractors (sec. 1511 of the Act and sec. 3402(t) of the Code)

### *Present Law*

For payments made after December 31, 2010, the Code imposes a withholding requirement at a three-percent rate on certain payments to persons providing property or services made by the Government of the United States, every State, every political subdivision thereof, and every instrumentality of the foregoing (including multi-State agencies). The withholding requirement applies regardless of whether the government entity making such payment is the recipient of the property or services. Political subdivisions of States (or any instrumentality thereof) with less than $100 million of annual expenditures for property or services that would otherwise be subject to withholding are exempt from the withholding requirement.

Payments subject to the three-percent withholding requirement include any payment made in connection with a government voucher or certificate program which functions as a payment for property or services. For example, payments to a commodity producer under a government commodity support program are subject to the withholding requirement. Present law also imposes information reporting requirements on the payments that are subject to withholding requirement.

The three-percent withholding requirement does not apply to any payments made through a Federal, State, or local government public assistance or public welfare program for which eligibility is determined by a needs or income test. The three-percent withholding requirement also does not apply to payments of wages or to any other payment with respect to which mandatory (e.g., U.S.-source income of foreign taxpayers) or voluntary (e.g., unemployment benefits) withholding applies under present law. Although the withholding requirement applies to payments that are potentially subject to backup withholding under section 3406, it does not apply to those payments from which amounts are actually being withheld under backup withholding rules.

The three-percent withholding requirement also does not apply to the following: payments of interest; payments for real property; payments to tax-exempt entities or foreign governments; intra-governmental payments; payments made pursuant to a classified or confidential contract (as defined in section 6050M(e)(3)), and payments to government employees that are not otherwise excludable from the new withholding proposal with respect to the employees' services as employees.

### *Reasons for Change*

The Congress believes that the three-percent withholding requirement was not appropriately targeted to the noncompliant taxpayers for whom it was originally intended and may impose significant and costly administrative burdens on State and local governments.

### *Explanation of Provision*

The provision delays the implementation of the three percent withholding requirement by one year to apply to payments after December 31, 2011.

### *Effective Date*

The provision is effective on the date of enactment (February 17, 2009).

## 11. Extend and modify the new markets tax credit (sec. 1403 of the Act and sec. 45D of the Code)

### *Present Law*

Section 45D provides a new markets tax credit for qualified equity investments made to acquire stock in a corporation, or a capital interest in a partnership, that is a qualified community development entity ("CDE").[213] The amount of the credit allowable to the investor (either the original purchaser or a subsequent holder) is (1) a five-percent credit for the year in which the equity interest is purchased from the CDE and for each of the following two years, and (2) a six-percent credit for each of the following four years. The credit is determined by applying the applicable percentage (five or six percent) to the amount paid to the CDE for the investment at its original issue, and is available for a taxable year to the taxpayer who holds the qualified equity investment on the date of the initial investment or on the respective anniversary date that occurs during the taxable year. The credit is recaptured if, at any time during the seven-year period that begins on the date of the original issue of the qualified equity investment, the issuing entity ceases to be a qualified CDE, the proceeds of the investment cease to be used as required, or the equity investment is redeemed.

A qualified CDE is any domestic corporation or partnership: (1) whose primary mission is serving or providing investment capital for low-income communities or low-income persons; (2) that maintains accountability to residents of low-income communities by providing them with representation on any governing board of or any advisory board to the CDE; and (3) that is certified by the Secretary as being a qualified CDE. A qualified equity investment means stock (other than nonqualified preferred stock) in a corporation or a capital interest in a partnership that is acquired directly from a CDE for cash, and includes an investment of a subsequent purchaser if such investment was a qualified equity investment in the hands of the prior holder. Substantially all of the investment

---

[213] Section 45D was added by section 121(a) of the Community Renewal Tax Relief Act of 2000, Pub. L. No. 106–554 (2000).

proceeds must be used by the CDE to make qualified low-income community investments. For this purpose, qualified low-income community investments include: (1) capital or equity investments in, or loans to, qualified active low-income community businesses; (2) certain financial counseling and other services to businesses and residents in low-income communities; (3) the purchase from another CDE of any loan made by such entity that is a qualified low-income community investment; or (4) an equity investment in, or loan to, another CDE.

A "low-income community" is a population census tract with either (1) a poverty rate of at least 20 percent or (2) median family income which does not exceed 80 percent of the greater of metropolitan area median family income or statewide median family income (for a non-metropolitan census tract, does not exceed 80 percent of statewide median family income). In the case of a population census tract located within a high migration rural county, low-income is defined by reference to 85 percent (rather than 80 percent) of statewide median family income. For this purpose, a high migration rural county is any county that, during the 20-year period ending with the year in which the most recent census was conducted, has a net out-migration of inhabitants from the county of at least 10 percent of the population of the county at the beginning of such period.

The Secretary has the authority to designate "targeted populations" as low-income communities for purposes of the new markets tax credit. For this purpose, a "targeted population" is defined by reference to section 103(20) of the Riegle Community Development and Regulatory Improvement Act of 1994 (12 U.S.C. 4702(20)) to mean individuals, or an identifiable group of individuals, including an Indian tribe, who (A) are low-income persons; or (B) otherwise lack adequate access to loans or equity investments. Under such Act, "low-income" means (1) for a targeted population within a metropolitan area, less than 80 percent of the area median family income; and (2) for a targeted population within a non-metropolitan area, less than the greater of 80 percent of the area median family income or 80 percent of the statewide non-metropolitan area median family income.[214] Under such Act, a targeted population is not required to be within any census tract. In addition, a population census tract with a population of less than 2,000 is treated as a low-income community for purposes of the credit if such tract is within an empowerment zone, the designation of which is in effect under section 1391, and is contiguous to one or more low-income communities.

A qualified active low-income community business is defined as a business that satisfies, with respect to a taxable year, the following requirements: (1) at least 50 percent of the total gross income of the business is derived from the active conduct of trade or business activities in any low-income community; (2) a substantial portion of the tangible property of such business is used in a low-income community; (3) a substantial portion of the services performed for such business by its employees is performed in a low-income community; and (4) less than five percent of the average of

---

[214] 12 U.S.C. sec. 4702(17) (defines "low-income" for purposes of 12 U.S.C. sec. 4702(20)).

the aggregate unadjusted bases of the property of such business is attributable to certain financial property or to certain collectibles.

The maximum annual amount of qualified equity investments is capped at $3.5 billion per year for calendar years 2006 through 2009. Lower caps applied for calendar years 2001 through 2005.

### *Explanation of Provision*[215]

For calendar years 2008 and 2009, the Act increases the maximum amount of qualified equity investments by $1.5 billion (to $5 billion for each year). The Act requires that the additional amount for 2008 be allocated to qualified CDEs that submitted an allocation application with respect to calendar year 2008 and either (1) did not receive an allocation for such calendar year, or (2) received an allocation for such calendar year in an amount less than the amount requested in the allocation application.

### *Effective Date*

The provision is effective on the date of enactment (February 17, 2009).

## D. Energy Incentives

### 1. Extension of the renewable electricity production credit (sec. 1101 of the Act and sec. 45 of the Code)

### *Present Law*

#### *In general*

An income tax credit is allowed for the production of electricity from qualified energy resources at qualified facilities (the "renewable electricity production credit").[216] Qualified energy resources comprise wind, closed-loop biomass, open-loop biomass, geothermal energy, solar energy, small irrigation power, municipal solid waste, qualified hydropower production, and marine and hydrokinetic renewable energy. Qualified facilities are, generally, facilities that generate electricity using qualified energy resources. To be eligible for the credit, electricity produced from qualified energy resources at qualified facilities must be sold by the taxpayer to an unrelated person.

#### *Credit amounts and credit period*

*In general*

The base amount of the electricity production credit is 1.5 cents per kilowatt-hour (indexed annually for inflation) of electricity produced. The amount of the credit was 2.1 cents per kilowatt-hour for 2008. A taxpayer may generally claim a credit during the 10-year period commencing with the date the qualified facility is placed in service. The credit is reduced for grants, tax-exempt bonds, subsidized energy financing, and other credits.

---

[215] The provision was subsequently amended by section 733 of the Tax Relief, Unemployment Insurance Reauthorization, and Job Creation Act of 2010, Pub. L. No. 111–312, described in Part Sixteen of this document.

[216] Sec. 45. In addition to the renewable electricity production credit, section 45 also provides income tax credits for the production of Indian coal and refined coal at qualified facilities.

*Credit phaseout*

The amount of credit a taxpayer may claim is phased out as the market price of electricity exceeds certain threshold levels. The electricity production credit is reduced over a 3-cent phaseout range to the extent the annual average contract price per kilowatt-hour of electricity sold in the prior year from the same qualified energy resource exceeds 8 cents (adjusted for inflation; 11.8 cents for 2008).

*Reduced credit periods and credit amounts*

Generally, in the case of open-loop biomass facilities (including agricultural livestock waste nutrient facilities), geothermal energy facilities, solar energy facilities, small irrigation power facilities, landfill gas facilities, and trash combustion facilities placed in service before August 8, 2005, the 10-year credit period is reduced to five years, commencing on the date the facility was originally placed in service. However, for qualified open-loop biomass facilities (other than a facility described in section 45(d)(3)(A)(i) that uses agricultural livestock waste nutrients) placed in service before October 22, 2004, the five-year period commences on January 1, 2005. In the case of a closed-loop biomass facility modified to co-fire with coal, to co-fire with other biomass, or to co-fire with coal and other biomass, the credit period begins no earlier than October 22, 2004.

In the case of open-loop biomass facilities (including agricultural livestock waste nutrient facilities), small irrigation power facilities, landfill gas facilities, trash combustion facilities, and qualified hydropower facilities the otherwise allowable credit amount is 0.75 cent per kilowatt-hour, indexed for inflation measured after 1992 (1 cent per kilowatt-hour for 2008).

*Other limitations on credit claimants and credit amounts*

In general, in order to claim the credit, a taxpayer must own the qualified facility and sell the electricity produced by the facility to an unrelated party. A lessee or operator may claim the credit in lieu of the owner of the qualifying facility in the case of qualifying open-loop biomass facilities and in the case of closed-loop biomass facilities modified to co-fire with coal, to co-fire with other biomass, or to co-fire with coal and other biomass. In the case of a poultry waste facility, the taxpayer may claim the credit as a lessee or operator of a facility owned by a governmental unit.

For all qualifying facilities, other than closed-loop biomass facilities modified to co-fire with coal, to co-fire with other biomass, or to co-fire with coal and other biomass, the amount of credit a taxpayer may claim is reduced by reason of grants, tax-exempt bonds, subsidized energy financing, and other credits, but the reduction cannot exceed 50 percent of the otherwise allowable credit. In the case of closed-loop biomass facilities modified to co-fire with coal, to co-fire with other biomass, or to co-fire with coal and other biomass, there is no reduction in credit by reason of grants, tax-exempt bonds, subsidized energy financing, and other credits.

The credit for electricity produced from renewable resources is a component of the general business credit.[217] Generally, the general business credit for any taxable year may not exceed the amount by which the taxpayer's net income tax exceeds the greater of the tentative minimum tax or 25 percent of so much of the net regular tax liability as exceeds $25,000. However, this limitation does not apply to section 45 credits for electricity or refined coal produced from a facility (placed in service after October 22, 2004) during the first four years of production beginning on the date the facility is placed in service.[218] Excess credits may be carried back one year and forward up to 20 years.

### *Qualified facilities*

*Wind energy facility*

A wind energy facility is a facility that uses wind to produce electricity. To be a qualified facility, a wind energy facility must be placed in service after December 31, 1993, and before January 1, 2010.

*Closed-loop biomass facility*

A closed-loop biomass facility is a facility that uses any organic material from a plant which is planted exclusively for the purpose of being used at a qualifying facility to produce electricity. In addition, a facility can be a closed-loop biomass facility if it is a facility that is modified to use closed-loop biomass to co-fire with coal, with other biomass, or with both coal and other biomass, but only if the modification is approved under the Biomass Power for Rural Development Programs or is part of a pilot project of the Commodity Credit Corporation.

To be a qualified facility, a closed-loop biomass facility must be placed in service after December 31, 1992, and before January 1, 2011. In the case of a facility using closed-loop biomass but also co-firing the closed-loop biomass with coal, other biomass, or coal and other biomass, a qualified facility must be originally placed in service and modified to co-fire the closed-loop biomass at any time before January 1, 2011.

A qualified facility includes a new power generation unit placed in service after October 3, 2008, at an existing closed-loop biomass facility, but only to the extent of the increased amount of electricity produced at the existing facility by reason of such new unit.

*Open-loop biomass (including agricultural livestock waste nutrients) facility*

An open-loop biomass facility is a facility that uses open-loop biomass to produce electricity. For purposes of the credit, open-loop biomass is defined as (1) any agricultural livestock waste nutrients or (2) any solid, nonhazardous, cellulosic waste material or any lignin material that is segregated from other waste materials and which is derived from:

- forest-related resources, including mill and harvesting residues, precommercial thinnings, slash, and brush;

[217] Sec. 38(b)(8).
[218] Sec. 38(c)(4)(B)(iii).

- solid wood waste materials, including waste pallets, crates, dunnage, manufacturing and construction wood wastes, and landscape or right-of-way tree trimmings; or
- agricultural sources, including orchard tree crops, vineyard, grain, legumes, sugar, and other crop by-products or residues.

Agricultural livestock waste nutrients are defined as agricultural livestock manure and litter, including bedding material for the disposition of manure. Wood waste materials do not qualify as open-loop biomass to the extent they are pressure treated, chemically treated, or painted. In addition, municipal solid waste, gas derived from the biodegradation of solid waste, and paper which is commonly recycled do not qualify as open-loop biomass. Open-loop biomass does not include closed-loop biomass or any biomass burned in conjunction with fossil fuel (co-firing) beyond such fossil fuel required for start up and flame stabilization.

In the case of an open-loop biomass facility that uses agricultural livestock waste nutrients, a qualified facility is one that was originally placed in service after October 22, 2004, and before January 1, 2009, and has a nameplate capacity rating which is not less than 150 kilowatts. In the case of any other open-loop biomass facility, a qualified facility is one that was originally placed in service before January 1, 2011. A qualified facility includes a new power generation unit placed in service after October 3, 2008, at an existing open-loop biomass facility, but only to the extent of the increased amount of electricity produced at the existing facility by reason of such new unit.

*Geothermal facility*

A geothermal facility is a facility that uses geothermal energy to produce electricity. Geothermal energy is energy derived from a geothermal deposit that is a geothermal reservoir consisting of natural heat that is stored in rocks or in an aqueous liquid or vapor (whether or not under pressure). To be a qualified facility, a geothermal facility must be placed in service after October 22, 2004, and before January 1, 2011.

*Solar facility*

A solar facility is a facility that uses solar energy to produce electricity. To be a qualified facility, a solar facility must be placed in service after October 22, 2004, and before January 1, 2006.

*Small irrigation facility*

A small irrigation power facility is a facility that generates electric power through an irrigation system canal or ditch without any dam or impoundment of water. The installed capacity of a qualified facility must be at least 150 kilowatts but less than five megawatts. To be a qualified facility, a small irrigation facility must be originally placed in service after October 22, 2004, and before October 3, 2008. Marine and hydrokinetic renewable energy facilities, described below, subsume small irrigation power facilities after October 2, 2008.

*Landfill gas facility*

A landfill gas facility is a facility that uses landfill gas to produce electricity. Landfill gas is defined as methane gas derived from the biodegradation of municipal solid waste. To be a qualified facility, a landfill gas facility must be placed in service after October 22, 2004, and before January 1, 2011.

*Trash combustion facility*

Trash combustion facilities are facilities that use municipal solid waste (garbage) to produce steam to drive a turbine for the production of electricity. To be a qualified facility, a trash combustion facility must be placed in service after October 22, 2004, and before January 1, 2011. A qualified trash combustion facility includes a new unit, placed in service after October 22, 2004, that increases electricity production capacity at an existing trash combustion facility. A new unit generally would include a new burner/boiler and turbine. The new unit may share certain common equipment, such as trash handling equipment, with other pre-existing units at the same facility. Electricity produced at a new unit of an existing facility qualifies for the production credit only to the extent of the increased amount of electricity produced at the entire facility.

*Hydropower facility*

A qualifying hydropower facility is (1) a facility that produced hydroelectric power (a hydroelectric dam) prior to August 8, 2005, at which efficiency improvements or additions to capacity have been made after such date and before January 1, 2011, that enable the taxpayer to produce incremental hydropower or (2) a facility placed in service before August 8, 2005, that did not produce hydroelectric power (a nonhydroelectric dam) on such date, and to which turbines or other electricity generating equipment have been added after such date and before January 1, 2011.

At an existing hydroelectric facility, the taxpayer may claim credit only for the production of incremental hydroelectric power. Incremental hydroelectric power for any taxable year is equal to the percentage of average annual hydroelectric power produced at the facility attributable to the efficiency improvement or additions of capacity determined by using the same water flow information used to determine an historic average annual hydroelectric power production baseline for that facility. The Federal Energy Regulatory Commission will certify the baseline power production of the facility and the percentage increase due to the efficiency and capacity improvements.

Nonhydroelectric dams converted to produce electricity must be licensed by the Federal Energy Regulatory Commission and meet all other applicable environmental, licensing, and regulatory requirements.

For a nonhydroelectric dam converted to produce electric power before January 1, 2009, there must not be any enlargement of the diversion structure, construction or enlargement of a bypass channel, or the impoundment or any withholding of additional water from the natural stream channel.

For a nonhydroelectric dam converted to produce electric power after December 31, 2008, the nonhydroelectric dam must (1) have been placed in service before October 3, 2008, (2) have been operated for flood control, navigation, or water supply purposes and (3) not have produced hydroelectric power on October 3, 2008. In addition, the hydroelectric project must be operated so that the water surface elevation at any given location and time that would have occurred in the absence of the hydroelectric project is maintained, subject to any license requirements imposed under applicable law that change the water surface elevation for the purpose of improving environmental quality of the affected waterway. The Secretary, in consultation with the Federal Energy Regulatory Commission, shall certify if a hydroelectric project licensed at a nonhydroelectric dam meets these criteria.

*Marine and hydrokinetic renewable energy facility*

A qualified marine and hydrokinetic renewable energy facility is any facility that produces electric power from marine and hydrokinetic renewable energy, has a nameplate capacity rating of at least 150 kilowatts, and is placed in service after October 2, 2008, and before January 1, 2012. Marine and hydrokinetic renewable energy is defined as energy derived from (1) waves, tides, and currents in oceans, estuaries, and tidal areas; (2) free flowing water in rivers, lakes, and streams; (3) free flowing water in an irrigation system, canal, or other man-made channel, including projects that utilize nonmechanical structures to accelerate the flow of water for electric power production purposes; or (4) differentials in ocean temperature (ocean thermal energy conversion). The term does not include energy derived from any source that uses a dam, diversionary structure (except for irrigation systems, canals, and other man-made channels), or impoundment for electric power production.

TABLE 1.—SUMMARY OF SECTION 45 CREDIT FOR ELECTRICITY PRODUCED FROM CERTAIN RENEWABLE RESOURCES

| Eligible electricity production activity | Credit amount for 2008 (cents per kilowatt-hour) | Credit period for facilities placed in service on or before August 8, 2005 (years from placed-in-service date) | Credit period for facilities placed in service after August 8, 2005 (years from placed-in-service date) |
|---|---|---|---|
| Wind | 2.1 | 10 | 10 |
| Closed-loop biomass | 2.1 | 10 [1] | 10 |
| Open-loop biomass (including agricultural livestock waste nutrient facilities) | 1.0 | 5 [2] | 10 |
| Geothermal | 2.1 | 5 | 10 |
| Solar (pre-2006 facilities only) | 2.1 | 5 | 10 |
| Small irrigation power | 1.0 | 5 | 10 |
| Municipal solid waste (including landfill gas facilities and trash combustion facilities) | 1.0 | 5 | 10 |
| Qualified hydropower | 1.0 | N/A | 10 |
| Marine and hydrokinetic | 1.0 | N/A | 10 |

[1] In the case of certain co-firing closed-loop facilities, the credit period begins no earlier than October 22, 2004.
[2] For certain facilities placed in service before October 22, 2004, the five-year credit period commences on January 1, 2005.

### *Taxation of cooperatives and their patrons*

For Federal income tax purposes, a cooperative generally computes its income as if it were a taxable corporation, with one exception: the cooperative may exclude from its taxable income distributions of patronage dividends. Generally, a cooperative that is subject to the cooperative tax rules of subchapter T of the Code[219] is permitted a deduction for patronage dividends paid only to the extent of net income that is derived from transactions with patrons who are members of the cooperative.[220] The availability of such deductions from taxable income has the effect of allowing the cooperative to be treated like a conduit with respect to profits derived from transactions with patrons who are members of the cooperative.

Eligible cooperatives may elect to pass any portion of the credit through to their patrons. An eligible cooperative is defined as a cooperative organization that is owned more than 50 percent by agricultural producers or entities owned by agricultural producers. The credit may be apportioned among patrons eligible to share in patronage dividends on the basis of the quantity or value of business done with or for such patrons for the taxable year. The election must be made on a timely filed return for the taxable year and, once made, is irrevocable for such taxable year.

## *Reasons for Change*

The Congress believes that additional incentives for the production of electricity from renewable resources will help limit the environmental consequences of continued reliance on power generated using fossil fuels. The Congress also believes that a multi-year extension of the present-law electricity production credit will encourage the development of renewable energy projects that will create new jobs for workers.

## *Explanation of Provision*

The provision extends for three years (generally, through 2013; through 2012 for wind facilities) the period during which qualified facilities producing electricity from wind, closed-loop biomass, open-loop biomass, geothermal energy, municipal solid waste, and qualified hydropower may be placed in service for purposes of the electricity production credit. The provision extends for two years (through 2013) the placed-in-service period for marine and hydrokinetic renewable energy resources.

The provision also makes a technical amendment to the definition of small irrigation power facility to clarify its integration into the definition of marine and hydrokinetic renewable energy facility.

## *Effective Date*

The extension of the electricity production credit is effective for property placed in service after the date of enactment (February 17, 2009). The technical amendment is effective as if included in section 102 of the Energy Improvement and Extension Act of 2008.

---

[219] Secs. 1381–1383.

[220] Sec. 1382.

## 2. Election of investment credit in lieu of production tax credits (sec. 1102 of the Act and secs. 45 and 48 of the Code)

### *Present Law*

#### *Renewable electricity credit*

An income tax credit is allowed for the production of electricity from qualified energy resources at qualified facilities.[221] Qualified energy resources comprise wind, closed-loop biomass, open-loop biomass, geothermal energy, solar energy, small irrigation power, municipal solid waste, qualified hydropower production, and marine and hydrokinetic renewable energy. Qualified facilities are, generally, facilities that generate electricity using qualified energy resources. To be eligible for the credit, electricity produced from qualified energy resources at qualified facilities must be sold by the taxpayer to an unrelated person. The credit amounts, credit periods, definitions of qualified facilities, and other rules governing this credit are described more fully in section D.1 of this document.

#### *Energy credit*

An income tax credit is also allowed for certain energy property placed in service. Qualifying property includes certain fuel cell property, solar property, geothermal power production property, small wind energy property, combined heat and power system property, and geothermal heat pump property.[222] The amounts of credit, definitions of qualifying property, and other rules governing this credit are described more fully in section D.3 of this document.

### *Reasons for Change*

The Congress believes that current economic circumstances are constraining investments in facilities that ordinarily would utilize the production tax credit, and wishes to give maximum flexibility to taxpayers to choose the tax incentive that will deliver the greatest benefit to them.

### *Explanation of Provision*

The Act allows the taxpayer to make an irrevocable election to have certain qualified facilities be treated as energy property eligible for a 30 percent investment credit under section 48. For this purpose, qualified facilities are facilities otherwise eligible for the section 45 production tax credit (other than refined coal, Indian coal, and solar facilities) with respect to which no credit under section 45 has been allowed. A taxpayer electing to treat a facility as energy property may not claim the production credit under section 45. Under the Act, facilities are eligible if placed in service during the extension period of section 45 as provided (generally, through 2013; through 2012 for wind facilities),

Property eligible for the credit is tangible personal or other tangible property (not including a building or its structural compo-

---

[221] Sec. 45. In addition to the electricity production credit, section 45 also provides income tax credits for the production of Indian coal and refined coal at qualified facilities.

[222] Sec. 48.

nents), and with respect to which depreciation or amortization is allowable, but only if such property is used as an integral part of the qualified facility. For example, in the case of a wind facility, the conferees intend that only property eligible for five-year depreciation under section 168(e)(3)(b)(vi) is treated as credit-eligible energy property under the election.

### *Effective Date*

The provision applies to facilities placed in service after December 31, 2008.

## 3. Modification of energy credit[223] (sec. 1103 of the Act and sec. 48 of the Code)

### *Present Law*

#### *In general*

A nonrefundable, 10-percent business energy credit[224] is allowed for the cost of new property that is equipment that either (1) uses solar energy to generate electricity, to heat or cool a structure, or to provide solar process heat, or (2) is used to produce, distribute, or use energy derived from a geothermal deposit, but only, in the case of electricity generated by geothermal power, up to the electric transmission stage. Property used to generate energy for the purposes of heating a swimming pool is not eligible solar energy property.

The energy credit is a component of the general business credit.[225] An unused general business credit generally may be carried back one year and carried forward 20 years.[226] The taxpayer's basis in the property is reduced by one-half of the amount of the credit claimed. For projects whose construction time is expected to equal or exceed two years, the credit may be claimed as progress expenditures are made on the project, rather than during the year the property is placed in service. The credit is allowed against the alternative minimum tax for credits determined in taxable years beginning after October 3, 2008.

Property financed by subsidized energy financing or with proceeds from private activity bonds is subject to a reduction in basis for purposes of claiming the credit. The basis reduction is proportional to the share of the basis of the property that is financed by the subsidized financing or proceeds. The term "subsidized energy financing" means financing provided under a Federal, State, or local program a principal purpose of which is to provide subsidized financing for projects designed to conserve or produce energy.

#### *Special rules for solar energy property*

The credit for solar energy property is increased to 30 percent in the case of periods prior to January 1, 2017. Additionally, equip-

---

[223] Additional provisions that (1) allow section 45 facilities to elect to be treated as section 48 energy property, and (2) allow section 45 and 48 facilities to elect to receive a grant from the Department of the Treasury rather than the section 45 production credit or the section 48 energy credit, are described by sections D.2 and D.4 of Part Two of this document.

[224] Sec. 48.

[225] Sec. 38(b)(1).

[226] Sec. 39.

ment that uses fiber-optic distributed sunlight to illuminate the inside of a structure is solar energy property eligible for the 30-percent credit.

### *Fuel cells and microturbines*

The energy credit applies to qualified fuel cell power plants, but only for periods prior to January 1, 2017. The credit rate is 30 percent.

A qualified fuel cell power plant is an integrated system composed of a fuel cell stack assembly and associated balance of plant components that (1) converts a fuel into electricity using electrochemical means, and (2) has an electricity-only generation efficiency of greater than 30 percent and a capacity of at least one-half kilowatt. The credit may not exceed $1,500 for each 0.5 kilowatt of capacity.

The energy credit applies to qualifying stationary microturbine power plants for periods prior to January 1, 2017. The credit is limited to the lesser of 10 percent of the basis of the property or $200 for each kilowatt of capacity.

A qualified stationary microturbine power plant is an integrated system comprised of a gas turbine engine, a combustor, a recuperator or regenerator, a generator or alternator, and associated balance of plant components that converts a fuel into electricity and thermal energy. Such system also includes all secondary components located between the existing infrastructure for fuel delivery and the existing infrastructure for power distribution, including equipment and controls for meeting relevant power standards, such as voltage, frequency and power factors. Such system must have an electricity-only generation efficiency of not less than 26 percent at International Standard Organization conditions and a capacity of less than 2,000 kilowatts.

### *Geothermal heat pump property*

The energy credit applies to qualified geothermal heat pump property placed in service prior to January 1, 2017. The credit rate is 10 percent. Qualified geothermal heat pump property is equipment that uses the ground or ground water as a thermal energy source to heat a structure or as a thermal energy sink to cool a structure.

### *Small wind property*

The energy credit applies to qualified small wind energy property placed in service prior to January 1, 2017. The credit rate is 30 percent. The credit is limited to $4,000 per year with respect to all wind energy property of any taxpayer. Qualified small wind energy property is property that uses a qualified wind turbine to generate electricity. A qualifying wind turbine means a wind turbine of 100 kilowatts of rated capacity or less.

### *Combined heat and power property*

The energy credit applies to combined heat and power ("CHP") property placed in service prior to January 1, 2017. The credit rate is 10 percent.

CHP property is property: (1) that uses the same energy source for the simultaneous or sequential generation of electrical power, mechanical shaft power, or both, in combination with the generation of steam or other forms of useful thermal energy (including heating and cooling applications); (2) that has an electrical capacity of not more than 50 megawatts or a mechanical energy capacity of no more than 67,000 horsepower or an equivalent combination of electrical and mechanical energy capacities; (3) that produces at least 20 percent of its total useful energy in the form of thermal energy that is not used to produce electrical or mechanical power, and produces at least 20 percent of its total useful energy in the form of electrical or mechanical power (or a combination thereof); and (4) the energy efficiency percentage of which exceeds 60 percent. CHP property does not include property used to transport the energy source to the generating facility or to distribute energy produced by the facility.

The otherwise allowable credit with respect to CHP property is reduced to the extent the property has an electrical capacity or mechanical capacity in excess of any applicable limits. Property in excess of the applicable limit (15 megawatts or a mechanical energy capacity of more than 20,000 horsepower or an equivalent combination of electrical and mechanical energy capacities) is permitted to claim a fraction of the otherwise allowable credit. The fraction is equal to the applicable limit divided by the capacity of the property. For example, a 45 megawatt property would be eligible to claim 15/45ths, or one third, of the otherwise allowable credit. Again, no credit is allowed if the property exceeds the 50 megawatt or 67,000 horsepower limitations described above.

Additionally, systems whose fuel source is at least 90 percent open-loop biomass and that would qualify for the credit but for the failure to meet the efficiency standard are eligible for a credit that is reduced in proportion to the degree to which the system fails to meet the efficiency standard. For example, a system that would otherwise be required to meet the 60-percent efficiency standard, but which only achieves 30-percent efficiency, is permitted a credit equal to one-half of the otherwise allowable credit (i.e., a 5-percent credit).

### *Reasons for Change*

The Congress believes the cap on the availability of the investment credit with respect to wind energy property is inconsistent with the objective of stimulating greater investment in such property. Therefore, the Congress believes it is appropriate to remove the cap on the amount of credit that may be claimed for wind energy property.

In order to protect the efficacy of both the energy credit and subsidized financing as means of stimulating investment in renewable technologies, the Congress believes taxpayers utilizing subsidized energy financing should not be required to reduce their otherwise allowable credit.

### *Explanation of Provision*

The Act eliminates the credit cap applicable to qualified small wind energy property. The Act also removes the rule that reduces the basis of the property for purposes of claiming the credit if the property is financed in whole or in part by subsidized energy financing or with proceeds from private activity bonds.

### *Effective Date*

The provision applies to periods after December 31, 2008, under rules similar to the rules of section 48(m) of the Code (as in effect on the day before the enactment of the Revenue Reconciliation Act of 1990).

## 4. Grants for specified energy property in lieu of tax credits (secs. 1104 and 1603 of the Act and secs. 45 and 48 of the Code)

### *Present Law*

#### *Renewable electricity production credit*

An income tax credit is allowed for the production of electricity from qualified energy resources at qualified facilities (the "renewable electricity production credit").[227] Qualified energy resources comprise wind, closed-loop biomass, open-loop biomass, geothermal energy, solar energy, small irrigation power, municipal solid waste, qualified hydropower production, and marine and hydrokinetic renewable energy. Qualified facilities are, generally, facilities that generate electricity using qualified energy resources. To be eligible for the credit, electricity produced from qualified energy resources at qualified facilities must be sold by the taxpayer to an unrelated person. The credit amounts, credit periods, definitions of qualified facilities, and other rules governing this credit are described more fully in section D.1 of this document.

#### *Energy credit*

An income tax credit is also allowed for certain energy property placed in service. Qualifying property includes certain fuel cell property, solar property, geothermal power production property, small wind energy property, combined heat and power system property, and geothermal heat pump property.[228] The amounts of credit, definitions of qualifying property, and other rules governing this credit are described more fully in section D.3 of this document.

### *Reasons for Change*

The Congress believes that incentives for the production of electricity from renewable resources will help limit the environmental consequences of continued reliance on power generated using fossil fuels. The Congress understands that some investors in renewable energy projects have suffered economic losses that prevent them from benefitting from the renewable electricity production credit

[227] Sec. 45. In addition to the renewable electricity production credit, section 45 also provides income tax credits for the production of Indian coal and refined coal at qualified facilities.

[228] Sec. 48.

and the energy credit. The Congress further believes that this situation, combined with current economic conditions, has the potential to jeopardize investment in renewable energy facilities. The Congress therefore believes that, in the short term, allowing renewable energy developers to elect to receive direct grants in lieu of the renewable electricity production credit and the energy credit is necessary for continued growth in this important industry.

### *Explanation of Provision*[229]

The provision authorizes the Secretary of the Treasury to provide a grant to each person who places in service energy property that is either (1) part of an electricity production facility otherwise eligible for the renewable electricity production credit or (2) qualifying property otherwise eligible for the energy credit. In general, the grant amount is 30 percent of the basis of the property that would (1) be eligible for credit under section 48 or (2) be part of a section 45 credit-eligible facility. For qualified microturbine, combined heat and power system, and geothermal heat pump property, the amount is 10 percent of the basis of the property.

Qualifying property must be depreciable or amortizable to be eligible for a grant. In addition, the property must be originally placed in service in 2009 or 2010 or construction of the property must begin in 2009 or 2010 and be completed prior to 2013 (in the case of wind facility property), 2014 (in the case of other renewable power facility property eligible for credit under section 45), or 2017 (in the case of any specified energy property described in section 48).

It is intended that the grant provision mimic the operation of the credit under section 48. For example, the amount of the grant is not includable in gross income. However, the basis of the property is reduced by fifty percent of the amount of the grant. In addition, some or all of each grant is subject to recapture if the grant eligible property is disposed of by the grant recipient within five years of being placed in service.

Nonbusiness property and property that would not otherwise be eligible for credit under section 48 or part of a facility that would be eligible for credit under section 45 is not eligible for a grant under the provision. The grant may be paid to whichever party would have been entitled to a credit under section 48 or section 45, as the case may be.

Under the provision, if a grant is paid, no renewable electricity credit or energy credit may be claimed with respect to the grant eligible property. In addition, no grant may be awarded to any Federal, State, or local government (or any political subdivision, agency, or instrumentality thereof) or any section 501(c) tax-exempt entity.

The provision appropriates to the Secretary of Energy the funds necessary to make the grants. No grant may be made unless the application for the grant has been received before October 1, 2011.

[229] The provision was subsequently amended by section 707 of the Tax Relief, Unemployment Insurance Reauthorization, and Job Creation Act of 2010, Pub. L. No. 111–312, described in Part Sixteen of this document.

### *Effective Date*

The provision is effective on the date of enactment (February 17, 2009).

## 5. Expand new clean renewable energy bonds (sec. 1111 of the Act and sec. 54C of the Code)

### *Present Law*

#### *New Clean Renewable Energy Bonds*

New clean renewable energy bonds ("New CREBs") may be issued by qualified issuers to finance qualified renewable energy facilities.[230] Qualified renewable energy facilities are facilities that: (1) qualify for the tax credit under section 45 (other than Indian coal and refined coal production facilities), without regard to the placed-in-service date requirements of that section; and (2) are owned by a public power provider, governmental body, or cooperative electric company.

The term "qualified issuers" includes: (1) public power providers; (2) a governmental body; (3) cooperative electric companies; (4) a not-for-profit electric utility that has received a loan or guarantee under the Rural Electrification Act; and (5) clean renewable energy bond lenders. The term "public power provider" means a State utility with a service obligation, as such terms are defined in section 217 of the Federal Power Act (as in effect on the date of the enactment of this paragraph). A "governmental body" means any State or Indian tribal government, or any political subdivision thereof. The term "cooperative electric company" means a mutual or cooperative electric company (described in section 501(c)(12) or section 1381(a)(2)(C)). A clean renewable energy bond lender means a cooperative that is owned by, or has outstanding loans to, 100 or more cooperative electric companies and is in existence on February 1, 2002 (including any affiliated entity which is controlled by such lender).

There is a national limitation for New CREBs of $800 million. No more than one third of the national limit may be allocated to projects of public power providers, governmental bodies, or cooperative electric companies. Allocations to governmental bodies and cooperative electric companies may be made in the manner the Secretary determines appropriate. Allocations to projects of public power providers shall be made, to the extent practicable, in such manner that the amount allocated to each such project bears the same ratio to the cost of such project as the maximum allocation limitation to projects of public power providers bears to the cost of all such projects.

New CREBs are a type of qualified tax credit bond for purposes of section 54A of the Code. As such, 100 percent of the available project proceeds of New CREBs must be used within the three-year period that begins on the date of issuance. Available project proceeds are proceeds from the sale of the bond issue less issuance costs (not to exceed two percent) and any investment earnings on such sale proceeds. To the extent less than 100 percent of the avail-

[230] Sec. 54C.

able project proceeds are used to finance qualified projects during the three-year spending period, bonds will continue to qualify as New CREBs if unspent proceeds are used within 90 days from the end of such three-year period to redeem bonds. The three-year spending period may be extended by the Secretary upon the qualified issuer's request demonstrating that the failure to satisfy the three-year requirement is due to reasonable cause and the projects will continue to proceed with due diligence.

New CREBs generally are subject to the arbitrage requirements of section 148. However, available project proceeds invested during the three-year spending period are not subject to the arbitrage restrictions (i.e., yield restriction and rebate requirements). In addition, amounts invested in a reserve fund are not subject to the arbitrage restrictions to the extent: (1) such fund is funded at a rate not more rapid than equal annual installments; (2) such fund is funded in a manner reasonably expected to result in an amount not greater than an amount necessary to repay the issue; and (3) the yield on such fund is not greater than the average annual interest rate of tax-exempt obligations having a term of 10 years or more that are issued during the month the New CREBs are issued.

As with other tax credit bonds, a taxpayer holding New CREBs on a credit allowance date is entitled to a tax credit. However, the credit rate on New CREBs is set by the Secretary at a rate that is 70 percent of the rate that would permit issuance of such bonds without discount and interest cost to the issuer.[231] The Secretary determines credit rates for tax credit bonds based on general assumptions about credit quality of the class of potential eligible issuers and such other factors as the Secretary deems appropriate. The Secretary may determine credit rates based on general credit market yield indexes and credit ratings.[232]

The amount of the tax credit is determined by multiplying the bond's credit rate by the face amount of the holder's bond. The credit accrues quarterly, is includible in gross income (as if it were an interest payment on the bond), and can be claimed against regular income tax liability and alternative minimum tax liability. Unused credits may be carried forward to succeeding taxable years. In addition, credits may be separated from the ownership of the underlying bond similar to how interest coupons can be stripped for interest-bearing bonds.

An issuer of New CREBs is treated as meeting the "prohibition on financial conflicts of interest" requirement in section 54A(d)(6) if it certifies that it satisfies (i) applicable State and local law requirements governing conflicts of interest and (ii) any additional conflict of interest rules prescribed by the Secretary with respect to any Federal, State, or local government official directly involved with the issuance of New CREBs.

### *Reasons for Change*

The Congress believes that the New CREBs program provides an efficient mechanism to finance qualified renewable energy facilities.

[231] Given the differences in credit quality and other characteristics of individual issuers, the Secretary cannot set credit rates in a manner that will allow each issuer to issue tax credit bonds at par.

[232] See Notice 2009–15, 2009–6 I.R.B. 449 (January 22, 2009).

Therefore, the Congress wishes to expand the New CREBs program by increasing the amount of the national bond volume limitation.

### *Explanation of Provision*[233]

#### *In general*

The provision expands the New CREBs program. The provision authorizes issuance of up to an additional $1.6 billion of New CREBs.

### *Effective Date*

The provision applies to obligations issued after the date of enactment (February 17, 2009).

## 6. Expand qualified energy conservation bonds (sec. 1112 of the Act and sec. 54D of the Code)

### *Present Law*

Qualified energy conservation bonds may be used to finance qualified conservation purposes.

The term "qualified conservation purpose" means:

1. Capital expenditures incurred for purposes of reducing energy consumption in publicly owned buildings by at least 20 percent; implementing green community programs; rural development involving the production of electricity from renewable energy resources; or any facility eligible for the production tax credit under section 45 (other than Indian coal and refined coal production facilities);
2. Expenditures with respect to facilities or grants that support research in: (a) development of cellulosic ethanol or other nonfossil fuels; (b) technologies for the capture and sequestration of carbon dioxide produced through the use of fossil fuels; (c) increasing the efficiency of existing technologies for producing nonfossil fuels; (d) automobile battery technologies and other technologies to reduce fossil fuel consumption in transportation; and (E) technologies to reduce energy use in buildings;
3. Mass commuting facilities and related facilities that reduce the consumption of energy, including expenditures to reduce pollution from vehicles used for mass commuting;
4. Demonstration projects designed to promote the commercialization of: (a) green building technology; (b) conversion of agricultural waste for use in the production of fuel or otherwise; (c) advanced battery manufacturing technologies; (D) technologies to reduce peak-use of electricity; and (d) technologies for the capture and sequestration of carbon dioxide emitted from combusting fossil fuels in order to produce electricity; and

---

[233] Section 301 of the Hiring Incentives to Restore Employment Act, Pub. L. No. 111–147, added a provision to section 6431, allowing the issuer of the bonds to elect to receive a direct payment from the Treasury in lieu of providing a tax credit to the holders of the bonds. For further discussion, see Part Seven of this document.

5. Public education campaigns to promote energy efficiency (other than movies, concerts, and other events held primarily for entertainment purposes).

There is a national limitation on qualified energy conservation bonds of $800 million. Allocations of qualified energy conservation bonds are made to the States with sub-allocations to large local governments. Allocations are made to the States according to their respective populations, reduced by any sub-allocations to large local governments (defined below) within the States. Sub-allocations to large local governments shall be an amount of the national qualified energy conservation bond limitation that bears the same ratio to the amount of such limitation that otherwise would be allocated to the State in which such large local government is located as the population of such large local government bears to the population of such State. The term "large local government" means: any municipality or county if such municipality or county has a population of 100,000 or more. Indian tribal governments also are treated as large local governments for these purposes (without regard to population).

Each State or large local government receiving an allocation of qualified energy conservation bonds may further allocate issuance authority to issuers within such State or large local government. However, any allocations to issuers within the State or large local government shall be made in a manner that results in not less than 70 percent of the allocation of qualified energy conservation bonds to such State or large local government being used to designate bonds that are not private activity bonds (i.e., the bond cannot meet the private business tests or the private loan test of section 141).

Qualified energy conservations bonds are a type of qualified tax credit bond for purposes of section 54A of the Code. As a result, 100 percent of the available project proceeds of qualified energy conservation bonds must be used for qualified conservation purposes. In the case of qualified conservation bonds issued as private activity bonds, 100 percent of the available project proceeds must be used for capital expenditures. In addition, qualified energy conservation bonds only may be issued by Indian tribal governments to the extent such bonds are issued for purposes that satisfy the present law requirements for tax-exempt bonds issued by Indian tribal governments (i.e., essential governmental functions and certain manufacturing purposes).

Under present law, 100 percent of the available project proceeds of qualified energy conservation bonds to be used within the three-year period that begins on the date of issuance. Available project proceeds are proceeds from the sale of the issue less issuance costs (not to exceed two percent) and any investment earnings on such sale proceeds. To the extent less than 100 percent of the available project proceeds are used to finance qualified conservation purposes during the three-year spending period, bonds will continue to qualify as qualified energy conservation bonds if unspent proceeds are used within 90 days from the end of such three-year period to redeem bonds. The three-year spending period may be extended by the Secretary upon the issuer's request demonstrating that the failure to satisfy the three-year requirement is due to reasonable cause and the projects will continue to proceed with due diligence.

Qualified energy conservation bonds generally are subject to the arbitrage requirements of section 148. However, available project proceeds invested during the three-year spending period are not subject to the arbitrage restrictions (i.e., yield restriction and rebate requirements). In addition, amounts invested in a reserve fund are not subject to the arbitrage restrictions to the extent: (1) such fund is funded at a rate not more rapid than equal annual installments; (2) such fund is funded in a manner reasonably expected to result in an amount not greater than an amount necessary to repay the issue; and (3) the yield on such fund is not greater than the average annual interest rate of tax-exempt obligations having a term of 10 years or more that are issued during the month the qualified energy conservation bonds are issued.

The maturity of qualified energy conservation bonds is the term that the Secretary estimates will result in the present value of the obligation to repay the principal on such bonds being equal to 50 percent of the face amount of such bonds, using as a discount rate the average annual interest rate of tax-exempt obligations having a term of 10 years or more that are issued during the month the qualified energy conservation bonds are issued.

As with other tax credit bonds, the taxpayer holding qualified energy conservation bonds on a credit allowance date is entitled to a tax credit. The credit rate on the bonds is set by the Secretary at a rate that is 70 percent of the rate that would permit issuance of such bonds without discount and interest cost to the issuer.[234] The Secretary determines credit rates for tax credit bonds based on general assumptions about credit quality of the class of potential eligible issuers and such other factors as the Secretary deems appropriate. The Secretary may determine credit rates based on general credit market yield indexes and credit ratings.[235] The amount of the tax credit is determined by multiplying the bond's credit rate by the face amount on the holder's bond. The credit accrues quarterly, is includible in gross income (as if it were an interest payment on the bond), and can be claimed against regular income tax liability and alternative minimum tax liability. Unused credits may be carried forward to succeeding taxable years. In addition, credits may be separated from the ownership of the underlying bond similar to how interest coupons can be stripped for interest-bearing bonds.

Issuers of qualified energy conservation bonds are required to certify that the financial disclosure requirements that applicable State and local law requirements governing conflicts of interest are satisfied with respect to such issue, as well as any other additional conflict of interest rules prescribed by the Secretary with respect to any Federal, State, or local government official directly involved with the issuance of qualified energy conservation bonds.

---

[234] Given the differences in credit quality and other characteristics of individual issuers, the Secretary cannot set credit rates in a manner that will allow each issuer to issue tax credit bonds at par.

[235] See Notice 2009–15, 2009–6 I.R.B. 449 (January 22, 2009).

### *Reasons for Change*

The Congress believes that an increase in the volume limitation for qualified energy conservation bonds is needed to help move the nation toward more energy-efficient policies. The Congress is aware that a number of communities have initiated low-interest loan and grant programs to encourage the adoption of energy conserving products as part of their green community programs. The Congress believes that incentives for the purchase and installation of energy-efficient property and energy-efficient improvements to residences are desirable to help reduce energy consumption in the household sector. Therefore, the Congress believes it is appropriate to allow the proceeds of qualified energy conservation bonds to be used for loans and grants to implement green community programs.

### *Explanation of Provision*[236]

The provision expands the present-law qualified energy conservation bond program. The provision authorizes issuance of an additional $2.4 billion of qualified energy conservation bonds. Also, the provision clarifies that capital expenditures to implement green community programs include grants, loans and other repayment mechanisms to implement such programs. For example, this expansion will enable States to issue these tax credit bonds to finance retrofits of existing private buildings through loans and/or grants to individual homeowners or businesses, or through other repayment mechanisms. Other repayment mechanisms can include periodic fees assessed on a government bill or utility bill that approximates the energy savings of energy efficiency or conservation retrofits. Retrofits can include heating, cooling, lighting, water-saving, storm water-reducing, or other efficiency measures.

Finally, the provision clarifies that any bond used for the purpose of providing grants, loans or other repayment mechanisms for capital expenditures to implement green community programs is not treated as a private activity bond for purposes of determining whether the requirement that not less than 70 percent of allocations within a State or large local government be used to designate bonds that are not private activity bonds (sec. 54D(e)(3)) has been satisfied.

### *Effective Date*

The provision is effective for bonds issued after the date of enactment (February 17, 2009).

---

[236] Section 301 of the Hiring Incentives to Restore Employment Act, Pub. L. No. 111–147, added a provision to section 6431, allowing the issuer of the bonds to elect to receive a direct payment from the Treasury in lieu of providing a tax credit to the holders of the bonds. For further discussion, see Part Seven of this document.

## 7. Modification to high-speed intercity rail facility bonds (sec. 1504 of the Act and sec. 142(i) of the Code)

### *Present Law*

#### *In general*

Under present law, gross income does not include interest on State or local bonds. State and local bonds are classified generally as either governmental bonds or private activity bonds. Governmental bonds are bonds the proceeds of which are primarily used to finance governmental functions or which are repaid with governmental funds. Private activity bonds are bonds in which the State or local government serves as a conduit providing financing to nongovernmental persons (e.g., private businesses or individuals). The exclusion from income for State and local bonds does not apply to private activity bonds unless the bonds are issued for certain permitted purposes ("qualified private activity bonds") and other Code requirements are met.

#### *High-speed rail*

An exempt facility bond is a type of qualified private activity bond. Exempt facility bonds can be issued for high-speed intercity rail facilities. A facility qualifies as a high-speed intercity rail facility if it is a facility (other than rolling stock) for fixed guideway rail transportation of passengers and their baggage between metropolitan statistical areas. The facilities must use vehicles that are reasonably expected to operate at speeds in excess of 150 miles per hour between scheduled stops and the facilities must be made available to members of the general public as passengers. If the bonds are to be issued for a nongovernmental owner of the facility, such owner must irrevocably elect not to claim depreciation or credits with respect to the property financed by the net proceeds of the issue.

The Code imposes a special redemption requirement for these types of bonds. Any proceeds not used within three years of the date of issuance of the bonds must be used within the following six months to redeem such bonds.

Seventy-five percent of the principal amount of the bonds issued for high-speed rail facilities is exempt from the volume limit. If all the property to be financed by the net proceeds of the issue is to be owned by a governmental unit, then such bonds are completely exempt from the volume limit.

### *Explanation of Provision*

#### *In general*

The provision modifies the requirement that high-speed intercity rail transportation facilities use vehicles that are reasonably expected to operate at speeds in excess of 150 miles per hour. Instead, under the provision such facilities must use vehicles capable of attaining a maximum speed in excess of 150 miles per hour.

### *Effective Date*

The provision is effective for obligations issued after the date of enactment (February 17, 2009).

## 8. Extension and modification of credit for nonbusiness energy property (sec. 1121 of the Act and sec. 25C of the Code)

### *Present Law*

Section 25C provides a 10-percent credit for the purchase of qualified energy efficiency improvements to existing homes. A qualified energy efficiency improvement is any energy efficiency building envelope component (1) that meets or exceeds the prescriptive criteria for such a component established by the 2000 International Energy Conservation Code as supplemented and as in effect on August 8, 2005 (or, in the case of metal roofs with appropriate pigmented coatings, meets the Energy Star program requirements); (2) that is installed in or on a dwelling located in the United States and owned and used by the taxpayer as the taxpayer's principal residence; (3) the original use of which commences with the taxpayer; and (4) that reasonably can be expected to remain in use for at least five years. The credit is nonrefundable.

Building envelope components are: (1) insulation materials or systems which are specifically and primarily designed to reduce the heat loss or gain for a dwelling; (2) exterior windows (including skylights) and doors; and (3) metal or asphalt roofs with appropriate pigmented coatings or cooling granules that are specifically and primarily designed to reduce the heat gain for a dwelling.

Additionally, section 25C provides specified credits for the purchase of specific energy efficient property. The allowable credit for the purchase of certain property is (1) $50 for each advanced main air circulating fan, (2) $150 for each qualified natural gas, propane, or oil furnace or hot water boiler, and (3) $300 for each item of energy-efficient building property.

An advanced main air circulating fan is a fan used in a natural gas, propane, or oil furnace originally placed in service by the taxpayer during the taxable year, and which has an annual electricity use of no more than two percent of the total annual energy use of the furnace (as determined in the standard Department of Energy test procedures).

A qualified natural gas, propane, or oil furnace or hot water boiler is a natural gas, propane, or oil furnace or hot water boiler with an annual fuel utilization efficiency rate of at least 95.

Energy-efficient building property is: (1) an electric heat pump water heater which yields an energy factor of at least 2.0 in the standard Department of Energy test procedure, (2) an electric heat pump which has a heating seasonal performance factor (HSPF) of at least 9, a seasonal energy efficiency ratio (SEER) of at least 15, and an energy efficiency ratio (EER) of at least 13, (3) a central air conditioner with energy efficiency of at least the highest efficiency tier established by the Consortium for Energy Efficiency as in effect on Jan. 1, 2006[237], (4) a natural gas, propane, or oil water heater which has an energy factor of at least 0.80 or thermal efficiency of at least 90 percent, and (5) biomass fuel property.

Biomass fuel property is a stove that burns biomass fuel to heat a dwelling unit located in the United States and used as a principal residence by the taxpayer, or to heat water for such dwelling unit, and that has a thermal efficiency rating of at least 75 percent. Biomass fuel is any plant-derived fuel available on a renewable or recurring basis, including agricultural crops and trees, wood and wood waste and residues (including wood pellets), plants (including aquatic plants), grasses, residues, and fibers.

Under section 25C, the maximum credit for a taxpayer with respect to the same dwelling for all taxable years is $500, and no more than $200 of such credit may be attributable to expenditures on windows.

The taxpayer's basis in the property is reduced by the amount of the credit. Special proration rules apply in the case of jointly owned property, condominiums, and tenant-stockholders in cooperative housing corporations. If less than 80 percent of the property is used for nonbusiness purposes, only that portion of expenditures that is used for nonbusiness purposes is taken into account.

For purposes of determining the amount of expenditures made by any individual with respect to any dwelling unit, expenditures which are made from subsidized energy financing are not taken into account. The term "subsidized energy financing" means financing provided under a Federal, State, or local program a principal purpose of which is to provide subsidized financing for projects designed to conserve or produce energy.

The credit applies to expenditures made after December 31, 2008, for property placed in service after December 31, 2008, and prior to January 1, 2010.

### *Reasons for Change*

The Congress believes that an immediate increase in the credit rate and the amount of the maximum credit that may be claimed is warranted to encourage additional investments that will help reduce reliance on fossil fuels.

### *Explanation of Provision*[238]

The Act raises the 10 percent credit rate to 30 percent. Additionally, all energy property otherwise eligible for the $50, $100, or $150 credit is instead eligible for a 30 percent credit on expenditures for such property.

The credit is extended for one year, through December 31, 2010. The $500 lifetime cap (and the $200 lifetime cap with respect to windows) is eliminated and replaced with an aggregate cap of $1,500 in the case of property placed in service after December 31,

---

[237] The highest tier in effect at this time was tier 2, requiring SEER of at least 15 and EER of at least 12.5 for split central air conditioning systems and SEER of at least 14 and EER of at least 12 for packaged central air conditioning systems.

[238] The provision was subsequently amended by section 710 of the Tax Relief, Unemployment Insurance Reauthorization, and Job Creation Act of 2010, Pub. L. No. 111–312, described in Part Sixteen of this document.

2008 and prior to January 1, 2011. The present law rule related to subsidized energy financing is eliminated.

The Act modifies the efficiency standards for qualifying property as follows.

Building insulation must follow the prescriptive criteria of the 2009 International Energy Conservation Code. Additionally, qualifying exterior windows, doors, and skylights must have a U-factor at or below 0.30 and a seasonal heat gain coefficient ("SHGC") at or below 0.30.

Electric heat pumps must achieve the highest efficiency tier of Consortium for Energy Efficiency, as in effect on January 1, 2009. These standards are a SEER greater than or equal to 15, EER greater than or equal to 12.5, and HSPF greater than or equal to 8.5 for split heat pumps, and SEER greater than or equal to 14, EER greater than or equal to 12, and HSPF greater than or equal to 8.0 for packaged heat pumps.

Central air conditioners must achieve the highest efficiency tier of Consortium for Energy Efficiency, as in effect on January 1, 2009. These standards are a SEER greater than or equal to 16 and EER greater than or equal to 13 for split systems, and SEER greater than or equal to 14 and EER greater than or equal to 12 for packaged systems.

Natural gas, propane, or oil water heaters must have an energy factor greater than or equal to 0.82 or a thermal efficiency of greater than or equal to 90 percent. Natural gas, propane, or oil water boilers must achieve an annual fuel utilization efficiency rate of at least 90. Qualified oil furnaces must achieve an annual fuel utilization efficiency rate of at least 90.

Lastly, the requirement that biomass fuel property have a thermal efficiency rating of at least 75 percent is modified to be a thermal efficiency rating of at least 75 percent as measured using a lower heating value.

### *Effective Date*

The provision is generally effective for taxable years beginning after December 31, 2008. The provisions that alter the efficiency standards of qualifying property, other than biomass fuel property, apply to property placed in service after the date of enactment, February 17, 2009. The modification with respect to biomass fuel property is effective for taxable years beginning after December 31, 2008.

## 9. Credit for residential energy efficient property (sec. 1122 of the Act and sec. 25D of the Code)

### *Present Law*

Section 25D provides a personal tax credit for the purchase of qualified solar electric property and qualified solar water heating property that is used exclusively for purposes other than heating swimming pools and hot tubs. The credit is equal to 30 percent of qualifying expenditures, with a maximum credit of $2,000 with respect to qualified solar water heating property. There is no cap with respect to qualified solar electric property.

Section 25D also provides a 30 percent credit for the purchase of qualified geothermal heat pump property, qualified small wind energy property, and qualified fuel cell power plants. The credit for geothermal heat pump property is capped at $2,000, the credit for qualified small wind energy property is limited to $500 with respect to each half kilowatt of capacity, not to exceed $4,000, and the credit for any fuel cell may not exceed $500 for each 0.5 kilowatt of capacity.

The credit with respect to all qualifying property may be claimed against the alternative minimum tax.

Qualified solar electric property is property that uses solar energy to generate electricity for use in a dwelling unit. Qualifying solar water heating property is property used to heat water for use in a dwelling unit located in the United States and used as a residence if at least half of the energy used by such property for such purpose is derived from the sun.

A qualified fuel cell power plant is an integrated system comprised of a fuel cell stack assembly and associated balance of plant components that (1) converts a fuel into electricity using electrochemical means, (2) has an electricity-only generation efficiency of greater than 30 percent and has a nameplate capacity of at least 0.5 kilowatt. The qualified fuel cell power plant must be installed on or in connection with a dwelling unit located in the United States and used by the taxpayer as a principal residence.

Qualified small wind energy property is property that uses a wind turbine to generate electricity for use in a dwelling unit located in the U.S. and used as a residence by the taxpayer.

Qualified geothermal heat pump property means any equipment which (1) uses the ground or ground water as a thermal energy source to heat the dwelling unit or as a thermal energy sink to cool such dwelling unit, (2) meets the requirements of the Energy Star program which are in effect at the time that the expenditure for such equipment is made, and (3) is installed on or in connection with a dwelling unit located in the United States and used as a residence by the taxpayer.

The credit is nonrefundable, and the depreciable basis of the property is reduced by the amount of the credit. Expenditures for labor costs allocable to onsite preparation, assembly, or original installation of property eligible for the credit are eligible expenditures.

Special proration rules apply in the case of jointly owned property, condominiums, and tenant-stockholders in cooperative housing corporations. If less than 80 percent of the property is used for nonbusiness purposes, only that portion of expenditures that is used for nonbusiness purposes is taken into account.

For purposes of determining the amount of expenditures made by any individual with respect to any dwelling unit, there shall not be taken into account expenditures which are made from subsidized energy financing. The term “subsidized energy financing” means financing provided under a Federal, State, or local program a principal purpose of which is to provide subsidized financing for projects designed to conserve or produce energy.

The credit applies to property placed in service prior to January 1, 2017.

### *Reasons for Change*

The Congress believes that an increase in the maximum credit that may be claimed for solar hot water, geothermal, and wind property is warranted to encourage additional investments that will help reduce reliance on fossil fuels. For the same reasons, the Congress believes it is appropriate to eliminate the rules that reduce available credits for property using subsidized energy financing.

### *Explanation of Provision*

The Act eliminates the credit caps for solar hot water, geothermal, and wind property and eliminates the reduction in credits for property using subsidized energy financing.

### *Effective Date*

The provision applies to taxable years beginning after December 31, 2008.

## 10. Temporary increase in credit for alternative fuel vehicle refueling property (sec. 1123 of the Act and sec. 30C of the Code)

### *Present Law*

Taxpayers may claim a 30-percent credit for the cost of installing qualified clean-fuel vehicle refueling property to be used in a trade or business of the taxpayer or installed at the principal residence of the taxpayer.[239] The credit may not exceed $30,000 per taxable year per location, in the case of qualified refueling property used in a trade or business and $1,000 per taxable year per location, in the case of qualified refueling property installed on property which is used as a principal residence.

Qualified refueling property is property (not including a building or its structural components) for the storage or dispensing of a clean-burning fuel or electricity into the fuel tank or battery of a motor vehicle propelled by such fuel or electricity, but only if the storage or dispensing of the fuel or electricity is at the point of delivery into the fuel tank or battery of the motor vehicle. The use of such property must begin with the taxpayer.

Clean-burning fuels are any fuel at least 85 percent of the volume of which consists of ethanol, natural gas, compressed natural gas, liquefied natural gas, liquefied petroleum gas, or hydrogen. In addition, any mixture of biodiesel and diesel fuel, determined without regard to any use of kerosene and containing at least 20 percent biodiesel, qualifies as a clean fuel.

Credits for qualified refueling property used in a trade or business are part of the general business credit and may be carried back for one year and forward for 20 years. Credits for residential qualified refueling property cannot exceed for any taxable year the difference between the taxpayer's regular tax (reduced by certain other credits) and the taxpayer's tentative minimum tax. Gen-

[239] Sec. 30C.

erally, in the case of qualified refueling property sold to a tax-exempt entity, the taxpayer selling the property may claim the credit.

A taxpayer's basis in qualified refueling property is reduced by the amount of the credit. In addition, no credit is available for property used outside the United States or for which an election to expense has been made under section 179.

The credit is available for property placed in service after December 31, 2005, and (except in the case of hydrogen refueling property) before January 1, 2011. In the case of hydrogen refueling property, the property must be placed in service before January 1, 2015.

### *Reasons for Change*

The Congress believes that widespread adoption of advanced technology and alternative-fuel vehicles is necessary to transform automotive transportation in the United States to be cleaner, more fuel efficient, and less reliant on petroleum fuels. The Congress further believes that one important method to encourage this trend is to provide additional tax incentives for the development and installation of the infrastructure necessary to deliver clean fuels to drivers of clean-fuel vehicles.

### *Explanation of Provision* [240]

For property placed in service in 2009 or 2010, the provision increases the maximum credit available for business property to $200,000 for qualified hydrogen refueling property and to $50,000 for other qualified refueling property. For nonbusiness property, the maximum credit is increased to $2,000. In addition, the credit rate is increased from 30 percent to 50 percent, except in the case of hydrogen refueling property.

### *Effective Date*

The provision is effective for taxable years beginning after December 31, 2008.

## 11. Modification of credit for carbon dioxide sequestration (sec. 1131 of the Act and sec. 45Q of the Code)

### *Present Law*

A credit of $20 per metric ton is available for qualified carbon dioxide captured by a taxpayer at a qualified facility and disposed of by such taxpayer in secure geological storage (including storage at deep saline formations and unminable coal seams under such conditions as the Secretary may determine).[241] In addition, a credit of $10 per metric ton is available for qualified carbon dioxide that is captured by the taxpayer at a qualified facility and used by such taxpayer as a tertiary injectant (including carbon dioxide augmented waterflooding and immiscible carbon dioxide displacement)

[240] The provision was subsequently amended by section 711 of the Tax Relief, Unemployment Insurance Reauthorization, and Job Creation Act of 2010, Pub. L. No. 111–312, described in Part Sixteen of this document.

[241] Sec. 45Q.

in a qualified enhanced oil or natural gas recovery project. Both credit amounts are adjusted for inflation after 2009.

Qualified carbon dioxide is defined as carbon dioxide captured from an industrial source that (1) would otherwise be released into the atmosphere as an industrial emission of greenhouse gas, and (2) is measured at the source of capture and verified at the point or points of injection. Qualified carbon dioxide includes the initial deposit of captured carbon dioxide used as a tertiary injectant but does not include carbon dioxide that is recaptured, recycled, and re-injected as part of an enhanced oil or natural gas recovery project process. A qualified enhanced oil or natural gas recovery project is a project that would otherwise meet the definition of an enhanced oil recovery project under section 43, if natural gas projects were included within that definition.

A qualified facility means any industrial facility (1) which is owned by the taxpayer, (2) at which carbon capture equipment is placed in service, and (3) which captures not less than 500,000 metric tons of carbon dioxide during the taxable year. The credit applies only with respect to qualified carbon dioxide captured and sequestered or injected in the United States [242] or one of its possessions.[243]

Except as provided in regulations, credits are attributable to the person that captures and physically or contractually ensures the disposal, or use as a tertiary injectant, of the qualified carbon dioxide. Credits are subject to recapture, as provided by regulation, with respect to any qualified carbon dioxide that ceases to be recaptured, disposed of, or used as a tertiary injectant in a manner consistent with the rules of the provision.

The credit is part of the general business credit. The credit sunsets at the end of the calendar year in which the Secretary, in consultation with the Administrator of the Environmental Protection Agency, certifies that 75 million metric tons of qualified carbon dioxide have been captured and disposed of or used as a tertiary injectant.

### *Explanation of Provision*

The provision requires that carbon dioxide used as a tertiary injectant and otherwise eligible for a $10 per metric ton credit must be sequestered by the taxpayer in permanent geological storage in order to qualify for such credit. The provision also clarifies that the term permanent geological storage includes oil and gas reservoirs in addition to unminable coal seams and deep saline formations. In addition, the provision requires that the Secretary of the Treasury consult with the Secretary of Energy and the Secretary of the Interior, in addition to the Administrator of the Environmental Protection Agency, in promulgating regulations relating to the permanent geological storage of carbon dioxide.

### *Effective Date*

The provision is effective for carbon dioxide captured after the date of enactment (February 17, 2009).

---

[242] Sec. 638(1).
[243] Sec. 638(2).

## 12. Modification of the plug-in electric drive motor vehicle credit (secs. 1141–1144 of the Act and secs. 30, 30B, and 30D of the Code)

### *Present Law*

#### *Alternative motor vehicle credit*

A credit is available for each new qualified fuel cell vehicle, hybrid vehicle, advanced lean burn technology vehicle, and alternative fuel vehicle placed in service by the taxpayer during the taxable year.[244] In general, the credit amount varies depending upon the type of technology used, the weight class of the vehicle, the amount by which the vehicle exceeds certain fuel economy standards, and, for some vehicles, the estimated lifetime fuel savings. The credit generally is available for vehicles purchased after 2005. The credit terminates after 2009, 2010, or 2014, depending on the type of vehicle. The alternative motor vehicle credit is not allowed against the alternative minimum tax.

#### *Plug-in electric drive motor vehicle credit*

A credit is available for each qualified plug-in electric drive motor vehicle placed in service. A qualified plug-in electric drive motor vehicle is a motor vehicle that has at least four wheels, is manufactured for use on public roads, meets certain emissions standards (except for certain heavy vehicles), draws propulsion using a traction battery with at least four kilowatt-hours of capacity, and is capable of being recharged from an external source of electricity.

The base amount of the plug-in electric drive motor vehicle credit is $2,500, plus another $417 for each kilowatt-hour of battery capacity in excess of four kilowatt-hours. The maximum credit for qualified vehicles weighing 10,000 pounds or less is $7,500. This maximum amount increases to $10,000 for vehicles weighing more than 10,000 pounds but not more than 14,000 pounds, to $12,500 for vehicles weighing more than 14,000 pounds but not more than 26,000 pounds, and to $15,000 for vehicle weighing more than 26,000 pounds.

In general, the credit is available to the vehicle owner, including the lessor of a vehicle subject to lease. If the qualified vehicle is used by certain tax-exempt organizations, governments, or foreign persons and is not subject to a lease, the seller of the vehicle may claim the credit so long as the seller clearly discloses to the user in a document the amount that is allowable as a credit. A vehicle must be used predominantly in the United States to qualify for the credit.

Once a total of 250,000 credit-eligible vehicles have been sold for use in the United States, the credit phases out over four calendar quarters. The phaseout period begins in the second calendar quarter following the quarter during which the vehicle cap has been reached. Taxpayers may claim one-half of the otherwise allowable credit during the first two calendar quarters of the phaseout period and twenty-five percent of the otherwise allowable credit during

---

[244] Sec. 30B.

the next two quarters. After this, no credit is available. Regardless of the phase-out limitation, no credit is available for vehicles purchased after 2014.

The basis of any qualified vehicle is reduced by the amount of the credit. To the extent a vehicle is eligible for credit as a qualified plug-in electric drive motor vehicle, it is not eligible for credit as a qualified hybrid vehicle under section 30B. The portion of the credit attributable to vehicles of a character subject to an allowance for depreciation is treated as part of the general business credit; the nonbusiness portion of the credit is allowable to the extent of the excess of the regular tax over the alternative minimum tax (reduced by certain other credits) for the taxable year.

### *Explanation of Provision*

#### *Credit for electric drive low-speed vehicles, motorcycles, and three-wheeled vehicles*

The provision creates a new 10-percent credit for low-speed vehicles, motorcycles, and three-wheeled vehicles that would otherwise meet the criteria of a qualified plug-in electric drive motor vehicle but for the fact that they are low-speed vehicles or do not have at least four wheels. The maximum credit for such vehicles is $2,500. Basis reduction and other rules similar to those found in section 30 apply under the provision. In the case of vehicles of a character subject to an allowance for depreciation, the new credit is part of the general business credit. The new credit is not available for vehicles sold after December 31, 2011.

#### *Credit for converting a vehicle into a plug-in electric drive motor vehicle*

The provision also creates a new 10-percent credit, up to $4,000, for the cost of converting any motor vehicle into a qualified plug-in electric drive motor vehicle. To be eligible for the credit, a qualified plug-in traction battery module must have a capacity of at least four kilowatt-hours. The credit is not available for conversions made after December 31, 2011.

#### *Modification of the plug-in electric drive motor vehicle credit*

The provision modifies the plug-in electric drive motor vehicle credit by limiting the maximum credit to $7,500 regardless of vehicle weight. The provision also eliminates the credit for low speed plug-in vehicles and for plug-in vehicles weighing 14,000 pounds or more.

The provision replaces the 250,000 total plug-in vehicle limitation with a 200,000 plug-in vehicles per manufacturer limitation. The credit phases out over four calendar quarters beginning in the second calendar quarter following the quarter in which the manufacturer limit is reached.

#### *Treatment of alternative motor vehicle credit as a personal credit allowed against the alternative minimum tax*

The provision provides that the alternative motor vehicle credit for nondepreciable property is a personal credit allowed against the alternative minimum tax.

### *Effective Date*

The new 10-percent credit for low-speed vehicles, motorcycles, and three-wheeled vehicles is effective for vehicles acquired after February 17, 2009. The credit for converting a vehicle into a plug-in electric drive motor vehicle is effective for property placed in service after February 17, 2009. The modification of the plug-in electric drive motor vehicle credit is effective for vehicles acquired after December 31, 2009. The allowance of the treatment of the alternative motor vehicle credit against the alternative minimum tax is effective for taxable years beginning after December 31, 2008.

## 13. Parity for qualified transportation fringe benefits (sec. 1151 of the Act and sec. 132 of the Code)

### *Present Law*

Qualified transportation fringe benefits provided by an employer are excluded from an employee's gross income for income tax purposes and from an employee's wages for payroll tax purposes.[245] Qualified transportation fringe benefits include parking, transit passes, vanpool benefits, and qualified bicycle commuting reimbursements. Up to $230 (for 2009) per month of employer-provided parking is excludable from income. Up to $120 (for 2009) per month of employer-provided transit and vanpool benefits are excludable from gross income. These amounts are indexed annually for inflation, rounded to the nearest multiple of $5. No amount is includible in the income of an employee merely because the employer offers the employee a choice between cash and qualified transportation fringe benefits. Qualified transportation fringe benefits also include a cash reimbursement by an employer to an employee. However, in the case of transit passes, a cash reimbursement is considered a qualified transportation fringe benefit only if a voucher or similar item which may be exchanged only for a transit pass is not readily available for direct distribution by the employer to the employee.

### *Explanation of Provision*[246]

The provision increases the monthly exclusion for employer-provided transit and vanpool benefits to the same level as the exclusion for employer-provided parking.

### *Effective Date*

The provision is effective for months beginning on or after date of enactment (February 17, 2009). The provision does not apply to tax years beginning after December 31, 2010.

---

[245] Secs. 132(f), 3121(b)(2), 3306(b)(16), and 3401(a)(19).

[246] The provision was subsequently amended by section 727 of the Tax Relief, Unemployment Insurance Reauthorization, and Job Creation Act of 2010, Pub. L. No. 111–312, described in Part Sixteen of this document.

### 14. Credit for investment in advanced energy property (sec. 1302 of the Act and new sec. 48C of the Code)

#### *Present Law*

An income tax credit is allowed for the production of electricity from qualified energy resources at qualified facilities.[247] Qualified energy resources comprise wind, closed-loop biomass, open-loop biomass, geothermal energy, solar energy, small irrigation power, municipal solid waste, qualified hydropower production, and marine and hydrokinetic renewable energy. Qualified facilities are, generally, facilities that generate electricity using qualified energy resources.

An income tax credit is also allowed for certain energy property placed in service. Qualifying property includes certain fuel cell property, solar property, geothermal power production property, small wind energy property, combined heat and power system property, and geothermal heat pump property.[248]

In addition to these, numerous other credits are available to taxpayers to encourage renewable energy production and energy conservation, including, among others, credits for certain biofuels, plug-in electric vehicles, and energy efficient appliances, and for improvements to heating, air conditioning, and insulation.

No credit is specifically designed under present law to encourage the development of a domestic manufacturing base to support the industries described above.

#### *Explanation of Provision*

The provision establishes a 30-percent allocated credit for investment in qualified property used in a qualified advanced energy manufacturing project. The provision authorizes the Secretary of the Treasury to allocate up to $2.3 billion of credits.

A qualified advanced energy project is a project that re-equips, expands, or establishes a manufacturing facility for the production of: (1) property designed to be used to produce energy from the sun, wind, or geothermal deposits (within the meaning of section 613(e)(2)), or other renewable resources; (2) fuel cells, microturbines, or an energy storage system for use with electric or hybrid-electric motor vehicles; (3) electric grids to support the transmission of intermittent sources of renewable energy, including storage of such energy; (4) property designed to capture and sequester carbon dioxide; (5) property designed to refine or blend renewable fuels (but not fossil fuels) or to produce energy conservation technologies (including energy-conserving lighting technologies and smart grid technologies); (6) property designed to manufacture any new qualified plug-in electric drive motor vehicle (as defined by section 30D(c)), any qualified plug-in electric vehicle (as defined by section 30(d)), or any component which is designed specifically for use with such vehicles, including any electric motor, generator, or power control unit; or (7) other advanced energy property designed

---

[247] Sec. 45. In addition to the electricity production credit, section 45 also provides income tax credits for the production of Indian coal and refined coal at qualified facilities.

[248] Sec. 48.

to reduce greenhouse gas emissions as may be determined by the Secretary.

Qualified property must be depreciable (or amortizable) property used in a qualified advanced energy project and must consist of tangible personal property or other tangible property (not including building or its structural components). Qualified property does not include property designed to manufacture equipment for use in the refining or blending of any transportation fuel other than renewable fuels. The basis of qualified property must be reduced by the amount of credit received.

Credits are available only for projects certified by the Secretary of the Treasury, in consultation with the Secretary of Energy. The Secretary of the Treasury must establish a certification program no later than 180 days after date of enactment, and may allocate up to $2.3 billion in credits.

In selecting projects, the Secretary may consider only those projects where there is a reasonable expectation of commercial viability. In addition, the Secretary must consider other selection criteria, including which projects (1) will provide the greatest domestic job creation; (2) will provide the greatest net impact in avoiding or reducing air pollutants or anthropogenic emissions of greenhouse gases; (3) have the greatest potential for technological innovation or commercial deployment; (4) have the lowest levelized cost of generated or stored energy, or of measured reduction in energy consumption or greenhouse gas emission; and (5) have the shortest project time from certification to completion.

Each project application must be submitted during the two-year period beginning on the date such certification program is established. An applicant for certification has one year from the date the Secretary accepts the application to provide the Secretary with evidence that the requirements for certification have been met. Upon certification, the applicant has three years from the date of issuance of the certification to place the project in service. Not later than four years after the date of enactment of the credit, the Secretary is required to review the credit allocations and redistribute any credits that were not used either because of a revoked certification or because of an insufficient quantity of credit applications.

### *Effective Date*

The provision is effective on the date of enactment (February 17, 2009).

## E. Other Provision

### 1. Application of certain labor standards to projects financed with certain tax-favored bonds (sec. 1601 of the Act)

### *Present Law*

The United States Code (Subchapter IV of Chapter 31 of Title 40) applies a prevailing wage requirement to certain contracts to which the Federal Government is a party.

### *Reasons for Change*

The Congress believes that it is appropriate to apply the prevailing wage requirement to a broader class of contracts including those financed with tax-favored bonds.

### *Explanation of Provision*

The provision provides that Subchapter IV of Chapter 31 of Title 40 of the U.S. Code shall apply to projects financed with the proceeds of:

1. any new clean renewable energy bond (as defined in sec. 54C of the Code) issued after the date of enactment;
2. any qualified energy conservation bond (as defined in sec. 54D of the Code) issued after the date of enactment;
3. any qualified zone academy bond (as defined in sec. 54E of the Code) issued after the date of enactment;
4. any qualified school construction bond (as defined in sec. 54F of the Code); and
5. any recovery zone economic development bond (as defined in sec. 1400U–2 of the Code).

### *Effective Date*

The provision is effective on the date of enactment (February 17, 2009).

## TITLE III—HEALTH INSURANCE ASSISTANCE

### A. Assistance for COBRA Continuation Coverage (sec. 3001 of the Act and new sec. 139C, sec. 4980B, and new secs. 6432 and 6720C of the Code)

### *Present Law*

#### *In general*

The Code contains rules that require certain group health plans to offer certain individuals ("qualified beneficiaries") the opportunity to continue to participate for a specified period of time in the group health plan ("continuation coverage") after the occurrence of certain events that otherwise would have terminated such participation ("qualifying events").[249] These continuation coverage rules are often referred to as "COBRA continuation coverage" or "COBRA," which is a reference to the acronym for the law that added the continuation coverage rules to the Code.[250]

The Code imposes an excise tax on a group health plan if it fails to comply with the COBRA continuation coverage rules with respect to a qualified beneficiary. The excise tax with respect to a qualified beneficiary generally is equal to $100 for each day in the noncompliance period with respect to the failure. A plan's noncompliance period generally begins on the date the failure first occurs and ends when the failure is corrected. Special rules apply

[249] Sec. 4980B.

[250] The COBRA rules were added to the Code by the Consolidated Omnibus Budget Reconciliation Act of 1985, Pub. L. No. 99–272. The rules were originally added as Code sections 162(i) and (k). The rules were later restated as Code section 4980B, pursuant to the Technical and Miscellaneous Revenue Act of 1988, Pub. L. No. 100–647.

that limit the amount of the excise tax if the failure would not have been discovered despite the exercise of reasonable diligence or if the failure is due to reasonable cause and not willful neglect.

In the case of a multiemployer plan, the excise tax generally is imposed on the group health plan. A multiemployer plan is a plan to which more than one employer is required to contribute, that is maintained pursuant to one or more collective bargaining agreements between one or more employee organizations and more than one employer, and that satisfies such other requirements as the Secretary of Labor may prescribe by regulation. In the case of a plan other than a multiemployer plan (a "single employer plan"), the excise tax generally is imposed on the employer.

### *Plans subject to COBRA*

A group health plan is defined as a plan of, or contributed to by, an employer (including a self-employed person) or employee organization to provide health care (directly or otherwise) to the employees, former employees, the employer, and others associated or formerly associated with the employer in a business relationship, or their families. A group health plan includes a self-insured plan. The term group health plan does not, however, include a plan under which substantially all of the coverage is for qualified long-term care services.

The following types of group health plans are not subject to the Code's COBRA rules: (1) a plan established and maintained for its employees by a church or by a convention or association of churches which is exempt from tax under section 501 (a "church plan"); (2) a plan established and maintained for its employees by the Federal government, the government of any State or political subdivision thereof, or by any instrumentality of the foregoing (a "governmental plan"); [251] and (3) a plan maintained by an employer that normally employed fewer than 20 employees on a typical business day during the preceding calendar year [252] (a "small employer plan").

### *Qualifying events and qualified beneficiaries*

A qualifying event that gives rise to COBRA continuation coverage includes, with respect to any covered employee, the following events which would result in a loss of coverage of a qualified beneficiary under a group health plan (but for COBRA continuation coverage): (1) death of the covered employee; (2) the termination (other than by reason of such employee's gross misconduct), or a reduction in hours, of the covered employee's employment; (3) divorce or legal separation of the covered employee; (4) the covered employee becoming entitled to Medicare benefits under title XVIII of the Social Security Act; (5) a dependent child ceasing to be a dependent child under the generally applicable requirements of the plan; and (6) a proceeding in a case under the U.S. Bankruptcy Code commencing

[251] A governmental plan also includes certain plans established by an Indian tribal government.

[252] If the plan is a multiemployer plan, then each of the employers contributing to the plan for a calendar year must normally employ fewer than 20 employees during the preceding calendar year.

on or after July 1, 1986, with respect to the employer from whose employment the covered employee retired at any time.

A "covered employee" is an individual who is (or was) provided coverage under the group health plan on account of the performance of services by the individual for one or more persons maintaining the plan and includes a self-employed individual. A "qualified beneficiary" means, with respect to a covered employee, any individual who on the day before the qualifying event for the employee is a beneficiary under the group health plan as the spouse or dependent child of the employee. The term qualified beneficiary also includes the covered employee in the case of a qualifying event that is a termination of employment or reduction in hours.

***Continuation coverage requirements***

Continuation coverage that must be offered to qualified beneficiaries pursuant to COBRA must consist of coverage which, as of the time coverage is being provided, is identical to the coverage provided under the plan to similarly situated non-COBRA beneficiaries under the plan with respect to whom a qualifying event has not occurred. If coverage under a plan is modified for any group of similarly situated non-COBRA beneficiaries, the coverage must also be modified in the same manner for qualified beneficiaries. Similarly situated non-COBRA beneficiaries means the group of covered employees, spouses of covered employees, or dependent children of covered employees who (i) are receiving coverage under the group health plan for a reason other than pursuant to COBRA, and (ii) are the most similarly situated to the situation of the qualified beneficiary immediately before the qualifying event, based on all of the facts and circumstances.

The maximum required period of continuation coverage for a qualified beneficiary (i.e., the minimum period for which continuation coverage must be offered) depends upon a number of factors, including the specific qualifying event that gives rise to a qualified beneficiary's right to elect continuation coverage. In the case of a qualifying event that is the termination, or reduction of hours, of a covered employee's employment, the minimum period of coverage that must be offered to the qualified beneficiary is coverage for the period beginning with the loss of coverage on account of the qualifying event and ending on the date that is 18 months[253] after the date of the qualifying event. If coverage under a plan is lost on account of a qualifying event but the loss of coverage actually occurs at a later date, the minimum coverage period may be extended by the plan so that it is measured from the date when coverage is actually lost.

The minimum coverage period for a qualified beneficiary generally ends upon the earliest to occur of the following events: (1) the date on which the employer ceases to provide any group health plan to any employee, (2) the date on which coverage ceases under the plan by reason of a failure to make timely payment of any premium required with respect to the qualified beneficiary, and (3) the

[253] In the case of a qualified beneficiary who is determined, under Title II or XVI of the Social Security Act, to have been disabled during the first 60 days of continuation coverage, the 18 month minimum coverage period is extended to 29 months with respect to all qualified beneficiaries if notice is given before the end of the initial 18 month continuation coverage period.

date on which the qualified beneficiary first becomes (after the date of election of continuation coverage) either (i) covered under any other group health plan (as an employee or otherwise) which does not include any exclusion or limitation with respect to any preexisting condition of such beneficiary or (ii) entitled to Medicare benefits under title XVIII of the Social Security Act. Mere eligibility for another group health plan or Medicare benefits is not sufficient to terminate the minimum coverage period. Instead, the qualified beneficiary must be actually covered by the other group health plan or enrolled in Medicare. Coverage under another group health plan or enrollment in Medicare does not terminate the minimum coverage period if such other coverage or Medicare enrollment begins on or before the date that continuation coverage is elected.

### *Election of continuation coverage*

The COBRA rules specify a minimum election period under which a qualified beneficiary is entitled to elect continuation coverage. The election period begins not later than the date on which coverage under the plan terminates on account of the qualifying event, and ends not earlier than the later of 60 days or 60 days after notice is given to the qualified beneficiary of the qualifying event and the beneficiary's election rights.

### *Notice requirements*

A group health plan is required to give a general notice of COBRA continuation coverage rights to employees and their spouses at the time of enrollment in the group health plan.

An employer is required to give notice to the plan administrator of certain qualifying events (including a loss of coverage on account of a termination of employment or reduction in hours) generally within 30 days of the qualifying event. A covered employee or qualified beneficiary is required to give notice to the plan administrator of certain qualifying events within 60 days after the event. The qualifying events giving rise to an employee or beneficiary notification requirement are the divorce or legal separation of the covered employee or a dependent child ceasing to be a dependent child under the terms of the plan. Upon receiving notice of a qualifying event from the employer, covered employee, or qualified beneficiary, the plan administrator is then required to give notice of COBRA continuation coverage rights within 14 days to all qualified beneficiaries with respect to the event.

### *Premiums*

A plan may require payment of a premium for any period of continuation coverage. The amount of such premium generally may not exceed 102 percent[254] of the "applicable premium" for such period and the premium must be payable, at the election of the payor, in monthly installments.

The applicable premium for any period of continuation coverage means the cost to the plan for such period of coverage for similarly

[254] In the case of a qualified beneficiary whose minimum coverage period is extended to 29 months on account of a disability determination, the premium for the period of the disability extension may not exceed 150 percent of the applicable premium for the period.

situated non-COBRA beneficiaries with respect to whom a qualifying event has not occurred, and is determined without regard to whether the cost is paid by the employer or employee. The determination of any applicable premium is made for a period of 12 months (the "determination period") and is required to be made before the beginning of such 12 month period.

In the case of a self-insured plan, the applicable premium for any period of continuation coverage of qualified beneficiaries is equal to a reasonable estimate of the cost of providing coverage during such period for similarly situated non-COBRA beneficiaries which is determined on an actuarial basis and takes into account such factors as the Secretary of the Treasury prescribes in regulations. A self-insured plan may elect to determine the applicable premium on the basis of an adjusted cost to the plan for similarly situated non-COBRA beneficiaries during the preceding determination period.

A plan may not require payment of any premium before the day which is 45 days after the date on which the qualified beneficiary made the initial election for continuation coverage. A plan is required to treat any required premium payment as timely if it is made within 30 days after the date the premium is due or within such longer period as applies to, or under, the plan.

### *Other continuation coverage rules*

Continuation coverage rules which are parallel to the Code's continuation coverage rules apply to group health plans under the Employee Retirement Income Security Act of 1974 (ERISA).[255] ERISA generally permits the Secretary of Labor and plan participants to bring a civil action to obtain appropriate equitable relief to enforce the continuation coverage rules of ERISA, and in the case of a plan administrator who fails to give timely notice to a participant or beneficiary with respect to COBRA continuation coverage, a court may hold the plan administrator liable to the participant or beneficiary in the amount of up to $110 a day from the date of such failure.

Although the Federal government and State and local governments are not subject to the Code and ERISA's continuation coverage rules, other laws impose similar continuation coverage requirements with respect to plans maintained by such governmental employers.[256] In addition, many States have enacted laws or promulgated regulations that provide continuation coverage rights that are similar to COBRA continuation coverage rights in the case of a loss of group health coverage. Such State laws, for example, may apply in the case of a loss of coverage under a group health plan maintained by a small employer.

---

[255] Secs. 601 to 608 of ERISA.

[256] Continuation coverage rights similar to COBRA continuation coverage rights are provided to individuals covered by health plans maintained by the Federal government. 5 U.S.C. sec. 8905a. Group health plans maintained by a State that receives funds under Chapter 6A of Title 42 of the United States Code (the Public Health Service Act) are required to provide continuation coverage rights similar to COBRA continuation coverage rights for individuals covered by plans maintained by such State (and plans maintained by political subdivisions of such State and agencies and instrumentalities of such State or political subdivision of such State). 42 U.S.C. sec. 300bb–1.

### *Reasons for Change*

The Congress is aware that the majority of Americans with health insurance coverage obtain such coverage heavily subsidized through their employers. As a result of the current economic crisis, a significant number of Americans have been, and are expected to be, involuntarily terminated from their employment and thus will lose their income and their subsidy toward health insurance coverage. While present law permits a terminated employee to continue to participate in his or her former employer's group health coverage at a rate of 102% of the premium for current employees, the Congress is concerned that such coverage is particularly unaffordable in the case of an individual who has been involuntarily terminated from employment. The Congress believes that a temporary subsidy should be made available to make COBRA continuation coverage more affordable for employees who involuntarily lose their jobs on account of the current economic crisis. The subsidy provided under the provision is estimated to benefit approximately 7 million people for some portion of 2009.[257]

### *Explanation of Provision*

#### *Reduced COBRA premium*

The provision provides that, for a period not exceeding 9 months,[258] an assistance eligible individual is treated as having paid any premium required for COBRA continuation coverage under a group health plan if the individual pays 35 percent of the premium.[259] Thus, if the assistance eligible individual pays 35 percent of the premium, the group health plan must treat the individual as having paid the full premium required for COBRA continuation coverage, and the individual is entitled to a subsidy for 65 percent of the premium. An assistance eligible individual is any qualified beneficiary who elects COBRA continuation coverage and satisfies three additional requirements. First, the qualifying event with respect to the covered employee for that qualified beneficiary must be a loss of group health plan coverage on account of an involuntary termination of the covered employee's employment.[260] However, a termination of employment for gross misconduct does not qualify (since such a termination under present law does not qualify for COBRA continuation coverage). Second, the qualifying event must occur during the period beginning September 1, 2008 and ending with December 31, 2009, and the qualified beneficiary must be eligible for COBRA continuation coverage during that pe-

---

[257] Joint Committee on Taxation, *Estimated Budget Effects of the Revenue Provisions contained in Title I and Title III of H.R. 598, the "American Recovery and Reinvestment Tax Act of 2009, Scheduled for Markup by the Committee on Ways and Means on January 22, 2009* (JCX-7-09), January 21, 2009, footnote 9.

[258] This provision was subsequently extended in sec. 1010(b) of the Department of Defense Appropriations Act, Pub. L. No. 111-118, described in Part Twenty-One of this document.

[259] For this purpose, payment by an assistance eligible individual includes payment by another individual paying on behalf of the individual, such as a parent or guardian, or an entity paying on behalf of the individual, such as a State agency or charity. Further, the amount of the premium used to calculate the reduced premium is the premium amount that the employee would be required to pay for COBRA continuation coverage absent this premium reduction (e.g. 102 percent of the "applicable premium" for such period).

[260] The provision was subsequently clarified in sec. 3(b) of the Temporary Extension Act of 2010, Pub. L. No. 111-144, described in Part Twenty-One of this document.

riod and elect such coverage.[261] Third, the assistance eligible individual must meet certain income threshold requirements.

The income threshold applies based on the modified adjusted gross income for an individual income tax return for the taxable year in which the subsidy is received with respect to which the assistance eligible individual is the taxpayer, the taxpayer's spouse or a dependent of the taxpayer (within the meaning of section 152 of the Code, determined without regard to sections 152(b)(1), (b)(2) and (d)(1)(B)). Modified adjusted gross income for this purpose means adjusted gross income as defined in section 62 of the Code increased by any amount excluded from gross income under section 911, 931, or 933 of the Code. Under this income threshold, if the premium subsidy is provided with respect to any COBRA continuation coverage which covers the taxpayer, the taxpayer's spouse, or any dependent of the taxpayer during a taxable year and the taxpayer's modified adjusted gross income exceeds $145,000 (or $290,000 for joint filers), then the amount of the premium subsidy for all months during the taxable year must be repaid. The mechanism for repayment is an increase in the taxpayer's income tax liability for the year equal to such amount. For taxpayers with adjusted gross income between $125,000 and $145,000 (or $250,000 and $290,000 for joint filers), the amount of the premium subsidy for the taxable year that must be repaid is reduced proportionately.

Under this income threshold, for example, an assistance eligible individual who is eligible for Federal COBRA continuation coverage based on the involuntary termination of a covered employee in August 2009 but who is not entitled to the premium subsidy for the periods of coverage during 2009 due to having income above the threshold, may nevertheless be entitled to the premium subsidy for any periods of coverage in the remaining period during 2010 to which the subsidy applies if the modified adjusted gross income for 2010 of the relevant taxpayer is not above the income threshold.

Under the provision an individual is allowed to make a permanent election (at such time and in such form as the Secretary of the Treasury may prescribe) to waive the right to the premium subsidy for all periods of coverage. For the election to take effect, the individual must notify the entity (to which premiums are reimbursed under section 6432(a) of the Code) of the election. This waiver provision allows an assistance eligible individual who is certain that the modified adjusted gross income limit prevents the individual from being entitled to any premium subsidy for any coverage period to decline the subsidy for all coverage periods and avoid being subject to the recapture tax. However, this waiver applies to all periods of coverage (regardless of the tax year of the coverage) for which the individual might be entitled to the subsidy. The premium subsidy for any period of coverage cannot later be claimed as a tax credit or otherwise be recovered, even if the individual later determines that the income threshold was not exceeded for a relevant tax year. This waiver is made separately by each

---

[261] The provision was subsequently extended in sec. 1010(a) of the Department of Defense Appropriations Act, Pub. L. No. 111–118, sec. 3(a) of the Temporary Extension Act of 2010, Pub. L. No. 111–144, and sec. 2(a) of the Continuing Extension Act of 2010, Pub. L. No. 111–157, described in Part Twenty-One of this document.

qualified beneficiary (who could be an assistance eligible individual) with respect to a covered employee.

An assistance eligible individual can be any qualified beneficiary associated with the relevant covered employee (e.g., a dependent of an employee who is covered immediately prior to a qualifying event), and such qualified beneficiary can independently elect COBRA (as provided under present law COBRA rules) and independently receive a subsidy. Thus, the subsidy for an assistance eligible individual continues after an intervening death of the covered employee.

Under the provision, any subsidy provided is excludible from the gross income of the covered employee and any assistance eligible individuals. However, for purposes of determining the gross income of the employer and any welfare benefit plan of which the group health plan is a part, the amount of the premium reduction is intended to be treated as an employee contribution to the group health plan. Finally, under the provision, notwithstanding any other provision of law, the subsidy is not permitted to be considered as income or resources in determining eligibility for, or the amount of assistance or benefits under, any public benefit provided under Federal or State law (including the law of any political subdivision).

### *Eligible COBRA continuation coverage*

Under the provision, continuation coverage that qualifies for the subsidy is not limited to coverage required to be offered under the Code's COBRA rules but also includes continuation coverage required under State law that requires continuation coverage comparable to the continuation coverage required under the Code's COBRA rules for group health plans not subject to those rules (e.g., a small employer plan) and includes continuation coverage requirements that apply to health plans maintained by the Federal government or a State government. Comparable continuation coverage under State law does not include every State law right to continue health coverage, such as a right to continue coverage with no rules that limit the maximum premium that can be charged with respect to such coverage. To be comparable, the right generally must be to continue substantially similar coverage as was provided under the group health plan (or substantially similar coverage as is provided to similarly situated beneficiaries) at a monthly cost that is based on a specified percentage of the group health plan's cost of providing such coverage.

The cost of coverage under any group health plan that is subject to the Code's COBRA rules (or comparable State requirements or continuation coverage requirement under health plans maintained by the Federal government or any State government) is eligible for the subsidy, except contributions to a health flexible spending account offered under a cafeteria plan within the meaning of section 125 of the Code.

A group health plan is permitted to provide a special enrollment right to assistance-eligible individuals to allow them to change coverage options under the plan in conjunction with electing COBRA continuation coverage. Under this special enrollment right, the assistance eligible individual must only be offered the option to change to any coverage option offered to employed workers that provides the same or lower health insurance premiums than the individual's group health plan coverage as of the date of the covered employee's qualifying event. If the individual elects a different coverage option under this special enrollment right in conjunction with electing COBRA continuation coverage, this is the coverage that must be provided for purposes of satisfying the COBRA continuation coverage requirement. However the coverage plan option into which the individual must be given the opportunity to enroll under this special enrollment right does not include the following: a coverage option providing only dental, vision, counseling, or referral services (or a combination of the foregoing); a health flexible spending account or health reimbursement arrangement; or coverage for treatment that is furnished in an on-site medical facility maintained by the employer and that consists primarily of first-aid services, prevention and wellness care, or similar care (or a combination of such care).

This special enrollment right only allows a group health plan to offer additional coverage options to assistance eligible individuals and does not change the basic requirement under Federal COBRA continuation coverage requirements that a group health plan must allow an assistance eligible individual to choose to continue with the coverage in which the individual is enrolled as of the qualifying event.[262] However, once the election of the other coverage is made, it becomes COBRA continuation coverage under the applicable COBRA continuation provisions. Thus, for example, under the Federal COBRA continuation coverage provisions, if a covered employee chooses different coverage pursuant to being provided this option, the different coverage elected must generally be permitted to be continued for the applicable required period (generally 18 months or 36 months, absent an event that permits coverage to be terminated under the Federal COBRA continuation provisions) even though the premium subsidy is only for nine months.

***Termination of eligibility for reduced premiums***

The assistance eligible individual's eligibility for the subsidy terminates with the first month beginning on or after the earlier of (1) the date which is 9 months after the first day of the first month for which the subsidy applies,[263] (2) the end of the maximum required period of continuation coverage for the qualified beneficiary under the Code's COBRA rules or the relevant State or Federal law (or regulation), or (3) the date that the assistance eligible individual becomes eligible for Medicare benefits under title XVIII of the Social Security Act or health coverage under another group health plan (including, for example, a group health plan maintained by the new employer of the individual or a plan maintained by the employer of the individual's spouse). However, eligibility for coverage under another group health plan does not terminate eligibility for the subsidy if the other group health plan provides only dental, vision, counseling, or referral services (or a combination of

---

[262] All references to "Federal COBRA continuation coverage" mean the COBRA continuation coverage provisions of the Code, ERISA, and PHSA.

[263] The provision was subsequently extended in sec. 101(b) of the Department of Defense Appropriations Act, Pub. L. No. 111–118, described in Part Twenty-One of this document.

the foregoing), is a health flexible spending account or health reimbursement arrangement, or is coverage for treatment that is furnished in an on-site medical facility maintained by the employer and that consists primarily of first-aid services, prevention and wellness care, or similar care (or a combination of such care).

If a qualified beneficiary paying a reduced premium for COBRA continuation coverage under this provision becomes eligible for coverage under another group health plan or Medicare, the provision requires the qualified beneficiary to notify, in writing, the group health plan providing the COBRA continuation coverage with the reduced premium of such eligibility under the other plan or Medicare. The notification by the assistance eligible individual must be provided to the group health plan in the time and manner as is specified by the Secretary of Labor. If an assistance eligible individual fails to provide this notification at the required time and in the required manner, and as a result the individual's COBRA continuation coverage continues to be subsidized after the termination of the individual's eligibility for such subsidy, a penalty is imposed on the individual equal to 110 percent of the subsidy provided after termination of eligibility.

This penalty only applies if the subsidy in the form of the premium reduction is actually provided to a qualified beneficiary for a month that the beneficiary is not eligible for the reduction. Thus, for example, if a qualified beneficiary becomes eligible for coverage under another group health plan and stops paying the reduced COBRA continuation premium, the penalty generally will not apply. As discussed below, under the provision, the group health plan is reimbursed for the subsidy for a month (65 percent of the amount of the premium for the month) only after receipt of the qualified beneficiary's portion (35 percent of the premium amount). Thus, the penalty generally will only arise when the qualified beneficiary continues to pay the reduced premium and does not notify the group health plan providing COBRA continuation coverage of the beneficiary's eligibility under another group health plan or Medicare.

***Special COBRA election opportunity***

The provision provides a special 60 day election period for a qualified beneficiary who is eligible for a reduced premium and who has not elected COBRA continuation coverage as of the date of enactment. The 60 day election period begins on the date that notice is provided to the qualified beneficiary of the special election period. However, this special election period does not extend the period of COBRA continuation coverage beyond the original maximum required period (generally 18 months after the qualifying event) and any COBRA continuation coverage elected pursuant to this special election period begins on the date of enactment and does not include any period prior to that date. Thus, for example, if a covered employee involuntarily terminated employment on September 10, 2008, but did not elect COBRA continuation coverage and was not eligible for coverage under another group health plan, the employee would have 60 days after date of notification of this new election right to elect the coverage and receive the subsidy. If the employee made the election, the coverage would begin with the date of enactment and would not include any period prior to that date. However, the coverage would not be required to last for 18 months. Instead the maximum required COBRA continuation coverage period would end not later than 18 months after September 10, 2008. This special COBRA election opportunity includes a qualified beneficiary who elected COBRA coverage but who is no longer enrolled on the date of enactment, for example, because the beneficiary was unable to continue paying the premium.

The special enrollment provision applies to a group health plan that is subject to the COBRA continuation coverage requirements of the Code, ERISA, Title 5 of the United States Code (relating to plans maintained by the Federal government), or the Public Health Service Act ("PHSA").

With respect to an assistance eligible individual who elects coverage pursuant to the special election period, the period beginning on the date of the qualifying event and ending with the day before the date of enactment is disregarded for purposes of the rules that limit the group health plan from imposing pre-existing condition limitations with respect to the individual's coverage.[264]

***Reimbursement of group health plans***

The provision provides that the entity to which premiums are payable (determined under the applicable COBRA continuation coverage requirement)[265] shall be reimbursed by the amount of the premium for COBRA continuation coverage that is not paid by an assistance eligible individual on account of the premium reduction. An entity is not eligible for subsidy reimbursement, however, until the entity has received the reduced premium payment from the assistance eligible individual. To the extent that such entity has liability for income tax withholding from wages[266] or FICA taxes[267] with respect to its employees, the entity is reimbursed by treating the amount that is reimbursable to the entity as a credit against its liability for these payroll taxes.[268] To the extent that such amount exceeds the amount of the entity's liability for these payroll taxes, the Secretary shall reimburse the entity for the excess directly (i.e., a tax refund). The provision requires any entity entitled to such reimbursement to submit such reports as the Secretary of the Treasury may require, including an attestation of the involun-

[264] Section 9801 provides that a group health plan may impose a pre-existing condition exclusion for no more than 12 months after a participant or beneficiary's enrollment date. Such 12-month period must be reduced by the aggregate period of creditable coverage (which includes periods of coverage under another group health plan). A period of creditable coverage can be disregarded if, after the coverage period and before the enrollment date, there was a 63-day period during which the individual was not covered under any creditable coverage. Similar rules are provided under ERISA and PHSA.

[265] Applicable continuation coverage that qualifies for the subsidy and thus for reimbursement is not limited to coverage required to be offered under the Code's COBRA rules but also includes continuation coverage required under State law that requires continuation coverage comparable to the continuation coverage required under the Code's COBRA rules for group health plans not subject to those rules (e.g., a small employer plan) and includes continuation coverage requirements that apply to health plans maintained by the Federal government or a State government. The person to whom the reimbursement is payable is either (1) the multiemployer group health plan, (2) the employer maintaining the group health plan subject to Federal COBRA continuation coverage requirements, and (3) the insurer providing coverage under an insured plan.

[266] Sec. 3401.

[267] Sec. 3102 (relating to FICA taxes applicable to employees) and sec. 3111 (relating to FICA taxes applicable to employers).

[268] In determining any amount transferred or appropriated to any fund under the Social Security Act, amounts credited against an employer's payroll tax obligations pursuant to the provision shall not be taken into account.

tary termination of employment of each covered employee on the basis of whose termination entitlement to reimbursement of premiums is claimed, and a report of the amount of payroll taxes offset for a reporting period and the estimated offsets of such taxes for the next reporting period. This report is required to be provided at the same time as the deposits of the payroll taxes would have been required, absent the offset, or such times as the Secretary specifies.

Overstatement of reimbursement is a payroll tax violation. For example, IRS can assert appropriate penalties for failing to truthfully account for the reimbursement. However, it is not intended that any portion of the reimbursement is taken into account when determining the amount of any penalty to be imposed against any person, required to collect, truthfully account for, and pay over any tax under section 6672 of the Code.

It is intended that reimbursement not be mirrored in the U.S. possessions that have mirror income tax codes (the Commonwealth of the Northern Mariana Islands, Guam, and the Virgin Islands). Rather, the intent of Congress is that reimbursement will have direct application to persons in those possessions. Moreover, it is intended that income tax withholding payable to the government of any possession (American Samoa, the Commonwealth of the Northern Mariana Islands, the Commonwealth of Puerto Rico, Guam, or the Virgin Islands) (in contrast with FICA withholding payable to the U.S. Treasury) will not be reduced as a result of the application of this provision. A person liable for both FICA withholding payable to the U.S. Treasury and income tax withholding payable to a possession government will be credited or refunded any excess of (1) the amount of FICA taxes treated as paid under the reimbursement rule of the provision over (2) the amount of the person's liability for those FICA taxes.

### *Notice requirements*

The notice of COBRA continuation coverage that a plan administrator is required to provide to qualified beneficiaries with respect to a qualifying event under present law must contain, under the provision, additional information including, for example, information about the qualified beneficiary's right to the premium reduction (and subsidy) and the conditions on the subsidy, and a description of the obligation of the qualified beneficiary to notify the group health plan of eligibility under another group health plan or eligibility for Medicare benefits under title XVIII of the Social Security Act, and the penalty for failure to provide this notification. The provision also requires a new notice to be given to qualified beneficiaries entitled to a special election period after enactment. A violation of the new notice requirements is also a violation of the notice requirements of the underlying COBRA provision. The new notice must be provided to all individuals who terminated employment during the applicable time period, and not just to individuals who were involuntarily terminated.

In the case of group health plans that are not subject to the COBRA continuation coverage requirements of the Code, ERISA, Title 5 of the United States Code (relating to plans maintained by the Federal government), or PHSA, the provision requires that notice be given to the relevant employees and beneficiaries as well, as specified by the Secretary of Labor. Within 30 days after enactment, the Secretary of Labor is directed to provide model language for the additional notification required under the provision.

The provision also provides an expedited 15-day review process by the Secretary of Labor or Health or the Secretary of Health and Human Services (both in consultation with the Secretary of the Treasury), under which an individual may request review of a denial of treatment as an assistance eligible individual by a group health plan. It is the intent of Congress to give the Secretaries the flexibility necessary to make determinations within 15 business days based upon evidence they believe, in their discretion, to be appropriate. Additionally, if an individual is denied treatment as an assistance eligible individual and also submits a claim for benefits to the plan that would be denied by reason of not being eligible for Federal COBRA continuation coverage (or failure to pay full premiums), the individual is eligible to proceed with expedited review irrespective of any claims for benefits that may be pending or subject to review under the provisions of ERISA 503. Either Secretary's determination upon review is de novo and is the final determination of such Secretary.

### *Regulatory authority*

The provision provides authority to the Secretary of the Treasury to issue regulations or other guidance as may be necessary or appropriate to carry out the provision, including any reporting requirements or the establishment of other methods for verifying the correct amounts of payments and credits under the provision. For example, the Secretary of the Treasury might require verification on the return of an assistance eligible individual who is the covered employee that the individual's termination of employment was involuntary. The provision directs the Secretary of the Treasury to issue guidance or regulations addressing the reimbursement of the subsidy in the case of a multiemployer group health plan. The provision also provides authority to the Secretary of the Treasury to promulgate rules, procedures, regulations, and other guidance as is necessary and appropriate to prevent fraud and abuse in the subsidy program, including the employment tax offset mechanism.

### *Reports*

The provision requires the Secretary of the Treasury to submit an interim and a final report regarding the implementation of the premium reduction provision. The interim report is to include information about the number of individuals receiving assistance, and the total amount of expenditures incurred, as of the date of the report. The final report, to be issued as soon as practicable after the last period of COBRA continuation coverage for which premiums are provided, is to include similar information as provided in the interim report, with the addition of information about the average dollar amount (monthly and annually) of premium reductions provided to such individuals. The reports are to be given to the Committee on Ways and Means, the Committee on Energy and Commerce, the Committee on Health Education, Labor and Pensions and the Committee on Finance.

### *Effective Date*

The provision is effective for periods of coverage beginning after the date of enactment (February 17, 2009). In addition, specific rules are provided in the case of an assistance eligible individual who pays 100 percent of the premium required for COBRA continuation coverage for any coverage period during the 60-day period beginning on the first day of the first coverage period after the date of enactment.

## B. Modify the Health Coverage Tax Credit (secs. 1899–1899L of the Act and secs. 35, 4980B, 7527, and 9801 of the Code)

### *Present Law*

#### *In general*

Under the Trade Act of 2002,[269] in the case of taxpayers who are eligible individuals, a refundable tax credit is provided for 65 percent of the taxpayer's premiums for qualified health insurance of the taxpayer and qualifying family members for each eligible coverage month beginning in the taxable year. The credit is commonly referred to as the health coverage tax credit ("HCTC"). The credit is available only with respect to amounts paid by the taxpayer. The credit is available on an advance basis.[270]

Qualifying family members are the taxpayer's spouse and any dependent of the taxpayer with respect to whom the taxpayer is entitled to claim a dependency exemption. Any individual who has other specified coverage is not a qualifying family member.

#### *Persons eligible for the credit*

Eligibility for the credit is determined on a monthly basis. In general, an eligible coverage month is any month if, as of the first day of the month, the taxpayer (1) is an eligible individual, (2) is covered by qualified health insurance, (3) does not have other specified coverage, and (4) is not imprisoned under Federal, State, or local authority.[271] In the case of a joint return, the eligibility requirements are met if at least one spouse satisfies the requirements.

An eligible individual is an individual who is (1) an eligible Trade Adjustment Assistance ("TAA") recipient, (2) an eligible alternative TAA recipient, or (3) an eligible Pension Benefit Guaranty Corporation ("PBGC") pension recipient.

An individual is an eligible TAA recipient during any month if the individual (1) is receiving for any day of such month a trade readjustment allowance[272] or who would be eligible to receive such an allowance but for the requirement that the individual exhaust unemployment benefits before being eligible to receive an allow-

---

[269] Pub. L. No. 107–210 (2002).

[270] An individual is eligible for the advance payment of the credit once a qualified health insurance costs credit eligibility certificate is in effect. Sec. 7527.

[271] An eligible month must begin after November 4, 2002. This date is 90 days after the date of enactment of the Trade Act of 2002, Pub. L. No. 107–210, which was August 6, 2002.

[272] The eligibility rules and conditions for such an allowance are specified in chapter 2 of title II of the Trade Act of 1974. Among other requirements, payment of a trade readjustment allowance is conditioned upon the individual enrolling in certain training programs or receiving a waiver of training requirements.

ance and (2) with respect to such allowance, is covered under a certification issued under subchapter A or D of chapter 2 of title II of the Trade Act of 1974. An individual is treated as an eligible TAA recipient during the first month that such individual would otherwise cease to be an eligible TAA recipient.

An individual is an eligible alternative TAA recipient during any month if the individual (1) is a worker described in section 246(a)(3)(B) of the Trade Act of 1974 who is participating in the program established under section 246(a)(1) of such Act, and (2) is receiving a benefit for such month under section 246(a)(2) of such Act. An individual is treated as an eligible alternative TAA recipient during the first month that such individual would otherwise cease to be an eligible TAA recipient.

An individual is a PBGC pension recipient for any month if he or she (1) is age 55 or over as of the first day of the month, and (2) is receiving a benefit any portion of which is paid by the PBGC. The IRS has interpreted the definition of PBGC pension recipient to also include certain alternative recipients and recipients who have received certain lump-sum payments on or after August 6, 2002. A person is not an eligible individual if he or she may be claimed as a dependent on another person's tax return.

An otherwise eligible taxpayer is not eligible for the credit for a month if, as of the first day of the month, the individual has other specified coverage. Other specified coverage is (1) coverage under any insurance which constitutes medical care (except for insurance substantially all of the coverage of which is for excepted benefits)[273] maintained by an employer (or former employer) if at least 50 percent of the cost of the coverage is paid by an employer[274] (or former employer) of the individual or his or her spouse or (2) coverage under certain governmental health programs. Specifically, an individual is not eligible for the credit if, as of the first day of the month, the individual is (1) entitled to benefits under Medicare Part A, enrolled in Medicare Part B, or enrolled in Medicaid or SCHIP, (2) enrolled in a health benefits plan under the Federal Employees Health Benefit Plan, or (3) entitled to receive benefits under chapter 55 of title 10 of the United States Code (relating to military personnel). An individual is not considered to be enrolled in Medicaid solely by reason of receiving immunizations.

A special rule applies with respect to alternative TAA recipients. For eligible alternative TAA recipients, an individual has other specified coverage if the individual is (1) eligible for coverage under any qualified health insurance (other than coverage under a

[273] Excepted benefits are: (1) coverage only for accident or disability income or any combination thereof; (2) coverage issued as a supplement to liability insurance; (3) liability insurance, including general liability insurance and automobile liability insurance; (4) worker's compensation or similar insurance; (5) automobile medical payment insurance; (6) credit-only insurance; (7) coverage for on-site medical clinics; (8) other insurance coverage similar to the coverages in (1)–(7) specified in regulations under which benefits for medical care are secondary or incidental to other insurance benefits; (9) limited scope dental or vision benefits; (10) benefits for long-term care, nursing home care, home health care, community-based care, or any combination thereof; and (11) other benefits similar to those in (9) and (10) as specified in regulations; (12) coverage only for a specified disease or illness; (13) hospital indemnity or other fixed indemnity insurance; and (14) Medicare supplemental insurance.

[274] An amount is considered paid by the employer if it is excludable from income. Thus, for example, amounts paid for health coverage on a salary reduction basis under an employer plan are considered paid by the employer. A rule aggregating plans of the same employer applies in determining whether the employer pays at least 50 percent of the cost of coverage.

COBRA continuation provision, State-based continuation coverage, or coverage through certain State arrangements) under which at least 50 percent of the cost of coverage is paid or incurred by an employer of the taxpayer or the taxpayer's spouse or (2) covered under any such qualified health insurance under which any portion of the cost of coverage is paid or incurred by an employer of the taxpayer or the taxpayer's spouse.

### *Qualified health insurance*

Qualified health insurance eligible for the credit is: (1) COBRA continuation[275] coverage; (2) State-based continuation coverage provided by the State under a State law that requires such coverage; (3) coverage offered through a qualified State high risk pool; (4) coverage under a health insurance program offered to State employees or a comparable program; (5) coverage through an arrangement entered into by a State and a group health plan, an issuer of health insurance coverage, an administrator, or an employer; (6) coverage offered through a State arrangement with a private sector health care coverage purchasing pool; (7) coverage under a State-operated health plan that does not receive any Federal financial participation; (8) coverage under a group health plan that is available through the employment of the eligible individual's spouse; and (9) coverage under individual health insurance if the eligible individual was covered under individual health insurance during the entire 30-day period that ends on the date the individual became separated from the employment which qualified the individual for the TAA allowance, the benefit for an eligible alternative TAA recipient, or a pension benefit from the PBGC, whichever applies.[276]

Qualified health insurance does not include any State-based coverage (i.e., coverage described in (2)–(7) in the preceding paragraph), unless the State has elected to have such coverage treated as qualified health insurance and such coverage meets certain requirements.[277] Such State coverage must provide that each qualifying individual is guaranteed enrollment if the individual pays the premium for enrollment or provides a qualified health insurance costs eligibility certificate and pays the remainder of the premium. In addition, the State-based coverage cannot impose any pre-existing condition limitation with respect to qualifying individuals. State-based coverage cannot require a qualifying individual to pay a premium or contribution that is greater than the premium or contribution for a similarly situated individual who is not a qualified individual. Finally, benefits under the State-based coverage must be the same as (or substantially similar to) benefits provided to similarly situated individuals who are not qualifying individuals.

A qualifying individual is an eligible individual who seeks to enroll in the State-based coverage and who has aggregate periods of

---

[275] COBRA continuation is defined by section 9832(d)(1).

[276] For this purpose, "individual health insurance" means any insurance which constitutes medical care offered to individuals other than in connection with a group health plan. Such term does not include Federal- or State-based health insurance coverage.

[277] For guidance on how a State elects a health program to be qualified health insurance for purposes of the credit, see Rev. Proc. 2004–12, 2004–1 C.B. 528.

creditable coverage[278] of three months or longer, does not have other specified coverage, and who is not imprisoned. In general terms, creditable coverage includes health care coverage without a gap of more than 63 days. Therefore, if an individual's qualifying coverage were terminated more than 63 days before the individual enrolled in the State-based coverage, the individual would not be a qualifying individual and would not be entitled to the State-based protections. A qualifying individual also includes qualified family members of such an eligible individual.

Qualified health insurance does not include coverage under a flexible spending or similar arrangement or any insurance if substantially all of the coverage is for excepted benefits.

### *Other rules*

Amounts taken into account in determining the credit may not be taken into account in determining the amount allowable under the itemized deduction for medical expenses or the deduction for health insurance expenses of self-employed individuals. Amounts distributed from a medical savings account or health savings accounts are not eligible for the credit. The amount of the credit available through filing a tax return is reduced by any credit received on an advance basis. Married taxpayers filing separate returns are eligible for the credit; however, if both spouses are eligible individuals and the spouses file separate returns, then the spouse of the taxpayer is not a qualifying family member.

The Secretary of the Treasury is authorized to prescribe such regulations and other guidance as may be necessary or appropriate to carry out the credit provision.

### *COBRA*

The Consolidated Omnibus Reconciliation Act of 1985 ("COBRA") requires that a group health plan must offer continuation coverage to qualified beneficiaries in the case of a qualifying event. An excise tax under the Code applies on the failure of a group health plan to meet the requirement.[279] Qualifying events include the death of the covered employee, termination of the covered employee's employment, divorce or legal separation of the covered employee, and certain bankruptcy proceedings of the employer. In the case of termination from employment, the coverage must be extended for a period of not less than 18 months. In certain other cases, coverage must be extended for a period of not less than 36 months. Under such period of continuation coverage, the plan may require payment of a premium by the beneficiary of up to 102 percent of the applicable premium for the period.

---

[278] Creditable coverage is determined under section 9801(c) of the Health Insurance Portability and Accountability Act, Pub. L. No. 104–191.

[279] Sec. 4980B.

### *Explanation of Provision*[280]

#### *Increase in credit percentage amount*

The provision increases the amount of the HCTC to 80 percent of the taxpayer's premiums for qualified health insurance of the taxpayer and qualifying family members.

*Effective date.*—The provision is effective for coverage months beginning on or after the first day of the first month beginning 60 days after date of enactment. The increased credit rate does not apply to months beginning after December 31, 2010.

#### *Payment for monthly premiums paid prior to commencement of advance payment of credit*

The provision provides that the Secretary of the Treasury shall make one or more retroactive payments on behalf of certified individuals equal to 80 percent of the premiums for coverage of the taxpayer and qualifying family members for qualified health insurance for eligible coverage months occurring prior to the first month for which an advance payment is made on behalf of such individual. The amount of the payment must be reduced by the amount of any payment made to the taxpayer under a national emergency grant pursuant to section 173(f) of the Workforce Investment Act of 1998 for a taxable year including such eligible coverage months.

*Effective date.*—The provision is effective for eligible coverage months beginning after December 31, 2008. The Secretary of the Treasury, however, is not required to make any payments under the provision until after the date that is six months after the date of enactment. The provision does not apply to months beginning after December 31, 2010.

#### *TAA recipients not enrolled in training programs eligible for credit*

The provision modifies the definition of an eligible TAA recipient to eliminate the requirement that an individual be enrolled in training in the case of an individual receiving unemployment compensation. In addition, the provision clarifies that the definition of an eligible TAA recipient includes an individual who would be eligible to receive a trade readjustment allowance except that the individual is in a break in training that exceeds the period specified in section 233(e) of the Trade Act of 1974, but is within the period for receiving the allowance.

*Effective date.*—The provision is effective for months beginning after the date of enactment in taxable years ending after such date. The provision does not apply to months beginning after December 31, 2010.

#### *TAA pre-certification period rule for purposes of determining whether there is a 63-day lapse in creditable coverage*

Under the provision, in determining if there has been a 63-day lapse in coverage (which determines, in part, if the State-based consumer protections apply), in the case of a TAA-eligible indi-

[280] The provision was subsequently amended by sections 111–118 of the Omnibus Trade Act of 2010, Pub. L. No. 111–344, described in Part Eighteen of this document.

vidual, the period beginning on the date the individual has a TAA-related loss of coverage and ending on the date which is seven days after the date of issuance by the Secretary (or by any person or entity designated by the Secretary) of a qualified health insurance costs credit eligibility certificate (under section 7527) for such individual is not taken into account.

*Effective date.*—The provision is effective for plan years beginning after the date of enactment. The provision does not apply to plan years beginning after December 31, 2010.

### *Continued qualification of family members after certain events*

The provision provides continued eligibility for the credit for family members after certain events. The rule applies in the case of (1) the eligible individual becoming entitled to Medicare, (2) divorce, and (3) death.

In the case of a month which would be an eligible coverage month with respect to an eligible individual except that the individual is entitled to benefits under Medicare Part A or enrolled in Medicare Part B, the month is treated as an eligible coverage month with respect to the individual solely for purposes of determining the amount of the credit with respect to qualifying family members (i.e., the credit is allowed for expenses paid for qualifying family members after the eligible individual is eligible for Medicare). Such treatment applies only with respect to the first 24 months after the eligible individual is first entitled to benefits under Medicare Part A or enrolled in Medicare Part B.

In the case of the finalization of a divorce between an eligible individual and the individual's spouse, the spouse is treated as an eligible individual for a period of 24 months beginning with the date of the finalization of the divorce. Under such rule, the only family members that may be taken into account with respect to the spouse as qualifying family members are those individuals who were qualifying family members immediately before such divorce finalization.

In the case of the death of an eligible individual, the spouse of such individual (determined at the time of death) is treated as an eligible individual for a period of 24 months beginning with the date of death. Under such rule, the only qualifying family members that may be taken into account with respect to the spouse are those individuals who were qualifying family members immediately before such death. In addition, any individual who was a qualifying family member of the decedent immediately before such death[281] is treated as an eligible individual for a period of 24 months beginning with the date of death, except that in determining the amount of the HCTC only such qualifying family member may be taken into account.

*Effective date.*—The provision is effective for months beginning after December 31, 2009. The provision does not apply to months that begin after December 31, 2010.

---

[281] In the case of a dependent, the rule applies to the taxpayer to whom the personal exemption deduction under section 151 is allowable.

### *Alignment of COBRA coverage*

The maximum required COBRA continuation coverage period is modified by the provision with respect to certain individuals whose qualifying event is a termination of employment or a reduction in hours. First, in the case of such a qualifying event with respect to a covered employee who has a nonforfeitable right to a benefit any portion of which is paid by the PBGC, the maximum coverage period must end not earlier than the date of death of the covered employee (or in the case of the surviving spouse or dependent children of the covered employee, not earlier than 24 months after the date of death of the covered employee). Second, in the case of such a qualifying event where the covered employee is a TAA eligible individual as of the date that the maximum coverage period would otherwise terminate, the maximum coverage period must extend during the period that the individual is a TAA eligible individual.

*Effective date.*—The provision is effective for periods of coverage that would, without regard to the provision, end on or after the date of enactment, provided that the provision does not extend any periods of coverage beyond December 31, 2010.

### *Addition of coverage through voluntary employees' beneficiary associations*

The provision expands the definition of qualified health insurance by including coverage under an employee benefit plan funded by a voluntary employees' beneficiary association ("VEBA," as defined in section 501(c)(9)) established pursuant to an order of a bankruptcy court, or by agreement with an authorized representative, as provided in section 1114 of title 11, United States Code.

*Effective date.*—The provision is effective on the date of enactment. The provision does not apply with respect to certificates of eligibility issued after December 31, 2010.

### *Notice requirements*

The provision requires that the qualified health insurance costs credit eligibility certificate provided in connection with the advance payment of the HCTC must include (1) the name, address, and telephone number of the State office or offices responsible for providing the individual with assistance with enrollment in qualified health insurance, (2) a list of coverage options that are treated as qualified health insurance by the State in which the individual resides, (3) in the case of a TAA-eligible individual, a statement informing the individual that the individual has 63 days from the date that is seven days after the issuance of such certificate to enroll in such insurance without a lapse in creditable coverage, and (4) such other information as the Secretary may provide.

*Effective date.*—The provision is effective for certificates issued after the date that is six months after the date of enactment. The provision does not apply to months beginning after December 31, 2010.

### *Survey and report on enhanced health coverage tax credit program*

*Survey*

The provision requires that the Secretary of the Treasury must conduct a biennial survey of eligible individuals containing the following information:

1. In the case of eligible individuals receiving the HCTC (including those participating in the advance payment program (the "HCTC program")) (A) demographic information of such individuals, including income and education levels, (B) satisfaction of such individuals with the enrollment process in the HCTC program, (C) satisfaction of such individuals with available health coverage options under the credit, including level of premiums, benefits, deductibles, cost-sharing requirements, and the adequacy of provider networks, and (D) any other information that the Secretary determines is appropriate.
2. In the case of eligible individuals not receiving the HCTC (A) demographic information on each individual, including income and education levels, (B) whether the individual was aware of the HCTC or the HCTC program, (C) the reasons the individual has not enrolled in the HCTC program, including whether such reasons include the burden of process of enrollment and the affordability of coverage, (D) whether the individual has health insurance coverage, and, if so, the source of such coverage, and (E) any other information that the Secretary determines is appropriate.

Not later than December 31 of each year in which a survey described above is conducted (beginning in 2010), the Secretary of the Treasury must report to the Committee on Finance and the Committee on Health, Education, Labor, and Pensions of the Senate and the Committee on Ways and Means and the Committee on Education and Labor of the House of Representatives the findings of the most recent survey.

*Report*

Not later than October 1 of each year (beginning in 2010), the Secretary of the Treasury must report to the Committee on Finance and the Committee on Health, Education, Labor, and Pensions of the Senate and the Committee on Ways and Means and the Committee on Education and Labor of the House of Representatives the following information with respect to the most recent taxable year ending before such date:

1. In each State and nationally (A) the total number of eligible individuals and the number of eligible individuals receiving the HCTC, (B) the total number of such eligible individuals who receive an advance payment of the HCTC through the HCTC program, (C) the average length of the time period of participation of eligible individuals in the HCTC program, and (D) the total number of participating eligible individuals in the HCTC program who are enrolled in each category of qualified health insurance with respect to each category of eligible individuals.

2. In each State and nationality, an analysis of (A) the range of monthly health insurance premiums, for self-only coverage and for family coverage, for individuals receiving the benefit of the HCTC and (B) the average and median monthly health insurance premiums, for self-only coverage and for family coverage, for individuals receiving the HCTC with respect to each category of qualified health insurance.

3. In each State and nationally, an analysis of the following information with respect to the health insurance coverage of individuals receiving the HCTC who are enrolled in State-based coverage: (A) deductible amounts, (B) other out-of-pocket cost-sharing amounts, and (C) a description of any annual or lifetime limits on coverage or any other significant limits on coverage services or benefits. The information must be reported with respect to each category of coverage.

4. In each State and nationally, the gender and average age of eligible individuals who receive the HCTC in each category of qualified health insurance with respect to each category of eligible individuals.

5. The steps taken by the Secretary of the Treasury to increase the participation rates in the HCTC program among eligible individuals, including outreach and enrollment activities.

6. The cost of administering the HCTC program by function, including the cost of subcontractors, and recommendations on ways to reduce the administrative costs, including recommended statutory changes.

7. After consultation with the Secretary of Labor, the number of States applying for and receiving national emergency grants under section 173(f) of the Workforce Investment Act of 1998, the activities funded by such grants on a State-by-State basis, and the time necessary for application approval of such grants.

***Other non-revenue provisions***

The provision also authorizes appropriations for implementation of the revenue provisions of the provision and provides grants under the Workforce Investment Act of 1998 for purposes related to the HCTC.

***GAO study***

The provision requires the Comptroller General of the United States to conduct a study regarding the HCTC to be submitted to Congress no later than March 31, 2010. The study is to include an analysis of (1) the administrative costs of the Federal government with respect to the credit and the advance payment of the credit and of providers of qualified health insurance with respect to providing such insurance to eligible individuals and their families, (2) the health status and relative risk status of eligible individuals and qualified family members covered under such insurance, (3) participation in the credit and the advance payment of the credit by eligible individuals and their qualifying family members, including the reasons why such individuals did or did not participate and the effects of the provision on participation, and (4) the extent to which eligible individuals and their qualifying family members obtained health insurance other than qualifying insurance or went without insurance coverage. The provision provides the Comptroller General access to the records within the possession or control of providers of qualified health insurance if determined relevant to the study. The Comptroller General may not disclose the identity of any provider of qualified health insurance or eligible individual in making information available to the public.

### *Effective Date*

The provision is generally effective upon the date of enactment (February 17, 2009), except as otherwise noted above.

# PART THREE: AIRPORT AND AIRWAY TRUST FUND EXTENSIONS (PUBLIC LAWS 111–12,[282] 111–69,[283] 111–116,[284] 111–153,[285] 111–161,[286] 111–197,[287] 111–216,[288] 111–249,[289] AND 111–329[290])

## *Present Law*

The Airport and Airway Trust Fund provides funding for capital improvements to the U.S. airport and airway system and funding for the Federal Aviation Administration ("FAA"), among other purposes. The excise taxes imposed to finance the Airport and Airway Trust Fund are:

- ticket taxes imposed on commercial, domestic passenger transportation by air;
- a use of international air facilities tax;
- a cargo tax imposed on freight transportation by air;
- fuels taxes imposed on gasoline used in commercial aviation and noncommercial aviation; and
- fuels taxes imposed on jet fuel (kerosene) and other aviation fuels used in commercial aviation and noncommercial aviation.

In general, except for 4.3 cents of the fuel tax rates, the excise taxes dedicated to the Airport and Airway Trust Fund did not apply after March 31, 2009. Expenditure authority for the Airport and Airway Trust Fund was scheduled to terminate after March 31, 2009.

## *Explanation of Provisions*

### *Pub. L. No. 111–12 (the "Federal Aviation Administration Extension Act of 2009")*

The provision extended the Airport and Airway Trust Fund excise taxes and expenditure authority through September 30, 2009.

---

[282] H.R. 1512. The House passed H.R. 1512 on March 18, 2009. The bill passed the Senate without amendment on March 18, 2009. The President signed the bill on March 30, 2009.

[283] H.R. 3607. The House passed H.R. 3607 on September 23, 2009. The bill passed the Senate without amendment on September 24, 2009. the President signed the bill on October 1, 2009.

[284] H.R. 4217. The House passed H.R. 4217 on December 8, 2009. The bill passed the Senate without amendment on December 10, 2009. The President signed the bill on December 16, 2009.

[285] H.R. 4957. The House passed H.R. 4957 on March 25, 2010. The bill passed the Senate without amendment on March 26, 2010. The President signed the bill on March 31, 2010.

[286] H.R. 5147. The House passed H.R. 5147 on April 28, 2010. The bill passed the Senate without amendment on April 28, 2010. The President signed the bill on April 30, 2010.

[287] H.R. 5611. The House passed H.R. 5611 on June 29, 2010. The bill passed the Senate without amendment on June 30, 2010. The President signed the bill on July 2, 2010.

[288] H.R. 5900. The House passed H.R. 5900 on July 29, 2010. The bill passed the Senate without amendment on July 30, 2010. The President signed the bill on August 1, 2010.

[289] H.R. 6190. The House passed H.R. 6190 on September 23, 2010. The bill passed the Senate without amendment on September 24, 2010. The President signed the bill on September 30, 2010.

[290] H.R. 6473. The House passed H.R. 6473 on December 2, 2010. The bill passed the Senate without amendment on December 18, 2010. The President signed the bill on December 22, 2010.

***Pub. L. No. 111–69 ("Fiscal Year 2010 Federal Aviation Administration Extension Act")***

The provision extended the Airport and Airway Trust Fund excise taxes and expenditure authority through December 31, 2009.

***Pub. L. No. 111–116 ("Fiscal Year 2010 Federal Aviation Administration Extension Act, Part II")***

The provisions extended the Airport and Airway Trust Fund excise taxes and expenditure authority through March 31, 2010.

***Pub. L. No. 111–153 (the "Federal Aviation Administration Extension Act of 2010")***

The provision extended the Airport and Airway Trust Fund excise taxes and expenditure authority through April 30, 2010.

***Pub. L. No. 111–161 (the "Airport and Airway Extension Act of 2010")***

The provision extended the Airport and Airway Trust Fund excise taxes and expenditure authority through July 3, 2010.

***Pub. L. No. 111–197 (the "Airport and Airway Extension Act of 2010, Part II")***

The provision extended the Airport and Airway Trust Fund excise taxes and expenditure authority through August 1, 2010.

***Pub. L. No. 111–216 (the "Airline Safety and Federal Aviation Administration Extension Act of 2010")***

The provision extended the Airport and Airway Trust Fund excise taxes and expenditure authority through September 30, 2010.

***Pub. L. No. 111–249 (the "Airport and Airway Extension Act of 2010, Part III")***

The provision extended the Airport and Airway Trust Fund excise taxes and expenditure authority through December 31, 2010.

***Pub. L. No. 111–329 (the "Airport and Airway Extension Act of 2010, Part IV")***

The provision extended the Airport and Airway Trust Fund excise taxes and expenditure authority through March 31, 2011.

# PART FOUR: HIGHWAY TRUST FUND (PUBLIC LAWS 111–46,[291] 111–68,[292] 111–118,[293] 111–144,[294] 111–147,[295] AND 111–322[296])

## A. Extension of Surface Transportation Act Expenditure Authority

### *Present Law*

Under present law, the Internal Revenue Code (sec. 9503) authorized expenditures (subject to appropriations) to be made from the Highway Trust Fund generally through September 30, 2009, for purposes provided in specified authorizing legislation as in effect on the date of enactment of the most recent authorizing Act (the Safe, Accountable, Flexible, Efficient Transportation Equity Act: A Legacy for Users ("SAFETEA–LU")).

### *Explanation of Provisions*

#### *Pub. L. No. 111–68 (the "Continuing Appropriations Resolution of 2010")*

This provision extends the authority to make expenditures (subject to appropriations) from the Highway Trust Fund through October 31, 2009. The Act also updates the cross-references to authorizing legislation to include expenditure purposes in this Act as in effect on the date of enactment. It also extends the expenditure authority for the Sport Fish Restoration and Boating Trust Fund through October 31, 2009.

---

[291] H.R. 3357. The bill passed the House on July 29, 2009. The Senate passed the bill on July 30, 2009, without amendment. The President signed the bill on August 7, 2009.

[292] H.R. 2918. The bill passed the House on June 19, 2009. The Senate passed the bill with an amendment on July 6, 2009. A conference report was filed on September 24, 2009 (H.R. Rep. No. 111–265) and passed the House on September 25, 2009, and the Senate on September 30, 2009. The President signed the bill on October 1, 2009.

[293] H.R. 3326. The bill passed the House on July 30, 2009. The Senate passed the bill with an amendment on October 6, 2009. The House agreed to the Senate amendment with an amendment on December 16, 2009. The Senate concurred in the House amendment to the Senate amendment on December 19, 2009. The President signed the bill on December 19, 2009.

[294] H.R. 4691. The bill passed the House on February 25, 2010. The Senate passed the bill without amendment on March 2, 2010. The President signed the bill on March 2, 2010.

[295] H.R. 2847. The bill passed the House on June 18, 2009. The Senate passed the bill with an amendment on November 5, 2009. The House agreed to the Senate amendment with an amendment on December 16, 2009. The Senate concurred in the House amendment to the Senate amendment with an amendment on February 24, 2010. The House agreed to the Senate amendment with an amendment to the House amendment to the Senate amendment on March 4, 2010. The Senate concurred in the House amendment to the Senate amendment to the House amendment to the Senate amendment on March 17, 2010. The President signed the bill on March 18, 2010.

[296] H.R. 3082. The bill passed the House on July 10, 2009. The Senate passed the bill with an amendment on November 17, 2009. The House agreed to the Senate Amendment with an amendment on December 8, 2010. The Senate concurred in the House amendment to the Senate amendment with an amendment on December 21, 2010. The House agreed to the Senate amendment to the House amendment to the Senate amendment on December 21, 2010. The President signed the bill on December 22, 2010.

### *Effective Date*

The provision is effective October 1, 2009.

### *Pub. L. No. 111–118 (the "Department of Defense Appropriations Act of 2010")*

This provision extends the authority to make expenditures (subject to appropriations) from the Highway Trust Fund (and Sport Fish Restoration and Boating Trust Fund) through February 28, 2010.

### *Effective Date*

The provision is effective October 1, 2009.

### *Pub. L. No. 111–144 (the "Temporary Extension Act of 2010")*

This provision extends the authority to make expenditures (subject to appropriations) from the Highway Trust Fund (and Sport Fish Restoration and Boating Trust Fund) through March 28, 2010.

### *Effective Date*

The provision is effective October 1, 2009.

### *Pub. L. No. 111–147 (the "Hiring Incentives to Restore Employment Act") (sec. 445)*

This provision extends the authority to make expenditures (subject to appropriations) from the Highway Trust Fund (and Sport Fish Restoration and Boating Trust Fund) through December 31, 2010. The Act also updates the cross-references to authorizing legislation to include expenditure purposes in this Act as in effect on the date of enactment.

### *Effective Date*

The provision is effective September 30, 2009.

### *Pub. L. No. 111–322 (the "Continuing Appropriations and Surface Transportation Extensions Act, 2011") (sec. 2401)*

This provision extends the authority to make expenditures (subject to appropriations) from the Highway Trust Fund (and Sport Fish Restoration and Boating Trust Fund) through March 4, 2011. The Act also updates the cross-references to authorizing legislation to include expenditure purposes in this Act as in effect on the date of enactment.

### *Effective Date*

The provision is effective December 31, 2010.

## B. Highway Trust Fund Restoration

### *Present Law*

Section 9004 of the Surface Transportation Revenue Act of 1998 (Title IX of the Transportation Equity Act for the 21st Century) provided that the Highway Trust Fund will not earn interest on unspent balances after September 30, 1998. Further, the balance in excess of $8 billion in the Highway Account of the Highway Trust Fund was cancelled on October 1, 1998 and transferred to the General Fund.

### *Explanation of Provision*

#### *Pub. L. No. 111–46*

The Act to restore funds to the Highway Trust Fund provided that out of the money in the Treasury not otherwise appropriated, $7,000,000,000 is appropriated to the Highway Trust Fund.

### *Effective Date*

The provision is effective on the date of enactment (August 7, 2009).

#### *Pub. L. No. 111–147 (the "Hiring Incentives to Restore Employment Act") (sec. 441, 442, 443, and 444)*

The provision repeals the requirement that obligations held by the Highway Trust Fund not be interest-bearing. The provision permits amounts in the Trust Fund to be invested in interest-bearing obligations of the United States and have the interest be credited to, and form a part of, the Highway Trust Fund. Thus, the Highway Trust Fund will accrue interest under the provision. The Act also provides that out of money in the Treasury not otherwise appropriated, $14,700,000,000 is appropriated to the Highway Account in the Highway Trust Fund and $4,800,000,000 is appropriated to the Mass Transit Account in the Highway Trust Fund, and makes those amounts available without fiscal year limitation. The Act terminated required transfers from the Highway Trust Fund into the general fund for certain repayments and credits, relating to amounts paid in respect of gasoline used on farms, amounts paid in respect of gasoline used for certain non-highway purposes or by local transit systems, amounts relating to fuels not used for taxable purposes, and income tax credits for certain uses of fuels.

### *Effective Date*

The provision is generally effective on the date of enactment (March 18, 2010). The provision terminating transfers from the Highway Trust Fund is effective for transfers relating to amounts paid and credits allowed after the date of enactment.

## PART FIVE: REVENUE PROVISIONS OF THE WORKER, HOMEOWNERSHIP, AND BUSINESS ASSISTANCE ACT OF 2009 (PUBLIC LAW 111–92)[297]

### A. Extension and Modification of First-Time Homebuyer Credit (secs. 11 and 12 of the Act and sec. 36 of the Code)

#### *Present Law*

***In general***

An individual who is a first-time homebuyer is allowed a refundable tax credit equal to the lesser of $8,000 ($4,000 for a married individual filing separately) or 10 percent of the purchase price of a principal residence. The credit is allowed for qualifying home purchases on or after April 9, 2008, and before December 1, 2009.[298]

The credit phases out for individual taxpayers with modified adjusted gross income between $75,000 and $95,000 ($150,000 and $170,000 for joint filers) for the year of purchase.

An individual is considered a first-time homebuyer if the individual had no ownership interest in a principal residence in the United States during the 3-year period prior to the purchase of the home.

An election is provided to treat a residence purchased after December 31, 2008, and before December 1, 2009, as purchased on December 31, 2008, so that the credit may be claimed on the 2008 income tax return.

No District of Columbia first-time homebuyer credit[299] is allowed to any taxpayer with respect to the purchase of a residence after December 31, 2008, and before December 1, 2009, if the national first-time homebuyer credit is allowable to such taxpayer (or the taxpayer's spouse) with respect to such purchase.

***Recapture***

For homes purchased on or before December 31, 2008, the credit is recaptured ratably over fifteen years with no interest charge beginning in the second taxable year after the taxable year in which the home is purchased. For example, if an individual purchases a home in 2008, recapture commences with the 2010 tax return. If the individual sells the home (or the home ceases to be used as the

[297] H.R. 3548. The bill passed the House on the suspension calendar on September 22, 2009. The Senate passed the bill with an amendment on November 4, 2009. The House agreed to the Senate amendment on the suspension calendar on November 5, 2009. The President signed the bill on November 6, 2009. For a technical explanation of the bill prepared by the staff of the Joint Committee on Taxation, see *Technical Explanation of Certain Revenue Provisions of the "Worker, Homeownership, and Business Assistance Act of 2009"* (JCX 44–09), November 3, 2009.

[298] For purchases before January 1, 2009, the dollar limits are $7,500 ($3,750 for a married individual filing separately).

[299] Sec. 1400C.

principal residence of the individual or the individual's spouse) prior to complete recapture of the credit, the amount of any credit not previously recaptured is due on the tax return for the year in which the home is sold (or ceases to be used as the principal residence).[300] However, in the case of a sale to an unrelated person, the amount recaptured may not exceed the amount of gain from the sale of the residence. For this purpose, gain is determined by reducing the basis of the residence by the amount of the credit to the extent not previously recaptured. No amount is recaptured after the death of an individual. In the case of an involuntary conversion of the home, recapture is not accelerated if a new principal residence is acquired within a two-year period. In the case of a transfer of the residence to a spouse or to a former spouse incident to divorce, the transferee spouse (and not the transferor spouse) will be responsible for any future recapture. Recapture does not apply to a home purchased after December 31, 2008 that is treated (at the election of the taxpayer) as purchased on December 31, 2008.

For homes purchased after December 31, 2008, and before December 1, 2009, the credit is recaptured only if the taxpayer disposes of the home (or the home otherwise ceases to be the principal residence of the taxpayer) within 36 months from the date of purchase.

### *Explanation of Provision*[301]

#### *Extension of application period*

In general, the credit is extended to apply to a principal residence purchased by the taxpayer before May 1, 2010. The credit applies to the purchase of a principal residence before July 1, 2010 by any taxpayer who enters into a written binding contract before May 1, 2010, to close on the purchase of a principal residence before July 1, 2010.

The waiver of recapture, except in the case of disposition of the home (or the home otherwise ceases to be the principal residence of the taxpayer) within 36 months from the date of purchase, is extended to any purchase of a principal residence after December 31, 2008.

The election to treat a purchase as occurring in a prior year is modified. In the case of a purchase of a principal residence after December 31, 2008, a taxpayer may elect to treat the purchase as made on December 31 of the calendar year preceding the purchase for purposes of claiming the credit on the prior year's tax return.

No District of Columbia first-time homebuyer credit[302] is allowed to any taxpayer with respect to the purchase of a residence after December 31, 2008, if the national first-time homebuyer credit is allowable to such taxpayer (or the taxpayer's spouse) with respect to such purchase.

---

[300] If the individual sells the home (or the home ceases to be used as the principal residence of the individual and the individual's spouse) in the same taxable year the home is purchased, no credit is allowed.

[301] This provision was subsequently amended by section 2 of the Homebuyer Assistance and Improvement Act of 2010, Pub. L. No. 111–98, described in Part Ten of this document.

[302] Sec. 1400C.

***Long-time residents of the same principal residence***

An individual (and, if married, the individual's spouse) who has maintained the same principal residence for any five-consecutive year period during the eight-year period ending on the date of the purchase of a subsequent principal residence is treated as a first-time homebuyer. The maximum allowable credit for such taxpayers is $6,500 ($3,250 for a married individual filing separately).

***Limitations***

The Act raises the income limitations to qualify for the credit. The credit phases out for individual taxpayers with modified adjusted gross income between $125,000 and $145,000 ($225,000 and $245,000 for joint filers) for the year of purchase.

No credit is allowed for the purchase of any residence if the purchase price exceeds $800,000.

No credit is allowed unless the taxpayer is 18 years of age as of the date of purchase. A taxpayer who is married is treated as meeting the age requirement if the taxpayer or the taxpayer's spouse meets the age requirement.

The definition of purchase excludes property acquired from a person related to the person acquiring such property or the spouse of the person acquiring the property, if married.

No credit is allowed to any taxpayer if the taxpayer is a dependent of another taxpayer.

No credit is allowed unless the taxpayer attaches to the relevant tax return a properly executed copy of the settlement statement used to complete the purchase.

***Waiver of recapture for individuals on qualified official extended duty***

In the case of a disposition of principal residence by an individual (or a cessation of use of the residence that otherwise would cause recapture) after December 31, 2008, in connection with Government orders received by the individual (or the individual's spouse) for qualified official extended duty service, no recapture applies by reason of the disposition of the residence,[303] and any 15-year recapture with respect to a home acquired before January 1, 2009, ceases to apply in the taxable year the disposition occurs.

Qualified official extended duty service means service on official extended duty as a member of the uniformed services, a member of the Foreign Service of the United States, or an employee of the intelligence community.[304]

Qualified official extended duty is any period of extended duty while serving at a place of duty at least 50 miles away from the taxpayer's principal residence or under orders compelling residence in government furnished quarters. Extended duty is defined as any period of duty pursuant to a call or order to such duty for a period in excess of 90 days or for an indefinite period.

---

[303] If the individual sells the home (or the home ceases to be used as the principal residence of the individual and the individual's spouse) in connection with such orders in the same taxable year the home is purchased, the credit is allowable.

[304] These terms have the same meaning as under the provision for exclusion of gain on the sale of certain principal residences (Sec. 121).

The uniformed services include: (1) the Armed Forces (the Army, Navy, Air Force, Marine Corps, and Coast Guard); (2) the commissioned corps of the National Oceanic and Atmospheric Administration; and (3) the commissioned corps of the Public Health Service.

The term "member of the Foreign Service of the United States" includes: (1) chiefs of mission; (2) ambassadors at large; (3) members of the Senior Foreign Service; (4) Foreign Service officers; and (5) Foreign Service personnel.

The term "employee of the intelligence community" means an employee of the Office of the Director of National Intelligence, the Central Intelligence Agency, the National Security Agency, the Defense Intelligence Agency, the National Geospatial-Intelligence Agency, or the National Reconnaissance Office. The term also includes employment with: (1) any other office within the Department of Defense for the collection of specialized national intelligence through reconnaissance programs; (2) any of the intelligence elements of the Army, the Navy, the Air Force, the Marine Corps, the Federal Bureau of Investigation, the Department of the Treasury, the Department of Energy, and the Coast Guard; (3) the Bureau of Intelligence and Research of the Department of State; and (4) the elements of the Department of Homeland Security concerned with the analyses of foreign intelligence information.

### *Extension of the first-time homebuyer credit for individuals on qualified official extended duty outside of the United States*

In the case of any individual (and, if married, the individual's spouse) who serves on qualified official extended duty service outside of the United States for at least 90 days during the period beginning after December 31, 2008, and ending before May 1, 2010, the expiration date of the first-time homebuyer credit is extended for one year, through May 1, 2011 (July 1, 2011, in the case of an individual who enters into a written binding contract before May 1, 2011, to close on the purchase of a principal residence before July 1, 2011).

### *Mathematical error authority*

The Act makes a number of changes to expand the definition of mathematical or clerical error for purposes of administration of the credit by the Internal Revenue Service ("IRS"). The IRS may assess additional tax without issuance of a notice of deficiency as otherwise required[305] in the case of: an omission of any increase in tax required by the recapture provisions of the credit; information from the person issuing the taxpayer identification number of the taxpayer that indicates that the taxpayer does not meet the age requirement of the credit; information provided to the Secretary by the taxpayer on an income tax return for at least one of the two preceding taxable years that is inconsistent with eligibility for such credit; or, failure to attach to the return a properly executed copy of the settlement statement used to complete the purchase.

---

[305] Sec. 6213.

### *Effective Date*

The extension of the first-time homebuyer credit and coordination with the first-time homebuyer credit for the District of Columbia apply to residences purchased after November 30, 2009.

Provisions relating to long-time residents of the same principal residence, and income, purchase price, age, related party, dependent, and documentation limitations apply for purchases after the date of enactment.

The waiver of recapture provision applies to dispositions and cessations after December 31, 2008.

The expansion of mathematical and clerical error authority applies to returns for taxable years ending on or after April 9, 2008.

## B. Five-Year Carryback of Operating Losses (sec. 13 of the Act and sec. 172 of the Code)

### *Present Law*

#### *In general*

Under present law, a net operating loss ("NOL") generally means the amount by which a taxpayer's business deductions exceed its gross income. In general, an NOL may be carried back two years and carried over 20 years to offset taxable income in such years.[306] NOLs offset taxable income in the order of the taxable years to which the NOL may be carried.[307]

For purposes of computing the alternative minimum tax ("AMT"), a taxpayer's NOL deduction cannot reduce the taxpayer's alternative minimum taxable income ("AMTI") by more than 90 percent of the AMTI.[308]

In the case of a life insurance company, present law allows a deduction for the operations loss carryovers and carrybacks to the taxable year, in lieu of the deduction for net operation losses allowed to other corporations.[309] A life insurance company is permitted to treat a loss from operations (as defined under section 810(c)) for any taxable year as an operations loss carryback to each of the three taxable years preceding the loss year and an operations loss carryover to each of the 15 taxable years following the loss year.[310]

#### *Temporary rule for small business*

Present law provides an eligible small business with an election[311] to increase the present-law carryback period for an "applicable 2008 NOL" from two years to any whole number of years elected by the taxpayer that is more than two and less than six. An eligible small business is a taxpayer meeting a $15,000,000 gross receipts test. An applicable 2008 NOL is the taxpayer's NOL for any taxable year ending in 2008, or if elected by the taxpayer, the NOL for any taxable year beginning in 2008. However, any

[306] Sec. 172(b)(1)(A). Different carryback periods apply with respect to NOLs arising in certain special circumstances.
[307] Sec. 172(b)(2).
[308] Sec. 56(d).
[309] Secs. 810, 805(a)(5).
[310] Sec. 810(b)(1).
[311] Sec. 172(b)(1)(H).

election under this provision may be made only with respect to one taxable year.

### *Explanation of Provision*

The provision provides an election[312] to increase the present-law carryback period for an applicable NOL from two years to any whole number of years elected by the taxpayer which is more than two and less than six. An applicable NOL is the taxpayer's NOL for a taxable year beginning or ending in either 2008 or 2009. Generally, a taxpayer may elect an extended carryback period for only one taxable year.

The amount of an NOL that may be carried back to the fifth taxable year preceding the loss year is limited to 50 percent of taxable income for such taxable year (computed without regard to the NOL for the loss year or any taxable year thereafter).[313] The limitation does not apply to the applicable 2008 NOL of an eligible small business with respect to which an election is made (either before or after the date of enactment of the Act (November 6, 2009)) under the provision as presently in effect. The amount of the NOL otherwise carried to taxable years subsequent to such fifth taxable year is to be adjusted to take into account that the NOL could offset only 50 percent of the taxable income in such year. Thus, in determining the excess of the applicable NOL over the sum of the taxpayer's taxable income for each of the prior taxable years to which the loss may be carried, only 50 percent of the taxable income for the taxable year for which the limitation applies is to be taken into account.

The provision also suspends the 90-percent limitation on the use of any alternative tax NOL deduction attributable to carrybacks of the applicable NOL for which an extended carryback period is elected.[314]

For life insurance companies, the provision provides an election to increase the present-law carryback period for an applicable loss from operations from three years to four or five years. An applicable loss from operations is the taxpayer's loss from operations for any taxable year beginning or ending in either 2008 or 2009. A 50-percent of taxable income limitation applies to the fifth taxable year preceding the loss year.

A taxpayer must make the election by the extended due date for filing the return for the taxpayer's last taxable year beginning in 2009, and in such manner as may be prescribed by the Secretary.[315] An election, once made, is irrevocable.

An eligible small business that timely made (or timely makes) an election under the provision as in effect on the day before the en-

[312] For all elections under this provision, the common parent of a group of corporations filing a consolidated return makes the election, which is binding on all such corporations.

[313] The taxable income limitation only applies to that portion of an applicable NOL that is carried back to the fifth preceding taxable year under subparagraph (H) of section 172(b)(1). The limitation does not apply to the portion of the loss carried back under another subparagraph of section 172(b)(1), such as a specified liability loss, farming loss, or qualified disaster loss.

[314] It is intended that in applying the 50-percent taxable income limitation with respect to the carryback of an alternative tax NOL deduction to the fifth preceding taxable year, the limitation is applied separately based on alternative minimum taxable income.

[315] It is anticipated that the procedures for making the election will be substantially similar to those prescribed for eligible small businesses under present law. See Rev. Proc. 2009–26, 2009–19 I.R.B. 935.

actment of the Act to carry back its applicable 2008 NOL may also elect to carry back a 2009 NOL under the amended provision.[316] It is intended that an eligible small business may continue to make the present-law election under procedures prescribed in Rev. Proc. 2009–26 following the enactment of the Act.

The provision generally does not apply to: (1) any taxpayer if (a) the Federal government acquired or acquires, at any time,[317] an equity interest in the taxpayer pursuant to the Emergency Economic Stabilization Act of 2008,[318] or (b) the Federal government acquired or acquires, at any time, any warrant (or other right) to acquire any equity interest with respect to the taxpayer pursuant to such Act; (2) the Federal National Mortgage Association and the Federal Home Loan Mortgage Corporation; and (3) any taxpayer that in 2008 or 2009[319] is a member of the same affiliated group (as defined in section 1504 without regard to subsection (b) thereof) as a taxpayer to which the provision does not otherwise apply. An equity interest (or right to acquire an equity interest) is disregarded for this purpose if acquired by the Federal government after the date of enactment from a financial institution[320] pursuant to a program established by the Secretary for the stated purpose of increasing the availability of credit to small businesses using funding made available under the Emergency Economic Stabilization Act of 2008.

### *Effective Date*

The provision is generally effective for net operating losses arising in taxable years ending after December 31, 2007. The modification to the alternative tax NOL deduction applies to taxable years ending after December 31, 2002. The modification with respect to operating loss deductions of life insurance companies applies to losses from operations arising in taxable years ending after December 31, 2007.

Under transition rules, a taxpayer may revoke any election to waive the carryback period under either section 172(b)(3) or section 810(b)(3) with respect to an applicable NOL or an applicable loss from operations for a taxable year ending before the date of enactment (November 6, 2009) by the extended due date for filing the tax return for the taxpayer's last taxable year beginning in 2009. Similarly, any application for a tentative carryback adjustment

---

[316] Present law section 172(b)(1)(H)(iii) provides that an eligible small business must make the election by the extended due date for filing its return for the taxable year of the NOL. An eligible small business that did not (or does not) timely elect to carryback its applicable 2008 NOL under present law is subject to the general provision (i.e., election available for either 2008 or 2009 NOL and 50 percent of taxable income limitation applies for the fifth taxable year preceding the loss year).

[317] For example, if the Federal government acquires an equity interest in the taxpayer during 2010, or in later years, the taxpayer is not entitled to the extended carryback rules under this provision. If the carryback has previously been claimed, amended filings may be necessary to reflect this disallowance. Additionally, if the Federal government acquired an equity interest in the taxpayer pursuant to the Emergency Economic Stabilization Act of 2008 and the taxpayer has repaid that investment, it is not entitled to the extended carryback rules under this provision.

[318] Pub. L. No. 110–343.

[319] For example, a taxpayer with an NOL in 2008 that in 2009 joins an affiliated group with a member in which the Federal government has acquired an equity interest pursuant to the Emergency Economic Stabilization Act of 2008 may not utilize the extended carryback rules under this provision with regard to the 2008 NOL. The taxpayer is required to amend prior filings to reflect the permitted carryback period.

[320] As defined in section 3 of the Emergency Economic Stabilization Act of 2008.

under section 6411(a) with respect to such loss is treated as timely filed if filed by the extended due date for filing the tax return for the taxpayer's last taxable year beginning in 2009.

## C. Exclusion from Gross Income of Qualified Military Base Realignment and Closure Fringe (sec. 14 of the Act and sec. 132 of the Code)

### *Present Law*

#### *Homeowners Assistance Program payment*

The Department of Defense Homeowners Assistance Program ("HAP") provides payments to certain employees and members of the Armed Forces to offset the adverse effects on housing values that result from a military base realignment or closure.

In general, under the HAP, eligible individuals receive either: (1) a cash payment as compensation for losses that may be or have been sustained in a private sale, in an amount not to exceed the difference between (a) 95 percent of the fair market value of their property prior to public announcement of intention to close all or part of the military base or installation and (b) the fair market value of such property at the time of the sale; or (2) as the purchase price for their property, an amount not to exceed 90 percent of the prior fair market value as determined by the Secretary of Defense, or the amount of the outstanding mortgages.

The American Recovery and Reinvestment Act of 2009[321] expands the HAP in various ways. It amends the Demonstration Cities and Metropolitan Development Act of 1966[322] to allow, under the HAP under such Act, the Secretary of Defense to provide assistance or reimbursement for certain losses in the sale of family dwellings by members of the Armed Forces living on or near a military installation in situations where: (1) there was a base closure or realignment; (2) the property was purchased before July 1, 2006, and sold between that date and September 30, 2012; (3) the property is the owner's primary residence; and (4) the owner has not previously received benefits under the HAP. Further, it authorizes similar HAP assistance or reimbursement with respect to: (1) wounded members and wounded civilian Department of Defense and Coast Guard employees (and their spouses); and (2) members permanently reassigned from an area at or near a military installation to a new duty station more than 50 miles away (with similar purchase and sale date, residence, and no-previous-benefit requirements as above). It allows the Secretary to provide compensation for losses from home sales by such individuals to ensure the realization of at least 90 percent (in some cases, 95 percent) of the pre-mortgage-crisis assessed value of such property.

#### *Tax treatment*

Present law generally excludes from gross income amounts received under the HAP (as in effect on November 11, 2003).[323] Amounts received under the program also are not considered wages

[321] Pub. L. No. 111–5.
[322] Pub. L. No. 89–754, 42 U.S.C. 3374.
[323] Sec. 132(n).

for FICA tax purposes (including Medicare). The excludable amount is limited to the reduction in the fair market value of property.

### *Explanation of Provision*

The Act expands the exclusion to HAP payments authorized under the American Recovery and Reinvestment Tax Act of 2009.

### *Effective Date*

The provision is effective for payments made after February 17, 2009 (the date of enactment of the American Recovery and Reinvestment Tax Act of 2009).

## D. Delay in Application of Worldwide Allocation of Interest (sec. 15 of the Act and sec. 864 of the Code)

### *Present Law*

#### *In general*

To compute the foreign tax credit limitation, a taxpayer must determine the amount of its taxable income from foreign sources. Thus, the taxpayer must allocate and apportion deductions between items of U.S.-source gross income, on the one hand, and items of foreign-source gross income, on the other.

In the case of interest expense, the rules generally are based on the approach that money is fungible and that interest expense is properly attributable to all business activities and property of a taxpayer, regardless of any specific purpose for incurring an obligation on which interest is paid.[324] For interest allocation purposes, all members of an affiliated group of corporations generally are treated as a single corporation (the so-called "one-taxpayer rule") and allocation must be made on the basis of assets rather than gross income. The term "affiliated group" in this context generally is defined by reference to the rules for determining whether corporations are eligible to file consolidated returns.

For consolidation purposes, the term "affiliated group" means one or more chains of includible corporations connected through stock ownership with a common parent corporation that is an includible corporation, but only if: (1) the common parent owns directly stock possessing at least 80 percent of the total voting power and at least 80 percent of the total value of at least one other includible corporation; and (2) stock meeting the same voting power and value standards with respect to each includible corporation (excluding the common parent) is directly owned by one or more other includible corporations.

Generally, the term "includible corporation" means any domestic corporation except certain corporations exempt from tax under section 501 (for example, corporations organized and operated exclusively for charitable or educational purposes), certain life insurance companies, corporations electing application of the possession tax credit, regulated investment companies, real estate investment

[324] However, exceptions to the fungibility principle are provided in particular cases, some of which are described below.

trusts, and domestic international sales corporations. A foreign corporation generally is not an includible corporation.

Subject to exceptions, the consolidated return and interest allocation definitions of affiliation generally are consistent with each other.[325] For example, both definitions generally exclude all foreign corporations from the affiliated group. Thus, while debt generally is considered fungible among the assets of a group of domestic affiliated corporations, the same rules do not apply as between the domestic and foreign members of a group with the same degree of common control as the domestic affiliated group.

*Banks, savings institutions, and other financial affiliates*

The affiliated group for interest allocation purposes generally excludes what are referred to in the Treasury regulations as "financial corporations."[326] A financial corporation includes any corporation, otherwise a member of the affiliated group for consolidation purposes, that is a financial institution (described in section 581 or section 591), the business of which is predominantly with persons other than related persons or their customers, and which is required by State or Federal law to be operated separately from any other entity that is not a financial institution.[327] The category of financial corporations also includes, to the extent provided in regulations, bank holding companies (including financial holding companies), subsidiaries of banks and bank holding companies (including financial holding companies), and savings institutions predominantly engaged in the active conduct of a banking, financing, or similar business.[328]

A financial corporation is not treated as a member of the regular affiliated group for purposes of applying the one-taxpayer rule to other nonfinancial members of that group. Instead, all such financial corporations that would be so affiliated are treated as a separate single corporation for interest allocation purposes.

***Worldwide interest allocation***

*In general*

The American Jobs Creation Act of 2004 ("AJCA")[329] modified the interest expense allocation rules described above (which generally apply for purposes of computing the foreign tax credit limitation) by providing a one-time election (the "worldwide affiliated group election") under which the taxable income of the domestic members of an affiliated group from sources outside the United States generally is determined by allocating and apportioning interest expense of the domestic members of a worldwide affiliated group on a worldwide-group basis (i.e., as if all members of the worldwide group were a single corporation). If a group makes this election, the taxable income of the domestic members of a worldwide affiliated group from sources outside the United States is de-

[325] One such exception is that the affiliated group for interest allocation purposes includes section 936 corporations (certain electing domestic corporations that have income from the active conduct of a trade or business in Puerto Rico or another U.S. possession) that are excluded from the consolidated group.

[326] Temp. Treas. Reg. sec. 1.861–11T(d)(4).

[327] Sec. 864(e)(5)(C).

[328] Sec. 864(e)(5)(D).

[329] Pub. L. No. 108–357, sec. 401.

termined by allocating and apportioning the third-party interest expense of those domestic members to foreign-source income in an amount equal to the excess (if any) of (1) the worldwide affiliated group's worldwide third-party interest expense multiplied by the ratio that the foreign assets of the worldwide affiliated group bears to the total assets of the worldwide affiliated group,[330] over (2) the third-party interest expense incurred by foreign members of the group to the extent such interest would be allocated to foreign sources if the principles of worldwide interest allocation were applied separately to the foreign members of the group.[331]

For purposes of the new elective rules based on worldwide fungibility, the worldwide affiliated group means all corporations in an affiliated group as well as all controlled foreign corporations that, in the aggregate, either directly or indirectly,[332] would be members of such an affiliated group if section 1504(b)(3) did not apply (i.e., in which at least 80 percent of the vote and value of the stock of such corporations is owned by one or more other corporations included in the affiliated group). Thus, if an affiliated group makes this election, the taxable income from sources outside the United States of domestic group members generally is determined by allocating and apportioning interest expense of the domestic members of the worldwide affiliated group as if all of the interest expense and assets of 80-percent or greater owned domestic corporations (i.e., corporations that are part of the affiliated group, as modified to include insurance companies) and certain controlled foreign corporations were attributable to a single corporation.

*Financial institution group election*

Taxpayers are allowed to apply the bank group rules to exclude certain financial institutions from the affiliated group for interest allocation purposes under the worldwide fungibility approach. The rules also provide a one-time "financial institution group" election that expands the bank group. At the election of the common parent of the pre-election worldwide affiliated group, the interest expense allocation rules are applied separately to a subgroup of the worldwide affiliated group that consists of (1) all corporations that are part of the bank group, and (2) all "financial corporations." For this purpose, a corporation is a financial corporation if at least 80 percent of its gross income is financial services income (as described in section 904(d)(2)(C)(i) and the regulations thereunder) that is derived from transactions with unrelated persons.[333] For these purposes, items of income or gain from a transaction or series of transactions are disregarded if a principal purpose for the transaction or transactions is to qualify any corporation as a financial corporation.

[330] For purposes of determining the assets of the worldwide affiliated group, neither stock in corporations within the group nor indebtedness (including receivables) between members of the group is taken into account.

[331] Although the interest expense of a foreign subsidiary is taken into account for purposes of allocating the interest expense of the domestic members of the electing worldwide affiliated group for foreign tax credit limitation purposes, the interest expense incurred by a foreign subsidiary is not deductible on a U.S. return.

[332] Indirect ownership is determined under the rules of section 958(a)(2) or through applying rules similar to those of section 958(a)(2) to stock owned directly or indirectly by domestic partnerships, trusts, or estates.

[333] See Treas. Reg. sec. 1.904–4(e)(2).

In addition, anti-abuse rules are provided under which certain transfers from one member of a financial institution group to a member of the worldwide affiliated group outside of the financial institution group are treated as reducing the amount of indebtedness of the separate financial institution group. Regulatory authority is provided with respect to the election to provide for the direct allocation of interest expense in circumstances in which such allocation is appropriate to carry out the purposes of these rules, to prevent assets or interest expense from being taken into account more than once, or to address changes in members of any group (through acquisitions or otherwise) treated as affiliated under these rules.

*Effective date of worldwide interest allocation*

The common parent of the domestic affiliated group must make the worldwide affiliated group election. It must be made for the first taxable year beginning after December 31, 2010, in which a worldwide affiliated group exists that includes at least one foreign corporation that meets the requirements for inclusion in a worldwide affiliated group.[334] The common parent of the pre-election worldwide affiliated group must make the election for the first taxable year beginning after December 31, 2010, in which a worldwide affiliated group includes a financial corporation. Once either election is made, it applies to the common parent and all other members of the worldwide affiliated group or to all members of the financial institution group, as applicable, for the taxable year for which the election is made and all subsequent taxable years, unless revoked with the consent of the Secretary of the Treasury.

*Phase-in rule*

HERA also provided a special phase-in rule in the case of the first taxable year to which the worldwide interest allocation rules apply. For that year, the amount of the taxpayer's taxable income from foreign sources is reduced by 70 percent of the excess of (i) the amount of its taxable income from foreign sources as calculated using the worldwide interest allocation rules over (ii) the amount of its taxable income from foreign sources as calculated using the present-law interest allocation rules. For that year, the amount of the taxpayer's taxable income from domestic sources is increased by a corresponding amount. Any foreign tax credits disallowed by virtue of this reduction in foreign-source taxable income may be carried back or forward under the normal rules for carrybacks and carryforwards of excess foreign tax credits.

[334] As originally enacted under AJCA, the worldwide interest allocation rules were effective for taxable years beginning after December 31, 2008. However, section 3093 of the Housing and Economic Recovery Act of 2008, Pub. L. No. 110–289, delayed the implementation of the worldwide interest allocation rules for two years, until taxable years beginning after December 31, 2010.

### *Explanation of Provision*[335]

The provision delays the effective date of the worldwide interest allocation rules for seven years, until taxable years beginning after December 31, 2017. The required dates for making the worldwide affiliated group election and the financial institution group election are changed accordingly.

The provision also eliminates the special phase-in rule that applies in the case of the first taxable year to which the worldwide interest allocation rules apply.

### *Effective Date*

The provision is effective for taxable years beginning after December 31, 2010.

## E. Modification of Penalty for Failure to File Partnership or S Corporation Returns (sec. 16 of the Act and secs. 6698 and 6699 of the Code)

### *Present Law*

Both partnerships and S corporations are generally treated as pass-through entities that do not incur an income tax at the entity level. Income earned by a partnership, whether distributed or not, is taxed to the partners. Distributions from the partnership generally are tax-free. The items of income, gain, loss, deduction or credit of a partnership generally are taken into account by a partner as allocated under the terms of the partnership agreement. If the agreement does not provide for an allocation, or the agreed allocation does not have substantial economic effect, then the items are to be allocated in accordance with the partners' interests in the partnership. To prevent double taxation of these items, a partner's basis in its interest is increased by its share of partnership income (including tax-exempt income), and is decreased by its share of any losses (including nondeductible losses). An S corporation generally is not subject to corporate-level income tax on its items of income and loss. Instead, the S corporation passes through its items of income and loss to its shareholders. The shareholders take into account separately their shares of these items on their individual income tax returns.

Under present law, both partnerships and S corporations are required to file tax returns for each taxable year.[336] The partnership's tax return is required to include the names and addresses of the individuals who would be entitled to share in the taxable income if distributed and the amount of the distributive share of each individual. The S corporation's tax return is required to include the following: the names and addresses of all persons owning stock in the corporation at any time during the taxable year; the number of shares of stock owned by each shareholder at all times during the taxable year; the amount of money and other property distributed by the corporation during the taxable year to each shareholder

[335] The effective date of the worldwide interest allocation rules was subsequently further delayed by section 551 of the Hiring Incentives to Restore Employment Act of 2010, Pub. L. No. 111–147, described in Part Seven of this document.

[336] Secs. 6031 and 6037, respectively.

and the date of such distribution; each shareholder's pro rata share of each item of the corporation for the taxable year; and such other information as the Secretary may require.

In addition to applicable criminal penalties, present law imposes assessable civil penalties for both the failure to file a partnership return and the failure to file an S corporation return.[337] Each of these penalties is currently $89 times the number of shareholders or partners for each month (or fraction of a month) that the failure continues, up to a maximum of 12 months for returns required to be filed after December 31, 2008.

### *Explanation of Provision*

Under the provision, the base amount on which a penalty is computed for a failure with respect to filing either a partnership or S corporation return is increased to $195 per partner or shareholder.

### *Effective Date*

The provision applies to returns for taxable years beginning after December 31, 2009.

## F. Expansion of Electronic Filing by Return Preparers (sec. 17 of the Act and sec. 6011(e) of the Code)

### *Present Law*

The Internal Revenue Service Restructuring and Reform Act of 1998[338] ("RRA 1998") states a Congressional policy to promote the paperless filing of Federal tax returns. Section 2001(a) of RRA 1998 sets a goal for the IRS to have at least 80 percent of all Federal tax and information returns filed electronically by 2007. Section 2001(b) of RRA 1998 requires the IRS to establish a 10-year strategic plan to eliminate barriers to electronic filing.

The Secretary has limited authority to issue regulations specifying which returns must be filed electronically.[339] First, it can apply only to persons required to file at least 250 returns during the calendar year.[340] Second, the Secretary is prohibited from requiring that income tax returns of individuals, estates, and trusts be submitted in any format other than paper (although these returns may be filed electronically by choice). Third, the Secretary, in determining which returns must be filed on magnetic media, must take into account relevant factors, including the ability of a taxpayer to comply with magnetic media filing at reasonable cost.[341] Finally, a failure to comply with the regulations mandating electronic filing cannot in itself establish the basis for assertion of a penalty for failure to file an information return, with certain exceptions for corporations and partnerships.[342]

---

[337] Secs. 6698 and 6699, respectively.

[338] Pub. L. No. 105–206.

[339] Sec. 6011(e).

[340] Partnerships with more than 100 partners are required to file electronically. Sec. 6011(e)(2).

[341] Sec. 6011(e).

[342] Sec. 6724(c). If a corporation fails to comply with the electronic filing requirements for more than 250 returns that it is required to file, it may be subject to the penalty for failure

Continued

Accordingly, the Secretary requires corporations and tax-exempt organizations that have assets of $10 million or more and file at least 250 returns during a calendar year, including income tax, information, excise tax, and employment tax returns, to file electronically their Form 1120/1120S income tax returns and Form 990 information returns for tax years ending on or after December 31, 2006.[343] Private foundations and charitable trusts that file at least 250 returns during a calendar year are required to file electronically their Form 990–PF information returns for tax years ending on or after December 31, 2006, regardless of their asset size. Taxpayers can request waivers of the electronic filing requirement if they cannot meet that requirement due to technological constraints, or if compliance with the requirement would result in undue financial burden on the taxpayer.

### *Explanation of Provision*

The provision generally maintains the current rule that regulations may not require any person to file electronically unless the person files at least 250 tax returns during the calendar year. However, the proposal provides an exception to this rule and mandates that the Secretary require electronic filing by specified tax return preparers. "Specified tax return preparers" are all return preparers except those who neither file nor reasonably expect to file more than ten individual income tax returns on behalf of clients in a calendar year. The term "individual income tax return" is defined to include returns for estates and trusts as well as individuals.

### *Effective Date*

The provision is effective for tax returns filed after December 31, 2010.

## G. Time for Payment of Corporate Estimated Taxes (sec. 18 of the Act and sec. 6655 of the Code)

### *Present Law*

In general, corporations are required to make quarterly estimated tax payments of their income tax liability.[344] For a corporation whose taxable year is a calendar year, these estimated tax payments must be made by April 15, June 15, September 15, and December 15. In the case of a corporation with assets of at least $1 billion (determined as of the end of the preceding tax year), payments due in July, August, or September, 2014, are increased to 100.25 percent of the payment otherwise due and the next required payment is reduced accordingly.[345]

---

to file information returns under section 6721. For partnerships, the penalty may be imposed only if the failure extends to more than 100 returns.

[343] Treas. Reg. secs. 301.6011–5, 301.6033–4, 301.6037–2.

[344] Sec. 6655.

[345] Joint resolution approving the renewal of import restrictions contained in the Burmese Freedom and Democracy Act of 2003, and for other purposes, Pub. L. No. 111–42, sec. 202(b)(1).

### *Explanation of Provision*[346]

The provision increases the required payment of estimated tax otherwise due in July, August, or September, 2014, by 33.00 percentage points.

### *Effective Date*

The provision is effective on the date of the enactment (November 6, 2009).

[346] All the public laws enacted in the 111th Congress affecting this provision are described in Part Twenty-One of this document.

## PART SIX: HAITI TAX RELIEF (PUBLIC LAW 111–126)[347]

### A. Accelerate the Income Tax Benefits for Charitable Cash Contributions for the Relief of Victims of the Earthquake in Haiti (sec. 1 of the Act)

#### *Present Law*

In general, under present law, taxpayers may claim an income tax deduction for charitable contributions. The charitable deduction generally is available for the taxable year in which the contribution is made. For taxpayers whose taxable year is the calendar year, the tax benefit of a charitable contribution made in January or February often is not realized until the following calendar year when the tax return is filed.

A donor who claims a charitable deduction for a charitable contribution of money, regardless of amount, must maintain as a record of the contribution a bank record or a written communication from the donee showing the name of the donee organization, the date of the contribution, and the amount of the contribution.[348] In addition to the foregoing recordkeeping requirements, substantiation requirements apply in the case of charitable contributions with a value of $250 or more. No charitable deduction is allowed for any contribution of $250 or more unless the taxpayer substantiates the contribution by a contemporaneous written acknowledgment of the contribution by the donee organization.

#### *Explanation of Provision*

The provision permits taxpayers to treat charitable contributions of cash made after January 11, 2010, and before March 1, 2010, as contributions made on December 31, 2009, if such contributions were for the purpose of providing relief to victims in areas affected by the earthquake in Haiti that occurred on January 12, 2010. Thus, the effect of the provision is to give calendar-year taxpayers who make Haitian earthquake-related charitable contributions of cash after January 11, 2010, and before March 1, 2010, the opportunity to accelerate their tax benefit. Under the provision, such taxpayers may realize the tax benefit of such contributions by taking a deduction on their 2009 tax return.

The provision also clarifies the recordkeeping requirement for monetary contributions eligible for the accelerated income tax benefits described above. With respect to such contributions, a tele-

[347] H.R. 4462. The bill passed the House on the suspension calendar on January 20, 2010. The Senate passed the bill by unanimous consent on January 21, 2010. The President signed the bill on January 22, 2010. For a technical explanation of the bill prepared by the staff of the Joint Committee on Taxation, see *Technical Explanation of H.R. 4462: A Bill to Accelerate the Income Tax Benefits for Charitable Cash Contributions for the Relief of Victims of the Earthquake in Haiti* (JCX–2–10), January 20, 2010.

[348] Sec. 170(f)(17).

phone bill will also satisfy the recordkeeping requirement if it shows the name of the donee organization, the date of the contribution, and the amount of the contribution. Thus, for example, in the case of a charitable contribution made by text message and chargeable to a telephone or wireless account, a bill from the telecommunications company containing the relevant information will satisfy the recordkeeping requirement.

### *Effective Date*

The provision is effective on the date of enactment (January 22, 2010).

## PART SEVEN: REVENUE PROVISIONS OF THE HIRING INCENTIVES TO RESTORE EMPLOYMENT ACT (PUBLIC LAW 111–147)[349]

## TITLE I—INCENTIVES FOR HIRING AND RETAINING UNEMPLOYED WORKERS

### A. Payroll Tax Forgiveness for Hiring Unemployed Workers (sec. 101 of the Act and new sec. 3111 of the Code)

#### *Present Law*

***In general***

Social security benefits and certain Medicare benefits are financed primarily by payroll taxes on wages.

***Federal Insurance Contributions Act ("FICA") tax***

The FICA tax applies to employers based on the amount of covered wages paid to an employee during the year. Generally, covered wages means all remuneration for employment, including the cash value of all remuneration (including benefits) paid in any medium other than cash. Certain exceptions from covered wages are also provided. The tax imposed is composed of two parts: (1) the old age, survivors, and disability insurance ("OASDI") tax equal to 6.2 percent of covered wages up to the taxable wage base ($106,800 in 2010); and (2) the Medicare hospital insurance ("HI") tax amount equal to 1.45 percent of covered wages. In addition to the tax on employers, each employee is subject to FICA taxes equal to the amount of tax imposed on the employer (the "employee portion"). The employee portion generally must be withheld and remitted to the Federal government by the employer.

***Self-Employment Contributions Act ("SECA") tax***

As a parallel to FICA taxes, the SECA tax applies to the net income from self-employment of self-employed individuals. The rate of the OASDI portion of SECA taxes is equal to the combined employee and employer OASDI FICA tax rates and applies to self-employment income up to the FICA taxable wage base. Similarly, the rate of the HI portion is the same as the combined employer and

[349] H.R. 2847. The bill originated as an appropriations bill and passed the House on June 18, 2009. The bill passed the Senate with an amendment on November 5, 2009. On December 16, 2009, the House agreed to the Senate amendment with an amendment containing revenue provisions. On February 24, 2010, the Senate concurred in the House amendment to the Senate amendment with an amendment substituting the text of the Hiring Incentives to Restore Employment Act. On March 4, 2010, the House agreed to the Senate amendment with an amendment. On March 17, 2010, the Senate concurred in the House amendment. The President signed the bill on March 18, 2010.

employee HI rates and there is no cap on the amount of self-employment income to which the rate applies.[350]

### *Railroad retirement tax*

The Railroad Retirement System has two main components. Tier I of the system is financed by taxes on employers and employees equal to the Social Security payroll tax and provides qualified railroad retirees (and their qualified spouses, dependents, widows, or widowers) with benefits that are roughly equal to Social Security. Covered railroad workers and their employers pay the Tier I tax instead of the Social Security payroll tax, and most railroad retirees collect Tier I benefits instead of Social Security. Tier II of the system replicates a private pension plan, with employers and employees contributing a certain percentage of pay toward the system to finance defined benefits to eligible railroad retirees (and qualified spouses, dependents, widows, or widowers) upon retirement; however, the Federal Government collects the Tier II payroll contribution and pays out the benefits.

## *Explanation of Provision*

### *In general*

The provision provides relief from the employer share of OASDI taxes (or railroad retirement taxes, if applicable) on wages paid by a qualified employer with respect to certain employment. The provision applies to wages paid beginning on the day after enactment (March 18, 2010) and ending on December 31, 2010. Under a special rule for the first calendar quarter of 2010, the exemption does not apply, but the amount by which the tax would have been reduced but for the special rule is credited to the employer in the second calendar quarter of 2010. The special rule was included in order to ease implementation of the payroll tax exemption.

Covered employment is limited to service performed by a qualified individual: (1) in a trade or business of a qualified employer; or (2) in furtherance of the activities related to the purpose or function constituting the basis of the employer's exemption under sec. 501 (in the case of a qualified employer that is exempt from tax under sec. 501(a)).

### *Qualified employer*

A qualified employer is any employer other than the United States, any State, any local government, or any instrumentality of the foregoing. Notwithstanding the forgoing, a qualified employer includes any employer that is a public higher education institution (as defined in sec. 101(b) of the Higher Education Act of 1965).

[350] For purposes of computing net earnings from self employment, taxpayers are permitted a deduction equal to the product of the taxpayer's earnings (determined without regard to this deduction) and one-half of the sum of the rates for OASDI tax (12.4 percent) and HI tax (2.9 percent), i.e., 7.65 percent of net earnings. This deduction reflects the fact that the FICA rates apply to an employee's wages, which do not include FICA taxes paid by the employer, whereas the self-employed individual's net earnings are economically equivalent to an employee's wages plus the employer share of FICA taxes.

### *Qualified individual*

A qualified individual is any individual who: (1) begins work for a qualified employer after February 3, 2010 and before January 1, 2011; (2) certifies by signed affidavit (under penalties of perjury) that he or she was employed for a total of 40 hours or less during the 60-day period ending on the date such employment begins; (3) is not employed to replace another employee of the employer unless such employee separated from employment voluntarily or for cause;[351] and (4) is not a related party (as defined under rules similar to sec. 51(i)) of the employer).

### *Employer election*

A qualified employer may elect to not have payroll tax forgiveness apply. The election is made in the manner required by the Secretary of the Treasury.

### *Coordination with work opportunity tax credit*

Under the provision, a qualified employer may not receive the work opportunity tax credit on any wages paid to a qualified individual during the one-year period beginning on the hiring date of such individual, if those wages qualify the employer for payroll tax forgiveness under this provision unless the employer makes an election not to have payroll tax forgiveness apply with respect to that individual.

### *Social Security trust funds*

The Federal Old-Age and Survivors Trust Fund and the Federal Disability Insurance Trust Fund will receive transfers from the General Fund of the United States Treasury equal to any reduction in payroll taxes attributable to the payroll tax forgiveness provided under the provision. The amounts will be transferred from the General Fund at such times and in such a manner as to replicate to the extent possible the transfers which would have occurred to the Trust Funds had the provision not been enacted.

## *Effective Date*

The provision applies to wages paid after the date of enactment (March 18, 2010).

---

[351] It is intended that an employer may qualify for the credit when it hires an otherwise qualified individual to replace an individual whose employment was terminated, for cause or due to other facts and circumstances. For example, an employer may qualify for the credit with respect to wages paid pursuant to the reopening of a factory which had been previously closed due to lack of demand for the product being produced (i.e., the employer may qualify by rehiring qualified individuals who had in the past worked for the employer but were terminated when the factory was closed or by hiring qualified individuals who had not previously worked for the employer). In contrast, an employer who terminates the employment of an individual not for cause, but rather to claim the credit with respect to the hiring of the same or another individual is not eligible for the credit under this rule.

## B. Business Credit for Retention of Certain Newly Hired Individuals in 2010 (sec. 102 of the Act and sec. 38(b) of the Code)

### *Present Law*

Present law does not provide a tax credit specifically for the retention of new employees.

However, present law provides for a general business credit consisting of various business tax credits.[352] The general business credit, to the extent it exceeds the relevant tax liability for the taxable year, may be carried back one year (but, in the case of a new credit, not to a taxable year before that credit is first allowable) and carried forward 20 years.[353]

### *Explanation of Provision*

#### *In general*

Under the provision, an employer's general business credit is increased by the lesser of $1,000 or 6.2 percent of wages for each retained worker that satisfies a minimum employment period. Generally, a retained worker is an individual who is a qualified individual as defined under the payroll tax forgiveness provision, above (new Code sec. 3111(d)). However, the credit is available only with respect to such an individual, if the individual: (1) is employed by the employer on any date during the taxable year; (2) continues to be employed by the employer for a period of not less than 52 consecutive weeks; and (3) receives wages for such employment during the last 26 weeks of such period that are least 80-percent of such wages during the first 26 weeks of such period.

The portion of the general business credit attributable to the retention credit may not be carried back to a taxable year that begins prior to the date of enactment of this provision (March 18, 2010).

#### *Treatment of the U.S. possessions*

*Mirror code possessions*[354]

The U.S. Treasury will make a payment to each mirror code possession in an amount equal to the aggregate amount of the credits allowable by reason of the provision to that possession's residents against its income tax. This amount will be determined by the Treasury Secretary based on information provided by the government of the respective possession. For purposes of this payment, a possession is a mirror code possession if the income tax liability of residents of the possession under that possession's income tax system is determined by reference to the U.S. income tax laws as if the possession were the United States.

---

[352] Sec. 38.

[353] Sec. 39.

[354] Possessions with mirror code tax systems are the United States Virgin Islands, Guam, and the Commonwealth of the Northern Mariana Islands.

*Non-mirror code possessions*[355]

To each possession that does not have a mirror code tax system, the U.S. Treasury will make a payment in an amount estimated by the Secretary as being equal to the aggregate credits that would have been allowed to residents of that possession if a mirror code tax system had been in effect in that possession. Accordingly, the amount of each payment to a non-mirror code possession will be an estimate of the aggregate amount of the credits that would be allowed to the possession's residents if the credit provided by the provision to U.S. residents were provided by the possession to its residents. This payment will not be made to any U.S. possession unless that possession has a plan that has been approved by the Secretary under which the possession will promptly distribute the payment to its residents.

*General rules*

No credit against U.S. income taxes is permitted under the provision for any person to whom a credit is allowed against possession income taxes as a result of the provision (for example, under that possession's mirror income tax). Similarly, no credit against U.S. income taxes is permitted for any person who is eligible for a payment under a non-mirror code possession's plan for distributing to its residents the payment described above from the U.S. Treasury.

For purposes of the rebate credit payment, the Commonwealth of Puerto Rico and the Commonwealth of the Northern Mariana Islands are considered possessions of the United States.

For purposes of the rule permitting the Treasury Secretary to disburse appropriated amounts for refunds due from certain credit provisions of the Internal Revenue Code of 1986, the payments required to be made to possessions under the provision are treated in the same manner as a refund due from the recovery rebate credit.

### *Effective Date*

The provision is effective for taxable years ending after the date of enactment (March 18, 2010).

## TITLE II—EXPENSING

### A. Increase in Expensing of Certain Depreciable Business Assets (sec. 201 of the Act and sec. 179 of the Code)

### *Present Law*

A taxpayer that satisfies limitations on annual investment may elect under section 179 to deduct (or "expense") the cost of qualifying property, rather than to recover such costs through depreciation deductions.[356] For taxable years beginning in 2009, the maximum amount that a taxpayer may expense is $250,000 of the cost of qualifying property placed in service for the taxable year. The

[355] Possessions that do not have mirror code tax systems are Puerto Rico and American Samoa.

[356] Additional section 179 incentives are provided with respect to qualified property meeting applicable requirements that is used by a business in an empowerment zone (sec. 1397A), a renewal community (sec. 1400J), or the Gulf Opportunity Zone (sec. 1400N(e)).

$250,000 amount is reduced (but not below zero) by the amount by which the cost of qualifying property placed in service during the taxable year exceeds $800,000.[357] For taxable years beginning in 2010, the maximum amount that a taxpayer may expense is $125,000 of the cost of qualifying property placed in service for the taxable year. The $125,000 amount is reduced (but not below zero) by the amount by which the cost of qualifying property placed in service during the taxable year exceeds $500,000. The $125,000 and $500,000 amounts are indexed for inflation. In general, qualifying property is defined as depreciable tangible personal property that is purchased for use in the active conduct of a trade or business. Off-the-shelf computer software placed in service in taxable years beginning before 2011 is treated as qualifying property.

The amount eligible to be expensed for a taxable year may not exceed the taxable income for a taxable year that is derived from the active conduct of a trade or business (determined without regard to this provision). Any amount that is not allowed as a deduction because of the taxable income limitation may be carried forward to succeeding taxable years (subject to similar limitations). No general business credit under section 38 is allowed with respect to any amount for which a deduction is allowed under section 179. An expensing election is made under rules prescribed by the Secretary.[358] An election under section 179 generally is revocable only with prior consent of the Secretary.[359]

For taxable years beginning in 2011 and thereafter, a taxpayer with a sufficiently small amount of annual investment may elect to deduct up to $25,000 of the cost of qualifying property placed in service for the taxable year. The $25,000 amount is reduced (but not below zero) by the amount by which the cost of qualifying property placed in service during the taxable year exceeds $200,000. The $25,000 and $200,000 amounts are not indexed. In general, qualifying property is defined as depreciable tangible personal property that is purchased for use in the active conduct of a trade or business (not including off-the-shelf computer software).

### *Explanation of Provision*[360]

The Act increases for one year the amount a taxpayer may deduct under section 179. The Act provides that the maximum amount a taxpayer may expense, for taxable years beginning after 2009 and before 2011, is $250,000 of the cost of qualifying property placed in service for the taxable year. The $250,000 amount is re-

---

[357] The temporary $250,000 and $800,000 amounts were enacted in the Economic Stimulus Act of 2008, Pub. L. No. 110–185, and extended for taxable years beginning in 2009 by the American Recovery and Reinvestment Act of 2009, Pub. L. No. 111–5.

[358] Sec. 179(c)(1). Under Treas. Reg. sec. 1.179–5, applicable to property placed in service in taxable years beginning after 2002 and before 2008, a taxpayer is permitted to make or revoke an election under section 179 without the consent of the Commissioner on an amended Federal tax return for that taxable year. This amended return must be filed within the time prescribed by law for filing an amended return for the taxable year. T.D. 9209, July 12, 2005.

[359] Section 179(c)(2) provides that with respect to any taxable year beginning after 2002 and before 2011, a taxpayer may revoke its section 179 election with respect to any property, and such revocation, once made is irrevocable.

[360] The provision was temporarily expanded and extended for taxable years beginning in 2010 and 2011 by section 2021 of the Small Business Jobs Act of 2010, Pub. L. No. 111–240, described in Part Fourteen. The provision was further modified and extended through 2012 by section 402 of the Tax Relief, Unemployment Insurance Reauthorization, and Job Creation Act of 2010, Pub. L. No. 111–312, described in Part Sixteen of this document.

duced (but not below zero) by the amount by which the cost of qualifying property placed in service during the taxable year exceeds $800,000.

### *Effective Date*

The provision is effective for taxable years beginning after December 31, 2009.

## TITLE III—QUALIFED TAX CREDIT BONDS

### A. Refundable Credit for Certain Qualified Tax Credit Bonds (sec. 301 of the Act and secs. 54F and 6431 of the Code)

### *Present Law*

#### *Build America Bonds*

Section 54AA, added to the Code by the American Recovery and Reinvestment Act of 2009 ("ARRA"),[361] permits an issuer to elect to have an otherwise tax-exempt bond, issued prior to January 1, 2011, treated as a "build America bond."[362] In general, build America bonds are taxable governmental bonds, the interest on which is subsidized by the Federal government by means of a tax credit to the holder ("tax-credit build America bonds") or, in the case of certain qualified bonds, a direct payment to the issuer ("direct-pay build America bonds").

*Definition and general requirements*

A build America bond is any obligation (other than a private activity bond) if the interest on such obligation would be (but for section 54AA) excludable from gross income under section 103, and the issuer makes an irrevocable election to have the rules in section 54AA apply.[363] In determining if an obligation would be tax-exempt under section 103, the credit (or the payment discussed below for direct-pay build America bonds) is not treated as a Federal guarantee.[364] Further, for purposes of the restrictions on arbitrage in section 148, the yield on a tax-credit build America bond is determined without regard to the credit;[365] the yield on a direct-pay build America bond is reduced by the payment made pursuant to section 6431.[366] A build America bond does not include any bond if the issue price has more than a de minimis amount of premium over the stated principal amount of the bond.[367]

*Treatment of holders of tax-credit build America bonds*

The holder of a tax-credit build America bond accrues a tax credit in the amount of 35 percent of the interest paid on the interest

[361] Pub. L. No. 111–5.
[362] Sec. 54AA.
[363] Sec. 54AA(d). Subject to updated IRS reporting forms or procedures, an issuer of build America bonds makes the election required by 54AA on its books and records on or before the issue date of such bonds. Notice 2009–26, 2009–16 I.R.B. 833.
[364] Sec. 54AA(d)(2)(A). Section 149(b) provides that section 103(a) shall not apply to any State or local bond if such bond is federally guaranteed.
[365] Sec. 54AA(d)(2)(B).
[366] Sec. 6431(c).
[367] Sec. 54AA(d)(2)(C).

payment dates of the bond during the calendar year.[368] The interest payment date is any date on which the holder of record of the build America bond is entitled to a payment of interest under such bond.[369] The sum of the accrued credits is allowed against regular and alternative minimum tax; unused credit may be carried forward to succeeding taxable years.[370] The credit, as well as the interest paid by the issuer, is included in gross income, and the credit may be stripped under rules similar to those provided in section 54A regarding qualified tax credit bonds.[371] Rules similar to those that apply for S corporations, partnerships and regulated investment companies with respect to qualified tax credit bonds also apply to the credit.[372]

*Special rules for direct-pay build America bonds*

Under the special rule for qualified bonds, in lieu of the tax credit to the holder, the issuer is allowed a credit equal to 35 percent of each interest payment made under such bond.[373] A "qualified bond," that is, a direct-pay build America bond, is any build America bond issued as part of an issue if 100 percent of the excess of available project proceeds of such issue over the amounts in a reasonably required reserve with respect to such issue are to be used for capital expenditures.[374] Direct-pay build America bonds also must be issued before January 1, 2011. The issuer must make an irrevocable election to have the special rule for qualified bonds apply.[375]

The payment by the Secretary is to be made contemporaneously with the interest payment made by the issuer, and may be made either in advance or as reimbursement.[376] In lieu of payment to the issuer, the payment may be made to a person making interest payments on behalf of the issuer.[377]

### *Qualified Tax Credit Bonds*

Qualified tax credit bonds include qualified forestry conservation bonds, new clean renewable energy bonds ("New CREBs"), qualified energy conservation bonds ("QECs"), qualified zone academy bonds issued after the date of enactment of the Tax Extenders and Alternative Minimum Tax Relief Act of 2008 ("QZABs"), and quali-

---

[368] Sec. 54AA(a) and (b). Original issue discount ("OID") is not treated as a payment of interest for purposes of determining the credit under the provision. OID is the excess of an obligation's stated redemption price at maturity over the obligation's issue price (section 1273(a)).

[369] Sec. 54AA(e).

[370] Sec. 54AA(c).

[371] Sec. 54AA(f).

[372] *Ibid.*

[373] Sec. 54AA(g)(1). OID is not treated as a payment of interest for purposes of calculating the refundable credit under the provision.

[374] Sec. 54AA(g). Under Treas. Reg. sec. 150–1(b), capital expenditure means any cost of a type that is properly chargeable to capital account (or would be so chargeable with a proper election or with the application of the definition of placed in service under Treas. Reg. sec. 1.150–2(c)) under general Federal income tax principles. For purposes of applying the "general Federal income tax principles" standard, an issuer should generally be treated as if it were a corporation subject to taxation under subchapter C of chapter 1 of the Code. An example of a capital expenditure would include expenditures made for the purchase of fiber-optic cable to provide municipal broadband service.

[375] Sec. 54AA(g)(2)(B). Subject to updated IRS reporting forms or procedures, an issuer of direct-pay build America bonds makes the election required by section 54AA(g)(2)(B) on its books and records on or before the issue date of such bonds. Notice 2009–26, 2009–16 I.R.B. 833.

[376] Sec. 6431.

[377] Sec. 6431(b)

fied school construction bonds ("QSCBs").[378] Qualified tax credit bonds generally are not interest-bearing obligations. Rather, the taxpayer holding a qualified tax credit bond on a credit allowance date is entitled to a tax credit.[379] The annual amount of the credit is determined by multiplying the bond's applicable credit rate by the outstanding face amount of the bond.[380] The credit rate for an issue of qualified tax credit bonds is determined by the Secretary and is estimated to be a rate that permits issuance of the qualified tax credit bonds without discount and interest cost to the qualified issuer.[381] The Secretary determines credit rates for tax credit bonds based on general assumptions about credit quality of the class of potential eligible issuers and such other factors as the Secretary deems appropriate. The Secretary may determine credit rates based on general credit market yield indices and credit ratings.[382] The credit accrues quarterly,[383] is includible in gross income (as if it were an interest payment on the bond),[384] and can be claimed against regular income tax liability and alternative minimum tax liability.[385] Unused credits may be carried forward to succeeding taxable years.[386] In addition, under regulations prescribed by the Secretary, credits may be stripped.[387]

Qualified tax credit bonds are subject to a maximum maturity limitation. The maximum maturity is the term which the Secretary estimates will result in the present value of the obligation to repay the principal on a qualified tax credit bond being equal to 50 percent of the face amount of such bond.[388] The discount rate used to determine the present value amount is the average annual interest rate of tax-exempt obligations having a term of 10 years or more which are issued during the month the qualified tax credit bonds are issued.

For qualified tax credit bonds, 100 percent of the available project proceeds must be used within the three-year period that begins on the date of issuance.[389] Available project proceeds are the sum of (1) the excess of the proceeds from the sale of the bond issue over issuance costs (not to exceed two percent) and (2) any investment earnings on such sale proceeds.[390] To the extent less than 100 percent of the available project proceeds are used to finance qualified projects during the three-year spending period, bonds will continue to qualify as qualified tax credit bonds if unspent proceeds are used within 90 days from the end of such three-year period to redeem bonds. The three-year spending period may be extended by the Secretary upon the qualified issuer's request demonstrating that the failure to satisfy the three-year requirement is due to rea-

---

[378] Sec. 54A(d).
[379] Sec. 54A(a).
[380] Sec. 54A(b)(2).
[381] Sec. 54A(b)(3). However, for New CREBs and QECs, the applicable credit rate is 70 percent of the otherwise applicable rate.
[382] See Notice 2009–15, 2009–6 I.R.B. 449 (January 22, 2009). Given the differences in credit quality and other characteristics of individual issuers, the Secretary cannot set credit rates in a manner that will allow each issuer to issue tax credit bonds at par.
[383] Sec. 54(A)(b)(1).
[384] Sec. 54A(f).
[385] Sec. 54A(c).
[386] *Ibid.*
[387] Sec. 54A(i).
[388] Sec. 54A(d)(5).
[389] Sec. 54A(d)(2).
[390] Sec. 54A(e)(4).

sonable cause and the projects will continue to proceed with due diligence.

Qualified tax credit bonds also are subject to the arbitrage requirements of section 148 that apply to traditional tax-exempt bonds.[391] Principles under section 148 and the regulations thereunder apply for purposes of determining the yield restriction and arbitrage rebate requirements applicable to qualified tax credit bonds. However, available project proceeds invested during the three-year spending period are not subject to the arbitrage restrictions (i.e., yield restriction and rebate requirements). In addition, amounts invested in a reserve fund are not subject to the arbitrage restrictions to the extent: (1) such fund is funded at a rate not more rapid than equal annual installments; (2) such fund is funded in a manner reasonably expected to result in an amount not greater than an amount necessary to repay the issue; and (3) the yield on such fund is not greater than the average annual interest rate of tax-exempt obligations having a term of 10 years or more that are issued during the month the qualified tax credit bonds are issued.

Issuers of qualified tax credit bonds are required to report issuance to the IRS in a manner similar to the information returns required for tax-exempt bonds.[392] In addition, issuers of qualified tax credit bonds are required to certify that applicable State and local law requirements governing conflicts of interest are satisfied with respect to an issue, and if the Secretary prescribes additional conflicts of interest rules governing the appropriate Members of Congress, Federal, State, and local officials, and their spouses, the issuer must certify compliance with such additional rules with respect to an issue.[393]

*New CREBs*

A New CREB is any bond issued as part of an issue if: (1) 100 percent of the available project proceeds of such issue are to be used for capital expenditures incurred by governmental bodies, public power providers, or cooperative electric companies for one or more qualified renewable energy facilities; (2) the bond is issued by a qualified issuer; and (3) the issuer designates such bond as a New CREB.[394] Qualified renewable energy facilities are facilities that: (1) qualify for the tax credit under section 45 (other than Indian coal and refined coal production facilities), without regard to the placed-in-service date requirements of that section; and (2) are owned by a public power provider, governmental body, or cooperative electric company.[395]

The term "qualified issuers" includes: (1) public power providers; (2) a governmental body; (3) cooperative electric companies; (4) a not-for-profit electric utility that has received a loan or guarantee under the Rural Electrification Act;[396] and (5) clean renewable en-

[391] Sec. 54A(d)(4).
[392] Sec. 54A(d)(3).
[393] Sec. 54A(d)(6).
[394] Sec. 54C(a).
[395] Sec. 54C(d)(1).
[396] Pub. L. No. 74–605.

ergy bond lenders.[397] The term "public power provider" means a State utility with a service obligation, as such terms are defined in section 217 of the Federal Power Act[398] (as in effect on the date of the enactment of this paragraph (March 18, 2010)).[399] A "governmental body" means any State or Indian tribal government, or any political subdivision thereof.[400] The term "cooperative electric company" means a mutual or cooperative electric company (described in section 501(c)(12) or section 1381(a)(2)(C)).[401] A clean renewable energy bond lender means a cooperative that is owned by, or has outstanding loans to, 100 or more cooperative electric companies and is in existence on February 1, 2002 (including any affiliated entity which is controlled by such lender).[402]

There is a national limitation for New CREBs of $2.4 billion.[403] No more than one third of the national limit may be allocated to projects of public power providers, governmental bodies, or cooperative electric companies.[404] Allocations to governmental bodies and cooperative electric companies may be made in the manner the Secretary determines appropriate. Allocations to projects of public power providers shall be made, to the extent practicable, in such manner that the amount allocated to each such project bears the same ratio to the cost of such project as the maximum allocation limitation to projects of public power providers bears to the cost of all such projects.[405]

As with other qualified tax credit bonds, a taxpayer holding New CREBs on a credit allowance date is entitled to a tax credit. However, the credit rate on New CREBs is set by the Secretary at a rate that is 70 percent of the rate that would permit issuance of such bonds without discount and interest cost to the issuer.[406]

*QECs*

A QEC is any bond issued as part of an issue if: (1) 100 percent of the available project proceeds of such issue are to be used for one or more qualified conservation purposes; (2) the bond is issued by a State or local government; and (3) the issuer designates such bond as a QEC.[407]

The term "qualified conservation purpose" means:

1. Capital expenditures incurred for purposes of reducing energy consumption in publicly owned buildings by at least 20 percent; implementing green community programs (including the use of loans, grants, or other repayment mechanisms to im-

---

397 Sec. 54C(d)(6).

398 16 U.S.C. 791a et seq.

399 Sec. 54C(d)(2).

400 Sec. 54C(d)(3).

401 Sec. 54C(d)(4). A mutual or cooperative electric company can be tax exempt under section 501(c)(12) only if 85 percent or more of its income consists of amounts collected from members for the sole purpose of meeting losses and expenses (the "85-percent income test"). Certain types of income, e.g., income from qualified pole rentals, are not taken into account for purposes of the 85-percent income test. Sec. 501(c)(12)(C).

402 Sec. 54C(d)(5).

403 Section 54C(c)(4) increases the original $800 million allocation by $1.6 billion for a total of $2.4 billion.

404 Secs. 54C(c)(2) and (c)(4).

405 Sec. 54C(c)(3).

406 Sec. 54C(b).

407 Sec. 54D(a).

plement such programs);[408] rural development involving the production of electricity from renewable energy resources; or any facility eligible for the production tax credit under section 45 (other than Indian coal and refined coal production facilities);[409]

2. Expenditures with respect to facilities or grants that support research in: (a) development of cellulosic ethanol or other nonfossil fuels; (b) technologies for the capture and sequestration of carbon dioxide produced through the use of fossil fuels; (c) increasing the efficiency of existing technologies for producing nonfossil fuels; (d) automobile battery technologies and other technologies to reduce fossil fuel consumption in transportation; or (e) technologies to reduce energy use in buildings;[410]

3. Mass commuting facilities and related facilities that reduce the consumption of energy, including expenditures to reduce pollution from vehicles used for mass commuting;[411]

4. Demonstration projects designed to promote the commercialization of: (a) green building technology; (b) conversion of agricultural waste for use in the production of fuel or otherwise; (c) advanced battery manufacturing technologies; (d) technologies to reduce peak use of electricity; or (e) technologies for the capture and sequestration of carbon dioxide emitted from combusting fossil fuels in order to produce electricity;[412] and

5. Public education campaigns to promote energy efficiency (other than movies, concerts, and other events held primarily for entertainment purposes).[413]

There is a national limitation on QECs of $3.2 billion.[414] Allocations of QECs are made to the States with sub-allocations to large local governments.[415] Allocations are made to the States according to their respective populations, reduced by any sub-allocations to large local governments (defined below) within the States. Sub-allocations to large local governments shall be an amount of the national QEC limitation that bears the same ratio to the amount of such limitation that otherwise would be allocated to the State in which such large local government is located as the population of such large local government bears to the population of such State. The term “large local government” means any municipality or county if such municipality or county has a population of 100,000 or more. Indian tribal governments also are treated as large local governments for these purposes (without regard to population).

Each State or large local government receiving an allocation of QECs may further allocate issuance authority to issuers within

[408] For example, States may issue QECs to finance retrofits of existing private buildings through loans and/or grants to individual homeowners or businesses, or through other repayment mechanisms. Other repayment mechanisms can include periodic fees assessed on a government bill or utility bill that approximates the energy savings of energy efficiency or conservation retrofits. Retrofits can include heating, cooling, lighting, water-saving, storm water-reducing, or other efficiency measures.

[409] Sec. 54D(f)(1)(A).

[410] Sec. 54D(f)(1)(B).

[411] Sec. 54D(f)(1)(C).

[412] Sec. 54D(f)(1)(D).

[413] Sec. 54D(f)(1)(E).

[414] Sec. 54D(d).

[415] Sec. 54D(e).

such State or large local government. However, any allocations to issuers within the State or large local government shall be made in a manner that results in not less than 70 percent of the allocation of QECs to such State or large local government being used to designate bonds that are not private activity bonds (i.e., the bond cannot meet the private business tests or the private loan test of section 141).[416]

As with other qualified tax credit bonds, the taxpayer holding QECs on a credit allowance date is entitled to a tax credit. However, the credit rate on the bonds is set by the Secretary at a rate that is 70 percent of the rate that would permit issuance of such bonds without discount and interest cost to the issuer.[417]

*QZABs*

A QZAB is any bond issued as part of an issue if: (1) 100 percent of the available project proceeds of such issue are to be used for a qualified purpose with respect to a qualified zone academy established by an eligible local education agency; (2) the bond is issued by a State or local government within the jurisdiction of which such academy is located; (3) the issuer designates such bond as a QZAB and certifies that (a) the private business contribution requirement will be met and (b) it has the written approval of the eligible local education agency for such bond issuance.[418]

A "qualified purpose" is: (1) rehabilitating or repairing the public school facility in which the qualified zone academy is established; (2) providing equipment for use at such academy; (3) developing course materials for education to be provided at such academy; and (4) training teachers and other school personnel in such academy.[419]

A public school (or academic program within a public school) is a "qualified zone academy" if: (1) the public school or program provides education and training below the college level; (2) the public school or program is designed in cooperation with business to enhance the academic curriculum, increase graduation and employment rates, and better prepare students for the rigors of college and the workforce; (3) students in such public school or program will be subject to the same academic standards and assessments as other students educated by the eligible local education agency; (4) the comprehensive education plan of such public school or program is approved by the eligible local education agency; and (5) either (a) the public school is located in an empowerment zone or enterprise community designated under the Code, or (b) it is reasonably expected that at least 35 percent of the students at the school will be eligible for free or reduced-cost lunches under the school lunch program established under the National School Lunch Act.[420]

In general, the private business contribution requirement is met where private entities have promised to contribute to the qualified

[416] Sec. 54D(e)(3). In the case of any bond used for the purpose of providing grants, loans or other repayment mechanisms for capital expenditures to implement green community programs, such bond shall not be treated as a private activity bond for purposes of determining whether this requirement is met. Sec. 54D(e)(4).

[417] Sec. 54D(b).

[418] Sec. 54E(a).

[419] Sec. 54E(d)(3).

[420] Sec. 54E(d)(1); Pub. L. No. 79–396.

zone academy certain equipment, technical assistance or training, employee services, or other property or services with a present value (as of the date of the issue) equal to at least 10 percent of the bond proceeds.[421]

There is a national QZAB limitation for each calendar year. For 2009 and 2010, the limitation is $1.4 billion.[422] The limitation is allocated by the Secretary among the States on the basis of their respective populations of individuals below the poverty line; each State education agency then make an allocation of its shares of the national limitation to qualified zone academies in the State.[423] Unused limitation may be carried only to the first two years following the unused limitation year.[424] For this purpose, a limitation amount shall be treated as used on a first-in first-out basis.

*QSCBs*

*In general*

QSCBs must meet three requirements: (1) 100 percent of the available project proceeds of the bond issue must be used for the construction, rehabilitation, or repair of a public school facility or for the acquisition of land on which such a bond-financed facility is to be constructed; (2) the bond must be issued by a State or local government within the jurisdiction of which such school is located; and (3) the issuer must designate such bonds as a QSCB.[425]

*National limitation*

There is a national limitation on qualified school construction bonds of $11 billion for calendar years 2009 and 2010, respectively.[426]

*Allocation to the States*

The national limitation is tentatively allocated among the States in proportion to respective amounts each such State is eligible to receive under section 1124 of the Elementary and Secondary Education Act of 1965[427] for the most recent fiscal year ending before such calendar year. Forty percent of the limitation is then allocated among the largest school districts, and the amount each State is allocated under the tentative allocation formula is then reduced by the amount received by any local large educational agency within the State.[428] The limitation amount allocated to a State is allocated by the State to issuers within such State.

For allocation purposes, a "State" includes the District of Columbia and any possession of the United States. The provision provides a special rule for allocation for possessions of the United States other than Puerto Rico under the national limitation for States.[429] Under this special rule, an allocation to a possession other than Puerto Rico is made on the basis of the respective populations of

[421] Sec. 54E(b).
[422] Sec. 54E(c)(1).
[423] Sec. 54E(c)(2).
[424] Sec. 54E(c)(4).
[425] Sec. 54F(a).
[426] Sec. 54F(c).
[427] Pub. L. No. 89–10.
[428] Sec. 54F(d).
[429] Sec. 54F(d)(3).

individuals below the poverty line (as defined by the Office of Management and Budget) rather than respective populations of children aged five through seventeen. This special allocation reduces the State allocation share of the national limitation otherwise available for allocation among the States. Under another special rule, the Secretary of the Interior may allocate $200 million of school construction bonds for 2009 and 2010, respectively, to Indian schools.[430] This special allocation for Indian schools is to be used for purposes of the construction, rehabilitation, and repair of schools funded by the Bureau of Indian Affairs. For purposes of such allocations Indian tribal governments are qualified issuers. The special allocation for Indian schools does not reduce the State allocation share of the national limitation otherwise available for allocation among the States.

If an amount allocated under this allocation to the States is unused for a calendar year it may be carried forward by the State to the next calendar year.[431]

*Allocation to large school districts*

Forty percent of the national limitation is allocated among large local educational agencies in proportion to the respective amounts each agency received under section 1124 of the Elementary and Secondary Education Act of 1965 for the most recent fiscal year ending before such calendar year.[432] With respect to a calendar year, the term large local educational agency means any local educational agency if such agency is: (1) among the 100 local educational agencies with the largest numbers of children aged five through 17 from families living below the poverty level, or (2) one of not more than 25 local educational agencies (other than in (1), immediately above) that the Secretary of Education determines are in particular need of assistance, based on a low level of resources for school construction, a high level of enrollment growth, or other such factors as the Secretary of Education deems appropriate. If any amount allocated to large local educational agency is unused for a calendar year the agency may reallocate such amount to the State in which the agency is located.

### *Explanation of Provision*

For bonds originally issued after the date of enactment, the provision allows an issuer of New CREBS, QECs, QZABs, or QSCBs to make an irrevocable election on or before the issue date of such bonds to receive a payment under section 6431 in lieu of providing a tax credit to the holder of the bonds.[433] The payment to the issuer on each payment date is equal to the lesser of (1) the amount of interest payable under such bond on such date, or (2) the amount of interest which would have been payable under such bond on such date if such interest were determined by the Secretary at the applicable credit rate under section 54A(b)(3) with re-

[430] Sec. 54F(d)(4).
[431] Sec. 54F(e).
[432] Sec. 54F(d)(2).
[433] It is anticipated that the election procedure will be similar to the procedure for making the election required under Sec. 54AA(g) for a direct-pay build America bond. See Notice 2009–26, 2009–16 I.R.B. 833.

spect to such bond. In the case of a New CREB or QEC, the amount determined pursuant to (2), immediately above, is 70 percent of such amount, without regard to sections 54C(b) and 54D(b). Bonds for which the election is made count against the national limitation in the same way that they would if no election were made.

The provision also adds a technical correction relating to QSCBs. The technical correction provides first that the limitation amount allocated to a State is to be allocated to issuers within such State by the State education agency (or such other agency as is authorized under State law to make such allocation). In addition, the technical correction provides that the rule in section 54F(e), permitting the carryover of unused QSCB limitation by a State or Indian tribal government, shall also apply to the 40 percent of QSCB limitation that is allocated among the largest school districts.

### *Effective Date*

The provision is effective for bonds issued after the date of enactment (March 18, 2010). The technical correction is effective as if it were included in section 1521 of ARRA.

# TITLE IV—EXTENSION OF CURRENT SURFACE TRANSPORTATON PROGRAMS

## A. Revenue Provisions Relating to the Highway Trust Fund (secs. 441–445 of the Act and secs. 9503 and 9504 of the Code)

### *Present Law*

#### *Extension of expenditure authority*

The Highway Trust Fund was established in 1956. It is divided into two accounts, a Highway Account and a Mass Transit Account, each of which is the funding source for specific transportation programs. The Highway Trust Fund is funded by taxes on motor fuels (gasoline, kerosene, diesel fuel, and certain alternative fuels), a tax on heavy vehicle tires, a retail sales tax on certain trucks, trailers and tractors, and an annual use tax for heavy highway vehicles. The current expenditure authority for the Highway Trust Fund generally expires on March 1, 2010.[434]

The Sport Fish Restoration and Boating Trust Fund is the funding source for certain coastal wetlands preservation, recreational boating safety, sport fish restoration and other programs. The current expenditure authority for the Sport Fish Restoration and Boating Trust Fund generally expires on March 1, 2010.

#### *Crediting of interest*

With respect to trust funds established by the Code, the Code requires that the Secretary invest the balances not needed to meet current withdrawals in interest-bearing obligations of the United States. The interest is credited to the respective Trust Fund.[435] However, as of September 30, 1998, the ability of the Highway

---

[434] The Department of Defense Appropriations Act of 2010, Pub. L. No. 111–118, Division B, sec. 1008 (2009).

[435] Sec. 9602(b).

Trust Fund to earn interest on its unexpended balances was terminated.[436]

### *Transfers from the Highway Trust Fund to the General Fund for certain payments and credits*

Under present law, revenues from the highway excise taxes generally are dedicated to the Highway Trust Fund. However, under section 9503(c)(2) of the Code, certain transfers are made from the Highway Trust Fund into the General Fund, relating to amounts paid in respect of gasoline used on farms, amounts paid in respect of gasoline used for certain nonhighway purposes or by local transit systems, amounts relating to fuels not used for taxable purposes, and income tax credits for certain uses of fuels.

## *Explanation of Provision*

### *Extension of expenditure authority*

The provision extends expenditure authority for the Highway Trust Fund through December 31, 2010. It also extends the expenditure authority for the Sport Fish Restoration and Boating Trust Fund through December 31, 2010.

### *Crediting of interest*

*Restoration of forgone interest*

The provision transfers $19.5 billion to the Highway Trust Fund, of that amount $14.7 billion is appropriated to the Highway Account of the Highway Trust Fund and $4.8 billion is appropriated to the Mass Transit Account. The amounts appropriated pursuant to this provision remain available without fiscal year limitation.

*Repeal of provision prohibiting the crediting of interest*

The provision repeals the requirement that obligations held by the Highway Trust Fund not be interest-bearing. The provision permits amounts in the Trust Fund to be invested in interest-bearing obligations of the United States and have the interest be credited to, and form a part of, the Highway Trust Fund. Thus, the Highway Trust Fund will accrue interest under the provision.

### *Termination of transfers from the Highway Trust Fund for certain repayments and credits*

The provision repeals section 9503(c)(2), eliminating the requirement that the Highway Trust Fund reimburse the General Fund for credits and payments related to nontaxable uses.

## *Effective Date*

The provisions are generally effective on the date of enactment (March 18, 2010). The expenditure authority provisions are effective September 30, 2009. The provision terminating transfers from the Highway Trust Fund is effective for transfers relating to amounts paid and credits allowed after the date of enactment (March 18, 2010).

---

[436] Sec. 9503(f)(2).

# TITLE V—OFFSET PROVISIONS

## A. Foreign Account Tax Compliance

### *1. Reporting on certain foreign accounts (sec. 501 of the Act and new secs. 1471–1474 and sec. 6611 of the Code)*

#### *Present Law*

#### *Withholding on payments to foreign persons*

Payments of U.S.-source fixed or determinable annual or periodical ("FDAP") income, including interest, dividends, and similar types of investment income, that are made to foreign persons are subject to U.S. withholding tax at a 30-percent rate, unless the withholding agent can establish that the beneficial owner of the amount is eligible for an exemption from withholding or a reduced rate of withholding under an income tax treaty.[437] The term "FDAP income" includes all items of gross income,[438] except gains on sales of property (including market discount on bonds and option premiums).[439]

Interest is derived from U.S. sources if it is paid by the United States or any agency or instrumentality thereof, a State or any political subdivision thereof, or the District of Columbia. Interest is also from U.S. sources if it is paid by a resident or a domestic corporation on a bond, note, or other interest-bearing obligation.[440] Dividend income is sourced by reference to the payor's place of incorporation.[441] Thus, dividends paid by a domestic corporation are generally treated as entirely U.S.-source income. Similarly, dividends paid by a foreign corporation are generally treated as entirely foreign-source income. Rental income is sourced by reference to the location or place of use of the leased property.[442] The nationality or the country of residence of the lessor or lessee does not affect the source of rental income. Rental income from property located or used in the United States (or from any interest in such property) is U.S.-source income, regardless of whether the property is real or personal, intangible or tangible. Royalties are sourced in the place of use (or the privilege of use) of the property for which the royalties are paid.[443] This source rule applies to royalties for the use of either tangible or intangible property, including patents, copyrights, secret processes, formulas, goodwill, trademarks, trade names, and franchises.

---

[437] Secs. 871, 881, 1441, 1442; Treas. Reg. sec. 1.1441–1(b). For purposes of the withholding tax rules applicable to payments to nonresident alien individuals and foreign corporations, a withholding agent is defined broadly to include any U.S. or foreign person that has the control, receipt, custody, disposal, or payment of an item of income of a foreign person subject to withholding. Treas. Reg. sec. 1.1441–7(a).

[438] Although technically insurance premiums paid to a foreign insurer or reinsurer are FDAP income, they are exempt from withholding under Treas. Reg. sec. 1.1441–2(a)(7) if the insurance contract is subject to the excise tax under section 4371.

[439] Treas. Reg. sec. 1.1441–2(b)(1)(i), –2(b)(2). However, gain on a sale or exchange of section 306 stock of a domestic corporation is FDAP income to the extent section 306(a) treats the gain as ordinary income. Treas. Reg. sec. 1.306–3(h).

[440] Sec. 861(a)(1); Treas. Reg. sec. 1.861–2(a)(1). Interest paid by the U.S. branch of a foreign corporation is also treated as U.S.-source interest under section 884(f)(1).

[441] Secs. 861(a)(2), 862(a)(2).

[442] Sec. 861(a)(4).

[443] *Ibid.*

The principal statutory exemptions from the 30-percent withholding tax apply to interest on bank deposits, portfolio interest, and gains derived from the sale of property. Since 1984, the United States has not imposed withholding tax on portfolio interest received by a nonresident individual or foreign corporation from sources within the United States.[444] Portfolio interest includes, generally, any interest (including original issue discount) other than interest received by a 10-percent shareholder,[445] certain contingent interest,[446] interest received by a controlled foreign corporation from a related person,[447] and interest received by a bank on an extension of credit made pursuant to a loan agreement entered into in the ordinary course of its trade or business.[448]

In the case of interest paid on a debt obligation that is in registered form,[449] the portfolio interest exemption is available only to the extent that the U.S. person otherwise required to withhold tax (the "withholding agent") has received a statement made by the beneficial owner of the obligation (or a securities clearing organization, bank, or other financial institution that holds customers' securities in the ordinary course of its trade or business) that the beneficial owner is not a U.S. person.[450]

Interest on deposits with foreign branches of domestic banks and domestic savings and loan associations is not treated as U.S.-source income and is thus exempt from U.S. withholding tax (regardless of whether the recipient is a U.S. or foreign person).[451] In addition, interest on bank deposits, deposits with domestic savings and loan associations, and certain amounts held by insurance companies are

---

[444] Secs. 871(h), 881(c). Congress believed that the imposition of a withholding tax on portfolio interest paid on debt obligations issued by U.S. persons might impair the ability of domestic corporations to raise capital in the Eurobond market (i.e., the global market for U.S. dollar-denominated debt obligations). Congress also anticipated that repeal of the withholding tax on portfolio interest would allow the Treasury Department direct access to the Eurobond market. See Joint Committee on Taxation, *General Explanation of the Revenue Provisions of the Deficit Reduction Act of 1984* (JCS–41–84), December 31, 1984, pp. 391–92.

[445] Sec. 871(h)(3). A 10-percent shareholder includes any person who owns 10 percent or more of the total combined voting power of all classes of stock of the corporation (in the case of a corporate obligor), or 10 percent or more of the capital or profits interest of the partnership (in the case of a partnership obligor). The attribution rules of section 318 apply for this purpose, with certain modifications.

[446] Sec. 871(h)(4). Contingent interest generally includes any interest if the amount of such interest is determined by reference to any receipts, sales, or other cash flow of the debtor or a related person; any income or profits of the debtor or a related person; any change in value of any property of the debtor or a related person; any dividend, partnership distributions, or similar payments made by the debtor or a related person; and any other type of contingent interest identified by Treasury regulation. Certain exceptions also apply.

[447] Sec. 881(c)(3)(C). A related person includes, among other things, an individual owning more than 50 percent of the stock of the corporation by value, a corporation that is a member of the same controlled group (defined using a 50-percent common ownership test), a partnership if the same persons own more than 50 percent in value of the stock of the corporation and more than 50 percent of the capital interests in the partnership, any U.S. shareholder (as defined in section 951(b) and generally including any U.S. person who owns 10 percent or more of the voting stock of the corporation), and certain persons related to such a U.S. shareholder.

[448] Sec. 881(c)(3)(A).

[449] An obligation is treated as in registered form if: (1) it is registered as to both principal and interest with the issuer (or its agent) and transfer of the obligation may be effected only by surrender of the old instrument and either the reissuance by the issuer of the old instrument to the new holder or the issuance by the issuer of a new instrument to the new holder; (2) the right to principal and stated interest on the obligation may be transferred only through a book entry system maintained by the issuer or its agent; or (3) the obligation is registered as to both principal and interest with the issuer or its agent and may be transferred through both of the foregoing methods. Treas. Reg. sec. 5f.103–1(c).

[450] Sec. 871(h)(2)(B), (5); Treas. Reg. sec. 1.871–14(e). This certification of non-U.S. ownership most commonly is made on an IRS Form W–8. This certification is not valid if the Secretary determines that statements from the person making the certification do not meet certain requirements.

[451] Sec. 861(a)(1)(B); Treas. Reg. sec. 1.1441–1(b)(4)(iii).

not subject to the U.S. withholding tax when paid to a foreign person, unless the interest is effectively connected with a U.S. trade or business of the recipient.[452] Similarly, interest and original issue discount on certain short-term obligations is also exempt from U.S. withholding tax when paid to a foreign person.[453] Additionally, there is no information reporting with respect to payments of such amounts.[454]

Gains derived from the sale of property by a nonresident alien individual or foreign corporation generally are exempt from U.S. tax, unless they are or are treated as effectively connected with the conduct of a U.S. trade or business. Gains derived by a nonresident alien individual generally are subject to U.S. taxation only if the individual is present in the United States for 183 days or more during the taxable year.[455] Foreign corporations are subject to tax with respect to certain gains on disposal of timber, coal, or domestic iron ore and certain gains from contingent payments made in connection with sales or exchanges of patents, copyrights, goodwill, trademarks, and similar intangible property.[456] Gain from the disposition of certain U.S. real property interests (which include interests in U.S. real property holding corporations) are treated as effectively connected with a U.S. trade or business.[457] Special rules apply in the case of interests in real estate investment trusts or interests in regulated investment companies that are or which would be, if not for certain exceptions, U.S. real property holding corporations.[458] Most gains realized by foreign investors on the sale of portfolio investment securities thus are exempt from U.S. taxation.

The 30-percent withholding tax may be reduced or eliminated by a tax treaty between the United States and the country in which the recipient of income otherwise subject to withholding is resident. Most U.S. income tax treaties provide a zero rate of withholding tax on interest payments (other than certain interest the amount of which is determined by reference to certain income items or other amounts of the debtor or a related person). Most U.S. income tax treaties also reduce the rate of withholding on dividends to 15 percent (in the case of portfolio dividends) and to five percent (in the case of "direct investment" dividends paid to a 10 percent-or-

---

[452] Secs. 871(i)(2)(A), 881(d); Treas. Reg. sec. 1.1441–1(b)(4)(ii). If the bank deposit interest is effectively connected with a U.S. trade or business, it is subject to regular U.S. income tax rather than withholding tax.

[453] Secs. 871(g)(1)(B), 881(a)(3); Treas. Reg. sec. 1.1441–1(b)(4)(iv).

[454] Treas. Reg. sec. 1.1461–1(c)(2)(ii)(A), (B). However, Treasury regulations require a bank to report interest if the recipient is a resident of Canada and the deposit is maintained at an office in the United States. Treas. Reg. secs. 1.6049–4(b)(5), 1.6049–8. This reporting is required to comply with the obligations of the United States under the U.S.-Canada income tax treaty. T.D. 8664, 1996–1 C.B. 292. In 2001, the IRS and the Treasury Department issued proposed regulations that would require annual reporting to the IRS of U.S. bank deposit interest paid to any foreign individual. 66 Fed. Reg. 3925 (Jan. 17, 2001). The 2001 proposed regulations were withdrawn in 2002 and replaced with proposed regulations that would require reporting with respect to payments made only to residents of certain specified countries (Australia, Denmark, Finland, France, Germany, Greece, Ireland, Italy, the Netherlands, New Zealand, Norway, Portugal, Spain, Sweden, and the United Kingdom). 67 Fed. Reg. 50,386 (Aug. 2, 2002). The proposed regulations have not been finalized.

[455] Sec. 871(a)(2). In most cases, however, an individual satisfying this presence test will be treated as a U.S. resident under section 7701(b)(3), and thus will be subject to full residence-based U.S. income taxation.

[456] Secs. 881(a), 631(b), (c).

[457] Sec. 897. Section 1445 imposes withholding requirements with respect to such dispositions.

[458] See sec. 897(h).

greater shareholder).[459] For royalties, the U.S. withholding rate is typically reduced to five percent or to zero. In each case, the reduced withholding rate is available only to a beneficial owner who is treated as a resident of the treaty country within the meaning of the treaty and satisfies all other treaty requirements including any applicable limitation on benefits provisions of the treaty.

***Refund or credits of taxes withheld from foreign persons***

A withholding agent that makes payments of U.S.-source amounts to a foreign person is required to report those payments, including any amounts of U.S. tax withheld, to the IRS on IRS Forms 1042 and 1042–S by March 15 of the calendar year following the year in which the payment is made.[460] To the extent that the withholding agent deducts and withholds an amount, the withheld tax is credited to the recipient of the income.[461] If the agent withholds more than is required, and results in an overpayment of tax, the excess may be refunded to the recipient of the income upon filing of a timely claim for refund.

*Payment of tax*

The date an amount is paid is relevant for determining the limitations period in which to claim a refund, the amount of refund available,[462] and the period for which interest may accrue on any overpayment.[463] An amount that is withheld, paid or credited as an estimate or deposit of tax generally does not count as the payment of tax until applied to a specific tax liability. To the extent that amounts previously withheld, paid or credited as an estimate or deposit of tax are applied to the tax liability for a year, they are deemed to have been paid as of the last day prescribed for payment of the tax, for both the recipient of the income[464] and the withholding agent.[465] Amounts that are refunded, credited to other periods, or offset against other liabilities are not considered as paid for this purpose.[466] Any amount that was previously paid but has been credited to a later year is considered credited on the last day prescribed for the payment of tax.[467]

---

[459] A number of recent U.S. income tax treaties eliminate withholding tax on dividends paid to a majority (typically 80-percent or greater) shareholder, including the present treaties with Australia, Belgium, Denmark, Finland, Germany, Japan, Mexico, the Netherlands, Sweden, and the United Kingdom.

[460] Treas. Reg. sec. 1.1461–1(b), (c). IRS Form 1042, "Annual Withholding Tax Return for U.S. Source Income of Foreign Persons," is the IRS form on which a withholding agent reports a summary of the total U.S.-source income paid and withholding tax withheld on foreign persons for the year. IRS Form 1042–S, "Foreign Person's U.S. Source Income Subject to Withholding," is the IRS form on which a withholding agent reports, to the foreign person and the IRS, a foreign person's U.S.-source income that is subject to reporting.

[461] Sec. 1462.

[462] See secs. 6511(a) (prescribing the period within which a claim must be filed) and 6511(b)(2) (limiting the amount that can be recovered if a claim is not filed within three years of filing a return). If a return is not filed, a claim for refund of any tax paid must be filed within two years of payment.

[463] Ses. 6611(b)(2), (d).

[464] Sec. 6513(b)(3).

[465] Sec. 6513(c)(2).

[466] Sec. 6513(d).

[467] Sec. 6513(d).

*Interest on overpayments*

The IRS is generally required to pay interest to a taxpayer whenever there is an overpayment of tax.[468] An overpayment of tax exists whenever more than the correct amount of tax is paid as of the last date prescribed for the payment of the tax. The last date prescribed for the payment of the income tax is the original due date of the return.[469] However, no interest is required to be paid by the IRS if it refunds or credits the amount due within 45 days of the filing of the return.[470] Notwithstanding these general rules, if a required return on which the payment should have been reported is either not filed, or is filed late, no interest on the overpayment accrues for any period prior to the filing of the return.[471]

Different interest rates are provided for the payment of interest depending upon the type of taxpayer, whether the interest relates to an underpayment or overpayment, and the size of the underpayment or overpayment. Interest on both underpayments and overpayments is compounded daily.[472] A special net interest rate of zero applies in situations where interest is both payable and allowable on offsetting amounts of overpayment and underpayment.[473] For individuals, interest on both underpayments and overpayments accrues at a rate equal to the short term applicable Federal rate ("AFR") plus three percentage points.[474] Interest on corporate overpayments generally accrues at a rate equal to the short term AFR plus two percentage points, unless the overpayment exceeds $10,000 in which case interest accrues at a rate equal to the short term AFR plus one-half percentage point.

*Period of overpayment*

If the overpayment is to be refunded to the taxpayer, interest accrues on the overpayment from the later of the due date of the return or the date the payment is made until a date that is not more than 30 days before the date of the refund check.[475] If the overpayment is to be credited or offset against some other liability, interest will accrue until the date it is so credited or offset.

A payment is not considered made by the taxpayer earlier than the time the taxpayer files a return showing the liability. However, in *MNOPF Trustees, Ltd.* v. *United States*,[476] the Federal Circuit held that overpayment interest accrued on the taxes unnecessarily withheld from the date that the withholdings were paid to the Service, because MNOPF was a tax-exempt organization, and, therefore, was not required to file tax returns. As a result, the court rejected arguments by the government that interest commenced no earlier than the filing of the refund claims. The court reasoned that sections 6611(d) and 6513(b)(3) did not apply because those sections only relate to taxable income and the taxpayer was exempt from Federal taxation. Instead, the court held that the or-

[468] Sec. 6611.
[469] Sec. 6601(b).
[470] Sec. 6611(e).
[471] Sec. 6611(b)(3).
[472] Sec. 6622.
[473] Sec. 6621(d).
[474] Sec. 6621.
[475] Sec. 6611(b)(2).
[476] 123 F.3d 1460, 1465 (Fed. Cir. 1997).

ganization's overpayment was deemed paid, pursuant to section 6611(b)(2), on the date the withholding agent filed the returns reporting the withheld taxes.

No interest accrues on an overpayment if the IRS makes the refund within 45 days of the later of the filing or the due date of the return showing the refund. If the IRS fails to make the refund within such 45-day period, interest is required to be paid for the entire period of the overpayment. For example, an individual taxpayer files his return on April 15, properly showing a refund due of $10,000. If the IRS pays the refund within 45 days, no interest on the overpayment will be required. However, if the IRS does not pay the refund until the 46th day, interest will be required from April 15.

***Certification of foreign status and reporting by U.S. withholding agents***

The U.S. withholding tax rules are administered through a system of self-certification. Thus, a nonresident investor seeking to obtain withholding tax relief for U.S.-source investment income typically must provide a certification, on IRS Form W–8 to the withholding agent to establish foreign status and eligibility for an exemption or reduced rate. Provision of the IRS Form W–8 also establishes an exemption from the rules that apply to many U.S. persons governing information reporting on IRS Form 1099 and backup withholding (discussed below).[477]

There are four relevant types of IRS Forms W–8.[478] Three of these forms are designed to be provided to the withholding agent by the beneficial owner of a payment of U.S.-source income:[479] (1) the IRS Form W–8BEN, which is provided by a beneficial owner of U.S.-source non-effectively-connected income; (2) the IRS Form W–8ECI, which is provided by a beneficial owner of U.S.-source effectively-connected income;[480] and (3) the IRS Form W–8EXP, which is provided by a beneficial owner of U.S.-source income that is an exempt organization or foreign government.[481] Each of these forms requires that the beneficial owner provide its name and address and certify that the beneficial owner is not a U.S. person. The IRS Form W–8BEN also includes a certification of eligibility for treaty benefits (for completion where applicable). All certifications on IRS Forms W–8 are made under penalties of perjury.

The fourth type of IRS Form W–8 is the IRS Form W–8IMY, which is provided by a payee that receives a payment of U.S.-

[477] See Treas. Reg. sec. 1.1441–1(b)(5).

[478] A fifth type of IRS Form W–8, the W–8CE, is filed to provide the payor with notice of a taxpayer's expatriation.

[479] The United States imposes tax on the beneficial owner of income, not its formal recipient. For example, if a U.S. citizen owns securities that are held in "street" name at a brokerage firm, that U.S. citizen (and not the brokerage firm nominee) is treated as the beneficial owner of the securities. A corporation (and not its shareholders) ordinarily is treated as the beneficial owner of the corporation's income. Similarly, a foreign complex trust ordinarily is treated as the beneficial owner of income that it receives, and a U.S. beneficiary or grantor is not subject to tax on that income unless and until he receives a distribution.

[480] The IRS Form W–8ECI requires that the beneficial owner specify the items of income to which the form is intended to apply and certify that those amounts are effectively connected with the conduct of a trade or business in the United States and includible in the beneficial owner's gross income for the taxable year.

[481] The IRS Form W–8EXP requires that the beneficial owner certify as to its qualification as a foreign government, an international organization, a foreign central bank of issue or a foreign tax-exempt organization, in each case meeting certain requirements.

source income as an intermediary for the beneficial owner of that income. The intermediary's IRS Form W–8IMY must be accompanied by an IRS Form W–8BEN, W–8EXP, or W–8ECI, as applicable,[482] furnished by the beneficial owner, unless the intermediary is a qualified intermediary ("QI"), a withholding foreign partnership, or a withholding foreign trust. The rules applicable to qualified intermediaries are discussed below. A withholding foreign partnership or trust is a foreign partnership or trust that has entered into an agreement with the IRS to collect appropriate IRS Forms W–8 from its partners or beneficiaries and act as a U.S. withholding agent with respect to those persons.[483]

***Information reporting and backup withholding with respect to U.S. persons***

Every person engaged in a trade or business must file with the IRS an information return on IRS Form 1099 (or, for wages or other compensation, on IRS Form W–2) for payments of certain amounts totaling at least $600 that it makes to another person in the course of its trade or business.[484] Detailed rules are provided for the reporting of various types of investment income, including interest, dividends, and gross proceeds from brokered transactions (such as a sale of stock).[485] In general, the requirement to file IRS Form 1099 applies with respect to amounts paid to U.S. persons and is linked to the backup withholding rules of section 3406. Thus, to avoid backup withholding, a U.S. payee (other than exempt recipients, including corporations and financial institutions) of interest, dividends, or gross proceeds generally must furnish to the payor an IRS Form W–9 providing that person's name and taxpayer identification number.[486] That information is then used to complete the IRS Form 1099.

If an IRS Form W–9 is not provided by a U.S. payee (other than payees exempt from reporting), the payor is required to impose a backup withholding tax of 28 percent of the gross amount of the payment.[487] The backup withholding tax may be credited by the payee against regular income tax liability.[488] This combination of reporting and backup withholding is designed to ensure that U.S. persons not exempt from reporting pay tax with respect to investment income, either by providing the IRS with the information that it needs to audit payment of the tax or, in the absence of such information, requiring collection of the tax on payment.

As described above, amounts paid to foreign persons are generally exempt from information reporting on IRS Form 1099. Foreign persons are subject to a separate information reporting requirement linked to the nonresident withholding provisions of chapter 3 of the Code.

---

[482] In limited cases, the intermediary may furnish documentary evidence, other than the IRS Form W–8, of the status of the beneficial owner.

[483] Rev. Proc. 2003–64, 2003–32 I.R.B. 306 (July 10, 2003), provides procedures for qualification as a withholding foreign partnership or withholding foreign trust in addition to providing model withholding agreements.

[484] Sec. 6041; Treas. Reg. secs. 1.6041–1, 1.6041–2.

[485] See secs. 6042 (dividends), 6045 (broker reporting), 6049 (interest), and the corresponding Treasury regulations.

[486] See Treas. Reg. secs. 31.3406(d)–1, 31.3406(h)–3.

[487] Sec. 3406(a)(1).

[488] Sec. 3406(h)(10).

In the case of U.S. source investment income, the information reporting, backup withholding and nonresident withholding rules apply broadly to any financial institution or other payor, including foreign financial institutions.[489] As a practical matter, however, these reporting and withholding requirements are difficult to enforce with respect to foreign financial institutions, unless these institutions have some connection to the United States, e.g., the institution is a foreign subsidiary of a U.S. financial institution, or the foreign financial institution is doing business in the United States. Moreover, to the extent that these rules apply to foreign financial institutions, the rules may also be modified by QI agreements between the institutions and the IRS, as described below.

***The qualified intermediary program***

A QI is defined as a foreign financial institution or a foreign clearing organization, other than a U.S. branch or U.S. office of such institution or organization, or a foreign branch of a U.S. financial institution that has entered into a withholding and reporting agreement (a "QI agreement") with the IRS.[490]

A foreign financial institution that becomes a QI is not required to forward beneficial ownership information with respect to its customers to a U.S. financial institution or other withholding agent of U.S.-source investment-type income to establish the customer's eligibility for an exemption from, or reduced rate of, U.S. withholding tax.[491] Instead, the QI is permitted to establish for itself the eligibility of its customers for an exemption or reduced rate, based on an IRS Form W–8 or W–9, or other specified documentary evidence, and information as to residence obtained under the know-your-customer rules to which the QI is subject in its home jurisdiction as approved by the IRS or as specified in the QI agreement.[492] The QI certifies as to eligibility on behalf of its customers, and provides withholding rate pool information to the U.S. withholding agent as to the portion of each payment that qualifies for an exemption or reduced rate of withholding.

The IRS has published a model QI agreement for foreign financial institutions.[493] A prospective QI must submit an application to

[489] See Treas. Reg. secs. 1.1441–7(a) (definition of withholding agent includes foreign persons), 31.3406(a)–2 (payor for backup withholding purposes means the person (the payor) required to file information returns for payments of interest, dividends, and gross proceeds (and other amounts)), 1.6049–4(a)(2) (definition of payor for interest reporting purposes does not exclude foreign persons), 1.6042–3(b)(2) (payor for dividend reporting purposes has the same meaning as for interest reporting purposes), 1.6045–1(a)(1) (brokers required to report include foreign persons). But see Treas. Reg. secs. 1.6049–5(b) (exception for interest from sources outside the U.S. paid outside the U.S. by a non-U.S. payor or a non-U.S. middleman), 1.6045–1(g)(1)(i) (exception for sales effected at an office outside the U.S. by a non-U.S. payor or a non-U.S. middleman), 1.6042–3(b)(1)(iv) (exceptions for distributions from sources outside the U.S. by a non-U.S. payor or a non-U.S. middleman).

[490] The definition also includes: a foreign branch or office of a U.S. financial institution or U.S. clearing organization; a foreign corporation for purposes of presenting income tax treaty claims on behalf of its shareholders; and any other person acceptable to the IRS, in each case that such person has entered into a withholding agreement with the IRS. Treas. Reg. sec. 1.1441–1(e)(5)(ii).

[491] U.S. withholding agents are allowed to rely on a QI's IRS Form W–8IMY without any underlying beneficial owner documentation. By contrast, nonqualified intermediaries are required both to provide an IRS Form W–8IMY to a U.S. withholding agent and to forward with that document IRS Forms W–8 or W–9 or other specified documentation for each beneficial owner.

[492] See Rev. Proc. 2000–12, 2000–1 C.B. 387, QI agreement secs. 2.12, 5.03, 6.01.

[493] Rev. Proc. 2000–12, 2000–1 C.B. 387, *supplemented by* Announcement 2000–50, 2000–1 C.B. 998, and *modified by* Rev. Proc. 2003–64, 2003–2 C.B. 306, and Rev. Proc. 2005–77, 2005–2 C.B. 1176. The QI agreement applies only to foreign financial institutions, foreign clearing or-

the IRS providing specified information, and any additional information and documentation requested by the IRS. The application must establish to the IRS's satisfaction that the applicant has adequate resources and procedures to comply with the terms of the QI agreement.

Before entering into a QI agreement that provides for the use of documentary evidence obtained under a country's know-your-customer rules, the IRS must receive (1) that country's know-your-customer practices and procedures for opening accounts and (2) responses to 18 related items.[494] If the IRS has already received this information, a particular prospective QI need not submit it again. The IRS has received such information and has approved know-your-customer rules in 59 countries.

A foreign financial institution or other eligible person becomes a QI by entering into an agreement with the IRS. Under the agreement, the financial institution acts as a QI only for accounts that the financial institution has designated as QI accounts. A QI is not required to act as a QI for all of its accounts; however, if a QI designates an account as one for which it will act as a QI, it must act as a QI for all payments made to that account.

The model QI agreement describes in detail the QI's withholding and reporting obligations. Certain key aspects of the model agreement are described below.[495]

*Withholding and reporting responsibilities*

As a technical matter, all QIs are withholding agents for purposes of the nonresident withholding and reporting rules, and payors (who are required to withhold and report) for purposes of the backup withholding and IRS Form 1099 information reporting rules. However, under the QI agreement, a QI may choose not to assume primary responsibility for nonresident withholding. In that case, the QI is not required to withhold on payments made to non-U.S. customers, or to report those payments on IRS Form 1042–S. Instead, the QI must provide a U.S. withholding agent with an IRS Form W–8IMY that certifies as to the status of its (unnamed) non-U.S. account holders and withholding rate pool information.

Similarly, a QI may choose not to assume primary responsibility for IRS Form 1099 reporting and backup withholding. In that case, the QI is not required to backup withhold on payments made to U.S. customers or to file IRS Forms 1099. Instead, the QI must provide a U.S. payor with an IRS Form W–9 for each of its U.S. non-exempt recipient account holders (i.e., account holders that are U.S. persons not generally exempt from IRS Form 1099 reporting and backup withholding).[496]

---

ganizations, and foreign branches or offices of U.S. financial institutions or U.S. clearing organizations. However, the principles of the QI agreement may be used to conclude agreements with other persons defined as QIs.

[494] See Rev. Proc. 2000–12, 2000–1 C.B. 387, sec. 3.02.

[495] Additional detail can be found in Joint Committee on Taxation, *Selected Issues Relating to Tax Compliance with Respect to Offshore Accounts and Entities* (JCX–65–08), July 23, 2008.

[496] Regardless of whether a QI assumes primary Form 1099 reporting and backup withholding responsibility, the QI is responsible for IRS Form 1099 reporting and backup withholding on certain reportable payments that are not reportable amounts. See Rev. Proc. 2000–12, 2001–1 C.B. 387, QI agreement secs. 2.43 (defining reportable amount), 2.44 (defining reportable payment), 3.05, 8.04. The reporting responsibility differs depending on whether the QI is a U.S. payor or a non-U.S. payor. Examples of payments for which the QI assumes primary IRS Form

Continued

A QI may elect to assume primary nonresident withholding and reporting responsibility, primary backup withholding and IRS Form 1099 reporting responsibility, or both.[497] A QI that assumes such responsibility is subject to all of the related obligations imposed by the Code on U.S. withholding agents or payors. The QI must also provide the U.S. withholding agent (or U.S. payor) additional information about the withholding rates to enable the withholding agent to appropriately withhold and report on payments made through the QI. These rates can be supplied with respect to withholding rate pools that aggregate payments of a single type of income (e.g., interest or dividends) that is subject to a single rate of withholding.

If a U.S. non-exempt recipient has not provided an IRS Form W–9, the QI must disclose the name, address, and taxpayer identification number ("TIN") (if available) to the withholding agent (and the withholding agent must apply backup withholding). However, no such disclosure is necessary if the QI is, under local law, prohibited from making the disclosure and the QI has followed certain procedural requirements (including providing for backup withholding, as described further below).

*Documentation of account holders*

A QI agrees to use its best efforts to obtain documentation regarding the status of their account holders in accordance with the terms of its QI agreement.[498] A QI must apply presumption rules[499] unless a payment can be reliably associated with valid documentation from the account holder. The QI agrees to adhere to the know-your-customer rules set forth in the QI agreement with respect to the account holder from whom the evidence is obtained.

A QI may treat an account holder as a foreign beneficial owner of an amount if the account holder provides a valid IRS Form W–8 (other than an IRS Form W–8IMY) or valid documentary evidence that supports the account holder's status as a foreign person.[500] With such documentation, a QI generally may treat an account holder as entitled to a reduced rate of withholding if all the requirements for the reduced rate are met and the documentation supports entitlement to a reduced rate. A QI may not reduce the

---

1099 reporting and backup withholding responsibility include certain broker proceeds from the sale of certain assets owned by a U.S. non-exempt recipient and payments of certain foreign-source income to a U.S. non-exempt recipient if such income is paid in the United States or to an account maintained in the United States.

[497] To the extent that a QI assumes primary responsibility for an account, it must do so for all payments made by the withholding agent to that account. See Rev. Proc. 2000–12, QI agreement sec. 3.

[498] See Rev. Proc. 2000–12, QI agreement sec. 5.

[499] The QI agreement contains its own presumption rules. See Rev. Proc. 2000–12, QI agreement sec. 5.13(C). An amount subject to withholding that is paid outside the United States to an account maintained outside the United States is presumed made to an undocumented foreign account holder (i.e., subject to 30-percent withholding). Payments of U.S. source deposit interest and certain other U.S. source interest and original issue discount paid outside of the United States to an offshore account is presumed made to an undocumented U.S. non-exempt account holder (i.e., subject to backup withholding). For payments of foreign source income, broker proceeds and certain other amounts, the QI can assume such payments are made to an exempt recipient if the amounts are paid outside the United States to an account maintained outside the United States.

[500] Documentary evidence is any documentation obtained under know-your-customer rules per the QI agreement, evidence sufficient to establish a reduced rate of withholding under Treas. Reg. sec. 1.1441–6, and evidence sufficient to establish status for purposes of chapter 61 under Treas. Reg. sec. 1.6049–5(c). See Rev. Proc. 2000–12, 2000–1 C.B. 387, QI agreement sec. 2.12.

rate of withholding if the QI knows that the account holder is not the beneficial owner of a payment to the account.

If a foreign account holder is the beneficial owner of a payment, then a QI may shield the account holder's identity from U.S. custodians and the IRS. If a foreign account holder is not the beneficial owner of a payment (for example, because the account holder is a nominee), the account holder must provide the QI with an IRS Form W–8IMY for itself along with specific information about each beneficial owner to which the payment relates. A QI that receives this information may shield the account holder's identity from a U.S. custodian, but not from the IRS.[501]

In general, if an account holder is a U.S. person, the account holder must provide the QI with an IRS Form W–9 or appropriate documentary evidence that supports the account holder's status as a U.S. person. However, if a QI does not have sufficient documentation to determine whether an account holder is a U.S. or foreign person, the QI must apply certain presumption rules detailed in the QI agreement. These presumption rules may not be used to grant a reduced rate of nonresident withholding; instead they merely determine whether a payment should be subject to full nonresident withholding (at a 30-percent rate), subject to backup withholding (at a 28-percent rate), or treated as exempt from backup withholding.

In general, under the QI agreement presumptions, U.S.-source investment income that is paid outside the United States to an offshore account is presumed to be paid to an undocumented foreign account holder. A QI must treat such a payment as subject to withholding at a 30-percent rate and report the payment to an unknown account holder on IRS Form 1042–S. However, most U.S.-source deposit interest and interest or original issue discount on short-term obligations that is paid outside the United States to an offshore account is presumed made to an undocumented U.S. nonexempt recipient account holder and thus is subject to backup withholding at a 28-percent rate.[502] Importantly, both foreign-source income and broker proceeds are presumed to be paid to a U.S. exempt recipient (and thus are exempt from both nonresident and backup withholding) when such amounts are paid outside the United States to an offshore account.

*QI information return requirements*

A QI must file IRS Form 1042 by March 15 of the year following any calendar year in which the QI acts as a QI. A QI is not required to file IRS Forms 1042–S for amounts paid to each separate account holder, but instead files a separate IRS Form 1042–S for each type of reporting pool.[503] A QI must file separate IRS Forms 1042–S for amounts paid to certain types of account holders, including: (1) other QIs which receive amounts subject to foreign

[501] This rule restricts one of the principal benefits of the QI regime, nondisclosure of account holders, to financial institutions that have assumed the documentation and other obligations associated with QI status.

[502] These amounts are statutorily exempt from nonresident withholding when paid to non-U.S. persons.

[503] A reporting pool consists of income that falls within a particular withholding rate and within a particular income code, exemption code, and recipient code as determined on IRS Form 1042–S.

withholding; (2) each foreign account holder of a nonqualified intermediary or other flow-through entity to the extent that the QI can reliably associate such amounts with valid documentation; and (3) unknown recipients of amounts subject to withholding paid through a nonqualified intermediary or other flow-through entity to the extent the QI cannot reliably associate such amounts with valid documentation. The IRS Form 1042 must also include an attachment setting forth the aggregate amounts of reportable payments paid to U.S. non-exempt recipient account holders, and the number of such account holders, whose identity is prohibited by foreign law (including by contract) from disclosure.[504]

A QI has specified IRS Form 1099[505] filing requirements including: (1) filing an aggregate IRS Form 1099 for each type of reportable amount paid to U.S. non-exempt recipient account holders whose identities are prohibited by law from being disclosed; (2) filing an aggregate IRS Form 1099 for reportable payments other than reportable amounts[506] paid to U.S. non-exempt recipient account holders whose identities are prohibited by law from being disclosed; (3) filing separate IRS Forms 1099 for reportable amounts paid to U.S. non-exempt recipient account holders for whom the QI has not provided an IRS Form W–9 or identifying information to a withholding agent; (4) filing separate IRS Forms 1099 for reportable payments other than reportable amounts paid to U.S. non-exempt recipient account holders; (5) filing separate IRS Forms 1099 for reportable amounts paid to U.S. non-exempt recipient account holders for which the QI has assumed primary IRS Form 1099 reporting and backup withholding responsibility; and (6) filing separate IRS Forms 1099 for reportable payments to an account holder that is a U.S. person if the QI has applied backup withholding and the amount was not otherwise reported on an IRS Form 1099.

*Foreign law prohibition of disclosure*

The QI agreement includes procedures to address situations in which foreign law (including by contract) prohibits the QI from disclosing the identities of U.S. non-exempt recipients (such as individuals). Separate procedures are provided for accounts established with a QI prior to January 1, 2001, and for accounts established on or after January 1, 2001.

*Accounts established prior to January 1, 2001.*—For accounts established prior to January 1, 2001, if the QI knows that the account holder is a U.S. non-exempt recipient, the QI must (1) request from the account holder the authority to disclose its name, address, TIN (if available), and reportable payments; (2) request from the account holder the authority to sell any assets that generate, or could generate, reportable payments; or (3) request that

[504] For undisclosed accounts, QIs must separately report each type of reportable payment (determined by reference to the types of income reported on IRS Forms 1099) and the number of undisclosed account holders receiving such payments.

[505] If the QI is required to file IRS Forms 1099, it must file the appropriate form for the type of income paid (e.g., IRS Form 1099–DIV for dividends, IRS Form 1099–INT for interest, and IRS Form 1099–B for broker proceeds).

[506] The term reportable amount generally includes those amounts that would be reported on IRS Form 1042–S if the amount were paid to a foreign account holder. The term reportable payment generally refers to amounts subject to backup withholding, but it has a different meaning depending upon the status of the QI as a U.S. or non-U.S. payor.

the account holder disclose itself by mandating the QI to provide an IRS Form W–9 completed by the account holder. The QI must make these requests at least two times during each calendar year and in a manner consistent with the QI's normal communications with the account holder (or at the time and in the manner that the QI is authorized to communicate with the account holder). Until the QI receives a waiver on all prohibitions against disclosure, authorization to sell all assets that generate, or could generate, reportable payments, or a mandate from the account holder to provide an IRS Form W–9, the QI must backup withhold on all reportable payments paid to the account holder and report those payments on IRS Form 1099 or, in certain cases, provide another withholding agent with all of the information required for that withholding agent to backup withhold and report the payments on IRS Form 1099.

*Accounts established on or after January 1, 2001.*—For any account established by a U.S. non-exempt recipient on or after January 1, 2001, the QI must (1) request from the account holder the authority to disclose its name, address, TIN (if available), and reportable payments; (2) request from the account holder, prior to opening the account, the authority to exclude from the account holder's account any assets that generate, or could generate, reportable payments; or (3) request that the account holder disclose itself by mandating the QI to transfer an IRS Form W–9 completed by the account holder.

If a QI is authorized to disclose the account holder's name, address, TIN, and reportable amounts, it must obtain a valid IRS Form W–9 from the account holder, and, to the extent the QI does not have primary IRS Form 1099 and backup withholding responsibility, provide the IRS Form W–9 to the appropriate withholding agent promptly after obtaining the form. If an IRS Form W–9 is not obtained, the QI must provide the account holder's name, address, and TIN (if available) to the withholding agents from whom the QI receives reportable amounts on behalf of the account holder, together with the withholding rate applicable to the account holder. If a QI is not authorized to disclose an account holder's name, address, TIN (if available), and reportable amounts, but is authorized to exclude from the account holder's account any assets that generate, or could generate, reportable payments, the QI must follow procedures designed to ensure that it will not hold any assets that generate, or could generate, reportable payments in the account holder's account.[507]

*External audit procedures*

The IRS generally does not audit a QI with respect to withholding and reporting obligations covered by a QI agreement if an approved external auditor conducts an audit of the QI. An external audit must be performed in the second and fifth full calendar years in which the QI agreement is in effect. In general, the IRS must

[507] Under both of these procedures, if the QI is a non-U.S. payor, a U.S. non-exempt recipient may effectively avoid disclosure and backup withholding by investing in assets that generate solely non-reportable payments such as foreign source income (such as bonds issued by a foreign government) paid outside of the United States.

receive the external auditor's report by June 30 of the year following the year being audited.

Requirements for the external audit are provided in the QI agreement. In general, the QI must permit the external auditor to have access to all relevant records of the QI, including information regarding specific account holders. In addition, the QI must permit the IRS to communicate directly with the external auditor, review the audit procedures followed by the external auditor, and examine the external auditor's work papers and reports.

In addition to the external audit requirements set forth in the QI agreement, the IRS has issued further guidance (the "QI audit guidance") for an external auditor engaged by a QI to verify the QI's compliance with the QI agreement.[508] An external auditor must conduct its audit in accordance with the procedures described in the QI agreement. However, the QI audit guidance is intended to assist the external auditor in understanding and applying those procedures. The QI audit guidance does not amend, modify, or interpret the QI agreement.

*Term of a QI agreement*

A QI agreement expires on December 31 of the fifth full calendar year after the year in which the QI agreement first takes effect, although it may be renewed. Either the IRS or the QI may terminate the QI agreement prior to its expiration by delivering a notice of termination to the other party. However, the IRS generally does not terminate a QI agreement unless there is a significant change in circumstances or an event of default occurs, and the IRS determines that the change in circumstance or event of default warrants termination. In the event that an event of default occurs, a QI is given an opportunity to cure it within a specified time.

***Know-your-customer due diligence requirements***

*United States*

The U.S. know-your-customer rules[509] require financial institutions[510] to develop and maintain a written customer identification program and anti-money laundering policies and procedures. Additionally, financial institutions must perform customer due diligence. The due diligence requirements are enhanced where the account or the financial institution has a higher risk profile.[511]

A customer identification program at a minimum requires the financial institution to collect the name, date of birth (for individuals), address,[512] and identification number[513] for new customers.

---

[508] Rev. Proc. 2002–55, 2002–2 C.B. 435.

[509] The U.S. know-your-customer rules are primarily found in the Bank Secrecy Act of 1970 and in Title III, The International Money Laundering Abatement and Anti-Terrorist Financing Act of 2001 of the USA PATRIOT Act.

[510] The term financial institution is broadly defined under 31 U.S.C. sec. 5312(a)(2) or (c)(1) and includes U.S. banks and agencies or branches of foreign banks doing business in the United States, insurance companies, credit unions, brokers and dealers in securities or commodities, money services businesses, and certain casinos.

[511] Relevant risks include the types of accounts held at the financial institution, the methods available for opening accounts, the types of customer identification information available, and the size, location, and customer base of the financial institution. 31 C.F.R. sec. 103.121(b)(2).

[512] For a person other than an individual the address is the principal place of business, local office, or other physical location. 31 C.F.R. sec. 103.121(b)(2)(i)(3)(iii).

[513] For a U.S. person the identification number is the TIN. For a non-U.S. person the identification number could be a TIN, passport number, alien identification number, or number and

In fulfilling their customer due diligence requirements, financial institutions are required to verify enough customer information to enable the financial institution to form a "reasonable belief that it knows the true identity of each customer."[514]

In many cases the know-your-customer rules do not require financial institutions to look through an entity to determine its ultimate ownership.[515] However, based on the financial institution's risk assessment, the financial institution may need to obtain information about individuals with authority or control over such an account in order to verify the identity of the customer.[516] A financial institution's customer due diligence must include gathering sufficient information on a business entity and its owners for the financial institution to understand and assess the risks of the account relationship.[517]

Enhanced due diligence is required if customers are deemed to be of higher risk, and is mandated for certain types of accounts including foreign correspondent accounts, private banking accounts, and accounts for politically exposed persons. Private banking accounts are considered to be of significant risk and enhanced due diligence requires identification of nominal and beneficial owners for these accounts.[518]

Financial institutions must maintain records for a minimum of five years after the account is closed or becomes dormant. They are required to monitor accounts including the frequency, size and ultimate destinations of transfers and must update customer due diligence and enhanced due diligence when there are significant changes to the customer's profile (for example, volume of transaction activity, risk level, or account type).

*European Union Third Money Laundering Directive*

The European Union ("EU") Third Money Laundering Directive[519] is also applicable to a broad range of persons including credit institutions and financial institutions as well as to persons acting in the exercise of certain professional activities.[520] It requires systems, adequate policies and procedures for customer due diligence, reporting, record keeping, internal controls, risk assessment, risk management, compliance management, and communication. Required customer due diligence measures go further than the

---

country of issuance of any other government-issued document evidencing nationality or residence and bearing a photograph or similar safeguard. 31 C.F.R. sec. 103.121(b)(2)(i)(4).

514 See 31 C.F.R. sec. 103.121(b)(2).

515 For example, a financial institution is not "required to look through trust, escrow, or similar accounts to verify the identities of beneficiaries and instead will only be required to verify the identity of the named accountholder." See 68 Fed. Reg. 25,090, 25,094 (May 9, 2003).

516 See 31 sec. 103.121(b)(2)(ii)(C).

517 In order to assess the risk of the account relationship, a financial institution may need to ascertain the type of business, the purpose of the account, the source of the account funds, and the source of the wealth of the owner or beneficial owner of the entity.

518 31 C.F.R. sec. 103.178. A private banking account is an account that (1) requires a minimum deposit of not less than 1 million dollars; (2) is established for the benefit of one or more non-U.S. persons who are direct or beneficial owners of the account; and (3) is administered or managed by an officer, employee or agent of the financial institution. Beneficial owner for these purposes is defined as an individual who has a level of control over, or entitlement to the funds or assets in the account. 31 C.F.R. secs. 103.175(b), 103.175(o).

519 Directive 2005/60/EC of the European Parliament and of the Council, October 26, 2005 ("EU Third Money Laundering Directive").

520 The directive applies to auditors, accountants, tax advisors, notaries, legal professionals, real estate agents, certain persons trading in goods (cash transactions in excess of EUR 15,000), and casinos.

know-your-customer rules in the United States in requiring identification and verification of the beneficial owner and an understanding of the ownership and control structure of the customer in addition to the basic customer identification program and customer due diligence requirements.

A beneficial owner is defined as the natural person who ultimately owns or controls the customer and/or the natural person on whose behalf a transaction or activity is being conducted. For corporations, beneficial owner includes: (1) the natural person or persons who ultimately owns or controls a legal entity through direct or indirect ownership or control over a sufficient percentage (25 percent plus one share) of the shares or voting rights in that legal entity; and 2) the natural person or persons who otherwise exercises control over the management of the legal entity.[521] For foundations, trusts, and like entities that administer and distribute funds, beneficial owner includes: (1) in cases in which future beneficiaries are determined, a natural person who is the beneficiary of 25 percent or more of the property; (2) in cases in which future beneficiaries have yet to be determined, the class of person in whose main interest the legal arrangement is set up or operates; and (3) natural person who exercises control over 25 percent or more of the property.[522] Under the EU Third Money Laundering Directive, EU member states generally must require identification of the customer and any beneficial owners before the establishment of a business relationship.[523]

The EU Third Money Laundering Directive requires ongoing account monitoring including scrutiny of transactions throughout the course of relationship to ensure that the transactions conducted are consistent with the customer and the business risk profile. It requires documents and other information to be updated and requires performance of customer due diligence procedures at appropriate times (such as a change in account signatories or change in the use of an account) for existing customers on a risk sensitive basis. Records must be maintained for up to five years after the customer relationship has ended.

### *Explanation of Provision*

The provision adds a new chapter 4 to the Code that provides for withholding taxes to enforce new reporting requirements on specified foreign accounts owned by specified United States persons or by United States owned foreign entities. The provision establishes rules for withholdable payments to foreign financial institutions and for withholdable payments to other foreign entities.

#### ***Withholdable payments to foreign financial institutions***

The provision requires a withholding agent to deduct and withhold a tax equal to 30 percent on any withholdable payment made to a foreign financial institution if the foreign financial institution does not meet certain requirements. Specifically, withholding is generally not required if an agreement is in effect between the for-

[521] EU Third Money Laundering Directive Art. 3(6)(a). Inquiries into beneficial ownership generally may stop at the level of any owner that is a company listed on a regulated market.
[522] EU Third Money Laundering Directive Art. 3(6)(b).
[523] EU Third Money Laundering Directive Art. 9.

eign financial institution and the Secretary of the Treasury (the "Secretary") under which the institution agrees to:

1. Obtain information regarding each holder of each account maintained by the institution as is necessary to determine which accounts are United States accounts;
2. Comply with verification and due diligence procedures as the Secretary requires with respect to the identification of United States accounts;
3. Report annually certain information with respect to any United States account maintained by such institution;
4. Deduct and withhold 30 percent from any pass-thru payment that is made to a (1) recalcitrant account holder or another financial institution that does not enter into an agreement with the Secretary, or (2) foreign financial institution that has elected to be withheld upon rather than to withhold with respect to the portion of the payment that is allocable to recalcitrant account holders or to foreign financial institutions that do not have an agreement with the Secretary.
5. Comply with requests by the Secretary for additional information with respect to any United States account maintained by such institution; and
6. Attempt to obtain a waiver in any case in which any foreign law would (but for a waiver) prevent the reporting of information required by the provision with respect to any United States account maintained by such institution, and if a waiver is not obtained from each account holder within a reasonable period of time, to close the account.

If the Secretary determines that the foreign financial institution is out of compliance with the agreement, the agreement may be terminated by the Secretary. The provision applies with respect to United States accounts maintained by the foreign financial institution and, except as provided by the Secretary, to United States accounts maintained by each other financial institution that is a member of the same expanded affiliated group (other than any foreign financial institution that also enters into an agreement with the Secretary).

It is expected that in complying with the requirements of this provision, the foreign financial institution and the other members of the same expanded affiliated group comply with know-your-customer, anti-money laundering, anti-corruption, or other similar rules to which they are subject, as well as with such procedures and rules as the Secretary may prescribe, both with respect to due diligence by the foreign financial institution and verification by or on behalf of the IRS to ensure the accuracy of the information, documentation, or certification obtained to determine if the account is a United States account. The Secretary may use existing know-your-customer, anti-money laundering, anti-corruption, and other regulatory requirements as a basis in crafting due diligence and verification procedures in jurisdictions where those requirements provide reasonable assurance that the foreign financial institution is in compliance with the requirements of this provision.

The provision allowing for withholding on payments made to an account holder that fails to provide the information required under this provision is not intended to create an alternative to information reporting. It is anticipated that the Secretary may require, under the terms of the agreement, that the foreign financial institution achieve certain levels of reporting and make reasonable attempts to acquire the information necessary to comply with the requirements of this section or to close accounts where necessary to meet the purposes of this provision. It is anticipated that the Secretary may also require, under the terms of the agreement that, in the case of new accounts, the foreign financial institution may not withhold as an alternative to collecting the required information.

A foreign financial institution may be deemed, by the Secretary, to meet the requirements of this provision if: (1) the institution complies with procedures prescribed by the Secretary to ensure that the institution does not maintain United States accounts, and meets other requirements as the Secretary may prescribe with respect to accounts of other foreign financial institutions, or (2) the institution is a member of a class of institutions for which the Secretary has determined that the requirements are not necessary to carry out the purposes of this provision. For instance, it is anticipated that the Secretary may provide rules that would permit certain classes of widely held collective investment vehicles, and to the limited extent necessary to implement these rules, the entities providing administration, distribution and payment services on behalf of those vehicles, to be deemed to meet the requirements of this provision. It is anticipated that a foreign financial institution that has an agreement with the Secretary may meet the requirements under this provision with respect to certain members of its expanded affiliated group if the affiliated foreign financial institution complies with procedures prescribed by the Secretary and does not maintain United States accounts. Additionally, the Secretary may identify classes of institutions that are deemed to meet the requirements of this provision if such institutions are subject to similar due diligence and reporting requirements under other provisions in the Code. Such institutions may include certain controlled foreign corporations owned by U.S. financial institutions and certain U.S. branches of foreign financial institutions that are treated as U.S. payors under present law.

Under the provision, a foreign financial institution may elect to have a U.S. withholding agent or a foreign financial institution that has entered into an agreement with the Secretary withhold on payments made to the electing foreign financial institution rather than acting as a withholding agent for the payments it makes to other foreign financial institutions that either do not enter into agreements with the Secretary or that themselves have elected not to act as a withholding agent, or for payments it makes to account holders that fail to provide required information. If the election under this provision is made, the withholding tax will apply with respect to any payment made to the electing foreign financial institution to the extent the payment is allocable to accounts held by foreign financial institutions that do not enter into an agreement with the Secretary or to payments made to recalcitrant account holders.

A payment may be allocable to accounts held by a recalcitrant account holder or a foreign financial institution that does not meet the requirements of this section either as a result of such person holding an account directly with the electing foreign financial institution, or in relation to an indirect account held through other foreign financial institutions that either do not enter into an agreement with the Secretary or are themselves electing foreign financial institutions.

The electing foreign financial institution must notify the withholding agent of its election and must provide information necessary for the withholding agent to determine the appropriate amount of withholding. The information may include information regarding the amount of any payment that is attributable to a withholdable payment and information regarding the amount of any payment that is allocable to recalcitrant account holders or to foreign financial institutions that have not entered into agreements with the Secretary. Additionally, the electing foreign financial institution must waive any right under a treaty with respect to an amount deducted and withheld pursuant to the election. To the extent provided by the Secretary, the election may be made with respect to certain classes or types of accounts.

A foreign financial institution meets the annual information reporting requirements under the provision by reporting the following information:

1. The name, address, and TIN of each account holder that is a specified United States person;
2. The name, address, and TIN of each substantial United States owner of any account holder that is a United States owned foreign entity;
3. The account number;
4. The account balance or value (determined at such time and in such manner as the Secretary provides); and
5. Except to the extent provided by the Secretary, the gross receipts and gross withdrawals or payments from the account (determined for such period and in such manner as the Secretary may provide).

This information is required with respect to each United States account maintained by the foreign financial institution and, except as provided by the Secretary, each United States account maintained by each other foreign financial institution that is a member of the same expanded affiliated group (other than any foreign financial institution that also enters into an agreement with the Secretary).

Alternatively, a foreign financial institution may make an election and report under sections 6041 (information at source), 6042 (returns regarding payments of dividends and corporate earnings and profits), 6045 (returns of brokers), and 6049 (returns regarding payments of interest), as if such foreign financial institution were a U.S. person (i.e., elect to provide full IRS Form 1099 reporting under these sections). Under this election, the foreign financial institution reports on each account holder that is a specified United States person or United States owned foreign entity as if the holder of the account were a natural person and citizen of the United States. As a result, both U.S.- and foreign-source amounts (including gross proceeds) are subject to reporting under this election regardless of whether the amounts are paid inside or outside the United States. If a foreign financial institution makes this election, the institution is also required to report the following information with respect to each United States account maintained by the institution: (1) the name, address, and TIN of each account holder that is a specified United States person; (2) the name, address, and TIN of each substantial United States owner of any account holder that is a United States owned foreign entity; and (3) the account number. This election can be made by a foreign financial institution even if other members of its expanded affiliated group do not make the election. The Secretary has authority to specify the time and manner of the election and to provide other conditions for meeting the reporting requirements of the election.

Foreign financial institutions that have entered into QI or similar agreements with the Secretary, under section 1441 and the regulations thereunder, are required to meet the requirements of this provision in addition to any other requirements imposed under the QI or similar agreement.

Under the provision, a United States account is any financial account held by one or more specified United States persons or United States owned foreign entities. Depository accounts are not treated as United States accounts for these purposes if (1) each holder of the account is a natural person and (2) the aggregate value of all depository accounts held (in whole or in part) by each holder of the account maintained by the financial institution does not exceed $50,000. A foreign financial institution may, however, elect to include all depository accounts held by U.S. individuals as United States accounts. To the extent provided by the Secretary, financial institutions that are members of the same expanded affiliated group may be treated as a single financial institution for purposes of determining the aggregate value of depository accounts maintained at the financial institution.

In addition, a financial account is not a United States account if the account is held by a foreign financial institution that has entered into an agreement with the Secretary or is otherwise subject to information reporting requirements that the Secretary determines would make the reporting duplicative. It is anticipated that the Secretary may exclude certain financial accounts held by bona fide residents of any possession of the United States maintained by a financial institution organized under the laws of the possession if the Secretary determines that such reporting is not necessary to carry out the purposes of this provision.

Except as otherwise provided by the Secretary, a financial account is any depository or custodial account maintained by a foreign financial institution and, any equity or debt interest in a foreign financial institution (other than interests that are regularly traded on an established securities market). Any equity or debt interest that is treated as a financial account with respect to any financial institution is treated for purposes of this provision as maintained by the financial institution. It is anticipated that the Secretary may determine that certain short-term obligations, or short-term deposits, pose a low risk of U.S. tax evasion and thus, may not treat such obligations or deposits as financial accounts for purposes of this provision.

A United States owned foreign entity is any foreign entity that has one or more substantial United States owners. A foreign entity is any entity that is not a U.S. person.

A foreign financial institution is any financial institution that is a foreign entity, and except as provided by the Secretary, does not include a financial institution organized under the laws of any possession of the United States. The Secretary may exercise its authority to issue guidance that it deems necessary to prevent financial institutions organized under the laws of U.S. possessions from being used as intermediaries in arrangements under which U.S. tax avoidance or evasion is facilitated.

Except as otherwise provided by the Secretary, a financial institution for purposes of this provision is any entity that (1) accepts deposits in the ordinary course of a banking or similar business; (2) as a substantial portion of its business, holds financial assets for the account of others; or (3) is engaged (or holding itself out as being engaged) primarily in the business of investing, reinvesting, or trading in securities,[524] interests in partnerships, commodities,[525] or any interest (including a futures or forward contract or option) in such securities, partnership interests, or commodities. Accordingly, the term financial institution may include among other entities, investment vehicles such as hedge funds and private equity funds. Additionally, the Secretary may provide exceptions for certain classes of institutions. Such exceptions may include entities such as certain holding companies, research and development subsidiaries, or financing subsidiaries within an affiliated group of non-financial operating companies. It is anticipated that the Secretary may prescribe special rules addressing the circumstances in which certain categories of companies, such as certain insurance companies, are financial institutions, or the circumstances in which certain contracts or policies, for example annuity contracts or cash value life insurance contracts, are financial accounts or United States accounts for these purposes.

For purposes of this provision, a recalcitrant account holder is any account holder that (1) fails to comply with reasonable requests for information necessary to determine if the account is a United States account; (2) fails to provide the name, address, and TIN of each specified United States person and each substantial United States owner of a United States owned foreign entity; or (3) fails to provide a waiver of any foreign law that would prevent the foreign financial institution from reporting any information required under this provision.

A passthru payment is any withholdable payment or other payment to the extent it is attributable to a withholdable payment.

The reporting requirements apply with respect to United States accounts maintained by a foreign financial institution and, except as otherwise provided by the Secretary, with respect to United States accounts maintained by each other foreign financial institution that is a member of the same expanded affiliated group as such foreign financial institution. An expanded affiliated group for these purposes is an affiliated group as defined in section 1504(a)

[524] As defined in section 475(c)(2), without regard to the last sentence thereof.
[525] As defined in section 475(e)(2).

except that "more than 50 percent" is substituted for "at least 80 percent" each place it appears in that section, and is determined without regard to paragraphs (2) and (3) of section 1504(b). A partnership or any other entity that is not a corporation is treated as a member of an expanded affiliated group if such entity is controlled by members of such group.[526]

This provision does not apply with respect to a payment to the extent that the beneficial owner of such payment is (1) a foreign government, a political subdivision of a foreign government, or a wholly owned agency of any foreign government or political subdivision; (2) an international organization or any wholly owned agency or instrumentality thereof; (3) a foreign central bank of issue; or (4) any other class of persons identified by the Secretary as posing a low risk of U.S. tax evasion.

Under the provision, a withholding agent includes any person, in whatever capacity, having the control, receipt, custody, disposal, or payment of any withholdable payment.

Except as provided by the Secretary, a withholdable payment is any payment of interest (including any original issue discount), dividends, rents, salaries, wages, premiums, annuities, compensations, remunerations, emoluments, and other fixed or determinable annual or periodical gains, profits, and income from sources within the United States. The term also includes any gross proceeds from the sale or other disposition of any property that could produce interest or dividends from sources within the United States, including dividend equivalent payments treated as dividends from sources in the United States pursuant to section 541 of the Act. Any item of income effectively connected with the conduct of a trade or business within the United States that is taken into account under sections 871(b)(1) or 882(a)(2) is not treated as a withholdable payment for purposes of the provision. In determining the source of a payment, section 861(a)(1)(B) (the rule for sourcing interest paid by foreign branches of domestic financial institutions) does not apply. The Secretary may determine that certain payments made with respect to short-term debt or short-term deposits, including gross proceeds paid pose little risk of United States tax evasion and may be excluded from withholdable payments for purposes of this provision.

A substantial United States owner is: (1) with respect to any corporation, any specified U.S. person that directly or indirectly owns more than 10 percent of the stock (by vote or value) of such corporation; (2) with respect to any partnership, a specified United States person that directly or indirectly owns more than 10 percent of the profits or capital interests of such partnership; and (3) with respect to any trust, any specified United States person treated as an owner of any portion of such trust under the grantor trust rules,[527] or to the extent provided by the Secretary, any specified United States person that holds, directly or indirectly, more than 10 percent of the beneficial interests of the trust. To the extent the foreign entity is a corporation or partnership engaged (or holding itself out as being engaged) primarily in the business of investing,

---

[526] Control for these purposes has the same meaning as control for purposes of section 954(d)(3).

[527] Subpart E of Part I of subchapter J of chapter 1.

reinvesting, or trading in securities, interests in partnerships, commodities, or any interest (including a futures or forward contract or option) in such securities, interests or commodities, the 10-percent threshold is reduced to zero percent. In determining whether an entity is a United States owned foreign entity (and whether any person is a substantial United States owner of such entity), only specified United States persons are considered.

Except as otherwise provided by the Secretary, a specified United States person is any U.S. person other than (1) a publicly traded corporation or a member of the same expanded affiliated group as a publicly traded corporation, (2) any tax-exempt organization or individual retirement plan, (3) the United States or a wholly owned agency or instrumentality of the United States, (4) a State, the District of Columbia, any possession of the United States, or a political subdivision or wholly owned agency of a State, the District of Columbia, or a possession of the United States, (5) a bank,[528] (6) a real estate investment trust,[529] (7) a regulated investment company,[530] (8) a common trust fund,[531] and (9) a trust that is exempt from tax under section 664(c)[532] or is described in section 4947(a)(1).[533]

### *Withholdable payments to other foreign entities*

The provision requires a withholding agent to deduct and withhold a tax equal to 30 percent of any withholdable payment made to a non-financial foreign entity if the beneficial owner of such payment is a non-financial foreign entity that does not meet specified requirements.

A non-financial foreign entity is any foreign entity that is not a financial institution under the provision. A non-financial foreign entity meets the requirements of the provision (i.e., payments made to such entity will not be subject to the imposition of 30-percent withholding tax) if the payee or the beneficial owner of the payment provides the withholding agent with either a certification that the foreign entity does not have a substantial United States owner, or provides the withholding agent with the name, address, and TIN of each substantial United States owner. Additionally, the withholding agent must not know or have reason to know that the certification or information provided regarding substantial United States owners is incorrect, and the withholding agent must report the name, address, and TIN of each substantial United States owner to the Secretary.

The provision does not apply to any payment beneficially owned by a publicly traded corporation or a member of an expanded affiliated group of a publicly traded corporation (defined as above but without the inclusion of partnerships or other non-corporate entities). Publicly traded corporations (and their affiliates) receiving payments directly from U.S. withholding agents may present a lower risk of U.S. tax evasion than other non-financial foreign entities. The provision also does not apply to any payment beneficially

[528] As defined in section 581.
[529] As defined in section 856.
[530] As defined in section 851.
[531] As defined in section 584(a).
[532] This includes charitable remainder annuity trusts and charitable remainder unitrusts.
[533] This includes certain charitable trusts not exempt under section 501(a).

owned by any: (1) entity that is organized under the laws of a possession of the United States and that is wholly owned by one or more bona fide residents of the possession; (2) foreign government, political subdivision of a foreign government, or wholly owned agency or instrumentality of any foreign government or political subdivision of a foreign government; (3) international organization or any wholly owned agency or instrumentality of an international organization; (4) foreign central bank of issue; (5) any other class of persons identified by the Secretary for purposes of the provision; or (6) class of payments identified by the Secretary as posing a low risk of U.S. tax evasion. It is anticipated that the Secretary may exclude certain payments made for goods, services, or the use of property if the payment is made pursuant to an arm's length transaction in the ordinary course of the payor's trade or business.

It is expected that the Secretary will provide coordinating rules for application of the withholding provisions applicable to foreign financial institutions and to foreign entities that are non-financial foreign entities under this provision.

***Credits and refunds***

In general, the determination of whether an overpayment of tax deducted and withheld under the provision results in an overpayment by the beneficial owner of the payment is made in the same manner as if the tax had been deducted and withheld under subchapter A of chapter 3 (withholding tax on nonresident aliens and foreign corporations). An amount of tax required to be withheld by a foreign financial institution under its agreement with the Secretary is treated the same as if it were required to be withheld on a withholdable payment made to a foreign financial institution that does not enter into an agreement with the Secretary. Under the provision, if a beneficial owner of a payment is entitled under an income tax treaty to a reduced rate of withholding tax on the payment, that beneficial owner may be eligible for a credit or refund of the excess of the amount withheld under the provision over the amount permitted to be withheld under the treaty. Similarly, if a payment is of an amount not otherwise subject to U.S. tax (because, for instance, the payment represents gross proceeds from the sale of stock or is interest eligible for the portfolio interest exemption), the beneficial owner of the payment generally is eligible for a credit or refund of the full amount of the tax withheld.

The Secretary has the authority to administer credit and refund procedures which may include requirements for taxpayers claiming credits or refunds of amounts withheld from payments to which the provision applies to supply appropriate documentation establishing that they are the beneficial owners of the payments from which tax was withheld, and that, in circumstances in which treaty benefits are being claimed, they are eligible for treaty benefits. No credit or refund is allowed with respect to tax properly deducted and withheld unless the beneficial owner of the payment provides the Secretary with such information as the Secretary may require to determine whether the beneficial owner of the payment is a United States owned foreign entity and the identity of any substantial United States owners of such entity. It is intended that any such guidance provided by the Secretary under this provision, including documentation and requirements to provide information, be consistent with existing income tax treaties.

If tax is withheld under the provision, this credit and refund mechanism ensures that the provisions are consistent with U.S. obligations under existing income tax treaties. U.S. income tax treaties do not require the United States and its treaty partners to follow a specific procedure for providing treaty benefits.[534] For example, in cases in which proof of entitlement to treaty benefits is demonstrated in advance of payment, the United States may permit reduced withholding or exemption at the time of payment. Alternatively, the United States may require withholding at the relevant statutory rate at the time of payment and allow treaty country residents to obtain treaty benefits through a refund process. The credit and refund mechanism ensures that residents of treaty partners continue to obtain treaty benefits in the event tax is withheld under the provision.

A special rule applies with respect to any tax properly deducted and withheld from a specified financial institution payment, which is defined as any payment with respect to which a foreign financial institution is the beneficial owner. Credits and refunds with respect to specified financial institution payments generally are not allowed. However, refunds and credits are allowed if, with respect to the payment, the foreign financial institution is entitled to an exemption or a reduced rate of tax by reason of any treaty obligation of the United States. In such a case, the foreign financial institution is entitled to an exemption or a reduced rate of tax only to the extent provided under the treaty. In no event will interest be allowed or paid with respect to any credit or refund of tax properly withheld on a specified financial institution payment.

Under the provision, the grace period for which the government is not required to pay interest on an overpayment is increased from 45 days to 180 days for overpayments resulting from excess amounts deducted and withheld under chapters 3 or 4 of the Code. The increased grace period applies to refunds of withheld taxes with respect to (1) returns due after the date of enactment (March 18, 2010), (2) claims for refund filed after date of enactment (March 18, 2010) and (3) IRS-initiated adjustments if the refunds are paid after the date of enactment (March 18, 2010) . It is anticipated that the Secretary may specify the proper form and information required for a claim for refund under section 6611(e)(2) and may pro-

[534] See, for example, the Commentaries on the OECD Model Tax Convention on Income and on Capital, which make clear that individual countries are free to establish procedures for providing any reduced tax rates agreed to by treaty partners. These procedures can include both relief at source and/or full withholding at domestic rates, followed by a refund. See, e.g., Commentary 26.2 to Article 1.

> A number of Articles of the Convention limit the right of a State to tax income derived from its territory. As noted in paragraph 19 of the Commentary on Article 10 as concerns the taxation of dividends, the Convention does not settle procedural questions and each State is free to use the procedure provided in its domestic law in order to apply the limits provided by the Convention. A State can therefore automatically limit the tax that it levies in accordance with the relevant provisions of the Convention, subject to possible prior verification of treaty entitlement, or it can impose the tax provided for under its domestic law and subsequently refund the part of that tax that exceeds the amount that it can levy under the provisions of the Convention.

*Ibid.* While Commentary 26.2 notes that a refund mechanism is not the preferred approach, the Act establishes such a mechanism for beneficial owners in certain circumstances. This approach serves to address, in part, observed difficulties in identifying U.S. persons who inappropriately seek treaty benefits to which they are not entitled.

vide that a purported claim that does not include such information is not considered filed.

### *General provisions*

Every person required to deduct and withhold any tax under the provision is liable for such tax and is indemnified against claims and demands of any person for the amount of payments made in accordance with the provision.

No person may use information under the provision except for the purpose of meeting any requirements under the provision or for purposes permitted under section 6103. However, the identity of foreign financial institutions that have entered into an agreement with the Secretary is not treated as return information for purposes of section 6103.

The Secretary is expected to provide for the coordination of withholding under this provision with other withholding provisions of the Code, including providing for the proper crediting of amounts deducted and withheld under this provision against amounts required to be deducted and withheld under other provisions of the Code. The Secretary may provide further coordinating rules to prevent double withholding, including in situations involving tiered U.S. withholding agents.

The provision makes several conforming amendments to other provisions in the Code. The provision grants authority to the Secretary to prescribe regulations necessary and appropriate to carry out the purposes of the provision, and to prevent the avoidance of this provision.

## *Effective Date*

The provision generally applies to payments made after December 31, 2012. The provision, however, does not require any amount to be deducted or withheld from any payment under any obligation outstanding on the date that is two years after the date of enactment (March 18, 2010), or from the gross proceeds from any disposition of such an obligation. It is anticipated that the Secretary may provide guidance as to the application of the material modification rules under section 1001 in determining whether an obligation is considered to be outstanding on the date that is two years after the date of enactment (March 18, 2010).

The interest provisions increasing the grace period for which the government is not required to pay interest on an overpayment from 45 to 180 days apply to: (1) returns with due dates after the date of enactment (March 18, 2010); (2) claims for credit or refund of overpayment filed after the date of enactment (March 18, 2010); and (3) refunds paid on adjustments initiated by the Secretary paid after the date of enactment (March 18, 2010).

## 2. Repeal of certain foreign exceptions to registered bond requirements (sec. 502 of the Act and secs. 149, 163, 165, 871, 881, 1287, and 4701 of the Code and 31 U.S.C. sec. 3121)

### *Present Law*

#### *Registration-required obligations and treatment of bonds not issued in registered form*

In general, a taxpayer may deduct all interest paid or accrued within the taxable year on indebtedness.[535] For registration-required obligations, a deduction for interest is allowed only if the obligation is in registered form. Generally, an obligation is treated as issued in registered form if the issuer or its agent maintains a registration of the identity of the owner of the obligation and the obligation can be transferred only through this registration system.[536] A registration-required obligation is any obligation other than one that: (1) is made by a natural person; (2) matures in one year or less; (3) is not of a type offered to the public; or (4) is a foreign targeted obligation.[537]

In applying this requirement, the IRS has adopted a flexible approach that recognizes that a debt obligation that is formally in bearer (i.e., not in registered) form is nonetheless "in registered form" for these purposes where there are arrangements that preclude individual investors from obtaining definitive bearer securities or that permit such securities to be issued only upon the occurrence of an extraordinary event.[538]

A foreign targeted obligation (to which the registration requirement does not apply) is any obligation satisfying the following requirements: (1) there are arrangements reasonably designed to ensure that such obligation will be sold (or resold in connection with the original issue) only to a person who is not a United States person; (2) interest is payable only outside the United States and its possessions; and (3) the face of the obligation contains a statement that any United States person who holds this obligation will be subject to limitations under the U.S. income tax laws.[539]

In addition to the denial of an interest deduction, interest on a State or local bond that is a registration-required obligation will

---

[535] Sec. 163(a).

[536] An obligation is treated as in registered form if (1) it is registered as to both principal and interest with the issuer (or its agent) and transfer of the obligation may be effected only by surrender of the old instrument and either the reissuance by the issuer of the old instrument to the new holder or the issuance by the issuer of a new instrument to the new holder, (2) the right to principal and stated interest on the obligation may be transferred only through a book entry system maintained by the issuer or its agent, or (3) the obligation is registered as to both principal and interest with the issuer or its agent and may be transferred through both of the foregoing methods. Treas. Reg. sec. 5f.103–1(c).

[537] Sec. 163(f)(2)(A). The registration requirement is intended to preserve liquidity while reducing opportunities for noncompliant taxpayers to conceal income and property from the reach of the income, estate and gift taxes. See Joint Committee on Taxation, *General Explanation of the Revenue Provisions of the Tax Equity and Fiscal Responsibility Act of 1982* (JCS–38–82), December 31, 1982, p. 190.

[538] Priv. Ltr. Rul. 1993–43–018 (1993); Priv. Ltr. Rul. 1993–43–019 (1993); Priv. Ltr. Rul. 1996–13–002 (1996). The IRS held that the registration requirement may be satisfied by "dematerialized book-entry systems" developed in some foreign countries, even if, under such a system, a holder is entitled to receive a physical certificate, tradable as a bearer instrument, in the event the clearing organization maintaining the system goes out of existence, because "cessation of operation of the book-entry system would be an extraordinary event." Notice 2006–99, 2006–2 C.B. 907.

[539] Sec. 163(f)(2)(B).

not qualify for the applicable tax exemption if the bond is not in registered form.[540] Also, an excise tax is imposed on the issuer of any registration-required obligation that is not in registered form.[541] The excise tax is equal to one percent of the principal amount of the obligation multiplied by the number of calendar years (or portions thereof) during the period beginning on the date of issuance of the obligation and ending on the date of maturity.

Moreover, any gain realized by the beneficial owner of a registration-required obligation that is not in registered form on the sale or other disposition of the obligation is treated as ordinary income (rather than capital gain), unless the issuer of the obligation was subject to the excise tax described above.[542] Finally, deductions for losses realized by beneficial owners of registration-required obligations that are not in a registered form are disallowed.[543] For the purposes of ordinary income treatment and denial of deduction for losses, a registration-required obligation is any obligation other than one that: (1) is made by a natural person; (2) matures in one year or less; or (3) is not of a type offered to the public.

***Treatment as portfolio interest***

Payments of U.S.-source "fixed or determinable annual or periodical" income, including interest, dividends, and similar types of investment income, that are made to foreign persons are subject to U.S. withholding tax at a 30-percent rate, unless the withholding agent can establish that the beneficial owner of the amount is eligible for an exemption from withholding or a reduced rate of withholding under an income tax treaty.[544] In 1984, the Congress repealed the 30-percent tax on portfolio interest received by a nonresident individual or foreign corporation from sources within the United States.[545]

The term "portfolio interest" means any interest (including original issue discount) that is (1) paid on an obligation that is in registered form and for which the beneficial owner has provided to the U.S. withholding agent a statement certifying that the beneficial owner is not a U.S. person, or (2) paid on an obligation that is not in registered form and that meets the foreign targeting requirements of section 163(f)(2)(B).[546] Portfolio interest, however, does

[540] Sec. 103(b)(3). For the purposes of this section, registration-required obligation is any obligation other than one that: (1) is not of a type offered to the public; (2) matures in one year or less; or (3) is a foreign targeted obligation.

[541] Sec. 4701.

[542] Sec. 1287.

[543] Sec. 165(j).

[544] Secs. 871, 881; Treas. Reg. sec. 1.1441–1(b). Generally, the determination by a withholding agent of the U.S. or foreign status of a payee and of its other relevant characteristics (e.g., as a beneficial owner or intermediary, or as an individual, corporation, or flow-through entity) is made on the basis of a withholding certificate that is a Form W–8 or a Form 8233 (indicating foreign status of the payee or beneficial owner) or a Form W–9 (indicating U.S. status of the payee).

[545] Secs. 871(h) and 881(c). Congress believed that the imposition of a withholding tax on portfolio interest paid on debt obligations issued by U.S. persons might impair the ability of U.S. corporations to raise capital in the Eurobond market (i.e., the global market for U.S. dollar-denominated debt obligations). Congress also anticipated that repeal of the withholding tax on portfolio interest would allow the U.S. Treasury Department direct access to the Eurobond market. See Joint Committee on Taxation, *General Explanation of the Revenue Provisions of the Deficit Reduction Act of 1984* (JCS–41–84), December 31, 1984, pp. 391–92.

[546] In repealing the 30-percent tax on portfolio interest, under the Deficit Reduction Act of 1984, Congress expressed concern about potential compliance problems in connection with obligations issued in bearer form. Given the foreign targeted exception to the registration requirement under section 163(f)(2)(A), U.S. persons intent on evading U.S. tax on interest income

not include interest received by a 10-percent shareholder,[547] certain contingent interest,[548] interest received by a controlled foreign corporation from a related person,[549] or interest received by a bank on an extension of credit made pursuant to a loan agreement entered into in the ordinary course of its trade or business.[550]

***Requirement that U.S. Treasury obligations be in registered form***

Under title 31 of the United States Code, every "registration-required obligation" of the U.S. Treasury must be in registered form.[551] For this purpose, a foreign targeted obligation is excluded from the definition of a registration-required obligation.[552] Thus, a foreign targeted obligation of the Treasury can be in bearer (rather than registered) form.

### *Explanation of Provision*

***Repeal of the foreign targeted obligation exception to the registration requirement***

The provision repeals the foreign targeted obligation exception to the denial of a deduction for interest on bonds not issued in registered form. Thus, under the provision, a deduction for interest is disallowed with respect to any obligation not issued in registered form, unless that obligation (1) is issued by a natural person, (2) matures in one year or less, or (3) is not of a type offered to the public.

Also, the provision repeals the foreign targeted obligation exception to the denial of the tax exemption on interest on State and local bonds not issued in registered form. Therefore, under the provision, interest paid on State and local bonds not issued in registered form will not qualify for tax exemption unless that obligation (1) is not of a type offered to the public, or (2) matures in one year or less.

The Act preserves the ordinary income treatment under present law of any gain realized by the beneficial owner from the sale or other disposition of a registration-required obligation that is not in registered form. Similarly, the Act does not change the present law rule disallowing deductions for losses realized by a beneficial owner of a registration-required obligation that is not in a registered form.

---

might attempt to buy U.S. bearer obligations overseas, claiming to be foreign persons. These persons might then claim the statutory exemption from withholding tax for the interest paid on the obligations and fail to declare the interest income on their U.S. tax returns, without concern that their ownership of the obligations would come to the attention of the IRS. Because of these concerns, Congress expanded the Treasury's authority to require registration of obligations deigned to be sold to foreign persons. See Joint Committee on Taxation, *General Explanation of the Revenue Provisions of the Deficit Reduction Act of 1984* (JCS–41–84), December 31, 1984, p. 393.

[547] Sec. 871(h)(3).

[548] Sec. 871(h)(4).

[549] Sec. 881(c)(3)(C).

[550] Sec. 881(c)(3)(A).

[551] 31 U.S.C. sec. 3121(g)(3). For purposes of title 31 of the United States Code, registration-required obligation is defined as any obligation except: (1) an obligation not of a type offered to the public; (2) an obligation having a maturity (at issue) of not more than one year; or (3) a foreign targeted obligation.

[552] 31 U.S.C. sec. 3121(g)(2).

### *Preservation of exception to the registration requirement for excise tax purposes*

Under the provision, the foreign targeted obligation exception is available with respect to the excise tax applicable to issuers of registration-required obligations that are not in registered form. Thus, the excise tax applies with respect to any obligation that is not in registered form unless the obligation (1) is issued by a natural person, (2) matures in one year or less, (3) is not of a type offered to the public, or (4) is a foreign targeted obligation.

### *Repeal of treatment as portfolio interest*

The provision repeals the treatment as portfolio interest of interest paid on bonds that are not issued in registered form but meet the foreign targeting requirements of section 163(f)(2)(B). Under the provision, interest qualifies as portfolio interest only if it is paid on an obligation that is issued in registered form and either (1) the beneficial owner has provided the withholding agent with a statement certifying that the beneficial owner is not a United States person (on IRS Form W–8), or (2) the Secretary has determined that such statement is not required in order to carry out the purposes of the subsection. It is anticipated that the Secretary may exercise its authority under this rule to waive the requirement of collecting Forms W–8 in circumstances in which the Secretary has determined there is a low risk of tax evasion and there are adequate documentation standards within the country of tax residency of the beneficial owner of the obligations in question or in the country where the book-entry system exists. Generally, however, as a result of the provision, interest paid to a foreign person on an obligation that is not issued in registered form is subject to U.S. withholding tax at a 30-percent rate, unless the withholding agent can establish that the beneficial owner of the amount is eligible for an exemption from withholding other than the portfolio interest exemption or for a reduced rate of withholding under an income tax treaty.

### *Dematerialized book-entry systems treated as registered form*

The provision provides that a debt obligation held through a dematerialized book entry system, or other book entry system specified by the Secretary, is treated, for purposes of section 163(f), as held through a book entry system for the purpose of treating the obligation as in registered form.[553] A debt obligation that is formally in bearer form is treated, for the purposes of section 163(f), as held in a book-entry system as long as the debt obligation may be transferred only through a dematerialized book entry system or other book entry system specified by the Secretary.

### *Repeal of exception to requirement that Treasury obligations be in registered form*

The provision includes a conforming change to title 31 of the United States Code that repeals the foreign targeted exception to

---

[553] By reason of cross references, this rule will also apply to sections 165(j), 312(m), 871(h), 881(c), 1287 and 4701.

the definition of a registration-required obligation. Thus, a foreign targeted obligation of the Treasury must be in registered form.

### *Effective Date*

The provision applies to debt obligations issued after the date which is two years after the date of enactment (March 18, 2010).

## 3. Disclosure of information with respect to foreign financial assets (sec. 511 of the Act and new sec. 6038D of the Code)

### *Present Law*

U.S. persons who transfer assets to, and hold interests in, foreign bank accounts or foreign entities may be subject to self-reporting requirements under both Title 26 (the Internal Revenue Code) and Title 31 (the Bank Secrecy Act) of the United States Code.

Since its enactment, the Bank Secrecy Act has been expanded beyond its original focus on large currency transactions, while retaining its broad purpose of obtaining self-reporting of information with "a high degree of usefulness in criminal, tax, or regulatory investigations or proceedings."[554] As the reporting regime has expanded,[555] reporting obligations have been imposed on both financial institutions and account holders. With respect to account holders, a U.S. citizen, resident, or person doing business in the United States is required to keep records and file reports, as specified by the Secretary, when that person enters into a transaction or maintains an account with a foreign financial agency.[556] Regulations promulgated pursuant to broad regulatory authority granted to the Secretary in the Bank Secrecy Act[557] provide additional guidance regarding the disclosure obligation with respect to foreign accounts. The Bank Secrecy Act specifies only that such disclosure contain the following information "in the way and to the extent the Secretary prescribes": (1) the identity and address of participants in a transaction or relationship; (2) the legal capacity in which a participant is acting; (3) the identity of real parties in interest; and (4) a description of the transaction.

Treasury Department Form TD F 90–22.1, "Report of Foreign Bank and Financial Accounts," (the "FBAR") must be filed by June 30 of the year following the year in which the $10,000 filing threshold is met.[558] The FBAR is filed with the Treasury Department at the IRS Detroit Computing Center. Failure to file the FBAR is sub-

---

[554] 31 U.S.C. sec. 5311.

[555] See, e.g., Title III of the USA PATRIOT Act, Pub. L. No. 107–56 (October 26, 2001) (sections 351 through 366 amended the Bank Secrecy Act as part of a series of reforms directed at international financing of terrorism).

[556] 31 U.S.C. sec. 5314. The term "agency" in the Bank Secrecy Act includes financial institutions.

[557] 31 U.S.C. sec. 5314(a) provides: "Considering the need to avoid impeding or controlling the export or import of monetary instruments and the need to avoid burdening unreasonably a person making a transaction with a foreign financial agency, the Secretary of the Treasury shall require a resident or citizen of the United States or a person in, and doing business in, the United States, to keep records, file reports, or keep records and file reports, when the resident, citizen, or person makes a transaction or maintains a relation for any person with a foreign financial agency."

[558] 31 C.F.R. sec. 103.27(c). The $10,000 threshold is the aggregate value of all foreign financial accounts in which a U.S. person has a financial interest or over which the U.S. person has signature or other authority.

ject to both criminal[559] and civil penalties.[560] Since 2004, the civil sanctions have included penalties not to exceed (1) $10,000 for failures that are not willful and (2) the greater of $100,000 or 50 percent of the balance in the account for willful failures. Although the FBAR is received and processed by the IRS, it is neither part of the income tax return filed with the IRS nor filed in the same office as that return. As a result, for purposes of Title 26, the FBAR is not considered "return information," and its distribution to other law enforcement agencies is not limited by the nondisclosure rules of Title 26.[561]

Although the obligation to file an FBAR arises under Title 31, individual taxpayers subject to the FBAR reporting requirements are alerted to this requirement in the preparation of annual Federal income tax returns. Part III ("Foreign Accounts and Trusts") of Schedule B of the 2008 IRS Form 1040 includes the question, "At any time during 2008, did you have an interest in or signatory or any other authority over a financial account in a foreign country, such as a bank account, securities account, or other financial account?" and directs taxpayers to "See page B–2 for exceptions and filing requirements for Form TD F 90–22.1." The Form 1040 instructions advise individuals who answer "yes" to this question to identify the foreign country or countries in which such accounts are located.[562] Responding to this question does not discharge one's obligations under Title 31 and constitutes "return information" protected from routine disclosure to those charged with enforcing Title 31. In addition, the Form 1040 instructions identify certain types of accounts that are not subject to disclosure, including those instances in which the combined value of all accounts held by the taxpayer did not exceed $10,000 at any point during the relevant tax year.

The FBAR requires disclosure of any account in which the filer has a financial interest or as to which the filer has signature or other authority (in which case the filer must identify the owner of the account). The Treasury Department and the IRS revised the FBAR and its accompanying instructions in October, 2008, to clarify the filing requirements for U.S. persons holding interests in foreign bank accounts.[563] The terminology has been updated to reflect

---

[559] 31 U.S.C. sec. 5322 (failure to file is punishable by a fine up to $250,000 and imprisonment for five years, which may double if the violation occurs in conjunction with certain other violations).

[560] 31 U.S.C. sec. 5321(a)(5).

[561] Section 6103 bars disclosure of return information, unless permitted by an exception.

[562] 31 C.F.R. sec. 103.24.

[563] Treasury Department Form TD F 90–22.1, Report of Foreign Bank and Financial Accounts, and its instructions states:

A financial interest in a bank, securities, or other financial account in a foreign country means an interest described in one of the following three paragraphs: 1. A United States person has a financial interest in each account for which such person is the owner of record or has legal title, whether the account is maintained for his or her own benefit or for the benefit of others including non-United States persons. 2. A United States person has a financial interest in each bank, securities, or other financial account in a foreign country for which the owner of record or holder of legal title is: (a) a person acting as an agent, nominee, attorney, or in some other capacity on behalf of the U.S. person; (b) a corporation in which the United States person owns directly or indirectly more than 50 percent of the total value of shares of stock or more than 50 percent of the voting power for all shares of stock; (c) a partnership in which the United States person owns an interest in more than 50 percent of the profits (distributive share of income, taking into account any special allocation agreement) or more than 50 percent of the capital of the partnership; or (d) a trust in which the United States person either has a present beneficial interest, either directly or indirectly, in more than 50 percent of the assets or from which such person receives more than 50 percent of the current income. 3. A United States per-new types of financial transactions. For example, "financial account" now specifies that debit or prepaid credit cards are financial accounts,[564] and the definition of "signature or other authority" now encompasses the ability to indirectly exercise this authority, even in the absence of written instructions.[565] The revised instructions also provide that foreign individuals doing business in the Unitod States may be required to file an FBAR.[566] In August, 2009, the IRS requested public comments to help determine the scope and nature of future additional guidance.[567]

The revised instructions explain the basis for reporting other information in more detail, and provide that (1) all foreign persons with an interest in the account must be identified (including foreign identification numbers for each), (2) the highest value held in the account at any point in the year must be disclosed, (3) corporate employees with signature authority but no financial interest are generally required to disclose the signature authority, unless the corporate Chief Financial Officer ("CFO") (or in the case of an employee of a subsidiary, the parent company's CFO) certifies that the account will be reported on the corporate filing and (4) any amended or delinquent filing should be identified as such, and accompanied by an explanatory statement.

In addition to the FBAR requirements under Title 31, there are additional reports required by the Code to be filed with the IRS by U.S. persons engaged in foreign activities, directly or indirectly, through a foreign business entity. Upon the formation, acquisition or ongoing ownership of certain foreign corporations, U.S. persons that are officers, directors, or shareholders must file a Form 5471, "Information Return of U.S. Persons with Respect to Certain For-

---

son has a financial interest in each bank, securities, or other financial account in a foreign country for which the owner of record or holder of legal title is a trust, or a person acting on behalf of a trust, that was established by such United States person and for which a trust protector has been appointed. A trust protector is a person who is responsible for monitoring the activities of a trustee, with the authority to influence the decisions of the trustee or to replace, or recommend the replacement of, the trustee. Correspondent or "nostro" accounts (international interbank transfer accounts) maintained by banks that are used solely for the purpose of bank-to-bank settlement need not be reported on this form, but are subject to other Bank Secrecy Act filing requirements. This exception is intended to encompass those accounts utilized for bank-to-bank settlement purposes only.

[564] See Chief Couns. Adv. 200603026 (January 20, 2006) for a discussion of whether payment card accounts constitute financial accounts.

[565] According to the instructions to the FBAR, a person has "signature authority" over an account "if such person can control the disposition of money or other property in it by delivery of a document containing his or her signature (or his or her signature and that of one or more other persons) to the bank or other person with whom the account is maintained." "Other authority" exists in a person "who can exercise comparable power over an account by communication to the bank or other person with whom the account is maintained, either directly or through an agent, nominee, attorney, or in some other capacity on behalf of the U.S. person, either orally or by some other means."

[566] Although the revised instructions currently track the language of the statute in stating that a person in or doing business in the United States is within its purview, and thus merely clarify what has long been required, the IRS announced that pending publication of guidance on the scope of the statute, people could rely on the earlier, unrevised instructions to determine whether they are required to file a FBAR. Announcement 2009–51, 2009–25 I.R.B. 1105. Subsequently, the IRS announced that persons with only signature authority over a foreign financial account as well as for signatories or owners of financial interest in a foreign commingled fund have until June 30, 2010 to file an FBAR for the 2008 and earlier calendar years with respect to those accounts. Notice 2009–62, 2009–35 I.R.B. 260.

[567] Notice 2009–62, 2009–35 I.R.B. 260, specifically requested comments concerning: (1) when a person having only signature authority or having an interest in a commingled fund should be relieved of filing an FBAR; (2) the circumstances under which the FBAR filing exceptions for officers and employees of banks and some publicly traded domestic corporations should be expanded; (3) when an interest in a foreign entity should be subject to FBAR reporting; and (4) whether the passive asset and passive income thresholds are appropriate and should apply conjunctively.

eign Corporations."[568] Similarly, an IRS Form 8865, "Return of U.S. Persons with Respect to Certain Foreign Partnerships," must be filed with respect to certain interests in a controlled foreign partnership; an IRS Form 3520, "Annual Return to Report Transactions with Foreign Trusts and Receipt of Certain Foreign Gifts," must be filed with respect to certain foreign trusts; and an IRS Form 8858, "Information Return of U.S. Persons With Respect To Foreign Disregarded Entities" must be filed with respect to a foreign disregarded entity.[569] To the extent that the U.S. person engages in such foreign activities indirectly through a foreign business entity, other self-reporting requirements may apply. In addition, a U.S. person that capitalizes a foreign entity generally is required to file an IRS Form 926, "Return by a U.S. Transferor of Property to a Foreign Corporation."[570]

With the exception of the questions included on Form 1040, Schedule B, there is no requirement to disclose the information includible on FBAR on an individual tax return.

*FBAR enforcement responsibility*

Until 2003, the Financial Crimes and Enforcement Network ("FinCEN"), an agency of the Department of the Treasury, had responsibility for civil penalty enforcement of FBAR.[571] As a result, persons who were more than 180 days delinquent in paying any FBAR penalties were referred for collection action to the Financial Management Service of the Treasury Department, which is responsible for such non-tax collections.[572] Continued nonpayment resulted in a referral to the Department of Justice for institution of court proceedings against the delinquent person. In 2003, the Secretary delegated civil enforcement to the IRS.[573] This change reflected the fact that a major purpose of the FBAR was to identify potential tax evasion, and therefore was not closely aligned with FinCEN's core mission.[574] The authority delegated to the IRS in 2003 included the authority to determine and enforce civil penalties,[575] as well as to revise the form and instructions. However, the collection and enforcement powers available to enforce the Internal Revenue Code under Title 26 are not available to the IRS in the enforcement of FBAR civil penalties, which remain collect-

---

[568] Secs. 6038, 6046.

[569] Form 8858 is used to satisfy reporting requirements of sections 6011, 6012, 6031, 6038, and related regulations.

[570] Sec. 6038B. The filing of this form may also be required upon future contributions to the foreign corporation.

[571] Treas. Directive 15–14 (December 1, 1992), in which the Secretary delegated to the IRS authority to investigate violations of the Bank Secrecy Act. If the IRS Criminal Investigation Division declines to pursue a possible criminal case, it is to refer the matter to FinCEN for civil enforcement.

[572] 31 U.S.C. sec. 3711(g).

[573] 31 C.F.R. sec. 103.56(g). Memorandum of Agreement and Delegation of Authority for Enforcement of FBAR Requirements (April 2, 2003); News Release, IR–2003–48 (April 10, 2003).

[574] Secretary of the Treasury, "A Report to Congress in Accordance with sec. 361(b) of the Uniting and Strengthening America by Providing Appropriate Tools Required to Intercept and Obstruct Terrorism Act of 2001 (USA Patriot Act)" (April 24, 2003).

[575] A penalty may be assessed before the end of the six-year period beginning on the date of the transaction with respect to which the penalty is assessed. 31 U.S.C. sec. 5321(b)(1). A civil action for collection may be commenced within two years of the later of the date of assessment and the date a judgment becomes final in any a related criminal action. 31 U.S.C. sec. 5321(b)(2).

ible only in accord with the procedures for non-tax collections described above.

In general, information reported on an FBAR is available to the IRS and other law enforcement agencies. In contrast, information on income tax returns—including the Schedule B information regarding foreign bank accounts—is not readily available to those within the IRS who are charged with administering FBAR compliance, despite the fact that Federal returns and return information may be the best source of information for this purpose.

The nondisclosure constraints on IRS personnel who examine income tax liability (i.e., Form 1040 reporting) generally preclude the sharing of tax return information with any other IRS personnel or Treasury officials, except for tax administration purposes.[576] Tax administration is defined as "the administration, management, conduct, direction, and supervision of the execution and application of the internal revenue laws or related statutes" and does not necessarily include administration of Title 31.[577] Because Title 31 includes enforcement of non-tax provisions of the Bank Secrecy Act, Title 31 is not, per se, a "related statute," for purposes of finding that a disclosure of such information would be for tax administration purposes. As a result, IRS personnel charged with investigating and enforcing the civil penalties under Title 31 are not routinely permitted access to Form 1040 information that would support or shed light on the existence of an FBAR violation. Instead, there must be a determination, in writing, that the FBAR violation was in furtherance of a Title 26 violation in order to support a finding that the statutes are "related statutes" for purposes of authorizing the disclosure. The effect of this prerequisite is to subsume the bank account information reported on Form 1040 under the scope of "return information" and therefore, the protection from disclosure provided under Title 26.[578]

*Penalties*

Failure to comply with the FBAR filing requirements is subject to penalties imposed under Title 31 of the United States Code, and may be both civil and criminal. Since the initial enactment of the Bank Secrecy Act, a willful failure to comply with the FBAR reporting requirement has been subject to a civil penalty. In 2004, the available penalties were expanded to include a reduced penalty for a non-willful failure to file.[579] Willful failure to file an FBAR may be subject to penalties in amounts not to exceed the greater of $100,000 or 50 percent of the amount in the account at the time of the violation.[580] A non-willful, but negligent, failure to file is subject to a penalty of $10,000 for each negligent violation.[581] The penalty may be waived if (1) there is reasonable cause for the failure to report and (2) the amount of the transaction or balance in the account was properly reported. In addition, serious violations

[576] Sec. 6103(h)(1). In essence, section 6103(h)(1) authorizes officers and employees of both the Treasury Department and IRS to have access to return information on the basis of a "need to know" in order to perform a tax administration function.

[577] Sec. 6103(b)(4).

[578] Internal Revenue Manual, paragraphs 4.26.14.2 and 4.26.14.2.1.

[579] American Jobs Creation Act of 2004, Pub. L. No. 108–357, sec. 821(b). This provision is codified in 31 U.S.C. sec. 5321(a)(5).

[580] 31 U.S.C. sec. 5321(a)(5)(C).

[581] 31 U.S.C. sec. 5321(a)(5)(B)(i), (ii).

are subject to criminal prosecution, potentially resulting in both monetary penalties and imprisonment. Civil and criminal sanctions are not mutually exclusive.

Failure to comply with information returns required by the Internal Revenue Code is subject to a variety of sanctions, including (1) suspension of the applicable statute of limitations,[582] (2) disallowance of otherwise permitted tax attributes, deductions or credits,[583] and (3) imposition of penalties. For most information returns, the failure to file penalty is $50 per return, up to a maximum of $250,000 per taxpayer.[584] Failures to disclose control of any foreign business entity,[585] foreign parties with 25-percent ownership interest in a domestic company,[586] domestic officers and 10-percent owners of a foreign corporation,[587] or change in ownership of a foreign partnership[588] are subject to penalties of $10,000, plus $10,000 for every 30 days the failure to file persists longer than 90 days after the taxpayer is informed of the failure. A failure to report a transfer to a foreign corporation is subject to a penalty equal to 10 percent of the value of the transfer, but is capped at $10,000 if the failure is not willful.[589] Failure to report the creation of a foreign trust is subject to a 35 percent penalty on the reportable amount (or five percent for a Form 3520–A report), plus $10,000 for every 30 days the failure to file persists after 90 days from the date on which the taxpayer is informed of the failure to file. The penalty is capped at the gross reportable amount.[590]

### *Explanation of Provision*

The provision requires individual taxpayers with an interest in a "specified foreign financial asset" during the taxable year to attach a disclosure statement to their income tax return for any year in which the aggregate value of all such assets is greater than $50,000. Although the nature of the information required is similar to the information disclosed on an FBAR, it is not identical. For example, a beneficiary of a foreign trust who is not within the scope of the FBAR reporting requirements because his interest in the trust is less than 50 percent may nonetheless be required to disclose the interest in the trust with his tax return under this provision if the value of his interest in the trust together with the value of other specified foreign financial assets exceeds the aggregate value threshold. Nothing in this provision is intended as a substitute for compliance with the FBAR reporting requirements, which are unchanged by this provision.

"Specified foreign financial assets" are depository or custodial accounts at foreign financial institutions and, to the extent not held in an account at a financial institution, (1) stocks or securities issued by foreign persons, (2) any other financial instrument or contract held for investment that is issued by or has a counterparty

[582] Sec. 6501(c)(8).
[583] Secs. 1295, 6038.
[584] Sec. 6721.
[585] Sec. 6038.
[586] Sec. 6038A.
[587] Sec. 6046.
[588] Sec. 6046A.
[589] Sec. 6038B.
[590] Sec. 6048.

that is not a U.S. person, and (3) any interest in a foreign entity. The information to be included on the statement includes identifying information for each asset and its maximum value during the taxable year. For an account, the name and address of the institution at which the account is maintained and the account number are required. For a stock or security, the name and address of the issuer, and any other information necessary to identify the stock or security and terms of its issuance must be provided. For all other instruments or contracts, or interests in foreign entities, the information necessary to identify the nature of the instrument, contract or interest must be provided, along with the names and addresses of all foreign issuers and counterparties. An individual is not required under this provision to disclose interests that are held in a custodial account with a U.S. financial institution nor is an individual required to identify separately any stock, security instrument, contract, or interest in a foreign financial account disclosed under the provision. In addition, the provision permits the Secretary to issue regulations that would apply the reporting obligations to a domestic entity in the same manner as if such entity were an individual if that domestic entity is formed or availed of to hold such interests, directly or indirectly.

Individuals who fail to make the required disclosures are subject to a penalty of $10,000 for the taxable year. An additional penalty may apply if the Secretary notifies an individual by mail of the failure to disclose and the failure to disclose continues. If the failure continues beyond 90 days following the mailing, the penalty increases by $10,000 for each 30 day period (or a fraction thereof), up to a maximum penalty of $50,000 for one taxable period. The computation of the penalty is similar to that applicable to failures to file reports with respect to certain foreign corporations under section 6038. Thus, an individual who is notified of his failure to disclose with respect to a single taxable year under this provision and who takes remedial action on the 95th day after such notice is mailed incurs a penalty of $20,000 comprising the base amount of $10,000, plus $10,000 for the fraction (i.e., the five days) of a 30-day period following the lapse of 90 days after the notice of noncompliance was mailed. An individual who postpones remedial action until the 181st day is subject to the maximum penalty of $50,000: the base amount of $10,000, plus $30,000 for the three 30-day periods, plus $10,000 for the one fraction (i.e., the single day) of a 30-day period following the lapse of 90 days after the notice of noncompliance was mailed.

No penalty is imposed under the provision against an individual who can establish that the failure was due to reasonable cause and not willful neglect. Foreign law prohibitions against disclosure of the required information cannot be relied upon to establish reasonable cause.

To the extent the Secretary determines that the individual has an interest in one or more foreign financial assets but the individual does not provide enough information to enable the Secretary to determine the aggregate value thereof, the aggregate value of such identified foreign financial assets will be presumed to have exceeded $50,000 for purposes of assessing the penalty.

The provision also grants authority to promulgate regulations necessary to carry out the intent. Such regulations may include exceptions for nonresident aliens and classes of assets identified by the Secretary, including those assets which the Secretary determines are subject to reporting requirements under other provisions of the Code. In particular, regulatory exceptions to avoid duplicative reporting requirements are anticipated.

### *Effective Date*

The provision is effective for taxable years beginning after the date of enactment (March 18, 2010).

## 4. Penalties for underpayments attributable to undisclosed foreign financial assets (sec. 512 of the Act and sec. 6662 of the Code)

### *Present Law*

The Code imposes penalties equal to 20 percent of the portion of any underpayments that are attributable to any of the following five grounds: (1) negligence or disregard of rules or regulations; (2) any substantial understatement[591] of income tax; (3) any substantial valuation misstatement; (4) any substantial overstatement of pension liabilities; and (5) any substantial estate or gift tax valuation understatement. With the exception of a penalty based on negligence or disregard of rules or regulations, these penalties are commonly referred to as accuracy-related penalties, because the imposition of the penalty does not require an inquiry into the culpability of the taxpayer. If the penalty is asserted, a taxpayer may defend against the penalty by demonstrating that (1) there was "reasonable cause" for the underpayment and (2) the taxpayer acted in good faith.[592] Regulations provide that reasonable cause exists in cases in which the taxpayer "reasonably relies in good faith on the opinion of a professional tax advisor, if the opinion is based on the tax advisor's analysis of the pertinent facts and authorities . . . and unambiguously states that the tax advisor concludes that there is a greater than 50-percent likelihood that the tax treatment of the item will be upheld if challenged" by the IRS.[593]

A penalty for a substantial understatement may be reduced to the extent of the portion of the understatement attributable to an item on the return for which the challenged tax treatment (1) is supported by substantial authority or (2) is adequately disclosed on the return and there was a reasonable basis for such treatment. The tax treatment is considered to have been adequately disclosed only if all relevant facts are disclosed with the return. Regardless of whether an item would otherwise meet either of these tests, this defense is not available with respect to penalties imposed on under-

[591] If the correct income tax liability exceeds that reported by the taxpayer by the greater of 10 percent of the correct tax or $5,000 (or, in the case of corporations, by the lesser of (1) 10 percent of the correct tax (or, if greater, $10,000) or (2) $10 million), then a substantial understatement exists.

[592] Sec. 6664(c).

[593] Treas. Reg. secs. 1.6662–4(g)(4)(i)(B), 1.6664–4(c).

statements arising from tax shelters.[594] The Secretary may prescribe a list of positions which the Secretary believes do not meet the requirements for substantial authority under this provision.

Under present law, failure to comply with the various information reporting requirements generally does not, in itself, determine the amount of the penalty imposed on an underpayment of tax. However, such failure to comply may be relevant to (1) establishing negligence under section 6662 or fraudulent intent,[595] (2) determining whether penalties based on culpability are applicable or (3) determining whether certain defenses are available.

In the context of transactions that are subject to the "reportable transaction" disclosure regime,[596] a separate accuracy-related penalty may apply.[597] That penalty applies to "listed transactions" and other "reportable transactions" that have a significant tax avoidance purpose (a "reportable avoidance transaction"). The penalty rate and defenses available to avoid the section 6662A penalty vary, based on the adequacy of disclosure. In general, a 20-percent accuracy-related penalty is imposed on any understatement attributable to an adequately disclosed listed transaction or reportable avoidance transaction.[598] An exception is available if the taxpayer satisfies a higher standard under the reasonable cause and good faith exception. This higher standard requires the taxpayer to demonstrate that there was (1) adequate disclosure of the relevant facts affecting the treatment on the taxpayer's return, (2) substantial authority for the treatment on the taxpayer's return, and (3) a reasonable belief that the treatment on the taxpayer's return was more likely than not the proper treatment.[599] If the transaction is not adequately disclosed, the reasonable cause exception is not available and the taxpayer is subject to a penalty equal to 30 percent of the understatement.[600]

### *Explanation of Provision*

The provision adds a new accuracy related penalty to section 6662. The new provision, which is subject to the same defenses as are otherwise available under section 6662, imposes a 40-percent penalty on any understatement attributable to an undisclosed foreign financial asset. The term "undisclosed foreign financial asset" includes all assets subject to certain information reporting requirements[601] for which the required information was not provided by

---

[594] A tax shelter is defined for this purpose as a partnership or other entity, an investment plan or arrangement, or any other plan or arrangement if a significant purpose of such partnership, other entity, plan, or arrangement is the avoidance or evasion of Federal income tax. Sec. 6662(d)(2)(C).

[595] Section 6663 imposes a penalty of 75 percent on that portion of the understatement attributable to fraud. If the government proves that such understatement was attributable to fraud, there is a rebuttable presumption that any other understatement is attributable to fraud.

[596] Secs. 6011 through 6112 require taxpayers and their advisers to disclose certain transactions determined to have the potential for tax avoidance. All such transactions are referred to as "reportable transactions," and include within that class of transactions, those that are "listed," that is, the subject of published guidance in which the Secretary announces his intent to challenge such transactions.

[597] Sec. 6662A.

[598] Sec. 6662A(a).

[599] Sec. 6664(d).

[600] Sec. 6662A(c).

[601] The information reporting requirements identified include sections 6038, 6038A, new 6038D, 6046A, and 6048.

the taxpayer as required under the applicable reporting provisions. An understatement is attributable to an undisclosed foreign financial asset if it is attributable to any transaction involving such asset. Thus, a U.S. person who fails to comply with the various self-reporting requirements for a foreign financial asset and engages in a transaction with respect to that asset incurs a penalty on any resulting underpayment that is double the otherwise applicable penalty for substantial understatements or negligence. For example, if a taxpayer fails to disclose amounts held in a foreign financial account, any underpayment of tax related to the transaction that gave rise to the income would be subject to the penalty provision, as would any underpayment related to interest, dividends or other returns accrued on such undisclosed amounts.

### *Effective Date*

The provision is effective for taxable years beginning after the date of enactment (March 18, 2010).

## 5. Modification of statute of limitations for significant omission of income in connection with foreign assets (sec. 513 of the Act and secs. 6229 and 6501 of the Code)

### *Present Law*

Taxes are generally required to be assessed within three years after a taxpayer's return was filed, whether or not it was timely filed.[602] Of the exceptions to this general rule, only section 6501(c)(8) is specifically targeted at the identification of, and collection of information about, cross-border transactions. Under this exception, the limitation period for assessment of any tax imposed under the Code with respect to any event or period to which information about certain cross-border transactions required to be reported relates does not expire any earlier than three years after the required information is actually provided to the Secretary by the person required to file the return.[603] In general, such information reporting is due with the taxpayer's return; thus, the three-year limitation period commences when a timely and complete (including all information reporting) return is filed. Without the inclusion of the information reporting with the return, the limitation period does not commence until such time as the information reports are subsequently provided to the Secretary, even though the return has been filed.

In the case of a false or fraudulent return filed with the intent to evade tax, or if the taxpayer fails to file a required return, the tax may be assessed, or a proceeding in court for collection of such tax may be begun without assessment, at any time.[604] The limitation period also may be extended by taxpayer consent.[605] If a tax-

---

[602] Sec. 6501(a). Returns that are filed before the date they are due are deemed filed on the due date. See sec. 6501(b)(1) and (2).

[603] Required information reporting subject to this three-year rule is reporting under sections 6038 (certain foreign corporations and partnerships), 6038A (certain foreign-owned corporations), 6038B (certain transfers to foreign persons), 6046 (organizations, reorganizations, and acquisitions of stock of foreign corporations), 6046A (interests in foreign partnerships), and 6048 (certain foreign trusts).

[604] Sec. 6501(c).

[605] Sec. 6501(c)(4).

payer engages in a listed transaction but fails to include any of the information required under section 6011 on any return or statement for a taxable year, the limitation period with respect to such transaction will not expire before the date which is one year after the earlier of (1) the date on which the Secretary is provided the information so required, or (2) the date that a "material advisor" (as defined in section 6111) makes its section 6112(a) list available for inspection pursuant to a request by the Secretary under section 6112(b)(1)(A).[606]

A special rule is provided where there is a substantial omission of income. If a taxpayer omits substantial income on a return, any tax with respect to that return may be assessed and collected within six years of the date on which the return was filed. In the case of income taxes, "substantial" means at least 25 percent of the amount that was properly includible in gross income; for estate and gift taxes, it means 25 percent of a gross estate or total gifts. For this purpose, the gross income of a trade or business means gross receipts, without reduction for the cost of sales or services.[607] An amount is not considered to have been omitted if the item properly includible in income is disclosed on the return.[608]

In addition to the exceptions described, there are also circumstances under which the three-year limitation period is suspended. For example, service of an administrative summons triggers the suspension either (1) beginning six months after service (in the case of John Doe summonses)[609] or (2) when a proceeding to quash a summons is initiated by a taxpayer named in a summons to a third-party record-keeper. Judicial proceedings initiated by the government to enforce a summons generally do not suspend the limitation period.

### *Explanation of Provision*[610]

The provision authorizes a new six-year limitations period for assessment of tax on understatements of income attributable to foreign financial assets. The present exception that provides a six-year period for substantial omission of an amount equal to 25 percent of the gross income reported on the return is not changed.

The new exception applies if there is an omission of gross income in excess of $5,000 and the omitted gross income is attributable to an asset with respect to which information reports are required under section 6038D, as applied without regard to the dollar threshold, the statutory exception for nonresident aliens and any exceptions provided by regulation. If a domestic entity is formed or availed of to hold foreign financial assets and is subject to the reporting requirements of section 6038D in the same manner as an individual, the six-year limitations period may also apply to that

[606] Sec. 6501(c)(10).

[607] Sec. 6501(e)(1)(A)(i).

[608] Sec. 6501(e)(1)(A)(ii) provides that, in determining whether an amount was omitted, any amounts that are disclosed in the return or in a statement attached to the return in a manner adequate to apprise the Secretary of the nature and amount of such item are not taken into account.

[609] Sec. 7609(e)(2).

[610] This provision was subsequently amended by section 218 of the ____ Act of ____, Pub. L. No. 111–226, to provide a reasonable cause exception under which the suspension of a limitations period under section 6501(c)(8) may not apply to the entire return. See Part Twelve for a description of the provision.

entity. The Secretary is permitted to assess the resulting deficiency at any time within six years of the filing of the income tax return.

In providing that the applicability of section 6038D information reporting requirements is to be determined without regard to the statutory or regulatory exceptions, the statute ensures that the longer limitation period applies to omissions of income with respect to transactions involving foreign assets owned by individuals. Thus, a regulatory provision that alleviates duplicative reporting obligations by providing that a report that complies with another provision of the Code may satisfy one's obligations under new section 6038D does not change the nature of the asset subject to reporting. The asset remains one that is subject to the requirements of section 6038D for purposes of determining whether the exception to the three-year statute of limitations applies.

The provision also suspends the limitations period for assessment if a taxpayer fails to provide timely information returns required with respect to passive foreign investment corporations[611] and the new self-reporting of foreign financial assets. The limitations period will not begin to run until the information required by those provisions has been furnished to the Secretary. The provision also clarifies that the extension is not limited to adjustments to income related to the information required to be reported by one of the enumerated sections.

### *Effective Date*

The provision applies to returns filed after the date of enactment (March 18, 2010) as well as for any other return for which the assessment period specified in section 6501 has not yet expired as of the date of enactment (March 18, 2010).

## 6. Reporting of activities with respect to passive foreign investment companies (sec. 521 of the Act and sec. 1298 of the Code)

### *Present Law*

In general, active foreign business income derived by a foreign corporation with U.S. owners is not subject to current U.S. taxation until the corporation makes a dividend distribution to those owners. Certain rules, however, restrict the benefit of deferral of U.S. tax on income derived through foreign corporations. One such regime applies to U.S. persons who own stock of passive foreign investment companies ("PFICs"). A PFIC generally is defined as any foreign corporation if 75 percent or more of its gross income for the taxable year consists of passive income, or 50 percent or more of its assets consist of assets that produce, or are held for the production of, passive income.[612] Various sets of income inclusion rules apply to U.S. persons that are shareholders in a PFIC, regardless of their percentage ownership in the company. One set of rules applies to PFICs under which U.S. shareholders pay tax on certain income or gain realized through the companies, plus an interest

[611] Sec. 1295(b), (f).
[612] Sec. 1297.

charge intended to eliminate the benefit of deferral.[613] A second set of rules applies to PFICs that are "qualified electing funds" ("QEF"), under which electing U.S. shareholders currently include in gross income their respective shares of the company's earnings, with a separate election to defer payment of tax, subject to an interest charge, on income not currently received.[614] A third set of rules applies to marketable PFIC stock, under which electing U.S. shareholders currently take into account as income (or loss) the difference between the fair market value of the stock as of the close of the taxable year and their adjusted basis in such stock (subject to certain limitations), often referred to as "marking to market."[615]

In general, a U.S. person that is a direct or indirect shareholder of a PFIC must file IRS Form 8621, "Return by a Shareholder of a Passive Foreign Investment Company or Qualifying Electing Fund" for each tax year in which that U.S. person (1) recognizes gain on a direct or indirect disposition of PFIC stock, (2) receives certain direct or indirect distributions from a PFIC, or (3) is making a reportable election.[616] The Code includes a general reporting requirement for certain PFIC shareholders which is contingent upon the issuance of regulations.[617] Although Treasury issued proposed regulations in 1992 requiring U.S. persons to file annually Form 8621 for each PFIC of which the person is a shareholder during the taxable year, such regulations have not been finalized and current IRS Form 8621 requires reporting only based on one of the triggering events described above.[618]

### *Explanation of Provision*

The provision requires that, unless otherwise provided by the Secretary, each U.S. person who is a shareholder of a PFIC must file an annual information return containing such information as the Secretary may require. A person that meets the reporting requirements of this provision may, however, also meet the reporting requirements of section 511 of the Act and new section 6038D of the Code requiring disclosure of information with respect to foreign financial assets. It is anticipated that the Secretary will exercise regulatory authority under this provision or new section 6038D to avoid duplicative reporting.

[613] Sec. 1291.

[614] Secs. 1293–1295.

[615] Sec. 1296.

[616] See Instructions to IRS Form 8621. According to the form, reportable elections include the following: (i) an election to treat the PFIC as a QEF; (ii) an election to recognize gain on the deemed sale of a PFIC interest on the first day of the PFIC's tax year as a QEF; (iii) an election to treat an amount equal to the shareholder's post-1986 earnings and profits of a CFC as an excess distribution on the first day of a PFIC's tax year as a QEF that is also a controlled foreign corporation under section 957(a); (iv) an election to extend the time for payment of the shareholder's tax on the undistributed earnings and profits of a QEF; (v) an election to treat as an excess distribution the gain recognized on the deemed sale of the shareholder's interest in the PFIC, or to treat such shareholder's share of the PFIC's post-1986 earnings and profits as an excess distribution, on the last day of its last tax year as a PFIC under section 1297(a) if eligible; or (vi) an election to mark-to-market the PFIC stock that is marketable within the meaning of section 1296(e).

[617] Sec. 1291(e) by reference to sec. 1246(f).

[618] Prop. Treas. Reg. sec. 1.1291–1(i).

### *Effective Date*

The provision is effective on the date of enactment (March 18, 2010).

## 7. Secretary permitted to require financial institutions to file certain returns related to withholding on foreign transfers electronically (sec. 522 of the Act and sec. 6011 of the Code).

### *Present Law*

#### *Withholding responsibility*

A withholding agent is any person required to withhold U.S. income tax under sections 1441, 1442, 1443, or 1461. For purposes of these sections, a withholding agent is any person, whether a U.S. or a foreign person, that has the control, receipt, custody, disposal, or payment of an item of income of a foreign person subject to withholding.[619] A withholding agent is personally liable for the tax required to be withheld.[620]

#### *Reporting liability of a withholding agent*

Every withholding agent must file an annual return with the IRS on Form 1042, "Annual Withholding Tax Return for U.S. Source Income of Foreign Persons," reporting all taxes withheld during the preceding year and remitting any taxes still owing for such preceding year.[621] IRS Form 1042 must be filed on or before March 15 of the year following the year of the payment. The form must be filled even though no tax has been withheld from income paid during the year.[622] A withholding agent must also file an information return, IRS Form 1042–S, which is entitled "Foreign Person's U.S. Source Income Subject to Withholding," on or before March 15 of the year succeeding the year of payment. IRS Form 1042–S requires the withholding agent to provide all items of income specified in section 1441(b) paid during the previous year to foreign persons.[623] IRS Form 1042–S must be filed for each foreign recipient to whom payments were made during the preceding year,[624] even if no tax was required to have been withheld. A copy of IRS Form 1042–S must be sent to the payee.

#### *IRS's authority to require electronic filing*

The Internal Revenue Service Restructuring and Reform Act of 1998 ("RRA 1998")[625] states that it is a congressional policy to promote the paperless filing of Federal tax returns. Section 2001(a) of RRA 1998 set a goal for the IRS to have at least 80 percent of all

---

[619] Treas. Reg. sec. 1.1441–7(a)(1).
[620] Sec. 1461.
[621] Treas. Reg. sec. 1.1461–1(b)(1).
[622] *Ibid.*
[623] Treas. Reg. sec. 1.1461–1(c)(1). IRS Form 1042–S filings provide information important for the Secretary's purposes in properly effecting refund claims and in meeting IRS's obligations under exchange of information agreements with various treaty partners. Also, the IRS has the ability to validate electronically filed Form 1042–S upon such filing, thereby serving to better ensure the reliability of information included in such filings.
[624] *Ibid.* If payments are made to a nominee or representative of a foreign payee, Form 1042–S must also be sent to the beneficial owner of such payments, if known to the withholding agent.
[625] Pub. L. No. 105–206 (1998).

Federal tax and information returns filed electronically by 2007. Section 2001(b) of RRA 1998 requires the IRS to establish a 10-year strategic plan to eliminate barriers to electronic filing.

The Secretary has limited authority to issue regulations specifying which returns must be filed electronically. First, in general, such regulations can only apply to persons required to file at least 250 returns during the year.[626] Second, the Secretary is generally prohibited from requiring that income tax returns of individuals, estates, and trusts be submitted in any format other than paper (although these returns may be filed electronically by choice).[627] Third, the Secretary, in determining which returns must be filed on magnetic media, must take into account relevant factors, including the ability of a taxpayer to comply with magnetic media filing at reasonable cost.[628] Finally, a failure to comply with the regulations mandating electronic filing cannot in itself support a penalty for failure to file an information return, with certain exceptions for corporations and partnerships.[629]

Accordingly, the Secretary requires corporations and tax-exempt organizations that have assets of $10 million or more and file at least 250 returns during a calendar year, including income tax, information, excise tax, and employment tax returns, to file electronically their Form IRS 1120/1120–S income tax returns and IRS Form 990 information returns for tax years ending on or after December 31, 2006. Private foundations and charitable trusts that file at least 250 returns during a calendar year are required to file electronically their IRS Form 990–PF information returns for tax years ending on or after December 31, 2006, regardless of their asset size. Taxpayers can request waivers of the electronic filing requirement if they cannot meet that requirement due to technological constraints, or if compliance with the requirement would result in undue financial burden.

### *Explanation of Provision*

The provision provides an exception to the general annual 250 returns threshold and permits the Secretary to issue regulations to require filing on magnetic media for any return filed by a "financial institution"[630] with respect to any taxes withheld by the "financial institution" for which it is personally liable.[631] Under the provision, the Secretary is authorized to require a financial institution to electronically file returns with respect to any taxes withheld by the fi-

[626] Partnerships with more than 100 partners are required to file electronically. Sec. 6011(e)(2).

[627] For returns filed after 12/31/2010, under the recently enacted Worker, Homeownership, and Business Act of 2009, Pub. L. No. 111–92, any individual tax return, including any return of the tax imposed by subtitle A on individuals, estates, or trusts, prepared by a tax return preparer, is required to be filed electronically unless the tax return preparer reasonably expects to file ten or fewer tax returns during such calendar year. Sec. 6011(e)(3).

[628] Sec. 6011(e).

[629] Sec. 6724(c). If a corporation fails to comply with the electronic filing requirements for more than 250 returns that it is required to file, it may be subject to the penalty for failure to file information returns under section 6721. For partnerships, the penalty may only be imposed if the failure extends to more than 100 returns.

[630] See section 1471(d)(5) in section 101 of the Act.

[631] The "financial institution" is personally liable for any tax withheld in accordance with section 1461 and section 1474(a) under section 101 of the Act.

nancial institution even though such financial institution would be required to file less than 250 returns during the year.

The provision also makes a conforming amendment to section 6724, permitting assertion of a failure to file penalty under section 6721 against a financial institution that fails to comply with the electronic filing requirements.

### *Effective Date*

The provision applies to returns the due date for which (determined without regard to extensions) is after the date of enactment (March 18, 2010).

## 8. Clarifications with respect to foreign trusts which are treated as having a United States beneficiary (sec. 531 of the Act and sec. 679 of the Code)

### *Present Law*

Under the grantor trust rules, a U.S. person that directly or indirectly transfers property to a foreign trust[632] is generally treated as the owner of the portion of the trust comprising the transferred property for any taxable year in which there is a U.S. beneficiary of any portion of the trust.[633] This treatment generally does not apply to transfers by reason of death, or to transfers of property to the trust in exchange for at least the fair market value of the transferred property.[634] A trust is treated as having a U.S. beneficiary for the taxable year unless (1) under the terms of the trust, no part of the income or corpus of the trust may be paid or accumulated during the taxable year to or for the benefit of a U.S. person, and (2) if the trust were terminated at any time during the taxable year, no part of the income or corpus of the trust could be paid to or for the benefit of a U.S. person.[635]

Regulations under section 679 employ a broad approach in determining whether a foreign trust is treated as having a U.S. beneficiary. The determination of whether the trust has a U.S. beneficiary is made for each taxable year of the transferor. The default rule under the statute and regulations is that a trust has a U.S. beneficiary unless during the U.S. transferor's taxable year the trust meets the two requirements as stated above. Income or corpus may be paid or accumulated to or for the benefit of a U.S. person if, directly or indirectly, income may be distributed to or accumulated for the benefit of a U.S. person, or corpus of the trust may be distributed to or held for the future benefit of a U.S. person.[636] The determination is made without regard to whether income or corpus is actually distributed, and without regard to whether a U.S. person's interest in the trust income or corpus is contingent on a future event. A person who is not a named beneficiary and

---

[632] A trust is a foreign trust if it is not a U.S. person. Sec. 7701(a)(31)(B). A trust is a U.S. person if (1) a U.S. court is able to exercise primary supervision over the administration of the trust, and (2) one or more U.S. persons have the authority to control all substantial decisions of the trust. Sec. 7701(a)(30)(E).

[633] Sec. 679(a)(1). This rule does not apply to transfers to trusts established to fund certain deferred compensation plan trusts or to trusts exempt from tax under section 501(c)(3).

[634] Sec. 679(a)(2).

[635] Sec. 679(c)(1).

[636] Treas. Reg. sec. 1.679–2(a)(2)(i).

is not a member of a class of beneficiaries will not be taken into account if the transferor can show that the person's contingent interest in the trust is so remote as to be negligible.[637] In considering whether a foreign trust has a U.S. beneficiary under the terms of the trust, the trust instrument must be read together with other relevant factors including (1) all written and oral agreements and understandings related to the trust, (2) memoranda or letters of wishes, (3) all records that relate to the actual distribution of income and corpus, and (4) all other documents that relate to the trust, whether or not of any purported legal effect.[638] Other factors taken into account in determining whether a foreign trust is deemed to have a U.S. beneficiary include whether (1) the terms of the trust allow the trust to be amended to benefit a U.S. person, (2) the trust instrument does not allow such an amendment, but the law applicable to the foreign trust may require payments or accumulations of income or corpus to a U.S. person, or (3) the parties to the trust ignore the terms of the trust, or it reasonably expected that they will do so to benefit a U.S. person.[639]

If a foreign trust that was not treated as a grantor trust acquires a U.S. beneficiary and is treated as a grantor trust under section 679 for the taxable year, the transferor is taxable on the trust's undistributed net income[640] computed at the end of the preceding taxable year.[641] Any additional amount included in the transferor's gross income as a result of this provision is subject to the interest charge rules of section 668.[642]

### *Explanation of Provision*

In determining whether, under section 679, a foreign trust has a U.S. beneficiary, the provision clarifies that an amount is treated as accumulated for the benefit of a U.S. person even if the U.S. person's interest in the trust is contingent on a future event. Under the provision, if any person has the discretion (by authority given in the trust agreement, by power of appointment, or otherwise) to make a distribution from the trust to, or for the benefit of, any person, the trust is treated as having a U.S. beneficiary unless (1) the terms of the trust specifically identify the class of persons to whom such distributions may be made, and (2) none of those persons is a U.S. person during the taxable year. The provision is meant to be consistent with existing regulations under section 679.

The provision clarifies that if any U.S. person who directly or indirectly transfers property to the trust is directly or indirectly involved in any agreement or understanding (whether written, oral, or otherwise) that may result in the income or corpus of the trust being paid or accumulated to or for the benefit of a U.S. person, such agreement or understanding is treated as a term of the trust. It is assumed for these purposes that a transferor of property to the trust is generally directly or indirectly involved with agree-

---

[637] Treas. Reg. sec. 1.679–2(a)(2)(ii).
[638] Treas. Reg. sec. 1.679–2(a)(4)(i).
[639] Treas. Reg. sec. 1.679–2(a)(4)(ii).
[640] Undistributed net income is defined in section 665(a).
[641] Sec. 679(b).
[642] Treas. Reg. sec. 1.679–2(c)(1).

ments regarding the accumulation or disposition of the income and corpus of the trust.

### *Effective Date*

The provision is effective on the date of enactment (March 18, 2010).

## 9. Presumption that foreign trust has United States beneficiary (sec. 532 of the Act and sec. 679 of the Code)

### *Present Law*

Under the grantor trust rules, a U.S. person that directly or indirectly transfers property to a foreign trust[643] is generally treated as the owner of the portion of the trust comprising that property for any taxable year in which there is a U.S. beneficiary of any portion of the trust.[644] This treatment generally does not apply to transfers by reason of death, or to transfers of property to the trust in exchange for at least the fair market value of the transferred property.[645] A trust is treated as having a U.S. beneficiary for the taxable year unless (1) under the terms of the trust, no part of the income or corpus of the trust may be paid or accumulated during the taxable year to or for the benefit of a U.S. person, and (2) if the trust were terminated at any time during the taxable year, no part of the income or corpus of the trust could be paid to or for the benefit of a U.S. person.[646]

Section 6048 imposes various reporting obligations on foreign trusts and persons creating, making transfers to, or receiving distributions from such trusts. Within 90 days after a U.S. person transfers property to a foreign trust, the transferor must provide written notice of the transfer to the Secretary.[647]

### *Explanation of Provision*

Under the provision, if a U.S. person directly or indirectly transfers property to a foreign trust,[648] the Secretary may treat the trust as having a U.S. beneficiary for purposes of section 679 unless such U.S. person submits information as required by the Secretary and demonstrates to the satisfaction of the Secretary that (1) under the terms of the trust, no part of the income or corpus of the trust may be paid or accumulated during the taxable year to or for the benefit of a U.S. person, and (2) if the trust were terminated during the taxable year, no part of the income or corpus of the trust could be paid to or for the benefit of a U.S. person.

---

[643] A trust is a foreign trust if it is not a U.S. person. Sec. 7701(a)(31)(B). A trust is a U.S. person if (1) a U.S. court is able to exercise primary supervision over the administration of the trust and (2) one or more U.S. persons have the authority to control all substantial decisions of the trust. Sec. 7701(a)(30)(E).

[644] Sec. 679(a)(1). This rule does not apply to transfers to trusts established to fund certain deferred compensation plan trusts or to trusts exempt from tax under section 501(c)(3).

[645] Sec. 679(a)(2).

[646] Sec. 679(c)(1).

[647] Sec. 6048(a).

[648] A foreign trust for this purpose does not include deferred compensation and charitable trusts described in section 6048(a)(3)(B)(ii).

### *Effective Date*

The provision applies to transfers of property after the date of enactment (March 18, 2010).

### 10. Uncompensated use of trust property (sec. 533 of the Act and secs. 643 and 679 of the Code)

### *Present Law*

Under section 643(i), a loan of cash or marketable securities made by a foreign trust to any U.S. grantor, U.S. beneficiary, or any other U.S. person who is related to a U.S. grantor or U.S. beneficiary generally is treated as a distribution by the foreign trust to such grantor or beneficiary. This rule applies for purposes of determining if the foreign trust is a simple or complex trust, computing the distribution deduction for the trust, determining the amount of gross income of the beneficiaries, and computing any accumulation distribution. Loans to tax-exempt entities are excluded from this rule.[649] A trust treated under this rule as making a distribution is not treated as a simple trust for the year of the distribution.[650] This rule does not apply for purposes of determining if a trust has a U.S. beneficiary under section 679.

A subsequent repayment, satisfaction, or cancellation of a loan treated as a distribution under section 643(i) is disregarded for tax purposes.[651] This section applies a broad set of related party rules that treat a loan of cash or marketable securities to a spouse, sibling, ancestor, descendant of the grantor or beneficiary, spouse of such family members, other trusts in which the grantor or beneficiary has an interest, and corporations or partnerships controlled by the beneficiary or grantor or by family members of the beneficiary or grantor, as a distribution to the related grantor or beneficiary.[652]

### *Explanation of Provision*

The provision expands section 643(i) to provide that any use of trust property by the U.S. grantor, U.S. beneficiary or any U.S. person related to a U.S. grantor or U.S. beneficiary is treated as a distribution of the fair market value of the use of the property to the U.S. grantor or U.S. beneficiary. The use of property is not treated as a distribution to the extent that the trust is paid the fair market value for the use of the property within a reasonable period of time. A subsequent return of property treated as a distribution under section 643(i) is disregarded for tax purposes.

For purposes of determining whether a foreign trust has a U.S. beneficiary under section 679, a loan of cash or marketable securities or the use of any other trust property by a U.S. person is treated as a payment from the trust to the U.S. person in the amount of the loan or the fair market value of the use of the property. A loan or use of property is not treated as a payment to the extent

[649] Sec. 643(i)(2)(C).

[650] Sec. 643(i)(2)(D).

[651] Sec. 643(i)(3).

[652] Section 643(i)(2)(B) treats a person as a related person if the relationship between such person would result in a disallowance of losses under sections 267 or 707(b), broadened to include the spouses of members of the family described in such sections.

that the U.S. person repays the loan at a market rate of interest or pays the fair market value for the use of the trust property within a reasonable period of time.

### *Effective Date*

The provision applies to loans made and uses of property after the date of enactment (March 18, 2010).

## 11. Reporting requirement of United States owners of foreign trusts (sec. 534 of the Act and sec. 6048 of the Code)

### *Present Law*

Section 6048 imposes various reporting obligations on foreign trusts and persons creating, making transfers to, or receiving distributions from such trusts. If a U.S. person is treated as the owner of any portion of a foreign trust under the rules of subpart E of part I of subchapter J of chapter 1 (grantor trust provisions), the U.S. person is responsible for ensuring that the trust files an information return for the year and that the trust provides other information as the Secretary may require to each U.S. person who (1) is treated as the owner of any portion of the trust, or (2) receives (directly or indirectly) any distribution from the trust.[653]

### *Explanation of Provision*

The provision requires a U.S. person that is treated as an owner of any portion of a foreign trust under the rules of subpart E of part I of subchapter J of chapter 1 (grantor trust provisions) to provide information as the Secretary may require with respect to the trust, in addition to ensuring that the trust complies with its reporting obligations.

### *Effective Date*

The provision applies to taxable years beginning after the date of enactment (March 18, 2010).

## 12. Minimum penalty with respect to failure to report on certain foreign trusts (sec. 535 of the Act and sec. 6677 of the Code)

### *Present Law*

#### ***Minimum penalty with respect to failure to report on certain foreign trusts***

Section 6048 imposes various reporting obligations on foreign trusts and persons creating, making transfers to, or receiving distributions from such trusts. Generally, a trust is a foreign trust unless a U.S. court is able to exercise primary supervision over the trust's administration and a U.S. trustee has authority to control all substantial decisions of the trust.[654] If a U.S. person creates or

---

[653] Sec. 6048(b)(1).

[654] Sec. 7701(a)(30)(E), (31)(B). In addition, for purposes of section 6048, the IRS can classify a trust as foreign if it "has substantial activities, or holds substantial property, outside the United States." Sec. 6048(d)(2).

transfers property to a foreign trust, the U.S. person generally must report this event and certain other information by the due date for the U.S. person's tax return, including extensions, for the tax year in which the creation of the trust or the transfer occurs.[655] Similar rules apply in the case of the death of a U.S. citizen or resident if the decedent was treated as the owner of any portion of a foreign trust under the grantor trust rules or if any portion of a foreign trust was included in the decedent's gross estate. If a U.S. person directly or indirectly receives a distribution from a foreign trust, the U.S. person generally must report the distribution by the due date for the U.S. person's tax return, including extensions, for the tax year during which the distribution is received.[656] If a U.S. person is the owner of any portion of a foreign grantor trust at any time during the year, the person is responsible for causing an information return to be filed for the trust, which must, among other things, give the name of a U.S. agent for the trust.[657]

If a notice or return required under the rules just described is not filed when due or is filed without all required information, the person required to file is generally subject to a penalty based on the "gross reportable amount."[658] The gross reportable amount is (1) the value of the property transferred to the foreign trust if the delinquency is failure to file notice of the creation of or a transfer to a foreign trust; (2) the value (on the last day of the year) of the portion of a grantor trust owned by a U.S. person who fails to cause an annual return to be filed for the trust; and (3) the amount distributed to a distributee who fails to report distributions.[659] The initial penalty is 35 percent of the gross reportable amount in cases (1) and (3) and five percent in case (2).[660] If the return is more than 90 days late, additional penalties are imposed of $10,000 for every 30 days the delinquency continues, except that the aggregate of the penalties may not exceed the gross reportable amount.[661]

#### *Maximum penalty with respect to failure to report on certain foreign trusts*

In no event may the penalties imposed with respect to any failure to report under section 6048 exceed the gross reportable amount.[662]

### *Explanation of Provision*

#### *Increase of the minimum penalty with respect to failure to report on certain foreign trusts*

Under the provision, the initial penalty for failing to report under section 6048 is the greater of $10,000 or 35 percent of the gross reportable amount in cases (1) and (3) and the greater of $10,000 or five percent of the gross reportable amount in case (2). Thus, an initial penalty of $10,000 may be imposed even where the

[655] Sec. 6048(a).
[656] Sec. 6048(c).
[657] Sec. 6048(b).
[658] Sec. 6677(a).
[659] Sec. 6677(c).
[660] Sec. 6677(b).
[661] Sec. 6677(a).
[662] *Ibid.*

Secretary has insufficient information to determine the gross reportable amount. The additional $10,000 penalty for every additional 30 days of delinquency continues to apply.

***Amendment to the maximum penalty with respect to failure to report on certain foreign trusts***

The provision provides that the penalties with respect to failure to report on certain foreign trusts may exceed the gross reportable amount. However, to the extent that a taxpayer provides sufficient information for the Secretary to determine that the aggregate amount of the penalties exceeds the gross reportable amount, the Secretary is required to refund such excess to the taxpayer.

### *Effective Date*

The provision applies to notices and returns required to be filed after December 31, 2009.

## 13. Substitute dividends and dividend equivalent payments received by foreign persons treated as dividends (sec. 541 of the Act and sec. 871 of the Code)

### *Present Law*

Payments of U.S.-source "fixed or determinable annual or periodical" income, including interest, dividends, and similar types of investment income, made to foreign persons are generally subject to U.S. tax, collected by withholding, at a 30-percent rate, unless the withholding agent can establish that the beneficial owner of the amount is eligible for an exemption from withholding or a reduced rate of withholding under an income tax treaty.[663] Dividends paid by a domestic corporation are generally U.S.-source[664] and therefore potentially subject to withholding tax when paid to foreign persons.

The source of notional principal contract income generally is determined by reference to the residence of the recipient of the income.[665] Consequently, a foreign person's income related to a notional principal contract that references stock of a domestic corporation, including any amount attributable to, or calculated by reference to, dividends paid on the stock, generally is foreign source and is therefore not subject to U.S. withholding tax.

In contrast, a substitute dividend payment made to the transferor of stock in a securities lending transaction or a sale-repurchase transaction is sourced in the same manner as actual dividends paid on the transferred stock.[666] Accordingly, because divi-

[663] Secs. 871, 881, 1441, 1442; Treas. Reg. sec. 1.1441–1(b). For purposes of the withholding tax rules applicable to payments to nonresident alien individuals and foreign corporations, a withholding agent is defined broadly to include any U.S. or foreign person that has the control, receipt, custody, disposal, or payment of an item of income of a foreign person subject to withholding. Treas. Reg. sec. 1.1441–7(a).

[664] Sec. 861(a)(2).

[665] Treas. Reg. sec. 1.863–7(b)(1). A notional principal contract is a financial instrument that provides for the payment of amounts by one party to another at specified intervals calculated by reference to a specified index upon a notional principal amount in exchange for specified consideration or a promise to pay similar amounts. Treas. Reg. sec. 1.446–3(c)(1).

[666] Treas. Reg. sec. 1.861–3(a)(6). This regulation defines a substitute dividend payment as a payment, made to the transferor of a security in a securities lending transaction or a sale-repurchase transaction, of an amount equivalent to a dividend distribution which the owner of the transferred security is entitled to receive during the term of the transaction.

dends paid with respect to the stock of a U.S. company are generally U.S. source, if a foreign person lends stock of a U.S. company to another person (or sells the stock to the other person and later repurchases the stock in a transaction treated as a loan for U.S. Federal income tax purposes) and receives substitute dividend payments from that other person, the substitute dividend payments are U.S. source and are generally subject to U.S. withholding tax.[667] In 1997, the Treasury and IRS issued Notice 97–66 to address concerns that the sourcing rule just described (and the accompanying character rule) could cause the total U.S. withholding tax imposed in a series of securities lending or sale-repurchase transactions to be excessive.[668] In that Notice, the Treasury and IRS also stated that they intended to propose new regulations to provide detailed guidance on how substitute dividend payments made by one foreign person to another foreign person were to be treated. To date, no regulations have been proposed.[669]

### *Explanation of Provision*

The provision treats a dividend equivalent as a dividend from U.S. sources for certain purposes, including the U.S. withholding tax rules applicable to foreign persons.

A dividend equivalent is any substitute dividend made pursuant to a securities lending or a sale-repurchase transaction that (directly or indirectly) is contingent upon, or determined by reference to, the payment of a dividend from sources within the United States or any payment made under a specified notional principal contract that directly or indirectly is contingent upon, or determined by reference to, the payment of a dividend from sources within the United States. A dividend equivalent also includes any other payment that the Secretary determines is substantially similar to a payment described in the immediately preceding sentence. Under this rule, for example, the Secretary may conclude that payments under certain forward contracts or other financial contracts that reference stock of U.S. corporations are dividend equivalents.

A specified notional principal contract is any notional principal contract that has any one of the following five characteristics: (1) in connection with entering into the contract, any long party to the contract transfers the underlying security to any short party to the contract; (2) in connection with the termination of the contract, any short party to the contract transfers the underlying security to any long party to the contract; (3) the underlying security is not readily tradable on an established securities market; (4) in connection with

[667] For purposes of the imposition of the 30-percent withholding tax, substitute dividend payments (and substitute interest payments) received by a foreign person under a securities lending or sale-repurchase transaction have the same character as dividend (and interest) income received in respect of the transferred security. Treas. Reg. secs. 1.871–7(b)(2), 1.881–2(b)(2).

[668] Notice 97–66, 1997–2 C.B. 328 (December 1, 1997).

[669] There is evidence that some taxpayers have taken the position that Notice 97–66 sanctions the elimination of withholding tax in certain situations. See United States Senate, Permanent Subcommittee on Investigations, Committee on Homeland Security and Governmental Affairs, *Dividend Tax Abuse: How Offshore Entities Dodge Taxes on U.S. Stock Dividends,* Staff Report, September 11, 2008, pp. 18–20, 22–23, 40, 47, 52. In the Obama administration's fiscal year 2010 budget, the Treasury Department has announced that, to address the avoidance of U.S. withholding tax through the use of securities lending transactions, it plans to revoke Notice 97–66 and issue guidance that eliminates the benefits of those transactions but minimizes overwithholding. Department of the Treasury, General Explanations of the Administration's Fiscal Year 2010 Revenue Proposals, May 2009, p. 37.

entering into the contract, any short party to the contract posts the underlying security as collateral with any long party to the contract; or (5) the Secretary identifies the contract as a specified notional principal contract.[670] For purposes of these characteristics, for any underlying security of any notional principal contract (1) a long party is any party to the contract that is entitled to receive any payment under the contract that is contingent upon or determined by reference to the payment of a U.S.-source dividend on the underlying security, and (2) a short party is any party to the contract that is not a long party in respect of the underlying security. An underlying security in a notional principal contract is the security with respect to which the dividend equivalent is paid. For these purposes, any index or fixed basket of securities is treated as a single security. In applying this rule, it is intended that such a security will be deemed to be regularly traded on an established securities market if every component of such index or fixed basket is a security that is readily tradable on an established securities market.

For payments made more than two years after the provision's date of enactment (March 18, 2010), a specified notional principal contract also includes any notional principal contract unless the Secretary determines that the contract is of a type that does not have the potential for tax avoidance.

No inference is intended as to whether the definition of specified notional principal contract, or any determination under this provision that a transaction does not have the potential for the avoidance of taxes on U.S.-source dividends (or, in the case of a debt instrument, U.S.-source interest), is relevant in determining whether an agency relationship exists under general tax principles or whether a foreign party to a contract should be treated as having beneficial tax ownership of the stock giving rise to U.S.-source dividends.

The payments that are treated as U.S.-source dividends under the provision are the gross amounts that are used in computing any net amounts transferred to or from the taxpayer. The example of a "total return swap" referencing stock of a domestic corporation (an example of a notional principal contract to which the provision generally applies), illustrates the consequences of this rule. Under a typical total return swap, a foreign investor enters into an agreement with a counterparty under which amounts due to each party are based on the returns generated by a notional investment in a specified dollar amount of the stock underlying the swap. The investor agrees for a specified period to pay to the counterparty (1) an amount calculated by reference to a market interest rate (such as the London Interbank Offered Rate ("LIBOR")) on the notional amount of the underlying stock and (2) any depreciation in the value of the stock. In return, the counterparty agrees for the specified period to pay the investor (1) any dividends paid on the stock and (2) any appreciation in the value of the stock. Amounts owed by each party under this swap typically are netted so that only one party makes an actual payment. The provision treats any dividend-

[670] Any notional principal contract identified by the Secretary as a specified notional principal contract will be subject to the provision's general effective date described below.

based amount under the swap as a payment even though any actual payment under the swap is a net amount determined in part by other amounts (for example, the interest amount and the amount of any appreciation or depreciation in value of the referenced stock). Accordingly, a counterparty to a total return swap may be obligated to withhold and remit tax on the gross amount of a dividend equivalent even though, as a result of a netting of payments due under the swap, the counterparty is not required to make an actual payment to the foreign investor.

If there is a chain of dividend equivalents (under, for example, transactions similar to those described in Notice 97–66), and one or more of the dividend equivalents is subject to tax under the provision or under section 881, the Secretary may reduce that tax, but only to the extent that the taxpayer either establishes that the tax has been paid on another dividend equivalent in the chain, or that such tax is not otherwise due, or as the Secretary determines is appropriate to address the role of financial intermediaries in such chain. An actual dividend is treated as a dividend equivalent for purposes of this rule.

For purposes of chapter 3 (withholding of tax on nonresident aliens and foreign corporations) and chapter 4 (taxes to enforce reporting on certain foreign accounts), each person that is a party to a contract or other arrangement that provides for the payment of a dividend equivalent is treated as having control of the payment. Accordingly, Treasury may provide guidance requiring either party to withhold tax on dividend equivalents.

The rule treating dividend equivalents as U.S.-source dividends is not intended to limit the authority of the Secretary (1) to determine the appropriate source of income from financial arrangements (including notional principal contracts) under present law section 863 or 865 or (2) to provide additional guidance addressing the source and characterization of substitute payments made in securities lending and similar transactions.

### *Effective Date*

The provision applies to payments made on or after the date that is 180 days after the date of enactment (March 18, 2010).

## B. Delay in Application of Worldwide Allocation of Interest (sec. 551 of the Act and sec. 864 of the Code)

### *Present Law*

#### *In general*

To compute the foreign tax credit limitation, a taxpayer must determine the amount of its taxable income from foreign sources. Thus, the taxpayer must allocate and apportion deductions between items of U.S.-source gross income, on the one hand, and items of foreign-source gross income, on the other.

In the case of interest expense, the rules generally are based on the approach that money is fungible and that interest expense is properly attributable to all business activities and property of a taxpayer, regardless of any specific purpose for incurring an obligation on which interest is paid.[671] For interest allocation purposes, all members of an affiliated group of corporations generally are treated as a single corporation (the so-called "one-taxpayer rule") and allocation must be made on the basis of assets rather than gross income. The term "affiliated group" in this context generally is defined by reference to the rules for determining whether corporations are eligible to file consolidated returns.

For consolidation purposes, the term "affiliated group" means one or more chains of includible corporations connected through stock ownership with a common parent corporation that is an includible corporation, but only if: (1) the common parent owns directly stock possessing at least 80 percent of the total voting power and at least 80 percent of the total value of at least one other includible corporation; and (2) stock meeting the same voting power and value standards with respect to each includible corporation (excluding the common parent) is directly owned by one or more other includible corporations.

Generally, the term "includible corporation" means any domestic corporation except certain corporations exempt from tax under section 501 (for example, corporations organized and operated exclusively for charitable or educational purposes), certain life insurance companies, corporations electing application of the possession tax credit, regulated investment companies, real estate investment trusts, and domestic international sales corporations. A foreign corporation generally is not an includible corporation.

Subject to exceptions, the consolidated return and interest allocation definitions of affiliation generally are consistent with each other.[672] For example, both definitions generally exclude all foreign corporations from the affiliated group. Thus, while debt generally is considered fungible among the assets of a group of domestic affiliated corporations, the same rules do not apply as between the domestic and foreign members of a group with the same degree of common control as the domestic affiliated group.

*Banks, savings institutions, and other financial affiliates*

The affiliated group for interest allocation purposes generally excludes what are referred to in the Treasury regulations as "financial corporations."[673] A financial corporation includes any corporation, otherwise a member of the affiliated group for consolidation purposes, that is a financial institution (described in section 581 or section 591), the business of which is predominantly with persons other than related persons or their customers, and which is required by State or Federal law to be operated separately from any other entity that is not a financial institution.[674] The category of financial corporations also includes, to the extent provided in regulations, bank holding companies (including financial holding companies), subsidiaries of banks and bank holding companies (includ-

---

[671] However, exceptions to the fungibility principle are provided in particular cases, some of which are described below.

[672] One such exception is that the affiliated group for interest allocation purposes includes section 936 corporations (certain electing domestic corporations that have income from the active conduct of a trade or business in Puerto Rico or another U.S. possession) that are excluded from the consolidated group.

[673] Temp. Treas. Reg. sec. 1.861–11T(d)(4).

[674] Sec. 864(e)(5)(C).

ing financial holding companies), and savings institutions predominantly engaged in the active conduct of a banking, financing, or similar business.[675]

A financial corporation is not treated as a member of the regular affiliated group for purposes of applying the one-taxpayer rule to other nonfinancial members of that group. Instead, all such financial corporations that would be so affiliated are treated as a separate single corporation for interest allocation purposes.

### *Worldwide interest allocation*

#### *In general*

The American Jobs Creation Act of 2004 ("AJCA")[676] modified the interest expense allocation rules described above (which generally apply for purposes of computing the foreign tax credit limitation) by providing a one-time election (the "worldwide affiliated group election") under which the taxable income of the domestic members of an affiliated group from sources outside the United States generally is determined by allocating and apportioning interest expense of the domestic members of a worldwide affiliated group on a worldwide-group basis (i.e., as if all members of the worldwide group were a single corporation). If a group makes this election, the taxable income of the domestic members of a worldwide affiliated group from sources outside the United States is determined by allocating and apportioning the third-party interest expense of those domestic members to foreign-source income in an amount equal to the excess (if any) of (1) the worldwide affiliated group's worldwide third-party interest expense multiplied by the ratio that the foreign assets of the worldwide affiliated group bears to the total assets of the worldwide affiliated group,[677] over (2) the third-party interest expense incurred by foreign members of the group to the extent such interest would be allocated to foreign sources if the principles of worldwide interest allocation were applied separately to the foreign members of the group.[678]

For purposes of the new elective rules based on worldwide fungibility, the worldwide affiliated group means all corporations in an affiliated group as well as all controlled foreign corporations that, in the aggregate, either directly or indirectly,[679] would be members of such an affiliated group if section 1504(b)(3) did not apply (i.e., in which at least 80 percent of the vote and value of the stock of such corporations is owned by one or more other corporations included in the affiliated group). Thus, if an affiliated group makes this election, the taxable income from sources outside the United States of domestic group members generally is determined by allocating and apportioning interest expense of the domestic

---

[675] Sec. 864(e)(5)(D).

[676] Pub. L. No. 108–357, sec. 401.

[677] For purposes of determining the assets of the worldwide affiliated group, neither stock in corporations within the group nor indebtedness (including receivables) between members of the group is taken into account.

[678] Although the interest expense of a foreign subsidiary is taken into account for purposes of allocating the interest expense of the domestic members of the electing worldwide affiliated group for foreign tax credit limitation purposes, the interest expense incurred by a foreign subsidiary is not deductible on a U.S. return.

[679] Indirect ownership is determined under the rules of section 958(a)(2) or through applying rules similar to those of section 958(a)(2) to stock owned directly or indirectly by domestic partnerships, trusts, or estates.

members of the worldwide affiliated group as if all of the interest expense and assets of 80-percent or greater owned domestic corporations (i.e., corporations that are part of the affiliated group, as modified to include insurance companies) and certain controlled foreign corporations were attributable to a single corporation.

*Financial institution group election*

Taxpayers are allowed to apply the bank group rules to exclude certain financial institutions from the affiliated group for interest allocation purposes under the worldwide fungibility approach. The rules also provide a one-time "financial institution group" election that expands the bank group. At the election of the common parent of the pre-election worldwide affiliated group, the interest expense allocation rules are applied separately to a subgroup of the worldwide affiliated group that consists of (1) all corporations that are part of the bank group, and (2) all "financial corporations." For this purpose, a corporation is a financial corporation if at least 80 percent of its gross income is financial services income (as described in section 904(d)(2)(C)(i) and the regulations thereunder) that is derived from transactions with unrelated persons.[680] For these purposes, items of income or gain from a transaction or series of transactions are disregarded if a principal purpose for the transaction or transactions is to qualify any corporation as a financial corporation.

In addition, anti-abuse rules are provided under which certain transfers from one member of a financial institution group to a member of the worldwide affiliated group outside of the financial institution group are treated as reducing the amount of indebtedness of the separate financial institution group. Regulatory authority is provided with respect to the election to provide for the direct allocation of interest expense in circumstances in which such allocation is appropriate to carry out the purposes of these rules, to prevent assets or interest expense from being taken into account more than once, or to address changes in members of any group (through acquisitions or otherwise) treated as affiliated under these rules.

*Effective date of worldwide interest allocation*

The common parent of the domestic affiliated group must make the worldwide affiliated group election. It must be made for the first taxable year beginning after December 31, 2017, in which a worldwide affiliated group exists that includes at least one foreign corporation that meets the requirements for inclusion in a worldwide affiliated group.[681] The common parent of the pre-election worldwide affiliated group must make the election for the first taxable year beginning after December 31, 2017, in which a worldwide affiliated group includes a financial corporation. Once either election is made, it applies to the common parent and all other mem-

---

[680] See Treas. Reg. sec. 1.904–4(e)(2). a

[681] As originally enacted under AJCA, the worldwide interest allocation rules were effective for taxable years beginning after December 31, 2008. However, section 3093 of the Housing and Economic Recovery Act of 2008, Pub. L. No. 110–289, delayed the implementation of the worldwide interest allocation rules for two years, until taxable years beginning after December 31, 2010. The implementation of the worldwide interest allocation rules was further delayed by seven years, until taxable years beginning after December 31, 2017, in section 15 of the Worker, Homeownership, and Business Assistance Act of 2009, Pub. L. No. 111–92.

bers of the worldwide affiliated group or to all members of the financial institution group, as applicable, for the taxable year for which the election is made and all subsequent taxable years, unless revoked with the consent of the Secretary of the Treasury.

### *Explanation of Provision*

The provision delays the effective date of the worldwide interest allocation rules for three year, until taxable years beginning after December 31, 2020. The required dates for making the worldwide affiliated group election and the financial institution group election are changed accordingly.

### *Effective Date*

The provision is effective on the date of enactment (March 18, 2010).

## C. Corporate Estimated Tax (sec. 561 of the Act and sec. 6655 of the Code)

### *Present Law*

In general, corporations are required to make quarterly estimated tax payments of their income tax liability.[682] For a corporation whose taxable year is a calendar year, these estimated tax payments must be made by April 15, June 15, September 15, and December 15. In the case of a corporation with assets of at least $1 billion (determined as of the end of the preceding tax year), payments due in July, August, or September, 2014, are increased to 134.75 percent of the payment otherwise due and the next required payment is reduced accordingly.[683]

### *Explanation of Provision*[684]

The provision increases the applicable percentage in 2014 by 23.00 percentage points, the applicable percentage in 2015 by 21.50 percentage points, and the applicable percentage in 2019 by 6.50 percentage points. For each of the periods impacted, the next required payment is reduced accordingly.

### *Effective Date*

The provision is effective on the date of enactment (March 18, 2010).

---

[682] Sec. 6655.

[683] Act to extend the Generalized System of Preferences and the Andean Trade Preference Act, and for other purposes, Pub. L. No. 111–124, sec. 4; Worker, Homeownership, and Business Assistance Act of 2009, Pub. L. No. 111–92, sec. 18; Joint resolution approving the renewal of import restrictions contained in the Burmese Freedom and Democracy Act of 2003, and for other purposes, Pub. L. No. 111–42, sec. 202(b)(1).

[684] All the public laws enacted in the 111th Congress affecting this provision are described in Part Twenty-One of this document.

# PART EIGHT: HEALTH CARE PROVISIONS

# PATIENT PROTECTION AND AFFORDABLE CARE ACT (PUBLIC LAW 111–148),[685] HEALTH CARE AND EDUCATION RECONCILIATION ACT OF 2010 (PUBLIC LAW 111–152),[686] AN ACT TO CLARIFY THE HEALTH CARE PROVIDED BY THE SECRETARY OF VETERANS AFFAIRS THAT CONSTITUTES MINIMUM ESSENTIAL COVERAGE (PUBLIC LAW 111–173),[687] AND MEDICARE AND MEDICAID EXTENDERS ACT OF 2010 (PUBLIC LAW 111–309)[688]

## PATIENT PROTECTION AND AFFORDABLE CARE ACT

## TITLE I—QUALITY, AFFORDABLE HEALTH CARE FOR ALL AMERICANS

### A. Tax Exemption for Certain Member-Run Health Insurance Issuers (sec. 1322[689] of the Act and new sec. 501(c)(29) and sec. 6033 of the Code)

[685] H.R. 3590. The bill originated as the Service Members Home Ownership Tax Act of 2009 and passed the House on the suspension calendar on October 8, 2009. The House Ways and Means Committee reported H.R. 3200 on October 14, 2009 (H.R. Rep. No. 111–299 (part II)). The Senate Finance Committee reported S. 1796 on October 19, 2009 (S. Rep. No. 111–89). The House passed H.R. 3962 on November 7, 2009. The Senate passed H.R. 3590 with an amendment substituting the text of the Patient Protection and Affordable Care Act on December 24, 2009. The House agreed to the Senate amendment on March 21, 2010. The President signed the bill on March 23, 2010.

[686] H.R. 4872. The bill passed the House on March 21, 2010. The Senate passed the bill with amendments on March 25, 2010. The House agreed to the Senate amendments on March 25, 2010. The President signed the bill on March 30, 2010.

For a technical explanation of the bills prepared by the staff of the Joint Committee on Taxation, see *Technical Explanation of the Revenue Provisions of the "Reconciliation Act of 2010," as Amended, in Combination with the "Patient Protection and Affordable Care Act"* (JCX–18–10), March 21, 2010.

[687] H.R. 5014. The bill passed the House on the suspension calendar on May 12, 2010. The Senate passed the bill by unanimous consent on May 18, 2010. The President signed the bill on May 27, 2010.

Pub. L. No. 111–173, which amends section 5000A(f)(1)(A) of the Code, as added by section 1501(b) of the Patient Protection and Affordable Care Act, is described *infra* in a footnote in section H of title I of the Patient Protection and Affordable Care Act of Part Eight.

[688] H.R. 4994. The bill passed the House on the suspension calendar on April 14, 2010. The Senate passed the bill with amendments by unanimous consent on December 8, 2010. The House agreed to the Senate amendments on the suspension calendar on December 9, 2010. The President signed the bill on December 15, 2010.

Pub. L. No. 111–309, which amends section 36B(f)(2)(B) of the Code, is described *infra* in section C of title I of the Patient Protection and Affordable Care Act of Part Eight.

[689] Section 1322 of the Patient Protection and Affordable Care Act, Pub. L. No. 111–148, as amended by section 10104.

## *Present Law*

### *In general*

Although present law provides that certain limited categories of organizations that offer insurance may qualify for exemption from Federal income tax, present law generally does not provide tax-exempt status for newly established, member-run nonprofit health insurers that are established and funded pursuant to the Consumer Oriented, Not-for-Profit Health Plan program created under the Act and described below.

### *Taxation of insurance companies*

*Taxation of stock and mutual companies providing health insurance*

Present law provides special rules for determining the taxable income of insurance companies (subchapter L of the Code). Both mutual insurance companies and stock insurance companies are subject to Federal income tax under these rules. Separate sets of rules apply to life insurance companies and to property and casualty insurance companies. Insurance companies are subject to Federal income tax at regular corporate income tax rates.

An insurance company that provides health insurance is subject to Federal income tax as either a life insurance company or as a property and casualty insurance company, depending on its mix of lines of business and on the resulting portion of its reserves that are treated as life insurance reserves. For Federal income tax purposes, an insurance company is treated as a life insurance company if the sum of its (1) life insurance reserves and (2) unearned premiums and unpaid losses on noncancellable life, accident or health contracts not included in life insurance reserves, comprise more than 50 percent of its total reserves.[690]

*Life insurance companies*

A life insurance company, whether stock or mutual, is taxed at regular corporate rates on its life insurance company taxable income (LICTI). LICTI is life insurance gross income reduced by life insurance deductions.[691] An alternative tax applies if a company has a net capital gain for the taxable year, if such tax is less than the tax that would otherwise apply. Life insurance gross income is the sum of (1) premiums, (2) decreases in reserves, and (3) other amounts generally includible by a taxpayer in gross income. Methods for determining reserves for Federal income tax purposes generally are based on reserves prescribed by the National Association of Insurance Commissioners for purposes of financial reporting under State regulatory rules.

Because deductible reserves might be viewed as being funded proportionately out of taxable and tax-exempt income, the net increase and net decrease in reserves are computed by reducing the ending balance of the reserve items by a portion of tax-exempt in-

[690] Sec. 816(a).
[691] Sec. 801.

terest (known as a proration rule).[692] Similarly, a life insurance company is allowed a dividends-received deduction for intercorporate dividends from nonaffiliates only in proportion to the company's share of such dividends.[693]

*Property and casualty insurance companies*

The taxable income of a property and casualty insurance company is determined as the sum of the amount earned from underwriting income and from investment income (as well as gains and other income items), reduced by allowable deductions.[694] For this purpose, underwriting income and investment income are computed on the basis of the underwriting and investment exhibit of the annual statement approved by the National Association of Insurance Commissioners.[695]

Underwriting income means premiums earned during the taxable year less losses incurred and expenses incurred.[696] Losses incurred include certain unpaid losses (reported losses that have not been paid, estimates of losses incurred but not reported, resisted claims, and unpaid loss adjustment expenses). Present law limits the deduction for unpaid losses to the amount of discounted unpaid losses, which are discounted using prescribed discount periods and a prescribed interest rate, to take account partially of the time value of money.[697] Any net decrease in the amount of unpaid losses results in income inclusion, and the amount included is computed on a discounted basis.

In calculating its reserve for losses incurred, a proration rule requires that a property and casualty insurance company must reduce the amount of losses incurred by 15 percent of (1) the insurer's tax-exempt interest, (2) the deductible portion of dividends received (with special rules for dividends from affiliates), and (3) the increase for the taxable year in the cash value of life insurance, endowment, or annuity contracts the company owns (sec. 832(b)(5)). This rule reflects the fact that reserves are generally funded in part from tax-exempt interest, from wholly or partially deductible dividends, or from other untaxed amounts.

***Tax exemption for certain organizations***

*In general*

Section 501(a) generally provides for exemption from Federal income tax for certain organizations. These organizations include: (1) qualified pension, profit sharing, and stock bonus plans described in section 401(a); (2) religious and apostolic organizations described

---

[692] Secs. 807(b)(2)(B) and (b)(1)(B).

[693] Secs. 805(a)(4), 812. Fully deductible dividends from affiliates are excluded from the application of this proration formula (so long as such dividends are not themselves distributions from tax-exempt interest or from dividend income that would not be fully deductible if received directly by the taxpayer). In addition, the proration rule includes in prorated amounts the increase for the taxable year in policy cash values of life insurance policies and annuity and endowment contracts owned by the company (the inside buildup on which is not taxed).

[694] Sec. 832.

[695] Sec. 832(b)(1)(A).

[696] Sec. 832(b)(3). In determining premiums earned, the company deducts from gross premiums the increase in unearned premiums for the year (sec. 832(b)(4)(B)). The company is required to reduce the deduction for increases in unearned premiums by 20 percent, reflecting the matching of deferred expenses to deferred income.

[697] Sec. 846.

in section 501(d); and (3) organizations described in section 501(c). Sections 501(c) describes 28 different categories of exempt organizations, including: charitable organizations (section 501(c)(3)); social welfare organizations (section 501(c)(4)); labor, agricultural, and horticultural organizations (section 501(c)(5)); professional associations (section 501(c)(6)); and social clubs (section 501(c)(7)).[698]

*Insurance organizations described in section 501(c)*

Although most organizations that engage principally in insurance activities are not exempt from Federal income tax, certain organizations that engage in insurance activities are described in section 501(c) and exempt from tax under section 501(a). Section 501(c)(8), for example, describes certain fraternal beneficiary societies, orders, or associations operating under the lodge system or for the exclusive benefit of their members that provide for the payment of life, sick, accident, or other benefits to the members or their dependents. Section 501(c)(9) describes certain voluntary employees' beneficiary associations that provide for the payment of life, sick, accident, or other benefits to the members of the association or their dependents or designated beneficiaries. Section 501(c)(12)(A) describes certain benevolent life insurance associations of a purely local character. Section 501(c)(15) describes certain small non-life insurance companies with annual gross receipts of no more than $600,000 ($150,000 in the case of a mutual insurance company). Section 501(c)(26) describes certain membership organizations established to provide health insurance to certain high-risk individuals.[699] Section 501(c)(27) describes certain organizations established to provide workmen's compensation insurance.

*Certain section 501(c)(3) organizations*

Certain health maintenance organizations (HMOs) have been held to qualify for tax exemption as charitable organizations described in section 501(c)(3). In *Sound Health Association v. Com-*

---

[698] Certain organizations that operate on a cooperative basis are taxed under special rules set forth in Subchapter T of the Code. The two principal criteria for determining whether an entity is operating on a cooperative basis are: (1) ownership of the cooperative by persons who patronize the cooperative (e.g., the farmer members of a cooperative formed to market the farmers' produce); and (2) return of earnings to patrons in proportion to their patronage. In general, cooperative members are those who participate in the management of the cooperative and who share in patronage capital. For Federal income tax purposes, a cooperative that is taxed under the Subchapter T rules generally computes its income as if it were a taxable corporation, with one exception—the cooperative may deduct from its taxable income distributions of patronage dividends. In general, patronage dividends are the profits of the cooperative that are rebated to its patrons pursuant to a preexisting obligation of the cooperative to do so. Certain farmers' cooperatives described in section 521 are authorized to deduct not only patronage dividends from patronage sources, but also dividends on capital stock and certain distributions to patrons from nonpatronage sources.

Separate from the Subchapter T rules, the Code provides tax exemption for certain cooperatives. Section 501(c)(12), for example, provides that certain rural electric and telephone cooperative are exempt from tax under section 501(a), provided that 85 percent or more of the cooperative's income consists of amounts collected from members for the sole purpose of meeting losses or expenses, and certain other requirements are met.

[699] When section 501(c)(26) was enacted in 1996, the House Ways and Means Committee, in reporting out the bill, stated as its reasons for change: "The Committee believes that eliminating the uncertainty concerning the eligibility of certain State health insurance risk pools for tax-exempt status will assist States in providing medical care coverage for their uninsured high-risk residents." H.R. Rep. No. 104–496, Part I, "Health Coverage Availability and Affordability Act of 1996," 104th Cong., 2d Sess., March 25, 1996, 124. See also Joint Committee on Taxation, *General Explanation of Tax Legislation Enacted in the 104th Congress* (JCS–12–96), December 18, 1996, p. 351.

*missioner,*[700] the Tax Court held that a staff model HMO qualified as a charitable organization. A staff model HMO generally employs its own physicians and staff and serves its subscribers at its own facilities. The court concluded that the HMO satisfied the section 501(c)(3) community benefit standard, as its membership was open to almost all members of the community. Although membership was limited to persons who had the money to pay the fixed premiums, the court held that this was not disqualifying, because the HMO had a subsidized premium program for persons of lesser means to be funded through donations and Medicare and Medicaid payments. The HMO also operated an emergency room open to all persons regardless of income. The court rejected the government's contention that the HMO conferred primarily a private benefit to its subscribers, stating that when the potential membership is such a broad segment of the community, benefit to the membership is benefit to the community.

In *Geisinger Health Plan v. Commissioner,*[701] the court applied the section 501(c)(3) community benefit standard to an individual practice association (IPA) model HMO. In the IPA model, health care generally is provided by physicians practicing independently in their own offices, with the IPA usually contracting on behalf of the physicians with the HMO. Reversing a Tax Court decision, the court held that the HMO did not qualify as charitable, because the community benefit standard requires that an HMO be an actual provider of health care rather than merely an arranger or deliverer of health care, which is how the court viewed the IPA model in that case.

More recently, in *IHC Health Plans, Inc. v. Commissioner,*[702] the court ruled that three affiliated HMOs did not operate primarily for the benefit of the community they served. The organizations in the case did not provide health care directly, but provided group insurance that could be used at both affiliated and non-affiliated providers. The court found that the organizations primarily performed a risk-bearing function and provided virtually no free or below-cost health care services. In denying charitable status, the court held that a health-care provider must make its services available to all in the community plus provide additional community or public benefits.[703] The benefit must either further the function of government-funded institutions or provide a service that would not likely be provided within the community but for the subsidy. Further, the additional public benefit conferred must be sufficient to give rise to a strong inference that the public benefit is the primary purpose for which the organization operates.[704]

*Certain organizations providing commercial-type insurance*

Section 501(m) provides that an organization may not be exempt from tax under section 501(c)(3) (generally, charitable organizations) or section 501(c)(4) (social welfare organizations) unless no substantial part of its activities consists of providing commercial-

[700] 71 T.C. 158 (1978), *acq.* 1981–2 C.B. 2.
[701] 985 F.2d 1210 (3rd Cir. 1993), *rev'g* T.C. Memo. 1991–649.
[702] 325 F.3d 1188 (10th Cir. 2003).
[703] *Ibid.* at 1198.
[704] *Ibid.*

type insurance. For this purpose, commercial-type insurance excludes, among other things: (1) insurance provided at substantially below cost to a class of charitable recipients; and (2) incidental health insurance provided by an HMO of a kind customarily provided by such organizations.

When section 501(m) was enacted in 1986, the following reasons for the provision were stated: "The committee is concerned that exempt charitable and social welfare organizations that engaged in insurance activities are engaged in an activity whose nature and scope is so inherently commercial that tax exempt status is inappropriate. The committee believes that the tax-exempt status of organizations engaged in insurance activities provides an unfair competitive advantage to these organizations. The committee further believes that the provision of insurance to the general public at a price sufficient to cover the costs of insurance generally constitutes an activity that is commercial. In addition, the availability of tax-exempt status . . . has allowed some large insurance entities to compete directly with commercial insurance companies. For example, the Blue Cross/Blue Shield organizations historically have been treated as tax-exempt organizations described in sections 501(c)(3) or (4). This group of organizations is now among the largest health care insurers in the United States. Other tax-exempt charitable and social welfare organizations engaged in insurance activities also have a competitive advantage over commercial insurers who do not have tax-exempt status. . . ."[705]

*Unrelated business income tax*

Most organizations that are exempt from tax under section 501(a) are subject to the unrelated business income tax rules of sections 511 through 515. The unrelated business income tax generally applies to income derived from a trade or business regularly carried on by the organization that is not substantially related to the performance of the organization's tax-exempt functions. Certain types of income are specifically exempt from the unrelated business income tax, such as dividends, interest, royalties, and certain rents, unless derived from debt-financed property or from certain 50-percent controlled subsidiaries.

### *Explanation of Provision*

#### *In general*

The provision authorizes $6 billion in funding for, and instructs the Secretary of Health and Human Services ("HHS") to establish, the Consumer Operated and Oriented Plan (the "program") to foster the creation of qualified nonprofit health insurance issuers to offer qualified health plans in the individual and small group markets in the States in which the issuers are licensed to offer such plans. Federal funds are to be distributed as loans to assist with start-up costs and grants to assist in meeting State solvency requirements.

[705] H.R. Rep. No. 99–426, "Tax Reform Act of 1985," Report of the Committee on Ways and Means, 99th Cong., 1st Sess., December 7, 1985, 664. See also Joint Committee on Taxation, *General Explanation of the Tax Reform Act of 1986* (JCS–10–87), May 4, 1987, p. 584.

Under the provision, the Secretary of HHS must require any person receiving a loan or grant under the program to enter into an agreement with the Secretary of HHS requiring the recipient of funds to meet and continue to meet any requirement under the provision for being treated as a qualified nonprofit health insurance issuer, and any requirements to receive the loan or grant. The provision also requires that the agreement prohibit the use of loan or grant funds for carrying on propaganda or otherwise attempting to influence legislation or for marketing.

If the Secretary of HHS determines that a grant or loan recipient failed to meet the requirements described in the preceding paragraph, and failed to correct such failure within a reasonable period from when the person first knew (or reasonably should have known) of such failure, then such person must repay the Secretary of HHS an amount equal to 110 percent of the aggregate amount of the loans and grants received under the program, plus interest on such amount for the period during which the loans or grants were outstanding. The Secretary of HHS must notify the Secretary of the Treasury of any determination of a failure that results in the termination of the grantee's Federal tax-exempt status.

***Qualified nonprofit health insurance issuers***

The provision defines a qualified nonprofit health insurance issuer as an organization that meets the following requirements:

1. The organization is organized as a nonprofit, member corporation under State law;
2. Substantially all of its activities consist of the issuance of qualified health plans in the individual and small group markets in each State in which it is licensed to issue such plans;
3. None of the organization, a related entity, or a predecessor of either was a health insurance issuer as of July 16, 2009;
4. The organization is not sponsored by a State or local government, any political subdivision thereof, or any instrumentality of such government or political subdivision;
5. Governance of the organization is subject to a majority vote of its members;
6. The organization's governing documents incorporate ethics and conflict of interest standards protecting against insurance industry involvement and interference;
7. The organization must operate with a strong consumer focus, including timeliness, responsiveness, and accountability to its members, in accordance with regulations to be promulgated by the Secretary of HHS;
8. Any profits made must be used to lower premiums, improve benefits, or for other programs intended to improve the quality of health care delivered to its members;
9. The organization meets all other requirements that other issuers of qualified health plans are required to meet in any State in which it offers a qualified health plan, including solvency and licensure requirements, rules on payments to providers, rules on network adequacy, rate and form filing rules, and any applicable State premium assessments. Additionally, the organization must coordinate with certain other State insurance reforms under the Act; and

10. The organization does not offer a health plan in a State until that State has in effect (or the Secretary of HHS has implemented for the State), the market reforms required by part A of title XXVII of the Public Health Service Act ("PHSA"), as amended by the Act.

***Tax exemption for qualified nonprofit health insurance issuers***

An organization receiving a grant or loan under the program qualifies for exemption from Federal income tax under section 501(a) of the Code with respect to periods during which the organization is in compliance with the above-described requirements of the program and with the terms of any program grant or loan agreement to which such organization is a party. Such organizations also are subject to organizational and operational requirements applicable to certain section 501(c) organizations, including the prohibitions on private inurement and political activities, the limitation on lobbying activities, taxation of excess benefit transactions (section 4958), and taxation of unrelated business taxable income under section 511.

Program participants are required to file an application for exempt status with the IRS in such manner as the Secretary of the Treasury may require, and are subject to annual information reporting requirements. In addition, such an organization is required to disclose on its annual information return the amount of reserves required by each State in which it operates and the amount of reserves on hand.

### *Effective Date*

The provision is effective on the date of enactment (March 23, 2010).

## B. Tax Exemption for Entities Established Pursuant to Transitional Reinsurance Program for Individual Market in Each State (sec. 1341[706] of the Act)

### *Present Law*

Although present law provides that certain limited categories of organizations that offer insurance may qualify for exemption from Federal income tax, present law does not provide tax-exempt status for transitional nonprofit reinsurance entities created under the Senate bill and described below.

### *Explanation of Provision*

In general, issuers of health benefit plans that are offered in the individual market would be required to contribute to a temporary reinsurance program for individual policies that is administered by a nonprofit reinsurance entity. Such contributions would begin January 1, 2014, and continue for a 36-month period. The provision requires each State, no later than January 1, 2014, to adopt a rein-

[706] Section 1341 of the Patient Protection and Affordable Care Act, Pub. L. No. 111–148, as amended by section 10104.

surance program based on a model regulation and to establish (or enter into a contract with) one or more applicable reinsurance entities to carry out the reinsurance program under the provision. For purposes of the provision, an applicable reinsurance entity is a not-for-profit organization (1) the purpose of which is to help stabilize premiums for coverage in the individual market in a State during the first three years of operation of an exchange for such markets within the State, and (2) the duties of which are to carry out the reinsurance program under the provision by coordinating the funding and operation of the risk-spreading mechanisms designed to implement the reinsurance program. A State may have more than one applicable reinsurance entity to carry out the reinsurance program in the State, and two or more States may enter into agreements to allow a reinsurer to operate the reinsurance program in those States.

An applicable reinsurance entity established under the provision is exempt from Federal income tax. Notwithstanding an applicable reinsurance entity's tax-exempt status, it is subject to tax on unrelated business taxable income under section 511 as if such entity were described in section 511(a)(2).

### *Effective Date*

The provision is effective on the date of enactment (March 23, 2010).

## C. Refundable Tax Credit Providing Premium Assistance for Coverage Under a Qualified Health Plan (secs. 1401, 1411, and 1412[707] of the Act and sec. 208 of Pub. L. No. 111–309 and new sec. 36B of the Code)

### *Present Law*

Currently there is no tax credit that is generally available to low or middle income individuals or families for the purchase of health insurance. Some individuals may be eligible for health coverage through State Medicaid programs which consider income, assets, and family circumstances. However, these Medicaid programs are not in the Code.

#### *Health coverage tax credit*

Certain individuals are eligible for the health coverage tax credit ("HCTC"). The HCTC is a refundable tax credit equal to 80 percent of the cost of qualified health coverage paid by an eligible individual. In general, eligible individuals are individuals who receive a trade adjustment allowance (and individuals who would be eligible to receive such an allowance but for the fact that they have not exhausted their regular unemployment benefits), individuals eligible for the alternative trade adjustment assistance program, and individuals over age 55 who receive pension benefits from the Pension Benefit Guaranty Corporation. The HCTC is available for "qualified health insurance," which includes certain employer-based

[707] Sections 1401, 1411, and 1412 of the Patient Protection and Affordable Care Act, Pub. L. No. 111–148, as amended by sections 10104, 10105, and 10107, are further amended by section 1001 of the Health Care and Education Reconciliation Act of 2010, Pub. L. No. 111–152.

insurance, certain State-based insurance, and in some cases, insurance purchased in the individual market.

The credit is available on an advance basis through a program established and administered by the Treasury Department. The credit generally is delivered as follows: the eligible individual sends his or her portion of the premium to the Treasury, and the Treasury then pays the full premium (the individual's portion and the amount of the refundable tax credit) to the insurer. Alternatively, an eligible individual is also permitted to pay the entire premium during the year and claim the credit on his or her income tax return.

Individuals entitled to Medicare and certain other governmental health programs, covered under certain employer-subsidized health plans, or with certain other specified health coverage are not eligible for the credit.

***COBRA continuation coverage premium reduction***

The Consolidated Omnibus Reconciliation Act of 1985 ("COBRA")[708] requires that a group health plan must offer continuation coverage to qualified beneficiaries in the case of a qualifying event (such as a loss of employment). A plan may require payment of a premium for any period of continuation coverage. The amount of such premium generally may not exceed 102 percent of the "applicable premium" for such period and the premium must be payable, at the election of the payor, in monthly installments.

Section 3001 of the American Recovery and Reinvestment Act of 2009,[709] as amended by the Department of Defense Appropriations Act, 2010,[710] and the Temporary Extension Act of 2010[711] provides that, for a period not exceeding 15 months, an assistance eligible individual is treated as having paid any premium required for COBRA continuation coverage under a group health plan if the individual pays 35 percent of the premium. Thus, if the assistance eligible individual pays 35 percent of the premium, the group health plan must treat the individual as having paid the full premium required for COBRA continuation coverage, and the individual is entitled to a subsidy for 65 percent of the premium. An assistance eligible individual generally is any qualified beneficiary who elects COBRA continuation coverage and the qualifying event with respect to the covered employee for that qualified beneficiary is a loss of group health plan coverage on account of an involuntary termination of the covered employee's employment (for other than gross misconduct).[712] In addition, the qualifying event must occur during the period beginning September 1, 2008, and ending March 31, 2010.

---

[708] Pub. L. No. 99–272.
[709] Pub. L. No. 111–5.
[710] Pub. L. No. 111–118.
[711] Pub. L. No. 111–144.
[712] TEA expanded eligibility for the COBRA subsidy to include individuals who experience a loss of coverage on account of a reduction in hours of employment followed by the involuntary termination of employment of the covered employee. For an individual entitled to COBRA because of a reduction in hours and who is then subsequently involuntarily terminated from employment, the termination is considered a qualifying event for purposes of the COBRA subsidy, as long as the termination occurs during the period beginning on the date following TEA's date of enactment and ending on date of enactment (March 31, 2010).

The COBRA continuation coverage subsidy also applies to temporary continuation coverage elected under the Federal Employees Health Benefits Program and to continuation health coverage under State programs that provide coverage comparable to continuation coverage. The subsidy is generally delivered by requiring employers to pay the subsidized portion of the premium for assistance eligible individuals. The employer then treats the payment of the subsidized portion as a payment of employment taxes and offsets its employment tax liability by the amount of the subsidy. To the extent that the aggregate amount of the subsidy for all assistance eligible individuals for which the employer is entitled to a credit for a quarter exceeds the employer's employment tax liability for the quarter, the employer can request a tax refund or can claim the credit against future employment tax liability.

There is an income limit on the entitlement to the COBRA continuation coverage subsidy. Taxpayers with modified adjusted gross income exceeding $145,000 (or $290,000 for joint filers), must repay any subsidy received by them, their spouse, or their dependant, during the taxable year. For taxpayers with modified adjusted gross incomes between $125,000 and $145,000 (or $250,000 and $290,000 for joint filers), the amount of the subsidy that must be repaid is reduced proportionately. The subsidy is also conditioned on the individual not being eligible for certain other health coverage. To the extent that an eligible individual receives a subsidy during a taxable year to which the individual was not entitled due to income or being eligible for other health coverage, the subsidy overpayment is repaid on the individual's income tax return as additional tax. However, in contrast to the HCTC, the subsidy for COBRA continuation coverage may only be claimed through the employer and cannot be claimed at the end of the year on an individual tax return.

## *Explanation of Provision*

### *Premium assistance credit*

The provision creates a refundable tax credit (the "premium assistance credit") for eligible individuals and families who purchase health insurance through an exchange.[713] The premium assistance credit, which is refundable and payable in advance directly to the insurer, subsidizes the purchase of certain health insurance plans through an exchange.

Under the provision, to receive advance payment of the premium assistance credit, an eligible individual enrolls in a plan offered through an exchange and reports his or her income to the exchange. Based on the information provided to the exchange, the individual receives a premium assistance credit based on income and the Treasury pays the premium assistance credit amount directly to the insurance plan in which the individual is enrolled. The individual then pays to the plan in which he or she is enrolled the dollar difference between the premium tax credit amount and the

[713] Individuals enrolled in multi-state plans, pursuant to section 1334 of the Patient Protection and Affordable Care Act, Pub. L. No. 111–148, are also eligible for the credit.

total premium charged for the plan.[714] Individuals who fail to pay all or part of the remaining premium amount are given a mandatory three-month grace period prior to an involuntary termination of their participation in the plan. Initial eligibility for the premium assistance credit is based on the individual's income for the tax year ending two years prior to the enrollment period. Individuals (or couples) who experience a change in marital status or other household circumstance, experience a decrease in income of more than 20 percent, or receive unemployment insurance, may update eligibility information or request a redetermination of their tax credit eligibility.

The premium assistance credit is generally available for individuals (single or joint filers) with household incomes between 100 and 400 percent of the Federal poverty level ("FPL") for the family size involved.[715] Individuals who are not eligible for certain other health insurance, including certain health insurance through an employer or a spouse's employer, may not be eligible for the credit. Household income is defined as the sum of: (1) the taxpayer's modified adjusted gross income, plus (2) the aggregate modified adjusted gross incomes of all other individuals taken into account in determining that taxpayer's family size (but only if such individuals are required to file a tax return for the taxable year). Modified adjusted gross income is defined as adjusted gross income increased by: (1) the amount (if any) normally excluded by section 911 (the exclusion from gross income for citizens or residents living abroad), plus (2) any tax-exempt interest received or accrued during the tax year. To be eligible for the premium assistance credit, taxpayers who are married (within the meaning of section 7703) must file a joint return. Individuals who are listed as dependents on a return are ineligible for the premium assistance credit.

As described in Table 1 below, premium assistance credits are available on a sliding scale basis for individuals and families with household incomes between 100 and 400 percent of FPL to help offset the cost of private health insurance premiums. The premium assistance credit amount is determined based on the percentage of income the cost of premiums represents, rising from two percent of income for those at 100 percent of FPL for the family size involved to 9.5 percent of income for those at 400 percent of FPL for the family size involved. Beginning in 2014, the percentages of income are indexed to the excess of premium growth over income growth for the preceding calendar year. Beginning in 2018, if the aggregate amount of premium assistance credits and cost-sharing reductions[716] exceeds 0.504 percent of the gross domestic product for that year, the percentage of income is also adjusted to reflect the excess (if any) of premium growth over the rate of growth in the consumer price index for the preceding calendar year. For purposes

[714] Although the credit is generally payable in advance directly to the insurer, individuals may choose to purchase health insurance out-of-pocket and claim the credit at the end of the taxable year. The amount of the reduction in premium is required to be included with each bill sent to the individual.

[715] Individuals who are lawfully present in the United States but are not eligible for Medicaid because of their immigration status are treated as having a household income equal to 100 percent of FPL (and thus eligible for the premium assistance credit) as long as their household income does not actually exceed 100 percent of FPL.

[716] As described in section 1402 of the Patient Protection and Affordable Care Act, Pub. L. No. 111–148.

of calculating family size, individuals who are in the country illegally are not included.

Premium assistance credits, or any amounts that are attributable to them, cannot be used to pay for abortions for which federal funding is prohibited. Premium assistance credits are not available for months in which an individual has a free choice voucher (as defined in section 10108 of the Act).

***The low income premium credit phase-out***

The premium assistance credit increases, on a sliding scale in a linear manner, as shown in the table below.

| Household Income (expressed as a percent of poverty line) | Initial Premium (percentage) | Final Premium (percentage) |
|---|---|---|
| 100% through 133% | 2.0 | 2.0 |
| 133% through 150% | 3.0 | 4.0 |
| 150% through 200% | 4.0 | 6.3 |
| 200% through 250% | 6.3 | 8.05 |
| 250% through 300% | 8.05 | 9.5 |
| 300% through 400% | 9.5 | 9.5 |

The premium assistance credit amount is tied to the cost of the second lowest-cost silver plan (adjusted for age) which: (1) is in the rating area where the individual resides, (2) is offered through an exchange in the area in which the individual resides, and (3) provides self-only coverage in the case of an individual who purchases self-only coverage, or family coverage in the case of any other individual. If the plan in which the individual enrolls offers benefits in addition to essential health benefits,[717] even if the State in which the individual resides requires such additional benefits, the portion of the premium that is allocable to those additional benefits is disregarded in determining the premium assistance credit amount.[718] Premium assistance credits may be used for any plan purchased through an exchange, including bronze, silver, gold and platinum level plans and, for those eligible,[719] catastrophic plans.

***Minimum essential coverage and employer offer of health insurance coverage***

Generally, if an employee is offered minimum essential coverage[720] in the group market, including employer-provided health insurance coverage, the individual is ineligible for the premium tax credit for health insurance purchased through a State exchange.

If an employee is offered unaffordable coverage by his or her employer or the plan's share of the total allowed cost of benefits is less than 60 percent of such costs, the employee can be eligible for the premium tax credit, but only if the employee declines to enroll in the coverage and satisfies the conditions for receiving a tax credit

[717] As defined in section 1302(b) of the Patient Protection and Affordable Care Act, Pub. L. No. 111–148.

[718] A similar rule applies to additional benefits that are offered in multi-State plans, under section 1334 of the Patient Protection and Affordable Care Act, Pub. L. No. 111–148.

[719] Those eligible to purchase catastrophic plans either must have not reached the age of 30 before the beginning of the plan year, or have certification of an affordability or hardship exemption from the individual responsibility payment, as described in new sections 5000A(e)(1) and 5000A(e)(5), respectively.

[720] As defined in section 5000A(f) of the Patient Protection and Affordable Care Act, Pub. L. No. 111–148.

through an exchange. Unaffordable is defined as coverage with a premium required to be paid by the employee that is more than 9.5 percent of the employee's household income, based on the self-only coverage.[721] The percentage of income that is considered unaffordable is indexed in the same manner as the percentage of income is indexed for purposes of determining eligibility for the credit (as discussed above). The Secretary of the Treasury is informed of the name and employer identification number of every employer that has one or more employees receiving a premium tax credit.

No later than five years after the date of the enactment of the provision the Comptroller General must conduct a study of whether the percentage of household income used for purposes of determining whether coverage is affordable is the appropriate level, and whether such level can be lowered without significantly increasing the costs to the Federal Government and reducing employer-provided health coverage. The Secretary reports the results of such study to the appropriate committees of Congress, including any recommendations for legislative changes.

***Procedures for determining eligibility***

In order to receive an advance payment of the premium assistance credit, exchange participants must provide to the exchange certain information from their tax return from two years prior during the open enrollment period for coverage during the next calendar year. For example, if an individual applies for a premium assistance credit for 2014, the individual must provide a tax return from 2012 during the 2103 open enrollment period. The Internal Revenue Service ("IRS") is authorized to disclose to HHS limited tax return information to verify a taxpayer's income based on the most recent return information available to establish eligibility for advance payment of the premium tax credit. Existing privacy and safeguard requirements apply. Individuals who do not qualify for advance payment of the premium tax credit on the basis of their prior year income may apply for the premium tax credit based on specified changes in circumstances. For individuals and families who did not file a tax return in the prior tax year, the Secretary of HHS will establish alternative income documentation that may be provided to determine income eligibility for advance payment of the premium tax credit.

The Secretary of HHS must establish a program for determining whether or not individuals are eligible to: (1) enroll in an exchange-offered health plan; (2) receive advance payment of a premium assistance credit; and (3) establish that their coverage under an employer-sponsored plan is unaffordable. The program must provide for the following: (1) the details of an individual's application process; (2) the details of how public entities are to make determinations of individuals' eligibility; (3) procedures for deeming individuals to be eligible; and, (4) procedures for allowing individuals with limited English proficiency to have proper access to exchanges.

In applying for enrollment in an exchange-offered health plan, an individual applicant is required to provide individually identifiable

[721] The 9.5 percent amount is indexed for calendar years beginning after 2014.

information, including name, address, date of birth, and citizenship or immigration status. In the case of an individual applying to receive advance payment of a premium assistance credit, the individual is required to submit to the exchange income and family size information and information regarding changes in marital or family status or income. Personal information provided to the exchange is submitted to the Secretary of HHS. In turn, the Secretary of HHS submits the applicable information to the Social Security Commissioner, Homeland Security Secretary, and Treasury Secretary for verification purposes. The Secretary of HHS is notified of the results following verification, and notifies the exchange of such results. The provision specifies actions to be undertaken if inconsistencies are found. The Secretary of HHS, in consultation with the Social Security Commissioner, the Secretary of Homeland Security, and the Treasury Secretary must establish procedures for appealing determinations resulting from the verification process, and redetermining eligibility on a periodic basis.

An employer must be notified if one of its employees is determined to be eligible for a premium assistance credit because the employer does not provide minimal essential coverage through an employer-sponsored plan, or the employer does offer such coverage but it is not affordable or does not provide minimum value. The notice must include information about the employer's potential liability for payments under section 4980H and that terminating or discriminating against an employee because he or she received a credit or subsidy is in violation of the Fair Labor Standards Act.[722] An employer is generally not entitled to information about its employees who qualify for the premium assistance credit. Employers may, however, be notified of the name of the employee and whether his or her income is above or below the threshold used to measure the affordability of the employer's health insurance coverage.

Personal information submitted for verification may be used only to the extent necessary for verification purposes and may not be disclosed to anyone not identified in this provision. Any person, who submits false information due to negligence or disregard of any rule, and without reasonable cause, is subject to a civil penalty of not more than $25,000. Any person who intentionally provides false information will be fined not more than $250,000. Any person who knowingly and willfully uses or discloses confidential applicant information will be fined not more than $25,000. Any fines imposed by this provision may not be collected through a lien or levy against property, and the section does not impose any criminal liability.

The provision requires the Secretary of HHS, in consultation with the Secretaries of the Treasury and Labor, to conduct a study to ensure that the procedures necessary to administer the determination of individuals' eligibility to participate in an exchange, to receive advance payment of premium assistance credits, and to obtain an individual responsibility exemption, adequately protect employees' rights of privacy and employers' rights to due process. The results of the study must be reported by January 1, 2013, to the appropriate committees of Congress.

[722] Pub. L. No. 75–718.

***Reconciliation***

If the premium assistance received through an advance payment exceeds the amount of credit to which the taxpayer is entitled, the excess advance payment is treated as an increase in tax. For persons with household income below 500% of the FPL, the amount of the increase in tax is limited as shown in the table below (one half of the applicable dollar amount shown below for unmarried individuals who are not surviving spouses or filing as heads of households).[723]

| Household income (expressed as a percent of poverty line) | Applicable dollar amount |
|---|---|
| Less than 200% | $600 |
| At least 200% but less than 250% | 1,000 |
| At least 250% but less than 300% | 1,500 |
| At least 300% but less than 350% | 2,000 |
| At least 350% but less than 400% | 2,500 |
| At least 400% but less than 450% | 3,000 |
| At least 450% but less than 500% | 3,500 |

If the premium assistance received through an advance payment is less than the amount of the credit to which the taxpayer is entitled, the shortfall is treated as a reduction in tax.

The eligibility for and amount of advance payment of premium assistance is determined in advance of the coverage year, on the basis of household income and family size from two years prior, and the monthly premiums for qualified health plans in the individual market in which the taxpayer, spouse and any dependent enroll in an exchange. Any advance premium assistance is paid during the year for which coverage is provided by the exchange. In the subsequent year, the amount of advance premium assistance is required to be reconciled with the allowable refundable credit for the year of coverage. Generally, this would be accomplished on the tax return filed for the year of coverage, based on that year's actual household income, family size, and premiums. Any adjustment to tax resulting from the difference between the advance premium assistance and the allowable refundable tax credit would be assessed as additional tax or a reduction in tax on the tax return.

Separately, the provision requires that the exchange, or any person with whom it contracts to administer the insurance program, must report to the Secretary with respect to any taxpayer's participation in the health plan offered by the Exchange. The information to be reported is information necessary to determine whether a person has received excess advance payments, identifying information about the taxpayer (such as name, taxpayer identification number, months of coverage) and any other person covered by that policy; the level of coverage purchased by the taxpayer; the total premium charged for the coverage, as well as the aggregate advance payments credited to that taxpayer; and information provided to the Exchange for the purpose of establishing eligibility for the program, including changes of circumstances of the taxpayer since first pur-

[723] Medicare and Medicaid Extenders Act of 2010, Pub. L. No. 111–309, sec. 208. Prior to the Medicare and Medicaid Extenders Act of 2010, for persons whose household income was below 400% of the FPL, the amount of the increase in tax was limited to $400 ($250 for unmarried individuals who are not surviving spouses or filing as heads of households).

chasing the coverage. Finally, the party submitting the report must provide a copy to the taxpayer whose information is the subject of the report.

### *Effective Date*

The provision is effective for taxable years ending after December 31, 2013.

## D. Reduced Cost-Sharing for Individuals Enrolling in Qualified Health Plans (secs. 1402, 1411, and 1412 of the Act[724])

### *Present Law*

Currently there is no tax credit that is generally available to low or middle income individuals or families for the purchase of health insurance. Some individuals may be eligible for health coverage through State Medicaid programs which consider income, assets, and family circumstances. However, these Medicaid programs are not in the Code.

#### *Health coverage tax credit*

Certain individuals are eligible for the HCTC. The HCTC is a refundable tax credit equal to 80 percent of the cost of qualified health coverage paid by an eligible individual. In general, eligible individuals are individuals who receive a trade adjustment allowance (and individuals who would be eligible to receive such an allowance but for the fact that they have not exhausted their regular unemployment benefits), individuals eligible for the alternative trade adjustment assistance program, and individuals over age 55 who receive pension benefits from the Pension Benefit Guaranty Corporation. The HCTC is available for "qualified health insurance," which includes certain employer-based insurance, certain State-based insurance, and in some cases, insurance purchased in the individual market.

The credit is available on an advance basis through a program established and administered by the Treasury Department. The credit generally is delivered as follows: the eligible individual sends his or her portion of the premium to the Treasury, and the Treasury then pays the full premium (the individual's portion and the amount of the refundable tax credit) to the insurer. Alternatively, an eligible individual is also permitted to pay the entire premium during the year and claim the credit on his or her income tax return.

Individuals entitled to Medicare and certain other governmental health programs, covered under certain employer-subsidized health plans, or with certain other specified health coverage are not eligible for the credit.

---

[724] Sections 1401, 1411 and 1412 of the Patient Protection and Affordable Care Act, Pub. L. No. 111–148, as amended by section 10104, is further amended by section 1001 of the Health Care and Education Reconciliation Act of 2010, Pub. L. No. 111–152.

### *COBRA continuation coverage premium reduction*

COBRA[725] requires that a group health plan must offer continuation coverage to qualified beneficiaries in the case of a qualifying event (such as a loss of employment). A plan may require payment of a premium for any period of continuation coverage. The amount of such premium generally may not exceed 102 percent of the "applicable premium" for such period and the premium must be payable, at the election of the payor, in monthly installments.

Section 3001 of the American Recovery and Reinvestment Act of 2009,[726] as amended by the Department of Defense Appropriations Act, 2010,[727] and the Temporary Extension Act of 2010[728] provides that, for a period not exceeding 15 months, an assistance eligible individual is treated as having paid any premium required for COBRA continuation coverage under a group health plan if the individual pays 35 percent of the premium. Thus, if the assistance eligible individual pays 35 percent of the premium, the group health plan must treat the individual as having paid the full premium required for COBRA continuation coverage, and the individual is entitled to a subsidy for 65 percent of the premium. An assistance eligible individual generally is any qualified beneficiary who elects COBRA continuation coverage and the qualifying event with respect to the covered employee for that qualified beneficiary is a loss of group health plan coverage on account of an involuntary termination of the covered employee's employment (for other than gross misconduct).[729] In addition, the qualifying event must occur during the period beginning September 1, 2008, and ending March 31, 2010.

The COBRA continuation coverage subsidy also applies to temporary continuation coverage elected under the Federal Employees Health Benefits Program and to continuation health coverage under State programs that provide coverage comparable to continuation coverage. The subsidy is generally delivered by requiring employers to pay the subsidized portion of the premium for assistance eligible individuals. The employer then treats the payment of the subsidized portion as a payment of employment taxes and offsets its employment tax liability by the amount of the subsidy. To the extent that the aggregate amount of the subsidy for all assistance eligible individuals for which the employer is entitled to a credit for a quarter exceeds the employer's employment tax liability for the quarter, the employer can request a tax refund or can claim the credit against future employment tax liability.

There is an income limit on the entitlement to the COBRA continuation coverage subsidy. Taxpayers with modified adjusted gross income exceeding $145,000 (or $290,000 for joint filers), must repay any subsidy received by them, their spouse, or their dependant,

[725] Pub. L. No. 99–272.

[726] Pub. L. No. 111–5.

[727] Pub. L. No. 111–118.

[728] Pub. L. No. 111–144.

[729] TEA expanded eligibility for the COBRA subsidy to include individuals who experience a loss of coverage on account of a reduction in hours of employment followed by the involuntary termination of employment of the covered employee. For an individual entitled to COBRA because of a reduction in hours and who is then subsequently involuntarily terminated from employment, the termination is considered a qualifying event for purposes of the COBRA subsidy, as long as the termination occurs during the period beginning on the date following TEA's date of enactment and ending on March 31, 2010.

during the taxable year. For taxpayers with modified adjusted gross incomes between $125,000 and $145,000 (or $250,000 and $290,000 for joint filers), the amount of the subsidy that must be repaid is reduced proportionately. The subsidy is also conditioned on the individual not being eligible for certain other health coverage. To the extent that an eligible individual receives a subsidy during a taxable year to which the individual was not entitled due to income or being eligible for other health coverage, the subsidy overpayment is repaid on the individual's income tax return as additional tax. However, in contrast to the HCTC, the subsidy for COBRA continuation coverage may only be claimed through the employer and cannot be claimed at the end of the year on an individual tax return.

### *Explanation of Provision*

#### *Cost-sharing subsidy*

A cost-sharing subsidy is provided to reduce annual out-of-pocket cost-sharing for individuals and households between 100 and 400 of percent FPL (for the family size involved). The reductions are made in reference to the dollar cap on annual deductibles for high deductable health plans in section 223(c)(2)(A)(ii) (currently $5,000 for self-only coverage and $10,000 for family coverage). For individuals with household income of more than 100 but not more than 200 percent of FPL, the out-of-pocket limit is reduced by two-thirds. For those between 201 and 300 percent of FPL by one-half, and for those between 301 and 400 percent of FPL by one-third.

The cost-sharing subsidy that is provided must buy out any difference in cost-sharing between the qualified health insurance purchased and the actuarial values specified below. For individuals between 100 and 150 percent of FPL (for the family size involved), the subsidy must bring the value of the plan to not more than 94 percent actuarial value. For those between 150 and 200 percent of FPL, the subsidy must bring the value of the plan to not more than 87 percent actuarial value. For those between 201 and 250 percent of FPL, the subsidy must bring the value of the plan to not more than 73 percent actuarial value. For those between 251 and 400 percent of FPL, the subsidy must bring the value of the plan to not more than 70 percent actuarial value. The determination of cost-sharing subsidies will be made based on data from the same taxable year as is used for determining advance credits under section 1412 of the Act (and not the taxable year used for determining premium assistance credits under section 36B). The amount received by an insurer as a cost-sharing subsidy on behalf of an individual, as well as any out-of-pocket spending by the individual, counts towards the out-of-pocket limit. Individuals enrolled in multi-state plans, pursuant to section 1334 of the Act, are eligible for the subsidy.

In addition to adjusting actuarial values, plans must further reduce cost-sharing for low-income individuals as specified below. For individuals between 100 and 150 percent of FPL (for the family size involved) the plan's share of the total allowed cost of benefits provided under the plan must be 94 percent. For those between 151 and 200 percent of FPL, the plan's share must be 87 percent, and for those between 201 and 250 percent of FPL the plan's share must be 73 percent.

The cost-sharing subsidy is available only for those months in which an individual receives an affordability credit under new section 36B.[730]

As with the premium assistance credit, if the plan in which the individual enrolls offers benefits in addition to essential health benefits,[731] even if the State in which the individual resides requires such additional benefits, the reduction in cost-sharing does not apply to the additional benefits. In addition, individuals enrolled in both a qualified health plan and a pediatric dental plan may not receive a cost-sharing subsidy for the pediatric dental benefits that are included in the essential health benefits required to be provided by the qualified health plan. Cost-sharing subsidies, and any amounts that are attributable to them, cannot be used to pay for abortions for which federal funding is prohibited.

The Secretary of HHS must establish a program for determining whether individuals are eligible to claim a cost-sharing credit. The program must provide for the following: (1) the details of an individual's application process; (2) the details of how public entities are to make determinations of individuals' eligibility; (3) procedures for deeming individuals to be eligible; and, (4) procedures for allowing individuals with limited English proficiency proper access to exchanges.

In applying for enrollment, an individual claiming a cost-sharing subsidy is required to submit to the exchange income and family size information and information regarding changes in marital or family status or income. Personal information provided to the exchange is submitted to the Secretary of HHS. In turn, the Secretary of HHS submits the applicable information to the Social Security Commissioner, Homeland Security Secretary, and Treasury Secretary for verification purposes. The Secretary of HHS is notified of the results following verification, and notifies the exchange of such results. The provision specifies actions to be undertaken if inconsistencies are found. The Secretary of HHS, in consultation with the Treasury Secretary, Homeland Security Secretary, and Social Security Commissioner, must establish procedures for appealing determinations resulting from the verification process, and redetermining eligibility on a periodic basis.

The Secretary of HHS notifies the plan that the individual is eligible and the plan reduces the cost-sharing by reducing the out-of-pocket limit under the provision. The plan notifies the Secretary of HHS of cost-sharing reductions and the Secretary of HHS makes periodic and timely payments to the plan equal to the value of the reductions in cost-sharing. The provision authorizes the Secretary of HHS to establish a capitated payment system with appropriate risk adjustments.

An employer must be notified if one of its employees is determined to be eligible for a cost-sharing subsidy. The notice must include information about the employer's potential liability for payments under section 4980H and explicit notice that hiring, termi-

---

[730] Section 1401 of the Patient Protection and Affordable Care Act, Pub. L. No. 111–148.

[731] As defined in section 1302(b) of the Patient Protection and Affordable Care Act, Pub. L. No. 111–148.

nating, or otherwise discriminating against an employee because he or she received a credit or subsidy is in violation of the Fair Labor Standards Act.[732] An employer is generally not entitled to information about its employees who qualify for the premium assistance credit or the cost-sharing subsidy. Employers may, however, be notified of the name of an employee and whether his or her income is above or below the threshold used to measure the affordability of the employer's health insurance coverage.

The Secretary of the Treasury is informed of the name and employer identification number of every employer that has one or more employees receiving a cost-sharing subsidy.

The provision implements special rules for Indians (as defined by the Indian Health Care Improvement Act) and undocumented aliens. The provision prohibits cost-sharing reductions for individuals who are not lawfully present in the United States, and such individuals are not taken into account in determining the family size involved.

The provision defines any term used in this section that is also used by section 36B as having the same meaning as defined by the latter. The provision also denies subsidies to dependents, with respect to whom a deduction under section 151 is allowable to another taxpayer for a taxable year beginning in the calendar year in which the individual's taxable year begins. Further, the provision does not permit a subsidy for any month that is not treated as a coverage month.

### *Effective Date*

The provision is effective on the date of enactment (March 23, 2010).

## E. Disclosures to Carry Out Eligibility Requirements for Certain Programs (Sec. 1414[733] of the Act and sec. 6103 of the Code)

### *Present Law*

Section 6103 provides that returns and return information are confidential and may not be disclosed by the IRS, other Federal employees, State employees, and certain others having access to such information except as provided in the Internal Revenue Code. Section 6103 contains a number of exceptions to the general rule of nondisclosure that authorize disclosure in specifically identified circumstances. For example, section 6103 provides for the disclosure of certain return information for purposes of establishing the appropriate amount of any Medicare Part B premium subsidy adjustment.

Section 6103(p)(4) requires, as a condition of receiving returns and return information, that Federal and State agencies (and certain other recipients) provide safeguards as prescribed by the Sec-

[732] Pub. L. No. 75–718.

[733] Section 1414 of the Patient Protection and Affordable Care Act, Pub. L. No. 111–148, is amended by section 1004 of the Health Care and Education Reconciliation Act of 2010, Pub. L. No. 111–152.

retary of the Treasury by regulation to be necessary or appropriate to protect the confidentiality of returns or return information. Unauthorized disclosure of a return or return information is a felony punishable by a fine not exceeding $5,000 or imprisonment of not more than five years, or both, together with the costs of prosecution.[734] The unauthorized inspection of a return or return information is punishable by a fine not exceeding $1,000 or imprisonment of not more than one year, or both, together with the costs of prosecution.[735] An action for civil damages also may be brought for unauthorized disclosure or inspection.[736]

### *Explanation of Provision*

Individuals will submit income information to an exchange as part of an application process in order to claim the cost-sharing reduction and the tax credit on an advance basis. The Department of HHS serves as the centralized verification agency for information submitted by individuals to the exchanges with respect to the reduction and the tax credit to the extent provided on an advance basis. The IRS is permitted to substantiate the accuracy of income information that has been provided to HHS for eligibility determination.

Specifically, upon written request of the Secretary of HHS, the IRS is permitted to disclose the following return information of any taxpayer whose income is relevant in determining the amount of the tax credit or cost-sharing reduction, or eligibility for participation in the specified State health subsidy programs (i.e., a State Medicaid program under title XIX of the Social Security Act, a State's children's health insurance program under title XXI of such Act, or a basic health program under section 2228 of such Act): (1) taxpayer identity; (2) the filing status of such taxpayer; (3) the modified adjusted gross income (as defined in new sec. 36B of the Code) of such taxpayer, the taxpayer's spouse and of any dependants who are required to file a tax return; (4) such other information as is prescribed by Treasury regulation as might indicate whether such taxpayer is eligible for the credit or subsidy (and the amount thereof); and (5) the taxable year with respect to which the preceding information relates, or if applicable, the fact that such information is not available. HHS is permitted to disclose to an exchange or its contractors, or to the State agency administering the health subsidy programs referenced above (and their contractors) any inconsistency between the information submitted and IRS records.

The disclosed return information may be used only for the purposes of, and only to the extent necessary in, establishing eligibility for participation in the exchange, verifying the appropriate amount of the tax credit, and cost-sharing subsidy, or eligibility for the specified State health subsidy programs.

Recipients of the confidential return information are subject to the safeguard protections and civil and criminal penalties for unau-

[734] Sec. 7213.
[735] Sec. 7213A.
[736] Sec. 7431.

thorized disclosure and inspection. The IRS is required to make an accounting for all disclosures.

### *Effective Date*

The provision is effective on the date of enactment (March 23, 2010).

## F. Premium Tax Credit and Cost-Sharing Reduction Payments Disregarded for Federal and Federally Assisted Programs (sec. 1415 of the Act)

### *Present Law*

There is no tax credit that is generally available to low or middle income individuals or families for the purchase of health insurance.

### *Explanation of Provision*

Any premium assistance tax credits and cost-sharing subsidies provided to an individual under the Act are disregarded for purposes of determining that individual's eligibility for benefits or assistance, or the amount or extent of benefits and assistance, under any Federal program or under any State or local program financed in whole or in part with Federal funds. Specifically, any amount of premium tax credit provided to an individual is not counted as income, and cannot be taken into account as resources for the month of receipt and the following two months. Any cost sharing subsidy provided on the individual's behalf is treated as made to the health plan in which the individual is enrolled and not to the individual.

### *Effective Date*

The provision is effective on the date of enactment (March 23, 2010).

## G. Small Business Tax Credit (sec. 1421 [737] of the Act and new sec. 45R of the Code)

### *Present Law*

The Code does not provide a tax credit for employers that provide health coverage for their employees. The cost to an employer of providing health coverage for its employees is generally deductible as an ordinary and necessary business expense for employee compensation.[738] In addition, the value of employer-provided health insurance is not subject to employer-paid Federal Insurance Contributions Act ("FICA") tax.

The Code generally provides that employees are not taxed on the value of employer-provided health coverage under an accident or

---

[737] Section 1421 of the Patient Protection and Affordable Care Act, Pub. L. No. 111–148, is amended by section 10105 of the Patient Protection and Affordable Care Act, Pub. L. No. 111–152.

[738] Sec. 162. However, see special rules in sections 419 and 419A for the deductibility of contributions to welfare benefit plans with respect to medical benefits for employees and their dependents.

health plan.[739] That is, these benefits are excluded from gross income. In addition, medical care provided under an accident or health plan for employees, their spouses, and their dependents generally is excluded from gross income.[740] Active employees participating in a cafeteria plan may be able to pay their share of premiums on a pre-tax basis through salary reduction.[741] Such salary reduction contributions are treated as employer contributions and thus also are excluded from gross income.

## *Reasons for Change*

The Congress supports additional incentives and assistance to encourage small business employers with low-wage employees to provide health insurance coverage to their employees. Providing health insurance coverage is particularly challenging for these small business employers. In particular, the cost of health insurance may be disproportionately large as a portion of payroll expenses. The tax credit for qualified employee health coverage expenses is designed to make the provision of health insurance coverage by small business employers of low-wage employees more affordable.

## *Explanation of Provisions*

### *Small business employers eligible for the credit*

Under the provision, a tax credit is provided for a qualified small employer for nonelective contributions to purchase health insurance for its employees. A qualified small employer for this purpose generally is an employer with no more than 25 full-time equivalent employees ("FTEs") employed during the employer's taxable year, and whose employees have annual full-time equivalent wages that average no more than $50,000. However, the full amount of the credit is available only to an employer with 10 or fewer FTEs and whose employees have average annual full-time equivalent wages from the employer of not more than $25,000. These wage limits are indexed to the Consumer Price Index for Urban Consumers ("CPI–U") for years beginning in 2014.

Under the provision, an employer's FTEs are calculated by dividing the total hours worked by all employees during the employer's tax year by 2080. For this purpose, the maximum number of hours that are counted for any single employee is 2080 (rounded down to the nearest whole number). Wages are defined in the same manner as under section 3121(a) (as determined for purposes of FICA taxes but without regard to the dollar limit for covered wages) and the average wage is determined by dividing the total wages paid by the small employer by the number of FTEs (rounded down to the nearest $1,000).

The number of hours of service worked by, and wages paid to, a seasonal worker of an employer is not taken into account in determining the full-time equivalent employees and average annual wages of the employer unless the worker works for the employer on more than 120 days during the taxable year. For purposes of the

---

[739] Sec 106.
[740] Sec. 105(b).
[741] Sec. 125.

credit the term 'seasonal worker' means a worker who performs labor or services on a seasonal basis as defined by the Secretary of Labor, including workers covered by 29 CFR sec. 500.20(s)(1) and retail workers employed exclusively during holiday seasons.

The contributions must be provided under an arrangement that requires the eligible small employer to make a nonelective contribution on behalf of each employee who enrolls in certain defined qualifying health insurance offered to employees by the employer equal to a uniform percentage (not less than 50 percent) of the premium cost of the qualifying health plan.

The credit is only available to offset actual tax liability and is claimed on the employer's tax return. The credit is not payable in advance to the taxpayer or refundable. Thus, the employer must pay the employees' premiums during the year and claim the credit at the end of the year on its income tax return. The credit is a general business credit, and can be carried back for one year and carried forward for 20 years. The credit is available for tax liability under the alternative minimum tax.

### *Years the credit is available*

Under the provision, the credit is initially available for any taxable year beginning in 2010, 2011, 2012, or 2013. Qualifying health insurance for claiming the credit for this first phase of the credit is health insurance coverage within the meaning of section 9832, which is generally health insurance coverage purchased from an insurance company licensed under State law.

For taxable years beginning in years after 2013, the credit is only available to a qualified small employer that purchases health insurance coverage for its employees through a State exchange and is only available for a maximum coverage period of two consecutive taxable years beginning with the first year in which the employer or any predecessor first offers one or more qualified plans to its employees through an exchange.[742]

The maximum two-year coverage period does not take into account any taxable years beginning in years before 2014. Thus a qualified small employer could potentially qualify for this credit for six taxable years, four years under the first phase and two years under the second phase.

### *Calculation of credit amount*

Only nonelective contributions by the employer are taken into account in calculating the credit. Therefore, any amount contributed pursuant to a salary reduction arrangement under a cafeteria plan within the meaning of section 125 is not treated as an employer contribution for purposes of this credit. The credit is equal to the lesser of the following two amounts multiplied by an applicable tax credit percentage: (1) the amount of contributions the employer made on behalf of the employees during the taxable year for the qualifying health coverage and (2) the amount of contributions that the employer would have made during the taxable year if each employee had enrolled in coverage with a small business benchmark

---

[742] Sec. 1301 of the Patient Protection and Affordable Care Act, Pub. L. No. 111–148, provides the requirements for a qualified health plan purchased through the exchange.

premium. As discussed above, this tax credit is only available if this uniform percentage is at least 50 percent.

For the first phase of the credit (any taxable years beginning in 2010, 2011, 2012, or 2013), the applicable tax credit percentage is 35 percent. The benchmark premium is the average total premium cost in the small group market for employer-sponsored coverage in the employer's State. The premium and the benchmark premium vary based on the type of coverage provided to the employee (e.g., single or family).

For taxable years beginning in years after 2013, the applicable tax credit percentage is 50 percent. The benchmark premium is the average premium cost in the small group market in the rating area in which the employee enrolls in coverage. The premium and the benchmark premium vary based on the type of coverage being provided to the employee (e.g., single or family).

The credit is reduced for an employer with between 10 and 25 FTEs. The amount of this reduction is equal to the amount of the credit (determined before any reduction) multiplied by a fraction, the numerator is the number of FTEs of the employer in excess of 10 and the denominator of which is 15. The credit is also reduced for an employer for whom the average wages per employee is between $25,000 and $50,000. The amount of this reduction is equal to the amount of the credit (determined before any reduction) multiplied by a fraction, the numerator of which is the average annual wages of the employer in excess of $25,000 and the denominator is $25,000. For an employer with both more than 10 FTEs and average annual wages in excess of $25,000, the reduction is the sum of the amount of the two reductions.

***Tax exempt organizations as qualified small employers***

Any organization described in section 501(c) which is exempt under section 501(a) that otherwise qualifies for the small business tax credit is eligible to receive the credit. However, for tax-exempt organizations, the applicable percentage for the credit during the first phase of the credit (any taxable year beginning in 2010, 2011, 2012, or 2013) is limited to 25 percent and the applicable percentage for the credit during the second phase (taxable years beginning in years after 2013) is limited to 35 percent. The small business tax credit is otherwise calculated in the same manner for tax-exempt organizations that are qualified small employers as the tax credit is calculated for all other qualified small employers. However, for tax-exempt organizations, instead of being a general business credit, the small business tax credit is a refundable tax credit limited to the amount of the payroll taxes of the employer during the calendar year in which the taxable year begins. For this purpose, payroll taxes of an employer means: (1) the amount of income tax required to be withheld from its employees' wages; (2) the amount of hospital insurance tax under section 3101(b) required to be withheld from its employees' wages; and (3) the amount of the hospital insurance tax under section 3111(b) imposed on the employer.

***Special rules***

The employer is entitled to a deduction under section 162 equal to the amount of the employer contribution minus the dollar amount of the credit. For example, if a qualified small employer pays 100 percent of the cost of its employees' health insurance coverage and the tax credit under this provision is 50 percent of that cost, the employer is able to claim a section 162 deduction for the other 50 percent of the premium cost.

The employer is determined by applying the employer aggregations rules in section 414(b), (c), and (m). In addition, the definition of employee includes a leased employee within the meaning of section 414(n).[743]

Self-employed individuals, including partners and sole proprietors, two percent share-holders of an S Corporation, and five percent owners of the employer (within the meaning of section 416(i)(1)(B)(i)) are not treated as employees for purposes of this credit. There is also a special rule to prevent sole proprietorships from receiving the credit for the owner and their family members. Thus, no credit is available for any contribution to the purchase of health insurance for these individuals and these individuals are not taken into account in determining the number of FTEs or average full-time equivalent wages.

The Secretary of is directed to prescribe such regulations as may be necessary to carry out the provisions of new section 45R, including regulations to prevent the avoidance of the two-year limit on the credit period for the second phase of the credit through the use of successor entities and the use of the limit on the number of employees and the amount of average wages through the use of multiple entities. The Secretary of the Treasury, in consultation with the Secretary of Labor, is directed to prescribe such regulations, rules, and guidance as may be necessary to determine the hours of service of an employee for purposes of determining FTEs, including rules for the employees who are not compensated on an hourly basis.

### *Effective Date*

The provision is effective for taxable years beginning after December 31, 2009.

## H. Excise Tax on Individuals Without Essential Health Benefits Coverage (sec. 1501[744] of the Act and sec. 1 of Pub. L. No. 111–173 and new sec. 5000A of the Code)

---

[743] Section 414(b) provides that, for specified employee benefit purposes, all employees of all corporations which are members of a controlled group of corporations are treated as employed by a single employer. There is a similar rule in section 414(c) under which all employees of trades or businesses (whether or not incorporated) which are under common are treated under regulations as employed by a single employer, and, in section 414(m), under which employees of an affiliated service group (as defined in that section) are treated as employed by a single employer. Section 414(n) provides that leased employees, as defined in that section, are treated as employees of the service recipient for specified purposes. Section 414(o) authorizes the Treasury to issue regulations to prevent avoidance of the certain requirement under sections 414(m) and (n).

[744] Section 1501 of the Patient Protection and Affordable Care Act, Pub. L. No. 111–148, as amended by section 10106, is further amended by section 1002 of the Health Care and Education Reconciliation Act of 2010, Pub. L. No. 111–152.

## *Present Law*

Federal law does not require individuals to have health insurance. Only the Commonwealth of Massachusetts, through its statewide program, requires that individuals have health insurance (although this policy has been considered in other states, such as California, Maryland, Maine, and Washington). All adult residents of Massachusetts are required to have health insurance that meets "minimum creditable coverage" standards if it is deemed "affordable" at their income level under a schedule set by the board of the Commonwealth Health Insurance Connector Authority ("Connector"). Individuals report their insurance status on State income tax forms. Individuals can file hardship exemptions from the mandate; persons for whom there are no affordable insurance options available are not subject to the requirement for insurance coverage.

For taxable year 2007, an individual without insurance and who was not exempt from the requirement did not qualify under Massachusetts law for a State income tax personal exemption. For taxable years beginning on or after January 1, 2008, a penalty is levied for each month an individual is without insurance. The penalty consists of an amount up to 50 percent of the lowest premium available to the individual through the Connector. The penalty is reported and paid by the individual with the individual's Massachusetts State income tax return at the same time and in the same manner as State income taxes. Failure to pay the penalty results in the same interest and penalties as apply to unpaid income tax.

## *Explanation of Provision*

### *Personal responsibility requirement*

Beginning January, 2014, non-exempt U.S. citizens and legal residents are required to maintain minimum essential coverage. Minimum essential coverage includes government sponsored programs, eligible employer-sponsored plans, plans in the individual market, grandfathered group health plans and grandfathered health insurance coverage, and other coverage as recognized by the Secretary of HHS in coordination with the Secretary of the Treasury. Government sponsored programs include Medicare, Medicaid, Children's Health Insurance Program, coverage for members of the U.S. military,[745] veterans health care,[746] and health care for Peace Corps volunteers.[747] Eligible employer-sponsored plans include: governmental plans,[748] church plans,[749] grandfathered plans and other group health plans offered in the small or large group market within a State. Minimum essential coverage does not include coverage that consists of certain HIPAA excepted benefits.[750] Other

[745] 10 U.S.C. sec. 55 and 38 U.S.C. sec. 1781.

[746] Section 5000A is amended by Pub. L. No. 111–173 to clarify that minimum essential coverage includes any health care program under section 17 or 18 of Title 38 of the United States Code, as determined by the Secretary of Veterans Affairs, in coordination with the Secretary of HHS and the Secretary of Treasury.

[747] 22 U.S.C. sec. 2504(e).

[748] ERISA sec. 3(32).

[749] ERISA sec. 3(33).

[750] 42 U.S.C. sec. 300gg–91(c)(1). HIPAA excepted benefits include: (1) coverage only for accident, or disability income insurance; (2) coverage issued as a supplement to liability insurance; (3) liability insurance, including general liability insurance and automobile liability insurance;

Continued

HIPAA excepted benefits that do not constitute minimum essential coverage if offered under a separate policy, certificate or contract of insurance include long term care, limited scope dental and vision benefits, coverage for a disease or specified illness, hospital indemnity or other fixed indemnity insurance or Medicare supplemental health insurance.[751]

Individuals are exempt from the requirement for months they are incarcerated, not legally present in the United States or maintain religious exemptions. Those who are exempt from the requirement due to religious reasons must be members of a recognized religious sect exempting them from self-employment taxes[752] and adhere to tenets of the sect. Individuals residing[753] outside of the United States are deemed to maintain minimum essential coverage. If an individual is a dependent[754] of another taxpayer, the other taxpayer is liable for any penalty payment with respect to the individual.

***Penalty***

Individuals who fail to maintain minimum essential coverage in 2016 are subject to a penalty equal to the greater of: (1) 2.5 percent of the excess of the taxpayer's household income for the taxable year over the threshold amount of income required for income tax return filing for that taxpayer under section 6012(a)(1);[755] or (2) $695 per uninsured adult in the household. The fee for an uninsured individual under age 18 is one-half of the adult fee for an adult. The total household penalty may not exceed 300 percent of the per adult penalty ($2,085). The total annual household payment may not exceed the national average annual premium for bronze level health plan offered through the Exchange that year for the household size.

This per adult annual penalty is phased in as follows: $95 for 2014; $325 for 2015; and $695 in 2016. For years after 2016, the $695 amount is indexed to CPI–U, rounded to the next lowest $50. The percentage of income is phased in as follows: one percent for 2014; two percent in 2015; and 2.5 percent beginning after 2015. If a taxpayer files a joint return, the individual and spouse are jointly liable for any penalty payment.

The penalty applies to any period the individual does not maintain minimum essential coverage and is determined monthly. The penalty is an excise tax that is assessed in the same manner as an assessable penalty under the enforcement provisions of subtitle F of the Code.[756] As a result, it is assessable without regard to the

---

(4) workers' compensation or similar insurance; (5) automobile medical payment insurance; (6) credit-only insurance; (7) coverage for on-site medical clinics; and (8) other similar insurance coverage, specified in regulations, under which benefits for medical care are secondary or incidental to other insurance benefits.

[751] 42 U.S.C. sec. 300gg–91(c)(2–4).

[752] Sec. 1402(g)(1).

[753] Sec. 911(d)(1).

[754] Sec. 152.

[755] Generally, in 2010, the filing threshold is $9,350 for a single person or a married person filing separately and is $18,700 for married filing jointly. IR–2009–93, Oct. 15, 2009.

[756] IRS authority to assess and collect taxes is generally provided in subtitle F, "Procedure and Administration" in the Code. That subtitle establishes the rules governing both how taxpayers are required to report information to the IRS and pay their taxes as well as their rights. It also establishes the duties and authority of the IRS to enforce the Code, including civil and criminal penalties.

restrictions of section 6213(b). Although assessable and collectible under the Code, the IRS authority to use certain collection methods is limited. Specifically, the filing of notices of liens and levies otherwise authorized for collection of taxes does not apply to the collection of this penalty. In addition, the statute waives criminal penalties for non-compliance with the requirement to maintain minimum essential coverage. However, the authority to offset refunds or credits is not limited by the provision.

Individuals who cannot afford coverage because their required contribution for employer-sponsored coverage or, with respect to whom, the lowest cost bronze plan in the local Exchange exceeds eight percent of household income for the year are exempt from the penalty.[757] In years after 2014, the eight percent exemption is increased by the amount by which premium growth exceeds income growth. For employees, and individuals who are eligible for minimum essential coverage through an employer by reason of a relationship to an employee, the determination of whether coverage is affordable to the employee and any such individual is made by reference to the required contribution of the employees for self-only coverage. Individuals are liable for penalties imposed with respect to their dependents (as defined in section 152). An individual filing a joint return with a spouse is jointly liable for any penalty imposed with respect to the spouse. Taxpayers with income below the income tax filing threshold[758] are also exempt from the penalty for failure to maintain minimum essential coverage. All members of Indian tribes[759] are exempt from the penalty.

No penalty is assessed for individuals who do not maintain health insurance for a period of three months or less during the taxable year. If an individual exceeds the three month maximum during the taxable year, the penalty for the full duration of the gap during the year is applied. If there are multiple gaps in coverage during a calendar year, the exemption from penalty applies only to the first such gap in coverage. The Secretary of the Treasury shall provide rules when a coverage gap includes months in multiple calendar years. Individuals may also apply to the Secretary of HHS for a hardship exemption due to hardship in obtaining coverage.[760] Residents of the possessions[761] of the United States are treated as being covered by acceptable coverage.

Family size is the number of individuals for whom the taxpayer is allowed a personal exemption. Household income is the sum of the modified adjusted gross incomes of the taxpayer and all individuals accounted for in the family size required to file a tax return for that year. Modified adjusted gross income means adjusted gross

[757] In the case of an individual participating in a salary reduction arrangement, the taxpayer's household income is increased by any exclusion from gross income for any portion of the required contribution to the premium. The required contribution to the premium is the individual contribution to coverage through an employer or in the purchase of a bronze plan through the Exchange.

[758] Generally, in 2010, the filing threshold is $9,350 for a single person or a married person filing separately and is $18,700 for married filing jointly. IR–2009–93, Oct. 15, 2009.

[759] Tribal membership is defined in section 45A(c)(6).

[760] Sec. 1311(d)(4)(H).

[761] Sec. 937(a).

income increased by all tax-exempt interest and foreign earned income.[762]

### *Effective Date*

The provision is effective for taxable years beginning after December 31, 2013.

## I. Reporting of Health Insurance Coverage (sec. 1502 of the Act and new sec. 6055 and sec. 6724(d) of the Code)

### *Present Law*

#### *Insurer reporting of health insurance coverage*

No provision.

#### *Penalties for failure to comply with information reporting requirements*

Present law imposes a variety of information reporting requirements on participants in certain transactions.[763] These requirements are intended to assist taxpayers in preparing their income tax returns and help the IRS determine whether such returns are correct and complete. Failure to comply with the information reporting requirements may result in penalties, including: a penalty for failure to file the information return,[764] a penalty for failure to furnish payee statements,[765] and a penalty for failure to comply with various other reporting requirements.[766]

The penalty for failure to file an information return generally is $50 for each return for which such failure occurs. The total penalty imposed on a person for all failures during a calendar year cannot exceed $250,000. Additionally, special rules apply to reduce the per-failure and maximum penalty where the failure is corrected within a specified period.

The penalty for failure to provide a correct payee statement is $50 for each statement with respect to which such failure occurs, with the total penalty for a calendar year not to exceed $100,000. Special rules apply that increase the per-statement and total penalties where there is intentional disregard of the requirement to furnish a payee statement.

### *Explanation of Provision*

Under the provision, insurers (including employers who self-insure) that provide minimum essential coverage[767] to any individual during a calendar year must report certain health insurance coverage information to both the covered individual and to the IRS. In the case of coverage provided by a governmental unit, or any agency or instrumentality thereof, the reporting requirement ap-

---

[762] Sec. 911.

[763] Secs. 6031 through 6060.

[764] Sec. 6721.

[765] Sec. 6722.

[766] Sec. 6723. The penalty for failure to comply timely with a specified information reporting requirement is $50 per failure, not to exceed $100,000 for a calendar year.

[767] As defined in section 5000A of the Patient Protection and Affordable Care Act, Pub. L. No. 111–148, as amended by section 10106, as further amended by section 1002 of the Health Care and Education Reconciliation Act of 2010, Pub. L. No. 111–152.

plies to the person or employee who enters into the agreement to provide the health insurance coverage (or their designee).

The information required to be reported includes: (1) the name, address, and taxpayer identification number of the primary insured, and the name and taxpayer identification number of each other individual obtaining coverage under the policy; (2) the dates during which the individual was covered under the policy during the calendar year; (3) whether the coverage is a qualified health plan offered through an exchange; (4) the amount of any premium tax credit or cost-sharing reduction received by the individual with respect to such coverage; and (5) such other information as the Secretary may require.

To the extent health insurance coverage is provided through an employer-sponsored group health plan, the insurer is also required to report the name, address and employer identification number of the employer, the portion of the premium, if any, required to be paid by the employer, and any other information the Secretary may require to administer the new tax credit for eligible small employers.

The insurer is required to report the above information, along with the name, address and contact information of the reporting insurer, to the covered individual on or before January 31 of the year following the calendar year for which the information is required to be reported to the IRS.

The provision amends the information reporting provisions of the Code to provide that an insurer who fails to comply with these new reporting requirements is subject to the penalties for failure to file an information return and failure to furnish payee statements, respectively.

The IRS is required, not later than June 30 of each year, in consultation with the Secretary of HHS, to provide annual notice to each individual who files an income tax return and who fails to enroll in minimum essential coverage. The notice is required to include information on the services available through the exchange operating in the individual's State of residence.

### *Effective Date*

The provision is effective for calendar years beginning after 2013.

## J. Shared Responsibility for Employers (sec. 1513[768] of the Act and new sec. 4980H of the Code)

### *Present Law*

Currently, there is no Federal requirement that employers offer health insurance coverage to employees or their families. However, as with other compensation, the cost of employer-provided health coverage is a deductible business expense under section 162 of the

[768] Section 1513 of the Patient Protection and Affordable Care Act, Pub. L. No. 111–148, as amended by section 10106, is further amended by section 1003 of the Health Care and Education Reconciliation Act of 2010, Pub. L. No. 111–152.

Code.[769] In addition, employer-provided health insurance coverage is generally not included in an employee's gross income.[770]

Employees participating in a cafeteria plan may be able to pay the portion of premiums for health insurance coverage not otherwise paid for by their employers on a pre-tax basis through salary reduction.[771] Such salary reduction contributions are treated as employer contributions for purposes of the Code, and are thus excluded from gross income.

One way that employers can offer employer-provided health insurance coverage for purposes of the tax exclusion is to offer to reimburse employees for the premiums for health insurance purchased by employees in the individual health insurance market. The payment or reimbursement of employees' substantiated individual health insurance premiums is excludible from employees' gross income.[772] This reimbursement for individual health insurance premiums can also be paid through salary reduction under a cafeteria plan.[773] However, this offer to reimburse individual health insurance premiums constitutes a group health plan.

The Employee Retirement Income Security Act of 1974 ("ERISA")[774] preempts State law relating to certain employee benefit plans, including employer-sponsored health plans. While ERISA specifically provides that its preemption rule does not exempt or relieve any person from any State law which regulates insurance, ERISA also provides that an employee benefit plan is not deemed to be engaged in the business of insurance for purposes of any State law regulating insurance companies or insurance contracts. As a result of this ERISA preemption, self-insured employer-sponsored health plans need not provide benefits that are mandated under State insurance law.

While ERISA does not require an employer to offer health benefits, it does require compliance if an employer chooses to offer health benefits, such as compliance with plan fiduciary standards, reporting and disclosure requirements, and procedures for appealing denied benefit claims. There are other Federal requirements for health plans which include, for example, rules for health care continuation coverage.[775] The Code imposes an excise tax on group health plans that fail to meet these other requirements.[776] The excise tax generally is equal to $100 per day per failure during the period of noncompliance and is imposed on the employer sponsoring the plan.

Under Medicaid, States may establish "premium assistance" programs, which pay a Medicaid beneficiary's share of premiums for employer-sponsored health coverage. Besides being available to the beneficiary through his or her employer, the coverage must be comprehensive and cost-effective for the State. An individual's enroll-

---

[769] Sec. 162. However see special rules in sections 419 and 419A for the deductibility of contributions to welfare benefit plans with respect to medical benefits for employees and their dependents.

[770] Sec. 106.

[771] Sec. 125.

[772] Rev. Rul. 61–146 (1961–2 CB 25).

[773] Prop. Treas. Reg. sec. 1.125–1(m).

[774] Pub. L. No. 93–406.

[775] These rules were added to ERISA and the Code by the Consolidated Omnibus Budget Reconciliation Act of 1985, Pub. L. No. 99–272.

[776] Sec. 4980B.

ment in an employer plan is considered cost-effective if paying the premiums, deductibles, coinsurance and other cost-sharing obligations of the employer plan is less expensive than the State's expected cost of directly providing Medicaid-covered services. States are also required to provide coverage for those Medicaid-covered services that are not included in the private plans. A 2007 analysis showed that 12 States had Medicaid premium assistance programs as authorized under current law.

### *Explanation of Provision*

An applicable large employer that does not offer coverage for all its full-time employees, offers minimum essential coverage that is unaffordable, or offers minimum essential coverage that consists of a plan under which the plan's share of the total allowed cost of benefits is less than 60 percent, is required to pay a penalty if any full-time employee is certified to the employer as having purchased health insurance through a state exchange with respect to which a tax credit or cost-sharing reduction is allowed or paid to the employee.

#### *Applicable large employer*

An employer is an applicable large employer with respect to any calendar year if it employed an average of at least 50 full-time employees during the preceding calendar year. For purposes of the provision, "employer" includes any predecessor employer. An employer is not treated as employing more than 50 full-time employees if the employer's workforce exceeds 50 full-time employees for 120 days or fewer during the calendar year and the employees that cause the employer's workforce to exceed 50 full-time employees are seasonal workers. A seasonal worker is a worker who performs labor or services on a seasonal basis (as defined by the Secretary of Labor), including retail workers employed exclusively during the holiday season and workers whose employment is, ordinarily, the kind exclusively performed at certain seasons or periods of the year and which, from its nature, may not be continuous or carried on throughout the year.[777]

In counting the number of employees for purposes of determining whether an employer is an applicable large employer, a full-time employee (meaning, for any month, an employee working an average of at least 30 hours or more each week) is counted as one employee and all other employees are counted on a pro-rated basis in accordance with regulations prescribed by the Secretary. The number of full-time equivalent employees that must be taken into account for purposes of determining whether the employer exceeds the threshold is equal to the aggregate number of hours worked by non-full-time employees for the month, divided by 120 (or such other number based on an average of 30 hours of service each week as the Secretary may prescribe in regulations).

The Secretary, in consultation with the Secretary of Labor, is directed to issue, as necessary, rules, regulations and guidance to de-

[777] 29 C.F.R. section 500.20(s)(1). Under section 5000.20(s)(1), a worker who moves from one seasonal activity to another, while employed in agriculture or performing agricultural labor, is employed on a seasonal basis even though he may continue to be employed during a major portion of the year.

termine an employee's hours of service, including rules that apply to employees who are not compensated on an hourly basis.

The aggregation rules of section 414(b), (c), (m), and (o) apply in determining whether an employer is an applicable large employer. The determination of whether an employer that was not in existence during the preceding calendar year is an applicable large employer is made based on the average number of employees that it is reasonably expected to employ on business days in the current calendar year.

***Penalty for employers not offering coverage***

An applicable large employer who fails to offer its full-time employees and their dependents the opportunity to enroll in minimum essential coverage under an employer-sponsored plan for any month is subject to a penalty if at least one of its full-time employees is certified to the employer as having enrolled in health insurance coverage purchased through a State exchange with respect to which a premium tax credit or cost-sharing reduction is allowed or paid to such employee or employees. The penalty for any month is an excise tax equal to the number of full-time employees over a 30-employee threshold during the applicable month (regardless of how many employees are receiving a premium tax credit or cost-sharing reduction) multiplied by one-twelfth of $2,000. In the case of persons treated as a single employer under the provision, the 30-employee reduction in full-time employees is made from the total number of full-time employees employed by such persons (i.e., only one 30-person reduction is permitted per controlled group of employers) and is allocated among such persons in relation to the number of full-time employees employed by each such person.

For example, in 2014, Employer A fails to offer minimum essential coverage and has 100 full-time employees, ten of whom receive a tax credit for the year for enrolling in a State exchange-offered plan. For each employee over the 30-employee threshold, the employer owes $2,000, for a total penalty of $140,000 ($2,000 multiplied by 70 ((100–30)). This penalty is assessed on an annual, monthly, or periodic basis as the Secretary may prescribe.

For calendar years after 2014, the $2,000 amount is increased by the percentage (if any) by which the average per capita premium for health insurance coverage in the United States for the preceding calendar year (as estimated by the Secretary of HHS no later than October 1 of the preceding calendar year) exceeds the average per capita premium for 2013 (as determined by the Secretary of HHS), rounded down to the nearest $10.

***Penalty for employees receiving premium credits***

An applicable large employer who offers, for any month, its full-time employees and their dependents the opportunity to enroll in minimum essential coverage under an employer-sponsored plan is subject to a penalty if any full-time employee is certified to the employer as having enrolled in health insurance coverage purchased through a State exchange with respect to which a premium tax credit or cost-sharing reduction is allowed or paid to such employee or employees.

The penalty is an excise tax that is imposed for each employee who receives a premium tax credit or cost-sharing reduction for health insurance purchased through a State exchange. For each full-time employee receiving a premium tax credit or cost-sharing subsidy through a State exchange for any month, the employer is required to pay an amount equal to one-twelfth of $3,000. The penalty for each employer for any month is capped at an amount equal to the number of full-time employees during the month (regardless of how many employees are receiving a premium tax credit or cost-sharing reduction) in excess of 30, multiplied by one-twelfth of $2,000. In the case of persons treated as a single employer under the provision, the 30-employee reduction in full-time employees for purposes of calculating the maximum penalty is made from the total number of full-time employees employed by such persons (i.e., only one 30-person reduction is permitted per controlled group of employers) and is allocated among such persons in relation to the number of full-time employees employed by each such person.

For example, in 2014, Employer A offers health coverage and has 100 full-time employees, 20 of whom receive a tax credit for the year for enrolling in a State exchange offered plan. For each employee receiving a tax credit, the employer owes $3,000, for a total penalty of $60,000. The maximum penalty for this employer is capped at the amount of the penalty that it would have been assessed for a failure to provide coverage, or $140,000 ($2,000 multiplied by 70 ((100–30)). Since the calculated penalty of $60,000 is less than the maximum amount, Employer A pays the $60,000 calculated penalty. This penalty is assessed on an annual, monthly, or periodic basis as the Secretary may prescribe.

For calendar years after 2014, the $3,000 and $2,000 amounts are increased by the percentage (if any) by which the average per capita premium for health insurance coverage in the United States for the preceding calendar year (as estimated by the Secretary of HHS no later than October 1 of the preceding calendar year) exceeds the average per capita premium for 2013 (as determined by the Secretary of HHS), rounded down to the nearest $10.

### *Time for payment, deductibility of excise taxes, restrictions on assessment*

The excise taxes imposed under this provision are payable on an annual, monthly or other periodic basis as the Secretary of the Treasury may prescribe. The excise taxes imposed under this provision for employees receiving premium tax credits are not deductible under section 162 as a business expense. The restrictions on assessment under section 6213 are not applicable to the excise taxes imposed under the provision.

### *Employer offer of health insurance coverage*

Under the provision, as under current law, an employer is not required to offer health insurance coverage. If an employee is offered health insurance coverage by his or her employer and chooses to enroll in the coverage, the employer-provided portion of the coverage is excluded from gross income. The tax treatment is the same whether the employer offers coverage outside of a State exchange or the employer offers a coverage option through a State exchange.

*Definition of coverage*

As a general matter, if an employee is offered affordable minimum essential coverage under an employer-sponsored plan, the individual is ineligible for a premium tax credit and cost sharing reductions for health insurance purchased through a State exchange.

*Unaffordable coverage*

If an employee is offered minimum essential coverage by their employer that is either unaffordable or that consists of a plan under which the plan's share of the total allowed cost of benefits is less than 60 percent, however, the employee is eligible for a premium tax credit and cost sharing reductions, but only if the employee declines to enroll in the coverage and purchases coverage through the exchange instead. Unaffordable is defined as coverage with a premium required to be paid by the employee that is more than 9.5 percent of the employee's household income (as defined for purposes of the premium tax credits), based on the self-only coverage. This percentage of the employee's income is indexed to the per capita growth in premiums for the insured market as determined by the Secretary of HHS. The employee must seek an affordability waiver from the State exchange and provide information as to family income and the lowest cost employer option offered to them. The State exchange then provides the waiver to the employee. The employer penalty applies for any employee(s) receiving an affordability waiver.

For purposes of determining if coverage is unaffordable, required salary reduction contributions are treated as payments required to be made by the employee. However, if an employee is reimbursed by the employer for any portion of the premium for health insurance coverage purchased through the exchange, including any reimbursement through salary reduction contributions under a cafeteria plan, the coverage is employer-provided and the employee is not eligible for premium tax credits or cost-sharing reductions. Thus, an individual is not permitted to purchase coverage through the exchange, apply for the premium tax credit, and pay for the individual's portion of the premium using salary reduction contributions under the cafeteria plan of the individual's employer.

An employer must be notified if one of its employees is determined to be eligible for a premium assistance credit or a cost-sharing reduction because the employer does not provide minimal essential coverage through an employer-sponsored plan, or the employer does offer such coverage but it is not affordable or the plan's share of the total allowed cost of benefits is less than 60 percent. The notice must include information about the employer's potential liability for payments under section 4980H. The employer must also receive notification of the appeals process established for employers notified of potential liability for payments under section 4980H. An employer is generally not entitled to information about its employees who qualify for the premium assistance credit or cost-sharing reductions; however, the appeals process must provide an employer the opportunity to access the data used to make the determination of an employee's eligibility for a premium assistance credit or cost-sharing reduction, to the extent allowable by law.

The Secretary is required to prescribe rules, regulations or guidance for the repayment of any assessable payment (including interest) if the payment is based on the allowance or payment of a premium tax credit or cost-sharing reduction with respect to an employee that is subsequently disallowed and with respect to which the assessable payment would not have been required to have been made in the absence of the allowance or payment.

*Effect of medicaid enrollment*

A Medicaid-eligible individual can always choose to leave the employer's coverage and enroll in Medicaid, and an employer is not required to pay a penalty for any employees enrolled in Medicaid.

***Study and reporting on employer responsibility requirements***

The Secretary of Labor is required to study whether employee wages are reduced by reason of the application of the employer responsibility requirements, using the National Compensation Survey published by the Bureau of Labor Statistics. The Secretary of Labor is to report the results of this study to the Committee on Ways and Means of the House of Representatives and the Committee on Finance of the Senate.

### *Effective Date*

The provision is effective for months beginning after December 31, 2013.

## K. Reporting of Employer Health Insurance Coverage (sec. 1514 of the Act and new sec. 6056 and sec. 6724(d) of the Code)

### *Present Law*

***Employer reporting of health insurance coverage***

No provision.

***Penalties for failure to comply with information reporting requirements***

Present law imposes a variety of information reporting requirements on participants in certain transactions.[778] These requirements are intended to assist taxpayers in preparing their income tax returns and help the IRS determine whether such returns are correct and complete. Failure to comply with the information reporting requirements may result in penalties, including: a penalty for failure to file the information return,[779] a penalty for failure to furnish payee statements,[780] and a penalty for failure to comply with various other reporting requirements.[781]

The penalty for failure to file an information return generally is $50 for each return for which such failure occurs. The total penalty imposed on a person for all failures during a calendar year cannot

[778] Secs. 6031 through 6060.
[779] Sec. 6721.
[780] Sec. 6722.
[781] Sec. 6723. The penalty for failure to comply timely with a specified information reporting requirement is $50 per failure, not to exceed $100,000 for a calendar year.

exceed $250,000. Additionally, special rules apply to reduce the per-failure and maximum penalty where the failure is corrected within a specified period.

The penalty for failure to provide a correct payee statement is $50 for each statement with respect to which such failure occurs, with the total penalty for a calendar year not to exceed $100,000. Special rules apply that increase the per-statement and total penalties where there is intentional disregard of the requirement to furnish a payee statement.

### *Explanation of Provision*

Under the provision, each applicable large employer subject to the employer responsibility provisions of new section 4980H and each "offering employer" must report certain health insurance coverage information to both its full-time employees and to the IRS. An offering employer is any employer who offers minimum essential coverage[782] to its employees under an eligible employer-sponsored plan and who pays any portion of the costs of such plan, but only if the required employer contribution of any employee exceeds eight percent of the wages paid by the employer to the employee. In the case of years after 2014, the eight percent is indexed to reflect the rate of premium growth over income growth between 2013 and the preceding calendar year. In the case of coverage provided by a governmental unit, or any agency or instrumentality thereof, the reporting requirement applies to the person or employee appropriately designated for purposes of making the returns and statements required by the provision.

The information required to be reported includes: (1) the name, address and employer identification number of the employer; (2) a certification as to whether the employer offers its full-time employees and their dependents the opportunity to enroll in minimum essential coverage under an eligible employer-sponsored plan; (3) the number of full-time employees of the employer for each month during the calendar year; (4) the name, address and taxpayer identification number of each full-time employee employed by the employer during the calendar year and the number of months, if any, during which the employee (and any dependents) was covered under a plan sponsored by the employer during the calendar year; and (5) such other information as the Secretary may require.

Employers who offer the opportunity to enroll in minimum essential coverage must also report: (1) in the case of an applicable large employer, the length of any waiting period with respect to such coverage; (2) the months during the calendar year during which the coverage was available; (3) the monthly premium for the lowest cost option in each of the enrollment categories under the plan; (4) the employer's share of the total allowed costs of benefits under the plan; and (5), in the case of an offering employer, the option for which the employer pays the largest position of the cost of the plan and the portion of the cost paid by the employer in each of the enrollment categories under each option.

---

[782] As defined in section 5000A of the Patient Protection and Affordable Care Act, Pub. L. No. 111–148, as amended by section 10106, as further amended by section 1002 of the Health Care and Education Reconciliation Act of 2010, Pub. L. No. 111–152.

The employer is required to report to each full-time employee the above information required to be reported with respect to that employee, along with the name, address and contact information of the reporting employer, on or before January 31 of the year following the calendar year for which the information is required to be reported to the IRS.

The provision amends the information reporting provisions of the Code to provide that an employer who fails to comply with these new reporting requirements is subject to the penalties for failure to file an information return and failure to furnish payee statements, respectively.

To the maximum extent feasible, the Secretary may provide that any information return or payee statement required to be provided under the provision may be provided as part of any return or statement required under new sections 6051 [783] or 6055 [784] and, in the case of an applicable large employer or offering employer offering health insurance coverage of a health insurance issuer, the employer may enter into an agreement with the issuer to include the information required by the provision with the information return and payee statement required under new section 6055.

The Secretary has the authority, in coordination with the Secretary of Labor, to review the accuracy of the information reported by the employer, including the employer's share of the total allowed costs of benefits under the plan.

### *Effective Date*

The provision is effective for periods beginning after December 31, 2013.

## L. Offering of Qualified Health Plans Through Cafeteria Plans (sec. 1515 of the Act and sec. 125 of the Code)

### *Present Law*

Currently, there is no Federal requirement that employers offer health insurance coverage to employees or their families. However, as with other compensation, the cost of employer-provided health coverage is a deductible business expense under section 162 of the Code.[785] In addition, employer-provided health insurance coverage is generally not included in an employee's gross income.[786]

#### *Definition of a cafeteria plan*

If an employee receives a qualified benefit (as defined below) based on the employee's election between the qualified benefit and a taxable benefit under a cafeteria plan, the qualified benefit gen-

---

[783] For additional information on new section 6051, see the explanation of section 9002 of the Patient Protection and Affordable Care Act, Pub. L. No. 111–148, "Inclusion of Employer-Sponsored Health Coverage on W–2."

[784] For additional information on new section 6055, see the explanation of section 1502 of the Patient Protection and Affordable Care Act, Pub. L. No. 111–148, "Reporting of Health Insurance Coverage."

[785] Sec. 162. However see special rules in sections 419 and 419A for the deductibility of contributions to welfare benefit plans with respect to medical benefits for employees and their dependents.

[786] Sec. 106.

erally is not includable in gross income.[787] However, if a plan offering an employee an election between taxable benefits (including cash) and nontaxable qualified benefits does not meet the requirements for being a cafeteria plan, the election between taxable and nontaxable benefits results in gross income to the employee, regardless of what benefit is elected and when the election is made.[788] A cafeteria plan is a separate written plan under which all participants are employees, and participants are permitted to choose among at least one permitted taxable benefit (for example, current cash compensation) and at least one qualified benefit. Finally, a cafeteria plan must not provide for deferral of compensation, except as specifically permitted in sections 125(d)(2)(B), (C), or (D).

### *Qualified benefits*

Qualified benefits under a cafeteria plan are generally employer-provided benefits that are not includable in gross income under an express provision of the Code. Examples of qualified benefits include employer-provided health insurance coverage, group term life insurance coverage not in excess of $50,000, and benefits under a dependent care assistance program. In order to be excludable, any qualified benefit elected under a cafeteria plan must independently satisfy any requirements under the Code section that provides the exclusion. However, some employer-provided benefits that are not includable in gross income under an express provision of the Code are explicitly not allowed in a cafeteria plan. These benefits are generally referred to as nonqualified benefits. Examples of nonqualified benefits include scholarships;[789] employer-provided meals and lodging;[790] educational assistance;[791] and fringe benefits.[792] A plan offering any nonqualified benefit is not a cafeteria plan.[793]

### *Payment of health insurance premiums through a cafeteria plan*

Employees participating in a cafeteria plan may be able to pay the portion of premiums for health insurance coverage not otherwise paid for by their employers on a pre-tax basis through salary reduction.[794] Such salary reduction contributions are treated as employer contributions for purposes of the Code, and are thus excluded from gross income.

One way that employers can offer employer-provided health insurance coverage for purposes of the tax exclusion is to offer to reimburse employees for the premiums for health insurance purchased by employees in the individual health insurance market. The payment or reimbursement of employees' substantiated individual health insurance premiums is excludible from employees'

---

[787] Sec. 125(a).
[788] Prop. Treas. Reg. sec. 1.125–1(b).
[789] Sec. 117.
[790] Sec. 119.
[791] Sec. 127.
[792] Sec. 132.
[793] Prop. Treas. Reg. sec. 1.125–1(q). Long-term care services, contributions to Archer Medical Savings Accounts, group term life insurance for an employee's spouse, child or dependent, and elective deferrals to section 403(b) plans are also nonqualified benefits.
[794] Sec. 125.

gross income.[795] This reimbursement for individual health insurance premiums can also be paid for through salary reduction under a cafeteria plan.[796] This offer to reimburse individual health insurance premiums constitutes a group health plan.

### *Explanation of Provision*

Under the provision, reimbursement (or direct payment) for the premiums for coverage under any qualified health plan (as defined in section 1301(a) of the Act) offered through an Exchange established under section 1311 of the Act is a qualified benefit under a cafeteria plan if the employer is a qualified employer. Under section 1312(f)(2) of the Act, a qualified employer is generally a small employer that elects to make all its full-time employees eligible for one or more qualified plans offered in the small group market through an Exchange.[797] Otherwise, reimbursement (or direct payment) for the premiums for coverage under any qualified health plan offered through an Exchange is not a qualified benefit under a cafeteria plan. Thus, an employer that is not a qualified employer cannot offer to reimburse an employee for the premium for a qualified plan that the employee purchases through the individual market in an Exchange as a health insurance coverage option under its cafeteria plan.

### *Effective Date*

This provision applies to taxable years beginning after December 31, 2013.

## M. Conforming Amendments (sec. 1563 of the Act and new sec. 9815 of the Code)

### *Present Law*

The Health Insurance Portability and Accountability Act of 1996 ("HIPAA")[798] imposes a number of requirements with respect to group health coverage that are designed to provide protections to health plan participants. These protections include limitations on exclusions from coverage based on pre-existing conditions; the prohibition of discrimination on the basis of health status; guaranteed renewability in multiemployer plans and certain employer welfare arrangements; standards relating to benefits for mother and newborns; parity in the application of certain limits to mental health benefits; and coverage of dependent students on medically necessary leave of absence. The requirements are enforced through the Code, ERISA,[799] and the PHSA.[800] The HIPAA requirements in the Code are in chapter 100 of Subtitle K, Group Health Plan Requirements.

---

[795] Rev. Rul. 61–146, 1961–2 CB 25.

[796] Prop. Treas. Reg. sec. 1.125–1(m).

[797] Beginning in 2017, each State may allow issuers of health insurance coverage in the large group market in a state to offer qualified plans in the large group market. In that event, a qualified employer includes a small employer that elects to make all its full-time employees eligible for one or more qualified plans offered in the large group market through an Exchange.

[798] Pub. L. No. 104–191.

[799] Pub. L. No. 93–406.

[800] 42 U.S.C. 6A.

A group health plan is defined as a plan (including a self-insured plan) of, or contributed to by, an employer (including a self-employed person) or employee organization to provide health care (directly or otherwise) to the employees, former employees, the employer, others associated or formerly associated with the employer in a business relationship, or their families.[801]

The Code imposes an excise tax on group health plans which fail to meet the HIPAA requirements.[802] The excise tax is equal to $100 per day during the period of noncompliance and is generally imposed on the employer sponsoring the plan if the plan fails to meet the requirements. The maximum tax that can be imposed during a taxable year cannot exceed the lesser of: (1) 10 percent of the employer's group health plan expenses for the prior year; or (2) $500,000. No tax is imposed if the Secretary determines that the employer did not know, and in exercising reasonable diligence would not have known, that the failure existed.

### *Explanation of Provision*

The provision adds new Code section 9815 which provides that the provisions of part A of title XXVII of the PHSA (as amended by the Act) apply to group health plans, and health insurance issuers providing health insurance coverage in connection with group health plans, as if included in Subchapter B of Chapter 100 of the Code. To the extent that any HIPAA provision of the Code conflicts with a provision of part A of title XXVII of the PHSA with respect to group health plans, or health insurance issuers providing health insurance coverage in connection with group health plans, the provisions of such part A generally apply.

The provisions of part A of title XXVII of the PHSA added by section 1001 of the Act that are incorporated by reference in new section 9815 include the following: section 2711 (No lifetime or annual limits); section 2712 (Prohibition on rescissions); section 2713 (Coverage of preventive health services); section 2714 (Extension of dependent coverage); section 2715 (Development and utilization of uniform explanation of coverage documents and standardized definitions); section 2716 (Prohibition of discrimination in favor of highly compensated individuals); section 2717 (Ensuring the quality of care); section 2718 (Bringing down the cost of health care coverage); and section 2719 (Appeals process). These new sections of the PHSA, which relate to individual and group market reforms, are effective six months after the date of enactment (March 23, 2010).

The provisions of part A of title XXVII of the PHSA added by section 1201 of the Act that are incorporated by reference in new section 9815 include the following: section 2704 (Prohibition of preexisting condition exclusions or other discrimination based on health status); section 2701 (Fair health insurance premiums); section 2702 (Guaranteed availability of coverage) section 2703 (Guaranteed renewability of coverage); section 2705 (Prohibiting discrimination against individual participants and beneficiaries based

---

[801] The requirements do not apply to any governmental plan or any group health plan that has fewer than two participants who are current employees.

[802] Sec. 4980D.

on health status); section 2706 (Non-discrimination in health care); section 2707 (Comprehensive health insurance coverage); and section 2708 (Prohibition on excessive waiting periods). These new sections of the PHSA, which relate to general health insurance reforms, are effective for plan years beginning on or after January 1, 2014.

New section 9815 specifies that section 2716 (Prohibition of discrimination based on salary) and 2718 (Bringing down the cost of health coverage) of title XXVII of the PHSA (as amended by the Act) do not apply under the Code provisions of HIPAA with respect to self-insured group health plans.

As a result of incorporating these PHSA provisions by reference, the excise tax that applies in the event of a violation of present law HIPAA requirements also applies in the event of a violation of these new requirements.

### *Effective Date*

This provision is effective on the date of enactment (March 23, 2010).

## TITLE III—IMPROVING THE QUALITY AND EFFICIENCY OF HEALTHCARE

### A. Disclosures to Carry Out the Reduction of Medicare Part D Subsidies for High Income Beneficiaries (sec. 3308(b)(2) of the Act and sec. 6103 of the Code)

### *Present Law*

Section 6103 provides that returns and return information are confidential and may not be disclosed by the IRS, other Federal employees, State employees, and certain others having access to such information except as provided in the Code. Section 6103 contains a number of exceptions to the general rule of nondisclosure that authorize disclosure in specifically identified circumstances. For example, section 6103 provides for the disclosure of certain return information for purposes of establishing the appropriate amount of any Medicare Part B premium subsidy adjustment.

Specifically, upon written request from the Commissioner of Social Security, the IRS may disclose the following limited return information of a taxpayer whose premium, according to the records of the Secretary, may be subject to adjustment under section 1839(i) of the Social Security Act (relating to Medicare Part B):

- Taxpayer identity information with respect to such taxpayer;
- The filing status of the taxpayer;
- The adjusted gross income of such taxpayer;
- The amounts excluded from such taxpayer's gross income under sections 135 and 911 to the extent such information is available;
- The interest received or accrued during the taxable year which is exempt from the tax imposed by chapter 1 to the extent such information is available;

- The amounts excluded from such taxpayer's gross income by sections 931 and 933 to the extent such information is available;
- Such other information relating to the liability of the taxpayer as is prescribed by the Secretary by regulation as might indicate that the amount of the premium of the taxpayer may be subject to an adjustment and the amount of such adjustment; and
- The taxable year with respect to which the preceding information relates.

This return information may be used by officers, employees, and contractors of the Social Security Administration only for the purposes of, and to the extent necessary in, establishing the appropriate amount of any Medicare Part B premium subsidy adjustment.

Section 6103(p)(4) requires, as a condition of receiving returns and return information, that Federal and State agencies (and certain other recipients) provide safeguards as prescribed by the Secretary by regulation to be necessary or appropriate to protect the confidentiality of returns or return information. Unauthorized disclosure of a return or return information is a felony punishable by a fine not exceeding $5,000 or imprisonment of not more than five years, or both, together with the costs of prosecution.[803] The unauthorized inspection of a return or return information is punishable by a fine not exceeding $1,000 or imprisonment of not more than one year, or both, together with the costs of prosecution.[804] An action for civil damages also may be brought for unauthorized disclosure or inspection.[805]

### *Explanation of Provision*

Upon written request from the Commissioner of Social Security, the IRS may disclose the following limited return information of a taxpayer whose Medicare Part D premium subsidy, according to the records of the Secretary, may be subject to adjustment:

- Taxpayer identity information with respect to such taxpayer;
- The filing status of the taxpayer;
- The adjusted gross income of such taxpayer;
- The amounts excluded from such taxpayer's gross income under sections 135 and 911 to the extent such information is available;
- The interest received or accrued during the taxable year which is exempt from the tax imposed by chapter 1 to the extent such information is available;
- The amounts excluded from such taxpayer's gross income by sections 931 and 933 to the extent such information is available;
- Such other information relating to the liability of the taxpayer as is prescribed by the Secretary by regulation as might indicate that the amount of the Part D premium of the tax-

[803] Sec. 7213.
[804] Sec. 7213A.
[805] Sec. 7431.

payer may be subject to an adjustment and the amount of such adjustment; and

- The taxable year with respect to which the preceding information relates.

This return information may be used by officers, employees, and contractors of the Social Security Administration only for the purposes of, and to the extent necessary in, establishing the appropriate amount of any Medicare Part D premium subsidy adjustment.

For purposes of both the Medicare Part B premium subsidy adjustment and the Medicare Part D premium subsidy adjustment, the provision provides that the Social Security Administration may redisclose only taxpayer identity and the amount of premium subsidy adjustment to officers and employees and contractors of the Centers for Medicare and Medicaid Services, and officers and employees of the Office of Personnel Management and the Railroad Retirement Board. This redisclosure is permitted only to the extent necessary for the collection of the premium subsidy amount from the taxpayers under the jurisdiction of the respective agencies.

Further, the Social Security Administration may redisclose the return information received under this provision to officers and employees of the Department of HHS to the extent necessary to resolve administrative appeals of the Part B and Part D subsidy adjustments and to officers and employees of the Department of Justice to the extent necessary for use in judicial proceedings related to establishing and collecting the appropriate amount of any Medicare Part B or Medicare Part D premium subsidy adjustments.

### *Effective Date*

The provision is effective on the date of enactment (March 23, 2010).

## TITLE VI—TRANSPARENCY AND PROGRAM INTEGRITY

### A. Patient-Centered Outcomes Research Trust Fund; Financing for Trust Fund (sec. 6301 of the Act and new secs. 4375, 4376, 4377, and 9511 of the Code)

#### *Present Law*

No provision.

#### *Reasons for Change*

The Congress believes that comparative effectiveness research is a public good and that a sustained investment in such research is needed to improve the quality of information about the relative strengths and weaknesses of various health care items, services and systems to allow physicians and patients to make more informed health care decisions. To insure that there are sufficient amounts of public and private funds dedicated to this purpose, and to insulate such funding from inappropriate outside influence, the Congress believes that it is appropriate to establish a trust fund, impose fees on health insurance plans and receive transfer payments from Medicare, and have such amounts in the fund dedicated to finance comparative effectiveness research.

### *Explanation of Provision*

#### *Patient-Centered Outcomes Research Trust Fund*

Under new section 9511, there is established in the Treasury of the United States a trust fund, the Patient Centered Outcomes Research Trust Fund ("PCORTF"), to carry out the provisions in the Act relating to comparative effectiveness research. The PCORTF is funded in part from fees imposed on health plans under new sections 4375 through 4377.

#### *Fee on insured and self-insured health plans*

*Insured plans*

Under new section 4375, a fee is imposed on each specified health insurance policy. The fee is equal to two dollars (one dollar in the case of policy years ending during fiscal year 2013) multiplied by the average number of lives covered under the policy. For any policy year beginning after September 30, 2014, the dollar amount is equal to the sum of: (1) the dollar amount for policy years ending in the preceding fiscal year, plus (2) an amount equal to the product of (A) the dollar amount for policy years ending in the preceding fiscal year, multiplied by (B) the percentage increase in the projected per capita amount of National Health Expenditures, as most recently published by the Secretary before the beginning of the fiscal year. The issuer of the policy is liable for payment of the fee. A specified health insurance policy includes any accident or health insurance policy[806] issued with respect to individuals residing in the United States.[807] An arrangement under which fixed payments of premiums are received as consideration for a person's agreement to provide, or arrange for the provision of, accident or health coverage to residents of the United States, regardless of how such coverage is provided or arranged to be provided, is treated as a specified health insurance policy. The person agreeing to provide or arrange for the provision of coverage is treated as the issuer.

*Self-insured plans*

In the case of an applicable self-insured health plan, new Code section 4376 imposes a fee equal to two dollars (one dollar in the case of policy years ending during fiscal year 2013) multiplied by the average number of lives covered under the plan. For any policy year beginning after September 30, 2014, the dollar amount is equal to the sum of: (1) the dollar amount for policy years ending in the preceding fiscal year, plus (2) an amount equal to the prod-

---

[806] A specified health insurance policy does not include insurance if substantially all of the coverage provided under such policy consists of excepted benefits described in section 9832(c). Examples of excepted benefits described in section 9832(c) are coverage for only accident, or disability insurance, or any combination thereof; liability insurance, including general liability insurance and automobile liability insurance; workers' compensation or similar insurance; automobile medical payment insurance; coverage for on-site medical clinics; limited scope dental or vision benefits; benefits for long term care, nursing home care, community based care, or any combination thereof; coverage only for a specified disease or illness; hospital indemnity or other fixed indemnity insurance; and Medicare supplemental coverage.

[807] Under the provision, the United States includes any possession of the United States.

uct of (A) the dollar amount for policy years ending in the preceding fiscal year, multiplied by (B) the percentage increase in the projected per capita amount of National Health Expenditures, as most recently published by the Secretary before the beginning of the fiscal year. The plan sponsor is liable for payment of the fee. For purposes of the provision, the plan sponsor is: the employer in the case of a plan established or maintained by a single employer or the employee organization in the case of a plan established or maintained by an employee organization. In the case of: (1) a plan established or maintained by two or more employers or jointly by one of more employers and one or more employee organizations, (2) a multiple employer welfare arrangement, or (3) a voluntary employees' beneficiary association described in Code section 501(c)(9) ("VEBA"), the plan sponsor is the association, committee, joint board of trustees, or other similar group of representatives of the parties who establish or maintain the plan. In the case of a rural electric cooperative or a rural telephone cooperative, the plan sponsor is the cooperative or association.

Under the provision, an applicable self-insured health plan is any plan providing accident or health coverage if any portion of such coverage is provided other than through an insurance policy and such plan is established or maintained: (1) by one or more employers for the benefit of their employees or former employees, (2) by one or more employee organizations for the benefit of their members or former members, (3) jointly by one or more employers and one or more employee organizations for the benefit of employees or former employees, (4) by a VEBA, (5) by any organization described in section 501(c)(6) of the Code, or (6) in the case of a plan not previously described, by a multiple employer welfare arrangement (as defined in section 3(40) of ERISA, a rural electric cooperative (as defined in section 3(40)(B)(iv) of ERISA), or a rural telephone cooperative association (as defined in section 3(40)(B)(v) of ERISA).

*Other special rules*

Governmental entities are generally not exempt from the fees imposed under the provision. There is an exception for exempt governmental programs including, Medicare, Medicaid, SCHIP, and any program established by Federal law for proving medical care (other than through insurance policies) to members of the Armed Forces, veterans, or members of Indian tribes.

No amount collected from the fee on health insurance and self-insured plans is covered over to any possession of the United States. For purposes of the Code's procedure and administration rules, the fee imposed under the provision is treated as a tax. The fees imposed under new sections 4375 and 4376 do not apply to plan years ending after September 31, 2019.

### *Effective Date*

The fee on health insurance and self-insured plans is effective with respect to policies and plans for portions of policy or plan years ending after September 30, 2012.

# TITLE IX—REVENUE PROVISIONS

## A. Excise Tax on High Cost Employer-Sponsored Health Coverage (sec. 9001[808] of the Act and new sec. 4980I of the Code)

### *Present Law*

#### *Taxation of insurance companies*

Current law provides special rules for determining the taxable income of insurance companies (subchapter L of the Code). Separate sets of rules apply to life insurance companies and to property and casualty insurance companies. Insurance companies generally are subject to Federal income tax at regular corporate income tax rates.

An insurance company that provides health insurance is subject to Federal income tax as either a life insurance company or as a property insurance company, depending on its mix of lines of business and on the resulting portion of its reserves that are treated as life insurance reserves. For Federal income tax purposes, an insurance company is treated as a life insurance company if the sum of its (1) life insurance reserves and (2) unearned premiums and unpaid losses on noncancellable life, accident or health contracts not included in life insurance reserves, comprise more than 50 percent of its total reserves.[809]

Some insurance providers may be exempt from Federal income tax under section 501(a) if specific requirements are satisfied. Section 501(c)(8), for example, describes certain fraternal beneficiary societies, orders, or associations operating under the lodge system or for the exclusive benefit of their members that provide for the payment of life, sick, accident, or other benefits to the members or their dependents. Section 501(c)(9) describes certain voluntary employees' beneficiary associations that provide for the payment of life, sick, accident, or other benefits to the members of the association or their dependents or designated beneficiaries. Section 501(c)(12)(A) describes certain benevolent life insurance associations of a purely local character. Section 501(c)(15) describes certain small non-life insurance companies with annual gross receipts of no more than $600,000 ($150,000 in the case of a mutual insurance company). Section 501(c)(26) describes certain membership organizations established to provide health insurance to certain high-risk individuals. Section 501(c)(27) describes certain organizations established to provide workmen's compensation insurance. A health maintenance organization that is tax-exempt under section 501(c)(3) or (4) is not treated as providing prohibited[810] commercial-type insurance, in the case of incidental health insurance provided by the health maintenance organization that is of a kind customarily provided by such organizations.

---

[808] Section 9001 of the Patient Protection and Affordable Care Act, Pub. L. No. 111–148, as amended by section 10901, is further amended by section 1401 of the Health Care and Education Reconciliation Act of 2010, Pub. L. No. 111–152.

[809] Sec. 816(a).

[810] Sec. 501(m).

### *Treatment of employer-sponsored health coverage*

As with other compensation, the cost of employer-provided health coverage is a deductible business expense under section 162.[811] Employer-provided health insurance coverage is generally not included in an employee's gross income.

In addition, employees participating in a cafeteria plan may be able to pay the portion of premiums for health insurance coverage not otherwise paid for by their employers on a pre-tax basis through salary reduction.[812] Such salary reduction contributions are treated as employer contributions for Federal income purposes, and are thus excluded from gross income.

Employers may agree to reimburse medical expenses of their employees (and their spouses and dependents), not covered by a health insurance plan, through flexible spending arrangements which allow reimbursement not in excess of a specified dollar amount (either elected by an employee under a cafeteria plan or otherwise specified by the employer). Reimbursements under these arrangements are also excludible from gross income as employer-provided health coverage.

A flexible spending arrangement for medical expenses under a cafeteria plan ("Health FSA") is an unfunded arrangement under which employees are given the option to reduce their current cash compensation and instead have the amount made available for use in reimbursing the employee for his or her medical expenses.[813] Health FSAs that are funded on a salary reduction basis are subject to the requirements for cafeteria plans, including a requirement that amounts remaining under a Health FSA at the end of a plan year must be forfeited by the employee (referred to as the "use-it-or-lose-it rule").[814]

Alternatively, the employer may specify a dollar amount that is available for medical expense reimbursement. These arrangements are commonly called Health Reimbursement Arrangements ("HRAs"). Some of the rules applicable to HRAs and Health FSAs are similar (e.g., the amounts in the arrangements can only be used to reimburse medical expenses and not for other purposes), but the rules are not identical. In particular, HRAs cannot be funded on a salary reduction basis and the use-it-or-lose-it rule does not apply. Thus, amounts remaining at the end of the year may be carried forward to be used to reimburse medical expenses in following years.[815]

Current law provides that individuals with a high deductible health plan (and generally no other health plan) may establish and make tax-deductible contributions to a health savings account ("HSA"). An HSA is subject to a condition that the individual is covered under a high deductible health plan (purchased either

[811] Sec. 162. However see special rules in section 419 and 419A for the deductibility of contributions to welfare benefit plans with respect to medical benefits for employees and their dependents.

[812] Sec. 125.

[813] Sec. 125. Prop. Treas. Reg. sec. 1.125–5 provides rules for Health FSAs. There is a similar type of flexible spending arrangement for dependent care expenses.

[814] Sec. 125(d)(2). A cafeteria plan is permitted to allow a grace period not to exceed two and one-half months immediately following the end of the plan year during which unused amounts may be used. Notice 2005–42, 2005–1 C.B. 1204.

[815] Guidance with respect to HRAs, including the interaction of FSAs and HRAs in the case of an individual covered under both, is provided in Notice 2002–45, 2002–2 C.B. 93.

through the individual market or through an employer). Subject to certain limitations,[816] contributions made to an HSA by an employer, including contributions made through a cafeteria plan through salary reduction, are excluded from income (and from wages for payroll tax purposes). Contributions made by individuals are deductible for income tax purposes, regardless of whether the individuals itemize. Like an HSA, an Archer MSA is a tax-exempt trust or custodial account to which tax-deductible contributions may be made by individuals with a high deductible health plan; however, only self-employed individuals and employees of small employers are eligible to have an Archer MSA. Archer MSAs provide tax benefits similar to, but generally not as favorable as, those provided by HSAs for individuals covered by high deductible health plans.[817]

ERISA[818] preempts State law relating to certain employee benefit plans, including employer-sponsored health plans. While ERISA specifically provides that its preemption rule does not exempt or relieve any person from any State law which regulates insurance, ERISA also provides that an employee benefit plan is not deemed to be engaged in the business of insurance for purposes of any State law regulating insurance companies or insurance contracts. As a result of this ERISA preemption, self-insured employer-sponsored health plans need not provide benefits that are mandated under State insurance law.

While ERISA does not require an employer to offer health benefits, it does require compliance if an employer chooses to offer health benefits, such as compliance with plan fiduciary standards, reporting and disclosure requirements, and procedures for appealing denied benefit claims. ERISA was amended (as well as the PHSA and the Code) by COBRA[819] and HIPAA,[820] which added other Federal requirements for health plans, including rules for health care continuation coverage, limitations on exclusions from coverage based on preexisting conditions, and a few benefit requirements such as minimum hospital stay requirements for mothers following the birth of a child.

COBRA requires that a group health plan offer continuation coverage to qualified beneficiaries in the case of a qualifying event (such as a loss of employment).[821] A plan may require payment of a premium for any period of continuation coverage. The amount of

[816] For 2010, the maximum aggregate annual contribution that can be made to an HSA is $3,050 in the case of self-only coverage and $6,150 in the case of family coverage. The annual contribution limits are increased for individuals who have attained age 55 by the end of the taxable year (referred to as "catch-up contributions"). In the case of policyholders and covered spouses who are age 55 or older, the HSA annual contribution limit is greater than the otherwise applicable limit by $1,000 in 2009 and thereafter. Contributions, including catch-up contributions, cannot be made once an individual is enrolled in Medicare.

[817] In addition to being limited to self-employed individuals and employees of small employers, the definition of a high deductible health plan for an Archer MSA differs from that for an HSA. After 2007, no new contributions can be made to Archer MSAs except by or on behalf of individuals who previously had made Archer MSA contributions and employees who are employed by a participating employer.

[818] Pub. L. No. 93–406.

[819] Pub. L. No. 99–272.

[820] Pub. L. No. 104–191.

[821] A group health plan is defined as a plan (including a self-insured plan) of, or contributed to by, an employer (including a self-employed person) or employee organization to provide health care (directly or otherwise) to the employees, former employees, the employer, others associated or formerly associated with the employer in a business relationship, or their families. The COBRA requirements are enforced through the Code, ERISA, and the PHSA.

such premium generally may not exceed 102 percent of the "applicable premium" for such period and the premium must be payable, at the election of the payor, in monthly installments. The applicable premium for any period of continuation coverage means the cost to the plan for such period of coverage for similarly situated non-COBRA beneficiaries with respect to whom a qualifying event has not occurred, and is determined without regard to whether the cost is paid by the employer or employee. There are special rules for determining the applicable premium in the case of self-insured plans. Under the special rules for self-insured plans, the applicable premium generally is equal to a reasonable estimate of the cost of providing coverage for similarly situated beneficiaries which is determined on an actuarial basis and takes into account such other factors as the Secretary of the Treasury may prescribe in regulations.

Current law imposes an excise tax on group health plans that fail to meet HIPAA and COBRA requirements.[822] The excise tax generally is equal to $100 per day per failure during the period of noncompliance and is imposed on the employer sponsoring the plan.

***Deduction for health insurance costs of self-employed individuals***

Under current law, self-employed individuals may deduct the cost of health insurance for themselves and their spouses and dependents.[823] The deduction is not available for any month in which the self-employed individual is eligible to participate in an employer-subsidized health plan. Moreover, the deduction may not exceed the individual's earned income from self-employment. The deduction applies only to the cost of insurance (i.e., it does not apply to out-of-pocket expenses that are not reimbursed by insurance). The deduction does not apply for self-employment tax purposes. For purposes of the deduction, a more-than-two-percent-shareholder-employee of an S corporation is treated the same as a self-employed individual. Thus, the exclusion for employer provided health care coverage does not apply to such individuals, but they are entitled to the deduction for health insurance costs as if they were self-employed.

***Deductibility of excise taxes***

In general, excise taxes may be deductible under section 162 of the Code if such taxes are paid or incurred in carrying on a trade or business, and are not within the scope of the disallowance of deductions for certain taxes enumerated in section 275 of the Code.

### *Explanation of Provision*

The provision imposes an excise tax on insurers if the aggregate value of employer-sponsored health insurance coverage for an employee (including, for purposes of the provision, any former employee, surviving spouse and any other primary insured individual) exceeds a threshold amount. The tax is equal to 40 percent of the aggregate value that exceeds the threshold amount. For 2018, the

[822] Secs. 4980B and 4980D.
[823] Sec. 162(l).

threshold amount is $10,200 for individual coverage and $27,500 for family coverage, multiplied by the health cost adjustment percentage (as defined below) and increased by the age and gender adjusted excess premium amount (as defined below).

The health cost adjustment percentage is designed to increase the thresholds in the event that the actual growth in the cost of U.S. health care between 2010 and 2018 exceeds the projected growth for that period. The health cost adjustment percentage is equal to 100 percent plus the excess, if any, of (1) the percentage by which the per employee cost of coverage under the Blue Cross/ Blue Shield standard benefit option under the Federal Employees Health Benefits Plan ("standard FEHBP coverage")[824] for plan year 2018 (as determined using the benefit package for standard FEHBP coverage for plan year 2010) exceeds the per employee cost of standard FEHBP coverage for plan year 2010; over (2) 55 percent. In 2019, the threshold amounts, after application of the health cost adjustment percentage in 2018, if any, are indexed to the CPI-U, as determined by the Department of Labor, plus one percentage point, rounded to the nearest $50. In 2020 and thereafter, the threshold amounts are indexed to the CPI-U as determined by the Department of Labor, rounded to the nearest $50.

For each employee (other than for certain retirees and employees in high risk professions, whose thresholds are adjusted under rules described below), the age and gender adjusted excess premium amount is equal to the excess, if any, of (1) the premium cost of standard FEHBP coverage for the type of coverage provided to the individual if priced for the age and gender characteristics of all employees of the individual's employer over (2) the premium cost, determined under procedures proscribed by the Secretary, for that coverage if priced for the age and gender characteristics of the national workforce.

For example, if the growth in the cost of health care during the period between 2010 and 2018, calculated by reference to the growth in the per employee cost of standard FEHBP coverage during that period (holding benefits under the standard FEBHP plan constant during the period) is 57 percent, the threshold amounts for 2018 will be $10,200 for individual coverage and $27,500 for family coverage, multiplied by 102 percent (100 percent plus the excess of 57 percent over 55 percent), or $10,404 for individual coverage and $28,050 for family coverage. In 2019, the new threshold amounts of $10,404 for individual coverage and $28,050 for family coverage are indexed for CPI–U, plus one percentage point, rounded to the nearest $50. Beginning in 2020, the threshold amounts are indexed to the CPI–U, rounded to the nearest $50.

The new threshold amounts (as indexed) are then increased for any employee by the age and gender adjusted excess premium amount, if any. For an employee with individual coverage in 2019, if standard FEHBP coverage priced for the age and gender characteristics of the workforce of the employee's employer is $11,400 and

[824] For purposes of determining the health cost adjustment percentage in 2018 and the age and gender adjusted excess premium amount in any year, in the event the standard Blue Cross/ Blue Shield option is not available under the Federal Employees Health Benefit Plan for such year, the Secretary will determine the health cost adjustment percentage by reference to a substantially similar option available under the Federal Employees Health Benefit Plan for that year.

the Secretary estimates that the premium cost for individual standard FEHBP coverage priced for the age and gender characteristics of the national workforce is $10,500, the threshold for that employee is increased by $900 ($11,400 less $10,500) to $11,304 ($10,404 plus $900).

The excise tax is imposed pro rata on the issuers of the insurance. In the case of a self-insured group health plan, a Health FSA or an HRA, the excise tax is paid by the entity that administers benefits under the plan or arrangement ("plan administrator"). Where the employer acts as plan administrator to a self-insured group health plan, a Health FSA or an HRA, the excise tax is paid by the employer. Where an employer contributes to an HSA or an Archer MSA, the employer is responsible for payment of the excise tax, as the insurer.

Employer-sponsored health insurance coverage is health coverage under any group health plan offered by an employer to an employee without regard to whether the employer provides the coverage (and thus the coverage is excludable from the employee's gross income) or the employee pays for the coverage with after-tax dollars. Employer-sponsored health insurance coverage includes coverage under any group health plan established and maintained primarily for the civilian employees of the Federal government or any of its agencies or instrumentalities and, except as provided below, of any State government or political subdivision thereof or by any of agencies or instrumentalities of such government or subdivision.

Employer-sponsored health insurance coverage includes both fully-insured and self-insured health coverage excludable from the employee's gross income, including, in the self-insured context, onsite medical clinics that offer more than a de minimis amount of medical care to employees and executive physical programs. In the case of a self-employed individual, employer-sponsored health insurance coverage is coverage for any portion of which a deduction is allowable to the self-employed individual under section 162(l).

In determining the amount by which the value of employer-sponsored health insurance coverage exceeds the threshold amount, the aggregate value of all employer-sponsored health insurance coverage is taken into account, including coverage in the form of reimbursements under a Health FSA or an HRA, contributions to an HSA or Archer MSA, and, except as provided below, other supplementary health insurance coverage. The value of employer-sponsored coverage for long term care and the following benefits described in section 9832(c)(1) that are excepted from the portability, access and renewability requirements of HIPAA are not taken into account in the determination of whether the value of health coverage exceeds the threshold amount: (1) coverage only for accident or disability income insurance, or any combination of these coverages; (2) coverage issued as a supplement to liability insurance; (3) liability insurance, including general liability insurance and automobile liability insurance; (4) workers' compensation or similar insurance; (5) automobile medical payment insurance; (5) credit-only insurance; and (6) other similar insurance coverage, specified in regulations, under which benefits for medical care are secondary or incidental to other insurance benefits.

The value of employer-sponsored health insurance coverage does not include the value of independent, noncoordinated coverage described in section 9832(c)(3) as excepted from the portability, access and renewability requirements of HIPAA if that coverage is purchased exclusively by the employee with after-tax dollars (or, in the case of a self-employed individual, for which a deduction under section 162(l) is not allowable). The value of employer-sponsored health insurance coverage does include the value of such coverage if any portion of the coverage is employer-provided (or, in the case of a self-employed individual, if a deduction is allowable for any portion of the payment for the coverage). Coverage described in section 9832(c)(3) is coverage only for a specified disease or illness or for hospital or other fixed indemnity health coverage. Fixed indemnity health coverage pays fixed dollar amounts based on the occurrence of qualifying events, including but not limited to the diagnosis of a specific disease, an accidental injury or a hospitalization, provided that the coverage is not coordinated with other health coverage.

Finally, the value of employer-sponsored health insurance coverage does not include any coverage under a separate policy, certificate, or contract of insurance which provides benefits substantially all of which are for treatment of the mouth (including any organ or structure within the mouth) or for treatment of the eye.

### *Calculation and proration of excise tax and reporting requirements*

#### *Applicable threshold*

In general, the individual threshold applies to any employee covered by employer-sponsored health insurance coverage. The family threshold applies to an employee only if such individual and at least one other beneficiary are enrolled in coverage other than self-only coverage under an employer-sponsored health insurance plan that provides minimum essential coverage (as determined for purposes of the individual responsibility requirements) and under which the benefits provided do not vary based on whether the covered individual is the employee or other beneficiary.

For all employees covered by a multiemployer plan, the family threshold applies regardless of whether the individual maintains individual or family coverage under the plan. For purposes of the provision, a multiemployer plan is an employee health benefit plan to which more than one employer is required to contribute, which is maintained pursuant to one or more collective bargaining agreements between one or more employee organizations and more than one employer.

#### *Amount of applicable premium*

Under the provision, the aggregate value of all employer-sponsored health insurance coverage, including any supplementary health insurance coverage not excluded from the value of employer-sponsored health insurance, is generally calculated in the same manner as the applicable premiums for the taxable year for the employee determined under the rules for COBRA continuation coverage, but without regard to the excise tax. If the plan provides for the same COBRA continuation coverage premium for both individual coverage and family coverage, the plan is required to calculate separate individual and family premiums for this purpose. In determining the coverage value for retirees, employers may elect to treat pre-65 retirees together with post-65 retirees.

*Value of coverage in the form of Health FSA reimbursements*

In the case of a Health FSA from which reimbursements are limited to the amount of the salary reduction, the value of employer-sponsored health insurance coverage is equal to the dollar amount of the aggregate salary reduction contributions for the year. To the extent that the Health FSA provides for employer contributions in excess of the amount of the employee's salary reduction, the value of the coverage generally is determined in the same manner as the applicable premium for COBRA continuation coverage. If the plan provides for the same COBRA continuation coverage premium for both individual coverage and family coverage, the plan is required to calculate separate individual and family premiums for this purpose.

*Amount subject to the excise tax and reporting requirement*

The amount subject to the excise tax on high cost employer-sponsored health insurance coverage for each employee is the sum of the aggregate premiums for health insurance coverage, the amount of any salary reduction contributions to a Health FSA for the taxable year, and the dollar amount of employer contributions to an HSA or an Archer MSA, minus the dollar amount of the threshold. The aggregate premiums for health insurance coverage include all employer-sponsored health insurance coverage including coverage for any supplementary health insurance coverage. The applicable premium for health coverage provided through an HRA is also included in this aggregate amount.

Under a separate rule,[825] an employer is required to disclose the aggregate premiums for health insurance coverage for each employee on his or her annual Form W–2.

Under the provision, the excise tax is allocated pro rata among the insurers, with each insurer responsible for payment of the excise tax on an amount equal to the amount subject to the total excise tax multiplied by a fraction, the numerator of which is the amount of employer-sponsored health insurance coverage provided by that insurer to the employee and the denominator of which is the aggregate value of all employer-sponsored health insurance coverage provided to the employee. In the case of a self-insured group health plan, a Health FSA or an HRA, the excise tax is allocated to the plan administrator. If an employer contributes to an HSA or an Archer MSA, the employer is responsible for payment of the excise tax, as the insurer. The employer is responsible for calculating the amount subject to the excise tax allocable to each insurer and plan administrator and for reporting these amounts to each insurer, plan administrator and the Secretary, in such form and at such time as the Secretary may prescribe. Each insurer and

[825] See the explanation of section 9002 of the Patient Protection and Affordable Care Act, Pub. L. No. 111–148, "Inclusion of Cost of Employer Sponsored Health Coverage on W–2."

plan administrator is then responsible for calculating, reporting and paying the excise tax to the IRS on such forms and at such time as the Secretary may prescribe.

For example, if in 2018 an employee elects family coverage under a fully-insured health care policy covering major medical and dental with a value of $31,000, the health cost adjustment percentage for that year is 100 percent, and the age and gender adjusted excess premium amount for the employee is $600, the amount subject to the excise tax is $2,900 ($31,000 less the threshold of $28,100 ($27,500 multiplied by 100 percent and increased by $600)). The employer reports $2,900 as taxable to the insurer, which calculates and remits the excise tax to the IRS.

Alternatively, if in 2018 an employee elects family coverage under a fully-insured major medical policy with a value of $28,500 and contributes $2,500 to a Health FSA, the employee has an aggregate health insurance coverage value of $31,000. If the health cost adjustment percentage for that year is 100 percent and the age and gender adjusted excess premium amount for the employee is $600, the amount subject to the excise tax is $2,900 ($31,000 less the threshold of $28,100 ($27,500 multiplied by 100 percent and increased by $600)). The employer reports $2,666 ($2,900 × $28,500/$31,000) as taxable to the major medical insurer which then calculates and remits the excise tax to the IRS. If the employer uses a third-party administrator for the Health FSA, the employer reports $234 ($2,900 × $2,500/$31,000) to the administrator and the administrator calculates and remits the excise tax to the IRS. If the employer is acting as the plan administrator of the Health FSA, the employer is responsible for calculating and remitting the excise tax on the $234 to the IRS.

***Penalty for underreporting liability for tax to insurers***

If the employer reports to insurers, plan administrators and the IRS a lower amount of insurance cost subject to the excise tax than required, the employer is subject to a penalty equal to the sum of any additional excise tax that each such insurer and administrator would have owed if the employer had reported correctly and interest attributable to that additional excise tax as determined under Code section 6621 from the date that the tax was otherwise due to the date paid by the employer. This may occur, for example, if the employer undervalues the aggregate premium and thereby lowers the amount subject to the excise tax for all insurers and plan administrators (including the employer, when acting as plan administrator of a self-insured plan).

The penalty will not apply if it is established to the satisfaction of the Secretary that the employer neither knew, nor exercising reasonable diligence would have known, that the failure existed. In addition, no penalty will be imposed on any failure corrected within the 30–day period beginning on the first date that the employer knew, or exercising reasonable diligence, would have known, that the failure existed, so long as the failure is due to reasonable cause and not to willful neglect. All or part of the penalty may be waived by the Secretary in the case of any failure due to reasonable cause and not to willful neglect, to the extent that the payment of the penalty would be excessive or otherwise inequitable relative to the failure involved.

The penalty is in addition to the amount of excise tax owed, which may not be waived.

***Increased thresholds for certain retirees and individuals in high-risk professions***

The threshold amounts are increased for an individual who has attained age of 55 who is non-Medicare eligible and receiving employer-sponsored retiree health coverage or who is covered by a plan sponsored by an employer the majority of whose employees covered by the plan are engaged in a high risk profession or employed to repair or install electrical and telecommunications lines. For these individuals, the threshold amount in 2018 is increased by (1) $1,650 for individual coverage or $3,450 for family coverage and (2) the age and gender adjusted excess premium amount (as defined above). In 2019, the additional $1,650 and $3,450 amounts are indexed to the CPI–U, plus one percentage point, rounded to the nearest $50. In 2020 and thereafter, the additional threshold amounts are indexed to the CPI–U, rounded to the nearest $50.

For purposes of this rule, employees considered to be engaged in a high risk profession are law enforcement officers, employees who engage in fire protection activities, individuals who provide out-of-hospital emergency medical care (including emergency medical technicians, paramedics, and first-responders), individuals whose primary work is longshore work, and individuals engaged in the construction, mining, agriculture (not including food processing), forestry, and fishing industries. A retiree with at least 20 years of employment in a high risk profession is also eligible for the increased threshold.

Under this provision, an individual's threshold cannot be increased by more than $1,650 for individual coverage or $3,450 for family coverage (indexed as described above) and the age and gender adjusted excess premium amount, even if the individual would qualify for an increased threshold both on account of his or her status as a retiree over age 55 and as a participant in a plan that covers employees in a high risk profession.

***Deductibility of excise tax***

Under the provision, the amount of the excise tax imposed is not deductible for Federal income tax purposes.

***Regulatory authority***

The Secretary is directed to prescribe such regulations as may be necessary to carry out the provision.

### *Effective Date*

The provision is effective for taxable years beginning after December 31, 2017.

## B. Inclusion of Cost of Employer-Sponsored Health Coverage on W–2 (sec. 9002 of the Act and sec. 6051 of the Code)

### *Present Law*

In many cases, an employer pays for all or a portion of its employees' health insurance coverage as an employee benefit. This benefit often includes premiums for major medical, dental, and other supplementary health insurance coverage. Under present law, the value of employer-provided health coverage is not required to be reported to the IRS or any other Federal agency. The value of the employer contribution to health coverage is excludible from an employee's income.[826]

Under current law, every employer is required to furnish each employee and the Federal government with a statement of compensation information, including wages, paid by the employer to the employee, and the taxes withheld from such wages during the calendar year. The statement, made on the Form W–2, must be provided to each employee by January 31 of the succeeding year. There is no requirement that the employer report the total value of employer-sponsored health insurance coverage on the Form W–2,[827] although some employers voluntarily report the amount of salary reduction under a cafeteria plan resulting in tax-free employee benefits in box 14.

### *Explanation of Provision*

Under the provision, an employer is required to disclose on each employee's annual Form W–2 the value of the employee's health insurance coverage sponsored by the employer. If an employee enrolls in employer-sponsored health insurance coverage under multiple plans, the employer must disclose the aggregate value of all such health coverage (excluding the value of any salary reduction contribution to a health flexible spending arrangement). For example, if an employee enrolls in employer-sponsored health insurance coverage under a major medical plan and a health reimbursement arrangement, the employer is required to report the total value of the combination of both of these health plans. For this purpose, employers generally use the same value for all similarly situated employees receiving the same category of coverage (such as single or family health insurance coverage).

To determine the value of employer-sponsored health insurance coverage, the employer calculates the applicable premiums for the taxable year for the employee under the rules for COBRA continuation coverage under section 4980B(f)(4) (and accompanying Treasury regulations), including the special rule for self-insured plans. The value that the employer is required to report is the portion of the aggregate premium. If the plan provides for the same COBRA continuation coverage premium for both individual coverage and family coverage, the plan would be required to calculate separate individual and family premiums for this purpose.

---

[826] Sec. 106.

[827] Any portion of employer sponsored coverage that is paid for by the employee with after-tax contributions is included as wages on the W–2 Form.

### *Effective Date*

The provision is effective for taxable years beginning after December 31, 2010.

## C. Distributions for Medicine Qualified Only if for Prescribed Drug or Insulin (sec. 9003 of the Act and secs. 105, 106, 220, and 223 of the Code)

### *Present Law*

#### *Individual deduction for medical expenses*

Expenses for medical care, not compensated for by insurance or otherwise, are deductible by an individual under the rules relating to itemized deductions to the extent the expenses exceed 7.5 percent of adjusted gross income ("AGI").[828] Medical care generally is defined broadly as amounts paid for diagnoses, cure, mitigation, treatment or prevention of disease, or for the purpose of affecting any structure of the body.[829] However, any amount paid during a taxable year for medicine or drugs is explicitly deductible as a medical expense only if the medicine or drug is a prescribed drug or is insulin.[830] Thus, any amount paid for medicine available without a prescription ("over-the-counter medicine") is not deductible as a medical expense, including any medicine recommended by a physician.[831]

#### *Exclusion for employer-provided health care*

The Code generally provides that employees are not taxed on (that is, may exclude from gross income) the value of employer-provided health coverage under an accident or health plan.[832] In addition, any reimbursements under an accident or health plan for medical care expenses for employees, their spouses, and their dependents generally are excluded from gross income.[833] An employer may agree to reimburse expenses for medical care of its employees (and their spouses and dependents), not covered by a health insurance plan, through a flexible spending arrangement ("FSA") which allows reimbursement not in excess of a specified dollar amount. Such dollar amount is either elected by an employee under a cafeteria plan ("Health FSA") or otherwise specified by the employer under an HRA. Reimbursements under these arrangements are also excludible from gross income as employer-provided health coverage. The general definition of medical care without the explicit limitation on medicine applies for purposes of the exclusion for employer-provided health coverage and medical care.[834] Thus, under an HRA or under a Health FSA, amounts paid for prescription and

---

[828] Sec. 213(a).

[829] Sec. 213(d). There are certain limitations on the general definition including a rule that cosmetic surgery or similar procedures are generally not medical care.

[830] Sec. 213(b).

[831] Rev. Rul. 2003–58, 2003–1 CB 959.

[832] Sec 106.

[833] Sec. 105(b).

[834] Sec. 105(b) provides that reimbursements for medical care within the meaning of section 213(d) pursuant to employer-provided health coverage are excludible from gross income. The definition of medical care in section 213(d) does not include the prescription drug limitation in section 213(b).

over-the-counter medicine are treated as medical expenses, and reimbursements for such amounts are excludible from gross income.

***Medical savings arrangements***

Present law provides that individuals with a high deductible health plan (and generally no other health plan) purchased either through the individual market or through an employer may establish and make tax-deductible contributions to a health savings account ("HSA").[835] Subject to certain limitations,[836] contributions made to an HSA by an employer, including contributions made through a cafeteria plan through salary reduction, are excluded from income (and from wages for payroll tax purposes). Contributions made by individuals are deductible for income tax purposes, regardless of whether the individuals itemize. Distributions from an HSA that are used for qualified medical expenses are excludible from gross income.[837] The general definition of medical care without the explicit limitation on medicine also applies for purposes of this exclusion.[838] Similar rules apply for another type of medical savings arrangement called an Archer MSA.[839] Thus, a distribution from a HSA or an Archer MSA used to purchase over-the-counter medicine also is excludible as an amount used for qualified medical expenses.

### *Explanation of Provision*

Under the provision, with respect to medicines, the definition of medical expense for purposes of employer-provided health coverage (including HRAs and Health FSAs), HSAs, and Archer MSAs, is conformed to the definition for purposes of the itemized deduction for medical expenses, except that prescribed drug is determined without regard to whether the drug is available without a prescription. Thus, under the provision, the cost of over-the-counter medicines may not be reimbursed with excludible income through a Health FSA, HRA, HSA, or Archer MSA, unless the medicine is prescribed by a physician.

### *Effective Date*

The provision is effective for expenses incurred after December 31, 2010.

---

[835] Sec. 223.

[836] For 2009, the maximum aggregate annual contribution that can be made to an HSA is $3,000 in the case of self-only coverage and $5,950 in the case of family coverage ($3,050 and $6,150 for 2010). The annual contribution limits are increased for individuals who have attained age 55 by the end of the taxable year (referred to as "catch-up contributions"). In the case of policyholders and covered spouses who are age 55 or older, the HSA annual contribution limit is greater than the otherwise applicable limit by $1,000 in 2009 and thereafter. Contributions, including catch-up contributions, cannot be made once an individual is enrolled in Medicare.

[837] Sec. 223(f).

[838] Sec. 223(d)(2).

[839] Sec. 220.

## D. Increase in Additional Tax on Distributions from HSAs Not Used for Medical Expenses (sec. 9004 of the Act and secs. 220 and 223 of the Code)

### *Present Law*

#### *Health savings account*

Present law provides that individuals with a high deductible health plan (and generally no other health plan) may establish and make tax-deductible contributions to a health savings account ("HSA").[840] An HSA is a tax-exempt account held by a trustee or custodian for the benefit of the individual. An HSA is subject to a condition that the individual is covered under a high deductible health plan (purchased either through the individual market or through an employer). The decision to create and fund an HSA is made on an individual-by-individual basis and does not require any action on the part of the employer.

Subject to certain limitations, contributions made to an HSA by an employer, including contributions made through a cafeteria plan through salary reduction, are excluded from income (and from wages for payroll tax purposes). Contributions made by individuals are deductible for income tax purposes, regardless of whether the individuals itemize their deductions on their tax return (rather than claiming the standard deduction). Income from investments made in HSAs is not taxable and the overall income is not taxable upon disbursement for medical expenses.

For 2010, the maximum aggregate annual contribution that can be made to an HSA is $3,050 in the case of self-only coverage and $6,150 in the case of family coverage. The annual contribution limits are increased for individuals who have attained age 55 by the end of the taxable year (referred to as "catch-up contributions"). In the case of policyholders and covered spouses who are age 55 or older, the HSA annual contribution limit is greater than the otherwise applicable limit by $1,000 in 2010 and thereafter. Contributions, including catch-up contributions, cannot be made once an individual is enrolled in Medicare.

A high deductible health plan is a health plan that has an annual deductible that is at least $1,200 for self-only coverage or $2,400 for family coverage for 2010 and that limits the sum of the annual deductible and other payments that the individual must make with respect to covered benefits to no more than $5,950 in the case of self-only coverage and $11,900 in the case of family coverage for 2010.

Distributions from an HSA that are used for qualified medical expenses are excludible from gross income. Distributions from an

[840] An individual with other coverage in addition to a high deductible health plan is still eligible for an HSA if such other coverage is "permitted insurance" or "permitted coverage." Permitted insurance is: (1) insurance if substantially all of the coverage provided under such insurance relates to (a) liabilities incurred under worker's compensation law, (b) tort liabilities, (c) liabilities relating to ownership or use of property (e.g., auto insurance), or (d) such other similar liabilities as the Secretary may prescribe by regulations; (2) insurance for a specified disease or illness; and (3) insurance that provides a fixed payment for hospitalization. Permitted coverage is coverage (whether provided through insurance or otherwise) for accidents, disability, dental care, vision care, or long-term care. With respect to coverage for years beginning after December 31, 2006, certain coverage under a Health FSA is disregarded in determining eligibility for an HSA.

HSA that are not used for qualified medical expenses are includible in gross income. An additional 10 percent tax is added for all HSA disbursements not made for qualified medical expenses. The additional 10-percent tax does not apply, however, if the distribution is made after death, disability, or attainment of age of Medicare eligibility (currently, age 65). Unlike reimbursements from a flexible spending arrangement or health reimbursement arrangement, distributions from an HSA are not required to be substantiated by the employer or a third party for the distributions to be excludible from income.

As in the case of individual retirement arrangements,[841] the individual is the beneficial owner of his or her HSA, and thus the individual is required to maintain books and records with respect to the expense and claim the exclusion for a distribution from the HSA on their tax return. The determination of whether the distribution is for a qualified medical expense is subject to individual self-reporting and IRS enforcement.

***Archer medical savings account***

An Archer MSA is also a tax-exempt trust or custodial account to which tax-deductible contributions may be made by individuals with a high deductible health plan.[842] Archer MSAs provide tax benefits similar to, but generally not as favorable as, those provided by HSAs for individuals covered by high deductible health plans. The main differences include: (1) only self-employed individuals and employees of small employers are eligible to have an Archer MSA; (2) for Archer MSA purposes, a high deductible health plan is a health plan with (a) an annual deductible for 2010 of at least $2,000 and no more than $3,000 in the case of self-only coverage and at least $4,050 and no more than $6,050 in the case of family coverage and (b) maximum out-of pocket expenses for 2010 of no more than $4,050 in the case of self-only coverage and no more than $7,400 in the case of family coverage; and (3) the additional tax on distributions not used for medical expenses is 15 percent rather than 10 percent. After 2007, no new contributions can be made to Archer MSAs except by or on behalf of individuals who previously had made Archer MSA contributions and employees who are employed by a participating employer.

### *Explanation of Provision*

The additional tax on distributions from an HSA or an Archer MSA that are not used for qualified medical expenses is increased to 20 percent of the disbursed amount.

### *Effective Date*

The change is effective for disbursements made during tax years starting after December 31, 2010.

---

[841] Sec. 408.
[842] Sec. 220.

## E. Limitation on Health Flexible Spending Arrangements under Cafeteria Plans (sec. 9005[843] of the Act and sec. 125 of the Code)

### *Present law*

#### *Exclusion from income for employer-provided health coverage*

The Code generally provides that the value of employer-provided health coverage under an accident or health plan is excludible from gross income.[844] In addition, any reimbursements under an accident or health plan for medical care expenses for employees, their spouses, and their dependents generally are excluded from gross income.[845] The exclusion applies both to health coverage in the case in which an employer absorbs the cost of employees' medical expenses not covered by insurance (i.e., a self-insured plan) as well as in the case in which the employer purchases health insurance coverage for its employees. There is no limit on the amount of employer-provided health coverage that is excludible. A similar rule excludes employer-provided health insurance coverage from the employees' wages for payroll tax purposes.[846]

Employers may also provide health coverage in the form of an agreement to reimburse medical expenses of their employees (and their spouses and dependents), not reimbursed by a health insurance plan, through flexible spending arrangements which allow reimbursement for medical care not in excess of a specified dollar amount (either elected by an employee under a cafeteria plan or otherwise specified by the employer). Health coverage provided in the form of one of these arrangements is also excludible from gross income as employer-provided health coverage under an accident or health plan.[847]

#### *Qualified benefits*

Qualified benefits under a cafeteria plan are generally employer-provided benefits that are not includable in gross income under an express provision of the Code. Examples of qualified benefits include employer-provided health coverage, group term life insurance coverage not in excess of $50,000, and benefits under a dependent care assistance program. In order to be excludable, any qualified benefit elected under a cafeteria plan must independently satisfy any requirements under the Code section that provides the exclusion. However, some employer-provided benefits that are not includable in gross income under an express provision of the Code are explicitly not allowed in a cafeteria plan. These benefits are generally referred to as nonqualified benefits. Examples of non-

[843] Section 9005 of the Patient Protection and Affordable Care Act, Pub. L. No. 111–148, as amended by section 10902, is further amended by section 1403 of the Health Care and Education Reconciliation Act of 2010, Pub. L. No. 111–152.

[844] Sec. 106. Health coverage provided to active members of the uniformed services, military retirees, and their dependents are excludable under section 134. That section provides an exclusion for "qualified military benefits," defined as benefits received by reason of status or service as a member of the uniformed services and which were excludable from gross income on September 9, 1986, under any provision of law, regulation, or administrative practice then in effect.

[845] Sec. 105(b).

[846] Secs. 3121(a)(2), and 3306(a)(2). See also section 3231(e)(1) for a similar rule with respect to compensation for purposes of Railroad Retirement Tax.

[847] Sec. 106.

qualified benefits include scholarships;[848] employer-provided meals and lodging;[849] educational assistance;[850] and fringe benefits.[851] A plan offering any nonqualified benefit is not a cafeteria plan.[852]

### *Flexible spending arrangement under a cafeteria plan*

A flexible spending arrangement for medical expenses under a cafeteria plan ("Health FSA") is health coverage in the form of an unfunded arrangement under which employees are given the option to reduce their current cash compensation and instead have the amount of the salary reduction contributions made available for use in reimbursing the employee for his or her medical expenses.[853] Health FSAs are subject to the general requirements for cafeteria plans, including a requirement that amounts remaining under a Health FSA at the end of a plan year must be forfeited by the employee (referred to as the "use-it-or-lose-it rule").[854] A Health FSA is permitted to allow a grace period not to exceed two and one-half months immediately following the end of the plan year during which unused amounts may be used.[855] A Health FSA can also include employer flex-credits which are non-elective employer contributions that the employer makes for every employee eligible to participate in the employer's cafeteria plan, to be used only for one or more tax excludible qualified benefits (but not as cash or a taxable benefit).[856]

A flexible spending arrangement including a Health FSA (under a cafeteria plan) is generally distinguishable from other employer-provided health coverage by the relationship between the value of the coverage for a year and the maximum amount of reimbursement reasonably available during the same period. A flexible spending arrangement for health coverage generally is defined as a benefit program which provides employees with coverage under which specific incurred medical care expenses may be reimbursed (subject to reimbursement maximums and other conditions) and the maximum amount of reimbursement reasonably available is less than 500 percent of the value of such coverage.[857]

### *Health reimbursement arrangement*

Rather than offering a Health FSA through a cafeteria plan, an employer may specify a dollar amount that is available for medical expense reimbursement. These arrangements are commonly called HRAs. Some of the rules applicable to HRAs and Health FSAs are similar (e.g., the amounts in the arrangements can only be used to reimburse medical expenses and not for other purposes), but the rules are not identical. In particular, HRAs cannot be funded on a salary reduction basis and the use-it-or-lose-it rule does not apply.

---

[848] Sec. 117.
[849] Sec. 119.
[850] Sec. 127.
[851] Sec. 132.
[852] Prop. Treas. Reg. sec. 1.125–1(q). Long-term care services, contributions to Archer Medical Savings Accounts, group term life insurance for an employee's spouse, child or dependent, and elective deferrals to section 403(b) plans are also nonqualified benefits.
[853] Sec. 125 and Prop. Treas. Reg. sec. 1.125–5.
[854] Sec. 125(d)(2) and Prop. Treas. Reg. sec. 1.125–5(c).
[855] Notice 2005–42, 2005–1 C.B. 1204 and Prop. Treas. Reg. sec. 1.125–1(e).
[856] Prop. Treas. Reg. sec. 1–125–5(b).
[857] Sec. 106(c)(2) and Prop. Treas. Reg. sec. 1.125–5(a).

Thus, amounts remaining at the end of the year may be carried forward to be used to reimburse medical expenses in following years.[858]

### *Explanation of Provision*

Under the provision, in order for a Health FSA to be a qualified benefit under a cafeteria plan, the maximum amount available for reimbursement of incurred medical expenses of an employee, the employee's dependents, and any other eligible beneficiaries with respect to the employee, under the Health FSA for a plan year (or other 12-month coverage period) must not exceed $2,500.[859] The $2,500 limitation is indexed to CPI–U, with any increase that is not a multiple of $50 rounded to the next lowest multiple of $50 for years beginning after December 31, 2013.

A cafeteria plan that does not include this limitation on the maximum amount available for reimbursement under any FSA is not a cafeteria plan within the meaning of section 125. Thus, when an employee is given the option under a cafeteria plan maintained by an employer to reduce his or her current cash compensation and instead have the amount of the salary reduction be made available for use in reimbursing the employee for his or her medical expenses under a Health FSA, the amount of the reduction in cash compensation pursuant to a salary reduction election must be limited to $2,500 for a plan year.

It is intended that regulations would require all cafeteria plans of an employer to be aggregated for purposes of applying this limit. The employer for this purpose is determined after applying the employer aggregation rules in section 414(b), (c), (m), and (o).[860] In the event of a plan year or coverage period that is less than 12 months, it is intended that the limit be required to be prorated.

The provision does not limit the amount permitted to be available for reimbursement under employer-provided health coverage offered through an HRA, including a flexible spending arrangement within the meaning of section 106(c)(2), that is not part of a cafeteria plan.

### *Effective Date*

The provision is effective for taxable year beginning after December 31, 2012.

---

[858] Guidance with respect to HRAs, including the interaction of FSAs and HRAs in the case of an individual covered under both, is provided in Notice 2002–45, 2002–2 C.B. 93.

[859] The provision does not change the present law treatment as described in Prop. Treas. Reg. section 1.125–5 for dependent care flexible spending arrangements or adoption assistance flexible spending arrangements.

[860] Section 414(b) provides that, for specified employee benefit purposes, all employees of all corporations which are members of a controlled group of corporations are treated as employed by a single employer. There is a similar rule in section 414(c) under which all employees of trades or businesses (whether or not incorporated) which are under common control are treated under regulations as employed by a single employer, and, in section 414(m), under which employees of an affiliated service group (as defined in that section) are treated as employed by a single employer. Section 414(o) authorizes the Treasury to issue regulations to prevent avoidance of the requirements under section 414(m). Section 125(g)(4) applies this rule to cafeteria plans.

## F. Expansion of Information Reporting Requirements (sec. 9006 of the Act and sec. 6041 of the Code)[861]

### *Present Law*

Present law imposes a variety of information reporting requirements on participants in certain transactions.[862] These requirements are intended to assist taxpayers in preparing their income tax returns and to help the IRS determine whether such returns are correct and complete.

The primary provision governing information reporting by payors requires an information return by every person engaged in a trade or business who makes payments aggregating $600 or more in any taxable year to a single payee in the course of that payor's trade or business.[863] Payments subject to reporting include fixed or determinable income or compensation, but do not include payments for goods or certain enumerated types of payments that are subject to other specific reporting requirements.[864] The payor is required to provide the recipient of the payment with an annual statement showing the aggregate payments made and contact information for the payor.[865] The regulations generally except from reporting, payments to corporations, exempt organizations, governmental entities, international organizations, or retirement plans.[866] However, the following types of payments to corporations must be reported: Medical and healthcare payments;[867] fish purchases for cash;[868] attorney's fees;[869] gross proceeds paid to an attorney;[870] substitute payments in lieu of dividends or tax-exempt interest;[871] and payments by a Federal executive agency for services.[872]

Failure to comply with the information reporting requirements results in penalties, which may include a penalty for failure to file the information return,[873] and a penalty for failure to furnish

[861] This description is based upon the discussion at page 334 in S. Rep. No. 111–89, *Final Committee Report of the Senate Finance Committee on "America's Healthy Future Act of 2009,"* published October 21, 2009.

[862] Secs. 6031 through 6060.

[863] Sec. 6041(a). The information return is generally submitted electronically as a Form–1099 or Form–1096, although certain payments to beneficiaries or employees may require use of Forms W–3 or W–2, respectively. Treas. Reg. sec. 1.6041–1(a)(2).

[864] Sec. 6041(a) requires reporting as to "other fixed or determinable gains, profits, and income (other than payments to which section 6042(a)(1), 6044(a)(1), 6047(c), 6049(a) or 6050N(a) applies and other than payments with respect to which a statement is required under authority of section 6042(a), 6044(a)(2) or 6045)[.]" These excepted payments include most interest, royalties, and dividends.

[865] Sec. 6041(d).

[866] Treas. Reg. sec. 1.6041–3(p). Certain for-profit health provider corporations are not covered by this general exception, including those organizations providing billing services for such companies.

[867] Sec. 6050T.

[868] Sec. 6050R.

[869] Sec. 6045(f)(1) and (2); Treas. Reg. secs. 1.6041–1(d)(2) and 1.6045–5(d)(5).

[870] *Ibid.*

[871] Sec. 6045(d).

[872] Sec. 6041(d)(3).

[873] Sec. 6721. The penalty for the failure to file an information return generally is $50 for each return for which such failure occurs. The total penalty imposed on a person for all failures during a calendar year cannot exceed $250,000. Additionally, special rules apply to reduce the per-failure and maximum penalty where the failure is corrected within a specified period.

payee statements[874] or failure to comply with other various reporting requirements.[875]

Detailed rules are provided for the reporting of various types of investment income, including interest, dividends, and gross proceeds from brokered transactions (such as a sale of stock).[876] In general, the requirement to file Form 1099 applies with respect to amounts paid to U.S. persons and is linked to the backup withholding rules of section 3406. Thus, a payor of interest, dividends or gross proceeds generally must request that a U.S. payee (other than certain exempt recipients) furnish a Form W–9 providing that person's name and taxpayer identification number.[877] That information is then used to complete the Form 1099.

### *Explanation of Provision*

Under the provision, a business is required to file an information return for all payments aggregating $600 or more in a calendar year to a single payee (other than a payee that is a tax-exempt corporation), notwithstanding any regulation promulgated under section 6041 prior to the date of enactment (March 23, 2010). The payments to be reported include gross proceeds paid in consideration for property or services. However, the provision does not override specific provisions elsewhere in the Code that except certain payments from reporting, such as securities or broker transactions as defined under section 6045(a) and the regulations thereunder.

### *Effective Date*

The provision is effective for payments made after December 31, 2011.

## G. Additional Requirements for Charitable Hospitals (sec. 9007[878] of the Act and sec. 501(c), new sec. 4959, and sec. 6033 of the Code)

### *Present Law*

#### *Tax exemption*

Charitable organizations, i.e., organizations described in section 501(c)(3), generally are exempt from Federal income tax, are eligible to receive tax deductible contributions,[879] have access to tax-exempt financing through State and local governments (described in

[874] Sec. 6722. The penalty for failure to provide a correct payee statement is $50 for each statement with respect to which such failure occurs, with the total penalty for a calendar year not to exceed $100,000. Special rules apply that increase the per-statement and total penalties where there is intentional disregard of the requirement to furnish a payee statement.

[875] Sec. 6723. The penalty for failure to timely comply with a specified information reporting requirement is $50 per failure, not to exceed $100,000 for a calendar year.

[876] Secs. 6042 (dividends), 6045 (broker reporting) and 6049 (interest) and the Treasury regulations thereunder.

[877] See Treas. Reg. sec. 31.3406(h)–3.

[878] Section 9007 of the Patient Protection and Affordable Care Act, Pub. L. No. 111–148, is amended by section 10903 of the Patient Protection and Affordable Care Act, Pub. L. No. 111–152.

[879] Sec. 170.

more detail below),[880] and generally are exempt from State and local taxes. A charitable organization must operate primarily in pursuit of one or more tax-exempt purposes constituting the basis of its tax exemption.[881] The Code specifies such purposes as religious, charitable, scientific, educational, literary, testing for public safety, to foster international amateur sports competition, or for the prevention of cruelty to children or animals. In general, an organization is organized and operated for charitable purposes if it provides relief for the poor and distressed or the underprivileged.[882]

The Code does not provide a per se exemption for hospitals. Rather, a hospital qualifies for exemption if it is organized and operated for a charitable purpose and otherwise meets the requirements of section 501(c)(3).[883] The promotion of health has been recognized by the IRS as a charitable purpose that is beneficial to the community as a whole.[884] It includes not only the establishment or maintenance of charitable hospitals, but clinics, homes for the aged, and other providers of health care.

Since 1969, the IRS has applied a "community benefit" standard for determining whether a hospital is charitable.[885] According to Revenue Ruling 69–545, community benefit can include, for example: maintaining an emergency room open to all persons regardless of ability to pay; having an independent board of trustees composed of representatives of the community; operating with an open medical staff policy, with privileges available to all qualifying physicians; providing charity care; and utilizing surplus funds to improve the quality of patient care, expand facilities, and advance medical training, education and research. Beginning in 2009, hospitals generally are required to submit information on community benefit on their annual information returns filed with the IRS.[886] Present law does not include sanctions short of revocation of tax-exempt status for hospitals that fail to satisfy the community benefit standard.

Although section 501(c)(3) hospitals generally are exempt from Federal tax on their net income, such organizations are subject to the unrelated business income tax on income derived from a trade or business regularly carried on by the organization that is not substantially related to the performance of the organization's tax-exempt functions.[887] In general, interest, rents, royalties, and annu-

[880] Sec. 145.

[881] Treas. Reg. sec. 1.501(c)(3)–1(c)(1).

[882] Treas. Reg. sec. 1.501(c)(3)–1(d)(2).

[883] Although nonprofit hospitals generally are recognized as tax-exempt by virtue of being "charitable" organizations, some might qualify for exemption as educational or scientific organizations because they are organized and operated primarily for medical education and research purposes.

[884] Rev. Rul. 69–545, 1969–2 C.B. 117; see also Restatement (Second) of Trusts secs. 368, 372 (1959); see Bruce R. Hopkins, *The Law of Tax-Exempt Organizations,* sec. 6.3 (8th ed. 2003) (discussing various forms of health-care providers that may qualify for exemption under section 501(c)(3)).

[885] Rev. Rul. 69–545, 1969–2 C.B. 117. From 1956 until 1969, the IRS applied a "financial ability" standard, requiring that a charitable hospital be "operated to the extent of its financial ability for those not able to pay for the services rendered and not exclusively for those who are able and expected to pay." Rev. Rul. 56–185, 1956–1 C.B. 202.

[886] IRS Form 990, Schedule H.

[887] Secs. 511–514.

ities are excluded from the unrelated business income of tax-exempt organizations.[888]

### *Charitable contributions*

In general, a deduction is permitted for charitable contributions, including charitable contributions to tax-exempt hospitals, subject to certain limitations that depend on the type of taxpayer, the property contributed, and the donee organization. The amount of deduction generally equals the fair market value of the contributed property on the date of the contribution. Charitable deductions are provided for income, estate, and gift tax purposes.[889]

### *Tax-exempt financing*

In addition to issuing tax-exempt bonds for government operations and services, State and local governments may issue tax-exempt bonds to finance the activities of charitable organizations described in section 501(c)(3). Because interest income on tax-exempt bonds is excluded from gross income, investors generally are willing to accept a lower pre-tax rate of return on such bonds than they might otherwise accept on a taxable investment. This, in turn, lowers the cost of capital for the users of such financing. Both capital expenditures and limited working capital expenditures of charitable organizations described in section 501(c)(3) generally may be financed with tax-exempt bonds. Private, nonprofit hospitals frequently are the beneficiaries of this type of financing.

Bonds issued by State and local governments may be classified as either governmental bonds or private activity bonds. Governmental bonds are bonds the proceeds of which are primarily used to finance governmental functions or which are repaid with governmental funds. Private activity bonds are bonds in which the State or local government serves as a conduit providing financing to nongovernmental persons (e.g., private businesses or individuals). For these purposes, the term "nongovernmental person" generally includes the Federal government and all other individuals and entities other than States or local governments, including section 501(c)(3) organizations. The exclusion from income for interest on State and local bonds does not apply to private activity bonds, unless the bonds are issued for certain permitted purposes ("qualified private activity bonds") and other Code requirements are met.

### *Reporting and disclosure requirements*

Exempt organizations are required to file an annual information return, stating specifically the items of gross income, receipts, disbursements, and such other information as the Secretary may prescribe.[890] Section 501(c)(3) organizations that are classified as public charities must file Form 990 (Return of Organization Exempt

---

[888] Sec. 512(b).

[889] Secs. 170, 2055, and 2522, respectively.

[890] Sec. 6033(a). An organization that has not received a determination of its tax-exempt status, but that claims tax-exempt status under section 501(a), is subject to the same annual reporting requirements and exceptions as organizations that have received a tax-exemption determination.

From Income Tax),[891] including Schedule A, which requests information specific to section 501(c)(3) organizations. Additionally, an organization that operates at least one facility that is, or is required to be, licensed, registered, or similarly recognized by a state as a hospital must complete Schedule H (Form 990), which requests information regarding charity care, community benefits, bad debt expense, and certain management company and joint venture arrangements of a hospital.

An organization described in section 501(c) or (d) generally is also required to make available for public inspection for a period of three years a copy of its annual information return (Form 990) and exemption application materials.[892] This requirement is satisfied if the organization has made the annual return and exemption application widely available (e.g., by posting such information on its website).[893]

## *Explanation of Provision*

### *Additional requirements for section 501(c)(3) hospitals*[894]

*In general*

The provision establishes new requirements applicable to section 501(c)(3) hospitals. The new requirements are in addition to, and not in lieu of, the requirements otherwise applicable to an organization described in section 501(c)(3). The requirements generally apply to any section 501(c)(3) organization that operates at least one hospital facility. For purposes of the provision, a hospital facility generally includes: (1) any facility that is, or is required to be, licensed, registered, or similarly recognized by a State as a hospital; and (2) any other facility or organization the Secretary of the Treasury (the "Secretary"), in consultation with the Secretary of HHS and after public comment, determines has the provision of hospital care as its principal purpose. To qualify for tax exemption under section 501(c)(3), an organization subject to the provision is required to comply with the following requirements with respect to each hospital facility operated by such organization.

*Community health needs assessment*

Each hospital facility is required to conduct a community health needs assessment at least once every three taxable years and adopt an implementation strategy to meet the community needs identified through such assessment. The assessment may be based on current information collected by a public health agency or non-profit organizations and may be conducted together with one or more other organizations, including related organizations. The assessment process must take into account input from persons who represent the broad interests of the community served by the hospital facility, including those with special knowledge or expertise of public health issues. The hospital must disclose in its annual informa-

[891] Social welfare organizations, labor organizations, agricultural organizations, horticultural organizations, and business leagues are subject to the generally applicable Form 990, Form 990–EZ, and Form 990–T annual filing requirements.
[892] Sec. 6104(d).
[893] Sec. 6104(d)(4); Treas. Reg. sec. 301.6104(d)-2(b).
[894] No inference is intended regarding whether an organization satisfies the present law community benefit standard.

tion report to the IRS (i.e., Form 990 and related schedules) how it is addressing the needs identified in the assessment and, if all identified needs are not addressed, the reasons why (e.g., lack of financial or human resources). Each hospital facility is required to make the assessment widely available. Failure to complete a community health needs assessment in any applicable three-year period results in a penalty on the organization equal to $50,000. For example, if a facility does not complete a community health needs assessment in taxable years one, two or three, it is subject to the penalty in year three. If it then fails to complete a community health needs assessment in year four, it is subject to another penalty in year four (for failing to satisfy the requirement during the three-year period beginning with taxable year two and ending with taxable year four). An organization that fails to disclose how it is meeting needs identified in the assessment is subject to existing incomplete return penalties.[895]

*Financial assistance policy*

Each hospital facility is required to adopt, implement, and widely publicize a written financial assistance policy. The financial assistance policy must indicate the eligibility criteria for financial assistance and whether such assistance includes free or discounted care. For those eligible for discounted care, the policy must indicate the basis for calculating the amounts that will be billed to such patients. The policy must also indicate how to apply for such assistance. If a hospital does not have a separate billing and collections policy, the financial assistance policy must also indicate what actions the hospital may take in the event of non-response or nonpayment, including collections action and reporting to credit rating agencies. Each hospital facility also is required to adopt and implement a policy to provide emergency medical treatment to individuals. The policy must prevent discrimination in the provision of emergency medical treatment, including denial of service, against those eligible for financial assistance under the facility's financial assistance policy or those eligible for government assistance.

*Limitation on charges*

Each hospital facility is permitted to bill for emergency or other medically necessary care provided to individuals who qualify for financial assistance under the facility's financial assistance policy no more than the amounts generally billed to individuals who have insurance covering such care. A hospital facility may not use gross charges (i.e., "chargemaster" rates) when billing individuals who qualify for financial assistance. It is intended that amounts billed to those who qualify for financial assistance may be based on either the best, or an average of the three best, negotiated commercial rates, or Medicare rates.

*Collection processes*

Under the provision, a hospital facility (or its affiliates) may not undertake extraordinary collection actions (even if otherwise permitted by law) against an individual without first making reason-

---

[895] Sec. 6652.

able efforts to determine whether the individual is eligible for assistance under the hospital's financial assistance policy. Such extraordinary collection actions include lawsuits, liens on residences, arrests, body attachments, or other similar collection processes. The Secretary is directed to issue guidance concerning what constitutes reasonable efforts to determine eligibility. It is intended that for this purpose, "reasonable efforts" includes notification by the hospital of its financial assistance policy upon admission and in written and oral communications with the patient regarding the patient's bill, including invoices and telephone calls, before collection action or reporting to credit rating agencies is initiated.

***Reporting and disclosure requirements***

The provision includes new reporting and disclosure requirements. Under the provision, the Secretary or the Secretary's delegate is required to review information about a hospital's community benefit activities (currently reported on Form 990, Schedule H) at least once every three years. The provision also requires each organization to which the provision applies to file with its annual information return (i.e., Form 990) a copy of its audited financial statements (or, in the case of an organization the financial statements of which are included in a consolidated financial statement with other organizations, such consolidated financial statements).

The provision requires the Secretary, in consultation with the Secretary of HHS, to submit annually a report to Congress with information regarding the levels of charity care, bad debt expenses, unreimbursed costs of means-tested government programs, and unreimbursed costs of non-means tested government programs incurred by private tax-exempt, taxable, and governmental hospitals, as well as the costs incurred by private tax-exempt hospitals for community benefit activities. In addition, the Secretary, in consultation with the Secretary of HHS, must conduct a study of the trends in these amounts, and submit a report on such study to Congress not later than five years from date of enactment (March 23, 2010).

## *Effective Date*

Except as provided below, the provision is effective for taxable years beginning after the date of enactment (March 23, 2010). The community health needs assessment requirement is effective for taxable years beginning after the date which is two years after the date of enactment (March 23, 2010).[896] The excise tax on failures to satisfy the community health needs assessment requirement is effective for failures occurring after the date of enactment (March 23, 2010).

[896] For example, assume the date of enactment is April 1, 2010. A calendar year taxpayer would test whether it meets the community health needs assessment requirement in the taxable year ending December 31, 2013. To avoid the penalty, the taxpayer must have satisfied the community health needs assessment requirements in 2011, 2012, or 2013.

## H. Imposition of Annual Fee on Branded Prescription Pharmaceutical Manufacturers and Importers (sec. 9008[897] of the Act)

### *Present Law*

There are two Medicare trust funds under present law, the Hospital Insurance ("HI") fund and the Supplementary Medical Insurance ("SMI") fund.[898] The HI trust fund is primarily funded through payroll tax on covered earnings. Employers and employees each pay 1.45 percent of wages, while self-employed workers pay 2.9 percent of a portion of their net earnings from self-employment. Other HI trust fund revenue sources include a portion of the Federal income taxes paid on Social Security benefits, and interest paid on the U.S. Treasury securities held in the HI trust fund. For the SMI trust fund, transfers from the general fund of the Treasury represent the largest source of revenue, but additional revenues include monthly premiums paid by beneficiaries, and interest paid on the U.S. Treasury securities held in the SMI trust fund.

Present law does not impose a fee creditable to the Medicare trust funds on companies that manufacture or import prescription drugs for sale in the United States.

### *Explanation of Provision*

The provision imposes a fee on each covered entity engaged in the business of manufacturing or importing branded prescription drugs for sale to any specified government program or pursuant to coverage under any such program for each calendar year beginning after 2010. Fees collected under the provision are credited to the Medicare Part B trust fund.

The aggregate annual fee for all covered entities is the applicable amount. The applicable amount is $2.5 billion for calendar year 2011, $2.8 billion for calendar years 2012 and 2013, $3 billion for calendar years 2014 through 2016, $4 billion for calendar year 2017, $4.1 billion for calendar year 2018, and $2.8 billion for calendar year 2019 and thereafter. The aggregate fee is apportioned among the covered entities each year based on such entity's relative share of branded prescription drug sales taken into account during the previous calendar year. The Secretary of the Treasury will establish an annual payment date that will be no later than September 30 of each calendar year.

The Secretary of the Treasury will calculate the amount of each covered entity's fee for each calendar year by determining the relative market share for each covered entity. A covered entity's relative market share for a calendar year is the covered entity's branded prescription drug sales taken into account during the preceding calendar year as a percentage of the aggregate branded prescription drug sales of all covered entities taken into account during the preceding calendar year. The percentage of branded pre-

---

[897] Section 9008 of the Patient Protection and Affordable Care Act, Pub. L. No. 111–148, is amended by section 1404 of the Health Care and Education Reconciliation Act of 2010, Pub. L. No. 111–152.

[898] See 2009 Annual Report of the Boards of Trustees of the Federal Hospital Insurance and Federal Supplementary Medical Insurance Trust Funds, available at *http://www.cms.hhs.gov/ReportsTrustFunds/downloads/tr2009.pdf*.

scription drug sales that are taken into account during any calendar year with respect to any covered entity is: (1) zero percent of sales not more than $5 million, (2) 10 percent of sales over $5 million but not more than $125 million, (3) 40 percent of sales over $125 million but not more than $225 million, (4) 75 percent of sales over $225 million but not more than $400 million, and (5) 100 percent of sales over $400 million.

For purposes of the provision, a covered entity is any manufacturer or importer with gross receipts from branded prescription drug sales. All persons treated as a single employer under section 52(a) or (b) or under section 414(m) or 414(o) will be treated as a single covered entity for purposes of the provision. In applying the single employer rules under 52(a) and (b), foreign corporations will not be excluded. If more than one person is liable for payment of the fee imposed by this provision, all such persons are jointly and severally liable for payment of such fee. It is anticipated that the Secretary may require each covered entity to identify each member of the group that is treated as a single covered entity under the provision.

Under the provision, branded prescription drug sales are sales of branded prescription drugs made to any specified government program or pursuant to coverage under any such program. The term branded prescription drugs includes any drug which is subject to section 503(b) of the Federal Food, Drug, and Cosmetic Act and for which an application was submitted under section 505(b) of such Act, and any biological product the license for which was submitted under section 351(a) of the Public Health Service Act. Branded prescription drug sales, as defined under the provision, does not include sales of any drug or biological product with respect to which an orphan drug tax credit was allowed for any taxable year under section 45C. The exception for orphan drug sales does not apply to any drug or biological product after such drug or biological product is approved by the Food and Drug Administration for marketing for any indication other than the rare disease or condition with respect to which the section 45C credit was allowed.

Specified government programs under the provision are: (1) the Medicare Part D program under part D of title XVIII of the Social Security Act; (2) the Medicare Part B program under part B of title XVIII of the Social Security Act; (3) the Medicaid program under title XIX of the Social Security Act; (4) any program under which branded prescription drugs are procured by the Department of Veterans Affairs; (5) any program under which branded prescription drugs are procured by the Department of Defense; and (6) the TRICARE retail pharmacy program under section 1074g of title 10, United States Code.

The Secretary of HHS, the Secretary of Veterans Affairs, and the Secretary of Defense will report to the Secretary of the Treasury, at a time and in such a manner as the Secretary of the Treasury prescribes, the total branded prescription drug sales for each covered entity with respect to each specified government program under such Secretary's jurisdiction. The provision includes specific information to be included in the reports by the respective Secretaries for each specified government program.

The fees imposed under the provision are treated as excise taxes with respect to which only civil actions for refunds under the provisions of subtitle F will apply. Thus, the fees may be assessed and collected using the procedures in subtitle F without regard to the restrictions on assessment in section 6213.

The Secretary of the Treasury has authority to publish guidance as necessary to carry out the purposes of this provision.[899] It is anticipated that the Secretary of the Treasury will publish guidance related to the determination of the fee under this section. For example, the Secretary may publish initial determinations, allow a notice and comment period, and then provide notice and demand for payment of the fee. It is also anticipated that the Secretary of the Treasury will provide guidance as to the determination of the fee in situations involving mergers, acquisitions, business divisions, bankruptcy, or any other situations where guidance is necessary to account for sales taken into account for determining the fee for any calendar year.

The fees imposed under the provision are not deductible for U.S. income tax purposes.

#### *Effective Date*

The provision is effective for calendar years beginning after December 31, 2010.

### I. Imposition of Annual Fee on Medical Device Manufacturers and Importers (sec. 9009[900] of the Act)

#### *Repeal*

The provision of the Patient Protection and Affordable Care Act imposing an annual fee on manufacturers and importers of medical devices is repealed by the Health Care and Education Reconciliation Act of 2010.

#### *Effective Date*

The repeal is effective as of the date of enactment (March 23, 2010) of the Patient Protection and Affordable Care Act.

### J. Imposition of Annual Fee on Health Insurance Providers (sec. 9010[901] of the Act)

#### *Present Law*

Present law provides special rules for determining the taxable income of insurance companies (subchapter L of the Code). Separate sets of rules apply to life insurance companies and to property and

[899] Notice 2010–71 provided initial guidance on the annual fee imposed under this provision, including procedures for filing Form 8947, Report of Branded Prescription Drug Information. Notice 2011–9 supersedes Notice 2010–71 and provides guidance on the methodology that will be used for calculating the allocation of the branded prescription drug fee and requests public comments.

[900] Section 9009 of the Patient Protection and Affordable Care Act, Pub. L. No. 111–148, is repealed by section 1405(d) of the Health Care and Education Reconciliation Act of 2010, Pub. L. No. 111–152.

[901] Section 9010 of the Patient Protection and Affordable Care Act, Pub. L. No. 111–148, as amended by section 10905, is further amended by section 1406 of the Health Care and Education Reconciliation Act of 2010, Pub. L. No. 111–152.

casualty insurance companies. Insurance companies are subject to Federal income tax at regular corporate income tax rates.

An insurance company that provides health insurance is subject to Federal income tax as either a life insurance company or as a property insurance company, depending on its mix of lines of business and on the resulting portion of its reserves that are treated as life insurance reserves. For Federal income tax purposes, an insurance company is treated as a life insurance company if the sum of its (1) life insurance reserves and (2) unearned premiums and unpaid losses on noncancellable life, accident or health contracts not included in life insurance reserves, comprise more than 50 percent of its total reserves.[902]

Some insurance providers may be exempt from Federal income tax under section 501(a) if specific requirements are satisfied. Section 501(c)(8), for example, describes certain fraternal beneficiary societies, orders, or associations operating under the lodge system or for the exclusive benefit of their members that provide for the payment of life, sick, accident, or other benefits to the members or their dependents. Section 501(c)(9) describes certain voluntary employees' beneficiary associations that provide for the payment of life, sick, accident, or other benefits to the members of the association or their dependents or designated beneficiaries. Section 501(c)(12)(A) describes certain benevolent life insurance associations of a purely local character. Section 501(c)(15) describes certain small non-life insurance companies with annual gross receipts of no more than $600,000 ($150,000 in the case of a mutual insurance company). Section 501(c)(26) describes certain membership organizations established to provide health insurance to certain high-risk individuals. Section 501(c)(27) describes certain organizations established to provide workmen's compensation insurance.

An excise tax applies to premiums paid to foreign insurers and reinsurers covering U.S. risks.[903] The excise tax is imposed on a gross basis at the rate of one percent on reinsurance and life insurance premiums, and at the rate of four percent on property and casualty insurance premiums. The excise tax does not apply to premiums that are effectively connected with the conduct of a U.S. trade or business or that are exempted from the excise tax under an applicable income tax treaty. The excise tax paid by one party cannot be credited if, for example, the risk is reinsured with a second party in a transaction that is also subject to the excise tax.

IRS authority to assess and collect taxes is generally provided in subtitle F of the Code (secs. 6001–7874), relating to procedure and administration. That subtitle establishes the rules governing both how taxpayers are required to report information to the IRS and to pay their taxes, as well as their rights. It also establishes the duties and authority of the IRS to enforce the Federal tax law, and sets forth rules relating to judicial proceedings involving Federal tax.

---

[902] Sec. 816(a).

[903] Secs. 4371–4374.

### *Explanation of Provision*

Under the provision, an annual fee applies to any covered entity engaged in the business of providing health insurance with respect to United States health risks. The fee applies for calendar years beginning after 2013. The aggregate annual fee for all covered entities is the applicable amount. The applicable amount is $8 billion for calendar year 2014, $11.3 billion for calendar years 2015 and 2016, $13.9 billion for calendar year 2017, and $14.3 billion for calendar year 2018. For calendar years after 2018, the applicable amount is indexed to the rate of premium growth.

The annual payment date for a calendar year is determined by the Secretary of the Treasury, but in no event may be later than September 30 of that year.

Under the provision, the aggregate annual fee is apportioned among the providers based on a ratio designed to reflect relative market share of U.S. health insurance business. For each covered entity, the fee for a calendar year is an amount that bears the same ratio to the applicable amount as (1) the covered entity's net premiums written during the preceding calendar year with respect to health insurance for any United States health risk, bears to (2) the aggregate net written premiums of all covered entities during such preceding calendar year with respect to such health insurance.

The provision requires the Secretary of the Treasury to calculate the amount of each covered entity's fee for the calendar year, determining the covered entity's net written premiums for the preceding calendar year with respect to health insurance for any United States health risk on the basis of reports submitted by the covered entity and through the use of any other source of information available to the Treasury Department. It is intended that the Treasury Department be able to rely on published aggregate annual statement data to the extent necessary, and may use annual statement data and filed annual statements that are publicly available to verify or supplement the reports submitted by covered entities.

Net written premiums is intended to mean premiums written, including reinsurance premiums written, reduced by reinsurance ceded, and reduced by ceding commissions. Net written premiums do not include amounts arising under arrangements that are not treated as insurance (i.e., in the absence of sufficient risk shifting and risk distribution for the arrangement to constitute insurance).[904]

The amount of net premiums written that are taken into account for purposes of determining a covered entity's market share is subject to dollar thresholds. A covered entity's net premiums written during the calendar year that are not more than $25 million are not taken into account for this purpose. With respect to a covered entity's net premiums written during the calendar year that are more than $25 million but not more than $50 million, 50 percent are taken into account, and 100 percent of net premiums written in excess of $50 million are taken into account.

After application of the above dollar thresholds, a special rule provides an exclusion, for purposes of determining an otherwise

[904] See *Helvering v. Le Gierse*, 312 U.S. 531 (1941).

covered entity's market share, of 50 percent of net premiums written that are attributable to the exempt activities[905] of a health insurance organization that is exempt from Federal income tax[906] by reason of being described in section 501(c)(3) (generally, a public charity), section 501(c)(4) (generally, a social welfare organization), section 501(c)(26) (generally, a high-risk health insurance pool), or section 501(c)(29) (a consumer operated and oriented plan ("CO-OP") health insurance issuer).

A covered entity generally is an entity that provides health insurance with respect to United States health risks during the calendar year in which the fee under this section is due. Thus for example, an insurance company subject to tax under part I or II of subchapter L, an organization exempt from tax under section 501(a), a foreign insurer that provides health insurance with respect to United States health risks, or an insurer that provides health insurance with respect to United States health risks under Medicare Advantage, Medicare Part D, or Medicaid, is a covered entity under the provision except as provided in specific exceptions.

Specific exceptions are provided to the definition of a covered entity. A covered entity does not include an employer to the extent that the employer self-insures the health risks of its employees. For example, a manufacturer that enters into a self-insurance arrangement with respect to the health risks of its employees is not treated as a covered entity. As a further example, an insurer that sells health insurance and that also enters into a self-insurance arrangement with respect to the health risks of its own employees is treated as a covered entity with respect to its health insurance business, but is not treated as a covered entity to the extent of the self-insurance of its own employees' health risks.

A covered entity does not include any governmental entity. For this purpose, it is intended that a governmental entity includes a county organized health system entity that is an independent public agency organized as a nonprofit under State law and that contracts with a State to administer State Medicaid benefits through local care providers or HMOs.

A covered entity does not include an entity that (1) qualifies as nonprofit under applicable State law, (2) meets the private inurement and limitation on lobbying provisions described in section 501(c)(3), and (3) receives more than 80 percent of its gross revenue from government programs that target low-income, elderly, or disabled populations (including Medicare, Medicaid, the State Children's Health Insurance Plan ("SCHIP"), and dual-eligible plans).

A covered entity does not include an organization that qualifies as a VEBA under section 501(c)(9) that is established by an entity other than the employer (i.e., a union) for the purpose of providing health care benefits. This exclusion does not apply to multi-employer welfare arrangements ("MEWAs").

---

[905] The exempt activities for this purpose are activities other than activities of an unrelated trade or business defined in section 513.

[906] Section 501(m) of the Code provides that an organization described in section 501(c)(3) or (4) is exempt from Federal income tax only if no substantial part of its activities consists of providing commercial-type insurance. Thus, an organization otherwise described in section 501(c)(3) or (4) that is taxable (under the Federal income tax rules) by reason of section 501(m) is not eligible for the 50-percent exclusion under the insurance fee.

For purposes of the provision, all persons treated as a single employer under section 52(a) or (b) or section 414(m) or (o) are treated as a single covered entity (or as a single employer, for purposes of the rule relating to employers that self-insure the health risks of employees), and otherwise applicable exclusion of foreign corporations under those rules is disregarded. However, the exceptions to the definition of a covered entity are applied on a separate entity basis, not taking into account this rule. If more than one person is liable for payment of the fee by reason of being treated as a single covered entity, all such persons are jointly and severally liable for payment of the fee.

A United States heath risk means the health risk of an individual who is a U.S. citizen, is a U.S. resident within the meaning of section 7701(b)(1)(A) (whether or not located in the United States), or is located in the United States, with respect to the period that the individual is located there. In general, it is intended that risks in the following lines of business reported on the annual statement as prescribed by the National Association of Insurance Commissioners and as filed with the insurance commissioners of the States in which insurers are licensed to do business constitute health risks for this purpose: comprehensive (hospital and medical), vision, dental, Federal Employees Health Benefit plan, title XVIII Medicare, title XIX Medicaid, and other health.

For purposes of the provision, health insurance does not include coverage only for accident, or disability income insurance, or a combination thereof. Health insurance does not include coverage only for a specified disease or illness, nor does health insurance include hospital indemnity or other fixed indemnity insurance. Health insurance does not include any insurance for long-term care or any Medicare supplemental health insurance (as defined in section 1882(g)(1) of the Social Security Act).

For purposes of procedure and administration under the rules of Subtitle F of the Code, the fee under this provision is treated as an excise tax with respect to which only civil actions for refund under Subtitle F apply. The Secretary of the Treasury may redetermine the amount of a covered entity's fee under the provision for any calendar year for which the statute of limitations remains open.

For purposes of section 275, relating to the nondeductibility of specified taxes, the fee is considered to be a nondeductible tax described in section 275(a)(6).

A reporting rule applies under the provision. A covered entity is required to report to the Secretary of the Treasury the amount of its net premiums written during any calendar year with respect to health insurance for any United States health risk.

A penalty applies for failure to report, unless it is shown that the failure is due to reasonable cause. The amount of the penalty is $10,000 plus the lesser of (1) $1,000 per day while the failure continues, or (2) the amount of the fee imposed for which the report was required. The penalty is treated as a penalty for purposes of subtitle F of the Code, must be paid on notice and demand by the Treasury Department and in the same manner as tax, and with respect to which only civil actions for refund under procedures of subtitle F apply. The reported information is not treated as taxpayer information under section 6103.

An accuracy-related penalty applies in the case of any understatement of a covered entity's net premiums written. For this purpose, an understatement is the difference between the amount of net premiums written as reported on the return filed by the covered entity and the amount of net premiums written that should have been reported on the return. The penalty is equal to the amount of the fee that should have been paid in the absence of an understatement over the amount of the fee determined based on the understatement. The accuracy-related penalty is subject to the provisions of subtitle F of the Code that apply to assessable penalties imposed under Chapter 68.

The provision provides authority for the Secretary of the Treasury to publish guidance necessary to carry out the purposes of the provision and to prescribe regulations necessary or appropriate to prevent avoidance of the purposes of the provision, including inappropriate actions taken to qualify as an exempt entity under the provision.

#### *Effective Date*

The annual fee is required to be paid in each calendar year beginning after December 31, 2013. The fee under the provision is determined with respect to net premiums written after December 31, 2012, with respect to health insurance for any United States health risk.

### K. Study and Report of Effect on Veterans Health Care (sec. 9011 of the Act)

#### *Present Law*

No provision.

#### *Explanation of Provision*

The provision requires the Secretary of Veterans Affairs to conduct a study on the effect (if any) of the fees assessed on manufacturers and importers of branded prescription drugs, manufacturers and importers of medical devices, and health insurance providers on (1) the cost of medical care provided to veterans and (2) veterans' access to branded prescription drugs and medical devices.

The Secretary of Veterans Affairs will report the results of the study to the Committee on Ways and Means of the House of Representatives and to the Committee on Finance of the Senate no later than December 31, 2012.

#### *Effective Date*

The provision is effective on the date of enactment (March 23, 2010).

## L. Repeal Business Deduction for Federal Subsidies for Certain Retiree Prescription Drug Plans (sec. 9012[907] of the Act and sec. 139A of the Code)

### *Present Law*

#### *In general*

Sponsors[908] of qualified retiree prescription drug plans are eligible for subsidy payments from the Secretary of HHS with respect to a portion of each qualified covered retiree's gross covered prescription drug costs ("qualified retiree prescription drug plan subsidy").[909] A qualified retiree prescription drug plan is employment-based retiree health coverage[910] that has an actuarial value at least as great as the Medicare Part D standard plan for the risk pool and that meets certain other disclosure and recordkeeping requirements.[911] These qualified retiree prescription drug plan subsidies are excludable from the plan sponsor's gross income for the purposes of regular income tax and alternative minimum tax (including the adjustment for adjusted current earnings).[912]

#### *Subsidy amounts*

For each qualifying covered retiree enrolled for a coverage year in a qualified retiree prescription drug plan, the qualified retiree prescription drug plan subsidy is equal to 28 percent of the portion of the allowable retiree costs paid by the plan sponsor on behalf of the retiree that exceed the cost threshold but do not exceed the cost limit. A "qualifying covered retiree" is an individual who is eligible for Medicare but not enrolled in either a Medicare Part D prescription drug plan or a Medicare Advantage-Prescription Drug plan, but who is covered under a qualified retiree prescription drug plan. In general, allowable retiree costs are, with respect to prescription drug costs under a qualified retiree prescription drug plan, the part of the actual costs paid by the plan sponsor on behalf of a qualifying covered retiree under the plan.[913] Both the threshold and limit are indexed to the percentage increase in Medicare per capita

---

[907] Section 9012 of the Patient Protection and Affordable Care Act, Pub. L. No. 111–148, is amended by section 1407 of the Health Care and Education Reconciliation Act of 2010, Pub. L. No. 111–152.

[908] The identity of the plan sponsor is determined in accordance with section 16(B) of ERISA, except that for cases where a plan is maintained jointly by one employer and an employee organization, and the employer is the primary source of financing, the employer is the plan sponsor.

[909] Sec. 1860D–22 of the Social Security Act (SSA), 42 U.S.C. sec. 1395w–132.

[910] Employment-based retiree health coverage is health insurance coverage or other coverage of health care costs (whether provided by voluntary insurance coverage or pursuant to statutory or contractual obligation) for Medicare Part D eligible individuals (their spouses and dependents) under group health plans based on their status as retired participants in such plans. For purposes of the subsidy, group health plans generally include employee welfare benefit plans (as defined in section 607(1) of ERISA) that provide medical care (as defined in section 213(d)), Federal and State governmental plans, collectively bargained plans, and church plans.

[911] In addition to meeting the actuarial value standard, the plan sponsor must also maintain and provide the Secretary of HHS access to records that meet the Secretary of HHS's requirements for purposes of audits and other oversight activities necessary to ensure the adequacy of prescription drug coverage and the accuracy of payments made to eligible individuals under the plan. In addition, the plan sponsor must disclose to the Secretary of HHS whether the plan meets the actuarial equivalence requirement and if it does not, must disclose to retirees the limitations of their ability to enroll in Medicare Part D and that non-creditable coverage enrollment is subject to penalties such as fees for late enrollment. 42 U.S.C. sec. 1395w–132(a)(2).

[912] Sec. 139A.

[913] For purposes of calculating allowable retiree costs, actual costs paid are net of discounts, chargebacks, and average percentage rebates, and exclude administrative costs.

prescription drug costs; the cost threshold was $250 in 2006 ($310 in 2010) and the cost limit was $5,000 in 2006 ($6,300 in 2010).[914]

### *Expenses relating to tax-exempt income*

In general, no deduction is allowed under any provision of the Code for any expense or amount which would otherwise be allowable as a deduction if such expense or amount is allocable to a class or classes of exempt income.[915] Thus, expenses or amount paid or incurred with respect to the subsidies excluded from income under section 139A would generally not be deductible. However, a provision under section 139A specifies that the exclusion of the qualified retiree prescription drug plan subsidy from income is not taken into account in determining whether any deduction is allowable with respect to covered retiree prescription drug expenses that are taken into account in determining the subsidy payment. Therefore, under present law, a taxpayer may claim a business deduction for covered retiree prescription drug expenses incurred notwithstanding that the taxpayer excludes from income qualified retiree prescription drug plan subsidies allocable to such expenses.

### *Explanation of Provision*

The provision eliminates the rule that the exclusion for subsidy payments is not taken into account for purposes of determining whether a deduction is allowable with respect to retiree prescription drug expenses. Thus, under the provision, the amount otherwise allowable as a deduction for retiree prescription drug expenses is reduced by the amount of the excludable subsidy payments received.

For example, assume a company receives a subsidy of $28 with respect to eligible drug expenses of $100. The $28 is excludable from income under section 139A, and the amount otherwise allowable as a deduction is reduced by the $28. Thus, if the company otherwise meets the requirements of section 162 with respect to its eligible drug expenses, it would be entitled to an ordinary business expense deduction of $72.

### *Effective Date*

The provision is effective for taxable years beginning after December 31, 2012.

## M. Modify the Itemized Deduction for Medical Expenses (sec. 9013 of the Act and sec. 213 of the Code)

### *Present Law*

### *Regular income tax*

For regular income tax purposes, individuals are allowed an itemized deduction for unreimbursed medical expenses, but only to the extent that such expenses exceed 7.5 percent of AGI.[916]

---

[914] *http://www.cms.hhs.gov/MedicareAdvtgSpecRateStats/Downloads/Announcement2010.pdf.* Retrieved on March 19, 2010.
[915] Sec. 265(a) and Treas. Reg. sec. 1.265–1(a).
[916] Sec. 213.

This deduction is available both to insured and uninsured individuals; thus, for example, an individual with employer-provided health insurance (or certain other forms of tax-subsidized health benefits) may also claim the itemized deduction for the individual's medical expenses not covered by that insurance if the 7.5 percent AGI threshold is met. The medical deduction encompasses health insurance premiums to the extent they have not been excluded from taxable income through the employer exclusion or self-insured deduction.

*Alternative minimum tax*

For purposes of the alternative minimum tax ("AMT"), medical expenses are deductible only to the extent that they exceed 10 percent of AGI.

### *Explanation of Provision*

This provision increases the threshold for the itemized deduction for unreimbursed medical expenses from 7.5 percent of AGI to 10 percent of AGI for regular income tax purposes. However, for the years 2013, 2014, 2015 and 2016, if either the taxpayer or the taxpayer's spouse turns 65 before the end of the taxable year, the increased threshold does not apply and the threshold remains at 7.5 percent of AGI. The provision does not change the AMT treatment of the itemized deduction for medical expenses.

### *Effective Date*

The provision is effective for taxable years beginning after December 31, 2012.

## N. Limitation on Deduction for Remuneration Paid by Health Insurance Providers (sec. 9014 of the Act and sec. 162 of the Code)

### *Present Law*

An employer generally may deduct reasonable compensation for personal services as an ordinary and necessary business expense. Section 162(m) provides explicit limitations on the deductibility of compensation expenses in the case of corporate employers.

*Section 162(m)*

*In general*

The otherwise allowable deduction for compensation paid or accrued with respect to a covered employee of a publicly held corporation[917] is limited to no more than $1 million per year.[918] The deduction limitation applies when the deduction would otherwise be taken. Thus, for example, in the case of compensation resulting from a transfer of property in connection with the performance of services, such compensation is taken into account in applying the

[917] A corporation is treated as publicly held if it has a class of common equity securities that is required to be registered under section 12 of the Securities Exchange Act of 1934.

[918] Sec. 162(m). This deduction limitation applies for purposes of the regular income tax and the alternative minimum tax.

deduction limitation for the year for which the compensation is deductible under section 83 (i.e., generally the year in which the employee's right to the property is no longer subject to a substantial risk of forfeiture).

*Covered employees*

Section 162(m) defines a covered employee as (1) the chief executive officer of the corporation (or an individual acting in such capacity) as of the close of the taxable year and (2) the four most highly compensated officers for the taxable year (other than the chief executive officer). Treasury regulations under section 162(m) provide that whether an employee is the chief executive officer or among the four most highly compensated officers should be determined pursuant to the executive compensation disclosure rules promulgated under the Securities Exchange Act of 1934 ("Exchange Act").

In 2006, the Securities and Exchange Commission amended certain rules relating to executive compensation, including which executive officers' compensation must be disclosed under the Exchange Act. Under the new rules, such officers consist of (1) the principal executive officer (or an individual acting in such capacity), (2) the principal financial officer (or an individual acting in such capacity), and (3) the three most highly compensated executive officers, other than the principal executive officer or financial officer. In response to the Securities and Exchange Commission's new disclosure rules, the IRS issued updated guidance on identifying which employees are covered by section 162(m).[919]

*Remuneration subject to the limit*

Unless specifically excluded, the deduction limitation applies to all remuneration for services, including cash and the cash value of all remuneration (including benefits) paid in a medium other than cash. If an individual is a covered employee for a taxable year, the deduction limitation applies to all compensation not explicitly excluded from the deduction limitation, regardless of whether the compensation is for services as a covered employee and regardless of when the compensation was earned. The $1 million cap is reduced by excess parachute payments (as defined in sec. 280G, discussed below) that are not deductible by the corporation.

Certain types of compensation are not subject to the deduction limit and are not taken into account in determining whether other compensation exceeds $1 million. The following types of compensation are not taken into account: (1) remuneration payable on a commission basis; (2) remuneration payable solely on account of the attainment of one or more performance goals if certain outside director and shareholder approval requirements are met ("performance-based compensation"); (3) payments to a tax-qualified retirement plan (including salary reduction contributions); (4) amounts that are excludable from the executive's gross income (such as employer-provided health benefits and miscellaneous fringe benefits[920]); and

[919] Notice 2007–49, 2007–25 I.R.B. 1429.
[920] Sec. 132.

(5) any remuneration payable under a written binding contract which was in effect on February 17, 1993.

Remuneration does not include compensation for which a deduction is allowable after a covered employee ceases to be a covered employee. Thus, the deduction limitation often does not apply to deferred compensation that is otherwise subject to the deduction limitation (e.g., is not performance-based compensation) because the payment of compensation is deferred until after termination of employment.

***Executive compensation of employers participating in the Troubled Assets Relief Program***

*In general*

Under section 162(m)(5), the deduction limit is reduced to $500,000 in the case of otherwise deductible compensation of a covered executive for any applicable taxable year of an applicable employer.

An applicable employer means any employer from which one or more troubled assets are acquired under the "troubled assets relief program" ("TARP") established by the Emergency Stabilization Act of 2008[921] ("EESA") if the aggregate amount of the assets so acquired for all taxable years (including assets acquired through a direct purchase by the Treasury Department, within the meaning of section 113(c) of Title I of EESA) exceeds $300,000,000. However, such term does not include any employer from which troubled assets are acquired by the Treasury Department solely through direct purchases (within the meaning of section 113(c) of Title I of EESA). For example, if a firm sells $250,000,000 in assets through an auction system managed by the Treasury Department, and $100,000,000 to the Treasury Department in direct purchases, then the firm is an applicable employer. Conversely, if all $350,000,000 in sales take the form of direct purchases, then the firm would not be an applicable employer.

Unlike section 162(m), an applicable employer under this provision is not limited to publicly held corporations (or even limited to corporations). For example, an applicable employer could be a partnership if the partnership is an employer from which a troubled asset is acquired. The aggregation rules of section 414(b) and (c) apply in determining whether an employer is an applicable employer. However, these rules are applied disregarding the rules for brother-sister controlled groups and combined groups in sections 1563(a)(2) and (3). Thus, this aggregation rule only applies to parent-subsidiary controlled groups. A similar controlled group rule applies for trades and businesses under common control.

The result of this aggregation rule is that all corporations in the same controlled group are treated as a single employer for purposes of identifying the covered executives of that employer and all compensation from all members of the controlled group are taken into account for purposes of applying the $500,000 deduction limit. Further, all sales of assets under the TARP from all members of the controlled group are considered in determining whether such sales exceed $300,000,000.

---

[921] Pub. L. No. 110–343.

An applicable taxable year with respect to an applicable employer means the first taxable year which includes any portion of the period during which the authorities for the TARP established under EESA are in effect (the "authorities period") if the aggregate amount of troubled assets acquired from the employer under that authority during the taxable year (when added to the aggregate amount so acquired for all preceding taxable years) exceeds $300,000,000, and includes any subsequent taxable year which includes any portion of the authorities period.

A special rule applies in the case of compensation that relates to services that a covered executive performs during an applicable taxable year but that is not deductible until a later year ("deferred deduction executive remuneration"), such as nonqualified deferred compensation. Under the special rule, the unused portion (if any) of the $500,000 limit for the applicable tax year is carried forward until the year in which the compensation is otherwise deductible, and the remaining unused limit is then applied to the compensation.

For example, assume a covered executive is paid $400,000 in cash salary by an applicable employer in 2008 (assuming 2008 is an applicable taxable year) and the covered executive earns $100,000 in nonqualified deferred compensation (along with the right to future earnings credits) payable in 2020. Assume further that the $100,000 has grown to $300,000 in 2020. The full $400,000 in cash salary is deductible under the $500,000 limit in 2008. In 2020, the applicable employer's deduction with respect to the $300,000 will be limited to $100,000 (the lesser of the $300,000 in deductible compensation before considering the special limitation, and $500,000 less $400,000, which represents the unused portion of the $500,000 limit from 2008).

Deferred deduction executive remuneration that is properly deductible in an applicable taxable year (before application of the limitation under the provision) but is attributable to services performed in a prior applicable taxable year is subject to the special rule described above and is not double-counted. For example, assume the same facts as above, except that the nonqualified deferred compensation is deferred until 2009 and that 2009 is an applicable taxable year. The employer's deduction for the nonqualified deferred compensation for 2009 would be limited to $100,000 (as in the example above). The limit that would apply under the provision for executive remuneration that is in a form other than deferred deduction executive remuneration and that is otherwise deductible for 2009 is $500,000. For example, if the covered executive is paid $500,000 in cash compensation for 2009, all $500,000 of that cash compensation would be deductible in 2009 under the provision.

*Covered executive*

The term covered executive means any individual who is the chief executive officer or the chief financial officer of an applicable employer, or an individual acting in that capacity, at any time during a portion of the taxable year that includes the authorities period. It also includes any employee who is one of the three highest compensated officers of the applicable employer for the applicable taxable year (other than the chief executive officer or the chief financial officer and only taking into account employees employed during any portion of the taxable year that includes the authorities period).[922]

*Executive remuneration*

The provision generally incorporates the present law definition of applicable employee remuneration. However, the present law exceptions for remuneration payable on commission and performance-based compensation do not apply for purposes of the $500,000 limit. In addition, the $500,000 limit only applies to executive remuneration which is attributable to services performed by a covered executive during an applicable taxable year. For example, assume the same facts as in the example above, except that the covered executive also receives in 2008 a payment of $300,000 in non-qualified deferred compensation that was attributable to services performed in 2006. Such payment is not treated as executive remuneration for purposes of the $500,000 limit.

***Taxation of insurance companies***

Present law provides special rules for determining the taxable income of insurance companies (subchapter L of the Code). Separate sets of rules apply to life insurance companies and to property and casualty insurance companies. Insurance companies are subject to Federal income tax at regular corporate income tax rates. An insurance company generally may deduct compensation paid in the course of its trade or business.

## *Explanation of Provision*

Under the provision, no deduction is allowed for remuneration which is attributable to services performed by an applicable individual for a covered health insurance provider during an applicable taxable year to the extent that such remuneration exceeds $500,000. As under section 162(m)(5) for remuneration from TARP participants, the exceptions for performance based remuneration, commissions, or remuneration under existing binding contracts do not apply. This $500,000 deduction limitation applies without regard to whether such remuneration is paid during the taxable year or a subsequent taxable year. In applying this rule, rules similar to those in section 162(m)(5)(A)(ii) apply. Thus in the case of remuneration that relates to services that an applicable individual performs during a taxable year but that is not deductible until a later year, such as nonqualified deferred compensation, the unused portion (if any) of the $500,000 limit for the year is carried forward until the year in which the compensation is otherwise deductible, and the remaining unused limit is then applied to the compensation.

[922] The determination of the three highest compensated officers is made on the basis of the shareholder disclosure rules for compensation under the Exchange Act, except to the extent that the shareholder disclosure rules are inconsistent with the provision. Such shareholder disclosure rules are applied without regard to whether those rules actually apply to the employer under the Exchange Act. If an employee is a covered executive with respect to an applicable employer for any applicable taxable year, the employee will be treated as a covered executive for all subsequent applicable taxable years (and will be treated as a covered executive for purposes of any subsequent taxable year for purposes of the special rule for deferred deduction executive remuneration).

In determining whether the remuneration of an applicable individual for a year exceeds $500,000, all remuneration from all members of any controlled group of corporations (within the meaning of section 414(b)), other businesses under common control (within the meaning of section 414(c)), or affiliated service group (within the meaning of sections 414(m) and (o)) are aggregated.

***Covered health insurance provider and applicable taxable year***

An insurance provider is a covered health insurance provider if at least 25 percent of the insurance provider's gross premium income from health business is derived from health insurance plans that meet the minimum creditable coverage requirements in the bill ("covered health insurance provider"). A taxable year is an applicable taxable year for an insurance provider if an insurance provider is a covered insurance provider for any portion of the taxable year. Employers with self-insured plans are excluded from the definition of covered health insurance provider.

***Applicable individual***

Applicable individuals include all officers, employees, directors, and other workers or service providers (such as consultants) performing services for or on behalf of a covered health insurance provider. Thus, in contrast to the general rules under section 162(m) and the special rules executive compensation of employers participating in the TARP program, the limitation on the deductibility of remuneration from a covered health insurance provided is not limited to a small group of officers and covered executives but generally applies to remuneration of all employees and service providers. If an individual is an applicable individual with respect to a covered health insurance provider for any taxable year, the individual is treated as an applicable individual for all subsequent taxable years (and is treated as an applicable individual for purposes of any subsequent taxable year for purposes of the special rule for deferred remuneration).

### *Effective Date*

The provision is effective for remuneration paid in taxable years beginning after 2012 with respect to services performed after 2009.

## O. Additional Hospital Insurance Tax on High Income Taxpayers (sec. 9015[923] of the Act and new secs. 1401 and 3101 of the Code)

### *Present Law*

***Federal Insurance Contributions Act tax***

The Federal Insurance Contributions Act imposes tax on employers based on the amount of wages paid to an employee during the year. The tax imposed is composed of two parts: (1) the old age, survivors, and disability insurance ("OASDI") tax equal to 6.2 per-

[923] Section 9015 of the Patient Protection and Affordable Care Act, Pub. L. No. 111–148, is amended by section 10906.

cent of covered wages up to the taxable wage base ($106,800 in 2010); and (2) the HI tax amount equal to 1.45 percent of covered wages. Generally, covered wages means all remuneration for employment, including the cash value of all remuneration (including benefits) paid in any medium other than cash. Certain exceptions from covered wages are also provided. In addition to the tax on employers, each employee is subject to FICA taxes equal to the amount of tax imposed on the employer.

The employee portion of the FICA tax generally must be withheld and remitted to the Federal government by the employer.[924] The employer generally is liable for the amount of this tax whether or not the employer withholds the amount from the employee's wages.[925] In the event that the employer fails to withhold from an employee, the employee generally is not liable to the IRS for the amount of the tax. However, if the employer pays its liability for the amount of the tax not withheld, the employer generally has a right to collect that amount from the employee. Further, if the employer deducts and pays the tax the employer is indemnified against the claims and demands of any person for the amount of any payment of the tax made by the employer.[926]

***Self-Employment Contributions Act tax***

As a parallel to FICA taxes, the Self-Employment Contributions Act ("SECA") imposes taxes on the net income from self employment of self employed individuals. The rate of the OASDI portion of SECA taxes is equal to the combined employee and employer OASDI FICA tax rates and applies to self employment income up to the FICA taxable wage base. Similarly, the rate of the HI portion is the same as the combined employer and employee HI rates and there is no cap on the amount of self employment income to which the rate applies.[927]

For purposes of computing net earnings from self employment, taxpayers are permitted a deduction equal to the product of the taxpayer's earnings (determined without regard to this deduction) and one-half of the sum of the rates for OASDI (12.4 percent) and HI (2.9 percent), i.e., 7.65 percent of net earnings. This deduction reflects the fact that the FICA rates apply to an employee's wages, which do not include FICA taxes paid by the employer, whereas the self-employed individual's net earnings are economically equivalent to an employee's wages plus the employer share of FICA taxes.

---

[924] Sec. 3102(a).

[925] Sec. 3102(b).

[926] *Ibid.*

[927] For purposes of computing net earnings from self employment, taxpayers are permitted a deduction equal to the product of the taxpayer's earnings (determined without regard to this deduction) and one-half of the sum of the rates for OASDI (12.4 percent) and HI (2.9 percent), i.e., 7.65 percent of net earnings. This deduction reflects the fact that the FICA rates apply to an employee's wages, which do not include FICA taxes paid by the employer, whereas the self-employed individual's net earnings are economically equivalent to an employee's wages plus the employer share of FICA taxes.

## *Explanation of Provision*

### *Additional HI tax on employee portion of HI tax*

*Calculation of additional tax*

The employee portion of the HI tax is increased by an additional tax of 0.9 percent on wages[928] received in excess of the threshold amount. However, unlike the general 1.45 percent HI tax on wages, this additional tax is on the combined wages of the employee and the employee's spouse, in the case of a joint return. The threshold amount is $250,000 in the case of a joint return or surviving spouse, $125,000 in the case of a married individual filing a separate return, and $200,000 in any other case.

*Liability for the additional HI tax on wages*

As under present law, the employer is required to withhold the additional HI tax on wages but is liable for the tax if the employer fails to withhold the amount of the tax from wages, or collect the tax from the employee if the employer fails to withhold. However, in determining the employer's requirement to withhold and liability for the tax, only wages that the employee receives from the employer in excess of $200,000 for a year are taken into account and the employer must disregard the amount of wages received by the employee's spouse. Thus, the employer is only required to withhold on wages in excess of $200,000 for the year, even though the tax may apply to a portion of the employee's wages at or below $200,000, if the employee's spouse also has wages for the year, they are filing a joint return, and their total combined wages for the year exceed $250,000.

For example, if a taxpayer's spouse has wages in excess of $250,000 and the taxpayer has wages of $100,000, the employer of the taxpayer is not required to withhold any portion of the additional tax, even though the combined wages of the taxpayer and the taxpayer's spouse are over the $250,000 threshold. In this instance, the employer of the taxpayer's spouse is obligated to withhold the additional 0.9-percent HI tax with respect to the $50,000 above the threshold with respect to the wages of $250,000 for the taxpayer's spouse.

In contrast to the employee portion of the general HI tax of 1.45 percent of wages for which the employee generally has no direct liability to the IRS to pay the tax, the employee is also liable for this additional 0.9-percent HI tax to the extent the tax is not withheld by the employer. The amount of this tax not withheld by an employer must also be taken into account in determining a taxpayer's liability for estimated tax.

### *Additional HI for self-employed individuals*

This same additional HI tax applies to the HI portion of SECA tax on self-employment income in excess of the threshold amount. Thus, an additional tax of 0.9 percent is imposed on every self-employed individual on self-employment income[929] in excess of the threshold amount.

---

[928] Sec. 3121(a).
[929] Sec. 1402(b).

As in the case of the additional HI tax on wages, the threshold amount for the additional SECA HI tax is $250,000 in the case of a joint return or surviving spouse, $125,000 in the case of a married individual filing a separate return, and $200,000 in any other case. The threshold amount is reduced (but not below zero) by the amount of wages taken into account in determining the FICA tax with respect to the taxpayer. No deduction is allowed under section 164(f) for the additional SECA tax, and the deduction under 1402(a)(12) is determined without regard to the additional SECA tax rate.

### *Effective Date*

The provision applies to remuneration received and taxable years beginning after December 31, 2012.

## P. Modification of Section 833 Treatment of Certain Health Organizations (sec. 9016 of the Act and sec. 833 of the Code)

### *Present Law*

A property and casualty insurance company is subject to tax on its taxable income, generally defined as its gross income less allowable deductions (sec. 832). For this purpose, gross income includes underwriting income and investment income, as well as other items. Underwriting income is the premiums earned on insurance contracts during the year, less losses incurred and expenses incurred. The amount of losses incurred is determined by taking into account the discounted unpaid losses. Premiums earned during the year is determined taking into account a 20-percent reduction in the otherwise allowable deduction, intended to represent the allocable portion of expenses incurred in generating the unearned premiums (sec. 832(b)(4)(B)).

Present law provides that an organization described in sections 501(c)(3) or (4) of the Code is exempt from tax only if no substantial part of its activities consists of providing commercial-type insurance (sec. 501(m)). When this rule was enacted in 1986,[930] special rules were provided under section 833 for Blue Cross and Blue Shield organizations providing health insurance that (1) were in existence on August 16, 1986; (2) were determined at any time to be tax-exempt under a determination that had not been revoked; and (3) were tax-exempt for the last taxable year beginning before January 1, 1987 (when the present-law rule became effective), provided that no material change occurred in the structure or operations of the organizations after August 16, 1986, and before the close of 1986 or any subsequent taxable year. Any other organization is eligible for section 833 treatment if it meets six requirements set forth in section 833(c): (1) substantially all of its activities involve providing health insurance; (2) at least 10 percent of

[930] See H. Rep. 99–426, Tax Reform Act of 1985, (December 7, 1985), p. 664. The Committee stated, "[T]he availability of tax-exempt status under [then-]present law has allowed some large insurance entities to compete directly with commercial insurance companies. For example, the Blue Cross/Blue Shield organizations historically have been treated as tax-exempt organizations described in sections 501(c)(3) or (4). This group of organizations is now among the largest health care insurers in the United States." See also Joint Committee on Taxation, *General Explanation of the Tax Reform Act of 1986,* JCS–10–87 (May 4, 1987), pp. 583–592.

its health insurance is provided to individuals and small groups (not taking into account Medicare supplemental coverage); (3) it provides continuous full-year open enrollment for individuals and small groups; (4) for individuals, it provides full coverage of pre-existing conditions of high-risk individuals and coverage without regard to age, income, or employment of individuals under age 65; (5) at least 35 percent of its premiums are community rated; and (6) no part of its net earnings inures to the benefit of any private shareholder or individual.

Section 833 provides a deduction with respect to health business of such organizations. The deduction is equal to 25 percent of the sum of (1) claims incurred, and liabilities incurred under cost-plus contracts, for the taxable year, and (2) expenses incurred in connection with administration, adjustment, or settlement of claims or in connection with administration of cost-plus contracts during the taxable year, to the extent this sum exceeds the adjusted surplus at the beginning of the taxable year. Only health-related items are taken into account.

Section 833 provides an exception for such an organization from the application of the 20-percent reduction in the deduction for increases in unearned premiums that applies generally to property and casualty companies.

Section 833 provides that such an organization is taxable as a stock property and casualty insurer under the Federal income tax rules applicable to property and casualty insurers.

### *Explanation of Provision*

The provision limits eligibility for the rules of section 833 to those organizations meeting a medical loss ratio standard of 85 percent for the taxable year. Thus, under the provision, an organization that does not meet the 85-percent standard is not allowed the 25-percent deduction and the exception from the 20-percent reduction in the unearned premium reserve deduction under section 833.

For this purpose, an organization's medical loss ratio is determined as the percentage of total premium revenue expended on reimbursement for clinical services that are provided to enrollees under the organization's policies during the taxable year, as reported under section 2718 of the PHSA.[931]

It is intended that the medical loss ratio under this provision be determined on an organization-by-organization basis, not on an affiliated or other group basis, and that Treasury Department guid-

[931] See Wednesday, March 24, 2010, Senate Floor statement of Senator Baucus relating to this provision, 156 Cong. Rec. S1989, stating in part, "First, it was our intention that, in calculating the medical loss ratios, these entities could include both the cost of reimbursement for clinical services provided to the individuals they insure and the cost of activities that improve health care quality. Determining the medical loss ratio under this provision using those two types of costs is consistent with the calculation of medical loss ratios elsewhere in the legislation. This determination would be made on an annual basis and would only affect the application of the special deductions for that year. Second, it was our intention that the only consequence for not meeting the medical loss ratio threshold would be that the 25 percent deduction for claims and expenses and the exception from the 20 percent reduction in the deduction for unearned premium reserves would not be allowed. The entity would still be treated as a stock property and casualty insurance company." A technical correction may be necessary so that the statute reflects this intent.

ance be promulgated promptly to carry out the purposes of the provision.

### *Effective Date*

The provision is effective for taxable years beginning after December 31, 2009.

## Q. Excise Tax on Indoor Tanning Services (sec. 9017[932] of the Act and new sec. 5000B of the Code)

### *Present Law*

There is no tax on indoor tanning services under present law.

### *Explanation of Provision*

#### *In general*

The provision imposes a tax on each individual on whom indoor tanning services are performed. The tax is equal to 10 percent of the amount paid for indoor tanning services.

For purposes of the provision, indoor tanning services are services employing any electronic product designed to induce skin tanning and which incorporate one or more ultraviolet lamps and intended for the irradiation of an individual by ultraviolet radiation, with wavelengths in air between 200 and 400 nanometers. Indoor tanning services do not include any phototherapy service performed by a licensed medical professional.

#### *Payment of tax*

The tax is paid by the individual on whom the indoor tanning services are performed. The tax is collected by each person receiving a payment for tanning services on which a tax is imposed. If the tax is not paid by the person receiving the indoor tanning services at the time the payment for the service is received, the person performing the procedure pays the tax.

Payment of the tax is remitted quarterly to the Secretary by the person collecting the tax. The Secretary is given discretion over the manner of the payment.

### *Effective Date*

The provision applies to tanning services performed on or after July 1, 2010.

[932] Section 9017 of the Patient Protection and Affordable Care Act, Pub. L. No. 111–148, as amended by section 10907.

## R. Exclusion of Health Benefits Provided by Indian Tribal Governments (sec. 9021 of the Act and new sec. 139D of the Code)

### *Present Law*

Present law generally provides that gross income includes all income from whatever source derived.[933] Exclusions from income are provided, however, for certain health care benefits.

#### *Exclusion from income for employer-provided health coverage*

Employees generally are not taxed on (that is, may "exclude" from gross income) the value of employer-provided health coverage under an accident or health plan.[934] In addition, any reimbursements under an accident or health plan for medical care expenses for employees, their spouses, and their dependents generally are excluded from gross income.[935] As with cash or other compensation, the amount paid by employers for employer-provided health coverage is a deductible business expense. Unlike other forms of compensation, however, if an employer contributes to a plan providing health coverage for employees (and the employees' spouses and dependents), the value of the coverage and all benefits (including reimbursements) in the form of medical care under the plan are excludable from the employees' income for income tax purposes.[936] The exclusion applies both to health coverage in the case in which an employer absorbs the cost of employees' medical expenses not covered by insurance (i.e., a self-insured plan) as well as in the case in which the employer purchases health insurance coverage for its employees. There is no limit on the amount of employer-provided health coverage that is excludable.

In addition, employees participating in a cafeteria plan may be able to pay the portion of premiums for health insurance coverage not otherwise paid for by their employers on a pre-tax basis through salary reduction.[937] Such salary reduction contributions are treated as employer contributions and thus also are excluded from gross income.

Employers may agree to reimburse medical expenses of their employees (and their spouses and dependents), not covered by a health insurance plan, through flexible spending arrangements which allow reimbursement not in excess of a specified dollar amount (either elected by an employee under a cafeteria plan or otherwise specified by the employer). Reimbursements under these arrangements are also excludible from gross income as employer-provided health coverage.

[933] Sec. 61.
[934] Sec 106.
[935] Sec. 105(b).
[936] Secs. 104, 105, 106, 125. A similar rule excludes employer provided health insurance coverage and reimbursements for medical expenses from the employees' wages for payroll tax purposes under sections 3121(a)(2), and 3306(a)(2). Health coverage provided to active members of the uniformed services, military retirees, and their dependents are excludable under section 134. That section provides an exclusion for "qualified military benefits," defined as benefits received by reason of status or service as a member of the uniformed services and which were excludable from gross income on September 9, 1986, under any provision of law, regulation, or administrative practice then in effect.
[937] Sec. 125.

***The general welfare exclusion***

Under the general welfare exclusion doctrine, certain payments made to individuals are excluded from gross income. The exclusion has been interpreted to cover payments by governmental units under legislatively provided social benefit programs for the promotion of the general welfare.[938]

The general welfare exclusion generally applies if the payments: (1) are made from a governmental fund, (2) are for the promotion of general welfare (on the basis of the need of the recipient), and (3) do not represent compensation for services.[939] A representative of the IRS recently expressed the view that the general welfare exclusion does not apply to persons with significant income or assets, and that any such extension would represent a departure from well-established administrative practice.[940] The representative further expressed the view that application of the general welfare exclusion to an Indian tribal government providing coverage or benefits to tribal members is dependent upon the structure and administration of the particular program.[941]

## *Explanation of Provision*

The provision allows an exclusion from gross income for the value of specified Indian tribe health care benefits. The exclusion applies to the value of: (1) health services or benefits provided or purchased by the Indian Health Service ("IHS"), either directly or indirectly, through a grant to or a contract or compact with an Indian tribe or tribal organization or through programs of third par-

---

[938] See, e.g., Rev. Rul. 78–170, 1978–1 C.B. 24 (government payments to assist low-income persons with utility costs are not income); Rev. Rul. 76–395, 1976–2 C.B. 16, 17 (government grants to assist low-income city inhabitants to refurbish homes are not income); Rev. Rul. 76–144, 1976–1 C.B. 17 (government grants to persons eligible for relief under the Disaster Relief Act of 1974 are not income); Rev. Rul. 74–153, 1974–1 C.B. 20 (government payments to assist adoptive parents with support and maintenance of adoptive children are not income); Rev. Rul. 74–205, 1974–1 C.B. 20 (replacement housing payments received by individuals under the Housing and Urban Development Act of 1968 are not includible in gross income); Gen. Couns. Mem. 34506 (May 26, 1971) (federal mortgage assistance payments excluded from income under general welfare exception); Rev. Rul. 57–102, 1957–1 C.B. 26 (government benefits paid to blind persons are not income). The courts have also acknowledged the existence of this doctrine. See, e.g., *Bailey v. Commissioner*, 88 T.C. 1293, 1299–1301 (1987) (new building façade paid for by urban renewal agency on taxpayer's property under façade grant program not considered payments under general welfare doctrine because awarded without regard to any need of the recipients); *Graff v. Commissioner*, 74 TC 743, 753–754 (1980) (court acknowledged that rental subsidies under Housing Act were excludable under general welfare doctrine but found that payments at issue made by HUD on taxpayer landlord's behalf were taxable income to him), *affd. per curiam* 673 F.2d 784 (5th Cir. 1982).

[939] See Rev. Rul. 98–19, 1998–1 C.B. 840 (excluding relocation payments made by local governments to those whose homes were damaged by floods). Recent guidance as to whether the need of the recipient (taken into account under the second requirement of the general welfare exclusion) must be based solely on financial means or whether the need can be based on a variety of other considerations including health, educational background, or employment status, has been mixed. Chief Couns. Adv. 200021036 (May 25, 2000) (excluding state adoption assistant payments made to individuals adopting special needs children without regard to financial means of parents; the children were considered to be the recipients); Priv. Ltr. Rul. 200632005 (April 13, 2006) (excluding payments made by Tribe to members based on multiple factors of need pursuant to housing assistance program); Chief Couns. Adv. 200648027 (Jul 25, 2006) (excluding subsidy payments based on financial need of recipient made by state to certain participants in state health insurance program to reduce cost of health insurance premiums).

[940] Testimony of Sarah H. Ingram, Commissioner, Tax Exempt and Government Entities, Internal Revenue Service, before the Senate Committee on Indian Affairs, *Oversight Hearing to Examine the Federal Tax Treatment of Health Care Benefits Provided by Tribal Governments to Their Citizens*, September 17, 2009.

[941] *Ibid.*

ties funded by the IHS;[942] (2) medical care (in the form of provided or purchased medical care services, accident or health insurance or an arrangement having the same effect, or amounts paid directly or indirectly, to reimburse the member for expenses incurred for medical care) provided by an Indian tribe or tribal organization to a member of an Indian tribe, including the member's spouse or dependents;[943] (3) accident or health plan coverage (or an arrangement having the same effect) provided by an Indian tribe or tribal organization for medical care to a member of an Indian tribe, including the member's spouse or dependents; and (4) any other medical care provided by an Indian tribe or tribal organization that supplements, replaces, or substitutes for the programs and services provided by the Federal government to Indian tribes or Indians.

This provision does not apply to any amount which is deducted or excluded from gross income under another provision of the Code.

No change made by the provision is intended to create an inference with respect to the exclusion from gross income of benefits provided prior to the date of enactment (March 23, 2010). Additionally, no inference is intended with respect to the tax treatment of other benefits provided by an Indian tribe or tribal organization not covered by this provision.

### *Effective Date*

The provision applies to benefits and coverage provided after the date of enactment (March 23, 2010).

## S. Establishment of SIMPLE Cafeteria Plans for Small Businesses (sec. 9022 of the Act and sec. 125 of the Code)

### *Present Law*

#### *Definition of a cafeteria plan*

If an employee receives a qualified benefit (as defined below) based on the employee's election between the qualified benefit and a taxable benefit under a cafeteria plan, the qualified benefit generally is not includable in gross income.[944] However, if a plan offering an employee an election between taxable benefits (including cash) and nontaxable qualified benefits does not meet the requirements for being a cafeteria plan, the election between taxable and nontaxable benefits results in gross income to the employee, re-

---

[942] The term "Indian tribe" means any Indian tribe, band, nation, pueblo, or other organized group or community, including any Alaska Native village, or regional or village corporation, as defined by, or established pursuant to, the Alaska Native Claims Settlement Act (43 U.S.C. 1601 et seq.), which is recognized as eligible for the special programs and services provided by the United States to Indians because of their status as Indians. The term "tribal organization" has the same meaning as such term in section 4(l) of the Indian Self-Determination and Education Assistance Act (25 U.S.C. 450b(1)).

[943] The terms "accident or health insurance" and "accident or health plan" have the same meaning as when used in section 105. The term "medical care" is the same as the definition under section 213. For purposes of the provision, dependents are determined under section 152, but without regard to subsections (b)(1), (b)(2), and (d)(1)(B). Section 152(b)(1) generally provides that if an individual is a dependent of another taxpayer during a taxable year such individual is treated as having no dependents for such taxable year. Section 152(b)(2) provides that a married individual filing a joint return with his or her spouse is not treated as a dependent of a taxpayer. Section 152(d)(1)(B) provides that a "qualifying relative" (i.e., a relative that qualifies as a dependent) does not include a person whose gross income for the calendar year in which the taxable year begins equals or exceeds the exempt amount (as defined under section 151).

[944] Sec. 125(a).

gardless of what benefit is elected and when the election is made.[945] A cafeteria plan is a separate written plan under which all participants are employees, and participants are permitted to choose among at least one permitted taxable benefit (for example, current cash compensation) and at least one qualified benefit. Finally, a cafeteria plan must not provide for deferral of compensation, except as specifically permitted in sections 125(d)(2)(B), (C), or (D).

### *Qualified benefits*

Qualified benefits under a cafeteria plan are generally employer-provided benefits that are not includable in gross income under an express provision of the Code. Examples of qualified benefits include employer-provided health insurance coverage, group term life insurance coverage not in excess of $50,000, and benefits under a dependent care assistance program. In order to be excludable, any qualified benefit elected under a cafeteria plan must independently satisfy any requirements under the Code section that provides the exclusion. However, some employer-provided benefits that are not includable in gross income under an express provision of the Code are explicitly not allowed in a cafeteria plan. These benefits are generally referred to as nonqualified benefits. Examples of nonqualified benefits include scholarships;[946] employer-provided meals and lodging;[947] educational assistance;[948] and fringe benefits.[949] A plan offering any nonqualified benefit is not a cafeteria plan.[950]

### *Employer contributions through salary reduction*

Employees electing a qualified benefit through salary reduction are electing to forego salary and instead to receive a benefit that is excludible from gross income because it is provided by employer contributions. Section 125 provides that the employee is treated as receiving the qualified benefit from the employer in lieu of the taxable benefit. For example, active employees participating in a cafeteria plan may be able to pay their share of premiums for employer-provided health insurance on a pre-tax basis through salary reduction.[951]

### *Nondiscrimination requirements*

Cafeteria plans and certain qualified benefits (including group term life insurance, self-insured medical reimbursement plans, and dependent care assistance programs) are subject to nondiscrimination requirements to prevent discrimination in favor of highly compensated individuals generally as to eligibility for benefits and as to actual contributions and benefits provided. There are also rules to prevent the provision of disproportionate benefits to key employees (within the meaning of section 416(i)) through a cafeteria

[945] Prop. Treas. Reg. sec. 1.125–1(b).
[946] Sec. 117.
[947] Sec. 119.
[948] Sec. 127.
[949] Sec. 132.
[950] Prop. Treas. Reg. sec. 1.125–1(q). Long-term care services, contributions to Archer Medical Savings Accounts, group term life insurance for an employee's spouse, child or dependent, and elective deferrals to section 403(b) plans are also nonqualified benefits.
[951] Sec. 125.

plan.[952] Although the basic purpose of each of the nondiscrimination rules is the same, the specific rules for satisfying the relevant nondiscrimination requirements, including the definition of highly compensated individual,[953] vary for cafeteria plans generally and for each qualified benefit. An employer maintaining a cafeteria plan in which any highly compensated individual participates must make sure that both the cafeteria plan and each qualified benefit satisfies the relevant nondiscrimination requirements, as a failure to satisfy the nondiscrimination rules generally results in a loss of the tax exclusion by the highly compensated individuals.

### *Explanation of Provision*

Under the provision, an eligible small employer is provided with a safe harbor from the nondiscrimination requirements for cafeteria plans as well as from the nondiscrimination requirements for specified qualified benefits offered under a cafeteria plan, including group term life insurance, benefits under a self insured medical expense reimbursement plan, and benefits under a dependent care assistance program. Under the safe harbor, a cafeteria plan and the specified qualified benefits are treated as meeting the specified nondiscrimination rules if the cafeteria plan satisfies minimum eligibility and participation requirements and minimum contribution requirements.

#### *Eligibility requirement*

The eligibility requirement is met only if all employees (other than excludable employees) are eligible to participate, and each employee eligible to participate is able to elect any benefit available under the plan (subject to the terms and conditions applicable to all participants). However, a cafeteria plan will not fail to satisfy this eligibility requirement merely because the plan excludes employees who (1) have not attained the age of 21 (or a younger age provided in the plan) before the close of a plan year, (2) have fewer than 1,000 hours of service for the preceding plan year, (3) have not completed one year of service with the employer as of any day during the plan year, (4) are covered under an agreement that the Secretary of Labor finds to be a collective bargaining agreement if there is evidence that the benefits covered under the cafeteria plan were the subject of good faith bargaining between employee rep-

---

[952] A key employee generally is an employee who, at any time during the year is (1) a five-percent owner of the employer, or (2) a one-percent owner with compensation of more than $150,000 (not indexed for inflation), or (3) an officer with compensation more than $160,000 (for 2010). A special rule limits the number of officers treated as key employees. If the employer is a corporation, a five-percent owner is a person who owns more than five percent of the outstanding stock or stock possessing more than five percent of the total combined voting power of all stock. If the employer is not a corporation, a five-percent owner is a person who owns more than five percent of the capital or profits interest. A one-percent owner is determined by substituting one percent for five percent in the preceding definitions. For purposes of determining employee ownership in the employer, certain attribution rules apply.

[953] For cafeteria plan purposes, a "highly compensated individual" is (1) an officer, (2) a five-percent shareholder, (3) an individual who is highly compensated, or (4) the spouse or dependent of any of the preceding categories. A "highly compensated participant" is a participant who falls in any of those categories. "Highly compensated" is not defined for this purpose. Under section 105(h), a self-insured medical expense reimbursement plan must not discriminate in favor of a "highly compensated individual," defined as (1) one of the five highest paid officers, (2) a 10–percent shareholder, or (3) an individual among the highest paid 25 percent of all employees. Under section 129 for a dependent care assistance program, eligibility for benefits, and the benefits and contributions provided, generally must not discriminate in favor of highly compensated employees within the meaning of section 414(q).

resentatives and the employer, or (5) are described in section 410(b)(3)(C) (relating to nonresident aliens working outside the United States). An employer may have a shorter age and service requirement but only if such shorter service or younger age applies to all employees.

***Minimum contribution requirement***

The minimum contribution requirement is met if the employer provides a minimum contribution for each nonhighly compensated employee (employee who is not a highly compensated employee[954] or a key employee (within the meaning of section 416(i))) in addition to any salary reduction contributions made by the employee. The minimum must be available for application toward the cost of any qualified benefit (other than a taxable benefit) offered under the plan. The minimum contribution is permitted to be calculated under either the nonelective contribution method or the matching contribution method, but the same method must be used for calculating the minimum contribution for all nonhighly compensated employees. The minimum contribution under the nonelective contribution method is an amount equal to a uniform percentage (not less than two percent) of each eligible employee's compensation for the plan year, determined without regard to whether the employees makes any salary reduction contribution under the cafeteria plan. The minimum matching contribution is the lesser of 100 percent of the amount of the salary reduction contribution elected to be made by the employee for the plan year or six percent of the employee's compensation for the plan year. Compensation for purposes of this minimum contribution requirement is compensation with the meaning of section 414(s).

A simple cafeteria plan is permitted to provide for the matching contributions in addition to the minimum required but only if matching contributions with respect to salary reduction contributions for any highly compensated employee or key employee are not made at a greater rate than the matching contributions for any nonhighly compensated employee. Nothing in this provision prohibits an employer from making contributions to provide qualified benefits under the plan in addition to the required contributions.

***Eligible employer***

An eligible small employer under the provision is, with respect to any year, an employer who employed an average of 100 or fewer employees on business days during either of the two preceding years. For purposes of the provision, a year may only be taken into account if the employer was in existence throughout the year. If an employer was not in existence throughout the preceding year, the determination is based on the average number of employees that it is reasonably expected such employer will employ on business days in the current year. If an employer was an eligible employer for any year and maintained a simple cafeteria plan for its employ-

[954] Section 414(q) generally defines a highly compensated employee as an employee (1) who was a five-percent owner during the year or the preceding year, or (2) who had compensation of $110,000 (for 2010) or more for the preceding year. An employer may elect to limit the employees treated as highly compensated employees based upon their compensation in the preceding year to the highest paid 20 percent of employees in the preceding year. Five-percent owner is defined by cross-reference to the definition of key employee in section 416(i).

ees for such year, then, for each subsequent year during which the employer continues, without interruption, to maintain the cafeteria plan, the employer is deemed to be an eligible small employer until the employer employs an average of 200 or more employees on business days during any year preceding any such subsequent year.

The determination of whether an employer is an eligible small employer is determined by applying the controlled group rules of sections 52(a) and (b) under which all members of the controlled group are treated as a single employer. In addition, the definition of employee includes leased employees within the meaning of sections 414(n) and (o).[955]

### *Effective Date*

The provision is effective for taxable years beginning after December 31, 2010.

## T. Investment Credit for Qualifying Therapeutic Discovery Projects (sec. 9023 of the Act and new sec. 48D of the Code)

### *Present Law*

Present law provides for a research credit equal to 20 percent (14 percent in the case of the alternative simplified credit) of the amount by which the taxpayer's qualified research expenses for a taxable year exceed its base amount for that year.[956] Thus, the research credit is generally available with respect to incremental increases in qualified research.

A 20-percent research tax credit is also available with respect to the excess of (1) 100 percent of corporate cash expenses (including grants or contributions) paid for basic research conducted by universities (and certain nonprofit scientific research organizations) over (2) the sum of (a) the greater of two minimum basic research floors plus (b) an amount reflecting any decrease in nonresearch giving to universities by the corporation as compared to such giving during a fixed-base period, as adjusted for inflation. This separate credit computation is commonly referred to as the "university basic research credit."[957]

Finally, a research credit is available for a taxpayer's expenditures on research undertaken by an energy research consortium. This separate credit computation is commonly referred to as the "energy research credit." Unlike the other research credits, the energy research credit applies to all qualified expenditures, not just those in excess of a base amount.

---

[955] Section 52(b) provides that, for specified purposes, all employees of all corporations which are members of a controlled group of corporations are treated as employed by a single employer. However, section 52(b) provides certain modifications to the control group rules including substituting 50 percent ownership for 80 percent ownership as the measure of control. There is a similar rule in section 52(c) under which all employees of trades or businesses (whether or not incorporated) which are under common control are treated under regulations as employed by a single employer. Section 414(n) provides rules for specified purposes when leased employees are treated as employed by the service recipient and section 414(o) authorizes the Treasury to issue regulations to prevent avoidance of the requirements of section 414(n).

[956] Sec. 41.

[957] Sec. 41(e).

The research credit, including the university basic research credit and the energy research credit, expired for amounts paid or incurred after December 31, 2009.[958]

Qualified research expenses eligible for the research tax credit consist of: (1) in-house expenses of the taxpayer for wages and supplies attributable to qualified research; (2) certain time-sharing costs for computer use in qualified research; and (3) 65 percent of amounts paid or incurred by the taxpayer to certain other persons for qualified research conducted on the taxpayer's behalf (so-called contract research expenses).[959] Notwithstanding the limitation for contract research expenses, qualified research expenses include 100 percent of amounts paid or incurred by the taxpayer to an eligible small business, university, or Federal laboratory for qualified energy research.

Present law also provides a 50-percent credit[960] for expenses related to human clinical testing of drugs for the treatment of certain rare diseases and conditions, generally those that afflict less than 200,000 persons in the United States. Qualifying expenses are those paid or incurred by the taxpayer after the date on which the drug is designated as a potential treatment for a rare disease or disorder by the Food and Drug Administration ("FDA") in accordance with section 526 of the Federal Food, Drug, and Cosmetic Act.

Present law does not provide a credit specifically designed to encourage investment in new therapies relating to diseases.

## *Explanation of Provision*

### *In general*

The provision establishes a 50-percent nonrefundable investment tax credit for qualified investments in qualifying therapeutic discovery projects. The provision allocates $1 billion during the two-year period 2009 through 2010 for the program. The Secretary, in consultation with the Secretary of HHS, will award certifications for qualified investments. The credit is available only to companies having 250 or fewer employees.[961]

A "qualifying therapeutic discovery project" is a project which is designed to develop a product, process, or therapy to diagnose, treat, or prevent diseases and afflictions by: (1) conducting pre-clinical activities, clinical trials, clinical studies, and research protocols, or (2) by developing technology or products designed to diagnose diseases and conditions, including molecular and companion drugs and diagnostics, or to further the delivery or administration of therapeutics.

---

[958] Sec. 41(h). The research credit, including the university basic research credit and the energy research credit, was extended for two years through 2011, in section 731 of the Tax Relief, Unemployment Insurance Reauthorization, and Job Creation Act of 2010, Pub. L. No. 111–312, described in Part Sixteen of this document.

[959] Under a special rule, 75 percent of amounts paid to a research consortium for qualified research are treated as qualified research expenses eligible for the research credit (rather than 65 percent under the general rule of section 41(b)(3) governing contract research expenses) if (1) such research consortium is a tax-exempt organization that is described in section 501(c)(3) (other than a private foundation) or section 501(c)(6) and is organized and operated primarily to conduct scientific research, and (2) such qualified research is conducted by the consortium on behalf of the taxpayer and one or more persons not related to the taxpayer. Sec. 41(b)(3)(C).

[960] Sec. 45C.

[961] The number of employees is determined taking into account all businesses of the taxpayer at the time it submits an application, and is determined taking into account the rules for determining a single employer under section 52(a) or (b) or section 414(m) or (o).

The qualified investment for any taxable year is the aggregate amount of the costs paid or incurred in such year for expenses necessary for and directly related to the conduct of a qualifying therapeutic discovery project. The qualified investment for any taxable year with respect to any qualifying therapeutic discovery project does not include any cost for: (1) remuneration for an employee described in section 162(m)(3), (2) interest expense, (3) facility maintenance expenses, (4) a service cost identified under Treas. Reg. Sec. 1.263A–1(e)(4), or (5) any other expenditure as determined by the Secretary as appropriate to carry out the purposes of the provision.

Companies must apply to the Secretary to obtain certification for qualifying investments.[962] The Secretary, in determining qualifying projects, will consider only those projects that show reasonable potential to: (1) result in new therapies to treat areas of unmet medical need or to prevent, detect, or treat chronic or acute disease and conditions, (2) reduce long-term health care costs in the United States, or (3) significantly advance the goal of curing cancer within a 30-year period. Additionally, the Secretary will take into consideration which projects have the greatest potential to: (1) create and sustain (directly or indirectly) high quality, high paying jobs in the United States, and (2) advance the United States' competitiveness in the fields of life, biological, and medical sciences.

Qualified therapeutic discovery project expenditures do not qualify for the research credit, orphan drug credit, or bonus depreciation.[963] If a credit is allowed for an expenditure related to property subject to depreciation, the basis of the property is reduced by the amount of the credit. Additionally, expenditures taken into account in determining the credit are nondeductible to the extent of the credit claimed that is attributable to such expenditures.

### *Election to receive grant in lieu of tax credit*

Taxpayers may elect to receive credits that have been allocated to them in the form of Treasury grants equal to 50 percent of the qualifying investment. Any such grant is not includible in the taxpayer's gross income.

In making grants under this section, the Secretary of the Treasury is to apply rules similar to the rules of section 50. In applying such rules, if an investment ceases to be a qualified investment, the Secretary of the Treasury shall provide for the recapture of the appropriate percentage of the grant amount in such manner as the Secretary of the Treasury determines appropriate. The Secretary of the Treasury shall not make any grant under this section to: (1) any Federal, State, or local government (or any political subdivision, agency, or instrumentality thereof), (2) any organization described in section 501(c) and exempt from tax under section 501(a), (3) any entity referred to in paragraph (4) of section 54(j), or (4) any partnership or other pass-thru entity any partner (or other

[962] The Secretary must take action to approve or deny an application within 30 days of the submission of such application.

[963] Any expenses for the taxable year that are qualified research expenses under section 41(b) are taken into account in determining base period research expenses for purposes of computing the research credit under section 41 for subsequent taxable years.

holder of an equity or profits interest) of which is described in paragraph (1), (2), or (3).

### *Effective Date*

The provision applies to expenditures paid or incurred after December 31, 2008, in taxable years beginning after December 31, 2008.

# TITLE X—STRENGTHENING QUALITY, AFFORDABLE HEALTH CARE FOR ALL AMERICANS

## A. Study of Geographic Variation in Application of FPL (sec. 10105 of the Act)

### *Present Law*

No provision.

### *Explanation of Provision*

The Secretary of HHS is instructed to conduct a study on the feasibility and implication of adjusting the application of the FPL under the provisions enacted in the Act for different geographical areas so as to reflect disparities in the cost of living among different areas in the United States, including the territories. If the Secretary deems such an adjustment feasible, then the study should include a methodology for implementing the adjustment. The Secretary is required to report the results of the study to Congress no later than January 1, 2013. The provision requires that special attention be paid to the impact of disparities between the poverty levels and the cost of living in the territories and the impact of this disparity on the expansion of health coverage in the territories. The territories are the Commonwealth of Puerto Rico, the U.S. Virgin Islands, Guam, the Commonwealth of the Northern Mariana Islands, American Samoa, and any other territory or possession of the United States.

### *Effective Date*

The provision is effective on the date of enactment (March 23, 2010).

## B. Free Choice Vouchers (sec. 10108 of the Act and sec. 139D of the Code)

### *Present Law*

No provision.

### *Explanation of Provision*

#### *Provision of vouchers*

Employers offering minimum essential coverage through an eligible employer-sponsored plan and paying a portion of that coverage must provide qualified employees with a voucher whose value can be applied to purchase of a health plan through the Exchange. Qualified employees are employees whose required contribution for employer sponsored minimum essential coverage exceeds eight percent, but does not exceed 9.8 percent of the employee's household income for the taxable year and the employee's total household income does not exceed 400 percent of the poverty line for the family. In addition, the employee must not participate in the employer's health plan.

The value of the voucher is equal to the dollar value of the employer contribution to the employer offered health plan. If multiple plans are offered by the employer, the value of the voucher is the dollar amount that would be paid if the employee chose the plan for which the employer would pay the largest percentage of the premium cost.[964] The value of the voucher is for self-only coverage unless the individual purchases family coverage in the Exchange. Under the provision, for purposes of calculating the dollar value of the employer contribution, the premium for any health plan is determined under rules similar to the rules of section 2204 of PHSA, except that the amount is adjusted for age and category of enrollment in accordance with regulations established by the Secretary.

In the case of years after 2014, the eight percent and the 9.8 percent are indexed to the excess of premium growth over income growth for the preceding calendar year.

### *Use of vouchers*

Vouchers can be used in the Exchange towards the monthly premium of any qualified health plan in the Exchange. The value of the voucher to the extent it is used for the purchase of a health plan is not includable in gross income. If the value of the voucher exceeds the premium of the health plan chosen by the employee, the employee is paid the excess value of the voucher. The excess amount received by the employee is includible in the employee's gross income.

If an individual receives a voucher, the individual is disqualified from receiving any tax credit or cost sharing credit for the purchase of a plan in the Exchange. Similarly, if any employee receives a free choice voucher, the employer is not be assessed a shared responsibility payment on behalf of that employee.[965]

### *Definition of terms*

The terms used for this provision have the same meaning as any term used in the provision for the requirement to maintain minimum essential coverage (section 1501 of the Act and new section 5000A). Thus for example, the terms "household income," "poverty line," "required contribution," and "eligible employer-sponsored plan" have the same meaning for both provisions. Thus, the re-

[964] For example, if an employer offering the same plans for $200 and $300 offers a flat $180 contribution for all plans, a contribution of 90 percent for the $200 plan and a contribution of 60 percent for the $300 plan, and the value of the voucher would equal the value of the contribution to the $200 since it received a 90 percent contribution, a value of $180. However, if the firm offers a $150 contribution to the $200 plan (75 percent) and a $200 contribution to the $300 plan (67 percent), the value of the voucher is based on the plan receiving the greater percentage paid by the employer and would be $150. If a firm offers health plans with monthly premiums of $200 and $300 and provides a payment of 60 percent of any plan purchased, the value of the voucher will be 60 percent the higher premium plan, in this case, 60 percent of $300 or $180.

[965] Section 1513 of the Patient Protection and Affordable Care Act, Pub. L. No. 111–148, and new Code section 4980H.

quired contribution includes the amount of any salary reduction contribution.

### *Effective Date*

The provision is effective after December 31, 2013.

## C. Exclusion for Assistance Provided to Participants in State Student Loan Repayment Programs for Certain Health Professionals (sec. 10908 of the Act and sec. 108(f)(4) of the Code)

### *Present Law*

Gross income generally includes the discharge of indebtedness of the taxpayer. Under an exception to this general rule, gross income does not include any amount from the forgiveness (in whole or in part) of certain student loans, provided that the forgiveness is contingent on the student's working for a certain period of time in certain professions for any of a broad class of employers.

Student loans eligible for this special rule must be made to an individual to assist the individual in attending an educational institution that normally maintains a regular faculty and curriculum and normally has a regularly enrolled body of students in attendance at the place where its education activities are regularly carried on. Loan proceeds may be used not only for tuition and required fees, but also to cover room and board expenses. The loan must be made by (1) the United States (or an instrumentality or agency thereof), (2) a State (or any political subdivision thereof), (3) certain tax-exempt public benefit corporations that control a State, county, or municipal hospital and whose employees have been deemed to be public employees under State law, or (4) an educational organization that originally received the funds from which the loan was made from the United States, a State, or a tax-exempt public benefit corporation.

In addition, an individual's gross income does not include amounts from the forgiveness of loans made by educational organizations (and certain tax-exempt organizations in the case of refinancing loans) out of private, nongovernmental funds if the proceeds of such loans are used to pay costs of attendance at an educational institution or to refinance any outstanding student loans (not just loans made by educational organizations) and the student is not employed by the lender organization. In the case of such loans made or refinanced by educational organizations (or refinancing loans made by certain tax-exempt organizations), cancellation of the student loan must be contingent upon the student working in an occupation or area with unmet needs, and such work must be performed for, or under the direction of, a tax-exempt charitable organization or a governmental entity.

Finally, an individual's gross income does not include any loan repayment amount received under the National Health Service Corps loan repayment program or certain State loan repayment programs.

### *Explanation of Provision*

The provision modifies the gross income exclusion for amounts received under the National Health Service Corps loan repayment program or certain State loan repayment programs to include any amount received by an individual under any State loan repayment or loan forgiveness program that is intended to provide for the increased availability of health care services in underserved or health professional shortage areas (as determined by the State).

### *Effective Date*

The provision is effective for amounts received by an individual in taxable years beginning after December 31, 2008.

## D. Expansion of Adoption Credit and the Exclusion from Gross Income for Employer-Provided Adoption Assistance (sec. 10909 of the Act and secs. 23 and 137 of the Code)

### *Present Law*

#### *Tax credit*

*Non-special needs adoptions*

Generally a nonrefundable tax credit is allowed for qualified adoption expenses paid or incurred by a taxpayer subject to the maximum credit. The maximum credit is $12,170 per eligible child for taxable years beginning in 2010. An eligible child is an individual who: (1) has not attained age 18; or (2) is physically or mentally incapable of caring for himself or herself. The maximum credit is applied per child rather than per year. Therefore, while qualified adoption expenses may be incurred in one or more taxable years, the tax credit per adoption of an eligible child may not exceed the maximum credit.

*Special needs adoptions*

In the case of a special needs adoption finalized during a taxable year, the taxpayer may claim as an adoption credit the amount of the maximum credit minus the aggregate qualified adoption expenses with respect to that adoption for all prior taxable years. A special needs child is an eligible child who is a citizen or resident of the United States whom a State has determined: (1) cannot or should not be returned to the home of the birth parents; and (2) has a specific factor or condition (such as the child's ethnic background, age, or membership in a minority or sibling group, or the presence of factors such as medical conditions, or physical, mental, or emotional handicaps) because of which the child cannot be placed with adoptive parents without adoption assistance.

*Qualified adoption expenses*

Qualified adoption expenses are reasonable and necessary adoption fees, court costs, attorneys fees, and other expenses that are: (1) directly related to, and the principal purpose of which is for, the legal adoption of an eligible child by the taxpayer; (2) not incurred in violation of State or Federal law, or in carrying out any surrogate parenting arrangement; (3) not for the adoption of the child of the taxpayer's spouse; and (4) not reimbursed (e.g., by an employer).

*Phase-out for higher-income individuals*

The adoption credit is phased out ratably for taxpayers with modified adjusted gross income between $182,520 and $222,520 for taxable years beginning in 2010. Under present law, modified adjusted gross income is the sum of the taxpayer's adjusted gross income plus amounts excluded from income under sections 911, 931, and 933 (relating to the exclusion of income of U.S. citizens or residents living abroad; residents of Guam, American Samoa, and the Northern Mariana Islands; and residents of Puerto Rico, respectively).

*EGTRRA sunset*[966]

For taxable years after 2010, the adoption credit will be reduced to a maximum credit of $6,000 for special needs adoptions and no tax credit for non-special needs adoptions. Also, the credit phase-out range will revert to the pre-EGTRRA levels (i.e., a ratable phase-out between modified adjusted gross income between $75,000 and $115,000). Finally, the adoption credit will be allowed only to the extent the individual's regular income tax liability exceeds the individual's tentative minimum tax, determined without regard to the minimum foreign tax credit.

***Exclusion for employer-provided adoption assistance***

An exclusion from the gross income of an employee is allowed for qualified adoption expenses paid or reimbursed by an employer under an adoption assistance program. For 2010, the maximum exclusion is $12,170. Also for 2010, the exclusion is phased out ratably for taxpayers with modified adjusted gross income between $182,520 and $222,520. Modified adjusted gross income is the sum of the taxpayer's adjusted gross income plus amounts excluded from income under Code sections 911, 931, and 933 (relating to the exclusion of income of U.S. citizens or residents living abroad; residents of Guam, American Samoa, and the Northern Mariana Islands; and residents of Puerto Rico, respectively). For purposes of this exclusion, modified adjusted gross income also includes all employer payments and reimbursements for adoption expenses whether or not they are taxable to the employee.

Adoption expenses paid or reimbursed by the employer under an adoption assistance program are not eligible for the adoption credit. A taxpayer may be eligible for the adoption credit (with respect to qualified adoption expenses he or she incurs) and also for the exclusion (with respect to different qualified adoption expenses paid or reimbursed by his or her employer).

Because of the EGTRRA sunset, the exclusion for employer-provided adoption assistance does not apply to amounts paid or incurred after December 31, 2010.

---

[966] "EGTRRA" refers to the Economic Growth and Tax Relief Reconciliation Act of 2001, Pub. L. No. 107–16.

### *Explanation of Provision*

#### *Tax credit*

For 2010, the maximum credit is increased to $13,170 per eligible child (a $1,000 increase). This increase applies to both non-special needs adoptions and special needs adoptions. Also, the adoption credit is made refundable.

The new dollar limit and phase-out of the adoption credit are adjusted for inflation in taxable years beginning after December 31, 2010.

The EGTRRA sunset is delayed for one year (i.e., the sunset becomes effective for taxable years beginning after December 31, 2011).

#### *Adoption assistance program*

The maximum exclusion is increased to $13,170 per eligible child (a $1,000 increase).

The new dollar limit and income limitations of the employer-provided adoption assistance exclusion are adjusted for inflation in taxable years beginning after December 31, 2010.

The EGTRRA sunset is delayed for one year (i.e., the sunset becomes effective for taxable years beginning after December 31, 2011).[967]

### *Effective Date*

The provisions generally are effective for taxable years beginning after December 31, 2009.

## HEALTH CARE AND EDUCATION RECONCILIATION ACT OF 2010

## A. Adult Dependents (sec. 1004 of the Act and secs. 105, 162, 401, and 501 of the Code)

### *Present Law*

#### *Definition of dependent for exclusion for employer-provided health coverage*

The Code generally provides that employees are not taxed on (that is, may "exclude" from gross income) the value of employer-provided health coverage under an accident or health plan.[968] This exclusion applies to coverage for personal injuries or sickness for employees (including retirees), their spouses and their dependents.[969] In addition, any reimbursements under an accident or health plan for medical care expenses for employees (including retirees), their spouses, and their dependents (as defined in section 152) generally are excluded from gross income.[970] Section 152 defines a dependent as a qualifying child or qualifying relative.

---

[967] Section 101(b) of the Tax Relief, Unemployment Insurance Reauthorization, and Job Creation Act of 2010 terminated the amendments made by this provision for taxable years beginning after December 31, 2011, without regard to the EGTRRA sunset.

[968] Sec 106.

[969] Treas. Reg. sec. 1.106–1.

[970] Sec. 105(b).

Under section 152(c), a child generally is a qualifying child of a taxpayer if the child satisfies each of five tests for the taxable year: (1) the child has the same principal place of abode as the taxpayer for more than one-half of the taxable year; (2) the child has a specified relationship to the taxpayer; (3) the child has not yet attained a specified age; (4) the child has not provided over one-half of their own support for the calendar year in which the taxable year of the taxpayer begins; and (5) the qualifying child has not filed a joint return (other than for a claim of refund) with their spouse for the taxable year beginning in the calendar year in which the taxable year of the taxpayer begins. A tie-breaking rule applies if more than one taxpayer claims a child as a qualifying child. The specified relationship is that the child is the taxpayer's son, daughter, stepson, stepdaughter, brother, sister, stepbrother, stepsister, or a descendant of any such individual. With respect to the specified age, a child must be under age 19 (or under age 24 in the case of a full-time student). However, no age limit applies with respect to individuals who are totally and permanently disabled within the meaning of section 22(e)(3) at any time during the calendar year. Other rules may apply.

Under section 152(d), a qualifying relative means an individual that satisfies four tests for the taxable year: (1) the individual bears a specified relationship to the taxpayer; (2) the individual's gross income for the calendar year in which such taxable year begins is less than the exemption amount under section 151(d); (3) the taxpayer provides more than one-half the individual's support for the calendar year in which the taxable year begins; and (4) the individual is not a qualifying child of the taxpayer or any other taxpayer for any taxable year beginning in the calendar year in which such taxable year begins. The specified relationship test for qualifying relative is satisfied if that individual is the taxpayer's: (1) child or descendant of a child; (2) brother, sister, stepbrother or stepsister; (3) father, mother or ancestor of either; (4) stepfather or stepmother; (5) niece or nephew; (6) aunt or uncle; (7) in-law; or (8) certain other individuals, who for the taxable year of the taxpayer, have the same principal place of abode as the taxpayer and are members of the taxpayer's household.[971]

Employers may agree to reimburse medical expenses of their employees (and their spouses and dependents), not covered by a health insurance plan, through flexible spending arrangements which allow reimbursement not in excess of a specified dollar amount (either elected by an employee under a cafeteria plan or otherwise specified by the employer). Reimbursements under these arrangements are also excludible from gross income as employer-provided health coverage. The same definition of dependents applies for purposes of flexible spending arrangements.

### *Deduction for health insurance premiums of self-employed individuals*

Under present law, self-employed individuals may deduct the cost of health insurance for themselves and their spouses and de-

[971] Generally, same-sex partners do not qualify as dependents under section 152. In addition, same-sex partners are not recognized as spouses for purposes of the Code. The Defense of Marriage Act, Pub. L. No. 104–199.

pendents. The deduction is not available for any month in which the self-employed individual is eligible to participate in an employer-subsidized health plan. Moreover, the deduction may not exceed the individual's self-employment income. The deduction applies only to the cost of insurance (i.e., it does not apply to out-of-pocket expenses that are not reimbursed by insurance). The deduction does not apply for self-employment tax purposes. For purposes of the deduction, a more than two percent shareholder-employee of an S corporation is treated the same as a self-employed individual. Thus, the exclusion for employer-provided health care coverage does not apply to such individuals, but they are entitled to the deduction for health insurance costs as if they were self-employed.

***Voluntary Employees' Beneficiary Associations***

A VEBA is a tax-exempt entity that is a part of a plan for providing life, sick or accident benefits to its members or their dependents or designated beneficiaries.[972] No part of the net earnings of the association inures (other than through the payment of life, sick, accident or other benefits) to the benefit of any private shareholder or individual. A VEBA may be funded with employer contributions or employee contributions or a combination of employer contributions and employee contributions. The same definition of dependent applies for purposes of receipt of medical benefits through a VEBA.

***Qualified plans providing retiree health benefits***

A qualified pension or annuity plan can establish and maintain a separate account to provide for the payment of sickness, accident, hospitalization, and medical expenses for retired employees, their spouses and their dependents ("401(h) account"). An employer's contributions to a 401(h) account must be reasonable and ascertainable, and retiree health benefits must be subordinate to the retirement benefits provided by the plan. In addition, it must be impossible, at any time prior to the satisfaction of all retiree health liabilities under the plan, for any part of the corpus or income of the 401(h) account to be (within the taxable year or thereafter) used for, or diverted to, any purpose other than providing retiree health benefits and, upon satisfaction of all retiree health liabilities, the plan must provide that any amount remaining in the 401(h) account be returned to the employer.

### ***Explanation of Provision***

The provision amends section 105(b) to extend the general exclusion for reimbursements for medical care expenses under an employer-provided accident or health plan to any child of an employee who has not attained age 27 as of the end of the taxable year. This change is also intended to apply to the exclusion for employer-proved coverage under an accident or health plan for injuries or sickness for such a child. A parallel change is made for VEBAs and 401(h) accounts.

The provision similarly amends section 162(l) to permit self-employed individuals to take a deduction for the cost of health insur-

[972] Secs. 419(e) and 501(c)(9).

ance for any child of the taxpayer who has not attained age 27 as of the end of the taxable year.

For purposes of the provision, "child" means an individual who is a son, daughter, stepson, stepdaughter or eligible foster child of the taxpayer.[973] An eligible foster child means an individual who is placed with the taxpayer by an authorized placement agency or by judgment, decree, or other order of any court of competent jurisdiction.

### *Effective Date*

The provision is effective as of the date of enactment (March 30, 2010).

## B. Unearned Income Medicare Contribution (sec. 1402 of the Act and new sec. 1411 of the Code)

### *Present Law*

Social Security benefits and certain Medicare benefits are financed primarily by payroll taxes on covered wages. FICA imposes tax on employers based on the amount of wages paid to an employee during the year. The tax imposed is composed of two parts: (1) the OASDI tax equal to 6.2 percent of covered wages up to the taxable wage base ($106,800 in 2010); and (2) the Medicare hospital insurance ("HI") tax amount equal to 1.45 percent of covered wages. In addition to the tax on employers, each employee is subject to FICA taxes equal to the amount of tax imposed on the employer. The employee level tax generally must be withheld and remitted to the Federal government by the employer.

As a parallel to FICA taxes, SECA imposes taxes on the net income from self-employment of self-employed individuals. The rate of the OASDI portion of SECA taxes is equal to the combined employee and employer OASDI FICA tax rates and applies to self-employment income up to the FICA taxable wage base. Similarly, the rate of the HI portion is the same as the combined employer and employee HI rates and there is no cap on the amount of self-employment income to which the rate applies.[974]

### *Explanation of Provision*

#### *In general*

In the case of an individual, estate, or trust an unearned income Medicare contribution tax is imposed. No provision is made for the transfer of the tax imposed by this provision from the General Fund of the United States Treasury to any Trust Fund.

---

[973] Sec. 152(f)(1). Under section 152(f)(1), a legally adopted child of the taxpayer or an individual who is lawfully placed with the taxpayer for legal adoption by the taxpayer is treated as a child of the taxpayer by blood.

[974] For purposes of computing net earnings from self employment, taxpayers are permitted a deduction equal to the product of the taxpayer's earnings (determined without regard to this deduction) and one-half of the sum of the rates for OASDI tax (12.4 percent) and HI tax (2.9 percent), i.e., 7.65 percent of net earnings. This deduction reflects the fact that the FICA rates apply to an employee's wages, which do not include FICA taxes paid by the employer, whereas the self-employed individual's net earnings are economically equivalent to an employee's wages plus the employer share of FICA taxes.

In the case of an individual, the tax is 3.8 percent of the lesser of net investment income or the excess of modified adjusted gross income over the threshold amount.

The threshold amount is $250,000 in the case of a joint return or surviving spouse, $125,000 in the case of a married individual filing a separate return, and $200,000 in any other case.

Modified adjusted gross income is adjusted gross income increased by the amount excluded from income as foreign earned income under section 911(a)(1) (net of the deductions and exclusions disallowed with respect to the foreign earned income).

In the case of an estate or trust, the tax is 3.8 percent of the lesser of undistributed net investment income or the excess of adjusted gross income (as defined in section 67(e)) over the dollar amount at which the highest income tax bracket applicable to an estate or trust begins.

The tax does not apply to a non-resident alien or to a trust all the unexpired interests in which are devoted to charitable purposes. The tax also does not apply to a trust that is exempt from tax under section 501 or a charitable remainder trust exempt from tax under section 664.

The tax is subject to the individual estimated tax provisions. The tax is not deductible in computing any tax imposed by subtitle A of the Internal Revenue Code (relating to income taxes).

### *Net investment income*

Net investment income is investment income reduced by the deductions properly allocable to such income.

Investment income is the sum of (i) gross income from interest, dividends, annuities, royalties, and rents (other than income derived in the ordinary course of any trade or business to which the tax does not apply), (ii) other gross income derived from any trade or business to which the tax applies, and (iii) net gain (to the extent taken into account in computing taxable income) attributable to the disposition of property other than property held in a trade or business to which the tax does not apply.[975]

In the case of a trade or business, the tax applies if the trade or business is a passive activity with respect to the taxpayer or the trade or business consists of trading financial instruments or commodities (as defined in section 475(e)(2)). The tax does not apply to other trades or businesses.

In the case of the disposition of a partnership interest or stock in an S corporation, gain or loss is taken into account only to the extent gain or loss would be taken into account by the partner or shareholder if the entity had sold all its properties for fair market value immediately before the disposition. Thus, only net gain or loss attributable to property held by the entity which is not property attributable to an active trade or business is taken into account.[976]

---

[975] Gross income does not include items, such as interest on tax-exempt bonds, veterans' benefits, and excluded gain from the sale of a principal residence, which are excluded from gross income under the income tax.

[976] For this purpose, a business of trading financial instruments or commodities is not treated as an active trade or business.

Income, gain, or loss on working capital is not treated as derived from a trade or business. Investment income does not include distributions from a qualified retirement plan or amounts subject to SECA tax.

### *Effective Date*

The provision applies to taxable years beginning after December 31, 2012.

## C. Excise Tax on Medical Device Manufacturers[977] (sec. 1405 of the Act and new sec. 4191 of the Code)

### *Present Law*

Chapter 32 imposes excise taxes on sales by manufacturers of certain products. Terms and procedures related to the imposition, payment, and reporting of these excise taxes are included in various provisions within the Code.

Certain sales are exempt from the excise tax imposed on manufacturers. Exempt sales include sales (1) for use by the purchaser for further manufacture, or for resale to a second purchaser in further manufacture, (2) for export or for resale to a second purchaser for export, (3) for use by the purchaser as supplies for vessels or aircraft, (4) to a State or local government for the exclusive use of a State or local government, (5) to a nonprofit educational organization for its exclusive use, or (6) to a qualified blood collector organization for such organization's exclusive use in the collection, storage, or transportation of blood.[978] If an article is sold free of tax for resale to a second purchaser for further manufacture or for export, the exemption will not apply unless, within the six-month period beginning on the date of sale by the manufacturer, the manufacturer receives proof that the article has been exported or resold for the use in further manufacturing.[979] In general, the exemptions will not apply unless the manufacturer, the first purchaser, and the second purchaser are registered with the Secretary of the Treasury.

The lease of an article is generally considered to be a sale of such article.[980] Special rules apply for the imposition of tax to each lease payment. Rules are also imposed that treat the use of articles subject to tax by manufacturers, producers, or importers of such articles, as sales for the purpose of imposition of certain excise taxes.[981]

There are also rules for determining the price of an article on which excise tax is imposed.[982] These rules provide for: (1) the inclusion of containers, packaging, and certain transportation charges in the price, (2) determining a constructive sales price if an article is sold for less than the fair market price, and (3) deter-

[977] The excise tax on medical devices as imposed by this provision replaces the annual fee on medical device manufacturers and importers under section 9009 of the Patient Protection and Affordable Care Act.

[978] Sec. 4221(a).

[979] Sec. 4221(b).

[980] Sec. 4217(a).

[981] Sec. 4218.

[982] Sec. 4216.

mining the tax due in the case of partial payments or installment sales.

A credit or refund is generally allowed for overpayments of manufacturers excise taxes.[983] Overpayments may occur when tax-paid articles are sold for export and for certain specified uses and resales, when there are price adjustments, and where tax paid articles are subject to further manufacture. Generally, no credit or refund of any overpayment of tax is allowed or made unless the person who paid the tax establishes one of four prerequisites: (1) the tax was not included in the price of the article or otherwise collected from the person who purchased the article; (2) the tax was repaid to the ultimate purchaser of the article; (3) for overpayments due to specified uses and resales, the tax has been repaid to the ultimate vendor or the person has obtained the written consent of such ultimate vendor; or (4) the person has filed with the Secretary of the Treasury the written consent of the ultimate purchaser of the article to the allowance of the credit or making of the refund.[984]

### *Explanation of Provision*

Under the provision, a tax equal to 2.3 percent of the sale price is imposed on the sale of any taxable medical device by the manufacturer, producer, or importer of such device. A taxable medical device is any device, defined in section 201(h) of the Federal Food, Drug, and Cosmetic Act,[985] intended for humans. The excise tax does not apply to eyeglasses, contact lenses, hearing aids, and any other medical device determined by the Secretary to be of a type that is generally purchased by the general public at retail for individual use. The Secretary may determine that a specific medical device is exempt under the provision if the device is generally sold at retail establishments (including over the internet) to individuals for their personal use. The exemption for such items is not limited by device class as defined in section 513 of the Federal Food, Drug, and Cosmetic Act. For example, items purchased by the general public at retail for individual use could include Class I items such as certain bandages and tipped applicators, Class II items such as certain pregnancy test kits and diabetes testing supplies, and Class III items such as certain denture adhesives and snake bite kits. Such items would only be exempt if they are generally designed and sold for individual use. It is anticipated that the Secretary will publish a list of medical device classifications[986] that are of a type generally purchased by the general public at retail for individual use.

---

[983] Sec. 6416.

[984] Sec. 6416(a).

[985] 21 U.S.C. 321. Section 201(h) defines device as an instrument, apparatus, implement, machine, contrivance, implant, in vitro reagent, or other similar or related article, including any component, part, or accessory, which is (1) recognized in the official National Formulary, or the United States Pharmacopeia, or any supplement to them, (2) intended for use in the diagnosis of disease or other conditions, or in the cure, mitigation, treatment, or prevention of disease, in man or other animals, or (3) intended to affect the structure or any function of the body of man or other animals, and which does not achieve its primary intended purposes through chemical action within or on the body of man or other animals and which is not dependent upon being metabolized for the achievement of its primary intended purposes.

[986] Medical device classifications are found in Title 21 of the Code of Federal Regulations, Parts 862–892.

The present law manufacturers excise tax exemptions for further manufacture and for export apply to tax imposed under this provision; however exemptions for use as supplies for vessels or aircraft, and for sales to State or local governments, nonprofit educational organizations, and qualified blood collector organizations are not applicable.

The provision repeals section 9009 of the Patient Protection and Affordable Care Act (relating to an annual fee on medical device manufacturers and importers).

### *Effective Date*

The provision applies to sales after December 31, 2012.

The repeal of section 9009 of Patient Protection and Affordable Care Act is effective on the date of enactment of the Patient Protection and Affordable Care Act (March 30, 2010).

## D. Elimination of Unintended Application of Cellulosic Biofuel Producer Credit (sec. 1408 of the Act and sec. 40 of the Code)

### *Present Law*

The "cellulosic biofuel producer credit" is a nonrefundable income tax credit for each gallon of qualified cellulosic fuel production of the producer for the taxable year. The amount of the credit is generally $1.01 per gallon.[987]

"Qualified cellulosic biofuel production" is any cellulosic biofuel which is produced by the taxpayer and which is: (1) sold by the taxpayer to another person (a) for use by such other person in the production of a qualified cellulosic biofuel mixture in such person's trade or business (other than casual off-farm production), (b) for use by such other person as a fuel in a trade or business, or (c) who sells such cellulosic biofuel at retail to another person and places such cellulosic biofuel in the fuel tank of such other person; or (2) used by the producer for any purpose described in (1)(a), (b), or (c).

"Cellulosic biofuel" means any liquid fuel that (1) is produced in the United States and used as fuel in the United States, (2) is derived from any lignocellulosic or hemicellulosic matter that is available on a renewable or recurring basis, and (3) meets the registration requirements for fuels and fuel additives established by the Environmental Protection Agency ("EPA") under section 211 of the Clean Air Act. The cellulosic biofuel producer credit cannot be claimed unless the taxpayer is registered by the IRS as a producer of cellulosic biofuel.

Cellulosic biofuel eligible for the section 40 credit is precluded from qualifying as biodiesel, renewable diesel, or alternative fuel for purposes of the applicable income tax credit, excise tax credit, or payment provisions relating to those fuels.[988]

Because it is a credit under section 40(a), the cellulosic biofuel producer credit is part of the general business credits in section 38.

---

[987] In the case of cellulosic biofuel that is alcohol, the $1.01 credit amount is reduced by the credit amount of the alcohol mixture credit, and for ethanol, the credit amount for small ethanol producers, as in effect at the time the cellulosic biofuel fuel is produced.

[988] See secs. 40A(d)(1), 40A(f)(3), and 6426(h).

However, the credit can only be carried forward three taxable years after the termination of the credit. The credit is also allowable against the alternative minimum tax. Under section 87, the credit is included in gross income. The cellulosic biofuel producer credit terminates on December 31, 2012.

The kraft process for making paper produces a byproduct called black liquor, which has been used for decades by paper manufacturers as a fuel in the papermaking process. Black liquor is composed of water, lignin and the spent chemicals used to break down the wood. The amount of the biomass in black liquor varies. The portion of the black liquor that is not consumed as a fuel source for the paper mills is recycled back into the papermaking process. Black liquor has ash content (mineral and other inorganic matter) significantly above that of other fuels.

In an informal Chief Counsel Advice ("CCA"), the IRS has concluded that black liquor is a liquid fuel from biomass and may qualify for the cellulosic biofuel producer credit, as well as the refundable alternative fuel mixture credit.[989] A taxpayer cannot claim both the alternative fuel mixture credit and the cellulosic biofuel producer credit. The alternative fuel credits and payment provisions expired December 31, 2009.

### *Explanation of Provision*

The provision modifies the cellulosic biofuel producer credit to exclude fuels with significant water, sediment, or ash content, such as black liquor. Consequently, credits will cease to be available for these fuels. Specifically, the provision excludes from the definition of cellulosic biofuel any fuels that (1) are more than four percent (determined by weight) water and sediment in any combination, or (2) have an ash content of more than one percent (determined by weight). Water content (including both free water and water in solution with dissolved solids) is determined by distillation, using for example ASTM method D95 or a similar method suitable to the specific fuel being tested. Sediment consists of solid particles that are dispersed in the liquid fuel and is determined by centrifuge or extraction using, for example, ASTM method D1796 or D473 or similar method that reports sediment content in weight percent. Ash is the residue remaining after combustion of the sample using a specified method, such as ASTM D3174 or a similar method suitable for the fuel being tested.

### *Effective Date*

The provision is effective for fuels sold or used on or after January 1, 2010.

[989] Chief Couns. Adv. 200941011 (June 30, 2009). The Code provides for a tax credit of 50 cents for each gallon of alternative fuel used to produce an alternative fuel mixture that is used or sold for use as a fuel. (sec. 6426(e)). Under Notice 2006–92, an alternative fuel mixture is a mixture of alternative fuel and a taxable fuel (such as diesel) that contains at least 0.1 percent taxable fuel. Liquid fuel derived from biomass is an alternative fuel (sec. 6426(d)(2)(G)). Diesel fuel has been added to black liquor to qualify for the alternative mixture credit and the mixture is burned in a recovery boiler as fuel. Persons that have an alternative fuel mixture credit amount in excess of their taxable fuel excise tax liability may make a claim for payment from the Treasury in the amount of the excess.

## E. Codification of Economic Substance Doctrine and Imposition of Penalties (sec. 1409 of the Act and secs. 6662, 6662A, 6664, 6676, and 7701 of the Code)

### *Present Law*

#### *In general*

The Code provides detailed rules specifying the computation of taxable income, including the amount, timing, source, and character of items of income, gain, loss, and deduction. These rules permit both taxpayers and the government to compute taxable income with reasonable accuracy and predictability. Taxpayers generally may plan their transactions in reliance on these rules to determine the Federal income tax consequences arising from the transactions.

In addition to the statutory provisions, courts have developed several doctrines that can be applied to deny the tax benefits of a tax-motivated transaction, notwithstanding that the transaction may satisfy the literal requirements of a specific tax provision. These common-law doctrines are not entirely distinguishable, and their application to a given set of facts is often blurred by the courts, the IRS, and litigants. Although these doctrines serve an important role in the administration of the tax system, they can be seen as at odds with an objective, "rule-based" system of taxation.

One common-law doctrine applied over the years is the "economic substance" doctrine. In general, this doctrine denies tax benefits arising from transactions that do not result in a meaningful change to the taxpayer's economic position other than a purported reduction in Federal income tax.[990]

*Economic substance doctrine*

Courts generally deny claimed tax benefits if the transaction that gives rise to those benefits lacks economic substance independent of U.S. Federal income tax considerations—notwithstanding that the purported activity actually occurred. The Tax Court has described the doctrine as follows:

> The tax law . . . requires that the intended transactions have economic substance separate and distinct from economic benefit achieved solely by tax reduction. The doctrine of economic substance becomes applicable, and a judicial remedy is warranted, where a taxpayer seeks to claim tax benefits, unin-

[990] See, e.g., *ACM Partnership v.* Commissioner, 157 F.3d 231 (3d Cir. 1998), *aff'g* 73 T.C.M. (CCH) 2189 (1997), *cert.* denied 526 U.S. 1017 (1999); *Klamath Strategic Investment Fund, LLC v. United States,* 472 F. Supp. 2d 885 (E.D. Texas 2007), *aff'd* 568 F.3d 537 (5th Cir. 2009); *Coltec Industries, Inc. v. United States,* 454 F.3d 1340 (Fed. Cir. 2006), *vacating and remanding* 62 Fed. Cl. 716 (2004) (slip opinion pp. 123–124, 128); *cert. denied,* 127 S. Ct. 1261 (Mem.) (2007).

Closely related doctrines also applied by the courts (sometimes interchangeable with the economic substance doctrine) include the "sham transaction doctrine" and the "business purpose doctrine." *See, e.g., Knetsch v. United States,* 364 U.S. 361 (1960) (denying interest deductions on a "sham transaction" that lacked "commercial economic substance"). Certain "substance over form" cases involving tax-indifferent parties, in which courts have found that the substance of the transaction did not comport with the form asserted by the taxpayer, have also involved examination of whether the change in economic position that occurred, if any, was consistent with the form asserted, and whether the claimed business purpose supported the particular tax benefits that were claimed. *See, e.g., TIFD III–E, Inc. v. United States,* 459 F.3d 220 (2d Cir. 2006); *BB&T Corporation v. United States,* 2007–1 USTC P 50,130 (M.D.N.C. 2007), aff'd 523 F.3d 461 (4th Cir. 2008). Although the Second Circuit found for the government in *TIFD III–E, Inc.*, on remand to consider issues under section 704(e), the District Court found for the taxpayer. See, *TIFD III–E Inc. v. United States,* No. 3:01–cv–01839, 2009 WL 3208650 (D. Conn. Oct. 23, 2009).

tended by Congress, by means of transactions that serve no economic purpose other than tax savings.[991]

*Business purpose doctrine*

A common law doctrine that often is considered together with the economic substance doctrine is the business purpose doctrine. The business purpose doctrine involves an inquiry into the subjective motives of the taxpayer—that is, whether the taxpayer intended the transaction to serve some useful non-tax purpose. In making this determination, some courts have bifurcated a transaction in which activities with non-tax objectives have been combined with unrelated activities having only tax-avoidance objectives, in order to disallow the tax benefits of the overall transaction.[992]

***Application by the courts***

*Elements of the doctrine*

There is a lack of uniformity regarding the proper application of the economic substance doctrine.[993] Some courts apply a conjunctive test that requires a taxpayer to establish the presence of both economic substance (i.e., the objective component) and business purpose (i.e., the subjective component) in order for the transaction to survive judicial scrutiny.[994] A narrower approach used by some courts is to conclude that either a business purpose or economic substance is sufficient to respect the transaction.[995] A third approach regards economic substance and business purpose as "simply more precise factors to consider" in determining whether a transaction has any practical economic effects other than the creation of tax benefits.[996]

One decision by the Court of Federal Claims questioned the continuing viability of the doctrine. That court also stated that "the use of the 'economic substance' doctrine to trump 'mere compliance

---

[991] *ACM Partnership v.* Commissioner, 73 T.C.M. at 2215.

[992] See, *ACM Partnership v.* Commissioner, 157 F.3d at 256 n.48.

[993] "The casebooks are glutted with [economic substance] tests. Many such tests proliferate because they give the comforting illusion of consistency and precision. They often obscure rather than clarify." *Collins v.* Commissioner, 857 F.2d 1383, 1386 (9th Cir. 1988).

[994] See, e.g., *Pasternak v.* Commissioner, 990 F.2d 893, 898 (6th Cir. 1993) ("The threshold question is whether the transaction has economic substance. If the answer is yes, the question becomes whether the taxpayer was motivated by profit to participate in the transaction."). See also, *Klamath Strategic Investment Fund v.* United States, 568 F. 3d 537, (5th Cir. 2009) (even if taxpayers may have had a profit motive, a transaction was disregarded where it did not in fact have any realistic possibility of profit and funding was never at risk).

[995] See, e.g., *Rice's Toyota World v.* Commissioner, 752 F.2d 89, 91–92 (4th Cir. 1985) ("To treat a transaction as a sham, the court must find that the taxpayer was motivated by no business purposes other than obtaining tax benefits in entering the transaction, and, second, that the transaction has no economic substance because no reasonable possibility of a profit exists."); *IES Industries v.* United States, 253 F.3d 350, 358 (8th Cir. 2001) ("In determining whether a transaction is a sham for tax purposes [under the Eighth Circuit test], a transaction will be characterized as a sham if it is not motivated by any economic purpose outside of tax considerations (the business purpose test), and if it is without economic substance because no real potential for profit exists (the economic substance test)."). As noted earlier, the economic substance doctrine and the sham transaction doctrine are similar and sometimes are applied interchangeably. For a more detailed discussion of the sham transaction doctrine, see, e.g., Joint Committee on Taxation, *Study of Present-Law Penalty and Interest Provisions as Required by Section 3801 of the Internal Revenue Service Restructuring and Reform Act of 1998 (including Provisions Relating to Corporate Tax Shelters* (JCS–3–99), p. 182.

[996] See, e.g., *ACM Partnership v. Commissioner,* 157 F.3d at 247; *James v. Commissioner,* 899 F.2d 905, 908 (10th Cir. 1995); *Sacks v. Commissioner,* 69 F.3d 982, 985 (9th Cir. 1995) ("Instead, the consideration of business purpose and economic substance are simply more precise factors to consider . . . We have repeatedly and carefully noted that this formulation cannot be used as a 'rigid two-step analysis'.")

with the Code' would violate the separation of powers" though that court also found that the particular transaction at issue in the case did not lack economic substance. The Court of Appeals for the Federal Circuit ("Federal Circuit Court") overruled the Court of Federal Claims decision, reiterating the viability of the economic substance doctrine and concluding that the transaction in question violated that doctrine.[997] The Federal Circuit Court stated that "[w]hile the doctrine may well also apply if the taxpayer's sole subjective motivation is tax avoidance even if the transaction has economic substance, [footnote omitted], a lack of economic substance is sufficient to disqualify the transaction without proof that the taxpayer's sole motive is tax avoidance."[998]

*Nontax economic benefits*

There also is a lack of uniformity regarding the type of non-tax economic benefit a taxpayer must establish in order to demonstrate that a transaction has economic substance. Some courts have denied tax benefits on the grounds that a stated business benefit of a particular structure was not in fact obtained by that structure.[999] Several courts have denied tax benefits on the grounds that the subject transactions lacked profit potential.[1000] In addition, some courts have applied the economic substance doctrine to disallow tax benefits in transactions in which a taxpayer was exposed to risk and the transaction had a profit potential, but the court concluded that the economic risks and profit potential were insignificant when compared to the tax benefits.[1001] Under this analysis, the taxpayer's profit potential must be more than nominal. Conversely, other courts view the application of the economic substance doctrine as requiring an objective determination of whether a "reasonable possibility of profit" from the transaction existed apart from the tax benefits.[1002] In these cases, in assessing whether a reason-

---

[997] *Coltec Industries, Inc. v.* United States, 62 Fed. Cl. 716 (2004) (slip opinion at 123–124, 128); *vacated and remanded,* 454 F.3d 1340 (Fed. Cir. 2006), *cert.* denied, 127 S. Ct. 1261 (Mem.) (2007).

[998] The Federal Circuit Court stated that "when the taxpayer claims a deduction, it is the taxpayer who bears the burden of proving that the transaction has economic substance." The Federal Circuit Court quoted a decision of its predecessor court, stating that *"Gregory v.* Helvering requires that a taxpayer carry an unusually heavy burden when he attempts to demonstrate that Congress intended to give favorable tax treatment to the kind of transaction that would never occur absent the motive of tax avoidance." The Court also stated that "while the taxpayer's subjective motivation may be pertinent to the existence of a tax avoidance purpose, all courts have looked to the objective reality of a transaction in assessing its economic substance." *Coltec Industries, Inc. v.* United States, 454 F.3d at 1355, 1356.

[999] See, e.g., *Coltec Industries v.* United States, 454 F.3d 1340 (Fed. Cir. 2006). The court analyzed the transfer to a subsidiary of a note purporting to provide high stock basis in exchange for a purported assumption of liabilities, and held these transactions unnecessary to accomplish any business purpose of using a subsidiary to manage asbestos liabilities. The court also held that the purported business purpose of adding a barrier to veil-piercing claims by third parties was not accomplished by the transaction. 454 F.3d at 1358–1360 (Fed. Cir. 2006).

[1000] See, e.g., *Knetsch,* 364 U.S. at 361; *Goldstein v.* Commissioner, 364 F.2d 734 (2d Cir. 1966) (holding that an unprofitable, leveraged acquisition of Treasury bills, and accompanying prepaid interest deduction, lacked economic substance).

[1001] See, e.g., *Goldstein v.* Commissioner, 364 F.2d at 739–40 (disallowing deduction even though taxpayer had a possibility of small gain or loss by owning Treasury bills); *Sheldon v. Commissioner*, 94 T.C. 738, 768 (1990) (stating that "potential for gain . . . is infinitesimally nominal and vastly insignificant when considered in comparison with the claimed deductions").

[1002] See, e.g., *Rice's Toyota World v.* Commissioner, 752 F.2d 89, 94 (4th Cir. 1985) (the economic substance inquiry requires an objective determination of whether a reasonable possibility of profit from the transaction existed apart from tax benefits); *Compaq Computer Corp. v.* Commissioner, 277 F.3d 778, 781 (5th Cir. 2001) (applied the same test, citing *Rice's Toyota World);*

Continued

able possibility of profit exists, it may be sufficient if there is a nominal amount of pre-tax profit as measured against expected tax benefits.

*Financial accounting benefits*

In determining whether a taxpayer had a valid business purpose for entering into a transaction, at least two courts have concluded that financial accounting benefits arising from tax savings do not qualify as a non-tax business purpose.[1003] However, based on court decisions that recognize the importance of financial accounting treatment, taxpayers have asserted that financial accounting benefits arising from tax savings can satisfy the business purpose test.[1004]

*Tax-indifferent parties*

A number of cases have involved transactions structured to allocate income for Federal tax purposes to a tax-indifferent party, with a corresponding deduction, or favorable basis result, to a taxable person. The income allocated to the tax-indifferent party for tax purposes was structured to exceed any actual economic income to be received by the tax indifferent party from the transaction. Courts have sometimes concluded that this particular type of transaction did not satisfy the economic substance doctrine.[1005] In other cases, courts have indicated that the substance of a transaction did not support the form of income allocations asserted by the taxpayer and have questioned whether asserted business purpose or other standards were met.[1006]

***Penalty regime***

*General accuracy-related penalty*

An accuracy-related penalty under section 6662 applies to the portion of any underpayment that is attributable to (1) negligence, (2) any substantial understatement of income tax, (3) any substantial valuation misstatement, (4) any substantial overstatement of pension liabilities, or (5) any substantial estate or gift tax valuation understatement. If the correct income tax liability exceeds that reported by the taxpayer by the greater of 10 percent of the correct tax or $5,000 (or, in the case of corporations, by the lesser of (a) 10 percent of the correct tax (or $10,000 if greater) or (b) $10 million), then a substantial understatement exists and a penalty may

*IES Industries v.* United States, 253 F.3d 350, 354 (8th Cir. 2001); *Wells Fargo & Company v.* United States, No. 06–628T, 2010 WL 94544, at *57–58 (Fed. Cl. Jan. 8, 2010).

[1003] See *American Electric Power, Inc. v.* United States, 136 F. Supp. 2d 762, 791–92 (S.D. Ohio 2001), *aff'd*, 326 F.3d.737 (6th Cir. 2003) and *Wells Fargo & Company v.* United States, No. 06–628T, 2010 WL 94544, at *59 (Fed. Cl. Jan. 8, 2010).

[1004] See, e.g., Joint Committee on Taxation, *Report of Investigation of Enron Corporation and Related Entities Regarding Federal Tax and Compensation Issues, and Policy Recommendations* (JSC–3–03), February, 2003 ("Enron Report"), Volume III at C–93, 289. Enron Corporation relied on *Frank Lyon Co. v.* United States, 435 U.S. 561, 577–78 (1978), and *Newman v.* Commissioner, 902 F.2d 159, 163 (2d Cir. 1990), to argue that financial accounting benefits arising from tax savings constitute a good business purpose.

[1005] See, e.g., *ACM Partnership v. Commissioner,* 157 F.3d 231 (3d Cir. 1998), *aff'g* 73 T.C.M. (CCH) 2189 (1997), *cert. denied* 526 U.S. 1017 (1999).

[1006] See, e.g., *TIFD III–E, Inc. v. United States,* 459 F.3d 220 (2d Cir. 2006). Although the Second Circuit found for the government in *TIFD III–E, Inc.*, on remand to consider issues under section 704(e), the District Court found for the taxpayer. See, *TIFD III–E Inc. v. United States,* No. 3:01–cv–01839, 2009 WL 3208650 (Oct. 23, 2009).

be imposed equal to 20 percent of the underpayment of tax attributable to the understatement.[1007] The section 6662 penalty is increased to 40 percent in the case of gross valuation misstatements as defined in section 6662(h). Except in the case of tax shelters,[1008] the amount of any understatement is reduced by any portion attributable to an item if (1) the treatment of the item is supported by substantial authority, or (2) facts relevant to the tax treatment of the item were adequately disclosed and there was a reasonable basis for its tax treatment. The Treasury Secretary may prescribe a list of positions which the Secretary believes do not meet the requirements for substantial authority under this provision.

The section 6662 penalty generally is abated (even with respect to tax shelters) in cases in which the taxpayer can demonstrate that there was "reasonable cause" for the underpayment and that the taxpayer acted in good faith.[1009] The relevant regulations for a tax shelter provide that reasonable cause exists where the taxpayer "reasonably relies in good faith on an opinion based on a professional tax advisor's analysis of the pertinent facts and authorities [that] . . . unambiguously concludes that there is a greater than 50-percent likelihood that the tax treatment of the item will be upheld if challenged" by the IRS.[1010] For transactions other than tax shelters, the relevant regulations provide a facts and circumstances test, the most important factor generally being the extent of the taxpayer's effort to assess the proper tax liability. If a taxpayer relies on an opinion, reliance is not reasonable if the taxpayer knows or should have known that the advisor lacked knowledge in the relevant aspects of Federal tax law, or if the taxpayer fails to disclose a fact that it knows or should have known is relevant. Certain additional requirements apply with respect to the advice.[1011]

### *Listed transactions and reportable avoidance transactions*

#### *In general*

A separate accuracy-related penalty under section 6662A applies to any "listed transaction" and to any other "reportable transaction" that is not a listed transaction, if a significant purpose of such transaction is the avoidance or evasion of Federal income

---

[1007] Sec. 6662.

[1008] A tax shelter is defined for this purpose as a partnership or other entity, an investment plan or arrangement, or any other plan or arrangement if a significant purpose of such partnership, other entity, plan, or arrangement is the avoidance or evasion of Federal income tax. Sec. 6662(d)(2)(C).

[1009] Sec. 6664(c).

[1010] Treas. Reg. sec. 1.6662–4(g)(4)(i)(B); Treas. Reg. sec. 1.6664–4(c).

[1011] See Treas. Reg. Sec. 1.6664–4(c). In addition to the requirements applicable to taxpayers under the regulations, advisors may be subject to potential penalties under section 6694 (applicable to return preparers), and to monetary penalties and other sanctions under Circular 230 (which provides rules governing persons practicing before the IRS). Under Circular 230, if a transaction is a "covered transaction" (a term that includes listed transactions and certain non-listed reportable transactions) a "more likely than not" confidence level is required for written tax advice that may be relied upon by a taxpayer for the purpose of avoiding penalties, and certain other standards must also be met. Treasury Dept. Circular 230 (Rev. 4–2008) Sec. 10.35. For other tax advice, Circular 230 generally requires a lower "realistic possibility" confidence level or a "non-frivolous" confidence level coupled with advising the client of any opportunity to avoid the accuracy related penalty under section 6662 by adequate disclosure. Treasury Dept. Circular 230 (Rev. 4–2008) Sec. 10.34.

tax[1012] (hereinafter referred to as a "reportable avoidance transaction"). The penalty rate and defenses available to avoid the penalty vary depending on whether the transaction was adequately disclosed.

Both listed transactions and other reportable transactions are allowed to be described by the Treasury Department under section 6011 as transactions that must be reported, and section 6707A(c) imposes a penalty for failure to adequately report such transactions under section 6011. A reportable transaction is defined as one that the Treasury Secretary determines is required to be disclosed because it is determined to have a potential for tax avoidance or evasion.[1013] A listed transaction is defined as a reportable transaction which is the same as, or substantially similar to, a transaction specifically identified by the Secretary as a tax avoidance transaction for purposes of the reporting disclosure requirements.[1014]

*Disclosed transactions*

In general, a 20-percent accuracy-related penalty is imposed on any understatement attributable to an adequately disclosed listed transaction or reportable avoidance transaction.[1015] The only exception to the penalty is if the taxpayer satisfies a more stringent reasonable cause and good faith exception (hereinafter referred to as the "strengthened reasonable cause exception"), which is described below. The strengthened reasonable cause exception is available only if the relevant facts affecting the tax treatment were adequately disclosed, there is or was substantial authority for the claimed tax treatment, and the taxpayer reasonably believed that the claimed tax treatment was more likely than not the proper treatment. A "reasonable belief" must be based on the facts and law as they exist at the time that the return in question is filed, and not take into account the possibility that a return would not be audited. Moreover, reliance on professional advice may support a "reasonable belief" only in certain circumstances.[1016]

*Undisclosed transactions*

If the taxpayer does not adequately disclose the transaction, the strengthened reasonable cause exception is not available (i.e., a strict liability penalty generally applies), and the taxpayer is subject to an increased penalty equal to 30 percent of the understatement.[1017] However, a taxpayer will be treated as having adequately disclosed a transaction for this purpose if the IRS Commissioner has separately rescinded the separate penalty under section 6707A for failure to disclose a reportable transaction.[1018] The IRS Commissioner is authorized to do this only if the failure does not relate to a listed transaction and only if rescinding the penalty would promote compliance and effective tax administration.[1019]

[1012] Sec. 6662A(b)(2).
[1013] Sec. 6707A(c)(1).
[1014] Sec. 6707A(c)(2).
[1015] Sec. 6662A(a).
[1016] Section 6664(d)(3)(B) does not allow a reasonable belief to be based on a "disqualified opinion" or on an opinion from a "disqualified tax advisor."
[1017] Sec. 6662A(c).
[1018] Sec. 6664(d).
[1019] Sec. 6707A(d).

A public entity that is required to pay a penalty for an undisclosed listed or reportable transaction must disclose the imposition of the penalty in reports to the SEC for such periods as the Secretary specifies. The disclosure to the SEC applies without regard to whether the taxpayer determines the amount of the penalty to be material to the reports in which the penalty must appear, and any failure to disclose such penalty in the reports is treated as a failure to disclose a listed transaction. A taxpayer must disclose a penalty in reports to the SEC once the taxpayer has exhausted its administrative and judicial remedies with respect to the penalty (or if earlier, when paid).[1020]

*Determination of the understatement amount*

The penalty is applied to the amount of any understatement attributable to the listed or reportable avoidance transaction without regard to other items on the tax return. For purposes of this provision, the amount of the understatement is determined as the sum of: (1) the product of the highest corporate or individual tax rate (as appropriate) and the increase in taxable income resulting from the difference between the taxpayer's treatment of the item and the proper treatment of the item (without regard to other items on the tax return);[1021] and (2) the amount of any decrease in the aggregate amount of credits which results from a difference between the taxpayer's treatment of an item and the proper tax treatment of such item.

Except as provided in regulations, a taxpayer's treatment of an item will not take into account any amendment or supplement to a return if the amendment or supplement is filed after the earlier of when the taxpayer is first contacted regarding an examination of the return or such other date as specified by the Secretary.[1022]

*Strengthened reasonable cause exception*

A penalty is not imposed under section 6662A with respect to any portion of an understatement if it is shown that there was reasonable cause for such portion and the taxpayer acted in good faith. Such a showing requires: (1) adequate disclosure of the facts affecting the transaction in accordance with the regulations under section 6011;[1023] (2) that there is or was substantial authority for such treatment; and (3) that the taxpayer reasonably believed that such treatment was more likely than not the proper treatment. For this purpose, a taxpayer will be treated as having a reasonable belief with respect to the tax treatment of an item only if such belief: (1) is based on the facts and law that exist at the time the tax return (that includes the item) is filed; and (2) relates solely to the taxpayer's chances of success on the merits and does not take into account the possibility that (a) a return will not be audited, (b) the

---

[1020] Sec. 6707A(e).

[1021] For this purpose, any reduction in the excess of deductions allowed for the taxable year over gross income for such year, and any reduction in the amount of capital losses which would (without regard to section 1211) be allowed for such year, will be treated as an increase in taxable income. Sec. 6662A(b).

[1022] Sec. 6662A(e)(3).

[1023] See the previous discussion regarding the penalty for failing to disclose a reportable transaction.

treatment will not be raised on audit, or (c) the treatment will be resolved through settlement if raised.[1024]

A taxpayer may (but is not required to) rely on an opinion of a tax advisor in establishing its reasonable belief with respect to the tax treatment of the item. However, a taxpayer may not rely on an opinion of a tax advisor for this purpose if the opinion (1) is provided by a "disqualified tax advisor" or (2) is a "disqualified opinion."

*Disqualified tax advisor*

A disqualified tax advisor is any advisor who: (1) is a material advisor[1025] and who participates in the organization, management, promotion, or sale of the transaction or is related (within the meaning of section 267(b) or 707(b)(1)) to any person who so participates; (2) is compensated directly or indirectly[1026] by a material advisor with respect to the transaction; (3) has a fee arrangement with respect to the transaction that is contingent on all or part of the intended tax benefits from the transaction being sustained; or (4) as determined under regulations prescribed by the Secretary, has a disqualifying financial interest with respect to the transaction.

A material advisor is considered as participating in the "organization" of a transaction if the advisor performs acts relating to the development of the transaction. This may include, for example, preparing documents: (1) establishing a structure used in connection with the transaction (such as a partnership agreement); (2) describing the transaction (such as an offering memorandum or other statement describing the transaction); or (3) relating to the registration of the transaction with any Federal, state, or local government body.[1027] Participation in the "management" of a transaction means involvement in the decision-making process regarding any business activity with respect to the transaction. Participation in the "promotion or sale" of a transaction means involvement in the marketing or solicitation of the transaction to others. Thus, an advisor who provides information about the transaction to a potential participant is involved in the promotion or sale of a transaction, as is any advisor who recommends the transaction to a potential participant.

---

[1024] Sec. 6664(d).

[1025] The term "material advisor" means any person who provides any material aid, assistance, or advice with respect to organizing, managing, promoting, selling, implementing, or carrying out any reportable transaction, and who derives gross income in excess of $50,000 in the case of a reportable transaction substantially all of the tax benefits from which are provided to natural persons ($250,000 in any other case). Sec. 6111(b)(1).

[1026] This situation could arise, for example, when an advisor has an arrangement or understanding (oral or written) with an organizer, manager, or promoter of a reportable transaction that such party will recommend or refer potential participants to the advisor for an opinion regarding the tax treatment of the transaction.

[1027] An advisor should not be treated as participating in the organization of a transaction if the advisor's only involvement with respect to the organization of the transaction is the rendering of an opinion regarding the tax consequences of such transaction. However, such an advisor may be a "disqualified tax advisor" with respect to the transaction if the advisor participates in the management, promotion, or sale of the transaction (or if the advisor is compensated by a material advisor, has a fee arrangement that is contingent on the tax benefits of the transaction, or as determined by the Secretary, has a continuing financial interest with respect to the transaction). See Notice 2005–12, 2005–1 C.B. 494, regarding disqualified compensation arrangements.

*Disqualified opinion*

An opinion may not be relied upon if the opinion: (1) is based on unreasonable factual or legal assumptions (including assumptions as to future events); (2) unreasonably relies upon representations, statements, findings or agreements of the taxpayer or any other person; (3) does not identify and consider all relevant facts; or (4) fails to meet any other requirement prescribed by the Secretary

*Coordination with other penalties*

Any understatement upon which a penalty is imposed under section 6662A is not subject to the accuracy related penalty for underpayments under section 6662.[1028] However, that understatement is included for purposes of determining whether any understatement (as defined in sec. 6662(d)(2)) is a substantial understatement under section 6662(d)(1).[1029] Thus, in the case of an understatement (as defined in sec. 6662(d)(2)), the amount of the understatement (determined without regard to section 6662A(e)(1)(A)) is increased by the aggregate amount of reportable transaction understatements for purposes of determining whether the understatement is a substantial understatement. The section 6662(a) penalty applies only to the excess of the amount of the substantial understatement (if any) after section 6662A(e)(1)(A) is applied over the aggregate amount of reportable transaction understatements.[1030] Accordingly, every understatement is penalized, but only under one penalty provision.

The penalty imposed under section 6662A does not apply to any portion of an understatement to which a fraud penalty applies under section 6663 or to which the 40-percent penalty for gross valuation misstatements under section 6662(h) applies.[1031]

*Erroneous claim for refund or credit*

If a claim for refund or credit with respect to income tax (other than a claim relating to the earned income tax credit) is made for an excessive amount, unless it is shown that the claim for such excessive amount has a reasonable basis, the person making such claim is subject to a penalty in an amount equal to 20 percent of the excessive amount.[1032]

The term "excessive amount" means the amount by which the amount of the claim for refund for any taxable year exceeds the amount of such claim allowable for the taxable year.

This penalty does not apply to any portion of the excessive amount of a claim for refund or credit which is subject to a penalty imposed under the accuracy related or fraud penalty provisions (including the general accuracy related penalty, or the penalty with respect to listed and reportable transactions, described above).

[1028] Sec. 6662(b) (flush language). In addition, section 6662(b) provides that section 6662 does not apply to any portion of an underpayment on which a fraud penalty is imposed under section 6663.

[1029] Sec. 6662A(e)(1).

[1030] Sec. 6662(d)(2)(A) (flush language).

[1031] Sec. 6662A(e)(2).

[1032] Sec. 6676.

### *Reasons for Change*

Tax avoidance transactions have relied upon the interaction of highly technical tax law provisions to produce tax consequences not contemplated by Congress. When successful, taxpayers who engage in these transactions enlarge the tax gap by gaining unintended tax relief and by undermining the overall integrity of the tax system.

A strictly rule-based tax system cannot efficiently prescribe the appropriate outcome of every conceivable transaction that might be devised and is, as a result, incapable of preventing all unintended consequences. Thus, many courts have long recognized the need to supplement tax rules with anti-tax-avoidance standards, such as the economic substance doctrine, in order to assure the Congressional purpose is achieved. The Congress recognizes that the IRS has achieved a number of recent successes in litigation. The Congress believes it is still desirable to provide greater clarity and uniformity in the application of the economic substance doctrine in order to improve its effectiveness at deterring unintended consequences.

The Congress believes that a stronger penalty under section 6662 should be imposed on understatements attributable to non-economic substance and similar transactions, to improve compliance by deterring taxpayers from entering such transactions. The Congress is concerned that under present law there is a potential to avoid penalties in such cases (based for example on certain levels of tax advice), and that the potential that a taxpayer in such cases may pay only the tax due plus interest is not a sufficient deterrent. The Congress therefore believes it is appropriate to impose a new strict liability penalty in such cases.

### *Explanation of Provision*

The provision clarifies and enhances the application of the economic substance doctrine. Under the provision, new section 7701(o) provides that in the case of any transaction[1033] to which the economic substance doctrine is relevant, such transaction is treated as having economic substance only if (1) the transaction changes in a meaningful way (apart from Federal income tax effects) the taxpayer's economic position, and (2) the taxpayer has a substantial purpose (apart from Federal income tax effects) for entering into such transaction. The provision provides a uniform definition of economic substance, but does not alter the flexibility of the courts in other respects.

The determination of whether the economic substance doctrine is relevant to a transaction is made in the same manner as if the provision had never been enacted. Thus, the provision does not change present law standards in determining when to utilize an economic substance analysis.[1034]

[1033] The term "transaction" includes a series of transactions.

[1034] If the realization of the tax benefits of a transaction is consistent with the Congressional purpose or plan that the tax benefits were designed by Congress to effectuate, it is not intended that such tax benefits be disallowed. See, e.g., Treas. Reg. sec. 1.269–2, stating that characteristic of circumstances in which an amount otherwise constituting a deduction, credit, or other allowance is not available are those in which the effect of the deduction, credit, or other allowance would be to distort the liability of the particular taxpayer when the essential nature

The provision is not intended to alter the tax treatment of certain basic business transactions that, under longstanding judicial and administrative practice are respected, merely because the choice between meaningful economic alternatives is largely or entirely based on comparative tax advantages. Among[1035] these basic transactions are (1) the choice between capitalizing a business enterprise with debt or equity;[1036] (2) a U.S. person's choice between utilizing a foreign corporation or a domestic corporation to make a foreign investment;[1037] (3) the choice to enter a transaction or series of transactions that constitute a corporate organization or reorganization under subchapter C;[1038] and (4) the choice to utilize a related-party entity in a transaction, provided that the arm's length standard of section 482 and other applicable concepts are satisfied.[1039] Leasing transactions, like all other types of transactions, will continue to be analyzed in light of all the facts and circumstances.[1040] As under present law, whether a particular transaction meets the requirements for specific treatment under any of these provisions is a question of facts and circumstances. Also, the fact that a transaction meets the requirements for specific treatment under any provision of the Code is not determinative of whether a transaction or series of transactions of which it is a part has economic substance.[1041]

The provision does not alter the court's ability to aggregate, disaggregate, or otherwise recharacterize a transaction when applying the doctrine. For example, the provision reiterates the present-law ability of the courts to bifurcate a transaction in which inde-

of the transaction or situation is examined in the light of the basic purpose or plan which the deduction, credit, or other allowance was designed by the Congress to effectuate. Thus, for example, it is not intended that a tax credit (e.g., section 42 (low-income housing credit), section 45 (production tax credit), section 45D (new markets tax credit), section 47 (rehabilitation credit), section 48 (energy credit), etc.) be disallowed in a transaction pursuant to which, in form and substance, a taxpayer makes the type of investment or undertakes the type of activity that the credit was intended to encourage.

[1035] The examples are illustrative and not exclusive.

[1036] See, e.g., *John Kelley Co. v. Commissioner,* 326 U.S. 521 (1946) (respecting debt characterization in one case and not in the other, based on all the facts and circumstances).

[1037] See, e.g., *Sam Siegel v. Commissioner,* 45. T.C. 566 (1966), acq. 1966–2 C.B. 3. But see *Commissioner v. Bollinger,* 485 U.S. 340 (1988) (agency principles applied to title-holding corporation under the facts and circumstances).

[1038] See, e.g., *Rev. Proc. 2010–3 2010–1 I.R.B. 110, Secs. 3.01(38), (39), (40), and (42)* (IRS will not rule on certain matters relating to incorporations or reorganizations unless there is a "significant issue"); *compare Gregory v. Helvering.* 293 U.S. 465 (1935).

[1039] See, e.g., *National Carbide v. Commissioner,* 336 U.S. 422 (1949), *Moline Properties v. Commissioner,* 319 U.S. 435 (1943); *compare, e.g. Aiken Industries, Inc. v. Commissioner,* 56 T.C. 925 (1971), acq., 1972–2 C.B. 1; *Commissioner v. Bollinger,* 485 U.S. 340 (1988); see also sec. 7701(l).

[1040] See, e.g., *Frank Lyon Co. v. Commissioner,* 435 U.S. 561 (1978); *Hilton v. Commissioner,* 74 T.C. 305, *aff'd,* 671 F. 2d 316 (9th Cir. 1982), *cert. denied,* 459 U.S. 907 (1982); *Coltec Industries v. United States,* 454 F.3d 1340 (Fed. Cir. 2006), *cert. denied,* 127 S. Ct. 1261 (Mem) (2007); *BB&T Corporation v. United States,* 2007–1 USTC P 50,130 (M.D.N.C. 2007), *aff'd,* 523 F.3d 461 (4th Cir. 2008); *Wells Fargo & Company v. United States,* No. 06–628T, 2010 WL 94544, at *60 (Fed. Cl. Jan. 8, 2010) (distinguishing leasing case *Consolidated Edison Company of New York,* No. 06–305T, 2009 WL 3418533 (Fed. Cl. Oct. 21, 2009) by observing that "considerations of economic substance are factually specific to the transaction involved").

[1041] As examples of cases in which courts have found that a transaction does not meet the requirements for the treatment claimed by the taxpayer under the Code, or does not have economic substance, See, e.g., *BB&T Corporation v. United States,* 2007–1 USTC P 50,130 (M.D.N.C. 2007) *aff'd,* 523 F.3d 461 (4th Cir. 2008); *Tribune Company and Subsidiaries v. Commissioner,* 125 T.C. 110 (2005); *H.J. Heinz Company and Subsidiaries v. United States,* 76 Fed. Cl. 570 (2007); *Coltec Industries, Inc. v. United States,* 454 F.3d 1340 (Fed. Cir. 2006), *cert. denied* 127 S. Ct. 1261 (Mem.) (2007); *Long Term Capital Holdings LP v. United States,* 330 F. Supp. 2d 122 (D. Conn. 2004), aff'd, 150 Fed. Appx. 40 (2d Cir. 2005); *Klamath Strategic Investment Fund, LLC v. United States,* 472 F. Supp. 2d 885 (E.D. Texas 2007); aff'd, 568 F. 3d 537 (5th Cir. 2009); *Santa Monica Pictures LLC v. Commissioner,* 89 T.C.M. 1157 (2005).

pendent activities with non-tax objectives are combined with an unrelated item having only tax-avoidance objectives in order to disallow those tax-motivated benefits.[1042]

### *Conjunctive analysis*

The provision clarifies that the economic substance doctrine involves a conjunctive analysis—there must be an inquiry regarding the objective effects of the transaction on the taxpayer's economic position as well as an inquiry regarding the taxpayer's subjective motives for engaging in the transaction. Under the provision, a transaction must satisfy both tests, i.e., the transaction must change in a meaningful way (apart from Federal income tax effects) the taxpayer's economic position and the taxpayer must have a substantial non-Federal-income-tax purpose for entering into such transaction, in order for a transaction to be treated as having economic substance. This clarification eliminates the disparity that exists among the Federal circuit courts regarding the application of the doctrine, and modifies its application in those circuits in which either a change in economic position or a non-tax business purpose (without having both) is sufficient to satisfy the economic substance doctrine.[1043]

### *Non-Federal-income-tax business purpose*

Under the provision, a taxpayer's non-Federal-income-tax purpose[1044] for entering into a transaction (the second prong in the analysis) must be "substantial." For purposes of this analysis, any State or local income tax effect which is related to a Federal income tax effect is treated in the same manner as a Federal income tax effect. Also, a purpose of achieving a favorable accounting treatment for financial reporting purposes is not taken into account as a non-Federal-income-tax purpose if the origin of the financial accounting benefit is a reduction of Federal income tax.[1045]

---

[1042] See, e.g., *Coltec Industries, Inc. v. United States,* 454 F.3d 1340 (Fed. Cir. 2006), *cert. denied* 127 S. Ct. 1261 (Mem.) (2007) ("the first asserted business purpose focuses on the wrong transaction—the creation of Garrison as a separate subsidiary to manage asbestos liabilities. . . . [W]e must focus on the transaction that gave the taxpayer a high basis in the stock and thus gave rise to the alleged benefit upon sale") 454 F.3d 1340, 1358 (Fed. Cir. 2006). See also *ACM Partnership v. Commissioner,* 157 F.3d at 256 n.48; *Minnesota Tea Co. v. Helvering,* 302 U.S. 609, 613 (1938) ("A given result at the end of a straight path is not made a different result because reached by following a devious path.").

[1043] The provision defines "economic substance doctrine" as the common law doctrine under which tax benefits under subtitle A with respect to a transaction are not allowable if the transaction does not have economic substance or lacks a business purpose. Thus, the definition includes any doctrine that denies tax benefits for lack of economic substance, for lack of business purpose, or for lack of both.

[1044] See, e.g., Treas. Reg. sec. 1.269–2(b) (stating that a distortion of tax liability indicating the principal purpose of tax evasion or avoidance might be evidenced by the fact that "the transaction was not undertaken for reasons germane to the conduct of the business of the taxpayer"). Similarly, in *ACM Partnership v. Commissioner,* 73 T.C.M. (CCH) 2189 (1997), the court stated:

> Key to [the determination of whether a transaction has economic substance] is that the transaction must be rationally related to a useful nontax purpose that is plausible in light of the taxpayer's conduct and useful in light of the taxpayer's economic situation and intentions. Both the utility of the stated purpose and the rationality of the means chosen to effectuate it must be evaluated in accordance with commercial practices in the relevant industry. A rational relationship between purpose and means ordinarily will not be found unless there was a reasonable expectation that the nontax benefits would be at least commensurate with the transaction costs. [citations omitted]

[1045] Claiming that a financial accounting benefit constitutes a substantial non-tax purpose fails to consider the origin of the accounting benefit (i.e., reduction of taxes) and significantly diminishes the purpose for having a substantial non-tax purpose requirement. *See, e.g., American Electric Power, Inc. v. United States,* 136 F. Supp. 2d 762, 791–92 (S.D. Ohio 2001) ("AEP's intended use of the cash flows generated by the [corporate-owned life insurance] plan is irrele-

***Profit potential***

Under the provision, a taxpayer may rely on factors other than profit potential to demonstrate that a transaction results in a meaningful change in the taxpayer's economic position or that the taxpayer has a substantial non-Federal-income-tax purpose for entering into such transaction. The provision does not require or establish a minimum return that will satisfy the profit potential test. However, if a taxpayer relies on a profit potential, the present value of the reasonably expected pre-tax profit must be substantial in relation to the present value of the expected net tax benefits that would be allowed if the transaction were respected.[1046] Fees and other transaction expenses are taken into account as expenses in determining pre-tax profit. In addition, the Secretary is to issue regulations requiring foreign taxes to be treated as expenses in determining pre-tax profit in appropriate cases.[1047]

***Personal transactions of individuals***

In the case of an individual, the provision applies only to transactions entered into in connection with a trade or business or an activity engaged in for the production of income.

***Other rules***

No inference is intended as to the proper application of the economic substance doctrine under present law. The provision is not intended to alter or supplant any other rule of law, including any common-law doctrine or provision of the Code or regulations or other guidance thereunder; and it is intended the provision be construed as being additive to any such other rule of law.

As with other provisions in the Code, the Secretary has general authority to prescribe rules and regulations necessary for the enforcement of the provision.[1048]

***Penalty for underpayments and understatements attributable to transactions lacking economic substance***

The provision imposes a new strict liability penalty under section 6662 for an underpayment attributable to any disallowance of claimed tax benefits by reason of a transaction lacking economic substance, as defined in new section 7701(o), or failing to meet the requirements of any similar rule of law.[1049] The penalty rate is 20 percent (increased to 40 percent if the taxpayer does not adequately disclose the relevant facts affecting the tax treatment in

---

vant to the subjective prong of the economic substance analysis. If a legitimate business purpose for the use of the tax savings 'were sufficient to breathe substance into a transaction whose only purpose was to reduce taxes, [then] every sham tax-shelter device might succeed,'") (citing Winn-Dixie v. Commissioner, 113 T.C. 254, 287 (1999)); aff'd, 326 F3d 737 (6th Cir. 2003).

[1046] See, e.g., *Rice's Toyota World v. Commissioner,* 752 F.2d at 94 (the economic substance inquiry requires an objective determination of whether a reasonable possibility of profit from the transaction existed apart from tax benefits); *Compaq Computer Corp. v. Commissioner,* 277 F.3d at 781 (applied the same test, *citing Rice's Toyota World);* IES Industries v. United States, 253 F.3d at 354 (the application of the objective economic substance test involves determining whether there was a "reasonable possibility of profit . . . apart from tax benefits.").

[1047] There is no intention to restrict the ability of the courts to consider the appropriate treatment of foreign taxes in particular cases, as under present law.

[1048] Sec. 7805(a).

[1049] It is intended that the penalty would apply to a transaction the tax benefits of which are disallowed as a result of the application of the similar factors and analysis that is required under the provision for an economic substance analysis, even if a different term is used to describe the doctrine.

the return or a statement attached to the return). An amended return or supplement to a return is not taken into account if filed after the taxpayer has been contacted for audit or such other date as is specified by the Secretary. No exceptions (including the reasonable cause rules) to the penalty are available. Thus, under the provision, outside opinions or in-house analysis would not protect a taxpayer from imposition of a penalty if it is determined that the transaction lacks economic substance or fails to meet the requirements of any similar rule of law. Similarly, a claim for refund or credit that is excessive under section 6676 due to a claim that is lacking in economic substance or failing to meet the requirements of any similar rule of law is subject to the 20 percent penalty under that section, and the reasonable basis exception is not available.

The penalty does not apply to any portion of an underpayment on which a fraud penalty is imposed.[1050] The new 40-percent penalty for nondisclosed transactions is added to the penalties to which section 6662A will not also apply.[1051]

As described above, under the provision, the reasonable cause and good faith exception of present law section 6664(c)(1) does not apply to any portion of an underpayment which is attributable to a transaction lacking economic substance, as defined in section 7701(o), or failing to meet the requirements of any similar rule of law. Likewise, the reasonable cause and good faith exception of present law section 6664(d)(1) does not apply to any portion of a reportable transaction understatement which is attributable to a transaction lacking economic substance, as defined in section 7701(o), or failing to meet the requirements of any similar rule of law.

### *Effective Date*

The provision applies to transactions entered into after the date of enactment and to underpayments, understatements, and refunds and credits attributable to transactions entered into after the date of enactment of the Act (March 30, 2010).

## F. Time for Payment of Corporate Estimated Taxes (sec. 1410 of the Act and sec. 6655 of the Code)

### *Present Law*

In general, corporations are required to make quarterly estimated tax payments of their income tax liability.[1052] For a corporation whose taxable year is a calendar year, these estimated tax payments must be made by April 15, June 15, September 15, and December 15. In the case of a corporation with assets of at least $1 billion (determined as of the end of the preceding taxable year), payments due in July, August, or September, 2014, are increased

[1050] As under present law, the penalties under section 6662 (including the new penalty) do not apply to any portion of an underpayment on which a fraud penalty is imposed.

[1051] As revised by the provision, new section 6662A(e)(2)(b) provides that section 6662A will not apply to any portion of an understatement due to gross valuation misstatement under section 6662(h) or nondisclosed noneconomic substance transactions under new section 6662(i).

[1052] Sec. 6655.

to 157.75 percent of the payment otherwise due and the next required payment is reduced accordingly.[1053]

### *Explanation of Provision* [1054]

The provision increases the required payment of estimated tax otherwise due in July, August, or September, 2014, by 15.75 percentage points.

### *Effective Date*

The provision is effective on the date of enactment (March 30, 2010).

[1053] Hiring Incentives to Restore Employment Act, Pub. L. No. 111–147, sec. 561, par. (1); Act to extend the Generalized System of Preferences and the Andean Trade Preference Act, and for other purposes, Pub. L. No. 111–124, sec. 4; Worker, Homeownership, and Business Assistance Act of 2009, Pub. L. No. 111–92, sec. 18; Joint resolution approving the renewal of import restrictions contained in the Burmese Freedom and Democracy Act of 2003, and for other purposes, Pub. L. No. 111–42, sec. 202(b)(1).

[1054] All of the public laws enacted in the 111th Congress affecting this provision are described in Part Twenty-One of this document.

## PART NINE: REVENUE PROVISIONS OF THE PRESERVATION OF ACCESS TO CARE FOR MEDICARE BENEFICIARIES AND PENSION RELIEF ACT OF 2010 (PUBLIC LAW 111–192)[1055]

### A. Authority to Disclose Return Information Concerning Outstanding Tax Debts for Purposes of Enhancing Medicare Program Integrity (sec. 103 of the Act and sec. 6103 of the Code)

#### *Present Law*

Section 6103 provides that returns and return information are confidential and may not be disclosed by the IRS, other Federal employees, State employees, and certain others having access to such information except as provided in the Internal Revenue Code. Section 6103 contains a number of exceptions to the general rule of nondisclosure that authorize disclosure in specifically identified circumstances. For example, section 6103 provides for the disclosure of certain return information for purposes of establishing the appropriate amount of any Medicare Part B premium subsidy adjustment.

Section 6103(p)(4) requires, as a condition of receiving returns and return information, that Federal and State agencies (and certain other recipients) provide safeguards as prescribed by the Secretary of the Treasury by regulation to be necessary or appropriate to protect the confidentiality of returns or return information. Unauthorized disclosure of a return or return information is a felony punishable by a fine not exceeding $5,000 or imprisonment of not more than five years, or both, together with the costs of prosecution.[1056] The unauthorized inspection of a return or return information is punishable by a fine not exceeding $1,000 or imprisonment of not more than one year, or both, together with the costs of prosecution.[1057] An action for civil damages also may be brought for unauthorized disclosure or inspection.[1058]

#### *Explanation of Provision*

Upon written request from the Secretary of Health and Human Services, the IRS is permitted to disclose to officers and employees of the Department of Health and Human Services the following information with respect to a taxpayer who has applied to enroll, or

[1055] H.R. 3962. The bill originated as the Affordable Health Care for America Act and passed the House on November 7, 2009. The Senate passed the bill with an amendment substituting the text of the Preservation of Access to Care for Medicare Beneficiaries and Pension Relief Act of 2010 by unanimous consent on June 18, 2010. The House agreed to the Senate amendment on June 24, 2010. The President signed the Act on June 25, 2010.

[1056] Sec. 7213.

[1057] Sec. 7213A.

[1058] Sec. 7431.

reenroll, as a provider of services or supplier under the Medicare program under title XVIII of the Social Security Act:

- Taxpayer identity information with respect to such person (i.e. the name of the person with respect to whom a return is filed, that person's mailing addresss, and taxpayer identifying number),
- The amount of the seriously delinquent tax debt owed by that taxpayer, and
- The taxable year to which the seriously delinquent debt relates.

For purposes of the provision, the term "seriously delinquent tax debt" means an outstanding debt under Title 26 for which a notice of lien has been filed. Such term does not include a debt that is being paid in a timely manner pursuant to an installment agreement (under section 6159) or offer in compromise (under section 7122). Nor does it include a debt for which a collection due process hearing (under section 6330) or innocent spouse relief (under subsections (a), (b) or (f) of section 6015) is requested or pending.

The information disclosed under the provision may be used by officers and employees of the Department of Health and Human Services only for the purposes of, and to the extent necessary in, establishing the taxpayer's eligibility for enrollment or reenrollment in the Medicare program, or in any administrative or judicial proceeding relating to, or arising from, a denial of such enrollment, or in determining the level of enhanced oversight to be applied with respect to such taxpayer pursuant to section 1866(j)(3) of the Social Security Act.

### *Effective Date*

The provision is effective on the date of enactment.

## B. Single Employer Plans

### 1. Extended period for single-employer defined benefit plans to amortize certain shortfall amortization bases (sec. 201 of the Act and sec. 430 of the Code)

### *Present Law*

#### *Minimum funding rules*

*In general*

Defined benefit pension plans generally are subject to minimum funding rules that require the sponsoring employer to periodically make contributions to fund plan benefits.[1059] The minimum fund-

[1059] Sec. 412. Similar rules apply to defined benefit pension plans under the Labor Code provisions of the Employee Retirement Income Security Act of 1974 ("ERISA"). A number of exceptions to the minimum funding rules apply. For example, governmental and church plans are not subject to the minimum funding rules. Under section 414(d), a governmental plan is generally a plan established and maintained for its employees by the Federal government, a State government or political subdivision, or an agency or instrumentality of the foregoing. A governmental plan also includes any plan to which the Railroad Retirement Act of 1935 or 1937 applies and which is financed by contributions required under that Act and any plan of an international organization that is exempt from taxation by reason of the International Organizations Immunities Act. A governmental plan includes a plan established and maintained by an Indian tribal government (as defined in section 7701(a)(40)), a subdivision of an Indian tribal govern-

Continued

ing rules for single-employer defined benefit pension plans were substantially revised by the Pension Protection Act of 2006 ("PPA").[1060] The PPA also revised the funding rules that apply to multiemployer defined benefit pension plans. The Worker, Retiree, and Employer Rccovery Act of 2008 ("WRERA")[1061] made a number of technical corrections to the PPA. In addition, WRERA made certain amendments to the PPA minimum funding rules to provide funding relief to defined benefit plans affected by the decline in global financial markets during 2008.

The PPA minimum funding rules are generally effective for plan years beginning after December 31, 2007. Delayed effective dates apply to single-employer plans sponsored by certain large defense contractors, multiple employer plans of some rural cooperatives, and single-employer plans affected by settlement agreements with the Pension Benefit Guaranty Corporation ("PBGC").[1062]

The minimum funding rules for single-employer and multiemployer plans are different. A single-employer plan is a plan that is not a multiemployer plan. A multiemployer plan is generally a plan to which more than one employer is required to contribute and which is maintained pursuant to a collective bargaining agreement. There are also multiple employer plans, which are plans maintained by more than one employer and to which more than one employer is required to contribute, but that are not maintained pursuant to a collective bargaining agreement. The single-employer plan funding rules generally apply to multiple employer plans.

The purpose of the minimum funding rules is to ensure that the sponsoring employer of a defined benefit pension plan makes periodic minimum contributions that will adequately fund benefits promised under the plan. The rules permit an employer to fund the plan over a period of time. Thus, it is possible that a plan may be terminated at a time when plan assets are not sufficient to provide all benefits accrued by employees under the plan.

The due date for the payment of a minimum required contribution for a plan year is generally eight and one-half months after the end of the plan year.[1063] If unpaid minimum funding contributions for a single-employer plan exceed $1,000,000, a lien arises in favor of the plan upon all property and rights to property (real or personal) belonging to the sponsoring employer (or member of the sponsoring employer's controlled group) in an amount equal to the unpaid minimum contributions.[1064] Notice must be given to the

---

ment (determined in accordance with section 7871(d)), or an agency or instrumentality of either, so long as all participants are employees of such entity, substantially all of whose services as employees are in the performance of essential governmental functions but not in the performance of commercial activities (whether or not an essential government function). Under section 414(e), a church plan is a plan established and maintained for its employee by a church or by a convention or association of churches which is exempt from tax under section 501. A church plan may elect to be subject to the minimum funding rules.

[1060] Pub. L. No. 109–280.

[1061] Pub. L. No. 110–458.

[1062] The PPA funding rules do not apply to eligible government contractor plans for plan years beginning before the earliest of: (1) the first plan year for which the plan ceases to be an eligible government contractor plan, (2) the effective date of the Cost Accounting Standards Pension Harmonization Rule, and (3) January 1, 2011. The new funding rules do not apply to eligible rural cooperative plans for plan years beginning before the earlier of: (1) the first plan year for which the plan ceases to be an eligible cooperative plan, or (2) January 1, 2017. The new funding rules do not apply to eligible PBGC settlement plans for plan years beginning before January 1, 2014.

[1063] Sec. 430(j).

[1064] Sec. 430(k).

PBGC[1065] of a funding failure that gives rise to a lien, and generally the lien is enforceable by the PBGC.

In the event of a failure to comply with the minimum funding rules, the Code imposes a two-level excise tax on the plan sponsor.[1066] The initial tax is 10 percent of aggregate unpaid contributions for single-employer plans and five percent of the plan's accumulated funding deficiency (as defined below) for multiemployer plans. An additional tax is imposed if the failure is not corrected before the date that a notice of deficiency with respect to the initial tax is mailed to the employer by the Internal Revenue Service ("IRS") or the date of assessment of the initial tax. The additional tax is equal to 100 percent of the unpaid contribution or the accumulated funding deficiency, whichever is applicable. Before issuing a notice of deficiency with respect to the excise tax, the Secretary must notify the Secretary of Labor and provide the Secretary of Labor with a reasonable opportunity to require the employer responsible for contributing to, or under, the plan to correct the deficiency or comment on the imposition of the tax.

*Funding target and shortfall amortization charges*

The minimum required contribution for a plan year for single-employer defined benefit plans generally depends on a comparison of the value of the plan's assets with the plan's funding target and target normal cost.[1067] The plan's funding target for a plan year is the present value of all benefits accrued or earned as of the beginning of the plan year. A plan's target normal cost for a plan year is the present value of benefits expected to accrue or to be earned during the plan year. WRERA clarified that a plan's target normal cost is increased by the amount of plan-related expenses expected to be paid from plan assets during the plan year, and is decreased by the amount of mandatory employee contributions expected to be made to the plan during the plan year.[1068]

A shortfall amortization base is determined for a plan year based on the plan's funding shortfall for the plan year.[1069] In general, a

[1065] The PBGC was established for the purpose of ensuring that benefits promised under a defined benefit pension plan are paid (up to specified annual limits) if the sponsoring employer is not able to fulfill its obligation to adequately fund the plan and the plan is terminated when it is underfunded. ERISA sec. 4002(a). The benefit protection function of the PBGC is carried out through an insurance program that applies to defined benefit pension plans. Sponsors of plans that are subject to the insurance program are liable to the PBGC for premium payments. PBGC termination insurance serves as a backstop to the minimum funding rules.

[1066] Sec. 4971.

[1067] Sec. 430.

[1068] This clarification is effective for plan years beginning after December 31, 2008, and is elective for the preceding plan year. Final regulations issued under section 430 reserve the issue of the definition of "plan-related expenses". The definition of the term is expected to be the subject of future proposed regulations. Treas. Reg. sec. 1.430(d)–1(b)(2)(iii)(B).

[1069] Under a special rule, a shortfall amortization base does not have to be established for a plan year if the value of a plan's assets is at least equal to the plan's funding target for the plan year. For purposes of the special rule, a transition rule applies for plan years beginning after 2007 and before 2011. The transition rule does not apply to a plan that (1) was not in effect for 2007, or (2) was subject to certain deficit reduction contribution rules for 2007 (i.e., a plan covering more than 100 participants and with a funded current liability below a specified threshold). Under the transition rule, a shortfall amortization base does not have to be established for a plan year during the transition period if the value of plan assets for the plan year is at least equal to the applicable percentage of the plan's funding target for the year. The applicable percentage is 92 percent for 2008, 94 percent for 2009, and 96 percent for 2010. While the PPA provided that the transition rule did not apply to a plan for any plan year after 2008 unless, for each preceding plan year after 2007, the plan's shortfall amortization base was zero (i.e., the plan was eligible for the special rule each preceding year), WRERA amended the PPA

Continued

plan has a funding shortfall for a plan year if the plan's funding target for the year exceeds the value of the plan's assets. The shortfall amortization base for a plan year is: (1) the plan's funding shortfall, minus (2) the present value, determined using the segment interest rates (discussed below), of the aggregate total of the shortfall amortization installments that have been determined for the plan year and any succeeding plan year with respect to any shortfall amortization bases for preceding plan years. As a result, in any given plan year, a plan may have a number of shortfall amortization installments that relate to the current or prior years. The aggregate of these installments is referred to as the shortfall amortization charge. In the case of a plan with a funding shortfall for a plan year, the minimum required contribution is generally equal to the sum of the plan's target normal cost and the shortfall amortization charge for that year.

A shortfall amortization base may be positive or negative, depending on whether the present value of remaining installments with respect to prior year amortization bases is more or less than the plan's funding shortfall. In either case, the shortfall amortization base is amortized over a seven-year period beginning with the current plan year. Shortfall amortization installments for a particular plan year with respect to positive and negative shortfall amortization bases are netted in determining the shortfall amortization charge for the plan year, but the resulting shortfall amortization charge cannot be less than zero (i.e., negative amortization installments may not offset normal cost).

If the value of the plan's assets exceeds the plan's funding target for a plan year, then the minimum required contribution is generally equal to the plan's target normal cost for the year. Target normal cost for this purpose is reduced (but not below zero) by the amount by which the value of the plan's assets exceed the plan's funding target.

*Actuarial assumptions*

The minimum funding rules for single-employer defined benefit pension plans specify the interest rates and other actuarial assumptions that must be used in determining a plan's target normal cost and funding target. Under the rules, present value is determined using three interest rates ("segment" rates), each of which applies to benefit payments expected to be made from the plan during a certain period. The first segment rate applies to benefits reasonably determined to be payable during the five-year period beginning on the first day of the plan year; the second segment rate applies to benefits reasonably determined to be payable during the 15-year period following the initial five-year period; and the third segment rate applies to benefits reasonably determined to be payable at the end of the 15-year period. Each segment rate is a single interest rate determined monthly by the Secretary on the basis of a corporate bond yield curve, taking into account only the portion of the yield curve based on corporate bonds maturing during the particular segment rate period. The corporate bond yield curve

---

rules to extend the transition rule to plan years beginning after 2008 even if, for each preceding plan year after 2007, the plan's shortfall amortization base was not zero.

used for this purpose reflects the average, for the 24-month period ending with the preceding month, of yields on investment grade corporate bonds with varying maturities and that are in the top three quality levels available.

The present value of liabilities under a plan is determined using the segment rates for the "applicable month" for the plan year. The applicable month is the month that includes the plan's valuation date for the plan year, or, at the election of the plan sponsor, any of the four months preceding the month that includes the valuation date. An election of a preceding month applies to the plan year for which it is made and all succeeding plan years unless revoked with the consent of the Secretary.

Solely for purposes of determining minimum required contributions, in lieu of the segment rates described above, a plan sponsor may elect to use interest rates on a yield curve based on the yields on investment grade corporate bonds for the month preceding the month in which the plan year begins (i.e., without regard to the 24-month averaging described above) ("spot" rates). In general, such an election may be revoked only with approval of the Secretary. However, Treasury regulations provide automatic approval for plan sponsors to make a new choice of interest rates for 2009 and 2010 (regardless of what choices were made for earlier years).[1070] In addition, for 2009, the IRS has indicated that it will allow plan sponsors to use the spot rate for the month that includes the plan's valuation date for the 2009 plan year, or, at the election of the plan sponsor, any of the four months preceding the month that includes the valuation date (rather than only for the month preceding the valuation date).[1071]

## *Explanation of Provision*

### *Election of extended amortization period*

The provision permits the plan sponsor of a single-employer defined benefit pension plan to elect to determine the shortfall amortization installments with respect to the shortfall amortization base for not more than two eligible plan years under two alternative extended amortization schedules.

Under the provision, the sponsor of a single-employer defined benefit plan may elect to amortize the shortfall amortization base for an eligible plan year over a nine-year period beginning with the election year ("two plus seven amortization schedule"). The shortfall amortization installments for the first two plan years in the nine-year period are equal to the interest on the shortfall amortization base for the election year, determined by using the effective interest rate for the election year.[1072] The shortfall amortization in-

[1070] Treas. Reg. sec. 1.430(h)(2)–1(h)(3). Final regulations under sections 430(d), 430(f), 430(g), 430(h)(2), 430(i), and 436 were issued on October 7, 2009 and published in the Federal Register on October 15, 2009. 74 Fed. Reg. 53004. The regulations are effective for plan years beginning on or after January 1, 2010, except for plans to which a delayed effective date applies. For plan years beginning before January 1, 2010, plans are permitted to rely on the final regulations or the proposed regulations (72 Fed. Reg. 74215) (December 31, 2007) for purposes of satisfying the requirements of sections 430 and 436.

[1071] Internal Revenue Service, Employee Plans News, March 2009 Special Edition.

[1072] The effective interest rate with respect to a plan for a plan year is the single rate of interest which, if used to determine the present value of the benefits taken into account in deter-

Continued

stallments for the last seven plan years in the nine-year period are equal to the amounts necessary to amortize the remaining balance of the shortfall amortization base for the election year in level annual installments over the seven-year period, determined by using the segment rates for the election year.

Alternatively, the sponsor of a single-employer defined benefit plan may elect to amortize the shortfall amortization base for an election year in level annual installments over a fifteen-year period beginning with the election year ("fifteen-year amortization schedule").

For purposes of the provision, an eligible plan year is a plan year beginning in 2008, 2009, 2010, or 2011, but only if the due date for the payment of the minimum required contribution for the plan year occurs on or after the date of enactment of the provision. A plan sponsor is not required to elect to use an extended amortization schedule for more than one eligible plan year or to make such election for consecutive eligible plan years; however, a plan sponsor who does make an election for two eligible plan years is required to elect the same extended amortization schedule for each year. For example, a plan sponsor who elects to use the fifteen-year amortization schedule for the plan year beginning in 2009 can make an election to use that same extended amortization schedule for the plan year beginning in 2010 or 2011; however, the plan sponsor is not permitted to elect the two plus seven amortization schedule for either of those subsequent eligible plan years.

Plans sponsored by certain government contractors that are not subject to the PPA minimum funding rules until the plan year beginning in 2011 may only elect an extended amortization schedule for the plan year beginning in 2011.

An election to use an extended amortization schedule may be revoked only with the consent of the Secretary. Prior to granting a revocation request the Secretary must provide the PBGC an opportunity to comment on the conditions applicable to the treatment of any portion of the election year shortfall amortization base that remains unamortized as of the revocation date.

### *Increase in required installments for certain plans*

#### *In general*

Under the provision, any plan year in a restriction period is a year in which the shortfall amortization installment otherwise determined and payable for that year pursuant to an election to use an extended amortization period may be increased, subject to certain limits described below, by an "installment acceleration amount". The length of the restriction period following an election to use an extended amortization schedule depends on the extended amortization schedule elected by the plan sponsor for the eligible plan year. For a plan sponsor who elects to use the two plus seven amortization schedule for an eligible plan year, the restriction period is the three year period beginning with the election year or, if later, the first plan year beginning after December 31, 2009. For

---

mining the plan's funding target for the year, would result in an amount equal to the plan's funding target (as determined using the first, second, and third segment rates). Sec. 430(h)(2)(A).

a plan sponsor who elects to use the fifteen-year amortization schedule for an eligible plan year, the restriction period is the five year period beginning with the election year or, if later, the first plan year beginning after December 31, 2009.

For example, for a plan sponsor who elects to use the two plus seven amortization schedule for the plan year beginning in 2009, the restriction period with respect to that election is the three year period during the 2010, 2011 and 2012 plan years. If the same plan sponsor then elects to use the two plus seven amortization schedule for the plan year beginning in 2011, the separate restriction period with respect to that election is the three year period during the 2011, 2012 and 2013 plan years.

*Installment acceleration amount*

The "installment acceleration amount" with respect to any plan year in a restriction period is the aggregate amount of excess employee compensation with respect to all employees for the plan year and the aggregate amount of extraordinary dividends and redemptions for the plan year. For purposes of the provision, "plan sponsor" includes any member of the plan sponsor's controlled group (as determined for purposes of the minimum funding rules).

*Excess employee compensation*

Excess employee compensation is compensation (as defined below) with respect to any employee (including a self-employed individual treated as an employee under section 401(c)) for any plan year in excess of $1,000,000. Beginning in 2011, the $1,000,000 threshold is indexed to the Consumer Price Index for Urban Consumers, rounded to the next lowest $1,000.

For purposes of determining excess employee compensation, "compensation" includes all amounts attributable to services performed by an employee for a plan sponsor after February 28, 2010 that are includable in the employee's income as remuneration during the calendar year in which the plan year begins, regardless of whether the services were performed during such calendar year. Compensation for any employee during a calendar year also includes any amount that the plan sponsor directly or indirectly sets aside or reserves in, or transfers to, a trust (or other arrangement specified by the Secretary) during the calendar year for purposes of paying deferred compensation to the employee under a nonqualified deferred compensation plan (as defined in section 409A) of the plan sponsor, unless such amount is otherwise includable in income as remuneration by the employee in that calendar year. To the extent that an amount is taken into account when set aside, reserved or transferred to a trust or other arrangement, that amount is not taken into account in calculating the excess employee compensation with respect to the employee in any subsequent calendar year. The rule for amounts set aside, reserved or transferred to a trust or other arrangement applies without regard to whether the related compensation is attributable to services performed by an employee for a plan sponsor before or after February 28, 2010.

Compensation does not include any amount otherwise includable in the employee's income with respect to the granting of service recipient stock (as defined for purposes of section 409A) after February 28, 2010 that is, at the time of grant, subject to a substantial risk of forfeiture (within the meaning of section 83(c)(1)) for at least five years following the date of grant. A grant would not fail to satisfy this requirement if the grant were vested upon death, disability, or involuntary termination of employment before the end of the five-year period. Under the provision, the Secretary may provide for the application of this exception for restricted service recipient stock to persons other than corporations. In addition, compensation does not include any remuneration payable to an employee on a commission basis solely on account of income directly generated by that employee's individual performance. Finally, compensation does not include any remuneration consisting of nonqualified deferred compensation, restricted stock, restricted stock units, stock options, or stock appreciation rights payable or granted under a binding written contract in effect on March 1, 2010 and not modified in any material respect before the remuneration is paid.

*Extraordinary dividends and redemptions*

The aggregate amount of extraordinary dividends and redemptions for a plan year is equal to the amount by which the sum of the dividends declared during the plan year by the plan sponsor and the aggregate amount paid for the redemption of stock of the plan sponsor redeemed during the plan year exceeds the greater of (1) the plan sponsor's adjusted net income (within the meaning of section 4043 of ERISA) for the preceding plan year, determined without regard for any reduction by reason of interest, taxes, depreciation or amortization or (2) for a plan sponsor who determined and declared dividends in the same manner for at least five consecutive years immediately preceding the plan year, the aggregate amount of dividends determined and declared for the plan year in that manner. It is intended that dividends would be deemed to be determined in the same manner for the prior five years if they are at the same level or rate as dividends in the previous five consecutive years. For purposes of the provision, only dividends declared and redemptions occurring after February 28, 2010 are taken into account in determining the amount of dividends and redemptions for a plan year.

In calculating the dividends declared and amounts paid for the redemption of stock during the plan year, the following amounts are disregarded: (1) dividends paid by one member of the plan sponsor's controlled group to another member of the controlled group; (2) redemptions made pursuant to an employee benefit plan or that are made on account of the death, disability or termination of employment of an employee or shareholder; and (3) dividends and redemptions with respect to applicable preferred stock on which dividends accrue at a specified rate in all events and without regard to the plan sponsor's income and with respect to which interest accrues on any unpaid dividends. Applicable preferred stock is preferred stock originally issued before March 1, 2010 (including any preferred stock originally issued prior to that date that is subsequently reissued with otherwise identical terms) and preferred stock issued after March 1, 2010 that is held by an employee benefit plan subject to Title I of ERISA.

*Limitations on installment acceleration amounts*

*Annual limitation*

Under the provision, the installment acceleration amount for a plan year is limited to the aggregate amount of funding relief received by the plan sponsor in prior years as a result of an election to use an extended amortization period for an eligible plan year. To the extent that an installment acceleration amount is limited by application of this rule, the excess installment acceleration amount is generally carried over to the succeeding plan year.

Thus, under the provision, the installment acceleration amount for any plan year may not exceed the excess (if any) of (1) the sum of the shortfall amortization installments for that plan year and all prior plan years in the nine or fifteen year amortization period, as elected, with respect to the shortfall amortization base for the election year, that would have been determined and payable by the plan sponsor with respect to that shortfall amortization base in the absence of an election to use an extended amortization period over (2) the sum of the shortfall amortization installments for such plan years, determined under the two and seven or fifteen year amortization schedule, as elected by the plan sponsor, including any installment acceleration amount from a preceding plan year ("annual limit").

To the extent that a carryover of excess installment acceleration amounts from a preceding plan year, when added to other installment acceleration amounts for a plan year (as determined prior to application of the annual limit on installment acceleration amounts) would cause the shortfall amortization installment for the plan year to exceed the annual limit, the excess is similarly carried over to the next succeeding plan year. Under the provision, the following ordering rule applies in applying the annual limit for a plan year: the installment acceleration amounts for the plan year, determined prior to the addition of any carryover installment acceleration amount from a preceding year, is applied first against the annual limit and then any installment acceleration amounts carried over to the plan year are applied against the annual limit on a first-in, first-out basis.

The carryover rules apply during the restriction period with respect to an election year and for a limited number of years following the expiration of the restriction period with respect to an election year. Under the provision, no amount is carried over to a plan year that begins after the first plan year following the last plan year in the restriction period applicable to a two plus seven amortization schedule and no amount is carried over to a plan year that begins after the second plan year following the last plan year in the restriction period applicable to a fifteen year amortization schedule.

*Total installments limited to the present value of the shortfall amortization base*

Two additional rules (subject to rules prescribed by the Secretary) apply under the provision to insure that the addition of an installment acceleration amount to a shortfall amortization installment for a plan year results only in an acceleration of the payment of amounts that would otherwise be included in subsequent shortfall amortization installments with respect to the shortfall amortization base for the election year and not in the amortization of an amount in excess of that shortfall amortization base.

Under the first rule, if the shortfall amortization installment with respect to the shortfall amortization base for an election year is required to be increased by any installment acceleration amount, the remaining shortfall amortization installments with respect that shortfall amortization base are reduced, in reverse order of the otherwise required installments, to the extent necessary to limit the present value of the remaining installments to the present value of the remaining unamortized shortfall amortization base. Under the second rule, the increase for any plan year is limited to the amount that does not cause the amount of the installment to exceed the present value of the installment and all succeeding installments with respect to the shortfall amortization base for the election year (determined without regard to the installment acceleration amount, but after application of the first rule reducing the remaining shortfall amortization installments to reflect any installment acceleration amount).

Under the provision, any installment acceleration amount is disregarded for purposes of determining a plan's quarterly contributions.

***Reporting requirement***

The provision requires a plan sponsor who elects to use an extended amortization schedule to give notice of the election to participants and beneficiaries of the plan and to inform the PBGC of the election in such form and manner as the Director of the PBGC may require.

***Regulations and guidance***

The Secretary is directed to provide rules for the application of the provisions governing installment acceleration amounts to plan sponsors who elect an extended amortization schedule for two or more plans, including rules for the ratable allocation of any installment acceleration amount among electing plans on the basis of each plan's relative reduction in its shortfall amortization installment for the first plan year in the extended amortization period. The Secretary is also directed to provide rules for the application of those provisions and the provisions governing the election of an extended amortization schedule in any case where there is a merger or acquisition involving an electing plan sponsor.

## *Effective Date*

The provision is effective for plan years beginning after December 31, 2007.

### 2. *Application of extended amortization period to plans subject to prior law funding rules (sec. 202 of the Act)*

#### *Present Law*

#### *In general*

Defined benefit pension plans generally are subject to minimum funding requirements under ERISA and the Code.[1073] PPA made significant changes to the minimum funding requirements for single-employer plans. Generally, those modifications became effective for plan years beginning after December 31, 2007. As discussed below, however, there are delayed effective dates for certain plans including multiple employer plans of certain cooperatives, certain PBGC settlement plans, and plans of certain government contractors.

*Multiple employer plans of certain cooperatives*

Section 104 of PPA provides a delayed effective date for the PPA's single-employer plan funding rules for any plan that was in existence on July 26, 2005, and was an eligible cooperative plan for the plan year including that date. A plan is treated as an eligible cooperative plan for a plan year if it is maintained by more than one employer and at least 85 percent of the employers are: (1) certain rural cooperatives;[1074] or (2) certain cooperative organizations that are more than 50-percent owned by agricultural producers or by cooperatives owned by agricultural producers, or organizations that are more than 50-percent owned, or controlled by, one or more such cooperative organizations. A plan is also treated as an eligible cooperative plan for any plan year for which it is maintained by more than one employer and is maintained by a rural telephone cooperative association.

The PPA's funding rules do not apply with respect to an eligible cooperative plan for plan years beginning before the earlier of: (1) the first plan year for which the plan ceases to be an eligible cooperative plan; or (2) January 1, 2017. In addition, in applying the pre-PPA funding rules to an eligible cooperative plan to such a plan for plan years beginning after December 31, 2007, and before the first plan year for which the PPA funding rules apply, the interest rate used is the interest rate applicable under the PPA funding rules with respect to payments expected to be made from the plan after the 20-year period beginning on the first day of the plan year (i.e., the third segment rate under the PPA funding rules).[1075]

---

[1073] Secs. 302 and 412 of ERISA. Multiemployer defined benefit pension plans are also subject to the minimum funding requirements, but the rules for multiemployer plans differ in various respects from the rules applicable to single-employer plans. Governmental plans and church plans are generally exempt from the minimum funding requirements.

[1074] This is as defined in Code section 401(k)(7)(B) without regard to (iv) thereof and includes (1) organizations engaged primarily in providing electric service on a mutual or cooperative basis, or engaged primarily in providing electric service to the public in its service area and which is exempt from tax or which is a State or local government, other than a municipality; (2) certain civic leagues and business leagues exempt from tax 80 percent of the members of which are described in (1); (3) certain cooperative telephone companies; and (4) any organization that is a national association of organizations described above.

[1075] PPA specifies the interest rates that must be used in determining a plan's target normal cost and funding target. Present value is determined using three interest rates ("segment" rates), each of which applies to benefit payments expected to be made from the plan during a certain period. The first segment rate applies to benefits reasonably determined to be payable

Continued

*Certain PBGC settlement plans*

The PPA provides a delayed effective date for its single-employer plan funding rules for any plan that was in existence on July 26, 2005, and was a "PBGC settlement plan" as of that date. The term "PBGC settlement plan" means a single-employer defined benefit plan: (1) that was sponsored by an employer in bankruptcy proceedings giving rise to a claim by the PBGC of not greater than $150 million, and the sponsorship of which was assumed by another employer (not a member of the same controlled group as the bankrupt sponsor) and the PBGC's claim was settled or withdrawn in connection with the assumption of the sponsorship; or (2) that, by agreement with the PBGC, was spun off from a plan subsequently terminated by the PBGC in an involuntary termination.

The PPA's funding rules do not apply with respect to a PBGC settlement plan for plan years beginning before January 1, 2014. In addition, in applying the pre-PPA funding rules to such a plan for plan years beginning after December 31, 2007, and before January 1, 2014, the interest rate used is the third segment rate under the PPA funding rules.

*Plans of certain government contractors*

The PPA provides a delayed effective date for its single-employer plan funding rules for any eligible government contractor plan. A plan is treated as an eligible government contractor plan if it is maintained by a corporation (or member of the same affiliated group): (1) whose primary source of revenue is derived from business performed under contracts with the United States that are subject to the Federal Acquisition Regulations[1076] and also to the Defense Federal Acquisition Regulation Supplement;[1077] (2) whose revenue derived from such business in the previous fiscal year exceeded $5 billion; and (3) whose pension plan costs that are assignable under those contracts are subject to certain provisions of the Cost Accounting Standards.[1078]

The PPA funding rules do not apply with respect to such a plan for plan years beginning before the earliest of: (1) the first plan year for which the plan ceases to be an eligible government contractor plan; (2) the effective date of the Cost Accounting Standards Pension Harmonization Rule;[1079] and (3) the first plan year beginning after December 31, 2010. In addition, in applying the pre-PPA funding rules to such a plan for plan years beginning after December 31, 2007, and before the first plan year for which the PPA

during the five-year period beginning on the first day of the plan year; the second segment rate applies to benefits reasonably determined to be payable during the 15-year period following the initial five-year period; and the third segment rate applies to benefits reasonably determined to be payable the end of the 15-year period. Each segment rate is a single interest rate determined monthly by the Secretary of the Treasury on the basis of a corporate bond yield curve, taking into account only the portion of the yield curve based on corporate bonds maturing during the particular segment rate period.

[1076] 48 C.F.R. 1.

[1077] 48 C.F.R. 2.

[1078] 48 C.F.R. 9904.412 and 9904.413.

[1079] Section 106(d) of PPA requires the Cost Accounting Standards Board to review and revise sections 412 and 413 of the Cost Accounting Standards (48 C.F.R. 9904.412 and 9904.413) to harmonize the minimum required contributions under ERISA of eligible government contractor plans and government reimbursable pension plan costs, not later than Jan. 1, 2010. Any final rule adopted by the Cost Accounting Standards Board will be considered the Cost Accounting Standards Pension Harmonization Rule.

funding rules apply, the interest rate used is the third segment rate under the PPA funding rules.

### *General minimum funding rules for plans with delayed PPA effective dates*

*Funding standard account*

As an administrative aid in the application of the pre-PPA funding requirements, a defined benefit pension plan is required to maintain a special account called a "funding standard account" to which specified charges and credits are made for each plan year, including a charge for normal cost and credits for contributions to the plan. Other charges or credits may apply as a result of decreases or increases in past service liability as a result of plan amendments, experience gains or losses, gains or losses resulting from a change in actuarial assumptions, or a waiver of minimum required contributions.

In determining plan funding under an actuarial cost method, a plan's actuary generally makes certain assumptions regarding the future experience of a plan. These assumptions typically involve rates of interest, mortality, disability, salary increases, and other factors affecting the value of assets and liabilities. If the plan's actual unfunded liabilities are less than those anticipated by the actuary on the basis of these assumptions, then the excess is an experience gain. If the actual unfunded liabilities are greater than those anticipated, then the difference is an experience loss. Experience gains and losses for a year are generally amortized as credits or charges to the funding standard account over five years.

If the actuarial assumptions used for funding a plan are revised and, under the new assumptions, the accrued liability of a plan is less than the accrued liability computed under the previous assumptions, the decrease is a gain from changes in actuarial assumptions. If the new assumptions result in an increase in the plan's accrued liability, the plan has a loss from changes in actuarial assumptions. The accrued liability of a plan is the actuarial present value of projected pension benefits under the plan that will not be funded by future contributions to meet normal cost or future employee contributions. The gain or loss for a year from changes in actuarial assumptions is amortized as credits or charges to the funding standard account over ten years.

If minimum required contributions are waived, the waived amount (referred to as a "waived funding deficiency") is credited to the funding standard account. The waived funding deficiency is then amortized over a period of five years, beginning with the year following the year in which the waiver is granted. Each year, the funding standard account is charged with the amortization amount for that year unless the plan becomes fully funded.

If, as of the close of a plan year, the funding standard account reflects credits at least equal to charges, the plan is generally treated as meeting the minimum funding standard for the year. If, as of the close of the plan year, charges to the funding standard account exceed credits to the account, then the excess is referred to as an "accumulated funding deficiency." Thus, as a general rule, the minimum contribution for a plan year is determined as the amount by which the charges to the funding standard account would exceed credits to the account if no contribution were made to the plan. For example, if the balance of charges to the funding standard account of a plan for a year would be $200,000 without any contributions, then a minimum contribution equal to that amount would be required to meet the minimum funding standard for the year to prevent an accumulated funding deficiency.

*Funding methods and general concepts*

A defined benefit pension plan is required to use an acceptable actuarial cost method to determine the elements included in its funding standard account for a year. Generally, an actuarial cost method breaks up the cost of benefits under the plan into annual charges consisting of two elements for each plan year. These elements are referred to as: (1) normal cost; and (2) supplemental cost.

The plan's normal cost for a plan year generally represents the cost of future benefits allocated to the year by the funding method used by the plan for current employees and, under some funding methods, for separated employees. Specifically, it is the amount actuarially determined that would be required as a contribution by the employer for the plan year in order to maintain the plan if the plan had been in effect from the beginning of service of the included employees and if the costs for prior years had been paid, and all assumptions as to interest, mortality, time of payment, etc., had been fulfilled. The normal cost will be funded by future contributions to the plan: (1) in level dollar amounts; (2) as a uniform percentage of payroll; (3) as a uniform amount per unit of service (e.g., $1 per hour); or (4) on the basis of the actuarial present values of benefits considered accruing in particular plan years.

The supplemental cost for a plan year is the cost of future benefits that would not be met by future normal costs, future employee contributions, or plan assets. The most common supplemental cost is that attributable to past service liability, which represents the cost of future benefits under the plan: (1) on the date the plan is first effective; or (2) on the date a plan amendment increasing plan benefits is first effective. Other supplemental costs may be attributable to net experience losses, changes in actuarial assumptions, and amounts necessary to make up funding deficiencies for which a waiver was obtained. Supplemental costs must be amortized (i.e., recognized for funding purposes) over a specified number of years, depending on the source. For example, the cost attributable to a past service liability is generally amortized over 30 years.

Normal costs and supplemental costs under a plan are computed on the basis of an actuarial valuation of the assets and liabilities of a plan. An actuarial valuation is generally required annually and is made as of a date within the plan year or within one month before the beginning of the plan year. However, a valuation date within the preceding plan year may be used if, as of that date, the value of the plan's assets is at least 100 percent of the plan's current liability (i.e., the present value of benefits under the plan, as described below).

For funding purposes, the actuarial value of plan assets may be used, rather than fair market value. The actuarial value of plan assets is the value determined on the basis of a reasonable actuarial valuation method that takes into account fair market value and is permitted under Treasury regulations. Any actuarial valuation method used must result in a value of plan assets that is not less than 80 percent of the fair market value of the assets and not more than 120 percent of the fair market value. In addition, if the valuation method uses average value of the plan assets, values may be used for a stated period not to exceed the five most recent plan years, including the current year.

In applying the funding rules, all costs, liabilities, interest rates, and other factors are required to be determined on the basis of actuarial assumptions and methods, each of which is reasonable (taking into account the experience of the plan and reasonable expectations), or which, in the aggregate, result in a total plan contribution equivalent to a contribution that would be determined if each assumption and method were reasonable. In addition, the assumptions are required to offer the actuary's best estimate of anticipated experience under the plan.[1080]

### *Additional contributions for underfunded plans with delayed PPA effective dates*

#### *In general*

Under special funding rules (referred to as the "deficit reduction contribution" rules),[1081] an additional charge to a plan's funding standard account is generally required for a plan year if the plan's funded current liability percentage for the plan year is less than 90 percent.[1082] A plan's "funded current liability percentage" is generally the actuarial value of plan assets as a percentage of the plan's current liability.[1083] In general, a plan's current liability means all liabilities to employees and their beneficiaries under the plan, determined on a present-value basis.

The amount of the additional charge required under the deficit reduction contribution rules is the sum of two amounts: (1) the excess, if any, of (a) the deficit reduction contribution (as described below), over (b) the contribution required under the normal funding rules; and (2) the amount (if any) required with respect to unpredictable contingent event benefits. The amount of the additional charge cannot exceed the amount needed to increase the plan's funded current liability percentage to 100 percent (taking into account the expected increase in current liability due to benefits accruing during the plan year).

---

[1080] Under present law, certain changes in actuarial assumptions that decrease the liabilities of an underfunded single-employer plan must be approved by the IRS.

[1081] The deficit reduction contribution rules apply to single-employer plans, other than single-employer plans with no more than 100 participants on any day in the preceding plan year. Single-employer plans with more than 100 but not more than 150 participants are generally subject to lower contribution requirements under these rules.

[1082] Under an alternative test, a plan is not subject to the deficit reduction contribution rules for a plan year if (1) the plan's funded current liability percentage for the plan year is at least 80 percent, and (2) the plan's funded current liability percentage was at least 90 percent for each of the two immediately preceding plan years or each of the second and third immediately preceding plan years.

[1083] In determining a plan's funded current liability percentage for a plan year, the value of the plan's assets is generally reduced by the amount of any credit balance under the plan's funding standard account. However, this reduction does not apply in determining the plan's funded current liability percentage for purposes of whether an additional charge is required under the deficit reduction contribution rules.

The deficit reduction contribution is generally the sum of: (1) the "unfunded old liability amount," (2) the "unfunded new liability amount," and (3) the expected increase in current liability due to benefits accruing during the plan year.[1084] The "unfunded old liability amount" is the amount needed to amortize certain unfunded liabilities under 1987 and 1994 transition rules. The "unfunded new liability amount" is the applicable percentage of the plan's unfunded new liability. Unfunded new liability generally means the unfunded current liability of the plan (i.e., the amount by which the plan's current liability exceeds the actuarial value of plan assets), but determined without regard to certain liabilities (such as the plan's unfunded old liability and unpredictable contingent event benefits). The applicable percentage is generally 30 percent, but decreases by .40 of one percentage point for each percentage point by which the plan's funded current liability percentage exceeds 60 percent. For example, if a plan's funded current liability percentage is 85 percent (i.e., it exceeds 60 percent by 25 percentage points), the applicable percentage is 20 percent (30 percent minus 10 percentage points (25 multiplied by .4)).[1085]

A plan may provide for unpredictable contingent event benefits, which are benefits that depend on contingencies that are not reliably and reasonably predictable, such as facility shutdowns or reductions in workforce. The value of any unpredictable contingent event benefit is not considered in determining additional contributions until the event has occurred. The event on which an unpredictable contingent event benefit is contingent is generally not considered to have occurred until all events on which the benefit is contingent have occurred.

## *Explanation of Provision*

### *In general*

The provision offers two types of funding relief to underfunded plans with delayed PPA effective dates.[1086] Under the provision a plan sponsor may elect either: (1) a two year look-back rule for purposes of calculating the plan's deficit reduction contribution; or (2) a 15-year amortization period for purposes of determining the plan's unfunded new liability.

Plan sponsors of eligible plans may elect relief for not more than two applicable years (one year for plans of certain government contractors). Plan sponsors electing two years of relief must elect the same type of relief for each year. Generally, relief may be elected for any two plan years beginning in 2008, 2009, 2010, or 2011. A plan year beginning in 2008 may be an applicable year, however, only if the due date for payment of the plan's minimum required contribution occurs on or after the provision's date of enactment. A plan sponsor is not required to make an election for more than one

---

[1084] The deficit reduction contribution may also include an additional amount as a result of the use of a new mortality table prescribed by the Secretary of the Treasury in determining current liability for plan years beginning after 2006.

[1085] In making these computations, the value of the plan's assets is reduced by the amount of any credit balance under the plan's funding standard account.

[1086] That is, multiple employer plans of certain cooperatives (as defined in section 104 of PPA), certain PBGC settlement plans (as defined in section 105 of PPA), and plans of certain government contractors (as defined in section 106 of PPA).

applicable plan year or to make such election for consecutive applicable plan years; however, a plan sponsor that does make an election for two plan years is required to elect the same relief provision for each year. For example, a plan sponsor that elects to use the two year look-back rule for the plan year beginning in 2009 can make an election to use that same rule for the plan year beginning in 2010 or 2011; however, the plan sponsor is not permitted to elect to use the 15-year amortization period for purposes of determining the plan's unfunded new liability for either of those subsequent eligible plan years. A "pre-effective date plan year" is any plan year prior to the first year to which the PPA funding rules apply to the plan.

The provision requires the Secretary of the Treasury to prescribe rules for making, and in appropriate circumstances revoking, elections. An election may be revoked only with the consent of the Secretary.

### *Look-back rule*

The provision permits plan sponsors of underfunded plans with delayed PPA effective dates to elect to use a two year look-back for purposes of determining their deficit reduction contribution. That is, an eligible underfunded plan may elect to use a plan's funded current liability percentage from the second plan year preceding the plan's first election year under the provision.

In determining its deficit reduction contribution, a plan that elects to use the two-year look-back rule is permitted to use the third segment rate under the PPA funding rules[1087] in calculating a portion of its unfunded new liability amount. Under the pre-PPA rules, the unfunded new liability amount is the applicable percentage of the plan's unfunded new liability. Under the provision, in calculating its unfunded new liability amount, an electing plan may use the PPA third segment rate as the applicable percentage rather than the pre-PPA applicable percentage (i.e., 30 percent decreased by .40 of one percentage point for each percentage point by which the plan's funded current liability exceeds 60 percent), but only with respect to the portion of the plan's unfunded new liability that is its "increased unfunded new liability." The electing plan continues to use the pre-PPA applicable percentage in calculating its unfunded new liability amount with respect to the excess of the unfunded new liability over the increased unfunded new liability. The increased unfunded new liability is the excess (if any) of the plan's unfunded new liability over the amount of unfunded new liability determined as if the value of the plan's assets equaled the product of the current liability of the plan for the year multiplied by the funded current liability percentage of the plan for the second plan year preceding the first election year of such plan.

### *15-year amortization*

The provision permits plan sponsors of underfunded plans with delayed PPA effective dates to elect to use a special applicable percentage for purposes of calculating a portion of their unfunded new

---

[1087] PPA secs. 104(b), 105(b), and 106(b). The third segment rate is derived from a corporate bond yield curve prescribed by the Secretary of the Treasury which reflects the yields on investment grade corporate bonds with varying maturities.

liability amount for any pre-effective date plan year beginning with or after the first election year. The special applicable percentage is the ratio of: (1) the annual installments payable in each year if the increased unfunded new liability for that plan year was amortized over 15 years, using an interest rate equal to the third segment rate under the PPA funding rules; to (2) the increased unfunded new liability for the plan year. This special applicable percentage applies with respect to the portion of the plan's unfunded new liability that is its increased unfunded new liability. The electing plan continues to use the pre-PPA applicable percentage in calculating its unfunded new liability amount with respect to the excess of the unfunded new liability over the increased unfunded new liability.

***Eligible charity plans***

The provision amends section 104 of PPA by making the section applicable to eligible charity plans. Under the provision, therefore, the delayed PPA effective date and special interest rates rules that apply to eligible cooperative plans apply to eligible charity plans. This provision was intended to allow plans of large national charities and their separately organized local chapters to have access to the relief whether or not they are treated as a single controlled group. An eligible charity plan that makes the election will not have violated the anti-cutback or other qualification requirements merely as a result of operating in accordance with the benefit limitation rules of section 436 for periods before the date of enactment.

A plan is an eligible charity plan for a plan year if it is maintained by more than one employer, 100 percent of whom are tax exempt organizations under section 501(c)(3).[1088] For purposes of the provision, the determination of whether a plan is maintained by more than one employer is determined without regard to the controlled group rules of section 414(c).

## *Effective Date*

In general, the provision is effective as if included in PPA. The provisions relating to eligible charity plans are effective for plan years beginning after December 31, 2007, except that a plan sponsor may elect to apply the provision to plan years beginning after December 31, 2008, pursuant to elections made at the time and in the manner prescribed by the Secretary. An election may be revoked only with the consent of the Secretary.

[1088] Generally, an organization is exempt under section 501(c)(3) if it is a corporation, community chest, fund, or foundation, organized and operated exclusively for religious, charitable, scientific, testing for public safety, literary, or educational purposes, or to foster national or international amateur sports competition, or for the prevention of cruelty to children or animals, no part of the net earnings of which inures to the benefit of any private shareholder or individual, no substantial part of the activities of which is carrying on propaganda, or otherwise attempting, to influence legislation, and which does not participate in, or intervene in, any political campaign of any candidate for public office.

## 3. Lookback for certain benefit restrictions (sec. 203 of the Act and sec. 436 of the Code)

### *Present Law*

#### *Benefit restrictions*

A single-employer defined benefit pension plan is required to comply with certain funding-based limits described in section 436 on benefits and benefit accruals if a plan's adjusted funding target attainment percentage is below a certain level.[1089] These limits were added by the PPA and are generally applicable to plan years beginning after December 31, 2007. The term "funding target attainment percentage" is defined in the same way as under the minimum funding rules applicable to single-employer defined benefit pension plans, and is the ratio, expressed as a percentage, that the value of the plan's assets (generally reduced by any funding standard carryover balance and prefunding balance) bears to the plan's funding target for the year (determined without regard to whether a plan is in at-risk status under the minimum funding rules). A plan's adjusted funding target attainment percentage is determined in the same way, except that the value of the plan's assets and the plan's funding target are both increased by the aggregate amount of purchases of annuities for employees other than highly compensated employees made by the plan during the two preceding plan years. Special rules apply for determining a plan's adjusted funding target attainment percentage in the case of a fully funded plan and for plan years beginning in 2007 and before 2011.

#### *Prohibited payments*

*General rule*

A plan must provide that, if the plan's adjusted funding target attainment percentage for a plan year is less than 60 percent, the plan will not make any "prohibited payments" after the valuation date for the plan year.[1090] For purposes of these limitations, a prohibited payment is (1) any payment in excess of the monthly amount paid under a single life annuity (plus any social security supplement provided under the plan) to a participant or beneficiary whose annuity starting date occurs during the period, (2) any payment for the purchase of an irrevocable commitment from an insurer to pay benefits (e.g., an annuity contract), (3) any transfer of assets and liabilities to another plan maintained by the same employer (or by any member of the employer's controlled group) that is made in order to avoid or terminate the application of the PPA benefit limitations; or (4) any other payment specified by the Secretary by regulations.

A plan must also provide that, if the plan's adjusted funding target attainment percentage for a plan year is 60 percent or greater, but less than 80 percent, the plan may not pay any prohibited payments exceeding the lesser of: (1) 50 percent of the amount otherwise payable under the plan; and (2) the present value of the maximum PBGC guarantee with respect to the participant (determined

---

[1089] Secs. 401(a)(29) and 436. Parallel rules apply under ERISA.
[1090] Sec. 436(d).

under guidance prescribed by the PBGC, using the interest rates and mortality table applicable in determining minimum lump-sum benefits). The plan must provide that only one payment under this exception may be made with respect to any participant[1091] during any period of consecutive plan years to which the limitation applies.

In addition, a plan must provide that, during any period in which the plan sponsor is in bankruptcy proceedings, the plan may not make any prohibited payment. This limitation does not apply on or after the date the plan's enrolled actuary certifies that the adjusted funding target attainment percentage of the plan is not less than 100 percent.

With respect to the prohibited payment rule, certain frozen plans, meaning plans that do not provide for any future benefit accruals, are grandfathered. The prohibited payment limitation does not apply to a plan for any plan year if the terms of the plan (as in effect for the period beginning on September 1, 2005, and ending with the plan year) provide for no benefit accruals with respect to any participant during the period. In addition, in the case of a terminated plan, while any benefit restriction in effect immediately before the termination of the plan continues to apply, the limitation on prohibited payments does not apply to payments made to carry out the termination of the plan in accordance with applicable law.[1092]

*Definition of social security supplement*

A social security supplement is an ancillary benefit that is permitted to be offered under a defined benefit plan. An ancillary benefit is benefit provided under the plan that is not a retirement-type subsidy or an optional form of payment of a participant's accrued benefit. It is benefit that is paid in addition to a participant's accrued benefit or any benefit treated as an accrued benefit. Specifically a social security supplement is a benefit for plan participants that commences before the age and terminates before the age when participants are entitled to old-age insurance benefits, unreduced on account of age, under title II of the Social Security Act, as amended (see section 202(a) and (g) of such Act), and does not exceed such old-age insurance benefit.[1093]

*Treatment of payments under Social Security leveling feature*

A Social Security leveling feature is a feature with respect to an optional form of payment of a participant's accrued benefit commencing prior to a participant's expected commencement of Social Security benefits that provides for a temporary period of higher payments which is designed to result in an approximately level amount of income when the participant's estimated old age benefits from Social Security are taken into account.[1094] Even though an

---

[1091] For purposes of the prohibited payment rules, the benefits provided with respect to a participant and any beneficiary of the participant (including an alternate payee) are aggregated. If the participant's accrued benefit is allocated to an alternate payee and one or more other persons, the amount that may be distributed is allocated in the same manner unless the applicable qualified domestic relations order provides otherwise.

[1092] Treas. Reg. sec. 1.436–1(a)(3)(ii).

[1093] Treas. Reg. sec. 1.411(a)–7(c)(4)

[1094] Treas. Reg. sec. 1.411(d)–3(g)(16)

optional form of benefit with this feature may provide the same stream of payments as a single life annuity plus a social security supplement, the amount in excess of a single life annuity paid before Social Security retirement age is a prohibited payment.

### *Limitation on future benefit accruals*

Among the benefit limitations is a requirement that if the plan's adjusted funding target attainment percentage is less than 60 percent for a plan year, all future benefit accruals under the plan must cease as of the valuation date for the plan year ("future benefit accrual limitation"). This future benefit accrual limitation applies only for purposes of the accrual of benefits; service during the freeze period is counted for other purposes. For example, if accruals are frozen pursuant to the limitation, service performed during the freeze period still counts for vesting purposes. Written notice must be provided to plan participants and beneficiaries if a future benefit accrual limitation or any other section 436 limitation provision applies to a plan.

A future benefit accrual limitation ceases to apply with respect to any plan year, effective as of the first day of the plan year, if the plan sponsor makes a contribution (in addition to any minimum required contribution for the plan year) equal to the amount sufficient to result in an adjusted funding target attainment percentage of 60 percent. The future benefit accrual limitation also does not apply for the first five years a plan (or a predecessor plan) is in effect.

If a future benefit accrual limitation ceases to apply to a plan, all such benefit accruals resume, effective as of the day following the close of the period for which the limitation applies. In addition, section 436 provides that nothing in the rules is to be construed as affecting a plan's treatment of benefits which would have been paid or accrued but for the limitation.

### *Temporary modification of application of limitation on benefit accruals under WRERA*

Under section 203 of WRERA, in the case of the first plan year beginning during the period of October 1, 2008, through September 30, 2009 ("WRERA relief plan year"), the future benefit accrual limitation rules under section 436 are applied by substituting the plan's adjusted funding target attainment percentage for the preceding plan year for the adjusted funding target attainment percentage for the WRERA relief plan year. Thus, the future benefit accrual limitation of section 436 is avoided if the plan's adjusted funding target attainment percentage for the preceding plan year is 60 percent or greater. This substitution of the plan's adjusted funding target attainment percentage is not intended to place a plan in a worse position with respect to the future benefit accrual limitation of section 436 than would apply absent the WRERA relief. Thus, the substitution does not apply if the adjusted funding target attainment percentage for the WRERA relief plan year is greater than the preceding year.

### *Explanation of Provision*

#### *Limitation on future benefit accruals*

The provision extends the temporary modification of the limitation on benefit accruals under section 203 of WRERA to the plan year beginning during the period of October 1, 2009 through September 30, 2010 and provides a special rule for any plan for which the valuation date is not the first day of the plan year. Under the provision, in the case of any plan year beginning during the period of October 1, 2008, through September 30, 2010, the future benefit accrual limitation rules under section 436 are applied by substituting the plan's adjusted funding target attainment percentage for any such plan year with the plan's adjusted funding target attainment percentage for the plan year beginning on or after October 1, 2007,[1095] and before October 1, 2008, as determined under rules prescribed by the Secretary. In the case of a plan for which the valuation date is not the first day of the plan year, for any plan years beginning after December 31, 2007, and before January 1, 2010, the future benefit accrual limitation rules under section 436 are applied by substituting the plan's adjusted funding target attainment percentage for any such plan year with the plan's adjusted funding target attainment percentage for the last plan year beginning before November 1, 2007, as determined under rules prescribed by the Secretary.

This substitution only applies if it results in a greater adjusted funding target attainment percentage for a plan for the relevant plan year. Thus, the future benefit accrual limitation of section 436 is avoided if the plan's adjusted funding target attainment percentage for the plan year beginning on or after October 1, 2007,[1096] and before October 1, 2008, is 60 percent or greater (or, in the case of a plan for which the valuation date is not the first day of the plan year, if the adjusted funding target attainment percentage for the plan year beginning before November 1, 2007 is 60 percent or greater). Because the provision applies to the same period as section 203 of WRERA, it explicitly provides that section 203 of WRERA applies to a plan for any plan year in lieu of the provision only to the extent that such section produces a higher adjusted funding target attainment percentage for such plan for such year.

#### *Prohibited payments*

Under the provision, in the case of any plan year beginning during the period of October 1, 2008, through September 30, 2010 (or, in the case of plan where the plan's valuation date is not the first day of the plan year, for any plan years beginning after December 31, 2007, and before January 1, 2010), the same substitution of the plan's adjusted funding target attainment percentage as applies for purposes of the limitation on benefit accruals also applies for purposes of determining whether a plan can pay a prohibited payment in the form of a social security leveling option. For this purpose,

[1095] A technical correction may be needed to make clear that the plan's adjusted funding target attainment percentage that is substituted is the percentage for the plan year beginning on or after (rather than after) October 1, 2007.

[1096] A technical correction may be needed to make clear that the plan's adjusted funding target attainment percentage that is substituted is the percentage for the plan year beginning on or after (rather than after) October 1, 2007.

a social security leveling option is a payment option which accelerates payments under the plan before, and reduces payments after, a participant starts receiving social security payments in order to provide substantially similar payments before and after such benefits are received.

### *Effective Date*

The provision generally is effective for plan years beginning on or after October 1, 2008. In the case of a plan for which the valuation date is not the first day of the plan year, the provision applies to plan years beginning after December 31, 2007.

## 4. Lookback for credit balance rule for plans maintained by charities (sec. 204 of the Act and sec. 430 of the Code)

### *Present Law*

*In general*

Under the PPA funding rules, credit balances that accumulated under pre-PPA law ("funding standard carryover balances") are preserved and, for plan years beginning after 2007, new credit balances (referred to as "prefunding balances") result if a plan sponsor makes contributions greater than those required under the PPA funding rules. In general, plan sponsors may choose whether to count funding standard carryover balances and prefunding balances in determining the value of plan assets or to use the balances to reduce required contributions, but not both.

*Funding standard carryover balance*

The funding standard carryover balance consists of a beginning balance in the amount of the positive balance in the funding standard account as of the end of the 2007 plan year, decreased (as described below) and adjusted to reflect the rate of net gain or loss on plan assets.

For each plan year beginning after 2008, the funding standard carryover balance is decreased (but not below zero) by the sum of: (1) any amount credited to reduce the minimum required contribution for the preceding plan year, plus (2) any amount elected by the plan sponsor as a reduction in the funding standard carryover balance (thus reducing the amount by which the value of plan assets must be reduced in determining minimum required contributions).

*Prefunding balance*

The prefunding balance consists of a beginning balance of zero for the 2008 plan year, increased and decreased (as described below) and adjusted to reflect the rate of net gain or loss on plan assets.

For subsequent years, i.e., as of the first day of plan year beginning after 2008 (the "current" plan year), the plan sponsor may increase the prefunding balance by an amount, not to exceed: (1) the excess (if any) of the aggregate total employer contributions for the preceding plan year, over (2) the minimum required contribution for the preceding plan year. For this purpose, any excess contribution for the preceding plan year is adjusted for interest accruing for the periods between the first day of the current plan year and the dates on which the excess contributions were made, determined using the effective interest rate of the plan for the preceding plan year and treating contributions as being first used to satisfy the minimum required contribution.

In determining the amount of the increase in a plan's prefunding balance, the amount by which the aggregate total employer contributions for the preceding plan year exceeds the minimum required contribution for the preceding plan year is reduced (but not below zero) by the amount of contributions an employer would need to make to avoid a benefit limitation that would otherwise be imposed for the preceding plan year under the rules relating to benefit limitations for single-employer plans (as discussed below).[1097]

For each plan year beginning after 2008, the prefunding balance of a plan is decreased (but not below zero) by the sum of: (1) any amount credited to reduce the minimum required contribution for the preceding plan year, plus (2) any amount elected by the plan sponsor as a reduction in the prefunding balance (thus reducing the amount by which the value of plan assets must be reduced in determining minimum required contributions).

*Application of balances to the value of plan assets or to reduce minimum required contributions*

If a plan sponsor elects to maintain a funding standard carryover balance or prefunding balance, the amount of those balances is generally subtracted from the value of plan assets for purposes of determining a plan's minimum required contributions, including a plan's funding shortfall, and a plan's funding target attainment percentage (defined as the ratio, expressed as a percentage, that the value of the plan's assets bears to the plan's funding target for the year). The value of a plan's assets is not reduced by these balances if a binding written agreement with the PBGC providing that all or a portion of the plan's funding standard carryover balance or prefunding balance is not available to offset the minimum required contribution for a plan year is in effect. In addition, for purposes of determining whether a plan is required to establish a shortfall amortization base for a plan year, the funding standard carryover balance is not subtracted from the value of plan assets and the prefunding balance is required to be subtracted from the value of plan assets only if an election has been made to use the balance to offset the plan's minimum required contribution for the plan year. However, the plan sponsor may elect to permanently reduce a funding standard carryover balance or prefunding balance, so that the value of plan assets is not required to be reduced by that amount in determining the minimum required contribution for the plan year.

If the value of the plan's assets (reduced by any prefunding balance but not by any funding standard carryover balance) is at least 80 percent of the plan's funding target for the preceding plan year, a plan sponsor is generally permitted to credit all or a portion of the funding standard carryover balance or prefunding balance

[1097] Any contribution that may be taken into account in satisfying the requirement to make additional contributions with respect to more than one type of benefit limitation is taken into account only once for purposes of this reduction.

against the minimum required contribution for the current plan year, thus reducing the amount that must be contributed for the current plan year.[1098] If a plan sponsor has elected to permanently reduce a funding standard carryover balance or prefunding balance, any reduction of such balances applies before determining the amount that is available for crediting against minimum required contributions for the plan year.

*Other rules*

In determining the prefunding balance or funding standard carryover balance as of the first day of a plan year, the plan sponsor must adjust the balance in accordance with regulations prescribed by the Secretary to reflect the rate of return on plan assets for the preceding year.[1099] The rate of return is determined on the basis of the fair market value of the plan assets and must properly take into account, in accordance with regulations, all contributions, distributions, and other plan payments made during the period.

To the extent that a plan has a funding standard carryover balance of more than zero for a plan year, none of the plan's prefunding balance may be credited to reduce a minimum required contribution, nor may an election be made to reduce the prefunding balance for purposes of determining the value of plan assets. Thus, the funding standard carryover balance must be used for these purposes before the prefunding balance may be used.

Any election relating to the prefunding balance and funding standard carryover balance is to be made in such form and manner as the Secretary prescribes.[1100]

### *Explanation of Provision*

Under the provision, for any plan year beginning on or after August 31, 2009, and before September 1, 2011, for purposes of determining whether the plan is sufficiently funded so as to be permitted to credit all or a portion of its funding standard carryover balance or prefunding balance against the minimum required contribution for the plan year, the plan may use the greater of: (1) its funding target attainment percentage (determined without regard to the provision) for the prior plan year, or (2) the funding target attainment percentage for the plan year beginning after August 31, 2007 and before September 1, 2008, as determined under rules prescribed by the Secretary. Thus, the provision temporarily permits plans whose funded status for the lookback year was at least equal to 80 percent to offset their minimum required contributions by a credit balance, even if the plan would not otherwise be permitted to do so.

For plans with valuation dates other than the first day of the plan year, the provision applies for any plan year beginning after December 31, 2007, and before January 1, 2010, and the plan may use the funding target attainment percentage for the last plan year

---

[1098] In the case of plan years beginning in 2008, the percentage for the preceding plan year may be determined using such methods of estimation as the Secretary of the Treasury may provide.

[1099] Treas. Reg. sec. 1.430(f)–1(b)(3).

[1100] See Treas. Reg. sec. 1.430(f)–1(f) for the rules governing elections relating to prefunding balances and funding standard carryover balances.

beginning before September 1, 2007, as determined under rules prescribed by the Secretary.

The provision applies only to plans maintained exclusively by one or more charitable organizations exempt from tax under section 501(c)(3).

### *Effective Date*

The provision is generally effective for plan years beginning after August 31, 2009. For plans with valuation dates other than the first day of the plan year, the provision is effective for plan years beginning after December 31, 2008.

## C. Multiemployer Plans

### 1. Adjustments to funding standard account rules (sec. 211 of the Act and sec. 431 of the Code)

### *Present Law*

Defined benefit pension plans generally are subject to minimum funding rules under the Code that require the sponsoring employer to periodically make contributions to fund plan benefits. Similar rules apply to defined benefit pension plans under the Labor Code provisions of ERISA.

The minimum funding rules for single-employer and multiemployer plans are different.[1101] A single-employer plan is a plan that is not a multiemployer plan. A multiemployer plan is generally a plan to which more than one employer is required to contribute and which is maintained pursuant to a collective bargaining agreement.[1102]

#### *Funding standard account*

A multiemployer defined benefit pension plan is required to maintain a special account called a "funding standard account" to which charges and credits (such as credits for plan contributions) are made for each plan year. If, as of the close of the plan year, charges to the funding standard account exceed credits to the account, the plan has an "accumulated funding deficiency" equal to the amount of such excess charges. For example, if the balance of charges to the funding standard account of a plan for a year would be $200,000 without any contributions, then a minimum contribution equal to that amount is required to meet the minimum funding standard for the year to prevent an accumulated funding deficiency. If credits to the funding standard account exceed charges, a "credit balance" results. The amount of the credit balance, increased with interest, can be used to reduce future required contributions.

#### *Amortization periods*

A plan is required to use an acceptable actuarial cost method to determine the elements included in its funding standard account for a year. Generally, an acceptable actuarial cost method breaks

[1101] The PPA modified the minimum funding rules for multiemployer defined benefit pension plans. These modifications are generally effective for plan years beginning after 2007.

[1102] Sec. 414(f).

up the cost of benefits under the plan into annual charges consisting of two elements for each plan year. These elements are referred to as the: (1) normal cost and (2) amortization of supplemental cost. The normal cost for a plan for a plan year generally represents the cost of future benefits allocated to the plan year under the funding method used by the plan for current employees. The supplemental cost for a plan year is the cost of future benefits that would not be met by future normal costs, future employee contributions, or plan assets, such as a net experience loss. Supplemental costs are amortized (i.e., recognized for funding purposes) over a specified number of years, depending on the source. The amortization period applicable to a multiemployer plan for most credits and charges is 15 years.[1103] Past service liability under the plan is amortized over 15 years;[1104] past service liability due to plan amendments is amortized over 15 years; and experience gains and losses resulting from a change in actuarial assumptions are amortized over 15 years. Experience gains and losses and waived funding deficiencies are also amortized over 15 years.

The Secretary, upon receipt of an application, is required to grant an extension of the amortization period for up to five years with respect to any unfunded past service liability, investment loss, or experience loss.[1105] There must be included with the application a certification by the plan's actuary that: (1) absent the extension, the plan would have an accumulated funding deficiency in the current plan year and any of the nine succeeding plan years; (2) the plan sponsor has adopted a plan to improve the plan's funding status; (3) taking into account the extension, the plan is projected to have sufficient assets to timely pay its expected benefit liabilities and other anticipated expenditures; and (4) required notice has been provided. The automatic extension provision does not apply with respect to any application submitted after December 31, 2014. The Secretary may also grant an additional extension of such amortization periods for an additional five years, using the same standards for determining whether such an extension may be granted as under the pre-PPA minimum funding rules.[1106]

### *Actuarial assumptions*

In applying the funding rules, all costs, liabilities, interest rates, and other factors are required to be determined on the basis of actuarial assumptions and methods, each of which must be reasonable (taking into account the experience of the plan and reasonable expectations), or which, in the aggregate, result in a total plan contribution equivalent to a contribution that would be obtained if each assumption and method were reasonable. In addition, the assumptions are required to offer the actuary's best estimate of anticipated experience under the plan.

---

[1103] Sec. 431(b)(2). Prior to the effective date of PPA, the amortization period was 30 years for past service liability, past service liability due to plan amendments, and losses and gains resulting from a change in actuarial assumptions.

[1104] In the case of a plan in existence on January 1, 1974, past service liability under the plan on the first day on which the plan was first subject to ERISA was amortized over 40 years. In the case of a plan which was not in existence on January 1, 1974, past service liability under the plan on the first day on which the plan was first subject to ERISA was amortized over 30 years. Past service liability due to plan amendments was amortized over 30 years.

[1105] Sec. 431(d)(1).

[1106] Sec. 431(d)(2).

### *Valuation of plan assets*

In determining the charges and credits to be made to the plan's funding standard account for a multiemployer plan, the value of plan assets may be determined on the basis of any reasonable actuarial method of valuation which takes into account fair market value and which is permitted under regulations prescribed by the Secretary.[1107] Thus, the actuarial value of a plan's assets under a reasonable actuarial valuation method can be used instead of fair market value. A reasonable actuarial valuation method generally can include a smoothing methodology that takes into account reasonable expected investment returns and average values of the plan assets, so long as the smoothing or averaging period does not exceed the five most recent plan years, including the current plan year. In addition, in order to be reasonable, any actuarial valuation method used by the plan is required to result in a value of plan assets that is not less than 80 percent of the current fair market value of the assets and not more than 120 percent of the current fair market value.[1108] In determining plan funding under an acceptable actuarial cost method, a plan's actuary generally makes certain assumptions regarding the future experience of a plan.

The actuarial valuation method is considered to be part of the plan's funding method. The same method must be used each plan year. If the valuation method is changed, the change is only permitted to take effect if approved by the Secretary of the Treasury.[1109]

### *Additional funding rules for plans in endangered or critical status*

Under section 432,[1110] additional funding rules apply to a multiemployer defined benefit pension plan that is in endangered or critical status. These rules require the adoption of and compliance with: (1) a funding improvement plan in the case of a multiemployer plan in endangered status; and (2) a rehabilitation plan in the case of a multiemployer plan in critical status. In the case of a plan in critical status, additional required contributions and benefit reductions apply and employers are relieved of liability for minimum required contributions under the otherwise applicable funding rules, provided that a rehabilitation plan is adopted and followed.

Section 432 is effective for plan years beginning after 2007. The additional funding rules for plans in endangered or critical status do not apply to plan years beginning after December 31, 2014, except that a plan operating under a funding improvement or rehabilitation plan for its last year beginning before January 1, 2015 must continue to operate under such plan until the funding improvement or rehabilitation period (as explained below) expires or the plan emerges from endangered or critical status.

[1107] Sec. 431(c)(2).

[1108] Treas. Reg. sec. 1.412(c)(2)–1(b). Rev. Proc. 2000–40, 2000–2 CB 357, generally indicates that only an averaging period that does not exceed five years will be approved by the IRS. The revenue procedure also indicates that for a funding valuation method to be approved, the asset value determined under the method must be adjusted to be no greater than 120 percent and no less than 80 percent of the fair market value.

[1109] Sec. 412(d)(1).

[1110] Parallel rules apply under ERISA.

***Failure to comply with minimum funding rules***

In the event of a failure to comply with the minimum funding rules, the Code imposes a two-level excise tax on the plan sponsor.[1111] The initial tax is five percent of the plan's accumulated funding deficiency for multiemployer plans. An additional tax is imposed if the failure is not corrected before the date that a notice of deficiency with respect to the initial tax is mailed to the employer by the IRS or the date of assessment of the initial tax. The additional tax is equal to 100 percent of the unpaid contribution or the accumulated funding deficiency, whichever is applicable. Before issuing a notice of deficiency with respect to the excise tax, the Secretary must notify the Secretary of Labor and provide the Secretary of Labor with a reasonable opportunity to require the employer responsible for contributing to, or under, the plan to correct the deficiency or comment on the imposition of the tax.

## *Explanation of Provision*

***Special funding relief rules***

A plan sponsor of a multiemployer plan that meets a solvency test is permitted to use either one or both of two special funding relief rules for either or both of two plan years.

*Amortization of net investment losses*

The first special funding relief rule allows the plan sponsor to treat the portion of its experience loss attributable to the net investment losses (if any) incurred in either or both of the first two plan years ending after August 31, 2008, as an item separate from other experience losses, to be amortized in equal annual installments (until fully amortized) over the period beginning with the plan year in which such portion is first recognized in the actuarial value of assets and ending in the 30-plan-year period beginning with the plan year in which the net investment loss was incurred. If this treatment is used for a plan year, the plan sponsor will not be eligible for an extension of this amortization period for this separate item, and if an extension was granted before electing this treatment of net investment losses, such extension must not result in such amortization period exceeding 30 years.

A plan sponsor is required to determine its net investment losses in the manner described by the Secretary, on the basis of the difference between actual and expected returns (including any difference attributable to any criminally fraudulent investment). The determination as to whether an arrangement is a criminally fraudulent investment arrangement shall be made under rules substantially similar to the rules prescribed by the Secretary for purposes of section 165.

*Expanded smoothing period and asset valuation corridor*

Under the other special funding relief rule, a multiemployer plan may change its asset valuation method in a manner which spreads the difference between the expected returns and actual returns for

[1111] Sec. 4971. Special rules apply under section 4971 for multiemployer plans in endangered or critical status.

either or both of the first two plan years ending after August 31, 2008 over a period of not more than 10 years. However, as under present law, spreading the difference between expected and actual returns under a plan's asset valuation method is only permitted if it does not result in a value of plan assets, when compared to the current fair market value of the plan assets, to be at any time outside an asset valuation corridor.

Under this special funding relief rule, the asset valuation corridor is expanded so that, for either or both of the first two plan years beginning after August 31, 2008, the plan's asset value must be adjusted under the valuation method being used so the value of plan assets is not less than 80 percent of the current fair market value of the assets and not more than 130 percent of the current fair market value (rather than 120 percent). This expanded valuation corridor is available whether or not the plan sponsor increases the period for spreading the difference between expected and actual returns under its asset valuation method.

If a plan sponsor uses either or both of the options (extending the spreading period and the expanded asset valuation corridor) under this special relief rule for one or both of these plan years, the Secretary will not treat the asset valuation method of the plan as unreasonable solely because of such change and the change will be deemed to be approved by the Secretary.

***Amortization of reduction in unfunded accrued liability***

To the extent a plan sponsor uses both of the two special funding relief rules for any plan year, the plan is required to treat any resulting reduction in the plan's unfunded accrued liability as a separate experience amortization base. This separate experience amortization base is amortized in annual installments (until fully amortized) over a period of 30 plan years (rather than the otherwise applicable amortization period).

***Solvency test***

The solvency test is satisfied only if the plan actuary certifies that the plan is projected to have sufficient assets to timely pay expected benefits and anticipated expenditures over the amortization period taking into account the changes in the funding standard account under the special funding relief rule elected.

***Benefit restriction***

If a plan sponsor of a multiemployer plan uses one, or both, of the special funding relief rules under this provision, then, in addition to any other applicable restrictions on benefit increases, the following limit also applies. A plan amendment increasing benefits may not go into effect during either of the two plan years immediately following any plan year to which such election first applies unless one of the following conditions is satisfied. Either (1) the plan actuary certifies that such increase is paid for out of additional contributions not allocated to the plan at the time the election was made, and the plan's funded percentage and projected credit balances for such two plan years are reasonably expected to be generally at the same levels as such percentage and balances would have been if the benefit increase had not been adopted, or

(2) the amendment is required to maintain the plan's status as a qualified retirement plan under the applicable provisions of the Code or to comply with other applicable law.

***Reporting***

A plan sponsor of a multiemployer plan that uses one or both of these special funding relief rules must give notice to participants and beneficiary of its use of the relief and must inform the PBGC of its use of the relief in such form and manner as the Director of the PBGC may prescribe.

## *Effective Date*

The provision takes effect as of the first day of the first plan year ending after August 31, 2008. However, if a plan sponsor uses either (or both) of the special funding relief provisions and such use affects the plan's funding standard account for the first plan year beginning after August 31, 2008, the use of the rule is disregarded for purposes of applying the provisions for additional funding for multiemployer plans in endangered or critical status under section 432 to such plan year. The restriction on plan amendments increasing benefits is effective on the date of enactment of this provision.

# PART TEN: REVENUE PROVISIONS OF THE HOMEBUYER ASSISTANCE AND IMPROVEMENT ACT OF 2010 (PUBLIC LAW 111–198) [1112]

## A. Homebuyer Credit (sec. 2 of the Act and sec. 36 of the Code)

### *Present Law*

***In general***

An individual who is a first-time homebuyer is allowed a refundable tax credit equal to the lesser of $8,000 ($4,000 for a married individual filing separately) or 10 percent of the purchase price of a principal residence. The credit is allowed for qualifying home purchases on or after April 9, 2008, and before May 1, 2010.[1113] The credit applies to the purchase of a principal residence before July 1, 2010 by any taxpayer who enters into a written binding contract before May 1, 2010, to close on the purchase of a principal residence before July 1, 2010.

An individual (and, if married, the individual's spouse) who has maintained the same principal residence for any five-consecutive year period during the eight-year period ending on the date of the purchase of a subsequent principal residence is treated as a first-time homebuyer. The maximum allowable credit for such taxpayers is $6,500 ($3,250 for a married individual filing separately).

The credit phases out for individual taxpayers with modified adjusted gross income between $125,000 and $145,000 ($225,000 and $245,000 for joint filers) for the year of purchase.

An individual is considered a first-time homebuyer if the individual had no ownership interest in a principal residence in the United States during the 3-year period prior to the purchase of the home.

In the case of a purchase of a principal residence after December 31, 2008, a taxpayer may elect to treat the purchase as made on December 31 of the calendar year preceding the purchase for purposes of claiming the credit on the prior year's tax return.

No District of Columbia first-time homebuyer credit[1114] is allowed to any taxpayer with respect to the purchase of a residence after December 31, 2008, if the national first-time homebuyer credit is allowable to such taxpayer (or the taxpayer's spouse) with respect to such purchase.

---

[1112] H.R. 5623. The bill passed the House on the suspension calendar on June 29, 2010. The Senate passed the bill by unanimous consent on June 30, 2010. The President signed the bill on July 2, 2010.

[1113] For purchases before January 1, 2009, the dollar limits are $7,500 ($3,750 for a married individual filing separately).

[1114] Sec. 1400C.

***Limitations***

No credit is allowed for the purchase of any residence if the purchase price exceeds $800,000.

No credit is allowed unless the taxpayer is 18 years of age as of the date of purchase. A taxpayer who is married is treated as meeting the age requirement if the taxpayer or the taxpayer's spouse meets the age requirement.

The definition of purchase excludes property acquired from a person related to the person acquiring such property or the spouse of the person acquiring the property, if married.

No credit is allowed to any taxpayer if the taxpayer is a dependent of another taxpayer.

No credit is allowed unless the taxpayer attaches to the relevant tax return a properly executed copy of the settlement statement used to complete the purchase.

***Recapture***

For homes purchased on or before December 31, 2008, the credit is recaptured ratably over fifteen years with no interest charge beginning in the second taxable year after the taxable year in which the home is purchased. For example, if an individual purchases a home in 2008, recapture commences with the 2010 tax return. If the individual sells the home (or the home ceases to be used as the principal residence of the individual or the individual's spouse) prior to complete recapture of the credit, the amount of any credit not previously recaptured is due on the tax return for the year in which the home is sold (or ceases to be used as the principal residence).[1115] However, in the case of a sale to an unrelated person, the amount recaptured may not exceed the amount of gain from the sale of the residence. For this purpose, gain is determined by reducing the basis of the residence by the amount of the credit to the extent not previously recaptured. No amount is recaptured after the death of an individual. In the case of an involuntary conversion of the home, recapture is not accelerated if a new principal residence is acquired within a two-year period. In the case of a transfer of the residence to a spouse or to a former spouse incident to divorce, the transferee spouse (and not the transferor spouse) will be responsible for any future recapture. Recapture does not apply to a home purchased after December 31, 2008 that is treated (at the election of the taxpayer) as purchased on December 31, 2008.

For homes purchased after December 31, 2008, the credit is recaptured only if the taxpayer disposes of the home (or the home otherwise ceases to be the principal residence of the taxpayer) within 36 months from the date of purchase.

***Waiver of recapture for individuals on qualified official extended duty***

In the case of a disposition of principal residence by an individual (or a cessation of use of the residence that otherwise would

[1115] If the individual sells the home (or the home ceases to be used as the principal residence of the individual and the individual's spouse) in the same taxable year the home is purchased, no credit is allowed.

cause recapture) after December 31, 2008, in connection with Government orders received by the individual (or the individual's spouse) for qualified official extended duty service, no recapture applies by reason of the disposition of the residence,[1116] and any 15-year recapture with respect to a home acquired before January 1, 2009, ceases to apply in the taxable year the disposition occurs.

Qualified official extended duty service means service on official extended duty as a member of the uniformed services, a member of the Foreign Service of the United States, or an employee of the intelligence community.[1117]

Qualified official extended duty is any period of extended duty while serving at a place of duty at least 50 miles away from the taxpayer's principal residence or under orders compelling residence in government furnished quarters. Extended duty is defined as any period of duty pursuant to a call or order to such duty for a period in excess of 90 days or for an indefinite period.

The uniformed services include: (1) the Armed Forces (the Army, Navy, Air Force, Marine Corps, and Coast Guard); (2) the commissioned corps of the National Oceanic and Atmospheric Administration; and (3) the commissioned corps of the Public Health Service.

The term "member of the Foreign Service of the United States" includes: (1) chiefs of mission; (2) ambassadors at large; (3) members of the Senior Foreign Service; (4) Foreign Service officers; and (5) Foreign Service personnel.

The term "employee of the intelligence community" means an employee of the Office of the Director of National Intelligence, the Central Intelligence Agency, the National Security Agency, the Defense Intelligence Agency, the National Geospatial-Intelligence Agency, or the National Reconnaissance Office. The term also includes employment with: (1) any other office within the Department of Defense for the collection of specialized national intelligence through reconnaissance programs; (2) any of the intelligence elements of the Army, the Navy, the Air Force, the Marine Corps, the Federal Bureau of Investigation, the Department of the Treasury, the Department of Energy, and the Coast Guard; (3) the Bureau of Intelligence and Research of the Department of State; and (4) the elements of the Department of Homeland Security concerned with the analyses of foreign intelligence information.

***Extension of the first-time homebuyer credit for individuals on qualified official extended duty outside of the United States***

In the case of any individual (and, if married, the individual's spouse) who serves on qualified official extended duty service outside of the United States for at least 90 days during the period beginning after December 31, 2008, and ending before May 1, 2010, the expiration date of the first-time homebuyer credit is extended for one year, through May 1, 2011 (July 1, 2011, in the case of an individual who enters into a written binding contract before May

[1116] If the individual sells the home (or the home ceases to be used as the principal residence of the individual and the individual's spouse) in connection with such orders in the same taxable year the home is purchased, the credit is allowable.

[1117] These terms have the same meaning as under the provision for exclusion of gain on the sale of certain principal residences. Sec. 121.

1, 2011, to close on the purchase of a principal residence before July 1, 2011).

### *Mathematical error authority*

The Act makes a number of changes to expand the definition of mathematical or clerical error for purposes of administration of the credit by the Internal Revenue Service ("IRS"). The IRS may assess additional tax without issuance of a notice of deficiency as otherwise required[1118] in the case of: an omission of any increase in tax required by the recapture provisions of the credit; information from the person issuing the taxpayer identification number of the taxpayer that indicates that the taxpayer does not meet the age requirement of the credit; information provided to the Secretary by the taxpayer on an income tax return for at least one of the two preceding taxable years that is inconsistent with eligibility for such credit; or, failure to attach to the return a properly executed copy of the settlement statement used to complete the purchase.

### *Explanation of Provision*

The Act extends the time for closing on a principal residence eligible for the first-time homebuyer credit through September 30, 2010 for any individual who entered into a written binding contract before May 1, 2010, to close on the purchase of a principal residence before July 1, 2010. The eligibility period for an individual who serves on qualified official extended duty outside of the United States who enters into a written binding contract before May 1, 2011, to close on the purchase of a principal residence before July 1, 2011, and who purchases such residence before July 1, 2011, is unchanged.

### *Effective Date*

The provision is effective for residences purchased after June 30, 2010.

## B. Revenue Offsets

### 1. Application of bad check penalty to electronic checks and other payment forms (sec. 3 of the Act and sec. 6657 of the Code)

### *Present Law*

### *In general*

Taxpayers may pay their tax liability by "any commercially acceptable means" that the Secretary deems appropriate.[1119] The Code authorizes the Secretary, with certain limitations, to specify when and how new media may be used to pay tax obligations.[1120]

[1118] Sec. 6213.
[1119] Sec. 6311(a).
[1120] Sec. 6311(d) requires that the Secretary identify such methods by regulations, and in doing so, specify when such payments are considered received, and provide means to ensure that tax matters may be resolved without involvement of financial institutions. The Secretary is also authorized to enter into contracts to obtain services related to receiving payment if it is cost-beneficial to the government, but may not pay "any fee or other consideration under such con-

Continued

The Secretary has long authorized the IRS to accept payments by check or money order, although personal checks may be refused if there is good reason to believe that the check will not be honored when presented to the financial institution on which it is drawn. Regulations authorize the acceptance of payments by debit or credit card, as well as electronic funds transfers, and also prescribe procedures for resolution of errors in processing payments by such means.[1121] Although the Secretary may permit and encourage tax payments by electronic funds transfers, credit card or debit card, the taxpayer's use of such means must be voluntary.[1122]

Taxpayers may pay their taxes by electronic funds transfers,[1123] either by initiating instructions to financial institutions at which they hold accounts (i.e., electronic funds withdrawal), or by enrolling in the Electronic Federal Tax Payment System ("EFTPS"),[1124] which is a tax payment system provided free by the Treasury, under which the taxpayer authorizes Treasury to initiate instructions for electronic transfers of funds from accounts held by the taxpayer to the IRS. Once enrolled, a taxpayer may pay all of its Federal taxes using EFTPS. Individuals can pay quarterly estimated taxes electronically using EFTPS, and can make payments weekly, monthly, or quarterly. Both business and individual payments can be scheduled in advance. Certain excise taxes are required to be paid by EFTPS.[1125]

Payments by checks or money orders are generally considered made on the date the financial instrument is received by the IRS, not the date that the financial institution on which payment is drawn remits the funds to the IRS. Thus, a check received by mail in an IRS office on April 15, 2010, is credited as of that date. Payments by debit or credit card are deemed received when the issuer of the card authorizes the transaction, provided that the payment is actually received by the United States in the ordinary course of business.[1126] The procedures under which the IRS accepts credit or debit card payment precludes the IRS from access to the card numbers, and instead require that such payments be provided through remittance with an electronically filed return, payment by phone or payment by internet. As a result, the card issuer authorization is contemporaneous with the IRS receiving notice of the payment. Payments by electronic funds transfer are considered paid on the date that funds are actually withdrawn from the taxpayer's account, i.e., the settlement date.[1127] The settlement date may be

---

tracts for the use of credit, debit or charge cards for the payment of taxes," such as the convenience fees charged for electronic tax payments. Sec. 6311(d)(2); Treas. Reg. sec. 301.6311–2(f).

[1121] Treas. Reg. sec. 1.6311–2.

[1122] Treas. Reg. sec. 301.6311–2(a)(1); Treas. Reg. sec. 31.3602–1(j).

[1123] Treas. Reg. sec. 301.6311–2(a)(2) provides that guidance on electronic funds transfers other than credit or debit cards is provided in regulations under section 6302, which defines electronic funds transfers generally to include any transfer of funds other than by check, draft or similar paper instrument, if initiated through an electronic media to instruct a financial institution or intermediary to debit or credit an account.

[1124] Treas. Reg. secs. 301.6311–1(b)(1) and 301.6311–2(b) provide that the underlying tax obligation is not considered satisfied until the check or money order is paid or the electronic payment has been authorized by the relevant financial institution and the payment actually received.

[1125] Secs. 5061(e) and 5703(b).

[1126] Treas. Reg. sec. 301.6311–2(b).

[1127] Treas. Reg. sec. 301.6311–2(a)(2) and Treas. Reg. sec. 31.6302–1(h)(8).

subsequent to the date on which the payment transaction is initiated.

***Bad check penalty***

Any taxpayer who attempts to satisfy a tax liability with a check or money order that is not duly paid is subject to a penalty. If the dishonored check or money order is equal to or greater than $1,250, the penalty is two percent of the face amount of the check or money order. If the dishonored check or money order is less than $1,250, the penalty is the lesser of $25 or the amount of the check or money order.[1128] The penalty is not applicable if the taxpayer establishes that payment was tendered in good faith and with reasonable cause to believe it would be paid.

The Code provides that this penalty applies to "any check or money order," without mention of payment by magnetic media, such as electronic funds transfers from a bank account, debit cards, and credit cards.

### *Explanation of Provision*

The provision expands the bad check penalty to cover all commercially acceptable instruments of payment that are not duly paid.

### *Effective Date*

The provision is effective for instruments tendered after the date of enactment (July 2, 2010).

## 2. Disclosure of prisoner return information to State prisons (sec. 4 of the Act and sec. 6103 of the Code)

### *Present Law*

Section 6103 provides that returns and return information are confidential and may not be disclosed by the IRS, other Federal employees, State employees, and certain others having access to the information except as provided in the Code.[1129] A "return" is any tax or information return, declaration of estimated tax, or claim for refund required by, or permitted under, the Code, that is filed with the Secretary by, on behalf of, or with respect to any person.[1130] "Return" also includes any amendment or supplement thereto, including supporting schedules, attachments, or lists which are supplemental to, or part of, the return so filed.

The definition of "return information" is very broad and includes any information gathered by the IRS with respect to a person's liability or possible liability under the Code.[1131] However, data in a

[1128] Sec. 6657.
[1129] Sec. 6103(a).
[1130] Sec. 6103(b)(1).
[1131] Sec. 6103(b)(2). Return information is:

• a taxpayer's identity, the nature, source, or amount of his income, payments, receipts, deductions, exemptions, credits, assets, liabilities, net worth, tax liability, tax withheld, deficiencies, overassessments, or tax payments, whether the taxpayer's return was, is being, or will be examined or subject to other investigation or processing, or any other data, received by, recorded by, prepared by, furnished to, or collected by the Secretary with respect to a return or with respect to the determination of the existence, or possible existence, of liability (or the

Continued

form that cannot be associated with, or otherwise identify, directly or indirectly a particular taxpayer is not "return information" for section 6103 purposes.

Section 6103 contains a number of exceptions to the general rule of confidentiality, which permit disclosure in specifically identified circumstances when certain conditions are satisfied.[1132] For example, the IRS is permitted to make investigative disclosures to the third parties to the extent such disclosure is necessary in obtaining information which is not otherwise reasonably available, with respect to the correct determination of tax, liability for tax, the amount to be collected or with respect to the enforcement of any other provision of the Code.

None of the exceptions permit the IRS to refer the tax-related misconduct of specific inmates to prison officials for imposition of administrative sanctions against such individuals. The IRS does publicize information from prosecutions which has been made part of the public record of such proceedings.

The Code permits disclosure of return information with respect to prisoners whom the Secretary has determined may have filed or facilitated the filing of false or fraudulent tax returns. The disclosures may be made to the head of the Federal Bureau of Prisons and redisclosed to officers and employees of the Federal Bureau of Prisons. The Secretary may only disclose such information as is necessary to permit effective tax administration. The authority terminates December 31, 2011. The Code requires the Treasury Inspector General for Tax Administration to report to Congress on the implementation of this provision no later than December 31, 2010.[1133]

The IRS is required to publish an annual report containing statistics relating to the number of false and fraudulent returns associated with each Federal and State prisons and such other information as the Secretary deems appropriate.

### *Explanation of Provision*

The provision extends the disclosure authority applicable to the Federal Bureau of Prisons to State prisons. The disclosure authority terminates December 31, 2011.

---

amount thereof) of any person under this title for any tax, penalty, interest, fine, forfeiture, or other imposition, or offense,

• any part of any written determination or any background file document relating to such written determination (as such terms are defined in section 6110(b)) which is not open to public inspection under section 6110,

• any advance pricing agreement entered into by a taxpayer and the Secretary and any background information related to such agreement or any application for an advance pricing agreement, and

• any closing agreement under section 7121, and any similar agreement, and any background information related to such an agreement or request for such an agreement.

[1132] Sec. 6103(c)–(o). Such exceptions include disclosures by consent of the taxpayer, disclosures to State tax officials, disclosures to the taxpayer and persons having a material interest, disclosures to Committees of Congress, disclosures to the President, disclosures to Federal employees for tax administration purposes, disclosures to Federal employees for nontax criminal law enforcement purposes and to the Government Accountability Office, disclosures for statistical purposes, disclosures for miscellaneous tax administration purposes, disclosures for purposes other than tax administration, disclosures of taxpayer identity information, disclosures to tax administration contractors and disclosures with respect to wagering excise taxes.

[1133] Sec. 7803(d)(3)(C). See Treasury Inspector General for Tax Administration, *Significant Problems Still Exist With Internal Revenue Service Efforts to Identify Prisoner Tax Refund Fraud* (Audit No. 2011–40–009) (December 29, 2010).

### *Effective Date*

The provision is effective on the date of enactment.

## PART ELEVEN: REVENUE PROVISIONS OF THE DODD-FRANK WALL STREET REFORM AND CONSUMER PROTECTION ACT (PUBLIC LAW 111–203) [1134]

### A. Certain Swaps, etc., Not Treated as Section 1256 Contracts (sec. 1601 of the Act and sec. 1256 of the Code)

#### *Present Law*

In general, section 1256 requires taxpayers to treat each section 1256 contract as if it were sold (and repurchased) for its fair market value on the last business day of the year (i.e., "marked to market"). Any gain or loss with respect to a section 1256 contract which is subject to the mark-to-market rule is treated as if 40 percent of the gain or loss were short-term capital gain or loss and 60 percent were long-term capital gain or loss.[1135] Gains and losses upon the termination (or transfer) of a section 1256 contract, by offsetting, taking or making delivery, by exercise or by being exercised, by assignment or being assigned, by lapse, or otherwise, also generally are treated as 40 percent short-term and 60 percent long-term capital gains or losses.[1136] Section 1256(b) provides that a "section 1256 contract" means (1) any regulated futures contract, (2) any foreign currency contract, (3) any nonequity option, (4) any dealer equity option, and (5) any dealer securities futures contract.

The rule in section 1256(a) treating gains and losses as 60 percent long-term capital gains and losses and 40 percent short-term capital gains and losses does not apply to (i) hedging transactions,[1137] (ii) section 1256 contracts that but for section 1256(a)(3) would be ordinary income property,[1138] (iii) a section 1256 contract that is part of a mixed straddle if the taxpayer elects to have section 1256 not apply to the section 1256 contract,[1139] or (iv) any section 1256 contract held by a dealer in commodities or by a trader in commodities that makes the mark-to-market election in section 475.[1140]

#### *Explanation of Provision*

The provision excludes from the definition of "section 1256 contract" any interest rate swap, interest rate cap, interest rate floor,

---

[1134] H.R. 4173. The bill passed the House on December 11, 2009. The Senate passed the bill with an amendment on May 20, 2010. The conference report was filed on June 29, 2010 (H.R. Rep. No. 111–517) and was passed by the House on June 30, 2010, and the Senate on July 15, 2010. The President signed the bill on July 21, 2010.

[1135] Sec. 1256(a)(3).

[1136] Sec. 1256(c)(1).

[1137] Sec. 1256(e)(1).

[1138] Sec. 1256(f)(2). Gain or loss from trading of section 1256 contracts is treated as gain or loss from the sale of a capital asset except to the extent the contract is held for purposes of hedging ordinary loss property. (Sec. 1256(f)(3)).

[1139] Sec. 1256(d).

[1140] See sec. 475(d)(1).

commodity swap, equity swap, equity index swap, credit default swap, or similar agreement.

### *Effective Date*

The provision is effective upon the date of enactment (July 21, 2010).

# PART TWELVE: REVENUE PROVISIONS OF THE ___ ACT OF ___ (PUBLIC LAW 111–226)[1141]

## A. Rules to Prevent Splitting Foreign Tax Credits from the Income to Which They Relate (sec. 211 of the Act and new sec. 909 of the Code)

### *Present Law*

The United States employs a worldwide tax system under which U.S. resident individuals and domestic corporations generally are taxed on all income, whether derived in the United States or abroad; the foreign tax credit provides relief from double taxation. Subject to the limitations discussed below, a U.S. taxpayer is allowed to claim a credit against its U.S. income tax liability for the foreign income taxes that it pays or accrues. A domestic corporation that owns at least 10 percent of the voting stock of a foreign corporation is allowed a deemed-paid credit for foreign income taxes paid by the foreign corporation that the domestic corporation is deemed to have paid when the foreign corporation's earnings are distributed or included in the domestic corporation's income under the provisions of subpart F.[1142]

A foreign tax credit is available only for foreign income, war profits, and excess profits taxes, and for certain taxes imposed in lieu of such taxes.[1143] Other foreign levies generally are treated as deductible expenses. Treasury regulations under section 901 provide detailed rules for determining whether a foreign levy is a creditable income tax.

The foreign tax credit is elective on a year-by-year basis. In lieu of electing the foreign tax credit, U.S. persons generally are permitted to deduct foreign taxes.[1144]

#### *Deemed-paid foreign tax credit*

Domestic corporations owning at least 10 percent of the voting stock of a foreign corporation are treated as if they had paid a share of the foreign income taxes paid by the foreign corporation

[1141] H.R. 1586. The bill originated as a bill imposing additional tax on bonuses received from certain TARP recipients and passed the House on the suspension calendar on March 19, 2009. The bill passed the Senate with an amendment substituting text relating to the FAA on March 22, 2010. The House agreed to the Senate amendment with an amendment on March 25, 2010. On August 5, 2010, the Senate concurred in the House amendment to the Senate amendment with an amendment substituting the text relating to education, jobs, and Medicaid for the previous language. On August 10, 2010, the House agreed to the Senate amendment to the House amendment to the Senate amendment. The President signed the bill on August 10, 2010. For a technical explanation of the bill prepared by the staff of the Joint Committee on Taxation, see *Technical Explanation of the Revenue Provisions of the Senate Amendment to the House Amendment to the Senate Amendment to H.R. 1586, Scheduled for Consideration by the House of Representatives on August 10, 2010* (JCX–46–10), August 10, 2010.

[1142] Secs. 901, 902, 960. Similar rules apply under sections 1291(g) and 1293(f) with respect to income that is includible under the passive foreign investment company ("PFIC") rules.

[1143] Secs. 901(b), 903.

[1144] Sec. 164(a)(3).

in the year in which that corporation's earnings and profits become subject to U.S. tax as dividend income of the U.S. shareholder.[1145] This credit is the deemed-paid or indirect foreign tax credit. A domestic corporation may also be deemed to have paid taxes paid by a second-, third-, fourth-, fifth-, or sixth-tier foreign corporation, if certain requirements are satisfied.[1146] Foreign taxes paid below the third tier are eligible for the deemed-paid credit only with respect to taxes paid in taxable years during which the payor is a controlled foreign corporation ("CFC"). Foreign taxes paid below the sixth tier are not eligible for the deemed-paid credit. In addition, a deemed-paid credit generally is available with respect to subpart F inclusions and inclusions under the PFIC provisions.[1147]

The amount of foreign tax eligible for the indirect credit is added to the actual dividend or inclusion (the dividend or inclusion is said to be "grossed-up") and is included in the domestic corporate shareholder's income; accordingly, the shareholder is treated as if it had received its proportionate share of pre-tax profits of the foreign corporation and paid its proportionate share of the foreign tax paid by the foreign corporation.[1148]

For purposes of computing the deemed-paid foreign tax credit, dividends (or other inclusions) are considered made first from the post-1986 pool of all the distributing foreign corporation's accumulated earnings and profits.[1149] Accumulated earnings and profits for this purpose include the earnings and profits of the current year undiminished by the current distribution (or other inclusion).[1150] Dividends in excess of the pool of post-1986 undistributed earnings and profits are treated as paid out of pre-1987 accumulated profits and are subject to the ordering principles of pre-1986 Act law.[1151]

### *Foreign tax credit limitation*

The foreign tax credit generally is limited to a taxpayer's U.S. tax liability on its foreign-source taxable income (as determined under U.S. tax accounting principles).[1152] This limit is intended to ensure that the credit serves its purpose of mitigating double taxation of foreign-source income without offsetting U.S. tax on U.S.-source income. The limit is computed by multiplying a taxpayer's total U.S. tax liability for the year by the ratio of the taxpayer's foreign-source taxable income for the year to the taxpayer's total taxable income for the year. If the total amount of foreign income taxes paid and deemed paid for the year exceeds the taxpayer's foreign tax credit limitation for the year, the taxpayer may carry back the excess foreign taxes to the previous taxable year or carry forward the excess taxes to one of the succeeding 10 taxable years.[1153]

The foreign tax credit limitation is generally applied separately for income in two different categories (referred to as "baskets"),

[1145] Sec. 902(a).
[1146] Sec. 902(b).
[1147] Secs. 960(a), 1291(g), 1293(f).
[1148] Sec. 78.
[1149] Sec. 902(c)(6)(B). Earnings and profits computations for these purposes are to be made under U.S. concepts. Secs. 902(c)(1), 964(a).
[1150] Sec. 902(c)(1).
[1151] Sec. 902(c)(6).
[1152] Secs. 901, 904.
[1153] Sec. 904(c).

passive basket income and general basket income.[1154] Passive basket income generally includes investment income such as dividends, interest, rents, and royalties.[1155] General basket income is all income that is not in the passive basket. Because the foreign tax credit limitation must be applied separately to income in these two baskets, credits for foreign tax imposed on income in one basket cannot be used to offset U.S. tax on income in the other basket.

Income that would otherwise constitute passive basket income is treated as general basket income if it is earned by a qualifying financial services entity (and certain other requirements are met).[1156] Passive income is also treated as general basket income if it is high-taxed income (i.e., if the foreign tax rate is determined to exceed the highest rate of tax specified in section 1 or 11, as applicable).[1157] Dividends (and subpart F inclusions), interest, rents, and royalties received from a CFC by a U.S. person that owns at least 10 percent of the CFC are assigned to a separate limitation basket by reference to the basket of income out of which the dividend or other payment is made.[1158] Dividends received by a 10-percent corporate shareholder from a foreign corporation that is not a CFC are also categorized on a look-through basis.[1159]

### *Explanation of Provision*

The provision adopts a matching rule to prevent the separation of creditable foreign taxes from the associated foreign income. In general, the provision states that when there is a foreign tax credit splitting event with respect to a foreign income tax paid or accrued by the taxpayer, the foreign income tax is not taken into account for Federal tax purposes before the taxable year in which the related income is taken into account by the taxpayer. In addition, if there is a foreign tax credit splitting event with respect to a foreign income tax paid or accrued by a section 902 corporation, that tax is not taken into account for purposes of section 902 or 960, or for purposes of determining earnings and profits under section 964(a), before the taxable year in which the related income is taken into account for Federal income tax purposes by the section 902 corporation, or a domestic corporation that meets the ownership requirements of section 902(a) or (b) with respect to the section 902 corporation. Thus, such tax is not added to the section 902 corporation's foreign tax pool, and its earnings and profits are not reduced by such tax.

In the case of a partnership, the provision's matching rule is applied at the partner level, and, except as otherwise provided by the

[1154] Sec. 904(d). Separate foreign tax credit limitations also apply to certain categories of income described in other sections. See, e.g., secs. 901(j), 904(h)(10), 865(h).

[1155] Sec. 904(d)(2)(B). Passive income is defined by reference to the definition of foreign personal holding company income in section 954(c), and thus generally includes dividends, interest, rents, royalties, annuities, net gains from certain property or commodities transactions, foreign currency gains, income equivalent to interest, income from notional principal contracts, and income from certain personal service contracts. Exceptions apply for certain rents and royalties derived in an active business and for certain income earned by dealers in securities or other financial instruments. Passive category income also includes amounts that are includible in gross income under section 1293 (relating to PFICs) and dividends received from certain DISCs and FSCs.

[1156] Sec. 904(d)(2)(C), (D).

[1157] Sec. 904(d)(2)(F).

[1158] Sec. 904(d)(3).

[1159] Sec. 904(d)(4).

Secretary, a similar rule applies in the case of any S corporation or trust. The Secretary may also issue regulations to establish the applicability of this matching rule to a regulated investment company that elects under section 853 for the foreign income taxes it pays to be treated as creditable to its shareholders under section 901.

For purposes of the provision, there is a "foreign tax credit splitting event" with respect to a foreign income tax if the related income is (or will be) taken into account for Federal income tax purposes by a covered person.[1160] A "foreign income tax" is any income, war profits, or excess profits tax paid or accrued to any foreign country or to any possession of the United States. This term includes any tax paid in lieu of such a tax within the meaning of section 903. "Related income" means, with respect to any portion of any foreign income tax, the income (or, as appropriate, earnings and profits), calculated under U.S. tax principles, to which such portion of foreign income tax relates. For purposes of determining related income, the Secretary may provide rules on the treatment of losses, deficits in earnings and profits, and certain timing differences between U.S. and foreign tax law. Moreover, it is not intended that differences in the timing of when income is taken into account for U.S. and foreign tax purposes (e.g., as a result of differences in the U.S. and foreign tax accounting rules) should create a foreign tax credit splitting event in cases in which the same person pays the foreign tax and takes into account the related income, but in different taxable periods.

With respect to any person who pays or accrues a foreign income tax (hereafter referred to in this paragraph as the "payor"), a "covered person" is: (1) any entity in which the payor holds, directly or indirectly, at least a 10-percent ownership interest (determined by vote or value); (2) any person that holds, directly or indirectly, at least a 10-percent ownership interest (determined by vote or value) in the payor; (3) any person that bears a relationship to the payor described in section 267(b) or 707(b) (including by application of the constructive ownership rules of section 267(c)); and (4) any other person specified by the Secretary. Accordingly, the Secretary may issue regulations that treat an unrelated counterparty as a covered person in certain sale-repurchase transactions and certain other transactions deemed abusive.

A "section 902 corporation" is any foreign corporation with respect to which one or more domestic corporations meets the ownership requirements of section 902(a) or (b).

Except as otherwise provided by the Secretary, in the case of any foreign income tax not currently taken into account by reason of the provision's matching rule, that tax is taken into account as a foreign income tax paid or accrued in the taxable year in which, and to the extent that, the taxpayer, the section 902 corporation, or a domestic corporation that meets the ownership requirements of section 902(a) or (b) with respect to the section 902 corporation

[1160] It is not intended that there be a foreign tax credit splitting event when, for example, a CFC pays or accrues a foreign income tax and takes into account the related income in the same year, even though the earnings and profits to which the foreign income tax relates may be distributed to a covered person as a dividend or included in such covered person's income under subpart F.

(as the case may be) takes the related income into account under chapter 1 of the Code. Accordingly, for purposes of determining the carryback and carryover of excess foreign tax credits under section 904(c), the deduction for foreign taxes paid or accrued under section 164(a), and the extended period for claim of a credit or refund under section 6511(d)(3)(A), foreign income taxes to which the provision applies are first taken into account, and treated as paid or accrued, in the year in which the related foreign income is taken into account. Notwithstanding the preceding rule, foreign taxes are translated into U.S. dollars in the year in which the taxes are paid or accrued under the general rules of section 986 rather than the year in which the related income is taken into account. The Secretary may issue regulations or other guidance providing additional exceptions.

The Secretary is also granted authority to issue regulations or other guidance as is necessary or appropriate to carry out the purposes of the provision. Such guidance may include providing successor rules addressing circumstances such as where, with respect to a foreign tax credit splitting event, the person who pays or accrues the foreign income tax or any covered person is liquidated. This grant of authority also allows the Secretary to provide appropriate exceptions from the application of the provision as well as to provide guidance as to how the provision applies in the case of any foreign tax credit splitting event involving a hybrid instrument. It is anticipated that the Secretary may also provide guidance as to the proper application of the provision in cases involving disregarded payments, group relief, or other arrangements having a similar effect.

An example of a foreign tax credit splitting event involving a hybrid instrument subject to the provision is as follows: U.S. Corp., a domestic corporation, wholly owns CFC1, a country A corporation. CFC1, in turn, wholly owns CFC2, a country A corporation. CFC2 is engaged in an active business that generates $100 of income. CFC2 issues a hybrid instrument to CFC1. This instrument is treated as equity for U.S. tax purposes but as debt for foreign tax purposes. Under the terms of the hybrid instrument, CFC2 accrues (but does not pay currently) interest to CFC1 equal to $100. As a result, CFC2 has no income for country A tax purposes, while CFC1 has $100 of income, which is subject to country A tax at a 30 percent rate. For U.S. tax purposes, CFC2 still has $100 of earnings and profits (the accrued interest is ignored since the United States views the hybrid instrument as equity), while CFC1 has paid $30 of foreign taxes. Under the provision, the related income with respect to the $30 of foreign taxes paid by CFC1 is the $100 of earnings and profits of CFC2.

### *Effective Date*

In general, the provision is effective with respect to foreign income taxes paid or accrued by U.S. taxpayers and section 902 corporations in taxable years beginning after December 31, 2010.

The provision also applies to foreign income taxes paid or accrued by a section 902 corporation in taxable years beginning on or before December 31, 2010 (and not deemed paid under section 902(a) or section 960 on or before such date), but only for purposes of applying sections 902 and 960 with respect to periods after such date (the "deemed-paid transition rule"). Accordingly, the deemed-paid transition rule applies for purposes of applying sections 902 and 960 to dividends paid, and inclusions under section 951(a) that occur, in taxable years beginning after December 31, 2010. However, no adjustment is made to a section 902 corporation's earnings and profits for the amount of any foreign income taxes suspended under the deemed-paid transition rule, either at the time of suspension or when such taxes are subsequently taken into account under the provision.

## B. Denial of Foreign Tax Credit with Respect to Foreign Income Not Subject to U.S. Taxation by Reason of Covered Asset Acquisitions (sec. 212 of the Act and sec. 901(m) of the Code)

### *Present Law*

#### *Foreign tax credit*

The United States employs a worldwide tax system under which U.S. resident individuals and domestic corporations generally are taxed on all income, whether derived in the United States or abroad; the foreign tax credit provides relief from double taxation. Subject to the limitations discussed below, a U.S. taxpayer is allowed to claim a credit against its U.S. income tax liability for the foreign income taxes that it pays. A domestic corporation that owns at least 10 percent of the voting stock of a foreign corporation is allowed a "deemed-paid" credit for foreign income taxes paid by the foreign corporation that the domestic corporation is deemed to have paid when the related income is distributed or is included in the domestic corporation's income under the provisions of subpart F.[1161]

The foreign tax credit is elective on a year-by-year basis. In lieu of electing the foreign tax credit, U.S. persons generally are permitted to deduct foreign taxes.[1162]

*Deemed-paid foreign tax credit*

U.S. corporations owning at least 10 percent of the voting stock of a foreign corporation are treated as if they had paid a share of the foreign income taxes paid by the foreign corporation in the year in which that corporation's earnings and profits ("E&P") become subject to U.S. tax as dividend income of the U.S. shareholder.[1163] This credit is the "deemed-paid" or "indirect" foreign tax credit. A U.S. corporation may also be deemed to have paid foreign income taxes paid by a second-, third-, fourth-, fifth-, or sixth-tier foreign corporation, if certain requirements are satisfied.[1164] Foreign income taxes paid below the third tier are eligible for the deemed-paid credit only with respect to foreign income taxes paid in taxable years during which the payor is a controlled foreign corporation ("CFC"). Foreign income taxes paid below the sixth tier are not

[1161] Secs. 901, 902, 960. Similar rules apply under sections 1291(g) and 1293(f) with respect to income that is includible under the passive foreign investment company ("PFIC") rules.
[1162] Sec. 164(a)(3).
[1163] Sec. 902(a).
[1164] Sec. 902(b).

eligible for the deemed-paid credit. In addition, a deemed-paid credit generally is available with respect to subpart F inclusions.[1165] Moreover, a deemed-paid credit generally is available with respect to inclusions under the PFIC provisions by U.S. corporations meeting the requisite ownership threshold.[1166]

The amount of foreign income tax eligible for the indirect credit is added to the actual dividend or inclusion (the dividend or inclusion is said to be "grossed-up") and is included in the U.S. corporate shareholder's income; accordingly, the shareholder is treated as if it had received its proportionate share of pre-tax profits of the foreign corporation and paid its proportionate share of the foreign income tax paid by the foreign corporation.[1167]

For purposes of computing the deemed-paid foreign tax credit, dividends (or other inclusions) are considered made first from the post-1986 pool of all the distributing foreign corporation's accumulated E&P.[1168] Accumulated E&P for this purpose include the E&P of the current year undiminished by the current distribution (or other inclusion).[1169] Dividends in excess of the accumulated pool of post-1986 undistributed E&P are treated as paid out of pre-1987 accumulated profits and are subject to the ordering principles of pre-1986 Act law.[1170]

*Foreign tax credit limitation*

The foreign tax credit generally is limited to a taxpayer's U.S. tax liability on its foreign-source taxable income (as determined under U.S. tax accounting principles).[1171] This limit is intended to ensure that the credit serves its purpose of mitigating double taxation of foreign-source income without offsetting U.S. tax on U.S.-source income. The limit is computed by multiplying a taxpayer's total U.S. tax liability for the year by the ratio of the taxpayer's foreign-source taxable income for the year to the taxpayer's total taxable income for the year. If the total amount of foreign income taxes paid and deemed paid for the year exceeds the taxpayer's foreign tax credit limitation for the year, the taxpayer may carry the excess back to the previous taxable year or forward to one of the succeeding 10 taxable years.[1172]

The foreign tax credit limitation is generally applied separately to two different categories of income (referred to as "baskets"), passive basket income and general basket income.[1173] Passive basket income generally includes investment income such as dividends, interest, rents, and royalties.[1174] General basket income is all income

[1165] Sec. 960(a).

[1166] Secs. 1291(g), 1293(f).

[1167] Sec. 78.

[1168] Sec. 902(c)(6)(B). Earnings and profits computations for these purposes are to be made under U.S. concepts. Secs. 902(c)(1), 964(a).

[1169] Sec. 902(c)(1).

[1170] Sec. 902(c)(6).

[1171] Secs. 901, 904.

[1172] Sec. 904(c).

[1173] Sec. 904(d). Separate foreign tax credit limitations also apply to certain categories of income described in other sections. See, e.g., secs. 901(j), 904(h)(10), 865(h).

[1174] Sec. 904(d)(2)(B). Passive income is defined by reference to the definition of foreign personal holding company income in section 954(c), and thus generally includes dividends, interest, rents, royalties, annuities, net gains from certain property or commodities transactions, foreign currency gains, income equivalent to interest, income from notional principal contracts, and income from certain personal service contracts. Exceptions apply for certain rents and royalties derived in an active business and for certain income earned by dealers in securities or other

that is not in the passive category. Because the foreign tax credit limitation must be applied separately to income in these two baskets, foreign tax imposed on income in one basket cannot be claimed as a credit against U.S. tax on income in the other basket.

Income that would otherwise constitute passive basket income is treated as general basket income if it is earned by a qualifying financial services entity (and certain other requirements are met).[1175] Passive income is also treated as general basket income if it is high-taxed income (i.e., if the foreign tax rate is determined to exceed the highest rate of tax specified in section 1 or 11, as applicable).[1176] Dividends (and subpart F inclusions), interest, rents, and royalties received from a CFC by a U.S. person that owns at least 10 percent of the CFC are assigned to a separate limitation basket by reference to the basket of income out of which the dividend or other payment is made.[1177] Dividends received by a 10-percent corporate shareholder from a foreign corporation that is not a CFC are also categorized on a look-through basis.[1178]

*Items giving rise to permanent basis differences*

In general, certain elections or transactions can result in the creation of additional asset basis eligible for cost recovery for U.S. tax purposes without a corresponding increase in the basis of such assets for foreign tax purposes. These include: (1) a qualifying stock purchase of a foreign corporation or domestic corporation with foreign assets for which a section 338 election is made; (2) an acquisition of an interest in a partnership holding foreign assets for which a section 754 election is in effect; and (3) certain other transactions involving an entity classification ("check-the-box") election in which a foreign entity is treated as a corporation for foreign tax purposes and as a partnership or disregarded entity for U.S. tax purposes.[1179]

*Section 338 elections*

In general, the basis of stock acquired by a U.S. taxpayer or a foreign subsidiary of a U.S. taxpayer is its cost,[1180] and there is no adjustment to the basis of the assets held by the acquired corporation.[1181] In certain circumstances, however, taxpayers may elect to treat a qualifying purchase of 80 percent of the stock of a target corporation (a "qualified stock purchase") as a purchase of the underlying assets of the target corporation.[1182] For this purpose, a "qualified stock purchase" is any transaction or series of transactions in which stock (meeting the requirements of section

financial instruments. Passive category income also includes amounts that are includible in gross income under section 1293 (relating to PFICs) and dividends received from certain DISCs and FSCs.

[1175] Sec. 904(d)(2)(C), (D).

[1176] Sec. 904(d)(2)(F).

[1177] Sec. 904(d)(3).

[1178] Sec. 904(d)(4).

[1179] Treas. Reg. sec. 301.7701–1, *et seq.*

[1180] Secs. 1011, 1012.

[1181] See sec. 1016.

[1182] Sec. 338(a).

1504(a)(2)) of one corporation is acquired by another corporation by purchase during the 12-month acquisition period.[1183]

Two alternatives exist for making a section 338 election when there is a qualifying stock purchase—one bilateral and one unilateral. A bilateral election, which is made pursuant to section 338(h)(10), requires a corporation to make a qualifying purchase of 80 percent of the stock of a domestic target corporation[1184] that is a member of a selling consolidated group (or affiliated group if no election to file a consolidated return has been made), or a qualifying purchase of 80 percent of the stock of an S corporation by a corporation from S corporation shareholders. The election is made jointly by the buyer and seller of the stock and must be made by the 15th day of the ninth month beginning after the month in which the acquisition date occurs. Pursuant to this election, the assets (rather than the stock) of the target corporation are deemed to have been sold in a single transaction at the close of the acquisition date, and the target corporation is deemed to have liquidated. The asset sale is taken into account by the target prior to its acquisition by the purchasing corporation.[1185]

With a unilateral election, which is made pursuant to section 338(g), the purchasing corporation treats a qualified stock purchase of a corporation (including a foreign corporation) as a deemed asset acquisition, whether or not the seller of the stock is a corporation. Pursuant to this election, the seller or sellers recognize gain or loss on the stock sale, and the target corporation also recognizes gain or loss on the deemed asset sale. The deemed asset acquisition also eliminates the historic E&P of the target corporation. In general, in cases in which the target corporation is foreign and the seller is a U.S. person or a CFC, the deemed asset sale has U.S. tax consequences.[1186] However, when the seller is neither a U.S. person nor a CFC, generally no U.S. tax consequences result from the deemed asset sale.[1187] The election is made by the purchasing corporation and must be made by the 15th day of the ninth month beginning after the month in which the acquisition date occurs.

Pursuant to a section 338 election, the target corporation is treated as (1) having sold all of its assets at the close of the acquisition date at fair market value in a single transaction, and (2) a new corporation that purchased all of the assets as of the begin-

[1183] Sec. 338(d)(3). Under section 1504(a)(2), the ownership of stock of any corporation meets the requirements of an affiliated group if it (A) possesses at least 80 percent of the total voting power of the stock of such corporation, and (B) has a value equal to at least 80 percent of the total value of the stock of such corporation. Further, section 1504(a)(4) states that for purposes of meeting the 80-percent requirement, the term stock does not include any stock which (A) is not entitled to vote, (B) is limited and preferred as to dividends and does not participate in corporate growth to any significant extent, (C) has redemption and liquidation rights which do not exceed the issue price of such stock, and (D) is not convertible into another class of stock.

[1184] A foreign corporation cannot be the target corporation in the case of a section 338(h)(10) election. See Treas. Reg. sec. 1.338(h)(10)–1(b)(1), (2), (3).

[1185] Sec. 338(h)(10); Treas. Regs. sec. 1.338(h)(10)–1(d)(3).

[1186] Section 338(h)(16) addresses the impact of the deemed asset sale on the E&P of the foreign target corporation for purposes of determining the source and character of any amount includible in gross income as a dividend under section 1248 to the seller.

[1187] When a domestic corporation or a CFC is the purchaser with respect to which a section 338(g) election is made for a foreign target corporation, the deemed asset sale may have U.S. tax consequences. For example, if the foreign target becomes a CFC for an uninterrupted period of 30 days or more during a taxable year pursuant to Section 951(a) prior to the purchasing corporation completing the qualified stock purchase, the deemed asset sale may generate subpart F income for any U.S. shareholder of the foreign target corporation. Treas. Reg. sec. 1.338–9(b).

ning of the day after the acquisition date.[1188] Accordingly, the aggregate basis of the assets of the target equals the sum of (1) the grossed-up basis of the purchasing corporation's recently purchased stock, and (2) the basis of the purchasing corporation's nonrecently purchased stock, with appropriate adjustments for liabilities and other relevant items under the regulations.[1189]

Since a section 338 election is relevant solely for U.S. tax purposes, the adjustment to the basis of the assets of a foreign target corporation (or a foreign branch of a domestic corporation) that increases the amount of depreciation, amortization, depletion, or gain for purposes of calculating U.S. taxable income or E&P results in no corresponding adjustment for foreign income tax purposes. As a result, cost recovery deductions attributable to such additional basis generally result in a permanent difference between (1) the foreign taxable income upon which foreign income tax is levied, and (2) the U.S. taxable income (or E&P) upon which U.S. tax is levied (whether currently or upon repatriation) and with respect to which a foreign tax credit may be allowed for any foreign income taxes paid.

*Section 754 election*

A partnership does not generally adjust the basis of partnership property following the transfer of a partnership interest unless the partnership has made a one-time election under section 754 for such purposes.[1190] If an election is in effect, adjustments to the basis of partnership property are made with respect to the transferee partner to account for the difference between the transferee partner's proportionate share of the adjusted basis of the partnership property and the transferee's basis in its partnership interest.[1191] These adjustments are intended to adjust the basis of partnership property to approximate the result of a direct purchase of the property by the transferee partner. Because a section 754 election has relevance only for U.S. tax purposes, to the extent that the underlying assets of the partnership include assets generating income subject to foreign tax, the basis adjustments made to these assets may also result in permanent differences between (1) the foreign taxable income upon which foreign income tax is levied, and (2) the U.S. taxable income (or E&P) upon which U.S. tax is levied (whether currently or upon repatriation) and with respect to which a foreign tax credit may be allowed for any foreign income taxes paid.

*Check-the-box election*

Comparable permanent differences between foreign taxable income and U.S. taxable income (or E&P) may also be achieved as a result of making a check-the-box election. Since a check-the-box election generally has no effect for foreign tax purposes, a sale of a wholly-owned foreign corporation for which an election to be disregarded is in effect will be respected as the sale of the corporation

[1188] Sec. 338(a).
[1189] Sec. 338(b).
[1190] Sec. 743(a). But see section 743(d) requiring a reduction to the basis of partnership property in certain cases where there is a substantial built-in loss.
[1191] Sec. 743(b).

for foreign tax purposes but treated as the sale of branch assets for U.S. tax purposes. If the purchaser is a U.S. taxpayer or a foreign entity owned by a U.S. taxpayer, the U.S. taxpayer may have additional asset basis eligible for cost recovery for U.S. tax purposes without a corresponding increase in the tax basis of such assets for foreign tax purposes. In this case, there would be a permanent difference between (1) the foreign taxable income upon which foreign income tax is levied, and (2) the U.S. taxable income (or E&P) upon which U.S. tax is levied (whether currently or upon repatriation) and with respect to which a foreign tax credit may be allowed. Similar results may be achieved through other transactions in which a check-the-box election has been made.

### *Explanation of Provision*

The provision denies a foreign tax credit for the disqualified portion of any foreign income tax paid or accrued in connection with a covered asset acquisition.

A "covered asset acquisition" means: (1) a qualified stock purchase (as defined in section 338(d)(3)) to which section 338(a) applies;[1192] (2) any transaction that is treated as the acquisition of assets for U.S. tax purposes and as the acquisition of stock (or is disregarded)[1193] for purposes of the foreign income taxes of the relevant jurisdiction;[1194] (3) any acquisition of an interest in a partnership that has an election in effect under section 754; and (4) to the extent provided by the Secretary, any other similar transaction. It is anticipated that the Secretary will issue regulations identifying other similar transactions that result in an increase to the basis of assets for U.S. tax purposes without a corresponding increase for foreign tax purposes.

The disqualified portion of any foreign income taxes paid or accrued with respect to any covered asset acquisition, for any taxable year, is the ratio (expressed as a percentage) of (1) the aggregate basis differences allocable to such taxable year with respect to all relevant foreign assets, divided by (2) the income on which the foreign income tax is determined. For this purpose, the income on which the foreign income tax is determined is the income as determined under the law of the relevant jurisdiction. If the taxpayer fails to substantiate such income to the satisfaction of the Secretary, then such income is determined by dividing the amount of such foreign income tax by the highest marginal tax rate applicable to such income in the relevant jurisdiction.

For purposes of determining the aggregate basis difference allocable to a taxable year, the term "basis difference" means, with re-

[1192] This includes transaction under section 338(g) and section 338(h)(10).

[1193] For example, the deemed liquidation of a CFC as the result of the making of an entity classification election pursuant to Treas. Reg. sec. 301.7701–3 may result in a section 331 liquidation for U.S. tax purposes that is disregarded for foreign income tax purposes.

[1194] Section 336(e) provides that, to the extent provided by the Secretary, in cases in which (1) a corporation owns at least 80 percent of the vote and value of stock of another corporation (as defined in section 1504(a)(2)), and (2) such corporation sells, exchanges, or distributes all of stock of such corporation, an election may be made to treat this sale, exchange, or distribution as a disposition of all of the assets of the other corporation, and no gain or loss is recognized on the sale, exchange, or distribution of the stock. To date, the Secretary has not promulgated regulations under section 336(e) so no election may be made. Nonetheless, to the extent regulations are promulgated under section 336(e) in the future permitting such an election to be made, a transaction to which the section 336(e) election relates would be a covered asset acquisition.

spect to any relevant foreign asset, the excess of (1) the adjusted basis of such asset immediately after the covered asset acquisition, over (2) the adjusted basis of such asset immediately before the covered asset acquisition. Thus, it is the tax basis for U.S. tax purposes that is relevant, and not the basis as determined under the law of the relevant foreign jurisdiction. Because CFCs are generally limited to straight-line cost recovery, it is anticipated that the basis difference applying U.S. tax principles generally is less than if the taxpayer were required to use the basis as determined under foreign law immediately before the covered asset acquisition. However, it is anticipated that the Secretary will issue regulations identifying those circumstances in which, for purposes of determining the adjusted basis of such assets immediately before the covered asset acquisition, it may be acceptable to utilize the basis of such asset under the law of the relevant jurisdiction or another reasonable method.

A built-in loss in a relevant foreign asset (i.e., in cases in which the fair market value of the asset is less than its adjusted basis immediately before the asset acquisition) is taken into account in determining the aggregate basis difference; however, a built-in loss cannot reduce the aggregate basis difference allocable to a taxable year below zero.

In the case of a qualified stock purchase to which section 338(a) applies, the covered asset acquisition is treated as occurring at the close of the acquisition date (as defined in section 338(h)(2)).

In general, the amount of the basis difference allocable to a taxable year with respect to any relevant foreign asset is determined using the applicable cost recovery method under U.S. tax rules. If there is a disposition of any relevant foreign asset before its cost has been entirely recovered or of any relevant foreign asset that is not eligible for cost recovery (e.g., land), the basis difference allocated to the taxable year of the disposition is the excess of the basis difference with respect to such asset over the aggregate basis difference with respect to such asset that has been allocated under this provision to all prior taxable years. Thus, any remaining basis difference is captured in the year of the sale, and there is no remaining basis difference to be allocated to any subsequent tax years. However, it is intended that this provision generally apply in circumstances in which there is a disposition of a relevant foreign asset and the associated income or gain is taken into account for purposes of determining foreign income tax in the relevant jurisdiction.

To illustrate, assume USP, a domestic corporation, acquires 100 percent of the stock of FT, a foreign target organized in Country F with a "u" functional currency, in a qualified stock purchase for which a section 338(g) election is made. The tax rate in Country F is 25 percent. Assume further that the aggregate basis difference in connection with the qualified stock purchase is 200u, including: (1) 150u that is attributable to Asset A, with a 15-year recovery period for U.S. tax purposes (10u of annual amortization); and (2) 50u that is attributable to Asset B, with a 5-year recovery period (10u of annual depreciation). In each of years 1 and 2, FT's taxable income is 100u for foreign tax purposes and FT pays foreign income tax of 25u (equal to $25 when translated at the average exchange rate for the year). As a result, the disqualified portion of foreign income tax in each of years 1 and 2 is \$5 ((10u + 10u of allocable basis difference / 100u of foreign taxable income) × \$25 foreign tax paid).

In year 3, FT's taxable income is 140u, 40u of which is attributable to gain on the sale of Asset B. FT's Country F tax is 35u (equal to \$35 translated at the average exchange rate for the year). Accordingly, the disqualified portion of its foreign income taxes paid is \$10 ((40u (including 10u of annual amortization on Asset A and 30u attributable to disposition of Asset B) of allocable basis difference / 140u of foreign taxable income) × \$35 foreign tax paid).

An asset is a "relevant foreign asset" with respect to any covered asset acquisition, whether the entity acquired is domestic or foreign, only if any income, deduction, gain, or loss attributable to the asset (including goodwill, going concern value, and any other intangible asset) is taken into account in determining foreign income tax in the relevant jurisdiction. For this purpose, the term "foreign income tax" means any income, war profits, or excess profits tax paid or accrued to any foreign country or to any possession of the United States, including any tax paid in lieu of such a tax within the meaning of section 903. In cases in which there has been a covered asset acquisition that involves either (1) both U.S. assets and relevant foreign assets, or (2) assets in multiple relevant jurisdictions, it is anticipated that the Secretary may issue regulations clarifying the manner in which any relevant foreign asset (such as intangible assets that may relate to more than one jurisdiction) are to be allocated between those jurisdictions. It is also anticipated that the Secretary may issue regulations to clarify the extent to which income is considered attributable to a relevant foreign asset, as well as the treatment of an asset that ceases to be taken into account in determining the foreign income tax in the relevant jurisdiction by some mechanism other than a disposition.

To the extent that a foreign tax credit is disallowed, the disqualified portion is allowed as a deduction to the extent otherwise deductible.[1195]

The Secretary may issue regulations or other guidance as is necessary or appropriate to carry out the purposes of this provision, including to provide (1) an exemption for certain covered asset acquisitions, and (2) an exemption for relevant foreign assets with respect to which the basis difference is de minimis. For example, it is anticipated that the Secretary will exclude covered asset acquisitions that are not taxable for U.S. purposes, or in which the basis of the relevant foreign assets is also increased for purposes of the tax laws of the relevant jurisdiction.

### *Effective Date*

In general, the provision is effective for covered asset acquisitions after December 31, 2010. However, the provision does not apply to any covered asset acquisition with respect to which the transferor and transferee are not related if the acquisition is (1) made pursuant to a written agreement that was binding on January 1, 2011,

[1195] Sec. 164(a)(3).

and at all times thereafter, (2) described in a ruling request[1196] submitted to the IRS on or before July 29, 2010, or (3) described in a public announcement or filing with the SEC on or before January 1, 2011.

For this purpose, a person is treated as related to another person if the relationship between such persons is described in section 267 or 707(b).

## C. Separate Application of Foreign Tax Credit Limitation, etc., to Items Resourced Under Treaties (sec. 213 of the Act and sec. 904(d) of the Code)

### *Present Law*

The United States taxes its citizens and residents (including domestic corporations) on worldwide income. Because the countries in which income is earned also may assert their jurisdiction to tax the same income on the basis of source, foreign-source income earned by U.S. persons may be subject to double taxation. Subject to limitations discussed below, a U.S. taxpayer is allowed to claim a credit against its U.S. income tax liability for foreign income taxes paid or accrued.[1197] A domestic corporation that owns at least 10 percent of the voting stock of a foreign corporation is allowed a "deemed-paid" credit for foreign income taxes paid by the foreign corporation that the domestic corporation is deemed to have paid when the foreign corporation's earnings are distributed or included in the domestic corporation's income under the provisions of subpart F.[1198]

A foreign tax credit is available only for foreign income, war profits, and excess profits taxes, and for certain taxes imposed in lieu of such taxes.[1199] Other foreign levies generally are treated as deductible expenses. The foreign tax credit is elective on a year-by-year basis. In lieu of electing the foreign tax credit, U.S. persons generally are permitted to deduct foreign taxes.[1200]

The foreign tax credit generally is limited to a taxpayer's U.S. tax liability on its foreign-source taxable income (as determined under U.S. tax accounting principles).[1201] This limit is intended to ensure that the credit serves its purpose of mitigating double taxation of foreign-source income without offsetting U.S. tax on U.S.-source income. The limit is computed by multiplying a taxpayer's total U.S. tax liability for the year by the ratio of the taxpayer's foreign-source taxable income for the year to the taxpayer's total taxable income for the year. If the total amount of foreign income taxes paid and deemed paid for the year exceeds the taxpayer's foreign tax credit limitation for the year, the taxpayer may carry back

[1196] A private letter ruling may be relied upon only by the taxpayer requesting the ruling. Transition relief is available only with respect to the transaction for which the ruling is requested.

[1197] Sec. 901.

[1198] Secs. 901, 902, 960. Similar rules apply under sections 1291(g) and 1293(f) with respect to income that is includible under the passive foreign investment company ("PFIC") rules.

[1199] Secs. 901(b), 903.

[1200] Sec. 164(a)(3).

[1201] Secs. 901, 904.

the excess foreign taxes to the previous taxable year or carry forward the excess taxes to one of the succeeding 10 taxable years.[1202]

The foreign tax credit limitation is generally applied separately for income in two different categories (referred to as "baskets"), passive category income and general category income.[1203] Passive category income generally includes investment income such as dividends, interest, rents, and royalties.[1204] General category income is all income that is not in the passive category. Because the foreign tax credit limitation must be applied separately to income in these two baskets, credits for foreign tax imposed on income in one basket cannot be used to offset U.S. tax on income in the other basket.

Income that would otherwise constitute passive basket income is treated as general basket income if it is earned by a qualifying financial services entity (and certain other requirements are met).[1205] Passive income is also treated as general basket income if it is high-taxed income (i.e., if the foreign tax rate is determined to exceed the highest rate of tax specified in section 1 or 11, as applicable).[1206] Dividends (and subpart F inclusions), interest, rents, and royalties received from a CFC by a U.S. person that owns at least 10 percent of the CFC are assigned to a separate basket by reference to the basket of income out of which the dividend or other payment is made.[1207] Dividends received by a 10-percent corporate shareholder from a foreign corporation that is not a CFC are also categorized on a look-through basis.[1208]

In general, amounts derived from a foreign corporation (such as interest and dividends) are treated as foreign-source income for U.S. foreign tax credit limitation purposes. A special sourcing rule applies to amounts (such as interest and dividends) derived from a U.S.-owned foreign corporation that are attributable to U.S.-source income of the foreign corporation. This special sourcing rule treats such amounts, which would otherwise be treated as foreign source, as U.S. source.[1209] For these purposes, a U.S.-owned foreign corporation is a foreign corporation that is at least 50-percent owned (directly or in certain cases indirectly) by vote or value by U.S. persons. The effect of sourcing what under the general rules would be foreign-source income as U.S.-source income under these special rules is to prevent taxpayers from routing U.S.-source in-

---

[1202] Sec. 904(c).

[1203] Sec. 904(d). Separate foreign tax credit limitations also apply to certain categories of income described in other sections. See, e.g., secs. 901(j), 904(h)(10), 865(h).

[1204] Sec. 904(d)(2)(B). Passive income is defined by reference to the definition of foreign personal holding company income in section 954(c), and thus generally includes dividends, interest, rents, royalties, annuities, net gains from certain property or commodities transactions, foreign currency gains, income equivalent to interest, income from notional principal contracts, and income from certain personal service contracts. Exceptions apply for certain rents and royalties derived in an active business and for certain income earned by dealers in securities or other financial instruments. Passive category income also includes amounts that are includible in gross income under section 1293 (relating to PFICs) and dividends received from certain DISCs and FSCs.

[1205] Sec. 904(d)(2)(C), (D).

[1206] Sec. 904(d)(2)(F).

[1207] Sec. 904(d)(3).

[1208] Sec. 904(d)(4).

[1209] Sec. 904(h). The special sourcing rule applies in the case of subpart F and passive foreign investment company inclusions to the extent that such amount is attributable to income of the U.S.-owned foreign corporation from U.S. sources; in the case of dividends, to the portion of the U.S.-owned foreign corporation's earnings and profits for the taxable year that are from U.S. sources; and in the case of interest paid to a U.S. shareholder or related person, to amounts properly allocable to the U.S.-owned foreign corporation's U.S.-source income. De minimis exceptions apply if the U.S.-owned foreign corporation has a small amount of U.S.-source income.

come through a foreign affiliate to increase the taxpayer's foreign-source income and, therefore, the taxpayer's foreign tax credit limitation.

A coordination rule applies in the case of an amount that would be treated as U.S.-source income under the special sourcing rule but which is treated as foreign source under a treaty. If (1) any amount derived from a U.S.-owned foreign corporation would be treated as U.S.-source income under the special sourcing rule described above, (2) a U.S. treaty obligation would treat such income as arising from sources outside the United States, and (3) the taxpayer chooses the benefits of this coordination rule, then the amount will be treated as foreign source. However, for foreign tax credit limitation purposes, a separate limitation applies to such amount and the associated foreign taxes. This coordination rule applies only to amounts derived from a U.S.-owned foreign corporation, and not to amounts derived from a foreign branch or disregarded entity.

For gains from the sale of certain stock or intangibles, a similar special sourcing rule applies to treat any such gain as foreign source, while requiring the taxpayer to assign any such gain and associated taxes to a separate limitation category for purposes of computing the foreign tax credit.[1210] This rule applies to the gain from sale of stock in a foreign corporation or an intangible that would be U.S. source but which under a U.S.-treaty obligation is treated as foreign source with respect to which the taxpayer chooses the benefits of this rule. This rule also applies to certain gains derived from a liquidating distribution from certain U.S.-possession corporations.

### *Explanation of Provision*

The provision applies a separate foreign tax credit limitation for each item (1) that is treated as derived from sources within the United States under U.S. tax law without regard to a treaty obligation, (2) that is treated as arising from sources outside the United States under a treaty obligation of the United States, and (3) for which the taxpayer chooses the benefits of the treaty.

The provision does not apply to items of income to which the coordination rule applicable to U.S.-owned foreign corporations or the rule for gains from the sale of certain stock or intangibles (discussed above) apply. The provision gives the Secretary authority to issue guidance as necessary or appropriate to carry out the purposes of the provision, including guidance providing that related items of income may be aggregated for purposes of the provision or grouping together items of income from the same trade or business.

### *Effective Date*

The provision is effective for taxable years beginning after the date of enactment (August 10, 2010).

---

[1210] Sec. 865(h).

## D. Limitation on the Amount of Foreign Taxes Deemed Paid with Respect to Section 956 Inclusions (sec. 214 of the Act and sec. 960 of the Code)

### *Present Law*

The United States employs a worldwide tax system under which U.S. resident individuals and domestic corporations generally are taxed on all income, whether derived in the United States or abroad; the foreign tax credit provides relief from double taxation. Income earned directly or through a pass-through entity (such as a partnership) is taxed on a current basis. By contrast, active foreign business earnings that a U.S. person derives indirectly through a foreign corporation generally are not subject to U.S. tax until such earnings are repatriated to the United States through a distribution of those earnings to the U.S. person. This ability of U.S. persons to defer income is circumscribed by various regimes intended to restrict or eliminate tax deferral with respect to certain categories of passive or highly mobile income. The main anti-deferral regimes are the controlled foreign corporation ("CFC") rules of subpart F[1211] and the passive foreign investment company rules.[1212]

***The subpart F CFC rules***

Under the subpart F CFC rules, a 10 percent-or-greater U.S. shareholder (a "U.S. Shareholder") of a CFC is subject to U.S. tax currently on (1) its pro rata share of certain income earned by the CFC[1213] and (2) certain untaxed earnings invested in United States property with respect to such shareholder.[1214] In each case, the U.S. Shareholder is subject to tax currently, whether or not such income is distributed. A CFC is defined generally as a foreign corporation with respect to which U.S. Shareholders own more than 50 percent of the combined voting power or total value of the stock of the corporation.[1215]

*United States property held by CFCs*

A U.S. Shareholder that owns stock in a CFC on the last day of the taxable year must include in its gross income the amount determined under section 956 with respect to such shareholder for such year (but only to the extent not previously taxed[1216]) (a "section 956 inclusion").[1217] The section 956 inclusion for any taxable year is generally the lesser of (1) the excess of such shareholder's pro rata share of the average of the amounts of United States property held (directly or indirectly) by the CFC as of the close of each quarter of such taxable year over the amount of previously taxed income from prior section 956 inclusions[1218] with respect to such

[1211] See secs. 951–965.
[1212] See secs. 1291–1298.
[1213] Sec. 951(a)(1)(A).
[1214] Sec. 951(a)(1)(B).
[1215] Sec. 957(a).
[1216] Sec. 959(a)(2).
[1217] Sec. 951(a)(1)(B).
[1218] See sec. 959(c)(1)(A).

shareholder, or (2) such shareholder's pro rata share of the applicable earnings of such CFC.[1219]

### *Foreign tax credits*

Subject to the limitations discussed below, a U.S. person is allowed to claim a credit against its U.S. income tax liability for the foreign income taxes that it pays. As discussed below, a domestic corporation may[1220] also be allowed a "deemed-paid" credit for foreign income taxes paid by a foreign corporation that the domestic corporation is deemed to have paid when the related income is distributed or is included in the domestic corporation's income under the provisions of subpart F, including section 956 inclusions.[1221]

A foreign tax credit is available only for foreign income, war profits, and excess profits taxes, and for certain taxes imposed in lieu of such taxes. Other foreign levies generally are treated as deductible expenses. The foreign tax credit is elective on a year-by-year basis. In lieu of electing the foreign tax credit, U.S. persons generally are permitted to deduct foreign taxes.[1222]

#### *Deemed-paid foreign tax credit*

Domestic corporations owning at least 10 percent of the voting stock of a foreign corporation are treated as if they had paid a share of the foreign income taxes paid by the foreign corporation in the year in which that corporation's earnings and profits ("E&P") become subject to U.S. tax as dividend income of the domestic corporation.[1223] This credit is the deemed-paid, or indirect, foreign tax credit. A domestic corporation may also be deemed to have paid taxes paid by a second-, third-, fourth-, fifth-, or sixth-tier foreign corporation, if certain requirements are satisfied.[1224] Foreign taxes paid below the third tier are eligible for the deemed-paid credit only with respect to taxes paid in taxable years during which the payor is a CFC and the corporation claiming the credit is a U.S. Shareholder of the CFC.[1225] Foreign taxes paid below the sixth tier are not eligible for the deemed-paid credit. In addition, a deemed-paid credit generally is available with respect to any inclusion of subpart F income or investments of earnings in United States property for the taxable year.[1226] The amount of the credit is determined by the same formula as under section 902, except that the numerator of the ratio is the amount of the inclusion, rather than the amount of dividends received during the taxable year.[1227]

E&P is determined under the same rules for purposes of the deemed-paid credit fraction with respect to subpart F and section

[1219] Sec. 956(a).

[1220] A U.S. Shareholder includes individuals and entities. Sec. 951(b). In contrast, only those U.S. Shareholders that are corporations are entitled to the deemed-paid credit.

[1221] Secs. 901, 902, 960. Similar rules apply under sections 1291(g) and 1293(f) with respect to income that is includible under the passive foreign investment company ("PFIC") rules.

[1222] Sec. 164(a)(3).

[1223] Sec. 902(a).

[1224] Sec. 902(b).

[1225] Sec. 902(b)(2).

[1226] Sec. 960(a).

[1227] Sec. 960(a)(1); Treas. Reg. sec. 1.960–1(i)(1).

956 inclusions as for dividends.[1228] These rules generally[1229] provide that the E&P of any foreign corporation is determined according to rules substantially similar to those applicable to domestic corporations, under regulations prescribed by the Secretary. The amount of foreign tax eligible for the indirect credit is added to the actual dividend or inclusion (the dividend or inclusion is said to be "grossed-up") and is included in the domestic corporation's income; accordingly, the domestic corporation is treated as if it had received its proportionate share of pre-tax profits of the foreign corporation and paid its proportionate share of the foreign tax paid by the foreign corporation.[1230]

For purposes of computing the deemed-paid foreign tax credit, distributions (or other inclusions) are considered made first from the post-1986 pool of all the distributing foreign corporation's accumulated E&P.[1231] Accumulated E&P for this purpose includes the E&P of the current year undiminished by the current distribution (or other inclusion).[1232] Distributions in excess of the accumulated pool of post-1986 undistributed E&P are treated as paid out of pre-1987 accumulated profits and are subject to the ordering principles of pre-1986 Act law.[1233]

*Foreign tax credit limitation*

The foreign tax credit generally is limited to a taxpayer's U.S. tax liability on its foreign-source taxable income (as determined under U.S. tax accounting principles).[1234] This limit is intended to ensure that the credit serves its purpose of mitigating double taxation of foreign-source income without offsetting U.S. tax on U.S.-source income. The limit is computed by multiplying a taxpayer's total U.S. tax liability for the year by the ratio of the taxpayer's foreign-source taxable income for the year to the taxpayer's total taxable income for the year. If the total amount of foreign income taxes paid and deemed paid for the year exceeds the taxpayer's foreign tax credit limitation for the year, the taxpayer may carry back the excess foreign taxes to the previous taxable year or carry forward the excess taxes to one of the succeeding 10 taxable years.[1235]

The foreign tax credit limitation is generally applied separately to two different categories of income, passive category income and general category income.[1236] Passive category income generally includes investment income such as dividends, interest, rents, and royalties.[1237] General category income is generally all income that

[1228] See secs. 902(c)(1), 964; Treas. Reg. sec. 1.964–1(a)(1).

[1229] For an exception, see sec. 312(k)(4).

[1230] Sec. 78.

[1231] Sec. 902(c)(6)(B). E&P computations for these purposes are to be made under U.S. tax principles. Secs. 902(c)(1), 964(a).

[1232] Sec. 902(c)(1).

[1233] Sec. 902(c)(6).

[1234] Secs. 901, 904.

[1235] Sec. 904(c).

[1236] Sec. 904(d). Separate foreign tax credit limitations also apply to certain categories of income described in other sections. See, e.g., secs. 901(j), 904(h)(10), 865(h).

[1237] Sec. 904(d)(2)(B). Passive income is defined by reference to the definition of foreign personal holding company income in section 954(c), and thus generally includes dividends, interest, rents, royalties, annuities, net gains from certain property or commodities transactions, foreign currency gains, income equivalent to interest, income from notional principal contracts, and income from certain personal service contracts. Exceptions apply for certain rents and royalties derived in an active business and for certain income earned by dealers in securities or other financial instruments. Passive category income also includes amounts that are includible in

is not in the passive category. Because the foreign tax credit limitation must be applied separately to income in these two categories, credits for foreign tax imposed on income in one category cannot be used to offset U.S. tax on income in the other category.

Income that would otherwise constitute passive category income is treated as general category income if it is earned by a qualifying financial services entity (and certain other requirements are met).[1238] Passive income is also treated as general category income if it is high-taxed income (i.e., if the foreign tax rate is determined to exceed the highest rate of tax specified in section 1 or 11, as applicable).[1239] Dividends (and subpart F inclusions), interest, rents, and royalties received from a CFC by a U.S. person are assigned to a separate limitation category by reference to the category of income out of which the dividend or other payment is made.[1240] Dividends received by a U.S. person from a foreign corporation that is not a CFC are also categorized on a look-through basis.[1241] For purposes of determining the foreign tax credit limitation, section 956 inclusions are treated as dividends.[1242]

Under the foreign tax credit limitation rules, the total amount of the credit taken into account cannot exceed the same proportion of the tax against which such credit is taken which the taxpayer's taxable income from sources without the United States (but not in excess of the taxpayer's taxable income) bears to his entire taxable income for the same taxable year.

### *Explanation of Provision*

The provision imposes a limit on the amount of foreign taxes that a U.S. Shareholder is deemed to pay with respect to any section 956 inclusion.

For section 956 inclusions attributable to United States property acquired by a CFC after the effective date, the amount of foreign taxes deemed paid in each separate category is determined by comparing the foreign taxes deemed paid with respect to the U.S. Shareholder's section 956 inclusion (determined without regard to the provision) (the "tentative credit") to its hypothetical amount of foreign taxes deemed paid as computed under the provision (the "hypothetical credit"). The U.S. Shareholder's hypothetical credit is the amount of foreign taxes it would have been deemed to have paid if cash in an amount equal to the section 956 inclusion had been distributed through the chain of ownership that begins with the foreign corporation that holds the investment in United States property and ends with the U.S. Shareholder. If the hypothetical credit is less than the tentative credit, then the amount of foreign taxes deemed paid with respect to the section 956 inclusion is limited to the hypothetical credit. However, the amount of the tentative credit is not increased if the hypothetical credit would have been greater than the tentative credit. This limitation applies

---

gross income under section 1293 (relating to PFICs) and dividends received from certain DISCs and FSCs.

[1238] Sec. 904(d)(2)(C),(D).

[1239] Sec. 904(d)(2)(F).

[1240] Sec. 904(d)(3).

[1241] Sec. 904(d)(4).

[1242] Sec. 904(d)(3)(G).

whether the U.S. Shareholder chooses to claim a credit[1243] for foreign taxes paid or accrued, or to deduct such taxes.[1244]

In general, present-law foreign tax credit rules apply in determining the hypothetical credit. The only exception is that, to the extent an actual distribution would be subject to any income or withholding tax, such taxes are not taken into account in determining the hypothetical credit.[1245] Thus, the generally applicable rules and definitions[1246] apply to each hypothetical distribution.

For example, assume that, for the relevant tax year, and before taking into account the hypothetical distribution under the provision, a U.S. parent ("USP") owns all of the vote and value of CFC1, a CFC organized in Country A with post-1986 undistributed earnings of 200u, and post-1986 foreign income taxes of $10.[1247] CFC1 owns all of the vote and value of CFC2, a CFC organized in Country B with post-1986 undistributed earnings of 100u, and post-1986 foreign income taxes of $50. If CFC2 makes a loan to USP that results in a section 956 inclusion of 100u, the tentative credit is $50 (equal to 100u/100u × $50).

The hypothetical distribution of 100u from CFC2 to CFC1 would increase CFC1's current E&P by 100u, from 200u to300u, and increase CFC1's foreign income taxes from $10 to $60. The 100u hypothetical distribution results in a dividend of 100u that is non-subpart F income of CFC1 under the subpart F look-through rules.[1248] Although Country B would impose a 10 percent withholding tax on an actual distribution of 100u to CFC1, for a total withholding tax of 10u, this amount is not taken into account in determining the hypothetical credit. Next, the 100u hypothetical distribution from CFC1 to USP would result in a dividend of 100u, on which USP would be deemed to have paid $20 in taxes.[1249] Because the hypothetical credit of $20 is less than the tentative credit of $50, USP's foreign taxes deemed paid with respect to its section 956 inclusion are limited to $20. USP's section 78 gross-up with respect to the section 956 inclusion is also $20.[1250]

---

1243 Sec. 901.

1244 Sec. 164(a)(3).

1245 Similarly, if this hypothetical distribution would be subject to a withholding tax upon distribution to USP, if it had been actually made, any such tax would not be taken into account in determining the hypothetical credit. However, this conclusion results because such taxes are described in section 901(b), thus they are outside the scope of the provision.

1246 See, e.g., secs. 902(b), (c), and 904(d)(3)(B), (D).

1247 For purposes of this example, assume that each CFC has: (1) a "u" functional currency; (2) E&P comprising solely post-1986 undistributed earnings or deficits in post-1986 undistributed earnings, such that there are no pre-1987 accumulated profits; (3) only post-1986 foreign income taxes; (4) no previously-taxed income; (5) only E&P and foreign income taxes in the section 904(d) general category; and (6) no other attributes than those listed. Except as provided in the example, there are no other distributions or inclusions during the taxable year. In addition, Country B imposes a 10-percent withholding tax on dividend payments to foreign shareholders.

1248 Sec. 954(c)(6). This assumes that the subpart F look-through rules of section 954(c)(6) are extended, and are therefore applicable to the hypothetical distribution. In the event the look-through rule of section 954(c)(6) expires, the 100u hypothetical distribution would result in a dividend of 100u that would be currently included in USP's income as a subpart F item at the level of CFC1.

1249 The hypothetical amount of foreign taxes deemed paid equals (100u/300u) × $60. The post-1986 undistributed earnings that is the denominator of the section 902(a) fraction for purposes of the provision equals CFC1's post-1986 undistributed earnings of 200u (determined without regard to the provision) plus the amount of the hypothetical dividend from CFC2, 100u.

1250 If, in the same taxable year, CFC1 were also to make an actual distribution of all its accumulated E&P of 200u, the 100u hypothetical distribution from CFC1 to USP would have no impact on the calculation of USP's actual deemed paid credit from CFC1's actual dividend. The deemed-paid credit on the 200u dividend would be $10, which equals (200u/200u × $10). In addition, the calculation of the hypothetical credit with respect to the hypothetical distribution of

The provision is applied with regard to earnings and taxes in each separate category. In addition, treatment of any foreign taxes over the limit imposed under the provision (the "excess taxes") is the same as the treatment of any other foreign taxes paid or accrued, but not yet deemed paid for purposes of the foreign tax credit rules. Thus, if a foreign corporation's excess taxes are in its general category post-1986 foreign income taxes pool, the foreign corporation's excess taxes are still considered general category post-1986 foreign income taxes.[1251] Accordingly, such taxes are included in the computation of foreign taxes deemed paid with respect to a subsequent distribution from, or income inclusion with respect to, that foreign corporation, subject to applicable limitations including the limitation of the provision. In the example above, excess taxes that remain at CFC2 equal $30.[1252]

The provision applies to United States property acquired by a CFC after December 31, 2010. Thus, for example, any section 956 inclusions from a CFC loan that was made to its U.S. parent on or before December 31, 2010, would not be subject to the limitation imposed by the provision. However, the limitation imposed by the provision would apply if, after December 31, 2010, there is a significant modification of the debt instrument such that the original debt instrument is considered as exchanged for a modified instrument that differs materially from the original.[1253]

The provision requires the Secretary to issue regulations or guidance to carry out the purposes of the provision, including regulations that prevent the inappropriate use of the foreign corporation's foreign income taxes not deemed paid by reason of the provision. It is anticipated that guidance will prohibit the inappropriate use of excess taxes, and will address attempted avoidance of the provision through a series of transactions.

### *Effective Date*

The provision is effective for acquisitions of United States property after December 31, 2010.

## E. Special Rule with Respect to Certain Redemptions by Foreign Subsidiaries (sec. 215 of the Act and sec. 304(b) of the Code)

### *Present Law*

Under section 304, if one corporation (the "acquiring corporation") purchases stock of a related corporation (the "target corporation") in exchange for property, the transaction generally is recharacterized as a redemption. To the extent a section 304(a)(1) transaction is treated as a distribution under section 301, the

100u from CFC2 would be the same (100u/300u × $60 = $20) whether or not CFC1 paid an actual dividend.

[1251] Sec. 902(c)(2).

[1252] The excess taxes equal the deemed paid foreign tax credit (determined without regard to the provision) of $50 minus the hypothetical credit of $20. Alternatively, if CFC2's E&P also included 125u in previously taxed income (which is taken into account in determining that the section 956 inclusion is 100u), then the excess taxes remaining at CFC2 would be $50, because the applicable ordering rules would prioritize the hypothetical distribution as coming first from the 125u in previously taxed income over the 100u in untaxed earnings. See sec. 959(c).

[1253] See Treas. Reg. sec. 1.1001–3.

transferor and the acquiring corporation are treated as if (1) the transferor had transferred the stock of the target corporation to the acquiring corporation in exchange for stock of the acquiring corporation in a transaction to which section 351(a) applies, and (2) the acquiring corporation had then transferred the property to the transferor in redemption of the stock it is deemed as having issued.[1254] In the case of a section 304 transaction, the amount and the source of a dividend are determined as if the property were distributed by the acquiring corporation to the extent of its earnings and profits ("E&P"), and then by the target corporation to the extent of its E&P.[1255] To the extent the dividend is sourced from the E&P of the acquiring corporation, the transferor is considered to receive the dividend directly from the acquiring corporation;[1256] this is commonly referred to as "hopscotching" because the dividend bypasses any intermediary shareholders.

Special rules apply if the acquiring corporation is foreign.[1257] For purposes of determining the amount of the dividend to the transferor, the foreign acquiring corporation's E&P that is taken into account is limited to the portion of such E&P that (1) is attributable to stock of the foreign acquiring corporation held by a corporation or individual who is the transferor (or a person related thereto) of the target corporation and who is a U.S. shareholder[1258] of the foreign acquiring corporation, and (2) was accumulated while such stock was owned by the transferor (or a person related thereto) and while the foreign acquiring corporation was a controlled foreign corporation ("CFC").[1259]

Section 1442 generally requires a 30-percent gross basis tax to be withheld on dividend payments to foreign persons unless reduced or eliminated pursuant to an applicable income tax treaty.

### *Explanation of Provision*

The provision generally imposes an additional limitation on the E&P of a foreign acquiring corporation that is taken into account in determining the amount (and source) of the distribution that is treated as a dividend.

Under the provision, if more than 50 percent of the dividends arising from acquisition would (without taking into account the provision) not be (1) subject to U.S. tax in the year in which the dividend arises, or (2) includible in the E&P of a CFC,[1260] then the E&P of the foreign acquiring corporation is not taken into account for this purpose.[1261]

If it is determined that the special rule applies, none of the foreign acquiring corporation's E&P is taken into account. In such case, the only E&P that is taken into account to determine the

---

[1254] Sec. 304(a)(1).

[1255] Sec. 304(b)(2).

[1256] See H.R. Rep. No. 98–861 (1984) (Conf. Rep.), 1222–1224; Rev. Rul. 80–189, 1980–2 C.B. 106.

[1257] Sec. 304(b)(5).

[1258] As that term is defined by section 951(b).

[1259] See sec. 304(b)(5).

[1260] For purposes of this rule, "CFC" is defined by reference to section 957, but without regard to section 953(c).

[1261] It is not intended that the provision apply if an amount is not subject to tax under this chapter for the taxable year in which the dividend arises solely as a result of the application of section 959.

amount constituting a dividend is the target corporation's E&P. The provision prevents the foreign acquiring corporation's E&P from permanently escaping U.S. taxation by being deemed to be distributed directly to a foreign person (i.e., the transferor) without an intermediate distribution to a domestic corporation in the chain of ownership between the acquiring corporation and the transferor corporation. Generally, if the transferor is a foreign corporation (and not a CFC) and the acquiring corporation is a CFC, it is not relevant whether the target corporation is a domestic or a foreign corporation. However, if the target is a U.S. corporation, the 30-percent gross basis withholding tax applies to the amount constituting a dividend from the target, unless reduced or eliminated by treaty.[1262]

It is anticipated that regulations will provide rules to prevent the avoidance of the provision, including through the use of partnerships, options, or other arrangements to cause a foreign corporation to be treated as a CFC.

### *Effective Date*

The provision is effective for acquisitions after the date of enactment (August 10, 2010).

## F. Modification of Affiliation Rules for Purposes of Rules Allocating Interest Expense (sec. 216 of the Act and sec. 864 of the Code)

### *Present Law*

#### *In general*

The United States employs a worldwide tax system under which U.S. resident individuals and domestic corporations generally are taxed on all income, whether derived in the United States or abroad; the foreign tax credit provides relief from double taxation. The foreign tax credit generally is limited to the U.S. tax liability on a taxpayer's foreign-source income, in order to ensure that the credit serves its purpose of mitigating double taxation of foreign-source income without offsetting the U.S. tax on U.S.-source income.[1263]

To compute the foreign tax credit limitation, a taxpayer must determine the amount of its taxable income from foreign sources by allocating and apportioning deductions between items of U.S.-source gross income, on the one hand, and items of foreign-source gross income, on the other. There are no specific rules for most types of deductions.[1264] Specific provisions govern the allocation and apportionment of interest.[1265]

For interest allocation purposes, all members of an affiliated group of corporations generally are treated as a single corporation

---

[1262] Sec. 1442; Rev. Rul. 92–85; 1992–2 C.B. 69.

[1263] Secs. 901, 904.

[1264] See, e.g., secs. 861(b), 862(b), and 863(a), which require that a taxpayer properly allocate and apportion expenses, losses, or other deductions, without containing any specific rules for allocating and apportioning particular types of deductions.

[1265] Sec. 864(e). In the case of interest expense, the rules generally are based on the premise that money is fungible and that interest expense is properly attributable to all business activities and property of a taxpayer, regardless of any specific purpose for incurring an obligation on which interest is paid. Temp. Treas. Reg. sec. 1.861–9T(a).

(the so-called "one-taxpayer rule") and allocation must be made on the basis of assets rather than gross income.[1266]

*Foreign corporations owned by an affiliated group of corporations*

The term "affiliated group" in this context generally is defined by reference to the rules for determining whether corporations are eligible to file consolidated returns.[1267] These rules exclude all foreign corporations from an affiliated group.[1268] Thus, while debt generally is considered fungible among the assets of a group of domestic affiliated corporations, the same rules do not apply as between the domestic and foreign members of a group with the same degree of common control as the domestic affiliated group.

Under Treasury regulations, however, certain foreign corporations are treated as affiliated corporations, in certain respects, if (1) at least 80 percent of either the vote or value of the corporation's outstanding stock is owned directly or indirectly by members of an affiliated group, and (2) more than 50 percent of the corporation's gross income for the taxable year is effectively connected with the conduct of a U.S. trade or business (also known as effectively connected income).[1269]

In the case of a foreign corporation that is treated as an affiliated corporation for interest allocation and apportionment purposes, the percentage of its assets and income that is taken into account varies depending on the percentage of the corporation's gross income that is effectively connected income. If 80 percent or more of the foreign corporation's gross income is effectively connected income, then all the corporation's assets and interest expense are taken into account. If, instead, between 50 percent and 80 percent of the foreign corporation's gross income is effectively connected income, then only the corporation's assets that generate effectively connected income and a percentage of its interest expense equal to the percentage of its assets that generate effectively connected income are taken into account.[1270]

### *Explanation of Provision*

The provision treats a foreign corporation as a member of an affiliated group, for interest allocation and apportionment purposes, if (1) more than 50 percent of the gross income of such foreign cor-

[1266] Secs. 864(e)(1), 864(e)(2).

[1267] Secs. 864(e)(5)(A), sec. 1504. The affiliated group for interest allocation purposes generally excludes certain corporations that are financial institutions. These corporate financial institutions are not treated as members of the regular affiliated group for purposes of applying the one-taxpayer rule to other non-financial members of that group. Instead, all such corporate financial institutions that would be so affiliated are treated as a separate single corporation for interest allocation purposes. Sec. 864(e)(5)(B).

[1268] Sec. 1504(b)(3).

[1269] Temp. Treas. Reg. sec. 1.861–11T(d)(6)(ii). The question as to whether a foreign person is engaged in a U.S. trade or business has generated a significant body of case law. Basic issues involved in the determination include whether the activity constitutes business rather than investing, whether sufficient activities in connection with the business are conducted in the United States, and whether the relationship between the foreign person and persons performing functions in the United States with respect to the business is sufficient to attribute those functions to the foreign person. Generally, only U.S.-source income is treated as effectively connected with the conduct of a U.S. trade or business. However, certain limited categories of foreign-source income are treated as effectively connected if the income is attributable to an office or other fixed place of business maintained by the foreign person in the United States. Sec. 864(c).

[1270] Temp. Treas. Reg. sec. 1.861–11T(d)(6)(ii).

poration for the taxable year is effectively connected income, and (2) at least 80 percent of either the vote or value of all outstanding stock of such foreign corporation is owned directly or indirectly by members of the affiliated group (determined with regard to this sentence). Thus, under the provision, if more than 50 percent of a foreign corporation's gross income is effectively connected income and at least 80 percent of either the vote or value of all outstanding stock of such foreign corporation is owned directly or indirectly by members of the affiliated group, then all of the foreign corporation's assets and interest expense are taken into account for the purposes of allocating and apportioning the interest expense of the affiliated group.

### *Effective Date*

The provision applies to taxable years beginning after the date of enactment (August 10, 2010).

## G. Termination of Special Rules for Interest and Dividends Received from Persons Meeting the 80-Percent Foreign Business Requirements (sec. 217 of the Act and secs. 861(a)(1)(A) and 871(i) of the Code)

### *Present Law*

The source of interest and dividend income generally is determined by reference to the country of residence of the payor.[1271] Thus, an interest or dividend payment from a U.S. payor to a foreign person generally is treated as U.S.-source income and is subject to the 30-percent gross-basis U.S. withholding tax.[1272] However, if a resident alien individual or domestic corporation satisfies an 80-percent active foreign business income requirement (the "80/20 test"), all or a portion of any interest paid by the resident alien individual or the domestic corporation (a so-called "80/20 company") is exempt from U.S. withholding tax. Interest paid by a resident alien individual that satisfies the 80/20 test or by an 80/20 company is treated as foreign-source income and is therefore exempt from the 30-percent withholding tax if it is paid to unrelated parties.[1273] When a resident alien individual or 80/20 company pays interest to a related party, the resourcing rule applies only to the percentage of the interest that is equal to the percentage of the resident alien individual's or 80/20 company's foreign-source income (described below) as a portion of the resident alien individual's or 80/20 company's total gross income during the three-year testing period (a so-called "look-through" approach).[1274]

In addition to interest, all or part of a dividend paid by an 80/20 company may also be exempt from U.S. withholding tax. The percentage of the dividend paid by an 80/20 company that equals the percentage of the 80/20 company's total gross income during the testing period that is foreign source is exempt from U.S. with-

[1271] Secs. 861(a)(1), (2), 862(a)(1), (2).
[1272] Secs. 871(a)(1)(A), 881(a)(1), 1441(b), and 1442(a).
[1273] Sec. 861(a)(1)(A).
[1274] Sec. 861(c)(2).

holding tax.[1275] Unlike interest, a dividend paid by an 80/20 company remains U.S. source (for example, for foreign tax credit limitation purposes).

In general, a resident alien individual or domestic corporation meets the 80/20 test if at least 80 percent of the gross income of the resident alien individual or corporation during the testing period is derived from foreign sources and is attributable to the active conduct of a trade or business in a foreign country (or a U.S. possession) by the resident alien individual or corporation or, in the case of a corporation, a 50-percent owned subsidiary of that corporation. The testing period generally is the three-year period preceding the year in which the interest or dividend is paid.[1276]

### *Explanation of Provision*

The provision repeals the present-law rule that treats as foreign-source all or a portion of any interest paid by a resident alien individual or domestic corporation that meets the 80/20 test. The provision also repeals the present-law rule that exempts from U.S. withholding tax all or a portion of any dividends paid by a domestic corporation that meets the 80/20 test.

The provision provides a grandfather rule for any domestic corporation that (1) meets the 80/20 test (as in effect before the enactment of this provision) (hereinafter "the present law 80/20 test") for its last taxable year beginning before January 1, 2011 ("an existing 80/20 company"), (2) meets a new 80/20 test with respect to each taxable year beginning after December 31, 2010, and (3) has not added a substantial line of business with respect to such corporation after the date of enactment of this provision. Any payment of dividend or interest after December 31, 2010 by an existing 80/20 company that meets the grandfather rule is exempt from withholding tax to the extent of the existing 80/20 company's active foreign business percentage. Nonetheless, any payment of interest will be treated as U.S.-source income.

As with the present law 80/20 test, a corporation meets the 80-percent foreign business requirements of the 80/20 test under the grandfather rule if it is shown to the satisfaction of the Secretary that at least 80-percent of the gross income from all sources of such corporation for the testing period is active foreign business income. This percentage—active foreign business income of the company for the testing period as a percentage of total gross income of the company for the testing period—is also the company's active foreign business percentage for purposes of determining the portion of any dividend or interest paid by an existing 80/20 company that is exempt from withholding tax. However, except as modified by the transition rule below, the existing 80/20 company and all of its subsidiaries are aggregated and treated as one corporation. For this purpose, a subsidiary means any corporation in which the existing 80/20 company owns (directly or indirectly) stock meeting the requirements of section 1504(a)(2), determined by substituting 50

[1275] Sec. 871(i).

[1276] Sec. 861(c)(1). The income of a subsidiary is attributed to the tested company only to the extent that the tested company actually receives income from the subsidiary in the form of dividends. *Conference Report to the 1986 Tax Reform Act,* Pub. L. No. 99–514, Vol. II, 602; see also Rev. Rul. 73–63, 1973–1 C.B. 336; P.L.R. 6905161160A (May 16, 1969).

percent for 80 percent and without regard to section 1504(b)(3). As a result, an existing 80/20 company must take into account the gross income of any domestic or foreign subsidiary. The Secretary may issue guidance as is necessary or appropriate to carry out the purpose of this provision, including guidance providing for the proper application of the aggregation rules.

Under the 80/20 test provided by the grandfather rule, the testing period is the three-year period ending with the close of the taxable year of the corporation preceding the payment (or such part of such period as may be applicable). If the corporation has no gross income for such three-year period (or part thereof), the testing period is the taxable year in which the payment is made.

The grandfather rule includes a transition rule that applies in the case of any taxable year for which the testing period includes one or more taxable years beginning before January 1, 2011. Under this transition rule, a corporation meets the 80-percent foreign business requirements if, and only if, the weighted average of (1) the percentage of the corporation's gross income from all sources that is active foreign business income (as defined in subparagraph (B) of section 861(c)(1) (as in effect before the date of enactment of this provision)) for the portion of the testing period that includes taxable years beginning before January 1, 2011,[1277] and (2) the percentage of the corporation's gross income from all sources that is active foreign business income for the portion of the testing period, if any, that includes taxable years beginning on or after January 1, 2011, is at least 80 percent. Accordingly, this transition rule applies instead of the new 80/20 test for the relevant tax years. This weighted average percentage is also treated as the active foreign business percentage for purposes of determining the amount of withholding for such taxable years.

The following example illustrates the operation of this transition rule. Assume a domestic corporation has $100 of active foreign business income and no other income on a separate company basis (i.e., without regard to the income of any affiliate) for each of the 2008, 2009, and 2010 tax years. For the 2011, 2012, and 2013 tax years, the domestic company has $700 of active foreign business income and $300 of other income on an aggregate basis (including the income of its 50-percent owned domestic and foreign subsidiaries). Under the provision, the domestic company's weighted average percentage for the 2011 tax year is 100 percent, determined by considering the 2008, 2009, and 2010 tax years on a separate company basis (($100 + $100 + $100)/($100 + $100 + $100)). Therefore, for the 2011 tax year, the domestic company meets the 80-percent active foreign business requirements, and its active foreign business percentage is 100 percent for the 2011 tax year.

For the 2012 tax year, the weighted average percentage is 90 percent, determined by considering the 2009 and 2010 tax years on a separate company basis (((\$100 + \$100)/(\$100 + \$100) × ⅔)) or 66.7 percent) and the 2011 tax year on an aggregate basis (((\$700/ \$1,000) × ⅓) or 23.3 percent). As a result, the domestic company meets the 80-percent active foreign business requirements, and its

[1277] Hence, this percentage is determined without application of the new aggregation rule.

active foreign business percentage is 90 percent for the 2012 tax year.

For the 2013 tax year, the weighted average percentage is 80 percent, determined by considering the 2010 tax year on a separate company basis ((($100/$100) × ⅓) or 33.3 percent) and the 2011 and 2012 tax years on an aggregate basis ((($700 + $700)/($1,000 + $1,000) × ⅔) or 46.7 percent). Therefore, for the 2013 tax year, the domestic company meets the 80-percent active foreign business requirements, and its active foreign business percentage is 80 percent.

For the 2014 tax year, the transition rule does not apply since none of the years within the three-year testing period begin before January 1, 2011. As a result, the domestic company does not meet the 80-percent foreign business requirements for the 2014 tax year since only 70 percent (($700 + $700 + $700)/($1,000 + $1,000 + $1,000)) of its gross income from all sources for the testing period is active foreign business income.

An existing 80/20 company does not meet the grandfather rule if there has been an addition of a substantial line of business with respect to such corporation after the date of enactment of this provision. For purposes of determining whether a substantial line of business has been added, rules similar to those of section 7704(g) and the Treasury regulations thereunder (relating to certain publicly-traded partnerships treated as corporations and including specifically Treas. Reg. section 1.7704–2(c) to (e)) apply. It is anticipated that the Secretary will issue guidance providing that the acquisition of foreign operating assets or stock of a foreign corporation by the existing 80/20 company for the purpose of increasing its active foreign business percentage will be treated as the addition of a substantial line of business.

### *Effective Date*

The provision is effective for taxable years beginning after December 31, 2010.

The repeal of the 80/20 company provisions relating to the payment of interest does not apply to payments of interest to persons not related to the 80/20 company (applying rules similar to those of section 954(d)(3)) on obligations issued before the date of enactment.[1278] For this purpose, a significant modification of the terms of any obligation (including any extension of the term of such obligation) is treated as the issuance of a new obligation.

[1278] A person will be treated as a related person with respect to a controlled foreign corporation if (A) such person is an individual, corporation, partnership, trust, or estate which controls, or is controlled by, the controlled foreign corporation, or (B) such person is a corporation, partnership, trust or estate which is controlled by the same person or persons which control the resident controlled foreign corporation. For purposes of the preceding sentence, control means, with respect to a corporation, the ownership, directly or indirectly, of stock possessing more than 50 percent of the total voting power of all classes of stock entitled to vote or of the total value of stock of such corporation. In the case of a partnership, trust, or estate, control means the ownership, directly or indirectly, of more than 50 percent (by value) of the beneficial interests in such partnership, trust, or estate. For purposes of this paragraph, rules similar to the rules of section 958 shall apply. Sec. 954(d)(3).

## H. Limitation on Extension of Statute of Limitations for Failure to Notify Secretary of Certain Foreign Transfers (sec. 218 of the Act and sec. 6501(c) of the Code)

### *Present Law*

Taxes are generally required to be assessed within three years after a taxpayer's return is filed, whether or not it was timely filed.[1279] In the case of a false or fraudulent return filed with the intent to evade tax, or if the taxpayer fails to file a required return, the tax may be assessed, or a proceeding in court for collection of such tax may be begun without assessment, at any time.[1280] The limitation period also may be extended by taxpayer consent.[1281] If a taxpayer engages in a listed transaction but fails to include any of the information required under section 6011 on any return or statement for a taxable year, the limitation period with respect to such transaction will not expire before the date which is one year after the earlier of (1) the date on which the Secretary is provided the information so required, or (2) the date that a "material advisor" (as defined in section 6111) makes its section 6112(a) list available for inspection pursuant to a request by the Secretary under section 6112(b)(1)(A).[1282] In addition to the exceptions described above, there are also circumstances under which the three-year limitation period is suspended.[1283]

Section 6501(c)(8) provides an exception to the three-year period of limitations due to failures to provide information about cross-border transactions or foreign assets. Under this exception, as amended by the Hiring Incentives to Restore Employment Act,[1284] the limitation period for assessment of tax does not expire any earlier than three years after the required information about certain cross-border transactions or foreign assets is actually provided to the Secretary by the person required to file the return.[1285] In general, such information reporting is due with the taxpayer's return; thus, the three-year limitation period commences when a timely and complete return (including all information reporting) is filed. Without the inclusion of the information reporting with the return, the limitation period does not commence until such time as the information reports are subsequently provided to the Secretary, even though the return has been filed. The taxes that may be assessed during this suspended or extended period are not limited to those

[1279] Sec. 6501(a). Returns that are filed before the date they are due are deemed filed on the due date. See sec. 6501(b)(1) and (2).

[1280] Sec. 6501(c).

[1281] Sec. 6501(c)(4).

[1282] Sec. 6501(c)(10).

[1283] For example, service of an administrative summons triggers the suspension either (1) beginning six months after service (in the case of John Doe summonses) or (2) when a proceeding to quash a summons is initiated by a taxpayer named in a summons to a third-party recordkeeper. Judicial proceedings initiated by the government to enforce a summons generally do not suspend the limitation period.

[1284] Sec. 513, Pub. L. No. 111–147.

[1285] Required information reporting subject to this three-year rule is reporting under sections 6038 (certain foreign corporations and partnerships), 6038A (certain foreign-owned corporations), 6038B (certain transfers to foreign persons), 6038D (individuals with foreign financial assets), 6046 (organizations, reorganizations, and acquisitions of stock of foreign corporations), 6046A (interests in foreign partnerships), and 6048 (certain foreign trusts), as well as information required with respect to elections under sections 1295(b) passive foreign investment corporations.

attributable to adjustments to items related to the information required to be reported by one of the enumerated sections.

### *Explanation of Provision*

The provision modifies the scope of the exception to the limitations period if a failure to provide information on cross-border transactions or foreign assets is shown to be due to reasonable cause and not willful neglect. In the absence of reasonable cause or the presence of willful neglect, the suspension of the limitations period and the subsequent three-year period that begins after information is ultimately supplied apply to all issues with respect to the income tax return. In cases in which a taxpayer establishes reasonable cause, the limitations period is suspended only for the item or items related to the failure to disclose. To prove reasonable cause, it is anticipated that a taxpayer must establish that the failure was objectively reasonable (i.e., the existence of adequate measures to ensure compliance with rules and regulations), and in good faith.

For example, the limitations period for assessing taxes with respect to a tax return filed on March 31, 2011 ordinarily expires on March 31, 2014. In order to assess tax with respect to any issue on the return after March 31, 2014, the IRS must be able to establish that one of the exceptions applies. If the taxpayer fails to attach to that return one of multiple information returns required, the limitations period does not begin to run unless and until that missing information return is supplied. Assuming that the missing report is supplied to the IRS on January 1, 2013, the limitations period for the entire return begins, and elapses no earlier than three years later, on January 1, 2016. All items are subject to adjustment during that time, unless the taxpayer can prove that reasonable cause for the failure to file existed. If the taxpayer establishes reasonable cause, the only adjustments to tax permitted after March 31, 2014 are those related to the failure to file the information return. For this purpose, related items include (1) adjustments made to the tax consequences claimed on the return with respect to the transaction that was the subject of the information return, (2) adjustments to any item to the extent the item is affected by the transaction even if it is otherwise unrelated to the transaction, and (3) interest and penalties that are related to the transaction or the adjustments made to the tax consequences.

### *Effective Date*

The provision is effective as if included in section 513 of the Hiring Incentives to Restore Employment Act.[1286] Thus, the provision applies for returns filed after March 18, 2010, the date of enactment of that Act, as well as for any other return for which the assessment period specified in section 6501 had not yet expired as of that date.

---

[1286] Pub. L. No. 111–147.

## I. Elimination of Advance Refundability of Earned Income Tax Credit (sec. 219 of the Act and secs. 32(g), 3507, and 6051(a) of the Code)

### *Present Law*

#### *Overview*

Low- and moderate-income workers may be eligible for the refundable earned income tax credit ("EITC"). Eligibility for the EITC is based on earned income, adjusted gross income, investment income, filing status, number of qualifying children and immigration and work status in the United States. The amount of the EITC is based on the presence and number of qualifying children in the worker's family, as well as on adjusted gross income and earned income.

The EITC generally equals a specified percentage of earned income [1287] up to a maximum dollar amount. The maximum amount applies over a certain income range and then diminishes to zero over a specified phaseout range. For taxpayers with earned income (or AGI, if greater) in excess of the beginning of the phaseout range, the maximum EITC amount is reduced by the phaseout rate multiplied by the amount of earned income (or AGI, if greater) in excess of the beginning of the phaseout range. For taxpayers with earned income (or AGI, if greater) in excess of the end of the phaseout range, no credit is allowed.

The EITC is a refundable credit, meaning that if the amount of the credit exceeds the taxpayer's Federal income tax liability, the excess is payable to the taxpayer as a direct transfer payment. Under an advance payment system, eligible taxpayers may elect to receive the credit in their paychecks, rather than waiting to claim a refund on their tax returns filed by April 15 of the following year.

#### *Advance payment system*

Under the advance payment system, available since 1979, eligible taxpayers may elect to receive the credit in their paychecks, rather than waiting to claim a refund on their tax return filed by April 15 of the following year. This means that the taxpayer's paycheck is adjusted to include not only the nonrefundable portion of the EITC (i.e., by reducing otherwise applicable tax liability) but also a portion of the refundable EITC (i.e., an outlay rather than a reduction in otherwise applicable tax liability). The portion of the EITC eligible for advance payment is limited to 60 percent of the maximum EITC for one qualifying child. A taxpayer electing the advance payment option is required to file a tax return for the taxable year (regardless of the otherwise applicable filing thresholds) in order to reconcile any advance payment with the actual allowable EITC.

Beginning in 1993, Congress required the IRS to notify eligible taxpayers of the advance payment option, but participation in the advance payment option has remained limited to a small percentage of eligible taxpayers.

---

[1287] Earned income is defined as (1) wages, salaries, tips, and other employee compensation, but only if such amounts are includible in gross income, plus (2) the amount of the individual's net self-employment earnings.

### *Explanation of Provision*

The provision repeals the advance payment option for the EITC. The taxpayer may still receive the nonrefundable portion of the EITC through the taxpayer's paycheck, by adjusting withholding, to the extent the taxpayer otherwise has positive tax liability.

### *Effective Date*

The provision is effective for taxable years beginning after December 31, 2010.

# PART THIRTEEN: FIREARMS EXCISE TAX IMPROVEMENT ACT OF 2010 (PUBLIC LAW 111–237) [1288]

## A. Time for Payment of Manufacturers' Excise Tax on Recreational Equipment (sec. 2 of the Act and sec. 6302 of the Code)

### *Present Law*

Excise tax is imposed on the sale by the manufacturer, producer or importer of firearms.[1289] The amount of the tax is 10 percent of the sales price of pistols and revolvers and 11 percent of the sales price of firearms (other than pistols and revolvers), shells, and cartridges. Sales made by small firearms manufacturers or importers (less than 50 firearms annually) and sales made to the Department of Defense are exempt from tax.

Firearms and ammunition manufacturers, importers, or producers are generally required to file quarterly excise tax returns if they have excise tax liability of more than $2,000 in a quarter and are generally required to make semimonthly deposits of excise tax.[1290]

### *Explanation of Provision*

The provision amends the due date for the payment of excise tax on firearms and ammunition to correspond with the due date for filing excise tax returns, generally requiring payments to be made by the last day of the first calendar month following the end of each calendar quarter.

### *Effective Date*

The provision applies to articles sold by the manufacturer, producer, or importer after the date of enactment (August 16, 2010).

## B. Allow Assessment of Criminal Restitution as Tax (sec. 3 of the Act and sec. 6213 of the Code)

### *Present Law*

The IRS has responsibility for investigation of criminal offenses under the Code[1291] as well as tax-related offenses under Title 18

[1288] H.R. 5552. The bill passed the House on the suspension calendar on June 29, 2010. The Senate passed the bill by unanimous consent on August 5, 2010. The President signed the bill on August 16, 2010.

[1289] Sec. 4181.

[1290] 27 CFR 53.159(b).

[1291] Secs. 7201 through 7275.

of the United States Code.[1292] Criminal investigations may involve income from legal sources or from illegal sources. When an investigation results in a recommendation to prosecute, after appropriate internal review, the case is referred to the Tax Division of the U.S. Department of Justice, where it is reviewed by prosecutors in one of the Criminal Enforcement Sections. If that office agrees with the recommendation and authorizes prosecution, the case may be handled by a prosecutor from that office or referred to a U.S. Attorney Office for prosecution.[1293]

Upon conviction after trial or as a result of a plea agreement, the taxpayer may be ordered to pay restitution, in addition to a fine, a term of incarceration, or as a condition of probation.[1294] Although the statutes do not specify that restitution is available for Code offenses, it is mandated in tax-related offenses arising under Title 18,[1295] and is permitted in any case concluded by plea agreement if the agreement so provides.[1296] In addition, the sentencing guidelines include restitution as a possible variable warranting a departure from the otherwise recommended sentence.[1297]

In criminal tax cases, the IRS is the victim to whom restitution is due.[1298] The amount of restitution is intended to compensate the IRS for the tax losses that arose from the charges, including interest. Because restitution is limited to the actual loss that the victim suffered,[1299] it does not include civil penalties. The amount to be paid is determined by the court, after a presentencing report is prepared by the probation office. The process by which restitution for a tax crime is collected is shared by the court that ordered restitution, the Financial Litigation Unit of the local U. S. Attorney's Office, and the IRS, working through Criminal Investigation and the Small-Business/Self-Employed Operating Division. The order of restitution gives rise to a lien, which may be filed and is entitled to the same priority as a Federal tax lien.[1300] Payments are made to the Financial Litigation Unit, which reports them to the Court and transfers the funds to the IRS. Return information from taxpayer delinquent account files of the defendant may be provided to a U.S. Probation Officer for the purpose of informing the court of noncompliance with the terms of the taxpayer's sentence or restitution order.[1301]

---

[1292] For example, aiding and abetting (18 U.S.C. sec 2); conspiracy to defraud the United States (18 U.S.C. sec. 286); false, fictitious or fraudulent claims (18 U.S.C. sec. 287); or conspiracy to commit an offense or to defraud the United States (18 U.S.C. sec. 371).

[1293] Internal Revenue Manual ("IRM") par. 9.5.12.4.1, July 25, 2007. Note that IRS investigators also support the development of financial crime investigations by Department of Justice related to organized crime, drug enforcement and counterterrorism programs.

[1294] 18 U.S.C. sec. 3556, which authorizes restitution orders both for cases in which restitution is mandatory as described in section 3663A and for those cases in which restitution is at the discretion of the court as described in section 3663. In either case, any order must comply with the procedures of section 3664.

[1295] 18 U.S.C. sec. 3663A(c)(A)(ii) requires restitution for all crimes against property arising under Title 18. Tax-related charges may arise under 18 U.S.C. secs. 286, 287, 371 and 1001.

[1296] 18 U.S.C. sec. 3663(a)(3).

[1297] 18 U.S.C. Appendix, Chapter 5E1.1, United States Sentencing Guidelines.

[1298] *United States v. Leahy*, 464 F.3d 773 (7th Cir. 2006); *United States v. Ekanem*, 383 F.3d 40 (2d Cir. 2004).

[1299] Dept. of Justice Criminal Tax Manual, par. 44.03 explains that in determining the principle amount to be paid as restitution, the court may include an amount representing pre-judgment interest to compensate for the failure to pay the tax when due under the Code, citing *United States v. Gordon*, 393 F. 3d 1044, 1057 (9th Cir. 2004); *United States v. Helmsley*, 941 F.2d 71 (2d Cir. 1991).

[1300] 18 U.S.C. secs. 3613(c) and 3613(d).

[1301] Sec. 6103(h)(4).

Although the amount of restitution ordered is computed by reference to the taxes that would have been owed but for the criminal offenses charged, restitution is not itself a determination of tax within the meaning of the Code and does not provide a basis on which tax may be assessed. The IRS must comply with the provisions of the Code to assess the proper tax, which may exceed the amounts on which a prosecution proceeded.[1302] Because work on the civil aspects of determining the tax liability is generally deferred until after the conclusion of criminal proceedings, unless the Department of Justice has agreed otherwise,[1303] the IRS often has not yet assessed the relevant civil tax liability at the time the restitution is ordered. Thus, the IRS has no account receivable against which the restitution payments can be credited. After the tax and any penalties are properly determined and assessed, either by agreement or at the conclusion of civil proceedings, payments that were received in satisfaction of a restitution order are applied to reduce the civil tax liability.[1304]

### *Explanation of Provision*

The provision allows the IRS and Treasury Department to immediately assess, without issuing a statutory notice of deficiency, and collect as a tax debt court-ordered restitution. The taxpayer may not collaterally attack the amount of restitution ordered by the court, but retains the ability to challenge the method of collection.

### *Effective Date*

The provision is effective for orders entered after date of enactment (August 16, 2010).

## C. Time for Payment of Corporate Estimated Taxes (sec. 4 of the Act and sec. 6655 of the Code)

### *Present Law*

In general, corporations are required to make quarterly estimated tax payments of their income tax liability.[1305] For a corporation whose taxable year is a calendar year, these estimated tax payments must be made by April 15, June 15, September 15, and December 15. In the case of a corporation with assets of at least $1 billion (determined as of the end of the preceding taxable year):

(i) payments due in July, August, or September, 2014, are increased to 174.25 percent of the payment otherwise due;[1306]

---

[1302] *Morse v. United States*, 419 F.3d 829 (8th Cir. 2005), held that the criminal prosecution did not require proof of a specific tax liability as an element of the crime, and therefore the government was not estopped from pursuing civil proceedings to collect an amount greater than any tax loss identified as part of the criminal sentence.

[1303] IRS Policy Statement 4–26 (formerly P–4–84), in IRM par. 5.1.5.2, explains the extent to which civil and criminal investigations may proceed in parallel. Once the IRS has referred a case and asked the Department of Justice to prosecute, authority to resolve the liabilities for the years that are the subject of the referral rests exclusively with the Department of Justice. Sec. 7122(a).

[1304] *United States v. Helmsley*, 941 F.2d 71 (2d Cir. 1991).

[1305] Sec. 6655.

[1306] Haiti Economic Lift Program of 2010, Pub. L. No. 111–171, sec. 12(a); Health Care and Education Reconciliation Act of 2010, Pub L. No. 111–152, sec. 1410; Hiring Incentives to Restore Employment Act, Pub. L. No. 111–147, sec.561(1); Act to extend the Generalized System

Continued

(ii) payments due in July, August or September, 2015, are increased to 123.00 percent of the payment otherwise due;[1307] and

(iii) payments due in July, August or September, 2019, are increased to 106.50 percent of the payment otherwise due.[1308]

For each of the periods impacted, the next required payment is reduced accordingly.

### *Explanation of Provision*[1309]

The provision increases the required payment of estimated tax otherwise due in July, August, or September, 2015, by 0.25 percentage points.

### *Effective Date*

The provision is effective on the date of enactment (August 16, 2010).

of Preferences and the Andean Trade Preference Act, and for other purposes, Pub. L. No. 111–124, sec. 4; Worker, Homeownership, and Business Assistance Act of 2009, Pub. L. No. 111–92, sec. 18; Joint resolution approving the renewal of import restrictions contained in the Burmese Freedom and Democracy Act of 2003, and for other purposes, Pub. L. No. 111–42, sec. 202(b)(1).

[1307] United States Manufacturing Enhancement Act of 2010, Pub. L. No. 111–227, sec. 4002; Joint resolution approving the renewal of import restrictions contained in the Burmese Freedom and Democracy Act of 2003, and for other purposes, Pub. L. No. 111–210; sec. 3; Haiti Economic Lift Program of 2010, Pub. L. No. 111–171, sec. 12(b); Hiring Incentives to Restore Employment Act, Pub. L. No. 111–147, sec. 561(2).

[1308] Hiring Incentives to Restore Employment Act, Pub. L. No. 111–147, sec. 561(3).

[1309] All the public laws enacted in the 111th Congress affecting this provision are described in Part Twenty-One of this document.

## PART FOURTEEN: REVENUE PROVISIONS OF THE SMALL BUSINESS JOBS ACT OF 2010 (PUBLIC LAW 111–240) [1310]

## I. SMALL BUSINESS RELIEF

### A. Providing Access to Capital

#### 1. Temporary exclusion of 100 percent of gain on certain small business stock (sec. 2011 of the Act and sec. 1202 of the Code)

##### *Present Law*

***In general***

Individuals generally may exclude 50 percent (60 percent for certain empowerment zone businesses) of the gain from the sale of certain small business stock acquired at original issue and held for at least five years.[1311] The amount of gain eligible for the exclusion by an individual with respect to any corporation is the greater of (1) ten times the taxpayer's basis in the stock or (2) $10 million. To qualify as a small business, when the stock is issued, the gross assets of the corporation may not exceed $50 million. The corporation also must meet certain active trade or business requirements.

The portion of the gain includible in taxable income is taxed at a maximum rate of 28 percent under the regular tax.[1312] A percentage of the excluded gain is an alternative minimum tax preference;[1313] the portion of the gain includible in alternative minimum taxable income is taxed at a maximum rate of 28 percent under the alternative minimum tax.

Gain from the sale of qualified small business stock generally is taxed at effective rates of 14 percent under the regular tax[1314] and (i) 14.98 percent under the alternative minimum tax for dispositions before January 1, 2011; (ii) 19.88 percent under the alter-

---

[1310] H.R. 5297. The House Committee on Ways and Means reported H.R. 4849 on March 19, 2010 (H.R. Rep. 111–447). The House passed H.R. 4849 on March 24, 2010. The House passed H.R. 5297 on June 17, 2010. The Senate passed H.R. 5297 with an amendment on September 16, 2010. On September 23, 2010, the House agreed to the Senate amendment. The President signed the bill on September 27, 2010. For a technical explanation of the bill prepared by the staff of the Joint Committee on Taxation, see *Technical Explanation of the Tax Provisions in Senate Amendment 4594 to H.R. 5297, the "Small Business Jobs Act of 2010," Scheduled for Consideration by the United States Senate on September 16, 2010* (JCX–47–10), September 16, 2010.

[1311] Sec. 1202.

[1312] Sec. 1(h).

[1313] Sec. 57(a)(7). In the case of qualified small business stock, the percentage of gain excluded from gross income which is an alternative minimum tax preference is (i) seven percent in the case of stock disposed of in a taxable year beginning before 2011; (ii) 42 percent in the case of stock acquired before January 1, 2001, and disposed of in a taxable year beginning after 2010; and (iii) 28 percent in the case of stock acquired after December 31, 2000, and disposed of in a taxable year beginning after 2010.

[1314] The 50 percent of gain included in taxable income is taxed at a maximum rate of 28 percent.

native minimum tax for dispositions after December 31, 2010, in the case of stock acquired before January 1, 2001; and (iii) 17.92 percent under the alternative minimum tax for dispositions after December 31, 2010, in the case of stock acquired after December 31, 2000.[1315]

***Temporary increase in exclusion***

The percentage exclusion for qualified small business stock acquired after February 17, 2009, and before January 1, 2011, is increased to 75 percent. As a result of the increased exclusion, gain from the sale of this qualified small business stock held at least five years is taxed at effective rates of seven percent under the regular tax[1316] and 12.88 percent under the alternative minimum tax.[1317]

### *Reasons for Change*

The Congress believes that increasing the exclusion of gain for small business stock will encourage new and additional investment in small businesses. Access to additional capital will help these small businesses expand and create jobs.

### *Explanation of Provision*[1318]

Under the provision, the percentage exclusion for qualified small business stock acquired during 2010 is increased to 100 percent and the minimum tax preference does not apply. Thus, no regular tax or alternative minimum tax is imposed on the sale of this stock held at least five years.

### *Effective Date*

The provision is effective for stock issued after the date of enactment (September 27, 2010) and before January 1, 2011.

## 2. Five-year carryback of general business credit of eligible small business (sec. 2012 of the Act and sec. 39 of the Code)

### *Present Law*

The general business credit generally may not exceed the excess of the taxpayer's net income tax over the greater of the taxpayer's tentative minimum tax or 25 percent of so much of the taxpayer's net regular tax liability as exceeds $25,000.[1319] General business

[1315] The amount of gain included in alternative minimum tax is taxed at a maximum rate of 28 percent. The amount so included is the sum of (i) 50 percent (the percentage included in taxable income) of the total gain and (ii) the applicable preference percentage of the one-half gain that is excluded from taxable income.

[1316] The 25 percent of gain included in taxable income is taxed at a maximum rate of 28 percent.

[1317] The 46 percent of gain included in alternative minimum tax is taxed at a maximum rate of 28 percent. Forty-six percent is the sum of 25 percent (the percentage of total gain included in taxable income) plus 21 percent (the percentage of total gain which is an alternative minimum tax preference).

[1318] The provision was subsequently amended by section 760 of the Tax Relief, Unemployment Insurance Reauthorization, and Job Creation Act of 2010, Pub. L. No. 111–312, described in Part Sixteen.

[1319] Sec. 38(c). The general business credit is the sum of the credits allowed under sec. 38(b).

credits in excess of this limitation may be carried back one year and forward up to 20 years.[1320]

### *Explanation of Provision*

The provision extends the carryback period for eligible small business credits from one to five years. Under the provision, eligible small business credits are defined as the sum of the general business credits determined for the taxable year with respect to an eligible small business. An eligible small business is, with respect to any taxable year, a corporation, the stock of which is not publicly traded, or a partnership which meets the gross receipts test of section 448(c), substituting $50 million for $5 million each place it appears.[1321] In the case of a sole proprietorship, the gross receipts test is applied as if it were a corporation. Credits determined with respect to a partnership or S corporation are not treated as eligible small business credits by a partner or shareholder unless the partner or shareholder meets the gross receipts test for the taxable year in which the credits are treated as current year business credits.

### *Effective Date*

The provision is effective for credits determined in the taxpayer's first taxable year beginning after December 31, 2009.

## 3. General business credit of eligible small business not subject to alternative minimum tax (sec. 2013 of the Act and sec. 38 of the Code)

### *Present Law*

For any taxable year, the general business credit, which is the sum of the various business credits, generally may not exceed the excess of the taxpayer's net income tax over the greater of the taxpayer's tentative minimum tax or 25 percent of so much of the taxpayer's net regular tax liability as exceeds $25,000. Any general business credit in excess of this limitation may be carried back one year and forward up to 20 years. The tentative minimum tax is an amount equal to specified rates of tax imposed on the excess of the alternative minimum taxable income over an exemption amount. However, in applying the tax liability limitation to certain specified credits that are part of the general business credit, the tentative minimum tax is treated as being zero.[1322] Thus, the specified credits may offset both regular and alternative minimum tax liability.

### *Explanation of Provision*

The Act provides that the tentative minimum tax is treated as being zero for eligible small business credits. Thus, an eligible small business credit may offset both regular and alternative min-

---

[1320] Sec. 39.

[1321] For example, a calendar year corporation meets the $50 million gross receipts test for the 2010 taxable year, if as of January 1, 2010, its average annual gross receipts for the 3-taxable-year period ending December 31, 2009, does not exceed $50 million. The aggregation and special rules under sections 448(c)(2) and (3) apply in applying the test.

[1322] See section 38(c)(4)(B) for a list of the specified credits.

imum tax liability. Under the provision, eligible small business credits are defined as the sum of the general business credits determined for the taxable year with respect to an eligible small business. An eligible small business is, with respect to any taxable year, a corporation, the stock of which is not publicly traded, or a partnership, which meets the gross receipts test of section 448(c), substituting $50 million for $5 million each place it appears.[1323] In the case of a sole proprietorship, the gross receipts test is applied as if it were a corporation. Credits determined with respect to a partnership or S corporation are not treated as eligible small business credits by a partner or shareholder unless the partner or shareholder meets the gross receipts test for the taxable year in which the credits are treated as current year business credits.

### *Effective Date*

The proposal is effective for credits determined in a taxpayer's first taxable year beginning after December 31, 2009.

## 4. Temporary reduction in recognition period for S corporation built-in gains tax (sec. 2014 of the Act and sec. 1374 of the Code)

### *Present Law*

A "small business corporation" (as defined in section 1361(b)) may elect to be treated as an S corporation. Unlike C corporations, S corporations generally pay no corporate-level tax. Instead, items of income and loss of an S corporation pass though to its shareholders. Each shareholder takes into account separately its share of these items on its individual income tax return.[1324]

A corporate level tax, at the highest marginal rate applicable to corporations (currently 35 percent) is imposed on an S corporation's gain that arose prior to the conversion of the C corporation to an S corporation and is recognized by the S corporation during the recognition period, i.e., the 10-year period beginning with the first day of the first taxable year for which the S election is in effect.[1325] For any taxable year beginning in 2009 and 2010, no tax is imposed on an S corporation under section 1374 if the seventh taxable year in the corporation's recognition period preceded such taxable year.[1326] Thus, with respect to gain that arose prior to the conversion of a C corporation to an S corporation, for taxable years beginning in 2009 and 2010, no tax is imposed under section 1374 after the seventh taxable year the S corporation election is in effect.

The built-in gains tax also applies to gains with respect to net recognized built-in gain attributable to property received by an S corporation from a C corporation in a carryover basis trans-

[1323] For example, a calendar year corporation meets the $50 million gross receipts test for the 2010 taxable year, if as of January 1, 2010, if its average annual gross receipts for the 3-taxable-year period ending December 31, 2009, does not exceed $50 million. The aggregation and special rules under sections 448(c)(2) and (3) apply for purposes of the test.

[1324] Sec. 1366.

[1325] Sec. 1374(d)(7)(A). The 10-year period refers to ten calendar years from the first day of the first taxable year for which the corporation was an S corporation.

[1326] Sec. 1374(d)(7)(B).

action.[1327] In the case of built-in gain attributable to an asset received by an S corporation from a C corporation in a carryover basis transaction, the recognition period rules are applied by substituting the date such asset was acquired by the S corporation in lieu of the beginning of the first taxable year for which the corporation was an S corporation.[1328]

Gains recognized in the recognition period are not built-in gains to the extent they are shown to have arisen while the S election was in effect or are offset by recognized built-in losses. The amount of the built-in gains tax is treated as a loss taken into account by the shareholders in computing their individual income tax.[1329]

### *Explanation of Provision*

For taxable years beginning in 2011, the provision provides that for purposes of computing the built-in gains tax, the "recognition period" is the five-year period[1330] beginning with the first day of the first taxable year for which the corporation was an S corporation.

### *Effective Date*

The provision is effective for taxable years beginning after December 31, 2010.

## B. Encouraging Investment

### 1. Increase and expand expensing of certain depreciable business assets (sec. 2021 of the Act and sec. 179 of the Code)

### *Present Law*

A taxpayer that satisfies limitations on annual investment may elect under section 179 to deduct (or "expense") the cost of qualifying property, rather than to recover such costs through depreciation deductions.[1331] For taxable years beginning in 2010, the maximum amount that a taxpayer may expense is $250,000 of the cost of qualifying property placed in service for the taxable year. The $250,000 amount is reduced (but not below zero) by the amount by which the cost of qualifying property placed in service during the taxable year exceeds $800,000.[1332] In general, qualifying property is defined as depreciable tangible personal property that is purchased for use in the active conduct of a trade or business. Off-the-

[1327] Sec. 1374(d)(8). With respect to such assets, the recognition period runs from the day on which such assets were acquired (in lieu of the beginning of the first taxable year for which the corporation was an S corporation). Sec. 1374(d)(8)(B).

[1328] Shareholders continue to take into account all items of gain and loss under section 1366.

[1329] Sec. 1366(f)(2).

[1330] The five-year period refers to five calendar years from the first day of the first taxable year for which the corporation was an S corporation.

[1331] Additional section 179 incentives are provided with respect to qualified property meeting applicable requirements that is used by a business in an enterprise zone (sec. 1397A), a renewal community (sec. 1400J), or the Gulf Opportunity Zone (sec. 1400N(e)).

[1332] The temporary $250,000 and $800,000 amounts were enacted in the Economic Stimulus Act of 2008, Pub. L. No. 110–185, extended for taxable years beginning in 2009 by the American Recovery and Reinvestment Act of 2009, Pub. L. No. 111–5, and extended for taxable years beginning in 2010 by the Hiring Incentives to Restore Employment Act of 2010, Pub. L. No. 111–147.

shelf computer software placed in service in taxable years beginning before 2011 is treated as qualifying property.

For taxable years beginning in 2011 and thereafter, a taxpayer with a sufficiently small amount of annual investment may elect to deduct up to $25,000 of the cost of qualifying property placed in service for the taxable year. The $25,000 amount is reduced (but not below zero) by the amount by which the cost of qualifying property placed in service during the taxable year exceeds $200,000. The $25,000 and $200,000 amounts are not indexed. In general, qualifying property is defined as depreciable tangible personal property that is purchased for use in the active conduct of a trade or business (not including off-the-shelf computer software).

The amount eligible to be expensed for a taxable year may not exceed the taxable income for a taxable year that is derived from the active conduct of a trade or business (determined without regard to this provision). Any amount that is not allowed as a deduction because of the taxable income limitation may be carried forward to succeeding taxable years (subject to similar limitations). No general business credit under section 38 is allowed with respect to any amount for which a deduction is allowed under section 179. An expensing election is made under rules prescribed by the Secretary.[1333]

### *Explanation of Provision*

The provision increases the maximum amount a taxpayer may expense under section 179 to $500,000 and increases the phase-out threshold amount to $2 million for taxable years beginning in 2010 and 2011.[1334] Thus, the provision provides that the maximum amount a taxpayer may expense, for taxable years beginning after 2009 and before 2012, is $500,000 of the cost of qualifying property placed in service for the taxable year. The $500,000 amount is reduced (but not below zero) by the amount by which the cost of qualifying property placed in service during the taxable year exceeds $2 million.

The provision permits a taxpayer to elect to temporarily expand the definition of property qualifying for section 179 to include certain real property—specifically, qualified leasehold improvement property, qualified restaurant property, and qualified retail improvement property—purchased by the taxpayer.[1335] The maximum amount with respect to real property that may be expensed under the proposal is $250,000.[1336] In addition, section 179 deduc-

---

[1333] Sec. 179(c)(1).

[1334] The provision was modified and extended for taxable years beginning in 2012 by section 402 of the Tax Relief, Unemployment Insurance Reauthorization, and Job Creation Act of 2010, Pub. L. No. 111–312, described in Part Sixteen.

[1335] For purposes of the provision, qualified leasehold improvement property has the meaning given such term under section 168(e)(6), qualified restaurant property has the meaning given such term under section 168(e)(7) (and includes a building described in section 168(e)(7)(A)(i) that is placed in service after December 31, 2009 and before January 1, 2012), and qualified retail improvement property has the meaning given such term under section 168(e)(8) (without regard to section 168(e)(8)(E)).

[1336] For example, assume that during 2010, a company's only asset purchases are section 179-eligible equipment costing $100,000 and qualifying leasehold improvements costing $350,000. Assuming the company has no other asset purchases during 2010, and is not subject to the taxable income limitation, the maximum section 179 deduction the company can claim for 2010 is $350,000 ($100,000 with respect to the equipment and $250,000 with respect to the qualifying leasehold improvements).

tions attributable to qualified real property that are disallowed under the trade or business income limitation may only be carried over to taxable years in which the definition of eligible section 179 property includes qualified real property. Thus under the provision, if a taxpayer's section 179 deduction for 2010 with respect to qualified real property is limited by the taxpayer's active trade or business income, such disallowed amount may be carried over to 2011 in the manner under present law. Any such amounts that are not used in 2011, plus any 2011 disallowed section 179 deductions attributable to qualified real property, are treated as property placed in service in 2011 for purposes of computing depreciation. The carryover amount from 2010 is considered placed in service on the first day of the 2011 taxable year.[1337]

### *Effective Date*

The provision is effective for taxable years beginning after December 31, 2009.

## 2. Extend the additional first-year depreciation allowance (sec. 2022 of the Act and sec. 168(k) of the Code)

### *Present Law*

#### *In general*

An additional first-year depreciation deduction is allowed equal to 50 percent of the adjusted basis of qualified property placed in service during 2008 and 2009 (2009 and 2010 for certain longer-lived and transportation property).[1338] The additional first-year depreciation deduction is allowed for both regular tax and alternative minimum tax purposes, but is not allowed for purposes of computing earnings and profits. The basis of the property and the depreciation allowances in the year of purchase and later years are appropriately adjusted to reflect the additional first-year depreciation deduction. In addition, there are no adjustments to the allowable amount of depreciation for purposes of computing a taxpayer's alternative minimum taxable income with respect to property to which the provision applies. The amount of the additional first-year depreciation deduction is not affected by a short taxable year. The taxpayer may elect out of additional first-year depreciation for any class of property for any taxable year.

The interaction of the additional first-year depreciation allowance with the otherwise applicable depreciation allowance may be illustrated as follows. Assume that in 2009, a taxpayer purchased new depreciable property and places it in service.[1339] The property's cost is $1,000, and it is five-year property subject to the half-year convention. The amount of additional first-year depreciation allowed is $500. The remaining $500 of the cost of the property is

---

[1337] For example, assume that during 2010, a company's only asset purchases are section 179-eligible equipment costing $100,000 and qualifying leasehold improvements costing $200,000. Assume the company has no other asset purchases during 2010, and has a taxable income limitation of $150,000. The maximum section 179 deduction the company can claim for 2010 is $150,000, which is allocated pro rata between the properties, such that the carryover to 2011 is allocated $100,000 to the qualified leasehold improvements and $50,000 to the equipment.

[1338] Sec. 168(k). The additional first-year depreciation deduction is subject to the general rules regarding whether an item must be capitalized under section 263 or section 263A.

[1339] Assume that the cost of the property is not eligible for expensing under section 179.

depreciable under the rules applicable to five-year property. Thus, 20 percent, or $100, is also allowed as a depreciation deduction in 2009. The total depreciation deduction with respect to the property for 2009 is $600. The remaining $400 adjusted basis of the property generally is recovered through otherwise applicable depreciation rules.

Property qualifying for the additional first-year depreciation deduction must meet all of the following requirements. First, the property must be (1) property to which MACRS applies with an applicable recovery period of 20 years or less; (2) water utility property (as defined in section 168(e)(5)); (3) computer software other than computer software covered by section 197; or (4) qualified leasehold improvement property (as defined in section 168(k)(3)).[1340] Second, the original use[1341] of the property must commence with the taxpayer after December 31, 2007.[1342] Third, the taxpayer must acquire the property within the applicable time period. Finally, the property must be placed in service after December 31, 2007, and before January 1, 2010. An extension of the placed in service date of one year (i.e., to January 1, 2011) is provided for certain property with a recovery period of ten years or longer and certain transportation property.[1343] Transportation property is defined as tangible personal property used in the trade or business of transporting persons or property.

The applicable time period for acquired property is (1) after December 31, 2007, and before January 1, 2010, but only if no binding written contract for the acquisition is in effect before January 1, 2008, or (2) pursuant to a binding written contract which was entered into after December 31, 2007, and before January 1, 2010.[1344] With respect to property that is manufactured, constructed, or produced by the taxpayer for use by the taxpayer, the taxpayer must begin the manufacture, construction, or production of the property after December 31, 2007, and before January 1, 2010. Property that is manufactured, constructed, or produced for the taxpayer by another person under a contract that is entered into prior to the manufacture, construction, or production of the property is considered to be manufactured, constructed, or produced by the taxpayer. For

[1340] The additional first-year depreciation deduction is not available for any property that is required to be depreciated under the alternative depreciation system of MACRS. The additional first-year depreciation deduction is also not available for qualified New York Liberty Zone leasehold improvement property as defined in section 1400L(c)(2).

[1341] The term "original use" means the first use to which the property is put, whether or not such use corresponds to the use of such property by the taxpayer.

If in the normal course of its business a taxpayer sells fractional interests in property to unrelated third parties, then the original use of such property begins with the first user of each fractional interest (i.e., each fractional owner is considered the original user of its proportionate share of the property).

[1342] A special rule applies in the case of certain leased property. In the case of any property that is originally placed in service by a person and that is sold to the taxpayer and leased back to such person by the taxpayer within three months after the date that the property was placed in service, the property would be treated as originally placed in service by the taxpayer not earlier than the date that the property is used under the leaseback.

If property is originally placed in service by a lessor, such property is sold within three months after the date that the property was placed in service, and the user of such property does not change, then the property is treated as originally placed in service by the taxpayer not earlier than the date of such sale.

[1343] Property qualifying for the extended placed in service date must have an estimated production period exceeding one year and a cost exceeding $1 million.

[1344] Property does not fail to qualify for the additional first-year depreciation merely because a binding written contract to acquire a component of the property is in effect prior to January 1, 2008.

property eligible for the extended placed in service date, a special rule limits the amount of costs eligible for the additional first-year depreciation. With respect to such property, only the portion of the basis that is properly attributable to the costs incurred before January 1, 2010, ("progress expenditures") is eligible for the additional first-year depreciation.[1345]

Property does not qualify for the additional first-year depreciation deduction when the user of such property (or a related party) would not have been eligible for the additional first-year depreciation deduction if the user (or a related party) were treated as the owner. For example, if a taxpayer sells to a related party property that was under construction prior to January 1, 2008, the property does not qualify for the additional first-year depreciation deduction. Similarly, if a taxpayer sells to a related party property that was subject to a binding written contract prior to January 1, 2008, the property does not qualify for the additional first-year depreciation deduction. As a further example, if a taxpayer (the lessee) sells property in a sale-leaseback arrangement, and the property otherwise would not have qualified for the additional first-year depreciation deduction if it were owned by the taxpayer-lessee, then the lessor is not entitled to the additional first-year depreciation deduction.

The limitation under section 280F on the amount of depreciation deductions allowed with respect to certain passenger automobiles is increased in the first year by $8,000 for automobiles that qualify (and for which the taxpayer does not elect out of the additional first-year deduction). The $8,000 increase is not indexed for inflation.

### *Explanation of Provision*

The provision extends the additional first-year depreciation deduction for one year to apply to qualified property acquired and placed in service during 2010 (or placed in service during 2011 for certain long-lived property and transportation property).[1346]

### *Effective Date*

The provision applies to property placed in service in taxable years ending after December 31, 2009.

---

[1345] For purposes of determining the amount of eligible progress expenditures, it is intended that rules similar to section 46(d)(3) as in effect prior to the Tax Reform Act of 1986 apply.

[1346] The provision was temporarily expanded and extended for two years generally through 2012 (through 2013 for certain longer-lived and transportation property) by section 401 of the Tax Relief, Unemployment Insurance Reauthorization, and Job Creation Act of 2010, Pub. L. No. 111–312, described in Part Sixteen of this document.

### 3. Disregard bonus depreciation in computing percentage completion (sec. 2023 of the Act and new sec. 460(c)(6) of the Code)

#### *Present Law*

*Percentage-of-completion method*

In general, in the case of a long-term contract, the taxable income from the contract is determined under the percentage-of-completion method.[1347] Under such method, the percentage of completion is determined by comparing costs allocated to the contract and incurred before the end of the taxable year with the estimated total contract costs. Costs allocated to the contract typically include all costs (including depreciation) that directly benefit or are incurred by reason of the taxpayer's long-term contract activities. The allocation of the costs to a contract is made in accordance with regulations.[1348]

*Additional first-year depreciation deduction ("bonus depreciation")*

A taxpayer is allowed to recover, through annual depreciation deductions, the cost of certain property used in a trade or business or for the production of income. The amount of the depreciation deduction allowed with respect to tangible property for a taxable year generally is determined under MACRS. Under MACRS, different types of property generally are assigned applicable recovery periods and depreciation methods. The recovery periods applicable to most tangible personal property (tangible property other than residential rental property and nonresidential real property) range from three to 25 years. The depreciation methods generally applicable to tangible personal property are the 200-percent and 150-percent declining balance methods, switching to the straight-line method for the taxable year in which the depreciation deduction would be maximized.[1349] In general, the recovery periods for real property are 39 years for non-residential real property and 27.5 years for residential rental property. The depreciation method for real property is the straight-line method.

An additional first-year depreciation deduction is allowed equal to 50 percent of the adjusted basis of qualified property placed in service during 2008 and 2009 (2009 and 2010 for certain longer-lived and transportation property),[1350] and for property placed in service in 2010 (2011 for certain longer-lived and transportation property) under section 2022 of the Act. The additional first-year depreciation deduction is allowed for both regular tax and alternative minimum tax purposes, but is not allowed for purposes of computing earnings and profits. The basis of the property and the depreciation allowances in the year of purchase and later years are

[1347] Sec. 460(a).

[1348] Treas. Reg. sec. 1.460–5.

[1349] For certain property, including tangible property used predominantly outside of the United States, tax-exempt use property, tax-exempt bond-financed property, and certain other property, the MACRS "alternative depreciation system" of section 168(g) applies, generally increasing recovery periods and requiring straight-line depreciation.

[1350] Sec. 168(k). The additional first-year depreciation deduction is subject to the general rules regarding whether an item must be capitalized under section 263 or section 263A.

appropriately adjusted to reflect the additional first-year depreciation deduction. In addition, there are no adjustments to the allowable amount of depreciation for purposes of computing a taxpayer's alternative minimum taxable income with respect to property to which the provision applies. The amount of the additional first-year depreciation deduction is not affected by a short taxable year. The taxpayer may elect out of additional first-year depreciation for any class of property for any taxable year.

Property qualifying for the additional first-year depreciation deduction must meet all of the following requirements. First, the property must be (1) property to which MACRS applies with an applicable recovery period of 20 years or less, (2) water utility property (as defined in section 168(e)(5)), (3) computer software other than computer software covered by section 197, or (4) qualified leasehold improvement property (as defined in section 168(k)(3)).[1351] Second, the original use[1352] of the property must commence with the taxpayer after December 31, 2007.[1353] Third, the taxpayer must purchase the property within the applicable time period. Finally, the property must be placed in service after December 31, 2007, and before January 1, 2011. An extension of the placed in service date of one year (i.e., to January 1, 2012) is provided for certain property with a recovery period of ten years or longer, and certain transportation property.[1354] Transportation property is defined as tangible personal property used in the trade or business of transporting persons or property.

The applicable time period for acquired property is (1) after December 31, 2008, and before January 1, 2011, but only if no binding written contract for the acquisition is in effect before January 1, 2010, or (2) pursuant to a binding written contract which was entered into after December 31, 2008, and before January 1, 2011.[1355] With respect to property that is manufactured, constructed, or produced by the taxpayer for use by the taxpayer, the taxpayer must begin the manufacture, construction, or production of the property after December 31, 2008, and before January 1, 2010. Property that is manufactured, constructed, or produced for the taxpayer by another person under a contract that is entered into prior to the man-

[1351] The additional first-year depreciation deduction is not available for any property that is required to be depreciated under the alternative depreciation system of MACRS. The additional first-year depreciation deduction is also not available for qualified New York Liberty Zone leasehold improvement property as defined in section 1400L(c)(2).

[1352] The term "original use" means the first use to which the property is put, whether or not such use corresponds to the use of such property by the taxpayer.

If in the normal course of its business a taxpayer sells fractional interests in property to unrelated third parties, then the original use of such property begins with the first user of each fractional interest (i.e., each fractional owner is considered the original user of its proportionate share of the property).

[1353] A special rule applies in the case of certain leased property. In the case of any property that is originally placed in service by a person and that is sold to the taxpayer and leased back to such person by the taxpayer within three months after the date that the property was placed in service, the property would be treated as originally placed in service by the taxpayer not earlier than the date that the property is used under the leaseback.

If property is originally placed in service by a lessor (including by operation of section 168(k)(2)(D)(i)), such property is sold within three months after the date that the property was placed in service, and the user of such property does not change, then the property is treated as originally placed in service by the taxpayer not earlier than the date of such sale.

[1354] Property qualifying for the extended placed in service date must have an estimated production period exceeding one year and a cost exceeding $1 million.

[1355] Property does not fail to qualify for the additional first-year depreciation merely because a binding written contract to acquire a component of the property is in effect prior to January 1, 2008.

ufacture, construction, or production of the property is considered to be manufactured, constructed, or produced by the taxpayer. For property eligible for the extended placed in service date, a special rule limits the amount of costs eligible for the additional first-year depreciation. With respect to such property, only the portion of the basis that is properly attributable to the costs incurred before January 1, 2011 ("progress expenditures") is eligible for the additional first-year depreciation.[1356]

Property does not qualify for the additional first-year depreciation deduction when the user of such property (or a related party) would not have been eligible for the additional first-year depreciation deduction if the user (or a related party) were treated as the owner. In addition, the limitation under section 280F on the amount of depreciation deductions allowed with respect to certain passenger automobiles is increased in the first year by $8,000 for automobiles that qualify (and for which the taxpayer does not elect out of the additional first-year deduction). The $8,000 increase is not indexed for inflation.

### *Explanation of Provision*

The Act provides that solely for purposes of determining the percentage of completion under section 460(b)(1)(A), the cost of qualified property is taken into account as a cost allocated to the contract as if bonus depreciation had not been enacted.[1357] Qualified property is property otherwise eligible for bonus depreciation that has a MACRS recovery period of 7 years or less and that is placed in service after December 31, 2009, and before January 1, 2011 (January 1, 2012, in the case of property described in section 168(k)(2)(B)[1358]).

### *Effective Date*

The provision is effective for property placed in service after December 31, 2009.

## C. Promoting Entrepreneurship

### 1. Increase amount allowed as deduction for start-up expenditures (sec. 2031 of the Act and sec. 195 of the Code)

### *Present Law*

#### *Start-up expenditures*

A taxpayer can elect to deduct up to $5,000 of start-up expenditures in the taxable year in which the active trade or business be-

[1356] For purposes of determining the amount of eligible progress expenditures, it is intended that rules similar to section 46(d)(3) as in effect prior to the Tax Reform Act of 1986 apply.

[1357] For example, assume a calendar year taxpayer is required to use the percentage-of-completion method to account for a long-term contract during 2010. Assume further that during 2010 the taxpayer purchases and places into service equipment with a cost basis of $500,000 and MACRS recovery period of 5 years. The taxpayer uses the equipment exclusively in performing its obligation under the contract. In computing the percentage of completion under section 460(b)(1)(A), the depreciation on the equipment (assuming a half-year convention) taken into account as a cost allocated to the contract for 2010 is $100,000 [$500,000/5*200%*.5]. The amount of the depreciation deduction that may be claimed by the taxpayer in 2010 with respect to the equipment is $300,000 [($500,000 * 50%) + (($500,000 − (500,000*50%))/5*200%*.5)].

[1358] Sec. 168(k)(2)(B) generally applies to property having longer production periods.

gins.[1359] However, the $5,000 amount is reduced (but not below zero) by the amount by which the cumulative cost of start-up expenditures exceeds $50,000.[1360] Start-up expenditures that are not deductible in the year in which the active trade or business begins are, at the taxpayer's election, amortized over a 15-year period beginning with the month the active trade or business begins.[1361] Start-up expenditures are amounts that would have been deductible as trade or business expenses, had they not been paid or incurred before business began, including amounts paid or incurred in connection with (1) investigating the creation or acquisition of an active trade or business, (2) creating an active trade or business, or (3) any activity engaged in for profit and for the production of income before the day on which the active trade or business begins, in anticipation of such activity becoming an active trade or business.[1362]

Treasury regulations[1363] provide that a taxpayer is deemed to have made an election under section 195(b) to amortize its start-up expenditures for the taxable year in which the active trade or business to which the expenditures relate begins. A taxpayer that chooses to forgo the deemed election must clearly elect to capitalize its start-up expenditures on its timely filed Federal income tax return for the taxable year the active trade or business commences. The election either to amortize or capitalize start-up expenditures is irrevocable and applies to all start-up expenditures related to the active trade or business.

### *Explanation of Provision*

For taxable years beginning in 2010, the provision increases the amount of start-up expenditures a taxpayer can elect to deduct from $5,000 to $10,000 and increases the deduction phase-out threshold such that the $10,000 is reduced (but not below zero) by the amount by which the cumulative cost of start-up expenditures exceeds $60,000.

### *Reasons for Change*

Congress believes that increasing the amount of start-up expenditures that a taxpayer can elect to deduct, rather than requiring their amortization, may help encourage the formation of new businesses.[1364]

### *Effective Date*

The provision is effective for taxable years beginning after December 31, 2009.

---

[1359] Sec. 195(b)(1)(A).
[1360] *Ibid.*
[1361] Sec. 195(b)(1)(B).
[1362] Sec. 195(c).
[1363] Temp. Treas. Reg. sec. 1.195–1T(b).
[1364] H.R. Rep. No. 111–447.

## D. Promoting Small Business Fairness

### 1. Limitation on penalty for failure to disclose certain information (sec. 2041 of the Act and sec. 6707A of the Code)

#### *Present Law*

The reporting requirements of sections 6011 through 6112 create interlocking disclosure obligations for both taxpayers and advisors. Each of these disclosure statutes has a parallel penalty provision that enforces it. Prior to enactment of the American Jobs Creation Act of 2004 ("AJCA"),[1365] no penalty was imposed on taxpayers who failed to disclose participation in transactions subject to section 6011. For disclosures that were due after enactment of that legislation, a strict liability penalty under section 6707A applies to any failure to disclose a reportable transaction.

Regulations under section 6011 require a taxpayer to disclose with its tax return certain information with respect to each "reportable transaction" in which the taxpayer participates.[1366] A reportable transaction is defined as one that the Secretary determines is required to be disclosed because it is determined to have a potential for tax avoidance or evasion.[1367] There are five categories of reportable transactions: listed transactions, confidential transactions, transactions with contractual protection, certain loss transactions and transactions of interest.[1368]

Transactions falling under the first and last categories of reportable transactions are transactions that are described in publications issued by the Treasury Department and identified as one of these types of transaction. A listed transaction is defined as a reportable transaction which is the same as, or substantially similar[1369] to, a transaction specifically identified by the Secretary as a tax avoidance transaction for purposes of the reporting disclosure requirements.[1370] A "transaction of interest" is one that is the same as or substantially similar to a transaction identified by the Secretary as one about which the Secretary is concerned but does not yet have sufficient knowledge to determine that the transaction is abusive.[1371]

The other categories of reportable transactions are not specifically identified in published guidance, but are defined as classes of transactions sharing certain characteristics. In general, a transaction is considered to be offered to a taxpayer under conditions of confidentiality if an advisor who is paid a minimum fee places a limitation on disclosure by the taxpayer of the tax treatment or tax structure of the transaction and the limitation on disclosure protects the confidentiality of that advisor's tax strategies (irrespective if such terms are legally binding).[1372] A transaction involves con-

---

[1365] Pub. L. No. 108–357.

[1366] Treas. Reg. sec. 1.6011–4.

[1367] Sec. 6707A(c)(1).

[1368] Treas. Reg. sec. 1.6011–4(b)(2)–(6).

[1369] The regulations clarify that the term "substantially similar" includes any transaction that is expected to obtain the same or similar types of tax consequences and that is either factually similar or based on the same or similar tax strategy. Further, the term must be broadly construed in favor of disclosure. Treas. Reg. sec. 1.6011–4(c)(4).

[1370] Sec. 6707A(c)(2).

[1371] Treas. Reg. sec. 1.6011–4(b)(6).

[1372] Treas. Reg. sec. 1.6011–4(b)(3).

tractual protection if (1) the taxpayer has the right to a full or partial refund of fees if the intended tax consequences from the transaction are not sustained, or (2) the fees are contingent on the intended tax consequences from the transaction being sustained.[1373] A reportable loss transaction generally includes any transaction that results in a taxpayer claiming a loss (under section 165) of at least (1) $10 million in any single year or $20 million in any combination of years by a corporate taxpayer or a partnership with only corporate partners; (2) $2 million in any single year or $4 million in any combination of years by all other partnerships, S corporations, trusts, and individuals; or (3) $50,000 in any single year for individuals or trusts if the loss arises with respect to foreign currency translation losses.[1374] Treasury has announced its intention to add a sixth category of reportable transactions, patented transactions, but has not yet done so.[1375]

Section 6707A imposes a penalty for failure to comply with the reporting requirements of 6011. A single reportable transaction may have to be reported by multiple taxpayers in connection with multiple tax returns. For example, a reportable transaction entered into by a partnership may have to be reported under section 6011 by both the partnership and its partners.[1376] The amount of the penalty due for each taxpayer's failure to comply varies depending upon whether or not the transaction is a listed transaction and whether the relevant taxpayer is an individual. For listed transactions, the maximum penalty is $100,000 for natural persons and $200,000 for all other persons. For reportable transactions other than listed transactions, the maximum penalty is $10,000 for natural persons and $50,000 for all other persons.

A public entity that is required to pay a penalty for an undisclosed listed or reportable transaction must disclose the imposition of the penalty in reports to the Securities and Exchange Commission ("SEC") for such periods specified by the Secretary. Disclosure to the SEC applies without regard to whether the taxpayer determines the amount of the penalty to be material to the reports in which the penalty must appear, and any failure to disclose such penalty in the reports is treated as a failure to disclose a listed transaction. A taxpayer must disclose a penalty in reports to the SEC once the taxpayer has exhausted its administrative and judicial remedies with respect to the penalty (or if earlier, when paid).[1377] However, the taxpayer is only required to report the penalty one time. A public entity that is subject to a gross valuation misstatement penalty under section 6662(h) attributable to a non-disclosed listed transaction or non-disclosed reportable avoidance transaction may also be required to make disclosures in its SEC filings.[1378]

For reportable transactions other than listed transactions, the Commissioner of the Internal Revenue ("Commissioner") or his delegate can rescind (or abate) the penalty only if rescinding the penalty would promote compliance with the tax laws and effective tax

[1373] Treas. Reg. sec. 1.6011–4(b)(4).
[1374] Treas. Reg. sec. 1.6011–4(b)(5).
[1375] Prop. Treas. Reg. sec. 1.6011–4(b)(7), published September 26, 2007 (REG–129916–07).
[1376] See, e.g., Treas. Reg. sec. 1.6011–4(c)(3)(ii), Example 2.
[1377] Sec. 6707A(e).
[1378] Sec. 6707A(e)(2)(C); Rev. Proc. 2005–51, 2005–2 CB 296.

administration.[1379] The decision to rescind a penalty must be accompanied by a record describing the facts and reasons for the action and the amount rescinded. Determinations by the Commissioner regarding rescission are not subject to judicial review.[1380] The Internal Revenue Service ("IRS") also is required to submit an annual report to Congress summarizing the application of the disclosure penalties and providing a description of each penalty rescinded under this provision and the reasons for the rescission. The section 6707A penalty cannot be waived with respect to a listed transaction.

The section 6707A penalty is assessed in addition to any accuracy-related penalties. If the taxpayer does not adequately disclose a reportable transaction, the strengthened reasonable cause exception to the accuracy-related penalty is not available, and the taxpayer is subject to an increased penalty equal to 30 percent of the understatement.[1381] However, a taxpayer will be treated as having adequately disclosed a transaction for this purpose if the Commissioner has separately rescinded the separate penalty under section 6707A for failure to disclose a reportable transaction.[1382] The Commissioner is authorized to do this only if the failure does not relate to a listed transaction and only if rescinding the penalty would promote compliance and effective tax administration.[1383]

### *Reasons for Change*

At the time that this penalty was enacted in 2004, Congress believed that a penalty for failing to make the required disclosures, when the imposition of such penalty is not dependent on the tax treatment of the underlying transaction ultimately being sustained, would provide an additional incentive for taxpayers to satisfy their reporting obligations under the new disclosure provisions.[1384] In the years since enactment, the Congress has learned that this penalty is very often applicable to small businesses and individuals in amounts that exceed the tax savings claimed on these returns, if any. These taxpayers often were not advised that the transactions are reportable to the IRS. In her annual report,[1385] the National Taxpayer Advocate informed Congress that the penalties cause unconscionable hardship on taxpayers as there are individuals facing bankruptcy and loss of a business as a result of the magnitude of the penalty for failure to disclose a reportable transaction. The

[1379] In determining whether to rescind (or abate) the penalty for failing to disclose a reportable transaction on the grounds that doing so would promote compliance with the tax laws and effective tax administration, it is intended that the Commissioner take into account whether: (1) the person on whom the penalty is imposed has a history of complying with the tax laws; (2) the violation is due to an unintentional mistake of fact; and (3) imposing the penalty would be against equity and good conscience.

[1380] This does not limit the ability of a taxpayer to challenge whether a penalty is appropriate (e.g., a taxpayer may litigate the issue of whether a transaction is a reportable transaction (and thus subject to the penalty if not disclosed) or not a reportable transaction (and thus not subject to the penalty)).

[1381] Sec. 6662A(c).

[1382] Sec. 6664(d).

[1383] Sec. 6707A(d).

[1384] See, "Reasons for Change" in discussion of section 811 of the American Jobs Creation Act of 2004 ("AJCA"), Pub. L. No. 108–357, p. 361 of the Joint Committee on Taxation, *General Explanation of Tax Legislation Enacted in the 108th Congress* (JCS–5–05), May 2005.

[1385] See, discussion of "Legislative Recommendations with Legislative Action: Modify Internal Revenue Code Section 6707A to Ameliorate Unconscionable Impact," Vol. 1 National Taxpayer Advocate 2008 Annual Report to Congress, p. 419.

statute allows penalties of up to $300,000 per year on taxpayers with no underpayment of tax and no knowledge that they entered into a transaction required to be reported. Such individuals generally invested in transactions (often a pension plan) that were required to be disclosed through their small businesses often organized as pass-through entities and claimed benefits for several years. Thus, once the IRS determined that the transaction should have been reported, the penalties applied to both the small business and the owner over several years, which resulted in some penalties exceeding over $1 million. The Congress believes that it is appropriate to provide a mechanism for establishing a penalty amount that will be proportionate to the misconduct to be penalized, without discouraging compliance with the requirement to disclose reportable transactions.

### *Explanation of Provision*

The provision changes the general rule for determining the amount of the applicable penalty to achieve proportionality between the penalty and the tax savings that were the object of the transaction, retains the current penalty amounts as the maximum penalty that may be imposed, and establishes a minimum penalty.

First, it provides a general rule that a participant in a reportable transaction who fails to disclose the reportable transaction as required under section 6011 is subject to a penalty equal to 75 percent of the reduction in tax reported on the participant's income tax return as a result of participation in the transaction, or that would result if the transaction were respected for federal tax purposes. Regardless of the amount determined under the general rule, the penalty for each such failure may not exceed certain maximum amounts. The maximum annual penalty that a taxpayer may incur for failing to disclose a particular reportable transaction other than a listed transaction is $10,000 in the case of a natural person and $50,000 for all other persons. The maximum annual penalty that a taxpayer may incur for failing to disclose a listed transaction is $100,000 in the case of a natural person and $200,000 for all other persons.

The provision also establishes a minimum penalty with respect to failure to disclose a reportable or listed transaction. That minimum penalty is $5,000 for natural persons and $10,000 for all other persons.

The following examples illustrate the operation of the maximum and minimum penalties with respect to a partnership or a corporation. First, assume that two individuals participate in a listed transaction through a partnership formed for that purpose. Both partners, as well as the partnership, are required to disclose the transaction. All fail to do so. The failure by the partnership to disclose its participation in a listed or otherwise reportable transaction is subject to the minimum penalty of $10,000, because income tax liability is not incurred at the partnership level nor reported on a partnership return. The individual partners in such partnership who also failed to comply with the reporting requirements of section 6011 are each subject to a penalty of no less than $5,000 and no more than $100,000, based on the reduction in tax reported on their respective returns.

In the second example, assume that a corporation participates in a single listed transaction over the course of three taxable years. The decrease in tax shown on the corporate returns is $1 million in the first year, $100,000 in the second year, and $10,000 in the third year. If the corporation fails to disclose the listed transaction in all three years, the corporation is subject to three separate penalties: a penalty of $200,000 in the first year (as a result of the cap on penalties), a $75,000 penalty in the second year (computed under the general rule) and a $10,000 penalty in the third year (as a result of the minimum penalty) for total penalties of $285,000.

### *Effective Date*

The provision applies to all penalties assessed under section 6707A after December 31, 2006.

## 2. Temporary deduction for health insurance costs in computing self-employment income (sec. 2042 of the Act and sec. 162(l) of the Code)

### *Present Law*

#### *Deduction for health insurance premiums of self-employed individuals*

In calculating adjusted gross income for income tax purposes, self-employed individuals may deduct the cost of health insurance for themselves and their spouses, dependents, and any children who have not attained age 27 as of the end of the taxable year.[1386] The deduction is not available for any month in which the self-employed individual is eligible to participate in an employer-subsidized health plan (maintained by the employer of the taxpayer or the taxpayer's spouse). Moreover, the deduction may not exceed the earned income (within the meaning of section 401(c)(2)) derived by the self-employed individual from the trade or business with respect to which the plan providing the health insurance coverage is established.[1387] The deduction applies only to the cost of insurance (i.e., it does not apply to out-of-pocket expenses that are not reimbursed by insurance).

#### *Self-Employment Contributions Act tax*

The Self-Employment Contributions Act ("SECA") imposes taxes on the net earnings from self-employment of self-employed individuals ("self-employment income"). The tax is composed of two parts: (1) the old age, survivors, and disability insurance ("OASDI") tax; and (2) the hospital insurance ("HI") tax. The rate of the OASDI portion of SECA taxes is equal to 12.4 percent of self-employment income and generally applies to self-employment income up to the Federal Insurance Contributions Act ("FICA") taxable wage base ($106,800 in 2010). The rate of the HI portion is equal to 2.9 percent[1388] of self-employment income and there is no cap on the

---

[1386] Sec. 162(l)(1). See Notice 2010–38 for a discussion of the deduction for children who have not attained age 27 as of the end of the taxable year.

[1387] Sec. 162(l)(2).

[1388] Sec. 1401. However, under section 9015 of the Patient Protection and Affordable Care Act, Pub. L. No. 111–148, for remuneration and self-employment income received for taxable years beginning after December 31, 2012, the HI tax under SECA is increased by an additional tax

amount of self-employment income to which the rate applies.[1389] The deduction allowable for the cost of health insurance for the self-employed individual and the individual's spouse, dependents, and children who have not attained age 27 as of the end of the taxable year for income taxes is not taken into account in determining an individual's net earnings from self-employment for purposes of SECA taxes.[1390]

### *Explanation of Provision*

Under the provision, the deduction for income tax purposes allowed to self-employed individuals for the cost of health insurance for themselves, their spouses, dependents, and children who have not attained age 27 as of the end of the taxable year is taken into account, and thus also allowed, in calculating net earnings from self-employment for purposes of SECA taxes.

It is intended that earned income within the meaning of section 401(c)(2) be computed without regard to this deduction for the cost of health insurance.[1391] Thus, earned income for purposes of the limitation applicable to the health insurance deduction is computed without regard to this deduction.

The provision only applies for the taxpayer's first taxable year beginning after December 31, 2009.

### *Effective Date*

The provision is effective for taxable years beginning after December 31, 2009.

## 3. Remove cellular phones and similar telecommunications equipment from the definition of listed property (sec. 2043 of the Act and sec. 280F of the Code)

### *Present Law*

#### *Employer deduction*

Property, including cellular telephones and similar telecommunications equipment (hereinafter collectively "cell phones"), used in carrying on a trade or business is subject to the general rules for deducting ordinary and necessary expenses under section 162. Under these rules, a taxpayer may properly claim depreciation deductions under the applicable cost recovery rules for only the portion of the cost of the property that is attributable to use in a trade

---

of 0.9 percent on self-employment income received in excess of a threshold amount. However, unlike the general 1.45 percent HI tax on self-employment income, this additional tax is on the combined wages and self-employment income of the self-employed individual and spouse, in the case of a joint return. The threshold amount is $250,000 in the case of a joint return or surviving spouse, $125,000 in the case of a married individual filing a separate return, and $200,000 in any other case.

[1389] For purposes of computing net earnings from self-employment, taxpayers are permitted a deduction equal to the product of the taxpayer's earnings (determined without regard to this deduction) and one-half of the sum of the rates for OASDI (12.4 percent) and HI (2.9 percent), i.e., 7.65 percent of net earnings. This deduction reflects the fact that the FICA rates apply to an employee's wages, which do not include FICA taxes paid by the employer, whereas the self-employed individual's net earnings are economically equivalent to an employee's wages plus the employer share of FICA taxes.

[1390] Sec. 162(l)(4).

[1391] A technical correction may be necessary so that the statute reflects this intent.

or business.[1392] Similarly, the business portion of monthly telecommunication service is generally deductible, subject to capitalization rules, as an ordinary and necessary expense of carrying on a trade or business.

In the case of certain listed property, special rules apply. Listed property generally is defined as (1) any passenger automobile; (2) any other property used as a means of transportation; (3) any property of a type generally used for purposes of entertainment, recreation, or amusement; (4) any computer or peripheral equipment; (5) any cellular telephone (or other similar telecommunications equipment);[1393] and (6) any other property of a type specified in Treasury regulations.[1394]

For listed property, no deduction is allowed unless the taxpayer adequately substantiates the expense and business usage of the property.[1395] A taxpayer must substantiate the elements of each expenditure or use of listed property, including (1) the amount (e.g., cost) of each separate expenditure and the amount of business or investment use, based on the appropriate measure (e.g., mileage for automobiles), and the total use of the property for the taxable period, (2) the date of the expenditure or use, and (3) the business purposes for the expenditure or use.[1396] The level of substantiation for business or investment use of listed property varies depending on the facts and circumstances. In general, the substantiation must contain sufficient information as to each element of every business or investment use.[1397]

With respect to the business use of listed property made available by an employer for use by an employee, the employer must substantiate that all or a portion of the use of the listed property is by employees in the employer's trade or business.[1398] If any employee used the listed property for personal use, the employer must substantiate that it included an appropriate amount in the employee's income.[1399] An employer generally may rely on adequate records maintained and retained by the employee or on the employee's own statement if it is corroborated by other sufficient evidence, unless the employer knows or has reason to know that the statement, records, or other evidence are not accurate.[1400]

### *Cost recovery*

A taxpayer is allowed to recover through annual depreciation deductions the cost of certain property used in a trade or business or for the production of income. The amount of the depreciation deduction allowed with respect to tangible property for a taxable year

[1392] Sec. 212 allows deductions for ordinary and necessary expenses paid or incurred for the production or collection of income.

[1393] Cellular telephones (or other similar telecommunications equipment) were added as listed property as in section 7643 of the Omnibus Budget Reconciliation Act of 1989, Pub. L. No. 101–239.

[1394] Sec. 280F(d)(4)(A).

[1395] Sec. 274(d)(4).

[1396] Temp. Treas. Reg. sec. 1.274–5T(b)(6).

[1397] Temp. Treas. Reg. sec. 1.274–5T(c)(2)(ii)(C).

[1398] Temp. Treas. Reg. sec. 1.274–5T(e)(2)(i)(A).

[1399] *Ibid.*

[1400] Temp. Treas. Reg. sec. 1.274–5T(e)(2)(ii). In Notice 2009–46, 2009–23 I.R.B. 1068, the Service requested comments regarding several proposals to simplify the procedures for employers to substantiate an employee's business use of certain employer-provided telecommunications equipment (including cellular telephones).

is determined under the modified accelerated cost recovery system ("MACRS"). Under MACRS, different types of property generally are assigned applicable recovery periods and depreciation methods. The recovery periods applicable to most tangible personal property range from three to 25 years. The depreciation methods generally applicable to tangible personal property are the 200-percent and 150-percent declining balance methods, switching to the straight-line method for the taxable year in which the taxpayer's depreciation deduction would be maximized.

In the case of certain listed property, special depreciation rules apply. First, if for the taxable year that the property is placed in service the use of the property for trade or business purposes does not exceed 50 percent of the total use of the property, then the depreciation deduction with respect to such property is determined under the alternative depreciation system.[1401] The alternative depreciation system generally requires the use of the straight-line method and a recovery period equal to the class life of the property.[1402] Second, if an individual owns or leases listed property that is used by the individual in connection with the performance of services as an employee, no depreciation deduction, expensing allowance, or deduction for lease payments is available with respect to such use unless the use of the property is for the convenience of the employer and required as a condition of employment.[1403]

### *Explanation of Provision*

The provision removes cell phones from the definition of listed property. Thus, under the provision, the heightened substantiation requirements and special depreciation rules that apply to listed property do not apply to cell phones.[1404]

### *Effective Date*

The provision is effective for taxable years ending after December 31, 2009.

---

[1401] Sec. 280F(b)(1). If for any taxable year after the year in which the property is placed in service the use of the property for trade or business purposes decreases to 50 percent or less of the total use of the property, then the amount of depreciation allowed in prior years in excess of the amount of depreciation that would have been allowed for such prior years under the alternative depreciation system is recaptured (i.e., included in gross income) for such taxable year.

[1402] Sec. 168(g).

[1403] Sec. 280F(d)(3).

[1404] The provision does not affect Treasury's authority to determine the appropriate characterization of cell phones as a working condition fringe benefit under section 132(d) or that the personal use of such devices that are provided primarily for business purposes may constitute a de minimis fringe benefit, the value of which is so small as to make accounting for it administratively impracticable, under section 132(e).

# II. REVENUE PROVISIONS

## A. Reducing the Tax Gap

### 1. Information reporting for rental property expense payments (sec. 2101 of the Act and sec. 6041 of the Code)

#### *Present Law*

A variety of information reporting requirements apply under present law.[1405] The primary provision governing information reporting by payors requires an information return by every person engaged in a trade or business who makes payments to any one payee aggregating $600 or more in any taxable year in the course of that payor's trade or business.[1406] Reportable payments include compensation for both goods and services, and may include gross proceeds. Certain enumerated types of payments that are subject to other specific reporting requirements are carved out of reporting under this general rule.[1407]

One such regulatory exception carved out payments to corporations,[1408] but was expressly overridden by the addition of new section 6041(h) by section 9006 of the Patient Protection and Affordable Health Care Act ("PPACA").[1409] New section 6041(h) expanded information reporting requirements to include gross proceeds paid in consideration for property and to subject payments to corporations to all of the reporting requirements under section 6041. The payor is required to provide the recipient of the payment with an annual statement showing the aggregate payments made and contact information for the payor.[1410] The regulations generally except from reporting payments to exempt organizations, governmental entities, international organizations, or retirement plans.[1411] Additionally, the requirement that businesses report certain payments is not applicable to persons engaged in a passive investment activity. Thus, a taxpayer whose rental real estate activity is a trade or business is subject to this reporting requirement, but a taxpayer whose rental real estate activity is not considered a trade or business is not subject to such requirement.

[1405] Secs. 6031 through 6060.

[1406] Sec. 6041(a). The information return is generally submitted electronically as a Form 1096 and Form 1099, although certain payments to beneficiaries or employees may require use of Forms W–3 and W–2, respectively. Treas. Reg. sec. 1.6041–1(a)(2).

[1407] Sec. 6041(a) requires reporting "other than payments to which section 6042(a)(1), 6044(a)(1), 6047(c), 6049(a) or 6050N(a) applies and other than payments with respect to which a statement is required under authority of section 6042(a), 6044(a)(2) or 6045[.]" The payments thus excepted include most interest, royalties, and dividends.

[1408] Treas. Reg. sec. 1.6041–3(p).

[1409] Pub. L. No. 111–148, sec. 9006 (effective for payments made after December 31, 2011).

[1410] Sec. 6041(d). Specifically, the recipient of the payment is required to provide a Form W–9 to the payor, which enables the payee to provide the recipient of the payment with an annual statement showing the aggregate payments made and contact information for the payor. If a Form W–9 is not provided, the payor is required to "backup withhold" tax at a rate of 28 percent of the gross amount of the payment unless the payee has otherwise established that the income is exempt from backup withholding. The backup withholding tax may be credited by the payee against regular income tax liability, i.e., it is effectively an advance payment of tax, similar to the withholding of tax from wages. This combination of reporting and backup withholding is designed to ensure that U.S. persons pay an appropriate amount of tax with respect to investment income, either by providing the IRS with the information that it needs to audit payment of the tax or, in the absence of such information, requiring collection of the tax on payment.

[1411] Treas. Reg. sec. 1.6041–3(p).

In addition, financial institutions are required to report to both taxpayers and the IRS the amount of interest taxpayers paid during the year on mortgages they held on their rental properties.[1412]

A person that fails to comply with the information reporting requirements is subject to penalties, which may include a penalty for failure to file the information return,[1413] for failure to furnish payee statements,[1414] or for failure to comply with other various reporting requirements.[1415]

### *Reasons for Change*

One of the principal methods of improving tax compliance is to require information reporting by the third-party payor. The Congress believes that requiring information reporting by taxpayers receiving rental income and deducting expenses on rental activities would improve tax compliance of both the payor and the recipient by reducing opportunities for error and fraud. If the payors are required to provide the IRS information with respect to taxable payments, the recipients are more likely to include the payment in income.[1416] The increased third-party reporting of payments to those who provide services with respect to rental property will assist such contractors in properly reporting their income.

### *Explanation of Provision*

Under the provision, recipients of rental income from real estate generally are subject to the same information reporting requirements as taxpayers engaged in a trade or business. In particular, rental income recipients making payments of $600 or more to a service provider (such as a plumber, painter, or accountant) in the course of earning rental income are required to provide an information return (typically Form 1099–MISC) to the IRS and to the service provider. Exceptions to this reporting requirement are made for (i) individuals who rent their principal residence on a temporary basis, including members of the military or employees of the intelligence community (as defined in section 121(d)(9)), (ii) individuals who receive only minimal amounts of rental income, as determined by the Secretary in accordance with regulations, and (iii) individuals for whom the requirements would cause hardship, as determined by the Secretary in accordance with regulations.

### *Effective Date*

The provision applies to payments made after December 31, 2010.

---

[1412] Sec. 6050H. This information is provided on Form 1098.

[1413] Sec. 6721.

[1414] Sec. 6722.

[1415] Sec. 6723. The penalty for failure to timely comply with a specified information reporting requirement is $50 per failure, not to exceed $100,000 for a calendar year.

[1416] See http://www.irs.gov/pub/irs-news/tax_gap_figures.pdf.

## 2. Increase in information return penalties (sec. 2102 of Act and secs. 6721 and 6722 of the Code)

### *Present Law*

Present law imposes information reporting requirements on participants in certain transactions. Under section 6721, any person who is required to file a correct information return who fails to do so on or before the prescribed filing date is subject to a penalty that varies based on when, if at all, the correct information return is filed. If a person files a correct information return after the prescribed filing date but on or before the date that is 30 days after the prescribed filing date, the amount of the penalty is $15 per return (the "first-tier penalty"), with a maximum penalty of $75,000 per calendar year. If a person files a correct information return after the date that is 30 days after the prescribed filing date but on or before August 1, the amount of the penalty is $30 per return (the "second-tier penalty"), with a maximum penalty of $150,000 per calendar year. If a correct information return is not filed on or before August 1 of any year, the amount of the penalty is $50 per return (the "third-tier penalty"), with a maximum penalty of $250,000 per calendar year. If a failure is due to intentional disregard of a filing requirement, the minimum penalty for each failure is $100, with no calendar year limit.

Special lower maximum levels for this penalty apply to small businesses. Small businesses are defined as firms having average annual gross receipts for the most recent three taxable years that do not exceed $5 million. The maximum penalties for small businesses are: $25,000 (instead of $75,000) if the failures are corrected on or before 30 days after the prescribed filing date; $50,000 (instead of $150,000) if the failures are corrected on or before August 1; and $100,000 (instead of $250,000) if the failures are not corrected on or before August 1.

Section 6722 imposes penalties for failing to furnish correct payee statements to taxpayers. The penalty amount is $50 for each failure to furnish a payee statement, up to a maximum of $100,000. If the failure is due to intentional disregard, the amount of the penalty per failure is increased[1417] and the cap on the penalty is not applicable. In addition, section 6723 imposes a penalty of $50 for failing to comply with other information reporting requirements, up to a maximum of $100,000.

### *Reasons for Change*

The amount of the penalties imposed for failure to file information returns was last amended in 1989.[1418] Since then, the importance of reliable third-party information reporting to the administration of the Code has greatly increased. The Congress believes

---

[1417] Section 6722(c)(1) provides that the penalty per failure is the greater of $100 or a fixed percentage of the aggregate items to be shown on the payee statements. The fixed amount is 10 percent for statements other than those required under sections 6045(b), 6041A(e), 6050H(d), 6050J(e), 6050K(b), or 6050L(c). The penalty is the greater of $100 or five percent of the amount required to be shown on statements required under sections 6045(b), 6050K(b) or 6050L(c).

[1418] The penalty was originally $50 for each failure, up to a maximum of $100,000 per year, as enacted by section 150 of the Tax Reform Act of 1986, Pub. L. No. 99–514. In 1989, the present penalty amounts in three tiers were enacted. Section 7711 of the Omnibus Budget Reconciliation Act of 1989, Pub. L. No. 101–239.

that it is important to increase the penalties to ensure that they encourage compliance with the reporting obligations.

### *Explanation of Provision*

The provision amends section 6721 to increase the first-tier penalty from $15 to $30, and increase the calendar year maximum from $75,000 to $250,000. The second-tier penalty is increased from $30 to $60, and the calendar year maximum is increased from $150,000 to $500,000. The third-tier penalty is increased from $50 to $100, and the calendar year maximum is increased from $250,000 to $1,500,000. For small business filers, the calendar year maximum is increased from $25,000 to $75,000 for the first-tier penalty, from $50,000 to $200,000 for the second-tier penalty, and from $100,000 to $500,000 for the third-tier penalty. The minimum penalty for each failure due to intentional disregard is increased from $100 to $250.

The penalty for failure to furnish a payee statement is revised to provide tiers and caps similar to those applicable to the penalty for failure to file the information return. A first-tier penalty is $30, subject to a maximum of $250,000; a second-tier penalty is $60 per statement, up to $500,000, and the third-tier penalty is $100, up to a maximum of $1,500,000. The penalty is also amended to provide limitations on penalties for small businesses and increased penalties for intentional disregard that parallel the penalty for failure to furnish information returns.

Both the failure to file and failure to furnish penalties will be adjusted to account for inflation every five years with the first adjustment to take place after 2012, effective for each year thereafter.

### *Effective Date*

The provision applies with respect to information returns required to be filed on or after January 1, 2011.

## 3. Annual reports on penalties and certain other enforcement actions (sec. 2103 of the Act)

### *Present Law*

Transactions that have the potential for tax avoidance are required to be disclosed by both the taxpayers who engage in the transaction and the various professionals who provide advice with respect to such transactions. Failure to comply with the reporting and disclosure requirements may result in assessment of penalties against both the taxpayer and material advisor and the use of special enforcement measures.

#### *Reporting obligations*

These disclosure requirements [1419] create interlocking disclosure obligations for both taxpayers and advisors. A taxpayer is required to disclose with its tax return certain information with respect to each "reportable transaction," as defined in regulations.[1420] Each

1419 Secs. 6011, 6111 and 6112.
1420 Treas. Reg. sec. 1.6011–4.

advisor who provides material advice with respect to any reportable transaction (including any listed transaction) is required to file an information return with the Secretary (in such form and manner as the Secretary may prescribe).[1421] Finally, the advisor is required to maintain a list of those persons he has advised with respect to a reportable transaction and to provide the list to the IRS upon request.[1422]

A reportable transaction is defined as one that the Secretary requires to be disclosed based on its potential for tax avoidance or evasion.[1423] There are five categories of reportable transactions: listed transactions, confidential transactions, transactions with contractual protection, certain loss transactions and transactions of interest.[1424]

### *Penalties and other enforcement tools related to reportable transactions*

Each of the disclosure statutes has a parallel penalty provision to aid enforcement. The taxpayer who participates in a reportable transaction and fails to disclose it is subject to a strict liability penalty.[1425] The penalty is assessed in addition to any accuracy-related penalties. It may be rescinded with respect to reportable transactions other than listed transactions. Rescission is discretionary and conditioned upon a determination by the Commissioner that rescinding the penalty would promote compliance and effective tax administration.[1426] The Code also imposes a penalty on any material advisor who fails to file an information return, or who files a false or incomplete information return, with respect to a reportable transaction (including a listed transaction). It may be rescinded, subject to limitations similar to those applicable to rescission of the penalty imposed on investors.[1427] The IRS may also submit a writ-

---

[1421] Sec. 6111.

[1422] Sec. 6112.

[1423] Sec. 6707A(c)(1) states that the term means "any transaction with respect to which information is required to be included with a return or statement because, as determined under regulations prescribed under section 6011, such transaction is of a type which the Secretary determines as having a potential for tax avoidance or evasion." Sections 6111(b)(2) and 6112 both define "reportable transaction" by reference to the definition in section 6707A(c). The definition of "listed transaction" similarly depends upon identification of transactions by the Secretary as tax avoidance transactions for purposes of section 6011.

[1424] Treas. Reg. sec. 1.6011–4(b)(2)–(6).

[1425] Section 6707A imposes a penalty for failure to comply with the reporting requirements of section 6011. A single reportable transaction may have to be reported by multiple taxpayers in connection with multiple tax returns. For example, a reportable transaction entered into by a partnership may have to be reported under section 6011 by both the partnership and its partners. The amount of the penalty due for each taxpayer's failure to comply varies depending upon whether or not the transaction is a listed transaction and whether the relevant taxpayer is an individual. For listed transactions, the maximum penalty is $100,000 for natural persons and $200,000 for all other persons. For reportable transactions other than listed transactions, the maximum penalty is $10,000 for natural persons and $50,000 for all other persons. A public entity that is required to pay a penalty for an undisclosed listed or reportable transaction must disclose the imposition of the penalty in reports to the SEC for such periods specified by the Secretary. Failure to comply with this reporting requirement may result in assessment of a second tier penalty.

[1426] Sec. 6707A(d). In determining whether to rescind (or abate) the penalty for failing to disclose a reportable transaction on the grounds that doing so would promote compliance with the tax laws and effective tax administration, it is intended that the Commissioner take into account whether: (1) the person on whom the penalty is imposed has a history of complying with the tax laws; (2) the violation is due to an unintentional mistake of fact; and (3) imposing the penalty would be against equity and good conscience.

[1427] Section 6707 provides a penalty in the amount of $50,000. If the penalty is with respect to a listed transaction, the amount of the penalty is increased to the greater of (1) $200,000, or (2) 50 percent of the gross income of such person with respect to aid, assistance, or advice which is provided with respect to the transaction before the date the information return that

ten request that a material advisor make available the list required to be maintained under section 6112(a). A failure to make the list available upon written request is subject to a penalty of $10,000 per day for as long as the failure continues, unless the advisor can establish reasonable cause for the failure.[1428]

In addition to the penalties that specifically address the failure to comply with the disclosure and reporting obligations, other special enforcement provisions are applicable to reportable transactions. An understatement arising from any listed transactions or from a reportable transaction for which a significant purpose is avoidance or evasion of Federal income tax will be subject to an accuracy-related penalty,[1429] unless the taxpayer can establish that the failure was due to reasonable cause as determined under a standard that is more stringent than that applicable to other accuracy-related penalties.[1430]

If the taxpayer does not adequately disclose a reportable transaction, the strengthened reasonable cause exception is not available and the taxpayer is subject to an increased penalty equal to 30 percent of the understatement.[1431] However, a taxpayer will be treated as having adequately disclosed a transaction for this purpose if the Commissioner has separately rescinded the separate penalty under section 6707A for failure to disclose a reportable transaction.[1432] Finally, a new exception to the statute of limitations provides that the period is suspended if a listed transaction is not properly disclosed.[1433] If the transaction is disclosed either because the taxpayer files the proper disclosure form or a material advisor identifies the transaction to the IRS in a list maintained under section 6112, the period will remain open for at least one year from the earlier of date of the disclosure by the investor or the disclosure by the material advisor with respect to that transaction.

The Code authorizes civil actions to enjoin any person from specified conduct relating to tax shelters or reportable transactions.[1434] The specified conduct includes failure to comply with respect to the requirements relating to the reporting of reportable transactions[1435] and the keeping of lists of investors by material advisors.[1436] Thus, an injunction may be sought against a material advisor to enjoin the advisor from (1) failing to file an information return with respect to a reportable transaction, or (2) failing to maintain, or to timely furnish upon written request by the Secretary, a list of investors with respect to each reportable transaction. In addition, injunctions, monetary penalties and suspension or disbarment are authorized with respect to violations of any of the rules under Circular 230, which regulates the practice of representatives of persons before the Department of the Treasury.

---

includes the transaction is filed. Intentional disregard by a material advisor of the requirement to disclose a listed transaction increases the penalty to 75 percent of the gross income.

[1428] Sec. 6708.
[1429] Sec. 6662A.
[1430] Sec. 6664(d).
[1431] Sec. 6662A(c).
[1432] Sec. 6664(d).
[1433] Sec. 6501(c)(10).
[1434] Sec. 7408.
[1435] Sec. 6707.
[1436] Sec. 6708.

***Reports to Congress by the Secretary***

The Secretary is required to maintain records and report on the administration of the penalties for failure to disclose a reportable transaction in two ways. First, each decision to rescind a penalty imposed under section 6707 or section 6707A must be memorialized in a record maintained in the Officer of the Commissioner.[1437] That record must include a description of the facts and circumstances of the violation, the reasons for the decision to rescind, and the amount rescinded. Second, the IRS is required to submit an annual report to Congress on the administration of the rescission authority under both sections 6707 and 6707A. The information with respect to the latter is to be in summary form, while the information on rescission of penalties imposed against material advisors is to be more detailed.[1438] The report is not required to address administration of the other enforcement tools described above.

### *Reasons for Change*

Since the enactment of a number of enforcement measures intended to support IRS efforts to combat abusive tax avoidance transactions, there has been little data available to determine whether the measures have the desired effect. Congress believes that an annual report on administrative experience with all of the enforcement measures modified or added by AJCA will better enable it to assess the efficacy of those measures.

### *Explanation of Provision*

The provision requires that the IRS, in consultation with the Secretary, submit an annual report on administration of certain penalty provisions of the Code to the Committee on Ways and Means of the House of Representatives and the Committee on Finance of the Senate. A summary of penalties assessed the preceding year is required. In addition, the Secretary must report actions taken against practitioners appearing before the Treasury or IRS with respect to a reportable transaction[1439] and instances in which the IRS attempted to rely on the exception to the limitations period for assessment based on failure to disclose a listed transaction.[1440] The penalties that are subject to this reporting requirement are those assessed in the preceding year with respect to (1) a participant's failure to disclose a reportable transaction,[1441] (2) reportable trans-

---

[1437] Section 6707(c) incorporates by reference the provisions of section 6707A(d), which details the extent of the Commissioner's authority to rescind the penalty.

[1438] AJCA provides:

"The Commissioner of Internal Revenue shall annually report to the Committee on Ways and Means of the House of Representatives and the Committee on Finance of the Senate—

"(1) a summary of the total number and aggregate amount of penalties imposed, and rescinded, under section 6707A of the Internal Revenue Code of 1986, and

"(2) a description of each penalty rescinded under section 6707(c) of such Code and the reasons therefor." Pub. L. No. 108–357, Title VIII, Subtitle B, Part I, 811(d), 118 Stat. 1577, Oct. 22, 2004.

[1439] 31 U.S.C. sec. 330(b) authorizes the Secretary to impose sanctions on those who appear before the Department, including monetary penalties and suspension or disbarment from practice before the Department.

[1440] Sec. 6501(c)(10) provides that the limitations period with respect to tax attributable to a listed transaction shall not expire less than one year after the required disclosure of that transaction is furnished by the taxpayer or by the material advisor, whichever is earlier.

[1441] Sec. 6707A.

action understatements,[1442] (3) promotion of abusive shelters,[1443] (4) failure of a material advisor to furnish information on a reportable transaction,[1444] and (5) material advisors' failure to maintain or produce a list of reportable transactions.[1445]

### *Effective Date*

The first annual report is required to be submitted not later than December 31, 2010.

## 4. Application of continuous levy to employment tax liability of certain Federal contractors (sec. 2104 of the Act and sec. 6330 of the Code)

### *Present Law*

#### *In general*

Levy is the IRS' administrative authority to seize a taxpayer's property or rights to property to pay the taxpayer's tax liability.[1446] Generally, the IRS is entitled to seize a taxpayer's property by levy if a Federal tax lien has attached to such property,[1447] and the IRS has provided both notice of intention to levy[1448] and notice of the right to an administrative hearing (referred to as a collections due process notice or "CDP" notice)[1449] at least thirty days before the levy is made. A Federal tax lien arises automatically when: (1) a tax assessment has been made; (2) the taxpayer has been given notice of the assessment stating the amount and demanding payment; and (3) the taxpayer has failed to pay the amount assessed within 10 days after the notice and demand.[1450]

The 30-day pre-levy notice requirements, the taxpayer's rights before, during, and following the CDP hearing, and the Federal payment levy program are discussed below.

#### *Pre-levy notice requirements*

The notice of intent to levy and the CDP notice must include a brief statement describing the following: (1) the statutory provisions and procedures for levy; (2) the administrative appeals available to the taxpayer; (3) the alternatives available to avoid levy; and (4) the provisions and procedures regarding redemption of levied property.[1451] In addition, the collection due process notice must include the following: (1) the amount of the unpaid tax; and (2) the right to request a hearing during the 30-day period before the IRS serves the levy.

[1442] Sec. 6662A.
[1443] Sec. 6700.
[1444] Sec. 6707.
[1445] Sec. 6708.
[1446] Sec. 6331(a). Levy specifically refers to the legal process by which the IRS orders a third party to turn over property in its possession that belongs to the delinquent taxpayer named in a notice of levy.
[1447] Sec. 6331(a).
[1448] Sec. 6331(d).
[1449] Sec. 6330. The administrative hearing is referred to as the CDP hearing.
[1450] Secs. 6321 and 6331(a).
[1451] Secs. 6330(a)(3) and 6331(d)(4). In practice, the notice of intent to levy and the collections due process notice is provided together in one document, Letter 1058, *Final Notice, Notice of Intent to Levy and Notice of Your Right to a Hearing.* Chief Couns. Adv. 2009041 (November 28, 2008).

Upon receipt of this information, the taxpayer may stay the levy action by requesting in writing a hearing before the IRS Appeals Office.[1452] Otherwise, the IRS will levy to collect the amount owed after expiration of 30 days from the notice.

The notice of intent to levy is not required if the Secretary finds that collection would be jeopardized by delay. The standard for determining whether jeopardy exists is similar to the standard applicable in permitting the IRS to assess a tax without following the normal deficiency procedures.[1453]

The CDP notice (and pre-levy CDP hearing) is not required if the Secretary finds that collection would be jeopardized by delay or the Secretary has served a levy on a State to collect a Federal tax liability from a State tax refund. In addition, a levy issued to collect Federal employment taxes is excepted from the CDP notice and the pre-levy CDP hearing requirement if the taxpayer subject to the levy requested a CDP hearing with respect to unpaid employment taxes arising in the two-year period before the beginning of the taxable period with respect to which the employment tax levy is served. The taxpayer, however, in each of these three cases, is provided an opportunity for a hearing within a reasonable period of time after the levy.[1454]

### *CDP hearing*

At the CDP hearing, the taxpayer may present defenses to collection as well as arguments disputing the merits of the underlying tax debt if the taxpayer had no prior opportunity to present such arguments.[1455] In addition, the taxpayer is required to be provided the opportunity to negotiate an alternative form of payment, such as an offer-in-compromise, under which the IRS would accept less than the full amount, or an installment agreement under which payments in satisfaction of the debt may be made over time rather than in one lump sum, or some combination of such measures.[1456] If a taxpayer exercises any of these rights in response to the notice of intent to levy, the IRS may not proceed with its levy.

After the CDP hearing, a taxpayer also has a right to seek, within 30 days, judicial review in the U.S. Tax Court of the determination of the CDP hearing to ascertain whether the IRS abused its discretion in reaching its determination.[1457] During this time period, the IRS may not proceed with its levy.

### *Federal payment levy program*

To help the IRS collect taxes more effectively, the Taxpayer Relief Act of 1997[1458] authorized the establishment of the Federal Payment Levy Program ("FPLP"), which allows the IRS to continuously levy up to 15 percent of certain "specified payments," such as government payments to Federal contractors that are delinquent

[1452] Sec. 6330(b).
[1453] Secs. 6331(d)(3) and 6861.
[1454] Sec. 6330(f).
[1455] Sec. 6330(c).
[1456] Sec. 6330(c)(2).
[1457] Sec. 6330(d).
[1458] Pub. L. No. 105–34.

on their tax obligations. The levy generally continues in effect until the liability is paid or the IRS releases the levy.[1459]

Under FPLP, the IRS matches its accounts receivable records with Federal payment records maintained by the Department of the Treasury's Financial Management Service ("FMS"), such as certain Social Security benefit and Federal wage records. When the records match, the delinquent taxpayer is provided both notice of intention to levy and notice of the right to the CDP hearing 30 days before the levy is made. If the taxpayer does not respond after 30 days, the IRS can instruct FMS to levy its Federal payments. Subsequent payments are continuously levied until the tax debt is paid or IRS releases the levy.

Upon receipt of this information, however, the taxpayer may stay the levy action by requesting in writing a hearing before the IRS Appeals Office. Following the CDP hearing, a taxpayer has a right to seek, within 30 days, judicial review in the U.S. Tax Court of the determination of the CDP hearing to ascertain whether the IRS abused its discretion in reaching its determination. During this time period, the IRS may not proceed with its levy.

### *Reasons for Change*

The Congress believes that permitting Federal contractors to delay collection until completion of CDP procedures may deprive the Federal government of the opportunity to levy payments because Treasury likely will have paid the Federal contractor before the CDP requirements are met. This lost opportunity is especially true in cases where taxpayers abuse CDP procedures and raise frivolous arguments simply for the purpose of delaying or evading collection of tax. By changing current law to allow the IRS to proceed with its levy for any Federal tax liabilities earlier in the debt collection process, the Congress believes that the IRS will collect more unpaid taxes.[1460]

To the extent that the delinquent taxes are employment tax liabilities, delay presents a greater risk to the government than delay may present in other contexts because employment tax liabilities continue to increase as ongoing wage payments are made to employees. In addition, much of an employer's employment tax liability consists of the employees' share of FICA tax withheld from employees' wages paid to the government on behalf of the employees. The risk for the government is that the employees are entitled to credits for amounts actually withheld, even if the employer ultimately fails to remit these amounts to the government.

### *Explanation of Provision*

The provision allows the IRS to issue levies prior to a CDP hearing with respect to Federal tax liabilities of Federal contractors identified under the Federal Payment Levy Program. When a levy is issued prior to a CDP hearing under this proposal, the taxpayer

[1459] Sec. 6331(h). With respect to Federal payments to vendors of goods or services (not defined), the continuous levy may be up to 100 percent of each payment. Sec. 6331(h)(3).

[1460] Government Accountability Office, *Tax Compliance: Thousands of Federal Contractors Abuse the Federal Tax System* (GAO–07–742T), April 19, 2007 (approximately 60,000 Federal contractors were delinquent on over $7 billion in Federal taxes).

has an opportunity for a CDP hearing within a reasonable time after the levy.

### *Effective Date*

The provision applies to levies issued after the date of enactment (September 27, 2010).

## B. Promoting Retirement Preparation

### 1. Allow participants in government section 457 plans to treat elective deferrals as Roth contributions (sec. 2111 of the Act and sec. 402A of the Code)

### *Present Law*

Section 401(k) plans and section 403(b) plans are permitted to have qualified Roth contribution programs under which participants may elect to make non-excludable contributions to "designated Roth accounts" and, if certain conditions are met, to exclude from gross income distributions from these accounts.

A qualified Roth contribution program is a program under which a participant may elect to make designated Roth contributions in lieu of all or a portion of the elective deferrals that he or she otherwise would be eligible to make under the applicable retirement plan. To qualify as a qualified Roth contribution program a plan must: (1) establish a separate designated Roth account for the designated Roth contributions of each participant (and for the earnings allocable to these contributions); (2) maintain separate records for each account; and (3) refrain from allocating to the designated Roth account amounts from non-designated Roth accounts.

Generally, if an "applicable retirement plan" includes a qualified Roth contribution program then any contribution that a participant makes under the program is treated as an "elective deferral," but is not excludable from gross income.[1461] For purposes of the qualified Roth contribution program rules, the term "applicable retirement plan" means: (1) an employee trust described in section 401(a) which is tax-exempt under section 501(a);[1462] and (2) a plan under which amounts are contributed by an individual's employer for a section 403(b) annuity contract.[1463] An "elective deferral" is any deferral described in: (1) section 402(g)(3)(A) (employer contributions to section 401(k) plans not includible in employee's gross income); or (2) section 402(g)(3)(C) (employer contributions to purchase an annuity contract under a section 403(b) salary reduction agreement).

### *Explanation of Provision*

The provision amends the definition of "applicable retirement plan" to include eligible deferred compensation plans (as defined under section 457(b)) maintained by a State, a political subdivision of a State, an agency or instrumentality of a State, or an agency

[1461] Sec. 402A(a)(1).

[1462] That is, a trust created or organized in the United States and forming part of a stock bonus, pension, or profit-sharing plan of an employer for the exclusive benefit of its employees or their beneficiaries.

[1463] That is, an annuity purchased by a section 501(c)(3) organization or a public school.

or instrumentality of a political subdivision of a State (collectively, "governmental 457(b) plans"). The provision also amends the definition of "elective deferral" in section 402A to include amounts deferred under governmental 457(b) plan.

### *Effective Date*

The provision is effective for taxable years beginning after December 31, 2010.

## 2. Allow rollovers from elective deferral plans to designated Roth accounts (sec. 2112 of the Act and sec. 402A of the Code)

### *Present law*

#### *Individual retirement arrangements*

*General rules*

There are two basic types of individual retirement arrangements ("IRAs") under present law: traditional IRAs,[1464] to which both deductible and nondeductible contributions may be made,[1465] and Roth IRAs, to which only nondeductible contributions may be made.[1466] The principal difference between these two types of IRAs is the timing of income tax inclusion. For a traditional IRA, an eligible contributor may deduct the contributions made for the year, but distributions are includible in gross income. For a Roth IRA, all contributions are after-tax (no deduction is allowed) but, if certain requirements are satisfied, distributions are not includable in gross income.

An annual limit applies to contributions to IRAs. The contribution limit is coordinated so that the aggregate maximum amount that can be contributed to all of an individual's IRAs (both traditional and Roth IRAs) for a taxable year is the lesser of a certain dollar amount ($5,000 for 2010)[1467] or the individual's compensation. In the case of a married couple, contributions can be made up to the dollar limit for each spouse if the combined compensation of the spouses is at least equal to the contributed amount.

An individual who has attained age 50 before the end of the taxable year may also make catch-up contributions to an IRA. For this purpose, the aggregate dollar limit is increased by $1,000. Thus for example, if an individual over age 50 contributes $6,000 to a Roth IRA for 2010 ($5,000 plus $1,000 catch-up), the individual will not be permitted to make any contributions to a traditional IRA for the year. In addition, deductible contributions to traditional IRAs and after tax contributions to Roth IRAs generally are subject to AGI limits. IRA contributions generally must be made in cash.

*Roth IRAs*

Individuals with adjusted gross income below certain levels may make nondeductible contributions to a Roth IRA. The maximum annual contribution that can be made to a Roth IRA is phased out

[1464] Sec. 408.
[1465] Sec. 219.
[1466] Sec. 408A.
[1467] The dollar limit is indexed for inflation.

for taxpayers with adjusted gross income for the taxable year over certain indexed levels. The adjusted gross income phase-out ranges for 2010 are: (1) for single taxpayers, $109,000 to $124,000; (2) for married taxpayers filing joint returns, $167,000 to $177,000; and (3) for married taxpayers filing separate returns, $0 to $10,000. Contributions to a Roth IRA may be made even after the account owner has attained age 70½.

Taxpayers generally may convert a traditional IRA into a Roth IRA.[1468] A conversion may be accomplished by means of a rollover, trustee-to-trustee transfer, or account redesignation. Regardless of the means used to convert, any amount converted from a traditional IRA to a Roth IRA is treated as distributed from the traditional IRA and rolled over to the Roth IRA. The amount converted is includible in income as if a withdrawal had been made, except that the 10-percent early withdrawal tax does not apply.

Amounts held in a Roth IRA that are withdrawn as a qualified distribution are not includible in income, or subject to the additional 10-percent tax on early withdrawals. A qualified distribution is a distribution that (1) is made after the five-taxable year period beginning with the first taxable year for which the individual made a contribution to a Roth IRA, and (2) is made after attainment of age 59½, on account of death or disability, or is made for first-time homebuyer expenses of up to $10,000.

Distributions from a Roth IRA that are not qualified distributions are includible in income to the extent attributable to earnings. Under special ordering rules, after-tax contributions are recovered before income.[1469] The amount includible in income is also subject to the 10-percent early withdrawal tax unless an exception applies. The same exceptions to the early withdrawal tax that apply to traditional IRAs apply to Roth IRAs.

***Cash or deferred arrangements***

*Section 401(k) plans and section 403(b) plans*

A qualified retirement plan[1470] that is a profit-sharing plan may allow an employee to make an election between cash and an employer contribution to the plan pursuant to a qualified cash or deferred arrangement. A plan with this feature is generally referred to as a section 401(k) plan. A section 403(b) plan may allow a similar salary reduction agreement under which an employee may make an election between cash and an employer contribution to the plan.[1471] Amounts contributed pursuant to these qualified cash or deferred arrangements and salary reduction agreements generally are referred to as elective contributions and generally are exclud-

---

[1468] For taxable years beginning before January 1, 2010, such a conversion is not permitted to be made by a taxpayer whose modified adjusted gross income for the year of the distribution exceeds $100,000 (or who, if married, does not file jointly). For taxable years beginning before January 1, 2010, a rollover from an eligible employer plan not made from a designated Roth account is available only to a taxpayer whose modified adjusted gross income for the year of the distribution does not exceed $100,000 (and who, if married, files jointly).

[1469] Sec. 408A(d)(4).

[1470] Qualified retirement plans include plans qualified under section 401(a) and section 403(a) annuity plans.

[1471] Section 403(b) plans may be maintained only by (1) tax-exempt charitable organizations, and (2) educational institutions of State or local governments (including public schools). Many of the rules that apply to section 403(b) plans are similar to the rules applicable to qualified retirement plans, including section 401(k) plans.

able from gross income. There is a dollar limit on the aggregate amount of elective contributions that an employee is permitted to contribute to either of these plans for a taxable year which is $16,500 for 2010. There is an additional catch up amount that employees over age 50 are allowed to contribute which is $5,500 for 2010.

Elective contributions under a section 401(k) plan are subject to distribution restrictions under the plan. Such contributions generally may only be distributed after attainment of age 59½, death of the employee, termination of the plan, or severance from employment with the employer maintaining the plan. These contributions are also permitted to be distributed on account of hardship. These limitations also apply to certain other contributions to the plan except that such distributions cannot be distributed on account of hardship. Similar distribution restrictions apply to salary reduction contributions under section 403(b) plans.

Amounts under a profit sharing plan that are not subject to these specific distribution restrictions are distributable only as permitted under the plan terms. In order to meet the definition of profit-sharing plan, the plan may allow distribution of an amount contributed to a profit sharing plan after a fixed number of years (but not less than two).[1472]

*Designated Roth accounts*

A qualified retirement plan or a section 403(b) plan with a cash or deferred arrangement can include a Designated Roth program under which an employee is permitted to designate any elective contribution as a designated Roth contribution in lieu of making a pre-tax elective contribution. Although such a plan is permitted to offer only the opportunity to make pre-tax elective contributions, a plan that allows designated Roth contributions must offer a choice of both pre-tax elective contributions and designated Roth contributions.[1473] The designated contributions are generally treated the same under the plan as pre-tax elective contributions (e.g. the nondiscrimination requirements and contribution limits) except a designated Roth contribution is not excluded from gross income.

All designated Roth contributions made under the plan must be maintained in a separate account (a designated Roth account). Any distribution from a designated Roth account (other than a qualified distribution) is taxable under section 402 by treating the designated Roth account as a separate contract for purpose of section 72. The distribution is included in the distributee's gross income to the extent allocable to income under the contract and excluded from gross income to the extent allocable to investment in the contract (commonly referred to as basis), taking into account only the designated Roth contributions as basis. The special basis-first recovery rule for Roth IRAs does not apply to distributions from designated Roth accounts.

A qualified distribution from a designated Roth account is excludable from gross income. A qualified distribution is a distribution that is made after completion of a specified 5-year period and

[1472] Rev. Rul. 71–295, 1971–2, C.B. 184 and Treas. Reg. sec. 1.401(b)(1)(ii).
[1473] Treas. Reg. sec. 1.401(k)–1(f)(1)(i).

the satisfaction of one of three other requirements. The three other requirements are the same as the other requirements for a qualified distribution from a Roth account except that the first-time home buyer provision does not apply.

Eligible rollover distributions from designated Roth accounts may only be rolled over tax free to another designated Roth account or a Roth IRA.

### *Rollovers from eligible retirement plans*

An eligible rollover distribution from an eligible employer plan that is not from a designated Roth account may be rolled over to an eligible retirement plan that is not a Roth IRA or a designated Roth account. An eligible employer plan is a qualified retirement plan, a section 403(b) plan, and a "governmental section 457(b) plan."[1474] In such a case, the distribution generally is not currently includible in the distributee's gross income. An eligible retirement plan means an individual retirement plan or an eligible employer plan. An eligible rollover distribution is any distribution from an eligible employer plan with certain exceptions. Distributions that are not eligible rollover distributions generally are certain periodic payments, any distribution to the extent the distribution is a minimum required distribution, and any distribution made on account of hardship of the employee.[1475] Only an employee or a surviving spouse of an employee is allowed to roll over an eligible rollover distribution from an eligible employer plan to another eligible employer plan.[1476]

Distributions from an eligible employer plan are also permitted to be rolled over into a Roth IRA, subject to the present law rules that apply to conversions from a traditional IRA into a Roth IRA.[1477] Thus, a rollover from an eligible employer plan into a Roth IRA is includible in gross income (except to the extent it represents a return of after-tax contributions), and the 10-percent early distribution tax does not apply.[1478] In the case of a distribution and rollover of property, the amount of the distribution for purposes of determining the amount includable in gross income is generally the fair market value of the property on the date of the distribution.[1479] The special rules relating to net unrealized appreciation and certain optional methods for calculating tax available to participants born on or before January 1, 1936 are not applicable.[1480] A special recapture rule relating to the 10-percent addi-

---

[1474] A governmental section 457(b) plan is an eligible section 457(b) plan maintained by a governmental employer described in section 457(e)(1)(A).

[1475] Sec. 402(c)(4).

[1476] Section 402(c)(10) allows nonspouse beneficiaries to make a direct rollover to an IRA but not another eligible employer plan.

[1477] For taxable years beginning before January 1, 2010, a rollover from an eligible employer plan not made from a designated Roth account is available only to a taxpayer whose modified adjusted gross income for the year of the distribution does not exceed $100,000 (and who, if married, files jointly).

[1478] Prior to enactment of section 824 of the Pension Protection Act of 2006, P.L. No. 109–280, an eligible rollover distribution from an eligible employer plan not made from a designated Roth account could be rolled over to a non-Roth IRA and then converted to a Roth IRA, but could not be rolled over to a Roth IRA without an intervening rollover to a non-Roth IRA followed by a conversion to a Roth IRA. See Notice 2008–30, 2008–12 I.R.B. 638.

[1479] Treas. Reg. sec. 1.402(a)–1(a)(iii).

[1480] Notice 2009–75, 2009–39 I.R.B. 436.

tional tax on early distributions applies for distributions made from a Roth IRA within a specified five-year period after a rollover.[1481]

***Special rule for 2010 conversions or rollovers***

In the case of a rollover from a tax-qualified retirement plan (other than a designated Roth account) into a Roth IRA, unless the taxpayer elects to include the distribution in income in 2010, any amount otherwise required to be included in gross income for the 2010 taxable year is not included in that taxable year but is instead included in gross income in equal amounts for the 2011 and 2012 taxable years. The same rule applies to a conversion of a traditional IRA into a Roth IRA in 2010. However, in both cases, the special recapture rule relating to the 10-percent additional tax on early distributions applies for distributions made from a Roth IRA within a specified five-year period after a rollover.

### *Explanation of Provision*

Under the provision, if a section 401(k) plan, section 403(b) plan, or governmental section 457(b) plan[1482] has a qualified designated Roth contribution program, a distribution to an employee (or a surviving spouse) from an account under the plan that is not a designated Roth account is permitted to be rolled over into a designated Roth account under the plan for the individual. However, a plan that does not otherwise have a designated Roth program is not permitted to establish designated Roth accounts solely to accept these rollover contributions. Thus, for example, a qualified employer plan that does not include a qualified cash or deferred arrangement with a designated Roth program cannot allow rollover contributions from accounts that are not designated Roth accounts to designated Roth accounts established solely for purposes of accepting these rollover contributions. Further, the distribution to be rolled over must be otherwise allowed under the plan. For example, an amount under a section 401(k) plan subject to distribution restrictions cannot be rolled over to a designated Roth account under this provision. However, if an employer decides to expand its distribution options beyond those currently allowed under its plan, such as by adding in-service distributions or distributions prior to normal retirement age, in order to allow employees to make the rollover contributions permitted under this provision, the plan may condition eligibility for such a new distribution option on an employee's election to have the distribution directly rolled over to the designated Roth program within that plan.

In the case of a permitted rollover contribution to a designated Roth account under this provision, the individual must include the distribution in gross income (subject to basis recovery) in the same manner as if the distribution were rolled over into a Roth IRA. Thus the special rule for distributions from eligible retirement plans (other than from designated Roth accounts) that are contributed to a Roth IRA in 2010 applies for these rollover contributions to a designated Roth account. Under this special rule, the taxpayer

---

[1481] Sec. 408A(d)(3)(F), Treas. Reg. sec. 1.408A-6 A-5, and Notice 2008-30, Q&A-3.

[1482] The bill includes a provision which adds governmental section 457(b) plans to the plans that are permitted to include a designated Roth program. See explanation of section 211 of the bill.

is allowed to include the amount in income in equal parts in 2011 and 2012. The special recapture rule for the 10-percent early distribution tax also applies if distributions are made from the designated Roth account in the relevant five year period.

This rollover contribution may be accomplished at the election of the employee (or surviving spouse) through a direct rollover (operationally through a transfer of assets from the account that is not a designated Roth account to the designated Roth account). However, such a direct rollover is only permitted if the employee (or surviving spouse) is eligible for a distribution in that amount and in that form (if property is transferred) and the distribution is an eligible rollover distribution. If the direct rollover is accomplished by a transfer of property to the designated Roth account (rather than cash), the amount of the distribution is the fair market value of the property on the date of the transfer.

A plan that includes a designated Roth program is permitted but not required to allow employees (and surviving spouses) to make the rollover contribution described in this provision to a designated Roth account. If a plan allows these rollover contributions to a designated Roth account, the plan must be amended to reflect this plan feature. It is intended that the IRS will provide employers with a remedial amendment period that allows the employers to offer this option to employees (and surviving spouses) for distributions during 2010 and then have sufficient time to amend the plan to reflect this feature.[1483]

### *Effective Date*

The provision is effective for distributions made after the date of enactment.

## 3. Permit partial annuitization of a nonqualified annuity contract (sec. 2113 of the Act and sec. 72 of the Code)

### *Present Law*

#### *Treatment of annuity contracts*

In general, earnings and gains on a deferred annuity contract are not subject to tax during the deferral period in the hands of the holder of the contract.[1484] When payout commences under a deferred annuity contract, the tax treatment of amounts distributed depends on whether the amount is received as an annuity (generally, as periodic payments under contract terms) or not.[1485]

For amounts received as an annuity by an individual, an exclusion ratio is provided for determining the taxable portion of each payment.[1486] The portion of each payment that is attributable to recovery of the taxpayer's investment in the contract is not taxed. The taxable portion of each payment is ordinary income. The exclusion ratio is the ratio of the taxpayer's investment in the contract

---

[1483] See section 401(b), Treas. Reg. sec 1.401(b)–1, and Rev. Proc. 2007–44, 2007–2 CB 54, regarding remedial amendment periods for plan amendments.

[1484] If an annuity contract is held by a corporation or by any other person that is not a natural person, the income on the contract is treated as ordinary income accrued by the contract owner and is subject to current taxation. The contract is not treated as an annuity contract. Sec. 72(u).

[1485] Sec. 72.

[1486] Sec. 72(b).

to the expected return under the contract, that is, the total of the payments expected to be received under the contract. The ratio is determined as of the taxpayer's annuity starting date. Once the taxpayer has recovered his or her investment in the contract, all further payments are included in income. If the taxpayer dies before the full investment in the contract is recovered, a deduction is allowed on the final return for the remaining investment in the contract. Section 72 uses the term "investment in the contract" in lieu of the more generally applicable term "basis."

Amounts not received as an annuity generally are included as ordinary income if received on or after the annuity starting date, and are included in income to the extent allocable to income on the contract if received before the annuity starting date (i.e., as income first).[1487]

Specific rules for recovering the investment in the contract for amounts received as an annuity are provided for plans qualified under section 401(a), plans described in section 403(a), and section 403(b) tax-deferred annuities.[1488] In addition, specific rules apply to amounts not received as an annuity under these plans and individual retirement plans.[1489]

***Tax-free exchanges of annuity contracts***

Present law provides for the exchange of certain insurance contracts without recognition of gain or loss.[1490] No gain or loss is recognized on the exchange of: (1) a life insurance contract for another life insurance contract or for an endowment or annuity contract or for a qualified long-term care insurance contract; or (2) an endowment contract for another endowment contract (that provides for regular payments beginning no later than under the exchanged contract) or for an annuity contract or for a qualified long-term care insurance contract; (3) an annuity contract for an annuity contract or for a qualified long-term care insurance contract; or (4) a qualified long-term care insurance contract for a qualified long-term care insurance contract. The basis of the contract received in the exchange generally is the same as the basis of the contract exchanged.[1491]

In interpreting section 1035, case law holds that an exchange of a portion of an annuity contract for another annuity contract qualifies as a tax-free exchange.[1492] Treasury guidance provides rules for determining whether a direct transfer of a portion of the cash surrender value of an annuity contract for a second annuity contract qualifies as a section 1035 tax-free exchange. Under the

---

[1487] Sec. 72(e). By contrast to distributions under an annuity contract, distributions from a life insurance contract (other than a modified endowment contract) that are made prior to the death of the insured generally are includible in income, to the extent that the amounts distributed exceed the taxpayer's basis in the contract; such distributions generally are treated first as a tax-free recovery of basis, and then as income (sec. 72(e)). In the case of a modified endowment contract, however, in general, distributions are treated as income first, loans are treated as distributions (i.e., income rather than basis recovery first), and an additional 10 percent tax is imposed on the income portion of distributions made before age 59½ and in certain other circumstances (secs. 72(e) and (v)). A modified endowment contract is a life insurance contract that does not meet a statutory "7-pay" test, i.e., generally is funded more rapidly than seven annual level premiums. Sec. 7702A.

[1488] Sec. 72(d).

[1489] Sec. 72(e)(8).

[1490] Sec. 1035.

[1491] Sec. 1031(d).

[1492] *Conway v. Comm'r*, 111 T.C. 350 (1998), *acq.*, 1999–2 C.B. xvi.

Treasury guidance, either the annuity contract received, or the contract partially exchanged, in the tax-free exchange may be annuitized without jeopardizing the tax-free exchange (or amounts withdrawn from it or received in surrender of it) after the period ending 12 months from the receipt of the premium in the exchange.[1493]

### *Explanation of Provision*

The provision permits a portion of an annuity, endowment, or life insurance contract to be annuitized while the balance is not annuitized, provided that the annuitization period is for 10 years or more, or is for the lives of one or more individuals.

The provision provides that if any amount is received as an annuity for a period of 10 years or more, or for the lives of one or more individuals, under any portion of an annuity, endowment, or life insurance contract, then that portion of the contract is treated as a separate contract for purposes of section 72.

The investment in the contract is allocated on a pro rata basis between each portion of the contract from which amounts are received as an annuity and the portion of the contract from which amounts are not received as an annuity. This allocation is made for purposes of applying the rules relating to the exclusion ratio, the determination of the investment in the contract, the expected return, the annuity starting date, and amounts not received as an annuity.[1494] A separate annuity starting date is determined with respect to each portion of the contract from which amounts are received as an annuity.

The provision is not intended to change the present-law rules with respect either to amounts received as an annuity, or to amounts not received as an annuity, in the case of plans qualified under section 401(a), plans described in section 403(a), section 403(b) tax-deferred annuities, or individual retirement plans.

### *Effective Date*

The provision is effective for amounts received in taxable years beginning after December 31, 2010.

## C. Closing Unintended Loopholes

### 1. Make crude tall oil ineligible for the cellulosic biofuel producer credit (sec. 2121 of the Act and sec. 40 of the Code)

### *Present Law*

The "cellulosic biofuel producer credit" is a nonrefundable income tax credit for each gallon of qualified cellulosic biofuel production

---

[1493] Rev. Proc. 2008–24, 2008–13 I.R.B. 684. The Rev. Proc. further provides that a transfer does not, however, qualify as a tax-free exchange if the payment is a distribution that is part of a series of substantially equal periodic payments, or if the payment is a distribution under an immediate annuity. The Treasury guidance further provides that if a direct transfer of a portion of an annuity contract for a second annuity contract does not qualify as a tax-free exchange under section 1035, it is treated as a taxable distribution followed by a payment for the second contract. The 2011 Priority Guidance Plan for the Treasury Department and IRS anticipates further guidance on this issue.

[1494] Secs. 72(b), (c), and (e).

of the producer for the taxable year. The amount of the credit is generally $1.01 per gallon.[1495]

"Qualified cellulosic biofuel production" is any cellulosic biofuel which is produced by the taxpayer and which is: (1) sold by the taxpayer to another person (a) for use by such other person in the production of a qualified cellulosic biofuel mixture in such person's trade or business (other than casual off-farm production), (b) for use by such other person as a fuel in a trade or business, or (c) who sells such cellulosic biofuel at retail to another person and places such cellulosic biofuel in the fuel tank of such other person; or (2) used by the producer for any purpose described in (1)(a), (b), or (c).

"Cellulosic biofuel" means any liquid fuel that (1) is produced in the United States and used as fuel in the United States, (2) is derived from any lignocellulosic or hemicellulosic matter that is available on a renewable or recurring basis, and (3) meets the registration requirements for fuels and fuel additives established by the Environmental Protection Agency ("EPA") under section 211 of the Clean Air Act. The cellulosic biofuel producer credit cannot be claimed unless the taxpayer is registered by the IRS as a producer of cellulosic biofuel.

Cellulosic biofuel does not include certain unprocessed fuel. Unprocessed fuels are fuels which (1) are more than four percent (determined by weight) water and sediment in any combination, or (2) have an ash content of more than one percent (determined by weight).[1496] Cellulosic biofuel eligible for the section 40 credit is precluded from qualifying as biodiesel, renewable diesel, or alternative fuel for purposes of the applicable income tax credit, excise tax credit, or payment provisions relating to those fuels.[1497]

Because it is a credit under section 40(a), the cellulosic biofuel producer credit is part of the general business credits in section 38. However, unlike other general business credits, the cellulosic biofuel producer credit can only be carried forward three taxable years after the termination of the credit. The credit is also allowable against the alternative minimum tax. Under section 87, the credit is included in gross income. The cellulosic biofuel producer credit terminates on December 31, 2012.

The kraft process for making paper produces a byproduct called black liquor, which has been used for decades by paper manufacturers as a fuel in the papermaking process. Black liquor is composed of water, lignin and the spent chemicals used to break down the wood. The amount of the biomass in black liquor varies. The portion of the black liquor that is not consumed as a fuel source for the paper mills is recycled back into the papermaking process. Black liquor has ash content (mineral and other inorganic matter) significantly above that of other fuels.

---

[1495] In the case of cellulosic biofuel that is alcohol, the $1.01 credit amount is reduced by the credit amount of the alcohol mixture credit, and for ethanol, the credit amount for small ethanol producers, as in effect at the time the cellulosic biofuel fuel is produced.

[1496] Water content (including both free water and water in solution with dissolved solids) is determined by distillation, using for example ASTM method D95 or a similar method suitable to the specific fuel being tested. Sediment consists of solid particles that are dispersed in the liquid fuel and is determined by centrifuge or extraction using, for example, ASTM method D1796 or D473 or similar method that reports sediment content in weight percent. Ash is the residue remaining after combustion of the sample using a specified method, such as ASTM D3174 or a similar method suitable for the fuel being tested.

[1497] See sections 40A(d)(1), 40A(f)(3), and 6426(h).

Crude tall oil is generated by reacting acid with black liquor soap. Crude tall oil is used in various applications, such as adhesives, resins and inks. It also can be burned and used as a fuel.

### *Explanation of Provision*

The provision modifies the cellulosic biofuel producer credit to exclude from the definition of cellulosic biofuel fuels with an acid number of greater than 25. The acid number is the amount of base required to neutralize the acid in the sample. The acid number is reported as weight of the base (typically potassium hydroxide) per weight of sample, or milligram ("mg") potassium hydroxide per gram. The normal acid number for crude tall oil is between 100 and 175. As a comparison, ASTM D6751 for biodiesel specifies that the acid number be less than 0.5 mg potassium hydroxide. ASTM D4806 for ethanol does not have acid value but instead limits "acidity" to 0.007 mg of acetic acid per liter, which is significantly below an acid number of 25.

### *Effective Date*

The provision is effective for fuels sold or used on or after January 1, 2010.

## 2. Source rules for income on guarantees (sec. 2122 of the Act and secs. 861, 862, and 864 of the Code)

### *Present Law*

The United States taxes U.S. citizens and residents (including domestic corporations) on their worldwide income, whether derived in the United States or abroad. The United States generally taxes nonresident alien individuals and foreign corporations engaged in a trade or business in the United States on income that is effectively connected with the conduct of such trade or business (sometimes referred to as "effectively connected income"). The United States also taxes nonresident alien individuals and foreign corporations on certain U.S.-source income that is not effectively connected with the conduct of a U.S. trade or business.

Income of a nonresident alien individual or foreign corporation that is effectively connected with the conduct of a trade or business in the United States generally is subject to U.S. tax in the same manner and at the same rates as income of a U.S. person. Deductions are allowed to the extent that they are connected with effectively connected income.[1498] A foreign corporation also is subject to a flat 30-percent branch profits tax on its "dividend equivalent amount," which is a measure of the effectively connected earnings and profits of the corporation that are removed in any year from the conduct of its U.S. trade or business.[1499] In addition, a foreign corporation is subject to a flat 30-percent branch-level excess interest tax on the excess of the amount of interest that is deducted by the foreign corporation in computing its effectively connected in-

[1498] Secs. 864(c), 871(b), 873, 882(a) and 882(c).
[1499] Sec. 884.

come over the amount of interest that is paid by its U.S. trade or business.[1500]

Subject to a number of exceptions, U.S.-source fixed or determinable, annual or periodical income ("FDAP") of a nonresident alien individual or foreign corporation that is not effectively connected with the conduct of a U.S. trade or business is subject to U.S. tax at a rate of 30 percent of the gross amount paid.[1501] Items of income within the scope of FDAP include, for example, interest, dividends, rents, royalties, salaries, and annuities. The tax generally is collected by means of withholding.[1502]

Present law provides detailed rules for the determination of whether income is from U.S. sources or foreign sources. For example, the source of compensation for services is generally determined by the location in which the services were performed, regardless of the country of residence of the payor.[1503] In contrast, the source of interest income is generally determined by reference to the country of residence of the obligor.[1504] As a result, interest paid by a U.S. obligor typically is considered U.S.-source income, while interest paid by a foreign obligor is treated as foreign-source income. Rents and royalties paid for the use of property located in the United States are considered to be U.S.-source income.[1505]

To the extent that the source of income is not specified in the statute, the Secretary may promulgate regulations that explain the appropriate treatment. Many items of income are not explicitly addressed by either the statute or the regulations. On several occasions, courts have determined the source of such items by applying the rule for the type of income to which the disputed income is most closely analogous, based on all facts and circumstances.[1506] Items as dissimilar as alimony and letters of credit commissions were sourced by analogy to interest.[1507] The U.S. Tax Court, in *Container Corp. v. Commissioner,* recently rejected IRS arguments that fees paid by a domestic corporation to its foreign parent with respect to guarantees issued by the parent for the debts of the domestic corporation were analogous to interest. The Tax Court held that the payments were more closely analogous to compensation for services, and determined that the source of the fees should be determined by reference to the residence of the foreign parent-guarantor. As a result, the income was treated as income from foreign sources.[1508]

---

[1500] Sec. 884(f).

[1501] Secs. 871(a), 881(a).

[1502] Secs. 1441 and 1442 provide for collection from nonresident aliens and foreign corporations, respectively.

[1503] Under section 861(a)(3), compensation for personal services performed in the United States is U.S. source, unless the individual performing the services is a nonresident alien who is temporarily present in the United States, receives no more than $3,000 of compensation and is performing the services for a foreign person not engaged in a U.S. trade or business. Conversely, section 862(a)(3) provides that compensation for labor or services performed outside the United States is foreign source.

[1504] Secs. 861(a)(1), 862(a)(1).

[1505] Sec. 861(a)(4).

[1506] *Hunt v. Commissioner*, 90 T.C. 1289 (1988).

[1507] *Manning v. Commissioner*, 614 F.2d 815 (1st Cir. 1980); *Bank of America v. United States*, 230 Ct. Cl. 679, 680 F.2d 142 (1982), aff'g in part, rev'g in part, 47 AFTR 2d 81–652 (Ct. Cl. 1981).

[1508] *Container Corp. v. Commissioner*, 134 T.C. No. 5 (February 17, 2010), *gov't notice of appeal filed* (5th Cir. June 1, 2010).

### *Explanation of Provision*

This provision effects a legislative override of the opinion in *Container Corp. v. Commissioner, supra,* by amending the source rules of section 861 and 862 to address income from guarantees issued after the date of enactment. Under new section 861(a)(9), income from sources within the United States includes amounts received, whether directly or indirectly, from a noncorporate resident or a domestic corporation for the provision of a guarantee of indebtedness of such person. The scope of the provision includes payments that are made indirectly for the provision of a guarantee. For example, the provision would treat as income from U.S. sources a guarantee fee paid by a foreign bank to a foreign corporation for the foreign corporation's guarantee of indebtedness owed to the bank by the foreign corporation's domestic subsidiary, where the cost of the guarantee fee is passed on to the domestic subsidiary through, for example, additional interest charged on the indebtedness.

Such U.S.-source income also includes amounts received from a foreign person, whether directly or indirectly, for the provision of a guarantee of indebtedness of that foreign person if the payments received are connected with income of such person which is effectively connected with conduct of a U.S. trade or business. A conforming amendment to section 862 provides that amounts received from a foreign person, whether directly or indirectly, for the provision of a guarantee of that person's debt, are treated as foreign source income if they are not from sources within the United States as determined under new section 861(a)(9).

For purposes of this provision, the phrase "noncorporate residents" has the same meaning as for purposes of section 861(a)(1), except that foreign partnerships are not included. Payments received from a foreign partnership for the provision of a guarantee of indebtedness of that foreign partnership are U.S. source if the amounts received are connected with income which is effectively connected with the conduct of a U.S. trade or business. A conforming amendment to section 864 provides that amounts received, whether directly or indirectly, for the provision of a guarantee are deemed to be effectively connected with the conduct of a U.S. trade or business if derived in the active conduct of a banking, financing or similar business.

Although this provision overturns the opinion in *Container Corp. v. Commissioner, supra,* no inference is intended with respect to the source of income received for the provision of a guarantee issued before the date of enactment. The Secretary may provide rules for determining the source of other types of payments that are not within the scope of this provision.

### *Effective Date*

The provision applies to guarantees issued after the date of enactment. No inference is intended with respect to the source of income received with respect to guarantees issued before the date of enactment.

## D. Time for Payment of Corporate Estimated Taxes (sec. 2131 of the Act and sec. 6655 of the Code)

### *Present Law*

In general, corporations are required to make quarterly estimated tax payments of their income tax liability.[1509] For a corporation whose taxable year is a calendar year, these estimated tax payments must be made by April 15, June 15, September 15, and December 15. In the case of a corporation with assets of at least $1 billion (determined as of the end of the preceding taxable year):

(iv) payments due in July, August, or September, 2014, are increased to 174.25 percent of the payment otherwise due;[1510]

(ii) payments due in July, August or September, 2015, are increased to 123.25 percent of the payment otherwise due;[1511] and

(v) payments due in July, August or September, 2019, are increased to 106.50 percent of the payment otherwise due.[1512]

For each of the periods impacted, the next required payment is reduced accordingly.

### *Explanation of Provision*[1513]

The provision increases the required payment of estimated tax otherwise due in July, August, or September, 2015, by 36.00 percentage points.

### *Effective Date*

The provision is effective on the date of enactment (September 26, 2010).

---

[1509] Sec. 6655.

[1510] Haiti Economic Lift Program of 2010, Pub. L. No. 111–171, sec. 12(a); Health Care and Education Reconciliation Act of 2010, Pub L. No. 111–152, sec. 1410; Hiring Incentives to Restore Employment Act, Pub. L. No. 111–147, sec.561(1); Act to extend the Generalized System of Preferences and the Andean Trade Preference Act, and for other purposes, Pub. L. No. 111–124, sec. 4; Worker, Homeownership, and Business Assistance Act of 2009, Pub. L. No. 111–92, sec. 18; Joint resolution approving the renewal of import restrictions contained in the Burmese Freedom and Democracy Act of 2003, and for other purposes, Pub. L. No. 111–42, sec. 202(b)(1).

[1511] Firearms Excise Tax Improvement Act of 2010, Pub. L. No. 111–237, sec. 4(a); United States Manufacturing Enhancement Act of 2010, Pub. L. No. 111–227, sec. 4002; Joint resolution approving the renewal of import restrictions contained in the Burmese Freedom and Democracy Act of 2003, and for other purposes, Pub. L. No. 111–210; sec. 3; Haiti Economic Lift Program of 2010, Pub. L. No. 111–171, sec. 12(b); Hiring Incentives to Restore Employment Act, Pub. L. No. 111–147, sec. 561(2).

[1512] Hiring Incentives to Restore Employment Act, Pub. L. No. 111–147, sec. 561(3).

[1513] All the public laws enacted in the 111th Congress affecting this provision are described in Part Twenty-One of this document.

## PART FIFTEEN: THE CLAIMS RESOLUTION ACT OF 2010 (PUBLIC LAW 111-291)[1514]

### A. The Individual Indian Money Account Litigation (sec. 101 of the Act)

#### *Present Law*

Under section 61 of the Code, gross income includes all income from whatever source derived. The Code includes a number of exceptions from this rule, including exceptions for amounts of any damages received on account of personal physical injuries under section 104(a)(2). There is no specific exclusion from gross income for amounts received by individual Indians pursuant to the proposed settlement reached on December 7, 2009 between Elouise Cobell, et al. and the Secretary of Interior, et al. (the "Settlement").

In general, individual Indians, regardless of tribal affiliation, are subject to Federal income taxes and section 61 of the Code, even if the income is distributed to individual Indians out of income otherwise immune from taxation when first received by the tribe.[1515] However, certain types of income earned by individual Indians are not subject to Federal tax such as income derived from certain fishing activities.[1516] As another example, income derived directly from individually allotted land held in trust by the Federal government for the benefit of an individual Indian is excluded.[1517] Income is derived directly from trust land if it is generated principally from the use of allotted land and resources rather than from capital improvements upon the land, and includes income from logging, mining, farming, or ranching activities.[1518]

---

[1514] H.R. 4783. The bill passed the House on March 10, 2010. The Senate passed the bill with amendments on November 19, 2010. The House agreed to the Senate amendments on November 30, 2010. The President signed the bill on December 8, 2010.

[1515] *Squire v. Capoeman,* 351 U.S. 1, 6 (1956). Per capita payments of net revenues from gaming activities conducted or licensed by any Indian tribe are specifically made subject to Federal taxes by the Indian Gaming Regulatory Act, 25 U.S.C. sec. 2710(b)(3)(D), Pub. L. No. 100–497 (Oct. 17, 1988).

[1516] Sec. 7873 (exemption of income from treaty fishing rights).

[1517] Section 5 of the General Allotment Act of 1887, as amended, provided for tribal lands to be allotted to individual Indians in trust for a period of years, after which the lands were to be conveyed to the allottees in fee "free of all charge or incumbrance whatsoever." 25 U.S.C. sec. 348. This provision has been interpreted to prevent taxation of income or capital gains "derived directly" from allotted land while it remains in trust. *Squire v. Capoeman,* 351 U.S. 1 (1956); Rev. Rul. 57–407, 1957–2 C.B. 45 (any gain from the sale or exchange of the land while it is still held in trust is not subject to tax); Rev. Rul. 67–284, 1967–2 C.B. 55 (lists several types of income that will be treated as "derived directly" from allotted land, including rentals (including crop rentals), royalties, and proceeds from the sale of natural resources from the land. A number of courts have held that the exclusion is only available for income derived from land allotted to the individual earning the income and is not available for income derived from land leased from the tribe or another individual to whom the land is allotted. See *Kieffer v. Comm'r,* T.C. 1998–202; *Anderson v. United States,* 845 F.2d 206 (9th Cir. 1988); *Holt v. Comm'r,* 364 F.2d 38 (8th Cir. 1966); but see *Campbell v. Comm'r,* T.C. Memo 1997–502 at 19. The exclusion does not extend to income derived from the reinvestment of income derived from allotted land. *Capoeman,* 351 U.S. at 9.

[1518] *Capoeman* applies to allotments issued pursuant to tribe-specific allotment statues, regardless of whether the General Allotment Act applies to those allotments. See *United States*

A proposed Settlement has been reached in a class action lawsuit filed in 1996 against the Federal government for mismanagement of individual Indian trust accounts and trust assets. The lawsuit seeks a complete historical accounting as well as the correction of all individual Indian trust account balances due to this mismanagement. The Settlement is with the Secretary of the Interior, the Assistant Secretary of the Interior—Indian Affairs, and the Secretary of the Treasury. The individual Indian trust accounts relate to land, oil, natural gas, mineral, timber, grazing, water and other resources and rights on or under individual Indian lands.

Under the terms of the Settlement, the government will create a $1.412 billion Accounting/Trust Administration Fund and a $2 billion Trust Land Consolidation Fund. The Settlement also creates a federal Indian Education Scholarship Fund of up to $60 million to improve access to higher education for Indian youth.

### *Explanation of Provision*

The provision approves the Settlement, including the appropriation and payment of Federal funds. As required under the Settlement, the provision confirms that the amounts received by an individual Indian as a lump sum or a periodic payment pursuant to the Settlement will not be included in gross income and will not be taken into consideration for purposes of applying any provision of the Code that takes into account excludible income in computing adjusted gross income or modified adjusted gross income. The provision also provides that for purposes of determining eligibility under any Federal assisted program, the amounts received will not be treated as income for the month during which the amounts were received or as a resource during the 1-year period beginning on the date of receipt.

### *Effective Date*

The provision is effective upon date of enactment (December 8, 2010).

## B. Collection of Past-Due, Legally Enforceable State Debts (sec. 801 of the Act and sec. 6402(f) of the Code)

### *Present Law*

Under present law, the IRS has the authority to credit Federal tax overpayments payable on or before September 30, 2018 against any other Federal tax liability owed by the person who made the overpayment. The balance of the overpayment is generally refunded, unless a claim has been made for payment of certain nontax debts of that person, including certain unemployment com-

*v. Hallam,* 304 F.2d 629 (10th Cir. 1962) (income from Quapaw allotments in form of rents, royalties, and proceeds from restricted allotted lands exempt); *Stevens v. Commissioner,* 452 F.2d 741 (9th Cir. 1971) (construing Ft. Belknap Allotment Act to find farming and ranching income exempt); *Big Eagle v. United States,* 300 F.2d 765 (Ct. Cl. 1962) (receiving royalties from tribal mineral deposits exempt by virtue of Osage Allotment Act); Rev. Rul. 74–13, 1974–1 C.B. 14 (exemption described as applying to restricted lands generally rather than specifically to General Allotment Act lands).

pensation debts.[1519] Unemployment compensation debts subject to offset include those arising from uncollected contributions due to the State's Federal Unemployment Insurance Trust Fund that remain unpaid due to fraud and erroneous payments of unemployment compensation that were obtained by fraud on the part of the taxpayer who made the overpayment of tax, as well as the penalty and interest attributable to these debts. If the debt is for an erroneous payment, the State must establish that the debt has become final and certified by the Secretary of Labor.[1520] In addition, a State may only seek an offset for unemployment compensation debts owed by residents of the requesting State.[1521]

Offsets for unemployment compensation and/or State income tax debts occur only after a taxpayer's overpayment has been reduced for any of the following debts, in the following order and before any amount is credited to estimated tax for a future Federal tax liability: (1) Federal tax debts, (2) past-due support within the meaning of the Social Security Act, and (3) debts owed to Federal agencies.[1522] If more than one unemployment compensation or State income tax debt is owed by the same resident to his State, the debts are satisfied by the overpayment in the order in which the debts accrued, without regard to whether they arise from State income tax or unemployment compensation. The actions of the IRS in reducing the overpayment to satisfy the foregoing debts are not subject to judicial review.[1523] In the event that a payment to a State is determined to have been made erroneously by the IRS in the exercise of its authority to offset for unemployment compensation debt, the State is required to promptly repay upon notice from the IRS.[1524]

Certain safeguards apply to the offset of unemployment compensation debt. Before submitting its claim to the IRS, the State must provide notice by certified mail with return receipt of its intent to the person owing the debt and provide at least 60 days for the person to submit a response, with any supporting evidence, which the State will then consider.[1525] Other conditions may be prescribed by the Secretary to ensure that the State has made reasonable efforts to obtain payment of the covered debt and that the State determination with respect to fraud is valid. If such a debt is claimed by the creditor agency to which the debt is owed, the IRS notifies the person who overpaid that the overpayment has been reduced by the amount of the debt and that such amount will be paid to the creditor agency.

### *Explanation of Provision*

The provision expands the ability of a State to collect benefit overpayments from a benefit recipient's Federal income tax over-

---

[1519] Sec. 6402(f) authorizes offsets of unemployment compensation debts against refunds payable for the ten year period beginning after September 30, 2008. Other non-Federal tax debts that may be claimed against overpayments of Federal tax liability include past-due support within the meaning of the Social Security Act, debts owed to Federal agencies and State income tax obligations. Sec. 6402(c)–(e).

[1520] Sec. 6402(f)(5)(A).

[1521] Sec. 6402(f)(3).

[1522] Sec. 6402(f)(2).

[1523] Sec. 6402(g).

[1524] Sec. 6402(f)(7).

[1525] Sec. 6402(f)(4).

payment in two ways. It removes the requirement that the excessive or erroneous payment of State benefits have been attributable to fraud. It also no longer requires that the State provide notice to the taxpayer by certified mail of the State's intent to submit a request for offset to the IRS.

In addition, the authority for such offsets is now permanent. The provision does not change the present-law provision under which a State's ability to request offset of unemployment compensation debts against Federal income tax refunds is limited to requests with respect to residents of the requesting State.

### *Effective Date*

The provision is effective with respect to refunds under section 6402 payable on or after the date of enactment (December 8, 2010).

# PART SIXTEEN: REVENUE PROVISONS OF THE TAX RELIEF, UNEMPLOYMENT INSURANCE REAUTHORIZATION, AND JOB CREATION ACT OF 2010 (PUBLIC LAW 111–312)[1526]

## TITLE I—TEMPORARY EXTENSION OF TAX RELIEF

### A. Marginal Individual Income Tax Rate Reductions (sec. 101 of the Act and sec. 1 of the Code)

#### *Present Law*

***In general***

The Economic Growth and Tax Relief Reconciliation Act of 2001[1527] ("EGTRRA") created a new 10-percent regular income tax bracket for a portion of taxable income that was previously taxed at 15 percent. EGTRRA also reduced the other regular income tax rates. The otherwise applicable regular income tax rates of 28 percent, 31 percent, 36 percent and 39.6 percent were reduced to 25 percent, 28 percent, 33 percent, and 35 percent, respectively. These provisions of EGTRRA shall cease to apply for taxable years beginning after December 31, 2010.

***Tax rate schedules***

To determine regular tax liability, a taxpayer generally must apply the tax rate schedules (or the tax tables) to his or her regular taxable income. The rate schedules are broken into several ranges of income, known as income brackets, and the marginal tax rate increases as a taxpayer's income increases. Separate rate schedules apply based on an individual's filing status. For 2010, the regular individual income tax rate schedules are as follows:

[1526] H.R. 4853. The Act originated as a bill relating to the Airport and Airway Trust Fund and passed the House on the suspension calendar on March 17, 2010. The Senate passed the bill with an amendment on September 23, 2010. The House agreed to the Senate amendment with an amendment substituting the text of the "Middle Class Tax Relief Act of 2010" on December 2, 2010. The Senate agreed to the House amendment to the Senate amendment with an amendment substituting the text of the "Tax Relief, Unemployment Insurance Reauthorization, and Jobs Creation Act of 2010" on December 15, 2010. The House agreed to the Senate amendment to the House amendment to the Senate amendment on December 16, 2010. The President signed the bill on December 17, 2010. For a technical explanation of the Act prepared by the staff of the Joint Committee on Taxation, see *Technical Explanation of the Revenue Provisions Contained in the "Tax Relief, Unemployment Insurance Reauthorization, and Jobs Creation Act of 2010" Scheduled for Consideration by the United States Senate* (JCX 55–10), December 10, 2010.

[1527] Pub. L. No. 107–16.

TABLE 1—FEDERAL INDIVIDUAL INCOME TAX RATES FOR 2010

| If taxable income is: | Then income tax equals: |
|---|---|
| **Single Individuals** | |
| Not over $8,375 | 10% of the taxable income. |
| Over $8,375 but not over $34,000 | $837.50 plus 15% of the excess over $8,375. |
| Over $34,000 but not over $82,400 | $4,681.25 plus 25% of the excess over $34,000. |
| Over $82,400 but not over $171,850 | $16,781.25 plus 28% of the excess over $82,400. |
| Over $171,850 but not over $373,650 | $41,827.25 plus 33% of the excess over $171,850. |
| Over $373,650 | $108,421.25 plus 35% of the excess over $373,650. |
| **Heads of Households** | |
| Not over $11,950 | 10% of the taxable income. |
| Over $11,950 but not over $45,550 | $1,195 plus 15% of the excess over $11,950. |
| Over $45,550 but not over $117,650 | $6,235 plus 25% of the excess over $45,550. |
| Over $117,650 but not over $190,550 | $24,260 plus 28% of the excess over $117,650. |
| Over $190,550 but not over $373,650 | $44,672 plus 33% of the excess over $190,550. |
| Over $373,650 | $105,095 plus 35% of the excess over $373,650. |
| **Married Individuals Filing Joint Returns and Surviving Spouses** | |
| Not over $16,750 | 10% of the taxable income. |
| Over $16,750 but not over $68,000 | $1,675 plus 15% of the excess over $16,750. |
| Over $68,000 but not over $137,300 | $9,362.50 plus 25% of the excess over $68,000. |
| Over $137,300 but not over $209,250 | $26,687.50 plus 28% of the excess over $137,300. |
| Over $209,250 but not over $373,650 | $46,833.50 plus 33% of the excess over $209,250. |
| Over $373,650 | $101,085.50 plus 35% of the excess over $373,650. |
| **Married Individuals Filing Separate Returns** | |
| Not over $8,375 | 10% of the taxable income. |
| Over $8,375 but not over $34,000 | $837.50 plus 15% of the excess over $8,375. |
| Over $34,000 but not over $68,650 | $4,681.25 plus 25% of the excess over $34,000. |
| Over $68,650 but not over $104,625 | $13,343.75 plus 28% of the excess over $68,650. |
| Over $104,625 but not over $186,825 | $23,416.75 plus 33% of the excess over $104,625. |
| Over $186,825 | $50,542.75 plus 35% of the excess over $186,825. |

## *Explanation of Provision*

The provision extends the 10-percent, 15-percent, 25-percent, 28-percent, 33-percent and 35-percent individual income tax rates for two years (through 2012).

The rate structure is indexed for inflation.

A comparison of Table 2, below, with Table 1, above, illustrates the tax rate changes. Note that Table 2 also incorporates the provision to retain the marriage penalty relief with respect to the size of the 15 percent rate bracket, as discussed below.

TABLE 2.—FEDERAL INDIVIDUAL INCOME TAX RATES FOR 2011

| If taxable income is: | Then income tax equals: |
|---|---|
| Single Individuals | |
| Not over $8,500 | 10% of the taxable income. |
| Over $8,500 but not over $34,500 | $850 plus 15% of the excess over $8,500. |
| Over $34,500 but not over $83,600 | $4,750 plus 25% of the excess over $34,500. |
| Over $83,600 but not over $174,400 | $17,025 plus 28% of the excess over $83,600. |
| Over $174,400 but not over $379,150 | $42,449 plus 33% of the excess over $174,400. |
| Over $379,150 | $110,016.50 plus 35% of the excess over $379,150. |
| Heads of Households | |
| Not over $12,150 | 10% of the taxable income. |
| Over $12,150 but not over $46,250 | $1,215 plus 15% of the excess over $12,150. |
| Over $46,250 but not over $119,400 | $6,330 plus 25% of the excess over $46,250. |
| Over $119,400 but not over $193,350 | $24,617.50 plus 28% of the excess over $119,400. |
| Over $193,350 but not over $379,150 | $45,323.50 plus 33% of the excess over $193,350. |
| Over $379,150 | $106,637.50 plus 35% of the excess over $379,150. |
| Married Individuals Filing Joint Returns and Surviving Spouses | |
| Not over $17,000 | 10% of the taxable income. |
| Over $17,000 but not over $69,000 | $1,700 plus 15% of the excess over $17,000. |
| Over $69,000 but not over $139,350 | $9,500 plus 25% of the excess over $69,000. |
| Over $139,350 but not over $212,300 | $27,087.50 plus 28% of the excess over $139,350. |
| Over $212,300 but not over $379,150 | $47,513.50 plus 33% of the excess over $212,300. |
| Over $379,150 | $102,574 plus 35% of the excess over $379,150. |
| Married Individuals Filing Separate Returns | |
| Not over $8,500 | 10% of the taxable income. |
| Over $8,500 but not over $34,500 | $850 plus 15% of the excess over $8,500. |
| Over $34,500 but not over $69,675 | $4,750 plus 25% of the excess over $34,500. |
| Over $69,675 but not over $106,150 | $13,543.75 plus 28% of the excess over $69,675. |
| Over $106,150 but not over $189,575 | $23,756.75 plus 33% of the excess over $106,150. |
| Over $189,575 | $51,287 plus 35% of the excess over $189,575. |

### *Effective Date*

The provision applies to taxable years beginning after December 31, 2010.

## B. The Overall Limitation on Itemized Deductions and the Personal Exemption Phase-Out (sec. 101 of the Act and secs. 68 and 151 of the Code)

### *Present Law*

#### *Overall limitation on itemized deductions ("Pease" limitation)*

Unless an individual elects to claim the standard deduction for a taxable year, the taxpayer is allowed to deduct his or her itemized deductions. Itemized deductions generally are those deductions which are not allowed in computing adjusted gross income ("AGI"). Itemized deductions include unreimbursed medical expenses, investment interest, casualty and theft losses, wagering losses, charitable contributions, qualified residence interest, State and local income and property taxes, unreimbursed employee business expenses, and certain other miscellaneous expenses.

Prior to 2010, the total amount of otherwise allowable itemized deductions (other than medical expenses, investment interest, and casualty, theft, or wagering losses) was limited for upper-income taxpayers. In computing this reduction of total itemized deductions, all limitations applicable to such deductions (such as the separate floors) were first applied and, then, the otherwise allowable total amount of itemized deductions was reduced by three percent of the amount by which the taxpayer's AGI exceeded a threshold amount which was indexed annually for inflation. The otherwise allowable itemized deductions could not be reduced by more than 80 percent.

EGTRRA repealed this overall limitation on itemized deductions with the repeal phased-in over five years. EGTRRA provided: (1) a one-third reduction of the otherwise applicable limitation in 2006 and 2007; (2) a two-thirds reduction in 2008, and 2009; and (3) no overall limitation on itemized deductions in 2010. Thus in 2009, for example, the total amount of otherwise allowable itemized deductions (other than medical expenses, investment interest, and casualty, theft, or wagering losses) was reduced by three percent of the amount of the taxpayer's AGI in excess of $166,800 ($83,400 for married couples filing separate returns). Then the overall reduction in itemized deductions was phased-down to 1/3 of the full reduction amount (that is, the limitation was reduced by two-thirds).

Pursuant to the general EGTRRA sunset, the phased-in repeal of the Pease limitation sunsets and the limitation becomes fully effective again in 2011. Adjusting for inflation, the AGI threshold is $169,550 for 2011.

***Personal exemption phase-out for certain taxpayers ("PEP")***

Personal exemptions generally are allowed for the taxpayer, his or her spouse, and any dependents. For 2010, the amount deductible for each personal exemption is $3,650. This amount is indexed annually for inflation.

Prior to 2010, the deduction for personal exemptions was reduced or eliminated for taxpayers with incomes over certain thresholds, which were indexed annually for inflation. Specifically, the total amount of exemptions that could be claimed by a taxpayer was reduced by two percent for each $2,500 (or portion thereof) by which the taxpayer's AGI exceeded the applicable threshold. (The phase-out rate was two percent for each $1,250 for married taxpayers filing separate returns.) Thus, the deduction for personal exemptions was phased out over a $122,500 range (which was not indexed for inflation), beginning at the applicable threshold.

In 2009, for example, the applicable thresholds were $166,800 for single individuals, $250,200 for married individuals filing a joint return and surviving spouses, $208,500 for heads of households, and $125,100 for married individuals filing separate returns.

EGTRRA repealed PEP with the repeal phased-in over five years. EGTRRA provided: (1) a one-third reduction of the otherwise applicable limitation in 2006 and 2007: (2) a two-thirds reduction in 2008, and 2009; and (3) no PEP in 2010. However, under the EGTRRA sunset, the PEP becomes fully effective again in 2011. Adjusted for inflation, the PEP thresholds for 2011 are: (1) $169,550 for unmarried individuals; (2) $254,350 for married couples filing joint returns; and (3) $211,950 for heads of households.

### *Explanation of Provision*

***Overall limitation on itemized deductions ("Pease" limitation)***

Under the provision the overall limitation on itemized deductions does not apply for two additional years (through 2012).

***Personal exemption phase-out for certain taxpayers ("PEP")***

Under the provision the personal exemption phase-out does not apply for two additional years (through 2012).

### *Effective Date*

The provision applies to taxable years beginning after December 31, 2010.

## C. Child Tax Credit (secs. 101 and 103 of the Act and sec. 24 of the Code)

### *Present Law*

An individual may claim a tax credit for each qualifying child under the age of 17. The maximum amount of the credit per child is $1,000 through 2010 and $500 thereafter. A child who is not a citizen, national, or resident of the United States cannot be a qualifying child.

The aggregate amount of child credits that may be claimed is phased out for individuals with income over certain threshold amounts. Specifically, the otherwise allowable aggregate child tax credit amount is reduced by $50 for each $1,000 (or fraction thereof) of modified adjusted gross income ("modified AGI") over $75,000 for single individuals or heads of households, $110,000 for married individuals filing joint returns, and $55,000 for married individuals filing separate returns. For purposes of this limitation, modified AGI includes certain otherwise excludable income earned by U.S. citizens or residents living abroad or in certain U.S. territories.

The credit is allowable against the regular tax and, for taxable years beginning before January 1, 2011, is allowed against the alternative minimum tax ("AMT"). To the extent the child tax credit exceeds the taxpayer's tax liability, the taxpayer is eligible for a refundable credit (the additional child tax credit) equal to 15 percent of earned income in excess of a threshold dollar amount (the "earned income" formula). EGTRRA provided, in general, that this threshold dollar amount is $10,000 indexed for inflation from 2001. The American Recovery and Reinvestment Act of 2009 ("ARRA")[1528] set the threshold at $3,000 for both 2009 and 2010. After 2010, the ability to determine the refundable child credit based on earned income in excess of the threshold dollar amount expires.

Families with three or more qualifying children may determine the additional child tax credit using the "alternative formula" if this results in a larger credit than determined under the earned income formula. Under the alternative formula, the additional child tax credit equals the amount by which the taxpayer's social secu-

[1528] Pub. L. No. 111–5.

rity taxes exceed the taxpayer's earned income tax credit ("EITC"). After 2010, due to the expiration of the earned income formula, this is the only manner of obtaining a refundable child credit.

Earned income is defined as the sum of wages, salaries, tips, and other taxable employee compensation plus net self-employment earnings. Unlike the EITC, which also includes the preceding items in its definition of earned income, the additional child tax credit is based only on earned income to the extent it is included in computing taxable income. For example, some ministers' parsonage allowances are considered self-employment income, and thus are considered earned income for purposes of computing the EITC, but are excluded from gross income for individual income tax purposes. Therefore, these allowances are not considered earned income for purposes of the additional child tax credit.

### *Explanation of Provision*

The provision extends the $1,000 child tax credit and allows the child tax credit against the individual's regular income tax and AMT for two years (through 2012). The provision also extends the EGTRRA repeal of a prior-law provision that reduced the refundable child credit by the amount of the AMT for two years (through 2012). The provision extends the earned income formula for determining the refundable child credit, with the earned income threshold of $3,000 (also, the provision stops indexation for inflation of the $3,000 earnings threshold) for two years (through 2012).[1529] Finally, the provision extends the rule that the refundable portion of the child tax credit does not constitute income and shall not be treated as resources for purposes of determining eligibility or the amount or nature of benefits or assistance under any Federal program or any State or local program financed with Federal funds for two years (through 2012).

### *Effective Date*

The provision applies to taxable years beginning after December 31, 2010.

## D. Marriage Penalty Relief and Earned Income Tax Credit Simplification (sec. 101 of the Act and secs. 1, 32, and 63 of the Code)

### *Present Law*

#### *Marriage penalty*

A married couple generally is treated as one tax unit that must pay tax on the couple's total taxable income. Although married couples may elect to file separate returns, the rate schedules and other provisions are structured so that filing separate returns usually results in a higher tax than filing a joint return. Other rate schedules apply to single persons and to single heads of households.

---

[1529] Section 101 of the Act extends the EGTRRA modifications to the provision. Section 103 of the Act extends the modifications to the provision (including reduction in the earnings threshold for the refundable portion of the child tax credit to $3,000). See Title I, section J for additional discussion of the child tax credit, below.

A "marriage penalty" exists when the combined tax liability of a married couple filing a joint return is greater than the sum of the tax liabilities of each individual computed as if they were not married. A "marriage bonus" exists when the combined tax liability of a married couple filing a joint return is less than the sum of the tax liabilities of each individual computed as if they were not married.

***Basic standard deduction***

EGTRRA increased the basic standard deduction for a married couple filing a joint return to twice the basic standard deduction for an unmarried individual filing a single return. The basic standard deduction for a married taxpayer filing separately continued to equal one-half of the basic standard deduction for a married couple filing jointly; thus, the basic standard deduction for unmarried individuals filing a single return and for married couples filing separately are the same.

***Fifteen percent rate bracket***

EGTRRA increased the size of the 15-percent regular income tax rate bracket for a married couple filing a joint return to twice the size of the corresponding rate bracket for an unmarried individual filing a single return.

***Earned income tax credit***

The earned income tax credit ("EITC") is a refundable credit available to certain low-income taxpayers. Generally, the amount of an individual's allowable earned income credit is dependent on the individual's earned income, adjusted gross income, the number of qualifying children and (through 2010) filing status.

## *Explanation of Provision*

***Basic standard deduction***

The provision increases the basic standard deduction for a married couple filing a joint return to twice the basic standard deduction for an unmarried individual filing a single return for two years (through 2012).

***Fifteen percent rate bracket***

The provision increases the size of the 15-percent regular income tax rate bracket for a married couple filing a joint return to twice the 15-percent regular income tax rate bracket for an unmarried individual filing a single return for two years (through 2012).

***Earned income tax credit***

The provision extends certain EITC provisions adopted by EGTRRA for two years (through 2012). These include: (1) a simplified definition of earned income; (2) a simplified relationship test; (3) use of AGI instead of modified AGI; (4) a simplified tie-breaking rule; (5) additional math error authority for the Internal Revenue Service; (6) a repeal of the prior-law provision that reduced an individual's EITC by the amount of his alternative minimum tax liability; and (7) increases in the beginning and ending points of the credit phase-out for married taxpayers by $5,000.[1530]

### *Effective Date*

The provision applies to taxable years beginning after December 31, 2010.

## E. Education Incentives (sec. 101 of the Act and secs. 117, 127, 142, 146–148, 221, and 530 of the Code)

### *Present Law*

#### *Income and wage exclusion for awards under the National Health Service Corps Scholarship Program and the F. Edward Hebert Armed Forces Health Professions Scholarship and Financial Assistance Program*

Section 117 excludes from gross income amounts received as a qualified scholarship by an individual who is a candidate for a degree and used for tuition and fees required for the enrollment or attendance (or for fees, books, supplies, and equipment required for courses of instruction) at a primary, secondary, or post-secondary educational institution. The tax-free treatment provided by section 117 does not extend to scholarship amounts covering regular living expenses, such as room and board. In addition to the exclusion for qualified scholarships, section 117 provides an exclusion from gross income for qualified tuition reductions for certain education provided to employees (and their spouses and dependents) of certain educational organizations. Amounts excludable from gross income under section 117 are also excludable from wages for payroll tax purposes.[1531]

The exclusion for qualified scholarships and qualified tuition reductions does not apply to any amount received by a student that represents payment for teaching, research, or other services by the student required as a condition for receiving the scholarship or tuition reduction. An exception to this rule applies in the case of the National Health Service Corps Scholarship Program (the "NHSC Scholarship Program") and the F. Edward Hebert Armed Forces Health Professions Scholarship and Financial Assistance Program (the "Armed Forces Scholarship Program").

The NHSC Scholarship Program and the Armed Forces Scholarship Program provide education awards to participants on the condition that the participants provide certain services. In the case of the NHSC Scholarship Program, the recipient of the scholarship is obligated to provide medical services in a geographic area (or to an underserved population group or designated facility) identified by the Public Health Service as having a shortage of health care professionals. In the case of the Armed Forces Scholarship Program, the recipient of the scholarship is obligated to serve a certain number of years in the military at an armed forces medical facility.

Under the sunset provisions of EGTRRA, the exclusion from gross income and wages for the NHSC Scholarship Program and

---

[1530] The $5,000 amount, which is indexed for inflation annually, also reflects the increase from $3,000 to $5,000 described more fully in Title I, section K of this document, below.

[1531] Sec. 3121(a)(20).

the Armed Forces Scholarship Program will no longer apply for taxable years beginning after December 31, 2010.

***Income and wage exclusion for employer-provided educational assistance***

If certain requirements are satisfied, up to $5,250 annually of educational assistance provided by an employer to an employee is excludable from gross income for income tax purposes and from wages for employment tax purposes.[1532] This exclusion applies to both graduate and undergraduate courses.[1533] For the exclusion to apply, certain requirements must be satisfied. The educational assistance must be provided pursuant to a separate written plan of the employer. The employer's educational assistance program must not discriminate in favor of highly compensated employees. In addition, no more than five percent of the amounts paid or incurred by the employer during the year for educational assistance under a qualified educational assistance program can be provided for the class of individuals consisting of more than five-percent owners of the employer and the spouses or dependents of such more than five-percent owners.

For purposes of the exclusion, educational assistance means the payment by an employer of expenses incurred by or on behalf of the employee for education of the employee including, but not limited to, tuition, fees, and similar payments, books, supplies, and equipment. Educational assistance also includes the provision by the employer of courses of instruction for the employee (including books, supplies, and equipment). Educational assistance does not include (1) tools or supplies that may be retained by the employee after completion of a course, (2) meals, lodging, or transportation, or (3) any education involving sports, games, or hobbies. The exclusion for employer-provided educational assistance applies only with respect to education provided to the employee (e.g., it does not apply to education provided to the spouse or a child of the employee).

In the absence of the specific exclusion for employer-provided educational assistance under section 127, employer-provided educational assistance is excludable from gross income and wages only if the education expenses qualify as a working condition fringe benefit.[1534] In general, education qualifies as a working condition fringe benefit if the employee could have deducted the education expenses under section 162 if the employee paid for the education. In general, education expenses are deductible by an individual under section 162 if the education (1) maintains or improves a skill required in a trade or business currently engaged in by the taxpayer, or (2) meets the express requirements of the taxpayer's employer, applicable law, or regulations imposed as a condition of con-

[1532] Secs. 127, 3121(a)(18).

[1533] The exclusion has not always applied to graduate courses. The exclusion was first made inapplicable to graduate-level courses by the Technical and Miscellaneous Revenue Act of 1988. The exclusion was reinstated with respect to graduate-level courses by the Omnibus Budget Reconciliation Act of 1990, effective for taxable years beginning after December 31, 1990. The exclusion was again made inapplicable to graduate-level courses by the Small Business Job Protection Act of 1996, effective for courses beginning after June 30, 1996. The exclusion for graduate-level courses was reinstated by EGTRRA, although that change does not apply to taxable years beginning after December 31, 2010 (under EGTRRA's sunset provision).

[1534] Sec. 132(d).

tinued employment. However, education expenses are generally not deductible if they relate to certain minimum educational requirements or to education or training that enables a taxpayer to begin working in a new trade or business. In determining the amount deductible for this purpose, the two-percent floor on miscellaneous itemized deductions is disregarded.

The specific exclusion for employer-provided educational assistance was originally enacted on a temporary basis and was subsequently extended 10 times.[1535] EGTRRA deleted the exclusion's explicit expiration date and extended the exclusion to graduate courses. However, those changes are subject to EGTRRA's sunset provision so that the exclusion will not be available for taxable years beginning after December 31, 2010. Thus, at that time, educational assistance will be excludable from gross income only if it qualifies as a working condition fringe benefit (i.e., the expenses would have been deductible as business expenses if paid by the employee). As previously discussed, to meet such requirement, the expenses must be related to the employee's current job.[1536]

***Deduction for student loan interest***

Certain individuals who have paid interest on qualified education loans may claim an above-the-line deduction for such interest expenses, subject to a maximum annual deduction limit.[1537] Required payments of interest generally do not include voluntary payments, such as interest payments made during a period of loan forbearance. No deduction is allowed to an individual if that individual is claimed as a dependent on another taxpayer's return for the taxable year.

A qualified education loan generally is defined as any indebtedness incurred solely to pay for the costs of attendance (including room and board) of the taxpayer, the taxpayer's spouse, or any dependent of the taxpayer as of the time the indebtedness was incurred in attending an eligible educational institution on at least a half-time basis. Eligible educational institutions are (1) post-secondary educational institutions and certain vocational schools defined by reference to section 481 of the Higher Education Act of 1965, or (2) institutions conducting internship or residency programs leading to a degree or certificate from an institution of higher education, a hospital, or a health care facility conducting postgraduate training. Additionally, to qualify as an eligible educational institution, an institution must be eligible to participate in Department of Education student aid programs.

The maximum allowable deduction per year is $2,500. For 2010, the deduction is phased out ratably for single taxpayers with AGI between $60,000 and $75,000 and between $120,000 and $150,000 for married taxpayers filing a joint return. The income phaseout ranges are indexed for inflation and rounded to the next lowest multiple of $5,000.

Effective for taxable years beginning after December 31, 2010, the changes made by EGTRRA to the student loan provisions no

[1535] The exclusion was first enacted as part of the Revenue Act of 1978 (with a 1983 expiration date).

[1536] Treas. Reg. sec. 1.162–5.

[1537] Sec. 221.

longer apply. The EGTRRA changes scheduled to expire are: (1) increases that were made in the AGI phaseout ranges for the deduction and (2) rules that extended deductibility of interest beyond the first 60 months that interest payments are required. With the expiration of EGTRRA, the phaseout ranges will revert to a base level of $40,000 to $55,000 ($60,000 to $75,000 in the case of a married couple filing jointly), but with an adjustment for inflation occurring since 2002.

***Coverdell education savings accounts***

A Coverdell education savings account is a trust or custodial account created exclusively for the purpose of paying qualified education expenses of a named beneficiary.[1538] Annual contributions to Coverdell education savings accounts may not exceed $2,000 per designated beneficiary and may not be made after the designated beneficiary reaches age 18 (except in the case of a special needs beneficiary). The contribution limit is phased out for taxpayers with modified AGI between $95,000 and $110,000 ($190,000 and $220,000 for married taxpayers filing a joint return); the AGI of the contributor, and not that of the beneficiary, controls whether a contribution is permitted by the taxpayer.

Earnings on contributions to a Coverdell education savings account generally are subject to tax when withdrawn.[1539] However, distributions from a Coverdell education savings account are excludable from the gross income of the distributee (i.e., the student) to the extent that the distribution does not exceed the qualified education expenses incurred by the beneficiary during the year the distribution is made. The earnings portion of a Coverdell education savings account distribution not used to pay qualified education expenses is includible in the gross income of the distributee and generally is subject to an additional 10-percent tax.[1540]

Tax-free (including free of additional 10-percent tax) transfers or rollovers of account balances from one Coverdell education savings account benefiting one beneficiary to another Coverdell education savings account benefiting another beneficiary (as well as redesignations of the named beneficiary) are permitted, provided that the new beneficiary is a member of the family of the prior beneficiary and is under age 30 (except in the case of a special needs beneficiary). In general, any balance remaining in a Coverdell education savings account is deemed to be distributed within 30 days after the date that the beneficiary reaches age 30 (or, if the beneficiary dies before attaining age 30, within 30 days of the date that the beneficiary dies).

Qualified education expenses include "qualified higher education expenses" and "qualified elementary and secondary education expenses."

The term "qualified higher education expenses" includes tuition, fees, books, supplies, and equipment required for the enrollment or attendance of the designated beneficiary at an eligible education in-

[1538] Sec. 530.

[1539] In addition, Coverdell education savings accounts are subject to the unrelated business income tax imposed by section 511.

[1540] This 10-percent additional tax does not apply if a distribution from an education savings account is made on account of the death or disability of the designated beneficiary, or if made on account of a scholarship received by the designated beneficiary.

stitution, regardless of whether the beneficiary is enrolled at an eligible educational institution on a full-time, half-time, or less than half-time basis.[1541] Moreover, qualified higher education expenses include certain room and board expenses for any period during which the beneficiary is at least a half-time student. Qualified higher education expenses include expenses with respect to undergraduate or graduate-level courses. In addition, qualified higher education expenses include amounts paid or incurred to purchase tuition credits (or to make contributions to an account) under a qualified tuition program for the benefit of the beneficiary of the Coverdell education savings account.[1542]

The term "qualified elementary and secondary education expenses," means expenses for: (1) tuition, fees, academic tutoring, special needs services, books, supplies, and other equipment incurred in connection with the enrollment or attendance of the beneficiary at a public, private, or religious school providing elementary or secondary education (kindergarten through grade 12) as determined under State law; (2) room and board, uniforms, transportation, and supplementary items or services (including extended day programs) required or provided by such a school in connection with such enrollment or attendance of the beneficiary; and (3) the purchase of any computer technology or equipment (as defined in section 170(e)(6)(F)(i)) or Internet access and related services, if such technology, equipment, or services are to be used by the beneficiary and the beneficiary's family during any of the years the beneficiary is in elementary or secondary school. Computer software primarily involving sports, games, or hobbies is not considered a qualified elementary and secondary education expense unless the software is predominantly educational in nature.

Qualified education expenses generally include only out-of-pocket expenses. Such qualified education expenses do not include expenses covered by employer-provided educational assistance or scholarships for the benefit of the beneficiary that are excludable from gross income. Thus, total qualified education expenses are reduced by scholarship or fellowship grants excludable from gross income under section 117, as well as any other tax-free educational benefits, such as employer-provided educational assistance, that are excludable from the employee's gross income under section 127.

Effective for taxable years beginning after December 31, 2010, the changes made by EGTRRA to Coverdell education savings accounts no longer apply. The EGTRRA changes scheduled to expire are: (1) the increase in the contribution limit to $2,000 from $500; (2) the increase in the phaseout range for married taxpayers filing jointly to $190,000–$220,000 from $150,000–$160,000; (3) the expansion of qualified expenses to include elementary and secondary education expenses; (4) special age rules for special needs beneficiaries; (5) clarification that corporations and other entities are permitted to make contributions, regardless of the income of the corporation or entity during the year of the contribution; (6) certain rules regarding when contributions are deemed made and extending the time during which excess contributions may be returned

[1541] Qualified higher education expenses are defined in the same manner as for qualified tuition programs.

[1542] Sec. 530(b)(2)(B).

without additional tax; (7) certain rules regarding coordination with the Hope and Lifetime Learning credits; and (8) certain rules regarding coordination with qualified tuition programs.

***Amount of governmental bonds that may be issued by governments qualifying for the "small governmental unit" arbitrage rebate exception***

To prevent State and local governments from issuing more Federally subsidized tax-exempt bonds than is necessary for the activity being financed or from issuing such bonds earlier than needed for the purpose of the borrowing, the Code includes arbitrage restrictions limiting the ability to profit from investment of tax-exempt bond proceeds.[1543] The Code also provides certain exceptions to the arbitrage restrictions. Under one such exception, small issuers of governmental bonds issued for local governmental activities are not subject to the rebate requirement.[1544] To qualify for this exception the governmental bonds must be issued by a governmental unit with general taxing powers that reasonably expects to issue no more than $5 million of tax-exempt governmental bonds in a calendar year.[1545] Prior to EGTRRA, the $5 million limit was increased to $10 million if at least $5 million of the bonds are used to finance public schools. EGTRRA provided the additional amount of governmental bonds for public schools that small governmental units may issue without being subject to the arbitrage rebate requirements is increased from $5 million to $10 million.[1546] Thus, these governmental units may issue up to $15 million of governmental bonds in a calendar year provided that at least $10 million of the bonds are used to finance public school construction expenditures. This increase is subject to the EGTRRA sunset.

***Issuance of tax-exempt private activity bonds for public school facilities***

Interest on bonds that nominally are issued by State or local governments, but the proceeds of which are used (directly or indirectly) by a private person and payment of which is derived from funds of such a private person is taxable unless the purpose of the borrowing is approved specifically in the Code or in a non-Code provision of a revenue act. These bonds are called "private activity bonds."[1547] The term "private person" includes the Federal government and all other individuals and entities other than State or local governments.

Only specified private activity bonds are tax-exempt. EGTRRA added a new type of private activity bond that is subject to the EGTRRA sunset. This category is bonds for elementary and sec-

---

[1543] The exclusion from gross income for interest on State and local bonds does not apply to any arbitrage bond (sec. 103(a), (b)(2)). A bond is an arbitrage bond if it is part of an issue that violates the restrictions against investing in higher-yielding investments under section 148(a) or that fails to satisfy the requirement to rebate arbitrage earnings under section 148(f).

[1544] Ninety-five percent or more of the net proceeds of governmental bond issue are to be used for local governmental activities of the issuer. Sec. 148(f)(4)(D).

[1545] Under the Treasury regulations, an issuer may apply a fact-based rather than an expectations-based test. Treas. Reg. sec. 1.148–8(c)(1).

[1546] Sec. 148(f)(4)(D)(vii).

[1547] The Code provides that the exclusion from gross income does not apply to interest on private activity bonds that are not qualified bonds within the meaning of section 141. See secs. 103(b)(1), 141.

ondary public school facilities that are owned by private, for-profit corporations pursuant to public-private partnership agreements with a State or local educational agency.[1548] The term school facility includes school buildings and functionally related and subordinate land (including stadiums or other athletic facilities primarily used for school events) and depreciable personal property used in the school facility. The school facilities for which these bonds are issued must be operated by a public educational agency as part of a system of public schools.

A public-private partnership agreement is defined as an arrangement pursuant to which the for-profit corporate party constructs, rehabilitates, refurbishes, or equips a school facility for a public school agency (typically pursuant to a lease arrangement). The agreement must provide that, at the end of the contract term, ownership of the bond-financed property is transferred to the public school agency party to the agreement for no additional consideration.

Issuance of these bonds is subject to a separate annual per-State private activity bond volume limit equal to $10 per resident ($5 million, if greater) in lieu of the present-law State private activity bond volume limits. As with the present-law State private activity bond volume limits, States can decide how to allocate the bond authority to State and local government agencies. Bond authority that is unused in the year in which it arises may be carried forward for up to three years for public school projects under rules similar to the carryforward rules of the present-law private activity bond volume limits.

### *Explanation of Provision*

The provision delays the EGTRRA sunset as it applies to the NHSC Scholarship Program and the Armed Forces Scholarship Program, the section 127 exclusion from income and wages for employer-provided educational assistance, the student loan interest deduction, and Coverdell education savings accounts for two years. The provision also delays the EGTRRA sunset as it applies to the expansion of the small government unit exception to arbitrage rebate and allowing issuance of tax-exempt private activity bonds for public school facilities. Thus, all of these tax benefits for education continue to be available through 2012.

### *Effective Date*

The provision is effective on the date of enactment.

[1548] Sec. 142(a)(13), (k).

## F. Other Incentives for Families and Children (includes extension of the adoption tax credit, employer-provided child care tax credit, and dependent care tax credit) (sec. 101 of the Act and secs. 21, 23, 36C, 45D, and 137 of the Code)

### *Present Law*

#### *Adoption credit and exclusion from income for employer-provided adoption assistance*

Present law for 2010 provides: (1) a maximum adoption credit of $13,170 per eligible child (both special needs and non-special needs adoptions); and (2) a maximum exclusion of $13,170 per eligible child (both special needs and non-special needs adoptions).[1549] These dollar amounts are adjusted annually for inflation. These benefits are phased-out over a $40,000 range for taxpayers with modified adjusted gross income ("modified AGI") in excess of certain dollar levels. For 2010, the phase-out range is between $182,520 and $222,520. The phase-out threshold is adjusted for inflation annually, but the phase-out range remains a $40,000 range.

For taxable years beginning after December 31, 2011, the adoption credit and employer-provided adoption assistance exclusion are available only to special needs adoptions and the maximum credit and exclusion are reduced to $6,000, respectively. The phase-out range is reduced to lower income levels (i.e., between $75,000 and $115,000). The maximum credit, exclusion, and phase-out range are not indexed for inflation.

#### *Employer-provided child care tax credit*

Taxpayers receive a tax credit equal to 25 percent of qualified expenses for employee child care and 10 percent of qualified expenses for child care resource and referral services. The maximum total credit that may be claimed by a taxpayer cannot exceed $150,000 per taxable year.

Qualified child care expenses include costs paid or incurred: (1) to acquire, construct, rehabilitate or expand property that is to be used as part of the taxpayer's qualified child care facility; (2) for the operation of the taxpayer's qualified child care facility, including the costs of training and certain compensation for employees of the child care facility, and scholarship programs; or (3) under a contract with a qualified child care facility to provide child care services to employees of the taxpayer. To be a qualified child care facility, the principal use of the facility must be for child care (unless it is the principal residence of the taxpayer), and the facility must meet all applicable State and local laws and regulations, including any licensing laws. A facility is not treated as a qualified child care facility with respect to a taxpayer unless: (1) it has open

[1549] EGTRRA increased the maximum credit and exclusion to $10,000 (indexed for inflation after 2002) for both non-special needs and special needs adoptions, increased the phase-out starting point to $150,000 (indexed for inflation after 2002), and allowed the credit against the AMT. Section 10909 of the Patient Protection and Affordable Care Act, Pub. L. No. 111–148: (1) extended the EGTRRA expansion of the adoption credit and exclusion from income for employer-provided adoption assistance for one year (for 2011); (2) increased by $1,000 (to $13,170, indexed for inflation) the maximum adoption credit and exclusion from income for employer-provided adoption assistance for two years (2010 and 2011); and (3) made the credit refundable for two years (2010 and 2011).

enrollment to the employees of the taxpayer; (2) use of the facility (or eligibility to use such facility) does not discriminate in favor of highly compensated employees of the taxpayer (within the meaning of section 414(q) of the Code); and (3) at least 30 percent of the children enrolled in the center are dependents of the taxpayer's employees, if the facility is the principal trade or business of the taxpayer. Qualified child care resource and referral expenses are amounts paid or incurred under a contract to provide child care resource and referral services to the employees of the taxpayer. Qualified child care services and qualified child care resource and referral expenditures must be provided (or be eligible for use) in a way that does not discriminate in favor of highly compensated employees of the taxpayer (within the meaning of section 414(q) of the Code).

Any amounts for which the taxpayer may otherwise claim a tax deduction are reduced by the amount of these credits. Similarly, if the credits are taken for expenses of acquiring, constructing, rehabilitating, or expanding a facility, the taxpayer's basis in the facility is reduced by the amount of the credits.

Credits taken for the expenses of acquiring, constructing, rehabilitating, or expanding a qualified facility are subject to recapture for the first ten years after the qualified child care facility is placed in service. The amount of recapture is reduced as a percentage of the applicable credit over the 10-year recapture period. Recapture takes effect if the taxpayer either ceases operation of the qualified child care facility or transfers its interest in the qualified child care facility without securing an agreement to assume recapture liability for the transferee. The recapture tax is not treated as a tax for purposes of determining the amount of other credits or determining the amount of the alternative minimum tax. Other rules apply.

This tax credit expires for taxable years beginning after December 31, 2010.

### *Dependent care tax credit*

The maximum dependent care tax credit is $1,050 (35 percent of up to $3,000 of eligible expenses) if there is one qualifying individual, and $2,100 (35 percent of up to $6,000 of eligible expenses) if there are two or more qualifying individuals. The 35-percent credit rate is reduced, but not below 20 percent, by one percentage point for each $2,000 (or fraction thereof) of adjusted gross income ("AGI") above $15,000. Therefore, the credit percentage is reduced to 20 percent for taxpayers with AGI over $43,000.

The level of this credit is reduced for taxable years beginning after December 31, 2010, under the EGTRRA sunset.

## *Explanation of Provision*

### *Adoption credit and exclusion from income for employer-provided adoption assistance*

The provision extends the EGTRRA expansion of these two benefits for one year (2012). Therefore, for 2012, the maximum benefit is $12,170 (indexed for inflation after 2010). The adoption credit and exclusion are phased out ratably for taxpayers with modified adjusted gross income between $182,520 and $222,520 (indexed for inflation after 2010).[1550]

***Employer-provided child care tax credit***

The provision extends this tax benefit for two years (through 2012).

***Expansion of dependent care tax credit***

The provision extends the dependent care tax credit EGTRRA expansion for two years (through 2012).

### *Effective Date*

The provisions apply to taxable years beginning after December 31, 2010.

## G. Alaska Native Settlement Trusts (sec. 101 of the Act and sec. 646 of the Code)

### *Present Law*

The Alaska Native Claims Settlement Act ("ANCSA")[1551] established Alaska Native Corporations to hold property for Alaska Natives. Alaska Natives are generally the only permitted common shareholders of those corporations under section 7(h) of ANCSA, unless an Alaska Native Corporation specifically allows other shareholders under specified procedures.

ANCSA permits an Alaska Native Corporation to transfer money or other property to an Alaska Native Settlement Trust ("Settlement Trust") for the benefit of beneficiaries who constitute all or a class of the shareholders of the Alaska Native Corporation, to promote the health, education and welfare of beneficiaries and to preserve the heritage and culture of Alaska Natives.[1552]

Alaska Native Corporations and Settlement Trusts, as well as their shareholders and beneficiaries, are generally subject to tax under the same rules and in the same manner as other taxpayers that are corporations, trusts, shareholders, or beneficiaries.

Special tax rules enacted in 2001 allow an election to use a more favorable tax regime for transfers of property by an Alaska Native Corporation to a Settlement Trust and for income taxation of the Settlement Trust. There is also simplified reporting to beneficiaries.

Under the special tax rules, a Settlement Trust may make an irrevocable election to pay tax on taxable income at the lowest rate specified for individuals (rather than the highest rate that is generally applicable to trusts) and to pay tax on capital gains at a rate consistent with being subject to such lowest rate of tax. As described further below, beneficiaries may generally thereafter ex-

[1550] The changes to the adoption credit and exclusion from employer-provided adoption assistance for 2010 and 2011 (relating to the $1,000 increase in the maximum credit and exclusion and the refundability of the credit) enacted as part of the Patient Protection and Affordable Care Act, Pub. L. No. 111–148, are not extended by the provision.

[1551] 43 U.S.C. 1601 *et. seq*.

[1552] With certain exceptions, once an Alaska Native Corporation has made a conveyance to a Settlement Trust, the assets conveyed shall not be subject to attachment, distraint, or sale or execution of judgment, except with respect to the lawful debts and obligations of the Settlement Trust.

clude from gross income distributions from a trust that has made this election. Also, contributions from an Alaska Native Corporation to an electing Settlement Trust generally will not result in the recognition of gross income by beneficiaries on account of the contribution. An electing Settlement Trust remains subject to generally applicable requirements for classification and taxation as a trust.

A Settlement Trust distribution is excludable from the gross income of beneficiaries to the extent of the taxable income of the Settlement Trust for the taxable year and all prior taxable years for which an election was in effect, decreased by income tax paid by the Trust, plus tax-exempt interest from State and local bonds for the same period. Amounts distributed in excess of the amount excludable is taxed to the beneficiaries as if distributed by the sponsoring Alaska Native Corporation in the year of distribution by the Trust, which means that the beneficiaries must include in gross income as dividends the amount of the distribution, up to the current and accumulated earnings and profits of the Alaska Native Corporation. Amounts distributed in excess of the current and accumulated earnings and profits are not included in gross income by the beneficiaries.

A special loss disallowance rule reduces (but not below zero) any loss that would otherwise be recognized upon disposition of stock of a sponsoring Alaska Native Corporation by a proportion, determined on a per share basis, of all contributions to all electing Settlement Trusts by the sponsoring Alaska Native Corporation. This rule prevents a stockholder from being able to take advantage of a decrease in value of an Alaska Native Corporation that is caused by a transfer of assets from the Alaska Native Corporation to a Settlement Trust.

The fiduciary of an electing Settlement Trust is obligated to provide certain information relating to distributions from the trust in lieu of reporting requirements under Section 6034A.

The earnings and profits of an Alaska Native Corporation are not reduced by the amount of its contributions to an electing Trust at the time of the contributions. However, the Alaska Native Corporation earnings and profits are reduced as and when distributions are thereafter made by the electing Trust that are taxed to the beneficiaries as dividends from the Alaska Native Corporation to the beneficiaries.

The election to pay tax at the lowest rate is not available in certain disqualifying cases: (a) where transfer restrictions have been modified either to allow a transfer of a beneficial interest that would not be permitted by section 7(h) of the Alaska Native Claims Settlement Act if the interest were Settlement Common stock, or (b) where transfer restrictions have been modified to allow a transfer of any Stock in an Alaska Native Corporation that would not be permitted by section 7(h) if it were Settlement Common Stock and the Alaska Native Corporation thereafter makes a transfer to the Trust. Where an election is already in effect at the time of such disqualifying situations, the special rules applicable to an electing trust cease to apply and rules generally applicable to trusts apply. In addition, the distributable net income of the trust is increased by undistributed current and accumulated earnings and profits of the trust, limited by the fair market value of trust assets at the date the trust becomes so disposable. The effect is to cause the trust to be taxed at regular trust rates on the amount of recomputed distributable net income not distributed to beneficiaries, and to cause the beneficiaries to be taxed on the amount of any distributions received consistent with the applicable tax rate bracket.[1553]

### *Explanation of Provision*

The provision delays for two years the EGTRRA sunset as it applies to electing Settlement Trusts.

### *Effective Date*

The provision is effective for taxable years of electing Settlement Trusts, their beneficiaries, and sponsoring Alaska Native Corporations beginning after December 31, 2010.

## H. Reduced Rate on Dividends and Capital Gains (sec. 102 of the Act and sec. 1(h) of the Code)

### *Present Law*

#### *Dividends*

*In general*

A dividend is the distribution of property made by a corporation to its shareholders out of its after-tax earnings and profits.

*Tax rates before 2011*

An individual's qualified dividend income is taxed at the same rates that apply to net capital gain. This treatment applies for purposes of both the regular tax and the alternative minimum tax. Thus, for taxable years beginning before 2011, an individual's qualified dividend income is taxed at rates of zero and 15 percent. The zero-percent rate applies to qualified dividend income which otherwise would be taxed at a 10- or 15-percent rate if the special rates did not apply.

Qualified dividend income generally includes dividends received from domestic corporations and qualified foreign corporations. The term "qualified foreign corporation" includes a foreign corporation that is eligible for the benefits of a comprehensive income tax treaty with the United States which the Treasury Department determines to be satisfactory and which includes an exchange of information program. In addition, a foreign corporation is treated as a qualified foreign corporation for any dividend paid by the corporation with respect to stock that is readily tradable on an established securities market in the United States.

If a shareholder does not hold a share of stock for more than 60 days during the 121-day period beginning 60 days before the ex-dividend date (as measured under section 246(c)), dividends received on the stock are not eligible for the reduced rates. Also, the

[1553] These provisions were enacted by section 671 of the Economic Growth and Tax Relief Reconciliation Act of 2001, Pub. L. No. 107–16, scheduled to sunset in taxable years beginning after December 31, 2010. See H.R. Rep. No. 107–84 (2001).

reduced rates are not available for dividends to the extent that the taxpayer is obligated to make related payments with respect to positions in substantially similar or related property.

Dividends received from a corporation that is a passive foreign investment company (as defined in section 1297) in either the taxable year of the distribution, or the preceding taxable year, are not qualified dividends.

Special rules apply in determining a taxpayer's foreign tax credit limitation under section 904 in the case of qualified dividend income. For these purposes, rules similar to the rules of section 904(b)(2)(B) concerning adjustments to the foreign tax credit limitation to reflect any capital gain rate differential will apply to any qualified dividend income.

If a taxpayer receives an extraordinary dividend (within the meaning of section 1059(c)) eligible for the reduced rates with respect to any share of stock, any loss on the sale of the stock is treated as a long-term capital loss to the extent of the dividend.

A dividend is treated as investment income for purposes of determining the amount of deductible investment interest only if the taxpayer elects to treat the dividend as not eligible for the reduced rates.

The amount of dividends qualifying for reduced rates that may be paid by a regulated investment company ("RIC") for any taxable year in which the qualified dividend income received by the RIC is less than 95 percent of its gross income (as specially computed) may not exceed the sum of (1) the qualified dividend income of the RIC for the taxable year and (2) the amount of earnings and profits accumulated in a non-RIC taxable year that were distributed by the RIC during the taxable year.

The amount of dividends qualifying for reduced rates that may be paid by a real estate investment trust ("REIT") for any taxable year may not exceed the sum of (1) the qualified dividend income of the REIT for the taxable year, (2) an amount equal to the excess of the income subject to the taxes imposed by section 857(b)(1) and the regulations prescribed under section 337(d) for the preceding taxable year over the amount of these taxes for the preceding taxable year, and (3) the amount of earnings and profits accumulated in a non-REIT taxable year that were distributed by the REIT during the taxable year.

The reduced rates do not apply to dividends received from an organization that was exempt from tax under section 501 or was a tax-exempt farmers' cooperative in either the taxable year of the distribution or the preceding taxable year; dividends received from a mutual savings bank that received a deduction under section 591; or deductible dividends paid on employer securities.[1554]

*Tax rates after 2010*

For taxable years beginning after 2010, dividends received by an individual are taxed at ordinary income tax rates.

---

[1554] In addition, for taxable years beginning before 2011, amounts treated as ordinary income on the disposition of certain preferred stock (sec. 306) are treated as dividends for purposes of applying the reduced rates; the tax rate for the accumulated earnings tax (sec. 531) and the personal holding company tax (sec. 541) is reduced to 15 percent; and the collapsible corporation rules (sec. 341) are repealed.

### *Capital gains*

#### *In general*

In general, gain or loss reflected in the value of an asset is not recognized for income tax purposes until a taxpayer disposes of the asset. On the sale or exchange of a capital asset, any gain generally is included in income. Any net capital gain of an individual generally is taxed at rates lower than rates applicable to ordinary income. Net capital gain is the excess of the net long-term capital gain for the taxable year over the net short-term capital loss for the year. Gain or loss is treated as long-term if the asset is held for more than one year.

Capital losses generally are deductible in full against capital gains. In addition, individual taxpayers may deduct capital losses against up to $3,000 of ordinary income in each year. Any remaining unused capital losses may be carried forward indefinitely to another taxable year.

A capital asset generally means any property except (1) inventory, stock in trade, or property held primarily for sale to customers in the ordinary course of the taxpayer's trade or business, (2) depreciable or real property used in the taxpayer's trade or business, (3) specified literary or artistic property, (4) business accounts or notes receivable, (5) certain U.S. publications, (6) certain commodity derivative financial instruments, (7) hedging transactions, and (8) business supplies. In addition, the net gain from the disposition of certain property used in the taxpayer's trade or business is treated as long-term capital gain. Gain from the disposition of depreciable personal property is not treated as capital gain to the extent of all previous depreciation allowances. Gain from the disposition of depreciable real property is generally not treated as capital gain to the extent of the depreciation allowances in excess of the allowances available under the straight-line method of depreciation.

#### *Tax rates before 2011*

Under present law, for taxable years beginning before January 1, 2011, the maximum rate of tax on the adjusted net capital gain of an individual is 15 percent. Any adjusted net capital gain which otherwise would be taxed at a 10- or 15-percent rate is taxed at a zero rate. These rates apply for purposes of both the regular tax and the AMT.

Under present law, the "adjusted net capital gain" of an individual is the net capital gain reduced (but not below zero) by the sum of the 28-percent rate gain and the unrecaptured section 1250 gain. The net capital gain is reduced by the amount of gain that the individual treats as investment income for purposes of determining the investment interest limitation under section 163(d).

The term "28-percent rate gain" means the excess of the sum of the amount of net gain attributable to long-term capital gains and losses from the sale or exchange of collectibles (as defined in section 408(m) without regard to paragraph (3) thereof) and the amount of gain equal to the additional amount of gain that would be excluded from gross income under section 1202 (relating to certain small business stock) if the percentage limitations of section

1202(a) did not apply, over the sum of the net short-term capital loss for the taxable year and any long-term capital loss carryover to the taxable year.

"Unrecaptured section 1250 gain" means any long-term capital gain from the sale or exchange of section 1250 property (i.e., depreciable real estate) held more than one year to the extent of the gain that would have been treated as ordinary income if section 1250 applied to all depreciation, reduced by the net loss (if any) attributable to the items taken into account in computing 28-percent rate gain. The amount of unrecaptured section 1250 gain (before the reduction for the net loss) attributable to the disposition of property to which section 1231 (relating to certain property used in a trade or business) applies may not exceed the net section 1231 gain for the year.

An individual's unrecaptured section 1250 gain is taxed at a maximum rate of 25 percent, and the 28-percent rate gain is taxed at a maximum rate of 28 percent. Any amount of unrecaptured section 1250 gain or 28-percent rate gain otherwise taxed at a 10- or 15-percent rate is taxed at the otherwise applicable rate.

*Tax rates after 2010*

For taxable years beginning after December 31, 2010, the maximum rate of tax on the adjusted net capital gain of an individual is 20 percent. Any adjusted net capital gain which otherwise would be taxed at the 15-percent rate is taxed at a 10-percent rate.

In addition, any gain from the sale or exchange of property held more than five years that would otherwise have been taxed at the 10-percent capital gain rate is taxed at an 8-percent rate. Any gain from the sale or exchange of property held more than five years and the holding period for which began after December 31, 2000, that would otherwise have been taxed at a 20-percent rate is taxed at an 18-percent rate.

The tax rates on 28-percent gain and unrecaptured section 1250 gain are the same as for taxable years beginning before 2011.

### *Explanation of Provision*

Under the provision, the regular and minimum tax rates for qualified dividend income and capital gain in effect before 2011 are extended for two additional years (through 2012).

### *Effective Date*

The provision applies to taxable years beginning after December 31, 2010.

## I. Extend American Opportunity Tax Credit (sec. 103 of the Act and sec. 25A of the Code)

### *Present Law*

#### ***Hope credit***

For taxable years beginning before 2009 and after 2010, individual taxpayers are allowed to claim a nonrefundable credit, the Hope credit, against Federal income taxes of up to $1,800 (for 2008) per eligible student per year for qualified tuition and related expenses paid for the first two years of the student's post-secondary education in a degree or certificate program. The Hope credit rate is 100 percent on the first $1,200 of qualified tuition and related expenses, and 50 percent on the next $1,200 of qualified tuition and related expenses; these dollar amounts are indexed for inflation, with the amount rounded down to the next lowest multiple of $100. Thus, for example, a taxpayer who incurs $1,200 of qualified tuition and related expenses for an eligible student is eligible (subject to the adjusted gross income phaseout described below) for a $1,200 Hope credit. If a taxpayer incurs $2,400 of qualified tuition and related expenses for an eligible student, then he or she is eligible for a $1,800 Hope credit.

The Hope credit that a taxpayer may otherwise claim is phased out ratably for taxpayers with modified AGI between $48,000 and $58,000 ($96,000 and $116,000 for married taxpayers filing a joint return) for 2008. The beginning points of the AGI phaseout ranges are indexed for inflation, with the amount rounded down to the next lowest multiple of $1,000. The size of the phaseout ranges are always $10,000 and $20,000 respectively.

The qualified tuition and related expenses must be incurred on behalf of the taxpayer, the taxpayer's spouse, or a dependent of the taxpayer. The Hope credit is available with respect to an individual student for two taxable years, provided that the student has not completed the first two years of post-secondary education before the beginning of the second taxable year.

The Hope credit is available in the taxable year the expenses are paid, subject to the requirement that the education is furnished to the student during that year or during an academic period beginning during the first three months of the next taxable year. Qualified tuition and related expenses paid with the proceeds of a loan generally are eligible for the Hope credit. The repayment of a loan itself is not a qualified tuition or related expense.

A taxpayer may claim the Hope credit with respect to an eligible student who is not the taxpayer or the taxpayer's spouse (e.g., in cases in which the student is the taxpayer's child) only if the taxpayer claims the student as a dependent for the taxable year for which the credit is claimed. If a student is claimed as a dependent, the student is not entitled to claim a Hope credit for that taxable year on the student's own tax return. If a parent (or other taxpayer) claims a student as a dependent, any qualified tuition and related expenses paid by the student are treated as paid by the parent (or other taxpayer) for purposes of determining the amount of qualified tuition and related expenses paid by such parent (or other taxpayer) under the provision. In addition, for each taxable year, a taxpayer may elect either the Hope credit, the Lifetime Learning credit, or an above-the-line deduction for qualified tuition and related expenses with respect to an eligible student.

The Hope credit is available for "qualified tuition and related expenses," which include tuition and fees (excluding nonacademic fees) required to be paid to an eligible educational institution as a condition of enrollment or attendance of an eligible student at the institution. Charges and fees associated with meals, lodging, insurance, transportation, and similar personal, living, or family expenses are not eligible for the credit. The expenses of education involving sports, games, or hobbies are not qualified tuition and related expenses unless this education is part of the student's degree program.

Qualified tuition and related expenses generally include only out-of-pocket expenses. Qualified tuition and related expenses do not include expenses covered by employer-provided educational assistance and scholarships that are not required to be included in the gross income of either the student or the taxpayer claiming the credit. Thus, total qualified tuition and related expenses are reduced by any scholarship or fellowship grants excludable from gross income under section 117 and any other tax-free educational benefits received by the student (or the taxpayer claiming the credit) during the taxable year. The Hope credit is not allowed with respect to any education expense for which a deduction is claimed under section 162 or any other section of the Code.

An eligible student for purposes of the Hope credit is an individual who is enrolled in a degree, certificate, or other program (including a program of study abroad approved for credit by the institution at which such student is enrolled) leading to a recognized educational credential at an eligible educational institution. The student must pursue a course of study on at least a half-time basis. A student is considered to pursue a course of study on at least a half-time basis if the student carries at least one half the normal full-time work load for the course of study the student is pursuing for at least one academic period that begins during the taxable year. To be eligible for the Hope credit, a student must not have been convicted of a Federal or State felony consisting of the possession or distribution of a controlled substance.

Eligible educational institutions generally are accredited post-secondary educational institutions offering credit toward a bachelor's degree, an associate's degree, or another recognized post-secondary credential. Certain proprietary institutions and post-secondary vocational institutions also are eligible educational institutions. To qualify as an eligible educational institution, an institution must be eligible to participate in Department of Education student aid programs.

Effective for taxable years beginning after December 31, 2010, the changes to the Hope credit made by EGTRRA no longer apply. The principal EGTRRA change scheduled to expire is the change that permits a taxpayer to claim a Hope credit in the same year that he or she claims an exclusion from a Coverdell education savings account. Thus, after 2010, a taxpayer cannot claim a Hope credit in the same year he or she claims an exclusion from a Coverdell education savings account.

### *American opportunity tax credit*

The American Opportunity Tax Credit refers to modifications to the Hope credit that apply for taxable years beginning in 2009 or 2010. The maximum allowable modified credit is $2,500 per eligible student per year for qualified tuition and related expenses paid for each of the first four years of the student's post-secondary education in a degree or certificate program. The modified credit rate is 100 percent on the first $2,000 of qualified tuition and related expenses, and 25 percent on the next $2,000 of qualified tuition and related expenses. For purposes of the modified credit, the definition of qualified tuition and related expenses is expanded to include course materials.

Under the provision, the modified credit is available with respect to an individual student for four years, provided that the student has not completed the first four years of post-secondary education before the beginning of the fourth taxable year. Thus, the modified credit, in addition to other modifications, extends the application of the Hope credit to two more years of post-secondary education.

The modified credit that a taxpayer may otherwise claim is phased out ratably for taxpayers with modified AGI between $80,000 and $90,000 ($160,000 and $180,000 for married taxpayers filing a joint return). The modified credit may be claimed against a taxpayer's AMT liability.

Forty percent of a taxpayer's otherwise allowable modified credit is refundable. However, no portion of the modified credit is refundable if the taxpayer claiming the credit is a child to whom section 1(g) applies for such taxable year (generally, any child who has at least one living parent, does not file a joint return, and is either under age 18 or under age 24 and a student providing less than one-half of his or her own support).

Bona fide residents of the U.S. possessions are not permitted to claim the refundable portion of the modified credit in the United States. Rather, a bona fide resident of a mirror code possession (Commonwealth of the Northern Mariana Islands, Guam, and the Virgin Islands) may claim the refundable portion of the credit in the possession in which the individual is a resident. Similarly, a bona fide resident of a non-mirror code possession (Commonwealth of Puerto Rico and American Samoa) may claim the refundable portion of the credit in the possession in which the individual is resident, but only if the possession establishes a plan for permitting the claim under its internal law. The U.S. Treasury will make payments to the possession in respect of credits allowable to their residents under their internal laws.

### *Explanation of Provision*

The provision extends for two years (through 2012) the temporary modifications to the Hope credit for taxable years beginning in 2009 and 2010 that are known as the American Opportunity Tax Credit, including the rules governing the treatment of the U.S. possessions.

### *Effective Date*

The provision is effective for taxable years beginning after December 31, 2010.

## J. Child Tax Credit (sec. 103 of the Act and sec. 24 of the Code)

### *Present Law*

An individual may claim a tax credit for each qualifying child under the age of 17. The maximum amount of the credit per child is $1,000 through 2010 and $500 thereafter. A child who is not a citizen, national, or resident of the United States cannot be a qualifying child.

The aggregate amount of child credits that may be claimed is phased out for individuals with income over certain threshold amounts. Specifically, the otherwise allowable aggregate child tax credit amount is reduced by $50 for each $1,000 (or fraction thereof) of modified adjusted gross income ("modified AGI") over $75,000 for single individuals or heads of households, $110,000 for married individuals filing joint returns, and $55,000 for married individuals filing separate returns. For purposes of this limitation, modified AGI includes certain otherwise excludable income earned by U.S. citizens or residents living abroad or in certain U.S. territories.

The credit is allowable against the regular tax and, for taxable years beginning before January 1, 2011, is allowed against the alternative minimum tax ("AMT"). To the extent the child tax credit exceeds the taxpayer's tax liability, the taxpayer is eligible for a refundable credit (the additional child tax credit) equal to 15 percent of earned income in excess of a threshold dollar amount (the "earned income" formula). EGTRRA provided, in general, that this threshold dollar amount is $10,000 indexed for inflation from 2001. The American Recovery and Reinvestment Act of 2009 set the threshold at $3,000 for both 2009 and 2010. After 2010, the ability to determine the refundable child credit based on earned income in excess of the threshold dollar amount expires.

Families with three or more qualifying children may determine the additional child tax credit using the "alternative formula" if this results in a larger credit than determined under the earned income formula. Under the alternative formula, the additional child tax credit equals the amount by which the taxpayer's social security taxes exceed the taxpayer's earned income tax credit ("EITC"). After 2010, due to the expiration of the earned income formula, this is the only manner of obtaining a refundable child credit.

Earned income is defined as the sum of wages, salaries, tips, and other taxable employee compensation plus net self-employment earnings. Unlike the EITC, which also includes the preceding items in its definition of earned income, the additional child tax credit is based only on earned income to the extent it is included in computing taxable income. For example, some ministers' parsonage allowances are considered self-employment income, and thus are considered earned income for purposes of computing the EITC, but the allowances are excluded from gross income for individual income tax purposes, and thus are not considered earned income for purposes of the additional child tax credit since the income is not included in taxable income.

### *Explanation of Provision*

The provision extends for two years the earned income threshold of $3,000. Also, the provision stops indexation for inflation of the $3,000 earnings threshold for that period.

### *Effective Date*

The provision applies to taxable years beginning after December 31, 2010.

## K. Increase in the Earned Income Tax Credit (sec. 103 of the Act and sec. 32 of the Code)

### *Present Law*

#### *Overview*

Low- and moderate-income workers may be eligible for the refundable earned income tax credit ("EITC"). Eligibility for the EITC is based on earned income, adjusted gross income, investment income, filing status, number of children, and immigration and work status in the United States. The amount of the EITC is based on the presence and number of qualifying children in the worker's family, as well as on adjusted gross income and earned income.

The EITC generally equals a specified percentage of earned income up to a maximum dollar amount. The maximum amount applies over a certain income range and then diminishes to zero over a specified phaseout range. For taxpayers with earned income (or adjusted gross income ("AGI"), if greater) in excess of the beginning of the phaseout range, the maximum EITC amount is reduced by the phaseout rate multiplied by the amount of earned income (or AGI, if greater) in excess of the beginning of the phaseout range. For taxpayers with earned income (or AGI, if greater) in excess of the end of the phaseout range, no credit is allowed.

An individual is not eligible for the EITC if the aggregate amount of disqualified income of the taxpayer for the taxable year exceeds $3,100 (for 2010). This threshold is indexed for inflation. Disqualified income is the sum of: (1) interest (both taxable and tax exempt); (2) dividends; (3) net rent and royalty income (if greater than zero); (4) capital gains net income; and (5) net passive income that is not self-employment income (if greater than zero).

The EITC is a refundable credit, meaning that if the amount of the credit exceeds the taxpayer's Federal income tax liability, the excess is payable to the taxpayer as a direct transfer payment.

#### *Filing status*

An unmarried individual may claim the EITC if he or she files as a single filer or as a head of household. Married individuals generally may not claim the EITC unless they file jointly. An exception to the joint return filing requirement applies to certain spouses who are separated. Under this exception, a married taxpayer who is separated from his or her spouse for the last six months of the taxable year is not considered to be married (and, accordingly, may file a return as head of household and claim the EITC), provided that the taxpayer maintains a household that constitutes the principal place of abode for a dependent child (including a son, stepson, daughter, stepdaughter, adopted child, or a foster child) for over half the taxable year, and pays over half the cost of maintaining the household in which he or she resides with the child during the year.

### *Presence of qualifying children and amount of the earned income credit*

Four separate credit schedules apply: one schedule for taxpayers with no qualifying children, one schedule for taxpayers with one qualifying child, one schedule for taxpayers with two qualifying children, and one schedule for taxpayers with three or more qualifying children.

Taxpayers with no qualifying children may claim a credit if they are over age 24 and below age 65. The credit is 7.65 percent of earnings up to $5,980, resulting in a maximum credit of $457 for 2010. The maximum is available for those with incomes between $5,980 and $7,480 ($12,490 if married filing jointly). The credit begins to phase out at a rate of 7.65 percent of earnings above $7,480 ($12,480 if married filing jointly) resulting in a $0 credit at $13,460 of earnings ($18,470 if married filing jointly).

Taxpayers with one qualifying child may claim a credit in 2010 of 34 percent of their earnings up to $8,970, resulting in a maximum credit of $3,050. The maximum credit is available for those with earnings between $8,970 and $16,450 ($21,460 if married filing jointly). The credit begins to phase out at a rate of 15.98 percent of earnings above $16,450 ($21,460 if married filing jointly). The credit is completely phased out at $35,535 of earnings ($40,545 if married filing jointly).

Taxpayers with two qualifying children may claim a credit in 2010 of 40 percent of earnings up to $12,590, resulting in a maximum credit of $5,036. The maximum credit is available for those with earnings between $12,590 and $16,450 ($21,460 if married filing jointly). The credit begins to phase out at a rate of 21.06 percent of earnings above $16,450 ($21,460 if married filing jointly). The credit is completely phased out at $40,363 of earnings ($45,373 if married filing jointly).

A temporary provision enacted by ARRA allows taxpayers with three or more qualifying children to claim a credit of 45 percent for 2009 and 2010. For example, in 2010 taxpayers with three or more qualifying children may claim a credit of 45 percent of earnings up to $12,590, resulting in a maximum credit of $5,666. The maximum credit is available for those with earnings between $12,590 and $16,450 ($21,460 if married filing jointly). The credit begins to phase out at a rate of 21.06 percent of earnings above $16,450 ($21,460 if married filing jointly). The credit is completely phased out at $43,352 of earnings ($48,362 if married filing jointly).

Under another provision of ARRA, the phase-out thresholds for married couples were raised to an amount $5,000 above that for other filers for 2009 (and indexed for inflation). The increase is $5,010 for 2010. Formerly, the phase-out thresholds for married couples were $3,000 (indexed for inflation from 2008) greater than those for other filers as provided for in EGTRRA.

If more than one taxpayer lives with a qualifying child, only one of these taxpayers may claim the child for purposes of the EITC. If multiple eligible taxpayers actually claim the same qualifying child, then a tiebreaker rule determines which taxpayer is entitled to the EITC with respect to the qualifying child. Any eligible taxpayer with at least one qualifying child who does not claim the EITC with respect to qualifying children due to failure to meet certain identification requirements with respect to such children (i.e., providing the name, age and taxpayer identification number of each of such children) may not claim the EITC for taxpayers without qualifying children.

### *Explanation of Provision*

The provision extends the EITC at a rate of 45 percent for three or more qualifying children for two years (through 2012).

The provision extends the higher phase-out thresholds for married couples filing joint returns enacted as part of ARRA for two years (through 2012).

### *Effective Date*

The provision applies to taxable years beginning after December 31, 2010.

## TITLE II—TEMPORARY EXTENSION OF INDIVIDUAL ALTERNATIVE MINIMUM TAX RELIEF

### A. Extension of Alternative Minimum Tax Relief for Nonrefundable Personal Credits and Increased Alternative Minimum Tax Exemption Amount (secs. 201 and 202 of the Act and secs. 26 and 55 of the Code)

### *Present Law*

Present law imposes an alternative minimum tax ("AMT") on individuals. The AMT is the amount by which the tentative minimum tax exceeds the regular income tax. An individual's tentative minimum tax is the sum of (1) 26 percent of so much of the taxable excess as does not exceed $175,000 ($87,500 in the case of a married individual filing a separate return) and (2) 28 percent of the remaining taxable excess. The taxable excess is so much of the alternative minimum taxable income ("AMTI") as exceeds the exemption amount. The maximum tax rates on net capital gain and dividends used in computing the regular tax are used in computing the tentative minimum tax. AMTI is the individual's taxable income adjusted to take account of specified preferences and adjustments.

The exemption amounts are: (1) $70,950 for taxable years beginning in 2009 and $45,000 in taxable years beginning after 2009 in the case of married individuals filing a joint return and surviving spouses; (2) $46,700 for taxable years beginning in 2009 and $33,750 in taxable years beginning after 2009 in the case of other unmarried individuals; (3) $35,475 for taxable years beginning in 2009 and $22,500 in taxable years beginning after 2009 in the case of married individuals filing separate returns; and (4) $22,500 in the case of an estate or trust. The exemption amount is phased out by an amount equal to 25 percent of the amount by which the individual's AMTI exceeds (1) $150,000 in the case of married individuals filing a joint return and surviving spouses, (2) $112,500 in the case of other unmarried individuals, and (3) $75,000 in the case of married individuals filing separate returns or an estate or a trust. These amounts are not indexed for inflation.

Present law provides for certain nonrefundable personal tax credits (i.e., the dependent care credit, the credit for the elderly and disabled, the child credit, the credit for interest on certain home mortgages, the Hope Scholarship and Lifetime Learning credits, the credit for savers, the credit for certain nonbusiness energy property, the credit for residential energy efficient property, the credit for certain plug-in electric vehicles, the credit for alternative motor vehicles, the credit for new qualified plug-in electric drive motor vehicles, and the D.C. first-time homebuyer credit).

For taxable years beginning before 2010, the nonrefundable personal credits are allowed to the extent of the full amount of the individual's regular tax and alternative minimum tax.

For taxable years beginning after 2009, the nonrefundable personal credits (other than the child credit, the credit for savers, the credit for residential energy efficient property, the credit for certain plug-in electric drive motor vehicles, the credit for alternative motor vehicles, and credit for new qualified plug-in electric drive motor vehicles) are allowed only to the extent that the individual's regular income tax liability exceeds the individual's tentative minimum tax, determined without regard to the minimum tax foreign tax credit. The remaining nonrefundable personal credits are allowed to the full extent of the individual's regular tax and alternative minimum tax.[1555]

### *Explanation of Provisions*

The provision allows an individual to offset the entire regular tax liability and alternative minimum tax liability by the nonrefundable personal credits for 2010 and 2011.

The provision provides that the individual AMT exemption amount for taxable years beginning in 2010 is (1) $72,450, in the case of married individuals filing a joint return and surviving spouses; (2) $47,450 in the case of other unmarried individuals; and (3) $36,225 in the case of married individuals filing separate returns.

The provision provides that the individual AMT exemption amount for taxable years beginning in 2011 is (1) $74,450, in the case of married individuals filing a joint return and surviving spouses; (2) $48,450 in the case of other unmarried individuals; and (3) $37,225 in the case of married individuals filing separate returns.

### *Effective Date*

The provision is effective for taxable years beginning after 2009.

[1555] The rule applicable to the child credit after 2010 is subject to the EGTRRA sunset. The adoption credit is refundable in 2010 and 2011 and beginning in 2012 is nonrefundable and treated for purposes of the AMT in the same manner as the child credit.

# TITLE III—TEMPORARY ESTATE TAX RELIEF

## A. Modify and Extend the Estate, Gift, and Generation Skipping Transfer Taxes After 2009 (sections 301–304 of the Act and sections 2001, 2010, 2502, 2505, 2511, 2631, and 6018 of the Code)

### *Present and Prior Law*

#### *In general*

In general, a gift tax is imposed on certain lifetime transfers and an estate tax is imposed on certain transfers at death. A generation skipping transfer tax generally is imposed on certain transfers, either directly or in trust or similar arrangement, to a "skip person" (i.e., a beneficiary in a generation more than one generation younger than that of the transferor). Transfers subject to the generation skipping transfer tax include direct skips, taxable terminations, and taxable distributions.

The estate and generation skipping transfers taxes are repealed for decedents dying and gifts made during 2010, but are reinstated for decedents dying and gifts made after 2010.

#### *Exemption equivalent amounts and applicable tax rates*

*In general*

Under present law in effect through 2009 and after 2010, a unified credit is available with respect to taxable transfers by gift and at death.[1556] The unified credit offsets tax computed at the lowest estate and gift tax rates.

Before 2004, the estate and gift taxes were fully unified, such that a single graduated rate schedule and a single effective exemption amount of the unified credit applied for purposes of determining the tax on cumulative taxable transfers made by a taxpayer during his or her lifetime and at death. For years 2004 through 2009, the gift tax and the estate tax continued to be determined using a single graduated rate schedule, but the effective exemption amount allowed for estate tax purposes was higher than the effective exemption amount allowed for gift tax purposes. In 2009, the highest estate and gift tax rate was 45 percent. The unified credit effective exemption amount was $3.5 million for estate tax purposes and $1 million for gift tax purposes.

For 2009 and after 2010, the generation skipping transfer tax is imposed using a flat rate equal to the highest estate tax rate on cumulative generation skipping transfers in excess of the exemption amount in effect at the time of the transfer. The generation skipping transfer tax exemption for a given year (prior to and after repeal, discussed below) is equal to the unified credit effective exemption amount for estate tax purposes.

*Repeal of estate and generation skipping transfer taxes in 2010; modifications to gift tax*

Under EGTRRA, the estate and generation skipping transfer taxes are repealed for decedents dying and generation skipping

[1556] Sec. 2010.

transfers made during 2010. The gift tax remains in effect during 2010, with a $1 million exemption amount and a gift tax rate of 35 percent. Also in 2010, except as provided in regulations, certain transfers in trust are treated as transfers of property by gift, unless the trust is treated as wholly owned by the donor or the donor's spouse under the grantor trust provisions of the Code.

*Reinstatement of the estate and generation skipping transfer taxes for decedents dying and generation skipping transfers made after December 31, 2010*

The estate, gift, and generation skipping transfer tax provisions of EGTRRA sunset at the end of 2010, such that those provisions (including repeal of the estate and generation skipping transfer taxes) do not apply to estates of decedents dying, gifts made, or generation skipping transfers made after December 31, 2010. As a result, in general, the estate, gift, and generation skipping transfer tax rates and exemption amounts that would have been in effect had EGTRRA not been enacted apply for estates of decedents dying, gifts made, or generation skipping transfers made in 2011 or later years. A single graduated rate schedule with a top rate of 55 percent and a single effective exemption amount of $1 million applies for purposes of determining the tax on cumulative taxable transfers by lifetime gift or bequest.

***Basis in property received***

*In general*

Gain or loss, if any, on the disposition of property is measured by the taxpayer's amount realized (i.e., gross proceeds received) on the disposition, less the taxpayer's basis in such property.[1557] Basis generally represents a taxpayer's investment in property, with certain adjustments required after acquisition. For example, basis is increased by the cost of capital improvements made to the property and decreased by depreciation deductions taken with respect to the property.

*Basis in property received by lifetime gift*

Property received from a donor of a lifetime gift generally takes a carryover basis.[1558] "Carryover basis" means that the basis in the hands of the donee is the same as it was in the hands of the donor. The basis of property transferred by lifetime gift also is increased, but not above fair market value, by any gift tax paid by the donor. The basis of a lifetime gift, however, generally cannot exceed the property's fair market value on the date of the gift. If the basis of property is greater than the fair market value of the property on the date of the gift, then, for purposes of determining loss, the basis is the property's fair market value on the date of the gift.

[1557] Sec. 1001.
[1558] Sec. 1015.

*Basis in property received from a decedent who died in 2009*

Property passing from a decedent who died during 2009 generally takes a "stepped-up" basis.[1559] In other words, the basis of property passing from such a decedent's estate generally is the fair market value on the date of thc decedent's death (or, if the alternate valuation date is elected, the earlier of six months after the decedent's death or the date the property is sold or distributed by the estate).[1560] This step up in basis generally eliminates the recognition of income on any appreciation of the property that occurred prior to the decedent's death. If the value of property on the date of the decedent's death was less than its adjusted basis, the property takes a stepped-down basis when it passes from a decedent's estate. This stepped-down basis eliminates the tax benefit from any unrealized loss.

*Basis in property received from a decedent who dies during 2010*

The rules providing for stepped-up basis in property acquired from a decedent are repealed for assets acquired from decedents dying in 2010, and a modified carryover basis regime applies.[1561] Under this regime, recipients of property acquired from a decedent at the decedent's death receive a basis equal to the lesser of the decedent's adjusted basis or the fair market value of the property on the date of the decedent's death. The modified carryover basis rules apply to property acquired by bequest, devise, or inheritance, or property acquired by the decedent's estate from the decedent, property passing from the decedent to the extent such property passed without consideration, and certain other property to which the prior law rules apply, other than property that is income in respect of a decedent. Property acquired from a decedent is treated as if the property had been acquired by gift. Thus, the character of gain on the sale of property received from a decedent's estate is carried over to the heir. For example, real estate that has been depreciated and would be subject to recapture if sold by the decedent will be subject to recapture if sold by the heir.

An executor generally may increase the basis in assets owned by the decedent and acquired by the beneficiaries at death, subject to certain special rules and exceptions. Under these rules, each decedent's estate generally is permitted to increase the basis of assets transferred by up to a total of $1.3 million. The $1.3 million is increased by the amount of unused capital losses, net operating losses, and certain "built-in" losses of the decedent. Nonresidents who are not U.S. citizens may be allowed to increase the basis of

---

[1559] Sec. 1014.

[1560] There is an exception to the rule that assets subject to the Federal estate tax receive stepped-up basis in the case of "income in respect of a decedent." Sec. 1014(c). The basis of assets that are "income in respect of a decedent" is a carryover basis (i.e., the basis of such assets to the estate or heir is the same as it was in the hands of the decedent) increased by estate tax paid on that asset. Income in respect of a decedent includes rights to income that has been earned, but not recognized, by the date of death (e.g., wages that were earned, but not paid, before death), individual retirement accounts (IRAs), and assets held in accounts governed by section 401(k).

In community property states, a surviving spouse's one-half share of community property held by the decedent and the surviving spouse generally is treated as having passed from the decedent and, thus, is eligible for stepped-up basis. Under 2009 law, this rule applies if at least one-half of the whole of the community interest is includible in the decedent's gross estate.

[1561] Sec. 1022.

property by up to $60,000. In addition, the basis of property transferred to a surviving spouse may be increased by an additional $3 million.

*Repeal of modified carryover basis regime for determining basis in property received from a decedent who dies after December 31, 2010*

As a result of the EGTRRA sunset at the end of 2010, the modified carryover basis regime in effect for determining basis in property acquired from a decedent who dies during 2010 does not apply for purposes of determining basis in property received from a decedent who dies after December 31, 2010. Instead, the law in effect prior to 2010, which generally provides for stepped-up basis in property passing from a decedent, applies.

***State death tax credit; deduction for State death taxes paid***

*State death tax credit under prior law*

Before 2005, a credit was allowed against the Federal estate tax for any estate, inheritance, legacy, or succession taxes ("death taxes") actually paid to any State or the District of Columbia with respect to any property included in the decedent's gross estate.[1562] The maximum amount of credit allowable for State death taxes was determined under a graduated rate table, the top rate of which was 16 percent, based on the size of the decedent's adjusted taxable estate. Most States imposed a "pick-up" or "soak-up" estate tax, which served to impose a State tax equal to the maximum Federal credit allowed.

*Phase-out of State death tax credit; deduction for State death taxes paid*

Under EGTRRA, the amount of allowable State death tax credit was reduced from 2002 through 2004. For decedents dying after 2004, the State death tax credit was repealed and replaced with a deduction for death taxes actually paid to any State or the District of Columbia, in respect of property included in the gross estate of the decedent.[1563] Such State taxes must have been paid and claimed before the later of: (1) four years after the filing of the estate tax return; or (2)(a) 60 days after a decision of the U.S. Tax Court determining the estate tax liability becomes final, (b) the expiration of the period of extension to pay estate taxes over time under section 6166, or (c) the expiration of the period of limitations in which to file a claim for refund or generally 60 days after a decision of a court in which such refund suit has become final.

*Reinstatement of State death tax credit for decedents dying after December 31, 2010*

As described above, the estate, gift, and generation skipping transfer tax provisions of EGTRRA sunset at the end of 2010, such that those provisions will not apply to estates of decedents dying, gifts made, or generation skipping transfers made after December 31, 2010. As a result, neither the EGTRRA modifications to the

[1562] Sec. 2011.
[1563] Sec. 2058.

State death tax credit nor the replacement of the credit with a deduction applies for decedents dying after December 31, 2010. Instead, the State death tax credit as in effect for decedents who died prior to 2002 applies.

## *Exclusions and deductions*

### *Gift tax annual exclusion*

Donors of lifetime gifts are provided an annual exclusion of $13,000 (for 2010 and 2011) on transfers of present interests in property to each donee during the taxable year.[1564] If the non-donor spouse consents to split the gift with the donor spouse, then the annual exclusion is $26,000 for 2010 and 2011. The dollar amounts are indexed for inflation.

### *Transfers to a surviving spouse*

*In general.*—A 100-percent marital deduction generally is permitted for estate and gift tax purposes for the value of property transferred between spouses.[1565] Transfers of "qualified terminable interest property" are eligible for the marital deduction. "Qualified terminable interest property" is property: (1) that passes from the decedent; (2) in which the surviving spouse has a "qualifying income interest for life"; and (3) to which an election applies. A "qualifying income interest for life" exists if: (1) the surviving spouse is entitled to all the income from the property (payable annually or at more frequent intervals) or has the right to use the property during the spouse's life; and (2) no person has the power to appoint any part of the property to any person other than the surviving spouse.

*Transfers to surviving spouses who are not U.S. citizens.*—A marital deduction generally is denied for property passing to a surviving spouse who is not a citizen of the United States.[1566] A marital deduction is permitted, however, for property passing to a qualified domestic trust of which the noncitizen surviving spouse is a beneficiary. A qualified domestic trust is a trust that has as its trustee at least one U.S. citizen or U.S. corporation. No corpus may be distributed from a qualified domestic trust unless the U.S. trustee has the right to withhold any estate tax imposed on the distribution.

For years when the estate tax is in effect, the estate tax is imposed on (1) any distribution from a qualified domestic trust before the date of the death of the noncitizen surviving spouse and (2) the value of the property remaining in a qualified domestic trust on the date of death of the noncitizen surviving spouse. The tax is computed as an additional estate tax on the estate of the first spouse to die.

### *Conservation easements*

For years when an estate tax is in effect, an executor generally may elect to exclude from the taxable estate 40 percent of the value of any land subject to a qualified conservation easement, up to a

[1564] Sec. 2503(b).
[1565] Secs. 2056 & 2523.
[1566] Secs. 2056(d)(1) & 2523(i)(1).

maximum exclusion of $500,000.[1567] The exclusion percentage is reduced by two percentage points for each percentage point (or fraction thereof) by which the value of the qualified conservation easement is less than 30 percent of the value of the land (determined without regard to the value of such easement and reduced by the value of any retained development right).

Before 2001, a qualified conservation easement generally was one that met the following requirements: (1) the land was located within 25 miles of a metropolitan area (as defined by the Office of Management and Budget) or a national park or wilderness area, or within 10 miles of an Urban National Forest (as designated by the Forest Service of the U.S. Department of Agriculture); (2) the land had been owned by the decedent or a member of the decedent's family at all times during the three-year period ending on the date of the decedent's death; and (3) a qualified conservation contribution (within the meaning of sec. 170(h)) of a qualified real property interest (as generally defined in sec. 170(h)(2)(C)) was granted by the decedent or a member of his or her family. Preservation of a historically important land area or a certified historic structure does not qualify as a conservation purpose.

Effective for estates of decedents dying after December 31, 2000, EGTRRA expanded the availability of qualified conservation easements by eliminating the requirement that the land be located within a certain distance of a metropolitan area, national park, wilderness area, or Urban National Forest. A qualified conservation easement may be claimed with respect to any land that is located in the United States or its possessions. EGTRRA also clarifies that the date for determining easement compliance is the date on which the donation is made.

As a result of the EGTRRA sunset at the end of 2010, the EGTRRA modifications to expand the availability of qualified conservation contributions do not apply for decedents dying after December 31, 2010.

***Provisions affecting small and family-owned businesses and farms***

*Special-use valuation*

For years when an estate tax is in effect, an executor may elect to value for estate tax purposes certain "qualified real property" used in farming or another qualifying closely-held trade or business at its current-use value, rather than its fair market value.[1568] The maximum reduction in value for such real property was $1 million for 2009. Real property generally can qualify for special-use valuation if at least 50 percent of the adjusted value of the decedent's gross estate consists of a farm or closely-held business assets in the decedent's estate (including both real and personal property) and at least 25 percent of the adjusted value of the gross estate consists of farm or closely-held business real property. In addition, the property must be used in a qualified use (e.g., farming) by the decedent

[1567] Sec. 2031(c).
[1568] Sec. 2032A.

or a member of the decedent's family for five of the eight years immediately preceding the decedent's death.

If, after a special-use valuation election is made, the heir who acquired the real property ceases to use it in its qualified use within 10 years of the decedent's death, an additional estate tax is imposed in order to recapture the entire estate-tax benefit of the special-use valuation.

*Family-owned business deduction*

Prior to 2004, an estate was permitted to deduct the adjusted value of a qualified family-owned business interest of the decedent, up to $675,000.[1569] A qualified family-owned business interest generally is defined as any interest in a trade or business (regardless of the form in which it is held) with a principal place of business in the United States if the decedent's family owns at least 50 percent of the trade or business, two families own 70 percent, or three families own 90 percent, as long as the decedent's family owns, in the case of the 70-percent and 90-percent rules, at least 30 percent of the trade or business.

To qualify for the deduction, the decedent (or a member of the decedent's family) must have owned and materially participated in the trade or business for at least five of the eight years preceding the decedent's date of death. In addition, at least one qualified heir (or member of the qualified heir's family) is required to materially participate in the trade or business for at least 10 years following the decedent's death. The qualified family-owned business rules provide a graduated recapture based on the number of years after the decedent's death within which a disqualifying event occurred.

In general, there is no requirement that the qualified heir (or members of his or her family) continue to hold or participate in the trade or business more than 10 years after the decedent's death. However, the 10-year recapture period can be extended for a period of up to two years if the qualified heir does not begin to use the property for a period of up to two years after the decedent's death.

EGTRRA repealed the qualified family-owned business deduction for estates of decedents dying after December 31, 2003. As a result of the EGTRRA sunset at the end of 2010, the qualified family-owned business deduction applies to estates of decedents dying after December 31, 2010.

*Installment payment of estate tax for closely held businesses*

Estate tax generally is due within nine months of a decedent's death. However, an executor generally may elect to pay estate tax attributable to an interest in a closely held business in two or more installments (but no more than 10).[1570] An estate is eligible for payment of estate tax in installments if the value of the decedent's interest in a closely held business exceeds 35 percent of the decedent's adjusted gross estate (i.e., the gross estate less certain de-

[1569] Sec. 2057. The qualified family-owned business deduction and the unified credit effective exemption amount are coordinated. If the maximum deduction amount of $675,000 is elected, then the unified credit effective exemption amount is $625,000, for a total of $1.3 million. Because of the coordination between the qualified family-owned business deduction and the unified credit effective exemption amount, the qualified family-owned business deduction would not provide a benefit in any year in which the applicable exclusion amount exceeds $1.3 million.

[1570] Sec. 6166.

ductions). If the election is made, the estate may defer payment of principal and pay only interest for the first five years, followed by up to 10 annual installments of principal and interest. This provision effectively extends the time for paying estate tax by 14 years from the original due date of the estate tax. A special two-percent interest rate applies to the amount of deferred estate tax attributable to the first $1.34 million[1571] (as adjusted annually for inflation occurring after 1998; the original amount for 1998 was $1 million) in taxable value of a closely held business. The interest rate applicable to the amount of estate tax attributable to the taxable value of the closely held business in excess of $1.34 million is equal to 45 percent of the rate applicable to underpayments of tax under section 6621 of the Code (i.e., 45 percent of the Federal short-term rate plus two percentage points). Interest paid on deferred estate taxes is not deductible for estate or income tax purposes.

Under pre-EGTRRA law, for purposes of these rules an interest in a closely held business was: (1) an interest as a proprietor in a sole proprietorship; (2) an interest as a partner in a partnership carrying on a trade or business if 20 percent or more of the total capital interest of such partnership was included in the decedent's gross estate or the partnership had 15 or fewer partners; and (3) stock in a corporation carrying on a trade or business if 20 percent or more of the value of the voting stock of the corporation was included in the decedent's gross estate or such corporation had 15 or fewer shareholders.

Under present and pre-EGTRRA law, the decedent may own the interest directly or, in certain cases, indirectly through a holding company. If ownership is through a holding company, the stock must be non-readily tradable. If stock in a holding company is treated as business company stock for purposes of the installment payment provisions, the five-year deferral for principal and the two-percent interest rate do not apply. The value of any interest in a closely held business does not include the value of that portion of such interest attributable to passive assets held by such business.

Effective for estates of decedents dying after December 31, 2001, EGTRRA expands the definition of a closely held business for purposes of installment payment of estate tax. EGTRRA increases from 15 to 45 the maximum number of partners in a partnership and shareholders in a corporation that may be treated as a closely held business in which a decedent held an interest, and thus will qualify the estate for installment payment of estate tax.

EGTRRA also expands availability of the installment payment provisions by providing that an estate of a decedent with an interest in a qualifying lending and financing business is eligible for installment payment of the estate tax. EGTRRA provides that an estate with an interest in a qualifying lending and financing business that claims installment payment of estate tax must make installment payments of estate tax (which will include both principal and interest) relating to the interest in a qualifying lending and financing business over five years.

[1571] Rev. Proc. 2009–50, I.R.B. 2009–45 (Nov. 9, 2009).

EGTRRA clarifies that the installment payment provisions require that only the stock of holding companies, not the stock of operating subsidiaries, must be non-readily tradable to qualify for installment payment of the estate tax. EGTRRA provides that an estate with a qualifying property interest held through holding companies that claims installment payment of estate tax must make all installment payments of estate tax (which will include both principal and interest) relating to a qualifying property interest held through holding companies over five years.

As a result of the EGTRRA sunset at the end of 2010, the EGTRRA modifications to the estate tax installment payment rules described above do not apply for estates of decedents dying after December 31, 2010.

***Generation-skipping transfer tax rules***

*In general*

For years before and after 2010, a generation skipping transfer tax generally is imposed on transfers, either directly or in trust or similar arrangement, to a "skip person" (as defined above).[1572] Transfers subject to the generation skipping transfer tax include direct skips, taxable terminations, and taxable distributions.[1573] An exemption generally equal to the estate tax effective exemption amount is provided for each person making generation skipping transfers. The exemption may be allocated by a transferor (or his or her executor) to transferred property.

A direct skip is any transfer subject to estate or gift tax of an interest in property to a skip person.[1574] Natural persons or certain trusts may be skip persons. All persons assigned to the second or more remote generation below the transferor are skip persons (e.g., grandchildren and great-grandchildren). Trusts are skip persons if (1) all interests in the trust are held by skip persons, or (2) no person holds an interest in the trust and at no time after the transfer may a distribution (including distributions and terminations) be made to a non-skip person. A taxable termination is a termination (by death, lapse of time, release of power, or otherwise) of an interest in property held in trust unless, immediately after such termination, a non-skip person has an interest in the property, or unless at no time after the termination may a distribution (including a distribution upon termination) be made from the trust to a skip person.[1575] A taxable distribution is a distribution from a trust to a skip person (other than a taxable termination or direct skip).[1576] If a transferor allocates generation skipping transfer tax exemption to a trust prior to the taxable distribution, generation skipping transfer tax may be avoided.

The tax rate on generation skipping transfers is a flat rate of tax equal to the maximum estate and gift tax rate in effect at the time of the transfer multiplied by the "inclusion ratio." The inclusion ratio with respect to any property transferred in a generation skipping transfer is a function of the amount of "generation skipping

[1572] Sec. 2601.
[1573] Sec. 2611.
[1574] Sec. 2612(c).
[1575] Sec. 2612(a).
[1576] Sec. 2612(b).

transfer tax exemption" allocated to a trust. The allocation of generation skipping transfer tax exemption effectively reduces the tax rate on a generation skipping transfer.

If an individual makes a direct skip during his or her lifetime, any unused generation-skipping transfer tax exemption is automatically allocated to a direct skip to the extent necessary to make the inclusion ratio for such property equal to zero. An individual can elect out of the automatic allocation for lifetime direct skips.

Under pre-EGTRRA law, for lifetime transfers made to a trust that were not direct skips, the transferor had to make an affirmative allocation of generation skipping transfer tax exemption; the allocation was not automatic. If generation skipping transfer tax exemption was allocated on a timely filed gift tax return, then the portion of the trust that was exempt from generation skipping transfer tax was based on the value of the property at the time of the transfer. If, however, the allocation was not made on a timely filed gift tax return, then the portion of the trust that was exempt from generation skipping transfer tax was based on the value of the property at the time the allocation of generation skipping transfer tax exemption was made.

An election to allocate generation skipping transfer tax to a specific transfer generally may be made at any time up to the time for filing the transferor's estate tax return.

*Modifications to the generation skipping transfer tax rules under EGTRRA*

Generally effective after 2000, EGTRRA modifies and adds certain mechanical rules related to the generation skipping transfer tax. First, EGTRRA generally provides that generation skipping transfer tax exemption will be allocated automatically to transfers made during life that are "indirect skips." An indirect skip is any transfer of property (that is not a direct skip) subject to the gift tax that is made to a generation skipping transfer trust, as defined in the Code. If any individual makes an indirect skip during the individual's lifetime, then any unused portion of such individual's generation skipping transfer tax exemption is allocated to the property transferred to the extent necessary to produce the lowest possible inclusion ratio for such property. An individual can elect out of the automatic allocation or may elect to treat a trust as a generation skipping transfer trust attracting the automatic allocation.

Second, EGTRRA provides that, under certain circumstances, generation skipping transfer tax exemption can be allocated retroactively when there is an unnatural order of death. In general, if a lineal descendant of the transferor predeceases the transferor, then the transferor can allocate any unused generation skipping transfer exemption to any previous transfer or transfers to the trust on a chronological basis.

Third, EGTRRA provides that a trust that is only partially subject to generation skipping transfer tax because its inclusion ratio is less than one can be severed in a "qualified severance." A qualified severance generally is defined as the division of a single trust and the creation of two or more trusts, one of which would be exempt from generation skipping transfer tax and another of which would be fully subject to generation skipping transfer tax, if (1) the single trust was divided on a fractional basis, and (2) the terms of the new trusts, in the aggregate, provide for the same succession of interests of beneficiaries as are provided in the original trust.

Fourth, EGTRRA provides that in connection with timely and automatic allocations of generation skipping transfer tax exemption, the value of the property for purposes of determining the inclusion ratio shall be its finally determined gift tax value or estate tax value depending on the circumstances of the transfer. In the case of a generation skipping transfer tax exemption allocation deemed to be made at the conclusion of an estate tax inclusion period, the value for purposes of determining the inclusion ratio shall be its value at that time.

Fifth, under EGTRRA, the Secretary of the Treasury generally is authorized and directed to grant extensions of time to make the election to allocate generation skipping transfer tax exemption and to grant exceptions to the time requirement, without regard to whether any period of limitations has expired. If such relief is granted, then the gift tax or estate tax value of the transfer to trust would be used for determining generation skipping transfer tax exemption allocation.

Sixth, EGTRRA provides that substantial compliance with the statutory and regulatory requirements for allocating generation skipping transfer tax exemption will suffice to establish that generation skipping transfer tax exemption was allocated to a particular transfer or a particular trust. If a taxpayer demonstrates substantial compliance, then so much of the transferor's unused generation skipping transfer tax exemption will be allocated as produces the lowest possible inclusion ratio.

*Sunset of EGTRRA modifications to the generation skipping transfer tax rules*

The estate and generation skipping transfer taxes are repealed for decedents dying and gifts made in 2010. As a result of the EGTRRA sunset at the end of 2010, the generation skipping transfer tax again will apply after December 31, 2010. However, the EGTRRA modifications to the generation skipping transfer tax rules described above do not apply to generation skipping transfers made after December 31, 2010. Instead, in general, the rules as in effect prior to 2001 apply.

### *Explanation of Provision*

#### *In general*

The provision reinstates the estate and generation skipping transfer taxes effective for decedents dying and transfers made after December 31, 2009. The estate tax applicable exclusion amount is $5 million under the provision and is indexed for inflation for decedents dying in calendar years after 2011, and the maximum estate tax rate is 35 percent. For gifts made in 2010, the applicable exclusion amount for gift tax purposes is $1 million, and the gift tax rate is 35 percent. For gifts made after December 31, 2010, the gift tax is reunified with the estate tax, with an applicable exclusion amount of $5 million and a top estate and gift tax rate of 35 percent.[1577]

The generation skipping transfer tax exemption for decedents dying or gifts made after December 31, 2009, is equal to the applicable exclusion amount for estate tax purposes (e.g., $5 million for 2010).[1578] Therefore, up to $5 million in generation skipping transfer tax exemption may be allocated to a trust created or funded during 2010, depending upon the amount of such exemption used by the taxpayer before 2010. Although the generation skipping transfer tax is applicable in 2010, the generation skipping transfer tax rate for transfers made during 2010 is zero percent. The generation skipping transfer tax rate for transfers made after 2010 is equal to the highest estate and gift tax rate in effect for such year (35 percent for 2011 and 2012).

The provision allows a deduction for certain death taxes paid to any State or the District of Columbia for decedents dying after December 31, 2009.

The provision generally repeals the modified carryover basis rules that, under EGTRRA, would apply for purposes of determining basis in property acquired from a decedent who dies in 2010. Under the provision, a recipient of property acquired from a decedent who dies after December 31, 2009, generally will receive fair market value basis (i.e., "stepped up" basis) under the basis rules applicable to assets acquired from decedents who died in 2009.[1579]

The provision extends the EGTRRA modifications to the rules regarding (1) qualified conservation easements, (2) installment payment of estate taxes, and (3) various technical aspects of the generation skipping transfer tax, described in the present-law section, above.

### *Election for decedents who die during 2010*

In the case of a decedent who dies during 2010, the provision generally allows the executor of such decedent's estate to elect to apply the Internal Revenue Code as if the new estate tax and basis step-up rules described in the preceding section had not been enacted. In other words, instead of applying the above-described new estate tax and basis step-up rules of the provision, the executor may elect to have present law (as enacted under EGTRRA) apply. In general, if such an election is made, the estate would not be subject to estate tax, and the basis of assets acquired from the decedent would be determined under the modified carryover basis rules

---

[1577] The provision clarifies current law regarding the computation of estate and gift taxes. Under present law, the gift tax on taxable transfers for a year is determined by computing a tentative tax on the cumulative value of current year transfers and all gifts made by a decedent after December 31, 1976, and subtracting from the tentative tax the amount of gift tax that would have been paid by the decedent on taxable gifts after December 31, 1976, if the tax rate schedule in effect in the current year had been in effect on the date of the prior-year gifts. Under the provision, for purposes of determining the amount of gift tax that would have been paid on one or more prior year gifts, the estate tax rates in effect under section 2001(c) at the time of the decedent's death are used to compute both (1) the gift tax imposed by chapter 12 with respect to such gifts, and (2) the unified credit allowed against such gifts under section 2505 (including in computing the applicable credit amount under section 2505(a)(1) and the sum of amounts allowed as a credit for all preceding periods under section 2505(a)(2)).

[1578] The $5 million generation skipping transfer tax exemption is available in 2010 regardless of whether the executor of an estate of a decedent who dies in 2010 makes the election described below to apply the EGTRRA 2010 estate tax rules and section 1022 basis rules.

[1579] See generally sec. 1014.

of section 1022.[1580] This election will have no effect on the continued applicability of the generation skipping transfer tax. In addition, in applying the definition of transferor in section 2652(a)(1), the determination of whether any property is subject to the tax imposed by chapter 11 of the Code is made without regard to an election made under this provision.

The Secretary of the Treasury or his delegate shall determine the time and manner for making the election. The election, once made, is revocable only with the consent of the Secretary or his delegate.

***Extension of certain filing deadlines***

The provision also provides for the extension of filing deadlines for certain transfer tax returns. Specifically, in the case of a decedent dying after December 31, 2009, and before the date of enactment, the due date shall not be earlier than the date which is nine months after the date of enactment for: (1) filing an estate tax return required under section 6018; (2) making the payment of estate tax under Chapter 11; and (3) making any disclaimer described in section 2518(b) of an interest in property passing by reason the death of such a decedent. In the case of a generation skipping transfer made after December 31, 2009, and before the date of enactment, the due date for filing any return required under section 2662 (including the making of any election required to be made on the return) shall not be earlier than the date which is nine months after the date of enactment.

***Portability of unused exemption between spouses***

Under the provision, any applicable exclusion amount that remains unused as of the death of a spouse who dies after December 31, 2010 (the "deceased spousal unused exclusion amount"), generally is available for use by the surviving spouse, as an addition to such surviving spouse's applicable exclusion amount.[1581]

If a surviving spouse is predeceased by more than one spouse, the amount of unused exclusion that is available for use by such surviving spouse is limited to the lesser of $5 million or the unused exclusion of the last such deceased spouse.[1582] A surviving spouse may use the predeceased spousal carryover amount in addition to such surviving spouse's own $5 million exclusion for taxable transfers made during life or at death.

A deceased spousal unused exclusion amount is available to a surviving spouse only if an election is made on a timely filed estate tax return (including extensions) of the predeceased spouse on which such amount is computed, regardless of whether the estate of the predeceased spouse otherwise is required to file an estate tax return. In addition, notwithstanding the statute of limitations for assessing estate or gift tax with respect to a predeceased spouse, the Secretary of the Treasury may examine the return of a pre-

[1580] Therefore, an heir who acquires an asset from the estate of a decedent who died in 2010 and whose executor elected application of the 2010 EGTRRA rules has a basis in the asset determined under the modified carryover basis rules of section 1022. Such basis is applicable for the determination of any gain or loss on the sale or disposition of the asset in any future year regardless of the status of the sunset provision described below.

[1581] The provision does not allow a surviving spouse to use the unused generation skipping transfer tax exemption of a predeceased spouse.

[1582] The last deceased spouse limitation applies whether or not the last deceased spouse has any unused exclusion or the last deceased spouse's estate makes a timely election.

deceased spouse for purposes of determining the deceased spousal unused exclusion amount available for use by the surviving spouse. The Secretary of the Treasury shall prescribe regulations as may be appropriate and necessary to carry out the rules described in this paragraph.

*Example 1.*—Assume that Husband 1 dies in 2011, having made taxable transfers of $3 million and having no taxable estate. An election is made on Husband 1's estate tax return to permit Wife to use Husband 1's deceased spousal unused exclusion amount. As of Husband 1's death, Wife has made no taxable gifts. Thereafter, Wife's applicable exclusion amount is $7 million (her $5 million basic exclusion amount plus $2 million deceased spousal unused exclusion amount from Husband 1), which she may use for lifetime gifts or for transfers at death.

*Example 2.*—Assume the same facts as in Example 1, except that Wife subsequently marries Husband 2. Husband 2 also predeceases Wife, having made $4 million in taxable transfers and having no taxable estate. An election is made on Husband 2's estate tax return to permit Wife to use Husband 2's deceased spousal unused exclusion amount. Although the combined amount of unused exclusion of Husband 1 and Husband 2 is $3 million ($2 million for Husband 1 and $1 million for Husband 2), only Husband 2's $1 million unused exclusion is available for use by Wife, because the deceased spousal unused exclusion amount is limited to the lesser of the basic exclusion amount ($5 million) or the unused exclusion of the last deceased spouse of the surviving spouse (here, Husband 2's $1 million unused exclusion). Thereafter, Wife's applicable exclusion amount is $6 million (her $5 million basic exclusion amount plus $1 million deceased spousal unused exclusion amount from Husband 2), which she may use for lifetime gifts or for transfers at death.

*Example 3.*—Assume the same facts as in Examples 1 and 2, except that Wife predeceases Husband 2. Following Husband 1's death, Wife's applicable exclusion amount is $7 million (her $5 million basic exclusion amount plus $2 million deceased spousal unused exclusion amount from Husband 1). Wife made no taxable transfers and has a taxable estate of $3 million. An election is made on Wife's estate tax return to permit Husband 2 to use Wife's deceased spousal unused exclusion amount, which is $4 million (Wife's $7 million applicable exclusion amount less her $3 million taxable estate). Under the provision, Husband 2's applicable exclusion amount is increased by $4 million, i.e., the amount of deceased spousal unused exclusion amount of Wife.

***Sunset provision***

Under the Act, the sunset of the EGTRRA estate, gift, and generation skipping transfer tax provisions, scheduled to apply to estates of decedents dying, gifts made, or generation skipping transfers after December 31, 2010, is extended to apply to estates of decedents dying, gifts made, or generation skipping transfers after December 31, 2012. The EGTRRA sunset, as extended by the Act, applies to the amendments made by the provision. Therefore, neither the EGTRRA rules nor the new rules of the provision will apply to estates of decedents dying, gifts made, or generation skipping transfers made after December 31, 2012.

### *Effective Date*

The estate and generation skipping transfer tax provisions generally are effective for decedents dying, gifts made, and generation skipping transfers made after December 31, 2009. The modifications to the gift tax exemption and rate generally are effective for gifts made after December 31, 2010. The new rules providing for portability of unused exemption between spouses generally are effective for decedents dying and gifts made after December 31, 2010.

## TITLE IV—TEMPORARY EXTENSION OF INVESTMENT INCENTIVES

### A. Extension of Bonus Depreciation; Temporary 100 Percent Expensing for Certain Business Assets (sec. 401 of the Act and sec. 168(k) of the Code)

### *Present Law*

#### *In general*

An additional first-year depreciation deduction is allowed equal to 50 percent of the adjusted basis of qualified property placed in service during 2008, 2009, and 2010 (2009, 2010, and 2011 for certain longer-lived and transportation property).[1583] The additional first-year depreciation deduction is allowed for both regular tax and alternative minimum tax purposes, but is not allowed for purposes of computing earnings and profits. The basis of the property and the depreciation allowances in the year of purchase and later years are appropriately adjusted to reflect the additional first-year depreciation deduction. In addition, there are no adjustments to the allowable amount of depreciation for purposes of computing a taxpayer's alternative minimum taxable income with respect to property to which the provision applies. The amount of the additional first-year depreciation deduction is not affected by a short taxable year. The taxpayer may elect out of additional first-year depreciation for any class of property for any taxable year.

The interaction of the additional first-year depreciation allowance with the otherwise applicable depreciation allowance may be illustrated as follows. Assume that in 2009, a taxpayer purchased new depreciable property and placed it in service.[1584] The property's cost is $1,000, and it is five-year property subject to the half-year convention. The amount of additional first-year depreciation allowed is $500. The remaining $500 of the cost of the property is depreciable under the rules applicable to five-year property. Thus, 20 percent, or $100, is also allowed as a depreciation deduction in 2009. The total depreciation deduction with respect to the property for 2009 is $600. The remaining $400 adjusted basis of the property

[1583] Sec. 168(k). The additional first-year depreciation deduction is subject to the general rules regarding whether an item must be capitalized under section 263 or section 263A.

[1584] Assume that the cost of the property is not eligible for expensing under section 179.

generally is recovered through otherwise applicable depreciation rules.

Property qualifying for the additional first-year depreciation deduction must meet all of the following requirements. First, the property must be (1) property to which MACRS applies with an applicable recovery period of 20 years or less; (2) water utility property (as defined in section 168(e)(5)); (3) computer software other than computer software covered by section 197; or (4) qualified leasehold improvement property (as defined in section 168(k)(3)).[1585] Second, the original use[1586] of the property must commence with the taxpayer after December 31, 2007.[1587] Third, the taxpayer must acquire the property within the applicable time period. Finally, the property must be placed in service after December 31, 2007, and before January 1, 2011. An extension of the placed in service date of one year (i.e., to January 1, 2012) is provided for certain property with a recovery period of 10 years or longer and certain transportation property.[1588] Transportation property is defined as tangible personal property used in the trade or business of transporting persons or property.

To qualify, property must be acquired (1) after December 31, 2007, and before January 1, 2011, but only if no binding written contract for the acquisition is in effect before January 1, 2008, or (2) pursuant to a binding written contract which was entered into after December 31, 2007, and before January 1, 2011.[1589] With respect to property that is manufactured, constructed, or produced by the taxpayer for use by the taxpayer, the taxpayer must begin the manufacture, construction, or production of the property after December 31, 2007, and before January 1, 2011. Property that is manufactured, constructed, or produced for the taxpayer by another person under a contract that is entered into prior to the manufacture, construction, or production of the property is considered to be manufactured, constructed, or produced by the taxpayer. For property eligible for the extended placed in service date, a special rule limits the amount of costs eligible for the additional first-year depreciation. With respect to such property, only the portion of the basis that is properly attributable to the costs incurred before Jan-

[1585] The additional first-year depreciation deduction is not available for any property that is required to be depreciated under the alternative depreciation system of MACRS. The additional first-year depreciation deduction is also not available for qualified New York Liberty Zone leasehold improvement property as defined in section 1400L(c)(2).

[1586] The term "original use" means the first use to which the property is put, whether or not such use corresponds to the use of such property by the taxpayer.

If in the normal course of its business a taxpayer sells fractional interests in property to unrelated third parties, then the original use of such property begins with the first user of each fractional interest (i.e., each fractional owner is considered the original user of its proportionate share of the property).

[1587] A special rule applies in the case of certain leased property. In the case of any property that is originally placed in service by a person and that is sold to the taxpayer and leased back to such person by the taxpayer within three months after the date that the property was placed in service, the property would be treated as originally placed in service by the taxpayer not earlier than the date that the property is used under the leaseback.

If property is originally placed in service by a lessor, such property is sold within three months after the date that the property was placed in service, and the user of such property does not change, then the property is treated as originally placed in service by the taxpayer not earlier than the date of such sale.

[1588] Property qualifying for the extended placed in service date must have an estimated production period exceeding one year and a cost exceeding $1 million.

[1589] Property does not fail to qualify for the additional first-year depreciation merely because a binding written contract to acquire a component of the property is in effect prior to January 1, 2008.

uary 1, 2011, ("progress expenditures") is eligible for the additional first-year depreciation.[1590]

Property does not qualify for the additional first-year depreciation deduction when the user of such property (or a related party) would not have been eligible for the additional first-year depreciation deduction if the user (or a related party) were treated as the owner. For example, if a taxpayer sells to a related party property that was under construction prior to January 1, 2008, the property does not qualify for the additional first-year depreciation deduction. Similarly, if a taxpayer sells to a related party property that was subject to a binding written contract prior to January 1, 2008, the property does not qualify for the additional first-year depreciation deduction. As a further example, if a taxpayer (the lessee) sells property in a sale-leaseback arrangement, and the property otherwise would not have qualified for the additional first-year depreciation deduction if it were owned by the taxpayer-lessee, then the lessor is not entitled to the additional first-year depreciation deduction.

The limitation under section 280F on the amount of depreciation deductions allowed with respect to certain passenger automobiles is increased in the first year by $8,000 for automobiles that qualify (and for which the taxpayer does not elect out of the additional first-year deduction). The $8,000 increase is not indexed for inflation.

***Election to accelerate certain credits in lieu of claiming bonus depreciation***

A corporation otherwise eligible for additional first year depreciation under section 168(k) may elect to claim additional research or minimum tax credits in lieu of claiming depreciation under section 168(k) for "eligible qualified property" placed in service after March 31, 2008, and before December 31, 2008.[1591] A corporation making the election forgoes the depreciation deductions allowable under section 168(k) and instead increases the limitation under section 38(c) on the use of research credits or section 53(c) on the use of minimum tax credits.[1592] The increases in the allowable credits are treated as refundable. The depreciation for qualified property is calculated for both regular tax and AMT purposes using the straight-line method in place of the method that would otherwise be used absent the election under this provision.

The research credit or minimum tax credit limitation is increased by the bonus depreciation amount, which is equal to 20 percent of bonus depreciation[1593] for certain eligible qualified property that could be claimed absent an election under this provision. Generally,

[1590] For purposes of determining the amount of eligible progress expenditures, it is intended that rules similar to section 46(d)(3) as in effect prior to the Tax Reform Act of 1986 apply.

[1591] Sec. 168(k)(4). In the case of an electing corporation that is a partner in a partnership, the corporate partner's distributive share of partnership items is determined as if section 168(k) does not apply to any eligible qualified property and the straight line method is used to calculate depreciation of such property.

[1592] Special rules apply to an applicable partnership.

[1593] For this purpose, bonus depreciation is the difference between (i) the aggregate amount of depreciation for all eligible qualified property determined if section 168(k)(1) applied using the most accelerated depreciation method (determined without regard to this provision), and shortest life allowable for each property, and (ii) the amount of depreciation that would be determined if section 168(k)(1) did not apply using the same method and life for each property.

eligible qualified property included in the calculation is bonus depreciation property that meets the following requirements: (1) the original use of the property must commence with the taxpayer after March 31, 2008; (2) the taxpayer must purchase the property either (a) after March 31, 2008, and before January 1, 2010, but only if no binding written contract for the acquisition is in effect before April 1, 2008,[1594] or (b) pursuant to a binding written contract which was entered into after March 31, 2008, and before January 1, 2010;[1595] and (3) the property must be placed in service after March 31, 2008, and before January 1, 2010 (January 1, 2011 for certain longer-lived and transportation property).

The bonus depreciation amount is limited to the lesser of: (1) $30 million, or (2) six percent of the sum of research credit carryforwards from taxable years beginning before January 1, 2006 and minimum tax credits allocable to the adjusted minimum tax imposed for taxable years beginning before January 1, 2006. All corporations treated as a single employer under section 52(a) are treated as one taxpayer for purposes of the limitation, as well as for electing the application of this provision.

A corporation may make a separate election to increase the research credit or minimum tax credit limitation by the bonus depreciation amount with respect to certain property placed in service in 2009 (2010 in the case of certain longer-lived and transportation property). The election applies with respect to extension property, which is defined as property that is eligible qualified property solely because it meets the requirements under the extension of the special allowance for certain property acquired during 2009.

A corporation that has made an election to increase the research credit or minimum tax credit limitation for eligible qualified property for its first taxable year ending after March 31, 2008, may choose not to make this election for extension property. Further, a corporation that has not made an election for eligible qualified property for its first taxable year ending after March 31, 2008, is permitted to make the election for extension property for its first taxable year ending after December 31, 2008, and for each subsequent year. In the case of a taxpayer electing to increase the research or minimum tax credit for both eligible qualified property and extension property, a separate bonus depreciation amount, maximum amount, and maximum increase amount is computed and applied to each group of property.[1596]

### *Explanation of Provision*

The provision extends and expands the additional first-year depreciation to equal 100 percent of the cost of qualified property placed in service after September 8, 2010, and before January 1, 2012, (before January 1, 2013, for certain longer-lived and trans-

---

[1594] In the case of passenger aircraft, the written binding contract limitation does not apply.

[1595] Special rules apply to property manufactured, constructed, or produced by the taxpayer for use by the taxpayer.

[1596] In computing the maximum amount, the maximum increase amount for extension property is reduced by bonus depreciation amounts for preceding taxable years only with respect to extension property.

portation property),[1597] and provides for a 50 percent first-year additional depreciation deduction for qualified property placed in service after December 31, 2011, and before January 1, 2013, (after December 31, 2012, and before January 1, 2014, for certain longer-lived and transportation property). Rules similar to those in section 168(k)(2)(A)(ii) and (iii), which provide that qualified property does not include property acquired pursuant to a written binding contract that was in effect prior to January 1, 2008, apply for purposes of determining whether property is eligible for the temporary 100 percent additional first-year depreciation deduction. Thus under the provision, property acquired pursuant to a written binding contract entered into after December 31, 2007, is qualified property for purposes of the 100 percent additional first-year depreciation deduction assuming all other requirements of section 168(k)(2) are met.

The provision also generally permits a corporation to increase the minimum tax credit limitation by the bonus depreciation amount with respect to certain property placed in service after December 31, 2010, and before January 1, 2013, (January 1, 2014 in the case of certain longer-lived and transportation property).[1598] The provision applies with respect to round 2 extension property, which is defined as property that is eligible qualified property solely because it meets the requirements under the extension of the additional first-year depreciation deduction for certain property placed in service after December 31, 2010.[1599]

Under the provision, a taxpayer that has made an election to increase the research credit or minimum tax credit limitation for eligible qualified property for its first taxable year ending after March 31, 2008 or for extension property may choose not to make this election for round 2 extension property. Further, the provision allows a taxpayer that has not made an election for eligible qualified property for its first taxable year ending after March 31, 2008, or for extension property, to make the election for round 2 extension property for its first taxable year ending after December 31, 2010, and for each subsequent year. In the case of a taxpayer electing to

[1597] It is intended that, in the case of qualified property that is acquired by the taxpayer after September 8, 2010 and placed in service by the taxpayer in 2012 and that is eligible for 100 percent bonus depreciation by reason of the extended placed in service date provided in section 168(k)(5), the 100 percent bonus deprecation applies only to the extent of the adjusted basis of the property attributable to manufacture, construction, or production before January 1, 2012. It is also intended that a taxpayer may elect 50 percent (rather than 100 percent) bonus depreciation with respect to all property in any class of property placed in service during a taxable year. Finally, it is intended that section 168(k)(5) does not apply to passenger automobiles subject to the limitations on depreciation provided in section 280F, but that such property continues to be eligible for 50-percent bonus depreciation. Technical corrections may be necessary so that the statute reflects this intent.

[1598] An electing taxpayer does not compute a bonus depreciation amount under section 168(k)(4)(C) for any bonus depreciation allowable with respect to property placed in service during 2010 except long-production period property (or certain transportation property) placed in service in 2010 that is extension property. For example, assume in its taxable year beginning October 1, 2010, and ending September 30, 2011, a corporation places into service qualified property with a total cost of $1,000,000, of which $250,000 was placed in service before December 31, 2010. The corporation computes its bonus depreciation amount under section 168(k)(4)(C) taking into account only the bonus depreciation computed with respect to the $750,000 of property placed in service after December 31, 2010.

[1599] An election under new section 168(k)(4)(I) with respect to round 2 extension property is binding for any property that is eligible qualified property solely by reason of the amendments made by section 401(a) of the Tax Relief, Unemployment Insurance Reauthorization, and Job Creation Act of 2010 (and the application of such extension to this paragraph pursuant to the amendment made by section 401(c)(1) of such Act), Pub. L. No. 111–312, even if such property is placed in service in 2012.

increase the research or minimum tax credit for eligible qualified property and/or extension property and the minimum tax credit for round 2 extension property, a separate bonus depreciation amount, maximum amount, and maximum increase amount is computed and applied to each group of property.[1600]

### *Effective Date*

The provision generally applies to property placed in service by the taxpayer after December 31, 2010, in taxable years ending after such date. The provision expanding the additional first-year depreciation deduction to 100 percent of the basis of qualified property applies to property placed in service by the taxpayer after September 8, 2010, in taxable years ending after such date.

## B. Temporary Extension of Increased Small Business Expensing (sec. 402 of the Act and sec. 179 of the Code)

### *Present Law*

Subject to certain limitations, a taxpayer that invests in certain qualifying property may elect under section 179 to deduct (or "expense") the cost of qualifying property, rather than to recover such costs through depreciation deductions.[1601] For taxable years beginning in 2010 and 2011, the maximum amount that a taxpayer may expense is $500,000 of the cost of qualifying property placed in service for the taxable year.[1602] The $500,000 amount is reduced (but not below zero) by the amount by which the cost of qualifying property placed in service during the taxable year exceeds $2,000,000.[1603] Off-the-shelf computer software placed in service in taxable years beginning before 2012 is treated as qualifying property.

The amount eligible to be expensed for a taxable year may not exceed the taxable income for a taxable year that is derived from the active conduct of a trade or business (determined without regard to this provision). Any amount that is not allowed as a deduction because of the taxable income limitation generally may be carried forward to succeeding taxable years (subject to similar limitations).[1604] No general business credit under section 38 is allowed with respect to any amount for which a deduction is allowed under

---

[1600] In computing the maximum amount, the maximum increase amount for extension property or for round 2 extension property is reduced by bonus depreciation amounts for preceding taxable years only with respect to extension property or round 2 extension property, respectively.

[1601] Additional section 179 incentives are provided with respect to qualified property meeting applicable requirements that is used by a business in an empowerment zone (sec. 1397A), a renewal community (sec. 1400J), or the Gulf Opportunity Zone (sec. 1400N(e)). In addition, section 179(e) provides for an enhanced section 179 deduction for qualified disaster assistance property.

[1602] The definition of qualifying property was temporarily (for 2010 and 2011) expanded to include up to $250,000 of qualified leasehold improvement property, qualified restaurant property, and qualified retail improvement property. See section 179(f)(2).

[1603] The temporary $500,000 and $2,000,000 amounts were enacted in Section 2021 of the Small Business Jobs Act of 2010, Pub. L. No. 111–240.

[1604] Special rules apply to limit the carryover of unused section 179 deductions attributable to qualified leasehold improvement property, qualified restaurant property, and qualified retail improvement property. See section 179(f)(4).

section 179. An expensing election is made under rules prescribed by the Secretary.[1605]

For taxable years beginning in 2012 and thereafter, a taxpayer with a sufficiently small amount of annual investment may elect to deduct up to $25,000 of the cost of qualifying property placed in service for the taxable year. The $25,000 amount is reduced (but not below zero) by the amount by which the cost of qualifying property placed in service during the taxable year exceeds $200,000. The $25,000 and $200,000 amounts are not indexed. In general, qualifying property is defined as depreciable tangible personal property that is purchased for use in the active conduct of a trade or business (not including off-the-shelf computer software).

### *Explanation of Provision*

Under the provision, for taxable years beginning in 2012, the maximum amount a taxpayer may expense is $125,000 of the cost of qualifying property placed in service for the taxable year. The $125,000 amount is reduced (but not below zero) by the amount by which the cost of qualifying property placed in service during the taxable year exceeds $500,000. The $125,000 and $500,000 amounts are indexed for inflation.

In addition, the provision extends the treatment of off-the-shelf computer software as qualifying property,[1606] as well as the provision permitting a taxpayer to amend or irrevocably revoke an election for a taxable year under section 179 without the consent of the Commissioner for one year (through 2012).

For taxable years beginning in 2013, and thereafter, the maximum amount a taxpayer may expense is $25,000 of the cost of qualifying property placed in service for the taxable year. The $25,000 amount is reduced (but not below zero) by the amount by which the cost of qualifying property placed in service during the taxable year exceeds $200,000.

### *Effective Date*

The provision is effective for taxable years beginning after December 31, 2011.

## TITLE VI—TEMPORARY EMPLOYEE PAYROLL TAX CUT

### A. Payroll Tax Cut (sec. 601 of the Act)

### *Present Law*

#### *Federal Insurance Contributions Act ("FICA") tax*

The FICA tax applies to employers based on the amount of covered wages paid to an employee during the year.[1607] Generally,

[1605] Sec. 179(c)(1). Under Treas. Reg. sec. 1.179–5, applicable to property placed in service in taxable years beginning after 2002 and before 2008, a taxpayer is permitted to make or revoke an election under section 179 without the consent of the Commissioner on an amended Federal tax return for that taxable year. This amended return must be filed within the time prescribed by law for filing an amended return for the taxable year. T.D. 9209, July 12, 2005.

[1606] The temporary extension of the definition of qualifying property to include qualified leasehold improvement property, qualified restaurant property, and qualified retail improvement property is not extended.

[1607] Sec. 3111.

covered wages means all remuneration for employment, including the cash value of all remuneration paid in any medium other than cash.[1608] Certain exceptions from covered wages are also provided. The tax imposed is composed of two parts: (1) the old age, survivors, and disability insurance ("OASDI") tax equal to 6.2 percent of covered wages up to the taxable wage base ($106,800 in 2010); and (2) the Medicare hospital insurance ("HI") tax amount equal to 1.45 percent of covered wages.

In addition to the tax on employers, each employee is subject to FICA taxes equal to the amount of tax imposed on the employer (the "employee portion").[1609] The employee portion generally must be withheld and remitted to the Federal government by the employer.

### *Self-Employment Contributions Act ("SECA") tax*

As a parallel to FICA taxes, the SECA tax applies to the self-employment income of self-employed individuals.[1610] The rate of the OASDI portion of SECA taxes is 12.4 percent, which is equal to the combined employee and employer OASDI FICA tax rates, and applies to self-employment income up to the FICA taxable wage base. Similarly, the rate of the HI portion is 2.9 percent, the same as the combined employer and employee HI rates under the FICA tax, and there is no cap on the amount of self-employment income to which the rate applies. [1611]

An individual may deduct, in determining net earnings from self-employment under the SECA tax, the amount of the net earnings from self-employment (determined without regard to this deduction) for the taxable year multiplied by one half of the combined OASDI and HI rates.[1612]

Additionally, a deduction, for purposes of computing the income tax of an individual, is allowed for one half of the amount of the SECA tax imposed on the individual's self-employment income for the taxable year.[1613]

### *Railroad retirement tax*

The Railroad Retirement System has two main components. Tier I of the system is financed by taxes on employers and employees equal to the Social Security payroll tax and provides qualified railroad retirees (and their qualified spouses, dependents, widows, or widowers) with benefits that are roughly equal to Social Security. Covered railroad workers and their employers pay the Tier I tax instead of the Social Security payroll tax, and most railroad retirees collect Tier I benefits instead of Social Security. Tier II of the system replicates a private pension plan, with employers and employees contributing a certain percentage of pay toward the system to finance defined benefits to eligible railroad retirees (and qualified spouses, dependents, widows, or widowers) upon retirement; however, the Federal Government collects the Tier II payroll contribution and pays out the benefits.

---

[1608] Sec. 3121.
[1609] Sec. 3101. For taxable years beginning after 2012, an additional HI tax applies.
[1610] Sec. 1401.
[1611] For taxable years beginning after 2012, an additional HI tax applies.
[1612] Sec. 1402(a)(12).
[1613] Sec. 164(f).

### *Explanation of Provision*

The provision reduces the employee OASDI tax rate under the FICA tax by two percentage points to 4.2 percent for one year (2011). Similarly, the provision reduces the OASDI tax rate under the SECA tax by two percentage points to 10.4 percent for taxable years of individuals that begin in 2011. A similar reduction applies to the railroad retirement tax.

The provision provides rules for coordination with deductions for employment taxes. The rate reduction is not taken into account in determining the SECA tax deduction allowed for determining the amount of the net earnings from self-employment for the taxable year. Thus, the deduction for 2011 remains at 7.65 percent of self-employment income (determined without regard to the deduction).

The income tax deduction allowed under section 164(f) for taxable years beginning in 2011 is computed at the rate of 59.6 percent of the OASDI tax paid, plus one half of the HI tax paid.[1614]

The provision provides that the Treasury Secretary is to notify employers of the payroll tax cut.

The Federal Old-Age and Survivors Trust Fund, the Federal Disability Insurance Trust Fund, and the Social Security Equivalent Benefit Account established under the Railroad Retirement Act of 1974[1615] will receive transfers from the General Fund of the United States Treasury equal to any reduction in payroll taxes attributable to this provision. The amounts will be transferred from the General Fund at such times and in such a manner as to replicate to the extent possible the transfers which would have occurred to the Trust Funds or Benefit Account had the provision not been enacted.

For purposes of applying any provision of Federal law other than the provisions of the Internal Revenue Code of 1986, the rate of tax in effect under section 3101(a) is determined without regard to the reduction in that rate under this provision.

### *Effective Date*

The provision is effective for remuneration received during 2011 and for self-employment income for taxable years beginning in 2011.

[1614] This percentage replaces the rate of one half (50 percent) allowed under present law for this portion of the deduction. The new percentage is necessary to continue to allow the self-employed taxpayer to deduct the full amount of the employer portion of SECA taxes. The employer OASDI tax rate remains at 6.2 percent, while the employee portion falls to 4.2 percent. Thus, the employer share of total OASDI taxes is 6.2 divided by 10.4, or 59.6 percent of the OASDI portion of SECA taxes.

[1615] 45 U.S.C. 231n–1(a).

# TITLE VII—TEMPORARY EXTENSION OF CERTAIN EXPIRING PROVISIONS

## A. Energy

### 1. Incentives for biodiesel and renewable diesel (sec. 701 of the Act and secs. 40A, 6426, and 6427 of the Code)

#### *Present Law*

***Biodiesel***

The Code provides an income tax credit for biodiesel fuels (the "biodiesel fuels credit").[1616] The biodiesel fuels credit is the sum of three credits: (1) the biodiesel mixture credit, (2) the biodiesel credit, and (3) the small agri-biodiesel producer credit. The biodiesel fuels credit is treated as a general business credit. The amount of the biodiesel fuels credit is includible in gross income. The biodiesel fuels credit is coordinated to take into account benefits from the biodiesel excise tax credit and payment provisions discussed below. The credit does not apply to fuel sold or used after December 31, 2009.

Biodiesel is monoalkyl esters of long chain fatty acids derived from plant or animal matter that meet (1) the registration requirements established by the EPA under section 211 of the Clean Air Act (42 U.S.C. sec. 7545) and (2) the requirements of the American Society of Testing and Materials ("ASTM") D6751. Agri-biodiesel is biodiesel derived solely from virgin oils including oils from corn, soybeans, sunflower seeds, cottonseeds, canola, crambe, rapeseeds, safflowers, flaxseeds, rice bran, mustard seeds, camelina, or animal fats.

Biodiesel may be taken into account for purposes of the credit only if the taxpayer obtains a certification (in such form and manner as prescribed by the Secretary) from the producer or importer of the biodiesel that identifies the product produced and the percentage of biodiesel and agri-biodiesel in the product.

*Biodiesel mixture credit*

The biodiesel mixture credit is $1.00 for each gallon of biodiesel (including agri-biodiesel) used by the taxpayer in the production of a qualified biodiesel mixture. A qualified biodiesel mixture is a mixture of biodiesel and diesel fuel that is (1) sold by the taxpayer producing such mixture to any person for use as a fuel, or (2) used as a fuel by the taxpayer producing such mixture. The sale or use must be in the trade or business of the taxpayer and is to be taken into account for the taxable year in which such sale or use occurs. No credit is allowed with respect to any casual off-farm production of a qualified biodiesel mixture.

Per IRS guidance a mixture need only contain 1/10th of one percent of diesel fuel to be a qualified mixture.[1617] Thus, a qualified

[1616] Sec. 40A.

[1617] Notice 2005–62, I.R.B. 2005–35, 443 (2005). "A biodiesel mixture is a mixture of biodiesel and diesel fuel containing at least 0.1 percent (by volume) of diesel fuel. Thus, for example, a mixture of 999 gallons of biodiesel and 1 gallon of diesel fuel is a biodiesel mixture." *Ibid.*

biodiesel mixture can contain 99.9 percent biodiesel and 0.1 percent diesel fuel.

*Biodiesel credit (B–100)*

The biodiesel credit is $1.00 for each gallon of biodiesel that is not in a mixture with diesel fuel (100 percent biodiesel or B–100) and which during the taxable year is (1) used by the taxpayer as a fuel in a trade or business or (2) sold by the taxpayer at retail to a person and placed in the fuel tank of such person's vehicle.

*Small agri-biodiesel producer credit*

The Code provides a small agri-biodiesel producer income tax credit, in addition to the biodiesel and biodiesel mixture credits. The credit is 10 cents per gallon for up to 15 million gallons of agri-biodiesel produced by small producers, defined generally as persons whose agri-biodiesel production capacity does not exceed 60 million gallons per year. The agri-biodiesel must (1) be sold by such producer to another person (a) for use by such other person in the production of a qualified biodiesel mixture in such person's trade or business (other than casual off-farm production), (b) for use by such other person as a fuel in a trade or business, or, (c) who sells such agri-biodiesel at retail to another person and places such agri-biodiesel in the fuel tank of such other person; or (2) used by the producer for any purpose described in (a), (b), or (c).

*Biodiesel mixture excise tax credit*

The Code also provides an excise tax credit for biodiesel mixtures.[1618] The credit is $1.00 for each gallon of biodiesel used by the taxpayer in producing a biodiesel mixture for sale or use in a trade or business of the taxpayer. A biodiesel mixture is a mixture of biodiesel and diesel fuel that (1) is sold by the taxpayer producing such mixture to any person for use as a fuel or (2) is used as a fuel by the taxpayer producing such mixture. No credit is allowed unless the taxpayer obtains a certification (in such form and manner as prescribed by the Secretary) from the producer of the biodiesel that identifies the product produced and the percentage of biodiesel and agri-biodiesel in the product.[1619]

The credit is not available for any sale or use for any period after December 31, 2009. This excise tax credit is coordinated with the income tax credit for biodiesel such that credit for the same biodiesel cannot be claimed for both income and excise tax purposes.

*Payments with respect to biodiesel fuel mixtures*

If any person produces a biodiesel fuel mixture in such person's trade or business, the Secretary is to pay such person an amount equal to the biodiesel mixture credit.[1620] The biodiesel fuel mixture credit must first be taken against tax liability for taxable fuels. To the extent the biodiesel fuel mixture credit exceeds such tax liability, the excess may be received as a payment. Thus, if the person has no section 4081 liability, the credit is refundable. The Sec-

[1618] Sec. 6426(c).
[1619] Sec. 6426(c)(4).
[1620] Sec. 6427(e).

retary is not required to make payments with respect to biodiesel fuel mixtures sold or used after December 31, 2009.

### *Renewable diesel*

"Renewable diesel" is liquid fuel that (1) is derived from biomass (as defined in section 45K(c)(3)), (2) meets the registration requirements for fuels and fuel additives established by the EPA under section 211 of the Clean Air Act, and (3) meets the requirements of the ASTM D975 or D396, or equivalent standard established by the Secretary. ASTM D975 provides standards for diesel fuel suitable for use in diesel engines. ASTM D396 provides standards for fuel oil intended for use in fuel-oil burning equipment, such as furnaces. Renewable diesel also includes fuel derived from biomass that meets the requirements of a Department of Defense specification for military jet fuel or an ASTM specification for aviation turbine fuel.

For purposes of the Code, renewable diesel is generally treated the same as biodiesel. In the case of renewable diesel that is aviation fuel, kerosene is treated as though it were diesel fuel for purposes of a qualified renewable diesel mixture. Like biodiesel, the incentive may be taken as an income tax credit, an excise tax credit, or as a payment from the Secretary.[1621] The incentive for renewable diesel is $1.00 per gallon. There is no small producer credit for renewable diesel. The incentives for renewable diesel expire after December 31, 2009.

## *Explanation of Provision*

The provision extends the income tax credit, excise tax credit and payment provisions for biodiesel and renewable diesel for two additional years (through December 31, 2011).

In light of the retroactive nature of the provision, the provision creates a special rule to address claims regarding excise credits and claims for payment associated with periods occurring during 2010. In particular the provision directs the Secretary to issue guidance within 30 days of the date of enactment. Such guidance is to provide for a one-time submission of claims covering periods occurring during 2010. The guidance is to provide for a 180-day period for the submission of such claims (in such manner as prescribed by the Secretary) to begin no later than 30 days after such guidance is issued. Such claims shall be paid by the Secretary of the Treasury not later than 60 days after receipt. If the claim is not paid within 60 days of the date of the filing, the claim shall be paid with interest from such date determined by using the overpayment rate and method under section 6621 of such Code.

## *Effective Date*

The provision is effective for sales and uses after December 31, 2009.

[1621] Secs. 40A(f), 6426(c), and 6427(e).

### 2. Credit for refined coal facilities (sec. 702 of the Act and sec. 45 of the Code)

#### *Present Law*

#### *In general*

A credit is available for refined coal. In general, refined coal is a fuel produced from coal that is (1) used to produce steam or (2) used to produce steel industry fuel.

#### *Refined coal used to produce steam*

An income tax credit is allowed for the production at qualified facilities of certain refined coal sold to an unrelated person for use to produce steam. The amount of the refined coal credit is $4.375 per ton (adjusted for inflation using 1992 as the base year; $6.27 for 2010). A taxpayer may generally claim the credit during the 10-year period commencing with the date the qualified facility is placed in service.

A qualifying refined coal facility is a facility producing refined coal that is placed in service after October 22, 2004, and before January 1, 2010. Refined coal is a qualifying liquid, gaseous, or solid synthetic fuel produced from coal (including lignite) or high-carbon fly ash, including such fuel used as a feedstock. A qualifying fuel is a fuel that, when burned, emits 20 percent less nitrogen oxides and either sulfur dioxide or mercury than the burning of feedstock coal or comparable coal predominantly available in the marketplace as of January 1, 2003, but only if the fuel sells at prices at least 50 percent greater than the prices of the feedstock coal or comparable coal. In addition, to be qualified refined coal, the taxpayer must sell the fuel with the reasonable expectation that it will be used for the primary purpose of producing steam.

The refined coal credit is reduced over an $8.75 phase-out range as the reference price of the fuel used as feedstock for the refined coal exceeds an amount equal to 1.7 times the reference price for such fuel in 2002 (adjusted for inflation). The amount of the credit a taxpayer may claim is reduced by reason of grants, tax-exempt bonds, subsidized energy financing, and other credits, but the reduction cannot exceed 50 percent of the otherwise allowable credit.

The credit is a component of the general business credit,[1622] allowing excess credits to be carried back one year and forward up to 20 years. The credit is also subject to the alternative minimum tax.

#### *Facilities placed in service after 2008 that make refined coal used to produce steam*

For refined coal facilities placed in service after 2008, the requirement that the qualified refined coal fuel sell at a price at least 50 percent greater than the price of the feedstock coal does not apply. However, to be credit-eligible, refined coal produced by such facilities must reduce by 40 percent (not 20 percent) the amount by which refined coal must reduce, when burned, emissions of either sulfur dioxide or mercury compared to the emissions released by

---

[1622] Sec. 38(b)(8).

the feedstock coal or comparable coal predominantly available in the marketplace as of January 1, 2003.

***Refined coal that is steel industry fuel***

Each barrel-of-oil equivalent (defined as 5.8 million British thermal units) of steel industry fuel produced at a qualified facility during the credit period receives a $2 credit (adjusted for inflation using 1992 as the base year, $2.87 for 2010). A qualified facility is any facility capable of producing steel industry fuel (or any modification to a facility making it so capable) that is placed in service before January 1, 2010. For facilities capable of producing steel industry fuel on or before October 1, 2008, the credit is available for fuel produced and sold on or after such date and before January 1, 2010. For facilities placed in service or modified to produce steel industry fuel after October 1, 2008, the credit period begins on the placed-in-service or modification date and ends one year after such date or December 31, 2009, whichever is later.

Steel industry fuel is defined as a fuel produced through a process of liquefying coal waste sludge, distributing the liquefied product on coal, and using the resulting mixture as a feedstock for the manufacture of coke. Coal waste sludge includes tar decanter sludge and related byproducts of the coking process.

#### *Explanation of Provision*

The provision extends for two years (through December 31, 2011) the placed-in-service period for new refined coal facilities other than refined coal facilities that produce steel industry fuel.

#### *Effective Date*

The modifications to the placed-in-service period are effective on the date of enactment.

### 3. New energy efficient home credit (sec. 703 of the Act and sec. 45L of the Code)

#### *Present Law*

The Code provides a credit to an eligible contractor for each qualified new energy-efficient home that is constructed by the eligible contractor and acquired by a person from such eligible contractor for use as a residence during the taxable year. To qualify as a new energy-efficient home, the home must be: (1) a dwelling located in the United States, (2) substantially completed after August 8, 2005, and (3) certified in accordance with guidance prescribed by the Secretary to have a projected level of annual heating and cooling energy consumption that meets the standards for either a 30-percent or 50-percent reduction in energy usage, compared to a comparable dwelling constructed in accordance with the standards of chapter 4 of the 2003 International Energy Conservation Code as in effect (including supplements) on August 8, 2005, and any applicable Federal minimum efficiency standards for equipment. With respect to homes that meet the 30-percent standard, one-third of such 30-percent savings must come from the building envelope, and with respect to homes that meet the 50-percent standard, one-fifth of such 50-percent savings must come from the building envelope.

Manufactured homes that conform to Federal manufactured home construction and safety standards are eligible for the credit provided all the criteria for the credit are met. The eligible contractor is the person who constructed the home, or in the case of a manufactured home, the producer of such home.

The credit equals $1,000 in the case of a new home that meets the 30-percent standard and $2,000 in the case of a new home that meets the 50-percent standard. Only manufactured homes are eligible for the $1,000 credit.

In lieu of meeting the standards of chapter 4 of the 2003 International Energy Conservation Code, manufactured homes certified by a method prescribed by the Administrator of the Environmental Protection Agency under the Energy Star Labeled Homes program are eligible for the $1,000 credit provided criteria (1) and (2), above, are met.

The credit applies to homes that are purchased prior to January 1, 2010. The credit is part of the general business credit.

### *Explanation of Provision*

The provision extends the credit to homes that are purchased prior to January 1, 2012.

### *Effective Date*

The provision applies to homes acquired after December 31, 2009.

## 4. Excise tax credits and outlay payments for alternative fuel and alternative fuel mixtures (sec. 704 of the Act and secs. 6426 and 6427(e) of the Code)

### *Present Law*

The Code provides two per-gallon excise tax credits with respect to alternative fuel: the alternative fuel credit, and the alternative fuel mixture credit. For this purpose, the term "alternative fuel" means liquefied petroleum gas, P Series fuels (as defined by the Secretary of Energy under 42 U.S.C. sec. 13211(2)), compressed or liquefied natural gas, liquefied hydrogen, liquid fuel derived from coal through the Fischer-Tropsch process ("coal-to-liquids"), compressed or liquefied gas derived from biomass, or liquid fuel derived from biomass. Such term does not include ethanol, methanol, or biodiesel.

For coal-to-liquids produced after September 30, 2009, through December 30, 2009, the fuel must be certified as having been derived from coal produced at a gasification facility that separates and sequesters 50 percent of such facility's total carbon dioxide emissions. The sequestration percentage increases to 75 percent for fuel produced after December 30, 2009.

The alternative fuel credit is allowed against section 4041 liability, and the alternative fuel mixture credit is allowed against section 4081 liability. Neither credit is allowed unless the taxpayer is registered with the Secretary. The alternative fuel credit is 50 cents per gallon of alternative fuel or gasoline gallon equivalents[1623] of nonliquid alternative fuel sold by the taxpayer for use as a motor fuel in a motor vehicle or motorboat, sold for use in aviation or so used by the taxpayer.

The alternative fuel mixture credit is 50 cents per gallon of alternative fuel used in producing an alternative fuel mixture for sale or use in a trade or business of the taxpayer. An "alternative fuel mixture" is a mixture of alternative fuel and taxable fuel that contains at least 1⁄10 of one percent taxable fuel. The mixture must be sold by the taxpayer producing such mixture to any person for use as a fuel, or used by the taxpayer producing the mixture as a fuel. The credits generally expired after December 31, 2009 (September 30, 2014 for liquefied hydrogen).

A person may file a claim for payment equal to the amount of the alternative fuel credit and alternative fuel mixture credits. These payment provisions generally also expired after December 31, 2009. With respect to liquefied hydrogen, the payment provisions expire after September 30, 2014. The alternative fuel credit and alternative fuel mixture credit must first be applied to the applicable excise tax liability for under section 4041 or 4081, and any excess credit may be taken as a payment.

### *Explanation of Provision*

The provision extends the alternative fuel credit, alternative fuel mixture credit, and related payment provisions, for two additional years (through December 31, 2011). For purposes of the alternative fuel credit, alternative fuel mixture credit and related payment provisions, the provision excludes fuel (including lignin, wood residues, or spent pulping liquors) derived from the production of paper or pulp.

In light of the retroactive nature of the provision, the provision creates a special rule to address claims regarding excise credits and claims for payment associated with periods occurring during 2010. In particular the provision directs the Secretary to issue guidance within 30 days of the date of enactment. Such guidance is to provide for a one-time submission of claims covering periods occurring during 2010. The guidance is to provide for a 180–day period for the submission of such claims (in such manner as prescribed by the Secretary) to begin no later than 30 days after such guidance is issued. Such claims shall be paid by the Secretary of the Treasury not later than 60 days after receipt. If the claim is not paid within 60 days of the date of the filing, the claim shall be paid with interest from such date determined by using the overpayment rate and method under section 6621 of such Code.

### *Effective Date*

The provision is effective for fuel sold or used after December 31, 2009.

[1623] "Gasoline gallon equivalent" means, with respect to any nonliquid alternative fuel (for example, compressed natural gas), the amount of such fuel having a Btu (British thermal unit) content of 124,800 (higher heating value).

### 5. Special rule for sales or dispositions to implement FERC or State electric restructuring policy for qualified electric utilities (sec. 705 of the Act and sec. 451(i) of the Code)

#### *Present Law*

A taxpayer selling property generally recognizes gain to the extent the sales price (and any other consideration received) exceeds the seller's basis in the property. The recognized gain is subject to current income tax unless the gain is deferred or not recognized under a special tax provision.

One such special tax provision permits taxpayers to elect to recognize gain from qualifying electric transmission transactions ratably over an eight-year period beginning in the year of sale if the amount realized from such sale is used to purchase exempt utility property within the applicable period[1624] (the "reinvestment property").[1625] If the amount realized exceeds the amount used to purchase reinvestment property, any realized gain is recognized to the extent of such excess in the year of the qualifying electric transmission transaction.

A qualifying electric transmission transaction is the sale or other disposition of property used by a qualified electric utility to an independent transmission company prior to January 1, 2010. A qualified electric utility is defined as an electric utility, which as of the date of the qualifying electric transmission transaction, is vertically integrated in that it is both (1) a transmitting utility (as defined in the Federal Power Act)[1626] with respect to the transmission facilities to which the election applies, and (2) an electric utility (as defined in the Federal Power Act).[1627]

In general, an independent transmission company is defined as: (1) an independent transmission provider[1628] approved by the Federal Energy Regulatory Commission ("FERC"); (2) a person (i) who the FERC determines under section 203 of the Federal Power Act (or by declaratory order) is not a "market participant" and (ii) whose transmission facilities are placed under the operational control of a FERC-approved independent transmission provider no later than four years after the close of the taxable year in which the transaction occurs; or (3) in the case of facilities subject to the jurisdiction of the Public Utility Commission of Texas, (i) a person which is approved by that Commission as consistent with Texas State law regarding an independent transmission organization, or (ii) a political subdivision, or affiliate thereof, whose transmission facilities are under the operational control of an organization described in (i).

---

[1624] The applicable period for a taxpayer to reinvest the proceeds is four years after the close of the taxable year in which the qualifying electric transmission transaction occurs.

[1625] Sec. 451(i).

[1626] Sec. 3(23), 16 U.S.C. 796, defines "transmitting utility" as any electric utility, qualifying cogeneration facility, qualifying small power production facility, or Federal power marketing agency which owns or operates electric power transmission facilities which are used for the sale of electric energy at wholesale.

[1627] Sec. 3(22), 16 U.S.C. 796, defines "electric utility" as any person or State agency (including any municipality) which sells electric energy; such term includes the Tennessee Valley Authority, but does not include any Federal power marketing agency.

[1628] For example, a regional transmission organization, an independent system operator, or an independent transmission company.

Exempt utility property is defined as: (1) property used in the trade or business of generating, transmitting, distributing, or selling electricity or producing, transmitting, distributing, or selling natural gas, or (2) stock in a controlled corporation whose principal trade or business consists of the activities described in (1). Exempt utility property does not include any property that is located outside of the United States.

If a taxpayer is a member of an affiliated group of corporations filing a consolidated return, the reinvestment property may be purchased by any member of the affiliated group (in lieu of the taxpayer).

### *Explanation of Provision*

The provision extends the treatment under the present-law deferral provision to sales or dispositions by a qualified electric utility that occur prior to January 1, 2012.

### *Effective Date*

The extension provision applies to dispositions after December 31, 2009.

## 6. Suspension of limitation on percentage depletion for oil and gas from marginal wells (sec. 706 of the Act and sec. 613A of the Code)

### *Present Law*

The Code permits taxpayers to recover their investments in oil and gas wells through depletion deductions. Two methods of depletion are currently allowable under the Code: (1) the cost depletion method, and (2) the percentage depletion method.[1629] Under the cost depletion method, the taxpayer deducts that portion of the adjusted basis of the depletable property which is equal to the ratio of units sold from that property during the taxable year to the number of units remaining as of the end of taxable year plus the number of units sold during the taxable year. Thus, the amount recovered under cost depletion may never exceed the taxpayer's basis in the property.

The Code generally limits the percentage depletion method for oil and gas properties to independent producers and royalty owners.[1630] Generally, under the percentage depletion method, 15 percent of the taxpayer's gross income from an oil- or gas-producing property is allowed as a deduction in each taxable year.[1631] The amount deducted generally may not exceed 100 percent of the net income from that property in any year (the "net-income limitation").[1632] The 100-percent net-income limitation for marginal production has been suspended for taxable years beginning before January 1, 2010.

Marginal production is defined as domestic crude oil and natural gas production from stripper well property or from property sub-

[1629] Secs. 611–613.
[1630] Sec. 613A.
[1631] Sec. 613A(c).
[1632] Sec. 613(a).

stantially all of the production from which during the calendar year is heavy oil. Stripper well property is property from which the average daily production is 15 barrel equivalents or less, determined by dividing the average daily production of domestic crude oil and domestic natural gas from producing wells on the property for the calendar year by the number of wells. Heavy oil is domestic crude oil with a weighted average gravity of 20 degrees API or less (corrected to 60 degrees Fahrenheit).[1633]

### *Explanation of Provision*

The provision extends the suspension of the 100-percent net-income limitation for marginal production for two years (to apply to tax years beginning before January 1, 2012).

### *Effective Date*

The provision is effective for taxable years beginning after December 31, 2009.

## 7. Extension of grants for specified energy property in lieu of tax credits (sec. 707 of the Act)

### *Present Law*

#### *Renewable electricity production credit*

An income tax credit is allowed for the production of electricity from qualified energy resources at qualified facilities (the "renewable electricity production credit").[1634] Qualified energy resources comprise wind, closed-loop biomass, open-loop biomass, geothermal energy, solar energy, small irrigation power, municipal solid waste, qualified hydropower production, and marine and hydrokinetic renewable energy. Qualified facilities are, generally, facilities that generate electricity using qualified energy resources. To be eligible for the credit, electricity produced from qualified energy resources at qualified facilities must be sold by the taxpayer to an unrelated person.

SUMMARY OF CREDIT FOR ELECTRICITY PRODUCED FROM CERTAIN RENEWABLE RESOURCES

| Eligible electricity production activity (sec. 45) | Credit amount for 2010[1] (cents per kilowatt-hour) | Expiration[2] |
|---|---|---|
| Wind | 2.2 | December 31, 2012. |
| Closed-loop biomass | 2.2 | December 31, 2013. |
| Open-loop biomass (including agricultural livestock waste nutrient facilities). | 1.1 | December 31, 2013. |
| Geothermal | 2.2 | December 31, 2013. |
| Solar (pre-2006 facilities only) | 2.2 | December 31, 2005. |
| Small irrigation power | 1.1 | December 31, 2013. |
| Municipal solid waste (including landfill gas facilities and trash combustion facilities). | 1.1 | December 31, 2013. |
| Qualified hydropower | 1.1 | December 31, 2013. |
| Marine and hydrokinetic | 1.1 | December 31, 2013. |

[1] In general, the credit is available for electricity produced during the first 10 years after a facility has been placed in service.
[2] Expires for property placed in service after this date.

[1633] The American Petroleum Institute gravity, or API gravity, is a measure of how heavy or light a petroleum liquid is compared to water.

[1634] Sec. 45. In addition to the renewable electricity production credit, section 45 also provides income tax credits for the production of Indian coal and refined coal at qualified facilities.

### *Energy credit*

An income tax credit is also allowed for certain energy property placed in service. Qualifying property includes certain fuel cell property, solar property, geothermal power production property, small wind energy property, combined heat and power system property, and geothermal heat pump property.[1635]

SUMMARY OF ENERGY INVESTMENT TAX CREDIT

| | | Credit rate (Percent) | Maximum credit | Expiration |
|---|---|---|---|---|
| **Energy credit (sec. 48)** | Equipment to produce energy from a geothermal deposit. | 10 | None | None. |
| | Equipment to use ground or ground water for heating or cooling. | 10 | None | December 31, 2016. |
| | Microturbine property (<2 Mw electrical generation power plants of >26% efficiency). | 10 | $200 per Kw of capacity. | December 31, 2016. |
| | Combined heat and power property (simultaneous production of electrical/mechanical power and useful heat > 60% efficiency). | 10 | None | December 31, 2016. |
| | Solar electric or solar hot water property. | 30% (10% after December 31, 2016). | None | None. |
| | Fuel cell property (generates electricity through electrochemical process). | 30 | $1,500 for each ½ Kw of capacity. | December 31, 2016. |
| | Small (<100 Kw capacity) wind electrical generation property. | 30 | None | December 31, 2016. |

### *Election to claim energy credit in lieu of renewable electricity production credit*

A taxpayer may make an irrevocable election to have certain property which is part of a qualified renewable electricity production facility be treated as energy property eligible for a 30 percent investment credit under section 48. For this purpose, qualified facilities are facilities otherwise eligible for the renewable electricity production credit with respect to which no credit under section 45 has been allowed. A taxpayer electing to treat a facility as energy property may not claim the renewable electricity production credit. The eligible basis for the investment credit for taxpayers making this election is the basis of the depreciable (or amortizable) property that is part of a facility capable of generating electricity eligible for the renewable electricity production credit.

### *Grants in lieu of credits*

The Secretary of the Treasury is authorized to provide a grant to each person who places in service depreciable property that is either (1) part of a qualified renewable electricity production facility or (2) qualifying property otherwise eligible for the energy credit. In general, the grant amount is 30 percent of the basis of the qualified property. For qualified microturbine, combined heat and power system, and geothermal heat pump property, the amount is 10 percent of the basis of the property. Otherwise eligible property

[1635] Sec. 48.

must be placed in service in calendar years 2009 or 2010, or its construction must begin during that period and must be completed prior to 2013 (in the case of wind facility property), 2014 (in the case of other renewable power facility property eligible for credit under section 45), or 2017 (in the case of any specified energy property described in section 48).

The grant provision mimics the operation of the energy credit. For example, the amount of the grant is not includable in gross income. However, the basis of the property is reduced by 50 percent of the amount of the grant. In addition, some or all of each grant is subject to recapture if the grant-eligible property is disposed of by the grant recipient within five years of being placed in service.

Under the provision, if a grant is paid, no renewable electricity credit or energy credit may be claimed with respect to the grant-eligible property. In general, tax-exempt entities are not eligible to receive a grant. No grant may be made unless the application for the grant has been received before October 1, 2011.

### *Description of Proposal*

The proposal extends the Secretary's authority to provide grants in lieu of credits for one year (through 2011). Otherwise eligible property must thus be placed in service in calendar years 2009, 2010, or 2011, or its construction must begin during that period and must be completed prior to 2013 (in the case of wind facility property), 2014 (in the case of other renewable power facility property eligible for credit under section 45), or 2017 (in the case of any specified energy property described in section 48).

### *Effective Date*

The proposal is effective on the date of enactment.

## 8. Extension of provisions related to alcohol used as fuel (sec. 708 of the Act and secs. 40, 6426, 6427(e) of the Code)

### *Present Law*

Sections 40, 6426 and 6427(e) provide per-gallon tax incentives for the sale, use and production of alcohol fuel and alcohol fuel mixtures. The incentives for alcohol generally do not apply after December 31, 2010. For cellulosic biofuel (discussed infra), the incentive is unavailable after December 31, 2012.

"Alcohol" includes methanol and ethanol, and the alcohol gallon equivalent of ethyl tertiary butyl ether, or other ethers produced from such alcohol. It does not include alcohol produced from petroleum, natural gas, or coal, or any alcohol with a proof of less than 150 (190 proof for purposes of the credit taken under 6426 or payment under section 6427). Denaturants (additives that make the alcohol unfit for human consumption) are disregarded for purposes of determining proof. However, denaturants are taken into account in determining the volume of alcohol eligible for the per-gallon incentive. In calculating alcohol volume, denaturants cannot exceed two percent of volume.

The section 40 alcohol fuels credit is an income tax credit comprised of four components: (1) the alcohol mixture credit, (2) the alcohol credit, (3) the small ethanol producer credit, and (4) the cellulosic biofuel producer credit. Sections 6426 and 6427(e) pertain to alcohol fuel mixtures only.

*Alcohol mixture credits and payments*

The alcohol fuel mixture credit may be taken as part of the section 40 income tax credit, the section 6426 excise tax credit, or as a payment under section 6427. For section 40, an alcohol fuel mixture is a mixture of alcohol and gasoline or alcohol and a special fuel. Since the excise tax credit is taken against the liability for taxable fuels (gasoline, kerosene, or diesel), for purposes of the excise tax payments and credits, an alcohol fuel mixture is a mixture of alcohol and a taxable fuel.

The fuel must be either sold for use as a fuel to another person or used as fuel in the mixture producer's trade or business. The addition of denaturants does not constitute production of a mixture. The credit is allowed only for the gallons of alcohol used to produce the mixture. For alcohol that is ethanol, the amount of the incentive is 45 cents per gallon. For other alcohol, the incentive is generally 60 cents per gallon.

The alcohol mixture credit is most often taken as an excise tax credit or payment. Persons who blend alcohol with gasoline, diesel fuel, or kerosene to produce an alcohol fuel mixture must pay tax on the volume of alcohol in the mixture when the mixture is sold or removed. The alcohol fuel mixture credit must first be taken to reduce excise tax liability for gasoline, diesel fuel or kerosene. Any excess credit may be taken as a payment or income tax credit.

*Alcohol credit (straight or "neat" alcohol)*

The second component of the section 40 income tax credit is the alcohol credit. The credit is available for alcohol (not in a mixture) that is either (1) used as a fuel in the taxpayer's trade or business, or (2) sold at retail and placed in the fuel tank of the retail buyer's vehicle. The credit cannot be claimed for alcohol bought at retail and placed in the fuel tank of the retail buyer's vehicle, even if the buyer uses it as a fuel in a trade or business. This credit is not available as an excise tax credit or payment.

*Small ethanol producer credit*

The third component of the section 40 income tax credit is the small ethanol producer credit. It is in addition to the credits described above and is an extra 10 cents per gallon available for up to 15 million gallons of qualified ethanol fuel production for any tax year. The 15 million gallon limitation is waived for ethanol that is cellulosic ethanol. The credit is available to eligible small ethanol producers, defined as producers who have an annual productive capacity of not more than 60 million gallons of any type of alcohol. Qualified ethanol fuel production is ethanol produced and sold by such producer to another person (a) for use by such other person in the production of a qualified alcohol fuel mixture in such person's trade or business (other than casual off-farm production), (b) for use by such other person as a fuel in a trade or business, or

(c) who sells such ethanol at retail to another person and places such ethanol in the fuel tank of such other person. Qualified ethanol fuel production also includes production for use or sale by the producer for any purpose described in (a), (b), or (c). A cooperative may pass through the small ethanol producer credit to its patrons. The small ethanol producer credit is not available as an excise tax credit or payment.

*Cellulosic biofuel producer credit*

The cellulosic biofuel producer credit is a nonrefundable income tax credit for each gallon of qualified cellulosic fuel production of the producer for the taxable year. The amount of the credit per gallon is $1.01, except in the case of cellulosic biofuel that is alcohol. In the case of cellulosic biofuel that is alcohol, the $1.01 credit amount is reduced by (1) the credit amount applicable for such alcohol under the alcohol mixture credit as in effect at the time cellulosic biofuel is produced and (2) in the case of cellulosic biofuel that is also ethanol, the credit amount for small ethanol producers as in effect at the time the cellulosic biofuel fuel is produced. The reduction applies regardless of whether the producer claims the alcohol mixture credit or small ethanol producer credit with respect to the cellulosic alcohol. When the alcohol mixture credit and small ethanol producer credit expire after December 31, 2010, cellulosic biofuel that is alcohol is entitled to the $1.01 without reduction.

***Duties on ethanol***

Heading 9901.00.50 of the Harmonized Tariff Schedule of the United States imposes a cumulative general duty of 14.27 cents per liter (approximately 54 cents per gallon) on imports of ethyl alcohol, and any mixture containing ethyl alcohol, if used as a fuel or in producing a mixture to be used as a fuel, that are entered into the United States prior to January 1, 2011. Heading 9901.00.52 of the Harmonized Tariff Schedule of the United States imposes a general duty of 5.99 cents per liter on imports of ethyl tertiary-butyl ether, and any mixture containing ethyl tertiary-butyl ether, that are entered into the United States prior to January 1, 2011.

## ***Explanation of Provision***

***Extension of income tax credit***

The provision extends the present-law income tax credit for alcohol fuels (other than the cellulosic biofuel producer credit) an additional year, through December 31, 2011.

***Extension of excise tax credit and outlay payment provisions for alcohol used as a fuel***

The provision extends the present-law excise tax credit and outlay payments for alcohol fuel mixtures for an additional year, through December 31, 2011.

***Extension of additional duties on ethanol***

The provision extends the present-law duties on ethanol and ethyl tertiary butyl ether for an additional year, through December 31, 2011.

### *Effective Date*

The extension of the income tax credit is effective for periods after December 31, 2010. The extension of excise tax credit for alcohol fuel mixtures applies to periods after December 31, 2010. The extension of the payment provisions for alcohol fuel mixtures applies to sales and uses after December 31, 2010. The extension of additional duties on ethanol takes effect on January 1, 2011.

## 9. Energy efficient appliance credit (sec. 709 of the Act and sec. 45M of the Code)

### *Present Law*

#### *In general*

A credit is allowed for the eligible production of certain energy-efficient dishwashers, clothes washers, and refrigerators. The credit is part of the general business credit.

The credits are as follows:

*Dishwashers*

$45 in the case of a dishwasher that is manufactured in calendar year 2008 or 2009 that uses no more than 324 kilowatt hours per year and 5.8 gallons per cycle, and

$75 in the case of a dishwasher that is manufactured in calendar year 2008, 2009, or 2010 and that uses no more than 307 kilowatt hours per year and 5.0 gallons per cycle (5.5 gallons per cycle for dishwashers designed for greater than 12 place settings).

*Clothes washers*

$75 in the case of a residential top-loading clothes washer manufactured in calendar year 2008 that meets or exceeds a 1.72 modified energy factor and does not exceed a 8.0 water consumption factor, and

$125 in the case of a residential top-loading clothes washer manufactured in calendar year 2008 or 2009 that meets or exceeds a 1.8 modified energy factor and does not exceed a 7.5 water consumption factor,

$150 in the case of a residential or commercial clothes washer manufactured in calendar year 2008, 2009, or 2010 that meets or exceeds a 2.0 modified energy factor and does not exceed a 6.0 water consumption factor, and

$250 in the case of a residential or commercial clothes washer manufactured in calendar year 2008, 2009, or 2010 that meets or exceeds a 2.2 modified energy factor and does not exceed a 4.5 water consumption factor.

*Refrigerators*

$50 in the case of a refrigerator manufactured in calendar year 2008 that consumes at least 20 percent but not more than 22.9 percent less kilowatt hours per year than the 2001 energy conservation standards,

$75 in the case of a refrigerator that is manufactured in calendar year 2008 or 2009 that consumes at least 23 percent but not more than 24.9 percent less kilowatt hours per year than the 2001 energy conservation standards,

$100 in the case of a refrigerator that is manufactured in calendar year 2008, 2009, or 2010 that consumes at least 25 percent but not more than 29.9 percent less kilowatt hours per year than the 2001 energy conservation standards, and

$200 in the case of a refrigerator manufactured in calendar year 2008, 2009, or 2010 that consumes at least 30 percent less energy than the 2001 energy conservation standards.

*Definitions*

A dishwasher is any residential dishwasher subject to the energy conservation standards established by the Department of Energy. A refrigerator must be an automatic defrost refrigerator-freezer with an internal volume of at least 16.5 cubic feet to qualify for the credit. A clothes washer is any residential clothes washer, including a residential style coin operated washer, that satisfies the relevant efficiency standard.

The term "modified energy factor" means the modified energy factor established by the Department of Energy for compliance with the Federal energy conservation standard.

The term "gallons per cycle" means, with respect to a dishwasher, the amount of water, expressed in gallons, required to complete a normal cycle of a dishwasher.

The term "water consumption factor" means, with respect to a clothes washer, the quotient of the total weighted per-cycle water consumption divided by the cubic foot (or liter) capacity of the clothes washer.

***Other rules***

Appliances eligible for the credit include only those produced in the United States and that exceed the average amount of U.S. production from the two prior calendar years for each category of appliance. The aggregate credit amount allowed with respect to a taxpayer for all taxable years beginning after December 31, 2007, may not exceed $75 million, with the exception that the $200 refrigerator credit and the $250 clothes washer credit are not limited. Additionally, the credit allowed in a taxable year for all appliances may not exceed two percent of the average annual gross receipts of the taxpayer for the three taxable years preceding the taxable year in which the credit is determined.

## ***Explanation of Provision***

The provision extends the credit for one year, for appliances manufactured in 2011, and changes the aggregate credit limitation to permit up to $25 million in credits to be claimed per manufacturer for appliances manufactured in 2011. Additionally, the provision changes the two percent gross receipts limitation on the credit to four percent. The credit modifies the standards and credit amounts as follows:

*Dishwashers*

$25 in the case of a dishwasher which is manufactured in calendar year 2011 and which uses no more than 307 kilowatt hours per year and 5.0 gallons per cycle (5.5 gallons per cycle for dishwashers designed for greater than 12 place settings),

$50 in the case of a dishwasher which is manufactured in calendar year 2011 and which uses no more than 295 kilowatt hours per year and 4.25 gallons per cycle (4.75 gallons per cycle for dishwashers designed for greater than 12 place settings), and

$75 in the case of a dishwasher which is manufactured in calendar year 2011 and which uses no more than 280 kilowatt hours per year and 4 gallons per cycle (4.5 gallons per cycle for dishwashers designed for greater than 12 place settings).

*Clothes washers*

$175 in the case of a top-loading clothes washer manufactured in calendar year 2011 which meets or exceeds a 2.2 modified energy factor and does not exceed a 4.5 water consumption factor, and

$225 in the case of a clothes washer manufactured in calendar year 2011 which (1) is a top-loading clothes washer and which meets or exceeds a 2.4 modified energy factor and does not exceed a 4.2 water consumption factor, or (2) is a front-loading clothes washer and which meets or exceeds a 2.8 modified energy factor and does not exceed a 3.5 water consumption factor.

*Refrigerators*

$150 in the case of a refrigerator manufactured in calendar year 2011 which consumes at least 30 percent less energy than the 2001 energy conservation standards, and

$200 in the case of a refrigerator manufactured in calendar year 2011 which consumes at least 35 percent less energy than the 2001 energy conservation standards.

### *Effective Date*

The provision applies to appliances produced after December 31, 2010. The provision related to the gross receipts limitation applies to taxable years beginning after December 31, 2010.

## 10. Credit for nonbusiness energy property (sec. 710 of the Act and sec. 25C of the Code)

### *Present Law*

#### *In general*

Section 25C provides a 30-percent credit for the purchase of qualified energy efficiency improvements to the envelope of existing homes. Additionally, section 25C provides a 30 percent credit for the purchase of (1) qualified natural gas, propane, or oil furnace or hot water boilers, (2) qualified energy efficient building property, and (3) advanced main air circulating fans.

The credit applies to expenditures made after December 31, 2008, for property placed in service after December 31, 2008, and prior to January 1, 2011.[1636] The aggregate amount of the credit

[1636] With the exception of biomass fuel property, property placed in service after December 31, 2008 and prior to February 17, 2009 qualifies for the new 30 percent credit rate (and $1,500 aggregate cap) if it met the efficiency standards of prior law for property placed in service during

Continued

allowed for a taxpayer for taxable years beginning in 2009 and 2010 is $1,500.

***Building envelope improvements***

A qualified energy efficiency improvement is any energy efficient building envelope component (1) that meets or exceeds the prescriptive criteria for such a component established by the 2000 International Energy Conservation Code[1637] as supplemented and as in effect on August 8, 2005 (or, in the case of metal roofs with appropriate pigmented coatings, meets the Energy Star program requirements); (2) that is installed in or on a dwelling located in the United States and owned and used by the taxpayer as the taxpayer's principal residence; (3) the original use of which commences with the taxpayer; and (4) that reasonably can be expected to remain in use for at least five years. The credit is nonrefundable.

Building envelope components are: (1) insulation materials or systems which are specifically and primarily designed to reduce the heat loss or gain for a dwelling and which meet the prescriptive criteria for such material or system established by the 2009 International Energy Conservation Code, as such Code (including supplements) is in effect on the date of the enactment of the American Recovery and Reinvestment Tax Act of 2009 (February 17, 2009); (2) exterior windows (including skylights) and doors provided such component has a U-factor and a seasonal heat gain coefficient ("SHGC") of 0.3 or less; and (3) metal or asphalt roofs with appropriate pigmented coatings or cooling granules that are specifically and primarily designed to reduce the heat gain for a dwelling.

***Other eligible property***

*Qualified natural gas, propane, or oil furnace or hot water boilers*

A qualified natural gas, propane, or oil hot water boiler is a natural gas, propane, or oil hot water boiler with an annual fuel utilization efficiency rate of at least 90. A qualified natural gas or propane furnace is a natural gas or propane furnace with an annual fuel utilization efficiency rate of at least 95. A qualified oil furnace is an oil furnace with an annual fuel utilization efficiency rate of at least 90.

*Qualified energy-efficient building property*

Qualified energy-efficient building property is: (1) an electric heat pump water heater which yields an energy factor of at least 2.0 in the standard Department of Energy test procedure, (2) an electric heat pump which achieves the highest efficiency tier established by the Consortium for Energy Efficiency, as in effect on January 1, 2009,[1638] (3) a central air conditioner which achieves the highest

ing 2009. Biomass fuel property placed in service at any point in 2009 is governed by the new efficiency standard.

[1637] This reference to the 2000 International Energy Conservation Code is superseded by the additional requirements described in the paragraph below regarding building envelope components.

[1638] These standards are a seasonal energy efficiency ratio ("SEER") greater than or equal to 15, an energy efficiency ratio ("EER") greater than or equal to 12.5, and heating seasonal performance factor ("HSPF") greater than or equal to 8.5 for split heat pumps, and SEER greater

efficiency tier established by the Consortium for Energy Efficiency as in effect on Jan. 1, 2009,[1639] (4) a natural gas, propane, or oil water heater which has an energy factor of at least 0.82 or thermal efficiency of at least 90 percent, and (5) biomass fuel property.

Biomass fuel property is a stove that burns biomass fuel to heat a dwelling unit located in the United States and used as a principal residence by the taxpayer, or to heat water for such dwelling unit, and that has a thermal efficiency rating of at least 75 percent as measured using a lower heating value. Biomass fuel is any plant-derived fuel available on a renewable or recurring basis, including agricultural crops and trees, wood and wood waste and residues (including wood pellets), plants (including aquatic plants), grasses, residues, and fibers.

*Advanced main air circulating fan*

An advanced main air circulating fan is a fan used in a natural gas, propane, or oil furnace and which has an annual electricity use of no more than two percent of the total annual energy use of the furnace (as determined in the standard Department of Energy test procedures).

### *Additional rules*

The taxpayer's basis in the property is reduced by the amount of the credit. Special proration rules apply in the case of jointly owned property, condominiums, and tenant-stockholders in cooperative housing corporations. If less than 80 percent of the property is used for nonbusiness purposes, only that portion of expenditures that is used for nonbusiness purposes is taken into account.

## *Explanation of Provision*

The provision extends the credits for one year but utilizes the credit structure and credit rates that existed prior to the enactment of the American Recovery and Reinvestment Act of 2009. The provision reinstates the rule that expenditures made from subsidized energy financing are not qualifying expenditures. Additionally, certain efficiency standards that were weakened in the American Recovery and Reinvestment Act are restored to their prior levels. Lastly, the provision provides that windows, skylights and doors that meet the Energy Star standards are qualified improvements.

The following describes the operation of the credit under the provision:

Section 25C provides a 10-percent credit for the purchase of qualified energy efficiency improvements to existing homes. A qualified energy efficiency improvement is any energy efficiency building envelope component (1) that meets or exceeds the prescriptive criteria for such a component established by the 2009 International Energy Conservation Code as such Code (including supplements) is in effect on the date of the enactment of the American Recovery and Reinvestment Tax Act of 2009 (February 17,

---

than or equal to 14, EER greater than or equal to 12, and HSPF greater than or equal to 8.0 for packaged heat pumps.

[1639] These standards are a SEER greater than or equal to 16 and EER greater than or equal to 13 for split systems, and SEER greater than or equal to 14 and EER greater than or equal to 12 for packaged systems.

2009) (or, in the case of windows, skylights and doors, and metal roofs with appropriate pigmented coatings or asphalt roofs with appropriate cooling granules, meets the Energy Star program requirements); (2) that is installed in or on a dwelling located in the United States and owned and used by the taxpayer as the taxpayer's principal residence; (3) the original use of which commences with the taxpayer; and (4) that reasonably can be expected to remain in use for at least five years. The credit is nonrefundable.

Building envelope components are: (1) insulation materials or systems which are specifically and primarily designed to reduce the heat loss or gain for a dwelling and which meet the prescriptive criteria for such material or system established by the 2009 International Energy Conservation Code, as such Code (including supplements) is in effect on the date of the enactment of the American Recovery and Reinvestment Tax Act of 2009 (February 17, 2009); (2) exterior windows (including skylights) and doors; and (3) metal or asphalt roofs with appropriate pigmented coatings or cooling granules that are specifically and primarily designed to reduce the heat gain for a dwelling.

Additionally, section 25C provides specified credits for the purchase of specific energy efficient property originally placed in service by the taxpayer during the taxable year. The allowable credit for the purchase of certain property is (1) $50 for each advanced main air circulating fan, (2) $150 for each qualified natural gas, propane, or oil furnace or hot water boiler, and (3) $300 for each item of energy efficient building property.

An advanced main air circulating fan is a fan used in a natural gas, propane, or oil furnace and which has an annual electricity use of no more than two percent of the total annual energy use of the furnace (as determined in the standard Department of Energy test procedures).

A qualified natural gas, propane, or oil furnace or hot water boiler is a natural gas, propane, or oil furnace or hot water boiler with an annual fuel utilization efficiency rate of at least 95.

Energy-efficient building property is: (1) an electric heat pump water heater which yields an energy factor of at least 2.0 in the standard Department of Energy test procedure, (2) an electric heat pump which achieves the highest efficiency tier established by the Consortium for Energy Efficiency, as in effect on January 1, 2009,[1640] (3) a central air conditioner which achieves the highest efficiency tier established by the Consortium for Energy Efficiency as in effect on Jan. 1, 2009,[1641] (4) a natural gas, propane, or oil water heater which has an energy factor of at least 0.82 or thermal efficiency of at least 90 percent, and (5) biomass fuel property.

Biomass fuel property is a stove that burns biomass fuel to heat a dwelling unit located in the United States and used as a principal residence by the taxpayer, or to heat water for such dwelling

[1640] These standards are a seasonal energy efficiency ratio ("SEER") greater than or equal to 15, an energy efficiency ratio ("EER") greater than or equal to 12.5, and heating seasonal performance factor ("HSPF") greater than or equal to 8.5 for split heat pumps, and SEER greater than or equal to 14, EER greater than or equal to 12, and HSPF greater than or equal to 8.0 for packaged heat pumps.

[1641] These standards are a SEER greater than or equal to 16 and EER greater than or equal to 13 for split systems, and SEER greater than or equal to 14 and EER greater than or equal to 12 for packaged systems.

unit, and that has a thermal efficiency rating of at least 75 percent. Biomass fuel is any plant-derived fuel available on a renewable or recurring basis, including agricultural crops and trees, wood and wood waste and residues (including wood pellets), plants (including aquatic plants), grasses, residues, and fibers.

Under section 25C, the maximum credit for a taxpayer for all taxable years is $500, and no more than $200 of such credit may be attributable to expenditures on windows.

The taxpayer's basis in the property is reduced by the amount of the credit. Special proration rules apply in the case of jointly owned property, condominiums, and tenant-stockholders in cooperative housing corporations. If less than 80 percent of the property is used for nonbusiness purposes, only that portion of expenditures that is used for nonbusiness purposes is taken into account.

For purposes of determining the amount of expenditures made by any individual with respect to any dwelling unit, expenditures which are made from subsidized energy financing are not taken into account. The term "subsidized energy financing" means financing provided under a Federal, State, or local program a principal purpose of which is to provide subsidized financing for projects designed to conserve or produce energy.

### *Effective Date*

The provision applies to property placed in service after December 31. 2010.

## 11. Alternative fuel vehicle refueling property (sec. 711 of the Act and sec. 30C of the Code)

### *Present Law*

Taxpayers may claim a 30-percent credit for the cost of installing qualified clean-fuel vehicle refueling property to be used in a trade or business of the taxpayer or installed at the principal residence of the taxpayer.[1642] The credit may not exceed $30,000 per taxable year per location, in the case of qualified refueling property used in a trade or business and $1,000 per taxable year per location, in the case of qualified refueling property installed on property which is used as a principal residence.

For property placed in service in 2009 or 2010, the maximum credit available for business property is increased to $200,000 for qualified hydrogen refueling property and to $50,000 for other qualified refueling property. For nonbusiness property, the maximum credit is increased to $2,000 for refueling property other than hydrogen refueling property. In addition, during these years, the credit rate is increased from 30 percent to 50 percent for refueling property other than hydrogen refueling property.

Qualified refueling property is property (not including a building or its structural components) for the storage or dispensing of a clean-burning fuel or electricity into the fuel tank or battery of a motor vehicle propelled by such fuel or electricity, but only if the storage or dispensing of the fuel or electricity is at the point of de-

[1642] Sec. 30C.

livery into the fuel tank or battery of the motor vehicle. The original use of such property must begin with the taxpayer.

Clean-burning fuels are any fuel at least 85 percent of the volume of which consists of ethanol, natural gas, compressed natural gas, liquefied natural gas, liquefied petroleum gas, or hydrogen. In addition, any mixture of biodiesel and diesel fuel, determined without regard to any use of kerosene and containing at least 20 percent biodiesel, qualifies as a clean fuel.

Credits for qualified refueling property used in a trade or business are part of the general business credit and may be carried back for one year and forward for 20 years. Credits for residential qualified refueling property cannot exceed for any taxable year the difference between the taxpayer's regular tax (reduced by certain other credits) and the taxpayer's tentative minimum tax. Generally, in the case of qualified refueling property sold to a tax-exempt entity, the taxpayer selling the property may claim the credit.

A taxpayer's basis in qualified refueling property is reduced by the amount of the credit. In addition, no credit is available for property used outside the United States or for which an election to expense has been made under section 179.

The credit is available for property placed in service after December 31, 2005, and (except in the case of hydrogen refueling property) before January 1, 2011. In the case of hydrogen refueling property, the property must be placed in service before January 1, 2015.

### *Explanation of Provision*

The provision extends through 2011 the 30-percent credit for alternative fuel refueling property (other than hydrogen refueling property, the credit for which continues under present law through 2014), subject to the pre-2009 maximum credit amounts.

### *Effective Date*

The provision is effective for property placed in service after December 31, 2010.

## B. Individual Tax Relief

### 1. Deduction for certain expenses of elementary and secondary school teachers (sec. 721 of the Act and sec. 62 of the Code)

### *Present Law*

In general, ordinary and necessary business expenses are deductible. However, unreimbursed employee business expenses generally are deductible only as an itemized deduction and only to the extent that the individual's total miscellaneous deductions (including employee business expenses) exceed two percent of adjusted gross income. With the exception of taxable years beginning in 2010, an individual's otherwise allowable itemized deductions may be further limited by the overall limitation on itemized deductions, which reduces itemized deductions for taxpayers with adjusted gross income in excess of a threshold amount. In addition, miscellaneous itemized deductions are not allowable under the alternative minimum tax.

Certain expenses of eligible educators are allowed as an above-the-line deduction. Specifically, for taxable years beginning prior to January 1, 2010, an above-the-line deduction is allowed for up to $250 annually of expenses paid or incurred by an eligible educator for books, supplies (other than nonathletic supplies for courses of instruction in health or physical education), computer equipment (including related software and services) and other equipment, and supplementary materials used by the eligible educator in the classroom.[1643] To be eligible for this deduction, the expenses must be otherwise deductible under section 162 as a trade or business expense. A deduction is allowed only to the extent the amount of expenses exceeds the amount excludable from income under section 135 (relating to education savings bonds), 529(c)(1) (relating to qualified tuition programs), and section 530(d)(2) (relating to Coverdell education savings accounts).

An eligible educator is a kindergarten through grade twelve teacher, instructor, counselor, principal, or aide in a school for at least 900 hours during a school year. A school means any school that provides elementary education or secondary education, as determined under State law.

The above-the-line deduction for eligible educators is not allowed for taxable years beginning after December 31, 2009.

### *Explanation of Provision*

The provision extends the deduction for eligible educator expenses for two years so that it is available for taxable years beginning before January 1, 2012.

### *Effective Date*

The provision is effective for expenses incurred in taxable years beginning after December 31, 2009.

## 2. Deduction of State and local sales taxes (sec. 722 of the Act and sec. 164 of the Code)

### *Present Law*

For purposes of determining regular tax liability, an itemized deduction is permitted for certain State and local taxes paid, including individual income taxes, real property taxes, and personal property taxes. The itemized deduction is not permitted for purposes of determining a taxpayer's alternative minimum taxable income. For taxable years beginning in 2004–2009, at the election of the taxpayer, an itemized deduction may be taken for State and local general sales taxes in lieu of the itemized deduction provided under present law for State and local income taxes. As is the case for State and local income taxes, the itemized deduction for State and local general sales taxes is not permitted for purposes of determining a taxpayer's alternative minimum taxable income. Taxpayers have two options with respect to the determination of the

[1643] Sec. 62(a)(2)(D).

sales tax deduction amount. Taxpayers may deduct the total amount of general State and local sales taxes paid by accumulating receipts showing general sales taxes paid. Alternatively, taxpayers may use tables created by the Secretary that show the allowable deduction. The tables are based on average consumption by taxpayers on a State-by-State basis taking into account number of dependents, modified adjusted gross income and rates of State and local general sales taxation. Taxpayers who live in more than one jurisdiction during the tax year are required to pro-rate the table amounts based on the time they live in each jurisdiction. Taxpayers who use the tables created by the Secretary may, in addition to the table amounts, deduct eligible general sales taxes paid with respect to the purchase of motor vehicles, boats and other items specified by the Secretary. Sales taxes for items that may be added to the tables are not reflected in the tables themselves.

The term "general sales tax" means a tax imposed at one rate with respect to the sale at retail of a broad range of classes of items. However, in the case of items of food, clothing, medical supplies, and motor vehicles, the fact that the tax does not apply with respect to some or all of such items is not taken into account in determining whether the tax applies with respect to a broad range of classes of items, and the fact that the rate of tax applicable with respect to some or all of such items is lower than the general rate of tax is not taken into account in determining whether the tax is imposed at one rate. Except in the case of a lower rate of tax applicable with respect to food, clothing, medical supplies, or motor vehicles, no deduction is allowed for any general sales tax imposed with respect to an item at a rate other than the general rate of tax. However, in the case of motor vehicles, if the rate of tax exceeds the general rate, such excess shall be disregarded and the general rate is treated as the rate of tax.

A compensating use tax with respect to an item is treated as a general sales tax, provided such tax is complementary to a general sales tax and a deduction for sales taxes is allowable with respect to items sold at retail in the taxing jurisdiction that are similar to such item.

### *Explanation of Provision*

The provision allowing taxpayers to elect to deduct State and local sales taxes in lieu of State and local income taxes is extended for two years (through December 31, 2011).

### *Effective Date*

The provision applies to taxable years beginning after December 31, 2009.

### 3. Contributions of capital gain real property made for conservation purposes (sec. 723 of the Act and sec. 170 of the Code)

#### *Present Law*

#### *Charitable contributions generally*

In general, a deduction is permitted for charitable contributions, subject to certain limitations that depend on the type of taxpayer, the property contributed, and the donee organization. The amount of deduction generally equals the fair market value of the contributed property on the date of the contribution. Charitable deductions are provided for income, estate, and gift tax purposes.[1644]

In general, in any taxable year, charitable contributions by a corporation are not deductible to the extent the aggregate contributions exceed 10 percent of the corporation's taxable income computed without regard to net operating or capital loss carrybacks. For individuals, the amount deductible is a percentage of the taxpayer's contribution base, (i.e., taxpayer's adjusted gross income computed without regard to any net operating loss carryback). The applicable percentage of the contribution base varies depending on the type of donee organization and property contributed. Cash contributions by an individual taxpayer to public charities, private operating foundations, and certain types of private nonoperating foundations may not exceed 50 percent of the taxpayer's contribution base. Cash contributions to private foundations and certain other organizations generally may be deducted up to 30 percent of the taxpayer's contribution base.

In general, a charitable deduction is not allowed for income, estate, or gift tax purposes if the donor transfers an interest in property to a charity while also either retaining an interest in that property or transferring an interest in that property to a noncharity for less than full and adequate consideration. Exceptions to this general rule are provided for, among other interests, remainder interests in charitable remainder annuity trusts, charitable remainder unitrusts, and pooled income funds, present interests in the form of a guaranteed annuity or a fixed percentage of the annual value of the property, and qualified conservation contributions.

#### *Capital gain property*

Capital gain property means any capital asset or property used in the taxpayer's trade or business the sale of which at its fair market value, at the time of contribution, would have resulted in gain that would have been long-term capital gain. Contributions of capital gain property to a qualified charity are deductible at fair market value within certain limitations. Contributions of capital gain property to charitable organizations described in section 170(b)(1)(A) (e.g., public charities, private foundations other than private non-operating foundations, and certain governmental units) generally are deductible up to 30 percent of the taxpayer's contribution base. An individual may elect, however, to bring all these

[1644] Secs. 170, 2055, and 2522, respectively.

contributions of capital gain property for a taxable year within the 50-percent limitation category by reducing the amount of the contribution deduction by the amount of the appreciation in the capital gain property. Contributions of capital gain property to charitable organizations described in section 170(b)(1)(B) (e.g., private non-operating foundations) are deductible up to 20 percent of the taxpayer's contribution base.

For purposes of determining whether a taxpayer's aggregate charitable contributions in a taxable year exceed the applicable percentage limitation, contributions of capital gain property are taken into account after other charitable contributions. Contributions of capital gain property that exceed the percentage limitation may be carried forward for five years.

***Qualified conservation contributions***

Qualified conservation contributions are not subject to the "partial interest" rule, which generally bars deductions for charitable contributions of partial interests in property.[1645] A qualified conservation contribution is a contribution of a qualified real property interest to a qualified organization exclusively for conservation purposes. A qualified real property interest is defined as: (1) the entire interest of the donor other than a qualified mineral interest; (2) a remainder interest; or (3) a restriction (granted in perpetuity) on the use that may be made of the real property. Qualified organizations include certain governmental units, public charities that meet certain public support tests, and certain supporting organizations. Conservation purposes include: (1) the preservation of land areas for outdoor recreation by, or for the education of, the general public; (2) the protection of a relatively natural habitat of fish, wildlife, or plants, or similar ecosystem; (3) the preservation of open space (including farmland and forest land) where such preservation will yield a significant public benefit and is either for the scenic enjoyment of the general public or pursuant to a clearly delineated Federal, State, or local governmental conservation policy; and (4) the preservation of an historically important land area or a certified historic structure.

Qualified conservation contributions of capital gain property are subject to the same limitations and carryover rules as other charitable contributions of capital gain property.

***Special rule regarding contributions of capital gain real property for conservation purposes***

*In general*

Under a temporary provision that is effective for contributions made in taxable years beginning after December 31, 2005,[1646] the 30-percent contribution base limitation on contributions of capital gain property by individuals does not apply to qualified conservation contributions (as defined under present law). Instead, individuals may deduct the fair market value of any qualified conservation contribution to an organization described in section 170(b)(1)(A) to the extent of the excess of 50 percent of the con-

---

[1645] Secs. 170(f)(3)(B)(iii) and 170(h).
[1646] Sec. 170(b)(1)(E).

tribution base over the amount of all other allowable charitable contributions. These contributions are not taken into account in determining the amount of other allowable charitable contributions.

Individuals are allowed to carry over any qualified conservation contributions that exceed the 50-percent limitation for up to 15 years.

For example, assume an individual with a contribution base of $100 makes a qualified conservation contribution of property with a fair market value of $80 and makes other charitable contributions subject to the 50 percent limitation of $60. The individual is allowed a deduction of $50 in the current taxable year for the non-conservation contributions (50 percent of the $100 contribution base) and is allowed to carry over the excess $10 for up to 5 years. No current deduction is allowed for the qualified conservation contribution, but the entire $80 qualified conservation contribution may be carried forward for up to 15 years.

*Farmers and ranchers*

In the case of an individual who is a qualified farmer or rancher for the taxable year in which the contribution is made, a qualified conservation contribution is allowable up to 100 percent of the excess of the taxpayer's contribution base over the amount of all other allowable charitable contributions.

In the above example, if the individual is a qualified farmer or rancher, in addition to the $50 deduction for non-conservation contributions, an additional $50 for the qualified conservation contribution is allowed and $30 may be carried forward for up to 15 years as a contribution subject to the 100-percent limitation.

In the case of a corporation (other than a publicly traded corporation) that is a qualified farmer or rancher for the taxable year in which the contribution is made, any qualified conservation contribution is allowable up to 100 percent of the excess of the corporation's taxable income (as computed under section 170(b)(2)) over the amount of all other allowable charitable contributions. Any excess may be carried forward for up to 15 years as a contribution subject to the 100-percent limitation.[1647]

As an additional condition of eligibility for the 100 percent limitation, with respect to any contribution of property in agriculture or livestock production, or that is available for such production, by a qualified farmer or rancher, the qualified real property interest must include a restriction that the property remain generally available for such production. (There is no requirement as to any specific use in agriculture or farming, or necessarily that the property be used for such purposes, merely that the property remain available for such purposes.) Such additional condition does not apply to contributions made on or before August 17, 2006.

A qualified farmer or rancher means a taxpayer whose gross income from the trade or business of farming (within the meaning of section 2032A(e)(5)) is greater than 50 percent of the taxpayer's gross income for the taxable year.

[1647] Sec. 170(b)(2)(B).

*Termination*

The special rule regarding contributions of capital gain real property for conservation purposes does not apply to contributions made in taxable years beginning after December 31, 2009.[1648]

### *Explanation of Provision*

The Act extends the special rule regarding contributions of capital gain real property for conservation purposes for two years for contributions made in taxable years beginning before January 1, 2012.

### *Effective Date*

The provision is effective for contributions made in taxable years beginning after December 31, 2009.

## 4. Above-the-line deduction for qualified tuition and related expenses (sec. 724 of the Act and sec. 222 of the Code)

### *Present Law*

An individual is allowed an above-the-line deduction for qualified tuition and related expenses for higher education paid by the individual during the taxable year.[1649] The term qualified tuition and related expenses is defined in the same manner as for the Hope and Lifetime Learning credits, and includes tuition and fees required for the enrollment or attendance of the taxpayer, the taxpayer's spouse, or any dependent of the taxpayer with respect to whom the taxpayer may claim a personal exemption, at an eligible institution of higher education for courses of instruction of such individual at such institution.[1650] The expenses must be in connection with enrollment at an institution of higher education during the taxable year, or with an academic period beginning during the taxable year or during the first three months of the next taxable year. The deduction is not available for tuition and related expenses paid for elementary or secondary education.

The maximum deduction is $4,000 for an individual whose adjusted gross income for the taxable year does not exceed $65,000 ($130,000 in the case of a joint return), or $2,000 for other individuals whose adjusted gross income does not exceed $80,000 ($160,000 in the case of a joint return). No deduction is allowed for an individual whose adjusted gross income exceeds the relevant adjusted gross income limitations, for a married individual who does not file a joint return, or for an individual with respect to whom a personal exemption deduction may be claimed by another taxpayer for the taxable year. The deduction is not available for taxable years beginning after December 31, 2009.

The amount of qualified tuition and related expenses must be reduced by certain scholarships, educational assistance allowances,

[1648] Secs. 170(b)(1)(E)(vi) and 170(b)(2)(B)(iii).

[1649] Sec. 222.

[1650] The deduction generally is not available for expenses with respect to a course or education involving sports, games, or hobbies, and is not available for student activity fees, athletic fees, insurance expenses, or other expenses unrelated to an individual's academic course of instruction.

and other amounts paid for the benefit of such individual,[1651] and by the amount of such expenses taken into account for purposes of determining any exclusion from gross income of: (1) income from certain U.S. savings bonds used to pay higher education tuition and fees; and (2) income from a Coverdell education savings account.[1652] Additionally, such expenses must be reduced by the earnings portion (but not the return of principal) of distributions from a qualified tuition program if an exclusion under section 529 is claimed with respect to expenses eligible for the qualified tuition deduction. No deduction is allowed for any expense for which a deduction is otherwise allowed or with respect to an individual for whom a Hope or Lifetime Learning credit is elected for such taxable year.

### *Explanation of Provision*

The provision extends the qualified tuition deduction for two years so that it is generally available for taxable years beginning before January 1, 2012.

### *Effective Date*

The provision is effective for taxable years beginning after December 31, 2009.

## 5. Tax-free distributions from individual retirement plans for charitable purposes (sec. 725 of the Act and sec. 408 of the Code)

### *Present Law*

#### *In general*

If an amount withdrawn from a traditional individual retirement arrangement ("IRA") or a Roth IRA is donated to a charitable organization, the rules relating to the tax treatment of withdrawals from IRAs apply to the amount withdrawn and the charitable contribution is subject to the normally applicable limitations on deductibility of such contributions. An exception applies in the case of a qualified charitable distribution.

#### *Charitable contributions*

In computing taxable income, an individual taxpayer who itemizes deductions generally is allowed to deduct the amount of cash and up to the fair market value of property contributed to the following entities: (1) a charity described in section 501(c)(3); (2) certain veterans' organizations, fraternal societies, and cemetery companies;[1653] and (3) a Federal, State, or local governmental entity, but only if the contribution is made for exclusively public purposes.[1654] The deduction also is allowed for purposes of calculating alternative minimum taxable income.

---

[1651] Secs. 222(d)(1) and 25A(g)(2).

[1652] Sec. 222(c). These reductions are the same as those that apply to the Hope and Lifetime Learning credits.

[1653] Secs. 170(c)(3)–(5).

[1654] Sec. 170(c)(1).

The amount of the deduction allowable for a taxable year with respect to a charitable contribution of property may be reduced depending on the type of property contributed, the type of charitable organization to which the property is contributed, and the income of the taxpayer.[1655]

A taxpayer who takes the standard deduction (i.e., who does not itemize deductions) may not take a separate deduction for charitable contributions.[1656]

A payment to a charity (regardless of whether it is termed a "contribution") in exchange for which the donor receives an economic benefit is not deductible, except to the extent that the donor can demonstrate, among other things, that the payment exceeds the fair market value of the benefit received from the charity. To facilitate distinguishing charitable contributions from purchases of goods or services from charities, present law provides that no charitable contribution deduction is allowed for a separate contribution of $250 or more unless the donor obtains a contemporaneous written acknowledgement of the contribution from the charity indicating whether the charity provided any good or service (and an estimate of the value of any such good or service provided) to the taxpayer in consideration for the contribution.[1657] In addition, present law requires that any charity that receives a contribution exceeding $75 made partly as a gift and partly as consideration for goods or services furnished by the charity (a "quid pro quo" contribution) is required to inform the contributor in writing of an estimate of the value of the goods or services furnished by the charity and that only the portion exceeding the value of the goods or services may be deductible as a charitable contribution.[1658]

Under present law, total deductible contributions of an individual taxpayer to public charities, private operating foundations, and certain types of private nonoperating foundations generally may not exceed 50 percent of the taxpayer's contribution base, which is the taxpayer's adjusted gross income for a taxable year (disregarding any net operating loss carryback). To the extent a taxpayer has not exceeded the 50-percent limitation, (1) contributions of capital gain property to public charities generally may be deducted up to 30 percent of the taxpayer's contribution base, (2) contributions of cash to private foundations and certain other charitable organizations generally may be deducted up to 30 percent of the taxpayer's contribution base, and (3) contributions of capital gain property to private foundations and certain other charitable organizations generally may be deducted up to 20 percent of the taxpayer's contribution base.

Contributions by individuals in excess of the 50-percent, 30-percent, and 20-percent limits generally may be carried over and deducted over the next five taxable years, subject to the relevant percentage limitations on the deduction in each of those years.

---

[1655] Secs. 170(b) and (e).

[1656] Sec. 170(a).

[1657] Sec. 170(f)(8). For any contribution of a cash, check, or other monetary gift, no deduction is allowed unless the donor maintains as a record of such contribution a bank record or written communication from the donee charity showing the name of the donee organization, the date of the contribution, and the amount of the contribution. Sec. 170(f)(17).

[1658] Sec. 6115.

In general, a charitable deduction is not allowed for income, estate, or gift tax purposes if the donor transfers an interest in property to a charity (e.g., a remainder) while also either retaining an interest in that property (e.g., an income interest) or transferring an interest in that property to a noncharity for less than full and adequate consideration.[1659] Exceptions to this general rule are provided for, among other interests, remainder interests in charitable remainder annuity trusts, charitable remainder unitrusts, and pooled income funds, and present interests in the form of a guaranteed annuity or a fixed percentage of the annual value of the property.[1660] For such interests, a charitable deduction is allowed to the extent of the present value of the interest designated for a charitable organization.

### *IRA rules*

Within limits, individuals may make deductible and nondeductible contributions to a traditional IRA. Amounts in a traditional IRA are includible in income when withdrawn (except to the extent the withdrawal represents a return of nondeductible contributions). Certain individuals also may make nondeductible contributions to a Roth IRA (deductible contributions cannot be made to Roth IRAs). Qualified withdrawals from a Roth IRA are excludable from gross income. Withdrawals from a Roth IRA that are not qualified withdrawals are includible in gross income to the extent attributable to earnings. Includible amounts withdrawn from a traditional IRA or a Roth IRA before attainment of age 59-½ are subject to an additional 10-percent early withdrawal tax, unless an exception applies. Under present law, minimum distributions are required to be made from tax-favored retirement arrangements, including IRAs. Minimum required distributions from a traditional IRA must generally begin by April 1 of the calendar year following the year in which the IRA owner attains age 70-½.[1661]

If an individual has made nondeductible contributions to a traditional IRA, a portion of each distribution from an IRA is nontaxable until the total amount of nondeductible contributions has been received. In general, the amount of a distribution that is nontaxable is determined by multiplying the amount of the distribution by the ratio of the remaining nondeductible contributions to the account balance. In making the calculation, all traditional IRAs of an individual are treated as a single IRA, all distributions during any taxable year are treated as a single distribution, and the value of the contract, income on the contract, and investment in the contract are computed as of the close of the calendar year.

In the case of a distribution from a Roth IRA that is not a qualified distribution, in determining the portion of the distribution attributable to earnings, contributions and distributions are deemed to be distributed in the following order: (1) regular Roth IRA contributions; (2) taxable conversion contributions;[1662] (3) nontaxable

---

[1659] Secs. 170(f), 2055(e)(2), and 2522(c)(2).

[1660] Sec. 170(f)(2).

[1661] Minimum distribution rules also apply in the case of distributions after the death of a traditional or Roth IRA owner.

[1662] Conversion contributions refer to conversions of amounts in a traditional IRA to a Roth IRA.

conversion contributions; and (4) earnings. In determining the amount of taxable distributions from a Roth IRA, all Roth IRA distributions in the same taxable year are treated as a single distribution, all regular Roth IRA contributions for a year are treated as a single contribution, and all conversion contributions during the year are treated as a single contribution.

Distributions from an IRA (other than a Roth IRA) are generally subject to withholding unless the individual elects not to have withholding apply.[1663] Elections not to have withholding apply are to be made in the time and manner prescribed by the Secretary.

***Qualified charitable distributions***

Present law provides an exclusion from gross income for otherwise taxable IRA distributions from a traditional or a Roth IRA in the case of qualified charitable distributions.[1664] The exclusion may not exceed $100,000 per taxpayer per taxable year. Special rules apply in determining the amount of an IRA distribution that is otherwise taxable. The otherwise applicable rules regarding taxation of IRA distributions and the deduction of charitable contributions continue to apply to distributions from an IRA that are not qualified charitable distributions. A qualified charitable distribution is taken into account for purposes of the minimum distribution rules applicable to traditional IRAs to the same extent the distribution would have been taken into account under such rules had the distribution not been directly distributed under the qualified charitable distribution provision. An IRA does not fail to qualify as an IRA as a result of qualified charitable distributions being made from the IRA.

A qualified charitable distribution is any distribution from an IRA directly by the IRA trustee to an organization described in section 170(b)(1)(A) (other than an organization described in section 509(a)(3) or a donor advised fund (as defined in section 4966(d)(2)). Distributions are eligible for the exclusion only if made on or after the date the IRA owner attains age 70-½ and only to the extent the distribution would be includible in gross income (without regard to this provision).

The exclusion applies only if a charitable contribution deduction for the entire distribution otherwise would be allowable (under present law), determined without regard to the generally applicable percentage limitations. Thus, for example, if the deductible amount is reduced because of a benefit received in exchange, or if a deduction is not allowable because the donor did not obtain sufficient substantiation, the exclusion is not available with respect to any part of the IRA distribution.

If the IRA owner has any IRA that includes nondeductible contributions, a special rule applies in determining the portion of a distribution that is includible in gross income (but for the qualified charitable distribution provision) and thus is eligible for qualified charitable distribution treatment. Under the special rule, the distribution is treated as consisting of income first, up to the aggregate amount that would be includible in gross income (but for the

[1663] Sec. 3405.

[1664] Sec. 408(d)(8). The exclusion does not apply to distributions from employer-sponsored retirement plans, including SIMPLE IRAs and simplified employee pensions ("SEPs").

qualified charitable distribution provision) if the aggregate balance of all IRAs having the same owner were distributed during the same year. In determining the amount of subsequent IRA distributions includible in income, proper adjustments are to be made to reflect the amount treated as a qualified charitable distribution under the special rule.

Distributions that are excluded from gross income by reason of the qualified charitable distribution provision are not taken into account in determining the deduction for charitable contributions under section 170.

The exclusion for qualified charitable distributions applies to distributions made in taxable years beginning after December 31, 2005. Under present law, the exclusion does not apply to distributions made in taxable years beginning after December 31, 2009.

### *Explanation of Provision*

The provision extends the exclusion for qualified charitable distributions to distributions made in taxable years beginning after December 31, 2009 and before January 1, 2012. The provision contains a special rule permitting taxpayers to elect (in such form and manner as the Secretary may prescribe) to have qualified charitable distributions made in January 2011 treated as having been made on December 31, 2010 for purposes of sections 408(a)(6), 408(b)(3), and 408(d)(8). Thus, a qualified charitable distribution made in January 2011 is permitted to be (1) treated as made in the taxpayer's 2010 taxable year and thus permitted to count against the 2010 $100,000 limitation on the exclusion, and (2) treated as made in the 2010 calendar year and thus permitted to be used to satisfy the taxpayer's minimum distribution requirement for 2010.

### *Effective Date*

The provision is effective for distributions made in taxable years beginning after December 31, 2009.

## 6. Look-thru of certain regulated investment company stock in determining gross estate of nonresidents (sec. 726 of the Act and sec. 2105 of the Code)

### *Present Law*

The gross estate of a decedent who was a U.S. citizen or resident generally includes all property—real, personal, tangible, and intangible—wherever situated.[1665] The gross estate of a nonresident non-citizen decedent, by contrast, generally includes only property that at the time of the decedent's death is situated within the United States.[1666] Property within the United States generally includes debt obligations of U.S. persons, including the Federal government and State and local governments, but does not include either bank deposits or portfolio obligations the interest on which

[1665] Sec. 2031. The Economic Growth and Tax Relief Reconciliation Act of 2001 ("EGTRRA") repealed the estate tax for estates of decedents dying after December 31, 2009. EGTRRA, however, included a termination provision under which EGTRRA's rules, including estate tax repeal, do not apply to estates of decedents dying after December 31, 2010.

[1666] Sec. 2103.

would be exempt from U.S. income tax under section 871.[1667] Stock owned and held by a nonresident non-citizen generally is treated as property within the United States if the stock was issued by a domestic corporation.[1668]

Treaties may reduce U.S. taxation of transfers of the estates of nonresident non-citizens. Under recent treaties, for example, U.S. tax generally may be eliminated except insofar as the property transferred includes U.S. real property or business property of a U.S. permanent establishment.

Although stock issued by a domestic corporation generally is treated as property within the United States, stock of a regulated investment company ("RIC") that was owned by a nonresident non-citizen is not deemed property within the United States in the proportion that, at the end of the quarter of the RIC's taxable year immediately before a decedent's date of death, the assets held by the RIC are debt obligations, deposits, or other property that would be treated as situated outside the United States if held directly by the estate (the "estate tax look-through rule for RIC stock").[1669] This estate tax look-through rule for RIC stock does not apply to estates of decedents dying after December 31, 2009.

### *Explanation of Provision*

The provision permits the estate tax look-through rule for RIC stock to apply to estates of decedents dying before January 1, 2012.

### *Effective Date*

The provision is effective for decedents dying after December 31, 2009.

## 7. Parity for exclusion from income for employer-provided mass transit and parking benefits (sec. 727 of the Act and sec. 132 of the Code)

### *Present Law*

#### *In general*

Qualified transportation fringe benefits provided by an employer are excluded from an employee's gross income for income tax purposes and from an employee's wages for payroll tax purposes.[1670] Qualified transportation fringe benefits include parking, transit passes, vanpool benefits, and qualified bicycle commuting reimbursements. No amount is includible in the income of an employee merely because the employer offers the employee a choice between cash and qualified transportation fringe benefits (other than a qualified bicycle commuting reimbursement). Qualified transportation fringe benefits also include a cash reimbursement by an employer to an employee. In the case of transit passes, however, a cash reimbursement is considered a qualified transportation fringe benefit only if a voucher or similar item which may be exchanged

[1667] Secs. 2104(c), 2105(b).
[1668] Sec. 2104(a); Treas. Reg. sec. 20.2104–1(a)(5)).
[1669] Sec. 2105(d).
[1670] Secs. 132(f), 3121(b)(2), and 3306(b)(16) and 3401(a)(19).

only for a transit pass is not readily available for direct distribution by the employer to the employee.

Prior to February 17, 2009, the amount that could be excluded as qualified transportation fringe benefits was limited to $100 per month in combined vanpooling and transit pass benefits and $175 per month in qualified parking benefits. All limits were adjusted annually for inflation, using 1998 as the base year (in 2009 the limits were $120 and $230, respectively). The American Recovery and Reinvestment Act of 2009, however, temporarily increased the monthly exclusion for employer-provided vanpool and transit pass benefits to the same level as the exclusion for employer-provided parking ($230 for 2010). The American Recovery and Reinvestment Act of 2009 limits are set to expire on December 31, 2010.

### *Explanation of Provision*

The provision extends the parity in qualified transportation fringe benefits for one year (through December 31, 2011).

### *Effective Date*

The provision is effective for months after December, 2010.

## 8. Refunds disregarded in the administration of Federal programs and Federally assisted programs (sec. 728 of the Act and sec. 6409 of the Code)

### *Present Law*

Qualifying individuals may receive refundable credits under various provisions in the Code. Some of these credits are not taken into account for purposes of determining eligibility for benefits or assistance under Federal programs, but the treatment of such credits is not uniform. For example, for purposes of determining an individual's eligibility under any Federal program or federally funded State or local program, the child tax credit[1671] is not considered a resource for the month of receipt and the following month,[1672] but the making work pay credit[1673] is not so considered for the month of receipt and the following two months.[1674] The earned income credit has a similar rule to the child tax credit but only with respect to certain specifically listed benefit programs.[1675]

### *Explanation of Provision*

Under this provision, any tax refund (or advance payment with respect to a refundable credit) received by an individual after December 31, 2009 begins a period of 12 months during which such refund may not be taken into account as a resource for purposes of determining the eligibility of such individual (or any other individual) for benefits or assistance (or the amount or extent of benefits or assistance) under any Federal program or under any State

[1671] Sec. 24.

[1672] Sec. 203 of the Economic Growth and Tax Relief Reconciliation Act of 2001, Pub. L. No. 107–16.

[1673] Sec. 36A.

[1674] Sec. 1001(c) of the American Recovery and Reinvestment Act of 2009, Pub. L. No. 111–5.

[1675] Sec. 32(l).

or local program financed in whole or in part with Federal funds. The provision terminates on December 31, 2012.

### *Effective Date*

The provision is effective for amounts received after December 31, 2009 and on or before December 31, 2012.

## C. Business Tax Relief

### 1. Research credit (sec. 731 of the Act and sec. 41 of the Code)

### *Present Law*

#### *General rule*

A taxpayer may claim a research credit equal to 20 percent of the amount by which the taxpayer's qualified research expenses for a taxable year exceed its base amount for that year.[1676] Thus, the research credit is generally available with respect to incremental increases in qualified research.

A 20-percent research tax credit is also available with respect to the excess of (1) 100 percent of corporate cash expenses (including grants or contributions) paid for basic research conducted by universities (and certain nonprofit scientific research organizations) over (2) the sum of (a) the greater of two minimum basic research floors plus (b) an amount reflecting any decrease in nonresearch giving to universities by the corporation as compared to such giving during a fixed-base period, as adjusted for inflation. This separate credit computation is commonly referred to as the university basic research credit.[1677]

Finally, a research credit is available for a taxpayer's expenditures on research undertaken by an energy research consortium. This separate credit computation is commonly referred to as the energy research credit. Unlike the other research credits, the energy research credit applies to all qualified expenditures, not just those in excess of a base amount.

The research credit, including the university basic research credit and the energy research credit, expires for amounts paid or incurred after December 31, 2009.[1678]

#### *Computation of allowable credit*

Except for energy research payments and certain university basic research payments made by corporations, the research tax credit applies only to the extent that the taxpayer's qualified research expenses for the current taxable year exceed its base amount. The base amount for the current year generally is computed by multiplying the taxpayer's fixed-base percentage by the average amount of the taxpayer's gross receipts for the four preceding years. If a taxpayer both incurred qualified research expenses and had gross receipts during each of at least three years from 1984 through 1988, then its fixed-base percentage is the ratio that its total quali-

[1676] Sec. 41.
[1677] Sec. 41(e).
[1678] Sec. 41(h).

fied research expenses for the 1984–1988 period bears to its total gross receipts for that period (subject to a maximum fixed-base percentage of 16 percent). All other taxpayers (so-called start-up firms) are assigned a fixed-base percentage of three percent.[1679]

In computing the credit, a taxpayer's base amount cannot be less than 50 percent of its current-year qualified research expenses.

To prevent artificial increases in research expenditures by shifting expenditures among commonly controlled or otherwise related entities, a special aggregation rule provides that all members of the same controlled group of corporations are treated as a single taxpayer.[1680] Under regulations prescribed by the Secretary, special rules apply for computing the credit when a major portion of a trade or business (or unit thereof) changes hands, under which qualified research expenses and gross receipts for periods prior to the change of ownership of a trade or business are treated as transferred with the trade or business that gave rise to those expenses and receipts for purposes of recomputing a taxpayer's fixed-base percentage.[1681]

### *Alternative simplified credit*

Taxpayers may elect to claim an alternative simplified credit for qualified research expenses. The alternative simplified research credit is equal to 14 percent of qualified research expenses that exceed 50 percent of the average qualified research expenses for the three preceding taxable years. The rate is reduced to six percent if a taxpayer has no qualified research expenses in any one of the three preceding taxable years. An election to use the alternative simplified credit applies to all succeeding taxable years unless revoked with the consent of the Secretary.

### *Eligible expenses*

Qualified research expenses eligible for the research tax credit consist of: (1) in-house expenses of the taxpayer for wages and supplies attributable to qualified research; (2) certain time-sharing costs for computer use in qualified research; and (3) 65 percent of amounts paid or incurred by the taxpayer to certain other persons for qualified research conducted on the taxpayer's behalf (so-called contract research expenses).[1682] Notwithstanding the limitation for

---

[1679] The Small Business Job Protection Act of 1996, Pub. L. No. 104–188, expanded the definition of start-up firms under section 41(c)(3)(B)(i) to include any firm if the first taxable year in which such firm had both gross receipts and qualified research expenses began after 1983. A special rule (enacted in 1993) is designed to gradually recompute a start-up firm's fixed-base percentage based on its actual research experience. Under this special rule, a start-up firm is assigned a fixed-base percentage of three percent for each of its first five taxable years after 1993 in which it incurs qualified research expenses. A start-up firm's fixed-base percentage for its sixth through tenth taxable years after 1993 in which it incurs qualified research expenses is a phased-in ratio based on the firm's actual research experience. For all subsequent taxable years, the taxpayer's fixed-base percentage is its actual ratio of qualified research expenses to gross receipts for any five years selected by the taxpayer from its fifth through tenth taxable years after 1993. Sec. 41(c)(3)(B).

[1680] Sec. 41(f)(1).

[1681] Sec. 41(f)(3).

[1682] Under a special rule, 75 percent of amounts paid to a research consortium for qualified research are treated as qualified research expenses eligible for the research credit (rather than 65 percent under the general rule under section 41(b)(3) governing contract research expenses) if (1) such research consortium is a tax-exempt organization that is described in section 501(c)(3) (other than a private foundation) or section 501(c)(6) and is organized and operated primarily

Continued

contract research expenses, qualified research expenses include 100 percent of amounts paid or incurred by the taxpayer to an eligible small business, university, or Federal laboratory for qualified energy research.

To be eligible for the credit, the research not only has to satisfy the requirements of present-law section 174 (described below) but also must be undertaken for the purpose of discovering information that is technological in nature, the application of which is intended to be useful in the development of a new or improved business component of the taxpayer, and substantially all of the activities of which constitute elements of a process of experimentation for functional aspects, performance, reliability, or quality of a business component. Research does not qualify for the credit if substantially all of the activities relate to style, taste, cosmetic, or seasonal design factors.[1683] In addition, research does not qualify for the credit: (1) if conducted after the beginning of commercial production of the business component; (2) if related to the adaptation of an existing business component to a particular customer's requirements; (3) if related to the duplication of an existing business component from a physical examination of the component itself or certain other information; or (4) if related to certain efficiency surveys, management function or technique, market research, market testing, or market development, routine data collection or routine quality control.[1684] Research does not qualify for the credit if it is conducted outside the United States, Puerto Rico, or any U.S. possession.

***Relation to deduction***

Under section 174, taxpayers may elect to deduct currently the amount of certain research or experimental expenditures paid or incurred in connection with a trade or business, notwithstanding the general rule that business expenses to develop or create an asset that has a useful life extending beyond the current year must be capitalized.[1685] However, deductions allowed to a taxpayer under section 174 (or any other section) are reduced by an amount equal to 100 percent of the taxpayer's research tax credit determined for the taxable year.[1686] Taxpayers may alternatively elect to claim a reduced research tax credit amount under section 41 in lieu of reducing deductions otherwise allowed.[1687]

## *Explanation of Provision*

The provision extends the research credit for two years, through December 31, 2011.

---

to conduct scientific research, and (2) such qualified research is conducted by the consortium on behalf of the taxpayer and one or more persons not related to the taxpayer. Sec. 41(b)(3)(C).

[1683] Sec. 41(d)(3).

[1684] Sec. 41(d)(4).

[1685] Taxpayers may elect 10-year amortization of certain research expenditures allowable as a deduction under section 174(a). Secs. 174(f)(2) and 59(e).

[1686] Sec. 280C(c).

[1687] Sec. 280C(c)(3).

### *Effective Date*

The provision is effective for amounts paid or incurred after December 31, 2009.

## 2. Indian employment tax credit (sec. 732 of the Act and sec. 45A of the Code)

### *Present Law*

In general, a credit against income tax liability is allowed to employers for the first $20,000 of qualified wages and qualified employee health insurance costs paid or incurred by the employer with respect to certain employees.[1688] The credit is equal to 20 percent of the excess of eligible employee qualified wages and health insurance costs during the current year over the amount of such wages and costs incurred by the employer during 1993. The credit is an incremental credit, such that an employer's current-year qualified wages and qualified employee health insurance costs (up to $20,000 per employee) are eligible for the credit only to the extent that the sum of such costs exceeds the sum of comparable costs paid during 1993. No deduction is allowed for the portion of the wages equal to the amount of the credit.

Qualified wages means wages paid or incurred by an employer for services performed by a qualified employee. A qualified employee means any employee who is an enrolled member of an Indian tribe or the spouse of an enrolled member of an Indian tribe, who performs substantially all of the services within an Indian reservation, and whose principal place of abode while performing such services is on or near the reservation in which the services are performed. An "Indian reservation" is a reservation as defined in section 3(d) of the Indian Financing Act of 1974[1689] or section 4(10) of the Indian Child Welfare Act of 1978.[1690] For purposes of the preceding sentence, section 3(d) is applied by treating "former Indian reservations in Oklahoma" as including only lands that are (1) within the jurisdictional area of an Oklahoma Indian tribe as determined by the Secretary of the Interior, and (2) recognized by such Secretary as an area eligible for trust land status under 25 C.F.R. Part 151 (as in effect on August 5, 1997).

An employee is not treated as a qualified employee for any taxable year of the employer if the total amount of wages paid or incurred by the employer with respect to such employee during the taxable year exceeds an amount determined at an annual rate of $30,000 (which after adjusted for inflation is currently $45,000 for 2009). In addition, an employee will not be treated as a qualified employee under certain specific circumstances, such as where the employee is related to the employer (in the case of an individual employer) or to one of the employer's shareholders, partners, or grantors. Similarly, an employee will not be treated as a qualified employee where the employee has more than a five percent ownership interest in the employer. Finally, an employee will not be considered a qualified employee to the extent the employee's services

[1688] Sec. 45A.
[1689] Pub. L. No. 93–262.
[1690] Pub. L. No. 95–608.

relate to gaming activities or are performed in a building housing such activities.

The wage credit is available for wages paid or incurred in taxable years that begin before January 1, 2010.

### *Explanation of Provision*

The provision extends for two years the present-law employment credit provision (through taxable years beginning on or before December 31, 2011).

### *Effective Date*

The provision is effective for taxable years beginning after December 31, 2009.

## 3. New markets tax credit (sec. 733 of the Act and sec. 45D of the Code)

### *Present Law*

Section 45D provides a new markets tax credit for qualified equity investments made to acquire stock in a corporation, or a capital interest in a partnership, that is a qualified community development entity ("CDE").[1691] The amount of the credit allowable to the investor (either the original purchaser or a subsequent holder) is (1) a five-percent credit for the year in which the equity interest is purchased from the CDE and for each of the following two years, and (2) a six-percent credit for each of the following four years.[1692] The credit is determined by applying the applicable percentage (five or six percent) to the amount paid to the CDE for the investment at its original issue, and is available to the taxpayer who holds the qualified equity investment on the date of the initial investment or on the respective anniversary date that occurs during the taxable year.[1693] The credit is recaptured if at any time during the seven-year period that begins on the date of the original issue of the investment the entity (1) ceases to be a qualified CDE, (2) the proceeds of the investment cease to be used as required, or (3) the equity investment is redeemed.[1694]

A qualified CDE is any domestic corporation or partnership: (1) whose primary mission is serving or providing investment capital for low-income communities or low-income persons; (2) that maintains accountability to residents of low-income communities by their representation on any governing board of or any advisory board to the CDE; and (3) that is certified by the Secretary as being a qualified CDE.[1695] A qualified equity investment means stock (other than nonqualified preferred stock) in a corporation or a capital interest in a partnership that is acquired directly from a CDE for cash, and includes an investment of a subsequent purchaser if such investment was a qualified equity investment in the

[1691] Section 45D was added by section 121(a) of the Community Renewal Tax Relief Act of 2000, Pub. L. No. 106–554.

[1692] Sec. 45D(a)(2).

[1693] Sec. 45D(a)(3).

[1694] Sec. 45D(g).

[1695] Sec. 45D(c).

hands of the prior holder.[1696] Substantially all of the investment proceeds must be used by the CDE to make qualified low-income community investments. For this purpose, qualified low-income community investments include: (1) capital or equity investments in, or loans to, qualified active low-income community businesses; (2) certain financial counseling and other services to businesses and residents in low-income communities; (3) the purchase from another CDE of any loan made by such entity that is a qualified low-income community investment; or (4) an equity investment in, or loan to, another CDE.[1697]

A "low-income community" is a population census tract with either (1) a poverty rate of at least 20 percent or (2) median family income which does not exceed 80 percent of the greater of metropolitan area median family income or statewide median family income (for a non-metropolitan census tract, does not exceed 80 percent of statewide median family income). In the case of a population census tract located within a high migration rural county, low-income is defined by reference to 85 percent (as opposed to 80 percent) of statewide median family income.[1698] For this purpose, a high migration rural county is any county that, during the 20-year period ending with the year in which the most recent census was conducted, has a net out-migration of inhabitants from the county of at least 10 percent of the population of the county at the beginning of such period.

The Secretary is authorized to designate "targeted populations" as low-income communities for purposes of the new markets tax credit.[1699] For this purpose, a "targeted population" is defined by reference to section 103(20) of the Riegle Community Development and Regulatory Improvement Act of 1994[1700] (the "Act") to mean individuals, or an identifiable group of individuals, including an Indian tribe, who are low-income persons or otherwise lack adequate access to loans or equity investments. Section 103(17) of the Act provides that "low-income" means (1) for a targeted population within a metropolitan area, less than 80 percent of the area median family income; and (2) for a targeted population within a non-metropolitan area, less than the greater of—80 percent of the area median family income, or 80 percent of the statewide non-metropolitan area median family income.[1701] A targeted population is not required to be within any census tract. In addition, a population census tract with a population of less than 2,000 is treated as a low-income community for purposes of the credit if such tract is within an empowerment zone, the designation of which is in effect under section 1391 of the Code, and is contiguous to one or more low-income communities.

A qualified active low-income community business is defined as a business that satisfies, with respect to a taxable year, the following requirements: (1) at least 50 percent of the total gross income of the business is derived from the active conduct of trade or business activities in any low-income community; (2) a substantial

[1696] Sec. 45D(b).
[1697] Sec. 45D(d).
[1698] Sec. 45D(e).
[1699] Sec. 45D(e)(2).
[1700] Pub. L. No. 103–325.
[1701] Pub. L. No. 103–325.

portion of the tangible property of the business is used in a low-income community; (3) a substantial portion of the services performed for the business by its employees is performed in a low-income community; and (4) less than five percent of the average of the aggregate unadjusted bases of the property of the business is attributable to certain financial property or to certain collectibles.[1702]

The maximum annual amount of qualified equity investments was $5.0 billion for calendar years 2008 and 2009. The new markets tax credit expired on December 31, 2009.

### *Explanation of Provision*

The provision extends the new markets tax credit for two years, through 2011, permitting up to $3.5 billion in qualified equity investments for each of the 2010 and 2011 calendar years. The provision also extends for two years, through 2016, the carryover period for unused new markets tax credits.

### *Effective Date*

The provision applies to calendar years beginning after December 31, 2009.

## 4. Railroad track maintenance credit (sec. 734 of the Act and sec. 45G of the Code)

### *Present Law*

Present law provides a 50-percent business tax credit for qualified railroad track maintenance expenditures paid or incurred by an eligible taxpayer during taxable years beginning before January 1, 2010.[1703] The credit is limited to the product of $3,500 times the number of miles of railroad track (1) owned or leased by an eligible taxpayer as of the close of its taxable year, and (2) assigned to the eligible taxpayer by a Class II or Class III railroad that owns or leases such track at the close of the taxable year.[1704] Each mile of railroad track may be taken into account only once, either by the owner of such mile or by the owner's assignee, in computing the per-mile limitation. The credit may also reduce a taxpayer's tax liability below its tentative minimum tax.[1705]

Qualified railroad track maintenance expenditures are defined as gross expenditures (whether or not otherwise chargeable to capital account) for maintaining railroad track (including roadbed, bridges, and related track structures) owned or leased as of January 1, 2005, by a Class II or Class III railroad (determined without regard to any consideration for such expenditure given by the Class II or Class III railroad which made the assignment of such track).[1706]

An eligible taxpayer means any Class II or Class III railroad, and any person who transports property using the rail facilities of a Class II or Class III railroad or who furnishes railroad-related property or services to a Class II or Class III railroad, but only

[1702] Sec. 45D(d)(2).
[1703] Sec. 45G(a).
[1704] Sec. 45G(b)(1).
[1705] Sec. 38(c)(4).
[1706] Sec. 45G(d).

with respect to miles of railroad track assigned to such person by such railroad under the provision.[1707]

The terms Class II or Class III railroad have the meanings given by the Surface Transportation Board.[1708]

### *Explanation of Provision*

The provision extends the present law credit for two years, for qualified railroad track maintenance expenses paid or incurred during taxable years beginning after December 31, 2009 and before January 1, 2012.

### *Effective Date*

The provision is effective for expenses paid or incurred in taxable years beginning after December 31, 2009.

## 5. Mine rescue team training credit (sec. 735 of the Act and sec. 45N of the Code)

### *Present Law*

An eligible employer may claim a general business credit against income tax with respect to each qualified mine rescue team employee equal to the lesser of: (1) 20 percent of the amount paid or incurred by the taxpayer during the taxable year with respect to the training program costs of the qualified mine rescue team employee (including the wages of the employee while attending the program); or (2) $10,000. A qualified mine rescue team employee is any full-time employee of the taxpayer who is a miner eligible for more than six months of a taxable year to serve as a mine rescue team member by virtue of either having completed the initial 20-hour course of instruction prescribed by the Mine Safety and Health Administration's Office of Educational Policy and Development, or receiving at least 40 hours of refresher training in such instruction. The credit is not allowable for purposes of computing the alternative minimum tax.[1709]

An eligible employer is any taxpayer which employs individuals as miners in underground mines in the United States. The term "wages" has the meaning given to such term by section 3306(b)[1710] (determined without regard to any dollar limitation contained in that section).

No deduction is allowed for the portion of the expenses otherwise deductible that is equal to the amount of the credit.[1711] The credit does not apply to taxable years beginning after December 31, 2009. Additionally, the credit may not offset the alternative minimum tax.

### *Explanation of Provision*

The provision extends the credit for two years through taxable years beginning on or before December 31, 2011.

---

[1707] Sec. 45G(c).
[1708] Sec. 45G(e)(1).
[1709] Sec. 38(c).
[1710] Section 3306(b) defines wages for purposes of Federal Unemployment Tax.
[1711] Sec. 280C(e).

### *Effective Date*

The provision generally is effective for taxable years beginning after December 31, 2009.

## 6. Employer wage credit for employees who are active duty members of the uniformed services (sec. 736 of the Act and sec. 45P of the Code)

### *Present Law*

#### *Differential pay*

In general, compensation paid by an employer to an employee is deductible by the employer under section 162(a)(1), unless the expense must be capitalized. In the case of an employee who is called to active duty with respect to the armed forces of the United States, some employers voluntarily pay the employee the difference between the compensation that the employer would have paid to the employee during the period of military service less the amount of pay received by the employee from the military. This payment by the employer is often referred to as "differential pay."

#### *Wage credit for differential pay*

If an employer qualifies as an eligible small business employer, the employer is allowed to take a credit against its income tax liability for a taxable year in an amount equal to 20 percent of the sum of the eligible differential wage payments for each of the employer's qualified employees for the taxable year.[1712]

An eligible small business employer means, with respect to a taxable year, any taxpayer which: (1) employed on average less than 50 employees on business days during the taxable year; and (2) under a written plan of the taxpayer, provides eligible differential wage payments to every qualified employee of the taxpayer. Taxpayers under common control are aggregated for purposes of determining whether a taxpayer is an eligible small business employer. The credit is not available with respect to a taxpayer who has failed to comply with the employment and reemployment rights of members of the uniformed services (as provided under Chapter 43 of Title 38 of the United States Code).

Differential wage payment means any payment which: (1) is made by an employer to an individual with respect to any period during which the individual is performing service in the uniformed services of the United States while on active duty for a period of more than 30 days; and (2) represents all or a portion of the wages that the individual would have received from the employer if the individual were performing services for the employer. The term eligible differential wage payments means so much of the differential wage payments paid to a qualified employee as does not exceed $20,000. A qualified employee is an individual who has been an employee for the 91-day period immediately preceding the period for which any differential wage payment is made.

No deduction may be taken for that portion of compensation which is equal to the credit. In addition, the amount of any other

[1712] Sec. 45P.

credit otherwise allowable under Chapter 1 (Normal Taxes and Surtaxes) of Subtitle A (Income Taxes) of the Code with respect to compensation paid to an employee must be reduced by the differential wage payment credit allowed with respect to such employee.

The differential wage payment credit is part of the general business credit, and thus this credit is subject to the rules applicable to business credits. For example, an unused credit generally may be carried back to the taxable year that precedes an unused credit year or carried forward to each of the 20 taxable years following the unused credit year. Any credit that is included in the general business credit, however, cannot be carried back to a tax year before the first tax year for which that credit is allowable under the effective date of that credit. Thus, the differential wage payment credit, if disallowed under section 38(c), cannot be carried back to tax years ending before June 18, 2008. In addition, unlike many of the other credits that are included in the general business credit, the differential wage payment credit is not a "qualified business credit" under section 196(c). Thus, a taxpayer cannot deduct under section 196(c) any differential wage payment credits that remain unused at the end of the 20-year carryforward period.

Rules similar to the rules in section 52(c), which bars the work opportunity tax credit for tax-exempt organizations other than certain farmer's cooperatives, apply to the differential wage payment credit. Additionally, rules similar to the rules in section 52(e), which limits the work opportunity tax credit allowable to regulated investment companies, real estate investment trusts, and certain cooperatives, apply to the differential wage payment credit.

The credit is not allowable against a taxpayer's alternative minimum tax liability. The amount of credit otherwise allowable under the income tax rules for compensation paid to any employee must be reduced by the differential wage payment credit with respect to that employee.

There are special rules for trusts and estates and their beneficiaries.

The credit is available with respect to amounts paid after June 17, 2008[1713] and before January 1, 2010.

### *Explanation of Provision*

The provision extends the availability of the credit to amounts paid before January 1, 2012.

### *Effective Date*

The provision applies to payments made after December 31, 2009.

[1713] This date is the date of enactment of the Heroes Earnings Assistance and Relief Tax Act of 2008, Pub. L. No. 110–245.

## 7. 15-year straight-line cost recovery for qualified leasehold improvements, qualified restaurant buildings and improvements, and qualified retail improvements (sec. 737 of the Act and sec. 168 of the Code)

### *Present Law*

#### *In general*

A taxpayer generally must capitalize the cost of property used in a trade or business and recover such cost over time through annual deductions for depreciation or amortization. Tangible property generally is depreciated under the modified accelerated cost recovery system ("MACRS"), which determines depreciation by applying specific recovery periods, placed-in-service conventions, and depreciation methods to the cost of various types of depreciable property.[1714] The cost of nonresidential real property is recovered using the straight-line method of depreciation and a recovery period of 39 years. Nonresidential real property is subject to the mid-month placed-in-service convention. Under the mid-month convention, the depreciation allowance for the first year property is placed in service is based on the number of months the property was in service, and property placed in service at any time during a month is treated as having been placed in service in the middle of the month.

#### *Depreciation of leasehold improvements*

Generally, depreciation allowances for improvements made on leased property are determined under MACRS, even if the MACRS recovery period assigned to the property is longer than the term of the lease. This rule applies regardless of whether the lessor or the lessee places the leasehold improvements in service. If a leasehold improvement constitutes an addition or improvement to nonresidential real property already placed in service, the improvement generally is depreciated using the straight-line method over a 39-year recovery period, beginning in the month the addition or improvement was placed in service. However, exceptions exist for certain qualified leasehold improvements, qualified restaurant property, and qualified retail improvement property.

#### *Qualified leasehold improvement property*

Section 168(e)(3)(E)(iv) provides a statutory 15-year recovery period for qualified leasehold improvement property placed in service before January 1, 2010. Qualified leasehold improvement property is recovered using the straight-line method and a half-year convention. Leasehold improvements placed in service after December 31, 2009 will be subject to the general rules described above.

Qualified leasehold improvement property is any improvement to an interior portion of a building that is nonresidential real property, provided certain requirements are met. The improvement must be made under or pursuant to a lease either by the lessee (or sublessee), or by the lessor, of that portion of the building to be occupied exclusively by the lessee (or sublessee). The improvement must be placed in service more than three years after the date the

---

[1714] Sec. 168.

building was first placed in service. Qualified leasehold improvement property does not include any improvement for which the expenditure is attributable to the enlargement of the building, any elevator or escalator, any structural component benefiting a common area, or the internal structural framework of the building.

If a lessor makes an improvement that qualifies as qualified leasehold improvement property, such improvement does not qualify as qualified leasehold improvement property to any subsequent owner of such improvement. An exception to the rule applies in the case of death and certain transfers of property that qualify for nonrecognition treatment.

***Qualified restaurant property***

Section 168(e)(3)(E)(v) provides a statutory 15-year recovery period for qualified restaurant property placed in service before January 1, 2010. Qualified restaurant property is any section 1250 property that is a building (if the building is placed in service after December 31, 2008 and before January 1, 2010) or an improvement to a building, if more than 50 percent of the building's square footage is devoted to the preparation of, and seating for on-premises consumption of, prepared meals.[1715] Qualified restaurant property is recovered using the straight-line method and a half-year convention. Additionally, qualified restaurant property is not eligible for bonus depreciation.[1716] Restaurant property placed in service after December 31, 2009 is subject to the general rules described above.

***Qualified retail improvement property***

Section 168(e)(3)(E)(ix) provides a statutory 15-year recovery period and for qualified retail improvement property placed in service after December 31, 2008 and before January 1, 2010. Qualified retail improvement property is any improvement to an interior portion of a building which is nonresidential real property if such portion is open to the general public[1717] and is used in the retail trade or business of selling tangible personal property to the general public, and such improvement is placed in service more than three years after the date the building was first placed in service. Qualified retail improvement property does not include any improvement for which the expenditure is attributable to the enlargement of the building, any elevator or escalator, or the internal structural framework of the building. In the case of an improvement made by the owner of such improvement, the improvement is a qualified retail improvement only so long as the improvement is held by such owner.

Retail establishments that qualify for the 15-year recovery period include those primarily engaged in the sale of goods. Examples of these retail establishments include, but are not limited to, grocery stores, clothing stores, hardware stores and convenience stores. Establishments primarily engaged in providing services, such as professional services, financial services, personal services, health serv-

---

[1715] Sec. 168(e)(7)(A).

[1716] Property that satisfies the definition of both qualified leasehold improvement property and qualified restaurant property is eligible for bonus depreciation.

[1717] Improvements to portions of a building not open to the general public (e.g., stock room in back of retail space) do not qualify under the provision.

ices, and entertainment, do not qualify. It is generally intended that businesses defined as a store retailer under the current North American Industry Classification System (industry sub-sectors 441 through 453) qualify while those in other industry classes do not qualify.

Qualified retail improvement property is recovered using the straight-line method and a half-year convention. Additionally, qualified retail improvement property is not eligible for bonus depreciation.[1718] Qualified retail improvement property placed in service on or after January 1, 2010 is subject to the general rules described above.

### *Explanation of Provision*

The present law provisions for qualified leasehold improvement property, qualified restaurant property, and qualified retail improvement property are extended for two years to apply to property placed in service on or before December 31, 2011.

### *Effective Date*

The provision is effective for property placed in service after December 31, 2009.

## 8. 7-year recovery period for motorsports entertainment complexes (sec. 738 of the Act and sec. 168 of the Code)

### *Present Law*

A taxpayer generally must capitalize the cost of property used in a trade or business and recover such cost over time through annual deductions for depreciation or amortization. Tangible property generally is depreciated under the modified accelerated cost recovery system ("MACRS"), which determines depreciation by applying specific recovery periods, placed-in-service conventions, and depreciation methods to the cost of various types of depreciable property.[1719] The cost of nonresidential real property is recovered using the straight-line method of depreciation and a recovery period of 39 years. Nonresidential real property is subject to the mid-month placed-in-service convention. Under the mid-month convention, the depreciation allowance for the first year property is placed in service is based on the number of months the property was in service, and property placed in service at any time during a month is treated as having been placed in service in the middle of the month. Land improvements (such as roads and fences) are recovered over 15 years. An exception exists for the theme and amusement park industry, whose assets are assigned a recovery period of seven years. Additionally, a motorsports entertainment complex placed in service before December 31, 2009 is assigned a recovery period of seven years.[1720] For these purposes, a motorsports entertainment complex means a racing track facility which is permanently situated on land and which during the 36-month period following its

---

[1718] Property that satisfies the definition of both qualified leasehold improvement property and qualified retail property is eligible for bonus depreciation.

[1719] Sec. 168.

[1720] Sec. 168(e)(3)(C)(ii).

placed-in-service date hosts a racing event.[1721] The term motorsports entertainment complex also includes ancillary facilities, land improvements (e.g., parking lots, sidewalks, fences), support facilities (e.g., food and beverage retailing, souvenir vending), and appurtenances associated with such facilities (e.g., ticket booths, grandstands).

### *Explanation of Provision*

The provision extends the present law seven-year recovery period for motorsports entertainment complexes two years to apply to property placed in service before January 1, 2012.

### *Effective Date*

The provision is effective for property placed in service after December 31, 2009.

## 9. Accelerated depreciation for business property on an Indian reservation (sec. 739 of the Act and sec. 168(j) of the Code)

### *Present Law*

With respect to certain property used in connection with the conduct of a trade or business within an Indian reservation, depreciation deductions under section 168(j) are determined using the following recovery periods:

| | |
|---|---|
| 3-year property | 2 years |
| 5-year property | 3 years |
| 7-year property | 4 years |
| 10-year property | 6 years |
| 15-year property | 9 years |
| 20-year property | 12 years |
| Nonresidential real property | 22 years |

"Qualified Indian reservation property" eligible for accelerated depreciation includes property described in the table above which is: (1) used by the taxpayer predominantly in the active conduct of a trade or business within an Indian reservation; (2) not used or located outside the reservation on a regular basis; (3) not acquired (directly or indirectly) by the taxpayer from a person who is related to the taxpayer;[1722] and (4) is not property placed in service for purposes of conducting gaming activities.[1723] Certain "qualified infrastructure property" may be eligible for the accelerated depreciation even if located outside an Indian reservation, provided that the purpose of such property is to connect with qualified infrastructure property located within the reservation (e.g., roads, power lines, water systems, railroad spurs, and communications facilities).[1724]

An "Indian reservation" means a reservation as defined in section 3(d) of the Indian Financing Act of 1974[1725] or section 4(10) of the Indian Child Welfare Act of 1978 (25 U.S.C. 1903(10)).[1726]

[1721] Sec. 168(i)(15).
[1722] For these purposes, related persons is defined in Sec. 465(b)(3)(C).
[1723] Sec. 168(j)(4)(A).
[1724] Sec. 168(j)(4)(C).
[1725] Pub. L. No. 93–262.
[1726] Pub. L. No. 95–608.

For purposes of the preceding sentence, section 3(d) is applied by treating "former Indian reservations in Oklahoma" as including only lands that are (1) within the jurisdictional area of an Oklahoma Indian tribe as determined by the Secretary of the Interior, and (2) recognized by such Secretary as an area eligible for trust land status under 25 C.F.R. Part 151 (as in effect on August 5, 1997).

The depreciation deduction allowed for regular tax purposes is also allowed for purposes of the alternative minimum tax. The accelerated depreciation for qualified Indian reservation property is available with respect to property placed in service on or after January 1, 1994, and before January 1, 2010.

### *Explanation of Provision*

The provision extends for two years the present-law accelerated MACRS recovery periods for qualified Indian reservation property to apply to property placed in service before January 1, 2012.

### *Effective Date*

The provision is effective for property placed in service after December 31, 2009.

## 10. Enhanced charitable deduction for contributions of food inventory (sec. 740 of the Act and sec. 170 of the Code)

### *Present Law*

#### *Charitable contributions in general*

In general, an income tax deduction is permitted for charitable contributions, subject to certain limitations that depend on the type of taxpayer, the property contributed, and the donee organization.[1727]

Charitable contributions of cash are deductible in the amount contributed. In general, contributions of capital gain property to a qualified charity are deductible at fair market value with certain exceptions. Capital gain property means any capital asset or property used in the taxpayer's trade or business the sale of which at its fair market value, at the time of contribution, would have resulted in gain that would have been long-term capital gain. Contributions of other appreciated property generally are deductible at the donor's basis in the property. Contributions of depreciated property generally are deductible at the fair market value of the property.

#### *General rules regarding contributions of food inventory*

Under present law, a taxpayer's deduction for charitable contributions of inventory generally is limited to the taxpayer's basis (typically, cost) in the inventory, or if less the fair market value of the inventory.

For certain contributions of inventory, C corporations may claim an enhanced deduction equal to the lesser of (1) basis plus one-half of the item's appreciation (i.e., basis plus one-half of fair market

[1727] Sec. 170.

value in excess of basis) or (2) two times basis.[1728] In general, a C corporation's charitable contribution deductions for a year may not exceed 10 percent of the corporation's taxable income.[1729] To be eligible for the enhanced deduction, the contributed property generally must be inventory of the taxpayer, contributed to a charitable organization described in section 501(c)(3) (except for private nonoperating foundations), and the donee must (1) use the property consistent with the donee's exempt purpose solely for the care of the ill, the needy, or infants, (2) not transfer the property in exchange for money, other property, or services, and (3) provide the taxpayer a written statement that the donee's use of the property will be consistent with such requirements.[1730] In the case of contributed property subject to the Federal Food, Drug, and Cosmetic Act, as amended, the property must satisfy the applicable requirements of such Act on the date of transfer and for 180 days prior to the transfer.[1731]

A donor making a charitable contribution of inventory must make a corresponding adjustment to the cost of goods sold by decreasing the cost of goods sold by the lesser of the fair market value of the property or the donor's basis with respect to the inventory.[1732] Accordingly, if the allowable charitable deduction for inventory is the fair market value of the inventory, the donor reduces its cost of goods sold by such value, with the result that the difference between the fair market value and the donor's basis may still be recovered by the donor other than as a charitable contribution.

To use the enhanced deduction, the taxpayer must establish that the fair market value of the donated item exceeds basis. The valuation of food inventory has been the subject of disputes between taxpayers and the IRS.[1733]

***Temporary rule expanding and modifying the enhanced deduction for contributions of food inventory***

Under a special temporary provision, any taxpayer, whether or not a C corporation, engaged in a trade or business is eligible to claim the enhanced deduction for donations of food inventory.[1734] For taxpayers other than C corporations, the total deduction for donations of food inventory in a taxable year generally may not exceed 10 percent of the taxpayer's net income for such taxable year from all sole proprietorships, S corporations, or partnerships (or other non C corporation) from which contributions of apparently wholesome food are made. For example, if a taxpayer is a sole proprietor, a shareholder in an S corporation, and a partner in a partnership, and each business makes charitable contributions of food inventory, the taxpayer's deduction for donations of food inventory is limited to 10 percent of the taxpayer's net income from the sole proprietorship and the taxpayer's interests in the S corporation and

[1728] Sec. 170(e)(3).
[1729] Sec. 170(b)(2).
[1730] Sec. 170(e)(3)(A)(i)–(iii).
[1731] Sec. 170(e)(3)(A)(iv).
[1732] Treas. Reg. sec. 1.170A–4A(c)(3).
[1733] *Lucky Stores Inc.* v. *Commissioner,* 105 T.C. 420 (1995) (holding that the value of surplus bread inventory donated to charity was the full retail price of the bread rather than half the retail price, as the IRS asserted).
[1734] Sec. 170(e)(3)(C).

partnership. However, if only the sole proprietorship and the S corporation made charitable contributions of food inventory, the taxpayer's deduction would be limited to 10 percent of the net income from the trade or business of the sole proprietorship and the taxpayer's interest in the S corporation, but not the taxpayer's interest in the partnership.[1735]

Under the temporary provision, the enhanced deduction for food is available only for food that qualifies as "apparently wholesome food." Apparently wholesome food is defined as food intended for human consumption that meets all quality and labeling standards imposed by Federal, State, and local laws and regulations even though the food may not be readily marketable due to appearance, age, freshness, grade, size, surplus, or other conditions.

The temporary provision does not apply to contributions made after December 31, 2009.

### *Explanation of Provision*

The provision extends the expansion of, and modifications to, the enhanced deduction for charitable contributions of food inventory to contributions made before January 1, 2012.

### *Effective Date*

The provision is effective for contributions made after December 31, 2009.

## 11. Enhanced charitable deduction for contributions of book inventories to public schools (sec. 741 of the Act and sec. 170 of the Code)

### *Present Law*

#### *Charitable contributions in general*

In general, an income tax deduction is permitted for charitable contributions, subject to certain limitations that depend on the type of taxpayer, the property contributed, and the donee organization.[1736]

Charitable contributions of cash are deductible in the amount contributed. In general, contributions of capital gain property to a qualified charity are deductible at fair market value with certain exceptions. Capital gain property means any capital asset or property used in the taxpayer's trade or business the sale of which at its fair market value, at the time of contribution, would have resulted in gain that would have been long-term capital gain. Contributions of other appreciated property generally are deductible at the donor's basis in the property. Contributions of depreciated

---

[1735] The 10 percent limitation does not affect the application of the generally applicable percentage limitations. For example, if 10 percent of a sole proprietor's net income from the proprietor's trade or business was greater than 50 percent of the proprietor's contribution base, the available deduction for the taxable year (with respect to contributions to public charities) would be 50 percent of the proprietor's contribution base. Consistent with present law, such contributions may be carried forward because they exceed the 50 percent limitation. Contributions of food inventory by a taxpayer that is not a C corporation that exceed the 10 percent limitation but not the 50 percent limitation could not be carried forward.

[1736] Sec. 170.

property generally are deductible at the fair market value of the property.

***General rules regarding contributions of book inventory***

Under present law, a taxpayer's deduction for charitable contributions of inventory generally is limited to the taxpayer's basis (typically, cost) in the inventory, or, if less, the fair market value of the inventory.

In general, for certain contributions of inventory, C corporations may claim an enhanced deduction equal to the lesser of (1) basis plus one-half of the item's appreciation (i.e., basis plus one-half of fair market value in excess of basis) or (2) two times basis.[1737] In general, a C corporation's charitable contribution deductions for a year may not exceed 10 percent of the corporation's taxable income.[1738] To be eligible for the enhanced deduction, the contributed property generally must be inventory of the taxpayer contributed to a charitable organization described in section 501(c)(3) (except for private nonoperating foundations), and the donee must (1) use the property consistent with the donee's exempt purpose solely for the care of the ill, the needy, or infants, (2) not transfer the property in exchange for money, other property, or services, and (3) provide the taxpayer a written statement that the donee's use of the property will be consistent with such requirements.[1739] In the case of contributed property subject to the Federal Food, Drug, and Cosmetic Act, as amended, the property must satisfy the applicable requirements of such Act on the date of transfer and for 180 days prior to the transfer.[1740]

A donor making a charitable contribution of inventory must make a corresponding adjustment to the cost of goods sold by decreasing the cost of goods sold by the lesser of the fair market value of the property or the donor's basis with respect to the inventory.[1741] Accordingly, if the allowable charitable deduction for inventory is the fair market value of the inventory, the donor reduces its cost of goods sold by such value, with the result that the difference between the fair market value and the donor's basis may still be recovered by the donor other than as a charitable contribution.

To use the enhanced deduction, the taxpayer must establish that the fair market value of the donated item exceeds basis.

***Special rule expanding and modifying the enhanced deduction for contributions of book inventory***

The generally applicable enhanced deduction for C corporations is expanded and modified to include certain qualified book contributions made after August 28, 2005, and before January 1, 2010.[1742] A qualified book contribution means a charitable contribution of books to a public school that provides elementary education or secondary education (kindergarten through grade 12) and that is an educational organization that normally maintains a reg-

---

[1737] Sec. 170(e)(3).
[1738] Sec. 170(b)(2).
[1739] Sec. 170(e)(3)(A)(i)–(iii)
[1740] Sec. 170(e)(3)(A)(iv).
[1741] Treas. Reg. sec. 1.170A–4A(c)(3).
[1742] Sec. 170(e)(3)(D).

ular faculty and curriculum and normally has a regularly enrolled body of pupils or students in attendance at the place where its educational activities are regularly carried on. The enhanced deduction for qualified book contributions is not allowed unless the donee organization certifies in writing that the contributed books are suitable, in terms of currency, content, and quantity, for use in the donee's educational programs and that the donee will use the books in such educational programs. The donee also must make the certifications required for the generally applicable enhanced deduction, i.e., the donee will (1) use the property consistent with the donee's exempt purpose solely for the care of the ill, the needy, or infants, (2) not transfer the property in exchange for money, other property, or services, and (3) provide the taxpayer a written statement that the donee's use of the property will be consistent with such requirements.

### *Explanation of Provision*

The provision extends the expansion of, and modifications to, the enhanced deduction for contributions of book inventory to contributions made before January 1, 2012.

### *Effective Date*

The provision is effective for contributions made after December 31, 2009.

## 12. Enhanced charitable deduction for corporate contributions of computer inventory for educational purposes (sec. 742 of the Act and sec. 170 of the Code)

### *Present Law*

In the case of a charitable contribution of inventory or other ordinary-income or short-term capital gain property, the amount of the charitable deduction generally is limited to the taxpayer's basis in the property. In the case of a charitable contribution of tangible personal property, the deduction is limited to the taxpayer's basis in such property if the use by the recipient charitable organization is unrelated to the organization's tax-exempt purpose. In cases involving contributions to a private foundation (other than certain private operating foundations), the amount of the deduction is limited to the taxpayer's basis in the property.[1743]

### *Explanation of Provision*

A taxpayer's deduction for charitable contributions of computer technology and equipment generally is limited to the taxpayer's basis (typically, cost) in the property. Under a special, temporary provision, certain corporations may claim a deduction in excess of basis for a "qualified computer contribution."[1744] This enhanced deduction is equal to the lesser of (1) basis plus one-half of the item's appreciation (i.e., basis plus one half of fair market value in excess of basis) or (2) two times basis. The enhanced deduction for quali-

---

[1743] Sec. 170(e)(1).
[1744] Sec. 170(e)(6).

fied computer contributions expires for any contribution made during any taxable year beginning after December 31, 2009.[1745]

A qualified computer contribution means a charitable contribution of any computer technology or equipment, which meets several requirements. The contribution must meet standards of functionality and suitability as established by the Secretary of the Treasury. The contribution must be to certain educational organizations or public libraries and made not later than three years after the taxpayer acquired the property (or, if the taxpayer constructed or assembled the property, the date construction or assembly of the property is substantially completed).[1746] The original use of the property must be by the donor or the donee,[1747] and substantially all of the donee's use of the property must be within the United States for educational purposes related to the function or purpose of the donee. The property must fit productively into the donee's education plan. The donee may not transfer the property in exchange for money, other property, or services, except for shipping, installation, and transfer costs. To determine whether property is constructed or assembled by the taxpayer, the rules applicable to qualified research contributions apply. Contributions may be made to private foundations under certain conditions.[1748]

### *Explanation of Provision*

The provision extends the enhanced deduction for computer technology and equipment to contributions made before January 1, 2012.

### *Effective Date*

The provision is effective for contributions made in taxable years beginning after December 31, 2009.

## 13. Election to expense mine safety equipment (sec. 743 of the Act and sec. 179E of the Code)

### *Present Law*

A taxpayer is allowed to recover, through annual depreciation deductions, the cost of certain property used in a trade or business or for the production of income. The amount of the depreciation deduction allowed with respect to tangible property for a taxable year is determined under the modified accelerated cost recovery system ("MACRS").[1749] Under MACRS, different types of property generally are assigned applicable recovery periods and depreciation methods. The recovery periods applicable to most tangible personal property (generally tangible property other than residential rental property and nonresidential real property) range from three to 20 years. The depreciation methods generally applicable to tangible

---

[1745] Sec. 170(e)(6)(G).

[1746] If the taxpayer constructed the property and reacquired such property, the contribution must be within three years of the date the original construction was substantially completed. Sec. 170(e)(6)(D)(i).

[1747] This requirement does not apply if the property was reacquired by the manufacturer and contributed. Sec. 170(e)(6)(D)(ii).

[1748] Sec. 170(e)(6)(C).

[1749] Sec. 168.

personal property are the 200-percent and 150-percent declining balance methods, switching to the straight-line method for the taxable year in which the depreciation deduction would be maximized.

In lieu of depreciation, a taxpayer with a sufficiently small amount of annual investment may elect to deduct (or "expense") such costs under section 179. Present law provides that the maximum amount a taxpayer may expense for taxable years beginning in 2010 is $500,000 of the cost of the qualifying property for the taxable year. In general, qualifying property is defined as depreciable tangible personal property that is purchased for use in the active conduct of a trade or business.[1750] The $500,000 amount is reduced (but not below zero) by the amount by which the cost of qualifying property placed in service during the taxable year exceeds $2,000,000.

A taxpayer may elect to treat 50 percent of the cost of any qualified advanced mine safety equipment property as an expense in the taxable year in which the equipment is placed in service.[1751] The deduction under section 179E is allowed for both regular and alternative minimum tax purposes, including adjusted current earnings. In computing earnings and profits, the amount deductible under section 179E is allowed as a deduction ratably over five taxable years beginning with the year the amount is deductible under section 179E.[1752]

"Qualified advanced mine safety equipment property" means any advanced mine safety equipment property for use in any underground mine located in the United States the original use of which commences with the taxpayer and which is placed in service before January 1, 2010.[1753]

Advanced mine safety equipment property means any of the following: (1) emergency communication technology or devices used to allow a miner to maintain constant communication with an individual who is not in the mine; (2) electronic identification and location devices that allow individuals not in the mine to track at all times the movements and location of miners working in or at the mine; (3) emergency oxygen-generating, self-rescue devices that provide oxygen for at least 90 minutes; (4) pre-positioned supplies of oxygen providing each miner on a shift the ability to survive for at least 48 hours; and (5) comprehensive atmospheric monitoring systems that monitor the levels of carbon monoxide, methane and oxygen that are present in all areas of the mine and that can detect smoke in the case of a fire in a mine.[1754]

The portion of the cost of any property with respect to which an expensing election under section 179 is made may not be taken into account for purposes of the 50-percent deduction under section 179E.[1755] In addition, a taxpayer making an election under section 179E must file with the Secretary a report containing information

---

[1750] The definition of qualifying property was temporarily (for 2010 and 2011) expanded to include up to $250,000 of qualified leasehold improvement property, qualified restaurant property, and qualified retail improvement property. See section 179(c).

[1751] Sec. 179E(a).

[1752] Sec. 312(k)(3). Section 56(g)(4)(C)(i) does not apply to a deduction under section 179E (or under sections 179, 179A, 179B, and 179D), as such deduction is permitted for purposes of computing earnings and profits.

[1753] Secs. 179E(c) and (g).

[1754] Sec. 179E(d).

[1755] Sec. 179E(e).

with respect to the operation of the mines of the taxpayer as required by the Secretary.[1756]

### *Explanation of Provision*

The provision extends for two years, to December 31, 2011, the present-law placed in service date relating to expensing of mine safety equipment.

### *Effective Date*

The provision applies to property placed in service after December 31, 2009.

## 14. Special expensing rules for certain film and television productions (sec. 744 of the Act and sec. 181 of the Code)

### *Present Law*

The modified accelerated cost recovery system ("MACRS") does not apply to certain property, including any motion picture film, video tape, or sound recording, or to any other property if the taxpayer elects to exclude such property from MACRS and the taxpayer properly applies a unit-of-production method or other method of depreciation not expressed in a term of years. Section 197 does not apply to certain intangible property, including property produced by the taxpayer or any interest in a film, sound recording, video tape, book or similar property not acquired in a transaction (or a series of related transactions) involving the acquisition of assets constituting a trade or business or substantial portion thereof. Thus, the recovery of the cost of a film, video tape, or similar property that is produced by the taxpayer or is acquired on a "standalone" basis by the taxpayer may not be determined under either the MACRS depreciation provisions or under the section 197 amortization provisions. The cost recovery of such property may be determined under section 167, which allows a depreciation deduction for the reasonable allowance for the exhaustion, wear and tear, or obsolescence of the property. A taxpayer is allowed to recover, through annual depreciation deductions, the cost of certain property used in a trade or business or for the production of income. Section 167(g) provides that the cost of motion picture films, sound recordings, copyrights, books, and patents are eligible to be recovered using the income forecast method of depreciation.

Under section 181, taxpayers may elect[1757] to deduct the cost of any qualifying film and television production, commencing prior to January 1, 2010, in the year the expenditure is incurred in lieu of capitalizing the cost and recovering it through depreciation allowances.[1758] Taxpayers may elect to deduct up to $15 million of the aggregate cost of the film or television production under this section.[1759] The threshold is increased to $20 million if a significant

[1756] Sec. 179E(f).

[1757] See Temp. Treas. Reg. section 1.181–2T for rules on making an election under this section.

[1758] For this purpose, a production is treated as commencing on the first date of principal photography.

[1759] Sec. 181(a)(2)(A).

amount of the production expenditures are incurred in areas eligible for designation as a low-income community or eligible for designation by the Delta Regional Authority as a distressed county or isolated area of distress.[1760]

A qualified film or television production means any production of a motion picture (whether released theatrically or directly to video cassette or any other format) or television program if at least 75 percent of the total compensation expended on the production is for services performed in the United States by actors, directors, producers, and other relevant production personnel.[1761] The term "compensation" does not include participations and residuals (as defined in section 167(g)(7)(B)).[1762] With respect to property which is one or more episodes in a television series, each episode is treated as a separate production and only the first 44 episodes qualify under the provision.[1763] Qualified property does not include sexually explicit productions as defined by section 2257 of title 18 of the U.S. Code.[1764]

For purposes of recapture under section 1245, any deduction allowed under section 181 is treated as if it were a deduction allowable for amortization.[1765]

### *Explanation of Provision*

The provision extends the present law expensing provision for two years, to qualified film and television productions commencing prior to January 1, 2012.

### *Effective Date*

The provision applies to qualified film and television productions commencing after December 31, 2009.

## 15. Expensing of environmental remediation costs (sec. 745 of the Act and sec. 198 of the Code)

### *Present Law*

Present law allows a deduction for ordinary and necessary expenses paid or incurred in carrying on any trade or business.[1766] Treasury regulations provide that the cost of incidental repairs that neither materially add to the value of property nor appreciably prolong its life, but keep it in an ordinarily efficient operating condition, may be deducted currently as a business expense.[1767] Section 263(a)(1) limits the scope of section 162 by prohibiting a current deduction for certain capital expenditures. Treasury regulations define "capital expenditures" as amounts paid or incurred to materially add to the value, or substantially prolong the useful life, of property owned by the taxpayer, or to adapt property to a new or different use.[1768] Amounts paid for repairs and maintenance do

[1760] Sec. 181(a)(2)(B).
[1761] Sec. 181(d)(3)(A).
[1762] Sec. 181(d)(3)(B).
[1763] Sec. 181(d)(2)(B).
[1764] Sec. 181(d)(2)(C).
[1765] Sec. 1245(a)(2)(C).
[1766] Sec. 162.
[1767] Treas. Reg. sec. 1.162–4.
[1768] Treas. Reg. sec. 1.263(a)–1(b).

not constitute capital expenditures. The determination of whether an expense is deductible or capitalizable is based on all relevant facts and circumstances.

Taxpayers may elect to treat certain environmental remediation expenditures paid or incurred before January 1, 2010, that would otherwise be chargeable to capital account as deductible in the year paid or incurred.[1769] The deduction applies for both regular and alternative minimum tax purposes. The expenditure must be incurred in connection with the abatement or control of hazardous substances at a qualified contaminated site. In general, any expenditure for the acquisition of depreciable property used in connection with the abatement or control of hazardous substances at a qualified contaminated site does not constitute a qualified environmental remediation expenditure. However, depreciation deductions allowable for such property that would otherwise be allocated to the site under the principles set forth in *Commissioner v. Idaho Power Co.*[1770] and section 263A are treated as qualified environmental remediation expenditures.

A "qualified contaminated site" (a so-called "brownfield") generally is any property that is held for use in a trade or business, for the production of income, or as inventory and is certified by the appropriate State environmental agency to be an area at or on which there has been a release (or threat of release) or disposal of a hazardous substance. Both urban and rural property may qualify. However, sites that are identified on the national priorities list under the Comprehensive Environmental Response, Compensation, and Liability Act of 1980 ("CERCLA")[1771] cannot qualify as targeted areas. Hazardous substances generally are defined by reference to sections 101(14) and 102 of CERCLA, subject to additional limitations applicable to asbestos and similar substances within buildings, certain naturally occurring substances such as radon, and certain other substances released into drinking water supplies due to deterioration through ordinary use, as well as petroleum products defined in section 4612(a)(3) of the Code.

In the case of property to which a qualified environmental remediation expenditure otherwise would have been capitalized, any deduction allowed under section 198 is treated as a depreciation deduction and the property is treated as section 1245 property. Thus, deductions for qualified environmental remediation expenditures are subject to recapture as ordinary income upon a sale or other disposition of the property. In addition, sections 280B (demolition of structures) and 468 (special rules for mining and solid waste reclamation and closing costs) do not apply to amounts that are treated as expenses under section 198.

### *Explanation of Provision*

The provision extends the present law expensing for two years to include expenditures paid or incurred before January 1, 2012.

[1769] Sec. 198.
[1770] 418 U.S. 1 (1974).
[1771] Pub. L. No. 96–510 (1980).

### *Effective Date*

The provision is effective for expenditures paid or incurred after December 31, 2009.

## 16. Deduction allowable with respect to income attributable to domestic production activities in Puerto Rico (sec. 746 of the Act and sec. 199 of the Code)

### *Present Law*

#### *General*

Present law provides a deduction from taxable income (or, in the case of an individual, adjusted gross income) that is equal to nine percent of the lesser of the taxpayer's qualified production activities income or taxable income for the taxable year. For taxpayers subject to the 35-percent corporate income tax rate, the nine-percent deduction effectively reduces the corporate income tax rate to just under 32 percent on qualified production activities income.

In general, qualified production activities income is equal to domestic production gross receipts reduced by the sum of: (1) the costs of goods sold that are allocable to those receipts; and (2) other expenses, losses, or deductions which are properly allocable to those receipts.

Domestic production gross receipts generally are gross receipts of a taxpayer that are derived from: (1) any sale, exchange, or other disposition, or any lease, rental, or license, of qualifying production property [1772] that was manufactured, produced, grown or extracted by the taxpayer in whole or in significant part within the United States; (2) any sale, exchange, or other disposition, or any lease, rental, or license, of qualified film [1773] produced by the taxpayer; (3) any lease, rental, license, sale, exchange, or other disposition of electricity, natural gas, or potable water produced by the taxpayer in the United States; (4) construction of real property performed in the United States by a taxpayer in the ordinary course of a construction trade or business; or (5) engineering or architectural services performed in the United States for the construction of real property located in the United States.

The amount of the deduction for a taxable year is limited to 50 percent of the wages paid by the taxpayer, and properly allocable to domestic production gross receipts, during the calendar year that ends in such taxable year.[1774] Wages paid to bona fide residents of Puerto Rico generally are not included in the definition of wages for purposes of computing the wage limitation amount.[1775]

---

[1772] Qualifying production property generally includes any tangible personal property, computer software, and sound recordings.

[1773] Qualified film includes any motion picture film or videotape (including live or delayed television programming, but not including certain sexually explicit productions) if 50 percent or more of the total compensation relating to the production of the film (including compensation in the form of residuals and participations) constitutes compensation for services performed in the United States by actors, production personnel, directors, and producers.

[1774] For purposes of the provision, "wages" include the sum of the amounts of wages as defined in section 3401(a) and elective deferrals that the taxpayer properly reports to the Social Security Administration with respect to the employment of employees of the taxpayer during the calendar year ending during the taxpayer's taxable year.

[1775] Section 3401(a)(8)(C) excludes wages paid to United States citizens who are bona fide residents of Puerto Rico from the term wages for purposes of income tax withholding.

### *Rules for Puerto Rico*

When used in the Code in a geographical sense, the term "United States" generally includes only the States and the District of Columbia.[1776] A special rule for determining domestic production gross receipts, however, provides that in the case of any taxpayer with gross receipts from sources within the Commonwealth of Puerto Rico, the term "United States" includes the Commonwealth of Puerto Rico, but only if all of the taxpayer's Puerto Rico-sourced gross receipts are taxable under the Federal income tax for individuals or corporations.[1777] In computing the 50-percent wage limitation, the taxpayer is permitted to take into account wages paid to bona fide residents of Puerto Rico for services performed in Puerto Rico.[1778]

The special rules for Puerto Rico apply only with respect to the first four taxable years of a taxpayer beginning after December 31, 2005 and before January 1, 2010.

### *Explanation of Provision*

The provision extends the special domestic production activities rules for Puerto Rico to apply for the first six taxable years of a taxpayer beginning after December 31, 2005 and before January 1, 2012.

### *Effective Date*

The provision is effective for taxable years beginning after December 31, 2009.

## 17. Modification of tax treatment of certain payments to controlling exempt organizations (sec. 747 of the Act and sec. 512 of the Code)

### *Present Law*

In general, organizations exempt from Federal income tax are subject to the unrelated business income tax on income derived from a trade or business regularly carried on by the organization that is not substantially related to the performance of the organization's tax-exempt functions.[1779] In general, interest, rents, royalties, and annuities are excluded from the unrelated business income of tax-exempt organizations.[1780]

Section 512(b)(13) provides special rules regarding income derived by an exempt organization from a controlled subsidiary. In general, section 512(b)(13) treats otherwise excluded rent, royalty, annuity, and interest income as unrelated business income if such income is received from a taxable or tax-exempt subsidiary that is 50-percent controlled by the parent tax-exempt organization to the extent the payment reduces the net unrelated income (or increases any net unrelated loss) of the controlled entity (determined as if the entity were tax exempt). However, a special rule provides that,

[1776] Sec. 7701(a)(9).
[1777] Sec. 199(d)(8)(A).
[1778] Sec. 199(d)(8)(B).
[1779] Sec. 511.
[1780] Sec. 512(b).

for payments made pursuant to a binding written contract in effect on August 17, 2006 (or renewal of such a contract on substantially similar terms), the general rule of section 512(b)(13) applies only to the portion of payments received or accrued in a taxable year that exceeds the amount of the payment that would have been paid or accrued if the amount of such payment had been determined under the principles of section 482 (i.e., at arm's length).[1781] In addition, the special rule imposes a 20-percent penalty on the larger of such excess determined without regard to any amendment or supplement to a return of tax, or such excess determined with regard to all such amendments and supplements.

In the case of a stock subsidiary, "control" means ownership by vote or value of more than 50 percent of the stock. In the case of a partnership or other entity, "control" means ownership of more than 50 percent of the profits, capital, or beneficial interests. In addition, present law applies the constructive ownership rules of section 318 for purposes of section 512(b)(13). Thus, a parent exempt organization is deemed to control any subsidiary in which it holds more than 50 percent of the voting power or value, directly (as in the case of a first-tier subsidiary) or indirectly (as in the case of a second-tier subsidiary).

The special rule does not apply to payments received or accrued after December 31, 2009.

### *Explanation of Provision*

The provision extends the special rule to payments received or accrued before January 1, 2012. Accordingly, under the provision, payments of rent, royalties, annuities, or interest income by a controlled organization to a controlling organization pursuant to a binding written contract in effect on August 17, 2006 (or renewal of such a contract on substantially similar terms), may be includible in the unrelated business taxable income of the controlling organization only to the extent the payment exceeds the amount of the payment determined under the principles of section 482 (i.e., at arm's length). Any such excess is subject to a 20-percent penalty on the larger of such excess determined without regard to any amendment or supplement to a return of tax, or such excess determined with regard to all such amendments and supplements.

### *Effective Date*

The provision is effective for payments received or accrued after December 31, 2009.

[1781] Sec. 512(b)(13)(E).

## 18. Treatment of certain dividends of regulated investment companies (sec. 748 of the Act and sec. 871(k) of the Code)

### *Present Law*[1782]

#### *In general*

A regulated investment company ("RIC") is an entity that meets certain requirements (including a requirement that its income generally be derived from passive investments such as dividends and interest and a requirement that it distribute at least 90 percent of its income) and that elects to be taxed under a special tax regime. Unlike an ordinary corporation, an entity that is taxed as a RIC can deduct amounts paid to its shareholders as dividends. In this manner, tax on RIC income is generally not paid by the RIC but rather by its shareholders. Income of a RIC distributed to shareholders as dividends is generally treated as an ordinary income dividend by those shareholders, unless other special rules apply. Dividends received by foreign persons from a RIC are generally subject to gross-basis tax under sections 871(a) or 881, and the RIC payor of such dividends is obligated to withhold such tax under sections 1441 and 1442.

Under present law, a RIC that earns certain interest income that would not be subject to U.S. tax if earned by a foreign person directly may, to the extent of such net income, designate a dividend it pays as derived from such interest income. A foreign person who is a shareholder in the RIC generally can treat such a dividend as exempt from gross-basis U.S. tax, as if the foreign person had earned the interest directly. Also, subject to certain requirements, the RIC is exempt from withholding the gross-basis tax on such dividends. Similar rules apply with respect to the designation of certain short term capital gain dividends. However, these provisions relating to certain dividends with respect to interest income and short term capital gain of the RIC do not apply to dividends with respect to any taxable year of a RIC beginning after December 31, 2009.

### *Explanation of Provision*

The provision extends the rules exempting from gross basis tax and from withholding tax the interest-related dividends and short term capital gain dividends received from a RIC, to dividends with respect to taxable years of a RIC beginning before January 1, 2012.

### *Effective Date*

The provision applies to dividends paid with respect to any taxable year of the RIC beginning after December 31, 2009.

---

[1782] Secs. 871(k), 881, 1441 and 1442.

### 19. RIC qualified investment entity treatment under FIRPTA (sec. 749 of the Act and secs. 897 and 1445 of the Code)

#### *Present law*

Special U.S. tax rules apply to capital gains of foreign persons that are attributable to dispositions of interests in U.S. real property. In general, although a foreign person (a foreign corporation or a nonresident alien individual) is not generally taxed on U.S. source capital gains unless certain personal presence or active business requirements are met, a foreign person who sells a U.S. real property interest ("USRPI") is subject to tax at the same rates as a U.S. person, under the Foreign Investment in Real Property Tax Act ("FIRPTA") provisions codified in section 897 of the Code. Withholding tax is also imposed under section 1445.

A USRPI includes stock or a beneficial interest in any domestic corporation unless such corporation has not been a U.S. real property holding corporation (as defined) during the testing period. A USRPI does not include an interest in a domestically controlled "qualified investment entity." A distribution from a "qualified investment entity" that is attributable to the sale of a USRPI is also subject to tax under FIRPTA unless the distribution is with respect to an interest that is regularly traded on an established securities market located in the United States and the recipient foreign corporation or nonresident alien individual did not hold more than 5 percent of that class of stock or beneficial interest within the 1-year period ending on the date of distribution.[1783] Special rules apply to situations involving tiers of qualified investment entities.

The term "qualified investment entity" includes a real estate investment trust ("REIT") and also includes a regulated investment company ("RIC") that meets certain requirements, although the inclusion of a RIC in that definition does not apply for certain purposes after December 31, 2009.[1784]

#### *Explanation of Provision*

The provision extends the inclusion of a RIC within the definition of a "qualified investment entity" under section 897 of the Code through December 31, 2011, for those situations in which that inclusion would otherwise have expired at the end of 2009.

#### *Effective Date*

The provision is generally effective on January 1, 2010.

The provision does not apply with respect to the withholding requirement under section 1445 for any payment made before the date of enactment, but a RIC that withheld and remitted tax under section 1445 on distributions made after December 31, 2009 and before the date of enactment is not liable to the distributee with respect to such withheld and remitted amounts.

[1783] Sections 857(b)(3)(F), 852(b)(3)(E), and 871(k)(2)(E) require dividend treatment, rather than capital gain treatment, for certain distributions to which FIRPTA does not apply by reason of this exception. See also section 881(e)(2).

[1784] Section 897(h).

## 20. Exceptions for active financing income (sec. 750 of the Act and secs. 953 and 954 of the Code)

### *Present Law*

Under the subpart F rules,[1785] 10-percent-or-greater U.S. shareholders of a controlled foreign corporation ("CFC") are subject to U.S. tax currently on certain income earned by the CFC, whether or not such income is distributed to the shareholders. The income subject to current inclusion under the subpart F rules includes, among other things, insurance income and foreign base company income. Foreign base company income includes, among other things, foreign personal holding company income and foreign base company services income (i.e., income derived from services performed for or on behalf of a related person outside the country in which the CFC is organized).

Foreign personal holding company income generally consists of the following: (1) dividends, interest, royalties, rents, and annuities; (2) net gains from the sale or exchange of (a) property that gives rise to the preceding types of income, (b) property that does not give rise to income, and (c) interests in trusts, partnerships, and real estate mortgage investment conduits ("REMICs"); (3) net gains from commodities transactions; (4) net gains from certain foreign currency transactions; (5) income that is equivalent to interest; (6) income from notional principal contracts; (7) payments in lieu of dividends; and (8) amounts received under personal service contracts.

Insurance income subject to current inclusion under the subpart F rules includes any income of a CFC attributable to the issuing or reinsuring of any insurance or annuity contract in connection with risks located in a country other than the CFC's country of organization. Subpart F insurance income also includes income attributable to an insurance contract in connection with risks located within the CFC's country of organization, as the result of an arrangement under which another corporation receives a substantially equal amount of consideration for insurance of other country risks. Investment income of a CFC that is allocable to any insurance or annuity contract related to risks located outside the CFC's country of organization is taxable as subpart F insurance income.[1786]

Temporary exceptions from foreign personal holding company income, foreign base company services income, and insurance income apply for subpart F purposes for certain income that is derived in the active conduct of a banking, financing, or similar business, as a securities dealer, or in the conduct of an insurance business (so-called "active financing income"). These provisions were enacted in the Taxpayer Relief Act of 1997 as one-year temporary exceptions, and in 1998, 1999, 2002, 2006, and 2008, the provisions were extended, and in some cases, modified.[1787]

---

[1785] Secs. 951–964.

[1786] Prop. Treas. Reg. sec. 1.953–1(a).

[1787] Temporary exceptions from the subpart F provisions for certain active financing income applied only for taxable years beginning in 1998. Taxpayer Relief Act of 1997, Pub. L. No. 105–34. Those exceptions were modified and extended for one year, applicable only for taxable years

Continued

With respect to income derived in the active conduct of a banking, financing, or similar business, a CFC is required to be predominantly engaged in such business and to conduct substantial activity with respect to such business in order to qualify for the active financing exceptions. In addition, certain nexus requirements apply, which provide that income derived by a CFC or a qualified business unit ("QBU") of a CFC from transactions with customers is eligible for the exceptions if, among other things, substantially all of the activities in connection with such transactions are conducted directly by the CFC or QBU in its home country, and such income is treated as earned by the CFC or QBU in its home country for purposes of such country's tax laws. Moreover, the exceptions apply to income derived from certain cross border transactions, provided that certain requirements are met. Additional exceptions from foreign personal holding company income apply for certain income derived by a securities dealer within the meaning of section 475 and for gain from the sale of active financing assets.

In the case of a securities dealer, the temporary exception from foreign personal holding company income applies to certain income. The income covered by the exception is any interest or dividend (or certain equivalent amounts) from any transaction, including a hedging transaction or a transaction consisting of a deposit of collateral or margin, entered into in the ordinary course of the dealer's trade or business as a dealer in securities within the meaning of section 475. In the case of a QBU of the dealer, the income is required to be attributable to activities of the QBU in the country of incorporation, or to a QBU in the country in which the QBU both maintains its principal office and conducts substantial business activity. A coordination rule provides that this exception generally takes precedence over the exception for income of a banking, financing or similar business, in the case of a securities dealer.

In the case of insurance, a temporary exception from foreign personal holding company income applies for certain income of a qualifying insurance company with respect to risks located within the CFC's country of creation or organization. In the case of insurance, temporary exceptions from insurance income and from foreign personal holding company income also apply for certain income of a qualifying branch of a qualifying insurance company with respect to risks located within the home country of the branch, provided certain requirements are met under each of the exceptions. Further, additional temporary exceptions from insurance income and from foreign personal holding company income apply for certain income of certain CFCs or branches with respect to risks located in a country other than the United States, provided that the requirements for these exceptions are met. In the case of a life insurance or annuity contract, reserves for such contracts are determined under rules specific to the temporary exceptions. Present law also

beginning in 1999. The Tax and Trade Relief Extension Act of 1998, Pub. L. No. 105–277. The Tax Relief Extension Act of 1999, Pub. L. No. 106–170, clarified and extended the temporary exceptions for two years, applicable only for taxable years beginning after 1999 and before 2002. The Job Creation and Worker Assistance Act of 2002, Pub. L. No. 107–147, modified and extended the temporary exceptions for five years, for taxable years beginning after 2001 and before 2007. The Tax Increase Prevention and Reconciliation Act of 2005, Pub. L. No. 109–222, extended the temporary provisions for two years, for taxable years beginning after 2006 and before 2009. The Energy Improvement and Extension Act of 2008, Pub. L. No. 110–343, extended the temporary provisions for one year, for taxable years beginning after 2008 and before 2010.

permits a taxpayer in certain circumstances, subject to approval by the IRS through the ruling process or in published guidance, to establish that the reserve of a life insurance company for life insurance and annuity contracts is the amount taken into account in determining the foreign statement reserve for the contract (reduced by catastrophe, equalization, or deficiency reserve or any similar reserve). IRS approval is to be based on whether the method, the interest rate, the mortality and morbidity assumptions, and any other factors taken into account in determining foreign statement reserves (taken together or separately) provide an appropriate means of measuring income for Federal income tax purposes.

### *Explanation of Provision*

The provision extends for two years (for taxable years beginning before 2012) the present-law temporary exceptions from subpart F foreign personal holding company income, foreign base company services income, and insurance income for certain income that is derived in the active conduct of a banking, financing, or similar business, or in the conduct of an insurance business.

### *Effective Date*

The provision is effective for taxable years of foreign corporations beginning after December 31, 2009, and for taxable years of U.S. shareholders with or within which such taxable years of such foreign corporations end.

## 21. Look-thru treatment of payments between related controlled foreign corporations under foreign personal holding company rules (sec. 751 of the Act and sec. 954(c)(6) of the Code)

### *Present Law*

#### *In general*

The rules of subpart F[1788] require U.S. shareholders with a 10-percent or greater interest in a controlled foreign corporation ("CFC") to include certain income of the CFC (referred to as "subpart F income") on a current basis for U.S. tax purposes, regardless of whether the income is distributed to the shareholders.

Subpart F income includes foreign base company income. One category of foreign base company income is foreign personal holding company income. For subpart F purposes, foreign personal holding company income generally includes dividends, interest, rents, and royalties, among other types of income. There are several exceptions to these rules. For example, foreign personal holding company income does not include dividends and interest received by a CFC from a related corporation organized and operating in the same foreign country in which the CFC is organized, or rents and royalties received by a CFC from a related corporation for the use of property within the country in which the CFC is organized. Interest, rent, and royalty payments do not qualify for this exclusion to the extent that such payments reduce the subpart F

[1788] Secs. 951–964.

income of the payor. In addition, subpart F income of a CFC does not include any item of income from sources within the United States that is effectively connected with the conduct by such CFC of a trade or business within the United States ("ECI") unless such item is exempt from taxation (or is subject to a reduced rate of tax) pursuant to a tax treaty.

***The "look-thru rule"***

Under the "look-thru rule" (sec. 954(c)(6)), dividends, interest (including factoring income that is treated as equivalent to interest under section 954(c)(1)(E)), rents, and royalties received by one CFC from a related CFC are not treated as foreign personal holding company income to the extent attributable or properly allocable to income of the payor that is neither subpart F income nor treated as ECI. For this purpose, a related CFC is a CFC that controls or is controlled by the other CFC, or a CFC that is controlled by the same person or persons that control the other CFC. Ownership of more than 50 percent of the CFC's stock (by vote or value) constitutes control for these purposes.

The Secretary is authorized to prescribe regulations that are necessary or appropriate to carry out the look-thru rule, including such regulations as are appropriate to prevent the abuse of the purposes of such rule.

The look-thru rule is effective for taxable years of foreign corporations beginning before January 1, 2010, and for taxable years of U.S. shareholders with or within which such taxable years of such foreign corporations end.

### *Explanation of Provision*

The provision extends for two years the application of the look-thru rule, to taxable years of foreign corporations beginning before January 1, 2012, and for taxable years of U.S. shareholders with or within which such taxable years of such foreign corporations end.

### *Effective Date*

The provision is effective for taxable years of foreign corporations beginning after December 31, 2009, and for taxable years of U.S. shareholders with or within which such taxable years of such foreign corporations end.

## 22. Basis adjustment to stock of S corps making charitable contributions of property (sec. 752 of the Act and sec. 1367 of the Code)

### *Present Law*

Under present law, if an S corporation contributes money or other property to a charity, each shareholder takes into account the shareholder's pro rata share of the contribution in determining its own income tax liability.[1789] A shareholder of an S corporation reduces the basis in the stock of the S corporation by the amount of

[1789] Sec. 1366(a)(1)(A).

the charitable contribution that flows through to the shareholder.[1790]

In the case of contributions made in taxable years beginning before January 1, 2010, the amount of a shareholder's basis reduction in the stock of an S corporation by reason of a charitable contribution made by the corporation is equal to the shareholder's pro rata share of the adjusted basis of the contributed property. For contributions made in taxable years beginning after December 31, 2009, the amount of the reduction is the shareholder's pro rata share of the fair market value of the contributed property.

### *Explanation of Provision*

The provision extends the rule relating to the basis reduction on account of charitable contributions of property for two years to contributions made in taxable years beginning before January 1, 2012.

### *Effective Date*

The provision applies to contributions made in taxable years beginning after December 31, 2009.

## 23. Empowerment zone tax incentives (sec. 753 of the Act and secs. 1202 and 1391 of the Code)

### *Present Law*

The Omnibus Budget Reconciliation Act of 1993 ("OBRA 93")[1791] authorized the designation of nine empowerment zones ("Round I empowerment zones") to provide tax incentives for businesses to locate within certain targeted areas[1792] designated by the Secretaries of the Department of Housing and Urban Development ("HUD") and the U.S Department of Agriculture ("USDA"). The Taxpayer Relief Act of 1997[1793] authorized the designation of two additional Round I urban empowerment zones, and 20 additional empowerment zones ("Round II empowerment zones"). The Community Renewal Tax Relief Act of 2000 ("2000 Community Renewal Act")[1794] authorized a total of ten new empowerment zones ("Round III empowerment zones"), bringing the total number of authorized empowerment zones to 40.[1795] In addition, the 2000 Com-

[1790] Sec. 1367(a)(2)(B).

[1791] Pub. L. No. 103–66.

[1792] The targeted areas are those that have pervasive poverty, high unemployment, and general economic distress, and that satisfy certain eligibility criteria, including specified poverty rates and population and geographic size limitations.

[1793] Pub. L. No. 105–34.

[1794] Pub. L. No. 106–554.

[1795] The urban part of the program is administered by the HUD and the rural part of the program is administered by the USDA. The eight Round I urban empowerment zones are Atlanta, GA; Baltimore, MD, Chicago, IL; Cleveland, OH; Detroit, MI; Los Angeles, CA; New York, NY; and Philadelphia, PA/Camden, NJ. Atlanta relinquished its empowerment zone designation in Round III. The three Round I rural empowerment zones are Kentucky Highlands, KY; Mid-Delta, MI; and Rio Grande Valley, TX. The 15 Round II urban empowerment zones are Boston, MA; Cincinnati, OH; Columbia, SC; Columbus, OH; Cumberland County, NJ; El Paso, TX; Gary/Hammond/East Chicago, IN; Ironton, OH/Huntington, WV; Knoxville, TN; Miami/Dade County, FL; Minneapolis, MN; New Haven, CT; Norfolk/Portsmouth, VA; Santa Ana, CA; and St. Louis, Missouri/East St. Louis, IL. The five Round II rural empowerment zones are Desert Communities, CA; Griggs-Steele, ND; Oglala Sioux Tribe, SD; Southernmost Illinois Delta, IL; and Southwest Georgia United, GA. The eight Round III urban empowerment zones are Fresno, CA; Jacksonville, FL; Oklahoma City, OK; Pulaski County, AR; San Antonio, TX; Syracuse, NY; Tuc-

Continued

munity Renewal Act conformed the tax incentives that are available to businesses in the Round I, Round II, and Round III empowerment zones, and extended the empowerment zone incentives through December 31, 2009.[1796]

The tax incentives available within the designated empowerment zones include a Federal income tax credit for employers who hire qualifying employees, accelerated depreciation deductions on qualifying equipment, tax-exempt bond financing, deferral of capital gains tax on sale of qualified assets sold and replaced, and partial exclusion of capital gains tax on certain sales of qualified small business stock.

The following is a description of the tax incentives.

***Employment credit***

A 20-percent wage credit is available to employers for the first $15,000 of qualified wages paid to each employee (i.e., a maximum credit of $3,000 with respect to each qualified employee) who (1) is a resident of the empowerment zone, and (2) performs substantially all employment services within the empowerment zone in a trade or business of the employer.[1797]

The wage credit rate applies to qualifying wages paid before January 1, 2010. Wages paid to a qualified employee who earns more than $15,000 are eligible for the wage credit (although only the first $15,000 of wages is eligible for the credit). The wage credit is available with respect to a qualified full-time or part-time employee (employed for at least 90 days), regardless of the number of other employees who work for the employer. In general, any taxable business carrying out activities in the empowerment zone may claim the wage credit, regardless of whether the employer meets the definition of an "enterprise zone business."[1798]

An employer's deduction otherwise allowed for wages paid is reduced by the amount of wage credit claimed for that taxable year.[1799] Wages are not to be taken into account for purposes of the wage credit if taken into account in determining the employer's work opportunity tax credit under section 51 or the welfare-to-work credit under section 51A.[1800] In addition, the $15,000 cap is reduced by any wages taken into account in computing the work opportunity tax credit or the welfare-to-work credit.[1801] The wage credit may be used to offset up to 25 percent of alternative minimum tax liability.[1802]

---

son, AZ; and Yonkers, NY. The two Round III rural empowerment zones are Aroostook County, ME; and Futuro, TX.

[1796] If an empowerment zone designation were terminated prior to December 31, 2009, the tax incentives would cease to be available as of the termination date.

[1797] Sec. 1396. The $15,000 limit is annual, not cumulative such that the limit is the first $15,000 of wages paid in a calendar year which ends with or within the taxable year.

[1798] Secs. 1397C(b) and 1397C(c). However, the wage credit is not available for wages paid in connection with certain business activities described in section 144(c)(6)(B), including a golf course, country club, massage parlor, hot tub facility, suntan facility, racetrack, or liquor store, or certain farming activities. In addition, wages are not eligible for the wage credit if paid to: (1) a person who owns more than five percent of the stock (or capital or profits interests) of the employer, (2) certain relatives of the employer, or (3) if the employer is a corporation or partnership, certain relatives of a person who owns more than 50 percent of the business.

[1799] Sec. 280C(a).

[1800] Secs. 1396(c)(3)(A) and 51A(d)(2).

[1801] Secs. 1396(c)(3)(B) and 51A(d)(2).

[1802] Sec. 38(c)(2).

***Increased section 179 expensing limitation***

An enterprise zone business is allowed an additional $35,000 of section 179 expensing (for a total of up to $285,000 in 2009)[1803] for qualified zone property placed in service before January 1, 2010.[1804] The section 179 expensing allowed to a taxpayer is phased out by the amount by which 50 percent of the cost of qualified zone property placed in service during the year by the taxpayer exceeds $500,000.[1805] The term "qualified zone property" is defined as depreciable tangible property (including buildings) provided that (i) the property is acquired by the taxpayer (from an unrelated party) after the designation took effect, (ii) the original use of the property in an empowerment zone commences with the taxpayer, and (iii) substantially all of the use of the property is in an empowerment zone in the active conduct of a trade or business by the taxpayer. Special rules are provided in the case of property that is substantially renovated by the taxpayer.

An enterprise zone business means any qualified business entity and any qualified proprietorship. A qualified business entity means, any corporation or partnership if for such year: (1) every trade or business of such entity is the active conduct of a qualified business within an empowerment zone; (2) at least 50 percent of the total gross income of such entity is derived from the active conduct of such business; (3) a substantial portion of the use of the tangible property of such entity (whether owned or leased) is within an empowerment zone; (4) a substantial portion of the intangible property of such entity is used in the active conduct of any such business; (5) a substantial portion of the services performed for such entity by its employees are performed in an empowerment zone; (6) at least 35 percent of its employees are residents of an empowerment zone; (7) less than five percent of the average of the aggregate unadjusted bases of the property of such entity is attributable to collectibles other than collectibles that are held primarily for sale to customers in the ordinary course of such business; and (8) less than 5 percent of the average of the aggregate unadjusted bases of the property of such entity is attributable to nonqualified financial property.[1806]

A qualified proprietorship is any qualified business carried on by an individual as a proprietorship if for such year: (1) at least 50 percent of the total gross income of such individual from such business is derived from the active conduct of such business in an empowerment zone; (2) a substantial portion of the use of the tangible property of such individual in such business (whether owned or leased) is within an empowerment zone; (3) a substantial portion of the intangible property of such business is used in the active conduct of such business; (4) a substantial portion of the services performed for such individual in such business by employees of such business are performed in an empowerment zone; (5) at least 35 percent of such employees are residents of an empowerment

[1803] For each of 2010 and 2011, the 179 expensing limitation will be a total of up to $535,000. The Small Business Jobs Act of 2010, Pub. L. No. 111–240, sec. 2021. See discussion in Part Fourteen of this document.

[1804] Secs. 1397A, 1397D.

[1805] Sec. 1397A(a)(2), 179(b)(2), (7). For 2008 and 2009, the limit is $800,000.

[1806] Sec. 1397C(b).

zone; (6) less than 5 percent of the average of the aggregate unadjusted bases of the property of such individual which is used in such business is attributable to collectibles other than collectibles that are held primarily for sale to customers in the ordinary course of such business; and (7) less than 5 percent of the average of the aggregate unadjusted bases of the property of such individual which is used in such business is attributable to nonqualified financial property.[1807]

A qualified business is defined as any trade or business other than a trade or business that consists predominantly of the development or holding of intangibles for sale or license or any business prohibited in connection with the employment credit.[1808] In addition, the leasing of real property that is located within the empowerment zone is treated as a qualified business only if (1) the leased property is not residential property, and (2) at least 50 percent of the gross rental income from the real property is from enterprise zone businesses. The rental of tangible personal property is not a qualified business unless at least 50 percent of the rental of such property is by enterprise zone businesses or by residents of an empowerment zone.

***Expanded tax-exempt financing for certain zone facilities***

States or local governments can issue enterprise zone facility bonds to raise funds to provide an enterprise zone business with qualified zone property.[1809] These bonds can be used in areas designated enterprise communities as well as areas designated empowerment zones. To qualify, 95 percent (or more) of the net proceeds from the bond issue must be used to finance: (1) qualified zone property whose principal user is an enterprise zone business, and (2) certain land functionally related and subordinate to such property.

The term enterprise zone business is the same as that used for purposes of the increased section 179 deduction limitation (discussed above) with certain modifications for start-up businesses. First, a business will be treated as an enterprise zone business during a start-up period if (1) at the beginning of the period, it is reasonable to expect the business to be an enterprise zone business by the end of the start-up period, and (2) the business makes bona fide efforts to be an enterprise zone business. The start-up period is the period that ends with the start of the first tax year beginning more than two years after the later of (1) the issue date of the bond issue financing the qualified zone property, and (2) the date this property is first placed in service (or, if earlier, the date that is three years after the issue date).[1810]

Second, a business that qualifies as at the end of the start-up period must continue to qualify during a testing period that ends three tax years after the start-up period ends. After the three-year testing period, a business will continue to be treated as an enter-

[1807] Sec. 1397C(c).

[1808] Sec. 1397C(d). Excluded businesses include any private or commercial golf course, country club, massage parlor, hot tub facility, sun tan facility, racetrack, or other facility used for gambling or any store the principal business of which is the sale of alcoholic beverages for off-premises consumption. Sec. 144(c)(6).

[1809] Sec. 1394.

[1810] Sec. 1394(b)(3).

prise zone business as long as 35 percent of its employees are residents of an empowerment zone or enterprise community.

The face amount of the bonds may not exceed $60 million for an empowerment zone in a rural area, $130 million for an empowerment zone in an urban area with zone population of less than 100,000, and $230 million for an empowerment zone in an urban area with zone population of at least 100,000.

***Elective roll over of capital gain from the sale or exchange of any qualified empowerment zone asset purchased after December 21, 2000***

Taxpayers can elect to defer recognition of gain on the sale of a qualified empowerment zone asset[1811] held for more than one year and replaced within 60 days by another qualified empowerment zone asset in the same zone.[1812] The deferral is accomplished by reducing the basis of the replacement asset by the amount of the gain recognized on the sale of the asset.

***Partial exclusion of capital gains on certain small business stock***

Individuals generally may exclude 50 percent (60 percent for certain empowerment zone businesses) of the gain from the sale of certain small business stock acquired at original issue and held for at least five years.[1813] The amount of gain eligible for the exclusion by an individual with respect to any corporation is the greater of (1) ten times the taxpayer's basis in the stock or (2) $10 million. To qualify as a small business, when the stock is issued, the gross assets of the corporation may not exceed $50 million. The corporation also must meet certain active trade or business requirements.

The portion of the gain includible in taxable income is taxed at a maximum rate of 28 percent under the regular tax.[1814] A percentage of the excluded gain is an alternative minimum tax preference;[1815] the portion of the gain includible in alternative minimum taxable income is taxed at a maximum rate of 28 percent under the alternative minimum tax.

---

[1811] The term "qualified empowerment zone asset" means any property which would be a qualified community asset (as defined in section 1400F, relating to certain tax benefits for renewal communities) if in section 1400F: (i) references to empowerment zones were substituted for references to renewal communities, (ii) references to enterprise zone businesses (as defined in section 1397C) were substituted for references to renewal community businesses, and (iii) the date of the enactment of this paragraph were substituted for "December 31, 2001" each place it appears. Sec. 1397B(b)(1)(A).

A "qualified community asset" includes: (1) qualified community stock (meaning original-issue stock purchased for cash in an enterprise zone business), (2) a qualified community partnership interest (meaning a partnership interest acquired for cash in an enterprise zone business), and (3) qualified community business property (meaning tangible property originally used in a enterprise zone business by the taxpayer) that is purchased or substantially improved after the date of the enactment of this paragraph.

For the definition of "enterprise zone business," see text accompanying *supra* note 1806. For the definition of "qualified business," see text accompanying *supra* note 1806.

[1812] Sec. 1397B.

[1813] Sec. 1202.

[1814] Sec. 1(h).

[1815] Sec. 57(a)(7). In the case of qualified small business stock, the percentage of gain excluded from gross income which is an alternative minimum tax preference is (i) seven percent in the case of stock disposed of in a taxable year beginning before 2011; (ii) 42 percent in the case of stock acquired before January 1, 2001, and disposed of in a taxable year beginning after 2010; and (iii) 28 percent in the case of stock acquired after December 31, 2000, and disposed of in a taxable year beginning after 2010.

Gain from the sale of qualified small business stock generally is taxed at effective rates of 14 percent under the regular tax[1816] and (i) 14.98 percent under the alternative minimum tax for dispositions before January 1, 2011; (ii) 19.88 percent under the alternative minimum tax for dispositions after December 31, 2010, in the case of stock acquired before January 1, 2001; and (iii) 17.92 percent under the alternative minimum tax for dispositions after December 31, 2010, in the case of stock acquired after December 31, 2000.[1817]

***Temporary increases in exclusion***

The percentage exclusion for qualified small business stock acquired after February 17, 2009, and on or before September 27, 2010, is increased to 75 percent.

The percentage exclusion for qualified small business stock acquired after September 27, 2010, and before January 1, 2011, is increased to 100 percent.[1818]

The temporary increases in the exclusion percentage apply for all qualified small business stock, including stock of empowerment zone businesses.[1819]

***Other tax incentives***

Other incentives not specific to empowerment zones but beneficial to these areas include the work opportunity tax credit for employers based on the first year of employment of certain targeted groups, including empowerment zone residents (up to $2,400 per employee), and qualified zone academy bonds for certain public schools located in an empowerment zone, or expected (as of the date of bond issuance) to have at least 35 percent of its students receiving free or reduced lunches.

## *Explanation of Provision*

The provision extends for two years, through December 31, 2011, the period for which the designation of an empowerment zone is in effect, thus extending for two years the empowerment zone tax incentives, including the wage credit, accelerated depreciation deductions on qualifying equipment, tax-exempt bond financing, and deferral of capital gains tax on sale of qualified assets sold and replaced. In the case of a designation of an empowerment zone the nomination for which included a termination date which is December 31, 2009, termination shall not apply with respect to such designation if the entity which made such nomination amends the nomination to provide for a new termination date in such manner as the Secretary may provide.

The provision extends for two years, through December 31, 2016, the period for which the percentage exclusion for qualified small business stock (of a corporation which is a qualified business enti-

[1816] The 50 percent of gain included in taxable income is taxed at a maximum rate of 28 percent.

[1817] The amount of gain included in alternative minimum tax is taxed at a maximum rate of 28 percent. The amount so included is the sum of (i) 50 percent (the percentage included in taxable income) of the total gain and (ii) the applicable preference percentage of the one-half gain that is excluded from taxable income.

[1818] Sec. 760 of the Act extends the January 1, 2011, date to January 1, 2012.

[1819] Secs. 1202(a)(3)(B) and 1202(a)(4)(B).

ty) acquired on or before February 17, 2009 is 60 percent. Gain attributable to periods after December 31, 2016 for qualified small business stock acquired on or before February 17, 2009 or after December 31, 2011 is subject to the general rule which provides for a percentage exclusion of 50 percent.

### *Effective Date*

The provision relating to the designation of an empowerment zone and the provision relating to the exclusion of gain from the sale or exchange of qualified small business stock held for more than five years applies to periods after December 31, 2009.

## 24. Tax incentives for investment in the District of Columbia (sec. 754 of the Act and secs. 1400, 1400A, 1400B, and 1400C of the Code)

### *Present Law*

#### *In general*

The Taxpayer Relief Act of 1997 designated certain economically depressed census tracts within the District of Columbia as the "District of Columbia Enterprise Zone," or "DC Zone," within which businesses and individual residents are eligible for special tax incentives. The census tracts that comprise the District of Columbia Enterprise Zone are (1) all census tracts that presently are part of the D.C. enterprise community designated under section 1391 (i.e., portions of Anacostia, Mt. Pleasant, Chinatown, and the easternmost part of the District of Columbia), and (2) all additional census tracts within the District of Columbia where the poverty rate is not less than 20 percent. The District of Columbia Enterprise Zone designation remains in effect for the period from January 1, 1998, through December 31, 2009.

The following tax incentives are available for businesses located in an empowerment zone and the District of Columbia Enterprise Zone is treated as an empowerment zone for this purpose: (1) 20-percent wage credit, (2) an additional $35,000 of section 179 expensing for qualified zone property, and (3) expanded tax-exempt financing for certain zone facilities. In addition, a zero-percent capital gains rate applies to capital gains from the sale of certain qualified DC Zone assets held for more than five years.

Present law also provides for a nonrefundable tax credit for first-time homebuyers of a principal residence in the District of Columbia.

#### *Employment credit*

A 20-percent wage credit is available to employers for the first $15,000 of qualified wages paid to each employee (i.e., a maximum credit of $3,000 with respect to each qualified employee) who (1) is a resident of the District of Columbia, and (2) performs substantially all employment services within an empowerment zone in a trade or business of the employer.

The wage credit rate applies to qualifying wages paid after December 31, 2001, and before January 1, 2010. Wages paid to a qualified employee who earns more than $15,000 are eligible for the wage credit (although only the first $15,000 of wages is eligible for the credit). The wage credit is available with respect to a qualified full-time or part-time employee (employed for at least 90 days), regardless of the number of other employees who work for the employer. In general, any taxable business carrying out activities in the empowerment zone may claim the wage credit, regardless of whether the employer meets the definition of an "enterprise zone business," as defined below.

An employer's deduction otherwise allowed for wages paid is reduced by the amount of wage credit claimed for that taxable year. Wages are not to be taken into account for purposes of the wage credit if taken into account in determining the employer's work opportunity tax credit under section 51 or the welfare-to-work credit under section 51A. In addition, the $15,000 cap is reduced by any wages taken into account in computing the work opportunity tax credit or the welfare-to-work credit. The wage credit may be used to offset up to 25 percent of alternative minimum tax liability.

***Increased section 179 expensing limitation***

An enterprise zone business is allowed an additional $35,000 of section 179 expensing (for a total of up to $285,000 in 2009) [1820] for qualified zone property placed in service after December 31, 2001, and before January 1, 2010. The section 179 expensing allowed to a taxpayer is phased out by the amount by which 50 percent of the cost of qualified zone property placed in service during the year by the taxpayer exceeds $500,000. The term "qualified zone property" is defined as depreciable tangible property (including buildings) provided that (i) the property is acquired by the taxpayer (from an unrelated party) after the designation took effect, (ii) the original use of the property in an empowerment zone commences with the taxpayer, and (iii) substantially all of the use of the property is in an empowerment zone in the active conduct of a trade or business by the taxpayer. For this purpose, special rules are provided in the case of property that is substantially renovated by the taxpayer.

An enterprise zone business means any qualified business entity and any qualified proprietorship. A qualified business entity means, any corporation or partnership if for such year: (1) every trade or business of such entity is the active conduct of a qualified business within an empowerment zone; (2) at least 50 percent of the total gross income of such entity is derived from the active conduct of such business; (3) a substantial portion of the use of the tangible property of such entity (whether owned or leased) is within an empowerment zone; (4) a substantial portion of the intangible property of such entity is used in the active conduct of any such business; (5) a substantial portion of the services performed for such entity by its employees are performed in an empowerment zone; (6) at least 35 percent of its employees are residents of an empowerment zone; (7) less than five percent of the average of the aggregate unadjusted bases of the property of such entity is attributable to collectibles other than collectibles that are held primarily for sale to customers in the ordinary course of such business; and

[1820] For each of 2010 and 2011, the 179 expensing limitation will be a total of up to $535,000. The Small Business Jobs Act of 2010, Pub. L. No. 111–240, sec. 2021. See discussion in Part Fourteen of this document.

(8) less than 5 percent of the average of the aggregate unadjusted bases of the property of such entity is attributable to nonqualified financial property.

A qualified proprietorship is any qualified business carried on by an individual as a proprietorship if for such year: (1) at least 50 percent of the total gross income of such individual from such business is derived from the active conduct of such business in an empowerment zone; (2) a substantial portion of the use of the tangible property of such individual in such business (whether owned or leased) is within an empowerment zone; (3) a substantial portion of the intangible property of such business is used in the active conduct of such business; (4) a substantial portion of the services performed for such individual in such business by employees of such business are performed in an empowerment zone; (5) at least 35 percent of such employees are residents of an empowerment zone; (6) less than 5 percent of the average of the aggregate unadjusted bases of the property of such individual which is used in such business is attributable to collectibles other than collectibles that are held primarily for sale to customers in the ordinary course of such business; and (7) less than 5 percent of the average of the aggregate unadjusted bases of the property of such individual which is used in such business is attributable to nonqualified financial property.

A qualified business is defined as any trade or business other than a trade or business that consists predominantly of the development or holding of intangibles for sale or license or any business prohibited in connection with the employment credit. In addition, the leasing of real property that is located within the empowerment zone is treated as a qualified business only if (1) the leased property is not residential property, and (2) at least 50 percent of the gross rental income from the real property is from enterprise zone businesses. The rental of tangible personal property is not a qualified business unless at least 50 percent of the rental of such property is by enterprise zone businesses or by residents of an empowerment zone.

***Expanded tax-exempt financing for certain zone facilities***

An enterprise zone business is permitted to borrow proceeds from the issuance of tax-exempt enterprise zone facility bonds (as defined in section 1394, without regard to the employee residency requirement) issued by the District of Columbia. To qualify, 95 percent (or more) of the net proceeds must be used to finance: (1) qualified zone property whose principal user is an enterprise zone business, and (2) certain land functionally related and subordinate to such property. Accordingly, most of the proceeds have to be used to finance certain facilities within the DC Zone. The aggregate face amount of all outstanding qualified enterprise zone facility bonds per enterprise zone business may not exceed $15 million and may be issued only while the DC Zone designation is in effect, from January 1, 1998 through December 31, 2009.

The term enterprise zone business is the same as that used for purposes of the increased section 179 deduction limitation with certain modifications for start-up businesses. First, a business will be treated as an enterprise zone business during a start-up period if

(1) at the beginning of the period, it is reasonable to expect the business to be an enterprise zone business by the end of the start-up period, and (2) the business makes bona fide efforts to be an enterprise zone business. The start-up period is the period that ends with the start of the first tax year beginning more than two years after the later of (1) the issue date of the bond issue financing the qualified zone property, and (2) the date this property is first placed in service (or, if earlier, the date that is three years after the issue date).

Second, a business that qualifies as at the end of the start-up period must continue to qualify during a testing period that ends three tax years after the start-up period ends. After the three-year testing period, a business will continue to be treated as an enterprise zone business as long as 35 percent of its employees are residents of an empowerment zone or enterprise community.

### *Zero-percent capital gains*

A zero-percent capital gains rate applies to capital gains from the sale of certain qualified DC Zone assets held for more than five years. In general, a "qualified DC Zone asset" means stock or partnership interests held in, or tangible property held by, a DC Zone business. For purposes of the zero-percent capital gains rate, the DC Zone is defined to include all census tracts within the District of Columbia where the poverty rate is not less than ten percent.

In general, gain eligible for the zero-percent tax rate is that from the sale or exchange of a qualified DC Zone asset that is (1) a capital asset or (2) property used in a trade or business, as defined in section 1231(b). Gain that is attributable to real property, or to intangible assets, qualifies for the zero-percent rate, provided that such real property or intangible asset is an integral part of a qualified DC Zone business. However, no gain attributable to periods before January 1, 1998, and after December 31, 2014, is qualified capital gain.

### *District of Columbia homebuyer tax credit*

First-time homebuyers of a principal residence in the District of Columbia qualify for a tax credit of up to $5,000. The $5,000 maximum credit amount applies both to individuals and married couples. The credit phases out for individual taxpayers with adjusted gross income between $70,000 and $90,000 ($110,000 and $130,000 for joint filers). The credit is available with respect to purchases of existing property as well as new construction.

A "first-time homebuyer" means any individual if such individual (and, if married, such individual's spouse) did not have a present ownership interest in a principal residence in the District of Columbia during the one-year period ending on the date of the purchase of the principal residence to which the credit applies. A taxpayer will be treated as a first-time homebuyer with respect to only one residence—i.e., a taxpayer may claim the credit only once. A taxpayer's basis in a property is reduced by the amount of any homebuyer tax credit claimed with respect to such property.

The first-time homebuyer credit is a nonrefundable personal credit and may offset the regular tax and the alternative minimum tax. Any credit in excess of tax liability may be carried forward indefinitely. The homebuyer credit is generally available for property purchased after August 4, 1997, and before January 1, 2010. However, the credit does not apply to the purchase of a residence after December 31, 2008 to which the national first-time homebuyer credit under Section 36 of the Code applies.

### *Explanation of Provision*

The provision extends for two years, through December 31, 2011, the designation of the District of Columbia Enterprise Zone. The provision also extends for two years through December 31, 2011, the special $15 million per-user bond limitation and the relief from resident and employee requirements for certain tax-exempt bonds issued in the District of Columbia Enterprise Zone.

The provision extends for two years the zero-percent capital gains rate applicable to capital gains from the sale or exchange of any DC Zone asset held for more than five years (and, as amended, acquired or substantially improved before January 1, 2012). The provision also extends for two years the period to which the term "qualified capital gain" refers. As amended, the term "qualified capital gain" shall not include any gain attributable to periods before January 1, 1998, or after December 31, 2016.

The provision extends the first-time D.C. homebuyer credit for two years (as amended, to apply to property purchased before January 1, 2012).

### *Effective Date*

The provision extending the period of designation of the District of Columbia Enterprise Zone and the provision extending the period for which the term "qualified capital gain" refers applies to periods after December 31, 2009. The provision extending tax-exempt financing for certain zone facilities applies to bonds issued after December 31, 2009. The provision amending the definitions of DC Zone business stock, DC Zone partnership interest, and DC Zone business property applies to property acquired or substantially improved after December 31, 2009. The provision extending the first-time homebuyer credit applies to homes purchased after December 31, 2009.

## 25. Temporary increase in limit on cover over of rum excise taxes to Puerto Rico and the Virgin Islands (sec. 755 of the Act and sec. 7652(f) of the Code)

### *Present Law*

A $13.50 per proof gallon[1821] excise tax is imposed on distilled spirits produced in or imported into the United States.[1822] The excise tax does not apply to distilled spirits that are exported from the United States, including exports to U.S. possessions (e.g., Puerto Rico and the Virgin Islands).[1823]

---

[1821] A proof gallon is a liquid gallon consisting of 50 percent alcohol. See secs. 5002(a)(10) and (11).

[1822] Sec. 5001(a)(1).

[1823] Secs. 5214(a)(1)(A), 5002(a)(15), 7653(b) and (c).

The Code provides for cover over (payment) to Puerto Rico and the Virgin Islands of the excise tax imposed on rum imported (or brought) into the United States, without regard to the country of origin.[1824] The amount of the cover over is limited under Code section 7652(f) to $10.50 per proof gallon ($13.25 per proof gallon before January 1, 2010).

Tax amounts attributable to shipments to the United States of rum produced in Puerto Rico are covered over to Puerto Rico. Tax amounts attributable to shipments to the United States of rum produced in the Virgin Islands are covered over to the Virgin Islands. Tax amounts attributable to shipments to the United States of rum produced in neither Puerto Rico nor the Virgin Islands are divided and covered over to the two possessions under a formula.[1825] Amounts covered over to Puerto Rico and the Virgin Islands are deposited into the treasuries of the two possessions for use as those possessions determine.[1826] All of the amounts covered over are subject to the limitation.

### *Explanation of Provision*

The provision suspends for two years the $10.50 per proof gallon limitation on the amount of excise taxes on rum covered over to Puerto Rico and the Virgin Islands. Under the provision, the cover over limitation of $13.25 per proof gallon is extended for rum brought into the United States after December 31, 2009 and before January 1, 2012. After December 31, 2011, the cover over amount reverts to $10.50 per proof gallon.

### *Effective Date*

The provision is effective for distilled spirits brought into the United States after December 31, 2009.

## 26. American Samoa economic development credit (sec. 756 of the Act and sec. 119 of Pub. L. No. 109–432)

### *Present Law*

A domestic corporation that was an existing credit claimant with respect to American Samoa and that elected the application of section 936 for its last taxable year beginning before January 1, 2006 is allowed a credit based on the corporation's economic activity-based limitation with respect to American Samoa. The credit is not part of the Code but is computed based on the rules of sections 30A and 936. The credit is allowed for the first four taxable years of a corporation that begin after December 31, 2005, and before January 1, 2010.

A corporation was an existing credit claimant with respect to American Samoa if (1) the corporation was engaged in the active conduct of a trade or business within American Samoa on October 13, 1995, and (2) the corporation elected the benefits of the posses-

[1824] Secs. 7652(a)(3), (b)(3), and (e)(1). One percent of the amount of excise tax collected from imports into the United States of articles produced in the Virgin Islands is retained by the United States under section 7652(b)(3).

[1825] Sec. 7652(e)(2).

[1826] Secs. 7652(a)(3), (b)(3), and (e)(1).

sion tax credit[1827] in an election in effect for its taxable year that included October 13, 1995.[1828] A corporation that added a substantial new line of business (other than in a qualifying acquisition of all the assets of a trade or business of an existing credit claimant) ceased to be an existing credit claimant as of the close of the taxable year ending before the date on which that new line of business was added.

The amount of the credit allowed to a qualifying domestic corporation under the provision is equal to the sum of the amounts used in computing the corporation's economic activity-based limitation with respect to American Samoa, except that no credit is allowed for the amount of any American Samoa income taxes. Thus, for any qualifying corporation the amount of the credit equals the sum of (1) 60 percent of the corporation's qualified American Samoa wages and allocable employee fringe benefit expenses and (2) 15 percent of the corporation's depreciation allowances with respect to short-life qualified American Samoa tangible property, plus 40 percent of the corporation's depreciation allowances with respect to medium-life qualified American Samoa tangible property, plus 65 percent of the corporation's depreciation allowances with respect to long-life qualified American Samoa tangible property.

The section 936(c) rule denying a credit or deduction for any possessions or foreign tax paid with respect to taxable income taken into account in computing the credit under section 936 does not apply with respect to the credit allowed by the provision.

The credit applies to the first four taxable years of a taxpayer which begin after December 31, 2005, and before January 1, 2010.

[1827] For taxable years beginning before January 1, 2006, certain domestic corporations with business operations in the U.S. possessions were eligible for the possession tax credit. Secs. 27(b), 936. This credit offset the U.S. tax imposed on certain income related to operations in the U.S. possessions. Subject to certain limitations, the amount of the possession tax credit allowed to any domestic corporation equaled the portion of that corporation's U.S. tax that was attributable to the corporation's non-U.S. source taxable income from (1) the active conduct of a trade or business within a U.S. possession, (2) the sale or exchange of substantially all of the assets that were used in such a trade or business, or (3) certain possessions investment. No deduction or foreign tax credit was allowed for any possessions or foreign tax paid or accrued with respect to taxable income that was taken into account in computing the credit under section 936.

Under the economic activity-based limit, the amount of the credit could not exceed an amount equal to the sum of (1) 60 percent of the taxpayer's qualified possession wages and allocable employee fringe benefit expenses, (2) 15 percent of depreciation allowances with respect to short-life qualified tangible property, plus 40 percent of depreciation allowances with respect to medium-life qualified tangible property, plus 65 percent of depreciation allowances with respect to long-life qualified tangible property, and (3) in certain cases, a portion of the taxpayer's possession income taxes. A taxpayer could elect, instead of the economic activity-based limit, a limit equal to the applicable percentage of the credit that otherwise would have been allowable with respect to possession business income, beginning in 1998, the applicable percentage was 40 percent.

To qualify for the possession tax credit for a taxable year, a domestic corporation was required to satisfy two conditions. First, the corporation was required to derive at least 80 percent of its gross income for the three-year period immediately preceding the close of the taxable year from sources within a possession. Second, the corporation was required to derive at least 75 percent of its gross income for that same period from the active conduct of a possession business. Sec. 936(a)(2). The section 936 credit generally expired for taxable years beginning after December 31, 2005.

[1828] A corporation will qualify as an existing credit claimant if it acquired all the assets of a trade or business of a corporation that (1) actively conducted that trade or business in a possession on October 13, 1995, and (2) had elected the benefits of the possession tax credit in an election in effect for the taxable year that included October 13, 1995.

### *Explanation of Provision*

The provision extends the credit to apply to the first six taxable years of a taxpayer beginning after December 31, 2005, and before January 1, 2012.

### *Effective Date*

The provision is effective for taxable years beginning after December 31, 2009.

## 27. Work opportunity credit (sec. 757 of the Act and sec. 51 of the Code)

### *Present Law*

#### *In general*

The work opportunity tax credit is available on an elective basis for employers hiring individuals from one or more of nine targeted groups. The amount of the credit available to an employer is determined by the amount of qualified wages paid by the employer. Generally, qualified wages consist of wages attributable to service rendered by a member of a targeted group during the one-year period beginning with the day the individual begins work for the employer (two years in the case of an individual in the long-term family assistance recipient category).

#### *Targeted groups eligible for the credit*

Generally, an employer is eligible for the credit only for qualified wages paid to members of a targeted group.

*(1) Families receiving TANF*

An eligible recipient is an individual certified by a designated local employment agency (e.g., a State employment agency) as being a member of a family eligible to receive benefits under the Temporary Assistance for Needy Families Program ("TANF") for a period of at least nine months part of which is during the 18-month period ending on the hiring date. For these purposes, members of the family are defined to include only those individuals taken into account for purposes of determining eligibility for the TANF.

*(2) Qualified veteran*

There are two subcategories of qualified veterans related to eligibility for food stamps and compensation for a service-connected disability.

*Food stamps*

A qualified veteran is a veteran who is certified by the designated local agency as a member of a family receiving assistance under a food stamp program under the Food Stamp Act of 1977 for a period of at least three months part of which is during the 12-month period ending on the hiring date. For these purposes, members of a family are defined to include only those individuals taken into account for purposes of determining eligibility for a food stamp program under the Food Stamp Act of 1977.

*Entitled to compensation for a service-connected disability*

A qualified veteran also includes an individual who is certified as entitled to compensation for a service-connected disability and: (1) having a hiring date which is not more than one year after having been discharged or released from active duty in the Armed Forces of the United States; or (2) having been unemployed for six months or more (whether or not consecutive) during the one-year period ending on the date of hiring.

*Definitions*

For these purposes, being entitled to compensation for a service-connected disability is defined with reference to section 101 of Title 38, U.S. Code, which means having a disability rating of 10 percent or higher for service connected injuries.

For these purposes, a veteran is an individual who has served on active duty (other than for training) in the Armed Forces for more than 180 days or who has been discharged or released from active duty in the Armed Forces for a service-connected disability. However, any individual who has served for a period of more than 90 days during which the individual was on active duty (other than for training) is not a qualified veteran if any of this active duty occurred during the 60-day period ending on the date the individual was hired by the employer. This latter rule is intended to prevent employers who hire current members of the armed services (or those departed from service within the last 60 days) from receiving the credit.

*(3) Qualified ex-felon*

A qualified ex-felon is an individual certified as: (1) having been convicted of a felony under any State or Federal law; and (2) having a hiring date within one year of release from prison or the date of conviction.

*(4) Designated community residents*

A designated community resident is an individual certified as being at least age 18 but not yet age 40 on the hiring date and as having a principal place of abode within an empowerment zone, enterprise community, renewal community or a rural renewal community. For these purposes, a rural renewal county is a county outside a metropolitan statistical area (as defined by the Office of Management and Budget) which had a net population loss during the five-year periods 1990–1994 and 1995–1999. Qualified wages do not include wages paid or incurred for services performed after the individual moves outside an empowerment zone, enterprise community, renewal community or a rural renewal community.

*(5) Vocational rehabilitation referral*

A vocational rehabilitation referral is an individual who is certified by a designated local agency as an individual who has a physical or mental disability that constitutes a substantial handicap to employment and who has been referred to the employer while receiving, or after completing: (a) vocational rehabilitation services under an individualized, written plan for employment under a State plan approved under the Rehabilitation Act of 1973;

(b) under a rehabilitation plan for veterans carried out under Chapter 31 of Title 38, U.S. Code; or (c) an individual work plan developed and implemented by an employment network pursuant to subsection (g) of section 1148 of the Social Security Act. Certification will be provided by the designated local employment agency upon assurances from the vocational rehabilitation agency that the employee has met the above conditions.

*(6) Qualified summer youth employee*

A qualified summer youth employee is an individual: (1) who performs services during any 90-day period between May 1 and September 15; (2) who is certified by the designated local agency as being 16 or 17 years of age on the hiring date; (3) who has not been an employee of that employer before; and (4) who is certified by the designated local agency as having a principal place of abode within an empowerment zone, enterprise community, or renewal community. As with designated community residents, no credit is available on wages paid or incurred for service performed after the qualified summer youth moves outside of an empowerment zone, enterprise community, or renewal community. If, after the end of the 90-day period, the employer continues to employ a youth who was certified during the 90-day period as a member of another targeted group, the limit on qualified first-year wages will take into account wages paid to the youth while a qualified summer youth employee.

*(7) Qualified food stamp recipient*

A qualified food stamp recipient is an individual at least age 18 but not yet age 40 certified by a designated local employment agency as being a member of a family receiving assistance under a food stamp program under the Food Stamp Act of 1977 for a period of at least six months ending on the hiring date. In the case of families that cease to be eligible for food stamps under section 6(o) of the Food Stamp Act of 1977, the six-month requirement is replaced with a requirement that the family has been receiving food stamps for at least three of the five months ending on the date of hire. For these purposes, members of the family are defined to include only those individuals taken into account for purposes of determining eligibility for a food stamp program under the Food Stamp Act of 1977.

*(8) Qualified SSI recipient*

A qualified SSI recipient is an individual designated by a local agency as receiving supplemental security income ("SSI") benefits under Title XVI of the Social Security Act for any month ending within the 60-day period ending on the hiring date.

*(9) Long-term family assistance recipients*

A qualified long-term family assistance recipient is an individual certified by a designated local agency as being: (1) a member of a family that has received family assistance for at least 18 consecutive months ending on the hiring date; (2) a member of a family that has received such family assistance for a total of at least 18 months (whether or not consecutive) after August 5, 1997 (the date of enactment of the welfare-to-work tax credit)[1829] if the individual is hired within two years after the date that the 18-month total is reached; or (3) a member of a family who is no longer eligible for family assistance because of either Federal or State time limits, if the individual is hired within two years after the Federal or State time limits made the family ineligible for family assistance.

*(10) Unemployed veterans and disconnected youth hired in 2009 and 2010*

Unemployed veterans and disconnected youth who begin work for the employer in 2009 or 2010 are treated as a targeted category under section 1221(a) of the American Recovery and Reinvestment Act of 2009.[1830]

An unemployed veteran is defined as an individual certified by the designated local agency as someone who: (1) has served on active duty (other than for training) in the Armed Forces for more than 180 days or who has been discharged or released from active duty in the Armed Forces for a service-connected disability; (2) has been discharged or released from active duty in the Armed Forces during the five-year period ending on the hiring date; and (3) has received unemployment compensation under State or Federal law for not less than four weeks during the one-year period ending on the hiring date.

A disconnected youth is defined as an individual certified by the designated local agency as someone: (1) at least age 16 but not yet age 25 on the hiring date; (2) not regularly attending any secondary, technical, or post-secondary school during the six-month period preceding the hiring date; (3) not regularly employed during the six-month period preceding the hiring date; and (4) not readily employable by reason of lacking a sufficient number of skills.

### *Qualified wages*

Generally, qualified wages are defined as cash wages paid by the employer to a member of a targeted group. The employer's deduction for wages is reduced by the amount of the credit.

For purposes of the credit, generally, wages are defined by reference to the FUTA definition of wages contained in sec. 3306(b) (without regard to the dollar limitation therein contained). Special rules apply in the case of certain agricultural labor and certain railroad labor.

### *Calculation of the credit*

The credit available to an employer for qualified wages paid to members of all targeted groups except for long-term family assistance recipients equals 40 percent (25 percent for employment of 400 hours or less) of qualified first-year wages. Generally, qualified first-year wages are qualified wages (not in excess of $6,000) attributable to service rendered by a member of a targeted group during the one-year period beginning with the day the individual began work for the employer. Therefore, the maximum credit per em-

---

[1829] The welfare-to-work tax credit was consolidated into the work opportunity tax credit in the Tax Relief and Health Care Act of 2006, Pub. L. No. 109–432, for qualified individuals who begin to work for an employer after December 31, 2006.

[1830] Pub. L. No. 111–5.

ployee is $2,400 (40 percent of the first $6,000 of qualified first-year wages). With respect to qualified summer youth employees, the maximum credit is $1,200 (40 percent of the first $3,000 of qualified first-year wages). Except for long-term family assistance recipients, no credit is allowed for second-year wages.

In the case of long-term family assistance recipients, the credit equals 40 percent (25 percent for employment of 400 hours or less) of $10,000 for qualified first-year wages and 50 percent of the first $10,000 of qualified second-year wages. Generally, qualified second-year wages are qualified wages (not in excess of $10,000) attributable to service rendered by a member of the long-term family assistance category during the one-year period beginning on the day after the one-year period beginning with the day the individual began work for the employer. Therefore, the maximum credit per employee is $9,000 (40 percent of the first $10,000 of qualified first-year wages plus 50 percent of the first $10,000 of qualified second-year wages).

In the case of a qualified veteran who is entitled to compensation for a service connected disability, the credit equals 40 percent of $12,000 of qualified first-year wages. This expanded definition of qualified first-year wages does not apply to the veterans qualified with reference to a food stamp program, as defined under present law.

### *Certification rules*

An individual is not treated as a member of a targeted group unless: (1) on or before the day on which an individual begins work for an employer, the employer has received a certification from a designated local agency that such individual is a member of a targeted group; or (2) on or before the day an individual is offered employment with the employer, a pre-screening notice is completed by the employer with respect to such individual, and not later than the 28th day after the individual begins work for the employer, the employer submits such notice, signed by the employer and the individual under penalties of perjury, to the designated local agency as part of a written request for certification. For these purposes, a pre-screening notice is a document (in such form as the Secretary may prescribe) which contains information provided by the individual on the basis of which the employer believes that the individual is a member of a targeted group.

### *Minimum employment period*

No credit is allowed for qualified wages paid to employees who work less than 120 hours in the first year of employment.

### *Other rules*

The work opportunity tax credit is not allowed for wages paid to a relative or dependent of the taxpayer. No credit is allowed for wages paid to an individual who is a more than fifty-percent owner of the entity. Similarly, wages paid to replacement workers during a strike or lockout are not eligible for the work opportunity tax credit. Wages paid to any employee during any period for which the employer received on-the-job training program payments with respect to that employee are not eligible for the work opportunity tax credit. The work opportunity tax credit generally is not allowed for wages paid to individuals who had previously been employed by the employer. In addition, many other technical rules apply.

***Expiration***

The work opportunity tax credit is not available for individuals who begin work for an employer after August 31, 2011.

### *Explanation of Provision*

The provision extends the work opportunity tax credit for four months (for individuals who begin work for an employer after August 31, 2011 before January 1, 2012).[1831]

### *Effective Date*

The provisions are effective for individuals who begin work for an employer after August 31, 2011.

## 28. Qualified zone academy bonds (sec. 758 of the Act and sec. 54E of the Code)

### *Present Law*

***Tax-exempt bonds***

Interest on State and local governmental bonds generally is excluded from gross income for Federal income tax purposes if the proceeds of the bonds are used to finance direct activities of these governmental units or if the bonds are repaid with revenues of the governmental units. These can include tax-exempt bonds which finance public schools.[1832] An issuer must file with the Internal Revenue Service certain information about the bonds issued in order for that bond issue to be tax-exempt.[1833] Generally, this information return is required to be filed no later the 15th day of the second month after the close of the calendar quarter in which the bonds were issued.

The tax exemption for State and local bonds does not apply to any arbitrage bond.[1834] An arbitrage bond is defined as any bond that is part of an issue if any proceeds of the issue are reasonably expected to be used (or intentionally are used) to acquire higher yielding investments or to replace funds that are used to acquire higher yielding investments.[1835] In general, arbitrage profits may be earned only during specified periods (e.g., defined "temporary periods") before funds are needed for the purpose of the borrowing or on specified types of investments (e.g., "reasonably required reserve or replacement funds"). Subject to limited exceptions, investment profits that are earned during these periods or on such investments must be rebated to the Federal Government.

---

[1831] The rule to allow unemployed veterans and disconnected youth who begin work for the employer in 2009 or 2010 to be treated as members of a targeted group is not extended.

[1832] Sec. 103.

[1833] Sec. 149(e).

[1834] Sec. 103(a) and (b)(2).

[1835] Sec. 148.

### *Qualified zone academy bonds*

As an alternative to traditional tax-exempt bonds, States and local governments were given the authority to issue "qualified zone academy bonds."[1836] A total of $400 million of qualified zone academy bonds is authorized to be issued annually in calendar years 1998 through 2008. That is increased to $1,400 million in 2009 and 2010. Each calendar year's bond limitation is allocated to the States according to their respective populations of individuals below the poverty line. Each State, in turn, allocates the credit authority to qualified zone academies within such State.

A taxpayer holding a qualified zone academy bond on the credit allowance date is entitled to a credit. The credit is includible in gross income (as if it were a taxable interest payment on the bond), and may be claimed against regular income tax and alternative minimum tax liability.

The Treasury Department sets the credit rate at a rate estimated to allow issuance of qualified zone academy bonds without discount and without interest cost to the issuer.[1837] The Secretary determines credit rates for tax credit bonds based on general assumptions about credit quality of the class of potential eligible issuers and such other factors as the Secretary deems appropriate. The Secretary may determine credit rates based on general credit market yield indexes and credit ratings. The maximum term of the bond is determined by the Treasury Department, so that the present value of the obligation to repay the principal on the bond is 50 percent of the face value of the bond.

"Qualified zone academy bonds" are defined as any bond issued by a State or local government, provided that (1) at least 95 percent of the proceeds are used for the purpose of renovating, providing equipment to, developing course materials for use at, or training teachers and other school personnel in a "qualified zone academy" and (2) private entities have promised to contribute to the qualified zone academy certain equipment, technical assistance or training, employee services, or other property or services with a value equal to at least 10 percent of the bond proceeds.

A school is a "qualified zone academy" if (1) the school is a public school that provides education and training below the college level, (2) the school operates a special academic program in cooperation with businesses to enhance the academic curriculum and increase graduation and employment rates, and (3) either (a) the school is located in an empowerment zone or enterprise community designated under the Code, or (b) it is reasonably expected that at least 35 percent of the students at the school will be eligible for free or reduced-cost lunches under the school lunch program established under the National School Lunch Act.

The arbitrage requirements which generally apply to interest-bearing tax-exempt bonds also generally apply to qualified zone academy bonds. In addition, an issuer of qualified zone academy bonds must reasonably expect to and actually spend 100 percent or more of the proceeds of such bonds on qualified zone academy prop-

---

[1836] See secs. 54E and 1397E.

[1837] Given the differences in credit quality and other characteristics of individual issuers, the Secretary cannot set credit rates in a manner that will allow each issuer to issue tax credit bonds at par.

erty within the three-year period that begins on the date of issuance. To the extent less than 100 percent of the proceeds are used to finance qualified zone academy property during the three-year spending period, bonds will continue to qualify as qualified zone academy bonds if unspent proceeds are used within 90 days from the end of such three-year period to redeem any nonqualified bonds. The three-year spending period may be extended by the Secretary if the issuer establishes that the failure to meet the spending requirement is due to reasonable cause and the related purposes for issuing the bonds will continue to proceed with due diligence.

Two special arbitrage rules apply to qualified zone academy bonds. First, available project proceeds invested during the three-year period beginning on the date of issue are not subject to the arbitrage restrictions (i.e., yield restriction and rebate requirements). Available project proceeds are proceeds from the sale of an issue of qualified zone academy bonds, less issuance costs (not to exceed two percent) and any investment earnings on such proceeds. Thus, available project proceeds invested during the three-year spending period may be invested at unrestricted yields, but the earnings on such investments must be spent on qualified zone academy property. Second, amounts invested in a reserve fund are not subject to the arbitrage restrictions to the extent: (1) such fund is funded at a rate not more rapid than equal annual installments; (2) such fund is funded in a manner reasonably expected to result in an amount not greater than an amount necessary to repay the issue; and (3) the yield on such fund is not greater than the average annual interest rate of tax-exempt obligations having a term of 10 years or more that are issued during the month the qualified zone academy bonds are issued.

Issuers of qualified zone academy bonds are required to report issuance to the Internal Revenue Service in a manner similar to the information returns required for tax-exempt bonds.

For bonds originally issued after March 18, 2010, an issuer of qualified zone academy bonds may make an irrevocable election on or before the issue date of such bonds to receive a payment under section 6431 in lieu of providing a tax credit to the holder of the bonds. The payment to the issuer on each payment date is equal to the lesser of (1) the amount of interest payable on such bond by such issuer with respect to such date or (2) the amount of the interest which would have been payable under such bond on such date if such interest were determined at the applicable tax credit bond rate.

## *Explanation of Provision*

### *In general*

The provision extends the qualified zone academy bond program for one year. The provision authorizes issuance of up to $400 million of qualified zone academy bonds for 2011.

The issuer election to receive a payment in lieu of providing a tax credit to the holder of the qualified zone academy bond is not available for bonds issued with the 2011 national limitation. The provision has no effect on bonds issued with limitation carried forward from 2009 or 2010.

### *Effective Date*

The provision applies to obligations issued after December 31, 2010.

## 29. Mortgage insurance premiums (sec. 759 of the Act and sec. 163 of the Code)

### *Present Law*

#### *In general*

Present law provides that qualified residence interest is deductible notwithstanding the general rule that personal interest is nondeductible (sec. 163(h)).

#### *Acquisition indebtedness and home equity indebtedness*

Qualified residence interest is interest on acquisition indebtedness and home equity indebtedness with respect to a principal and a second residence of the taxpayer. The maximum amount of home equity indebtedness is $100,000. The maximum amount of acquisition indebtedness is $1 million. Acquisition indebtedness means debt that is incurred in acquiring constructing, or substantially improving a qualified residence of the taxpayer, and that is secured by the residence. Home equity indebtedness is debt (other than acquisition indebtedness) that is secured by the taxpayer's principal or second residence, to the extent the aggregate amount of such debt does not exceed the difference between the total acquisition indebtedness with respect to the residence, and the fair market value of the residence.

#### *Private mortgage insurance*

Certain premiums paid or accrued for qualified mortgage insurance by a taxpayer during the taxable year in connection with acquisition indebtedness on a qualified residence of the taxpayer are treated as interest that is qualified residence interest and thus deductible. The amount allowable as a deduction is phased out ratably by 10 percent for each $1,000 by which the taxpayer's adjusted gross income exceeds $100,000 ($500 and $50,000, respectively, in the case of a married individual filing a separate return). Thus, the deduction is not allowed if the taxpayer's adjusted gross income exceeds $110,000 ($55,000 in the case of married individual filing a separate return).

For this purpose, qualified mortgage insurance means mortgage insurance provided by the Veterans Administration, the Federal Housing Administration,[1838] or the Rural Housing Administration, and private mortgage insurance (defined in section 2 of the Homeowners Protection Act of 1998 as in effect on the date of enactment of the provision).

Amounts paid for qualified mortgage insurance that are properly allocable to periods after the close of the taxable year are treated

[1838] The Veterans Administration and the Rural Housing Administration have been succeeded by the Department of Veterans Affairs and the Rural Housing Service, respectively.

as paid in the period to which they are allocated. No deduction is allowed for the unamortized balance if the mortgage is paid before its term (except in the case of qualified mortgage insurance provided by the Department of Veterans Affairs or Rural Housing Service).

The provision does not apply with respect to any mortgage insurance contract issued before January 1, 2007. The provision terminates for any amount paid or accrued after December 31, 2010, or properly allocable to any period after that date.

Reporting rules apply under the provision.

### *Explanation of Provision*

The provision extends the deduction for private mortgage insurance premiums for one year (only with respect to contracts entered into after December 31, 2006). Thus, the provision applies to amounts paid or accrued in 2011 (and not properly allocable to any period after 2011).

### *Effective Date*

The provision is effective for amounts paid or accrued after December 31, 2010.

## 30. Temporary exclusion of 100 percent of gain on certain small business stock (sec. 760 of the Act and sec. 1202 of the Code)

### *Present Law*

#### *In general*

Individuals generally may exclude 50 percent (60 percent for certain empowerment zone businesses) of the gain from the sale of certain small business stock acquired at original issue and held for at least five years.[1839] The amount of gain eligible for the exclusion by an individual with respect to any corporation is the greater of (1) ten times the taxpayer's basis in the stock or (2) $10 million. To qualify as a small business, when the stock is issued, the gross assets of the corporation may not exceed $50 million. The corporation also must meet certain active trade or business requirements.

The portion of the gain includible in taxable income is taxed at a maximum rate of 28 percent under the regular tax.[1840] A percentage of the excluded gain is an alternative minimum tax preference;[1841] the portion of the gain includible in alternative minimum taxable income is taxed at a maximum rate of 28 percent under the alternative minimum tax.

---

[1839] Sec. 1202.

[1840] Sec. 1(h).

[1841] Sec. 57(a)(7). In the case of qualified small business stock, the percentage of gain excluded from gross income which is an alternative minimum tax preference is (i) seven percent in the case of stock disposed of in a taxable year beginning before 2011; (ii) 42 percent in the case of stock acquired before January 1, 2001, and disposed of in a taxable year beginning after 2010; and (iii) 28 percent in the case of stock acquired after December 31, 2000, and disposed of in a taxable year beginning after 2010. Section 102 of the Act extends the 2010 and 2011 dates by two years.

Gain from the sale of qualified small business stock generally is taxed at effective rates of 14 percent under the regular tax[1842] and (i) 14.98 percent under the alternative minimum tax for dispositions before January 1, 2011; (ii) 19.88 percent under the alternative minimum tax for dispositions after December 31, 2010, in the case of stock acquired before January 1, 2001; and (iii) 17.92 percent under the alternative minimum tax for dispositions after December 31, 2010, in the case of stock acquired after December 31, 2000.[1843]

***Temporary increases in exclusion***

The percentage exclusion for qualified small business stock acquired after February 17, 2009, and on or before September 27, 2010, is increased to 75 percent. As a result of the increased exclusion, gain from the sale of this qualified small business stock held at least five years is taxed at effective rates of seven percent under the regular tax [1844] and 12.88 percent under the alternative minimum tax.[1845]

The percentage exclusion for qualified small business stock acquired after September 27, 2010, and before January 1, 2011, is increased to 100 percent and the minimum tax preference does not apply.[1846] The minimum tax preference does not apply.

### *Explanation of Provision*

The provision extends the 100-percent exclusion and the exception from minimum tax preference treatment for one year (for stock acquired before January 1, 2012).

### *Effective Date*

The provision is effective for stock acquired after December 31, 2010.

## D. Temporary Disaster Relief Provisions

### 1. New York Liberty Zone tax-exempt bond financing (sec. 761 of the Act and sec. 1400L of the Code)

### *Present Law*

An aggregate of $8 billion in tax-exempt private activity bonds is authorized for the purpose of financing the construction and repair of infrastructure in New York City ("Liberty Zone bonds"). The bonds must be issued before January 1, 2010.

---

[1842] The 50 percent of gain included in taxable income is taxed at a maximum rate of 28 percent.

[1843] The amount of gain included in alternative minimum tax is taxed at a maximum rate of 28 percent. The amount so included is the sum of (i) 50 percent (the percentage included in taxable income) of the total gain and (ii) the applicable preference percentage of the one-half gain that is excluded from taxable income.

[1844] The 25 percent of gain included in taxable income is taxed at a maximum rate of 28 percent.

[1845] The 46 percent of gain included in alternative minimum tax is taxed at a maximum rate of 28 percent. Forty-six percent is the sum of 25 percent (the percentage of total gain included in taxable income) plus 21 percent (the percentage of total gain which is an alternative minimum tax preference).

[1846] Sec. 1202(a)(4)(A) and (C).

### *Explanation of Provision*

The provision extends authority to issue Liberty Zone bonds for two years (through December 31, 2011).

### *Effective Date*

The provision is effective for bonds issued after December 31, 2009.

## 2. Increase in rehabilitation credit in the Gulf Opportunity Zone (sec. 762 of the Act and sec. 1400N(h) of the Code)

### *Present Law*

Present law provides a two-tier tax credit for rehabilitation expenditures.

A 20-percent credit is provided for qualified rehabilitation expenditures with respect to a certified historic structure. For this purpose, a certified historic structure means any building that is listed in the National Register, or that is located in a registered historic district and is certified by the Secretary of the Interior to the Secretary of the Treasury as being of historic significance to the district.

A 10-percent credit is provided for qualified rehabilitation expenditures with respect to a qualified rehabilitated building, which generally means a building that was first placed in service before 1936. The pre-1936 building must meet requirements with respect to retention of existing external walls and internal structural framework of the building in order for expenditures with respect to it to qualify for the 10-percent credit. A building is treated as having met the substantial rehabilitation requirement under the 10-percent credit only if the rehabilitation expenditures during the 24-month period selected by the taxpayer and ending within the taxable year exceed the greater of (1) the adjusted basis of the building (and its structural components), or (2) $5,000.

The provision requires the use of straight-line depreciation or the alternative depreciation system in order for rehabilitation expenditures to be treated as qualified under the provision.

Present law increases from 20 to 26 percent, and from 10 to 13 percent, respectively, the credit under section 47 with respect to any certified historic structure or qualified rehabilitated building located in the Gulf Opportunity Zone, provided the qualified rehabilitation expenditures with respect to such buildings or structures are incurred on or after August 28, 2005, and before January 1, 2010. The provision is effective for expenditures incurred on or after August 28, 2005, for taxable years ending on or after August 28, 2005.

### *Explanation of Provision*

The provision extends for two additional years the increase in the rehabilitation credit from 20 to 26 percent, and from 10 to 13 percent, respectively, with respect to any certified historic structure or qualified rehabilitated building located in the Gulf Opportunity Zone. Thus, the increase applies for qualified rehabilitation expenditures with respect to such buildings or structures incurred before January 1, 2012.

### *Effective Date*

The provision is effective for amounts paid or incurred after December 31, 2009.

## 3. Low-income housing credit rules for buildings in Gulf Opportunity Zones (sec. 763 and sec. 1400N(c)(5) of the Code)

### *Present Law*

#### *In general*

The low-income housing credit may be claimed over a 10-year period for the cost of rental housing occupied by tenants having incomes below specified levels. The amount of the credit for any taxable year in the credit period is the applicable percentage of the qualified basis of each qualified low-income building. The qualified basis of any qualified low-income building for any taxable year equals the applicable fraction of the eligible basis of the building.

The credit percentage for newly constructed or substantially rehabilitated housing that is not Federally subsidized is adjusted monthly by the Internal Revenue Service so that the 10 annual installments have a present value of 70 percent of the total qualified basis. The credit percentage for newly constructed or substantially rehabilitated housing that is Federally subsidized and for existing housing that is substantially rehabilitated is calculated to have a present value of 30 percent of qualified basis. These are referred to as the 70-percent credit and 30-percent credit, respectively.

#### *Volume limit*

Generally, a low-income housing credit is allowable only if the owner of a qualified building receives a housing credit allocation from the State or local housing credit agency. Each State has a limited amount of low-income housing credit available to allocate. This amount is called the aggregate housing credit dollar amount (or the "State housing credit ceiling"). For each State, the State housing credit ceiling is the sum of four components: (1) the unused housing credit ceiling, if any, of such State from the prior calendar year; (2) the credit ceiling for the year (either a per capital amount or the small State minimum annual cap); (3) any returns of credit ceiling to the State during the calendar year from previous allocations; and (4) the State's share, if any, of the national pool of unused credits from other States that failed to use them (only States which allocated their entire credit ceiling for the preceding calendar year are eligible for a share of the national pool. For calendar year 2010, each State's credit ceiling is $2.10 per resident, with a minimum annual cap of $2,430,000 for certain small population States.[1847] These amounts are indexed for inflation. These limits do not apply in the case of projects that also receive financing with proceeds of

[1847] Rev. Proc. 2009–50.

tax-exempt bonds issued subject to the private activity bond volume limit.

Under section 1400N(c) of the Code, the otherwise applicable State housing credit ceiling is increased for each of the States within the Gulf Opportunity Zone. This increase applies to calendar years 2006, 2007, and 2008. The additional volume for each of the affected States equals $18.00 times the number of such State's residents within the Gulf Opportunity Zone. This amount is not adjusted for inflation. This additional volume limit expires unless the applicable low-income buildings are placed in service before January 1, 2011.

### *Explanation of Provision*

The provision extends the placed-in-service deadline (for one year) to December 31, 2011.

### *Effective Date*

The provision is effective on the date of enactment.

## 4. Tax-exempt bond financing for the Gulf Opportunity Zones (sec. 764 of the Act and sec. 1400N(a) of the Code)

### *Present Law*

#### *In general*

Under present law, gross income does not include interest on State or local bonds. State and local bonds are classified generally as either governmental bonds or private activity bonds. Governmental bonds are bonds which are primarily used to finance governmental functions or which are repaid with governmental funds. Private activity bonds are bonds with respect to which the State or local government serves as a conduit providing financing to nongovernmental persons (e.g., private businesses or individuals). The exclusion from income for State and local bonds does not apply to private activity bonds, unless the bonds are issued for certain permitted purposes ("qualified private activity bonds"). The definition of a qualified private activity bond includes an exempt facility bond and a qualified mortgage bond.

#### *Exempt facility bonds*

The definition of exempt facility bond includes bonds issued to finance certain transportation facilities (airports, ports, mass commuting, and high-speed intercity rail facilities); qualified residential rental projects; privately owned and/or operated utility facilities (sewage, water, solid waste disposal, and local district heating and cooling facilities, certain private electric and gas facilities, and hydroelectric dam enhancements); public/private educational facilities; qualified green building and sustainable design projects; and qualified highway or surface freight transfer facilities (sec. 142(a)).

Residential rental property may be financed with exempt facility bonds if the financed project is a "qualified residential rental project." A project is a qualified residential rental project if 20 percent or more of the residential units in such project are occupied by individuals whose income is 50 percent or less of area median gross income (the "20–50 test"). Alternatively, a project is a qualified residential rental project if 40 percent or more of the residential units in such project are occupied by individuals whose income is 60 percent or less of area median gross income (the "40–60 test").

### *Qualified mortgage bonds*

Qualified mortgage bonds are tax-exempt bonds issued to make mortgage loans to eligible mortgagors for the purchase, improvement, or rehabilitation of owner-occupied residences. The Code imposes several limitations on qualified mortgage bonds, including income limitations for eligible mortgagors, purchase price limitations on the home financed with bond proceeds, and a "first-time homebuyer" requirement. In addition, bond proceeds generally only can be used for new mortgages, i.e., proceeds cannot be used to acquire or replace existing mortgages.

Exceptions to the new mortgage requirement are provided for the replacement of construction period loans, bridge loans, and other similar temporary initial financing. In addition, qualified rehabilitation loans may be used, in part, to replace existing mortgages. A qualified rehabilitation loan means certain loans for the rehabilitation of a building if there is a period of at least 20 years between the date on which the building was first used (the "20 year rule") and the date on which the physical work on such rehabilitation begins and the existing walls and basis requirements are met. The existing walls requirement for a rehabilitated building is met if 50 percent or more of the existing external walls are retained in place as external walls, 75 percent or more of the existing external walls are retained in place as internal or external walls, and 75 percent or more of the existing internal structural framework is retained in place. The basis requirement is met if expenditures for rehabilitation are 25 percent or more of the mortgagor's adjusted basis in the residence, determined as of the later of the completion of the rehabilitation or the date on which the mortgagor acquires the residence.

Qualified mortgage bonds also may be used to finance qualified home-improvement loans. Qualified home-improvement loans are defined as loans to finance alterations, repairs, and improvements on an existing residence, but only if such alterations, repairs, and improvements substantially protect or improve the basic livability or energy efficiency of the property. Qualified home-improvement loans may not exceed $15,000, and may not be used to refinance existing mortgages.

As with most qualified private activity bonds, issuance of qualified mortgage bonds is subject to annual State volume limitations (the "State volume cap").

### *Gulf Opportunity Zone Bonds*

The Gulf Opportunity Zone Act of 2005 authorizes Alabama, Louisiana, and Mississippi (or any political subdivision of those States) to issue qualified private activity bonds to finance the construction and rehabilitation of residential and nonresidential property located in the Gulf Opportunity Zone ("Gulf Opportunity Zone Bonds"). Gulf Opportunity Zone Bonds are not subject to the State volume cap. Rather, the maximum aggregate amount of Gulf Opportunity Zone Bonds that may be issued in any eligible State is limited to $2,500 multiplied by the population of the respective State within the Gulf Opportunity Zone.

Depending on the purpose for which such bonds are issued, Gulf Opportunity Zone Bonds are treated as either exempt facility bonds or qualified mortgage bonds. Gulf Opportunity Zone Bonds are treated as exempt facility bonds if 95 percent or more of the net proceeds of such bonds are to be used for qualified project costs located in the Gulf Opportunity Zone. Qualified project costs include the cost of acquisition, construction, reconstruction, and renovation of nonresidential real property (including buildings and their structural components and fixed improvements associated with such property), qualified residential rental projects (as defined in section 142(d) with certain modifications), and public utility property. Bond proceeds may not be used to finance movable fixtures and equipment.

Rather than applying the 20–50 and 40–60 test from section 142, a project is a qualified residential rental project under the provision if 20 percent or more of the residential units in such project are occupied by individuals whose income is 60 percent or less of area median gross income or if 40 percent or more of the residential units in such project are occupied by individuals whose income is 70 percent or less of area median gross income.

Gulf Opportunity Zone Bonds issued to finance residences located in the Gulf Opportunity Zone are treated as qualified mortgage bonds if the general requirements for qualified mortgage bonds are met. The Code also provides special rules for Gulf Opportunity Zone Bonds issued to finance residences located in the Gulf Opportunity Zone. For example, the first-time homebuyer rule is waived and the income and purchase price rules are relaxed for residences financed in the GO Zone, the Rita GO Zone, or the Wilma GO Zone. In addition, the Code increases from $15,000 to $150,000 the amount of a qualified home-improvement loan with respect to residences located in the specified disaster areas.

Also, a qualified GO Zone repair or reconstruction loan is treated as a qualified rehabilitation loan for purposes of the qualified mortgage bond rules. Thus, such loans financed with the proceeds of qualified mortgage bonds and Gulf Opportunity Zone Bonds may be used to acquire or replace existing mortgages, without regard to the existing walls or 20 year rule under present law. A qualified GO Zone repair or reconstruction loan is any loan used to repair damage caused by Hurricane Katrina, Hurricane Rita, or Hurricane Wilma to a building located in the GO Zones (or reconstruction of such building in the case of damage constituting destruction) if the expenditures for such repair or reconstruction are 25 percent or more of the mortgagor's adjusted basis in the residence. For these purposes, the mortgagor's adjusted basis is determined as of the later of (1) the completion of the repair or reconstruction or (2) the date on which the mortgagor acquires the residence.

Gulf Opportunity Zone Bonds must be issued before January 1, 2011.

### *Explanation of Provision*

The provision extends authority to issue Gulf Opportunity Zone Bonds for one year (through December 31, 2011).

### *Effective Date*

The provision is effective on the date of enactment.

## 5. Bonus depreciation deduction applicable to specified Gulf Opportunity Zone extension property (sec. 765 of the Act and sec. 1400N(d)(6) of the Code)

### *Present Law*

#### *In general*

An additional first-year depreciation deduction is allowed equal to 50 percent of the adjusted basis of qualified property placed in service during 2008, 2009, and 2010 (2009, 2010, and 2011 for certain longer-lived and transportation property).[1848] The additional first-year depreciation deduction is allowed for both regular tax and alternative minimum tax purposes, but is not allowed for purposes of computing earnings and profits. The basis of the property and the depreciation allowances in the year of purchase and later years are appropriately adjusted to reflect the additional first-year depreciation deduction. In addition, there are no adjustments to the allowable amount of depreciation for purposes of computing a taxpayer's alternative minimum taxable income with respect to property to which the provision applies. The amount of the additional first-year depreciation deduction is not affected by a short taxable year. The taxpayer may elect out of additional first-year depreciation for any class of property for any taxable year.

Property qualifying for the additional first-year depreciation deduction must meet all of the following requirements. First, the property must be (1) property to which MACRS applies with an applicable recovery period of 20 years or less; (2) water utility property (as defined in section 168(e)(5)); (3) computer software other than computer software covered by section 197; or (4) qualified leasehold improvement property (as defined in section 168(k)(3)).[1849] Second, the original use[1850] of the property must commence with the taxpayer after December 31, 2007.[1851] Third,

---

[1848] Sec. 168(k). The additional first-year depreciation deduction is subject to the general rules regarding whether an item must be capitalized under section 263 or section 263A.

[1849] The additional first-year depreciation deduction is not available for any property that is required to be depreciated under the alternative depreciation system of MACRS. The additional first-year depreciation deduction is also not available for qualified New York Liberty Zone leasehold improvement property as defined in section 1400L(c)(2).

[1850] The term "original use" means the first use to which the property is put, whether or not such use corresponds to the use of such property by the taxpayer.

If in the normal course of its business a taxpayer sells fractional interests in property to unrelated third parties, then the original use of such property begins with the first user of each fractional interest (i.e., each fractional owner is considered the original user of its proportionate share of the property).

[1851] A special rule applies in the case of certain leased property. In the case of any property that is originally placed in service by a person and that is sold to the taxpayer and leased back to such person by the taxpayer within three months after the date that the property was placed in service, the property would be treated as originally placed in service by the taxpayer not earlier than the date that the property is used under the leaseback.

If property is originally placed in service by a lessor, such property is sold within three months after the date that the property was placed in service, and the user of such property

the taxpayer must acquire the property within the applicable time period. Finally, the property must be placed in service after December 31, 2007, and before January 1, 2011. An extension of the placed in service date of one year (i.e., to January 1, 2012) is provided for certain property with a recovery period of 10 years or longer and certain transportation property.[1852] Transportation property is defined as tangible personal property used in the trade or business of transporting persons or property.

The applicable time period for acquired property is (1) after December 31, 2007, and before January 1, 2011, but only if no binding written contract for the acquisition is in effect before January 1, 2008, or (2) pursuant to a binding written contract which was entered into after December 31, 2007, and before January 1, 2011.[1853] With respect to property that is manufactured, constructed, or produced by the taxpayer for use by the taxpayer, the taxpayer must begin the manufacture, construction, or production of the property after December 31, 2007, and before January 1, 2011. Property that is manufactured, constructed, or produced for the taxpayer by another person under a contract that is entered into prior to the manufacture, construction, or production of the property is considered to be manufactured, constructed, or produced by the taxpayer. For property eligible for the extended placed in service date, a special rule limits the amount of costs eligible for the additional first-year depreciation. With respect to such property, only the portion of the basis that is properly attributable to the costs incurred before January 1, 2011 ("progress expenditures") is eligible for the additional first-year depreciation.[1854]

### *Gulf Opportunity Zone Additional Depreciation*

Present law provides an additional first-year depreciation deduction equal to 50 percent of the adjusted basis of specified qualified Gulf Opportunity Zone extension property. To qualify, property generally must be placed in service on or before December 31, 2010. Specified Gulf Opportunity Zone extension property is defined as property substantially all the use of which is in one or more specified portions of the Gulf Opportunity Zone and which is either: (1) nonresidential real property or residential rental property which is placed in service by the taxpayer on or before December 31, 2010, or (2) in the case of a taxpayer who places in service a building described in (1), property described in section 168(k)(2)(A)(i),[1855] if substantially all the use of such property is in such building and such property is placed in service within 90 days of the date the building is placed in service. However, in the case

---

does not change, then the property is treated as originally placed in service by the taxpayer not earlier than the date of such sale.

[1852] Property qualifying for the extended placed in service date must have an estimated production period exceeding one year and a cost exceeding $1 million.

[1853] Property does not fail to qualify for the additional first-year depreciation merely because a binding written contract to acquire a component of the property is in effect prior to January 1, 2008.

[1854] For purposes of determining the amount of eligible progress expenditures, it is intended that rules similar to section 46(d)(3) as in effect prior to the Tax Reform Act of 1986 apply.

[1855] Generally, property described in section 168(k)(2)(A)(i) is (1) property to which the general rules of the Modified Accelerated Cost Recovery System ("MACRS") apply with an applicable recovery period of 20 years or less, (2) computer software other than computer software covered by section 197, (3) water utility property (as defined in section 168(e)(5)), or (4) certain leasehold improvement property.

of nonresidential real property or residential rental property, only the adjusted basis of such property attributable to manufacture, construction, or production before January 1, 2010 is eligible for the additional first-year depreciation.

The specified portions of the Gulf Opportunity Zone are defined as those portions of the Gulf Opportunity Zone which are in a county or parish which is identified by the Secretary of the Treasury (or his delegate) as being a county or parish in which hurricanes occurring in 2005 damaged (in the aggregate) more than 60 percent of the housing units in such county or parish which were occupied (determined according to the 2000 Census).

### *Explanation of Provision*

The provision extends for one year through December 31, 2011, the date by which specified Gulf Opportunity Zone extension property must be placed in service to be eligible for the additional first-year depreciation deduction. In the case of nonresidential real property or residential rental property, the adjusted basis of such property attributable to manufacture, construction, or production before January 1, 2012 is eligible for the additional first-year depreciation.

### *Effective Date*

The provision applies to property placed in service after December 31, 2009.

# PART SEVENTEEN: REGULATED INVESTMENT COMPANY MODERNIZATION ACT OF 2010 (PUBLIC LAW 111–325)[1856]

## I. OVERVIEW OF REGULATED INVESTMENT COMPANIES

In general, a regulated investment company ("RIC") is an electing domestic corporation that either meets (or is excepted from) certain registration requirements under the Investment Company Act of 1940,[1857] that derives at least 90 percent of its ordinary income from specified sources considered passive investment income,[1858] that has a portfolio of investments that meet certain diversification requirements,[1859] and meets certain other requirements.[1860]

Many RICs are "open-end" companies (mutual funds), which have a continuously changing number of shares that are bought from, and redeemed by, the company and are not otherwise available for purchase or sale in the secondary market. Shareholders of open-end RICs generally have the right to have the company redeem shares at "net asset value." Other RICs are "closed-end" companies, which have a fixed number of shares that are normally traded on national securities exchanges or in the over-the-counter market and generally are not redeemable upon the demand of the shareholder.

In the case of a RIC that distributes at least 90 percent of its net ordinary income and net tax-exempt interest to its shareholders, a deduction for dividends paid is allowed to the RIC in computing its tax.[1861] Thus, no corporate income tax is imposed on income distributed to its shareholders. Dividends of a RIC generally are includible in the income of the shareholders; a RIC can pass through the character of (1) its long-term capital gain income, by paying "capital gain dividends" and (2) in certain cases, tax-exempt interest, by paying "exempt-interest dividends." A RIC may also pass through certain foreign tax credits and credits on tax-credit bonds, as well as the character of certain other income received by the RIC.

---

[1856] H.R. 4337. The House passed H.R. 4337 on September 28, 2010. The Senate passed the bill with an amendment on December 8, 2010. The House agreed to the Senate amendment on December 15, 2010. The President signed the bill on December 22, 2010. For a technical explanation of the bill prepared by the staff of the Joint Committee on Taxation, see *Technical Explanation of H.R. 4337, "The Regulated Investment Company Modernization Act of 2010," For Consideration on the Floor of the House of Representatives* (JCX–49-10), September 28, 2010.

[1857] Secs. 851(a) and (b)(1).

[1858] Sec. 851(b)(2).

[1859] Sec. 851(b)(3).

[1860] Secs. 851 and 852.

[1861] Sec. 852(a) and (b).

## II. CAPITAL LOSS CARRYOVERS OF RICS

### A. Capital Loss Carryovers of RICs (sec. 101 of the Act and sec. 1212(a) of the Code)

#### *Present Law*

***Limitation on capital losses***

Losses from the sale or exchange of capital assets are allowed only to the extent of the taxpayer's gains from the sale or exchange of capital assets plus, in the case of a taxpayer other than a corporation, $3,000.[1862]

***Carryover of net capital losses***

*RICs*

If a RIC has a net capital loss (i.e., losses from the sale or exchanges of capital assets in excess of gains from sales or exchanges of capital assets) for any taxable year, the amount of the net capital loss is a capital loss carryover to each of the eight taxable years following the loss year, and is treated as a short-term capital loss in each of those years.[1863] The entire amount of a net capital loss is carried over to the first taxable year succeeding the loss year and the portion of the loss which may be carried to each of the next seven years is the excess of the net capital loss over the net capital gain income[1864] (determined without regard to any net capital loss for the loss year or taxable year thereafter) for each of the prior taxable year to which the loss may be carried.

*Corporations other than RICs*

In the case of a corporation other than a RIC, a net capital loss generally is treated as a capital loss carryback to each of the three taxable years preceding the loss year and a capital loss carryover to each of the five taxable years following the loss year and is treated as a short-term capital loss in each of those years.[1865] The carryover amount is reduced in a manner similar to that described above applicable to RICs. A net capital loss may not be carried back to a taxable year for which a corporation is a RIC.[1866]

*Individual taxpayers*

If a taxpayer other than a corporation has a net capital loss for any taxable year, the excess (if any) of the net short-term capital loss over the net long-term capital gain is treated as a short-term capital loss in the succeeding taxable year, and the excess (if any) of the net long-term capital loss over the net short-term capital gain is treated as a long-term capital loss in the succeeding taxable year.[1867] There is no limitation on the number of taxable years that a net capital loss may be carried over.

---

[1862] Sec. 1211.
[1863] Sec. 1212(a)(1)(C)(i).
[1864] Capital gain net income is the excess of gains from the sale or exchange of capital assets over losses from such sales or exchanges. Sec. 1222(9).
[1865] Sec. 1212(a)(1)(A).
[1866] Sec. 1212(a)(3)(A).
[1867] Sec. 1212(b). Adjustments are made to take account of the $3,000 amount allowed against ordinary income.

### *Explanation of Provision*

#### *In general*

The Act provides capital loss carryover treatment for RICs similar to the present-law treatment of net capital loss carryovers applicable to individuals. Under the Act, if a RIC has a net capital loss for a taxable year, the excess (if any) of the net short-term capital loss over the net long-term capital gain is treated as a short-term capital loss arising on the first day of the next taxable year, and the excess (if any) of the net long-term capital loss over the net short-term capital gain is treated as a long-term capital loss arising on the first day of the next taxable year.[1868] The number of taxable years that a net capital loss of a RIC may be carried over under the provision is not limited.

#### *Coordination with present-law carryovers*

The Act provides for the treatment of net capital loss carryovers under the present law rules to taxable years of a RIC beginning after the date of enactment (December 22, 2010). These rules apply to (1) capital loss carryovers from taxable years beginning on or before the date of enactment (December 22, 2010) and (2) capital loss carryovers from other taxable years prior to the taxable year the corporation became a RIC.

Amounts treated as a long-term or short-term capital loss arising on the first day of the next taxable year under the provision are determined without regard to amounts treated as a short-term capital loss under the present-law carryover rule. In determining the amount by which a present-law carryover is reduced by capital gain net income for a prior taxable year, any capital loss treated as arising on the first day of the prior taxable year under the provision is taken into account in determining capital gain net income for the prior year.

The following example illustrates these rules:

Assume a calendar year RIC has no net capital loss for any taxable year beginning before 2010, a net capital loss of $2 million for 2010; a net capital loss of $1 million for 2011, all of which is a long-term capital loss; and $600,000 gain from the sale of a capital asset held less than one year on July 15, 2012.

For 2012, the RIC has (1) $600,000 short-term capital gain from the July 15 sale, (2) $2 million carryover from 2010 which is treated as a short-term capital loss,[1869] and (3) $1 million long-term capital loss from 2011 treated as arising on January 1, 2012. The capital loss allowed in 2012 is limited to $600,000, the amount of capital gain for the taxable year.

For purposes of determining the amount of the $2 million net capital loss that may be carried over from 2010 to 2013, there is no capital gain net income for 2012 because the $600,000 gain does not exceed the $1 million long-term loss treated as arising on January 1, 2012; therefore the entire 2010 net capital loss is carried over to 2013 and treated as a short-term capital loss in 2013. $400,000 (the excess of the $1 million long-term capital loss treated

---

[1868] For earnings and profits treatment of a RIC's net capital loss, see section 302 of the Act.

[1869] The present-law treatment of net capital losses arising in taxable years beginning before the date of enactment (December 22, 2010) continues to apply.

as arising on January 1, 2012, over the $600,000 short-term capital gain for 2012) is treated as a long-term capital loss on January 1, 2013. The 2010 net capital loss may continue to be carried over through 2018, subject to reduction by capital gain net income; no limitation applies on the number of taxable years that the 2011 net capital loss may be carried over.

### *Effective Date*

The provision generally applies to net capital losses for taxable years beginning after the date of enactment (December 22, 2010). The provision relating to the treatment of present-law carryovers applies to taxable years beginning after the date of enactment (December 22, 2010).

## III. MODIFICATION OF GROSS INCOME AND ASSET TESTS OF RICS

### A. Savings Provisions for Failures of RICs to Satisfy Gross Income and Asset Tests (sec. 201 of the Act and sec. 851(d) and (i) of the Code)

### *Present Law*

#### *Asset tests*

In general, at the close of each quarter of the taxable year, at least 50 percent of the value of a RIC's total assets must be represented by (i) cash and cash items (including receivables), Government securities and securities of other RICs, and (ii) other securities, generally limited in respect of any one issuer to an amount not greater in value than five percent of the value of the total assets of the RIC and to not more than 10 percent of the outstanding voting securities of such issuer.[1870]

In addition, at the close of each quarter of the taxable year, not more than 25 percent of the value of a RIC's total assets may be invested in (i) the securities (other than Government securities or the securities of other RICs) of any one issuer, (ii) the securities (other than the securities of other RICs) of two or more issuers which the taxpayer controls and which are determined, under regulations prescribed by the Secretary, to be engaged in the same or similar trades or businesses or related trades or businesses, or (iii) the securities of one or more qualified publicly traded partnerships (as defined in section 851(h)).[1871]

A RIC meeting both asset tests at the close of any quarter will not lose its status as a RIC because of a discrepancy during a subsequent quarter between the value of its various investments and the asset test requirements, unless such discrepancy exists immediately after the acquisition of any security or other property and is wholly or partly the result of such acquisition.[1872] This rule protects a RIC against inadvertent failures of the asset tests that may be caused by fluctuations in the relative values of its assets. A second rule (the "30-day rule") gives a RIC 30 days following the end

[1870] Sec. 851(b)(3)(A).
[1871] Sec. 851(b)(3)(B).
[1872] Sec. 851(d).

of a quarter in which it fails an asset test to cure the failure, if the failure is by reason of a discrepancy, between the value of its various investments and the asset test requirements, that exists immediately after the acquisition of any security or other property which is wholly or partly the result of such acquisition during such quarter.[1873] Failure of any asset test (except where the failure is cured pursuant to the 30-day rule) will prevent a corporation from qualifying as a RIC.

### *Gross income test*

A RIC must derive 90 percent of its gross income for a taxable year from certain types of income.[1874] These types of income ("qualifying income") are (1) dividends, interest, payments with respect to securities loans (as defined in section 512(a)(5)), and gains from the sale or other disposition of stock or securities (as defined in section 2(a)(36) of the Investment Company Act of 1940, as amended)[1875] or foreign currencies, or other income (including but not limited to gains from options, futures or forward contracts) derived with respect to the business of investing in such stock, securities, or currencies, and (2) net income derived from an interest in a qualified publicly traded partnership.[1876]

Thus, a RIC meets the gross income test provided its gross income that is not qualifying income does not exceed one-ninth of the portion of its gross income that is qualifying income. For example, a RIC with $90x of gross income from qualifying income can have up to $10x of gross income from other sources without failing the test. Failure to meet the gross income test for a taxable year prevents a corporation from qualifying as a RIC for that year.

## *Explanation of Provision*

### *Saving provision for asset test failures*

The Act provides a special rule for *de minimis* asset test failures and a mechanism by which a RIC can cure other asset test failures and pay a penalty tax. The rule for *de minimis* asset test failures applies if a RIC fails to meet one of the asset tests in section 851(b)(3) due to the ownership of assets the total value of which does not exceed the lesser of (i) one percent of the total value of the RIC's assets at the end of the quarter for which the assets are valued, and (ii) $10 million. Where the *de minimis* rule applies, the RIC shall nevertheless be considered to have satisfied the asset

---

[1873] *Ibid.*

[1874] Sec. 851(b)(2).

[1875] Section 2(a)(36) of the Investment Company Act of 1940 defines a "security" as "any note, stock, treasury stock, security future, bond, debenture, evidence of indebtedness, certificate of interest or participation in any profit-sharing agreement, collateral-trust certificate, preorganization certificate or subscription, transferable share, investment contract, voting-trust certificate, certificate of deposit for a security, fractional undivided interest in oil, gas, or other mineral rights, any put, call, straddle, option, or privilege on any security (including a certificate of deposit) or on any group or index of securities (including any interest therein or based on the value thereof), or any put, call, straddle, option, or privilege entered into on a national securities exchange relating to foreign currency, or, in general, any interest or instrument commonly known as a "security," or any certificate of interest or participation in, temporary or interim certificate for, receipt for, guarantee of, or warrant or right to subscribe to or purchase, any of the foregoing."

[1876] A "qualified publicly traded partnership" means a publicly traded partnership (within the meaning of section 7704(b)), other than a publicly traded partnership whose gross income is qualifying income (other than income of another publicly traded partnership). Sec. 851(h).

tests if, within six months of the last day of the quarter in which the RIC identifies that it failed the asset test (or such other time period provided by the Secretary) the RIC: (i) disposes of assets in order to meet the requirements of the asset tests, or (ii) the RIC otherwise meets the requirements of the asset tests.

In the case of other asset test failures, a RIC shall nevertheless be considered to have met the asset tests if: (i) the RIC sets forth in a schedule filed in the manner provided by the Secretary a description of each asset that causes the RIC to fail to satisfy the asset test; (ii) the failure to meet the asset tests is due to reasonable cause and not due to willful neglect; and (iii) within six months of the last day of the quarter in which the RIC identifies that it failed the asset test (or such other time period provided by the Secretary) the RIC (I) disposes of the assets which caused the asset test failure, or (II) otherwise meets the requirements of the asset tests. In cases of asset test failures other than *de minimis* failures, the provision imposes a tax in an amount equal to the greater of (i) $50,000 or (ii) the amount determined (pursuant to regulations promulgated by the Secretary) by multiplying the highest rate of tax specified in section 11 (currently 35 percent) by the net income generated during the period of asset test failure by the assets that caused the RIC to fail the asset test. For purposes of subtitle F, the tax imposed for an asset test failure is treated as excise tax with respect to which the deficiency procedures apply.

These provisions added by the Act do not apply to any quarter in which a corporation's status as a RIC is preserved under the provision of present law.

***Saving provision for gross income test failures***

The Act provides that a corporation that fails to meet the gross income test shall nevertheless be considered to have satisfied the test if, following the corporation's failure to meet the test for the taxable year, the corporation (i) sets forth in a schedule, filed in the manner provided by the Secretary, a description of each item of its gross income and (ii) the failure to meet the gross income test is due to reasonable cause and is not due to willful neglect.

In addition, under the Act, a tax is imposed on any RIC that fails to meet the gross income test equal to the amount by which the RIC's gross income from sources which are not qualifying income exceeds one-ninth of its gross income from sources which are qualifying income. For example, if a RIC has $90x of gross income of sources which are qualifying income and $15x of gross income from other sources, a tax of $5x is imposed. The tax is the amount by which the $15x gross income from sources which are not qualifying income exceeds the $10x permitted under present law.

***Calculation of investment company taxable income***

Taxes imposed for failure of the asset or income tests are deductible for purposes of calculating investment company taxable income.

### *Effective Date*

The provision applies to taxable years with respect to which the due date (determined with regard to extensions) of the return of tax is after the date of enactment (December 22, 2010).

## IV. MODIFICATION OF RULES RELATED TO DIVIDENDS AND OTHER DISTRIBUTIONS

### A. Modification of Dividend Designation Requirements and Allocation Rules for RICs (sec. 301 of the Act and sec. 852(b) of the Code)

#### *Present Law*

***Capital gain dividends***

*In general*

In general, a capital gain dividend paid by a RIC is treated by the RIC's shareholders as long-term capital gain.[1877] In addition, a RIC is allowed a dividend paid deduction for its capital gain dividends in computing the tax imposed on its net capital gain.[1878]

A capital gain dividend is any dividend, or part thereof, which is designated by the RIC as a capital gain dividend in a written notice mailed to the RIC's shareholders not later than 60 days after the close of the RIC's taxable year,[1879] except that in the event a RIC designates an aggregate amount of capital gain dividends for a taxable year that exceeds the RIC's net capital gain, the portion of each distribution that is a capital gain dividend is only that proportion of the designated amount that the RIC's net capital gain bears to the total amount so designated by the RIC. For example, assume a RIC makes quarterly distributions of $30, designated entirely as capital gain dividends. If the RIC has only $100 of net capital gain for its taxable year, only $25 of each quarterly distribution is a capital gain dividend (i.e., $30 × ($100/$120) = $25).

***Other designated items***

*Exempt-interest dividends*

A RIC may designate any portion of a dividend (other than a capital gain dividend) as an "exempt-interest dividend," if at least half of the RICs assets consist of tax-exempt State and local bonds. The shareholder treats an exempt-interest dividend as an item of tax-exempt interest.[1880]

---

[1877] Sec. 852(b)(3)(B). This provision applies only with respect to RICs which meet the requirements of section 852(a) for the taxable year.

[1878] Sec. 852(b)(3)(A).

[1879] Sec. 852(b)(3)(C). If there is an increase in the amount by which a RIC's net capital gain exceeds the deduction for dividends paid (determined with reference to capital gain dividends only) as a result of a "determination," the RIC has 120 days after the date of the determination to make a designation with respect to such increase. A determination is defined in section 860(e) as: (1) a decision by the Tax Court, or a judgment, decree, or other order by any court of competent jurisdiction, which has become final; (2) a closing agreement made under section 7121; (3) under regulations prescribed by the Secretary, an agreement signed by the Secretary and by, or on behalf of, the qualified investment entity relating to the liability of such entity for tax; or (4) a statement by the taxpayer attached to its amendment or supplement to a return of tax for the relevant tax year. See Rev. Proc. 2009–28, 2009–20 I.R.B. 1011.

[1880] Sec. 852(b)(5)(B).

Exempt-interest dividends are defined as any dividend, or part thereof, which is designated by the RIC as an exempt interest dividend in a written notice mailed to the RIC's shareholders not later than 60 days after the close of the RIC's taxable year,[1881] except that in the event a RIC designates an aggregate amount of exempt-interest dividends for a taxable year that exceeds the RIC's tax exempt interest (net of related deductions disallowed under sections 265 and 171(a)(2) by reason of the interest being tax exempt), the portion of each distribution that will be an exempt interest dividend is only that proportion of the designated amount that net exempt interest bears to the amount so designated.

*Foreign tax credits; credits for tax-credit bonds; dividends received by RIC*

RICs may pass through to shareholders certain foreign tax credits, credits for tax-credit bonds, and dividends received by the RIC that qualify, in the case of corporate shareholders, for the dividends received deduction, or, in the case of individual shareholders, the capital gain rates in effect for dividends received in taxable years beginning before January 1, 2013. In each case the qualifying amount must be designated in a written notice mailed to its shareholders not later than 60 days after the close of the RIC's taxable year.

*Dividends paid to certain foreign persons.*

Certain dividends paid to nonresident alien individuals and foreign corporations in taxable years of the RIC beginning before January 1, 2012, are treated as interest or short term-capital gain.[1882] These dividends must be designated in a written notice mailed to its shareholders not later than 60 days after the close of the RIC's taxable year. Rules similar to the rules described above relating to capital gain dividends and exempt-interest dividends apply to designated amounts in excess of the maximum amounts permitted to be so designated.

### *Explanation of Provision*

#### *Capital gain dividends*

*Reporting requirements*

The provision replaces the present-law designation requirement for a capital gain dividend with a requirement that a capital gain dividend be *reported* by the RIC in written statements furnished to its shareholders. A written statement furnishing this information to a shareholder may be a Form 1099.

*Allocation by fiscal year RICs*

The provision provides a special rule allocating the excess reported amount[1883] for taxable year RICs in order to reduce the need for RICs to amend Form 1099s and shareholders to file amended income tax returns. This special allocation rule applies to

[1881] Sec. 852(b)(5)(A).
[1882] Secs. 871(k) and 881(e).
[1883] The "excess reported amount" is the excess of the aggregate amount reported as capital gain dividends for the taxable year over the RIC's net capital gain for the taxable year.

a taxable year of a RIC which includes more than one calendar year if the RIC's post-December reported amount [1884] exceeds the excess reported amount for the taxable year.

For example, assume a RIC for its taxable year ending June 30, 2012, makes quarterly distributions of $30,000 on September 30, 2011, December 31, 2011, March 31, 2012, and June 30, 2012, and reports the amounts as capital gain dividends. If the RIC has only $100,000 net capital gain for its taxable year, the excess reported amount is $20,000. Because the post-December reported amount ($60,000) exceeds the excess reported amount ($20,000), the excess reported amount is allocated among the post-December reported capital gain dividends in proportion to the amount of each such distribution reported as a capital gain dividend. Thus, one-half of the excess reported amount (i.e., 1/2 of $20,000 = $10,000) is allocated to each post-December distribution, reducing the amount of each post-December distribution treated as a capital gain dividend from $30,000 to $20,000. Because no excess reported amount is allocated to either of the quarterly distributions made on or before December 31, 2011, the entire $30,000 of each of the distributions retains its character as a capital gain dividend.

If, in the above example, the RIC has only $40,000 net capital gain for its taxable year, the excess reported amount is $80,000. Because the post-December reported amount ($60,000) does not exceed the excess reported amount ($80,000), the excess reported amount is allocated among all the reported capital gain dividends for the taxable year in proportion to the amount of each distribution reported as a capital gain dividend. Thus, one-fourth of the excess reported amount (i.e., 1/4 of $80,000 = $20,000) is allocated to each distribution, reducing the amount of each distribution treated as a capital gain dividend from $30,000 to $10,000.

***Other designated items***

The provision replaces the other designation requirements described under present law with a requirement that amounts be reported by the RIC in written statements furnished to its shareholders.[1885]

The provision also provides allocation rules for excess reported amounts of exempt-interest dividends and certain dividends paid to nonresident alien individuals and foreign corporations by fiscal year RICs similar to the rule described above applicable capital gain dividends.

### *Effective Date*

The provision applies to taxable years beginning after the date of enactment (December 22, 2010).[1886]

---

[1884] The "post-December reported amount" is the aggregate amount reported with respect to items arising after December 31 of the RIC's taxable year.

[1885] The Act does not change the method of designation of undistributed capital gain taken into account by shareholders under section 852(b)(3)(D)(i).

[1886] Each amendment to a provision relating to qualified dividends of individual shareholders will sunset when the provision to which the amendment was made sunsets pursuant to section 303 of the Jobs and Growth Tax Relief Reconciliation Act. Under present law, these provisions sunset in taxable years beginning after December 31, 2012.

## B. Earnings and Profits of RICs (sec. 302 of the Act and sec. 852(c)(1) of the Code)

### *Present Law*

The current earnings and profits of a RIC are not reduced by any amount that is not allowable as a deduction in computing taxable income for the taxable year.[1887]

*Application to net capital loss*

Thus, under the general rule, the current earnings and profits of a RIC are not reduced by a net capital loss either in the taxable year the loss arose or any taxable year to which the loss is carried.[1888] The accumulated earnings and profits are reduced in the taxable year the net capital loss arose.

*Application to exempt-interest expenses*

Because the general rule denies deductions in computing current earnings and profits for amounts disallowed for expenses, interest, and amortizable bond premium relating to tax-exempt interest,[1889] the current earnings and profits of a RIC with tax-exempt interest may exceed the amount which the RIC can distribute as exempt-interest dividends.[1890] Thus, distributions by a RIC with only tax-exempt interest income may result in taxable dividends to its shareholders. For example, assume a RIC has $1 million gross tax-exempt interest and $10,000 expenses disallowed under section 265 (and no accumulated earnings and profits and no other item of current earnings and profits). If the RIC were to distribute $1 million to its shareholders during its taxable year (which is $10,000 more than its economic income for the year), $990,000 may be designated as exempt-interest dividends, and the remaining $10,000 is taxable as ordinary dividends.

### *Explanation of Provision*

#### *Net capital loss*

The rules applicable to the taxable income treatment of a net capital loss of a RIC apply for purposes of determining earnings and profits (both current earnings and profits and accumulated earnings and profits). Thus, a net capital loss for a taxable year is not taken into account in determining earnings and profits, but any capital loss treated as arising on the first day of the next taxable year is taken into account in determining earnings and profits for the next taxable year (subject to the application of the net capital loss rule for that year).

[1887] Sec. 852(c)(1). The provision applies to a RIC without regard to whether it meets the requirements of section 852(a) for the taxable year.

[1888] See explanation of section 101 of the Act for the treatment of carryovers of a net capital loss under present law and as amended by the Act.

[1889] Secs. 171(a)(2) and 265.

[1890] For a description of exempt-interest dividends, see explanation of section 301 of the Act.

***Exempt-interest expenses***

The deductions disallowed in computing investment company taxable income relating to tax-exempt interest are allowed in computing current earnings and profits of a RIC.

In the example under present law, the provision reduces the RIC's current earnings and profits from $1 million to $990,000 and if the RIC were to distribute $1 million to its shareholders during the taxable year, $990,000 may be reported as exempt-interest dividends and the remaining $10,000 is treated as a return of capital (or gain to the shareholder).

### *Effective Date*

The provision applies to taxable years beginning after the date of enactment (December 22, 2010).

## C. Pass-thru of Exempt-interest Dividends and Foreign Tax Credits in Fund of Funds Structures (sec. 303 of the Act and sec. 852(g) of the Code)

### *Present Law*

In a so-called "fund of funds" structure, one RIC ("upper-tier fund") holds stock in one or more other RICs ("lower-tier funds"). Generally, the character of certain types of income and gain, such as capital gain and qualified dividends, of a lower-tier fund pass through from the lower-tier RIC to the upper-tier RIC and then pass through to the shareholders of the upper-tier RIC.

Exempt-interest dividends may be paid by a RIC, and foreign tax credits may be passed through a RIC, only if at least 50 percent of the value of the total assets of a RIC consist of tax-exempt obligations (in the case of exempt-interest dividends) or more than 50 percent of the value of the total assets consist of stock or securities in foreign corporations (in the case of the foreign tax credits). Because an upper-tier RIC holds stock in other RICs, it does not meet the 50-percent asset requirements. As a result, it may not pass through these items to its shareholders, even if the items were passed through to it by a lower tier RIC meeting these requirements.

### *Explanation of Provision*

Under the provision, in the case of a qualified fund of funds, the RIC may (1) pay exempt-interest dividends without regard to the requirement that at least 50 percent of the value of its total assets consist of tax-exempt State and local bonds and (2) elect to allow its shareholders the foreign tax credit without regard to the requirement that more than 50 percent of the value of its total assets consist of stock or securities in foreign corporations.

For this purpose, a qualified fund of funds means a RIC at least 50 percent of the value of the total assets of which (at the close of each quarter of the taxable year) is represented by interests in other RICs.

### *Effective Date*

The provision applies to taxable years beginning after the date of enactment (December 22, 2010).

## D. Modification of Rules for Spillover Dividends of RICs (sec. 304 of the Act and sec. 855 of the Code)

### *Present Law*

A RIC may elect to have certain dividends paid after the close of a taxable year considered as having been paid during that year for purposes of the RIC distribution requirements and determining the taxable income of the RIC.[1891] These dividends are referred to as "spillover dividends." In order to qualify as a spillover dividend, the dividend must be declared prior to the time prescribed for filing the tax return for the taxable year (determined with regard to extensions) and the distribution must be made in the 12-month period following the close of the taxable year and not later than the date of the first dividend payment made after the declaration.

### *Explanation of Provision*

The time for declaring a spillover dividend is the later of the 15th day of the 9th month following the close of the taxable year or the extended due date for filing the return. Also, the requirement that the distribution be made not later than the date of the first dividend payment after the declaration is changed. The provision provides that the distribution must be made not later than the date of the first dividend payment of the same type of dividend (for example, an ordinary income dividend or a capital gain dividend) made after the declaration. For this purpose, a dividend attributable to short-term capital gain with respect to which a notice is required under the Investment Company Act of 1940 shall be treated as the same type of dividend as a capital gain dividend.[1892]

### *Effective Date*

The provision applies to distributions in taxable years beginning after the date of enactment (December 22, 2010).

## E. Return of Capital Distributions of RICs (sec. 305 of the Act and sec. 316 of the Code)

### *Present Law*

A dividend is a distribution of property by a corporation (1) out of its earnings and profits accumulated after February 28, 1913 ("accumulated earnings and profits"), and (2) out of its earnings and profits of the taxable year ("current earnings and profits").[1893] The current earnings and profits are prorated among current year distributions.[1894] Distributions of property which are not a dividend reduce the adjusted basis of a shareholder's stock and are

[1891] Sec. 855.
[1892] See section 19 of the Investment Company Act of 1940, as amended, for rules requiring notice to shareholders identifying source of distribution.
[1893] Sec. 316.
[1894] Treas. Reg. sec. 1.316–2(b).

treated as gain to the extent in excess of the stock's adjusted basis.[1895]

For example, assume a RIC, with a taxable year ending June 30 and with no accumulated earnings and profits, has current earnings and profits of $4 million and distributes $3 million to its shareholders on September 15 and $3 million on March 15. Under present law, $2 million of each distribution is out of current earnings and profits and is treated as dividend income to its shareholders. The remaining amounts are applied against the adjusted basis of each shareholder's stock or taken into account as gain by the shareholders.

### *Explanation of Provision*

In the case of a non-calendar year RIC which makes distributions of property with respect to the taxable year in an amount in excess of the current and accumulated earnings and profits, the current earnings and profits are allocated first to distributions made on or before December 31 of the taxable year.

Thus, under the provision, in the above example, all $3 million of the distribution made on September 15 is out of current earnings and profits and thus treated as dividend income. Only $1 million of the distribution made on March 15 is out of current earnings and profits and treated as dividend income. The remaining $2 million of the March 15 distribution is applied against the adjusted basis of each shareholder's stock or taken into account as gain by the shareholders.

In the case of a RIC with more than one class of stock, the provision applies separately to each class of stock.[1896]

### *Effective Date*

The provision applies to distributions made in taxable years beginning after the date of enactment (December 22, 2010).

## F. Distributions in Redemption of Stock of RICs (sec. 306 of the Act and secs. 267 and 302 of the Code)

### *Present Law*

#### *Exchange treatment*

The redemption of stock by a corporation is treated as an exchange of stock if the redemption fits into one of four categories of transactions.[1897] If the redemption does not fit into one of these categories, the redemption is treated as a distribution of property. One of the four categories of transactions is that the redemption "is not essentially equivalent to a dividend."[1898] A redemption "is not essentially equivalent to a dividend" if the redemption results in a "meaningful reduction in the shareholder's proportionate ownership in the corporation."[1899] Other categories include a substantially disproportionate redemption, a redemption that terminates the

[1895] Sec. 301(c).
[1896] See Rev. Rul. 69–440.
[1897] Sec. 302.
[1898] Sec. 302(b)(1).
[1899] *United States v. Davis,* 397 U.S. 301 (1970).

shareholder's interest in the corporation, and a partial liquidation (if the redeemed shareholder is not a corporation).[1900]

The Code provides no specific rule regarding the application of the "not essentially equivalent to a dividend" test in the case of an open-end RIC whose shareholders "sell" their shares by having them redeemed by the issuing RIC and where multiple redemptions by different shareholders may occur daily.

#### *Loss deferral*

Any deduction in respect of a loss from the sale or exchange of property between members of a controlled group of corporations is deferred until the transfer of the property outside the group.[1901] In the case of a fund of funds, a lower-tier fund may be required to redeem shares in an upper-tier fund when the upper-tier fund shareholders demand redemption of their shares. Because the upper-tier fund and lower-tier fund may be members of the same controlled group of corporations, any loss by the upper-tier fund on the disposition of the lower-tier fund shares may be deferred.

### *Explanation of Provision*

#### *Exchange treatment*

The Act provides that, except to the extent provided in regulations, the redemption of stock of a publicly offered RIC is treated as an exchange if the redemption is upon the demand of the shareholder and the company issues only stock which is redeemable upon the demand of the shareholder. A publicly offered RIC is a RIC the shares of which are (1) continuously offered pursuant to a public offering, (2) regularly traded on an established securities market, or (3) held by no fewer than 500 persons at all times during the taxable year.

#### *Loss disallowance*

The Act provides that, except to the extent provided in regulations, the loss deferral rule does not apply to any redemption of stock of a RIC if the RIC issues only stock which is redeemable upon the demand of the shareholder and the redemption is upon the demand of a shareholder which is another RIC.

### *Effective Date*

The provision applies to distributions after the date of enactment (December 22, 2010).

## G. Repeal of Preferential Dividend Rule for Publicly Offered RICs (sec. 307 of the Act and sec. 562 of the Code)

### *Present Law*

RICs are allowed a deduction for dividends paid to their shareholders. In order to qualify for the deduction, a dividend must not be a "preferential dividend."[1902] For this purpose, a dividend is

[1900] Sec. 302(b)(2)–(4).
[1901] Sec. 267(f).
[1902] Sec. 562(c).

preferential unless it is distributed pro rata to shareholders, with no preference to any share of stock compared with other shares of the same class, and with no preference to one class as compared with another except to the extent the class is entitled to a preference. A distribution by a RIC to a shareholder whose initial investment was $10 million or more is not treated as preferential if the distribution is increased to reflect reduced administrative cost of the RIC with respect to the shareholder.

Securities law, administered by the Securities Exchange Commission, provides strict limits on the ability of RICs to issue shares with preferences.[1903]

### *Explanation of Provision*

The provision repeals the preferential dividend rule for publicly offered RICs. For this purpose, a RIC is publicly offered if its shares are (1) continuously offered pursuant to a public offering, (2) regularly traded on an established securities market, or (3) held by no fewer than 500 persons at all times during the taxable year.

### *Effective Date*

The provision applies to distributions in taxable years beginning after the date of enactment (December 22, 2010).

## H. Elective Deferral of Certain Late-Year Losses of RICs (sec. 308 of the Act and sec. 852(b)(8) of the Code)

### *Present Law*

#### *Capital gains and losses*

*In general*

In general, a RIC may pay a capital gain dividend to its shareholders to the extent of the RIC's net capital gain for the taxable year. The shareholders treat capital gain dividends as long-term capital gain.[1904]

Under present law, an excise tax is imposed on a RIC for a calendar year equal to four percent of the excess (if any) of the required distribution over the distributed amount. The required distribution is the sum of 98 percent of the RIC's ordinary income for the calendar year and 98 percent of the capital gain net income for the one-year period ending October 31 of such calendar year. The distributed amount is the sum of the deduction for dividends paid during the calendar year and the amount on which a corporate income tax is imposed on the RIC for taxable years ending during the calendar year.[1905]

*Deferral of net capital losses and long-term capital losses*

Under present law, for purposes of determining the amount of a net capital gain dividend, the amount of net capital gain for a taxable year is determined without regard to any net capital loss or net long-term capital loss attributable to transactions after October

[1903] See, for example, section 18 of the Investment Company Act of 1940.
[1904] See explanation of section 301 of the Act.
[1905] Sec. 4982.

31 of the taxable year, and the post-October net capital loss or net long term capital loss is treated as arising on the first day of the RIC's next taxable year.[1906]

Present law provides that to the extent provided in regulations, the above rules relating to post-October net capital losses also apply for purposes of computing taxable income of a RIC.[1907] Regulations have been issued allowing RICs to elect to defer all or part of any net capital loss (or if there is no such net capital loss, any net long-term capital loss) attributable to the portion of the taxable year after October 31 to the first day of the succeeding taxable year.[1908]

The following example illustrates the application of the post-October capital loss rules.

Assume a RIC with a taxable year ending June 30, 2011, recognizes a long-term capital gain of $1,000,000 on September 15, 2010. In order to avoid the excise tax, the RIC distributes $980,000 on December 15, 2010, which it designates as a capital gain dividend. On January 15, 2011, the RIC recognizes a $600,000 long-term capital loss. The RIC has no other income or loss during 2010 and 2011, and has no accumulated earnings and profits.

Absent the post-October loss rule, the RIC would have a net capital gain (and current earnings and profits) of only $400,000 for the taxable year ending June 30, 2011. Only $400,000 of the December 15, 2010, distribution would be a capital gain dividend; the remaining $580,000 of the $980,000 distributed on December 15 would be a return of capital. Because the "distributed amount" for excise tax purposes takes into account only those distributions for which a deduction for dividends paid is allowed, the RIC's distributed amount for calendar year 2010 would be $400,000, which is less than the distributed amount required to avoid the excise tax. In addition, the shareholders may have improperly reported the distribution as a capital gain dividend on the 2010 income tax returns.

By "pushing" the post-October long-term capital loss to July 1, 2011, in the above example the entire $980,000 paid on December 15, 2010, is a capital gain dividend. The distribution is fully deductible in computing the excise tax. No excise tax is imposed for 2010 because the RIC has no undistributed income.

*Short-term capital losses not deferred*

No special rule applies to short-term capital losses arising after October 31 of the taxable year for purposes of defining a capital gain dividend.

The following example illustrates the present-law treatment of a RIC with a post-October 31 short-term capital loss:

Assume a RIC with a taxable year ending June 30, 2011, recognizes a short-term capital gain of $1 million on September 15, 2010. In order to avoid the excise tax, the RIC distributes $980,000 on December 15, 2010. On May 15, 2011, the RIC recognizes a $1 million long-term capital gain and $1 million short-term capital

---

[1906] Section 852(b)(3)(C). Certain RICs with taxable years ending with the month of November or December are not subject to this rule.

[1907] The last sentence of Sec. 852(b)(3)(C).

[1908] Treas. Reg. 1.852–11.

loss. The RIC has no other income or loss during 2010, 2011, or 2012 (and has no accumulated earnings and profits).

Under present law, the shareholders receive Forms 1099 for 2010 reporting the dividends as other than capital gain dividends and they report the dividends accordingly on their 2010 income tax returns. Because the RIC has only $1 million of current earnings and profits for its taxable year, the RIC may not pay an additional distribution designated as a capital gain dividend for its taxable year in order to be allowed a dividend paid deduction in computing the RIC's tax on net capital gain. Instead, the RIC could designate the December 15 distribution as a capital gain dividend, but that would require shareholders to file amended income tax returns for 2010.

*Deferral partly elective*

Under present law, for purposes of determining capital gain dividends, the "push" forward of post-October capital losses is automatic, rather than elective; in contrast the push forward of these losses is elective for RIC taxable income purposes. Assume for example that a RIC has no net capital gain for the portion of its taxable year on or before October 31, and makes no distributions before January 1 of the taxable year. For the remainder of its taxable year, the RIC has a $1 million short-term capital gain and a $1 million long-term capital loss. Under present law, for purposes of determining the amount of capital gain dividends, the $1 million long-term capital loss is automatically pushed forward to the next taxable year. But for purposes of determining its taxable income, the capital loss is pushed forward only if the RIC elects. If no election is made and the RIC has a $1 million long-term capital gain in the next taxable year and pays a $1 million dividend, the dividend may not be designated a capital gain dividend, although the RIC had $1 million long-term capital gain that year. If an election is made, the RIC must distribute the $1 million of short-term capital gain as an ordinary dividend in the current taxable year although the gains were economically offset by the long-term capital loss.

***Ordinary gains and losses***

*Net foreign currency losses and losses on stock in a passive foreign investment company*

In applying the excise tax described above, net foreign currency losses and gains and ordinary loss or gain from the disposition of stock in a passive foreign investment company ("PFIC") properly taken into account after October 31 are "pushed" to the following calendar year for purposes of the tax.[1909]

Under present law, to the extent provided in regulations, a RIC may elect to push the post-October net foreign currency losses and the net reduction in the value of stock in a PFIC with respect to which an election is in effect under section 1296(k) forward to the next taxable year.[1910] Regulations have been issued allowing RICs to elect to defer all or part of any post-October net foreign currency

[1909] Sec. 4982(e)(5) and (6).
[1910] Sec. 852(b)(8) and (10).

losses for the portion of the taxable year after October 31 to the first day of the succeeding taxable year.[1911]

*Other ordinary losses*

Other ordinary losses of a RIC may not be "pushed" forward. As a result, in the event that a RIC has net ordinary losses for the portion of the taxable year after December 31 (other than a net foreign currency loss or loss on stock of a PFIC), the RIC may have insufficient earnings and profits to pay a dividend during the calendar year ending in the taxable year in order to reduce or eliminate the excise tax.

For example, assume a RIC for its taxable year ending June 30, 2012, has ordinary income of $1 million for the portion of its taxable year ending on December 31, 2011. In order to avoid the excise tax, the RIC distributes $980,000 on December 15, 2011. The RIC has no accumulated earnings and profits. For the period beginning January 1, 2012, and ending on June 30, 2012, the RIC has a net ordinary loss of $1 million. Because the RIC has no earnings and profits, the distribution in 2011 is not a dividend; the distributed amount for calendar year 2011 is zero; and an excise tax is imposed.

## *Explanation of Provision*

### *Post-October capital losses*

Under the provision, except to the extent provided in regulations, a RIC may elect to "push" to the first day of the next taxable year part or all of any post-October capital loss. The post-October capital loss means the greatest of the RIC's net capital loss, net long-term capital loss, or the net short-term capital loss (attributable to the portion of the taxable year after October 31).[1912]

The election[1913] applies for all purposes of the Code, including determining taxable income, net capital gain, net short-term capital gain, and earnings and profits.

The application of the provision to short-term capital losses may be illustrated by the following example:

Assume a RIC for its taxable year ending June 30, 2012, recognizes a short-term capital gain of $1 million on September 15, 2011. In order to avoid the excise tax, the RIC distributes $980,000 on December 15, 2011. On May 15, 2012, the RIC recognizes a $1 million long-term capital gain and $1 million short-term capital loss. The RIC has no other income or loss during 2011, 2012, or 2013 (and has no accumulated earnings and profits).

The RIC may elect to treat the short-term capital loss as arising on July 1, 2012. If the RIC so elects and makes an additional $1 million distribution before July 1, 2012, it may report the distribution as a capital gain dividend and be allowed a dividends paid deduction in computing the tax on its net capital gain for the 2011–

[1911] Treas. Reg. sec. 1.852–11.

[1912] Special rules apply to certain RICs with taxable years ending with the month of November or December.

[1913] The principles of Treasury Regulation section 1.852–11 are to apply to a qualified late-year loss for which an election is made under this provision, subject to any subsequent change in the regulations.

2012 taxable year. No amended Forms 1099 and no amended tax returns by the shareholders are required.

***Late-year ordinary losses***

Under the provision, except to the extent provided in regulations, a RIC may elect to "push" to the first day of the next taxable year part or all of any qualified late-year ordinary loss. The qualified late year ordinary loss is the excess of (1) the sum of the specified losses attributable to the portion of the taxable year after October 31 and other ordinary losses attributable to the portion of the taxable year after December 31, over (2) the sum of the specified gains attributable to the portion of the taxable year after October 31 and other ordinary income attributable to the portion of the taxable year after December 31. Specified losses and gains have the same meaning as used for purposes of the excise tax under section 4982.[1914]

The election applies for all purposes of the Code.

### *Effective Date*

The provision applies to taxable years beginning after the date of enactment (December 22, 2010).

## I. Exception to Holding Period Requirement for Exempt-Interest Dividends Declared on Daily Basis (sec. 309 of the Act and sec. 852(b)(4) of the Code)

### *Present Law*

If a shareholder receives an exempt-interest dividend with respect to a share of RIC stock held for 6 months or less, any loss on the sale or exchange of the stock, to the extent of the amount of the exempt-interest dividend, is disallowed. To the extent provided by regulations, the loss disallowance rule does not apply to losses on shares which are sold or exchanged pursuant to a plan which involves the periodic liquidation of the shares. In the case of a RIC which regularly distributes at least 90 percent of its net tax-exempt interest, the Secretary may by regulations prescribe a shorter holding period not shorter than the greater of 31 days or the period between the regular distributions.

### *Explanation of Provision*

The provision makes the loss disallowance rule inapplicable, except as otherwise provided by regulations, with respect to a regular dividend paid by a RIC that declares exempt-interest dividends on a daily basis in an amount equal to at least 90 percent of its net tax-exempt interest and distributes the dividends on a monthly or more frequent basis.

### *Effective Date*

The provision applies to stock for which the taxpayer's holding period begins after the date of enactment (December 22, 2010).

[1914] See explanation of section 402 of the Act.

# V. MODIFICATIONS RELATED TO EXCISE TAX APPLICABLE TO RICS

## A. Excise Tax Exemption for Certain RICs Owned by Tax Exempt Entities (sec. 401 of the Act and sec. 4982(f) of the Code)

### *Present Law*

An excise tax is imposed on a RIC for a calendar year equal to four percent of the excess (if any) of the required distribution over the distributed amount. The required distribution is the sum of 98 percent of the RIC's ordinary income for the calendar year and 98 percent of the capital gain net income for the one-year period ending October 31 of such calendar year. The distributed amount is the sum of the deduction for dividends paid during the calendar year and the amount on which a corporate income tax is imposed on the RIC for taxable years ending during the calendar year.[1915]

The excise tax does not apply to a RIC for any calendar year if at all times during the calendar year each shareholder in the RIC is either a qualified pension plan exempt from tax or a segregated asset account of a life insurance company held in connection with variable contracts.

### *Explanation of Provision*

The provision adds tax-exempt entities whose ownership of beneficial interests in the RIC would not preclude the application of section 817(h)(4) (regarding segregated asset accounts of a variable annuity or life insurance contract) to the list of persons who may hold stock in a RIC that is exempt from the excise tax. These persons include qualified annuity plans described in section 403, IRAs, including Roth IRAs, certain government plans described in section 414(d) or 457, and a pension plan described in section 501(c)(18).[1916] Also, another RIC to which section 4982 does not apply may hold stock in a RIC exempt from the excise tax.

### *Effective Date*

The provision applies to calendar years beginning after the date of enactment (December 22, 2010).

## B. Deferral of Certain Gains and Losses of RICs for Excise Tax Purposes (sec. 402 of the Act and sec. 4982(e) of the Code)

### *Present Law*

Special rules apply to certain items of income and loss in computing the excise tax under section 4982.[1917] Any foreign currency gains and losses attributable to a section 988 transaction properly taken into account after October 31 of any calendar year generally

---

[1915] Sec. 4982.

[1916] See Rev. Rul. 94–62, 1994–2 C.B. 164, as supplemented by Rev. Rul. 2007–58, I.R.B. 2007–37 (Sept. 10, 2007).

[1917] See present-law explanation of section 401 for a description of the tax.

are "pushed" to the following calendar year.[1918] Any post-October positive or negative adjustments, and income or loss, on contingent payment debt instruments is treated in the same manner as foreign currency gain or loss from a section 988 transaction.[1919] Any gain recognized under section 1296 (relating to mark-to-market for marketable stock in a passive foreign investment company ("PFIC")) generally is determined as if the RIC's taxable year ends October 31, and any gain or loss from an actual disposition of stock in an electing PFIC after October 31 generally is "pushed" to the following calendar year.[1920]

To the extent provided in regulations, any net foreign currency loss of a RIC and any net reduction in the value of the stock of a PFIC held by a RIC attributable to transactions after October 31 of the taxable year may be "pushed" to the first day of the following taxable year for purposes of computing taxable income.[1921] Similar rules apply for purposes of computing earnings and profits in order to allow a RIC a distribution deduction for purposes of the excise tax.[1922]

### *Explanation of Provision*

Under the provision, the present-law excise tax "push" rules applicable to foreign currency gains and losses are expanded to include all "specified gains and losses," i.e., ordinary gains and losses from the sale, exchange, or other disposition of (or termination of a position with respect to) property, including foreign currency gain and loss, and amounts marked-to-market under section 1296. Thus, these post-October 31 gains and losses are "pushed" to the next calendar year.[1923]

The provision also provides that, for purposes of determining a RIC's ordinary income, the present-law rule treating PFIC stock as disposed of on October 31 is made applicable to all property held by a RIC which under any provision of the Code (including regulations thereunder) is treated as disposed of on the last day of the taxable year.

Finally, for purposes of the excise tax, the provision allows a RIC with a taxable year other than the calendar year, except as provided in regulations, to elect to "push" any net ordinary loss (determined without regard to ordinary gains and losses which are automatically "pushed" to the next calendar year) attributable to the portion of the calendar year after the beginning of the taxable year which begins in the calendar year to the first day of the next calendar year.

For example, assume a RIC for its taxable year ending June 30, 2012, has ordinary loss of $1 million for the portion of its taxable year ending on December 31, 2011, and $1 million ordinary income for the remainder of the taxable year. The RIC has no other items of income or loss in 2011, 2012, or 2013. The RIC must distribute

[1918] Sec. 4982(e)(5).

[1919] See Treas. Reg. sec. 1.1275–4(b)(9)(v).

[1920] Sec. 4982(e)(6).

[1921] Sec. 852(b)(8) and (10). See Treas. Reg. sec. 1.852–11 for rules relating to the treatment of losses attributable to periods after October 31 of a taxable year.

[1922] Sec. 852(c)(2).

[1923] For treatment of these losses for income tax purposes, see section 852(b)(8) of the Code, as amended by section 308 of the Act.

$980,000 in 2012 to avoid the excise tax, notwithstanding that it has no taxable income (or earnings and profits) for a taxable year which includes any portion of 2012. Under the provision, if the RIC makes an election, the $1 million ordinary loss will be treated as arising on January 1, 2012, for purposes of the excise tax and the RIC will not be required to make a distribution in 2012 to avoid the excise tax.

### *Effective Date*

The provision applies to calendar years beginning after the date of enactment (December 22, 2010).

## C. Distributed Amount for Excise Tax Purposes Determined on Basis of Taxes Paid by RIC (sec. 403 of the Act and sec. 4982(c)(4) of the Code)

### *Present Law*

In computing the excise tax under section 4982,[1924] a RIC is treated as having distributed amounts on which a tax is imposed on the RIC during the calendar year in which the taxable year of the RIC ends, regardless of the calendar year in which estimated tax payments are made.[1925]

### *Explanation of Provision*

Under the provision, a RIC making estimated tax payments of the taxes imposed on investment company taxable income and undistributed net capital gain for a taxable year beginning (but not ending) during any calendar year may elect to increase the distributed amount for that calendar year by the amount on which the estimated tax payments of these taxes are made during that calendar year. The distributed amount for the following calendar year is reduced by the amount of the prior year's increase.

### *Effective Date*

The provision applies to calendar years beginning after the date of enactment (December 22, 2010).

## D. Increase in Required Distribution of Capital Gain Net Income (sec. 404 of the Act and sec. 4982(b)(1) of the Code)

### *Present Law*

An excise tax is imposed on a RIC for a calendar year equal to four percent of the excess (if any) of the required distribution over the distributed amount. The required distribution is the sum of 98 percent of the RIC's ordinary income for the calendar year and 98 percent of the capital gain net income for the one-year period ending October 31 of such calendar year. The distributed amount is the sum of the deduction for dividends paid during the calendar

[1924] See present-law explanation of section 401 for a description of the tax.
[1925] Sec. 4982(c)(1)(B).

year and the amount on which a corporate income tax is imposed on the RIC for taxable years ending during the calendar year.[1926]

### *Explanation of Provision*

The provision increases the required distribution percentage of the capital gain net income from 98 percent to 98.2 percent.

### *Effective Date*

The provision applies to calendar years beginning after the date of enactment (December 22, 2010).

# VI. OTHER PROVISIONS

## A. Repeal of Assessable Penalty with Respect to Liability for Tax of RICs (sec. 501 of the Act and sec. 6697 of the Code)

### *Present Law*

If there is a determination that a RIC has a tax deficiency with respect to a prior taxable year, the RIC can distribute a "deficiency dividend."[1927] A deficiency dividend is treated by the RIC as a dividend paid with respect to the prior taxable year. As a result, the deficiency dividend increases the RIC's deduction for dividends paid for that year and eliminates the deficiency. A RIC making a deficiency dividend is subject to an interest charge as if the entire amount of the deficiency dividend were the amount of the tax deficiency. An additional penalty is also imposed equal to the lesser of (1) the amount of the interest charge, or (2) one-half of the amount of the deficiency dividend.[1928]

### *Explanation of Provision*

The provision repeals the additional penalty with respect to deficiency dividends.

### *Effective Date*

The provision applies to taxable years beginning after the date of enactment (December 22, 2010).

## B. Modification of Sale Load Basis Deferral Rule for RICs (sec. 502 of the Act and sec. 852(f)(1) of the Code)

### *Present Law*

If (1) a taxpayer incurs a load charge in acquiring stock in a RIC and by reason of incurring the charge or making the acquisition, acquires a reinvestment right, (2) the stock is disposed of within 90 days of the acquisition, and (3) the taxpayer subsequently acquires stock in a RIC and the otherwise applicable load charge is reduced by reason of the reinvestment right, the load charge (to the extent it does not exceed the reduction) is not taken into account

[1926] Sec. 4982.
[1927] Sec. 860.
[1928] Sec. 6697.

in determining gain or loss of the original stock but is treated as incurred in acquiring the subsequently acquired stock.[1929]

### *Explanation of Provision*

The provision limits the applicability of the provision described under present law to cases where the taxpayer subsequently acquires stock before January 31 of the calendar year following the calendar year the original stock is disposed of.

### *Effective Date*

The provision applies to charges incurred in taxable years beginning after the date of enactment (December 22, 2010).

[1929] Sec. 852(f).

## PART EIGHTEEN: REVENUE PROVISIONS OF THE OMNIBUS TRADE ACT OF 2010 (PUBLIC LAW 111–344) [1930]

### A. Extension of Health Coverage Tax Credit Improvements (secs. 111–118 of the Act and secs. 35 and 7527 of the Code)

#### *Present Law*

***In general***

Under the Trade Act of 2002,[1931] in the case of taxpayers who are eligible individuals,[1932] a refundable tax credit is provided for 65 percent of the taxpayer's premiums for qualified health insurance of the taxpayer and qualifying family members [1933] for each eligible coverage month beginning in the taxable year.[1934] The credit is commonly referred to as the health coverage tax credit ("HCTC"). The credit is available only with respect to amounts paid by the taxpayer. The credit is available on an advance payment basis.[1935]

***The American Recovery and Reinvestment Act of 2009***

Sections 1899 to 1899L of the American Recovery and Reinvestment Act of 2009 ("ARRA") made a number of temporary changes to the HCTC and related provisions that are generally effective for months beginning after February 17, 2009 and before January 1, 2011, or with respect to certain events occurring between those dates:

ARRA increases the amount of the HCTC to 80 percent of the taxpayer's premiums for qualified health insurance of the taxpayer and qualifying family members.

ARRA provides that the Secretary of the Treasury shall make one or more retroactive payments on behalf of certified individuals for qualified health insurance coverage of the taxpayer and qualifying family members.[1936] For this purpose, a retroactive advance payment is an advance payment for eligible coverage months occur-

---

[1930] H.R. 6517. The House passed H.R. 6517 on December 15, 2010. The Senate passed the bill with an amendment on December 22, 2010. The House agreed to the Senate amendment on December 22, 2010. The President signed the bill on December 29, 2010.

[1931] Pub. L. No. 107–210.

[1932] An eligible individual is an individual who is (1) an eligible Trade Adjustment Assistance ("TAA") recipient, (2) an eligible alternative TAA recipient, or (3) an eligible Pension Benefit Guaranty Corporation ("PBGC") pension recipient.

[1933] Qualifying family members are the taxpayer's spouse and any dependent of the taxpayer with respect to whom the taxpayer is entitled to claim a dependency exemption. Any individual who has other specified coverage is not a qualifying family member.

[1934] Please see Part Two, Section III.B, above for a discussion of eligible coverage months and a more lengthy discussion of persons eligible for the health coverage tax credit and the definition of qualified health insurance under the Trade Act of 2002.

[1935] Under section 7527, an individual is eligible for the advance payment of the credit once a qualified health insurance costs credit eligibility certificate is in effect.

[1936] This ARRA provision generally applies to months beginning after December 31, 2009 (rather than February 17, 2009) and before January 1, 2011.

ring prior to the first month for which an advance payment is otherwise made on behalf of such individual.

ARRA requires that the qualified health insurance costs credit eligibility certificate provided in connection with the advance payment of the HCTC must include certain additional information.[1937]

ARRA modifies the definition of eligible individual by modifying the definition of an eligible Trade Adjustment Assistance ("TAA") recipient. Specifically, the ARRA eliminates the requirement that an individual be enrolled in training in the case of an individual receiving unemployment compensation.[1938]

ARRA provides continued eligibility for the credit for family members after the following events: (1) the eligible individual becoming entitled to Medicare, (2) divorce, and (3) death.[1939]

ARRA expands the definition of qualified health insurance by including coverage under an employee benefit plan funded by a voluntary employees' beneficiary association ("VEBA," as defined in section 501(c)(9)) established pursuant to an order of a bankruptcy court, or by agreement with an authorized representative, as provided in section 1114 of title 11, United States Code.

Under ARRA, in determining if there has been a 63-day lapse in coverage (which determines, in part, if the State-based consumer protections apply), in the case of a TAA-eligible individual, the period beginning on the date the individual has a TAA-related loss of coverage and ending on the date which is seven days after the date of issuance by the Secretary (or by any person or entity designated by the Secretary) of a qualified health insurance costs credit eligibility certificate (under section 7527) for such individual is not taken into account.

ARRA modifies the maximum required COBRA continuation coverage period[1940] with respect to certain individuals whose qualifying event is a termination of employment or a reduction in hours to coordinate with eligibility for HCTC as an eligible individual or a qualifying family member.[1941]

### *Explanation of Provision*

Sections 111 through 118 of the Omnibus Trade Act of 2010 extends the temporary changes to the HCTC and related provisions made by ARRA so that the ARRA changes also apply to generally

---

[1937] The provision applies for certificates issued after August 17, 2009 and months beginning before January 1, 2011.

[1938] ARRA also clarifies that the definition of an eligible TAA recipient includes an individual who would be eligible to receive a trade readjustment allowance except that the individual is in a break in training that exceeds the period specified in section 233(e) of the Trade Act of 1974, but is within the period for receiving the allowance.

[1939] This ARRA provision generally applies to months beginning after December 31, 2008 (rather than February 17, 2009) and before January 2011.

[1940] The Consolidated Omnibus Reconciliation Act of 1985 ("COBRA") requires that a group health plan must offer continuation coverage to qualified beneficiaries in the case of a qualifying event. An excise tax under the Code applies on the failure of a group health plan to meet the requirement. Qualifying events include the death of the covered employee, termination of the covered employee's employment, divorce or legal separation of the covered employee, and certain bankruptcy proceedings of the employer. In the case of termination from employment, the coverage must be extended for a period of not less than 18 months. In certain other cases, coverage must be extended for a period of not less than 36 months. Under such period of continuation coverage, the plan may require payment of a premium by the beneficiary of up to 102 percent of the applicable premium for the period.

[1941] This ARRA provision is effective for periods of coverage that would, without regard to the provision, end on or after February 17, 2010, provided that the provision does not extend any periods of coverage beyond December 31, 2010.

months beginning (or, for certain provisions, plan years beginning or events occurring) after December 31, 2010 and before February 13, 2011.[1942]

### *Effective Date*

The provision is generally effective for months beginning (or, for certain provisions, plan years beginning or events occurring) after December 31, 2010.

## B. Time for Payment of Corporate Estimated Taxes (sec. 10002 of the Act and sec. 6655 of the Code)

### *Present Law*

In general, corporations are required to make quarterly estimated tax payments of their income tax liability.[1943] For a corporation whose taxable year is a calendar year, these estimated tax payments must be made by April 15, June 15, September 15, and December 15. In the case of a corporation with assets of at least $1 billion (determined as of the end of the preceding taxable year):

(i) payments due in July, August, or September, 2014, are increased to 174.25 percent of the payment otherwise due;[1944]

(ii) payments due in July, August or September, 2015, are increased to 159.25 percent of the payment otherwise due;[1945] and

(iii) payments due in July, August or September, 2019, are increased to 106.50 percent of the payment otherwise due.[1946]

For each of the periods impacted, the next required payment is reduced accordingly.

### *Explanation of Provision*[1947]

The provision increases the required payment of estimated tax otherwise due in July, August, or September, 2015, by 4.50 percentage points.

---

[1942] The expansion of the definition of qualified health insurance to include coverage under an employee benefit plan funded by certain VEBAs is extended to apply to months beginning before February 13, 2012.

[1943] Sec. 6655.

[1944] Haiti Economic Lift Program of 2010, Pub. L. No. 111–171, sec. 12(a); Health Care and Education Reconciliation Act of 2010, Pub. L. No. 111–152, sec. 1410; Hiring Incentives to Restore Employment Act, Pub. L. No. 111–147, sec. 561, par. (1); Act to extend the Generalized System of Preferences and the Andean Trade Preference Act, and for other purposes, Pub. L. No. 111–124, sec. 4; Worker, Homeownership, and Business Assistance Act of 2009, Pub. L. No. 111–92, sec. 18; Joint resolution approving the renewal of import restrictions contained in the Burmese Freedom and Democracy Act of 2003, and for other purposes, Pub. L. No. 111–42, sec. 202(b)(1).

[1945] Small Business Jobs Act of 2010, Pub. L. No. 111–240, sec. 2131; Firearms Excise Tax Improvements Act of 2010, Pub. L. No. 111–237, sec. 4(a); United States Manufacturing Enhancement Act of 2010, Pub. L. No. 111–227, sec. 4002; Joint resolution approving the renewal of import restrictions contained in the Burmese Freedom and Democracy Act of 2003, and for other purposes, No. 111–210, sec. 3; Haiti Economic Lift Program of 2010, Pub. L. No. 111–171, sec. 12(b); Hiring Incentives To Restore Employment Act, Pub. L. No. 111–147, sec. 561, par. (2).

[1946] Hiring Incentives to Restore Employment Act, Pub. L. No. 111–147, sec. 561, par. (3).

[1947] All the public laws enacted in the 111th Congress affecting this provision are described in Part Twenty-One of this document.

### *Effective Date*

The provision is effective on the date of enactment (December 29, 2010).

# PART NINETEEN: JAMES ZADROGA 9/11 HEALTH AND COMPENSATION ACT OF 2010 (PUBIC LAW 111–347)[1948]

## A. Excise Tax on Foreign Procurement (sec. 301 of the Act and new sec. 5000C of the Code)

### *Present Law*

The United States taxes U.S. citizens and residents (including domestic corporations) on their worldwide income, whether derived in the United States or abroad. The United States generally taxes nonresident alien individuals and foreign corporations engaged in a trade or business in the United States on income that is effectively connected with the conduct of such trade or business (sometimes referred to as "effectively connected income"). The United States also taxes nonresident alien individuals and foreign corporations on certain U.S.-source income that is not effectively connected with the conduct of a U.S. trade or business.

Income of a nonresident alien individual or foreign corporation that is effectively connected with the conduct of a trade or business in the United States generally is subject to U.S. tax in the same manner and at the same rates as income of a U.S. person. Deductions are allowed to the extent that they are connected with effectively connected income.[1949] A foreign corporation also is subject to a flat 30-percent branch profits tax on its "dividend equivalent amount," which is a measure of the effectively connected earnings and profits of the corporation that are removed in any year from the conduct of its U.S. trade or business.[1950] In addition, a foreign corporation is subject to a flat 30-percent branch-level excess interest tax on the excess of the amount of interest that is deducted by the foreign corporation in computing its effectively connected income over the amount of interest that is paid by its U.S. trade or business.[1951]

Subject to a number of exceptions, U.S.-source fixed or determinable, annual or periodical income ("FDAP") of a nonresident alien individual or foreign corporation that is not effectively connected with the conduct of a U.S. trade or business is subject to U.S. tax at a rate of 30 percent of the gross amount paid.[1952] Items of income within the scope of FDAP include, for example, interest, dividends, rents, royalties, salaries, and annuities. The tax generally is collected by means of withholding.[1953]

Treaties generally provide that neither country may subject nationals of the other country (or permanent establishments of enterprises of the other country) to taxation more burdensome than the tax it imposes on its own nationals (or on its own enterprises). Similarly, in general, neither treaty country may discriminate against enterprises owned by residents of the other country. The

[1948] H.R. 847. The House passed H.R. 847 on September 29, 2010. The Senate passed the bill with an amendment on December 22, 2010. The House agreed to the Senate amendment on December 22, 2010. The President signed the bill on January 2, 2011.

[1949] Secs. 864(c), 871(b), 873, 882(a), 882(c).

[1950] Sec. 884.

[1951] Sec. 884(f).

[1952] Secs. 871(a), 881(a).

[1953] Secs. 1441 and 1442 provide for withholding from payments to nonresident aliens and foreign corporations, respectively.

scope of the nondiscrimination provisions vary: Many older treaties provide protection only with respect to those taxes that are identified as covered taxes under the treaty. More recently, and consistent with the U.S. negotiating position since 1996,[1954] some nondiscrimination articles apply broadly to any tax imposed by one of the contracting states.

In addition to complying with tax laws, parties engaged in cross-border transactions are required to comply with relevant trade agreements of the jurisdictions in which they operate. To the extent that the purchaser is a governmental entity, such transactions are generally described in a subset of trade regulations known as government procurement agreements. The United States includes government procurement obligations in its free trade agreements ("FTA") with the aim of ensuring that U.S. goods, services and suppliers are afforded non-discriminatory opportunities to compete in the government procurement of U.S. trading partners.

The first major government procurement agreement was the 1979 Government Procurement Agreement ("GPA"), which entered into force in 1981. Since the formation of the World Trade Agreement in 1996, the United States has been a party to the "plurilateral" GPA that is an annex to the WTO agreement. This agreement is open only to members of WTO who either signed upon formation of the WTO in 1996, or subsequently acceded both to WTO and the GPA. At present, there are 41 members of the GPA, including all members of the European Union, the United States, Canada, Hong Kong, China, Iceland, Israel, Japan, the Republic of Korea, Liechtenstein, the Netherlands with respect to Aruba, Norway, Singapore, Switzerland, and Taiwan (Chinese Taipei).

### *Explanation of Provision*

Under this provision, foreign persons are subject to an excise tax of two percent on any specified procurement payment. A specified procurement payment is a payment made by the United States government or its agents, pursuant to a contract under which the United States purchases goods or services from a source in a country that is not party to an international procurement agreement with the United States. Goods are from such a source if produced or manufactured in such country. Payments for services are subject to the tax if the services are provided in a country that is not a party to such an agreement with the United States. If the origin of the goods or services is in a country that is not a member of the GPA, payments made to a foreign parent located in a country that is a member of the GPA are subject to the excise tax.

[1954] U.S. Department of the Treasury, U.S. Model Income Tax Convention of November 15, 2006, available at http://www.treasury.gov/offices/tax-policy/library/model006.pdf, updated an earlier model treaty published September 20, 1996. The Technical Explanation of the 1996 draft included a brief history of its provenance, explaining that it was drawn from a number of sources, including the U.S. Treasury Department's draft Model Income Tax Convention published on June 16, 1981, and withdrawn as an official U.S. Model on July 17, 1992, the Model Double Taxation Convention on Income and Capital, and its Commentaries, published by the OECD, as updated in 1995 (the "OECD Model"), existing U.S. income tax treaties, recent U.S. negotiating experience, current U.S. tax laws and policies and comments received from tax practitioners and other interested parties. U.S. Department of the Treasury, U.S. Model Income Tax Convention: Technical Explanation (September 20, 1996), available at 96 Tax Notes Today 186–7.

The excise tax is imposed on the gross amount of the payment. For purposes of subtitle F of the Internal Revenue Code, it is treated as an income tax, permitting assessment and collection of the amounts in a manner similar to the withholding taxes under chapter 3.

Executive agencies are required to ensure that funds disbursed to foreign contractors are not used to reimburse the tax imposed by this section. Contracting activities are to be monitored and reviewed annually to comply with this provision. Finally, the statute requires that the provision be administered in a manner consistent with U.S. obligations under international agreements.[1955]

### *Effective Date*

The provision applies to payments received under contracts entered into on or after the date of enactment (January 2, 2011).

[1955] Sec. 301(c) of the Act.

# PART TWENTY: AUTHORITY OF TAX COURT TO APPOINT EMPLOYEES (PUBLIC LAW 111–366)[1956]

## A. Authority of Tax Court to Appoint Employees (sec. 1 of the Act and sec. 7471 of the Code)

### *Present Law*

The United States Tax Court is an independent court of record established by Congress under Article I of the Constitution.[1957] Generally, the Tax Court is authorized to retain and compensate employees under the rules applicable to executive branch competitive service appointments.[1958]

### *Explanation of Provision*

The provision authorizes the Tax Court to establish an independent personnel management system that generally is not subject to the rules applicable to executive branch competitive service appointments. To the extent feasible, the Tax Court is directed to compensate employees at rates consistent with those for employees holding comparable positions in courts established under Article III of the Constitution.

The provision requires that the Tax Court preserve certain rights available to executive branch competitive service employees and prohibits employment discrimination on the basis of race, color, religion, age, gender, national origin, political affiliation, marital status, or handicapping condition. In addition, Tax Court employees employed prior to the effective date of the provision retain their appeal rights to the Merit Systems Protection Board and the Equal Employment Opportunity Commission so long as they are continuously employed by the court.

### *Effective Date*

The provision is effective on the date the United States Tax Court adopts a personnel management system after the date of enactment (January 4, 2011).

---

[1956] H.R. 5901. The House passed H.R. 5901 on July 30, 2010. The Senate passed the bill with an amendment on December 17, 2010. The House agreed to the Senate amendment on December 22, 2010. The President signed the bill on January 4, 2011.

[1957] Sec. 7441.

[1958] Sec. 7471.

## PART TWENTY-ONE: CUSTOMS USER FEES, CORPORATE ESTIMATED TAXES, AND ASSISTANCE FOR COBRA CONTINUATION COVERAGE

### A. Extension of Customs User Fees

#### *Present Law*

Section 13031 of the Consolidated Omnibus Budget Reconciliation Act of 1985 ("COBRA")[1959] authorized the Secretary of the Treasury to collect certain service fees. Section 412 of the Homeland Security Act of 2002[1960] authorized the Secretary of the Treasury to delegate such authority to the Secretary of Homeland Security. These fees include: processing fees for air and sea passengers, commercial trucks, rail cars, private aircraft and vessels, commercial vessels, dutiable mail packages, barges and bulk carriers, merchandise, and Customs broker permits.[1961] COBRA was amended on several occasions but most recently prior to the start of the 111th Congress by the Andean Tax Preference Act of 2008,[1962] which extended authorization for the collection of the passenger and conveyance fees through January 31, 2018 and the merchandise processing fees through February 14, 2018.

#### *Explanation of Provision*

The renewal of the Burmese Freedom and Democracy Act of 2003 extends the passenger and conveyance processing fees authorized under COBRA through February 7, 2018.[1963]

#### *Effective Date*

The provision is effective on July 26, 2009.

#### *Explanation of Provision*

The extension of the Andean Trade Preference Act extends: (1) the passenger and conveyance processing fees authorized under COBRA through June 7, 2008; and (2) the merchandise processing fees authorized under COBRA through May 14, 2008.[1964]

#### *Effective Date*

The provision is effective on date of enactment (December 28, 2009).

[1959] Pub. L. No. 99–272.
[1960] Pub. L. No. 107–296.
[1961] 19 U.S.C. sec. 58c.
[1962] Pub. L. No. 110–436.
[1963] Pub. L. No. 111–42.
[1964] Pub. L. No. 111–124.

### *Explanation of Provision*

The Haiti Economic Lift Program Act of 2010 extends: (1) the passenger and conveyance processing fees authorized under COBRA through August 17, 2018; and (2) the merchandise processing fees authorized under COBRA though November 10, 2018.[1965]

### *Effective Date*

The provision is effective on date of enactment (May 24, 2010).

### *Explanation of Provision*

The renewal of the Burmese Freedom and Democracy Act of 2003 extends the passenger and conveyance processing fees authorized under COBRA through August 24, 2018.[1966]

### *Effective Date*

The provision is effective on date of enactment (July 27, 2010).

### *Explanation of Provision*

The United States Manufacturing Enhancement Act of 2010 extends: (1) the passenger and conveyance processing fees authorized under COBRA through November 30, 2018; and (2) the merchandise processing fees authorized under COBRA through December 10, 2018.[1967]

### *Effective Date*

The provision is effective on date of enactment (August 11, 2010).

## B. Modifications to Corporate Estimated Tax Payments Due in July, August, and September, 2010, 2011, 2013, 2014, 2015, and 2019

### *Prior and Present Law*

In general, corporations are required to make quarterly estimated tax payments of their income tax liability. For a corporation whose taxable year is a calendar year, these estimated tax payments must be made by April 15, June 15, September 15, and December 15.

Under Section 401 of the Tax Increase Prevention Act of 2005 ("TIPRA") (including amendments that are contained in other provisions of law),[1968] in the case of a corporation with assets of at least $1 billion:

(i) payments due in July, August, or September, 2010, are increased to 120.50 percent of the payment otherwise due;

---

[1965] Pub. L. No. 111–171.

[1966] Pub. L. No. 111–210.

[1967] Pub. L. No. 111–227.

[1968] For additional detail, see Joint Committee on Taxation, *General Explanation of Tax Legislation Enacted in the 109th Congress* (JCS–1–00), January 17, 2007; see also Joint Committee on Taxation, *General Explanation of Tax Legislation Enacted in the 110th Congress* (JCS–1–09), March 2009.

(ii) payments due in July, August or September, 2011, are increased to 127.50 percent of the payment otherwise due; and

(iii) payments due in July, August or September, 2013, are increased to 120.00 percent of the payment otherwise due.

For each of the periods impacted, the next required payment is reduced accordingly.

### *Explanation of Provision*

The Children's Health Insurance Program Reauthorization Act of 2009[1969] increases the applicable percentage in 2013 (120.00 percent) by 0.50 percentage points.

### *Effective Date*

The provision is effective on the date of enactment (March 4, 2009).

### *Explanation of Provision*

The Corporate Estimated Tax Shift Act of 2009[1970] reduces the applicable percentage for 2010 (120.50 percent), 2011 (127.50 percent), and 2013 (120.50 percent) to 100 percent. Thus corporations will make estimated tax payments in 2010, 2011, and 2013 as if the TIPRA legislation had never been enacted or amended. The bill also increases the payments otherwise due in July, August, or September, 2014 (100 percent) by 0.25 percentage points. The next required payment is reduced accordingly.

### *Effective Date*

The provision is effective on the date of enactment (July 28, 2009).

### *Explanation of Provision*

The Worker, Homeownership, and Business Assistance Act of 2009[1971] increases the applicable percentage in 2014 (100.25 percent) by 33.00 percentage points.

### *Effective Date*

The provision is effective on the date of enactment (November 6, 2009).

### *Explanation of Provision*

The extension of the General System of Preferences and the Andean Trade Preference Act[1972] increases the applicable percentage in 2014 (133.25 percent) by 1.50 percentage points.

### *Effective Date*

The provision is effective on the date of enactment (December 28, 2009).

---

[1969] Pub. L. No. 111–3.
[1970] Pub. L. No. 111–42.
[1971] Pub. L. No. 111–92.
[1972] Pub. L. No. 111–124.

### *Explanation of Provision*

The Hiring Incentives to Restore Employment Act[1973] increases the applicable percentage in 2014 (134.75 percent) by 23.00 percentage points, the applicable percentage in 2015 (100 percent) by 21.50 percentage points, and the applicable percentage in 2019 (100 percent) by 6.50 percentage points. For each of the periods impacted, the next required payment is reduced accordingly.

### *Effective Date*

The provision is effective on the date of enactment (March 18, 2010).

### *Explanation of Provision*

The Health Care and Education Reconciliation Act of 2010[1974] increases the applicable percentage in 2014 (157.75 percent) by 15.75 percentage points.

### *Effective Date*

The provision is effective on the date of enactment (March 30, 2010).

### *Explanation of Provision*

The Haiti Economic Lift Program Act of 2010[1975] increases the applicable percentage in 2014 (173.50 percent) by 0.75 percentage points and the applicable percentage in 2015 (121.50 percent) by 0.75 percentage points.

### *Effective Date*

The provision is effective on the date of enactment (May 24, 2010).

### *Explanation of Provision*

The renewal of the Burmese Freedom and Democracy Act of 2003[1976] increases the applicable percentage in 2015 (122.25 percent) by 0.25 percentage points.

### *Effective Date*

The provision is effective on the date of enactment (July 27, 2010).

### *Explanation of Provision*

The United States Manufacturing Enhancement Act of 2010[1977] increases the applicable percentage in 2015 (122.50 percent) by 0.50 percentage points.

[1973] Pub. L. No. 111–147.
[1974] Pub. L. No. 111–152.
[1975] Pub. L. No. 111–171.
[1976] Pub. L. No. 111–210.
[1977] Pub. L. No. 111–227.

### *Effective Date*

The provision is effective on the date of enactment (August 11, 2010).

### *Explanation of Provision*

The Firearms Excise Tax Improvement Act of 2010 [1978] increases the applicable percentage in 2015 (123.00 percent) by 0.25 percentage points.

### *Effective Date*

The provision is effective on the date of enactment (August 16, 2010).

### *Explanation of Provision*

The Small Business Jobs and Credit Act of 2010 [1979] increases the applicable percentage in 2015 (123.25 percent) by 36.00 percentage points.

### *Effective Date*

The provision is effective on the date of enactment (September 27, 2010).

### *Explanation of Provision*

The Omnibus Trade Act of 2010 [1980] increases the applicable percentage in 2015 (159.25 percent) by 4.50 percentage points.

### *Effective Date*

The provision is effective on the date of enactment (December 29, 2010).

## C. Extension of Assistance for COBRA Continuation Coverage

### *Present Law*

The American Recovery and Reinvestment Act of 2009 provides that, for a period not exceeding nine months, an assistance eligible individual is treated as having paid any premium required for COBRA continuation coverage under a group health plan if the individual pays 35 percent of the premium.[1981] Thus, if the assistance eligible individual pays 35 percent of the premium, the group health plan must treat the individual as having paid the full premium required for COBRA continuation coverage, and the individual is entitled to a subsidy for 65 percent of the premium. An

[1978] Pub. L. No. 111–237.
[1979] Pub. L. No. 111–240.
[1980] Pub. L. No. 111–344.
[1981] For this purpose, payment by an assistance eligible individual includes payment by another individual paying on behalf of the individual, such as a parent or guardian, or an entity paying on behalf of the individual, such as a State agency or charity. Further, the amount of the premium used to calculate the reduced premium is the premium amount that the employee would be required to pay for COBRA continuation coverage absent this premium reduction (e.g. 102 percent of the "applicable premium" for such period).

assistance eligible individual is any qualified beneficiary who elects COBRA continuation coverage and satisfies three additional requirements. First, the qualifying event with respect to the covered employee for that qualified beneficiary must be a loss of group health plan coverage on account of an involuntary termination of the covered employee's employment (other than for gross misconduct). Second, the qualifying event must occur during the period beginning September 1, 2008 and ending with December 31, 2009, and the qualified beneficiary must be eligible for COBRA continuation coverage during that period and elect such coverage. Third, the assistance eligible individual must meet certain income threshold requirements.

### *Explanation of Provision*

The Department of Defense Appropriations Act, 2010 [1982] extends the maximum period an individual is eligible for the COBRA premium subsidy from nine months to 15 months. Specific transitions rules are provided for individuals who are eligible for the premium subsidy because of the extension of the period from nine to 15 months.

The provision also extends the time period during which the COBRA qualifying event must occur by two months so that it ends on February 28, 2010 (rather than December 31, 2009). Thus, in order to be an assistance-eligible individual for purposes of the premium subsidy, involuntary termination from employment must have occurred during the period beginning September 1, 2008, and ending February 28, 2010.

The provision contains notice requirements regarding the extensions to assistance eligible individuals who experience a qualifying event on or after October 31, 2009.

### *Effective Date*

The provision is effective as if included in the American Recovery and Reinvestment Act of 2009 (February 17, 2009).

### *Explanation of Provision*

The Temporary Extension Act of 2010 [1983] extends the time period during which the COBRA qualifying event must occur from February 28, 2010, to March 31, 2010.

The provision also clarifies that an assistance eligible individual can have experienced a qualifying event consisting of a reduction in hours of employment followed by an involuntary termination of employment (other than for gross misconduct) and still be eligible for the COBRA subsidy. If such individual did not elect continuation coverage after experiencing the reduction in hours, he or she must be given the chance to do so following termination of employment. In such circumstances, however, the individual's period of continuation coverage is determined as if it began immediately following the reduction in hours. The provision also clarifies the pre-

[1982] Pub. L. No. 111–118.
[1983] Pub. L. No. 111–144.

existing condition rules relating to such individuals. The provision contains notice requirements regarding the clarifications.

The provision permits the Secretary of Labor or the Secretary of Health and Human Services, whichever appropriate, or an affected individual, to bring a civil action to enforce a determination that the individual is an eligible individual for purposes of the subsidy and for appropriate relief. In addition, the appropriate Secretary may asses a penalty against a plan sponsor or health insurance issuer of not more than $100 per day for each failure to comply with a determination of eligibility (but only beginning 10 days after the sponsor's or issuer's receipt of the determination).

The provision deems an event to be an involuntary termination in all cases in which an employer reasonably determines it to be such and maintains supporting documentation of the determination (including an attestation by the employer).

The provision also makes certain technical clarifications to the period of assistance as defined in the American Recovery and Reinvestment Act of 2009, and to the Department of Defense Appropriations Act, 2010.

### *Effective Date*

The provision is generally effective as if included in the American Recovery and Reinvestment Act of 2009 (February 17, 2009).

The clarification regarding COBRA continuation coverage resulting from a reduction in hours is effective for periods of coverage after date of enactment (March 2, 2010).

The technical clarifications to the Department of Defense Appropriations Act, 2010 are effective as if included in the Department of Defense Appropriations Act, 2010 (February 17, 2009, because the Department of Defense Appropriations Act is effective as if included in the American Recovery and Reinvestment Act of 2009).

The provisions relating to enforcement and the clarification of period of assistance are effective on date of enactment (March 2, 2010).

### *Explanation of Provision*

The Continuing Extension Act of 2010 [1984] extends the time period during which the COBRA qualifying event must occur to May 31, 2010. In addition, specific transitions rules are provided for individuals who are eligible for the premium subsidy in April and May of 2010 because of the extension of the period.

### *Effective Date*

The provision is effective as if included in the American Recovery and Reinvestment Act of 2009 (February 17, 2009).

[1984] Pub. L. No. 111–157.

# APPENDIX: ESTIMATED BUDGET EFFECTS OF TAX LEGISLATION ENACTED IN THE 111TH CONGRESS

**APPENDIX:**
**ESTIMATED BUDGET EFFECTS OF TAX LEGISLATION ENACTED IN THE 111TH CONGRESS**

**Fiscal Years 2009 - 2020**

*[Millions of Dollars]*

| Provision | Effective | 2009 | 2010 | 2011 | 2012 | 2013 | 2014 | 2015 | 2016 | 2017 | 2018 | 2019 | 2020 | 2009-20 |
|---|---|---|---|---|---|---|---|---|---|---|---|---|---|---|
| **PART ONE: THE CHILDREN'S HEALTH INSURANCE PROGRAM REAUTHORIZATION ACT OF 2009 (P.L. 111-3, signed into law by the President on February 4, 2009)** | | | | | | | | | | | | | | |
| I. Requirements for Group Health Plans [1] [2] | DOE | --- | -150 | -275 | -325 | -350 | -375 | -375 | -425 | -450 | -475 | --- | --- | -3,200 |
| II. Other Revenue Provisions | | | | | | | | | | | | | | |
| A. Increase in Excise Tax Rate on Tobacco Products and Cigarette Papers and Tubes [3] | | | | | | | | | | | | | | |
| 1. Small Cigars | ara 3/31/09 | 46 | 108 | 91 | 91 | 91 | 92 | 92 | 92 | 92 | 92 | --- | --- | 886 |
| 2. Large Cigars | ara 3/31/09 | 75 | 424 | 419 | 425 | 433 | 442 | 451 | 458 | 466 | 474 | --- | --- | 4,070 |
| 3. Cigarettes | ara 3/31/09 | 3,489 | 6,479 | 6,173 | 6,117 | 6,066 | 6,014 | 5,960 | 5,906 | 5,849 | 5,795 | --- | --- | 57,850 |
| 4. All other tobacco products | ara 3/31/09 | 145 | 307 | 289 | 286 | 285 | 283 | 281 | 279 | 276 | 274 | --- | --- | 2,705 |
| B. Modify Definition of Roll-Your-Own Tobacco | ara 3/31/09 | [4] | [4] | [4] | [4] | [4] | [4] | [4] | [4] | [4] | [4] | --- | --- | 2 |
| C. Permit, Reporting, and Recordkeeping Requirements for Manufacturers and Importers of Processed Tobacco | 4/1/09 | *Negligible Revenue Effect* | | | | | | | | | | | | |
| D. Broaden Authority to Deny, Suspend, and Revoke Tobacco Permits | DOE | *Negligible Revenue Effect* | | | | | | | | | | | | |
| E. Clarify Statute of Limitations Pertaining to Excise Taxes Imposed on Imported Alcohol, Tobacco Products, and Cigarette Papers and Tubes | aiiUSa DOE | *Negligible Revenue Effect* | | | | | | | | | | | | |
| F. Impose Immediate Tax on Unlawfully Manufactured Tobacco Products and Cigarette Papers and Tubes | DOE | *Negligible Revenue Effect* | | | | | | | | | | | | |
| G. Use of Tax Information in Tobacco Transition Payment Assessments [5] | DOE | [4] | 1 | [4] | [4] | [4] | [4] | [4] | [4] | [4] | [4] | --- | --- | 2 |
| H. Study Concerning Magnitude of Tobacco Smuggling in the United States | [6] | *No Revenue Effect* | | | | | | | | | | | | |
| I. Modify Timing for Corporate Estimated Tax Payment [7] | DOE | --- | --- | --- | --- | 302 | -302 | --- | --- | --- | --- | --- | --- | --- |
| **TOTAL OF PART ONE** | | **3,755** | **7,169** | **6,697** | **6,594** | **6,827** | **6,154** | **6,409** | **6,310** | **6,233** | **6,160** | **---** | **---** | **62,315** |
| **PART TWO: THE AMERICAN RECOVERY AND REINVESTMENT TAX ACT OF 2009 (P.L. 111-5, signed into law by the President on February 17, 2009)** | | | | | | | | | | | | | | |
| I. Tax Provisions | | | | | | | | | | | | | | |
| A. Tax Relief for Individuals and Families | | | | | | | | | | | | | | |
| 1. Making Work Pay Credit - credit of 6.2% of earned income up to a maximum of $400 single ($800 joint) for tax years 2009 and 2010; phaseout for taxpayers with modified AGI in excess of $75,000 ($150,000 joint); and treatment of the U.S. Possessions [8] | tyba 12/31/08 | -19,900 | -66,133 | -30,166 | --- | --- | --- | --- | --- | --- | --- | --- | --- | -116,199 |

| Provision | Effective | 2009 | 2010 | 2011 | 2012 | 2013 | 2014 | 2015 | 2016 | 2017 | 2018 | 2019 | 2020 | 2009-20 |
|---|---|---|---|---|---|---|---|---|---|---|---|---|---|---|
| 2. $250 Refundable Credit for Federal and State Pensioners not Eligible for Social Security Benefits for Tax Year 2009 [9] [10] | tyba 12/31/08 | -44 | -174 | --- | --- | --- | --- | --- | --- | --- | --- | --- | --- | -218 |
| 3. Temporary increase in earned income tax credit for taxable years 2009 and 2010 | tyba 12/31/08 | -23 | -2,349 | -2,291 | --- | --- | --- | --- | --- | --- | --- | --- | --- | -4,663 |
| 4. Temporarily reduce the earnings threshold for the refundable portion of the child tax credit for taxable years 2009 and 2010 to $3,000 | tyba 12/31/08 | [11] | -7,489 | -7,342 | --- | --- | --- | --- | --- | --- | --- | --- | --- | -14,830 |
| 5. American Opportunity Tax Credit | | | | | | | | | | | | | | |
| a. Amend the HOPE scholarship credit for taxable years 2009 and 2010 so that it is available for four years at a rate of 100% of first $2,000 of expenses and 25% of next $2,000; phaseout for taxpayers with modified AGI between $80,000 - $90,000 ($160,000- $180,000 joint); make textbooks a qualifying expense; allow against the AMT [9] | tyba 12/31/08 | -791 | -4,425 | -5,040 | --- | --- | --- | --- | --- | --- | --- | --- | --- | -10,256 |
| b. Make 40% of the allowable American Opportunity Tax Credit refundable; and treatment of the U.S. Possessions [9] | tyba 12/31/08 | -331 | -1,725 | -1,595 | --- | --- | --- | --- | --- | --- | --- | --- | --- | -3,651 |
| 6. Temporarily allow computer technology and equipment as a qualified higher education expense for qualified tuition programs for 2009 and 2010 | epoia 12/31/08 | [11] | [11] | [11] | -1 | -1 | -1 | -1 | -1 | -1 | -1 | -1 | --- | -6 |
| 7. Extension of first-time homebuyer credit; increase maximum credit to $8,000; waiver of requirement to repay first-time homebuyer credit unless home is sold within 36 months of purchase (sunset 11/30/09) | qhpa 12/31/08 | -1,115 | -3,261 | 235 | 38 | -102 | -680 | -597 | -514 | -384 | -154 | -94 | --- | -6,638 |
| 8. Grants to States for low-income housing projects in lieu of low-income housing credit allocations for 2009 [12] | DOE | -3,006 | 28 | 150 | 309 | 350 | 350 | 350 | 350 | 350 | 350 | 350 | --- | -69 |
| 9. Provide that certain Federal grant monies do not reduce basis for purposes of determining the applicable low-income housing tax credit for such building [10] | DOE | -1 | -3 | -8 | -12 | -14 | -16 | -17 | -18 | -18 | -18 | -18 | --- | -143 |
| 10. Exclude up to $2,400 of unemployment insurance benefits from gross income for taxable year 2009 | tyba 12/31/08 | -948 | -3,792 | --- | --- | --- | --- | --- | --- | --- | --- | --- | --- | -4,740 |
| 11. Sales tax deduction for purchase (up to $49,500) of new cars, light trucks, motorcycles, and motor homes; phaseout for taxpayers with modified AGI in excess of $125,000 ($250,000 joint) (sunset 12/31/09) | po/a DOE | -424 | -1,269 | 9 | --- | --- | --- | --- | --- | --- | --- | --- | --- | -1,684 |
| 12. Increase individual AMT exemption amount to $46,700 ($70,950 joint) and allow personal credits against the AMT (sunset 12/31/09) | tyba 12/31/08 | -2,054 | -82,720 | 15,015 | --- | --- | --- | --- | --- | --- | --- | --- | --- | -69,759 |
| B. Tax Incentives for Business | | | | | | | | | | | | | | |
| 1. Special allowance for certain property acquired during 2009: | | | | | | | | | | | | | | |
| a. One-year extension of special allowance | ppisa 12/31/08 | -23,503 | -14,301 | 8,047 | 6,501 | 5,574 | 4,553 | 3,046 | 1,941 | 1,217 | 929 | 922 | --- | -5,074 |
| b. One-year extension of election to accelerate AMT and R&E credits in lieu of bonus depreciation | tyea 12/31/08 | -20 | -984 | 49 | 47 | 33 | 21 | 15 | 10 | 8 | 8 | 8 | --- | -805 |

| Provision | Effective | 2009 | 2010 | 2011 | 2012 | 2013 | 2014 | 2015 | 2016 | 2017 | 2018 | 2019 | 2020 | 2009-20 |
|---|---|---|---|---|---|---|---|---|---|---|---|---|---|---|
| 2. One-year extension of temporary increase in limitation on expensing of certain depreciable business assets | tyba 12/31/08 | -642 | -425 | 352 | 222 | 162 | 125 | 79 | 45 | 22 | 10 | 10 | --- | -41 |
| 3. 5-year carryback of 2008 NOLs for businesses with gross receipts of $15 million or less | [13] | -4,741 | 708 | 753 | 648 | 486 | 365 | 274 | 205 | 154 | 115 | 87 | --- | -947 |
| 4. Reduce required estimated tax payments in 2009 for certain small businesses | tybi 2009 | -275 | 275 | --- | --- | --- | --- | --- | --- | --- | --- | --- | --- | --- |
| 5. Modification of the work opportunity tax credit - incentives to hire unemployed veterans and disconnected youth | iwbwa 12/31/08 & [14] | -32 | -81 | -70 | -28 | -11 | -6 | -2 | [11] | --- | --- | --- | --- | -231 |
| 6. Clarification of regulations related to limitations on certain built-in losses following an ownership change | DOE | 1,437 | 1,775 | 646 | 261 | 225 | 304 | 419 | 457 | 470 | 484 | 499 | --- | 6,977 |
| 7. Treatment of certain ownership changes of manufacturing firms for purposes of limitation on net operating loss carryforwards and certain built-in losses | oca DOE | --- | --- | -19 | -19 | -181 | -289 | -289 | -491 | -625 | -625 | -625 | --- | -3,163 |
| 8. Deferral and ratable inclusion of income arising from business indebtedness discharged by the reacquisition of a debt instrument, and temporary AHYDO exception for debt exchange or modification | ra 12/31/08 & before 1/1/11; [15] | -12,113 | -22,803 | -7,479 | -483 | -269 | 4,948 | 8,349 | 8,328 | 8,306 | 8,285 | 3,310 | --- | -1,622 |
| 9. Special rules applicable to qualified small business stock for 2009 and 2010 | saa DOE | 2 | 6 | 2 | --- | --- | -207 | -360 | -163 | -50 | -36 | -22 | --- | -829 |
| 10. Temporarily reduce the S corporation built-in gains holding period from 10 to 7 years | tyba 12/31/08 and before 1/1/11 | -31 | -154 | -73 | -32 | -28 | -19 | -20 | -16 | -14 | -13 | -15 | --- | -415 |
| C. Fiscal Relief for State and Local Governments | | | | | | | | | | | | | | |
| 1. Modification of rules applicable to financial institutions for interest expense relating to tax-exempt income | oia 12/31/08 & before 1/1/11 | -79 | -239 | -326 | -340 | -336 | -331 | -326 | -321 | -317 | -312 | -307 | --- | -3,234 |
| 2. For bonds issued during 2009 and 2010, suspend alternative minimum tax limitations on private-activity tax-exempt bonds and modify ACE to exclude interest from all tax-exempt bonds; and provide AMT relief for current refundings of certain private activity bonds during 2009 and 2010 (refundings of private activity bonds issued since 1/1/04) | oia 12/31/08 | -27 | -69 | -76 | -49 | -49 | -49 | -49 | -48 | -47 | -46 | -46 | --- | -555 |
| 3. For bonds issued in 2009 and 2010, expand industrial development bonds to include creation of intangible property and eliminate 25% of proceeds restriction for facilities functionally related and subordinate to a manufacturing facility | oia DOE & before 1/1/11 | -1 | -6 | -16 | -23 | -24 | -23 | -23 | -23 | -22 | -22 | -21 | --- | -203 |
| 4. Qualified school construction bonds ($11 billion in 2009 and 2010) | oia DOE | -19 | -110 | -315 | -611 | -918 | -1,179 | -1,345 | -1,390 | -1,362 | -1,325 | -1,303 | --- | -9,877 |
| 5. Extend and expand qualified zone academy bonds ($1.4 billion in 2009 and 2010) | oia 12/31/08 | -1 | -10 | -40 | -90 | -130 | -140 | -137 | -131 | -125 | -121 | -120 | --- | -1,045 |
| 6. Build America Bonds - general rule: 35% credit to bondholders for bonds issued in 2009 and 2010 35% refundable credit to issuers for bonds issued 2009 and 2010 | oia DOE | -53 | -323 | -506 | -495 | -475 | -455 | -436 | -417 | -406 | -396 | -386 | --- | -4,348 |

| Provision | Effective | 2009 | 2010 | 2011 | 2012 | 2013 | 2014 | 2015 | 2016 | 2017 | 2018 | 2019 | 2020 | 2009-20 |
|---|---|---|---|---|---|---|---|---|---|---|---|---|---|---|
| 7. Recovery zone bonds ($15 billion private activity bond allocation; $10 billion allocation for refundable issuer credit bonds, credit rate 45%)........ | oia DOE & before 1/1/11 | -175 | -313 | -503 | -565 | -568 | -561 | -554 | -545 | -537 | -529 | -521 | --- | -5,371 |
| 8. Tribal economic development bonds - create a national pool of tax-exempt bonds for use by Indian tribes for economic development ($2 billion allocation)........ | oia DOE | -1 | -4 | -15 | -31 | -39 | -39 | -39 | -38 | -37 | -36 | -36 | --- | -315 |
| 9. Specify treatment of tax-credit bonds held by regulated investment companies........ | tyea DOE | ---------- | ---------- | ---------- | ---------- | ---------- | ---------- | *No Revenue Effect* | ---------- | ---------- | ---------- | ---------- | ---------- | ---------- |
| 10. Delay 3% withholding on government contracts by one year........ | DOE | --- | --- | -5,819 | 5,528 | --- | --- | --- | --- | --- | --- | --- | --- | -291 |
| 11. Extend and modify the new markets tax credit - increase new markets tax credit equity limitation to a total of $5 billion for calendar years 2008 and 2009........ | DOE | -51 | -31 | -48 | -103 | -115 | -138 | -131 | -117 | -86 | --- | 4 | --- | -815 |
| D. Energy Incentives | | | | | | | | | | | | | | |
| 1. Extend by three years the placed-in-service date for each section 45 qualified facility, (two years for marine renewables), excluding coal and solar facilities........ | ppisa 12/31/09 & 12/31/10 | --- | -127 | -440 | -921 | -1,365 | -1,603 | -1,649 | -1,700 | -1,743 | -1,788 | -1,806 | --- | -13,143 |
| 2. Election of investment credit for section 45 facilities in lieu of production credits........ | ppisa 12/31/08 | -96 | -131 | -71 | -16 | 9 | 12 | 6 | 2 | 1 | 1 | --- | --- | -285 |
| 3. Modify section 48 energy credit – remove cap for small wind systems, and remove cutback to credit for subsidized energy financing........ | pa 12/31/08 | -31 | -33 | -42 | -50 | -59 | -71 | -87 | -104 | -66 | -3[illegible] | -26 | --- | -604 |
| 4. Grants for specified energy property in lieu of tax credits [12]........ | ppisa 12/31/08 & before 1/1/11 | -27 | -77 | -18 | 41 | 41 | 27 | 8 | --- | --- | --- | --- | --- | -5 |
| 5. Increased limitation on issuance of new clean renewable energy bonds ($1.6 billion additional allocation)........ | DOE | -1 | -4 | -15 | -36 | -59 | -73 | -78 | -78 | -78 | -78 | -78 | --- | -578 |
| 6. Increased limitation on issuance of qualified energy conservation bonds ($2.4 billion additional allocation); and clarify green community programs for purposes of loans, grants and other repayment mechanisms........ | DOE | -1 | -5 | -17 | -41 | -69 | -95 | -111 | -116 | -116 | -116 | -116 | --- | -803 |
| 7. Modify speed requirement for high-speed rail exempt facility bonds........ | oia DOE | [11] | -1 | -3 | -7 | -13 | -20 | -29 | -38 | -48 | -58 | -71 | --- | -288 |
| 8. Extension and temporary increase to 30% ($1,500 per residence cap) credit for all section 25C nonbusiness energy property, repeal reduction in section 25C credits by reason of receipt of subsidized energy financing, and modify definition of qualified energy property and wood stoves (sunset 12/31/10)........ | tyba 12/31/08 [16] | -186 | -1,006 | -842 | --- | --- | --- | --- | --- | --- | --- | --- | --- | -2,034 |
| 9. Credit for residential energy efficient property - remove credit cap for residential wind, geothermal property, and residential solar thermal property under section 25D, repeal reduction in all section 25D credits (residential solar, geothermal, wind, fuel cells) by reason of receipt of subsidized energy........ | tyba 12/31/08 | -7 | -29 | -30 | -32 | -33 | -34 | -36 | -37 | -28 | --- | --- | --- | -268 |

| Provision | Effective | 2009 | 2010 | 2011 | 2012 | 2013 | 2014 | 2015 | 2016 | 2017 | 2018 | 2019 | 2020 | 2009-20 |
|---|---|---|---|---|---|---|---|---|---|---|---|---|---|---|
| 10. Temporarily increase credit rate for nonhydrogen refueling property to 50%; increase max credit to $50,000 for business property ($200,000 in the case of hydrogen) and $2,000 for nonbusiness property (sunset 12/31/10) | tyba 12/31/08 | -11 | -21 | -14 | -6 | -4 | -2 | 1 | 1 | 1 | 1 | 1 | --- | -54 |
| 11. Modify carbon dioxide sequestration credit to require permanent geologic storage for CO2 used as a tertiary injectant | DOE | *Negligible Revenue Effect* | | | | | | | | | | | | |
| 12. Modification of the alternative motor vehicle credit and the credit for qualified plug-in electric drive motor vehicles | generally DOE [17] | -3 | -20 | -39 | -74 | -39 | 4 | -85 | -232 | -383 | -540 | -589 | --- | -2,002 |
| 13. Credit for plug-in electric vehicle conversion (sunset 12/31/11) | ppisa DOE | *Estimate Included in C.12.* | | | | | | | | | | | | |
| 14. Treatment of alternative motor vehicle credit as a personal credit allowed against AMT | tyba 12/31/08 | *Estimate Included in C.12.* | | | | | | | | | | | | |
| 15. Equalize tax-free transit and parking benefits, set both at $230 for 2009 and then index equally in 2010 | mbo/a DOE | -57 | -106 | -29 | --- | --- | --- | --- | --- | --- | --- | --- | --- | -192 |
| 16. Credit for investment in advanced energy property ($2.3 billion of credits to allocate) | ppisa DOE | --- | -168 | -281 | -319 | -193 | -152 | -159 | -152 | -126 | -72 | -26 | --- | -1,647 |
| E. Other Provisions | | | | | | | | | | | | | | |
| 1. Prohibition on Collection of Certain Payments Made Under the Continued Dumping and Subsidy Offset Act of 2000 [5] [10] | DOE | -10 | -30 | -30 | -10 | -10 | --- | --- | --- | --- | --- | --- | --- | -90 |
| 2. Economic Recovery Payments to Certain Individuals - economic recovery payments to recipients of Social Security, supplemental security income, railroad retirement benefits, and veterans disability compensation or pension benefits [5] [10] | DOE | -14,041 | -169 | -15 | --- | --- | --- | --- | --- | --- | --- | --- | --- | -14,225 |
| III. Health Insurance Assistance | | | | | | | | | | | | | | |
| A. Premium Assistance for COBRA Continuation Coverage for Unemployed Workers and Their Families - 65% subsidy for up to 9 months; phased out for taxpayers with AGI above $125,000 single ($250,000 joint) [18] [19] | [20] | -14,302 | -9,154 | -1,407 | 26 | 75 | 46 | 29 | 10 | 1 | --- | --- | --- | -24,677 |
| B. Modifications to Health Coverage Tax Credit, including increase to 80% (sunset 12/31/10) [21] | generally DOE | -108 | -267 | -80 | -1 | --- | --- | --- | --- | --- | --- | --- | --- | -457 |
| **TOTAL OF PART TWO** | | **-97,843** | **-221,749** | **-39,862** | **9,226** | **1,851** | **4,572** | **6,016** | **4,659** | **3,911** | **3,855** | **-1,036** | **---** | **-326,412** |
| **PART THREE: AIRPORT AND AIRWAY TRUST FUND EXTENSIONS (P.L. 111-12, signed into law by the President on March 30, 2009; P.L. 111-69, signed into law by the President on October 1, 2009; P.L. 111-116, signed into law by the President on December 16, 2009; P.L. 111-153, signed into law by the President on March 31, 2010; P.L. 111-161, signed into law by the President on April 30, 2010; P.L. 111-197, signed into law by the President on July 2, 2010; P.L. 111-216, signed into law by the President on August 1, 2010; P.L. 11-249, signed into law by the President on September 30, 2010; and P.L. 111-329, signed into law by the President on December 22, 2010)** | **DOE** | ***No Revenue Effect*** | | | | | | | | | | | | |

| Provision | Effective | 2009 | 2010 | 2011 | 2012 | 2013 | 2014 | 2015 | 2016 | 2017 | 2018 | 2019 | 2020 | 2009-20 |
|---|---|---|---|---|---|---|---|---|---|---|---|---|---|---|
| **PART FOUR: THE HIGHWAY TRUST FUND PURPOSES (P.L. 111-46, signed into law by the President on August 7, 2009; P.L. 111-68, signed into law by the President on October 1, 2009; P.L. 111-118, signed into law by the President on December 19, 2009; P.L. 111-144, signed into law by the President on March 2, 2010; P.L. 111-147, signed into law by the President on March 18, 2010; and P.L. 111-322 signed into law by the President on December 22, 2010)** | **various** | ---------------------------------------- *No Revenue Effect* ---------------------------------------- | | | | | | | | | | | | |
| **PART FIVE: THE WORKER, HOMEOWNERSHIP, AND BUSINESS ASSISTANCE ACT OF 2009 (P.L. 111-92, signed into law by the President on November 6, 2009)** | | | | | | | | | | | | | | |
| A. Extension and Modification of First-Time Homebuyer Credit (sunset 4/30/10) | [22] | --- | -9,960 | -2,755 | 678 | 668 | 473 | 30 | 24 | 11 | 4 | 3 | --- | -10,823 |
| B. Increase Carryback Period to Five Years for Net Operating Losses Arising in Either 2008 or 2009 | [23] | --- | -33,197 | 5,870 | 5,202 | 3,808 | 2,673 | 1,877 | 1,319 | 928 | 653 | 461 | --- | -10,407 |
| C. Exclude From Gross Income Qualified Military Base Realignment and Closure Fringe | pma 2/17/09 | --- | -119 | -41 | -15 | -12 | -11 | -11 | -8 | -8 | -8 | -9 | --- | -243 |
| D. Delay in Application of Worldwide Allocation of Interest Until 2018 | tyba 12/31/10 | --- | --- | 494 | 1,362 | 3,077 | 3,200 | 3,328 | 3,361 | 3,475 | 1,826 | --- | --- | 20,123 |
| E. Modification of Penalty for Failure to File Partnership or S Corporation Returns | | | | | | | | | | | | | | |
| 1. Increase the penalty for failure to file partnership return by $106 to $195 | tyba 12/31/09 | --- | --- | --- | 2 | 39 | 92 | 95 | 98 | 102 | 105 | 109 | --- | 642 |
| 2. Increase the penalty for failure to file an S Corporation return by $106 to $195 | tyba 12/31/09 | --- | --- | --- | 2 | 36 | 84 | 87 | 90 | 93 | 96 | 99 | --- | 587 |
| F. Expansion of Electronic Filing by Return Preparers | rfa 12/31/10 | ---------------------------------------- *Negligible Revenue Effect* ---------------------------------------- | | | | | | | | | | | | |
| G. Increase the Required Corporate Estimated Tax Payments Factor for Corporations with Assets of at Least $1 Billion for Payments Due in July, August, and September 2014 by 33 Percentage Points | DOE | --- | --- | --- | --- | --- | 18,298 | -18,298 | --- | --- | --- | --- | --- | --- |
| **TOTAL OF PART FIVE** | | **---** | **-43,276** | **3,568** | **7,231** | **7,616** | **24,809** | **-12,892** | **4,884** | **4,601** | **2,676** | **663** | **---** | **-121** |
| **PART SIX: HAITI TAX RELIEF - ACCELERATE THE INCOME TAX BENEFITS FOR CHARITABLE CASH CONTRIBUTIONS FOR THE RELIEF OF VICTIMS OF EARTHQUAKE IN HAITI (P.L. 111-126, signed into law by the President on January 22, 2010)** | **cma 1/11/10 & before 3/1/20** | ---------------------------------------- ***Loss of Less Than $2 Million*** ---------------------------------------- | | | | | | | | | | | | |
| **PART SEVEN: THE HIRING INCENTIVES TO RESTORE EMPLOYMENT ACT (P.L. 111-147, signed into law by the President on March 18, 2010)** | | | | | | | | | | | | | | |
| A. Incentives for Hiring and Retaining Unemployed Workers | | | | | | | | | | | | | | |
| 1. Payroll tax forgiveness for hiring unemployed workers (sunset 12/31/10) [24] | wpa DOE | --- | -4,184 | -3,432 | --- | --- | --- | --- | --- | --- | --- | --- | --- | -7,616 |
| 2. Business credit for retention of certain newly hired individuals in 2010 | wpa DOE | --- | --- | -2,169 | -2,467 | -428 | -196 | -114 | -49 | --- | --- | --- | --- | -5,422 |
| B. Expensing - Increase in Expensing of Certain Depreciable Business Assets (sunset 12/31/10) | tyba 12/31/09 | --- | -556 | -368 | 305 | 192 | 140 | 108 | 68 | 39 | 19 | 9 | 8 | -35 |

| Provision | Effective | 2009 | 2010 | 2011 | 2012 | 2013 | 2014 | 2015 | 2016 | 2017 | 2018 | 2019 | 2020 | 2009-20 |
|---|---|---|---|---|---|---|---|---|---|---|---|---|---|---|
| C. Qualified Tax Credit Bonds - Allow a Refundable Credit to the Issuers of Qualified Zone Academy Bonds, Qualified School Construction Bonds, New Clean Renewable Energy Bonds, and Qualified Energy Credit Bonds (Refundable at 100% of Applicable Tax Credit Bond Rate) [25]...................... | bia DOE | --- | -81 | -559 | -813 | -895 | -713 | -550 | -393 | -260 | -159 | -81 | -57 | -4,561 |
| D. Revenue Provisions Contained in Extension of Current Surface Transportation Programs - Extend Highway Trust Fund (sunset 12/31/10), Provide for Interest and Certain Fund Transfers [26]............... | DOE | ---------- No Revenue Effect ---------- | | | | | | | | | | | | |
| E. Offset Provisions | | | | | | | | | | | | | | |
| 1. Foreign account tax compliance.......................... | various | --- | 343 | 448 | 710 | 769 | 804 | 840 | 878 | 917 | 958 | 1,001 | 1046 | 8,714 |
| 2. Delay implementation of worldwide interest allocation until 2021.................................................... | tyba 12/31/17 | --- | --- | --- | --- | --- | --- | 12 | 97 | 131 | 1,897 | 3,811 | 3,963 | 9,911 |
| 3. Increase the required corporate estimated tax payments due in July, August, and September 2014 to 157.75% of the payment otherwise due for corporations with assets of at least $1 billion [27]..................................................... | DOE | --- | --- | --- | --- | --- | 13,611 | -13,611 | --- | --- | --- | --- | --- | --- |
| 4. Increase the required corporate estimated tax payments due in July, August, and September 2015 to 121.5% of the payment otherwise due for corporations with assets of at least $1 billion.......................................................... | DOE | --- | --- | --- | --- | --- | --- | 13,267 | -13,267 | --- | --- | --- | --- | --- |
| 5. Increase the required corporate estimated tax payments due in July, August, and September 2019 to 106.5% of the payment otherwise due for corporations with assets of at least $1 billion.......................................................... | DOE | --- | --- | --- | --- | --- | --- | --- | --- | --- | --- | 4,428 | -4,428 | --- |
| **TOTAL OF PART SEVEN.................................................................** | | **---** | **-4,478** | **-6,080** | **-2,265** | **-362** | **13,646** | **-48** | **-12,666** | **827** | **2,715** | **9,168** | **532** | **991** |
| **PART EIGHT: HEALTH CARE PROVISIONS** | | | | | | | | | | | | | | |
| I. THE PATIENT PROTECTION AND AFFORDABLE CARE ACT (P.L. 111-148 signed into law by the President on March 23, 2010) IN COMBINATION WITH THE HEALTH CARE AND EDUCATION RECONCILIATION ACT OF 2010 (P.L. 111-152, signed into law by the President on March 30, 2010) THE PATIENT PROTECTION AND AFFORDABLE CARE ACT | | | | | | | | | | | | | | |
| Title I. Quality, Affordable Health Care for All Americans | | | | | | | | | | | | | | |
| 1. Tax exemption for certain member-run health insurance issuers.......................................................... | DOE | ---------- *Estimate Provided by the Congressional Budget Office in Collaboration with the Joint Committee on Taxation [28]* ---------- | | | | | | | | | | | | |
| 2. Tax exemption for entities established pursuant to transitional reinsurance program for individual market in each State.................................................... | DOE | ---------- *Estimate Provided by the Congressional Budget Office in Collaboration with the Joint Committee on Taxation [28]* ---------- | | | | | | | | | | | | |
| 3. Refundable tax credit providing premium assistance for coverage under a qualified health plan................. | tyea 12/31/13 | --- | --- | --- | --- | --- | -5,000 | -11,000 | -18,000 | -22,000 | -24,000 | -26,000 | --- | -107,000 |
| 4. Reduced cost-sharing for individuals enrolling in qualified health plans.................................................. | DOE | ---------- *Estimate Provided by the Congressional Budget Office in Collaboration with the Joint Committee on Taxation [28]* ---------- | | | | | | | | | | | | |
| 5. Disclosures to carry out eligibility requirements for certain programs......................................................... | DOE | ---------- *Estimate Provided by the Congressional Budget Office in Collaboration with the Joint Committee on Taxation [28]* ---------- | | | | | | | | | | | | |

| Provision | Effective | 2009 | 2010 | 2011 | 2012 | 2013 | 2014 | 2015 | 2016 | 2017 | 2018 | 2019 | 2020 | 2009-20 |
|---|---|---|---|---|---|---|---|---|---|---|---|---|---|---|
| 6. Premium tax credit and cost-sharing reduction payments disregarded for Federal and federally assisted programs | DOE | --- | Estimate Provided by the Congressional Budget Office in Collaboration with the Joint Committee on Taxation [28] | | | | | | | | | | | |
| 7. Small business tax credit | tyba 12/31/09 | --- | -2,000 | -4,000 | -5,000 | -6,000 | -5,000 | -4,000 | -3,000 | -3,000 | -4,000 | -4,000 | --- | -40,000 |
| 8. Excise tax on individuals without essential health benefits coverage | tyba 12/31/13 | --- | --- | --- | --- | --- | --- | 2,000 | 3,000 | 4,000 | 4,000 | 4,000 | --- | 17,000 |
| 9. Reporting of health insurance coverage | cyba 2013 | --- | Estimate Provided by the Congressional Budget Office in Collaboration with the Joint Committee on Taxation [28] | | | | | | | | | | | |
| 10. Shared responsibility for employers | mba 12/31/13 | --- | --- | --- | --- | --- | 3,000 | 8,000 | 10,000 | 10,000 | 10,000 | 11,000 | --- | 52,000 |
| 11. Reporting of employer health insurance coverage | pba 12/31/13 | --- | Estimate Provided by the Congressional Budget Office in Collaboration with the Joint Committee on Taxation [28] | | | | | | | | | | | |
| 12. Offering of qualified health plans through cafeteria plans | tyba 12/31/13 | --- | Estimate Provided by the Congressional Budget Office in Collaboration with the Joint Committee on Taxation [28] | | | | | | | | | | | |
| 13. Conforming amendments | DOE | --- | Estimate Provided by the Congressional Budget Office in Collaboration with the Joint Committee on Taxation [28] | | | | | | | | | | | |
| Title III. Improving the Quality and Efficiency of Health Care | | | | | | | | | | | | | | |
| 1. Disclosures to carry out the reduction of Medicare Part D subsidies for high income beneficiaries | DOE | --- | Estimate Provided by the Congressional Budget Office in Collaboration with the Joint Committee on Taxation [28] | | | | | | | | | | | |
| Title VI. Transparency and Program Integrity | | | | | | | | | | | | | | |
| 1. Impose Fee on Insured and Self-Insured Health Plans; Patient- Centered Outcomes Research Trust Fund | [29] | --- | --- | --- | --- | 110 | 267 | 325 | 360 | 418 | 512 | 659 | --- | 2,649 |
| Title IX. Revenue Provisions | | | | | | | | | | | | | | |
| 1. 40% excise tax on health coverage in excess of $10,200/$27,500 (subject to adjustment for unexpected increase in medical costs prior to effective date) and increased thresholds of $1,650/$3,450 for over age 55 retirees or certain high-risk professions, both indexed for inflation by CPI-U plus 1%; adjustment based on age and gender profile of employees; vision and dental excluded from excise tax; levied at insurer level; employer aggregates and issues information return for insurers indicating amount subject to the excise tax; nondeductible [30] | tyba 12/31/17 | --- | --- | --- | --- | --- | --- | --- | --- | --- | 12,200 | 19,800 | --- | 32,000 |
| 2. Employer W-2 reporting of value of health benefits | tyba 12/31/10 | --- | Negligible Revenue Effect | | | | | | | | | | | |
| 3. Conform the definition of medical expenses for health savings accounts, Archer MSAs, health flexible spending arrangements, and health reimbursement arrangements to the definition of the itemized deduction for medical expenses (excluding over-the-counter medicines prescribed by a physician) | eia 12/31/10 | --- | --- | 400 | 600 | 600 | 600 | 600 | 600 | 600 | 600 | 600 | --- | 5,000 |
| 4. Increase in additional tax on distributions from HSAs and Archer MSAs not used for qualified medical expenses to 20% | dma 12/31/10 | --- | --- | [31] | [31] | 100 | 100 | 100 | 200 | 200 | 300 | 300 | --- | 1,400 |
| 5. Limit health flexible spending arrangements in cafeteria plans to $2,500; indexed to CPI-U after 2013 [30] [32] | tyba 12/31/12 | --- | --- | --- | --- | 1,500 | 2,100 | 2,100 | 2,000 | 1,900 | 1,700 | 1,700 | --- | 13,000 |
| 6. Require information reporting on payments to corporations | pma 12/31/11 | --- | --- | --- | 400 | 3,300 | 2,000 | 2,100 | 2,200 | 2,300 | 2,400 | 2,500 | --- | 17,100 |
| **7. Additional requirements for section 501(c)(3) hospitals** | tyba DOE | --- | Negligible Revenue Effect | | | | | | | | | | | |

| Provision | Effective | 2009 | 2010 | 2011 | 2012 | 2013 | 2014 | 2015 | 2016 | 2017 | 2018 | 2019 | 2020 | 2009-20 |
|---|---|---|---|---|---|---|---|---|---|---|---|---|---|---|
| 8. Impose annual fee on manufacturers and importers of branded drugs ($2.5 billion for 2011, $2.8 billion per year for 2012 and 2013, $3.0 billion per year for 2014 through 2016, $4.0 billion for 2017, $4.1 billion for 2018, and $2.8 billion for 2019 and thereafter) [30] | cyba 12/31/10 | --- | --- | 2,200 | 2,900 | 2,900 | 2,900 | 2,900 | 2,900 | 3,400 | 4,000 | 2,900 | --- | 27,000 |
| 9. Impose annual fee on manufacturers and importers of certain medical devices ($2 billion per year for 2011 through 2017; and $3 billion per year thereafter) | DOE | --- | *Provision Repealed by Enactment of the "Health Care Education Reconciliation Act of 2010"* | | | | | | | | | | | |
| 10. Impose annual fee on health insurance providers ($8 billion in 2014, $11.3 billion in 2015 and 2016, $13.9 billion in 2017, $14.3 billion in 2018, and indexed to medical cost growth thereafter) [30] | [33] | --- | --- | --- | --- | --- | 6,100 | 9,300 | 9,500 | 11,400 | 11,700 | 12,100 | --- | 60,100 |
| 11. Study and report of effect on veterans health care | DOE | --- | *No Revenue Effect* | | | | | | | | | | | |
| 12. Eliminate deduction for expenses allocable to Medicare Part D subsidy [30] | tyba 12/31/12 | --- | --- | --- | --- | 400 | 600 | 600 | 600 | 700 | 700 | 800 | --- | 4,500 |
| 13. Raise 7.5% AGI floor on medical expenses deduction to 10%; AGI floor for individuals age 65 and older (and their spouses) remains at 7.5% through 2016 | tyba 12/31/12 | --- | --- | --- | --- | 400 | 1,500 | 1,600 | 1,700 | 2,500 | 3,700 | 3,900 | --- | 15,200 |
| 14. $500,000 deduction limitation on taxable year remuneration to officers, employees, directors, and service providers of covered health insurance providers | [34] | --- | --- | --- | --- | 100 | 100 | 100 | 100 | 100 | 100 | 100 | --- | 600 |
| 15. Broaden Medicare Hospital Insurance Tax Base for High-Income Taxpayers - additional HI tax of of 0.9% on earned income in excess of $200,000/$250,000 (unindexed) | tyba 12/31/12 | --- | --- | --- | --- | 13,300 | 6,000 | 10,400 | 13,100 | 14,100 | 14,700 | 15,200 | --- | 86,800 |
| 16. Modification of section 833 treatment of certain health organizations | tyba 12/31/09 | --- | [31] | 100 | 100 | [31] | [31] | [31] | [31] | [31] | [31] | [31] | --- | 400 |
| 17. Impose 10% excise tax on indoor tanning services | tspo/a 7/1/10 | --- | [31] | 200 | 200 | 300 | 300 | 300 | 300 | 300 | 300 | 300 | --- | 2,700 |
| 18. Provide income exclusion for specified Indian tribe health benefits | [35] | --- | --- | [36] | [36] | [36] | [36] | [36] | [36] | [36] | [36] | [36] | --- | [36] |
| 19. Simple cafeteria plan nondiscrimination safe harbor for certain small employers | tyba 12/31/10 | --- | *Negligible Revenue Effect* | | | | | | | | | | | |
| 20. Qualifying therapeutic discovery project credit (sunset 12/31/10) | [37] | --- | -400 | -200 | -100 | -100 | [36] | [36] | --- | --- | --- | --- | --- | -900 |
| Title X. Strengthening Qualify, Affordable Health Care for All Americans | | | | | | | | | | | | | | |
| 1. Study of geographic variation in application of FPL | DOE | --- | *No Revenue Effect* | | | | | | | | | | | |
| 2. Free choice vouchers | after 12/31/13 | --- | *Estimate Provided by the Congressional Budget Office in Collaboration with the Joint Committee on Taxation [28]* | | | | | | | | | | | |
| 3. Exclusion for assistance provided to participants in State student loan repayment programs for certain health professionals | tyba 12/31/08 | --- | [36] | [36] | [36] | [36] | [36] | [36] | [36] | [36] | [36] | [36] | --- | -100 |
| 4. Make the adoption credit refundable; increase qualifying expenses threshold, and extend the adoption credit through 2011 | tyba 12/31/09 | --- | -168 | -586 | -452 | [31] | --- | --- | --- | --- | --- | --- | --- | -1,206 |
| THE HEALTH CARE AND EDUCATION RECONCILIATION ACT OF 2010 | | | | | | | | | | | | | | |
| 1. Adult dependents | DOE | --- | *Estimate Provided by the Congressional Budget Office in Collaboration with the Joint Committee on Taxation [28]* | | | | | | | | | | | |

| Provision | Effective | 2009 | 2010 | 2011 | 2012 | 2013 | 2014 | 2015 | 2016 | 2017 | 2018 | 2019 | 2020 | 2009-20 |
|---|---|---|---|---|---|---|---|---|---|---|---|---|---|---|
| 2. Unearned Income Medicare Contribution on 3.8% on investment income for taxpayers with AGI in excess of $200,000/$250,000 (unindexed)................ | tyba 12/31/12 | --- | --- | --- | 1,300 | 7,200 | 10,600 | 18,900 | 19,600 | 20,700 | 21,900 | 23,300 | --- | 123,400 |
| 3. Impose 2.3% excise tax on manufacturers and importers of certain medical devices......................... | sa 12/31/12 | --- | --- | --- | --- | 1,800 | 2,700 | 2,800 | 3,000 | 3,100 | 3,200 | 3,400 | --- | 20,000 |
| 4. Exclusion of unprocessed fuels from the cellulosic biofuel producer credit.............................................. | fsouo/a 1/1/10 | --- | --- | 6,600 | 6,500 | 5,500 | 3,000 | 1,500 | 400 | --- | --- | --- | --- | 23,600 |
| 5. Codify economic substance doctrine and impose penalties for underpayments...................................... | teia DOE | --- | 67 | 316 | 409 | 471 | 505 | 523 | 536 | 551 | 566 | 601 | --- | 4,545 |
| 6. Increase by 15.75 percentage points the required corporate estimated tax payments factor for corporations with assets of at least $1 billion for payments due in July, August, and September 2014............................................................................ | DOE | --- | --- | --- | --- | --- | 8,800 | -8,800 | --- | --- | --- | --- | --- | --- |
| II. CLARIFICATION THAT THE HEALTH CARE PROVIDED BY THE SECRETARY OF VETERANS AFFAIRS CONSTITUTES MINIMUM ESSENTIAL COVERAGE - (P.L. 111-173, signed into law by the President on May 27, 2010)................................ | [38] | --- | ------------------------------------- | | | | | | *No Revenue Effect* ----------------------------------- | | | | | |
| III. MEDICARE AND MEDICAID EXTENDERS ACT OF 2010 - LIMITATIONS ON AGGREGATE AMOUNT RECOVERED ON RECONCILIATION OF THE HEALTH INSURANCE TAX CREDIT AND THE ADVANCE OF THAT CREDIT (P.L. 111-309, signed into law by the President on December 15, 2010) [1] [25]................................................ | tyba 12/31/13 | --- | --- | --- | --- | --- | 546 | 1416 | 2425 | 3181 | 3533 | 3787 | 4106 | 18,995 |
| **TOTAL OF PART EIGHT**.............................................................. | | **---** | **-2,501** | **5,030** | **6,857** | **31,881** | **41,718** | **41,764** | **51,521** | **54,450** | **68,111** | **76,947** | **4,106** | **378,783** |
| **PART NINE: PRESERVATION OF ACCESS TO CARE FOR MEDICARE BENEFICIARIES AND PENSION RELIEF ACT OF 2010 COVERAGE (P.L. 111-192, signed into law by the President on June 25, 2010)** | | | | | | | | | | | | | | |
| A. Authority to Disclose Return Information Concerning Outstanding Tax Debts for Purposes of Enhancing Medicare Program Integrity [5] [25]........ | DOE | --- | --- | --- | 38 | 38 | 50 | 50 | 50 | 50 | 50 | 50 | 50 | 425 |
| B. Pension Funding Relief | | | | | | | | | | | | | | |
| 1. Single-employer plans [39]...................................... | various | --- | 110 | 777 | 1,595 | 1,524 | 859 | 468 | 239 | -134 | -1,006 | -1,743 | -1,380 | 1,309 |
| 2. Multiemployer plans [39]......................................... | various | --- | 9 | 34 | 56 | 79 | 99 | 117 | 134 | 132 | 99 | 40 | -2 | 797 |
| **TOTAL OF PART NINE**.............................................................. | | **---** | **119** | **811** | **1,689** | **1,641** | **1,008** | **635** | **423** | **48** | **-857** | **-1,653** | **-1,332** | **2,531** |
| **PART TEN: THE HOMEBUYER ASSISTANCE AND IMPROVEMENT ACT OF 2010 (P.L. 111-198, signed into law by the President on July 2, 2010)** | | | | | | | | | | | | | | |
| A. Extend the Time for Closing on a Principal Residence Eligible for the First-Time Homebuyer Credit (Sunset 9/30/10)............................................ | rpa 6/30/10 | --- | -26 | -114 | --- | --- | --- | --- | --- | --- | --- | --- | --- | -140 |
| B. Revenue Offsets | | | | | | | | | | | | | | |
| 1. Application of bad checks penalty to electronic payments................................................................ | ita DOE | --- | 1 | 4 | 4 | 4 | 5 | 5 | 5 | 5 | 5 | 5 | 5 | 48 |
| 2. Disclosure of prisoner return information to State prisons [40]........................................................ | Dma DOE | --- | [4] | [4] | [4] | 1 | 1 | 1 | 1 | 1 | 1 | 1 | 1 | 6 |

| Provision | Effective | 2009 | 2010 | 2011 | 2012 | 2013 | 2014 | 2015 | 2016 | 2017 | 2018 | 2019 | 2020 | 2009-20 |
|---|---|---|---|---|---|---|---|---|---|---|---|---|---|---|
| 3. Amendment of the Travel Promotion Act of 2009 [5] [10] | DOE | --- | 6 | -14 | -6 | 23 | 7 | 120 | -30 | -10 | --- | --- | --- | 95 |
| **TOTAL OF PART TEN** | | **---** | **-19** | **-124** | **-2** | **28** | **13** | **126** | **-24** | **-4** | **6** | **6** | **6** | **9** |
| **PART ELEVEN: THE DODD-FRANK WALL STREET REFORM AND CONSUMER PROTECTION ACT - CERTAIN SWAPS, ETC., NOT TREATED AS SECTION 1256 CONTRACTS (P.L. 111-203, signed into law by the President on July 21, 2010)** | **tyba DOE** | **---** | **---** | **1** | **6** | **7** | **8** | **11** | **13** | **15** | **18** | **19** | **21** | **120** |
| **PART TWELVE: THE _____ ACT OF _____ (P.L. 111-226, signed into law by the President on August 10, 2010)** | | | | | | | | | | | | | | |
| A. Rules to Prevent Splitting Foreign Tax Credits from the Income to Which They Relate | generally fitpoaa 12/31/10 | --- | --- | 170 | 240 | 375 | 390 | 575 | 600 | 550 | 500 | 450 | 400 | 4,250 |
| B. Denial of Foreign Tax Credit With Respect to Foreign Income Not Subject to United States Taxation by Reason of Covered Asset Acquisitions | generally caaa 12/31/10 | --- | --- | 45 | 400 | 400 | 400 | 400 | 400 | 400 | 400 | 400 | 400 | 3,645 |
| C. Separate Application of Foreign Tax Credit Limitation, etc., to Items Resourced Under Treaties | tyba DOE | --- | --- | 25 | 25 | 25 | 25 | 25 | 25 | 25 | 25 | 25 | 25 | 250 |
| D. Limitation on the Amount of Foreign Taxes Deemed Paid with Respect to Section 956 Inclusions | [41] | --- | --- | 5 | 20 | 40 | 60 | 80 | 99 | 100 | 100 | 100 | 100 | 704 |
| E. Special Rule with Respect to Certain Redemptions by Foreign Subsidiaries | aa DOE | --- | --- | 25 | 25 | 25 | 25 | 25 | 25 | 25 | 25 | 25 | 25 | 250 |
| F. Modification of Affiliation Rules for Purposes of Rules Allocating Interest Expense | tyba DOE | --- | --- | 225 | 150 | 10 | 5 | [4] | [4] | [4] | [4] | [4] | [4] | 390 |
| G. Termination of Special Rules for Interest and Dividends Received from Persons Meeting the 80% Foreign Business Requirements | generally tyba 12/31/10 | --- | --- | 1 | 2 | 6 | 9 | 12 | 15 | 21 | 25 | 29 | 33 | 153 |
| H. Limitation on Extension of Statute of Limitations for Failure to Disclose Certain Foreign Transactions | [42] | --- | *No Revenue Effect* | | | | | | | | | | | |
| I. Elimination of Advanced Refundability of Earned Income Credit | tyba 12/31/10 | --- | --- | 153 | 122 | 102 | 102 | 103 | 105 | 107 | 110 | 112 | 114 | 1,131 |
| **TOTAL OF PART TWELVE** | | **---** | **---** | **649** | **984** | **983** | **1,016** | **1,220** | **1,269** | **1,228** | **1,185** | **1,141** | **1,097** | **10,773** |
| **PART THIRTEEN: THE FIREARMS EXCISE TAX IMPROVEMENT ACT OF 2010 (P.L. 111-237, signed into law by the President on August 17, 2010)** | | | | | | | | | | | | | | |
| A. Time For Payment Of Manufacturers' Excise Tax On Recreational Equipment [43] | [44] | --- | -82 | 31 | 29 | 10 | 5 | 1 | 1 | 1 | [4] | [4] | [11] | -5 |
| B. Assessment Of Certain Criminal Restitution | [45] | --- | [4] | 1 | 1 | 1 | 1 | 1 | 1 | 1 | 1 | 1 | 1 | 9 |
| C. Increase by 0.25 Percentage Points the Required Corporate Estimated Tax Payments Factor for Corporations with Assets of at Least $1 Billion for Payments Due in July, August, and September 2015 | DOE | --- | --- | --- | --- | --- | --- | 153 | -153 | --- | --- | --- | --- | --- |
| **TOTAL OF PART THIRTEEN** | | **---** | **-82** | **32** | **30** | **11** | **6** | **155** | **-151** | **2** | **1** | **1** | **1** | **4** |

| Provision | Effective | 2009 | 2010 | 2011 | 2012 | 2013 | 2014 | 2015 | 2016 | 2017 | 2018 | 2019 | 2020 | 2009-20 |
|---|---|---|---|---|---|---|---|---|---|---|---|---|---|---|
| **PART FOURTEEN: THE SMALL BUSINESS JOBS ACT OF 2010 (P.L. 111-240, signed into law by the President on September 27, 2010)** | | | | | | | | | | | | | | |
| I. Small Business Relief | | | | | | | | | | | | | | |
| A. Providing Access to Capital | | | | | | | | | | | | | | |
| 1. Modification to exclusion for gain from certain small business stock (sunset 12/31/10)........ | saa DOE | --- | --- | 2 | --- | --- | --- | -276 | -155 | -34 | -26 | -17 | -9 | -518 |
| 2. Five-year carryback of general business credit of eligible small business (sunset 12/31/10)........ | [46] | --- | --- | -1,440 | 241 | 192 | 180 | 156 | 144 | 132 | 114 | 96 | 78 | -107 |
| 3. General business credits of eligible small business not subject to alternative minimum tax (sunset 12/31/10)........ | [46] | --- | --- | -1,031 | 8 | 4 | 4 | 3 | 5 | 6 | 4 | 7 | 12 | -977 |
| 4. Reduction in recognition period for built-in gains tax (sunset 12/31/11)........ | tyba 12/31/10 | --- | --- | -45 | -23 | -2 | --- | --- | --- | --- | --- | --- | --- | -70 |
| B. Encouraging Investment | | | | | | | | | | | | | | |
| 1. Expand definition of eligible section 179 property to include certain real property and increase maximum amount and phase-out thresholds to $500,000 and $2,000,000, respectively........ | tyba 12/31/09 & before 1/1/12 | --- | --- | -9,735 | -3,024 | 3,441 | 2,280 | 1,705 | 1,291 | 838 | 509 | 302 | 215 | -2,177 |
| 2. One-year extension of bonus depreciation........ | ppisa 12/31/09 | --- | --- | -40,065 | 10,571 | 7,120 | 5,620 | 4,427 | 2,848 | 1,736 | 981 | 668 | 641 | -5,454 |
| 3. Special rule for long-term contract accounting........ | ppisa 12/31/09 | --- | --- | -1,785 | 751 | 463 | 276 | 163 | 82 | 38 | 12 | --- | --- | --- |
| C. Promoting Entrepreneurship | | | | | | | | | | | | | | |
| 1. Increase in amount allowed as a deduction for start-up expenditures........ | apoii tyba 12/31/09 | --- | --- | -347 | 4 | 18 | 17 | 16 | 15 | 14 | 13 | 11 | 9 | -230 |
| D. Promoting Small Business Fairness | | | | | | | | | | | | | | |
| 1. Limitation on penalty for failure to disclose reportable transactions based on resulting tax benefits........ | paa 12/31/06 | --- | --- | -85 | -21 | -16 | -8 | -8 | -8 | -8 | -8 | -8 | -8 | -176 |
| 2. Deduction for health insurance costs in computing self-employment taxes [47]........ | tyba 12/31/09 & before 1/1/11 | --- | --- | -1,754 | -165 | --- | --- | --- | --- | --- | --- | --- | --- | -1,919 |
| 3. Remove cellular telephones and similar telecommunications equipment from listed property........ | tyba 12/31/09 | --- | --- | -29 | -25 | -31 | -34 | -38 | -42 | -46 | -51 | -55 | -59 | -410 |
| II. Revenue Provisions | | | | | | | | | | | | | | |
| A. Reducing the Tax Gap | | | | | | | | | | | | | | |
| 1. Require information reporting for rental property expense payments........ | pma 12/31/10 | --- | --- | [48] | 227 | 247 | 259 | 269 | 284 | 294 | 309 | 324 | 335 | 2,546 |
| 2. Increase penalties related to information returns and payee statements........ | rtbfo/a 1/1/11 | --- | --- | 30 | 41 | 42 | 42 | 43 | 43 | 43 | 44 | 45 | 47 | 421 |
| 3. Annual reports on certain penalties and other enforcement tools........ | DOE [49] | --- | *No Revenue Effect* | | | | | | | | | | | |
| 4. Application of continuous levy to tax liabilities of certain Federal contractors........ | lia DOE | --- | --- | 127 | 98 | 100 | 102 | 104 | 106 | 108 | 10 | 112 | 114 | 1,080 |
| B. Promoting Retirement Preparation | | | | | | | | | | | | | | |
| 1. Allow participants in governmental 457 plans to treat elective deferrals as Roth contributions........ | tyba 12/31/10 | --- | --- | 12 | 17 | 25 | 36 | 48 | 56 | 60 | 69 | 83 | 100 | 506 |
| 2. Allow rollovers from elective deferral plans to Roth designated accounts........ | da DOE | --- | --- | 226 | 529 | 486 | 389 | 487 | 596 | 711 | 561 | 494 | 520 | 5,099 |
| 3. Permit partial annuitization of a nonqualified annuity contract........ | tyba 12/31/10 | --- | --- | 5 | 20 | 37 | 56 | 77 | 99 | 124 | 149 | 179 | 210 | 956 |

| Provision | Effective | 2009 | 2010 | 2011 | 2012 | 2013 | 2014 | 2015 | 2016 | 2017 | 2018 | 2019 | 2020 | 2009-20 |
|---|---|---|---|---|---|---|---|---|---|---|---|---|---|---|
| C. Closing Unintended Loopholes | | | | | | | | | | | | | | |
| 1. Crude tall oil ineligible for cellulosic biofuel producer credit | fsouo/a 1/1/10 | --- | --- | 523 | 512 | 425 | 237 | 118 | 34 | --- | --- | --- | --- | 1,849 |
| 2. Source rules for income on guarantees | gia DOE | --- | --- | 200 | 200 | 200 | 200 | 200 | 200 | 200 | 200 | 200 | 200 | 2,000 |
| D. Increase by 36 percentage points the required corporate estimated tax payments factor for corporations with assets of at least $1 billion for payments due in July, August, and September 2015 [50] | DOE | --- | --- | --- | --- | --- | --- | 21,234 | -21,234 | --- | --- | --- | --- | --- |
| **TOTAL OF PART FOURTEEN** | | **---** | **---** | **-55,191** | **9,961** | **12,751** | **9,656** | **28,728** | **-15,636** | **4,216** | **3,090** | **2,441** | **2,405** | **2,419** |
| **PART FIFTEEN: THE CLAIMS RESOLUTION ACT OF 2010 (P.L. 111-291, signed into law by the President on December 8, 2010)** | | | | | | | | | | | | | | |
| A. The Individual Indian Money Account Litigation | DOE | --- | *No Revenue Effect* | | | | | | | | | | | |
| B. Collection of Past-Due, Legally Enforceable State Debts [25] [51] | [52] | --- | --- | --- | 1,308 | 960 | 211 | 7 | -67 | -60 | -28 | 152 | 178 | 2,662 |
| **TOTAL OF PART FIFTEEN** | | **---** | **---** | **---** | **1,308** | **960** | **211** | **7** | **-67** | **-60** | **-28** | **152** | **178** | **2,662** |
| **PART SIXTEEN: THE TAX RELIEF, UNEMPLOYMENT INSURANCE REAUTHORIZATION, AND JOB CREATION ACT OF 2010 (P.L. 111-312, signed into law by the President on December 17, 2010)** | | | | | | | | | | | | | | |
| I. Temporary Extension of Tax Relief | | | | | | | | | | | | | | |
| A. Marginal Individual Income Tax Rate Reductions | | | | | | | | | | | | | | |
| 1. Retain 10% income tax bracket (sunset 12/31/12) [25] | tyba 12/31/10 | --- | --- | -30,990 | -44,807 | -13,511 | [11] | --- | --- | --- | --- | --- | --- | -89,308 |
| 2. Retain the 25% and the 28% income tax brackets (sunset 12/31/12) | tyba 12/31/10 | --- | --- | -12,792 | -18,376 | -5,526 | [11] | --- | --- | --- | --- | --- | --- | -36,693 |
| 3. Retain the 33% and the 35% income tax brackets (sunset 12/31/12) | tyba 12/31/10 | --- | --- | -19,714 | -31,276 | -9,783 | [11] | --- | --- | --- | --- | --- | --- | -60,774 |
| B. Repeal Overall Limitation on Itemized Deduction and the Personal Exemption Phaseout (sunset 12/31/12) | tyba 12/31/10 | --- | --- | -4,862 | -10,384 | -5,489 | [11] | --- | --- | --- | --- | --- | --- | -20,735 |
| C. Child Tax Credit - retain the child tax credit at $1,000; refundable up to greater of 15% of earned income in excess of $10,000 (indexed from 2001) or the taxpayer's social security tax liability to the extent that it exceeds the taxpayer's earned income credit; allow credit against the AMT; repeal AMT offset of refundable credits (sunset 12/31/12) [25] | tyba 12/31/10 | --- | --- | -7,075 | -35,565 | -29,056 | --- | --- | --- | --- | --- | --- | --- | -71,697 |
| D. Marriage Penalty Relief and Earned Income Tax Credit Simplification | | | | | | | | | | | | | | |
| 1. Standard deduction and 15% rate bracket set at 2 times single for married filing jointly (sunset 12/31/12) [25] | tyba 12/31/10 | --- | --- | -6,287 | -8,962 | -2,686 | [11] | --- | --- | --- | --- | --- | --- | -17,935 |

| Provision | Effective | 2009 | 2010 | 2011 | 2012 | 2013 | 2014 | 2015 | 2016 | 2017 | 2018 | 2019 | 2020 | 2009-20 |
|---|---|---|---|---|---|---|---|---|---|---|---|---|---|---|
| 2. EIC modification and simplification - increase in joint returns beginning and ending income level for phaseout by $3,000 indexed after 2008; simplify definition of earned income; use AGI instead of modified AGI; simplify definition of qualifying child and tie-breaker rules; and allow math error procedure with Federal Case registry data beginning in 2004 (sunset 12/31/12) [25] | tyba 12/31/10 | --- | --- | -44 | -4,424 | -4,469 | --- | --- | --- | --- | --- | --- | --- | -8,937 |
| E. Education Incentives | | | | | | | | | | | | | | |
| 1. Coverdell Education Savings Accounts ("ESAs") - increase the annual contribution limit to $2,000; allow ESA contributions for special needs beneficiaries above the age of 18; allow corporations and other entities to contribute to ESAs; allow contributions until April 15 of the following year; allow a taxpayer to exclude ESA distributions from gross income and claim the HOPE or Lifetime Learning credits as long as they are not used for the same expenses; repeal excise tax on contributions made to ESA when contribution made by anyone on behalf of same beneficiary to QTP; modify phaseout range for married taxpayers; allow tax-free expenditures for elementary and secondary school expenses; expand the definition of qualified expenses to include certain computers and related items (sunset 12/31/12) | tyba 12/31/10 | --- | --- | -11 | -17 | -5 | --- | --- | --- | --- | --- | --- | --- | -32 |
| 2. Employer provided educational assistance - extend the exclusion for undergraduate courses and graduate level courses (sunset 12/31/12) [53] | cba 12/31/10 | --- | --- | -707 | -964 | -243 | --- | --- | --- | --- | --- | --- | --- | -1,914 |
| 3. Student loan interest deduction - eliminate the 60-month rule and the disallowance for voluntary payments; increase phaseout ranges to $50,000-$65,000 single/ $100,000-$130,000 joint, indexed for inflation (sunset 12/31/12) | ipa 12/31/10 | --- | --- | -63 | -631 | -560 | --- | --- | --- | --- | --- | --- | --- | -1,254 |
| 4. Eliminate the tax on awards under the National Health Service Corps Scholarship program and F. Edward Hebert Armed Forces Health Professions Scholarship and Financial Assistance Program (sunset 12/31/12) | tyba 12/31/10 | --- | --- | -9 | -35 | -27 | --- | --- | --- | --- | --- | --- | --- | -70 |
| 5. Increase arbitrage rebate exception for governmental bonds used to finance qualified school construction from $10 million to $15 million (sunset 12/31/12) | bia 12/31/10 | --- | --- | [11] | -1 | -2 | -3 | -3 | -3 | -3 | -3 | -3 | -3 | -24 |
| 6. Issuance of tax-exempt private activity bonds for qualified education facilities with annual State volume caps the greater of $10 per resident or $5 million (sunset 12/31/12) | bia 12/31/10 | --- | --- | [11] | -1 | -3 | -5 | -5 | -5 | -5 | -5 | -5 | -5 | -39 |

| Provision | Effective | 2009 | 2010 | 2011 | 2012 | 2013 | 2014 | 2015 | 2016 | 2017 | 2018 | 2019 | 2020 | 2009-20 |
|---|---|---|---|---|---|---|---|---|---|---|---|---|---|---|
| F. Other Incentives for Families and Children | | | | | | | | | | | | | | |
| 1. Dependent care tax credit - increase the credit rate to 35%, increase the eligible expenses to $3,000 for one child and $6,000 for two or more children (not indexed), and increase the start of the phase-out to $15,000 of AGI (sunset 12/31/12) [25] | tyba 12/31/10 | --- | --- | -76 | -302 | -222 | --- | --- | --- | --- | --- | --- | --- | -600 |
| 2. Adoption credit - increase the expense limit and the exclusion to $10,000 for both non-special needs and special needs adoptions, make the credit independent of expenses for special needs adoptions, extend the credit and the exclusion, increase the phase-out start point to $150,000, index for inflation the expenses limit and the phase-out start point for both the credit and the exclusion, and allow the credit to apply to the AMT (sunset 12/31/12) [25] | tyba 12/31/10 | --- | --- | --- | -95 | -221 | --- | --- | --- | --- | --- | --- | --- | -315 |
| 3. Employer-provided child care credit of 25% for childcare expenditures and 10% for child care resource (sunset 12/31/12) | tyba 12/31/10 | --- | --- | -11 | -33 | -15 | --- | --- | --- | --- | --- | --- | --- | -58 |
| G. Allow Electing Alaska Native Settlement Trusts to Tax Income to the Trust not the Beneficiaries (sunset 12/31/12) | tyba 12/31/10 | --- | --- | -2 | -5 | -2 | --- | --- | --- | --- | --- | --- | --- | -9 |
| H. Reduced Rate on Dividends and Capital Gains | | | | | | | | | | | | | | |
| 1. Tax capital gains with a 0%/15% rate structure (sunset 12/31/12) | tyba 12/31/10 | --- | --- | -10,477 | 2,355 | -1,915 | -15,840 | --- | --- | --- | --- | --- | --- | -25,877 |
| 2. Tax dividends with a 0%/15% rate structure (sunset 12/31/12) | tyba 12/31/10 | --- | --- | -4,677 | -13,555 | -9,042 | --- | --- | --- | --- | --- | --- | --- | -27,274 |
| I. Extension of American Opportunity Tax Credit (sunset 12/31/12) [25] | tyba 12/31/10 | --- | --- | -1,194 | -7,094 | -9,277 | --- | --- | --- | --- | --- | --- | --- | -17,566 |
| J. Reduce the Earnings Threshold for the Refundable Portion of the Child Tax Credit to $3,000 (sunset 12/31/12) [25] | tyba 12/31/10 | --- | --- | --- | -9,826 | -9,917 | --- | --- | --- | --- | --- | --- | --- | -19,743 |
| K. Earned Income Credit | | | | | | | | | | | | | | |
| 1. Increase in earned income tax credit percentage (sunset 12/31/12) [25] | tyba 12/31/10 | --- | --- | -18 | -1,845 | -1,822 | --- | --- | --- | --- | --- | --- | --- | -3,685 |
| 2. EIC modification and simplification - increase in joint returns beginning and ending income level for phaseout by $5,000 indexed after 2008 (sunset 12/31/12) [25] | tyba 12/31/10 | --- | --- | -16 | -1,553 | -1,532 | --- | --- | --- | --- | --- | --- | --- | -3,101 |
| II. Temporary Alternative Minimum Tax Relief - Set the AMT Exemption Amount at $47,450 ($72,450 Joint) in 2010 and $48,450 ($74,450 Joint) in 2011 and Allow Personal Credits against the AMT (sunset 12/31/11) | tyba 12/31/09 | --- | --- | -85,833 | -67,597 | 16,754 | --- | --- | --- | --- | --- | --- | --- | -136,676 |
| III. Temporary Estate and Gift Tax Relief - $5 Million Unified and Indexed Exemption Amount; 35% Maximum Rate; Portability of Exemption Amount; and Decedents Dying in 2010 Can Elect into EGTRRA (sunset 12/31/12) | dda/gsta 12/31/09 & gma 12/31/10 | --- | --- | -4,546 | -28,050 | -29,349 | -3,483 | -2,088 | -981 | -53 | 130 | 135 | 136 | -68,149 |
| IV. Temporary Extension of Investment Incentives | | | | | | | | | | | | | | |
| A. Increase Additional First-Year Depreciation to 100 Percent (sunset 12/31/11); Extend 50 Percent Additional First-Year Depreciation for Property Placed in Service after 12/31/11 (sunset 12/31/12) | ppisa 9/8/10 | --- | --- | -55,419 | -54,422 | 2,687 | 25,519 | 19,778 | 15,671 | 11,161 | 7,071 | 4,297 | 2,775 | -20,883 |

| Provision | Effective | 2009 | 2010 | 2011 | 2012 | 2013 | 2014 | 2015 | 2016 | 2017 | 2018 | 2019 | 2020 | 2009-20 |
|---|---|---|---|---|---|---|---|---|---|---|---|---|---|---|
| B. Election To Accelerate AMT Credit in Lieu of Additional First-Year Depreciation (sunset 12/31/12) | [54] | --- | --- | -11 | -536 | -212 | 37 | 29 | 19 | 13 | 9 | 7 | 6 | -639 |
| C. Section 179 Expensing Amounts and Threshold Limits $125,000/ $500,000 (sunset 12/31/12) | tyba 12/31/11 | --- | --- | --- | -3,266 | -2,160 | 1,791 | 1,131 | 822 | 636 | 401 | 227 | 110 | -307 |
| V. Temporary Extension of Unemployment Insurance and Related Matters [5] [25] [10] | various | --- | --- | -34,515 | -21,642 | -100 | -102 | -76 | -41 | -29 | -4 | --- | --- | -56,510 |
| VI. Temporary Payroll Tax Reduction (Employee Side of OASDI) by 2 Percentage Points (sunset 12/31/11) [55] | tyba 12/31/10 | --- | --- | -67,239 | -44,414 | --- | --- | --- | --- | --- | --- | --- | --- | -111,653 |
| VII. Temporary Extension of Certain Expiring Provisions | | | | | | | | | | | | | | |
| A. Energy | | | | | | | | | | | | | | |
| 1. Incentives for biodiesel and renewable diesel (sunset 12/31/11) | fsoua 12/31/09 | --- | --- | -1,677 | -300 | --- | --- | --- | --- | --- | --- | --- | --- | -1,977 |
| 2. Placed-in-service date for facilities eligible to claim the refined coal production credit (excluding steel industry fuel) (sec. 45(d)) (sunset 12/31/11) | ppisa 12/31/09 | --- | --- | -15 | -20 | -23 | -24 | -24 | -24 | -25 | -26 | -26 | -24 | -230 |
| 3. Credit for construction of energy efficient new homes (sunset 12/31/11) | haa 12/31/09 | --- | --- | -66 | -25 | -12 | -11 | -9 | -8 | -5 | -1 | --- | --- | -138 |
| 4. Incentives for alternative fuel and alternative fuel mixtures (modified to exclude black liquor) (sunset 12/31/11) | fsoua 12/31/09 | --- | --- | -176 | -26 | --- | --- | --- | --- | --- | --- | --- | --- | -202 |
| 5. Special rule to implement electric transmission restructuring (sunset 12/31/11) | Da 12/31/09 | --- | --- | -232 | -92 | 51 | 51 | 51 | 51 | 51 | 51 | 18 | --- | --- |
| 6. Extension of suspension of 100 percent-of-net-income limitation on percentage depletion for oil and natural gas from marginal properties (sunset 12/31/11) | tyba 12/31/09 | --- | --- | -182 | -42 | --- | --- | --- | --- | --- | --- | --- | --- | -224 |
| 7. Grants for specified energy property in lieu of tax credits (sunset 12/31/11) [25] | ppisa DOE | --- | --- | -1,941 | -1,045 | --- | --- | --- | --- | --- | --- | --- | --- | -2,987 |
| 8. Extension of provisions related to alcohol used as fuel (extension of present law): | | | | | | | | | | | | | | |
| a. Extension of income tax credits for alcohol fuels; and extension of excise tax credits and outlay payments for alcohol fuel mixtures (sunset 12/31/11) | pa 12/31/10 & saua 12/31/10 | --- | --- | -3,558 | -1,311 | --- | --- | --- | --- | --- | --- | --- | --- | -4,869 |
| b. Extension of additional duties on ethanol (sunset 12/31/11) [5] | 1/1/11 | --- | --- | 8 | 3 | --- | --- | --- | --- | --- | --- | --- | --- | 10 |
| 9. Credit for energy efficient appliances (sunset 12/31/11) | apa 12/31/10 | --- | --- | -7 | -17 | -14 | -9 | -8 | -6 | -5 | -4 | -4 | -3 | -78 |
| 10. Extension and modification of section 25C nonbusiness energy property (sunset 12/31/11) | ppisa 12/31/10 | --- | --- | -119 | -477 | --- | --- | --- | --- | --- | --- | --- | --- | -596 |
| 11. Alternative fuel vehicle refueling property (non-hydrogen refueling property) (sunset 12/31/11) | ppisa 12/31/10 | --- | --- | -7 | -6 | -2 | -1 | -1 | [4] | [4] | [4] | [4] | [4] | -16 |
| B. Individual Tax Relief | | | | | | | | | | | | | | |
| 1. Above-the-line deduction of up to $250 for teacher classroom expenses (sunset 12/31/11) | tyba 12/31/09 | --- | --- | -39 | -195 | -156 | --- | --- | --- | --- | --- | --- | --- | -390 |
| 2. Deduction of State and local general sales taxes (sunset 12/31/11) | tyba 12/31/09 | --- | --- | -2,829 | -2,393 | -314 | --- | --- | --- | --- | --- | --- | --- | -5,536 |
| 3. Contributions of capital gain real property made for qualified conservation purposes (sunset 12/31/11) | cmi tyba 12/31/09 | --- | --- | -63 | -48 | --- | --- | --- | --- | --- | --- | --- | --- | -111 |
| 4. Deduction for qualified tuition and related expenses (sunset 12/31/11) [56] | tyba 12/31/09 | --- | --- | -711 | -450 | --- | --- | --- | --- | --- | --- | --- | --- | -1,161 |

| Provision | Effective | 2009 | 2010 | 2011 | 2012 | 2013 | 2014 | 2015 | 2016 | 2017 | 2018 | 2019 | 2020 | 2009-20 |
|---|---|---|---|---|---|---|---|---|---|---|---|---|---|---|
| 5. Tax-free distributions from IRAs to certain public charities for individuals age 70 1/2 or older, not to exceed $100,000 per taxpayer per year; distributions made in January 2011 may count against the 2010 $100,000 limit and satisfy the 2010 minimum distribution requirement (sunset 12/31/11) | dmi tyba 12/31/09 | --- | --- | -517 | -197 | -29 | -30 | -31 | -32 | -34 | -35 | -36 | -38 | -979 |
| 6. Estate tax look-through for certain RIC stock held by nonresidents (sunset 12/31/11) | dda 12/31/09 | --- | --- | -5 | -5 | --- | --- | --- | --- | --- | --- | --- | --- | -10 |
| 7. Parity for exclusion for employer-provided mass transit and parking benefits (sunset 12/31/11) [1] | ma 12/31/10 | --- | --- | -102 | -34 | --- | --- | --- | --- | --- | --- | --- | --- | -136 |
| 8. Refunds disregarded in the administration of Federal programs and federally assisted programs (sunset 12/31/12) [5] [25] | Ara 12/31/09 | --- | --- | -4 | -4 | --- | --- | --- | --- | --- | --- | --- | --- | -8 |
| C. Business Tax Relief | | | | | | | | | | | | | | |
| 1. Tax credit for research and experimentation expenses (sunset 12/31/11) | apoia 12/31/09 | --- | --- | -5,984 | -2,055 | -923 | -813 | -715 | -631 | -575 | -547 | -530 | -501 | -13,272 |
| 2. Indian employment tax credit (sunset 12/31/11) | tyba 12/31/09 | --- | --- | -59 | -33 | -9 | -1 | --- | --- | --- | --- | --- | --- | -102 |
| 3. New markets tax credit ($3.5 billion allocation for 2010 and $3.5 billion allocation for 2011) (sunset 12/31/11) | cyba 12/31/09 | --- | --- | -5 | -29 | -94 | -180 | -221 | -252 | -279 | -288 | -267 | -194 | -1,810 |
| 4. 50% tax credit for certain expenditures for maintaining railroad tracks (sunset 12/31/11) | epoid tyba 12/31/09 | --- | --- | -232 | -99 | [11] | --- | --- | --- | --- | --- | --- | --- | -331 |
| 5. Mine rescue team training credit (sunset 12/31/11) | tyba 12/31/09 | --- | --- | -2 | -1 | -1 | [11] | [11] | [11] | --- | --- | --- | --- | -5 |
| 6. Employer wage credit for activated military reservists (sunset 12/31/11) | pma 12/31/09 | --- | --- | -2 | -1 | [11] | [11] | [11] | [11] | [11] | [11] | [11] | [11] | -3 |
| 7. 15-year straight-line cost recovery for qualified leasehold, restaurant, and retail improvements and new restaurants (sunset 12/31/11) | ppisa 12/31/09 | --- | --- | -281 | -359 | -397 | -395 | -389 | -385 | -380 | -369 | -350 | -324 | -3,629 |
| 8. 7-year recovery period for certain motorsports racing track facilities (sunset 12/31/11) | ppisa 12/31/09 | --- | --- | -40 | -3 | -1 | --- | --- | -1 | 1 | 3 | 3 | 3 | -36 |
| 9. Accelerated depreciation for business property on Indian reservations (sunset 12/31/11) | ppisa 12/31/09 | --- | --- | -98 | -23 | 5 | 17 | 27 | 22 | 12 | 1 | -2 | -1 | -41 |
| 10. Enhanced charitable deduction for contributions of food inventory (sunset 12/31/11) | cma 12/31/09 | --- | --- | -92 | -42 | --- | --- | --- | --- | --- | --- | --- | --- | -134 |
| 11. Enhanced charitable deduction for contributions of book inventories to public schools (sunset 12/31/11) | cma 12/31/09 | --- | --- | -37 | -16 | --- | --- | --- | --- | --- | --- | --- | --- | -53 |
| 12. Enhanced charitable deduction for corporate contributions of computer inventory for educational purposes (sunset 12/31/11) | cmd tyba 12/31/09 | --- | --- | -245 | -105 | --- | --- | --- | --- | --- | --- | --- | --- | -350 |
| 13. Election to expense mine safety equipment (sunset 12/31/11) | ppisa 12/31/09 | --- | --- | -20 | 1 | 5 | 4 | 3 | 3 | 2 | 1 | [4] | --- | -1 |
| 14. Special expensing rules for certain film and television productions (sunset 12/31/11) | qfatpca 12/31/09 | --- | --- | -162 | -158 | 39 | 45 | 34 | 29 | 23 | 21 | 16 | 12 | -101 |
| 15. Expensing of "Brownfields" environmental remediation costs (sunset 12/31/11) | epoia 12/31/09 | --- | --- | -493 | -536 | -66 | 83 | 91 | 86 | 77 | 67 | 57 | 50 | -583 |
| 16. Deduction allowable with respect to income attributable to domestic production activities in Puerto Rico (sunset 12/31/11) | tyba 12/31/09 | --- | --- | -229 | -186 | --- | --- | --- | --- | --- | --- | --- | --- | -415 |
| 17. Modify tax treatment of certain payments under existing arrangements to controlling exempt organizations (sunset 12/31/11) | proaa 12/31/09 | --- | --- | -34 | -5 | --- | --- | --- | --- | --- | --- | --- | --- | -40 |

| Provision | Effective | 2009 | 2010 | 2011 | 2012 | 2013 | 2014 | 2015 | 2016 | 2017 | 2018 | 2019 | 2020 | 2009-20 |
|---|---|---|---|---|---|---|---|---|---|---|---|---|---|---|
| 18. Treatment of certain dividends of regulated investment companies ("RICs") (sunset 12/31/11)..... | [57] | --- | --- | -108 | -66 | --- | --- | --- | --- | --- | --- | --- | --- | -174 |
| 19. Extend the treatment of RICs as "qualified investment entities" under section 897 (FIRPTA) (sunset 12/31/11)........ | 1/1/10 | --- | --- | -23 | -36 | --- | --- | --- | --- | --- | --- | --- | --- | -59 |
| 20. Exception under subpart F for active financing income (sunset 12/31/11)........ | tyba 12/31/09 | --- | --- | -5,200 | -3,957 | --- | --- | --- | --- | --- | --- | --- | --- | -9,157 |
| 21. Look-through treatment of payments between related CFCs under foreign personal holding company income rules (sunset 12/31/11)........ | tyba 2009 | --- | --- | -814 | -691 | --- | --- | --- | --- | --- | --- | --- | --- | -1,505 |
| 22. Basis adjustment to stock of S corporations making charitable contributions of property (sunset 12/31/11)........ | cmi tyba 12/31/09 | --- | --- | -19 | -36 | -6 | -3 | -3 | -3 | -3 | -3 | -3 | -3 | -82 |
| 23. Empowerment zone tax incentives (sunset 12/31/11)........ | pa 12/31/09 | --- | --- | -330 | -46 | 3 | 1 | --- | -4 | -1 | -4 | -4 | -4 | -387 |
| 24. Tax incentives for investment in the District of Columbia (sunset 12/31/11)........ | pa 12/31/09 | --- | --- | -88 | -21 | -2 | -1 | -4 | -7 | -4 | -4 | -4 | -4 | -138 |
| 25. Temporary increase in limit on cover over of rum excise tax revenues (from $10.50 to $13.25 per proof gallon) to Puerto Rico and the Virgin Islands (sunset 12/31/11) [58]........ | abiUSa 12/31/09 | --- | --- | -235 | -27 | --- | --- | --- | --- | --- | --- | --- | --- | -262 |
| 26. Economic development credit for American Samoa (sunset 12/31/11)........ | tyba 12/31/09 | --- | --- | -15 | -12 | --- | --- | --- | --- | --- | --- | --- | --- | -27 |
| 27. Work opportunity tax credit (sunset 12/31/11)........ | wpoifibwa 8/31/11 | --- | --- | [11] | -131 | -16 | -8 | -5 | -2 | --- | --- | --- | --- | -162 |
| 28. Qualified zone academy bonds ($400 million allocation) (sunset 12/31/11)........ | oia 12/31/10 | --- | --- | [11] | -3 | -8 | -16 | -21 | -22 | -22 | -21 | -19 | -19 | -151 |
| 29. Premiums for mortgage insurance deductible as interest that is qualified residence interest (sunset 12/31/11)........ | apoaa 12/31/10 | --- | --- | -261 | -87 | --- | --- | --- | --- | --- | --- | --- | --- | -348 |
| 30. Special rules applicable to qualified small business stock (sunset 12/31/11)........ | saa 12/31/10 | --- | --- | 15 | 6 | --- | --- | -62 | -768 | -420 | -97 | -74 | -47 | -1,445 |
| D. Temporary Disaster Relief Provisions | | | | | | | | | | | | | | |
| 1. New York Liberty Zone - tax-exempt bond financing (sunset 12/31/11)........ | bia 12/31/09 | --- | --- | -8 | -12 | -12 | -12 | -12 | -12 | -12 | -12 | -12 | -12 | -116 |
| 2. GO Zone: | | | | | | | | | | | | | | |
| a. Increase in rehabilitation credit (sunset 12/31/11)........ | apoia 12/31/09 | --- | --- | -39 | -21 | [11] | 1 | 1 | 1 | 2 | 2 | 2 | 1 | -50 |
| b. Extend the placed-in-service deadline for GO Zone low-income housing credits (sunset 12/31/11)........ | ppisa 12/31/10 | --- | --- | -8 | -34 | -34 | -34 | -34 | -34 | -34 | -34 | -34 | -34 | -314 |
| c. Tax-exempt bond financing (sunset 12/31/11)........ | DOE | --- | --- | -5 | -18 | -26 | -26 | -26 | -26 | -25 | -25 | -25 | -25 | -226 |
| d. Bonus depreciation for specified GO Zone extension property (sunset 12/31/11)........ | ppisa 12/31/09 | --- | --- | -171 | -61 | -4 | -1 | 2 | 4 | 6 | 7 | 7 | 7 | -202 |
| **TOTAL OF PART SIXTEEN**........ | | --- | --- | **-374,154** | **-422,910** | **-119,751** | **6,551** | **17,410** | **13,461** | **10,070** | **6,282** | **3,371** | **1,859** | **-857,806** |
| **PART SEVENTEEN: THE REGULATED INVESTMENT COMPANY MODERNIZATION ACT OF 2010 (P.L. 111-325, signed into law by the President on December 22, 2010)** | | | | | | | | | | | | | | |
| I. Capital Loss Carryovers of Regulated Investment Companies ("RICs")........ | [59] | --- | --- | 3 | 22 | 34 | 39 | 43 | 48 | 53 | 59 | 65 | -262 | 104 |

| Provision | Effective | 2009 | 2010 | 2011 | 2012 | 2013 | 2014 | 2015 | 2016 | 2017 | 2018 | 2019 | 2020 | 2009-20 |
|---|---|---|---|---|---|---|---|---|---|---|---|---|---|---|
| II. Modification of Gross Income and Asset Tests of RICs - savings provisions for failures of regulated investment companies to satisfy gross income and asset tests.......... | [60] | --- | --- | [4] | [4] | [4] | [4] | [4] | [4] | [4] | [4] | [4] | [4] | [4] |
| III. Modification of Rules Related to Dividends and Other Distributions | | | | | | | | | | | | | | |
| A. Modification of Dividend Designation Requirements and Allocation Rules for RICs.................................. | di tyba DOE | --- | --- | [11] | [11] | [11] | [11] | [11] | [11] | [11] | [11] | [11] | [11] | [11] |
| B. Earnings and Profits of RICs.................................. | tyba DOE | --- | --- | [11] | [11] | [11] | [11] | [11] | [11] | [11] | [11] | [11] | [11] | [11] |
| C. Pass-Thru of Exempt-Interest Dividends and Foreign Tax Credits in Fund of Funds Structure.................... | tyba DOE | --- | --- | -2 | -4 | -4 | -4 | -4 | -4 | -4 | -5 | -5 | -5 | -41 |
| D. Modification of Rules for Spillover Dividends of RICs.................................................................. | di tyba DOE | --- | --- | [11] | [11] | [11] | [11] | [11] | [11] | [11] | [11] | [11] | [11] | [11] |
| E. Return of Capital Distributions of RICs.................... | di tyba DOE | --- | --- | [4] | [4] | [4] | [4] | [4] | [4] | [4] | [4] | [4] | [4] | [4] |
| F. Distributions in Redemption of Stock of a RIC......... | da DOE | --- | --- | -5 | -9 | -9 | -10 | -10 | -10 | -11 | -11 | -12 | -12 | -99 |
| G. Repeal Preferential Dividend Rule for Publicly Offered RICs.............................................................. | di tyba DOE | --- | Negligible Revenue Effect | | | | | | | | | | | |
| H. Elective Deferral of Certain Late-Year Losses of RICs.................................................................. | tyba DOE | --- | --- | [11] | [11] | [11] | [11] | [11] | [11] | [11] | [11] | [11] | [11] | [11] |
| I. Exception to Holding Period Requirement for Certain Regularly Declared Exempt-Interest Dividends........ | [61] | --- | --- | [11] | [11] | [11] | [11] | [11] | [11] | [11] | [11] | [11] | [11] | [11] |
| IV. Modifications Related to Excise Tax Applicable to RICs | | | | | | | | | | | | | | |
| A. Excise Tax Exemption for Certain RICs Owned by Tax Exempt Entities.................................................. | cyba DOE | --- | Negligible Revenue Effect | | | | | | | | | | | |
| B. Deferral of Certain Gains and Losses of RICs for Excise Tax Purposes............................................ | cyba DOE | --- | --- | [11] | [11] | [11] | [11] | [11] | [11] | [11] | [11] | [11] | [11] | [11] |
| C. Distributed Amount for Excise Tax Purposes Determined on Basis of Taxes Paid by RICs............ | cyba DOE | --- | --- | [11] | [11] | [11] | [11] | [11] | [11] | [11] | [11] | [11] | [11] | [11] |
| D. Increase from 98% to 98.2% the Required Distribution Rate on Capital Gain Income by RICs... | cyba DOE | --- | --- | 29 | 23 | 10 | 4 | 4 | 4 | 4 | 4 | 4 | 5 | 92 |
| V. Other Provisions | | | | | | | | | | | | | | |
| A. Repeal of Assessable Penalty with Respect to Liability for Tax of RICs........................................... | tyba DOE | --- | --- | [11] | [11] | [11] | [11] | [11] | [11] | [11] | [11] | [11] | [11] | [11] |
| B. Modification of Sale Load Basis Deferral Rule for RICs.......................................................................... | cii tyba DOE | --- | --- | -6 | -8 | -5 | -2 | -1 | -1 | -1 | -1 | -1 | -1 | -26 |
| **TOTAL OF PART SEVENTEEN**......................................................... | | **---** | **---** | **19** | **24** | **26** | **27** | **32** | **37** | **41** | **46** | **51** | **-275** | **30** |
| **PART EIGHTEEN: THE OMNIBUS TRADE ACT OF 2010 (P.L. 111-344, signed into law by the President on December 29, 2010)** | | | | | | | | | | | | | | |
| A. Extension of Health Coverage Tax Credit Improvements (sunset 2/13/11) [25]........................... | [62] | --- | --- | -19 | -11 | --- | --- | --- | --- | --- | --- | --- | --- | -31 |
| B. Increase by 4.5 Percentage Points the Required Corporate Estimated Tax Payments Factor for Corporations With Assets of at Least $1 Billion for Payments Due in July, August, and September 2015 [63]................................................................... | DOE | --- | --- | --- | --- | --- | --- | 2,475 | -2,475 | --- | --- | --- | --- | --- |
| **TOTAL OF PART EIGHTEEN**......................................................... | | **---** | **---** | **-19** | **-11** | **---** | **---** | **2,475** | **-2,475** | **---** | **---** | **---** | **---** | **-31** |

| Provision | Effective | 2009 | 2010 | 2011 | 2012 | 2013 | 2014 | 2015 | 2016 | 2017 | 2018 | 2019 | 2020 | 2009-20 |
|---|---|---|---|---|---|---|---|---|---|---|---|---|---|---|
| **PART NINTEEN: THE JAMES ZADROGA 9/11 HEALTH AND COMPENSATION ACT OF 2010 - EXCISE TAX ON FOREIGN PROCUREMENT (P.L. 111-347, signed into law by the President on January 2, 2011)** | **pruceio/a DOE** | **---** | **---** | **305** | **495** | **490** | **485** | **480** | **475** | **471** | **466** | **461** | **457** | **4,585** |
| **PART TWENTY: AUTHORITY OF TAX COURT TO APPOINT EMPLOYEES (P.L. 111-366, signed into law by the President on January 4, 2011)** | **[64]** | **---** | ***No Revenue Effect*** | | | | | | | | | | | |
| **PART TWENTY-ONE: CUSTOMS USER FEES, CORPORATE ESTIMATED TAXES, AND EXTENSION OF ASSISTANCE FOR COBRA CONTINUATION COVERAGE [65]** | | | | | | | | | | | | | | |
| A. Extension of Customs User Fees [66] | various | *Estimated by the Congressional Budget Office* | | | | | | | | | | | | |
| B. Modifications to Corporate Estimated Tax Payments | | | | | | | | | | | | | | |
| 1. Repeal 2010, 2011, and 2013 corporate estimated tax adjustments and add new 0.25 percentage point adjustment for payments due in July, August, and September 2014; applies to corporations with assets of at least $1 billion (P.L. 111-42, signed into law by the President on July 28, 2009 | DOE | --- | 6,864 | 3,024 | -9,888 | -11,850 | 11,994 | -144 | --- | --- | --- | --- | --- | --- |
| 2. Increase by 1.50 percentage points the required corporate estimated tax payments factor for corporations with assets of at least $1 billion for payments due in July, August, and September 2014 (P.L. 111-124, signed into law by the President on December 28, 2009 | DOE | --- | --- | --- | --- | --- | 806 | -806 | --- | --- | --- | --- | --- | --- |
| 3. Increase the required corporate estimated tax payments otherwise due in July, August, or September 2014 by 0.75 percentage points and July, August, or September 2015 by 0.75 percentage points (P.L. 111-171, signed into law by the President on May 24, 2010) | DOE | --- | --- | --- | --- | --- | 356 | 107 | -463 | --- | --- | --- | --- | --- |
| 4. Increase by 0.75 percentage points the required corporate estimated tax payments factor for corporations with assets of at least $1 billion for payments due in July, August, and September 2015 (P.L. 111-171, signed into law by the President on May 24, 2010) | DOE | --- | --- | --- | --- | --- | --- | 463 | -463 | --- | --- | --- | --- | --- |
| 5. Increase by 0.25 percentage points the required corporate estimated tax payments factor for corporations with assets of at least $1 billion for payments due in July, August, and September 2015 (P.L. 111-210, signed into law by the President on August 11, 2010) | DOE | --- | --- | --- | --- | --- | --- | 153 | -153 | --- | --- | --- | --- | --- |

| Provision | Effective | 2009 | 2010 | 2011 | 2012 | 2013 | 2014 | 2015 | 2016 | 2017 | 2018 | 2019 | 2020 | 2009-20 |
|---|---|---|---|---|---|---|---|---|---|---|---|---|---|---|
| 6. Increase by 0.50 percentage points the required corporate estimated tax payments factor for corporations with assets of at least $1 billion for payments due in July, August, and September 2015 (P.L. 111-227, signed into law by the President on August 11, 2010) | DOE | --- | --- | --- | --- | --- | --- | 305 | -305 | --- | --- | --- | --- | --- |
| 7. Increase by 4.5 percentage points the required corporate estimated tax payments factor for corporations with assets of at least $1 billion for payments due in July, August, and September 2015 (P.L. 111-344, signed into law by the President on December 29, 2010) | DOE | --- | --- | --- | --- | --- | --- | 2,475 | -2,475 | --- | --- | --- | --- | --- |
| C. Extension of Assistance for COBRA Continuation Coverage | | | | | | | | | | | | | | |
| 1. COBRA credit in Department of Defense Appropriations Act, 2010 (P.L. 111-118, signed into law by the President on December 19, 2009) [25] | [67] | --- | -4,473 | -1,673 | -330 | -15 | --- | --- | --- | --- | --- | --- | --- | -6,490 |
| 2. COBRA credit in the Temporary Extension Act of 2010 (P.L. 111-144, signed into law by the President on March 2, 2010) [25] | [68] | --- | -735 | -339 | -11 | --- | --- | --- | --- | --- | --- | --- | --- | -1,085 |
| 3. COBRA credit in the Continuing Extension Act of 2010 (P.L. 111-157, signed into law by the President on April 15, 2010) [25] | [67] | --- | -1,391 | -642 | -21 | --- | --- | --- | --- | --- | --- | --- | --- | -2,054 |
| **TOTAL OF PART TWENTY-ONE** | | **---** | **265** | **370** | **-10,250** | **-11,865** | **13,156** | **2,553** | **-3,859** | **---** | **---** | **---** | **---** | **-9,629** |

Joint Committee on Taxation

-----------------------------------

NOTE: Details may not add to totals due to rounding.

*[Legand and Footnotes for the Appendix appear on the following pages]*

**Legend and Footnotes for the Appendix:**

Legend for "Effective" column:

aa = acquisitions after
abiUSa = articles brought into the United States after
aiiUSa = articles imported into the United States after
apa = appliances produced after
apoaa = amounts paid or accrued after
apoia = amounts paid or incurred after
apoii = amounts paid or incurred in
ara = articles removed after
Ara = amounts received after
bia = bonds issued after
caaa = covered asset acquisitions after
cba = courses beginning after
cii = charges incurred in
cma = contributions made after
cmd = contributions made during
cmi = contributions made in
cyba = calendar years beginning after
da = distributions after
Da = dispositions after
dda = decedents dying after
dda/gsta = decedents dying after and generation-skipping transfers after
di = distributions in
dma = distributions made after
Dma = disclosures made after
dmi = distributions made in
DOE = date of enactment
eia = expenses incurred after
epoia = expenses paid or incurred after
epoid = expenses paid or incurred during
fitpoaa = foreign income taxes paid or accrued after
fsoua = fuel sold or used after
fsouo/a = fuels sold or used on or after
gma = gifts made after
gia = guarantees issued after
haa = homes acquired after
ipa = interest paid after
ita = instruments tendered after
iwbwa = individuals who begin work after
lia = levies issued after
ma = months after
mba = months beginning after
mbo/a = months beginning on or after
oca = ownership changes after
oia = obligations issued after
pa = periods after
paa = penalties assessed after
pba = periods beginning after
pma = payments made after
po/a = purchases on or after
ppisa = property placed in service after
proaa = payments received or accrued after
pruceio/a = payments received under contracts entered into on or after
qfatpca = qualified film and television productions commencing after
qhpa = qualified homes purchased after
ra = repurchases after
rfa = returns filed after
rpa = residences purchased after
rtbfo/a = returns to be filed on or after
sa = sales after
saa = stock acquired after
saua = sales and uses after
teia = transactions entered into after
tspo/a = tanning services performed on or after
tyba = taxable years beginning after
tybi = taxable years beginning in
tyea = taxable years ending after
wpa = wages paid after
wpoifibwa = wages paid or incurred for individuals beginning work after

| | 2009 | 2010 | 2011 | 2012 | 2013 | 2014 | 2015 | 2016 | 2017 | 2018 | 2019 | 2020 | 2009-20 |
|---|---|---|---|---|---|---|---|---|---|---|---|---|---|
| [1] Estimate includes the following off-budget effects: | | | | | | | | | | | | | |
| Requirements for Group Health Plans | --- | -50 | -100 | -125 | -125 | -125 | -125 | -150 | -150 | -150 | --- | --- | -1,100 |
| Limitations on aggregate amount recovered on reconciliation of the health insurance tax credit and the advance of that credit | --- | --- | --- | --- | --- | -14 | -24 | -40 | -44 | -49 | -51 | -52 | -275 |
| Parity for exclusion for employer-provided mass transit and parking benefits | --- | --- | -34 | -11 | --- | --- | --- | --- | --- | --- | --- | --- | -45 |

| | 2009 | 2010 | 2011 | 2012 | 2013 | 2014 | 2015 | 2016 | 2017 | 2018 | 2019 | 2020 | 2009-20 |
|---|---|---|---|---|---|---|---|---|---|---|---|---|---|
| [2] Estimate does not include the following effects on Medicaid outlays | --- | 30 | 60 | 70 | 70 | 80 | 90 | 90 | 100 | 110 | --- | --- | 700 |

[3] The excise tax rates on tobacco products and cigarette papers and tubes would be as follows:

| | |
|---|---|
| Cigars weighing not more than three pounds per thousand ("small cigars") | $50.33 per thousand ($1.0066 per pack) |
| Cigars weighing more than three pounds per thousand ("large cigars") | 52.75% of the manufacture's or importer's sales price but not more than $0.4026 per cigar |
| Cigarettes weighing not more than three pounds per thousand ("small cigarettes") | $50.33 per thousand ($1.0066 per pack) |
| Cigarettes weighing more than three pounds per thousand ("large cigarettes") | $105.69 per thousand |
| Cigarette papers | $0.0315 for each 50 papers |
| Cigarette tubes | $0.0630 for each 50 tubes |
| Snuff | $1.51 per pound |
| Chewing tobacco | $0.5033 per pound |
| Pipe tobacco | $2.8311 per pound |
| Roll-your-own tobacco | $24.78 per pound |

[4] Gain of less than $500,000.
[5] Estimate provided by the Congressional Budget Office.
[6] The study will be completed no later than one year after the date of enactment.
[7] Increase by 0.5 percentage points the required corporate estimated tax payments factor for corporations with assets of at least $1 billion for payments due in July, August, and September 2013.
[8] Estimated outlay effects as a result of U.S. possessions provision provided by the Joint Committee on Taxation in consultation with the Congressional Budget Office.

*[Footnotes for the Appendix are continued on the following pages]*

**Footnotes for the Appendix continued:**

[9] Estimate includes interaction with Making Work Pay Credit and Additional Tax Relief for Families With Children.
[10] This item does not have a separate description in the text of the document.
[11] Loss of less than $500,000.
[12] Estimate includes outlay effects provided by the Congressional Budget Office.
[13] Effective for net operating losses generated in either a taxable year beginning in 2008 or a taxable year ending in 2008.
[14] Effective for any unemployed veteran hired in 2009 and 2010 within five years (but not less than two months) of the date of discharge.
[15] The temporary suspension of section 163(e)(5) applies to obligations issued after August 31, 2008, in taxable years ending after such date. The additional authority granted to the Secretary to use a rate higher than the applicable Federal rate for purposes of applying section 163(e)(5) applies to obligations issued after December 31, 2009, in taxable years ending after such date.
[16] Modifications to the definitions of qualified energy property are effective for property placed in service after the date of enactment.
[17] The neighborhood electric vehicle and motorcycle rule is effective for vehicles acquired after date of enactment. The elimination of neighborhood vehicles and heavy plug-ins from section 30D and the 200,000 vehicle/manufacturer cap is effective for vehicles acquired after December 31, 2009.
[18] Estimate includes indirect effects of COBRA subsidy on Unemployment Insurance program.
[19] We estimate that approximately 7 million people, including COBRA policyholders and their dependents, would benefit from this credit for some portion of 2009.
[20] Effective for premiums for months of coverage beginning after the date of enactment.
[21] Estimate includes indirect revenue effects of Trade Adjustment Assistance Reauthorization; estimate does not include outlay effects of TAA.
[22] In general, the modifications apply to residences purchased after November 30, 2009. The waiver of recapture for individuals on qualified official extended duty applies to dispositions and cessations after December 31, 2008. The mathematical error authority applies to returns for taxable years ending on or after April 9, 2008. Provisions relating to long-time residents of the same principal residence, and income, purchase price, age, related party, dependent, and documentation limitations apply for purchases after the date of enactment.
[23] Generally effective for net operating losses arising in taxable years ending after December 31, 2007.
[24] The proposal also appropriates a transfer from the General Fund to the Social Security Trust Fund to keep the trust fund whole. Thus, the reported estimate is all on-budget.
[25] Estimate includes the following outlay effects:

| | 2009 | 2010 | 2011 | 2012 | 2013 | 2014 | 2015 | 2016 | 2017 | 2018 | 2019 | 2020 | 2009-20 |
|---|---|---|---|---|---|---|---|---|---|---|---|---|---|
| Qualified Tax Credit Bonds | --- | 98 | 694 | 1,091 | 1,314 | 1,441 | 1,441 | 1,441 | 1,441 | 1,441 | 1,441 | 1,441 | 13,284 |
| Limitations on aggregate amount recovered on reconciliation of the health insurance tax credit and the advance of that credit | --- | --- | --- | --- | --- | -610 | -1,297 | -2,167 | -2,639 | -2,893 | -3,081 | -3,283 | -15,969 |
| Authority to disclose return information concerning outstanding tax debts for purposes of enhancing Medicare Program Integrity [5] | --- | --- | --- | -38 | -38 | -50 | -50 | -50 | -50 | -50 | -50 | -50 | -425 |
| Collection of past-due, legally enforceable State debts [51] | --- | --- | --- | -1,308 | -1,076 | -455 | -337 | -291 | -270 | -276 | -416 | -433 | -4,863 |
| Retain 10% bracket | --- | --- | --- | 1,198 | 1,239 | --- | --- | --- | --- | --- | --- | --- | 2,437 |
| Retain the child tax credit at $1,000; refundable; AMT rules | --- | --- | --- | 16,457 | 16,530 | --- | --- | --- | --- | --- | --- | --- | 32,987 |
| Marriage penalty - standard deduction and 15% rate | --- | --- | --- | 2,000 | 2,030 | --- | --- | --- | --- | --- | --- | --- | 4,030 |
| EIC modification and simplification ($3,000) | --- | --- | --- | 3,724 | 3,781 | --- | --- | --- | --- | --- | --- | --- | 7,505 |
| Dependent care tax credit | --- | --- | --- | 49 | 146 | --- | --- | --- | --- | --- | --- | --- | 195 |
| Adoption credit | --- | --- | --- | --- | 53 | --- | --- | --- | --- | --- | --- | --- | 53 |
| American opportunity tax credit | --- | --- | --- | 2,086 | 2,172 | --- | --- | --- | --- | --- | --- | --- | 4,258 |
| Reduce the earnings threshold for the refundable portion of the child tax credit to $3,000 | --- | --- | --- | 9,826 | 9,917 | --- | --- | --- | --- | --- | --- | --- | 19,743 |
| Increase in earned income tax credit percentage | --- | --- | --- | 1,694 | 1,688 | --- | --- | --- | --- | --- | --- | --- | 3,382 |
| EIC modification and simplification ($5,000) | --- | --- | --- | 1,270 | 1,250 | --- | --- | --- | --- | --- | --- | --- | 2,520 |
| Temporary extension of unemployment insurance and related matters [5] | --- | --- | 34,515 | 21,565 | --- | --- | --- | --- | --- | --- | --- | --- | 56,080 |
| Grants for specified energy property in lieu of tax credits | --- | --- | 1,941 | 1,045 | --- | --- | --- | --- | --- | --- | --- | --- | 2,987 |
| Refunds disregarded in the administration of Federal programs and Federally assisted programs [5] | --- | --- | 4 | 4 | --- | --- | --- | --- | --- | --- | --- | --- | 8 |
| Extension of health coverage tax credit improvements | --- | --- | 15 | 9 | --- | --- | --- | --- | --- | --- | --- | --- | 24 |
| COBRA credit in DOD Act | --- | --- | --- | 313 | 157 | 27 | 8 | --- | --- | --- | --- | --- | 504 |
| COBRA credit in TEA | --- | --- | --- | 51 | 34 | 8 | --- | --- | --- | --- | --- | --- | 94 |
| COBRA credit in CEA | --- | --- | --- | 97 | 64 | 16 | --- | --- | --- | --- | --- | --- | 177 |

[26] Estimates for the rest of this title were provided by the Congressional Budget Office.
[27] Present law provides for a corporate estimated payments factor of 134.75 percent.

*[Footnotes for the Appendix are continued on the following page]*

**Footnotes for the Appendix continued:**

[28] Estimate included with estimate of associated effects of coverage provisions on revenues and other revenue provisions as reported by the Congressional Budget Office, Congressional Budget Office, cost estimate for the amendment in the nature of a substitute for H.R. 4782, the "Reconciliation Act of 2010," incorporating a proposed manager's amendment made public on March 20, 2010, available at http://www.cbo.gov/ftpdocs/113xx/doc11379/AmendReconProp.pdf.
[29] The fee on health insurance and self-insurance plans is effective with respect to policies and plans for portions of policy or plan years beginning on or after October 1, 2012.
[30] The description and revenue estimate of the provision reflects the modifications made by the "Health Care and Education Reconciliation Act of 2010."
[31] Gain of less than $50 million.
[32] Estimate includes interaction with the high premium excise tax.
[33] Effective for calendar years beginning after December 31, 2013; fee is allocated based on market share of net premiums written for any United States health risk for calendar years beginning after December 31, 2012.
[34] Effective for remuneration paid in taxable years beginning after 2012 with respect to services performed after 2009.
[35] Effective for health benefits and coverage provided after the date of enactment.
[36] Loss of less than $50 million.
[37] Effective for expenditures paid or incurred after December 31, 2008, in taxable years beginning after December 31, 2008.
[38] Effective as if included in section 1501(b) of the Patient Protection and Affordable Care Act.
[39] Estimate does not include Congressional Budget Office outlay effects. These effects were provided by the Congressional Budget Office separately.
[40] The provision amends Internal Revenue Code section 6103(k)(10), which sunsets December 31, 2011. Revenue effects after the sunset date are due to a decrease in the growth rate of prisoner fraud prior to the sunset. Although the present-law growth rate resumes after the sunset, the level of fraud remains lower due to preventive measures assumed to take place prior to the sunset.
[41] Effective for acquisitions of U.S. property determined under section 956(c) after December 31, 2010.
[42] Effective as if included in section 513 of the "Hiring Incentives to Restore Employment Act."
[43] Estimate includes effects on outlays from the Pittman-Robertson Aid to Wildlife Trust Fund (provided by the Congressional Budget Office).
[44] Effective for articles sold by the manufacturer, producer, or importer after the date of enactment.
[45] Effective for restitution ordered after the date of enactment.
[46] Effective for credits determined in the taxpayer's first taxable year beginning after December 31, 2009.
[47] Estimate includes effects on the Social Security trust fund.
[48] Negligible revenue effect.
[49] First report shall be submitted not later than December 31, 2010.
[50] Estimate is based on a 36 percentage point increase to the 2015 corporate estimated tax shift under paragraph (2) of section 561 of the "Hiring Incentives to Restore Employment Act," in effect on September 16, 2010.
[51] Estimate provided by the Joint Committee on Taxation in collaboration with the Congressional Budget Office.
[52] Effective with respect to refunds under section 6402 payable on or after the date of enactment.
[53] Estimate includes the following effects:

| | 2009 | 2010 | 2011 | 2012 | 2013 | 2014 | 2015 | 2016 | 2017 | 2018 | 2019 | 2020 | 2009-20 |
|---|---|---|---|---|---|---|---|---|---|---|---|---|---|
| Total Revenue Effects | --- | --- | -707 | -964 | -243 | --- | --- | --- | --- | --- | --- | --- | -1,914 |
| On-budget effects | --- | --- | -460 | -653 | -164 | --- | --- | --- | --- | --- | --- | --- | -1,277 |
| Off-budget effects | --- | --- | -246 | -311 | -79 | --- | --- | --- | --- | --- | --- | --- | -636 |

[54] Effective for property placed in service after December 31, 2010, in taxable years ending after such date.
[55] Estimate includes the following effects:

| | 2009 | 2010 | 2011 | 2012 | 2013 | 2014 | 2015 | 2016 | 2017 | 2018 | 2019 | 2020 | 2009-20 |
|---|---|---|---|---|---|---|---|---|---|---|---|---|---|
| Total Revenue Effects | --- | --- | -67,239 | -44,414 | --- | --- | --- | --- | --- | --- | --- | --- | -111,653 |
| On-budget effects | --- | --- | 1,293 | 1,274 | --- | --- | --- | --- | --- | --- | --- | --- | 2,567 |
| Off-budget effects | --- | --- | -68,532 | -45,688 | --- | --- | --- | --- | --- | --- | --- | --- | -114,220 |

[56] Estimate includes interaction with the extension of the American opportunity tax credit.
[57] Effective for dividends with respect to taxable years of regulated investment companies beginning after December 31, 2009.
[58] Estimate provided by the Congressional Budget Office and is preliminary and subject to change.
[59] The provision generally applies to net capital losses for taxable years beginning after the date of enactment. The provision relating to the treatment of present-law carryovers applies to taxable years beginning after the date of enactment.
[60] The provision applies to taxable years with respect to which the due date (determined with regard to extensions) of the return of tax is after the date of enactment.
[61] Effective for stock for which the taxpayer's holding period begins after the date of enactment.
[62] Effective for months beginning (or, for certain provisions, plan years beginning or events occurring) after December 31, 2010.
[63] Estimate is based on a 4.5 percentage point increase to the 2015 corporate estimated tax shift under paragraph (2) of section 561 of the "Hiring Incentives to Restore Employment Act," in effect on December 21, 2010.
[64] Effective on the date the United States Tax Court adopts a personnel management system after the date of enactment.
[65] Not elsewhere included.
[66] For the details relating to Custom User Fees, see Part Twenty-One of the General Explanation. For the estimates relating to the Custom User Fees, see the Congressional Budget Office website, www.CBO.gov.
[67] Effective as if included in the American Recovery and Reinvestment Act of 2009.
[68] Generally effective as if included in the American Recovery and Reinvestment Act of 2009.